ALSO BY FRANK TRENTMANN

Empire of Things: How We Became a World of Consumers from the Fifteenth Century to the Twenty-first

Free Trade Nation: Consumption, Civil Society, and Commerce in Modern Britain

Out of the Darkness

Out of the Darkness

THE GERMANS, 1942–2022

Frank Trentmann

ALFRED A. KNOPF | NEW YORK | 2024

THIS IS A BORZOI BOOK
PUBLISHED BY ALFRED A. KNOPF

 Published in the United States by Alfred A. Knopf, a division of Penguin Random House LLC, New York. Originally published in hardcover in Great Britain by Allen Lane, an imprint of Penguin Press, a division of Penguin Random House Ltd., London, in 2023.

www.aaknopf.com

Library of Congress Cataloging-in-Publication Data
Names: Trentmann, Frank, author.
Title: Out of the darkness : the Germans, 1942–2022 / Frank Trentmann.
Description: First edition. | New York : Alfred A. Knopf, 2024.
| Includes bibliographical references and index.
Identifiers: LCCN 2023013874 (print) | LCCN 2023013875 (ebook) |
ISBN 9781524732912 (hardcover) | ISBN 9781524732929 (ebook)
Subjects: LCSH: Germany—History—1945– | Germany (East)—History. |
Group identity—Germany. | National characteristics, German. |
Collective memory—Germany.
Classification: LCC DD257 .T74 2024 (print) | LCC DD257 (ebook) |
DDC 943.08—dc23/eng/20230417
LC record available at https://lccn.loc.gov/2023013874
LC ebook record available at https://lccn.loc.gov/2023013875

Jacket photograph of the twenty-fifth anniversary of German reunification,
October 3, 2015, Berlin, Germany, by Sean Gallup / Getty Images
Jacket design by Keenan

Manufactured in the United States of America
First United States Edition

For my mother

The realm of history is fertile and comprehensive:
it embraces the whole moral world.

FRIEDRICH SCHILLER, 1789

Contents

Preface and Acknowledgments

I started this book in the autumn of 2015, shortly after Chancellor Angela Merkel opened Germany's borders to hundreds of thousands of refugees. I completed it in the autumn of 2022, nine months after Russian president Vladimir Putin's invasion of Ukraine prompted Chancellor Olaf Scholz to announce a *Zeitenwende*—a "new era." This book, however, draws on decades of working out what it means to be German after Adolf Hitler. This is an unavoidable question, and one that gains special resonance when one lives abroad. I was born and raised in Hamburg, before leaving the country, in 1986, first to England to study, and then to the United States for a doctoral degree and my first teaching post. Since 2000, I have again lived in London, with a few stints elsewhere. While I have retained close ties with my home country and visit frequently, I have mainly observed its momentous changes from the outside—from the fall of the Berlin Wall to the soul-searching about Germany's role today. Being an émigré is not easy, even when it is voluntary, but it has this advantage: it teaches you to switch back and forth between being an insider and an outsider, still sympathetic to the country of one's birth and yet with enough distance to view it critically. What can seem natural and normal at home is revealed as something special, even strange, from abroad. Living in a foreign culture—with an American wife, and two children with eight passports among them—has been excellent training for this intercultural sensibility.

I have written with two readerships in mind. The first is foreigners, who are often bewildered, and sometimes frightened, by Germany. Most of what they know is about the Nazi years. Awareness of the Holocaust is as important as ever, but this should not entail ignorance about what has happened since. It is appalling and alarming how little is known about Germany after Hitler both in the Allied countries, which shed so much blood to defeat him, and in the societies that were ravaged and massacred by his regime and are now the nation's neighbors in the European Union. The victims, too, deserve a broader history. This book tries to fill some of that gap, question easy stereotypes, and inspire readers to find out more. It is also, however, written for the Germans themselves. While many will be familiar with the main events of their history, the book's distinctive vantage point will, I hope, also defamiliarize part of that history, and let them see their past and present in a new light. In the past eighty years, the Federal Republic of Germany has mastered many challenges, but it is too convenient to tell it as a success story, and at no time more so than now, when the country is searching for a new direction and needs to confront problems and shortcomings. It is time for a more self-critical look at the recent past. Inevitably, some readers will find me too harsh in places, while others will think me not harsh enough. To be clear, my goal has been to understand and explain, not to pass judgment.

Writing this new history would have been impossible without the generous support of many individuals and institutions. My first thanks must go to the Alexander von Humboldt Foundation for awarding me their Forschungspreis, which supported a much-needed longer stay at the Humboldt Universität in Berlin and the University of Konstanz, and to the two institutions for being generous hosts. A collective thanks to the many archivists who shared their knowledge as well as their collections with me. When I conceived this project, I was fortunate to have the advice and encouragement of two great historians: Ian Kershaw and Axel Schildt. It is very sad that the latter did not live long enough to see the end result. I am extremely grateful to a number of scholars whose work has been an inspiration and who kindly commented on draft chapters: Paul Betts, Frank Biess, Marcus Böick, David Feldman, Constantin Goschler, Rüdiger Graf, Christina von Hodenberg, Maren Möhring, Alexander Nützenadel, Till van Rahden, Laura Rischbieter, and Felix Römer. Benjamin Ziemann kindly gave his time and thought to the entire manuscript. Several seminars and conferences gave me a chance to discuss emerging arguments, including at the Humboldt, Konstanz/Reichenau, London, Paris, Helsinki, Caltech, and the Center for the History of Emotions at the Max Planck Institute for Human Development (Berlin). Collectively, they helped me make this a better book.

Contemporary history is thriving in Germany, and my debt to the research of many younger as well as older scholars will be apparent from the endnotes. Libraries in Berlin, the Forschungsstelle in Hamburg, the Hamburg Institute for Social Research (HIS), and the Institute for Contemporary History (IfZ) in Munich provided me with the most obscure as well as the most recent literature on numerous visits. Thanks also to everyone (past and present) at the Leibniz Centre for Contemporary History (ZZF), Potsdam. In Britain, the German Historical Institute London remains a precious oasis of tolerance and learning, and I would not have been able to finish this work without its superb and supportive library.

At several stages, I was fortunate to have ingenious and genial research assistants who tracked down scattered material and gathered complex data: Heather Chappells, Riitta Matilainen, Rasmus Randig, and Jasper Stange. Many others gave me help and advice along the way, including: Günther Bachmann, Patrick Bernhard, Ute Frevert, Gerhard Haupt, Ulrich Herbert, Säde Hormio, Ilja Kavonius, Volker Nowosadtko, Helge Pösche, Martin Sabrow, Andreas Schönfelder, Gunter Scholz, Bernd Schrage, Elke Seefried, Bärbel Spengler, Nicholas Stargardt, Agnes Stieda and family, the Taghizadeh family, Malte Thießen, Dieter Thomä, and Klaus Töpfer. At Birkbeck, the history department remains a rare haven of collegiality and imagination. *Kiitos* also to everyone at the Center for Consumer Society Research, Helsinki, for supporting my forays into morality. I gratefully acknowledge a grant on Material Cultures of Energy by the Arts and Humanities Research Council in the United Kingdom, which proved serendipitous when the energy crisis returned, and helped me with the last chapter. David Godwin, my agent, emboldened me to tackle the Germans, and I was lucky to have from start to finish the support, wisdom, and patience of Stuart Proffitt at Allen Lane/Penguin and Jonathan Segal at Knopf. Nina Sillem gave the book its German home at Fischer, where Tanja Hommen took it under her expert wing. At Knopf, additional thanks to Kevin Bourke, Sarah Perrin, Isabel Ribeiro, and Amy Stackhouse.

In addition to their private struggle with civilizing a German, my wife and children had to live with the German people since Hitler for the past few years. As with previous books, words are not enough to express my thanks to my wife, Elizabeth Ruddick, for her support, intelligence, and care for words. Not only did she make me clarify arguments, she also read multiple drafts and helped me polish the text. No author (or husband) could hope for more. This book, however, is dedicated to the person who has been there for me from the very beginning: my mother.

London
January 2023

Maps and Illustrations

MAPS

ILLUSTRATIONS

Nazi Germany and Europe, 1942
NORWAY
Oslo
SWEDEN
Stockholm
Glasgow
North Sea
DENMARK
Copenhagen
Baltic Sea
Königsberg (Kaliningrad)
Danzig (Gdansk)
Stolp (Słupsk)
Inste (Chernyakh
Lübeck
Hamburg
Neuengamme
Pomerania
Stettin (Szczecin)
Danzig-West Prussia
East Pruss
GREAT BRITAIN
London
Amsterdam
NETHERLANDS
Bergen-Belsen
Hanover
Ravensbrück
Berlin
Frankfurt
Posen (Poznań)
Chelmno
Treblinka
Warsa
Münster
Essen
Warstein
NAZI GERMANY
Reichsgau Wartheland
Brussels
BELGIUM
Wuppertal
Cologne
Aachen
Halle
Leipzig
Buchenwald
Erfurt
Dresden
Breslau (Wrocław)
Silesia
Channel Islands
Frankfurt
Schweinfurt
Theresienstadt
Sudetenland
Prague
Bohemia and Moravia
Auschwitz
Luxembourg
Würzburg
Saarbrücken
Nuremberg
Paris
Brünn
SLOVAK
FRANCE
Stuttgart
Regensburg
Strasbourg
Bratislava
Nantes
Dachau
Munich
Linz
Vienna
Basel
Bern
Ostmark
Anschluss Austria
13.3.1938
Budapes
HUNGA
SWITZERLAND
Vichy
Bordeaux
VICHY-FRANCE
(occupied from Nov. 1942)
Lyon
Milan
Zagreb
Venice
CROATIA
Genoa
Toulouse
Jajce
Kistanje
Marseille
ITALY
Adriatic Sea
MONTE NEGRO
SPAIN
Corsica
Rome
Mediterranean Sea
Tirana
ALBAN
Naples
Sardinia
Balearic Islands
Corf

Nazi Germany with incorporated areas in 1942
German occupied territories
Allies of Nazi Germany and their occupied territories
Neutral states
Front line December 1941
Front line November 1942
1937 borders
1941/42 borders
Extermination camps
Concentration camps
NLAND
Lake Ladoga
Leningrad (St Petersburg)
elsinki
AREAS UNDER MILITARY ADMINISTRATION
al (Tallinn)
Novgorod
Pskov
Rzhev
Moscow
iga
Tula
Wjasma (Vyazma)
Kaluga
Katyn
REICHS MMISSARIAT OSTLAND
Vitebsk
Smolensk
SOVIET UNION
nas
Vilnius
Mogilev
Bryansk
Oryol
Minsk
Kursk
Voronezh
lystok
Gomel
AREAS UNDER MILITARY ADMINISTRATION
istrict lystok
Chernihiv
Belgorod
Stalingrad (Volgograd)
Brest-Litovsk
Kharkiv (Kharkov)
Sobibor
Lublin
ajdanek
Rowno
Kiev (Kyiv)
AREAS UNDER MILITARY ADMINISTRATION
lzec
REICHSKOMMISSARIAT UKRAINE
Rostov
Lemberg (Lviv)
Kirovograd (Kropyvntsky)
vernment
Sea of Azoz
Kishinev (Chişinău)
Krasnodar
Odessa
Kerch
Crimea
Simferopol
Eupatoria (Yevpatoriya)
Yalta
Sevastopol
ROMANIA
Black Sea
Bucharest
BULGARIA
Sofia
Istanbul
TURKEY
Ankara
Aegean Sea
REECE
ommeno
SYRIA
0 50 100 150 km

Germany since 1945
DENMARK
SWEDE
Sylt
North Sea
Husum
Schleswig
Kiel
Schleswig-Holstein
Stralsund
Rostock
Brokdorf
Lübeck
Wismar
Mecklenburg-Vorpommern
Hamburg
Hamburg
Bremerhaven
Schwerin
Campen
Nordenham
Strelitz
Bremen
Oldenburg
Bremen
Lüneburg
Wendland
Gorleben
NETHERLANDS
Lower Saxony
Belsen
Havelberg
Celle
Berlin
Berlin
Amsterdam
Hanover
Wolfsburg
Saxony-Anhalt
Potsdam
Osnabrück
Wolfenbüttel
Salzhemmendorf
Magdeburg
Wusterhau
Münster
Bielefeld
Bad Harzburg
Halberstadt
Dessau
North Rhine-Westphalia
Bitterfeld
Göttingen
Harz Mountains
Essen
Bochum
Halle
Duisburg
Dortmund
Friedland
Bischofferode
Leipzig
Düsseldorf
Kassel
Merseburg
Espenhain
Cologne
Erfurt
Chemnit
Aachen
Eisenach
Karl-Marx-St
Bonn
Thuringia
Jena
Zwickau
Saxony
Hesse/Hessen
Saalfeld
BELGIUM
Plauen
Vogtland
Koblenz
Hof
Lower Franconia
Upper Franconia
Sudetenla
Hanau
Wiesbaden
Frankfurt
Mainz
Darmstadt
Bayreuth
Luxembourg
Würzburg
Rheinland-Palatinate
Erlangen
Saarland
Zirndorf
Nuremburg
Saarbrücken
Wackersdorf
Regensburg
Karlsruhe
Mutlangen
Ludwigsburg
Bavaria
Stuttgart
Strasbourg
Vilshofen
Offenburg
Dornstadt
Tübingen
Ulm
FRANCE
Black Forest
Baden-Württemberg
Augsburg
Wyhl
Munich
Freiburg
Landsberg
Salzbu
Lake Constance
Basel
SWITZERLAND

Baltic Sea
Sovetsk (Tilsit)
Oblast Kaliningrad
(USSR/Russia)
Kaliningrad (Königsberg)
Chernyakhovsk (Insterburg)
Gdańsk (Danzig)
East Prussia
Pomerania
Szczecin (Stettin)
Bydgoszcz (Bromberg)
POLAND
Poznań (Posen)
Eisenhüttenstadt
Silesia
Görlitz
Zittau
Wrocław (Breslau)
Giant Mountains
Opole (Oppeln)
Gliwice (Gleiwitz)
Kraków (Krakau)
Auschwitz
Sudetenland
Prague
CZECHOSLOVAKIA
(from 1.1.1993 Czech Republic and Slovakia)
Vienna
AUSTRIA
0 50 100 150 km
American Zone
British Zone
French Zone
Federal Republic of Germany from 1949
Soviet Zone (from 1949 GDR)
Formerly German eastern territories under Polish and Soviet administration (Potsdam Agreement)
from 1946 French Customs and economic area (since 1957 to the Federal Republic of Germany)
Borders after 1945
Oder-Neisse line
German borders since 1990
Border between West and East Germany until 1990
Borders of the federal states 2023
Capitals of the federal states
PANKOW
Crossing points
French Zone
Berlin Wall
BERLIN
Tegel
Bornholmer Str.
Havel
PRENZLAUER BERG
Soviet Zone
British Zone
FRIEDRICHSHAIN
CHARLOTTENBURG
Checkpoint Charlie
Spree
American Zone
NEUKÖLLN
0 5 10 15 km
Schönefeld

Out of the Darkness

Introduction

In 1945, Germany lay in ruins, morally and materially. Germans had waged the most brutal war in history and were responsible for genocide and mass murder. Seventy years later, the same country welcomed nearly 1 million refugees. To sympathetic observers, Germany had become the moral voice of Europe. To others, it was a reckless agent of moral imperialism, so keen to do good that it put the interests of strangers above its own. The return of a far-right party to parliament in 2017 revived long-standing fears that Germans had never really changed.

In February 2022, Putin invaded Ukraine and the concern was reversed: perhaps Germans had changed too much. For the first time since 1945, a war of conquest had returned to Europe. It called into question the dual strategy with which Germany had built its strength: global exports and military restraint. Many Germans had come to believe that as long as they reformed themselves, Europe would be spared war. The Russian attack on Ukraine exploded that assumption. On February 27, 2022, Chancellor Olaf Scholz announced a *Zeitenwende* pledging 100 billion euros for Germany's depleted army.[1] What kind of support the country should give Ukraine, however, remained deeply controversial. In May, in a letter to the chancellor, a group of well-known intellectuals and artists invoked their country's special "historical responsibility" to oppose calls for heavy weapons.[2] Having worked through their country's bloody past, some felt uniquely qualified to offer moral guidance to others, even to Ukrainians who had been the victims of Nazi Germany. By the end of the summer, Germany had sent ten self-propelled howitzers but mostly money, aid, and helmets.[3] It was only after mounting pressure from its allies that Germany, in January 2023, agreed to send battle tanks as part of a joint NATO effort. The invasion laid bare how the country had become dangerously dependent on authoritarian regimes, buying gas, oil, and coal from Russia and trading with China.

In its classic form, "the German problem" is about how a country of poets and philosophers produced the Holocaust. It has inspired libraries of studies on the German path to modernity, the failure of the Weimar Republic, Adolf Hitler's rise to power, the workings of the Nazi regime, and the road to the Final Solution. But this problem also has a sequel. How did a people emerge from totalitarianism, conquest, and genocide, and where did they go from there? This book follows Germans from the Second World War through the partition of their country and reunification (in 1990) to the present, navigating a series of moral challenges and contradictions. This process was set in motion by the war and its legacies but went much further and would carve its way through family, work, foreign policy, and the environment until effectively all spheres of life were framed in terms of right and wrong. This is a story of conflicts about guilt, shame, and making amends; rearmament and pacifism; tolerance and racism; rights and duties; fairness and inequality; and material comfort and care for the natural world.

My book begins that story not at the end of the war but in the middle, in the winter of 1942–43. Germany's unconditional surrender to the Allies on May 8, 1945, marked the formal end of the war in Europe. In many respects, it was not, however, "Hour Zero," as it came to be known. Hearts and minds were not uniforms that could simply be taken off. People carried their experiences of the war with them into peacetime. Starting the story in 1942 allows us to observe the Nazis' *Volksgemeinschaft*—the people's racial community—at a critical juncture, the year when Germany turned from bullets to gas chambers to exterminate the Jews, and when the tide of war began to turn against the Reich.

The Nazis' power was formidable because they ruled through consent as well as coercion.[4] They enjoyed broad support from the middle class and sections of the working class as well as from landed elites and big business, in addition to terrorizing "enemies" with the Gestapo (Geheime Staatspolizei, or secret police) and the SS (Schutzstaffel), the brutal paramilitary body. By 1939, most "Aryan" Germans belonged to one Nazi organization or another. Order, discipline, and the restoration of national honor and strength were popular ideals, as was the exclusion of racial, political, and social "misfits" from "the people's community." While not everyone cheered the outbreak of another war, almost everyone saw it as necessary and just. Yet SS units began to execute Jews and prisoners of war from the moment of the attack on Poland on September 1, 1939, and the invasion of the Soviet Union (Operation Barbarossa) on June 22, 1941, was launched as a war of extermination. In September of that year, Hitler ordered the deportation of all Jews remaining in the Reich. It was now that the Nazis scaled up the gas chambers they had used to murder people with disabilities inside Germany and created extermination camps in Poland where Jews from across the continent were killed on arrival. Chelmno, the first of these killing centers, started operating in December 1941; Belzec, Sobibor, Treblinka, and Auschwitz, the largest, would follow. Behind the 200,000 Germans who became perpetrators of genocide and other war crimes stood the regular army, which often assisted and colluded in mass murder, and behind them was in turn a population that overwhelmingly supported the regime. For millions of Germans, then, the Third Reich was not an external stranglehold on their otherwise good selves, as many liked to pretend after 1945: they were part of it and had to redefine themselves in order to regain a sense of being good.

It was the reversal of fortunes beginning in 1942 that made some Germans take their first step. In the Reich, cities were subject to ever more relentless Allied bombing from the air, while on the Eastern Front the German war effort ground to a halt, ending with the surrender of the 6th Army at Stalingrad on February 2, 1943. Parents began to ask what their sons were dying for. Stories about Nazi atrocities acquired a new significance as vulnerability prompted fear of accountability. Today we know that area bombing had military objectives. At the time, however, many Germans believed that it was directly related to the persecution of the Jews, sparking radically different thoughts about right and wrong. Were the bombings retribution for the deportations of their Jewish neighbors, a sign of divine wrath, or, rather, proof that Jews were scheming to destroy the German *Volk* and therefore further justification for their elimination? Soul searching was not enough to overthrow the Nazis—that needed Allied tanks and soldiers—but cracks were emerging in the *Volksgemeinschaft*.

The way out of the darkness was long and difficult, winding through a thicket of moral challenges. Defeat, death, and destruction raised momentous problems of crime, punishment, and reparation. Nazi Germany had murdered 6 million Jews; 3 million Soviet prisoners of war; 8 million non-Jewish Soviet, Polish, and Serbian civilians; nearly half a million Sinti and Roma; a quarter of a million disabled people; and many thousands of political opponents, "asocials," homosexuals, and Jehovah's Witnesses.[5] German troops had laid waste to the Balkans and Eastern Europe. Whose fault was this, and who should be made to pay—Hitler's henchmen, Nazi Party members, or the German population as a whole? Guilt vied with shame and denial, and denazification with antisemitism and calls for amnesty. Transitional justice—how a society responds to the legacy of conflict and massive human rights violations—faces the intrinsic difficulty of seeking to balance accountability and punishment with reconciliation. In Germany's case, its democratic West and socialist East were additionally trying to rebuild and reposition themselves on opposite sides in the Cold War. Making amends looked different on either side of the border. Communists had been among the Nazis' first victims, and the German Democratic Republic (East Germany, or the GDR) saw itself as the fruit of their heroic victory. The Federal Republic of Germany (West Germany, or the FRG), meanwhile, defined itself as the lawful successor of the German Reich, which meant taking on its liabilities. That, though, still left wide open the question of who qualified as victims of the Nazis, and which groups and countries were eligible for compensation—German Jews, or all Jews; political prisoners; homosexuals; Sinti and Roma; foreigners; foreign states? Not everyone believed that it was right to offer or accept money as reparation for Nazi crimes.

Today, Germans define themselves through a critical confrontation with their past. In the words of President Joachim Gauck in 2015: "There is no German identity without Auschwitz."[6] Immediately outside the Reichstag and Brandenburg Gate stand large memorials to the murdered Jews and Sinti and Roma. When it comes to reckoning with a murderous past, Germany has been a world leader and is frequently held up as a model from which others can learn. A few countries have taken up the baton—in 2018, Belgium moved toward an apology for its colonial crimes in the Congo. None, however, have turned past sins into a source of civic pride like Germany.[7] By comparison, the reckoning with fascism in Italy and Spain has been slow and patchy—Francisco Franco was only evicted from his mausoleum in 2019—while in Japan war criminals continue to be honored in Tokyo's Yasukuni Shrine. In Poland, anyone claiming that Poles shared responsibility for crimes committed by Nazi Germany is threatened with prison. Americans and Britons are bitterly divided over how to remember and make amends for the crimes of slavery and empire.

Coming to terms with Nazi crimes played an integral part in the moral transformation of Germany, but it happened halfway through our story and was only one source of change. It's true that already in the 1950s youth groups were taking trips to the Belsen concentration camp, the first camp survivors started speaking to students in schools, and the Ulm trial against the killing squads (Einsatzgruppen) in 1958 raised public awareness. Contemporaries began to call for *Vergangenheitsbewältigung*, one of those capacious compound words favored by the German language. It can mean both coping with the past and overcoming it (something that is, strictly speaking, impossible, since what has happened cannot be undone). The philosopher Theodor Adorno, in 1963, proposed *Aufarbeitung* ("working through" the past), and many writers since have followed him.[8] At that time, though, the past that most Germans cared to remember was *their* "good war" and *their* suffering, not what they did to others. Critical remembrance only gathered momentum in the 1970s and 1980s, when the Holocaust gradually moved to the center of public memory.

There is a popular view that it must have been their eventual reckoning with the past that made Germans moral crusaders in the present. After guilt had been initially repressed, it is said, a new generation in 1960s West Germany began to call their parents to account for their sins. The more they learned about their crimes, the more they realized how lightly their country had gotten off. Doing good made up for having been spared the punishment they deserved and demonstrated to themselves and the world that one was reformed. A nation of sinners turned into saints. From recycling glass and paper to helping the global poor, ultimately everything they do, in this view, springs from this bad conscience.[9]

The moral remaking of Germany is a much richer and more surprising story than this, and it is my ambition to unpack and explain its complexity, instead of reducing all motivation to guilt. That memory of the Holocaust is central to German identity does not mean that everything Germans do and care for is because of that remembrance. Volunteering, caregiving, and environmentalism, to name just a few examples, have their own histories. Family and work, getting and spending, wealth and welfare, industry and nature—all these spheres were charged with ideas about right and wrong, worthy and unworthy behavior, what counts as fair, and what people owe each other and the world. Together, these produced a thick morality. This process received a boost from "working through" the past from the 1960s, but it was more than that and already underway. It continues to the present.

Between 1949 and 1990, Germany was two countries, each with its own ideas about the type of society it wanted to build but each seeking to change its citizens' outlook and behavior. In East Germany, lessons in socialist morality pervaded everyday life—children's first day in school, the workplace with its "brigades" (socialist teams), "tenant communities" (*Hausgemeinschaften*) at home, "pensioner brigades" in old age. How close did they come to molding a new person who did "good deeds for socialism," as the fourth of the socialist Ten Commandments required? West Germany was born a liberal democracy with a parliament and free elections, but it needed to foster tolerance, debate, and civic engagement, the very opposite of what had been cultivated under the Nazis. Both countries faced historic challenges of social justice, having to integrate, in addition to the few surviving Jews who stayed, millions of citizens whose lives lay in ruins: disabled veterans; war widows; bombed-out residents; returning and missing POWs;

and the 12 million ethnic Germans who had been driven out of East Prussia, Silesia, the Sudetenland, and other territories. Their victim talk was often self-righteous and can look hypocritical, since most of them had cheered Hitler and supported the war that led to their plight. Still, it would be a mistake to reduce their stories of suffering to an attempt to cover up their guilt. They were competing for recognition and assistance, making claims about fairness, entitlement, and solidarity. What individuals could expect from the state was the subject of tense debate, with different answers in East and West Germany. In reverse, there was the question of what the state could expect from its citizens, and rearmament in a nuclear age made it an existential one. How to reconcile a soldier's duty and sacrifice (some added honor) with a citizen's conscience divided barracks as well as the nation.

In their constitutions, both states promised equality. For women, minorities, and people with disabilities, however, reality often fell short, and their struggles shed an interesting light on what was considered "normal" on each side of the border. So does the treatment of strangers. In 1989, West Germany, a country with 63 million citizens, was home to 5 million foreigners, mainly so-called guest workers from southern Europe who had arrived in the 1950s and 1960s and decided to stay. The GDR, with 16 million citizens, had a smaller contingent, 160,000 foreigners, mostly students and contract laborers from Vietnam, Poland, and Mozambique. Unlike earlier groups arriving from Silesia or the Sudetenland, these strangers were excluded from German citizenship, which had been defined by blood since 1913. The guests played their part in the remaking of Germany, and their experiences let us see the hosts' difficulties with race, religion, and living with difference. Migration and asylum have been especially explosive topics because they go to the heart of what it meant (and means) to be German.

For decades, the partition of Germany looked like the verdict of history. The unexpected fall of the Berlin Wall in 1989 opened a new chapter in the country's search for itself. Reunification rearranged biographies as well as borders. East Germans saw their world turned upside down. What had been right or wrong, good or bad, fair or unfair, suddenly was no longer so. Millions of Germans saw the country in which they had grown up, worked, and raised their families condemned as an unlawful, inhumane dictatorship. In the autumn of 1989, East Germans had initially challenged the regime with the chant "We are the people." It was soon replaced by "We are *one* people." More than three decades later, how close to unity is the new Germany?

For the millions of Turkish, Greek, and other migrants who had made Cologne or West Berlin their home, as for Vietnamese workers in Rostock or East Berlin, the chorus "We are one people" had a more ominous ring. Citizenship was opened up in 2000 but national identity far less so, in part because the collective memory of Nazi crimes meant that it was ethnic Germans who were remembering the sins of *their* fathers. Cultural openness and recognition of people with "a migration background," as they officially came to be called, had to compete with violence, racism, and antisemitism, which had never disappeared in either part of the country.

Reunification was just as disorienting internationally. In Europe, Germany's lectures about good housekeeping to supposedly lazy and profligate Mediterranean people during the debt crises (2010–15) almost broke up the European Union, to whose building West Germany had contributed so diligently over the previous half century. The end of the Cold War widened the gulf between Germany's economic ambition and its strategic-military reticence. While German companies pushed into Eastern Europe and China, German governments stayed on the sidelines of international affairs. Now and then a politician would say the country needed to fight for democracy, but the army was shrunk and foreign engagement rare and limited. Germans prided themselves on having learned from history, but it was becoming less clear what that lesson was. Did saying "Never again" to a Hitler-like ruler and concentration camps mean an automatic veto on sending German soldiers into battle? Or did it mean the opposite—sending them to prevent a repeat of conquest and genocide? Germans were increasingly divided on that question, as the Bosnian and Kosovo wars in the 1990s would demonstrate.

It is not just the grand themes of war and peace and the Nazi past that in Germany are discussed in moral terms. The final part of this book explores three crucial areas where moral ideals are acted out in daily life, with different results: money, welfare, and the environment. Each of these comes with national ideals and stereotypes about German virtues that need to be tested and evaluated.

Thrift is often portrayed as a defining German character trait, but after savings had been wiped out first in the hyperinflation of 1923 and then in the currency conversion of 1948, it hardly came naturally, and needed sustained preaching and incentives from government, banks, and schools to make it look attractive. What people actually did with their money and whether they were really more responsible than their neighbors are issues that require investigation. The rise in inequality since the 1980s was nothing peculiar to Germany: what made it so troubling was that it clashed with deeply held notions of merit and fairness. The *Wirtschaftswunder* ("economic miracle") of the postwar decades had convinced people to see their success as proof of a national ethos of *Leistung* ("performance"), where hard work paid off. What happened to those ideals when poor people with a job had to turn to benefits while wealthy heirs were getting richer and richer?

What people owe each other goes to the core of a society's moral self-understanding and is manifested in who cares for whom. In Germany, welfare has taken a distinctive form, that of *subsidiarity*, in which the duty of care proceeds outward from the family to the local community and churches before calling on the state. Germany is a *Sozialstaat* ("social state"), where the constitution requires the state to look after its citizens, but one that has been leaning heavily on the family, with profound consequences for gender inequality, since women continue to do most of the caregiving.

Germans, finally, see themselves as devoted to nature and with the *Energiewende* ("energy transition") have tried to become the vanguard of renewable power. At the same time, they love their cars, comfort, and sausages, and burn coal and emit more carbon dioxide than the average European. Today, it is that contradiction, not German soldiers, that poses the greatest danger to the world.

Putting morality at the center of Germany's transformation over the past eighty years raises challenges of definition, method, and sources. Morality is traditionally the preserve of philosophy and theology. Its core dilemma has been with us since the ancients: How do we know what is good and right? Moral philosophers try to understand why humans project ideas of right and wrong onto the world and how they should live with each other in it. For one school of thought, morality is hardwired into human nature: we intrinsically want to do good. People act on "moral sentiments," as the Enlightenment thinkers David Hume and Adam Smith put it. In recent years, brain scans have detected neural discharges when people give to charity, and anthropologists have traced altruism and empathy to an early stage in evolution when cooperation boosted chances of survival. For another school, morality is grounded in reason and requires dispassionate analysis. Moral philosophers differ fundamentally about what makes an action right or wrong. One group, following Aristotle, sees the goal of life in human flourishing and focuses on virtue. For another (so-called consequentialists), what matters is whether an action promotes good outcomes. For a third group (deontologists, from the Greek word for "duty"), what is decisive is the moral merit of the act itself. Some acts, they point out, are required (such as a duty of care) while others are forbidden (killing or cheating) regardless of their consequences.[10]

How far apart these schools are is a matter of debate. The philosopher Derek Parfit pictured their followers "climbing the same mountain on different sides."[11] Whether philosophers invoke concrete examples or thought experiments, however, they are in search of universal truths. The historian, by contrast, is interested in the changing moral landscape over time, trying to understand the rise and fall of moral concerns and what people in the past considered right and wrong, however flawed by today's standards or those of philosophy. Altruism, for example, may well have deep roots in our biology, but evidently its scope has changed enormously over the course of history. The historian is not hiking up "the same mountain" but navigating a river, deep in some places and shallow in others, with currents here and eddies there, always in flux and never the same. Historians should not try to compete with moral philosophers in offering normative accounts of the world.[12] What they can do is illuminate how people in real life have steered between the call for duty (treat human beings as an end, never only as a means, in the words of Immanuel Kant) and utility (the greatest good for the greatest number, Jeremy Bentham's maxim), and show how their moral compass has changed and sometimes failed altogether.

When Germans confront thorny decisions, they tend to turn for help not to philosophers but to their most famous sociologist, Max Weber, who, a century ago, contrasted an "ethic of conviction" (*Gesinnungsethik*) with an "ethic of responsibility" (*Verantwortungsethik*). The concepts have been subject to many uses (and abuses). Time and again, ruling politicians have invoked the ethic of responsibility. Chancellor Helmut Schmidt used it to justify the stationing of American nuclear warheads on German soil in 1979. More recently, in 2022, the premier of Saxony (in the former GDR) criticized sanctions against Russia as an abdication of responsibility for the national interest, putting jobs and social peace at risk.[13] In such views, a messy world of conflicting interests calls for realpolitik, not conviction. This is not, however, what Weber said. He did not draw a sharp divide between value and instrumental rationality. The true politician was not a cold, calculating pragmatist but someone acting out of devotion to "a cause," who, Weber hoped, would reach a point where, feeling his responsibility with "heart and soul," he would say, "Here I stand, I can do no other." Those were the famous words of Martin Luther, the Protestant reformer, at the Diet of Worms in 1521, when he refused to recant. What could be more principled than that?[14]

There are three moral concerns that will recur throughout this book: conscience, compassion, and complicity. Conscience is a mighty inner regulator of our conduct, with a long history.[15] It is our conscience that makes us evaluate our actions and our self against what we believe to be right and wrong, and failing to abide by them creates a bad conscience. Seneca, in ancient Rome, believed that people carried God in themselves. In the High Middle Ages, monks likened conscience to the face of the soul and a mirror that looked back on the individual. Luther replaced the external authority of the priesthood with the divine inner voice that established a direct line between sinner and God. Protestant elites turned conscience into a form of soft power, using it to discipline their subjects to adhere to social norms. It was the Enlightenment that gave conscience a more autonomous role. For Kant, it was both an "inner court" and the sense that its judgments must be followed.

It would be a mistake to assume that conscience intrinsically does "good" work. Its history is a tug of war between heeding norms and transgressing them in pursuit of an ideal that is felt to command a higher loyalty. Such ideals can be illiberal as well as liberal. In Germany, duty to the state came to occupy an especially large place. Conscience was weaponized, first when German soldiers took their oath to God, then, after 1934, in a "holy oath" (*diesen heiligen Eid*) to carry out the Führer's commands. With the supreme destiny of the German *Volk* and Hitler its savior, the Nazis created their own good conscience that could brush aside older moral concerns. In the famous words attributed to Reichsmarschall Hermann Göring: "My conscience is Adolf Hitler." As we shall see, some soldiers constantly interrogated their conscience, but in ways and with results that are alien and shocking to us. After the war, conscience would turn into a major battleground of what it meant to be a good German, and between the competing pull of duty to the state and resistance to it. In the 1950s, this pitted millions of veterans who felt they had followed their conscience by honoring their oath against the group of senior officers whose failed assassination attempt of Hitler on July 20, 1944, was now commemorated as the "uprising of the conscience" for which they had paid with their lives. In mass demonstrations against rearmament, protestors carried placards with Luther's famous words. The growing number of conscientious objectors led to heated debates about how to express and test the "inner voice."

If conscience listens inward, compassion looks outward. For Arthur Schopenhauer, in 1840, it was the basis of morality. What creates this fellow-feeling? For Aristotle, in ancient Greece, compassion derived from an awareness that we, too, might someday experience undeserved pain. Jean-Jacques Rousseau, in the eighteenth century, urged tutors to cultivate *pitié* among their pupils so that through an awareness of other people's suffering they would discover their own moral worth. The philosopher Martha Nussbaum goes one step further. Compassion, she says, requires that someone see another person's ill as harming their own flourishing: they must make themselves "vulnerable in the person of another."[16] Ideally, then, compassion involves three steps: an ability to see and feel another person's pain; the thought that this could happen to us; and a sense that the suffering of others diminishes our own well-being, even if we ourselves are spared.

Where Germans were at different moments in this process will be a recurrent concern of this book. Nussbaum has likened compassion to "the eye through which people see the good and ill of others." Learning once more to see with the eye of compassion, after the Nazi years, was an enormous challenge and faced coldheartedness (and worse) toward surviving Jews, forced laborers and displaced persons (DPs), and German refugees, too. In the 1960s, peace and development groups began to teach people to put themselves in the shoes of the less fortunate of the world—the poor in Latin American slums, children starving in Africa, and disabled people in Israel. Sympathy for marginalized groups at home was another matter. Compassion has had to compete with inwardness and solipsism.

While philosophers have had plenty to say about conscience and compassion, complicity has bedeviled the greatest of them. Kant and his followers have focused on the critical reason of individuals and their accountability for harm over which they had some control—either you are accountable, or you are not. In complicity in collective harms, however, individual accountability is dispersed. Utilitarians who follow Bentham concern themselves with the good or bad consequences of individual actions. How do you assess the moral significance of a collective wrong where the contribution of an individual is marginal because several million other people are involved? In recent years, the philosopher Christopher Kutz has proposed a way of linking individual accountability to collective action. Personal motive, in this view, is not decisive. It is enough that a person is intentionally participating in a collective project. Complicity takes seriously that individuals are and can be held accountable for collective harms.[17] The war and genocide left Germans with a huge problem of complicity, and how they understood and responded to it tells us a lot about their moral reorientation and its limits. Complicity, though, is not exclusive to the Holocaust, although this is where the focus of attention has rightly been. Germans have participated in many other collective projects since, notably reunification, a consumer society, and the energy transition.

Writing a history of the Germans through a moral lens raises a basic question: Why do modern societies have morality at all? The most influential answers have come from Marxists and early sociologists. For Marxists, moral ideas express the material basis of development and the interests of the class in command during that particular stage. With its social norms, the bourgeoisie disguised how, far from advancing universal happiness, it was enriching itself at the expense of the many. Inside the factory there was brutal exploitation; outside, pity for children and animals.[18] The ruling class, Leon Trotsky wrote in 1938, "could not have endured for a week through force alone"; it needed "the cement of morality."[19] The sociologist Émile Durkheim focused more on how dos and don'ts enable complex societies to function without falling to pieces.[20] For a history of morality, these two perspectives raise as many problems as they solve. Of course, norms facilitate social order and it matters whether those who propagate them are powerful or not. The weakness these accounts share is that they tend to picture morality as simple, stable, and top-down, which makes it difficult to explain national differences, change over time, and conflict at any given point. Morality is not the monopoly of the powerful. It can be the weapon of the powerless, a point made by Friedrich Nietzsche in *On the Genealogy of Morals* (1887). Our ideas about good versus evil, he said, were a historical invention, and came from subjugated groups who elevated altruism to an ideal with which to challenge the nobility—he called it the "slave revolt in morality." He saw it as the origin of a sense of guilt that stood in the way of humans reaching their greatness. We do not have to follow Nietzsche's plea to throw off morality to appreciate that good and evil and right and wrong can be the battleground of rival groups, ideals, and practices.

Morality is a tool of social discipline and order, but it can also be empowering. Morality orients us in our search for meaning and identity, providing us with a map of where we should be going and where we came from. Durkheim, in fact, was not the functionalist he is often made out to be, and in his later lectures he held up society as a "moral power" that inspired its members to aim higher.[21] As the authority of church and monarchy was coming under pressure in the seventeenth and eighteenth centuries, morality was gaining in significance for the individual self. Cultivating sympathy, learning to reason, consulting one's conscience, and developing a duty to others in this life began to take the place of striving for rewards in the next. Literature, the stage, and, indeed, history were agents of moral improvement—as in Friedrich Schiller's famous words that preface this book.[22] People found their selves through wanting to do good. While moral prescriptions and policing limit the sphere of action, moral values therefore also open up new vistas. Values are social, but individuals adapt and fit them together in ways that help them make sense of their own experiences. Put simply, people do not just follow the morality of their society; they create it, too.

This history of the remaking of Germany would have been impossible without the existing rich scholarship, but it breaks with the success story with which we have become familiar. The appeal of that story is not hard to understand. From the depths of Nazi hell, the only way was up. The Federal Republic has proved enormously robust and by 2023 had outlived the German Empire, Weimar, and the Third Reich put together. West German historians have favored grand narratives of Westernization and liberalization.[23] While each has its own merits, they share a teleological bent of progressing toward a better present. The problem with the story of the "road to the West" is that the West is not a single destination—is it the land of liberty or empire, welfare or riches, Barack Obama or Donald Trump? West Germany became more tolerant in the 1960s and 1970s toward single mothers and people with diverse sexual identities. Yet liberal trends have had countertrends, including racism, terrorism (right and left), and limits on abortion. Violence has mutated, not disappeared, from daily life. The economic miracle looks less miraculous from the perspective of the environment. Teleological hindsight tends to favor winners over losers and can blind us to how contemporaries experienced their own times. Attention to moral conflicts restores the balance and creates room for unresolved conflicts and contradictions that continue to this day. Conservative ethos, family virtues, provincial pride, soldiers, and supporters of nuclear power are at least as much part of contemporary Germany as progressive metropolitan circles, conscientious objectors, and anti-nuclear protestors. It is important to remember that in fifty-two out of its seventy-four years, the Federal Republic had a Christian Democrat as chancellor.

Above all, these narratives hit a roadblock with East Germany. The GDR can risk ending up as little more than an inconvenient detour that, with reunification, rejoins the main road to the liberal democratic West. Understandably, East Germans take offense when their own past is reduced to the historiographical version of a stuttering Trabant next to a West German Mercedes. One way around this is to stick to separate histories for what, after all, were countries separated at birth and, from 1961, by the Berlin Wall. The opposite strategy is to compare throughout.[24] This can be especially fruitful when looking at the two Germanies as variants of modern society undergoing dynamic change—both with an industrial core, similar traditions of welfare, and (from the 1970s also in the GDR) rising consumption and a parallel erosion of class. The difficulty is that, in the last instance, the East was always a dictatorship and the West a democracy—never perfect, but a democracy nonetheless.

My solution to this problem has been pragmatic. Where it is instructive, developments in East and West are compared directly, including with regard to denazification, the treatment of strangers, care for children and the elderly, and the approach to energy and the environment. Their rival systems and people's place within them, however, are the subject of two separate chapters. Democracy and socialism created radically different moral orbits for their citizens, with their own pressures and temptations. The GDR should not be reduced to a Stasi-land, but nor should it be normalized because many people felt that they led perfectly ordinary lives. The creation of a socialist normality was integral to dictatorial rule.

This book does not, of course, claim that morality is unique to Germans, let alone that it makes them somehow better. Several of their causes and convictions can be found in other societies, and where possible I have tried to place German developments in their international context. It is not a provincial story. German pacifists looked to Martin Luther King Jr. and Mahatma Gandhi for inspiration. Danes care at least as much about the environment. Global poverty, human rights, and animal rights are international causes. What is distinctive is not the particular concerns, it is the German habit of turning all social, economic, and political problems into moral ones. War and peace, personal lifestyle, whether someone works or not, saves money or is in debt, dutifully recycles, looks after their elderly parents: all of these are seen to reflect moral qualities. This does not mean they always avoid double standards, contradictions, and failures, not least when it comes to equality and the environment. It does mean, though, that life and politics are conducted in a moral tone. How that register established itself is one theme of this book.

Telling this story over the course of eighty years breaks also with a popular fixation on the 1960s as a watershed. In the immediate wake of the protests of 1968, the conservative thinker Arnold Gehlen lambasted students and intellectuals for spreading a new "hypermorality" with their feminist and humanitarian talk.[25] What this ignored was how family, war and peace, and many other subjects had already been supercharged, just not necessarily with radical energy. Political scientists meanwhile found in attitudinal surveys signs of a "silent revolution" from "material values" (food on the table, a job, law and order) to "post-material values" (freedom, environmentalism, and self-fulfillment) sweeping across the West as younger generations came under the spell of affluence, welfare, and higher education.[26] There are many problems with this thesis, but one is that it assumes a simplistic hierarchy of needs, where people only begin to care for higher things once they have filled their stomachs. For our purposes, this simultaneously misses how many Germans (East and West) cared for nature, freedom, and other "post-material" values before the 1960s, and how they have continued to attach huge importance to material security, work, and performance since.

This history, then, shares some ground with studies of values, emotions, and memory, but it also goes beyond them.[27] Emotions left to themselves can distort moral judgment, as Adam Smith and many others have recognized, and to guide what we do, reason, conscience, and duty are needed. In this book, I have tried to apply the insight of social theorists that our identities are embedded in action to the moral identity of the Germans, following their changing sense of right and wrong through what they actually did.[28] Volunteering, self-help, caregiving, saving, spending, and many other practices have played a vital role in shaping that identity. To capture morality in action we need to move beyond the words of priests and philosophers into the thick of life and follow families, charities and their clients, informers and their victims, soldiers and conscientious objectors, and many others. Since morality is dispersed and in motion, capturing it raises formidable challenges of research. Morality does not have its own separate sphere but is acted out in the family, at the workplace, and in public life. It consequently does not have an archive of its own. Tracing conscience, compassion, and complicity requires investigating social, political, and economic subjects and sources, and from the top of society to the bottom and back. I have especially seized on moments of fracture where views about right and wrong came under pressure and were contested, when people were reflecting on their actions or being made to do so.

Recent sociologists and anthropologists have called for new studies of morality better to understand how societies distinguish between right and wrong and live that difference.[29] What history can do is trace the evolution of a moral universe and show how seemingly natural norms and practices have emerged as the result of historical forces. Anthropologists, to give one example, have shown how humanitarian policies today increasingly draw on compassion rather than justice, asking refugees and the poor to display their suffering to prove they are worthy of help.[30] This "compassionate moment" might have certain neoliberal elements, but it also has a longer past reaching back to the campaigns against slavery in the late eighteenth century. After the Second World War, German refugees used stories of their expulsion and rape to document their moral worth to foreign donors. Duty, fairness, tolerance, sacrifice, and solidarity similarly have histories. The scholarly literature continues to be fragmented, with rich studies on the rise of humanitarianism in the eighteenth century at one end, and works about the care for strangers, animals, and the planet in more recent decades at the other, with case studies on charity, sex, and drugs scattered in between. Instead of splitting them up, this book tries to look at the interplay of moral concerns in the life of one society over the course of eighty years. I hope it will inspire others to follow and go further.

The sources for this book are, consequently, rich and diverse, and extend from state papers to the records of churches and charities, private letters and diaries, petitions and boycotts, court cases and debt statistics, children's essays, plays and movies. We will hear from a great number of voices: German soldiers and German Jews trying to make sense of what had happened to them and their country; expellees torn between revenge and settling down; young people tending war graves in France and trying to make amends in Israel; shopkeepers grumbling about energy shortages in the GDR; women fighting for the right to abortion and those fearing a new euthanasia of the disabled; foreign workers struggling to build new lives; environmental activists and coal miners; and many others. Moral debates had conservative and reactionary as well as liberal and progressive voices, and I have tried hard to listen to all of them, and to understand why they thought about right and wrong as they did, especially those whose judgments now look alien or outright dangerous. We need to hear all sides to make sense of the remaking of Germany. It is this great multiplicity of voices, and the tensions and contradictions between ideals and actions, that made and make the Germans who they are.

PART ONE

THE GERMAN WAR AND ITS LEGACIES

1942-60s

1

Parzival at War: The Troubled Conscience

It was not meant to be like this.

On June 22, 1941, the German army had invaded the Soviet Union. By November, German troops stood roughly twenty-two miles from the Kremlin. In Erfurt, in the center of Hitler's Reich, the schoolboy Reinhold Reichardt, one month shy of his eighteenth birthday, could wait no longer—he rushed to register as a cadet officer. On February 1, 1943, he was finally called up to join the reserve battalion of an infantry regiment. The evening he arrived at the barracks in Frankfurt (Oder), the last messages of the 6th Army, which had been lost at Stalingrad and included many men from his new regiment, were broadcast on the radio. In the following days, officers tried their best to boost morale among the new recruits by repeating the Nazi line about the "necessary sacrifice of the Stalingrad fighters," but it sounded rather labored and hollow, Reichardt confided to his diary, and could not hide the "mourning, anger, and rage about the senseless sacrifice of comrades."[1]

In July 1943, death came to his own family. Rainer, his older brother, was killed by a grenade north of Belgorod, Russia, in the battle of Kursk, the largest tank battle in the history of the world, which handed the strategic advantage to the Red Army. "He is dead—he is dead—he is dead!" Reinhold wrote. Yet "I feel, I know; I will find him again, he will come to me... Perhaps when I myself will be in the midst of the storm... For us... there is no death, no infinite nothingness. He fell for our shared love of the fatherland... But no, he did not 'fall,' did not sink into the underworld, he took wing and ascended to the sun throne—he came home!"[2]

As a boy, Reichardt had sometimes dreamed of a romantic life in a fishing hut on the North Sea or, perhaps, in an isolated farmhouse in southwest Africa. Now, he knew that "my goal in life cannot be to escape to the idyll of an island founded solely on my own inner peace." He needed to confront the "real forces of this world." He was destined to be a warrior. In writing his diary, he took his inspiration from Friedrich Hölderlin, the great German romantic poet, and his epistolary novel *Hyperion* (1797), about a hero who fights to free Greece from Turkish rule. Reichardt chose to address the letters in his diary to Patroclus, Achilles' close companion, who died fighting in the Trojan War. Reichardt explained that he had joined the struggle for "the freedom and spiritual purity of the fatherland" for his own happiness and peace of mind. Not to do so, he wrote, would "dishonor my spiritual fatherland." He had one great hope: "to take on the quest of battle, in the fellowship of Parsifal and his round table."[3]

In January 1944, he joined an infantry unit in Sarajevo,[4] arriving in one of the more brutal theaters of the Second World War. In the hills and mountains of Bosnia, the German army was fighting alongside the SS and Croatian fascist Ustashe against Josip Tito's partisans. Barely two weeks into his posting, Reichardt was in despair and unburdened himself to his diary, for once addressing his mother, not Patroclus. "*Liebes Muttchen*, I know it is not right that I write to you about these things, but I need to get it off my chest. For my comrades it is not an issue!" All around him, there were "burning, destroyed villages, dead animals, mutilated horses, and people who have been killed... Our fatherland can thank God that, notwithstanding the bombing terror, it has so far been spared such a gruesome war." The German soldiers fought hard, he said, but they also robbed and mistreated the locals. They stole their knives and clothes with the "flimsy remark that 'we are allowed to do that, we are bombed out at home.'" Their officers did nothing to stop such excesses. "The worst is when prisoners or 'supposed partisans' were captured" and because it might be "tiresome" to transport them back to base, they were executed with a shot in the neck, "with a smile, as if it was great fun." The soldiers would divide up the meager spoils.

A few days earlier, Reichardt had inquired about what had happened to the local nurse with a Red Cross armband. An eyewitness told him how a Sergeant Walz had stopped her on her horse, took her pistol, and shot her with it. "Such a beautiful woman!" he had shouted to the other soldiers, before pulling down her underwear, spreading her legs, and saying, "Come on, she's still warm!" Reichardt was "disgusted." He asked whether anyone had intervened: "No, no one," he was told.[5]

"The German soldier ought to be far too proud for such deeds," his diary continued, "since he prides himself everywhere for being superior to those of other nations." He was meant to be an "unsullied soldier for a holy cause." Sadly, he wrote, army life had taught him that until he had his own command he would have to look the other way when such things happened. These events could only have been meant to spur him on to greater tasks and duties, to reach the high ideal of soldiery that had made him volunteer in the first place. "It must be my consolation and pride to know that I am needed by the fatherland to reach this goal."[6]

A few days later, on January 17, 1944, he and his squad were in the mountains near Jajce when their truck came under fire. Reichardt quickly ordered his men to get out of the van, regroup in the bushes, and advance to the village where the shots were coming from. He spotted one of the partisans. "For the first time in my life, I consciously take aim at a shooting enemy." Reichardt's shot hit its target. The man was thrown in the air, then collapsed in the snow. Reichardt ran up to him. "There he is lying, bleeding heavily from the right hip. What should I do?" His orders were to "take no prisoners." "Could I simply leave the badly wounded man lying in the snow bleeding to death?" Suddenly, Sergeant Walz arrived on the scene, accompanied by his driver. "Now we've got one of these pigs!" the sergeant shouted, kicking the whimpering man in his wounded hip. He ordered the partisan to identify himself, took his papers, crumpled them up, and laughed. Meanwhile, the driver had picked up the partisan's rifle, opened its chamber, and found that there were four bullets left. "He aimed at the right shoulder of the wounded man and fired, then at the left, then at the right knee, then at the left. I stared at him in horror and called out: 'Now, please, a shot in the heart or the head!' " The sergeant yelled at him: "Are you crazy, we have to save ammunition!" and then walked away with his driver. Reichardt was left alone with the dying man. "I lifted my pistol, closed my eyes, and gave him the coup de grâce."[7]

Atrocities happen in almost any war. What set Nazi Germany apart was that war crimes were an integral feature of German warfare, not an aberration. The 1929 Geneva Convention, which Germany ratified in February 1934, a year after Hitler came to power, prohibited reprisals and required the humane treatment of prisoners. The Führer and his generals brushed these rules aside in their war of extermination. The execution of prisoners and civilians started the moment Germany attacked Poland in September 1939. Reichardt knew at least a little about the disregard for civilian life there. In April 1943 he was briefly in an army hospital in Frankfurt (Oder) for diphtheria and heard a grim story from an older soldier who had served in occupied Poland. Signs had been put up at railroad tracks, bridges, and roads warning people not to cross them. Instead of shouting at or shooing away little boys and girls who crossed them because they could not read, the guard on duty would gun them down, explaining with a laugh, "He had to execute his orders conscientiously, and a few Polish brats more or less did not matter."[8] The SS and police shootings of Polish intelligentsia and Jews were on a far larger scale. A few senior officers, such as Colonel General Johannes Blaskowitz, protested to Hitler about that in November 1939, although Blaskowitz was more concerned about the disorderly nature of the killings and the effect on the morale of his troops than about the victims. The Führer exploded: his generals had to let go of their "Salvation Army" mentality.[9]

In May and June 1941, with the launch of Operation Barbarossa, they did so. With the Barbarossa Decree, the Guidelines for the Conduct of Troops, and the Commissar Order, the German army's High Command laid down the ground rules for a new kind of war. The German people were fighting against their "mortal enemy," Bolshevism, the guidelines explained. "This battle demands ruthless and energetic measures against Bolshevik agitators, irregulars, saboteurs, and Jews, and the total eradication of any active or passive resistance."[10] Red Army commissars were to be separated from other prisoners and shot. If German troops were attacked by partisans, hostages were to be taken in reprisal and shot. While the execution of partisans and hostages was not illegal as such in international law, they were meant to be put on trial first. By contrast, Wehrmacht soldiers were now given free rein to kill civilians and suspected partisans. They would go unpunished, they were assured, even if they had committed a military crime. Revenge, reprisal, and retaliation escalated. The number of hostages and noncombatants killed by the Germans skyrocketed, out of all proportion to the number of German soldiers shot. And this included in Jajce, where Reichardt was. Just over a year earlier, German infantry had fought hard to recapture the town. On October 30, 1942, for example, German soldiers killed 257 "partisans," including women, in retaliation for the loss of one German soldier. Here, as elsewhere, the number of dead bodies outweighed the number of rifles by multiples, indicating that many of those killed were probably noncombatants.[11]

Reinhold Reichardt is not presented here as a "typical" soldier or a "typical" German. Morality was never monolithic. There were competing views of right and wrong, even in the darkest hours of Nazi Germany. Nor, however, are moralities random. There were distinctly German patterns, and Reichardt shared several of them. A Protestant child of the educated middle classes, the *Bildungsbürgertum*, he joined the Hitler Youth like almost all German boys his age. He and his friends not only quoted Hölderlin and Goethe to each other but had also absorbed the militarist memoirs so popular in the interwar years. His diary gives us a window on a moral universe shared by many recruits. He clearly had some freedom to choose one course of action over another—what we call "individual agency"; he might, for example, have joined in the execution of civilians, or he might have protested far more than beyond the pages in his diary; he did neither. In reflecting on his actions and those of others, however, he did not rely on purely personal convictions, either. His diary lets us see the social ideals and ways of looking at oneself and the world that circulated widely in Germany at the time: duty to the fatherland and the nobility of sacrifice; faith in God's plan and the workings of a world spirit; being hard and soulful in equal measure; cultivating the inwardness that made German *Kultur* superior to materialist civilization.

Reichardt is interesting not because he was the prototype of a perpetrator, but rather because he stands for a group that is just as troubling: young soldiers who flocked to fight for the fatherland, who were not Nazi fanatics, and whose consciences were troubled by certain atrocities, but who nonetheless fought until the bitter end. Reichardt's extensive and explicit diary gives us a chance to reconstruct not only what he did, but also *how* he thought about his actions, *what* he thought he should (and could not) do, and *why* he connected his actions to certain consequences but not to others. In short, it helps explain how a German soldier managed to separate his own heroic war from the atrocities around him.

Reichardt's view of the world blended humanism, romanticism, nationalism, and Christianity with a dash of pantheism. It provided him with a clear sense of his own position in a long, even cosmic, chain of events that connected individual and nation, past, present, and future, this world and the next. This had fundamental consequences for how he looked at the cause and effect of actions, and how he understood his own place in the war.

In his diary, war featured as a series of local skirmishes with identifiable soldiers and victims. But then there was also "the war," a fury of cosmic force that was sweeping across the world with its own supernatural logic. War was "the ruler of the world which, with inevitable violence, tightens its noose around the neck of people and nations."[12] Like most Germans at the time, Reichardt saw the Second World War as a continuation of a thirty-year-long drama that had begun in 1914. It was a "just war" to wipe away the "ignominious" peace of Versailles. The mantra of a "just war" ran so deep that he never felt the need to specify its aims other than with generic references to the survival of the fatherland. Ultimately, these historical events were the effects of a bigger metaphysical storm. His friend Horst, who joined the air force, expressed this well in a letter to him in April 1944. The world had a "soul" and a "will" that ruled over events. War and peace were like the tide, following an evolutionary course that they, perhaps, could not yet understand. Notwithstanding any evidence to the contrary, their instinctive sense of the workings of the world spirit had to become a matter of faith: they were fighters for the "holy cause." Horst closed his letter with the communion song of the knights of the Grail from Richard Wagner's *Parsifal*: "Take of the bread... true until death, steadfast in effort, to work the Savior's will!"[13]

The soldier, in this view, was a link in the chain between this world and the great beyond—a servant of a cosmic logic and simultaneously a medium between the dead and the living. Reichardt's lament for his dead brother echoed the spirit of one of the best sellers of the interwar years, Walter Flex's *The Wanderer Between the Two Worlds* (1916). The book idealized the soldier at the front as a new type of man whose proximity to death made him equally close to heaven and earth. Through their sacrifice, the dead lived on in the young. "Don't turn us into ghosts, give us our right to our homeland [*Heimrecht*]," Reichardt quoted Flex in his diary: "Your deeds and your dead keep you young and mature."[14]

On his first visit home from training in May 1943, Reichardt noted how quickly the army had made "a new man" of him. He felt like "Gulliver in a world of dwarves." For the rest of the war, he tried to hold on to this sense of power and destiny. Being a soldier was, in the first place, about cultivating and defending that new higher self. He framed his diary with his personal motto: "Great is the time of peace... even greater are the demands on you made by war: be hard toward yourself, and always with a courageous heart!" The soldier, he wrote, stripped himself of material possessions and the "numbing desire" for peace, order, and a comfortable, petty life.[15] Naked, he stepped forward to God and put on His armor to do battle for the triumph of His design. That echoed what was preached from pulpits across Germany. After his confirmation, Reichardt had continued to attend a Protestant youth group at St. Thomas in Erfurt, one of the united Protestant Churches; his local pastor there, Johannes Mebus, was a member of the Confessing Church wing and had been arrested in 1936 by the Gestapo for challenging the Nazi German Christians in his previous congregation.[16] In June 1943, Reichardt summarized one such sermon he had heard. The war was not about money, power, or glory, nor about "nations bleeding each other to death" but rather a "struggle for the purity of the human soul." Through sacrifice, the warrior purged his soul and "finds his way back to God as his humble Son."[17] The soldier was Christ, and death on the battlefield, resurrection.

Reichardt was not coldhearted, as we have seen. Still, his sympathy was truncated. If there was horror at the growing brutality, there was limited compassion for its victims. He did not ask himself how it felt to have one's entire village burned down, or to be the wife or child of an old peasant such as the one killed by a German soldier in cold blood on the off chance that he might be a partisan, as happened on January 20, 1944; afterward, when the soldiers went through the man's pockets, and took his cash, they found that his papers were perfectly in order.[18] Even for someone like Reichardt who constantly searched his conscience and tried to live up to his ethical ideals, these questions never arose. The closest he came was to express his relief that Germany and his family had been spared similar mayhem.

This does not mean Reichardt did not have a conscience. In effect, his diary expressed an inner voice that constantly watched and judged him. Sometimes he observed himself from the outside, as on the fateful day he shot the partisan. But his inner voice was not that of the "impartial spectator" that Adam Smith identified as the source of empathy, reason, and conscience. Reichardt's way of looking was not reflexive, traveling back and forth between one person's imagination and another's. It was self-referential. In the end, this young officer was always looking back at himself. "I am surrounded by repulsive cruelty, badness, betrayal, and cowardice," he wrote on February 5, 1944; "nonetheless there is no iron law that makes the heart grow cold, and I take comfort from that." Ultimately it was not medals but the "heart of the soldier facing God" that decided whether one was "a hero or common murderer."[19] Reichardt had little doubt how he would face his Maker. His agitation about the brutal killings, plunder, and mayhem arose not from a concern about the suffering of others but from the challenge it posed to his own self-image as a pure, noble knight. His moral vision was solipsistic.

By viewing the war as a struggle of cosmic proportions with a hidden metaphysical logic, Reichardt made questions of political responsibility irrelevant. The Nazis were marginal figures in his war. War aims or military options did not feature either. Since it was a war of destiny, it was sufficient to believe that it was a "just cause" and subordinate oneself to its higher logic. Faith took the place of critical reason. Reichardt knew that atrocities happened under the noses of many officers, but his idealism made it impossible to appreciate that extreme violence was an integral part of the German war. Instead, he found the answer in individual character flaws and a lack of *Kultur*, a diagnosis common among the educated German *Bürgertum*. On February 8, 1944, for example, Reichardt and his comrades again came under enemy fire, this time near Kistanje. When they took the enemy position, the wounded raised their hands and begged for mercy. "All of them were immediately shot," he wrote. "I turned away from the scene and left that business to those who think nothing of it or even experience pleasure, hatred, revenge, and satisfaction in such handiwork."[20] It was only the uncultured who succumbed to such animalistic passions. His own dignity and "just cause" remained unblemished. That, as a participant in the German war, he might share some responsibility for its consequences was a thought that never occurred to him.

All of this left Reichardt with few options for stemming the tide of violence. He vacillated between despair at the coarseness of many soldiers and faith in his ability to instill culture and ethics in his men. On February 5, 1944, one soldier in his squad started humming a Schubert song. Reichardt's despair immediately lifted. Many of the soldiers might be rough on the outside, he wrote, but they had a sensitive core. They could be made receptive to the biggest question of all: life and death. But how? He felt that if he played Beethoven's Ninth Symphony for them he could become the "interpreter between God and their soul."[21] How this would have stopped German soldiers from killing the locals is unclear.

Two months later, he was again in despair, troubled by the brutality and selfishness among the troops. He was now in Wischau (Vyskov), in Moravia, on an officer training course for Panzertruppen, the tank units. He recalled how after another battle with partisans one soldier had ordered the captured young women to undress and then shot them. Such violent outbursts were dangerous, he wrote, because they betrayed "our claim to courage, heroism, and idealism as justification for our struggle." He felt "deep human disappointment" about the lack of quality among the new aspiring lieutenants. They were like automatons, not officers, he confided to his captain. The captain agreed but explained that recent losses had inevitably led to a "lowering of intellectual-ethical criteria."[22] Reichardt was encountering the new generation of Hitler's "people's officers," who were more ruthless and ideological, promoted for their fanaticism and blind obedience to the Führer instead of their skill or seniority.

Once again, Reichardt tried to shield his ideals from the reality around him, and kept fighting. It was still possible to be "hard" but stay "clean," he wrote on May 21, 1944. But blind obedience and coercion were only justified in extreme situations. A different ethos was needed if soldiers were to give their lives.[23] Reichardt took comfort in the fact that he sometimes managed to rouse his men out of their stupor. To prepare them for "moral-ethical action"—that, for him, was "the most important and difficult duty of a military leader": "leading men into the inferno but giving them a chance to hold on to their moral justification for their struggle, so that they can consciously throw themselves into battle and bleed for their highest goal with a pure heart."[24]

Notwithstanding the collapse of the front and the war crimes he had witnessed, Reichardt continued to look inward. He took the hope of spiritual purification back with him to the front. In December 1944—now a lieutenant—he was fighting with his tank unit in Hungary. Soviet loudspeakers urged German soldiers to desert, promising social assistance and "sex every Thursday."[25] How primitive, Reichardt wrote. He preferred to distribute among the men Rainer Maria Rilke's prose poem *Cornet* (1912) and Goethe's homoerotic poem *Ganymed* (1774) about a beautiful youth who is taken to heaven by Zeus:

> Up, up, lies my course.
> While downward the clouds
> Are hovering, the clouds
> Are bending to meet yearning love.
> For me,
> Within thine arms
> Upward!
> Embraced and embracing!
> Upward into thy bosom,
> Oh Father all-loving![26]

That a German soldier who had seen what Reichardt had seen, and done what he had done, could still imagine himself pure and virtuous displayed a stunning capacity for self-deception. What would happen to this solipsistic sense of moral superiority is a major theme of this book.

2

The Wages of Sin: From Stalingrad to the End

Between December 1942 and July 1943 many Germans began to look at the war in a new light. Militarily, the balance had already tilted the previous year, when the United States entered the war (December 7, 1941) and the Wehrmacht's advance ground to a halt outside Moscow. As late as autumn 1942, though, Germans looking at a map of the world could only marvel at the territorial reach of their empire. Little pins of swastikas stretched from Norway in the north to Egypt in the south, from France in the west to Ukraine and the Caucasus in the East. Hitler had steeled the country for war, and most Germans believed that it was right and inevitable, but there had been little enthusiasm when it actually came, with the German attack on Poland on September 1, 1939. This changed with the string of unprecedented successes in the first two years of conflict, which left them with enormous pride in their army and silenced any doubts about the Führer's vision.

Things started to change with the attack on the Soviet Union in 1941. Nothing illustrates the dramatic reversal of fortune more starkly than the number of German fatalities. Between the invasion of Poland in September 1939 and Operation Barbarossa in June 1941, the German army had suffered a total of 125,000 fatalities. In December 1942 and January 1943 combined, the number was 269,000, 144,000 of whom died in the cauldron of Stalingrad, where the Red Army lost a staggering 486,000 troops. Another 100,000 German soldiers were taken prisoner when the remnants of the 6th Army finally surrendered on February 2, 1943. The war also came home with unprecedented force. The Royal Air Force had dropped bombs on German soil since the start of the war but mainly on industry and infrastructure. In March 1943, the British Bomber Command launched a sustained attack on all cities in the Ruhr Valley. On July 24, 1943, British and American bombers began Operation Gomorrah. For the next ten days and nights, some three thousand aircraft dropped nine thousand tons of bombs on Hamburg. By the end, a quarter of a million homes had been reduced to rubble. Forty-three thousand people died in the firestorm. Nearly one million took flight to the countryside.[1]

Together, the events that took place at Stalingrad and Hamburg shook the Nazis' *Volksgemeinschaft* to the core. The Nazis ruled with violence and terror, but ultimately their power rested on popular support. Nazi Germany was a "consensual dictatorship."[2] After 1933, enemies of the regime were imprisoned, terrorized, or murdered, but the majority of Germans were co-opted, including doctors, lawyers, and civil servants. Some feared losing their jobs, but for many more the Nazis spoke to preexisting beliefs, especially nationalism, antisemitism, and anti-Bolshevism. The working-class milieu—home to the largest labor movement in the world before 1933—was first broken up and then absorbed. Most Germans did not enjoy violence and coercion as such, but they were prepared to support or at least tolerate them as long as they served what seemed desirable ends. Order, national regeneration, and economic stability were the pillars of that consensus. Defeat at the front and bombs from the sky shook its foundations. The war was not yet lost, but Stalingrad raised the prospect that it might be. It was one thing to lose a son in the victorious Blitzkrieg, quite another to sacrifice a whole generation in a war where the outcome was uncertain. What happened at Stalingrad and Hamburg cracked the German soul, releasing competing emotions of fear and revenge and leading Germans to reexamine unspoken assumptions and confront inconvenient truths. This was the moral turning point of the war.

STALINGRAD: SACRIFICE FOR WHAT?

The battle of Stalingrad revealed all the weaknesses of the German army that would come to haunt it: ideological arrogance, blind loyalty, and poor logistics. Belief in their racial superiority made Hitler and his generals underestimate the fighting power of the Soviets and their ability, with American help, to replenish their resources. In September 1942, the Red Army first drew the Wehrmacht into the pocket of Stalingrad and then "hugged" them to defeat, keeping them so close that they rendered the Luftwaffe ineffective. German logistics and the Army Group South were overstretched. So was leadership.[3] Hitler had no patience with generals who had their own strategic ideas. A former frontline soldier himself, he belittled them as deskbound officers. Critics were humiliated or fired. Their successors were servile sycophants and careerists. Field Marshal Erich von Manstein, who was given the job of relieving the encircled troops, was a case in point. As vain as he was ambitious, he completely overestimated the forces at his command and failed to see that the air force could not possibly supply the encircled troops. Inside the cauldron, General Friedrich Paulus was out of his depth; prior to taking charge of the 6th Army, he had only ever led a battalion. Desperate, he tried to bomb the enemy from the air, a waste of the few resources at his command, because the Soviets would simply hide in the sewers. By December 1942, the 6th Army's supplies were exhausted, and soldiers started eating their horses and, indeed, considered eating each other. A culture of unquestioning obedience eliminated strategic options until it was too late. The one exception among the generals was Walther von Seydlitz, but he only told Hitler that it was impossible to hold Stalingrad at the end of November; up to that point he had loyally followed a strategy that he knew was disastrous.[4] After the war, Manstein would claim that he had given an order for a breakout that could have saved the army, but, in truth, he had been unwilling to confront Hitler and gave Paulus ambivalent signals as to whether to prepare for a breakout or not.

German soldiers at Stalingrad responded to their fate in different ways. One wrote home on New Year's Eve: "How bleak and hopeless everything is here." They hadn't had a slice of bread for four days. A sip of coffee in the morning and evening was all they got, plus a small tin of meat and cheese out of a tube every other day. "Hunger, hunger, hunger, and then lice and dirt," and at night dreams of "cake, cake, cake."

> Sometimes I pray and sometimes I curse my fate, but, ultimately, everything is pointless. When will deliverance come, and how? Will death come in the form of a bomb, a grenade, disease, or a debilitating illness... How can anyone possibly bear this? Is all the suffering a punishment by God?... I beg you, please do not cry too much when the news reaches you that I am no more.[5]

Others were defiant, driven on by faith in their invincibility and a sense of duty to dead comrades, as well as by fear of what the Russians might do to them. On January 13, 1943, a corporal noted the fate of one comrade who had recently been taken prisoner: he had been executed with a shot in the neck. However desperate the situation, the corporal was not giving up hope: "In this war we will have to be the winners, because otherwise all the hardship and sacrifice of so many comrades would have been for nothing." "We will fight to the last bullet," another soldier wrote a week later, "I will not go into captivity." As late as the end of January, some believed that the Führer would somehow miraculously save them.

For Hitler, surrender was out of the question. The 6th Army needed to demonstrate to the world that Germans were prepared to fight to the last man. On January 30, he promoted Paulus to field marshal in the knowledge that none of his predecessors had ever surrendered. If Paulus wanted to avoid eternal shame, he would fall on his sword. Paulus did not oblige. He was a Catholic, so instead of committing suicide, he surrendered, on February 2. Hitler was furious. Paulus had violated the Nazis' central tenet: the nation (*Volk*) was everything, the individual nothing. "What, after all, is 'life'?" Hitler raged. "Life is the *Volk*. The individual has to die anyway. The only thing that survives him is the *Volk* into which he is born."[6]

Stalingrad exposed the Nazis' and the German army's ruthless disregard for life. Overall, they murdered 20 million Jews, Soviet prisoners, and civilians, as well as "misfits" who had to be "weeded out" of the *Volksgemeinschaft*. But the disregard for life did not stop there. Since they called themselves "National *Socialists*" it is sometimes incorrectly assumed that the Nazis must have been egalitarian. In fact, one thing they hated about Bolshevism was that it bred "*Vermassung*," an artificial leveling of society into a homogeneous mass. While the Nazis believed that Germans were the master race, they also had a hierarchical view of their own nation, with an elite of "great men" at the top leading ordinary Germans. Hitler himself was *the* Führer, but other leading Nazis saw themselves as mini-Führers, only a step down from the greatest man in history and equally endowed with special vision and fighting spirit, chosen by destiny to lead the nation in its historic struggle. They were the actors who made history; other Germans were to follow and obey. This elitism also made them attractive to many bourgeois supporters. As long as the leaders were leading, Nazis and officers believed, a few hundred thousand dead Germans more or less didn't matter. In any case, their blood was not lost, because it enriched the soil out of which future generations of the *Volk* would grow (*die Aussaat*). It is no coincidence that Nazi organizations had their own finely graded hierarchies of *Führer*—from the Hitler Youth (*Rottenführer*, or squad leader) to the SS (*Obergruppenführer*/general, *Untersturmführer*/lieutenant, and so on).

The glorification of leadership was not just propaganda. It shaped actions. Battle was the true test of struggle (*Kampf*) and leadership. In contrast to, say, the British army, the Wehrmacht prized a particularly aggressive and costly style of close combat, the so-called *Sturm*, with troop leaders in the vanguard of daredevil attacks, setting a heroic example for their men, an energetic but not exactly sophisticated type of warfare.[7]

On January 30, 1943, Hermann Göring, the supreme commander of the Luftwaffe, gave a speech on German radio, which could be heard in Stalingrad, where the remaining soldiers listened to their own funeral oration.

He placed the Stalingrad fighters in a long line of selfless heroes stretching back to those outnumbered Spartans whose last stand had held back the Persian "hordes" for a few days at Thermopylae in 480 BC. Göring was speaking on the tenth anniversary of Hitler's seizure of power, and the cult of heroic sacrifice followed on logically from a reaffirmation of the Führer. Göring asked his listeners to cast their mind back to 1933 to appreciate the "Herculean task" Hitler had accomplished. Then, Germany had been weakened by internal enemies. Now, the same opponents—"Plutocracy and Bolshevism"—that had been defeated within were threatening them from without. Two things had made it possible to restore the German nation to its rightful greatness: the courage of its people and "a leader who is the greatest German in history." If it had not been for the Führer and his providential foresight, Germany would already have been overrun by the Bolshevik hordes. The fighters in Stalingrad now had played their vital part in stopping them from sweeping across Europe. The soldiers had "obeyed the law which everyone must obey: the law to die for Germany." It was not for the people to question whether this was necessary or not. Hitler had called on the nation to mobilize all forces and the nation would naturally obey. The struggle had reached an existential stage. It was about nothing less than the very life or death of the German people. The enemy, "led by the Jews," had only destruction on their mind. Germans needed to look to their Führer—always. "Could you possibly believe that the Almighty had led this man, a God-sent man, to pass through innumerable dangers and become greater and greater, all for nothing?" "Providence" had sent Germany their Führer to make them the strongest nation in the world—these were guarantees that justified their belief in victory.[8]

For the Nazi faithful, Göring was articulating basic truths. Theodor Habicht, one of the "old fighters," had joined the party in 1926 when it was at the fringes of politics and was their leader in Wiesbaden. He was a fairly typical Nazi functionary. Born in 1898, he fought in the First World War, and then, in 1919, as a member of the paramilitary right, against the communists at home. In civilian life he worked in a department store, but he knew he was chosen for greater things. In his view, history had taken a temporary wrong turn with Weimar before switching back to its destined track in 1933. The following year Habicht was the wirepuller behind the Nazis' attempt to overthrow the Austrian Republic, a coup d'état that failed. The true place for a leader like him, he decided, was on the battlefield, so in 1940, he volunteered for the front.

When Habicht listened to Göring's speech, he was encircled in the pocket of Demyansk, south of Leningrad. What a wonderful speech, he wrote in his diary—if the German people had the smallest bit of honor left, the speech was bound to have an effect. He was convinced that the Führer would enter the history books as "the political Clausewitz of the German people." "Germany has become one army poorer, but one heroic tale richer... Once 'the sun rises' and we are unleashed again, we will attack with new momentum." What troubled him about Stalingrad, he confessed a few months later, were the generals. They had failed the test of leadership and set a dangerous example to the rank and file. Sure, surrender might save the lives of a few thousand men. But what would happen if millions followed their example and suddenly put their own lives over and above their orders?[9] Stalingrad threatened to undermine the blind faith in obedience and self-sacrifice.

At home, the news from Stalingrad was greeted with shock and confusion. Two days after Paulus's surrender, the security service of the SS (the Sicherheitsdienst) reported rumors that the number of dead was as high as 300,000. Some said that Soviet captivity was worse than death, while others were praying that some soldiers might still be alive. It raised question after question: How could such a disaster possibly have been allowed to happen? Why had the Soviet forces been underestimated? Why did the Germans not retreat? Some put their faith in the total mobilization of the home front, which Hitler, Göring, and Joseph Goebbels now preached, and hoped that, in the end, final victory would be theirs. For others, though, Stalingrad was "the beginning of the end."[10]

These remained the two poles of public opinion for the rest of February. Many intelligence reports cited signs of a national awakening. "With one blow, Stalingrad had opened the eyes of the entire nation." Yet, total war and the call for women to do war work were also sowing division. Instead of "fusing together the *Volksgemeinschaft* and orienting it toward a single goal," the security service noted, there was a rise in "envy, suspicion, and prejudice." Some working-class and middle-class women threatened to make their contribution to the war effort contingent on "fine ladies" entering the factories as well. Just as worrying, foreign forced laborers were working less hard and becoming uppity: "Tomorrow me master and you serf," in the words of one observer. On a Berlin tram, a man was reported to have told other passengers, "I can assure you one hundred percent that we do not any longer need to lose this war, we have already lost it." This from someone allegedly working in a government office.

Stalingrad triggered contradictory emotions. Ursula von Kardorff was a journalist writing for the feuilleton of the *Deutsche Allgemeine Zeitung* in Berlin. She came from a cultured, aristocratic background and had initially supported Hitler for saving Germany from the left, but began to deplore the brutality of the regime. She, too, wrote antisemitic articles, but the Nazis were going too far. Still, by the end of 1942, her younger brother Jürgen was fighting with a tank unit in the eastern Ukraine. On January 31, she wrote in her diary, "Full of despair. Playing again and again on the gramophone the Bach aria: 'O Schmerz, wie zittert das gequälte Herz' ['O pain! Here trembleth the tormented heart']." She sarcastically commented on the speeches the day before: "How marvelous that the Führer had saved them [the Germans] from their downfall, Jews, and Bolshevism. On the other hand, Stalingrad,... the flight of the army in the Caucasus. The deportations of the Jews. Is it still possible to pray? I cannot anymore."[11] A few days later, the news came that her brother had died in battle. In the early stages of the war, obituaries in newspapers typically proclaimed the death as for "*Führer, Volk und Vaterland*." Now, Jürgen von Kardorff's death notice read: "died the way he had lived, a brave man and faithful Christian." This would become a growing pattern in the course of 1943. Many families chose the simple phrase "died far away from the homeland..." Among the living, "Good-bye" now sometimes replaced "Heil Hitler."[12]

What was the reaction of Germans who had joined the Nazi Party *after* 1933? The diary of Rudolf Tjaden shows how this middle school teacher in Oldenburg in the north of the country was making sense of the change in Germany's fortunes. He had been one of the few survivors at Langemarck in November 1914, one of the mythical battles of self-sacrifice invoked by Göring in his speech. In the Weimar years, Tjaden became a member of the Liberal Democrats (DDP) and of the German Peace Society (DFG). Like many civil servants, he joined the Nationalsozialistische Deutsche Arbeiterpartei (NSDAP, the Nazi Party) in spring 1933, shortly after Hitler seized control of the state. The initial string of victories in the Blitzkrieg made Tjaden delirious. Finally, Germany was able to right the "wrong" of 1918. On August 15, 1941, he wrote to a fellow teacher who was fighting in the East about how "wonderfully skilful" the Führer was! His "clever politics" had defeated one enemy after the other.[13] That autumn, the eastern campaign would be finished, he hoped. When spring 1942 came, Tjaden began to worry: Might Germany once again be "winning itself to death" (*totsiegen*)? It was around this time that he started to work as an informer (*V-Mann*) for the Sicherheitsdienst of the SS and filed fortnightly reports on local opinion.

In August 1942, his eighteen-year-old son, Enno, his eldest, was on his way to the Eastern Front. A month later, Tjaden heard that the war had claimed the first of his son's classmates—at Stalingrad. By November, his own son had reached the city. After three sorties, Enno's tank was disabled. Beginning on December 23, he was in a bunker. In his letters, he told his parents about his hunger and his despair: "I am completely at a loss how it will all end." His parents were sick with fear. On January 22, 1943, Tjaden was beginning to "imagine the worst." He took sleeping pills, only to wake up in fear a few hours later. "Ah, how awful, how infinitely sad it all is!" he confided in his diary. "Why must our dear, beautiful, intelligent, and pure boy be taken away from us by such madness? Is that the meaning of war, that the best must fall so that the riffraff can live?" On January 30, he, too, listened to Göring's speech. It was clear evidence, he concluded, that the soldiers "had been consciously sacrificed! Our Enno among them!" He asked himself why. It could only be for one of two reasons: "incompetence—or reckless leadership."[14]

That same day, Tjaden also listened on his radio to Goebbels, who read out a proclamation by the Führer and stressed that the word *"Kapitulation"* did not exist in the Nazi vocabulary. Perhaps, Tjaden thought, it was now a battle of "To be or not to be" for each and every German. "But who is responsible that it came to this?" he wondered. "Is it the Führer's fault with his 'push to the east' or Stalin's with his idea of Bolshevik world domination?"[15]

Tjaden did not suddenly wish for peace, let alone join the resistance, but he had lost faith in the Nazi leadership. Was Enno dead or was he still alive, in Russian hands? Tjaden assumed he was dead. Agnes, his wife, wished him dead rather than captured. For the moment, Tjaden looked for answers in the "madness that rules the world and with which so-called 'leaders' [here he used the word *Führer*] had indoctrinated it." Here was a flicker of his former liberal mind from the 1920s. On February 1, 1943, he noted, "Many people now have terrible thoughts about the future. How can we possibly win?" His wife began ranting in public against the "brown shirts" for "stirring up our youth and sending them to the front, while they themselves were hanging around at home." If the war in the East continued as it was, with an advance in the summer and retreat in the winter, Tjaden feared that the German troops would bleed to death first. That would mean Bolshevik rule. What would happen to their youngest, Karl? If everything people said about the Soviets was true, life would no longer be worth living.

Patriotism and fear of Bolshevism kept Tjaden supporting the German war effort, but he began to distinguish the "just" war from the Nazis' war. And as he did, he also began to step away from the Nazis in his own life. Sometime in February, he stopped wearing his Nazi Party badge. On April 20, 1943, Hitler's birthday, Tjaden decided he would not fly his swastika flag as long as his son was missing in action. Two weeks later, he refused to do any more work for the Sicherheitsdienst. By September 1944, he had convinced himself that he had always viewed Hitler's foreign policy with the "greatest distrust" and his treatment of the Jews with "the greatest abhorrence." To stay in power for a few days longer, the Nazis were prepared to sacrifice the entire nation. He did not feel obliged to sacrifice himself for that gang. Erased from memory were the days when he had cheered Hitler and reported to the security service. It would be a common refrain as the war was nearing its end. He and the rest of the German nation were now the Nazis' victims, not collaborators.[16]

There was hardly a family in Germany that did not know someone killed at Stalingrad or missing in action there. It was not a discrete event that could be relegated to the past. The battle informed an entire generation's view of the present and the future. When Tunis fell on May 12, 1943, people spoke of "Tunisgrad." This time, a quarter of a million German and Italian troops were taken prisoner in a decisive defeat of the Axis powers in North Africa. The only thing that improved as the war worsened was the Germans' gallows humor. The day after Tunis, Tjaden copied a joke that was making the rounds. Their neighbor had asked his wife: "Do you know the shortest joke? *Wir siegen*"—We are winning.[17]

The Nazi response to Stalingrad was to turn on the Jews and call publicly for their extermination. In his call for total war on February 18, 1943, Goebbels presented the German people with a radical analysis of the situation and an equally radical response. He told the crowds at the Berlin Sportpalast that the battle at Stalingrad proved what they had known for a long time: "Bolshevism had turned 200 million people into a tool of 'Jewish Terror' ready to attack Europe." Bolshevism had a single goal: "world revolution by the Jews." Jews would impose their "capitalist tyranny." It would mean the enslavement of all Germans and the end of Western civilization. The Jews were an "infectious disease that is contagious." Now in full swing, Goebbels called for their "complete and radical extermi—" before correcting this slip of the tongue, and finishing with "—elimination" ("*vollkommener und radikalster Ausrott—*" "*—schaltung*").[18] The Führer, he said, was absolutely right that this war was "no longer about winners and losers but those who would survive and those who would be annihilated... The dictate of the hour was total war." The time had come "for the gloves to come off and to bandage our fist." The crowd responded with a "thunderous applause," according to official reports. Ten days later, the Nazis arrested the few remaining thousand Jews who were still in Berlin, including most of those in mixed marriages. Their non-Jewish partners went to protest outside Rosenstrasse, where they were detained, and managed to get two thousand released. Seven thousand others were deported to Auschwitz.[19] In the Breendonk camp in Belgium, SS guards threw eighteen Jews and two "Aryan" prisoners in the water and beat them until they drowned as punishment for Stalingrad.[20]

Until Goebbels's speech there had been widespread rumors of atrocities, but they were never officially acknowledged. With the stumble about the extermination of the Jews, Goebbels made the Germans accomplices to murder.[21] Unlike some of his contemporaries, Tjaden was silent about the deportation of the Jews from Germany, which had begun in earnest in autumn 1941. Tjaden himself had first heard of a massacre in 1942. In June that year, his former pupil Gretel was back visiting from the Ukraine. She told him that six thousand Jews had been "eliminated" there. "Cursed times!" Tjaden wrote in his diary, and wondered what God would have to say about "the extinction of the Jewish race." Two months later, his son Enno was writing from Lemberg, on his way to the Eastern Front: "I am so lucky that I am not responsible for what happened here," he wrote, a coded reference to the massacre of children and the deportations of forty thousand Jews to Belzec. The news did not prompt a comment in his father's diary.

On February 25, 1943, the anniversary of the founding of the NSDAP, Tjaden listened on his radio to Hitler calling for the "extermination of European Jewry." Tjaden exploded: "Why does he not keep his mouth shut about such things! As if he had not already made himself enough enemies, and at a moment when he has the greatest difficulty to save his own people from destruction... And for something like that we are meant to sacrifice our sons!"

Tjaden's outburst shows the kind of moral reasoning that was starting to gain ground. By broadcasting to the world his intention to murder all the Jews, Hitler was encouraging the Allies to fight even harder. There had been massacres before Stalingrad, as Tjaden knew. But after Stalingrad they appeared to put non-Jewish German lives at risk.

The Nazi myth that the German Stalingrad soldiers were heroes who went to their death rather than surrender did not allow for any information to the contrary. In that vacuum, rumors began to circulate about survivors. Perhaps the soldiers had not all been killed or committed suicide but were prisoners of war? Perhaps their Soviet captors were not all brutes? A few postcards from the Soviet Union slipped through the net of Nazi censorship. Parents received letters with bits and pieces of news about their sons from comrades who had been evacuated. (There were also fraudsters who pretended to have been comrades, peddling false news.) Parents tried to get information via Turkey, Japan, and Switzerland.

For many, Goebbels's tirade provided just the right outlet for their grief: they wanted revenge. Since the Jews were behind the Bolsheviks, all the Jews in German hands needed to be killed. Or, at least, they should threaten to kill all the Jews in reprisal if German prisoners of war were harmed.

Others, however, reached the very opposite conclusion. An extraordinary case is that of Christian Schöne, a doctor of internal medicine who headed a small field hospital in Frankfurt (Oder), just outside annexed Poland. His youngest brother, Konrad, was among those missing in action at Stalingrad. Their father was a Lutheran pastor. Christian himself had been a prisoner of war in Siberia in the First World War, and highly decorated. In spring 1943, he joined an informal network that circulated news among relatives of those missing in action. He also wrote directly to the Foreign Ministry suggesting that if Soviet POWs were allowed to write home, then Moscow might reciprocate. On his brother's birthday—May 3, 1943—Christian Schöne contributed to a new chain letter that went a big step further. A reliable source had told his brother Konrad that sixty-four thousand Jews had been killed in Kiev by the Germans, and "not only men, but women and children." The removal of their corpses had been so poorly organized that, when the snow melted, piles of bodies resurfaced everywhere. Christian said that he himself was treating an SS man who suffered from nightmares and who wondered whether the "150 executions a day were perhaps too much." He concluded that "our prisoners will have to pay for this." The relatives needed to condemn these shootings as a matter of "morality and honor." He considered possible objections: Wouldn't this be undue interference? What if ending the massacre of the Jews did nothing for the German prisoners? He brushed them aside. "It is never too late to stop a moral wrong, and to contribute to that can only be honorable." Christian urged the other families to petition the Nazi Party and ministries to hand over military operations to "responsible experts" and to stop the murder of the Jews.

Two of the recipients immediately returned his chain letter with a note saying they did not agree with it. Christian Schöne was duly arrested. In November 1943, a military court sentenced him to one year in prison for undermining military morale (*Wehrkraftzersetzung*)—a mild sentence by the standards of the time. In his verdict, the judge noted that Schöne was a "dreamer," "out of touch with reality," and considered his intense worry for his brother an "honorable motive."

Christian Schöne survived the war. In the summer of 1947, his brother was finally able to send him a sign of life from Siberia. A couple of months earlier, Dr. Christian Schöne had died.[22]

Christian Schöne was one of thirty thousand people during the war who were sentenced for demoralization of the troops.[23] After Stalingrad, denunciations started to rise sharply, registering the increasingly bitter tensions in

German society. If there were more defeatists, there were also more informers. Contrary to popular stereotype, the Gestapo was not all-powerful. In fact, it was relatively small—in Lower Franconia, for example, a region with 840,000 inhabitants surrounding Würzburg, the Nazi secret state police had only twenty-two officers; its ability to strike terror into the heart of people was reliant on Germans spying on each other.[24] Contrary to a second stereotype, informers were mostly not gossipy women: three quarters were men, and most of them were everyday Germans who stubbornly refused to accept the change in military fortune.[25] Final victory would be theirs! Hitler had to be right! Denouncing internal "enemies" (*Volksfeinde*) was one way to keep that faith and self-image intact. It cultivated a sense of importance, of performing a national duty. After all, was defeatism not a betrayal of the nation, in the words of Roland Freisler, president of the Volksgerichtshof (the Nazis' special People's Court) since August 1942? The more fanatical the belief in final victory, the wider the interpretation of treason. In 1943, a soldier on leave told a neighbor that the war could not be won. A military court sentenced him to two years in prison, followed by service in Strafbataillon 999, the infamous penal unit sent on dangerous frontline missions; he would die on one of these in Poland. Employees informed on bosses who disputed that the Russians would kill them all. Others denounced those who questioned what Germany was doing in the East or wanted "defeatists" sent to concentration camps. As the war worsened, so the number of death sentences rose. In 1941, the People's Court had passed 102 death sentences. In 1943, under the ferocious Freisler, 1,662 would be condemned.

GOMORRAH: PUNISHED FOR WHAT?

Aerial bombing of cities was not new in 1943.[26] The German air force had bombed Warsaw at the end of September 1939, the Royal Air Force industry and oil plants in the Ruhr in May 1940. On September 7, 1940, Germany launched the Blitz with a first wave of direct attacks on London, and then, on November 14, 1940, on Coventry. Between Christmas 1940 and New Year 1941, London was subjected to another wave of heavy bombing. One might have expected that accounts of the bombing "would have incredibly shaken people," Tjaden wrote in his diary. "Far from it! One has become so used to them that one almost no longer pays attention when they take place." The bombing of German cities would change that, raising emotions to new heights.

The first raid on Hamburg took place during the night of May 17–18, 1940. It was the first time that Allied bombers had dared to target a major German city. Thirty-four people died. In the next three years, bombing Hamburg would become a matter of routine—137 raids and the loss of 1,431 lives.[27]

Operation Gomorrah was on an entirely different scale. In Hamburg, fifty-nine-year-old Renate Bock kept a diary to record for posterity "what we are going through." During the night of July 24–25, 1943, she was woken by the first attack. The attack on July 28, 1943, would be ten times worse. The alarm was sounded at 10:30 p.m. German anti-aircraft guns fired as Bock and her neighbors ran down to the basement to seek shelter. The floor was shaking. "Then all hell broke loose," she wrote. Two phosphorous bombs hit her street and spread fire everywhere. "The nine-year-old neighbors' son is screaming without restraint. I am cradling the eighty-year-old Mrs. Eigenbroot in my arm. We are kneeling on the floor; our eyes are covered with chalk and dust, our hearts racing." There was a brief moment of quiet, then a couple came running into their cellar. "The woman is half mad with fear!" Three days earlier she had been buried in her cellar and had to be dug out. "She is raving and screaming." It was like the end of the world.[28]

Blockbuster bombs blew off roofs and incendiaries created a firestorm, turning the city into one gigantic furnace. Extreme heat, high pressure, and raging flames swept through the streets. An air raid warden described the events of that same night in Hammerbrook, east of the old port. His block of apartment houses was hit by a phosphorous bomb. The third floor went up in flames. Then a second bomb threw him down the stairs. The flames were now approaching the gas cellar. The entire staircase collapsed, and the fire raged with "a wind speed of 10 on the Beaufort scale," like a gale. The warden and neighbors fought their way to the air raid shelter. People there were caught between the prospect of suffocation inside and the firestorm outside. Such was the force of the fire, the warden said, that "three men were unable to keep the door shut." He ordered people to cover their heads with coats and blankets and leave. The residents "had great trust in me, but they did not know what awaited them outside and how they still had to fight their way through a flaming hell." But not everyone left. He hurried back for the remaining women. An old man on canes "had to be left to his fate." Fire raged in the streets outside. On their knees, the group pressed themselves against the wall of the local schoolyard for five hours, until 7 a.m., waiting for the fire and heat to die down. The warden used all his powers of persuasion to make people wait with him. Some did, but others went out. "In the morning, I found their bodies, burned."[29] The extreme heat (up to almost 1,500°F) and pressure left behind a scene from hell: some bodies were reduced to charcoal, others were swollen beyond recognition, with male genitals "about as big as the head of a two-year-old child."[30] Over the city lay a cloud of smoke five miles high, and dust covered the city. There would be no light that day.

Göring had promised that no enemy aircraft would ever fly over the Reich. Allied bombers had attacked Lübeck a year earlier, in March 1942, and Cologne in May. Those had been single-night attacks. Göring had his own Stalingrad speech disrupted by two well-timed attacks from British Mosquitoes on Berlin, in broad daylight. The relentless weeklong bombing of Hamburg drove home the absolute vulnerability of the civilian population. Neither the German air force nor anti-aircraft defenses managed to protect them. The Hamburg inferno was followed by attacks on Vienna, Schweinfurt, Regensburg, and scores of other cities. By March 1944, daytime raids were a matter of routine, and they reached their climax in the winter of 1944–45.

In the wake of the bombings, people struggled to impose their meaning on the events. Their analyses differed greatly and reveal a new phase in the polarization of public opinion and moral judgments, between a fanatical hardening on one end and soul-searching on the other. One view interpreted the bombing as proof of Germany's innocence and wanted revenge. By mid-July, a few weeks before Operation Gomorrah, an intelligence report already noted that people in Hamburg "had for some time now been convinced of England's responsibility for the war in general and her responsibility for the bombing of civilians in particular. Since the English will not let themselves be impressed by the amorality of their actions and do not stop them, there can only be one option, that is, ruthless retaliation."[31] Similar views were reported in Berlin.[32] At the front, many soldiers shared that view. Heinz Sartorio was with the 18th Tank Division in Russia and wrote to his sister Elly, in Berlin, on August 7, 1943: "I am in a rage about the nasty way in which German civilians have been treated. I hope retaliation will strike soon, even if it smashes all of Europe into ruins. If people cannot get along, then they ought to kill each other." A feeling that the war might be lost only increased his lust for revenge. "What do I care. Bolshevism will triumph anyhow." Before that, though, he hoped that England would be hit by such force that "within a few days, there would be no England left."[33]

The problem was that Germany was now incapable of striking back. Almost 1 million Hamburg residents were homeless and spread a sense of despair and defeatism across the neighboring provinces. True, some poured their faith into miracle weapons, such as the V-1 flying bomb, the *Vergeltungs* ("vengeance") cruise missiles. But these would not be launched until June 1944, and, when they were, they were greeted with cynicism. Their real name, one joke went, was "*Verrücktheit 1* [Craziness 1] . . . effect zero. In London, one concert had to be canceled."[34]

Goebbels grasped that it would be counterproductive to play on calls for revenge. It could only raise expectations that the air force was unable to deliver. From December 1943, he prohibited the word "retaliation" from official use. Pinning the barbarism of the bombings exclusively on the British was also increasingly unconvincing. In addition to bombs, the Allies dropped fliers reminding Germans of their own bombing raids. The Nazis therefore decided to exploit the resilience of the local population as a sign of the newfound strength of the *Volksgemeinschaft*. Many later writers have assumed that the firestorm was so traumatic that it struck survivors speechless.[35] That is untrue. Such was the scale of death and destruction that people inevitably shared their loss and fear with each other. Rumors circulated that a quarter of a million had perished—the true number was closer to thirty-five thousand—and that the police and the Storm Troopers had to be called to suppress an uprising. The Nazis knew they could not silence talk, but they could still try to shape its direction.

The smoke had barely lifted when the regime's propaganda machine resumed. Ruined churches, in particular, received attention, partly to distract from the damage to docks and factories important to the war effort, partly to highlight the barbaric attack on cultural heritage. The biggest meeting took place in Adolf Hitler Square outside Hamburg's city hall, on November 21, 1943, the last Sunday before Advent—*Totensonntag*—the day traditionally reserved by Protestants for commemorating the dead. Tens of thousands watched as mourning gave way to a rallying cry to fight to the end. The bombing had been a historic test, the local Nazi leader, Gauleiter Karl Kaufmann, told them, and the people of Hamburg, with their Hanseatic spirit, had shown all Germans that they could withstand it. It had brought out the best in them: sacrifice, courage, and mutual help. Death had not been for nothing. The raids were like the "flames of a blacksmith," Kaufmann said, forging a genuine people's community, stronger than ever. For the dead, "there can only be one way to thank them for what they gave: victory."[36]

If punishing England was impossible, there was one enemy within reach: the Jews. Jews had been targets of revenge in earlier stages of the war. After the bombings of cities, they were blamed for the suffering of innocent Germans, women, and children. Wuppertal, on the Wupper River at the edge of the Ruhr Valley, was heavily bombed in May and June 1943. A month later, several hundred miles to the east, in Suhl, a poem made the rounds among the local workforce. It was called "Retaliation":

The day will come, when the crime of Wuppertal will
be bitterly avenged and you will break down under a
hail of iron in all your lands.
You murderers carried a lot of grief into this city and
fire, even the child at the mother's breast, the old and
the father you beat to death.
It drives us on to hate you with the wildest doggedness,
because you with all the Jewish races carry the stigma
of the Wupper.[37]

Elsewhere, people said they should not have driven out the Jews but instead created ghettos in German cities to hold them as human shields.[38] Some wrote directly to Hitler and Goebbels saying that for every "Aryan," ten or twenty Jews ought to be shot or hanged.[39] The brutal mathematical calculus of the military front had reached the home front.

The bombings pushed other Germans to follow a radically different chain of moral causation. The bombings, many believed, were a sign of divine wrath, retribution for sins committed by the Germans. This may not have been a majority view, but after the bombings it was no longer exceptional, either. In Hamburg, several pastors sensed a "feeling of guilt" among their flock.[40] One year earlier, in March 1942, the pastor of the Lutheran church in nearby Lübeck had pronounced an earlier raid a "divine judgment." (He was arrested, found guilty of undermining the morale of the troops, and guillotined.) On July 8, 1943, the security service of the SS reported that people in Berlin saw the bombing of Cologne cathedral as "punishment by God" for the burning of the synagogues in 1938.[41]

Not everyone believed that they were being punished by the hand of God, but a growing number certainly interpreted their own fate as a response to the treatment of the Jews. "Notwithstanding the rage at the English and Americans for their inhuman conduct of war," a Hamburg merchant wrote to a friend after Operation Gomorrah, "one has to acknowledge dispassionately that common people, the middle classes, and other groups repeatedly—and in larger as well as intimate settings—characterize the attacks as retaliation for our treatment of the Jews."[42] To members of small resistance groups, too, Allied bombings were fair retaliation for the deportations of their Jewish friends. "The English have avenged the misdeed with a big attack on Berlin," Ruth Andreas-Friedrich wrote in her diary on March 2, 1943; she belonged to the underground group Emil, which hid Jews in the metropole, and was a freelance journalist in Berlin. She was reminded of Goethe's "Sorcerer's Apprentice": the "broom which swept Germany clean of Jews will now no longer move back to the corner. And the spirits one called forth can no longer be gotten rid of."[43]

A SENSE OF COMPLICITY

We know today that the Allies bombed German cities to break the home front, not to avenge the murder of the Jews. For many Germans at the time, however, these two issues were linked. Intelligence reports in 1943–44 cited a growing number of these voices. In Schweinfurt, a center of the armaments industry in northern Bavaria, locals said they were being bombed in August 1943 in revenge for the Kristallnacht pogrom of 1938. In Bad Brückenau, a spa town in the rolling hills of the Rhön Mountains to the north, some said that the "whole attitude to the Jewish question" and its solution had been "fundamentally wrong." Now "the German population had to pay the price for it."[44] A Berliner put it succinctly in November 1943: "Do you actually know why our cities are being bombed? Because we have bumped off the Jews."[45]

What did he mean by "we"? The question of complicity in these statements is a tricky one. Some of the people quoted above might have taken refuge in the thought: *we* are being bombed because *others* (Nazis) maltreated the Jews in ways *we* never approved of. In medieval Rothenburg ob der Tauber, the local Nazi Party training center complained in October 1943 of a revival of the "fairy tale of the 'decent Jew'": many people believed that "the party had been too hard on the Jews, and now they had to pay the price."[46] Still, there was also a sense that the war was a collective project. The deportations were the final step on the road to mass murder, but steps leading up to them had been discrimination, exclusion, robbery, and assault. All of these had taken place in public and often involved public participation. Many Germans now lived in the homes of Jews, slept in Jewish beds, ate off Jewish porcelain. With the war turning against them, there was growing unease about how Jews might respond to the seizure of their property.

Germans have a saying: "*Mitgefangen, mitgehangen*"—caught together, hanged together. That, of course, is an extreme view of complicity since it punishes everyone equally regardless of the degree of their participation. The Nazis practiced a perverse cult of collective retribution. Hostages and civilians could be executed because they were guilty by extension for sabotage or the killing of individual German soldiers in their community, a policy enforced in colonial wars that had now been radicalized. Collective punishment reflected the lack of regard for individual life. The Nazis revived the medieval concept of *Sippenhaft* ("kin liability"), in which a whole family shared the responsibility for an act by one of its members—from late 1942, this would be applied to the wives, children, and brothers of deserters and, then, to the families of those who tried to assassinate Hitler on July 20, 1944. *After* 1945, the sense of guilt would undergo major changes. Here it is worth stressing that from 1943 to 1945, complicity for crimes committed in their name was not an alien concept for many Germans.

Knowledge of German atrocities undermined condemnation of Soviet crimes. In the spring of 1943, Nazi propaganda tried to exploit the discovery of mass graves in the Katyn forest, where the Soviets had executed Polish officers and intelligentsia, by presenting the killings as the "work of Jewish butchers." The public reaction ranged from aggressive antisemitism to critical self-examination. In Berlin, the security service reported the gist of opinions that, it said, circulated especially among educated and religious groups: "We do not have the right to get upset about Soviet measures, because Germans have eliminated far more Poles and Jews." Similar views were uttered in rural Lower Franconia. In Halle (in the Prussian province of Saxony), opinion was split between those who wanted to "kill the Jews" and those who said if the Germans had not attacked the Jews in the first place, they would already be enjoying peace. The "shock of Stalingrad has still not faded away," the district president of Swabia observed in June 1943, and there was fear that Russians might kill German POWs "in revenge for alleged German mass executions of Jews in the East."[47] By November 1944, the security branch in Stuttgart criticized Nazi propaganda about the Red Army massacre of German civilians in Nemmersdorf (today Mayakovskoye, Lithuania), the first village in East Prussia to fall to the Soviets, because it so easily backfired. "Numerous voices" in the population were saying:

> Every thinking person who sees this blood sacrifice will immediately think of the atrocities that we have committed in enemy lands, indeed, even in Germany itself. Have we not slaughtered the Jews in their thousands? Do soldiers not report again and again that Jews in Poland had to dig their own graves? And what we have done to the Jews in Alsace in the concentration camp? Jews are human, too. Thus, we have shown the enemies how they can treat us if they win.[48]

That was a lot of "we"s. A sense of complicity for crimes committed in their name was spreading among those on the home front.

Where did the churches position themselves in this landscape of retaliation, revenge, and retribution? Religion has traditionally laid claim to moral leadership. Under the Nazis, the Protestant and Catholic Churches all but forfeited that role. In 1933, both rallied to Hitler, the Lutherans especially so. Modernity and secularization were undermining religious faith and authority. The National Socialists, it was hoped, would revive Christianity as well as the country. The churches could not have been more mistaken. From youth groups and charity drives to public rituals and the cult of Hitler, the Nazis' totalitarianism ate further into the churches' shrinking place in society. Antisemitism and anti-Bolshevism were widespread among priests and pastors. The only two instances where the churches resisted were the Confessing Church's battle with the rabid German Christians over the exclusion of converted Jews from the ministry in 1934,[49] and Catholic and Protestant protests against euthanasia in 1941 that, briefly, made Hitler suspend the murder of disabled people; by that time, some 100,000 people had already been killed in the so-called Aktion T4. The latter protest, in particular, led by the Catholic bishop of Münster, Clemens von Galen, took courage. Still, these religious leaders' concerns were limited to their own flock. Converted Jews were members of their congregations, and the disabled were largely cared for in church-run asylums, and both groups had family members who could speak up on their behalf. Similar courage was almost completely missing when it came to outsiders, the deportation and murder of the Jews, the killings of Soviet prisoners and civilians, and other atrocities. The churches were actively engaged in the war, the propaganda against the Bolshevik enemy, and systems of coercion; some twelve thousand forced laborers, for example, worked in Protestant hospitals and vicarages.[50]

The Protestant bishop Theophil Wurm was one of the earliest and most vocal critics of Nazi mass murder. He sent letters of protest regarding both Kristallnacht and the euthanasia murders in 1940. He was hardly free of antisemitism—he believed Jews were a "dangerous" element and the state had a right to fight them—but the Nazis went too far. In 1941, he protested to Heinrich Himmler against mass killings. The deportation of mixed-race Jews—the "*Mischlinge*"—made him send off letters of protest in March 1943 to government ministers and, in July, to Hitler himself. "Killing without a military necessity and without judicial sentence is in contravention of God's commandment even if it is ordered by the authorities."[51] The "policy of exterminating Jewry," he wrote, "is a grave injustice and fateful for the German people." As with so many other statements, the main concern was not the murder of Jews but that "Aryan" Germans would end up having to pay for it. The bombings were divine retribution. Did the Bible not say, "As you sow, so shall you reap"? "Woe to the people," the Silesian Synod in Breslau declared at the end of August 1943, "who think it justified to kill other humans because they see them as worthless or belonging to another race."[52]

In the Protestant Church as a whole, however, other interpretations of the bombing gained hold, and nowhere more so than in Hamburg itself. It was the British who had chosen the name Operation Gomorrah, but local pastors and their congregations, too, turned to the Book of Genesis to make sense of the wrath of God. Did their fate not resemble that of Lot's wife? In this biblical story, before God punished the people of Sodom and Gomorrah, an angel had warned the faithful Lot and his people, "Flee for your lives! Don't look back, and don't stop... Flee to the mountains or you will be swept away!" Then the Lord rained "brimstone and fire" on the two cities. Lot listened, but his wife did not: she "looked back, and she became a pillar of salt" (Genesis 19:26). The lesson was to not dwell on your past sins, free yourself from them, look ahead and follow Christ. A pastor in the district of Hamm wrote a circular letter to his surviving flock around the story of Lot. The bombing was a warning to them all: "Do not look backward but upward." The German people were being punished because they had chosen worldly temptations over salvation. "Shall we accuse the Royal Air Force?" another pastor asked. It would not accomplish anything, he told his congregation.[53] Ultimately, the bombing was not about the British. It was a question by God to the Germans: When would their own godlessness come to an end?

Simon Schöffel was the senior pastor in Hamburg's main church, St. Michael's (the "Michel"), which was the landmark of the city. In 1933, he had urged all Lutherans to support the National Socialists in their fight against liberalism, secularism, and the pollution of the German nation with alien blood. Now, after the raids, he preached that the bombing was a message to shake off existing ties and to look to the future and follow Christ instead. On Easter Sunday 1944, in the middle of the service, another raid hit the city and the congregation had to take cover in the vault until one o'clock in the morning. When Schöffel resumed his sermon on Easter Monday, he assured those in attendance that the Resurrection now had greater meaning than ever. It was not just about tomorrow or the next year. Faith in Christ gave them an eternal future that could never become the past. The bombings were cleansing their souls. Suffering, he explained time and again, was not for nothing: it opened them up to the spirit of the Lord.[54]

All these interpretations led to the same conclusion. Yes, the Germans had been punished, and rightly so, but not for sins they had committed against the Jews or other "enemies" of the *Volk*. They were punished for their weak Christian faith. "There is suffering," Schöffel preached, "that is not imposed because of our sins, but—let's say it openly—for the sake of God's reign, for Jesus." In Catholic regions, church leaders similarly presented the bombings as the wrath of God directed toward a world gone mad with money, technology, and modernity. Such diagnoses also addressed a sort of complicity, but it was transcendental and looked to heaven, absolving the faithful from thinking about their responsibility for the consequences of their actions for others in the here and now. For these groups, the bombings meant turning away from Mammon, not Hitler.[55]

THE *VOLK* DIVIDED

Bombing, flight, and evacuation put a moral as well as material strain on the *Volksgemeinschaft.* The Nazis had created an extensive welfare network. Mutual aid was a central plank in the Nazi regime and created a glow of compassion in the hearts of many Germans, especially younger ones who helped the elderly and collected donations and scrap metal for the nation. The Winterhilfswerk (a donation drive for winter aid), with more than a million volunteers, organized mattresses, clothes, and food for those in need.[56] Its motto was that a people helps itself. A female charity worker explained its appeal. Unlike liberal Britain, with its bits and pieces of preventative aid, the Nazis attacked social diseases at their roots. Instead of relying on alms, the Nazis had made the "positive and constructive care of the *Volk*... the ethos of national self-preservation." Religious charity of the "love thy neighbor" kind was based on a "pure you-and-I relationship."[57] She hoped that it would survive but only to complement *Fernstenliebe*, the love of distant others. Of course, this wider circle of empathy was drawn around an "Aryan" nation and excluded the Jews, who were not allowed to contribute to these relief schemes, let alone benefit from them. The Nazis also challenged head-on the personal, spiritual idea of charity. In 1937, religious charities were no longer allowed to run their own street collections.

Nazi welfarism, in fact, was never genuinely voluntary. It relied on social pressure and compulsion. In March 1943, miners were effectively ordered to put in a "voluntary tank shift" to assist the war effort. A year later, all employees automatically had 10 percent of their wage tax deducted for winter aid.[58] When donations shot up again, it was partly because of inflation and a sense that money had lost its value.

Initially, bombed-out victims were able to rely on considerable help from the regime. By spring 1942, the city of Hamburg had registered 180,000 applications for 100 million Reichsmark worth of war damage—roughly 400 million euros in today's money. People received aid to buy new pots and pans. The homeless were moved into the apartments of deported Jews and received their share of confiscated Jewish furniture, although only after party bigwigs had helped themselves to the best pickings. Aid and welfare were important sinews of the Nazi *Volksgemeinschaft*. By summer 1943, however, the scale of destruction was such that local governments were no longer able to cope. The Nazis were now fearful that appeals to self-help would be a public confession of defeat.[59]

Mass evacuations produced further tensions. In Westphalia, in the northwestern part of the country, mothers openly protested against the evacuation order for children. The authorities threatened to take their food rations away. "My children will not leave, and if I do not have anything to eat, then at least I can perish together with them," one mother said.[60] Those people bombed out of the cities received the greatest understanding in regions that had their own experience with migration, such as the East. Elsewhere in the south the arrival of evacuated women and children made locals draw the circle of empathy more tightly around their own community. Intelligence reports in August 1943 warned of the "cool, even unfriendly reception" that greeted families from Hamburg in Austria and Bavaria, the "air raid shelter" of the Reich. When Munich and Nuremberg were bombed, one local among many blamed it on the people from Hamburg "because you do not go to church!"[61] In some towns, residents with large apartments refused to open their doors to bombed-out families and were arrested. In rural communities, hosts felt that the new arrivals from the cities were spoiled, and treated them like servants. Evacuated young mothers complained that their landladies would not allow them to wash diapers or warm up milk for their babies. There was a clash of different local cuisines, dialects, and ways of life. For evacuees in the Alps, the local diet of dumplings was judged to be "pigs' fodder."[62] Many evacuees felt so unwelcome that they decided to return home without permission. Even a damp cellar in bombed-out Hamburg was preferable. "No one here in Austria has any sympathy," one mother complained. "I wished they would get a taste of bombing, too."[63] The attacks clearly shattered the solidarity of the *Volksgemeinschaft*.

The bombing tested the bonds within families, too, with radically different outcomes. Being subject to "terror attacks," as the regime called them, provided many people at the home front with a sense of purpose and shared sacrifice with their sons on the battlefields. Two parents wrote to their son Helmut in May 1943, "No other city has had to go through such attacks as the people of Essen ... The purple heart for the wounded has been awarded, even the Iron Cross. That says everything ... We have become almost as humble as our brave soldiers at the front. We do not want you to be ashamed of us and we will always do our duty, until final victory."[64] Some soldiers were outraged when they heard that their families had fled their hometown. Martin Meier, a bank clerk from Berlin, was fighting with the 14th Tank Division in France and Ukraine, one of the divisions that had been lost at Stalingrad and had to be reassembled. In August 1943 he wrote to his wife: Was she "mad"? To flee Berlin was the worst possible thing she could have done: it was "disloyalty toward the Führer and our cause." She should be ashamed of herself. She and other Berliners deserved to be "sent to a concentration camp and face hunger for a few weeks." It was high treason, a stab in the back, just as in 1918. He would return victorious from Russia, and then he would sort out these selfish, narrow-minded people. He could count on one hand the times he had shouted "Heil," but still he could only spit on such behavior. If she had read the orders of evacuation correctly, it was only the elderly, children, and the sick who were meant to leave, because in autumn the Germans would flatten London and then it would be impossible to look after such "rubbish" if the British retaliated.[65]

Other families were torn apart. A tragic case was that of the docker Konrad H., who worked at the Blohm and Voss shipyard in Hamburg. At the very end of 1942, he was visiting his sick father in the Ruhr region and told the family that the war was being lost. In a local pub, surprised that people still gave the Hitler salute, he said that party members would be the first to lose their heads once the enemy had won. A few weeks later, his younger brother Willi arrived home on leave from the front and Fritz, the eldest, mentioned what had happened in the pub. Willi was with the Waffen-SS and said he needed to report the statement to his commanding officer. The fragmentary court records that survive do not say whether he did so. In February 1943, however, Konrad was arrested on suspicion of having been involved in sabotage that sank a ship. He was released the following day. In September he was arrested again, this time for undermining military morale. At work, he had reportedly said that "in Siberia, the cities were better than in America," "the war is being lost and the Russians would soon arrive in Hamburg," and, when it came to a wedding present for a coworker, that "a cooking pot would be better than a bust of Hitler." In March 1944, the People's Court met in a private home to reach its verdict. Those giving evidence included Fritz H. and his wife, although, as family members, they had been given the option of remaining silent. The door to the meeting room did not shut properly and those waiting outside heard Fritz H.'s testimony: "People like him must be weeded out [*ausgemerzt*]. We do not want to have another 1918"—referring to the alleged "stab in the back" by which the German home front had betrayed the army and lost the First World War. Konrad H. was sentenced to death. Fritz was in tears. "That is not what I had intended," he told other witnesses. "I did not expect it to come to this." On May 20, 1944, his brother was executed.[66]

The ideological divides that had torn the Weimar Republic apart were running straight through this working-class family. Though not a member of the Communist Party, Konrad was leaning in that direction, as his brothers knew. Willi and two other brothers were with the Waffen-SS. They all died in the last year of the war. Fritz H. had fought in France in the First World War. He then joined the right-wing paramilitary organization Stahlhelm and, in 1933, the NSDAP, but he never became an activist. Neither of his children was in a Nazi youth group. Fritz H. worked as a machine operator at the local copper-smelting plant, and, after the war, coworkers swore that, although he knew of oppositional views at work, he would not denounce them. At the time of the incident, his own son was at the front; he, too, would die in the war. By all accounts, Fritz and Konrad H. had been on friendly terms.

Fritz H. was one of a number of informers whose actions were considered by German courts after the war. He was tried three times and was acquitted, convicted, and then acquitted again. At the final trial in 1953, the jury found that Fritz H.'s actions were to be condemned on moral grounds, but did not amount to a crime.[67] His shock at hearing the verdict was seen as proof that he had neither intended his brother's execution nor been able to imagine that this might be the outcome. When he had called for the "weeding out" of his defeatist brother, he was using a "swear word" widespread at the time. His distress at the sentence, moreover, was treated as evidence that "wide circles" of the German population did not know of the Nazis' violation of justice or of other crimes "such as the KZ [concentration camp] horrors and murder of the Jews." Even if Fritz H. had not intended or been able to foresee his brother's execution, the troubling fact remains that he had willingly incriminated him and believed he should (at least) be locked up. By calling for "weeding out," Fritz H. had consciously or unconsciously accepted the Nazis' extension of a word normally used for eradicating weeds and vermin to people, including his own brother.

For others, the loss of loved ones in the raids broke their faith in the regime. Fritz Lang was a sergeant in the navy. In 1944, he sat in Fort Hunt, the U.S. prisoner-of-war camp in Virginia. Unlike many of his comrades, he no longer believed in Hitler. Both his parents had been killed in the bombing of Karlsruhe. His wife, too, was dead. He had nothing left in Germany. He blamed the Nazis for that.[68]

Hugo Manz, a doctor in the town of Waiblingen, on the outskirts of Stuttgart, did not know whether his son Werner was dead or alive. Werner was a fighter pilot, and had been shot down near Belgorod in the battle of Kursk in early August 1943. On August 15, his father started to write letters to him. If Werner returned, he would know what had happened while he was gone. If he did not, the letters would be "an eternal monument" for the family. Initially weekly, then monthly, these letters became a way for the father to hold on to his son and to express his own feelings. They also made him imagine himself in his son's position. In a way, his son served as an "impartial spectator." Hugo Manz's first letter described the horror of the bombings: "They were more heinous, ghastly, and inhuman than anything imaginable... Many, many thousand innocent men, women, children, and elderly, and the sick and frail, were doused with burning phosphorus and carbonized beyond recognition." Then the Allied planes "tortured" the survivors who had gathered at soup kitchens or to bury their dead with machine-gun fire. It was "more horrible than the Last Judgment in medieval paintings." He tried to cling to his son's image as a flying hero. But the ongoing raids on Stuttgart made him wonder whether his son's sacrifice had been worth it. Werner had written that he was willing to bear everything so that "afterward Germany would be better." To Hugo, it seemed "completely pointless and tragic that the courageous young generation... was being sacrificed without their hopes being fulfilled." In September, he learned from the army that his son had flown 148 enemy sorties, shot down four enemy planes, and been decorated twice. He had also been strafing defenseless people.[69] He comforted himself with the thought that the strafing must have been hardest for his son. His brother, a priest, gave him hope: Christianity was ultimately about love, not power. Hugo kept writing letters to his missing son until his own death in 1971. In 1988 the German Red Cross concluded that Werner "most probably" died in the crash after being shot down.

Stalingrad and area bombing shook Germans' moral certainties as much as their military confidence. Their own vulnerability and fear of retribution, even defeat, put what their country had done to others in a new light. Again, though, the sense of complicity pulled the population in opposing directions. One was to harden their fighting spirit, now that the war was all or nothing. As Goebbels noted in spring 1943, "Experience shows that once a movement and a people have burned the bridges behind them, they will fight more unrestrainedly than if they still have the possibility of retreat."[70] Both the Allied bombings and the Germans' own culpability helped the Nazis forge a "community of destiny" (*Schicksalsgemeinschaft*) that would fight on. That, however, was no longer the whole *Volksgemeinschaft* they had had behind them in the first half of the war. Growing numbers were blaming the regime for the lack of civilian defense, having doubts about the war and the sacrifices of their loved ones, and worrying that their own suffering was a retribution for German crimes. The soul-searching did not prompt rebellion, but it did lead to a gradually accelerating distancing and withdrawal.

GERMAN JEWS AND OTHER GERMANS

In the course of the Second World War, Nazi Germany and its collaborators murdered 6 million Jews, 3 million Soviet POWs, 500,000 Sinti and Roma, and 9 million non-Jewish civilians, especially Russians, Ukrainians, and Poles.[71] The vast majority of victims were from central and eastern Europe. German POWs died in Soviet hands as well, but this was primarily because Germans had destroyed the harvest or because the prisoners were already exhausted and sick when captured, such as the 100,000 Stalingrad fighters of whom only 5,000 survived. The Soviets did not intentionally exterminate their German prisoners; they were interested in their labor. The German strategy, by contrast, was one of calculated murder. The gas chambers of Auschwitz were the culmination of a killing spree that advanced via the gassing of the disabled in hospital rooms inside Germany (first tested in January 1940 by Aktion T4) and in mobile vans in the annexed Warthegau (Poland) as well as executions in the East by the Einsatzgruppen with a shot to the head (the "Holocaust by bullets"). The first five thousand Jews were in fact gassed in Germany, in Grafeneck Castle, outside Stuttgart, and Brandenburg an der Havel, outside Berlin.[72] The SS made up the vanguard of violence, but the sheer scale of the killings was only possible because of more or less direct support from regular troops, who helped with logistics, rounding up prisoners, and executions. In Belarus, for example, 1.6 million POWs and civilians were murdered, half of them by army units.[73] By the end of the war, the Nazis had exterminated two thirds of all Jews in Europe, including German Jews.

In this period, "Germans" and "German morality" were not terms referring to all Germans. The Nazis ejected certain Germans from their *Volksgemeinschaft*. In 1933, the country was home to half a million German Jews. The vast majority had converted and were assimilated. They were citizens and had fought in the First World War, taught in universities, ran businesses, sewed dresses, cured the sick, listened to Bach, and quoted Goethe. The Nuremberg racial laws in 1935, boycotts, and the removal from public offices and civic associations excluded them step by step from their own nation. During Kristallnacht, on November 29, 1938, 91 Jews were killed and another 30,000 taken to concentration camps. By the end of 1939,

300,000 German Jews had left their homeland; another 117,000 had fled Austria. Of these, 100,000 moved to neighboring countries that were soon occupied by the Nazis. In total, Germans murdered 170,000 of their Jewish fellow citizens. The majority had been deported to concentration camps. When the camps were liberated, a mere 10,000 German Jews were still alive. Another 20,000 had managed to survive in privileged mixed marriages and in the underground. Berlin had been one of the great centers of Jewish life, home to 161,000 German Jews in 1933. Twelve years later, there would be only 8,300 left.

Ernst Richard Neisser was born in 1863 in Liegnitz (Legnica) in Lower Silesia, in what is today Poland, into an assimilated family of German Jews. After medical school, he rose to director of the municipal hospital in Stettin, where he established a pioneering tuberculosis hospital.[74] A member of the Goethe Society, he was typical of so many German Jews: cultured and patriotic. He and his daughter would play the piano together, especially Mozart transcribed for four hands by Busoni. At sixty-eight, he took over a heart sanatorium. When the National Socialists came to power in 1933 and forced him out, he and his wife moved to Berlin. On September 30, 1942, he was told to prepare for his deportation the following morning at eight. His daughter had managed to secure a Swedish entry visa, but by then it was impossible to get out. Neisser's heart was weak, and he would rather commit suicide than be deported and die at the hands of murderers. He and his sister Lise were prepared. They called together their nearest and dearest in his apartment. He brought out an especially fine bottle of wine he had kept for a special occasion. They each took a sip. A colleague from a Berlin sanatorium handed him the poison he had asked for. Ernst Neisser said he felt no hatred. He had lived a good life. It was time to go.[75]

When the Gestapo came for him the following morning, they found his sister dead and Neisser unconscious, his heart still beating. They moved him to the Jewish hospital. It took four days for him to die. At the funeral, his daughter was joined by a few remaining "Aryan" friends. A quartet from the state opera played Mozart's "Ave Verum" and Bach's "Komm süsser Tod" ("Come Sweet Death"). A pastor from the Confessing Church, who himself had been in prison, gave the funeral oration. Ernst Neisser lay in his coffin wrapped in a plain shroud. The Nazis had robbed him of his last suit and watch.

A year earlier, Neisser had lost his wife, Margarethe, who was from the Jewish Pauly family. She, too, committed suicide, after three years of depression, which started after Kristallnacht. His sister-in-law and her two daughters were seized in the Breslau deportations in 1941 and would die two years later in Theresienstadt (Terezín) and in Grüssau, one of the many transit camps. In Germany, only Neisser's daughter and granddaughter survived, protected by the daughter's marriage to an "Aryan" German.

The Neisser family story illustrates the tragic ways in which German Jews responded to the noose tightening around their necks. Suicides were sometimes the result of despair and depression, as in the case of Neisser's wife, but often they stemmed from a position of pride and defiance, as in his own case.[76] Here it was not so much the self that had lost its meaning but the society around them. Suicide was a final assertion of a life well lived and an attempt to carry memories of their beloved Germany to the grave. It was mainly elderly Jews who were more rooted in Germany and less mobile who committed suicide; almost four thousand took their own lives between 1941 and 1943. Exclusion and discrimination robbed them of their reputation and titles as well as their jobs. Beginning in September 1941, German Jews had to wear the yellow star. By 1942, anti-Jewish measures targeted virtually every aspect of daily life with pathological German attention to detail.[77] From May 15, 1942, on, they were no longer allowed to have pets. A month later, they were forbidden to buy cigarettes unless they lived in a privileged mixed marriage, where the husband was not Jewish. On June 19, they had to hand over all electrical appliances, including hot plates. On July 7, the last remaining Jewish schools were shut, and German Jews were prohibited from entering cafés and waiting rooms in train stations. Three days later, they were banned from sending gifts to those already deported. On July 13, blind and deaf German Jews were no longer allowed to wear the customary arm bands that had encouraged people to help them. Then, in September 1942, came the big wave of deportations that Neisser escaped by taking his own life. In early October, all Jews in concentration camps within the Reich were deported to Auschwitz.

Mathilde Bing was fifty-three years old when she tried to escape to Sweden in spring 1943. She was arrested in Rostock, on the Baltic coast, and detained in the main assembly camp in Berlin. On June 27 she wrote to her two sons, who had made it to Britain in 1939. "My beloved boys! The time has come: tomorrow we will be taken away. Whether I will ever reappear, I do not know." She had "tried everything to survive" and promised to "continue to do so": "only when it becomes too horrible, will I make an end." Her longing to see them again kept her going. "In these terrible times, it was always a big, indeed the only comfort that both of you were safe and happy abroad." It was said that they were being deported "to a work camp in Upper Silesia, to Auschwitz, and from there to work in Birkenau or Monowitz." "Farewell, I cannot go on, otherwise I will cry and I want to remain strong to the end . . .

A thousand kisses... Mutti." On June 29, 1943, the 39th Osttransport reached Auschwitz, where Mathilde Bing was murdered. Her husband had suffered the same fate a few months earlier.[78]

The German-Jewish Mayer family had fled to the Netherlands after Kristallnacht. In September 1944, they were deported from the Westerbrok assembly camp to Theresienstadt (Terezín) in Bohemia. At the end of the month, the sons were moved to Auschwitz. The older of the two, twelve-year-old Leopold, wrote to his parents to reassure them. "I can guarantee you that I will make it through—inevitabilities excepted. I have the talent to seal myself off from the outside world like a hedgehog who curls up to protect itself against a hostile environment." He had learned to be frugal, and he believed that he was rising to the challenge God had chosen him for: "to do my bit and help that such tragedy which the Jewish people in particular and other peoples across the earth are currently going through will not repeat itself." He would be resilient, soak up the good, repel all evil, and wait for "the gate to freedom to open." "Dear parents," he begged, "please, do not bury yourself in tears but have faith in our reunion and the future... have the strength to live for us, your sons. *Chisku we imzu lanu* ["Make us strong and embolden us"—from the penitential prayer]." Barely a month later, their father was sent to Auschwitz and killed. Leopold and his brother lived to see the gates to freedom open when Auschwitz was liberated at the end of January 1945. Like thousands of others, they would both die from malnutrition shortly thereafter, in Dachau. Only their mother survived.[79]

SHAME, COMPASSION, INDIFFERENCE, FEAR

By 1942, many contemporaries were aware of mass shootings. Yet hardly anyone, not even that most astute observer Victor Klemperer, the author of *I Will Bear Witness*, was able to put the pieces together into a general picture of a genocide. Klemperer, a professor of eighteenth-century French literature, had been hounded out of his university in Dresden but survived thanks to his "Aryan" wife. In his diary, he described how his world was shrinking in these years, yet, the darker the hour, the brighter the patriotic memories of some surviving Jews. In January 1943, he recorded a meeting of three friends. "For all three, the First World War is the greatest and most beautiful event. They always hark back to it, as an adventure and a collective experience shared with the Germans; yet, all three are proud that they have remained Jews—as if it were a Kantian fulfilment of duty!"[80]

The intensification of antisemitic propaganda after the events at Stalingrad and Hamburg was having its effect. In August 1943, a "well-dressed and intelligent-looking" twelve-year-old boy shouted at Klemperer, "Kill him! You old Jew, you old Jew."[81] Klemperer, though, like many others in his increasingly desperate situation, kept taking comfort from small acts of kindness. The sixty-one-year-old Klemperer was forced to work in a factory. One day he was lifting a heavy chest of tea. An "Aryan" worker came up to him and relieved him of the task, saying, "Come on now, hand it over... you do not get that much meat."[82] Every new step of victimization by the Nazis set off a new search by the victim for a "decent" German. This was even truer for the non-Jewish partner in mixed marriages. Personalizing matters in this way often blinded them to the complicity of the state apparatus, justice system, and civil service in the persecution of the Jews—from their expulsion from public office to the deportations and mass murder. In Hamburg, the retired teacher Luise Solmitz went back and forth to the local authorities on behalf of her Jewish husband and took hope from officials who expressed at least some sympathy with their situation: "As little as we will be humiliated by all that is being done to us, as much can we be lifted up by friendliness and kindness—the decent people we have come to know thanks to the whole thing. To know that they exist is a big plus next to the many, many losses."[83]

In 1933, many non-Jewish Germans still made a special point of going to their German-Jewish doctor or lawyer in open defiance of a Nazi boycott. In the following years such displays of solidarity began to disappear. Empathy steadily narrowed. The Nuremberg race laws of 1935 had popular support, and during Kristallnacht ordinary Germans joined the SA in beating up Jewish shopkeepers. Some were horrified by the disorderly violence, but often less out of concern for the victims than for the destruction of property that could have been confiscated. The majority settled down into a mode of passivity.[84] When the deportations began in 1941, some cheered them on, pleased to see "all the useless mouths" gone and gladly helping themselves to their possessions, sold cheap in public auctions A few felt it was unchristian and unduly harsh on elderly Jews. In Hamburg, some firms anonymously donated packages of food for the journey. Most, however, simply looked on.[85]

While never universal, knowledge of atrocities was certainly widespread. On November 1, 1941, the diplomat Ulrich von Hassell recorded the "revulsion on the part of all decent people for the shameless measures" against Jews and prisoners in the East and against Jews in Germany.[86] Soldiers took pictures of executions and mentioned them to their families, sometimes approvingly. On November 16, 1941, the twenty-six-year-old Anton Böhrer, an infantry sergeant, wrote to his sister from near Kharkiv, Ukraine, that Jews had been hanged in reprisal for an attack on a building. One had to be "harsh and merciless," he explained. "The Jews here have been finished off very quickly, and that is how one should do it everywhere. Then we will finally be left in peace by this trash people [*Mistvolk*]."[87]

Hans Albring was more perturbed by what he had seen in Belorussia. In March 1942, he wrote to a friend from the Catholic youth movement about how the killings were becoming more systematic. Previously, Jews were just shot and left in a heap, he wrote, but now they were sorted and lime was spread across their bodies. Eugen Altrogge replied from his infantry unit near Dnipropetrovsk, Ukraine: "Yesterday evening we sat together talking about those things that make one ashamed to be German ... This has nothing any longer to do with antisemitism. It is inhumanity ... How it will have to be atoned one day! When I hear such stories—and firsthand—I want to despair. But what can we do? Keep our mouth shut and continue to serve."[88]

For anyone prepared to listen, there were many channels that delivered gruesome news back to the home front. Karl Dürkefälden worked as an engineer in a machine factory in Celle, in northern Germany, and kept a private record of what he heard in 1942. In February, a German soldier told him on a train that "such mass executions had not happened in the previous war." A few days later, Dürkefälden read in a newspaper article that Hitler promised the Jews would be "exterminated." In June, his brother-in-law returned from the Ukraine and reported that there were no Jews left after mass executions by German police. In the same month, he heard from other soldiers that entire villages had been wiped out, including women and children. In August, his mother-in-law told him that a soldier had mentioned the murder of ten thousand Jews in Russia. In October 1942, a colleague at work sighed, "the poor Jews ..."; according to his brother-in-law, who was visiting from the front, all Jews in the Caucasus had been killed, "regardless whether pregnant women, children, or babies." Among the troops, knowledge of atrocities was sufficiently widespread that soldiers often did not act surprised when they were mentioned.[89]

It was around this time that concerned Germans began to whisper about gassing and speculate about the fate that awaited German Jews after their deportation. "Terrible rumors are circulating about the fate of the evacuees," Ruth Andreas-Friedrich wrote in her diary in December 1942: "of mass executions and starvation, torture and gassing."[90] The extermination camps—Auschwitz, Treblinka, and others—were in the East, but signs of violence were already becoming widespread inside the old Reich before the death marches in the final months of the war. In May 1942, for example, the Gestapo organized a public hanging of nineteen Polish inmates from the concentration camp Buchenwald in a field in Thuringia, with several hundred curious spectators, including women and children; it was to avenge the murder of a German policeman and two affairs the prisoners allegedly had with German women.[91] The deportations in 1941–43 happened in full view of the public. By then Germany was peppered with a vast network of satellite camps; Buchenwald alone had 139 sub-camps. In many cities, concentration camp inmates were a ubiquitous presence, used for the most dangerous jobs, such as clearing bomb sites. The few people, like Klemperer, who somehow evaded deportation were made to do hard labor in German firms, their increasingly dire condition plainly visible to their "Aryan" bosses and coworkers. Beginning in summer 1944, Hungarian Jews were moved from Auschwitz to the Reich to work in the armaments industry.

There was not much weeping among the population about what happened to their Jewish fellow citizens. This lack of compassion signaled both a tacit acknowledgment of complicity and fear of retaliation.

If people showed some reaction, it was one of shame. When Jews were required to wear the Star of David beginning in September 1941, Andreas-Friedrich noted how children were publicly taunting Jews in the streets of Berlin. Her partner slapped two of them and said they "should be ashamed of" themselves. Onlookers smiled approvingly. "Almost everyone we meet," she wrote, "is unhappy about the new regulation: they are ashamed, as we are."[92] But her circle of friends and critics was hardly representative of society at large.

In June 1942, the Scholl siblings, Hans and Sophie, and their fellow students in the White Rose resistance circle, in their first flyer appealed to their compatriots' sense of shame to try to shake them out of their "apathy." "Every honest German today is ashamed of their government," they wrote. They quoted Schiller's critique of Sparta's constitution for treating human beings as means, not ends, and finished with Goethe's call for "freedom!" Just as important as humanism and Kantian reason was their Christian faith. Shame was linked to a moral duty to defend human dignity and freedom against the Nazis' "atheist state." The fight against the Nazi regime had to go into the "metaphysical" causes of the war, they wrote. "Behind all objective, logical considerations lurks the irrational element, that is, the struggle against the demon, against the messengers of the Antichrist." "Hitler," they wrote in a flyer in January 1943, "cannot win the war, only extend it." Now guilt and fear of retribution rather than shame were invoked to rouse Germans: "Germans! Do you and your children want to suffer the same fate that happened to the Jews?" they asked. Germans had to wake from their deep sleep, turn against the Nazis, and sabotage them if they did not want to be judged alongside their leaders. The students hoped for "freedom and honor," a future federal state that guaranteed freedom of speech and conscience and that protected citizens against criminal violence. Above all, they hoped for a spiritual renewal. On February 18, 1943, Hans and Sophie Scholl were caught by a university porter as they were distributing copies of their sixth flyer. They were handed over to the Gestapo, sentenced to death, and beheaded four days later.[93]

Andreas-Friedrich and the students of the White Rose showed that compassion was possible, even at the height of Nazi power, but their resistance circles were very small. For almost all Germans, the main concern was the war and its impact on them, not the fate of the Jews. Since the 1960s, the Holocaust has been seen as the defining event of the war. During the war, it was not. Allied surveillance of German POWs revealed that many soldiers were aware of mass murder, even if they had not participated in it, but it was a subject that basically did not interest them.[94] While shocking to us now, it is not surprising in retrospect: step by step, Jews had been further driven out of society until they were stripped of their humanity.

In Fort Hunt, American intelligence was listening in on conversations among German prisoners. Their transcripts show that knowledge of atrocities was widespread, while giving us a snapshot of German soldiers' ideological prejudices and the psychological strategies they fell back on when trying to square the murder of the Jews and other civilians with the belief that they were fighting a just war. One of the earliest moments the topic came up was on June 13, 1943, in a conversation among three young submarine crew members who had been captured in the North Atlantic: Drechsel, Meissle, and Schulz. Drechsel started talking about Jews from Lithuania and Poland:

> D:... They are dangerous people. How I have executed Jews there.
> M: Why executed?
> D: Every German soldier... [whispering], with the help of German police...
> M: There are pigs among the Germans just as there are pigs among the Jews, but there are also good Jews...
> D: I am sure the foreigners, too, know that so many Jews have been killed... sixteen-, seventeen-, eighteen-year-olds. They had to undress down to their shirt... and then they were shot. They did not even know why they were shot...

D: [whispering about an internment camp for Jews] There was a twenty-three-year-old pregnant woman and she had to do hard labor, my friend. And fourteen-year-old children too.
M: How many did they shoot?
D: Oh, it was incredible, and 60 percent were German...
M: That is not just. If we lose the war, then the Jews will make us pay the price... In my town [Vöhringen in Swabia], they dragged the Jews from the shops, and shaved the heads of women and girls and then paraded them through the streets. The Russian is not human, but there are also some wild beasts among us...
S: They will make us pay the price for what we have done. Hundreds and thousands of innocent men, women, and children murdered.
D: How could we help it, my boy?
S: Was it the fault of the Jews that they were murdered?
D: No, that is what's so sad about it.
S: Yes, that is sad... [But] Germany did not start the war out of its own volition.
D: We would have been attacked by the communists.
M: What for?
S: Well, there were many reasons, and that's why we started the war. Every great nation should have the right to defend itself; if the others see that they have not got anything, then they will be outdone.[95]

When the three talked it was still possible for them, as for many of their comrades, to think that Germany might not lose. In the final stages of the war, as the probability of defeat increased, so did concern about retaliation for what Germans had done to the Jews. Mass executions very rarely came up in the conversations among the POWs in Fort Hunt, but when they did, prisoners' instinctive response was disgust mixed with shame and fear. "Was that human?" one asked in early April 1945 when recalling how women and children had to dig their own graves. "Ugh, one is ashamed to be German," his comrade added. "How can that possibly be highly cultured, undressing women!" Another confessed, "I felt sorry for the people." But when his Catholic cellmate suggested that they were complicit, he responded, "One could not swim against the current."[96]

If there was shame and occasional pity, it tended to be drowned out by fear of revenge. Heinrich Voigtel, the son of a Protestant pastor, grew up in a liberal nationalist household in Thuringia. In October 1944, he was twenty-eight years old and, after tours in France and Russia, fighting in the Apennines. In his diary, he noted how the mood among the troops was shifting. There were still a few fanatics who believed in final victory. More and more soldiers, however, were consumed by fear for their families and what would happen to them once communist gangs ravaged their homeland. "Even greater" still, he wrote, "is their fear of the Jews and Poles. Here, in the face of their own existential fear the burden of past injustice rises to the top of their consciousness." The treatment of Jews and Poles was "not only a fateful political mistake, but a human injustice that increasingly burdens the national conscience." Voigtel now routinely overheard statements such as "Once they are unleashed, they will have some accounts to settle," "One overdid it, it really was no longer human"—even from members of the Nazi Party who would never have dared say such things a year earlier.[97]

The few thousand mainly elderly German Jews who managed to escape the deportations were more and more at the mercy of small groups of actors, with vicious Nazis on one side and an underground network of helpers on the other. The day after the abortive attempt on Hitler's life on July 20, 1944, an electrician and a plumber got together in Berlin and decided to avenge the attack. One had joined the NSDAP in 1932, the other the SS in 1937. Their group leader refused to be part of it, but the two went ahead regardless. They paid a visit to the Jewish tailor F., dragging him to a bridge across the Panke River, where someone had painted a Soviet star. F. was ordered to remove the graffiti, initially with his bare hand, then with a stone. In full view of onlookers, the two tormentors burned cigarettes on his back, pushed him against the railing, and beat him with fists and sticks. F. eventually collapsed and was thrown into the river. The plumber waded into the Panke and tried to drown him. F. was saved by an air raid and was moved to the Jewish hospital. He had been so badly beaten that his wife was barely able to recognize him. He died a few days later. In 1953, the two assailants would be sentenced to ten years in prison.[98]

Only a few lucky ones were able to seize a helping hand. About ten thousand to fifteen thousand German Jews went underground during the Second World War—the so-called *U-Boote*, or submarines. Around four thousand of them survived.[99] Often it was mixed Christian-Jewish couples who provided a hiding space, but the network extended to "Aryan" friends, former business associates, and members of the criminal underworld; in February 1942, during the *Fabrikaktion*—the roundup of the last Jews—it was neighbors, employers, and in some cases policemen who warned Jews of their impending deportation and urged them to hide. When we think of their experience, we tend to think of Anne Frank's ordeal, hidden away in Prinsengracht 263 in Amsterdam for two years before being discovered and deported to Auschwitz. That was atypical, though. For most, the underground was a revolving sofa. To evade the Nazis, most *U-Boote* had to be able to move quickly from one hiding place to another. On average, each Jew was dependent on ten helpers—a small minority of the German population. They needed not just a place to hide, but also food, clothing, and medicine. In Berlin, Andreas-Friedrich and her friends in the resistance group Emil counterfeited ration cards and fake papers for bombed-out Jewish friends, with the help of a stolen Nazi stamp.[100]

The number of helpers was small, but they came from all walks of life and included cleaning ladies as well as doctors, businessmen, and communists. Many years after the war, in autobiographies and interviews, helpers discussed their motivations. Some did not remember agonizing over their choices when they decided to act. They felt a moral imperative to help, triggered not so much by pity for the suffering Jews as by their own self-esteem. They saw themselves as "decent" Germans, unlike the barbaric Nazis. "To have turned away from the Jews," the philosopher Kristen Renwick Monroe has written, "would have meant turning away from one's self."[101]

Post facto interviews are a difficult source. They almost inevitably tell us about the self-image of historical actors after the event, not at the time. In the Nazi years there were plenty of Germans who turned away from the Jews without necessarily sacrificing their self-esteem. Nor were all the "unsung heroes" humanitarians. Motives varied. Anti-Nazism could be mixed with profiteering, neighborly solidarity with a more selfish eye on the future—the closer the defeat, the wiser to have a Jewish friend who could testify on one's behalf after the war. Helpers put themselves in danger, and sometimes ended up denouncing Jews for fear of their own life. Others took advantage of Jews' vulnerability and helped themselves to the few assets they had left. In some cases, it was Nazi Party members who offered a hiding space. The Munich lawyer Benno Schülein, for example, hid among a network of gentile friends that included Otto Jordan, a merchant and member of the Nazi Party since 1933. Jordan wanted to help, but he also profited from the arrangement. Help rarely came free. Underground networks depended on opportunism as well as courage and sympathy. Jordan's cook naturally knew the number of mouths she was feeding. Schülein survived, in part, because the cook agreed to keep her mouth shut instead of denouncing him to her friend in the SS. In exchange, her boss looked the other way when she helped herself to food, linen, and other valuables.[102] In Lenggries, Dr. Sophie Mayer survived thanks to the local police commissioner, who shared his family's ration cards with her. She lived in their sitting room. Yes, she told the denazification tribunal in 1946, he was a party member but also a "good brave man who was forced to wear a party badge." "They always comforted me and lifted up my spirits," she said.[103]

MORALS, HARD AND CLEAN

If the Nazi regime rested on broad popular foundations, its aims and methods relied on an extensive system of violence. At its center was the SS, which personified death, a skull gracing its uniforms. But it had many helpers. Ultimately, the deadliness of the Nazi regime lay in its ability to recruit some 200,000 perpetrators actively involved in mass murder.[104]

Under Heinrich Himmler, the Reichsführer SS, the Schutzstaffel, originally little more than Hitler's bodyguard, grew into a vast paramilitary organization, 1 million men strong, a state within the state that absorbed the secret police and security forces. The SS terrorized political opponents and defeatists at home, staffed the feared Einsatzgruppen who carried out mass executions in the East, and ran the concentration camps. The sickly Himmler, an agronomist by training, was the pinwheel of terror. Wherever he went, violence escalated. He joined the SS in 1925 as member number 168. In 1929, he became its head. After the seizure of power in 1933, Himmler set up the concentration camps in order to suppress and silence political opponents. In 1938, after the annexation of Austria, Einsatzgruppen were set up and began to operate in the Sudetenland. In October 1939, Himmler was tasked with overseeing the "Germanization" of the East. At this stage, forced migration (rather than extermination) still dominated Nazi policy. This would change with the attack on the Soviet Union in June 1941. In early August of that year, after Himmler's visit to the Eastern Front, the SS was ordered to execute not only Jewish men but all Jews in the Soviet Union; Jewish women were to be driven into "the swamps."[105] By the end of the year, the Einsatzgruppen had killed several hundred thousand Jews.

Mass murder did not simply follow from Himmler's orders. The Nazi regime was a jumble of competing Nazi and state structures with a Führer at the center who had an aversion to act. It led to what the historian Hans Mommsen called a "cumulative radicalization," with eager officers and officials on the ground and leaders and bureaucrats at the top pushing each other along the road to extermination.[106] On January 20, 1942, at the Wannsee conference, Nazi leaders decided to deport all Polish and Western European Jews to camps, work them to death, and murder them instead of sending them to Russia after victory.

Half a year later, in July 1942, it was Himmler who gave the order to clear all ghettos and send all Jews from occupied Poland to new extermination camps at Belzec, Sobibor, and Treblinka; the SS had first used mobile gas vans—a killing technology they had developed in their euthanasia program—before the installation of gas chambers. In December, Himmler ordered that thousands of Sinti and Roma be deported to Auschwitz. In April 1943, he explained how German troops should retreat in order to maximize the damage for the advancing Soviet enemy: any space vacated was to be emptied of people, who were to be either killed or enslaved. In summer 1943, Himmler also absorbed the Ministry of the Interior into his empire of violence. The death sentences for subverting military morale immediately shot up.[107]

Himmler did not think of himself or his SS charges as immoral. Quite the contrary. This appears shocking to us: Himmler's values and actions of course defy our own basic notions of morality. Nonetheless, it is important to recognize that the Nazis had their own moral code. On October 4, 1943, Himmler addressed SS leaders in Posen in a two-hour-long speech that mixed an analysis of the war with ideological ranting and an appeal to the virtues of the SS. One principle, he stressed, had to hold absolutely true for an SS man: "We have to be honest, decent, loyal, and comradely toward members of our own blood but to no one else." They would never be "raw or heartless, where it was not necessary." But "whether other peoples live in comfort or die of famine, I only care about as far as we can use them as slaves for our *Kultur*." In any case, Russians were not full humans but *Menschentiere* ("human beasts"). It did not interest him if ten thousand Russian women died in the course of digging anti-tank ditches as long as these were completed for Germany. It was "a crime against our own blood" to lament the treatment of others as inhumane. If you did, you were "a murderer of your own blood." Himmler then turned to the "extermination of the Jewish people," a "very heavy chapter," he said. Most of the SS men knew what it meant to leave behind five hundred or one thousand corpses. He praised those soldiers for having gone through with the executions, for being "hard" yet "decent," without giving in to sentiment. They had contributed a glorious new chapter of honor to German history, he assured them, for they had saved the nation from the dangerous enemy and secret agent that had sabotaged them in the First World War. Everyone in the SS needed to remember its guiding principle: "blood, selection, hardness." They adhered to the law of nature: "What is hard is good; what is powerful is good; what wins out in the struggle of existence physically, in willpower and ethically, that is the good." The virtues of the SS man were, consequently: loyalty, duty, courage, honesty, justice, respect for property, sincerity, integrity. They should all act as comrades, take on responsibility, work hard, and avoid alcohol.[108]

This was, of course, wishful thinking. Drunkenness, corruption, and sadism were rife in the SS.[109] Still, Himmler spelled out the image that SS men drew on for a moral justification of immoral acts. The virtuous German was a warrior—hard but "clean," racially and ethically. The essence of all life was struggle, not comfort, and only the strongest survived.[110] Since racial inequality was natural, it would be wrong to try and rectify it. The motto, then, was "To each his own," the words that appeared on the gate to Buchenwald. The Jews lived outside the circle of moral concern. They were bourgeois, strove for profit and comfort, and were driven by envy and selfishness. For the Nazis, morality was rooted in action, not reflection or compassion. Here was a crucial difference from liberal humanitarianism, which assumes that moral judgment can be trained and developed through critical reflection. For the Nazis, morality was fixed in nature and threatened by modernity; a "good" German acted out the law of nature. In any case, critical judgment was unnecessary, because the Führer knew what was best. Individual lives were only means to an end: the survival of the *Volk*. The Nazis did not throw off all bourgeois virtues—honesty, thrift, hard work, decency, responsibility, and self-sacrifice remained important. But they were now subordinated to the survival of the German race. The Fifth Commandment ceased to be absolute. Germans could—indeed should—kill enemies of the *Volk*. They remained "clean" and "decent" as long as they were orderly killers instead of sadistic beasts. In May 1943, an SS man was sentenced to ten years in prison for exterminating Jews without orders, allowing his men to descend into "vile brutalization" and taking "shameless and disgusting" pictures.[111] One reason SS commanders moved to gas chambers was concern about how mass executions by bullets were unhinging their men.

In a way, the Nazis turned the Golden Rule around. Instead of the command to "treat others as you want to be treated," their motto was: Do to other races what you do not want them to do to your own. The murder of Jews and other "enemies" was morally justified as a preventative act of racial self-defense.

Exterminating millions of people requires not only ideological fanaticism but logistics. This was the expertise of Adolf Eichmann, who since 1939 had been in charge of organizing the mass deportations. Eichmann worked in the Reich's main security office and was not a policy maker. His job was to get things done. Thanks to his spectacular capture in Argentina in 1960 and the subsequent televised trial in Jerusalem, Eichmann became the face of the Holocaust—the exemplar of the "banality of evil," as the philosopher Hannah Arendt famously called it in her eyewitness account of the trial. Eichmann, she wrote, was the very type of person the Nazis needed to carry out their genocidal plan: conscientious yet thoughtless; efficient and loyal but not fanatical; a family man who wanted his peace and quiet, happy to deceive himself that ultimately he was just carrying out orders.[112] He was what the Germans call a "*Schreibtischtäter*," in this case an administrator of death who signed the execution orders without looking up from his desk. Arendt was an original thinker who wrote brilliantly about the human condition and the nature of totalitarianism, but in her portrayal of Eichmann she fell victim to deception—Eichmann was not only a logistical mastermind but a talented actor as well, and the trial in Jerusalem was his stage. Eichmann was playing to the audience trying to save his neck, performing as the intelligent yet nonideological bureaucrat whose sole duty was to do his job, and who since 1945 had changed. He even had the nerve to quote Immanuel Kant. It was all for show.

In 1956–57, in Argentina, Eichmann had written notes and given taped interviews to a right-wing author that give a picture of his true state of mind. There was no such thing as universal morality, he said. War had its own morality, and it was natural to kill one's enemies. Eichmann argued that "the instinct for self-preservation is stronger than any ethical claim"; Kant probably turned in his grave at the thought. Eichmann had only contempt for Nazis who claimed that they had just been following orders—that was "cheap nonsense." The Jews were responsible for the war and thus had to be exterminated. The concentration camps were the real battlegrounds in the struggle with the racial enemy, and Eichmann felt he deserved more recognition for his role from those who tended to glorify military battles. The gas wagons, the executions, and the deportations—he acknowledged that he found it difficult to watch them at times. If he had any regrets, though, it was for not being "hard" enough to get the whole job done. "I must honestly tell you," he said to his interviewer, "had we killed all 10.3 million Jews... then I would have been satisfied, and would say that we have annihilated the enemy." But, sadly, many were saved by "the trick of destiny."

At his trial in Jerusalem, Eichmann's acting skills were not good enough. He was found guilty on fifteen counts of crimes against humanity and against the Jewish people, and hanged on June 1, 1962.[113]

It is tempting to assume a divide between a "modern" bureaucratic mode marked by efficiency and rationality and an atavistic ideology driven by faith and conviction. But this would be an "ideal-typical" distinction, in the words of Max Weber. In reality, many perpetrators had no problem being both: they were bureaucrats *and* ideologues, especially in the upper echelons of the regime. The life of Werner Best reveals many of the typical stepping stones that led a generation of highly educated professionals to become Nazi functionaries.[114] It was Best who built up the Reich's main security office, in which Eichmann had his department, and who steered the deportations of Jews from France to Auschwitz in 1942. Born in 1903, Best, like Himmler (who was three years older), missed out fighting in the First World War, but overcompensated with a faith in struggle as the essence of life. That war had brought social decline as well as national shame. Best's father, a civil servant with the postal service, died fighting in France in 1914, and left young Werner a dual legacy: to look after his mother and to restore Germany's pride. Political humiliation was personal. His mother, a mayor's daughter, had to make ends meet on a small widow's pension. Worse, their hometown, Mainz, was in the occupied Rhineland and half their house had been taken over by French soldiers.

Bright and ambitious, Best finished at the top of his class in school and studied law in Frankfurt. He was fascinated by ideas, but not those of the Enlightenment. Germany's crisis illustrated to him the bankruptcy of liberalism and its ideals of individualism and progress. Humanity was not universal, Best believed, and history was always a conflict between peoples. Instead of being independent agents, individuals acted out their *Volk*'s natural interest. In 1926, Best wrote an article entitled "Conscience" for a student magazine, in which he explained that this did not have to mean one was amoral: "We can respect those we are fighting against, perhaps even those we need to annihilate." But it was impossible to fight destiny. The best one could do was to abstain from "hatred and vulgarity" and adopt instead a "sober objectivity" to minimize any problems in the course of the struggle.[115]

In turning to the *Volk*, Best was turning against his father's generation, with their weepy nostalgia for the Kaiser and the good old times before the war. The *Volk* was best served by self-discipline and rationality. It was these core beliefs that guided him in his career as he expanded the police apparatus of terror. Best personified the technocratic Nazi, cold and functional. The Jews had to go, he agreed. But he abhorred antisemitism driven by hatred, lust, or envy. Emotions only got in the way of a rational handling of the Jewish question. Best prided himself on being "*korrekt*." Like so many others in his generation of professional lawyers and administrators who made their career under the Nazis, Best's moral compass had shrunk to an assessment of *how* actions were carried out—objective, knightly, proper: "good" versus impassioned and irrational, which were "bad." The substance of actions, however, was no longer subject to moral judgment. How could it be otherwise? Since the *Volk* was the supreme value, the only ethical command was that it lived on. Self-preservation became an end in itself.

On the ground, mass murder was mainly carried out by the SS, but it would have been impossible without the tacit approval, logistical support, and sometimes direct involvement of the regular army. Most generals shared the view that the war in the East was different and had to be fought with whatever means necessary. This, it needs to be stressed, was the creed even before Operation Barbarossa was launched, and not a reaction to later losses. General Gotthard Heinrici moved to the Eastern Front in June 1941 and a few months later took command of the 4th Army. Raised in Wilhelmine Germany in the 1880s in an aristocratic family of officers and pastors, he was convinced that Weimar was a conspiracy of Jews and Bolsheviks. From the outset, he ordered his troops to show "no mercy."[116] Von Manstein, the field marshal who failed to rescue the Stalingrad fighters, similarly believed that he was fighting a war of annihilation between rival ideologies. On November 20, 1941, Manstein issued an order to all his troops that echoed the one General von Reichenau had given to the 6th Army a month earlier: they were fighting "a crusade against the Jewish-Bolshevik system." Their aim was the "eradication of the Asiatic influence in civilized Europe." It required each soldier to go beyond the conventional rules of war. He had "to avenge the bestial acts" committed against the German people and appreciate the need for "hard but fair atonement for the subhuman Jewry." Such measures, he added, would also sniff out sabotage, which, "experience had shown, was plotted by the Jews."[117] On Christmas, Manstein's 11th Army provided the Einsatzgruppen with troops, weapons, and trucks to murder the Jews of Simferopol. After New Year, a rumor made the rounds that partisans had slit the throats of some wounded German soldiers. Von Manstein's troops conducted a punitive raid in western Crimea, rounded up 1,200 arbitrarily selected civilians in Eupatoria, and killed them.

On the Eastern Front, 90 percent of all army units carried out the Commissar Order to execute any captured Soviet political commissar.[118] When the German army began its retreat, some units, such as the 35th Infantry Division, used civilians as human shields against the Red Army.[119] Massacres and reprisals against civilians were routine in the Balkans as well as on the Eastern front, as we have seen. Those fighting only in France produced nothing like the orgy of violence that rolled over the East. Even France, though, was not spared atrocities; the Waffen-SS tank division "Das Reich" wiped out the entire village of Oradour-sur-Glane on June 10, 1944. Antisemitism, too, took its toll in France, as German officers decided to go along with the deportations of Jews in exchange for Hitler letting them run a less harsh occupation policy toward the rest of the French population.[120] Even some of the officers plotting to assassinate Hitler in July 1944 had been implicated in Nazi crimes. Henning von Tresckow played a key role in planning the military operations of the Army Group Center (Heeresgruppe Mitte). In the summer and autumn of 1941, he and fellow officers learned of the killing spree unleashed by the SS in their rear. They closed their eyes to that and pressed on with their military objectives. It was only when the advance ground to a halt and a lightning victory was no longer possible that Tresckow's conscience began to wake up to the massacre in Borissow on October 20, 1941, in which thousands of Jewish women and children were killed along with the men.[121] It was then that he joined the resistance.

First Lieutenant Hellmuth Stieff, another member of the July 20 plot, wrote to his wife at the end of November 1941 from outside Moscow. He felt he had become "the tool of a despotic will to exterminate which ignored all rules of humanity and basic decency." "These days," he told her a week later, "I unconsciously give orders to execute so-and-so many commissars or partisans, he or me—it is as simple as that." On January 10, 1942, he confessed, "We have taken on so much guilt, for we are jointly responsible. To me, the approaching Judgment appears a fair punishment for all the foul crimes we Germans have committed or tolerated in the last few years... I am so tired of this horror without end."[122] Wilhelm Speidel, the commander in Greece, also found his way to the resistance. He felt that mass reprisals against the population were counterproductive, but ordered them regardless. Such was war, he appeased his conscience, and in any case, he said, "the German population is suffering incomparably heavier losses from English and American terror flights on German towns"—as if the two were morally linked and the suffering of the latter excused the former.[123]

Hitler and his generals provided a license to kill, but soldiers pulled the trigger. Mass murder was not completely anonymous and bureaucratized. Of the 6 million murdered Jews, Germans shot almost 2 million in mass executions. The number of those directly involved in murder was therefore considerable. Who they were and what made them do it have been the subjects of heated debates among scholars. Did they arrive at the killing fields intent and ready to kill, driven by an "eliminationist" antisemitism, as Daniel Goldhagen maintains? Or were they "ordinary men" who were turned into murderers by the brutalizing experience of war and peer pressure, as Christopher Browning argued in his study of Police Battalion 101?[124]

Because of this controversy, a number of studies have examined particular atrocities and the biographies of soldiers. It is, they suggest, probably unwise to look for the answer in either the social situation of battle or the mental predisposition of the individual. What mattered was their interplay, as illustrated by the massacre in Kommeno in western Greece on August 16, 1943. There had been no attacks on German troops from that village. But that did not stop the 98th Mountain Infantry Regiment from going on a killing spree. At dawn, they launched grenades and then broke into the locals' houses and killed 317 people. The man in charge was Lieutenant Willibald Röser. Born in 1914, he advanced from Hitler Youth leader to protégé of General Ferdinand Schörner, a ruthless proponent of iron discipline and no mercy. Röser was handed the command of the regiment's 12th Company in the Caucasus in 1942 and acquired the nickname "Nero of the 12./98" for his brutality. Röser was a "150-percent Nazi," to quote one of his men. For the attack on Kommeno, he called for volunteers. Some stepped forward but not enough, so others were ordered to join; tellingly, only one of them refused and stayed behind. During the massacre, some soldiers shot into the ground and told locals to flee to the orange groves. But most followed the order ruthlessly and murdered children, the elderly, and anyone else they could find, making jokes and mutilating the bodies. The regiment's priest noted afterward how some soldiers struggled with their conscience: on the one hand, it was wrong to kill women and children; on the other, they felt it was wrong to disobey an order. Killing male civilians had already become normal. Most of the German soldiers had been brutalized on the Eastern Front, others in the war with partisans in Montenegro. In addition, Röser gave them a moral justification: killing women and children was just revenge for the British bombing of Cologne.[125]

It was not necessary to be a young indoctrinated Nazi to commit murder. Nor were all atrocities committed by soldiers who had served on the Eastern Front; none of the Hermann Göring Division that killed 250 innocent men, women, and children in Tuscany on June 29, 1944, had fought in the East, for example.[126] But when one or both of these factors were present, the probability of producing pure killers certainly increased; significantly, most of the soldiers involved in the Tuscan massacre were young hotheads. Peer pressure played a role in escalating violence, too. It often needed particularly vicious leaders like Röser to pull the others along. The war progressively lowered moral thresholds—once it became normal to round up and shoot Jews, it was a short step to killing other male civilians; once it became normal to kill male civilians, it was a short step to murdering women and children as well. The SS and Waffen-SS were particularly vicious, but elite troops among the regular army, such as the tank and mountain divisions, also carried out atrocities. They had a special hatred for partisans—an irregular enemy that threatened their own self-image. The Eastern Front was a particularly brutal school of violence, but some enrolled as more eager pupils and were more ready to kill than others.

Beliefs do not explain everything, but to ignore them altogether would be a big mistake. Devout Catholics and older soldiers could take moral principles with them into the war or had grown up before Hitler and often saw in the eyes of enemy women and children the faces of their own. Virulent antisemitism and anti-Bolshevism meant that many looked at Eastern Europeans from the moment they arrived as subhuman, threatening, and alien, seeing racial and ideological enemies lurking in every field and village.[127] This was very different from the German gaze in France or North Africa and had significant consequences for how they treated their respective enemies.

During and after the war, many officers and soldiers invoked "military necessity" to justify atrocities. But this was really a self-fulfilling prophecy, not a response to an objective situation. Executions, reprisals, and starvation appeared a "necessity" because of a prior racist perception of Jewish and "Asiatic" enemies plotting Germany's downfall. Ideology legitimated action. This was important not least for the psychology of the perpetrators themselves. It enabled them to shift the blame onto the victims.[128]

Not all Germans were willing perpetrators. In a few cases, German officers defied orders and held on to the basic rules of war. One dramatic incident took place in September 1942, when Werner Hartenstein, the commander of submarine U-156, began a rescue operation when he realized that the RMS *Laconia*, which they had just sunk, carried two thousand civilians and POWs; he and nearby German submarines had to abandon the rescue when they came under attack by U.S. bombers but still managed to save more than a thousand people. In the big picture, though, these were rare interventions. A week later Admiral Dönitz ordered that enemy soldiers were no longer to be rescued.[129] One dramatic incident occurred in Corfu in April 1944, when the commander of the island, Emil Jäger, in a rare intervention, tried to stop the deportations of the local Jews; he argued that it would destroy the occupiers' "ethical prestige" with the islanders. By June, the Jews of Corfu were being shipped to Auschwitz.[130] Even in concentration camps there were options. Fritz Bringmann was an apprentice plumber and medical orderly (*Sanitäter*) in KZ Neuengamme, at the outskirts of Hamburg. In 1942, he was told to inject and kill Soviet POWs who had typhus. He refused, and was let off.

After the war, perpetrators on trial routinely invoked the concept of "*Befehlsnotstand*": their hands were tied, they said, and to refuse an order would have been suicidal. We need to distinguish between a "putative" necessity—a subjective fear that disobedience would be followed by punishment—and an objective one. In the light of the growing number of executions of defeatists and deserters, a sense of putative necessity is not entirely implausible; certainly Röser's men knew that he had punished a soldier for refusing to shoot women.[131] Bringmann told the court in 1946 that he expected to be punished and was surprised when he was not. Still, the number of people who suffered serious consequences for refusing to commit murder was tiny. In July 1942, for example, the reserve officer Albert Battel tried to prevent the SS from rounding up Jews in Przemyśl, in southeastern Poland, evacuated several of them, and placed them under the protection of the army; again, while a member of the Nazi Party since 1933, Battel belonged to an older generation—he was born in 1891—was Catholic and a lawyer, and had been reprimanded for his friendly relations with Jews before the war. Himmler was furious and promised to arrest him the moment the war was over. Instead, in 1944, Battel was discharged with heart disease.[132]

A study of eighty-five cases found that for forty-nine men there were no negative consequences for refusing to carry out murder. Fifteen received reprimands or were threatened with being sent to a concentration camp—but these remained threats. Fourteen were transferred to another unit or sent back to Germany. Seven were not promoted. Five were briefly put under house arrest. Four were made to dig pits or seal off an area. Three resigned from their commission. Another three were sent to the more dangerous combat units. Only one was sent to a concentration camp, but even here there were no life-threatening consequences. This was the case of First Lieutenant Klaus Hornig, the officer in charge of Police Battalion 306 in Zamośĉ (Poland) in October 1941. He told his men that to shoot 780 defenseless Soviet POWs would be a breach of military law and smacked of methods used by the Soviet secret police. He would have no truck with it. He, too, was a Catholic and a lawyer. Another unit took over the killing. Hornig was sent to Buchenwald, but not as a regular prisoner; he was placed instead under investigative arrest and continued to receive his officer pay. Eventually he was sentenced to five years in prison. His crime was not a refusal to kill but subverting the morale of the troops by lecturing his soldiers that they had the right to refuse orders that were illegal. He would be liberated by the Americans on April 11, 1945.[133]

The majority of these cases involved officers who had some knowledge of military law. Several asked for a transfer from a concentration camp or the Einsatzgruppen to a combat unit. A few others shot wide intentionally or let Jewish captives escape. Almost half of these individuals did not specify a reason for their action. Among those who did, concern for the victims was not necessarily paramount. Fifteen justified their acts because the orders were illegal. For seven, executions did not fit with their ethos as soldiers. Another seven cited emotional distress. Two worried about political consequences. Only twenty-three invoked reasons of conscience—some religious, some humanist—and even here sometimes there were specific personal factors that triggered their conscience rather than a general concern for life. One soldier said he refused to kill women and children because he was thinking of his own wife and children. Another could not bring himself to pull the trigger because he knew one of the Jews lined up before him.

The tragic conclusion is that Nazi leaders did not need to terrorize soldiers for them to carry out mass executions. Many more could have refused to take part if they had wanted to, without serious risk to their own lives. There may have been a putative fear of being punished, but other enabling factors were at least as important: a widespread belief that orders were orders and had be carried out regardless of their criminal content; faith in Nazi leadership; shared antisemitism; peer pressure; and fear of being ostracized.

TERRIBLE CHOICES

The concentration camps were their own universe of violence, with a powerful gravitational pull difficult to withstand for all those involved, inmates as well as guards. Violence was the currency of daily life in the concentration camps and distributed via a hierarchical division of labor from camp commanders at the top to kapos (prisoner functionaries) at the bottom who kept fellow prisoners in check.[134] Golleschau (Goleszów), a cement factory, was one of the satellite work camps of Auschwitz and the site of a particularly vicious double act that illustrates the ease with which violence could escalate into sadism. Its commander was Johannes Mirbeth; the kapo, Josef Kierspel. Born in Munich in 1905, Mirbeth came from a family of artisans and was a trained carpenter. He joined the SS and Nazi Party in 1931. Early in 1941, he started to work as a guard in Auschwitz. Two years later, in April 1943, Rudolf Höss made him commander of Golleschau. Nine years his senior, Kierspel also came from a family of artisans but drifted into a criminal career that evolved from petty theft to armed robbery. In and out of prison in the 1920s, he ended up a criminal prisoner—inmates marked by a "green" badge—first in Buchenwald and Flossenbürg, then from autumn 1942 in Golleschau, where he quickly rose to camp kapo. One of Mirbeth's tasks was to increase productivity in the camp. According to the trial records after the war, he initially improved nutritional standards and prevented the execution of five Jewish bricklayers he needed for external works. This attitude did not last very long. The slightest breach of discipline sent Mirbeth into a rage. He whipped one Jew senseless, seriously damaging his spine and kidneys, simply for hanging up his laundry at the wrong time. After evening roll calls, Mirbeth would beat prisoners until he was exhausted, then he handed them over to Kierspel. Mirbeth took particular pleasure in showing the kapos how to whip properly by bending his knees to maximize the force of the swing so that it pierced the skin. Mirbeth also shot individual prisoners. And he selected prisoners unfit to work for the extermination camp next door. In 1953, the court sentenced him to six years; Kierspel, by contrast, received a life sentence. Kierspel, the court concluded, had always had a criminal mind-set, while Mirbeth had been turned into a criminal by the Nazi regime.[135]

No doubt, Kierspel was a sadist, but he was also a kapo and prisoner who received his orders from Mirbeth. Of course, Golleschau and the entire camp system had not been Mirbeth's creation. At the same time, when he passed through the gates of the camp he did so as a free man, unlike the prisoners. Mirbeth had chosen to join the SS in 1931. He could have turned down Golleschau and served at the front. Clearly, Mirbeth entered a place of violence with its own rules and abuses. Just as clearly, though, he had been an ardent supporter of a regime that openly practiced violence. Golleschau would not have existed without people like Mirbeth in the first place.

The SS controlled the camps through a strategy of divide and rule. From work discipline to medical care, most aspects of camp life were administered by the inmates themselves; Golleschau, for example, had a total of one thousand prisoners and a mere fifty-two SS men. This created enormous moral dilemmas for prisoners. A privileged position as a kapo could mean access to less dangerous work, better food, and vital medicine for oneself and one's friends—the difference between life and death. On the other hand, becoming a tool for the Nazis meant betraying other prisoners and selling one's soul. These were extraordinarily hard choices, but they were not impossible ones. People steered different paths through the moral thicket, depending in part on their personal willpower and social networks, in part on their moral sense of right and wrong. In the process, the sharp distinction between victims and perpetrators became blurred.

Unlike the "green" Kierspel, many kapos wore a "red" badge. These were political prisoners, especially communists. For camp commanders, this had many attractions: German communists were tightly organized, spoke their language, and, while ideological enemies, still were deemed racially superior to Jewish and Slavic inmates; at the end of 1944, Buchenwald had fifty-nine thousand prisoners, of whom only five thousand were German. For the "red" kapos, their privileged position created an opportunity for potential resistance within the camp. One technique was to get comrades into the hospital by swapping them with existing patients. Helmut Thiemann was a nurse in the sick bay in Buchenwald. In a note to the Communist Party immediately after the war, he explained the reasoning that guided him and his comrades in their actions: "The SS doctors murdered, and several comrades including myself had to assist them." Initially he resisted, but "after the party had pointed out the necessity of these tasks to me, I had to act accordingly." To them, the choice was simple. They could refuse the job, but that would have made them "indirect murderers of our own comrades." "Since we value our comrades more than the rest, we had to go along one step with the SS and, that is, destroy the sick without hope and people who had lost all strength." Such collaboration enabled them to run special wards and administer medicine exclusively for comrades from various countries. With regard to everyone else, Thiemann wrote, "we had to be ruthless."[136] Structural violence governed daily life and was part of the Nazis' design: work was backbreaking, food and hygiene insufficient, and medicine limited. The communists were victims caught in that web of violence. They had limited agency. But they used the little they had according to their own moral calculus. For the Nazis, the *Volk* was everything, the individual nothing. For the communists, it was the Communist Party. Some lives—Jews, Sinti and Roma, homosexuals, criminals—were more expendable than others.

Klara Pförtsch was thirty years old when she was arrested by the Gestapo in 1936. A communist, she had spent half her life working in a textile factory in Bavaria. Although initially acquitted of resistance activities, she was kept behind bars until 1940, when the People's Court charged her again, now for allegedly passing state secrets to a Czech lover. In April 1941, she was sent to Ravensbrück, the concentration camp for women and children north of Berlin. Within a year she worked her way up to camp elder and police guard. In October 1942, she was moved to Auschwitz-Birkenau, where she again advanced to camp elder, or head kapo. She contracted typhus and spent three months in the prison block for breaking camp rules. In summer 1944, she was transferred to the Geislingen camp. Initially, in Ravensbrück, she was inconspicuous. She would not pass on reports to overseers to spare fellow prisoners serious punishment. But then she started beating prisoners for no apparent reason. By autumn 1942, she was known as "Leo," feared for her violent outbursts. She made prisoners run around carrying heavy rocks with outstretched arms or squat with knees bent for hours. In Birkenau, she joined the SS in the selection of prisoners for the gas chambers, pointing out those least able to work and those she personally wanted to get rid of, including prisoners who were in the infirmary thanks to her beatings. On May 29, 1949, a French court sentenced the *bête humaine* ("human beast") to death for murder. A year later, the sentence was commuted to life imprisonment out of consideration for her as a woman. She was released early, in 1957.[137]

Most survivors wanted to see Pförtsch dead. One of the few who pleaded for mercy was Rosa Jochmann, who had been block elder when Pförtsch arrived in Ravensbrück. Jochmann pointed out that Pförtsch had at first helped prisoners. It was all too much and came too quickly for Pförtsch, in Jochmann's assessment. She lacked the psychological resilience to shoulder the moral responsibility placed on her. Nothing in her life had prepared her for the role of kapo.

Jochmann's own experience in Ravensbrück serves as a reminder that even in the hell of the camps there was room for another morality.[138] Jochmann was a socialist (not a communist), and adopted a two-faced strategy the moment she became elder in Block 1: follow SS orders but also act stupid and shield their victims. Fellow prisoners remembered how she brought warm stockings to the sick and protected young children from beatings. She forged papers and obtained sugar, bread, and sausages for Soviet women in the camp. In 1943, she and thirty-two others were denounced by a German prisoner for stealing food from the SS. She was put in the "bunker" with no food for twenty-one days, in complete darkness, but able to hear the whippings nearby. Life in the camps is often said to have followed the law of the jungle, pitting "beast against other beasts," in the words of Primo Levi, who survived the Monowitz labor camp in the Auschwitz complex.[139] Tadeusz Borowski, who also survived Auschwitz, but took his own life in 1951, wrote that "morality . . . and the ideals of freedom, justice, and human dignity had all slid off man like a rotten rag."[140] Amid all the horror, though, the camps were also sites of extraordinary kindness. Like food and medicine, compassion and care were limited and had to be rationed—there could be no help for the "*Muselmänner*," the name given to those emaciated prisoners who had resigned themselves to their impending death. Yet, among those strong enough, there was mutual aid. Levi described how the conscript laborer Lorenzo procured extra bowls of soup for him and others.[141] Medical prisoners helped the sick even at risk to themselves. Nurses changed the test results of inmates with syphilis to save them from being sent to their deaths. Survivors lived a daily struggle between a self-regarding focus on their own health and a crust of bread, and a selfless concern for others, trying to hold on to their own human dignity in the face of Nazi barbarity.[142] "Even if it is hard to believe for outsiders," Jochmann wrote later, "even in this hell it was possible to prevent a lot of evil and help many others."[143] What sustained her was her faith that Nazi rule would come to an end.

THE END

When it came, the end was protracted, bitter, and bloody. Italy capitulated in September 1943, but the German Reich fought on. In the West, the Allies landed in Normandy in June 1944. In the East, the Red Army annihilated the one formidable military asset the Germans had left: Army Group Center. And the Allies controlled the skies. A joke was making the rounds: for the remainder of the war, Adolf Hitler and Franklin D. Roosevelt had reached a gentlemen's agreement—the American president would provide the bombers, Hitler the airspace.[144] On January 29, 1945, the Soviets reached Königsberg (Kaliningrad). Dresden was flattened by bombing two weeks later. On March 6, the Americans took Cologne. Still, Germany neither collapsed nor rebelled. Even now, pockets were fighting back. The end only came with unconditional surrender on May 8, 1945.

The toll of the final struggle was immense, for Germans as well as for their victims and the Allies. Of the 5.3 million German soldiers killed in the war, half died in the final ten months. The Nazis threw Hitler Youth, women, and old men into battle. Some 7 million Germans fled from east to west between January and May 1945. At the beginning of 1945, concentration camps still held 700,000 prisoners, only half of whom would survive to see liberation.

For Germans, these final months were an emotional pressure cooker. The Nazis escalated their terror. As the hardened Nazis were pulling together, the rest of society was pulling apart. Many Germans might have been yearning for the war to end, but they possessed neither the resources nor the courage to challenge their rulers. The Nazis had all but eliminated the space for opposition. But the German people had also become more inward looking themselves, succumbing to a self-regarding attitude that by 1944 had become habitual. It diminished the capacity for looking outward and joining others in acts of resistance. Moral detachment from the Nazi regime was private. Care and concern now centered on the survival of one's family and friends but found no public outlet.

There were a few exceptions. On July 20, 1944, a group of officers around Claus Count Schenk von Stauffenberg, tried to assassinate Hitler in the

Wolf's Lair, the Führer's field headquarters in East Prussia. The bomb in Stauffenberg's briefcase exploded, but Hitler survived, shielded by a heavy leg of the conference table. Seven thousand officers and civil servants were arrested, most of whom were executed. Their courageous assassination attempt would become important for the new Federal Republic's collective identity after 1949. At the time, however, the abortive attack tells us more about the marginal role of resistance. The assassins were an exclusive group. The leaders were from aristocratic families, joined by a few old professors, civil servants, and theologians. The draft declaration of their provisional government promised to restore morality in public and private life and root out Nazi corruption and profiteering. While the murder of the Jews was condemned as "inhumane and merciless, deeply shameful," many in the resistance shared a sense that there was a "Jewish problem" that called for legal discrimination.[145] Their main concern was to stop Hitler from bleeding the German army to death—to prevent "the destruction of the material and blood-based substance" of the nation, as Stauffenberg called it. With a strong army, Germany might be able to strike a deal with the Western powers. Most resisters were conservative. They wanted to restore the rule of law but were distrustful of democracy, equality, and modernity. In his personal oath, Stauffenberg swore to fight social envy and restore power to the "natural ranks" of society.[146] A few of his collaborators dreamed of a federal Europe. By and large, however, their vision was backward looking. They were "neither capitalist nor communist but German," as the historian Ulrich Herbert has summed it up.[147] We might add "Prussian." Erwin von Witzleben, Helmuth James Graf von Moltke, and other members of the inner circle hailed from the Prussian province of Silesia; Henning von Tresckow—from Prussian Brandenburg—could count two dozen Prussian generals among his family tree; and even the Catholic Stauffenberg, who had grown up in a castle in southern Germany, had noble Baltic-German roots on his mother's side. Their imagined *Volksgemeinschaft* without the storm troopers was ultimately a larger version of the well-ordered community of their Prussian estates. There were anti-fascist groups with more modern ideas—Social Democrats and Communists—but those were mainly émigrés, operating from Scandinavia and the Soviet Union. Within Germany itself, resistance was largely limited to elite circles. The failed assassination attempt effectively wiped it out.

Even if Stauffenberg had managed to move the bomb to Hitler's side of the table leg, it is far from clear that the coup would have been successful. There might have been a mutiny, but most of the army was either loyal to

Hitler or at least loyal to their oath to serve him. To kill the commander, in their view, was treason, and could only destabilize the German war effort further. The bombings and military defeats may have damaged the reputation of many Nazi functionaries, but most people clung to their quasi-messianic faith in the Führer. Regardless what one thought about the Nazis, one soldier wrote to his wife a few days after the bomb, it was "a true stab in the back" and a "crime against the nation" to try to eliminate the leader at such a critical moment. As Germans, they needed to thank providence that Hitler had survived.[148] Even among non-Nazis the mood was split: while some regretted the lost chance of bringing the war to an end, others were relieved, because they feared civil war.[149] Dictatorship still seemed a price worth paying for social order.

Among the troops, discipline was crumbling. Martin Bormann, Hitler's secretary, reckoned that there were 600,000 shirkers in February 1945 who were avoiding frontline service.[150] The number of deserters rose too—15,000 were executed in the last year of the war. Still, in an army of 8 million men, this meant the vast majority continued to fight, and not only out of fear of being court-martialed. They had plenty of reasons: ideological conviction, fear of the Soviets, soldiery pride, a duty to comrades, and the routine of battle. And 1918 cast its shadow over 1943–45. In this view, lack of unity had cost Germany the earlier world war. Only collective sacrifice could save the German nation now—it was Stalingrad writ large. Hitler and Goebbels took this catastrophic logic to its deadly conclusion: national resurrection required self-destruction. There would be spiritual triumph in military defeat.[151]

In January 1945, 60 percent of German prisoners of war still believed in their Führer; as late as April it was still 20 percent, although hardly anyone thought Germany could win the war.[152] "For me, my Führer is my Führer," an SS *Sturmbannführer* summed it up in the prisoner-of-war camp Fort Hunt in Virginia in December 1944. His oath to Hitler "was the most beautiful event in my life... He is an outstanding man."[153] For many, the war had reduced their lives to a simple choice between life and death, just as Goebbels had predicted. There were no more in-betweens or compromises. A lieutenant fighting "in the West" wrote to his wife in Berlin in October 1944 that it was better to keep fighting than to end up as "slaves to foreign peoples." The army needed to hold out to the last man. Only then was there a chance that his wife and their children would walk toward a brighter future.[154]

By spring 1945, a growing number of soldiers on the Western Front thought differently: they'd rather be taken prisoner by the Americans and British than fight to their death. For hardened soldiers, though, disobedience was an alien concept. Their uniforms were a second skin. It was impossible to shed them without giving up their identity. Captain Jürgen von Samson, in an American POW camp in spring 1945, was outraged to see that some troops had taken off their medals. He continued to use the Hitler greeting and turned a silver coin into oak leaves, which he tied to his Iron Cross first class to restore his medal to its full glory.[155]

With the Nazis' emphasis on willpower and struggle, they had from the start encouraged a distorted view of reality, where determination and wishful thinking, if strong enough, could bend objective facts. A person in the resistance compared Germans to a violent child who abused a chair or a tree because it would not obey.[156] Many soldiers brushed away inconvenient news with the stubborn attitude that defeat could not happen as long as they did not want it to happen. Others bridged the widening gulf between faith and reality with fantastical hopes of miracle weapons. Yet others felt that since so much already lay in ruins, there was not much to lose from fighting a little longer.[157] Many had been socialized into brutal warfare by hardened fighters in their regiments. Peer pressure and family bonds reinforced the expectation to hold out. How could one possibly let down one's comrades, many of whom had sacrificed their lives for oneself, or one's father who had fought in the First World War?

That all the bloodletting could not have been in vain remained a matter of faith for many, as if German blood counted more than other blood. Even those who had suffered at the hand of the Nazis shared the sense of belonging to an elect people. Heinz Zabel served with the occupying forces in Denmark. His wife, Inge, was arrested in Mecklenburg after July 20, 1944, when a neighbor denounced her for calling Hitler "the greatest criminal and murderer in world history." She was sentenced to death. Heinz wrote to her in prison in December. He urged her not to despair. He and his comrades were sure that they would win the war, "because in our opinion the Creator could not really allow for so much courageous blood to have flowed for nothing."[158] He proved wrong about victory, but was lucky enough to see his wife survive a concentration camp.

By 1944, many soldiers had been fighting for three or even four years, and fighting had become a way of life from which they no longer knew how to escape. Willy Peter Reese—from Duisburg—joined the eastern campaign in 1941 after finishing high school. In his war diary, he captured how a regular soldier became gradually alienated from himself. Initially he fought for God and country. By the winter of 1942–43 it had become war for war's sake. Comradeship lost its heroic flair. They were not only "unwashed, unshaven, lice-eaten, and sick," he wrote, "but spiritually decayed, nothing more than a sum of blood, intestines, and bones." They had plundered and burned villages. He had been reduced to a "spiritual nothing." The war had turned his life into a lie, and he felt as if he were wearing a "mask." After his second winter in Russia, he felt like a "stranger," "a poor wanderer whom no one loves and no one knows." In July 1943, he was wounded and sent to Lake Constance to recover. Instead of making the most of his time away from the battlefield, he felt estranged and volunteered to return to the front. He wanted to "beat fire with fire, defeat the war through war... I threw myself away, because I lost my faith in the spirit and the soul." He drifted into the "idling motion of the soul" and felt his "last values disintegrating; the good, the noble, the beautiful was dying." The thick armor he had put on to shield himself against horror and fear had ended up "oppressing the delicate movements inside me, breaking the seeds of hope, faith, and love of humanity, turning my heart into stone. I was coming to an end and laughed at myself." In January 1944, he wrote, he no longer felt fear, just "numb, resigned despair" and a sense that everything was in vain. The more meaningless the war became politically, "the easier it is for me to play my role in it, for that way I do not enter into conflict with my conscience." He retreated behind his "mask" and kept fighting, not for *"Volk und Führer,"* but for the time after Hitler, ready to sacrifice himself for a "future, spiritually free Germany." In late June 1944, Reese was killed near Vitebsk in Belarus.[159]

Younger soldiers especially were driven on by their faith in the Führer, but for others it was their faith in God. If there was one soldier who should have had reason to throw down his gun it was Helmut Giesen. In 1941, he was thrown in prison for meeting with other Catholics in a youth group. After two years of hard labor in a quarry he was sent to the Balkans with Strafbataillon 999. Yet, rather than grumbling or resisting, he endured, even embraced, his ordeal. The swearing-in was a "beautiful, serious hour." He remembered his dead brother and fallen friends. "It is a big obligation they have left behind for us... I will try to fulfill it, as best as I can." In August 1944, he was on guard duty and took time to reflect on the meaning of war. The sky was dark with heavy clouds, the air thick. Then lightning struck and rain brought relief. "Wars are the same," he wrote in his diary. "Once the tension between peoples becomes too big, it must somehow find a way to release itself. A thunderstorm sweeps away the darkness, and then everything is quiet and relaxed again. They are visitations by God."

But why did God make Giesen suffer, for he had done no wrong? Giesen had hit on the problem of evil. His was the same question that had been asked by Job, God's most righteous servant, in the Old Testament. In the biblical story, Satan challenged God to see how long Job would keep his faith once his good fortune turned into calamity. God accepted the wager and killed Job's children and his sheep. Why retain faith in God if He made bad things happen to good people? Giesen, like Job, found the answer in the redemptive purpose of God's seemingly unjust interventions. Suffering, Giesen was convinced, was not pointless, but a sign of divine mercy. It freed the spirit: "Through suffering man reaches his inner fulfillment." But why did God take this detour? Giesen asked himself. Why give humans free will if it produced so much pain? It was, he wrote, because God wanted humans to share in his creation but also recognized that it was difficult for humans to give themselves over to His will. Suffering was the price they had to pay for God's mercy. Giesen accepted it by fighting on.[160] In the Bible, God ultimately shows himself to Job, who accepts his infinite power. All we know about Giesen is that his suffering came to an end on Christmas Eve 1944, when he was killed during the German retreat from Croatia.

On the home front, the mood swung violently between hope and despair. Eva Schwedhelm turned eighteen in 1943. As for many young women, the war opened up a world of new responsibilities. She began work as a nurse in a military hospital at the outskirts of Cologne. Life had never been more dramatic. On December 28, 1943, she had watched a movie before learning that her cousin Georg had died a "hero's death" in his submarine. Three days later she was in her basement suffering "deadly agony" during an aerial attack. At this point, she still hoped for a retaliatory strike soon. There were plenty of distractions. She went to the opera to hear *The Magic Flute*, saw *Tonelli* at the cinema (an outlandish melodrama mixing circus drama, jealousy, and murder), and listened to *Tosca* on the radio. In April 1944, the house next door took a direct hit, killing the owners. On the last Sunday of April, she sat in her "freezing flat": "If one goes out, all one sees is rubble and smells fire... If one did not have faith that the war would be over soon, then, I'd wished I'd be where Georg is already." But then she would pull herself together again and think of the day ahead. "A wonderful morning," she wrote at the end of June 1944: the sun was shining, and she and a fellow nurse, Gerti, agreed about the ethical importance of their work—as nurses they were giving the wounded "spiritual values" as well as pills and bandages. Three weeks later she was again in despair. "How long have we got left to live, and how will we die?" she wondered. "Sometimes the misery is overwhelming, for us young people the good times are over for ever... The time ahead is all bleak! To keep living is no longer worthwhile." Then, after another attack, she picked herself up: "Life continues after all, it has to, but for what?" She was no longer convinced that they were suffering for future generations: "They cannot thank us anyhow, because they cannot judge our situation."

The future narrowed to tomorrow. Eva lived from moment to moment. The days at the hospital were exciting, and so was the attractive Dr. Geiger, who worked there. By October 1944, she had abandoned all hope in miracle weapons. The Americans were now outside Aachen, only forty-three miles away. On October 17, she asked, "When will we finally be relieved by a painless death?!" Three days later, the doctor was telling her, "Enjoy the war, because the end will be horrible!"—something being heard across Germany. "I would so much love to believe in something else—one keeps hoping until the end regardless." Aachen fell the following day, after nineteen days of street fighting, the first city in western Germany to do so. On November 1, Eva Schwedhelm fled Cologne for a little village together with her mother and grandmother, but she was back at the hospital by the end of the month, reminiscing about "the most beautiful time." Cologne was taken by the Americans on March 6, 1945.[161]

In October 1944, Himmler gave the order for a *Volkssturm*, a people's militia composed of Hitler Youth, the elderly, and women to dig trenches, feed the aircraft defenses, and fight the enemy on German soil. Army regiments were freshened up with untrained teenagers. Not everyone had a problem with mobilizing children. In the middle of March 1945, a newspaper reported how a boy had been approached by a Canadian soldier for a friendly chat, whereupon the boy pulled out a pistol, and shot the Canadian. A German soldier stationed in Bohemia was horrified that German youth could do such a thing. How could the Germans possibly expect mercy from the enemy now? Except for two comrades, all the others applauded the deed and expressed admiration for the boy.[162]

For many Germans, however, the mobilization of women and children crossed a line. It broke a moral ground rule central to their self-understanding as a *Kulturnation* superior to the "barbarians" of the East. For years, the Nazis had condemned the Soviets for putting women into uniform and partisans for not fighting like proper soldiers. By November 1944, Hugo Manz—the doctor writing letters to his missing son—started to attack Hitler's moral double standard. First he had criticized "partisan women," now he was calling up Manz's daughter Annemarie to dig anti-tank ditches and man antiaircraft defenses. He managed to get her a job with the Red Cross instead. By February 1945, he was no longer looking for higher forces to explain the bombings but pinned them squarely on "the errors of the political and military leadership."[163] That same month, Captain Siegfried Käss decided that his war was over, too. He deserted. "Having a company, and then a battalion, gave me so much joy," he told fellow POWs two months later. "To see all the good it aroused in the men, their sacrifice . . . but—in the end—for what?

Comradeship was a really positive ideal. But toward the end I had eighteen- and even seventeen-year-old boys—splendid boys—... it was such a pity to see how they were murdered." It was when the regime armed their own boys and women that war turned into murder for many Germans. "They say that women are being recruited now," another POW said, "I can barely believe it, I do not understand it. That is not war, it is mass murder." The Nazis were "criminals."[164] In the chaos after the Dresden bombing, Victor Klemperer tore off his Jewish star and managed to escape to the Bavarian countryside. He noted the growing divide in local opinion. While some were still hoping that the Americans would fall out with the Soviets to give Germany one final chance, others were denouncing the call-up of Hitler Youth as "child murder."[165]

The Nazi regime now faced two enemies: the Allied troops pressing deeper into the Reich from the outside, and its crumbling authority on the inside. Its response followed its ruling mentality: an appeal to willpower and the brutal punishment of anyone who stepped out of line. Since 1933, the Nazis had used violence against "enemies" of the *Volk.* In spring 1945, the escalating violence reached the *Volk* itself. General Ferdinand Schörner, Hitler's favorite, introduced ruthless discipline. Any deserter, marauder, or shirker was hanged or shot. There was to be no "advancing backward." A German soldier had to fight to the last bullet. Schörner would ultimately exempt himself from that rule and flee by plane to the Alps, abandoning his men on the day of surrender.[166]

In early April 1945, Himmler gave the order to shoot all male inhabitants in any house that hoisted a white flag. The response in Heilbronn on the morning of April 6 was typical. American troops had already entered parts of the city. The local Nazi head, Richard Drauz, together with the Hitler Youth leader, Oskar Bordt, who commanded the people's militia, noticed white sheets hanging from the window of a block of apartments in Schweinsbergerstrasse. Drauz ordered his men to "shoot them, shoot them all." In the space of a few minutes, six shots were fired. A town official and his wife were found in a pool of blood, shot through the head and neck. Their neighbor, a pastor, had tried to escape to the basement but stumbled. He was shot in the heart and fell dead into the arms of his wife. Bordt then ran upstairs to the apartment where the white flag was hanging. A single fifty-two-year-old woman answered the door. Yes, she had put out the white sheet. Should she remove it? she asked. He fired at her, but, luckily, she fell down the stairs and survived. Bordt was not finished. In the garden, he stopped another neighbor trying to escape who pleaded with Bordt: he had nothing to do with the flag, he said—to no avail. Bordt shot him point-blank.

The house opposite had a white flag hanging from a window, too. The wife of a doctor told Bordt that she had hoisted the flag herself. Bordt shot her in the chest. In 1948, a German court would sentence Bordt to fifteen years in prison for premeditated and attempted murder.[167]

To the fear of the advancing Russians was now added fear of Nazi fanatics and marauding German soldiers. "All I fear now is the *German* soldier," a female schoolteacher in rural Bavaria said in April 1945.[168] In Berlin, Christa Ronke, one of the many thousands of refugees from the East, reached the metropolis in January 1945. "Everyone is railing at the government," she told her diary in March. "They should finally call it a day and save blood and rubble." The Nazis were trying to scare people with stories that "the enemies will kill everyone etc. The enemy radio says the opposite. One can no longer trust anyone. Perhaps the truth lies in the middle." The call for so-called Werewolf guerrilla groups, she wrote, showed that the regime had gone "completely mad." "I cannot say how angry I am at this gang of criminals." She was hoping that the Americans would advance quickly and bring the war to an end.

It was the Red Army, though, who took Berlin one month later. Ronke was sixteen years old and one of the many girls and women, perhaps 1 million, who were raped by soldiers of the Red Army. Contrary to the popular idea of complete silence, women did talk to each other about their ordeal. Back in school, Ronke learned that some of her friends had been raped six or seven times. Pregnancies were difficult to hide. Ronke also confided to her diary what happened to her. A "disgusting" Russian soldier with a wounded eye took her to a sofa. Her mother tried to stop him, in vain. "Amazingly, I was not afraid at all. I had to take off my trousers and then he put himself on top of me and did that thing!!! It hurt a little. In any case, it was awful." A month later, she wrote that life was becoming bearable and the Russians were behaving "half decently... Our SS behaved far worse."[169] It was a telling comparison. The escalation of violence in the final struggle had shifted the balance of evil.

Nothing in this inferno compared to what concentration camp inmates and foreign workers had to go through in the final months of the war. On Himmler's orders, KZs were evacuated so as not to fall into enemy hands. Tens of thousands of prisoners were moved toward the interior in brutal death marches. The weak were shot along the way. Of those who made it to Bergen-Belsen and other camps in the interior, many died of typhoid soon thereafter. In Gardelegen, west of Berlin, a thousand prisoners were locked in a barn by the local official with the help of the army and the last-ditch militia (*Volkssturm*), and set on fire.

At the end of 1944, there were 7 million displaced persons in Nazi Germany—2 million POWs and 5 million slave laborers, mostly young women from the Soviet Union and Poland. The bombings and the advancing front robbed them of their work, shelter, and food and made them fair game for the Gestapo, retreating troops, and locals terrified of plunder and revenge. Spring 1945 was a season of massacres. When the Americans reached Warstein, east of the Ruhr, at the end of April 1945, they found a gruesome site. On April 26, 1945, a local reported a mass grave he had come across in the nearby forest. Two days later, another pointed out two further trenches. In total, 208 forced laborers had been killed, men, women, and children, all "shot in the back of the head." The Soviet and Polish workers had been marched to the town ahead of the advancing American troops and put up in the local clubhouse. The first of the massacres took place on March 21. The SS officer in command gave the order to "decimate" the foreign workers. A mix of army and SS soldiers called together the foreigners and told those who wanted a better life to step forward. Thirty-five men and twenty-one women did, one of them cradling her nine-month-old child. They were put on a truck and driven to the forest. In Russian, they were told not to worry, everything would be fine. Then they were shot in the back of their heads and robbed of their few valuables. The regular soldiers had for the most part carried out their orders, but when it came to shooting the baby, they refused. The SS man Anton Boos took the baby by its legs and smashed its head against a tree.[170]

And how did the war end for the young Parzival, Reinhold Reichardt? In February 1945, in spite of a drunk and "macabre" imitation of a Goebbels speech, he was promoted to National Socialist leadership officer, charged with spreading the Nazi message, not romantic poetry, among his troops. Their mission to recapture Budapest was a complete disaster. They came under heavy fire from Soviet planes, infantry, and rocket launchers. Reichardt was hit by shrapnel in his right knee and went down, but managed to raise his pistol to stop his men from running away in headless flight. He next wrote to his parents from a field hospital near Prague, on Easter Sunday. They needed to remember, he told them, why as a family they had enjoyed so many wonderful years. They had resisted "narrow-minded egotism" and preserved their "faith in our God and fatherland." It was that faith alone that made them "free and happy people." To abandon it now, he wrote, would turn "us into cowardly traitors." No one knew what the future would hold. What he was sure about was that "there could not be a final downfall, a fall into nothingness for us and our *Volk*." "God is watching over us." All injustices in this world would collapse in the face of His omnipotent justice, "but only for the faithful who dare to remain his immaculate warriors."[171]

On April 30, 1945, Hitler shot himself in his bunker in Berlin. By now, Reichardt was back with his men in southern Bohemia. He told them to show bravery in their next mission. On May 7, he and fellow officers were called to their captain, who informed them of the general order of surrender for the following day. They were caught between the fronts, and the captain advised them to cross the Danube and walk toward Enns, in Austria, to reach the Americans. He added that if anyone felt that surrender was against their "soldier's conscience," he could show them on the map how to reach Field Marshal Schörner, who had pledged to fight to the last drop of blood. No one took him up on the offer.

On the morning of May 8, 1945, Reichardt and his men marched to the Danube, keeping the Soviets at bay with their remaining machine guns. On the bridge they were captured by the Americans and walked into town. Rumors reached them that the Americans might hand them over to the Soviets. He and two fellow officers decided to make their escape. They removed all their badges and medals from their uniforms and threw their revolvers into the Danube. In exchange for a carton of cigarettes, a local rowed them across the river. They continued on to Linz. Reichardt was warned that KZ Mauthausen was nearby, and former inmates were killing any soldier suspected to be from the SS. At night, Reichardt was surprised by a small group but was let go after showing them his regular army papers. Their fate barely registered with him, except that they asked him for bread and took one of his bags. Outside a POW camp he managed to sell his services as an English translator and jumped on a Red Cross ambulance, which seemed like a stroke of luck. In it, however, were seven men from the Waffen-SS. When he was stopped by an American patrol, he pulled together his scraps of French and English and pretended to be a forced laborer from Flanders trying to get back to Ghent. He was allowed to pass and crossed the Austrian border back into Germany, and walked home. On May 21, 1945, two and a half years and many million dead later, he was back in Erfurt.[172]

While Reichardt was leading his men to the Danube, Renate Bock, a victim of Operation Gomorrah, sat amid the ruins in Hamburg. Combat commander Alwin Wolz handed over the city to the British on May 1, 1945, one week before the general surrender. Bock tried to make sense of the historic day: "Once again all finished, and all sacrifices and suffering for nothing? Our poor, beautiful Germany! The dream is over. What will await us, the *VOLK*?"[173] It was a good question.

3

The Murderers Are Among Us: From Guilt to Amnesty

In the spring of 1947, Susanne Vogel picked up her pen and wrote to her cousin in America. "I do not believe," she told her, "it is necessary to return once again to the question of guilt that has been talked to death." "I wish that the world out there knew a little bit more of the pain that we all suffered, including some Nazis." Her cousin needed to understand: such pain shook a person to the core and robbed them of their "innocence" forever. The whole approach to denazification reminded her of one of those fairy tales where old women miraculously turned into innocent virgins. "But that is not what reality is like... In real life there is always evil as well as good." At the end of the war, Germany had had one "asset," Vogel felt: "The land of the 'Nazis' was also a land of sufferers." Christian countries especially should have given greater recognition to German suffering. The Allies had missed the opportunity to heal wounds and reform the Germans. Instead, in their "anger" and "will to destroy an—in their eyes—entire inhuman people," they punished them.[1]

It is tempting to dismiss the letter as just another instance of the German self-pity that Allied observers recorded in the ruins of the Reich—except for the fact that Susanne Vogel was a German Jew. She was the daughter of Ernst Neisser, the doctor who took his own life in Berlin in 1942 rather than allow the Nazis to take it. Like most German-Jewish families, the Neissers and the Paulys (on her mother's side) had been assimilated for generations and had converted to Protestantism. Her maternal aunt and cousins died in concentration camps. Liselotte, her cousin on her father's side, to whom these letters were addressed, had emigrated to America before the war. Susanne survived because of her marriage to an "Aryan" German who refused to give in to pressure from his "Uber-Nazi" nephew to divorce her. Her husband had lost his left thumb in battle in the First World War, which saved him from risking his life in the Second. At the start of the war, they put their daughter in a Moravian boarding school. Toward its end, Vogel had two narrow escapes, both times assisted by German neighbors. The first time, the mayor of their small Silesian town had warned her that the Gestapo were on their way. The second time, neighbors took her secretly with them on their flight from the advancing Red Army. She had just enough minutes to spare to pack her father's beloved sheet music of Bach and Brahms, some Goethe, and the Bible she had given her daughter on her confirmation day; a Kandinsky painting had to stay behind. When the Red Army raised the red flag over the Reichstag in Berlin on May 2, 1945, Vogel was on the outskirts, in Potsdam.

When she sat down to write to her cousin in 1947, she had also survived two years under Soviet occupation, before fleeing to Kassel in the American zone. Unlike many German women, Vogel and her daughter evaded rape, once by spitting "poisonous vapor" at a Russian soldier, as she put it ("when did I recently have the chance to brush my teeth") and declaring that she was "sick" (a lie). Ironically, it was the Soviets who made her pin a yellow star on her door, to mark her as a victim of the Nazis and protect her family from attack. In short, when Susanne Vogel wrote of pain and suffering she knew what she was talking about. In her six long letters to Liselotte she relayed what had happened to her and her family during the war. In the process, she gives us her personal moral view of the German catastrophe, of good and evil, and of the nature of guilt and what to do about it.

Germans had committed many crimes, but guilt, for Vogel, was neither a uniquely German problem nor a discrete historical phenomenon. Guilt was universal, and it concerned not just what people did to each other in this world but also their relationship with God.

When she told officials in the American zone in 1947 of the rape and murder she had witnessed in the Soviet zone, she received the response, "What did you expect?" "Personally," she wrote to her cousin, "I would never subscribe to such reasoning. Of course—the SS man who raped Jewish girls before killing them, I find even more horrible than the Russian who beat to death a school friend of my daughter's when she refused to hand over her briefcase to him." But the effect was the same, whether "dehumanized Nazi criminal or not-quite-human Asiatic hordes!" Vogel's Jewish descent did not make her immune to the German middle classes' fear that European civilization was under threat from the East. What mattered to her were consequences, not motivations. "As a woman, I have to deal exclusively with the results themselves, not with the evaluations of their causes or justifications." The virtue that was called for was charity. She reminded her cousin of the saying made famous by Seneca, the Roman Stoic philosopher: Charity looks to the plight, not its cause.[2]

Collective attributions of guilt were equally suspect. "One should never generalize!" Vogel said, citing the case of a young woman who had come to seek her advice. The woman had been raped, but the Russian soldier later apologized and promised to take care of the young woman and her family if she took him in. The mother was hard-up and famished; the young soldier sounded nice enough. Vogel urged the young woman to take up the offer. She herself entrusted her daughter to a Russian soldier for protection on the dangerous daily walks to school. His wife and his three children had been murdered by German troops, but he assured her, "I no longer want evil." All he asked for was for Susanne to play Russian folk songs on the piano while he sat in a corner and cried. When the police came to round up Nazis, she refused to denounce neighbors who had been party members. "Who should I have denounced as a Nazi?" she asked her cousin. The single old woman downstairs with her fanatical faith in "our beloved Führer" who had made their lives miserable but whose own daughter had recently died of flu? Or perhaps the tenant who was quartered with them, who was a longtime Nazi but also a devout Christian who had hidden Jews? Or the young Nazi seamstress—who was going out with an SS man—who could have squealed on Vogel and her family in the final stages of the war but did not? No, Vogel would not be part of such Nazi methods. They only bred suspicion and a disregard for individual life. One should concern oneself with the deeds that a person had actually committed. "We should leave it to God to 'look into someone's heart.'"[3]

Susanne Vogel did not try to equate or cancel out German atrocities with other crimes. Her moral calculus resembled more a pyramid of guilt. It was, "of course, terrible," she wrote, to be the helpless victim of an "ice-cold" strafing attack by enemy planes. It was "a thousand times more horrible" to be exposed to the blood lust of the victorious Red Army. Worse still was when, "in cold blood and in the name of an ideology, people seized other humans in order to torture and annihilate them," as did the Nazis: "This is the worst that can happen on this earth." For the death of the victim brought about the "inner death" of the perpetrator as well.[4]

Guilt manifested itself in a moment in time, but, for Vogel, its source was timeless. Everyone carried some guilt, because all people were born sinners. Guilt blazed forth "in the individual, in a nation, in the whole world, and then drops down as a nuclear bomb." Guilt, she wrote, "lives in the victim as well as the hangman."[5]

Morality, therefore, was a matter for the spirit, not reason. Her cousin might ask herself how her father, a doctor, could possibly have taken his own life. "You don't have to understand it," Vogel explained. "It is something that needs to be accepted and endured." All the suffering, she was convinced, had a divine purpose because it taught the need for love and redemption. It was in vain for governments to think they could exorcize dangerous ideologies. Evil "spirits" could not be driven out, only redeemed, and this required fearless love and the freedom to believe in God. Those who were calling for revenge would never be able to free themselves from the chain of violence. The lesson she had learned from her ordeal under the Nazis and was now, in 1947, passing on to her American cousin, quoting from the New Testament, was this: Learn to forgive and "love your enemies," and "Behold, I make all things new."[6]

THE MORAL TURN

There continues to be a widespread view that after the Germans' defeat they retreated into silence. This idea has come in various guises. One is that, hungry and homeless, Germans did not have the energy to worry about right and wrong. We can call this the Brechtian view, after the communist poet Bertold Brecht, who declared, "First feed the face, then talk right and wrong" in his *Threepenny Opera* (1928). A second is a Freudian view made famous by the psychoanalysts Alexander and Margarete Mitscherlich in the late 1960s; Alexander had observed the Nuremberg trials and written in 1949 about Nazi doctors' contempt for human life. Here, the Germans were portrayed as a neurotic child for whom the loss of their idealized father (Hitler) triggered a traumatic devaluation of their own self. They retreated into a protective shell of silence and self-pity. Incapable of mourning and working through their experience, they produced a numb, obedient, and authoritarian habitus. Other writers have argued that the Allies' accusation of "collective guilt" traumatized the Germans.[7]

These views are deeply misleading. They each have internal problems. First, ethics is not a luxury only of the well fed—the poor all over the world have moral concerns, too. Second, Germans were not incapable of mourning, but focused on their own loved ones, not on Jewish victims. Third, the Allies did not formally hold the German people responsible—although many Germans felt they did.[8] More fundamentally, it is simply wrong to think that Germans were silent. They had plenty to say after 1945, just not always what we, today, might have expected or wished for. Far too little was said about the suffering of the Jews. Given how widespread antisemitism was, this is hardly surprising. Even this relative silence was not something peculiar to the Germans—it applied to Britain and the Soviet Union as well as to France and Italy into the 1960s. It is true that after the war most Germans failed to show an understanding of the road from Weimar to Auschwitz, but, again, neither did professional historians before the 1970s.

We know what the Germans did not say, but we should pay more attention to what they did. For all the lack of political analysis, contemporaries did try to make sense of the catastrophe and identify the values and actions that could help them climb out of it. They spoke of good and evil, guilt and shame, suffering and charity, penance and forgiveness. The dominant language of moral renewal was cast in individual and spiritual, not political, terms, and it was mainly addressed to themselves—the Germans—not their victims.

We also need to pay attention to when and how they said what they did and to whom. In a much-cited article, Hannah Arendt commented on how the Germans she met all tended to suffer from a "general lack of emotion."[9] Who would not expect members of a nation of perpetrators to behave awkwardly in the presence of a Jewish author who had fled Nazi Germany? It does not automatically mean that the same people showed no emotion in other contexts or had difficulty expressing suffering as such. Moreover, Arendt was writing in 1950. Five years can be a long time in history, and rarely more so than in these five. They include the Nuremberg trials; the arrival of millions of German refugees and foreign displaced persons; the beginning of the Cold War; the shift from denazification to amnesty in the Western and Soviet zones; currency reform; and, in 1949, the establishment of two separate states, the Federal Republic of Germany in the West, and the communist German Democratic Republic in the East.

These years saw a major shift in the registers of morality in which Germans talked about the war and their crimes. Guilt gave way to shame and prosecution to amnesty. By the early 1950s, impunity ruled the courts. Outside, however, there were also growing protests demanding an end to "Nazi justice."

Self-pity was one of these registers, and there was plenty of it from the start. When James Stern, an Anglo-Irish writer who had known Germany before the war, returned to Munich in May 1945 as an intelligence officer with the U.S. Bombing Survey, he was stunned not so much by the few remaining stubborn Nazis but by the many "opportunists" who instinctively dwelled on their own misery and tried to shift all blame onto the Allies, pointing to their fatherland in ruins, the "terror" from the air, and their own deprivation. Stern, repulsed by such talk, retorted that he had been across Europe and that the Germans had murdered 6 million Jews, yet were the only "healthy-looking people left on the continent."

Self-pity, though, never had a monopoly on German feelings. When Stern reached Nuremberg a few weeks later, he found people "who expressed deep-seated feelings of guilt over the treatment of Jews." The massacres of Jews in Poland, one resident who had served there told Stern, were a "*Kulturschande*," a shameful deed against all cultural norms. "No nation capable of such atrocities could possibly win the war," the man added.[10]

Guilt, shame, remorse, and forgiveness are moral and emotional states, but they are also shaped by politics, law, and administration. They were competing with each other, and the balance between them was shifting in the postwar years. A major tilt occurred in 1947, the year in which Susanne Vogel was writing to her cousin in America, just as the momentum behind denazification was giving way to a drive for amnesty. As far as the punishment of former Nazis was concerned, this was a big step backward, but it did not mark the end of the debate about how to deal with German crimes and their victims. The year 1949 saw another dramatic shift. Until then the criminal prosecution of Nazis had been a significant praxis, but now justice all but lost its drive, in East and West Germany alike. In both countries, the reckoning with the Nazi era was increasingly handed over to the state and began to reflect each regime's interests, with radically different outcomes.

Socialist East Germany understood itself as a new state, unstained by the Nazi past. Anti-fascism—its founding ethos—served to exonerate its citizens. It was not responsible for the crimes against Jews, and consequently also owed them nothing. The only victims who deserved reparations were the Soviet people and German communists who had fought Hitler.

Capitalist West Germany, by contrast, found its identity in the idea of continuity: the Nazi regime died on May 8, 1945, but the German state lived on, and so did the German nation. West Germany accepted public liability for crimes and losses under the Nazis. This view of a state's responsibility was not without its moral pitfalls either. War damage and Nazi atrocities became tangled in a competitive victimization. Were the bombed-out German widow, the Silesian refugee, and the disabled soldier not victims of war and terror, too? If the East German conception of victims was too narrow, West Germany's became so large that it sometimes risked losing sight of the distinction between innocent victims of Nazi crimes and Germans who had lost their home or an arm in a war they had, after all, started and supported. Still, West Germany in the early 1950s began to pay reparations, first to Israel and to German Jewish survivors elsewhere, then to Western European countries it had invaded, as well as compensation to many (though not all) victims.

The scope of these payments and their limitations remain subjects of heated debate. But it should not distract from their historical significance:

morality took a major turn in the young Federal Republic. Within less than a decade, a concern with private conscience, personal guilt, and acts of redemption and forgiveness had largely moved into public hands in the form of international treaties, debt payments, and local administrators converting the days spent in concentration camps into monthly checks to survivors. Private guilt had given way to public liability. What was left over was collective shame.

A COUNTRY OF CAMPS

Germany in 1945 was the site of a humanitarian catastrophe. More than 6 million soldiers were dead or missing. Almost a third of homes had been destroyed. The land resembled one giant transit station for uprooted people. Almost 10 million former concentration camp inmates, forced laborers, and Eastern Europeans fleeing the Soviets were trying to find their feet.[11] There were also the many millions of Germans who had been bombed out or fled the eastern provinces of the Reich which had been lost. The war would cast a long shadow. In 1955, West Germany counted 4.3 million recognized war victims—war widows and orphans, and disabled soldiers; ten years later, the number was still a formidable 2.8 million. With the eastern provinces chopped off, the remaining rump of the country was placed under Allied occupation and carved up into four zones: the Soviet zone in the East, the American in the south, the British in the north, and the French in the western Rhineland and Saar. Berlin was split into four sectors.

In all the zones there were camps: for the former KZ inmates; newly arriving foreign displaced persons (DPs) from Poland and Eastern Europe; prisoners of war; German refugees from the East; and arrested Nazis. A quarter of a million Nazi officials spent the summer of 1945 in internment camps in the Western zones alone. Some of these were former concentration camps. Ten years after the war, the main Protestant charity, Evangelisches Hilfswerk, still looked after a quarter of a million people in four thousand camps in the Western zones. Food shortages and a public health crisis made things dramatically worse. Whereas during the war Germans had feasted on food plundered from the East, now there was hunger; 1946–47 would be remembered as "the hunger winter." In July 1946, the average German man in his twenties weighed 130 pounds. By February 1948, that had dropped to 114 pounds. For many, foreign CARE packages and local charity meant the difference between life and death. The only market that was booming in postwar Germany was the black market.[12]

In the face of this devastation, and given the violence of the Nazi regime, the social peace of postwar Germany is astonishing. Millions of victims were living in the land of their former perpetrators. Revenge killings were rare, and were mostly carried out by foreign prisoners and forced laborers. In early May 1945, for example, a train full of KZ inmates came to a stop at Lake Starnberg near Munich as the American troops were closing in. A group of Lithuanian prisoners overwhelmed a particularly brutal SS guard and killed him with his own bayonet. They rounded up the other SS men, locked them in a railway car, and handed them over to the Americans.[13] Three months later, one hundred DPs surrounded a farm near Münster in Westphalia, beat up the farmer, and set the farmhouse on fire; two children died in the blaze. The investigation revealed that three of the Polish DPs had previously been attacked by a group of Germans. Some DPs justified theft and plunder by saying they were only doing what German soldiers had done in the East. Still, while such incidents were not unknown, the DPs' crime rate was hardly exceptional and no higher than that of Germans. Indeed, in several cases former forced laborers helped protect German farmers from plunder.[14]

By contrast, the end of the war unleashed a wave of revenge killings in other countries. In France, Italy, Norway, and the Netherlands, some 100,000 collaborators were killed in bloody acts of "purification" (*epurazione*). These were civil conflicts, with resistance fighters settling scores with compatriots who had collaborated with the fascist occupiers. Germany avoided both large-scale violence and civil war for several reasons. Unlike France or Norway, Germany was not freed of a foreign yoke but the original aggressor. It consequently lacked the internal divisions that came with occupation. For most Germans, May 8, 1945, was a national defeat by foreign powers, not a liberation. There could be no myth of a victorious resistance as in Italy or France. In Germany, resistance groups were a tiny minority and knew it. The *epurazione* of a few thousand hated collaborators was one thing; blood revenge against an entire nation of complicit supporters would have been something altogether different. Defeat had been so crushing and comprehensive that it eliminated any serious challenge from the extreme right and extreme left. Most fanatical Nazis had died in the final battle, committed suicide, or been interned by the Allies. Many other former Nazi supporters had already refashioned themselves in the latter stages of the war as secret critics or betrayed victims. Unconditional surrender and Allied occupation meant there could be no myth of a stab in the back or talk of an unfairly imposed, shameful peace, as at Versailles. All of this set 1945 apart from 1918. If they were not in a prisoner-of-war camp, most soldiers were happy to be alive and had no appetite for joining a paramilitary organization; the few partisan Werewolf attacks on the Allies only confirmed people's sense that Nazism was no longer for them. What lust for revenge there might have been in May 1945 had abated by the time many hated Nazis were released from internment in 1946 and 1947. For German communists, meanwhile, there was no need to pick up arms: the Soviets established a communist zone for them. The division of Germany effectively separated left- and right-wing extremists from each other and thus prevented a return to civil war that had marked the years after the First World War.

Social peace was not a foregone conclusion, though. Immediately after liberation the situation was volatile. Locals outside camps were fearful and established guards to protect themselves from potential attacks by freed prisoners. Earl G. Harrison, an immigration lawyer, was sent by President Harry S. Truman to inspect the camps for Nazi victims in the American zone in July 1945. He was shocked by what he found. Inmates were still wearing their striped KZ pajamas or bleached SS uniforms. They were given black bread and the same rations as their torturers. Camps were organized by nationality, which meant Jews were thrown together with non-Jewish DPs, who often hated Jews. German police entered the camps as they pleased, exacerbating tensions. General George S. Patton, the military governor of Bavaria, had little sympathy with either Jews or DPs, but Harrison and younger officers (who included German exiles) succeeded in improving the situation. Jewish survivors were given their own camps—for example, Landsberg—self-government, and special rations.[15]

Just as important was the victims' restraint. The driving force behind the Central Committee of Liberated Jews and first chairman was Zalman Grinberg, a doctor. In June 1945, during the commemoration of their liberation, Grinberg told the assembled victims of the Landsberg camp why revenge was not the answer: "If we took revenge, we would descend into the lowest depth of ethics and morality to which the German nation has fallen during the past ten years. We are not able to slaughter women and children... We are not able to burn millions of people."[16] Self-respect and the chance to rebuild their lives demanded restraint. For some, the reversal of roles was satisfaction enough. Jews now had access to better food and resources than many local Germans and, instead of slaving for them, had Germans do work for them. "Revenge did not only mean killing Germans," a survivor remembered. "We got our revenge, when we saw Germans working as water carriers... when we saw them cleaning Jewish homes, [and] the Jewish school or paying for their cigarettes with gold—gold, which undoubtedly had been taken off Jews."[17]

The Nazis had been so brutally efficient that Jewish survivors were a minority in the camps. Far larger in number were new Jewish refugees from the Soviet Union and Poland, who arrived alongside many non-Jewish DPs from Eastern Europe in 1945 and 1946. Their enemy was the Bolsheviks, not the Nazis or the Germans. Most Jews, regardless of whether they were concentration camp survivors or recent DPs from the Soviet Union, did not want to have any association with the local population. They wanted to leave Germany for good. In the next few years, 700,000 of them would emigrate to the United States and to Palestine. By 1955, there were just 15,000 Jews in Germany. The history of postwar Germany might have been far more antagonistic if more victims had decided to stay.

Nazi victims received some local support in the summer of 1945. Konrad Adenauer, the mayor of Cologne, sent buses to Dachau, Buchenwald, and Theresienstadt (Terezín) to bring those liberated home. Elsewhere, inhabitants welcomed home Jewish neighbors with flowers and put up plaques in honor of those murdered. Town halls established special welfare units. In Stuttgart, each returnee received 30 Reichsmark on top of the regular welfare payment. The city also gave many an honorary gift (*Ehrengabe*) worth 250 RM. (Reichsmark would only be replaced by Deutschmark in 1948.) Public recognition of their special status as Nazi victims set them above the many ordinary Germans who had cheered for Hitler and were now lining up outside the welfare office.[18] There was self-help, too. Communists, Social Democrats, and other anti-fascists founded the Union of Persecutees of the Nazi Regime (Vereinigung der Verfolgten des Naziregimes, VVN), which assisted political prisoners and distributed food, clothing, and toys to their children; Adenauer himself was initially a member. There were unofficial and official donation drives for Nazi victims; in North Rhine–Westphalia these produced 1.9 million RM in autumn 1945.

Some perpetrators also had to pay directly. Cities confiscated clothes, furniture, and bicycles from Nazi Party members and gave them to their victims. In Münster, Maria K. received in this way a summer coat, one pair of summer shoes, a blouse, a hat, an umbrella, three pillow cases, and one mosquito net.[19] The champion of this direct approach was Philipp Auerbach, the commissioner for racial, religious, and political persecutees in Bavaria, himself an Auschwitz survivor. Auerbach worked tirelessly on behalf of the victims and found them apartments, jobs, and university places. In 1946, he set up a special fund that enabled Bavaria to pay them a pension and help them with medical aid.[20] His main goal was to reduce the huge number of victims and DPs in the camps by helping those who wanted to stay in Germany to find their feet, and those who did not to emigrate quickly. For Auerbach, financial help was tied to a principle of restorative justice between victim and perpetrator, and not only because public funds were limited. Reparation involved moral repair work. It not only offered relief to the victim but demanded punishment of the wrongdoer. This strategy, of course, raised the big question of who should pay: convicted Nazis only, everyone who had cheered Hitler, the German people as a whole? Auerbach's answer in Bavaria was to levy a fine (*Sühnegeld*) on former Nazis while also pressing for national retribution. Both German states would have to confront this thorny question on their foundation in 1949.

GUILT AND SHAME

These were the survivors, but Germans were also forced to confront the dead, and it was this encounter that brought them face-to-face with the question of guilt. Bergen-Belsen, the concentration camp near Hanover, was liberated by British troops on April 15, 1945. Pictures and stories of the piles of corpses soon filled the newspapers. British soldiers made SS guards, including SS women, haul the dead bodies into mass graves and bury them with their bare hands. Civilians from nearby towns were marched out and made to watch. Similar scenes took place across Germany. The country was peppered with camps, and there were plenty of civilians living in their vicinity. Ravensbrück, a camp for women, was liberated on April 30. Erika Buchmann, a communist who had been imprisoned there since 1940, walked with soldiers from the Red Army to nearby Fürstenberg, rounded up twenty locals, and took them to see the crematorium. Soviet soldiers forced inhabitants at gunpoint to carry the dead bodies from the camp to the local cemetery, climb into the graves to bury them, and, finally, place flowers on them. The soldiers themselves added a red star.[21] Sandbostel was one of the satellite camps of Neuengamme, near Hamburg. On May 1, 1945, secondary school children were told to present themselves at the camp the next morning. A fifteen-year-old wrote in her diary, "I have terrible fear of tomorrow."[22] She had heard that the inmates were half dead. She and other locals were ordered to wash the bodies of liberated prisoners.

Elsewhere, locals were taken to nearby killing fields to rebury the forced laborers who had been murdered in the final stages of the war. In Warstein, some ten thousand people—anyone able to walk, including children and the elderly—were force-marched in rows of four through the forest, flanked by military police. They were made to look at the bloated corpses before giving them a fitting reburial in individual coffins. Documentary film footage shows the somber expressions on their faces, with women trying to shield the eyes of their children and covering their noses because of the stench. The horrible images would stay with many for the rest of their lives. Fifty years later, a woman recalled her impressions from when she was thirteen:

> Heads, sometimes. Blue, red, and without skin. Eyes out of place. No eyes at all. Faces without eyes. I started feeling sick... A woman behind me fainted. Children were screaming, men were crying. My wilted bunch of wildflowers dropped onto a small, bloated corpse. I was afraid of the many soldiers and of the foreigners without uniform, who watched and made sure that each one of us was looking at their dead fellow countrymen.[23]

In the population at large, immediate reactions to the news of atrocities varied greatly. For some, their former sense of national entitlement now turned into national self-pity. "It is always us who get our alleged sins rubbed in our face," Renate Bock from Hamburg, who had survived Operation Gomorrah, reported angrily on May 20, 1945. The sins were "alleged," she insisted, because how could she be held responsible for something she did not know about? She pushed away German guilt by pointing at the guilt of others. "We are subject now to 'special laws' and are punished for things that the other countries can do to us without any consequences." The day before, Allied vans had driven through the streets with the slogan: "German women, German pigs"—a reference, probably, to brutal SS women in Belsen. "We constantly get to hear what the others have suffered," Bock added four days later, "but no one is allowed to talk of our own terrible suffering."[24] Stephen Spender, the English poet who had fallen in love with Germany (and young Germans) in 1929, received a similar response in a small town in Westphalia in July 1945 when he tried to impress on a woman the enormity of Nazi crimes in occupied countries. "I can well imagine that things are bad there," the woman said, "but our poor Germany is always hit hardest."[25]

Not everyone tried to hide behind stubborn denial. Five days after the end of the war, the bishop of Holstein called on Germans to acknowledge "the guilt of our people." By knowing the truth but not speaking out, he said, they had become "entangled in guilt."[26] For socialists and communists, Allied treatment was payback for what the Germans had done to Jews as well as to them and Russians. Some denounced German women. Four weeks after liberation, Erika Buchmann addressed several hundred women in Fürstenberg: "All of us, and every single one of us," she told them, "carry our share of responsibility for this war." Women in armament factories as well as soldiers were "jointly responsible for the misery of our people."[27] In prisoner-of-war camps, many German soldiers were in denial. But there were also socialists like Walter S. who had seen the death marches and felt it was only right and fair that "the Allied whip was now swinging over the heads of the German people." "It is not true," he wrote to his wife, "that only a few megalomaniac political adventurers carry the guilt for these crimes." Ordinary Germans including people they knew might not have been Nazis initially, but the "bacillus of racial megalomania" had already been slumbering within them.[28] He knew what Germans had done to Russian forced laborers and brushed aside stories of Soviet deportations of German prisoners as wild rumors; he was wrong on the last count. Mathilde Wolff-Mönckeberg, from a patrician family in Hamburg, also felt that the German people were all in the same boat. On June 1, she wrote to her children, it "serves us right that we are now daily reproached with the atrocities of the concentration camps. We all have to carry the responsibility for those horrible crimes and no one should close their mind to it."[29]

The face-to-face confrontation with terror in the camps was imposed, but it was easy for Germans to convince themselves of Nazi violence if they wanted to. Erich Schmalenberg was fourteen at the end of the war and lived at the outskirts of Dortmund. He was a lucky boy. Not only had he survived the bombing of the Ruhr, but at his own initiative he had joined the confirmation class of the local Protestant church and was just young enough to avoid the Hitler Youth. It freed him up to play the role of a self-styled reporter in the ruins. Schmalenberg was among those Germans who greeted the arrival of American troops warmly. His diary entry for April 13, 1945, was: "The day of freedom is here!" Five days later, he noted the gruesome discoveries that had been made in Belsen, Buchenwald, and Nordhausen: "Women, children, old people, and innocent men were tortured in a bestial way by the Nazis, Gestapo, and the SS . . . every day 200 inmates died." The next day, in Rombergspark, just a little over a mile from his home, a mass grave was uncovered with 132 corpses, including women and children. His father voluntarily went to satisfy himself of the "Gestapo murder of innocent people." Hitler was still alive. On April 20 ("the Führer's birthday"), Erich wrote, "Today, I had an opportunity to see the bestialities myself." He chose to watch how local Nazis were made to rebury their victims: "The corpses were beaten blue, and some women had half their fingers missing." The next day, Eric read in the newspaper how in "the Belsen concentration camp, they skinned people and made lampshades and bookbindings." On the 22nd, he was listening to broadcasts from London and learned of the murder of priests in Dachau. A day later, he visited the "torture chamber" of the Gestapo in his hometown and saw "three large butcher knives, which were at least 1/2 to 3/4 meters long." By the end of June, he had decided he would write a book on the "past, present, and future" that would reveal the "consequences we should draw from National Socialism."[30] That didn't happen. But, with such a critical fourteen-year-old observer, there was hope for the future.

In May, Allied posters appeared in shop windows with several pictures of heaps of corpses. The headline announced, "These vile deeds: your guilt!"[31] By June, however, the British were trying to win over Germans for a democratic future. In July, half a million magazines were distributed to German civilians and POWs in which "guilt" (*Schuld*) had been watered down to "complicity" (*Mitschuld*). The following month, at Potsdam, the Allies made clear that their intention was to give the German people "the opportunity to prepare for the eventual reconstruction of their life on a democratic and peaceful basis," not to "destroy or enslave" them.[32] At Nuremberg, in November 1945, the prosecution went out of its way to stress that they were charging particular individuals with crimes, not the German people at large.

If the Allies rapidly abandoned the charge of collective guilt, why did Germans continue to be so defensive about it? One reason is that Germans had been increasingly afraid of the charge since 1943. As we have seen, Allied bombing was widely interpreted as retaliation for German crimes against Jews and foreign civilians. Nazi propaganda, furthermore, had helped to stoke fear of retribution in case of defeat. A soldier in Russia spelled it out for his sister in the summer of 1943. "The entire people," he wrote, "will be held accountable for the horrors of the war that they have brought upon humanity. The German people must be completely destroyed so that they can never again be a threat for England. Thus speaks England."[33] When Germany surrendered, the Allies did not need to say much about collective guilt to confirm these predictions.

The first footage of the camps appeared in short newsreels, but by the summer of 1945, the Allies were showing longer documentaries to audiences of civilians and POWs. *Death Mills*, an American film, was completed in July. The Soviets produced *Majdanek* in August, a Polish co-production. Today, the word "KZ" evokes Auschwitz. While gas chambers and the crematorium of Auschwitz did appear in *Death Mills*, these films were not focused on genocide. The American and British took most of their footage from Belsen, Dachau, and other camps in their zones, which had not been extermination camps, but where prisoners had been worked to death, died of disease, or had ended up after death marches. Some of the films made the point that

Germans had been victims of concentration camps, too. The Soviets, meanwhile, were primarily interested in political prisoners, not Jews, and edited out Jewish prayer objects from *Majdanek.*

We know most about the Western films. Their main purpose was to shock and reeducate. This required balancing atrocity and accusation with the prospect of redemption and a better future. The camps thus became part of an Allied history lesson. *Deutschland Erwache* (*Germany Awake*) contrasted the promise of the thousand-year Reich with its twelve years of brutality. The film made a point that the Allies appreciated Goethe and Beethoven. They did not hate the Germans, only the Nazis with their murderous lust. For those whose hearts were open to the laws of humanity, there was a future of work and peace. The film ended not in the gas chambers but in San Francisco, with the founding of the United Nations.[34]

To reflect how German audiences reacted, we have two caches of documents—one with responses from prisoners of war in British camps, the other surveys of civilians conducted by the American Information Control Division. Both, of course, carried biases. These were not conversations among equals. The Allies were in power and the Germans at their mercy. Still, the responses were not entirely strategic, either. In fact, some were startingly honest. For all their limitations, they shed some light on the moral views at the time and how initial shock gave way to shame.

The film *KZ*, the first documentary on the camps, was shown to 202,404 POWs in 136 British camps. A prologue was meant to be read out before each screening describing the victims as the "silent or living witnesses of German guilt" and referring to the "inseparable guilt between the Nazis and the German people." However, British camp commandants decided to speak to their audiences only of "these crimes" instead of "their own crimes."[35] Some of the POWs had themselves been camp inmates, and the commandants felt that the requested change in wording was entirely appropriate. Most prisoners were "deeply shocked" and sat "in absolute silence, broken only by exclamations of disgust." Several commandants reported prisoners "weeping." A few young people believed that it had to be propaganda, but the majority accepted that the film was true, or at least most of it. These screenings were, of course, opportunities for prisoners to distance themselves from the Nazis in the eyes of their captors. In a dozen camps, prisoners passed general resolutions to that effect. But they were divided on what such condemnation entailed for themselves. Some accepted responsibility and pledged to do their utmost "to make good the injustices done." In one camp, prisoners raised a collection for the victims of Belsen. In others, prisoners condemned the atrocities but rejected any national responsibility.[36]

Several prisoners wrote individual letters that ranged from protestations of innocence to collective guilt by omission. "I do not think that Germany as a whole should be held responsible," a Corporal Eggemann said, because he and other Germans did not know and could not do anything against the Nazi government. Others protested their innocence with fascist or racist justification. H. Nellesser from cage 28 in the Cairo POW camp said, "I cannot accept that every one of us Germans should feel guilty for what was going on in the camps. Many of us thought and believed that inmates of these camps deserved punishment because they were politically dangerous." A Corporal Dober went one step further: he accepted that part of the film was true, but said, "I do not believe that any but Polish and Russian prisoners were treated as shown in the film." And those, after all, were not on "the same level of civilization [*Kultur*]" as Germans. What was criminal was not the murder of foreign prisoners but that the German government had had "such things done before they had made sure they were going to win the war." Interestingly, Dober identified himself as a "non-Nazi."

Many others, however, wanted the government and Nazi "criminals" to be punished. One soldier extended it to all Nazi members and suggested sending ten thousand National Socialist girls "to wait on the black soldiers or work on farms in Egypt" for ten years without pay. P. Mocha in cage 29 went further: "Every one of us who gave his vote to these murderers bears full responsibility for such bestialities." And a Corporal Fuchs went further still and found guilt by omission: "All Germans are responsible in that they did nothing to prevent such happenings." It was difficult to get closer to a sense of collective guilt than that.[37]

While guilt is about a wrong done to others, there was virtually no concern in these letters for the victims themselves. For many, it was not the Nazis' crimes as such that troubled their conscience but that these had also taken place inside their own country, carried out by Germans against Germans. A Sergeant Jung wrote that all those in his cage were "deeply shocked and discussed the film throughout the night." What was so shocking to him was not the murder of innocent civilians in general. He had seen what he euphemistically called the "ill-treatment of civilians in occupied Poland by SS guards," but he "never expected that such atrocities could be committed on a large scale inside Germany."[38] Where POWs did express sympathy with victims, it concerned the Allied treatment of German expellees.[39]

If guilt drew on nationalist self-regard and pride, so did shame. The introductory remarks the Allies gave to these atrocity films in July 1945 raised a clear expectation that viewers would see the pictures with "feelings of shame—and rightly so, for you, as former supporters of the Nazi regime, carry your individual share of responsibility for these crimes."[40] For the Allies, guilt and shame were closely connected. But were they for the Germans, too?

For many POWs watching the film *KZ* in British camps, shame was a substitute for guilt, not its cousin. Hugo Krause wrote that he knew camps existed before the film but now he felt "deeply ashamed to have fought for such a regime."[41] In cage 16, thirty-three soldiers signed a collective statement of shame that included "our comrades" who had sacrificed their lives for such a regime: "Everybody felt the disgrace of the profanation of the German nation of moral[ity] and honor." Those responsible, they argued, needed to be brought to justice. For themselves, this left shame.

This was also the overwhelming reaction among the civilian population who went to see the films. In Erlangen, in July 1945, American observers noted that the audience was "stunned" by the film *KZ*: "Many people went so far to declare that they were ashamed to be Germans" and even considered giving up their citizenship.[42] Between January and April 1946, the film *Death Mills* was shown in the American zone. In Bad Kissingen, the local mayor made viewing compulsory. Elsewhere, though, it was voluntary, at least on paper. In Bavaria, about half the population watched it. In Berlin, it was only one in six. A debate erupted about whether Germans did not attend because they were emotionally numb. One woman wondered why she should want to show her shame in public: "Is not every German already blushing with shame when reading reports of the movie? But to watch something that one is not personally guilty of—no. It is enough having to do penance for it." German journalists praised *Death Mills* for documenting the mountain of guilt the nation had to live down. Those who attended left with a different conclusion. According to an American audience survey, 88 percent of viewers felt no responsibility, and only 10 percent complicity.[43]

Shame expresses the sense of being powerless and inadequate in the eyes of someone else. In ancient Greece, it literally meant being naked with one's genitals exposed. It is often assumed that Germans showed shame in 1945 because they were trying to hide from the Allied gaze. That certainly happened—for example, during forced visits to the camps, when Germans turned away or covered their faces to avoid the stare of Allied soldiers. But German shame was about more than that. Whereas in empathy we resort to an "impartial spectator" to look at ourselves from the outside, in shame we rely on an "internalized other," in the words of the philosopher Bernard Williams. Instead of putting ourselves in the shoes of another person, shame records that we feel uncomfortable in our own shoes. It is introspective and results from the embarrassment of having failed by a standard we took to be our yardstick. Williams assigned shame an important role as a mediator between good and bad. Morality does not emerge through reason alone, as Immanuel Kant believed. Shame, Williams pointed out, is reciprocal in nature, about what we expect from the world, and what the world expects from us. By expressing one's feelings toward others, their desires and expectations, "shame can understand guilt."[44]

This did not happen in the case of the Germans after 1945. While shame is universal, people's sense of shame is different in different times and places. Germans did not feel they had failed to live up to the expectation of humanity as a whole, or that of the Jews or other victims of the Nazis. They were concerned with the German nation, with its supposedly higher *Kultur* that set it apart from lower races, not that of the English and Americans and their grubby materialist *Zivilisation.* Recent philosophers have pointed out that shame does not necessarily have to register a failure to live up to a standard. It can also express a gulf between a person's self-image and their identity—feeling shame for belonging to a poor family, for example.[45] For postwar Germans, shame extended this tension to one between self-image and national identity. As individuals, they were not perpetrators, but as members of the German people they inextricably belonged to a nation that had committed mass murder. When the German teenage girl who'd been victim of Soviet rape learned of the mass murder of the Jews from a Jewish American officer, her instinctive response was "I am ashamed to be a German."[46]

For many Germans, shame thus simultaneously expressed two negative feelings: that they belonged to a nation of mass murderers and that an idealized Germany was looking down on them. "I was once proud to be a German," the twenty-five-year-old POW H. Monneckes wrote, but after watching an atrocity film, "I feel I must lower my eyes in deepest shame before God and Mankind."[47] Such universal references to mankind were quite exceptional. Much more common were national ones. A Berliner felt that so few went to watch atrocity films in April 1946 because honest people were "carrying for some time a sense of shame that such things were even possible for a German"—implying that mass murder carried out by other people would have been less shameful.[48] The POW K. Bork wondered, "How can the German uniform ever free itself from that most awful shame?"[49] In 1945, shame was most often tied to national honor, not an understanding of guilt. It pointed away from personal complicity by directing attention to those Nazi "criminals" who had given the nation a bad name. In 1949, Theodor Heuss, the first president of the Federal Republic, would make "collective shame" a key term in the new country's political lexicon. But the ingredients were already there in 1945. On November 25, 1945, the liberal Heuss gave a memorial speech to victims of the Nazi regime in the state theater in Stuttgart. Barely half a year since defeat, some voices were already calling for an end to all the talk about Nazi atrocities. Heuss brushed them aside. Victims had a right to be remembered. But, he said, memorials were just as important for the moral future of the nation. After singling out Social Democrats and old elites who had died in the resistance, he told the audience what had been "the gravest and most precious victim of the Nazis." It was, he said, "the honor of the German name which had been pulled into the dirt." They should speak out in rage, as "shamed, defenseless contemporaries" and fulfill their duty of cleansing it.[50]

DEMONIC FORCES

After the summer of 1945, the debate about guilt changed. Whereas in May, the Allies had confronted Germans, from October it was German writers, pastors, and philosophers who did.

On November 11, 1945, Ernst Wiechert gave his "speech to German youth" to a full house in the Munich Kammerspiele theater. Forgotten today, Wiechert was part of the canon of German literature in the interwar years. His mythical musings about moors and forests as spiritual retreats from modernity made him a favorite with young Germans, for whom his tearful literary voice had shamanic qualities. Wiechert was a romantic nationalist. He hated democracy, cities, and materialism and initially welcomed the vision of the Third Reich. His problem with the Nazis was their methods, not their goals. Culture should be in the hands of ethereal poets, not violent street fighters. Morality and national interest demanded a respect for the law. This was the gist of two acclaimed speeches he gave to German youth in 1933 and 1935, courageous interventions, although they hardly forced him into "inner emigration," as he conveniently claimed later. Wiechert's *Simple Life* sold a quarter of a million copies and was adored by young men such as Reichardt, our Parzival, as well as by Hans Frank, the governor general of occupied Poland, who phased in the mass murder of the Jews. The true break came in 1938, when Wiechert stood up for Martin Niemöller, the submarine commander-turned-pastor who was sent first to Sachsenhausen, then to the Dachau camp, where he was kept as Hitler's personal prisoner. For Wiechert the arrest was a breach of honor as well as justice; a highly decorated officer was being treated like a common criminal. He announced that he would no longer contribute to the Nazi winter aid fund and would, instead, send his donation to Niemöller's family. Wiechert was immediately sent to Buchenwald, where the then fifty-year-old was made to carry heavy stones before being given a job darning socks. After two months he was freed and placed under Gestapo surveillance. In 1939, he wrote a fictionalized account of his time in Buchenwald (*The Forest of the Dead*) and buried it in his garden. It would be one of the first books to appear about the camps after the war. Susanne Vogel quoted from it to her cousin in America about the "freezing cold" that swept across the soul during the Nazi years.[51]

Wiechert took to the stage in November 1945 with the aura of the pure "inner Germany." For many contemporaries, Wiechert was the good German conscience that had withstood the Nazis. At the same time, he was one of the few Germans who had been praying for an Allied victory since 1939. He started work on his speech the moment Germany surrendered. His "message to the living" mixed an indictment of national complicity with a vision of love and redemption. "Let us recognize," Wiechert said, "that we are guilty and that perhaps one hundred years will not be enough to wash the guilt from our hands." "We will have to face hunger, because they died of hunger." "An eye for an eye, tooth for tooth, blood for blood" was the harsh law that applied to them. For Wiechert, there were only a few heroes, and these were not the returning soldiers but the victims behind barbed wire. Virtually everyone else was complicit. Where were the thinkers and poets, he asked? They had prostituted the spirit and collaborated with the Nazis. Teachers, doctors, lawyers, and priests—they all turned to "a new cross" on which was written "Death to the Jews." This did not mean that Wiechert himself was free from antisemitism. The Jewish people, he wrote in *The Forest of the Dead*, were "guiltier than other peoples," but "in the camps their guilt dissolved into nothing before the guilt of those who praised themselves as the new people."[52] The German generals were rotten to the core, too. "The *Volk* knew that it was a criminal war." "We also knew . . . what happened in the camps. We trembled in shock and horror, but we looked on." For people to deny their own guilt would only double it, he warned. "Never before have a people been so alone on this earth—so much so, that even the animals flee like they flee from a murderer."[53]

Nazi murderers, Wiechert argued, should receive as little mercy as they had shown to their victims. Everyone else, though, should be shown forgiveness as long as they promised not to sin again. National rebirth required a cleansing of the heart. "Don't believe in the age-old lie that shame can be washed off with blood," he told the audience, but "in the young truth that shame can only be washed away with honor and repentance." Revenge needed to be replaced by love: "As long as they do not have blood on their hands, do not push them away."[54]

Wiechert's speech articulated the power of evil that was readily understood by his audience but is so alien from our own way of thinking about Nazi Germany. Since the 1960s, the dynamics of the Nazi regime have been historicized with major debates about the role of intentions versus structures, the power of the Führer and his charismatic leadership, the backing of old elites and the bourgeoisie, and whether National Socialism belonged to the family of fascism or totalitarianism.[55] While differing in their conclusions, these approaches have established a clear understanding of the years 1933 to 1945, with identifiable causes and consequences, actors and institutions, ideas and interests. In 1945, however, few Germans thought in these categories. Significantly, in a land of eminent historians, even the most eminent, Friedrich Meinecke, failed to live up to the task and, except for criticizing the German bourgeoisie and the Prussian ethos of duty, took refuge in a fantasy of "Goethe loving communities" as a way out of the "German catastrophe." The Nazis, in this view, were an alien force, and Jews were jointly responsible for antisemitism; Leo Baeck, the rabbi at the head of the Jewish community in Germany before his deportation in 1943, called Meinecke's *German Catastrophe* a "miserable book by a distinguished man."[56]

Ernst Wiechert's prescription for national redemption drew on a spiritual interpretation of the German past. Leaders, institutions, and social classes were entirely absent from his address. Tellingly, Wiechert never mentioned Hitler by name and referred to him only as a liar, prophet, and dilettante in everything except the "art of evil." Some time after the First World War, he said, "the clock of our fate" started ticking. History did not result from the interplay between identifiable individuals, interests, and institutions, but from deeper spiritual forces. The German people, in this view, were like the Hebrews who had adored the Golden Calf in the Old Testament. The Germans allowed themselves to be corrupted by the Nazis and their cheap tunes, shiny uniforms, and "mass soul." They had traded in God and Goethe, faith and humanity, for a "magician" who promised them victory and greatness. Now, in the autumn of 1945, they needed to "dig out God from underneath the rubble of the Antichrist."[57] There were metaphysical elements in this perspective, but it would be too simple to brush them aside as an otherworldly apologia for inaction by hiding behind God. Wiechert called for actions in this world. Since guilt sprang from sources deeper than politics, renewal needed individual acts of love. Here was a moral understanding of German guilt that did not look outward toward courts and governments but inward to the soul.

Nazi crimes, in this view, were crimes committed by Germans, but resulted from a universal crisis of modernity, not German history. Demonic forces had been taking over the world. Hitler wore the mask of the devil. In the words of one Catholic priest in 1947, the international military tribunal at Nuremberg was merely a sideshow: "The whole world is a court. The prosecutor and judge is God. The main accused is Satan with his demonic power."[58] From here it was a short step to turning complicit Germans into victims. The historian Dan Diner has called the Nazi genocide a "rupture in civilization."[59] After the war, Germans thought in a radically different time frame. To them, the Nazis were not a caesura but the culmination of a long spiritual crisis. The events of 1933 to 1945 did not appear as a series of concrete causes but as manifestations of a deep and universal battle between good and evil.

The demonic interpretation would become a fixed part of the mental furniture in the young Federal Republic. In its selection of books for the summer of 1948, for example, the newspaper *Die Zeit* singled out for praise *The Demon and His Image* by Erwin Reisner, who told readers that satanic forces continued to exist whether they liked it or not; after 1939, Reisner had worked for the Büro Grüber, an organization which helped Protestants of Jewish descent.[60] In 1950, during an investigation of the changing nature of the family, sociologists asked one couple what they expected from the future. The husband, a mid-ranking civil servant who had refused to join the Nazi Party, was deeply pessimistic. He feared a "spiritual and physical" clash with the East. The interviewer asked who they felt was responsible for the situation. The wife responded "like a shot: Hitler!" The husband hushed her and then explained: "No one. It is the result of a very long development." Did he mean the French Revolution? the interviewer wanted to know. No, the husband replied, "it comes from much further away, more like the Renaissance. Hitler and similar phenomena were exponents of demons... They were forces over which humans had no power, and that made the story so sinister."[61]

The diagnosis was even shared by victims of the Nazis. In late July 1945, Samuel Beer interviewed Bavarian mayors on behalf of the U.S. military government. "You will not discover much about Nazism studying German history," the mayor of Bayreuth, Josef Kauper, assured him. "It could have happened anywhere." Unemployment, social distress, and internal conflict—any other society would have given in to the Nazis under similar pressures. People did Hitler's will, Kauper told Beer, to protect their families. "In addition to natural good there is natural evil. There is inherited sin."[62] Kauper was the new "clean" mayor appointed by the Americans. His mother was Jewish. He had been ostracized by the Nazis and spent several months doing forced labor. But he was also anti-Bolshevik and a proud veteran of the First World War who had joined the Free Corps that quashed the red republic in Munich in 1919.

Of course, not everyone subscribed to this view in all its aspects. For communists, fascism was the child of industrial capitalism A few others pointed to defects in German history. The Swiss theologian Karl Barth, for example, visited Germany in 1945, ten years after he had been removed from his chair at Bonn University for refusing to swear the oath to Hitler. A leading voice in the Confessing Church, Barth now helped in establishing the Council of German Protestant Churches (Evangelische Kirche in Deutschland, EKD) after the war. For Barth, the real problem was those Germans who treated Hitler as a "regrettable incident" in their otherwise glorious history; the historian Gerhard Ritter would become their spokesperson.[63] For Barth, the crumbling plaster of the Nazis revealed the nationalist masonry underneath. Hitler had followed in the footsteps of Otto von Bismarck and his militarist policy of blood and iron. But Barth's was a minority voice, and it narrowed the circle of guilt. Barth was convinced that the majority of Germans had never been Nazis: their "sole guilt stemmed from their passivity of not having been heroes." They did not need reeducation. Those who did, he argued, were the smaller number who continued to look back to 1871—German unification—with a glowing heart.

Another critic of Prussianism was Theodor Steltzer, who had been an officer with the high command in occupied Norway and close to the Kreisau resistance circle. He became the first minister-president of Schleswig-Holstein in 1946. Prussian "self-discipline" and "blind obedience" had come at the expense of "individual will and thought," he said during a commemoration for the victims of fascism in November 1945. He traced the problem back to Bismarck and Frederick the Great. All Germans shared responsibility for not averting Nazi crimes, himself included. But even Steltzer, who preached self-government, ended up looking for the source of evil in modernity at large. It was materialism that had eroded community spirit and led to the "ethical confusion" that enabled the demonic forces released by the Nazis to enslave the German people. After listing the various groups of Nazi victims—Jews were mentioned in passing—he concluded that "essentially the entire German *Volk*" were victims. The German people had strayed from their true self, but their core was good.[64]

For many contemporaries, Germany and the rest of the world were caught in a vicious cycle of violence. The mass murder of the Jews, in this view, was not unique but one manifestation of this universal cycle. Today, Hitler is commonly referred to as the face of evil, but the term is used casually. For many Germans after 1945, he literally was the incarnation of evil. Since then, we have made significant advances in understanding the mechanics of the Nazi regime, but we have also largely lost that deeper, more metaphysical sense of evil.

Today, 1945 marks peace in Europe. For Germans at the time that was far from clear. Hitler was dead, but for how much longer would the weapons be silent, with the country divided, millions of forced migrants and POWs, and Stalin eying Europe? After two world wars and Nazi rule, there was little faith in political solutions. It is therefore not so surprising that contemporaries looked to love, penance, and forgiveness to stop the cycle of violence. Many Germans in 1945 put an almost utopian faith in the Allies to usher in a new moral universe, and then sank into bitter frustration and anger when they were instead subjected to denazification and expulsions. It did not help that the nation now calling for peace and forgiveness had been the one that had started the war and murdered millions of innocent people.

CHURCHES DIVIDED

Guilt suggests sin, and this placed the churches, as the mediators between actions in this world and salvation in the next, in a central position. Anyone expecting a clear word of guidance from them was soon disappointed. In August 1945, German Catholic bishops still lamented that many compatriots, including their own flock, had participated in Nazi crimes. At large, though, the Catholic Church turned its back on the debate. The same bishop (Galen of Münster) who had challenged the Nazis over their euthanasia killings publicly denounced Nuremberg as a "show trial."[65] In Germany as in Rome, the Catholic Church fell silent over its own complicity during the Nazi years and hid behind a myth of resistance.

The Protestant Churches, by contrast, accepted guilt but came close to tearing themselves apart over its precise meaning. The clash was about politics and personalities as well as theology. Tensions were apparent from the outset, when, on October 19, 1945, the Council of the German Protestant Churches signaled its remorse to their foreign brethren at an ecumenical meeting in Stuttgart. In their "confession of guilt," German Protestants acknowledged that "through us infinite suffering had been brought over many peoples and countries"; an official reference to the murder of the Jews had to wait until 1950. At the same time, they insisted, "we have fought for long years in the name of Jesus Christ against the [Nazi] spirit."[66]

The two statements represented the rival camps fighting over the very identity of Protestantism. Historically, power lay with strong regional churches (*Landeskirchen*), which had their own distinct styles of faith and government following the Reformation. Loyalty to the state had been a core principle ever since Martin Luther. For reformers such as Niemöller and Barth, the lesson of the Nazi years was that the church of the future should never again play the role of the obedient servant to a regime. To retreat into the realm of the spirit—as the two had done in the Confessing Church—had been discredited. Protestants, they believed, had to play a more active political role in protecting law and liberty. Instead of a loose federation of churches, they wanted one church that cut across old territorial and confessional lines. For Niemöller, greater moral and political responsibility went hand in hand. The church, he argued, carried even greater guilt than the Nazis, for the Nazis at least believed they were on the right path, whereas they, the pastors, had known that the path was leading to ruin.[67]

The problem was that many bishops and pastors in their regional churches saw the situation rather differently. Partly, this stemmed from a genuine concern with pastoral care. German refugees and war victims in their parishes wanted to talk about their own suffering, not hear about their responsibility for the suffering of others. More practically, the regional churches had little interest in handing over historic powers to the center. Opposition, however, also arose from their own complicity. In northern Germany, one in four pastors had belonged to the Nazi Party before 1933. Many more joined thereafter; in Bremen it was a staggering 90 percent. Thuringia, in the Soviet zone, was a hotbed of the fascist German Christians.[68] In their search for local collaborators, the Allies had naively bought into the Churches' exaggerated self-presentation as islands of resistance. Almost all priests with a brown past thus stayed in their pulpits after 1945, in both East and West Germany. These men had little interest in following Niemöller and examining their own far greater guilt.

The Stuttgart confession caused anger and confusion among pastors and their flocks alike. A few churches were supportive. In the Rhineland, the synod asked its congregations whether they had raised their voices when "Jews, mentally disabled, and innocent were handed over to their hangmen." The fact that the Allies were committing sins, it said, did not absolve Germans of their own. For some priests, the confession was a mark of national honor, a sign that the *Volk* was going "up," not "down."[69] Overall, though, there was a public outcry. Many condemned it as an unacceptable declaration that Germany alone had been responsible for the war. The theologian Helmut Thielicke accepted the Stuttgart confession but added that guilt was always reciprocal: Versailles and the Allies' initial recognition of Hitler were responsible, too. Church leaders were attacked for doing the enemy's work. The bishop of Bavaria rejected outright the idea that those who spoke at Stuttgart spoke for the German nation. A POW likened it to a "kick in the face... of every patriotic German."[70] There was a storm of protest over the confession's silence about the Allied crimes committed against Germans and refugees, in particular; at Stuttgart, Otto Dibelius, the bishop of Berlin-Brandenburg, had tried to insert a reference to Allied crimes but it was diplomatically left out for fear of incensing the foreign delegates. What had made sense in spring 1945 no longer did now, the head of the church in Schleswig-Holstein Präses Wilhelm Halfmann wrote in October. "The enemies have pushed the word of penance back down our throats. Any German talking about guilt right now ought to bear in mind that our *Volk* is being murdered."[71] It was difficult enough to win back the souls of suffering Germans, but for some of them the Stuttgart confession was proof that Hitler had been right all along: the church could not be trusted. What was required, Halfmann insisted, was a solidarity of need, not guilt.

Many Protestants felt lost: How could their Evangelische Kirche have resisted the Nazis and be guilty at the same time? Why did it not focus on the real wire-pullers, the politicians, capitalists, and militarists? The Stuttgart confession was vocal about German guilt but vague about its exact nature and the expected response from individuals. The church leadership in Saxony wanted to know what it meant in practice. "Should we as civil servants, pastors, judges, and soldiers have refused to swear the oath to Hitler?... Should we have refused to do military service? Should a Christian have followed the martyrs of 20 July 1944 and committed treason?"[72]

Hans Asmussen, the head of the church chancellery at the EKD and someone who had consistently resisted Nazi attempts to take over the church, tried to calm the waters. In a commentary in December 1945, he expanded on the meaning of the Stuttgart confession. He warned against those who were pointing at the guilt of others: "Unadmitted guilt seals our mouth and closes the ear of the victors." Their own confession of guilt, he wrote, had been misunderstood. It was addressed to God, not to foreign peoples or Allied governments. Only a few Germans had been murderers, he said, but they all shared responsibility because Hitler, Goering, and SS guards were "of our own blood." The church would not defend Nazi leaders and party members, but it would not turn them away, either. "We are ashamed of their deeds, but we are not ashamed to call them our brothers." What exactly did Germans' complicity consist of, then? It was not the specific wrongs they had committed during the Nazi years. Rather, their guilt was their apostasy. They had sinned against the First Commandment—"You shall have no other gods before me." The root evil was secularization, which had created false gods in the form of ideologies. National Socialism was just one among others. Modern history, Asmussen wrote, was "an apocalyptic history." God was using history to punish man. He would forget neither the murdered Jews nor the murdered German refugees. The practical advice that followed was that people should be active in charity and public life. But, Asmussen warned, on its own this was "barely worth mentioning" and accomplished nothing. Germans had to rediscover God. "Who does not learn to serve God, will neither please God with their service to their neighbor, nor benefit the neighbor." The first step of repentance was to serve Christ in this world.[73]

Martin Niemöller crossed the country preaching a very different message. On January 22, 1946, he spoke to a packed church of young people in Erlangen in Bavaria. He recognized that it was difficult for soldiers who had served with good intentions to face up to the fact that they had been misused in pursuit of a criminal war. Other nations were not innocent, he agreed. Still, Germans had to accept that the disease which turned into crime had broken out in *their* nation. The only way to a new life was through confessing their guilt to the victims. He gave the example of his own meeting with a Jew who had lost his entire family: "Dear brother, human being, and Jew, before you say anything, I will tell you: I confess my guilt and beg you; forgive me and my people this guilt." Germans also needed to confess before God. "There were five to six million murdered Jews . . . on our national guilt account [*Schuldkonto*]." He himself was responsible, since he did not speak out against Nazi violence when he still could in the mid-1930s. Niemöller then admonished people for not talking about the immense suffering Germans had caused in the East, "about what happened in Poland, about the depopulation of Russia." It was at this point that members of the audience began shuffling their feet and heckling him: "And the guilt of the others?" When Niemöller tried to continue and quoted the Stuttgart confession, the audience became so unruly that the student pastor had to call for order and remind them they were in a place of worship.[74]

Even Niemöller only went so far. Acknowledgment of guilt did not translate into empathy for all the victims. In his speeches, German suffering received far more attention than that of the Jews. The "brother" and "human being" just mentioned happened to be a baptized Protestant of Jewish descent from his old congregation at Dahlem. The other Jews only featured as an anonymous number. Niemöller did not believe in collective guilt—that would have required a collective conscience, he said. But Germans had a "collective liability" to take on the consequences of Nazi crimes. The principal aim of such public exhortations was to get the German Protestant Church back on its feet. In order to renew itself, the church needed to shoulder that burden. It could not just tell Nazi Party members to carry their guilt on their own. National pride and ideological prejudice made such confessions difficult enough in 1945. A year later, any existing space for them shrank further under the pressure of denazification. A public confession of guilt now risked one's livelihood. An antisemite, Niemöller himself emerged as one of the most vocal critics of denazification and would call for its boycott. Denazification and Washington were run by Jews, he said.[75]

In the hands of the Protestant Church, guilt narrowed from a public into a spiritual concern, a matter between the individual sinner and God. The theologian Helmut Thielicke, who talked to officers and students, said tellingly that "where the question of guilt was taken really seriously, public discussion stopped." It called for faith, not action in this world. A few regional churches, such as Hessen-Nassau, where Niemöller presided, made a point that they had known of the "persecution and deportation of the Jews." The provincial synod in Oldenburg reminded congregations that they had been more than bystanders: they had taken an active part when their Jewish neighbors and political undesirables had been deprived of their "property and bread."[76] But, in general, the debate about guilt was one without the victims. Under the Nazis, Jews had been pushed further and further out of Aryan Germans' circle of sympathy. The end of the war did not suddenly reverse that. In December 1945, Heinrich Held, one of the signatories of the Stuttgart confession, declared categorically that "Jews are not suffering any need in Germany."[77] This stunning statement came from a theologian who had helped dozens of Jews survive in hiding. The spiritual interpretation of guilt directed Germans' eyes firmly on God and kept victims where they were: out of sight. In February 1946, a POW and theology student wrote from Naples to Bishop Wurm of Württemberg. The Stuttgart confession threatened to undo all his hard Bible study work in the camp. "What is more important," he asked the bishop, "a confession of guilt before people of other nations or a confession before God" that would also send a light to all those searching among "one's own people"?[78] It did not dawn on him that the two might not be mutually exclusive and that the former might help with the latter.

If the Protestant Church saw Jews at all, it was as potential converts in their mission work. This otherworldly orientation of guilt and penance, it needs to be stressed, was not something typically Protestant but something distinctly German. Sin and atonement have mobilized millions of Christians into action in other contexts; the antislavery movements and social work in the slums are just two examples. Hans Asmussen talked of the apocalypse, but after the war German Protestants lacked human empathy and a sense of millennial urgency to try to save themselves by saving others.

At the end of 1946, Asmussen sent a memorandum to all German bishops hoping to settle the question of guilt once and for all. It was an extraordinary step. Churches, he wrote, should announce that God forgave everyone their sins who had confessed "their own guilt and that of our *Volk*" and who believed in Jesus Christ. God's forgiveness, he added, would extend to those still awaiting their earthly judge, undergoing denazification, or being held in an internment camp. In other words, it would extend to SS men, Nazi functionaries, and even convicted war criminals. His fellow brethren on the Council of the German Protestant Churches were appalled. They wondered whether there had been a single congregation in Germany in which guilt had been sufficiently confessed to warrant such a general absolution. It was unheard of, they reminded him, that the one who confessed a sin and the one who forgave it were one and the same person.[79] Nonetheless, the wind was clearly blowing in the direction of a self-amnesty.

GUILT TURNED INWARD

The philosopher Karl Jaspers—"the only successor Kant has ever had" in Germany,[80] in the words of his student Hannah Arendt—tried to impose some order on the debate about guilt in a series of lectures at the University of Heidelberg, published in April 1946. Jaspers's wife was Jewish, and he had been forcibly retired in 1937. But he was also a patriot and refused to leave his country. In March 1945, he was sitting with his wife and two capsules of cyanide expecting deportation to the camps. Luckily, the Americans arrived before the Gestapo. Now, he worked his way through the different registers of guilt: moral, metaphysical, judicial, and political. Jaspers rejected collective guilt as meaningless. A nation, he said, did not have a moral character, only a common language. What Germans did have to accept as a whole was political liability. As for metaphysical guilt, it might, perhaps, be a subject of revelation "in the works of poets and philosophers, but hardly one for personal communication." Morality was ultimately individual. Individuals needed to act for themselves.

Just as interesting as what Jaspers did say was what he did not, and the reactions he triggered. Jaspers accepted that Germany alone was responsible for the war but then criticized foreign powers for turning a blind eye to "the satanic forces of the Nazis."[81] Allied foreign policy received more space in his lectures than Hitler and the internal history of Nazi Germany combined. Germans appear either as the first victims of Nazi terror or as passive bystanders. Kristallnacht, he said, happened "without the participation of the local population"—a far cry from the truth. He acknowledged war crimes but at the same time exonerated individual soldiers. Hitler's accomplices were only in the "ten thousands."[82] Even at the time, these were questionable views. The Social Democrat Willy Brandt, for example, returned from Norwegian exile in November 1945 and wrote a report on Germany in which he noted the army's role in atrocities and counted those complicit in Nazi crimes in the millions.[83] However mild Jasper's verdict, it still struck most contemporaries as far too harsh. He had never encountered such hostile audiences in all his life, he told Arendt. "Publicly, they leave me alone. But, on the quiet, I am abused: by the communists as a pacesetter for National Socialism, by the defiant as a traitor."[84]

While agreeing with him on many points, Arendt had her reservations, too, among them that Jaspers was too fixated on individual guilt. Yes, she wrote to Jaspers from New York, hang Göring and the rest. But guilt was more than the sum of judicial crimes. Nazi policies were so "monstrous" that they could no longer be grasped by the articles of criminal justice. For Arendt, metaphysical guilt was not just for poets and philosophers. It concerned our human solidarity with everyone else in the here and now, making it the foundation of a republic. Arendt wanted a more "positive political declaration of will addressed to the victims" that stressed their equal rights in a future German state.[85]

Today, we tend to think that it would have been better had the Germans talked more of their guilt. At the time, though, many reached the opposite conclusion, and not only former Nazis who wanted to obfuscate their past. Heinrich Blücher, Arendt's communist husband and a philosopher himself, felt Jaspers was trying too hard to redeem the German soul, as if Germans just needed to rediscover their private virtue. All the talk about guilt, Blücher wrote to Arendt, was blurring a sense of political responsibility. Guilt tended toward the universal, but that also made it politically meaningless. If everyone was guilty, no one was. Blücher preferred to focus on shame, instead. While everyone might be a sinner, some lived with honor yet others with shame. Unlike guilt, he wrote, "shame is a thing of this world and can be washed off with blood." The Germans did not need to save themselves from guilt but from shame.[86]

Niemöller, Jaspers, and Wiechert—leading voices calling on Germans to confront their guilt—had all initially supported or tolerated the Nazis before they fell victim to them. Exiles, by contrast, were greeted with vitriolic attacks when they tried to address the German catastrophe. Thomas Mann, for example, the Nobel laureate author of *Buddenbrooks* and other works of renown, had left Germany in 1935, first going to Switzerland, then, in 1939, to the United States (New Jersey, then California). There, he made a series of anti-Nazi broadcasts. On the day of surrender, his radio message stressed that the terrifying scenes of the liberated camps were not the work of a "small number of criminals but of several hundred thousand members of a so-called German elite, men, boys, and dehumanized women."[87] By August 1945, eminent German authors publicly called on him to return to the fatherland and join them in their search for truth as a "soul expert": it would be a sign of faith in people's "sympathy with their fellow men."[88] Nothing lay further from Mann's mind than such a joint enterprise with authors who had been bystanders or, worse, supporters of the Nazis. Before Mann had finished his response, he and other exiles were subjected to an orchestrated nationalist attack in the press. Those who had chosen to watch the German tragedy from comfortable "box seats... in a foreign country" were disqualified from lecturing the millions of Germans who had loyally stayed behind in their country's hour of greatest need; that this charge came from an author (Frank Thiess) who himself had moved to Rome and Vienna and hardly qualified as someone who had gone into "inner emigration" only added insult to injury.[89] Mann would not return until 1949, and then only to commemorate Goethe's two-hundredth birthday. He spent his last years in Switzerland, where he died in 1955. None of these charges could be levied against Niemöller, who was held for over six years in Sachsenhausen, then Dachau, concentration camps, yet offered to fight and die for Germany, or against Jaspers or Wiechert, both of whom had opportunities to emigrate, even though the idea of deserting their fatherland was inconceivable to them.

The first wave of public soul-searching lasted until 1947–48. In the first three years after the war, Northwest German Radio (NWDR) broadcast in the British zone a program on National Socialism almost every second day. Guilt and responsibility were discussed, although the Nuremberg trials received most attention. Some broadcasts now identified the camps as systems of mass killing with many willing helpers, rejecting the idea of "necessity" and acting under duress, both of which would become a convenient fiction in court trials in the 1950s. Most programs, though, reflected the ideas we have explored. Nazi leaders received the most attention, followed by the German resistance, and only then came German society. Jews and foreign victims were barely mentioned. Programs had titles such as "I—You—All of Us." There was a general consensus that people needed to confront the Nazi years, but only one journalist went so far as to say that they were all complicit because they had voted for Hitler. The others settled for collective liability for what a few others had done. They blamed cowardice, fear, and an inferiority complex that allowed the "demons of the deep" to rise in Germans' hearts and make them throw themselves into the arms of "villains." Every German carried "in his heart a secret diary of these dark years," the journalist Axel Eggebrecht said.[90] They needed to take stock, not destroy it. Here, again, the main appeal was for private introspection, not a public reckoning. Ultimately, these programs were forward, not backward, looking. And this is what listeners took away, judging from their mostly positive responses. A self-critical look back was to give people the assurance needed for reconstruction. These broadcasts were not invitations to atone for crimes against their victims; they were, rather, for the Germans to rebuild their own lives.

In 1947–48, the international context for reconstruction changed fundamentally. In the spring of 1947, President Truman pledged to contain Soviet expansion. A year later, the Marshall Plan started giving U.S. aid to Western Europe. Germany was now at the center of the Cold War. And as it intensified, the terms of the debate about guilt also changed. Instead of fascism, West German radio began to talk of totalitarianism. The national specifics of German guilt disappeared further as Nazis and Bolsheviks came to be seen as symptoms of the same disease.

Niemöller, Jaspers, and Wiechert were now swimming against the current. Germany's emerging division into a capitalist West and a socialist East made Niemöller's vision of a united nation look irrelevant. For him, Catholicism was a greater threat than socialism; paranoid, he believed that the Americans were behind a popish plot.[91] That did not endear him to Protestants, East or West, confronted with the hardening communist line in the Soviet zone. His suspicions of parliamentary democracy did not help either. At the first synod of the Council of German Protestant Churches in January 1949, Niemöller was standing again for the position of deputy chair. He received a mere two votes. For the moment, he was isolated.

In the case of Jaspers and Wiechert, postwar Germans managed to do what the Nazis had not: they pushed them away. Jaspers received antisemitic hate mail warning him that the "rats are leaving the sinking ship." Just as hurtful was the general apathy he encountered everywhere. Some students responded to his call for self-reflection, but he felt that pride and indifference dominated. In 1948, he and Gertrud, his Jewish wife, emigrated to Switzerland, where he took up a chair at Basel University.[92]

Wiechert felt let down by the Allies and Germans alike. Justice from the Allies was not to be expected, he wrote in 1946. The British had suffered "under the brutality of our conduct of war," the French were full of sadistic revenge, the Russians had the souls of children but also "the wildness of their Asiatic heritage," and the Americans were "masters of civilization but did not know much of *Kultur*."[93] The Germans, meanwhile, had wasted an entire year in "idle talk" about guilt, deaf to his call for love and an embrace of suffering. The "corpse of humanity" lay "violated" in front of them crying out for acts of mercy. Instead the Germans "played philosophy with it."[94] During a memorial at the Dachau concentration camp in 1947 he told the assembled 1,500 former prisoners—other Germans were notable by their absence—that they needed to embrace their suffering. They had lost everything—"the Reich, the war, their home, clothes, bread, and wine"—but these were earthly things and could be sacrificed. The one thing they should not give up was their experience of suffering. It was the only path leading to a new community of man.[95] It would be the theme of his final novel, *Tidings* (*Missa Sine Nomine*), in which Baron Amadeus returns from a concentration camp, where he had shot the executioner to save a French fellow prisoner. After leading a trek of German refugees to safety in the Western zone, he withdraws to a shepherd hut and learns to forgive the forester, who had denounced him, and his fascist daughter. Here was a pre-democratic story of redemption with aristocratic leaders, loyal servants, and mystical moors. Good and evil fatally coexisted in nature and the divine. Evil could never be eliminated. "For we need evil to become good," as the priest tells Amadeus. Nor did good people have a right to look down on their evil cousins, since "deep down they had the same source."[96] Only suffering, remorse, and forgiveness made it possible to restore natural harmony.

Wiechert himself was hardly a paragon of charity—he refused to take in German refugees. But he was also not used to open attacks on his moral and literary authority. That he welcomed defeat as liberation from the Nazis was for many unforgivable. A new generation of authors—his German youth—parodied his speeches as those of a vain old man who was out of touch.[97] How dare he present himself as their self-appointed visionary? He was a hypocrite, they said, who talked of suffering he had never experienced himself and who knew nothing of theirs. For someone who had spent time in Buchenwald, however short, that was a blow below the belt. More generally, it signaled how the focus on suffering, instead of fostering solidarity, was fueling a competitive victim politics. In 1947, Wiechert told a Swedish journalist that the German people were doomed: he would "never again speak to Germany, nor to German youth."[98] The following summer, he, too, moved to Switzerland.

ON TRIAL

On November 19, 1945, the Allies put twenty-four leading members of Nazi Germany before the world's first International Military Court, at Nuremberg. For the next eleven months, the court deliberated their share in conspiracies against peace, wars of aggression, war crimes, and crimes against humanity. In addition, the prosecution charged the main Nazi bodies as well as the Army High Command with being criminal organizations. On September 30 and October 1, the verdicts were read. The SS, Gestapo, the Security Service (SD), and the leadership of the Nazi Party were declared to be criminal organizations. The Army High Command and the Storm Troopers were not. Three of the individuals charged were acquitted—Franz von Papen, Weimar's penultimate chancellor and Hitler's vice chancellor in 1933; Hjalmar Schacht, the economics minister until 1938; and Hans Fritzsche, the head of broadcasting under Goebbels. Seven of those charged received lengthy prison sentences, including Hitler's deputy, Rudolf Hess (life), and Albert Speer (twenty years), Hitler's favorite architect, who was in charge of armaments and slave labor after 1942. In two cases, the court was unable to reach a decision.

Twelve men were sentenced to death by hanging. They included Hans Frank, the governor general of occupied Poland; Ernst Kaltenbrunner, the man in charge of the security service and its Einsatzgruppen; Wilhelm Keitel, head of the Army High Command; and Joachim von Ribbentrop, the foreign minister. Martin Bormann, Hitler's secretary, was sentenced in absentia but, it turned out, was already dead. Hermann Göring beat the hangman by swallowing a capsule of cyanide the evening before his scheduled execution. The others met their fate shortly after midnight on October 16, 1946.

The day before the hangings, a different story of crime and punishment had its premiere on Unter den Linden in the Soviet zone of Berlin. Normally the home of the state opera, the Admiralspalast was showing Wolfgang Staudte's *The Murderers Are Among Us*, the first German movie made after the war. In the film, a mix of melodrama and noir, the surgeon Hans Mertens meets his former captain, Brückner, on Christmas Eve, 1945. The baubles and lights trigger memories of Brückner's order, exactly three years earlier, to shoot civilians in a Polish village, ignoring Mertens's appeals for mercy. A newspaper headline flickers across the screen about 2 million people gassed, reminding audiences of the scale of Nazi crimes. Unlike Mertens, who is traumatized by the past, Brückner has moved on and successfully set himself up in business. He is a slimy opportunist and capitalist, not a fanatical Nazi. Instead of showing any remorse, he tells Mertens, "Whether you make steel helmets out of pots or turn helmets into pots, who cares? What matters is that one manages well."[99] In the original screenplay, Mertens kills the captain, but the Soviet authorities had no interest in inciting vigilante justice. To get permission to shoot the film, Wolfgang Staudte, the director, changed the story. The innocent and angelic Susanne Wallner, a mysterious camp survivor, saves the tormented Mertens from drink, despair, and murder. He drops his plan to kill the captain. "We do not have the right to pass sentence," she tells him. Hans responds: "We have the duty to press charges."[100] The final scene shows Brückner behind bars.

So close in time, the trials and the film were also miles apart in their approach to justice. At Nuremberg, the Allied prosecutors deliberately focused on the inner circle of Nazi Germany. The army was let off the hook; General Hans Röttiger gave a witness statement that acknowledged army involvement in war crimes, but later withdrew it after concerted pressure from the generals on trial. In the film, the murderer on trial is an ordinary army captain. More than that, the film leaves open the possibility that responsibility for the crime extends to the soldiers killing the civilians, and perhaps even to Hans Mertens himself. "We are all murderers," one reviewer wrote, and that included Mertens, "for he allowed the bloodbath to take place. He clicked his heels in resignation, once he saw that his intervention was in vain. He did what we all did: he capitulated in the face of force."[101] At Nuremberg, Allied prosecutors pressed charges. In the film, Susanne (a victim) dissuades Hans from taking justice into his own hands. But, in the final moments, the call for accountability comes from Hans, the former soldier, not Susanne, the camp survivor.

How many Brückners were there out there who should be put on trial? The question haunted Germany in the postwar years. Nuremberg raised thorny issues of legal interpretation. It violated the positivist principle against retroactive punishment—a crime was only a crime if it violated a law at the time it was committed. Von Ribbentrop rejected Nuremberg as a trial without law; it did not save him from the gallows. The Allies, by contrast, invoked a higher universal law that applied to war crimes and crimes against humanity across time. This, it needs to be noted, was also the position endorsed by Gustav Radbruch, the eminent German legal mind, a

Social Democrat and minister of justice in the Weimar Republic, who translated the American prosecution's speech at Nuremberg. Where a statutory law ignored the equality at the heart of all justice, a judge needed to put aside such law and rule in favor of the higher principle of justice. Simply put, an act did not become legal because Hitler said it was.

These differences would come to matter *after* the Allies handed sovereignty back to German authorities in 1949. In the immediate postwar years, however, they were a subordinate question. Dr. Hugo Manz summarized the popular reaction to the Nuremberg verdicts in one of his letters to his missing pilot son. They stretched from communist protest strikes against the acquittals to "complete indifference."[102] For some it was "a disgrace" to see officers and politicians at the mercy of the victors, and "tasteless" that the ashes of the executed were strewn into the wind. Still, Manz noted, except for a handful of stubborn individuals, no one was standing up for the Nazis. Complaints about "victor's justice" were vocal but should not be given undue importance. American opinion polls showed that more than three in four Germans thought the trials were fair.[103] Harsh sentences for Nazi leaders were easy to agree on. Nuremberg confirmed the convenient story of deception and betrayal by a gang of "criminals." Here were the men who had "gagged" the innocent German people and misled their honorable soldiers. Far more troubling was the scope of criminal accountability beyond the Nazi leadership. There were millions of Germans between Hermann Göring and Hans Mertens. Where should the line of justice be drawn?

Putting Germans on trial had major consequences for the debate about guilt. Instead of hovering in metaphysical air, in the courtroom guilt was pulled down to earth and made tangible and personal. It was individuals who were sentenced or acquitted. Justice always concerns individuals—criminals and their victims. But how justice is administered also reflects a society's values and priorities, and in the wake of Nazi Germany's enormous crimes, it was an extraordinary challenge. Justice is a balancing act between competing objectives: retribution (making the criminal pay); reparation (compensating the victim); rehabilitation (reforming the criminal); deterrence (protecting society as a whole); and vindication (applying the law so the law is respected). Between 1945 and the late 1950s, the balance between these principles shifted in both West and East Germany, reflecting not just the two countries' verdict on their past, but also how they wanted to see themselves in the present.

Justice came in a variety of forms between 1945 and 1949. The main Nuremberg trial was followed by twelve trials of industrialists, camp doctors, judges, senior civil servants, and police officers. In addition, the Allies had their own system of criminal justice and military tribunals in their respective zones. The Allies also granted a series of amnesties.

But justice was not entirely in Allied hands. German prosecutors and judges were already reentering courtrooms in the first year after the war. At the end of 1945, the British zone introduced a so-called piggy-back clause that allowed for each innocent jurist one former Nazi Party member to return to the bench. The legal basis was the Allied Control Council Law No. 10 (Kontrollratsgesetz Nr. 10), or CCL10. It applied the Nuremberg principle of a higher law to minor as well as major Nazi criminals. The highest court in Berlin (*Kammergericht*) defended its rationale in 1947. The idea of "no crime without law" was meant to protect citizens against arbitrary treatment by a state trying to hold them responsible for deeds that had not been illegal at the time. But now they were dealing with individuals who had committed crimes protected and encouraged by a criminal regime. The Allied directive, the court explained, was not an alien import but restored the certainty of justice broken by the Nazis. It formed the basis for courts in the British, French, and Soviet zones. The Americans, by contrast, did without it, partly worrying that it would complicate proceedings already underway in their zone. The Allied directive remained in effect until 1951.

FROM DENAZIFICATION TO AMNESTY

Denazification is now mainly remembered as a failure, and, as we shall see, there was no shortage of failings. Still, we get a distorted picture from judging the subject only by its end result, and not looking at the process itself. For Germans caught up in it, the future looked highly uncertain—they did not know that amnesties were around the corner.

In its first phase, Allied occupation came close to a social revolution. Defeat did not only mean the internment of surviving Nazi functionaries. There was a sweep of the local elites who had continued to serve the Nazi state—mayors, town treasurers, judges, policemen. In July 1945, the United States ruled (partly in response to popular opinion back home) that anyone who had been a member of the Nazi Party before 1937 was to be removed from public administration. In September, Law No. 8 made it illegal for party members to run a private business, leading to fears that the Americans might, after all, follow the Morgenthau Plan, which, in 1944, had proposed eliminating Germany's military potential forever by deindustrializing the country and turning it into one giant farm. The majority of Germans were not affected by these measures, but the elites were. In the Marburg area, almost every mayor and every second official was sacked.[104] In many communities, the end of the Nazis marked a bigger break in the social hierarchy than their coming to power. A pastor's wife in Celle, in northern Germany, thought the new "regime of terror" by the Social Democrats, who had seized many vacant posts, was worse than the Nazis.[105]

In spring 1946, denazification began to be handed over to German tribunals (*Spruchkammern*), watched over scrupulously by the Allies. Initial sentences were tough, in both the American and the Soviet zones. The tribunals had the job of placing an individual in one of five categories, depending on his role in Nazi organizations: "principally guilty" (I, war criminals); "guilty" (II, activists, militarists, profiteers); "minor incrimination" (III); "opportunist" (IV); "uncompromised" (V). In Bayreuth, for example, the businessman Hans A. had been a leading official in the SA. In August 1946, the local tribunal placed him in group I and sentenced him to five years in a labor camp. Eighty percent of his property was confiscated.[106] A year later, the deputy mayor of Ansbach, Albert Böhm, found himself on trial there. He was an "old fighter" who had joined the Nazi Party in 1926. He was a fanatic, corrupt, and responsible for some locals ending up in Dachau. He, too, was sent to a camp for hard labor for two and a half years, and all his property was confiscated.[107]

In the course of 1947, though, the taste for thorough denazification was fast disappearing. A joke captured the changing mood:

> A man goes to the local police office and asks to be registered as a Nazi. The surprised officer tells him that he should have reported himself a year and a half earlier. The man responds: "But I was not a Nazi a year and a half ago!"[108]

Was denazification leading to renazification? The turn against the tribunals came from several directions at once: the population, the Allies, and German political parties. The process had a major design flaw in that it relied on self-reporting and self-incrimination. In order to obtain a "clean" certificate that enabled people to apply for jobs or receive a pension, they were asked to fill in a questionnaire about their political past. Lying on the questionnaire could have serious consequences. In Bayreuth, the deputy district administrator had left out his membership in the Nazi Party and was sentenced to four years in prison as a result.[109] Not surprisingly, those with the murkiest CV and independent means were the slowest to come forward. This meant only the little fish ended up in the net. Tribunals were swamped with cases from ordinary party members. Towns ran out of questionnaires or did not have the manpower to handle those they received. Those people who could not afford to wait would downplay their support for the Nazis or lie outright to protest their innocence. In many cases, moreover, party membership was a poor shorthand for complicity. Some officials who had signed deportation orders had never become party members. A former Social Democrat, by contrast, had been a member of the SA for one year in 1934—under pressure from his employer, he claimed. He was classified as an opportunist and handed a 300 Reichsmark fine. He was outraged to be put in the same group as many lifelong Nazis and spent two years appealing the decision.[110] There were also ex-Nazis, such as Hansjoerg Maurer, who fell out with Hitler after the abortive 1923 coup and in the late 1930s helped victims. He fought for fourteen months to be reclassified as innocent.[111] Minor offenders experienced the process as a disgrace and public humiliation. Unlike several of his colleagues, Dr. Manz, the father of the missing pilot, was allowed to continue his medical practice, since he had only joined the NSDAP in 1937. In November 1946, it emerged that he had not reported the fact that he had given first-aid training to the SA in 1933. Manz had to appear before the American military tribunal and was fined 1,500 RM, almost as much as a worker brought home in an entire year. Two years later, he was still pained by the "shame" (*Kulturschande*) of having been tried by a prosecutor who was a dockworker from New York.[112]

By 1947, letters of good character were no longer signed freely solely by pastors and colleagues, but by victims, too. Surviving victims who did not emigrate were a small minority, scarred, stigmatized, and isolated, without power to impose claims on the majority. Instead of pulling communities apart, denazification pulled most of them together. Especially in provincial Germany, social networks went back generations. There was a basic sense that one would have to live with the people one knew in the future. Denazification therefore tended to strike outsiders rather than insiders. In East Frisia, for example, a Nazi official, an outsider, was sentenced by the tribunal, while the local butcher who had been in the SS was protected by his peers, quickly recategorized as "uncompromised," and reinstated in his job.[113]

By the end of 1947, some 12 million questionnaires had been submitted in the American zone, but only 631,000 cases had been completed. Forty-one percent were amnestied, cleared, or suspended; 47 percent were classified as opportunists and 10 percent as minor figures. Only 2 percent were in the activist category and only 0.1 percent found chiefly guilty.[114]

The Western Allies pursued a zigzag course. On the one hand, the U.S. military governor, Lucius D. Clay, threatened to take back control of denazification if the Germans were too soft on each other. On the other, Clay was worried about destroying the seeds of democracy before they had a chance to sprout by alienating too many "little" party members, opportunists, or the young; the first free elections for local government in the American zone were in January 1946. The delays, frustrations, and uncertainty of denazification interfered with everyone's priority: reconstruction. Town halls adopted elaborate schemes, such as appointing the wives of officials undergoing denazification, who then handed the work to their husbands back at home.[115] The Soviets, meanwhile, primarily saw denazification as a vehicle for regime change, and this meant getting rid of fascist-capitalist elites, not alienating the German people as a whole.

German political parties had no interest in mass purges either. None of the party leaders had any doubt about the degree of complicity with the Nazis. In private letters, Konrad Adenauer of the Christian Democrats blamed bishops, businessmen, and Prussian militarists alike.[116] But in public, his priority was to win over former Nazi supporters. Max Brauer, the Social Democratic mayor of Hamburg, put it bluntly in December 1946: "Ninety-five percent of the German people had worked in one way or another with the Nazi regime. With just 5 percent, though, it is not possible to build a state."[117] Christian Democrats and Social Democrats feared both communist control of the tribunals and that alienating former Nazi supporters would drive them into the arms of Bolsheviks. The strategy of the Socialist Unity Party (SED)—the result of a communist takeover of the Social Democrats in the Soviet zone in April 1946—was, similarly, to win over former Nazi backers. As early victims of the Nazis, communists knew better than most how widespread Nazi support had been in the population. Since communists saw big business as pulling the strings behind Hitler, however, they tended to downplay popular responsibility. After the Nuremberg verdict, Otto Grotewohl, the SED leader, compared the "acquitted criminals of banking capital, Messrs. Schacht and von Papen," to the "more innocent," "oppressed, abused, and . . . persecuted German people."[118] In neither East nor West were political interests boding well for a reckoning with complicity and guilt.

The parallels in the initial speed and subsequent collapse of denazification were remarkable. An American analysis in September 1946 found that 178,111 persons had been dismissed in their zone by that date, and 180,356 in the Soviet zone. In both sectors, almost every second public official had been removed.[119] Just as in the American zone, denazification came to a halt in the Soviet zone in 1948. The difference lay in their political priorities and strategies of rehabilitation.

For communists, denazification was a chance to complete their control of the state. The exchange of personnel was therefore highly uneven across the professions. Compared to the West, the eastern approach was more radical in public administration, justice, and policing, although more Nazis managed to hang on than is sometimes realized. Of the 828 cases reviewed in public meetings in the town of Saalfeld in Thuringia, for example, two thirds went scot-free. Barely two dozen public officials were demoted or dismissed. The few sentenced were mainly people who had their shop or private business sequestered. The new mayor had served in the Waffen-SS, which the regime conveniently overlooked in exchange for secret intelligence from him.[120] In schools and hospitals across East Germany, former Nazis largely continued in their posts.[121]

In the West, rehabilitation was linked to a professional ethos. It was a form of anti-politics: do your job and stay clear of extremism. In the Soviet zone, by contrast, it required political conversion. Since ordinary Nazi Party members had simply been "betrayed" by fascism, there was no need for atonement. Except for perpetrators, the key test was not what people had done in the Nazi era but what they were prepared to do for the socialist future. Demonstrations and newspapers gave former Nazis an opportunity to declare their commitment to the anti-fascist struggle. In 1948, an entire new party was created, the National-Demokratische Partei Deutschlands, to provide a socialist home for former Nazis. Denazification turned into an opportunity for expropriating businessmen and other class enemies, although local protests would see to it that at least some owners got their sequestered companies and properties back a couple of years later.[122] In Schwerin, northern Germany, the head of customs, who had not even been in the Nazi Party, was sentenced to eighteen months in prison and a loss of his pension and civil rights on the pretext of a swastika being found in the building.[123] Someone who kept the duchy's coat of arms on display in his office could not be trusted with the socialist project. Denazification in the eastern zone should, perhaps, be called pro-Sovietization.

The Cold War sealed the fate of denazification. The pressure for amnesty, however, was already mounting before the Western Allies failed to agree on a peace treaty with the Soviet Union at the Moscow conference in March 1947. Amnesties came in a series of waves. In August 1946, the Americans granted an amnesty to young Germans born after 1918. This was followed in December by one for the disabled and the poor (serious offenders were excluded). Doctors began freely handing out 50 percent disability certificates. In 1949, West Germany extended amnesty to everyone with a prison sentence of no more than six months—800,000 people walked free. This time, it did not only cover petty criminals and people who had been caught trading in the black market, it also benefited some 30,000 perpetrators who had committed grievous bodily harm and homicide—these had minimum sentences of only three to six months. The Soviets granted a "peasant amnesty" in 1947 and followed a year later with a bigger one, in honor of the 1848 revolution, for anyone with a prison sentence shorter than a year.[124] Italy, France, and the Netherlands had their own amnesties.

In East as in West Germany, the spirit behind these amnesties was reconstruction, not reparation. This forward-looking orientation reflected a widespread sense that, with their own suffering after 1945, Germans had more than served their sentence. Barely one and a half years after defeat, the rising star of the German literary scene Alfred Andersch declared that German guilt had been compensated for by Allied bombing, expulsion, and the "Babylonian imprisonment" of German POWs. It was time to draw a line under the past. Hans Werner Richter, a fellow member of the "Group 47" that would transform German literature, likened German soldiers to slaves and concentration camp inmates.[125] Such statements revealed not only traces of antisemitism but a troubling notion of justice, as if the crime of others somehow canceled out one's own and, with it, the need for any atonement.

German youth occupied a special role in these debates. Young Germans had been especially fanatical Nazis, yet arguably it had been their parents' generation who had raised them to be monsters. Youth was no excuse, the writer Manfred Haussmann (born in 1898) argued in 1946. They could have known about Nazi crimes if they had wanted to. Instead they "kept on believing and drumming." The article triggered a storm of protests. Members of the older generation were hypocrites, with their talk of "inner emigration," the writer Wolfdietrich Schnurre (born in 1920) responded. "You said nothing. You waited. And when it was all over, you stepped out of your idyllic villas . . . and offered yourself for 'democratic reconstruction,' and talked to us about guilt, us who returned from captivity with burning eyes and dried-up hearts."[126] Youth was a flexible term, and amnesty stretched it to those who were twenty-seven in 1945, which made for a large cohort.

The young generation found its voice in November 1947 with the character of Beckmann in Wolfgang Borchert's play *The Man Outside* (*Draussen vor der Tür*). Its fame was sealed by the tragic death from liver failure of the twenty-six-year-old playwright and poet (and former Wehrmacht soldier) the day before the premiere. In the expressionist play, the young corporal Beckmann—captured at Stalingrad—returns from Russia to bombed-out Hamburg, caught in a nightmare of his own guilt and unable to reenter peacetime society. It pains him that he cannot undo his colonel's order for a reconnaissance that ended in the loss of eleven of his men. His own parents, he learns, had been outspoken Nazis, hated Jews, and committed suicide after the war. No one shows any empathy with anyone; the only thing that saddens his old neighbor is that precious cooking gas has been wasted in Beckmann's parents' suicide. The director of a cabaret tells him that the war was "long past" and to "be positive, my dear! Think of Goethe! Think of Mozart!" The play closes with a question: "Is no one, no one giving an answer???"[127] The ending is sometimes treated as a mystery: an answer to what? In fact, Beckmann raises a whole string of critical questions: "I? The murdered... am I the murderer?" "Do I not have a right to my own suicide?" "You say I shall live! For what? For whom?" The emphasis of the final line is on "no one." Even God is silent. And so are people passing death in the street with indifference. Elsewhere Borchert called his age group a "generation without farewell... without God... ties, past, or recognition."[128]

The success of the play on stage and radio lay in its very solipsism: past and present evolved around the figure of Beckmann, onto whom young Germans were able to project their own lives. At last, some listeners wrote, they were being heard. For many, Borchert was the conscience of a generation. He was not a nihilist, some pupils wrote in their school newspaper in 1948: he was "'the other' who always warns, affirms, drives on, and shakes up."[129] Only a few listeners pointed out that it was the Beckmanns who were the aggressors in the war and that, in the words of one listener, "our youth... had often been a more than willing instrument of the tyrants who wanted to destroy mankind."[130]

Amnesty is known as the sister of arbitrariness. The winding down of denazification saved the neck of many Nazis. In Bavaria, only a fifth of the principal offenders (*Hauptbelastete*) had been tried by the summer of 1947. More than a thousand Nazi officials used the amnesties of 1949 and 1954 to resurface and return to their true identity; how many others continued to live under a false name is unknown. In 1951, the so-called 131 law reopened the door for civil servants and professional soldiers to resume their old jobs and pensions.

It is tempting to see the whole messy chapter as a revolving door, but it was one that did not operate smoothly. Many were stuck inside it for several years, and when they came out they were different people from when they entered. Two years after the war, there were still 100,000 people interred in the Western zones. After their release, many never found their way back into their old lives. Christian Hansen had studied engineering and worked in his father's firm when, in 1933, he was recruited to the SS Leibstandarte, Hitler's bodyguards. In the war, he fought in the East with the SS tank corps. On his release from internment in February 1948, the only work he could find was as an agricultural laborer. It was six years after the war before he managed to set himself up as a freelance architect.[131] Walter Fandrey had been a Nazi district leader (*Kreisleiter*) in Altötting, Bavaria, until 1941 when the visiting *Gauleiter* took offense at not being welcomed with a big feast and had him transferred to the army. In 1948, Fandrey was one of the many who were reclassified as an "opportunist." As was common in the American zone—but not in the Soviet one—he had his three-year internment taken into account and walked free. He could only find work as a casual laborer. Franz Emmer, the local Nazi district leader in Fürstenfeldbruck, also Bavaria, suffered a steeper fall. In October 1948, the tribunal sentenced him as a main offender to six years of hard labor and the loss of his pension, all moveable property, the right to vote, and the right to work in his profession. Twenty percent of his income was taken to pay for reparations. Emmer appealed, but the verdict was confirmed in 1949. He appealed again and in 1957 was given a general pardon and had his fine lowered. For several years, this former bigwig was destitute and dependent on welfare benefits. His wife waited on tables in a restaurant while he became a liquor salesman. Eventually, he got his house back. Occasionally he would rant in the local pub, but the locals ignored him. In 1956, he attended a few meetings of the right-wing Deutsche Reichspartei, but his energy for activism was spent.

Emmer's was a comparatively harsh fate.[132] Most civil servants and army officers only lost their job and pension, and it was they who led the campaign for rehabilitation in 1951. The results, though, were similar. In addition to providing the country with breathing space between 1945 and 1948 by locking up hard-core Nazis, denazification cured any taste for political adventurism thereafter. Those who had been through it all were relieved to be granted a second chance. They wanted to put on slippers, not jackboots.

On October 1, 1951, the town council of Stadtoldendorf in Lower Saxony assembled at the municipal gasworks and burned all its denazification files and Nazi Party membership lists. They were the first city to "draw a line" under denazification, the local mayor, a Social Democrat, proudly declared. He defended it as a well-thought-through decision. It was a "demonstration for the peace of the town." The resident British officer, he noted, had told him he would have done exactly the same: "What is past, one should leave behind as past." In the wrong hands, these files would result in bad blood. The eight thousand local inhabitants needed to look forward. The decision had been made by the town council on the fiftieth anniversary of the municipal hospital, which, it just so happened, had been generously founded by Max Lewy, a Jewish factory owner. The locals got their amnesty, the Jewish cemetery a wreath.[133] Before 1933, the town had been home to seventy Jews. Only two escaped deportation and death, thanks to being in "mixed" marriages.

Here as elsewhere, the voices of the victims were drowned out by the call for social peace and reintegration. When Bonn decided to rehabilitate civil servants and army officers in 1951, it understandably left behind a bad taste among survivors. "Marvelous!" a reader wrote sarcastically to the weekly Jewish newspaper. In 1945, all Nazi Party members had magically disappeared. Now they received reparation. "What a shame that I was not in the party. I believe I would be better off today!"[134]

The turn from denazification to rehabilitation was part of a broader shift in the mental atmosphere of the late 1940s. Culture and literature, as we have seen, were principal sites where Germans confronted the past after 1945. On the stage, the most popular play in 1948 by far was Carl Zuckmayer's *The Devil's General* (*Des Teufels General*). Written in American exile in 1942, it had its German premiere in Frankfurt in November 1947. It was performed several thousand times across West Germany in the following two years (it was prohibited in the Soviet zone) and widely used in schools. A film adaptation followed in 1955. Instead of the spineless officer of *The Murderers Are Among Us*, the central figure of this play is a tragic hero, the smart, likeable General Harras, a veteran flying ace whose love for planes, women, and wine is stronger than his distaste for the Nazis. "The first two years of the war," he reminisces, "they had real style."[135] Then, in the winter of 1941–42, he realizes that he is serving a criminal regime. As he investigates mysterious plane crashes, he discovers that they are the result of sabotage by a friend and anti-Hitler officer. The SS challenges Harras to either reveal the saboteur or to resign and incriminate himself. The general takes off in the manipulated plane and crashes it into the control tower.

There was some morality for everyone: the pitfalls of opportunism, the evil of fanaticism, the courage of resistance, and self-sacrifice. There is even selfless concern for Jewish victims when Harras is preparing to smuggle out his old Jewish doctor and wife, only to find they have committed suicide. Like Thomas Mann, Zuckmayer had fled Nazi Germany. Unlike Mann, he was convinced that Germans could be re-civilized. In 1946, in a tour for the American government, he held dialogues with schoolchildren. Denazification, he argued, got things wrong: instead of punishing Nazi Party members, they should honor those who had put up resistance.[136]

That was not, however, what many audiences and reviewers took away from his play. They perceived the idealized honest soldier turned victim that they wanted to see in themselves: good patriotic Germans trapped by the evil Nazis. A soldier sabotaging the war effort went too far for many. When, in the third act, Harras's officer friend declares that defeat should be pursued by any means necessary to get rid of the satanic Nazi regime, audiences made their disagreement heard. Reviewers considered it in Zuckmayer's favor that he, unlike Mann and other authors in exile, had abstained from passing collective verdicts on their "unfortunate German homeland." But to put a speech about justice and freedom into the mouth of a saboteur was unacceptable. "Countless Germans had longed for the collapse of the regime, but... not at any price." Unlike Claus von Stauffenberg, who had attempted to blow up Hitler in July 1944, the officer-saboteur sent "fellow decent soldiers to a pointless death," no different from the Nazis. By spring 1949, a reviewer felt that the original message of the play had been transformed by events. The "devil's power" had not been eliminated: it had shifted its "geographic position." For "us Germans," the play was "a terrible memory, for our European neighbors a warning." The devil was now the communists.[137] For Zuckmayer, the reception came as a shock, and, in the early 1960s, he barred any future performances.

By 1950, such contemporary drama had all but vanished, together with the genre of "rubble film" and rubble poetry. That year, the literary Group 47 awarded its prize to Günter Eich. In 1947, Eich had written "Inventory," a poem that reduced his self to his few belongings as a prisoner of war: "This is my cap, this is my coat, here is my shaving stuff, in a linen bag."[138] Now, in 1950, he was celebrated for the rather different tone of his new poems, including the "Franconian-Tibetan Cherry Orchard." "Prayer in the ear of the starlings," it began, "from the cells of the cloister town, above the cherry hills, the vein in the leaf."[139] Writers were dropping the wreckage left behind by the war and escaping into ethereal aesthetics. Literature in the early 1950s became, in the words of one literary critic, "a kind of sanatorium stay in higher regions."[140]

A GATHERING IMPUNITY

Along with the denazification tribunals, there were two additional organs of transitional justice: Allied military tribunals and German courts. It was here that serious Nazi criminals and perpetrators were tried. The number of convictions was tiny. In the six decades after the war, West German authorities investigated 172,294 individuals. Charges were brought against only 10 percent of them. A mere 6,656 were convicted, and most of them received mild sentences. Of the 1,770 members of the Einsatzgruppen, barely a dozen were successfully convicted. No army officer was convicted for crimes against Jews, and not a single Nazi judge, either.[141]

These figures are a damning verdict on justice overall. In Auschwitz alone, some 6,000 perpetrators had been at work. The long view, though, can distort the record in the short run. The first five years after the war saw a rising wave of prosecutions. In the Soviet zone, it peaked in 1948 when German courts passed 4,549 sentences for Nazi crimes. In addition, Soviet tribunals sentenced 37,000 Germans and Austrians, of whom 436 were executed. West German courts were similarly active, at least initially. Between 1945 and 1951, they investigated 17,000 crimes and passed 5,500 sentences. In their military tribunals, the Western Allies sentenced a further 5,000 people—794 to death, although half of these sentences would be commuted. The rising number of prosecutions was one reason people turned against denazification. It was no longer just Nazi bosses who found themselves on trial, but ordinary Germans, including those who had denounced, plundered, or beat up their neighbors.

East Germany passed more sentences proportionally than the larger West Germany, although direct comparisons are difficult. In the Western zones, crimes were sometimes handled by denazification tribunals and the special courts (*Spruchgerichte*) appointed by the British to investigate membership in a criminal organization. In the East, some cases involved summary justice, most notoriously the show trial at Waldheim, in Saxony, in 1950, which sentenced 3,400 persons in one fell swoop, some without evidence or legal defense. Still, the two countries broadly followed a parallel trend. The drop came after 1950 and followed from the new political realities, a focus on consolidation and reintegration at all costs, and a return to the German criminal code. By 1956, the number of cases investigating Nazi crimes had fallen to 276 in the West. In the East, there was just one.[142]

While the handling of Nazi crimes was far from perfect in the immediate postwar years, it was poles apart from the failure it became thereafter. The years 1948 and 1949 saw, among others, the first trial of an Auschwitz kapo (in Berlin) and prosecutions of those involved in the deportations to Belzec (in Munich) and crimes in the Minsk Ghetto (in Karlsruhe). Gerhard Peters, the former general manager of the company that had developed Zyklon B for the gas chambers at Auschwitz, was sentenced by the jury in Frankfurt to five years in prison for being an accessory to murder.[143] Although lacking a systematic approach and often resulting in mild sentences, virtually every German prosecutor was involved in investigations of Nazi crimes. If West and East Germany had continued along these early tracks after 1950, our verdict of transitional justice would be more positive today.

While courts were active on either side of the Iron Curtain in the late 1940s, they diverged in their legal reasoning, sentences, and the types of crimes that attracted their interest. East German courts paid greater attention to crimes committed against political prisoners in the camps, Soviet POWs, and forced labor.[144] West German courts were more preoccupied with Nazi crimes against German civilians, especially euthanasia of the disabled; denunciations; SA crimes before 1939, including Kristallnacht; and executions in the final months of the war. The murder of the Jews attracted little interest in either West or East or, for that matter, in the rest of Europe. East German courts passed tougher sentences than those in West Germany and worked with a collective as well as an individual definition of guilt. In 1948, for example, the district court in Schwerin heard the case of a guard from the Ravensbrück camp. She had been conscripted in the final months of the war, and the court found no evidence of "personal guilt." Nonetheless, she was sentenced to eighteen months in prison for "collective responsibility." The same court sentenced a police commissioner who had worked in the personnel department of the Gestapo, without being directly involved in a crime, to two years and nine months in prison. To put this in perspective, a Gestapo officer who had participated in the execution of Polish workers received a prison sentence of two years in another court in East Germany in 1950.[145] Such a notion of collective responsibility was entirely alien both to Nuremberg and liberal principles of justice; after German reunification in 1990, these sentences would be overthrown for violating the rule of law.

Western courts were more lenient. In the British zone, most SS men were let off with a fine, and the one third who were sent to prison were sentenced to only two years on average.[146] Still, until 1951, courts were taking a broad view of perpetrators and of the nature of criminal responsibility. In the British zone, German courts upheld and applied the human rights principles of the Control Council Law 10—that a person who had not himself pulled the trigger did not exempt him from criminal conviction, nor did the fact that he was following orders. The Supreme Special Court (*Oberster Spruchgerichtshof*) ruled in several cases that the establishment of concentration camps was a crime against humanity. Conviction did not require evidence of personal brutality toward inmates. Similarly, involvement in deportations was considered sufficient proof of guilt, because the goal of the deed was elimination, not resettlement. Josef Grohé, the Nazi leader in Cologne-Aachen, was sentenced to four and a half years because of his knowledge of the deportations from that city; he was freed after the proceedings, however, because he had already served his time in internment.[147]

Common design and complicity still had a place in postwar legal justice. The courts caught up with the Treblinka SS guard Josef Hirtreiter in early 1951. Hirtreiter claimed that he had only overseen the clothes-changing station and thus was innocent of murder. Witnesses spoke of his brutality, his use of a whip with added lead, and how he had smashed children's heads against the walls. He was sentenced to life in prison for being an accomplice to extreme violence. The district court in Frankfurt ruled that where someone worked in Treblinka made a difference. But it only affected the severity of the sentence, not culpability as such. As far as criminal responsibility was concerned, in a system like a concentration camp, it was irrelevant whether someone "turned on the gas for the gas chambers... or supervised the kitchen personnel":

> In such an organized collective criminal act, all those actions which were individual acts of a collective event were causal for the intended result—the extermination of many people—because its success was only made possible through the interaction of these individual actions, and would have not happened, if these had not been carried out.[148]

Hirtreiter would not be released until 1977, and he died the year after.

The problem in West Germany was that for each court that punished complicity, there was another that did not. Allied zones were divided in their legal philosophy and practice. The American zone did not follow CCL 10. Courts there were more likely to follow the conventional criminal code and base their verdicts on individual deeds and intentions, and judge them according to the law at the time. This could lead to radically different rulings. In Bavaria, a woman had been denounced and executed at the end of April 1945 while eagerly awaiting the arrival of the American troops. Her sister pleaded with the American legal officer to punish the "indirect murderers," the Nazi mayor and local Gestapo leader.[149] In the British zone they would have been punished. In the American, the courts followed the principle of no retrospective punishment. Since local officials responsible for executing "defeatists" or "deserters" during the "final struggle" had carried out orders and not broken the law at the time, it was difficult to convict them. The idea of an ever-present superior spirit of justice championed by the leading jurist Gustav Radbruch and his followers was expressly challenged. The eminent criminal lawyer Hellmuth von Weber argued that Nazi-era punishments such as execution for treason did not amount to "inhuman consequences" at the time, regardless of whether they might appear "excessive" under subsequent laws.[150] In 1948, several courts went so far as to rule that the "displacement" of Jews was in itself not something criminal and that emigration was voluntary.[151]

In 1952, the "alien" CCL 10 was replaced by the old German criminal code. The end of Allied occupation spelled the end of a universalist view of justice with transcending principles. The shifting balance of power between legal norms, however, was already discernible on the eve of West German independence. The case of Paul Schraermeyer is instructive. Schraermeyer had been the district administrator (*Landrat*) of Hechingen in Swabia. Today the town is a popular spot for excursions to the nearby Hohenzollern castle. In 1941–42, it was the site for the deportation of 290 Jews. They were robbed of their property and deported to Riga, where most of them were killed. Five years later, Schraermeyer found himself in the local district court. He was innocent, he insisted. He was conservative but not antisemitic. He oversaw the local deportation but was only following orders. He did not know that they might end in people's deaths. If he was guilty, he argued, that would mean so too was any typist or train driver involved in the deportations. Had he not acted, he maintained, he would have ended up in a concentration camp.

The first court hearing the case, in 1947, rejected his argument. A local official, it said, was different from a typist. As a civil servant he was responsible for protecting the population against the violation of their legal rights and for upholding morality. While not responsible for murder, he was responsible for robbery and racial persecution as defined by CCL 10. A few months later, the case was reviewed by the Supreme District Court in Tübingen, which twisted CCL 10 to require an accomplice to have shared the mind-set of the actual perpetrators, and looked at Schraermeyer's character and motivations. He had protected Catholic processions and sought to preserve his position and influence in order to prevent Nazi repression in the future. Indeed, the court agreed with him that the Jews themselves saw evacuation as preferable to staying in Germany; that they had been driven to this by persecution was ignored. It also accepted, without any supporting evidence, Schraermeyer's claim that he would have ended up in a camp had he declined to take part. The district court, moreover, had prematurely rejected his self-defense of acting on orders under duress (*Notstand*). It had confused law and morality. Resisting injustice without consideration of the damage to one's own life might have been virtuous. "Still, in law we are not dealing with what may be expected from a hero or a saint but what can and must be demanded from the average morally disposed law-abiding citizen," the higher court said.[152] On January 20, 1948, Schraermeyer was acquitted.

Schraermeyer's arguments would become the standard chorus repeated ad nauseam in West German courts in the 1950s in support of mild sentences for perpetrators: an otherwise good character, an alleged motivation to prevent worse harm, a lack of criminal intent, and, above all, acting on orders under duress.

Throughout most of the world, the postwar years are often celebrated for the embrace of human rights as fundamental principles of international law. In Germany, however, the record was mixed. The Federal Republic passed the Basic Law (Grundgesetz) on May 8, 1949, which declared "human dignity ... inviolable." This step forward was soon followed by a step back. The abolition of the special court and the replacement of CCL 10 by the old German criminal code meant the end of retroactive sentences. In 1950, the European Human Rights Convention upheld the principle of "no punishment without law" (Article 7-1), but followed it with a second paragraph that explicitly allowed for the punishment of any act that, at the time it was committed, "was criminal according to the general principles of law recognised by civilised nations" (Article 7-2). When the Federal Republic signed on to the convention two years later, it only did so by registering a reservation to the second paragraph: "Any act is only punishable if it was so by law before the offense was committed."[153]

These changes amounted to a profound metamorphosis of crime and liability. The 1871 criminal code had been written to protect society against ordinary criminals, not to respond to state-sponsored mass murder. In German courts, war crimes and crimes against humanity became ordinary crimes. Mass murder was treated as an unrelated act carried out by potentially but not necessarily culpable individuals. The key questions in committing a crime now concerned personal motive and intention. Courts applied a narrow "test of subjective participation" (*subjektive Teilnahmelehre*) to determine whether an individual saw himself as the willing and responsible author of a deed at the time of carrying it out. The circle of guilt narrowed further in 1954–55 when West Germany became fully sovereign. An amnesty was instituted for crimes committed in the "final phase" of the war, which stretched from October 1944 to July 1945. There was an added provision that, even if new evidence arose, no one could be tried twice for the same Nazi-related crime. It was only in 1979, after repeated debate, that the German parliament excluded genocide from the statute of limitations.

It was very difficult to try perpetrators; it required an energetic prosecutor and clear evidence, ideally from victims who were alive and willing to face their tormentors in court. Judicial changes in the 1950s made convictions for murder all but impossible. In the words of the historian Norbert Frei, a "fatal fog" was spreading through the corridors of West German justice.[154] Bank robbers received harsher sentences than Nazi murderers, who were classified as accessories or acquitted altogether. The head of police in Nuremberg, Benno Martin, for example, had been responsible for the deportation of one thousand Jews to Riga, where most were killed. The court accepted his claim that he was acting under orders and duress and, in 1953, found him not guilty. The remaining war criminals were released from the Landsberg prison in the following years. And when they were, like Martin Sandberger, the head of Einsatzkommando 1a, a unit of the SS Einsatzgruppen, they could not be prosecuted again even if new evidence emerged.

There were some limits. Parliamentarians refused to give the Waffen-SS the same rights and amnesties as the army. In 1953, the Constitutional Court overruled the Federal Court of Justice (Bundesgerichtshof) and declared that by playing an integral role in the Nazi state, civil servants lost their rights (and pension claims) when the German Reich surrendered. When, two years later, the district court in Bochum decided that Paul-Werner Hoppe, the commandant who had introduced the use of Zyklon B gas in train wagons in the Stutthoff camp, was only a small cog in the wheel and sentenced him to five years, the Federal Court of Justice intervened. This interpretation of subjective participation was going too far. The question, it ruled in 1956, was whether Hoppe had a decisive influence on the execution of a criminal act. It was irrelevant whether he was a faithful Nazi and believed in racial extermination. His influence as a commandant was sufficient. The Federal Court increased his sentence to nine years. Yet even then Hoppe was found guilty only as an accomplice to murder. Twelve years after the war, he was still the only camp commandant sentenced by a German court, and he would be released early, in 1960.[155] Several newspapers aptly dubbed the situation "justice by chance."[156]

Why did it come to this? After all, leading politicians had personally suffered under the Nazis. Thomas Dehler, the Liberal minister of justice, had a Jewish wife. His permanent secretary, Walter Strauss, had lost both his Jewish parents in Theresienstadt. Partly, it was due to the shift in political priorities with the Cold War. Adenauer was elected chancellor in 1949. He worried about communists, not former Nazis; the business of "sniffing out" Nazis needed to stop, he said in 1952. The following year, the minister of expellees (as the German refugees from the eastern territories came to be called), Hans Lukaschek, a resistance fighter, was replaced with a former SA officer, Theodor Oberländer. That Adenauer's chief of staff, Hans Globke, had given the 1935 race laws his judicial stamp of approval was an irrelevant detail compared to the chancellor's overall goal of integrating the Federal Republic into the West. What mattered was that Globke was ultra-loyal, a workaholic who knew everyone's personnel file inside out; Adenauer intervened in 1961 to have a criminal investigation against him moved to Bonn in order to stall it. The two batted away challenges until October 1963, when they both retired. A few months earlier, Globke had been sentenced in absentia in the GDR to life imprisonment for being an accomplice to murder and crimes against humanity.[157]

Anti-communism was a central strand of the DNA of the new Federal Republic. It also eased relations with Western Allies who wanted West Germany as a military ally. The Americans and British, once the main drivers behind denazification, now switched to reintegration. In 1949, Winston Churchill personally contributed £25 to the defense fund for General Manstein, a war criminal. A year later, U.S. High Commissioner for Germany John McCloy, with grinding teeth, gave in to pressure from former German generals and declared that he was not aware that "any good German soldiers had lost their honor."[158] Even the pacifist philosopher Bertrand Russell said it was important to look to the future and work with the Germans, and not constantly remind them of their war crimes. Former Nazis were kept from ministerial positions—Oberländer was the exception to the rule—but they recaptured the level below, the apparatus of state power. In 1950, minister of the interior Gustav Heinemann wanted to exclude former Nazi Party members from top ministerial and civil service posts, but none of the other cabinet members agreed. The Ministry of Justice and the Foreign Ministry, in particular, became their natural home. In the daunting task of getting the legal system back on its feet, Dehler considered work experience under the Nazis a plus, not a minus. In one of many ironies, the law for the new Constitutional Court was coauthored by a former Nazi prosecutor. Above all, though, the judicial backsliding resulted from an elective affinity between personnel politics and legal culture. The takeover by judges and prosecutors with a Nazi past was eased by a bourgeois mind-set that approached crime as a matter of individual character rather than sociopolitical structures.

The extent of self-amnesty in the West German justice system is hard to exaggerate. By the end of the 1950s, entire departments in the Ministry of Justice, including the one for criminal law, were in the hands of former National Socialist jurists, and so were many district courts. The head of the department responsible for constitutional and administrative law was Walter Roemer, who had handed down many death sentences in the Third

Reich, including against the students of the White Rose resistance group. At the Federal Court of Justice, three out of every four lawyers had practiced under the Nazis. Here was a major difference from East Germany. The GDR had its own problem with inherited Nazis; the SS man and camp guard Ernst Grossmann, for example, mutated into a "hero of labor" and sat on the central committee of the Socialist Unity Party of Germany (SED) in the late 1950s. Still, Nazi prosecutors such as Richard Jacob had to leave the justice system before they could make a career in the socialist regime. Most Nazi judges were dismissed and replaced with fast-tracked people's judges. Ernst Melsheimer, a successful judge under the Nazis, who advanced to attorney general (1949–60), was an exception. In the GDR, 80 percent of Nazi army judges were let go. In West Germany, almost that same proportion stayed on. In Bremen and Berlin nearly every second judge and prosecutor in 1953 had worked under the Nazis; in Cologne and Karlsruhe it was three quarters.[159] An inquiry into Nazi Party membership only became compulsory for civil service applicants in 1965.

Since the anti-fascist GDR absolved itself of any responsibility for Nazi crimes and effectively stopped investigations of its own citizens, the overhaul of judges had little consequence for Nazi trials there; East Germany focused on exposing Nazis in West Germany in so-called brown books that documented their criminal past. In West Germany, however, the continuity in personnel cast a dark shadow over justice. Fritz Bauer, the tireless Frankfurt state prosecutor and one of the few Nazi victims working in the courts, compared stepping out of his office to crossing into enemy country. It was Bauer who, in 1957, would relay crucial information about Adolf Eichmann to Israeli intelligence. Former Nazi jurists shielded themselves behind a "professional protective wall," in Bauer's phrase.[160] They hid behind the myth that they had shielded the law from worse abuses by the Nazis. In reality, many had helped to legalize injustice, and in several cases had passed death sentences that were unlawful even by Nazi laws. It was not surprising that they joined in a general self-amnesty after 1949 and chose not to investigate each other. It needed a rare force like Bauer to start investigations—in 1960—against judges for being accessories to murder in the euthanasia killings, which the vast majority of judges had gone along with in spite of there being no law to support them.

Legal positivism, which treats law as a matter of social fact and rejects universally binding norms and human rights, provided amnesties with intellectual respectability. Often it was little more than a convenient excuse; several lawyers had rejected positivism when they were fighting progressive rulings in Weimar. Where there was a will there was a way to a tougher handling of perpetrators even within traditional German law. In the Frankfurt trials against mid-ranking officers at Auschwitz in 1963, Bauer presented the killings at the camp as an organically unified deed (*einheitliche Tat*) and not as a sum of disparate individual actions. The trials against individual perpetrators, he hoped, would reveal wider social responsibility. What was lacking were "judges, not laws," as Adolf Arndt, a member of Parliament for the Social Democratic Party (SDP) put it in 1959.[161] The few Nazi criminals remaining in prisons abroad received more support than their many victims; the four SS men held in Breda in the Netherlands, for their role in the deportations of Jews from that country to the extermination camps, enjoyed entertainment and specially imported sardines in addition to counsel from top lawyers, all paid for by the German taxpayer.[162] Judges worked with a narrow legal mind-set that initially treated the Basic Law as just another law, not its foundation. From inside the Ministry of Justice, drafts emerged for a state of emergency that would have bypassed parliament and overstepped the constitution. Roma, homosexuals, and victims of forced sterilization could not expect sympathy from these quarters. Sinti and Roma continued to be treated as criminals, "deserters" as traitors. Victims of Nazi eugenics and court-martials only received posthumous justice in 1998 and 2002, and those who had been convicted of treason only had their sentences quashed in 2009.

In the courtroom, the approach to perpetrators mirrored the legal profession's social ideal that they were protecting a respectable, law-abiding society against a few criminal elements. Where the GDR had a socialist blind spot, with its anti-fascist origin myth, West German justice suffered from a bourgeois one. Perpetrators were judged for their character, motives, and emotional profile. Nazi crimes appeared to flow from the deranged psyche and sadistic lust of "pathological" individuals rather than from inside the "normal," educated middle-class society, which had, in fact, freely provided the Nazis with so many officers, teachers, and lawyers.

The type of justice this produced can be gleaned from the differential treatment of Kierspel and Mirbeth, the brutal duo of kapo and commandant of the Auschwitz satellite camp Golleschau. The court in Bremen in 1953 found Kierspel to be "an asocial human being with a pronounced propensity to commit crime." He had committed a string of petty crimes and fraud, then armed robbery, before ending up in Nazi camps. After the war, he was arrested for drug dealing. In its verdict, the court ruled that a "devilish system had left this morally depraved person" in charge of hundreds of Jewish prisoners and given him "the opportunity to commit crimes without punishment." That the Nazis had poisoned the atmosphere against Jews was a mitigating circumstance. His criminal character, on the other hand, was an aggravating factor. He was a "weak-willed... psychopath" and utterly unpredictable. The "ugly way" in which he carried out homicide and the "nullity" behind it were the unmistakable signs of his "brutal disposition, his common mind-set, and the inferiority of his character." The examining psychiatrist found no inherited nervous disease. Kierspel's emotional state, though, was found to be underdeveloped. He was "evil, rough, and brutal," and showed no emotional reaction to the charges. He was "asocial"—a Nazi term for "misfits" who needed to be banished from the people's community. "Special preventative considerations demand palpable punishment." That he shouted out at witnesses, "This is the revenge of Jewry against the German man!" did not help him. Kierspel was sentenced to life in prison and the lifelong loss of his civil rights.[163]

Johann Mirbeth, by contrast, received far more sympathetic treatment. Mirbeth had been born in Munich in 1905 to a family of respectable artisans. Unlike the kapo under his command, he completed school and became a carpenter, a job to which he returned in 1949. "Ultimately he was turned into a criminal by an irresponsible government," the court ruled. Kierspel represented the textbook criminal, Mirbeth the good, law-abiding German who had unintentionally and mysteriously fallen victim to an external, superior force. The Nazi years were treated almost as a footnote on his CV, similar to how contemporaries saw German history as a whole. That he had spent a solid fifteen years in the NSDAP and SS barely received notice. For the court, it was the commandant who came under the unfortunate influence of the psychopath kapo. Unlike Kierspel, Mirbeth showed "deep remorse" in court. He found the courage to admit "the inhumanity of his harsh punishments" and he asked witnesses for forgiveness. The court found what it was looking for: Mirbeth showed "signs of understanding" (*Einsicht*) and a willingness "to think and act in a principled and decent manner." Mirbeth was sentenced for homicide—not murder—to six years in prison, and his civil rights were taken away for only three. He would be released early after serving three years.[164]

Many perpetrators were skillful practitioners of deception. Allied internment camps did not share information with denazification tribunals, and in the general chaos of the immediate postwar years, it was easy to slip under the radar. But their success in evading courts and tougher sentences also relied on many fellow Germans wanting to be deceived. Bernhard Fischer-Schweder, for example, had been the head of police in Lithuania and in charge of mass executions of Jews in 1941. Under a false name, he rose to be head of a refugee camp in 1953. After he was dismissed for providing false information, he had the audacity to challenge the decision in court. In a local newspaper he presented himself as a friend of Jews. It was only when a former policeman saw the article and reported him that he was prosecuted.[165] In numerous cases, neighbors and employers closed ranks around one of their own. Franz Behrendt, responsible for atrocities in the Baltic region, received a letter of support from his Christian trombone choir: he was a respectable member of the community and "had loyally stood by the flag of our Lord Jesus Christ and played in praise of God." Another leader of the Einsatzgruppen, Werner Schmidt-Hammer, carried out three mass executions of Jews, on Fischer-Schweder's orders. He himself gave the final shots to the head when needed. But he had also qualified as a master optician at Carl Zeiss in 1930 and returned there in 1949, and that was what finally took precedence over his wartime career as a murderer. In 1957, he was arrested at work. Without a second thought, the firm put up 20,000 DM bail–four times the average annual income. Out of detention, he continued to work unofficially from home. The director and workers' council jointly petitioned the court to show mercy: it was only "through a tragic chain of events without his personal contribution" that their esteemed colleague had ended up "in the Nazi system of command, which through deception and coercion abused him for execrable ends." Schmidt-Hammer was an accessory to the murder of 526 people. He was sentenced to only three years in prison.[166]

We can see here social networks at work. Just as important was the desire to believe in the good core of friends and peers—and, by extension, in oneself. They could not possibly be murderers or ready accomplices, but rather were soldiers and civil servants who did their duty, tried to prevent worse from happening, or were deceived or acted on orders. Exculpatory appeals to duty became so expansive, and those hearing them so receptive, that even those who had given the orders were excused. In the end, all orders were the responsibility of Hitler and Himmler. This moral self-deception was especially widespread in the milieu that struggled hardest to reconcile its own ideals with the reality of complicity under the Nazis: the *Bürgertum*, the educated middle classes.

If anyone invoked high moral standards in postwar West Germany, it was Theodor Heuss, the first president. In countless speeches, he extolled the importance of being true to oneself, responsible, upright, and "noble" (*edel*). Self-discipline, and a duty to oneself and one's family and community, were core *bürgerliche* values. Heuss acknowledged German atrocities and felt a sense of personal and collective shame for not having stood up to the Nazis. But he had also lost two nephews fighting in the war and wanted to preserve their place in family memory. In 1954, he was asked to intervene by distant family friends on behalf of their son. Martin Sandberger had been the head of the Einsatzkommando 1a in Estonia between 1941 and 1943. He was responsible for thousands of executions and confessed to having personally murdered hundreds. Initially sentenced to death in 1947, his sentence was commuted to life imprisonment by the U.S. high commissioner in 1951. Heuss had only met Sandberger once, in 1919. Still, he was the son of an old acquaintance, a retired director of the chemical giant IG Farben whom he remembered from their time together in the German Democratic Party in the Weimar years. Heuss appealed to the American ambassador for mercy and asked for parole after ten years. Sandberger might not be very bright, Heuss said, but he was not an "evil" or "ignoble person."[167] He had simply been caught in dangerous times and deceived. He had been punished and proved his good character in prison. Carlo Schmid, a Social Democrat and one of the drafters of the German constitution, similarly obliged. Schmid had taught law at Tübingen and remembered Sandberger as a "diligent, intelligent, and talented" student. For Schmid, Sandberger was pulled between the "intellectual nihilism of the times" and his frantic efforts to hold on to the "bourgeois forms... and traditions of his family." Without the "invasion" of Nazi rule, he would have become a "proper, hardworking, and ambitious civil servant."[168]

Schmid and Heuss were part of a whole industry of petitions for war criminals. The fact that Sandberger (like Mirbeth and many others) had actively fought to install the terror regime and then personally carried out crimes against humanity barely registered. In the end, Sandberger did not even have to wait ten years. He was released early with the other three remaining war criminals in the Landsberg prison in 1958. Unlike his many victims, he was gifted another fifty-two years to live, dying in 2010.

"AWAY WITH NAZI JUSTICE"

Public opinion became sharply divided in West Germany in the 1950s. War criminals were received with flowers on their release from prison. Martin Heidegger, depending on one's philosophical taste either the greatest thinker of the twentieth century or its greatest charlatan, stubbornly refused to distance himself from his flirtation with the Nazis. "He who thinks big, must err big," he declared, as if a grave error is proof of a great mind.[169] In court, many perpetrators showed limited or no remorse. One man saw no problem in having thrown explosives among Soviet POWs in a perverse medical experiment and distinguished it from killing "absolutely innocent people." Another said he had come to appreciate that mass executions were "completely wrong," only to add, "One should have looked for other ways to annihilate the Jews." Yet another invoked the pressure to carry out orders when executing partisans; that he afterward also shot their children was a humanitarian act, "since they could not exist without father and mother."[170] Each of these three statements was made seventeen years after the war.

The mild sentences and accidental character of such trials increasingly galvanized popular outrage. It is sometimes thought that the critical reactions started with the Auschwitz trials in Frankfurt in 1963 or the generational revolt of 1968. This is misleading. There was no sharp break between amnesia one year and a confrontation with the past the next. Rather, justice and popular reaction followed each other like a rising tide from the 1950s onward. After a trial, public interest would ebb away, but each new tide would rise higher. Democratic institutions and a free press provided a favorable setting, but ultimately it was political protests, social movements, and courageous individuals who insisted on a more critical confrontation with the past.

Adenauer's Germany (1949–63) is often portrayed as stiff and dull, like Bonn, its provincial capital. It is true that Adenauer ruled like an autocrat. Democracy to him meant people going to the polls every four years to select a ruling party headed by himself, who knew what was best for them. Their role was to be one of acclamation, not public debate, let alone interference with the affairs of state. Adenauer, equally true, got his way in setting the decisive strategic course of these years: integration into the West, rearmament, and membership in NATO in 1955. Success, however, came at a price. The new army, the Bundeswehr, was only pushed through against mass agitation. Ironically, Adenauer ended up politicizing millions of citizens. A dynamic protest culture was gaining ground. This was a mix of old and new, the revived milieu of trade unions and youth groups, such as the socialist Falken (Falcons), and a new grassroots movement against conscription and nuclear weapons. They fed the public challenges to official justice.

In 1950, for example, forty thousand people marched in Bielefeld in northwestern Germany and workers put down their tools in protest at the leniency of an eighteen-month prison sentence for a member of the Gestapo convicted of torture. Their banners demanded "Away with Nazi Justice"; it was the largest demonstration in the history of that city.[171] In September that year, the press officer of the Hamburg senate, the critical journalist Erich

Lüth, opened the "week of German film" by calling on cinema owners to show their "*Charakter*" and boycott the latest film by Veit Harlan, the director of the Nazis' infamous antisemitic propaganda film *Jud Süss*.[172]

The case is now remembered as a milestone in constitutional history. Harlan had been charged in 1949 under CCL 10 for being an accessory to persecution. The case had been initiated by Social Democrats and victims of the Nazi regime. A Hamburg court found no direct causal link between Harlan filming *Jud Süss*, which was watched by 19 million Germans, and the murder of the Jews. The Supreme Court in the British zone, however, declared the film inflammatory. In April 1950, a new trial found that Harlan's actions did indeed satisfy the criteria of crimes against humanity but, in its verdict, the court fell back on the German criminal code (Article 52) and conceded that he had acted under duress. Harlan was free, but stood morally condemned.

The movie company sued Lüth for saying that showing the new film would be a sign of indecency. In 1951, a Hamburg court threatened Lüth with fines and prison if he did not retract his accusation. Seven years later, in 1958, the Constitutional Court finally found in Lüth's favor and ruled that basic rights such as freedom of speech outweighed the norms of civil law such as "common decency" (*gute Sitten*).[173]

Just as important was what happened outside the courts. Lüth, who had spent the years under the Nazis writing copy for an engineering firm, had no intention of giving in. He refused to settle out of court with the movie company. It was a question of ethics, not money, he explained. Harlan's new film, *Immortal Beloved* (*Unsterbliche Geliebte*), might be a harmless romantic drama, but his Nazi past made him morally unfit to play a role in German film. A film under his name would be painful for millions of victims. Lüth felt it would interfere with the moral reconstruction of Germany.[174] In the course of the following year, there were sixty demonstrations against Harlan across the country; some young protestors stormed cinemas and physically disrupted the screening.[175] In Hamburg, Frankfurt, and Cologne, several officials endorsed the boycott. In 1954, Harlan tried to show remorse by burning what appeared to be the last surviving copy of the negative of *Jud Süss* in a field outside Zurich. The invited representatives of Jewish organizations refused to attend. This was not his last controversial appearance, however. In 1957, the German Federation of Artists called for another boycott, this time of his film *Anders als Du und ich* (*Different from You and Me*), not for its defamation of homosexuals but because the film presented modern artists as "decadent," which was reminiscent of Nazi attacks on them.[176]

The Harlan case illustrates the competing forces in 1950s West Germany, between the Allies' broad conception of crimes against humanity, on the one hand, and the German criminal code, on the other, and finally the unequivocal assertion of the supremacy of the new Basic Law. Above all, it reveals the centrality of public agitation and moral pressure in between, which, by responding to the first, set in motion the latter.

The 1950s, then, saw a tug of war between those clinging stubbornly to the idea of a "regular war" and those seeking to confront the past. In opinion polls in 1951, only 32 percent of those surveyed accepted that Germany bore sole responsibility for the Second World War. Ten years later it was 53 percent. In 1955, 48 percent of Germans still answered that "without the war," Hitler would have been one of the greatest German statesmen of all time. Five years later that number was down to 36 percent.[177]

Newspapers helped keep Nazi crimes in the public eye. Initially, trials attracted mainly local attention. By 1957–58, though, they were regularly covered in regional and national media. This exposed the myth that all Nazi criminals were deviant and pathological characters. They included "normal" family men and "cultured" Germans, too. In its coverage of the Warstein massacre of Soviet and Polish forced laborers and their families, *Der Spiegel* appropriately took its headline from Staudte's 1946 film: *The Murderers Are Among Us*. One of those accused of murder was Wolfgang Wetzling. Newspapers described how the SS officer had been let off as a mere "opportunist" in his 1950 denazification process and settled with his wife and children at the outskirts of Lüneburg in northern Germany, where he worked as the legal counsel of the regional health insurance body. "It was a wonderful time," he was quoted as saying of the Nazi years, "my wife at the grand piano, and I with the violin, playing the classical composers under candlelight." "Does acting on orders cover 208 murders?" a regional paper asked.[178] Local witnesses turned against the accused.

By the late 1950s, soft sentences caused media outrage. According to opinion surveys, most Germans wanted to see perpetrators punished severely. In 1958, West Germany held its own first major trial of Nazi crimes, charging ten members of an Einsatzkommando with the murder of more than five thousand Jewish men, women, and children in Lithuania in 1941. The Ulm trial triggered a furious reaction. In addition to giving greater voice to victims, it highlighted the randomness of prosecutions and ushered in a more systematic and coordinated approach to the investigation of Nazi crimes. A national central office was established at Ludwigsburg.[179]

It was in this charged atmosphere that Eichmann went on trial in Jerusalem. In June 1960, barely a month after his capture, the conservative newspaper *Die Welt* stressed that it was not possible to draw a line under the Nazi crimes like a merchant might under his accounts. Germans could not bury the past. They had to confront it honestly if they wanted to free themselves from their "own awkwardness."[180] Eichmann's trial, it said, should prompt each German to give an account of their own actions in the Nazi years. To be true, West Germans continued to be primarily concerned with themselves, not with the victims and their suffering. Still, in terms of confronting their own past, this change in sensibility was a big step forward.

JUSTICE AND COMPROMISE

Transitional justice is by its very nature imperfect. It tries to balance peace and reconstruction with accountability and punishment, to reconcile victims with their former enemies, and to honor the interests of past, present, and future. Nazi Germany's crimes were unique. That does not mean we should not put the record of transitional justice after 1945 into a comparative perspective. To compare is not necessarily to equate. Comparison can help inject a dose of historical realism into normative ideals. In the age-old history of violence, humans have yet to discover a model of transitional justice that works. In other words, there is no general yardstick against which we can measure postwar Germany. Transitional justice has been guided by radically different ideals. Today, the remembrance of past crimes is assumed to be a natural way forward. But this only became accepted in the last two generations. Since Aristotle and St. Augustine, there have been many voices advocating forgetting as the road to harmony. After Franco, Spain followed a policy of silence that has only been changing in recent years. Greece, in 1989, destroyed all security and surveillance files, in the same spirit that German towns burned theirs in 1951. Amnesty can leave behind an open wound that never heals.

Judgments of Germany's postwar record have differed in the extreme. At the time, Adenauer defended amnesty as the only realistic option available. "'You do not pour out dirty water, if you do not have any that is clean,'" he said, quoting a saying from Cologne.[181] To have a chance of success, he believed, reconstruction needed to draw on the civil servants, experts, and businessmen available, regardless of their Nazi past. With amnesty, Adenauer took a big gamble. Democratic institutions were young and respect for the law fragile. It was far from certain that they would flourish with former Nazis in positions of authority. While the GDR did a superior job in cleaning out its justice system, its overall approach was not so different. As one socialist leader told old comrades in 1946, they could only build a new state with "the human material that we currently have" and that meant working with some of the "human material that had been contaminated by Nazism for twelve years."[182] By contrast, some recent historians have pronounced postwar justice an abject failure that sponsored the rehabilitation of Nazis at the expense of their victims, especially in the West.[183]

The late 1940s showed that there were possibilities between the twin poles of punishing millions and letting virtually everyone go free. Belgium and the Netherlands punished 1 percent of their population for collaboration, Norway 2 percent—taking away their property, right to vote, and right to work as doctors, lawyers, teachers, and priests; the punishment also extended to their wives.[184] None of these countries ended up poor and backward countries. For Germany, an equivalent figure would have meant "civic death" for more than a million people. This did not happen because the primary pressure for justice in Germany was external (the Allies), not internal (the resistance). At the same time, Germany avoided the worst of vigilante justice, such as the twenty-two thousand revenge killings in France and Italy. Again, Allied occupation made the decisive difference.

In an ideal world, perpetrators would step forward, confess their crimes, ask forgiveness, and receive amnesty. This was the spirit behind the South African Truth and Reconciliation Commission. Most Nazi perpetrators, however, showed no remorse, and the majority of their victims were either dead or, understandably, preferred to have nothing more to do with Germany. While most Germans were in favor of punishing Nazi atrocities, they simultaneously tried to hold on to the idea of a just war and a "clean army," downplaying crimes against civilians and POWs. East Germany made former Nazi supporters publicly announce their conversion to socialism, but whether they would have been prepared to confess actual crimes to their victims is doubtful. The sheer number of Nazi supporters and perpetrators, on the one hand, and the mass annihilation of victims, on the other, left postwar Germany a much more uneven stage for transitional justice than societies emerging from civil wars and apartheid. Even in South Africa, it is worth remembering, only 7,000 people applied to the Truth and Reconciliation Commission and a mere 849 amnesties were granted.[185] Most perpetrators did not make themselves known.

German courts followed a different spirit of reconciliation. Here (as in the rest of Europe) the focus was not on Jewish victims, nor was it primarily on punishing the individual and extracting remorse. Rather, it was on demonstrating that society as a whole was willing to repent and give those who had come around to see their Nazi "mistake" a second chance. For all its deficits, West Germany compares favorably to its former fascist allies on several points. Unlike in Italy, rehabilitation in Adenauer's Germany happened in tandem with a prohibition of neofascist politics. After 1945, denazification and the temporary loss of a job provided hundreds of thousands of Germans with an object lesson they did not forget. In Japan, the Americans kept the emperor on the throne and not even a thousand civil servants were dismissed. Here the prosecution of war criminals came to a complete halt in 1952.[186] Initially, the differences may have been largely due to greater Allied pressure on Germany. Once that was removed, though, internal pressure came to fill the space. In West Germany, several large trials came late (Ulm/Einsatzgruppen, 1958; Frankfurt/Auschwitz, 1963–65; Dusseldorf/Majdanek, 1975–81), but they did happen eventually. And when they did, they served as moral lessons for society at large, in addition to dispensing justice. In spite of the many interests trying to pull the curtain shut, it never fully closed on the past.

4

Making (Some) Amends: Reparation and Atonement

On September 20, 1949, Konrad Adenauer took to the floor of the Bundestag to deliver his first declaration as chancellor of the new Federal Republic of Germany. Bonn, he assured everyone, would not turn out like Weimar. The new democracy was built on stronger foundations: the protection of personal liberties, the relative autonomy of federal states, respect for parliamentary opposition, and a social market economy. The war and the "turmoil" of the postwar years had been such a "hard test" and come with so many "temptations" that one had to show understanding for "some mistakes and lapses"—Adenauer here responded to the popular backlash against denazification by lumping actions under Hitler together with those under the Allies and keeping "temptations" so vague that they captured everything from involvement in the black market after 1945 to opportunistic support of the Nazis before then. It was time, the chancellor said, to bring denazification to a close and move on. The government, he announced, was considering a general amnesty. It drew shouts of "Bravo!" from the assembly. His government, Adenauer said, was determined "to let bygones be bygones" ("*Vergangenes vergangen sein zu lassen*") but would not tolerate anyone threatening the foundations of the new state. He condemned recent antisemitic incidents as "undignified and unthinkable" after "all that has happened under the Nazis." The real enemy to democracy now, however, was communism. There was a commitment to punishing those "truly guilty of the crimes committed in the National Socialist era and during the war," but no mention of the Jews. The victims whom Adenauer acknowledged were other Germans: the "heavy fate" of the millions of German prisoners of war in the East and the "suffering" of their relatives back home; the expellees who had been driven from their homes or died during their flight; the bombed out, the disabled, the war widows, and the civil servants who had lost their posts. All these people, he promised, would receive the attention of his government.[1]

It was only seven weeks later, in an interview he had requested with the *Allgemeine Wochenzeitung der Juden in Deutschland*, the weekly German-Jewish newspaper, in which he hoped to dispel a potential misunderstanding of what he had said about antisemitism, that Adenauer extended his consideration to Jewish victims. The German *Volk*, he said, was determined to "make good the wrong done to the Jews in its name by a criminal regime, as far as this is still possible after millions of lives have been irreversibly destroyed [*unwiederbringlich vernichtet*]. We consider such reparation as our duty." "Moral reparation," he added, "is part of our reconstruction of the rule of law."[2]

These two statements—and their sequence—set the scene for what follows. We have seen how the prosecution of perpetrators all but came to a halt with the founding of the two new German states. While it is natural to think of perpetrators and victims at the same time—after all, neither would exist without the other—this was not how the two Germanies approached the matter. Adenauer's interview was typical of the indirect and passive constructions to which Germans resorted to avoid naming perpetrators—what has been called a "grammar of exculpation."[3] Mass murder tended to be cast as a "wrong done to the Jews" and other civilians, but the murderers mostly remained nameless or were subsumed into a nebulous "criminal regime." There was continued reference to non-Jewish German victims. In his inaugural speech, Adenauer effectively made the German people the victims of the Nazis. Jewish victims had their place only within that larger context. Postwar Germans had difficulty in naming the murderers in their midst. Crimes tended to be committed "in the name of the German people," rarely by specific Germans, except for a few who were characterized as "abnormal" sadists. This indirect formulation, however, was not all about deflection. While vague on agency and guilt, it was explicit in accepting the state's collective liability and accountability. As Adenauer stressed in his interview with the German-Jewish newspaper, his government regarded reparations to Jewish victims "as our duty." On this point, West and East Germany would diverge fundamentally. That duty, however, extended primarily to German Jews, not to the Jewish people in general, and excluded the millions of other foreign victims.

In West Germany, Adenauer (the chancellor) and Theodor Heuss (the president) personified the historic spirit of the "good Germany" that supposedly persisted in spite of the barbaric interlude of Nazism. The two were children of German unification and grew up when Otto von Bismarck was chancellor and William I sat on the throne; Adenauer was born in 1876, Heuss eight years later. For Heuss, the sense of collective shame articulated the lofty ideals of German *Kultur*. For Adenauer, it was right for West Germany to take on the collective accountability for debts and crimes committed by its predecessor just as an upright son took on the debts of his bankrupt fraudulent father. The Federal Republic was a legal continuation of the German Reich, as the Basic Law explicitly stressed. (That was, of course, also the argument made by the many denazified civil servants and professional soldiers who lobbied to get back their posts and pensions.) Taking over prewar debts and taking on new indemnities for the many victims of Nazi crimes were essential elements of this continuity. Socialist East Germany, by contrast, saw itself as a new state, free from such legal, financial, and historic responsibility.

Instead of a binary axis that runs from perpetrator to victim, then, in West Germany there was a triangular relationship between Jewish victims, German victims, and the state. In his interview, Adenauer also said that his government would shoulder reparations, a first step on the road to the Luxembourg Agreement in 1952, in which the country pledged to pay Israel and the Jewish Claims Conference (JCC) 3.5 billion Deutschmark. Making amends was no longer a private matter, with individual punishment and atonement, but a public affair with monthly pension checks going to Jewish victims. This was very different from the immediate postwar years, when the focus had been on confiscating property from convicted Nazis and handing it to their victims, the restitution of stolen assets, and fines for individual criminals (*Sühnegeld*).

Our view of postwar Germany has been strongly tied to a particular idea about guilt, where morality appears as the property of the individual, not a collective. Karl Jaspers (and many others) rejected the idea of passing judgment on the morality of an entire society. What happens to morality, though, when a state assumes public accountability for wrongs committed on behalf of a nation? Did the conversion of individual guilt (*Schuld*) into public liability (*Schulden*) give Germans more, or less, of a sense of responsibility and remorse for wrongs committed? That is the essential question.

WIEDERGUTMACHUNG

Few German words have given rise to so much debate as *Wiedergutmachung*, the umbrella term for German efforts to put right the wrong done to Nazi victims, especially Jews. It literally translates as "making good again," but to avoid adding to the confusion it is important to note that when Germans used this term they did not imagine that this was actually possible, just as paying damages does not fix what is broken. Adenauer, as we have seen, referred to lives that had been "irreversibly destroyed." The term was well established by 1945 and signaled replacement, compensation, payment, or expiation. It was aspirational.

There was a broad consensus that Germany ought to provide *Wiedergutmachung.* There was just as wide a disagreement, however, about who should provide it, who should receive it, how much, and in what form. English translations vary between reparation, indemnity, compensation, and restitution. It would be a mistake to settle instantly for one of these, since the postwar years were a struggle over the term's precise meaning, one that broadly went through two phases. In the first, from 1945 to 1952, *Wiedergutmachung* referred to a patchwork of measures that ranged from voluntary donations and welfare services to fining Nazis to raise money for their victims. The initiatives involved local authorities and committees, staffed by Germans. The restitution of property, however, was mainly an Allied project, driven by the Americans and overseen by a court with Allied as well as German members. The return of property to Jewish victims was very rare in the Soviet zone. For East Germany, *Wiedergutmachung* meant paying reparations to the Soviet Union, which formally came to an end in 1953. West Germany, on the other hand, entered a second phase in 1952. Now *Wiedergutmachung* became a federal matter and primarily came to mean both individual compensation (especially in the form of pensions) for victims of the Nazis who had suffered persecution for their "race," religion, or politics, and collective *Wiedergutmachung* with Israel and the Jewish Claims Conference.

Before the end of the war, Social Democrats in exile had already listed *Wiedergutmachung* in their plans for a future Germany. In view of the scale of Nazi crimes and the potentially ruinous costs, the idea was to make the Nazis pay, not the German people as a whole. After the war, Bavarian prime minister Wilhelm Hoegner, a Social Democrat, saw denazification and *Wiedergutmachung* as two sides of the same coin. In March 1946, the Law for the Liberation from National Socialism empowered regional authorities to confiscate property and impose special levies to compensate victims. Effectively, the state took from the Nazis and gave to the Jews and to communists and Social Democrats who had been imprisoned. The problem was that a lot of National Socialist property was not in the hands of individual Nazis but belonged to the state itself. By June 1948, only 104 million Reichsmark had been collected, a drop in the ocean of historic suffering. Victim committees organized street collections. (Some of the collection cans still bore the Nazi logo.) In North Rhine–Westphalia, such donation drives produced

1.9 million RM for Nazi victims in the autumn of 1945, when giving was still considered the decent thing to do.[4]

Financial aid was complemented by the confiscation of furniture, clothes, and flats from local Nazis. In Münster, the *Wiedergutmachung* committee took away blankets, bicycles, radios, and household appliances and handed them out to their victims. Elsewhere, victims and the homeless moved into apartments occupied by former Nazis. That was easily done when the occupants sat in an internment or prisoner-of-war camp. By 1948, however, many of them had come back and crowded the courts to get their flats back.[5]

In Frankfurt, the welfare office provided the "seventy-nine star wearers still alive" with emergency aid. The city also found money for Rabbi Leopold Neuhaus to restore the Westend synagogue and cemetery and for rehabilitation and care, including for the additional sixty-three Jews returning from Theresienstadt; Neuhaus was one of the survivors. In total, 548 victims of the Nazis received 139,253 RM to purchase clothes and household goods. Forty-five Polish Jews also received money to buy clothes.[6]

In general, though, the needs of victims vastly exceeded the financial and charitable resources available to the local authorities of the ruined cities of postwar Germany. The mayor described the situation in nearby Hanau at the end of October 1945. In May, a care center had been set up for Nazi victims. In August, it got its first paid employee, a man who had spent eleven years in a concentration camp. He was responsible for looking after 220 residents and another 200 who were passing through the town. All he was able to give them were a few Reichsmark, some firewood, and vouchers for potatoes. Furniture was confiscated in twenty-four parishes "on a voluntary basis." Many of the victims were left without shoes or a change of clothes. It was a far cry from *Wiedergutmachung*, the mayor said. He wanted the benefits currently reserved for the severely disabled to be extended to everyone who had been in a concentration camp as well as to their bereaved dependents.[7]

By 1948–49, it appeared that Germany was further away from *Wiedergutmachung* than ever. Who counted as an officially recognized victim eligible for aid and compensation was not clear-cut. The best-organized groups of victims were the political prisoners: communists and Social Democrats. It was often they who advised local authorities and gave their stamp of approval to victims applying for help. Flensburg, near the Danish border, was typical. In 1945–46, special aid was granted to Nazi victims but limited to those who had spent time in a concentration camp, and not even all of them. It was only renewed pressure from the British Military Government that made the committee extend their consideration to "half-Jews" and widows of those persecuted. For local authorities it depended on why someone had been in a camp. Political motives counted; being a Rom, homosexual, or criminal did not. Evaluations of an applicant's character and way of life often ended up echoing that of the Nazis, with "gypsies" classified as "asocial" and, hence, unworthy of support. Similarly, alcoholics or criminals had little chance of a sympathetic hearing.[8]

The care department (*Betreuungsstelle*) in Frankfurt routinely rejected applications that did not fit the political, social, and gendered box of a "proper" Nazi victim. Johanna Hescher, a worker born in 1920, was married by proxy (*ferngetraut*) to a soldier at the Eastern Front in 1941. Shortly thereafter, she was seen entering a hotel with a French POW. At the factory where they both worked, she was repeatedly spotted handing him "cigarettes, sandwiches, and pieces of cake" as well as a wallet. In April 1942, she was arrested for aiding him in an abortive escape, and sent to prison. Her application for assistance was rejected in January 1948 because her actions did not show a "political motive"—that she had suffered in a Nazi prison did not matter.

The widow of Heinrich Heusser was turned away for the same reason. Her husband had been sentenced to death for refusing to follow orders in battle in 1941. After psychiatric examination, he was placed in a psychiatric institution instead, where he died on January 26, 1945. "Pulmonary tuberculosis," the authorities told her, "developed quite often in such cases of mental disorder." She was furious. "Deliberate starvation" and locking someone up in a "stinking room" that made the body so weak that it became susceptible to infections was "organized murder," she complained in the summer of 1946. Wasn't the fact that he had been sentenced to death enough proof that her husband was a victim of the Nazis? For the authorities, it was not.

Other prisoners fell victim to a narrow view of what counted as resistance. Else Hodapp was thirty-two when, in October 1942, she was arrested trying to help a Jewish woman cross the Swiss border. She spent the next six months in the Ravensbrück camp. In March 1948, she appealed to the Frankfurt care department for help. After consulting with the local court in Lörrach, near the Swiss border, where she had been arrested, officials decided to reject her application because it lacked evidence of political persecution. She appealed, providing the names of three witnesses. This was not considered sufficient, and she was asked to provide testimony from the woman. That woman was dead, however, so the application was rejected again. Hodapp appealed once more. In March 1949, the senior official in charge rejected her final appeal because there was "no proof that she had acted as an accessory of the persecuted Jew out of principled opposition to the Nazi regime." The official speculated that she probably did it for money or "some other form of payment." The fact that she had been sent to a concentration camp was irrelevant.[9]

Even for victims who could show that they had suffered racial persecution, the road to *Wiedergutmachung* was littered with obstacles. Bernard Hess was "half Jewish." Both his parents had been deported to a concentration camp and their property confiscated. He himself spent six weeks in a camp, and then went into hiding until the end of the war. He was now destitute and asked for help and some clothing. He was rejected because he failed to meet the minimum requirement of a six-month stay in a camp.[10]

Political prisoners were the best-organized lobby—with the Union of Persecutees of the Nazi Regime (Vereinigung der Verfolgten des Naziregimes, VVN)—but even they soon lost the little political clout they had. Victims of the Nazis, they now became victims of the Cold War. The communist takeover of the left in the Soviet zone meant the Social Democrats in the Western zones came to look at the VVN as a Trojan horse steered by Moscow. In 1948, the SPD excluded all VVN members from their party. Three years later, the VVN's council was banned in the West. While in East Germany communist members of the resistance were feted as heroes, they were stigmatized and criminalized in the West.[11] In 1953, active communists lost their claims to compensation in the Federal Republic altogether. The state took away their pensions and passports and launched criminal investigations of more than 100,000 of them. In 1950, Doris Maase, a doctor and a communist, was certified as 60 percent disabled as a consequence of her time in a camp. In 1960, the pension authorities no longer considered her disabled, although they later agreed to raise her disability to 30 percent. She felt like "half a human being." Instead of receiving compensation for her suffering, she had to refund part of her pension, while old Nazis continued to receive theirs.[12]

The GDR, meanwhile, on the twentieth anniversary of liberation, passed a pension law in honor of "veteran fighters" against the Nazis. Beginning in 1965 they would receive 800 DM a month, at a time when the average income was only 490 DM. But generosity in the East had its limits. Old communists had been angry for some time, because prior to 1965 pensions were based on victims' former incomes. This was said to favor Jews who had worked as lawyers and professionals, rather than communists, who had been dockers or unemployed. In response, East Germany created an exclusive club of hero-victims. Whereas in West Germany, claimants for *Wiedergutmachung* exceeded several million people by the mid-1960s, East Germany recognized a mere twenty-five thousand individuals as victims of Nazism; fifteen thousand of these were honored with a medal as "fighters against fascism."[13] To qualify as a member of this elite, one needed to have suffered at the hands of the Nazis before 1945 as well as demonstrated one's commitment to socialism after 1945. The fight against fascism never stopped. Privileged victims paid dearly for their pensions by having to give endless lectures about their anti-fascist struggle to young pioneers and party conferences.

Tensions between communists and Social Democrats had a long history, but why did the Social Democrats not do more for victims in their own ranks? After all, many had been in camps, in exile, or underground. Kurt Schumacher, the party leader, had spent ten years in concentration camps. Partly, the reason was that the SPD, like the communists, saw themselves as a party of resistance. The focus was on the collective, not individuals. After boycotting the VVN, the Social Democrats did set up their own Campaign Group of Persecuted Social Democrats (AG verfolgter Sozialdemokraten), but mainly to control and contain victim politics. A second reason was that Nazism had eaten into the working class. After the war, there were many working-class families in which Social Democrats and former Nazis sat around the same coffee table. *Wiedergutmachung* was a sensitive subject. For example, a woman who had been a Nazi victim died childless in 1956. Her late brother and his surviving children had joined the Nazi Party. Were they to inherit her claims to compensation?[14] A final reason was the popular association of the camps with criminals, which made it difficult for political prisoners to speak of their experience.

Above all, Nazi victims were a political liability in the battle for votes. The Nazis had been so efficient that only a minority was still alive, and, of those, many either had emigrated or were planning to. Altogether, there were around 300,000 German victims in the Western zones, a tiny number compared to the millions of Germans who, in one way or another, bore the scars of the war and saw themselves as its primary victims. In other words, among the rank and file of the SPD and voters more generally, the few Social Democratic victims faded into insignificance next to bombed-out residents, the families of prisoners of war, the disabled, war widows, and expellees. The SPD was trying to reinvent itself as a party of the people. In 1952–53, in opposition, it would lend Adenauer crucial support for his agreements with Israel and the JCC. At the same time, SPD leaders knew that reparations had little support among its members. A survey in 1952 found that only 13 percent of SPD members fully supported the Luxembourg Agreement between Germany and Israel. Thirty percent supported it but thought that too much money was being paid out. Almost half saw no need for *Wiedergutmachung* at all.[15]

Nothing better illustrates the role reversal in victim politics in these years than that of restitution. In 1933, the half-million German Jews owned 16 billion Reichsmark (roughly 65 billion euros today). They only managed to move a quarter of these assets abroad. The rest was either "Aryanized" or confiscated. Homes, paintings, jewelry, silverware, and furniture all passed into non-Jewish German hands, in most cases well below market prices. In November 1946, the Bavarian state commissar called on all those who had acquired Jewish possessions second- or thirdhand to return the property to the victims. Many heeded the call or settled with the owners out of court.[16] It was one thing to make such an appeal when Germany was occupied. It was something quite different after 1949, when West Germany had regained part of its sovereignty and political parties were competing for voters. It was largely thanks to the pressure from the Americans, who sat alongside Germans in the Supreme Court of Appeal, that in the American zone around 60 percent of all restitution cases were settled by 1951. In total, though, West Germans would return only 7 billion DM (roughly $3.8 billion today) to their rightful Jewish owners in the first forty years after the war.[17]

Restitution was political dynamite because Jewish possessions had gone through so many German hands that millions of people were entangled in the sorry business. During the occupation, Germans swallowed their anger and blamed the Allies. After 1949, however, it became an internal German political issue. There were some cases where business partners or neighbors had paid Jewish friends a decent price to enable them to emigrate and rescue part of their property. Many more, though, took advantage of the situation and profiteered directly—or indirectly by later acquiring such "Aryanized" goods at an artificially low price. It was this last group of "third-party" owners who proved particularly troublesome. They complained that they were treated as thieves, even though they had engaged in what they considered good faith in a commercial transaction with the seller. Politicians distinguished between "loyal" and "malicious" purchasers. The conservative CSU (Christlich-Soziale Union), the Bavarian sister party of Adenauer's Christian Democratic Union (CDU), and the Liberal FDP (Freie Demokratische Partei) warned that restitution to Jews was endangering the economic recovery and the very principle of private property. There was little recognition of the original violation of private property that Germans from across society had been complicit in. The Association for Loyal Restitution (Vereinigung für loyale Restitution) bombarded members of parliament with letters. The "destiny of the German people" was at stake, it argued in 1951. If restitution was not scaled back, West Germany would face bankruptcy. The association deployed antisemitic imagery to argue that even "fair-thinking Jews" were "horrified by the stain of '*Wiedergutmachung*'" while the law allowed others "to enrich themselves in a shameless and completely unjustified manner" and pocket "billions from the impoverished German *Volk*."[18] The tax authorities routinely received letters telling them that Jews were "by nature swindlers."[19]

Jewish survivors faced so much hostility and distrust that, in Nuremberg in 1947, they refused to take advantage of the extra meat rations the Americans granted them for fear of prompting an antisemitic backlash.[20] In this climate, Jewish groups in Germany opposed proposals to make Nazis pay victims directly. The dramatic fall of Philipp Auerbach, the champion of that approach in Bavaria, revealed the diminishing political space for this kind of *Wiedergutmachung*. A corruption scandal sealed his downfall in 1951, and he was imprisoned, abandoned by Jewish organizations as well as German officials. He felt like a German Dreyfus, he said, and committed suicide; he would be posthumously rehabilitated in 1956.[21]

The matter of restitution indicated how many Germans thought about right and wrong five years after Hitler. Denial about persecution ran deep, as did the belief that one had acted honorably in the transaction. Some argued that Jews ended up selling property because they were bad businessmen, others that they had ultimately profited from emigrating because it saved them from losing their homes in the bombings. When Nazi persecution was acknowledged, it was often to minimize the role of everyday Germans. As one commentator put it, if they had refused to buy, then "the only road left for quite a few emigrants would have been the road to Auschwitz."[22] Irma B. from Upper Franconia wrote to the president of the Bavarian parliament in November 1949 about the Allied court order to hand over her farm or pay for it in cash. In 1938, she explained, she had bought it from a Jewish owner, only to help him emigrate. In 1945, the farm was confiscated and placed in the hands of a Polish trustee. "First, our refugees are driven out [of the Eastern provinces]," Irma wrote, "and now they even take our home and farm in our own country. Does this not exceed even the methods of the Third Reich?" How could "normal people" pass such laws and call it "democracy"? They "who had helped the Jews and, to a degree, saved their lives, now had to pay for that by having their farm taken from them." Her husband meticulously itemized the damage caused by the Polish trustee, down to wear and tear on the electric water pump resulting from her "excessive" water consumption. He then added the costs he had incurred in the denazification process as a member of the Nazi Party. In his moral ledger, denazification and *Wiedergutmachung* were equivalent, and he could not be expected to pay the same debt twice.[23]

Those who tried to reclaim their property faced an uphill battle, as was illustrated by the Rosenthal family's fight to regain control of their internationally renowned porcelain firm in Upper Franconia.[24] In 1933, in anticipation of a forced fusion of his two companies, Philipp Rosenthal passed 60 percent of the shares to his "Aryan" son-in-law. A year later, Philipp was excluded from the board of directors. He died in 1937. After the war, his son launched a legal challenge to regain the family property. For two years, the board fought the restitution claim. The transfer of shares and other transactions, they argued, had been purely commercial and had nothing to do with the Nazi persecution of the Jewish owners. Did Philipp not die a peaceful death, and did his wife Maria, a Catholic and "Aryan," not survive the Nazis unharmed? The board had lawyers, money, and, above all, time. They also had political allies, including Ludwig Erhard, the future chancellor, who stood up for them and lobbied the American authorities. In 1950, after a two-year legal battle, Philip Rosenthal—the son—settled for 1 million Deutschmark, barely one fifth of his initial claim, plus a seat on the board. The son had the tenacity and resources to wage his fight. Most emigrants and survivors had neither.

The situation was even worse in Austria and worst in East Germany. Austria, playing the role of victim, felt that neither restitution nor reparation was its responsibility—had the Allies at the Moscow conference in November 1943 not declared Austria the first free country to fall victim to Nazi aggression?

In the Soviet zone, the persecution of the Jews initially attracted attention. Victim groups published accounts of what had transpired in the Warsaw Ghetto and some local authorities did hand back property to Nazi victims. But the only region in the future GDR to pass a *Wiedergutmachung* law was Thuringia, which had initially been occupied by the Americans. When it was handed over to the Soviets in July 1945, the preparations for the law were well underway, and it was passed just two months later. Some within the Thuringian administration saw it as "an ethical duty" not only to return stolen property but also to compensate Jewish victims for "their loss of freedom and the destruction of their material existence."[25] The Soviet authorities did not care much about restitution one way or another, but the official deputy in charge, Georg Chaim, a Jewish survivor of the Buchenwald camp, did. In 1933, Thuringia had been home to just under three thousand Jews. By 1949, more than a thousand restitution cases had been filed. Of the cases that reached the regional court, almost two thirds were successful, and several hundred pieces of real estate were returned to their rightful owners, who had mainly emigrated.

Thuringia was exceptional, though, and short-lived in its generosity. In 1948, Paul Merker, a member of the Politburo, and Leo Zuckermann, a senior official, drafted a national bill for *Wiedergutmachung*. An internal statement by the central committee of the ruling Socialist Unity Party (SED) recorded the many objections to compensation: "Jewish emigrants do not belong to the working class"; "the emigrants no longer have any claims—why should we throw money after them?"; "the expellees do not get anything either, why should the Jews get something?" To think a Jewish state had claims was the equivalent of recognizing "the claims of monopolists and trust-mongers." Merker was excluded from the Politburo in 1950 and two years later arrested for conspiracy; he would not be rehabilitated until six years later. Zuckermann, who had helped write the East German constitution, was tried as a "Zionist agent," but managed to flee to West Berlin. Restitution in Thuringia was terminated in 1951.

The purges in East Berlin were part of the antisemitic show trials across the Eastern bloc that began with Stalin's campaign against "rootless" cosmopolitan Jews in 1948. Anyone supporting *Wiedergutmachung* was now branded a traitor seeking to move public property to the class enemy. In 1952, Adenauer told Nahum Goldmann, who headed the JCC, that West Germany would take on two thirds of Jewish claims; the remaining third would be East Germany's responsibility. This never stood a chance. Otto Grotewohl, then the prime minister of the GDR, was strongly pro-Arab and condemned West German reparations as funding Zionist imperialism. The party line was that East Germany had already taken on more than its fair share by paying reparations to the Soviet Union. Admittedly, East Germany shouldered fifteen times as much of the Allied reparations as did West Germany, per person. The Soviets took away the equivalent of $15 billion from East Germany in the shape of railway tracks, machinery, and goods; one fifth of production went to Moscow. But that was of little help to Jewish survivors. After the June 17, 1953, uprising, which almost toppled the GDR, the Soviet Union formally ended its own reparations and also saw to it that Poland withdrew its demands. Its priority now lay in stabilizing its ally in East Berlin, not burdening its fragile economy with fresh claims.

The GDR even reversed restitutions and seized back property from Jewish owners. There was no place for either them or their private businesses in the new "progressive" social order of the GDR. As the justice department of the SED Central Committee explained, to hand back what now were nationalized firms to Jewish individuals "would mean that socialization stopped short of Jewish capital, and that Jewish capitalists would be granted special favors over all other capitalists."[26] If Hitler had not already dispossessed the Jews, it was argued, then the GDR would have had to do it. In exchange for losing the right to their properties, Jews only received welfare benefits due to other victims of fascism. The GDR now "administered" Jewish property for a better socialist future. Unlike West Germany, it did not even prosecute the profiteers (so-called Ariseure) who had taken advantage of the plight facing the Jews under the Nazis to help themselves cheaply to their possessions. It was only after the Berlin Wall came down in 1989 that the victims were finally able to start the process of reclaiming the ten thousand firms and forty-five thousand homes that had been taken from them east of the Elbe.[27]

VICTIM POLITICS

Germany after the war was a home to murderers, but Germans at the time saw themselves as a nation of victims, and the relationships among the victims were not harmonious. In recent years, philosophers have turned to human vulnerability as a unifying experience. In this view, appeals to the Enlightenment and universal reason perished with the Holocaust, and a new humanist biopolitics should look to our shared vulnerability. After all, all humans suffer pain and die. In the words of Judith Butler, a leading proponent of this idea, our bodies "are not self-enclosed kinds of entities," but are "always in some sense outside themselves" and get "lost in another": we all experience "dispossession." This shared vulnerability can remind us of our mutual dependence and help us "overcome precarity in the name of livable lives."[28] In short, our morality stems from our mortality.

This way of looking at vulnerability has many things to commend it and sets out an attractive path to overcome injustices. Unfortunately, postwar German reality could not have been further from this ideal. Instead it produced a competitive politics of lamentation and battle for recognition. War widows, disabled soldiers, expellees, and bombed-out residents all wanted to be heard, and they shouted louder and louder about their plight. Vulnerability might be universal, but the resources a community has to help reduce suffering are limited, and in the ruins of postwar Germany they were especially so. Authorities were confronted with disability pensions for soldiers, social benefits to war widows, new homes for the expellees, and compensation for Nazi victims. Not everyone received his or her fair share. Beginning in the mid-1950s, the economic miracle would dramatically broaden what was feasible, but in the late 1940s, politicians and victims alike knew that funds were limited and that any winner entailed a loser. Instead of encouraging empathy, the awareness that almost everyone was suffering bred rivalry.

This does not mean Germans were completely indifferent to the plight of the Jews. In August 1949, a survey asked, "Do you believe that Germany has a duty for *Wiedergutmachung* for the surviving German Jews?" Fifty-four percent answered yes, 31 percent said no, and 15 percent were undecided. More revealing of the state of popular opinion at the time is when the duty is set in relationship to duties to other groups. An Allied survey in December 1946 asked Germans who they wanted most to receive aid. Sixty-three percent wanted to see disabled soldiers get help and compensation, 57 percent people who had been bombed out, and 48 percent war widows. Only 25 percent picked the political victims of the Nazis, and only 18 percent Jews.[29] Five years later, Germans seemed more generous, with 68 percent supporting aid to Jews. Yet, again, this was well below the level of sympathy for war widows and expellees; even the surviving family members of the failed assassination attempt on July 20, 1944—a group that for many remained traitors—enjoyed more support, with 73 percent.[30] There was a hierarchy of empathy, and German Jews continued to find themselves at the bottom—though it needs to be said that other groups that had been excluded from the *Volksgemeinschaft*, such as homosexuals and Sinti and Roma, were not even included in questionnaires, and Jewish victims from Poland or Ukraine were completely outside the bounds of compassion.

The various lobbies of war victims had their eyes on state resources, and their main rivalry was with each other, not with the victims of the Nazis. The bombed-out evacuees, for example, felt that too much attention and money was showered on the expellees from the East. The expellees, in turn, were fighting for the same few homes, jobs, and benefits as the returning POWs. The crumbs that would be left for the few Jewish survivors was a secondary matter. It was only in 1952, with the agreement between West Germany and Israel and the Jewish Claims Conference (JCC), that compensation for Jewish victims became an important item. West Germany had more than 4 million recognized "war victims" who were entitled to special benefits and pensions. This included 1.5 million war disabled, and 2.5 million widows, widowers, orphans, and half-orphans.[31] In addition, there were 12 million expellees and more than 20 million who had lost their homes in the bombings. The main conflict about who would get what was between these

TOP, LEFT 1. The Holocaust by bullets: a member of the Einsatzgruppen, the death squad of the SS, executing a Jew in Vinnytsia, Ukraine, after the German occupation in mid-1941.

TOP, RIGHT 2. Members of the Wehrmacht, the regular army, assassinating civilians in Pančevo, Serbia, in April 1941 in retaliation for the killing of an SS soldier.

3. A German soldier took this photograph of the mass murder of Jews at Babyn Yar, Ukraine, on September 29–30, 1941.

ABOVE 4. A police photo of the deportation of Jews from Würzburg, Germany, in 1942.

LEFT 5. Some of the c. 100,000 German prisoners of war who surrendered at Stalingrad, February 1943.

BELOW 6. Survivors walk through the ruins of Hamburg Altona, Germany, on July 26, 1943, after the second night of Operation Gomorrah, during which three thousand British bombers dropped nine thousand tons of bombs on that city over ten days and nights. Forty-three thousand people died in the firestorm and nearly one million fled to the countryside. Cities across Germany were routinely subject to similar area bombings in the second half of World War II.

RIGHT 7. On May 3, 1945, five days before Germany surrendered, this German civilian was ordered by troops of the U.S. Ninth Army to hold the corpse of a Russian baby killed in a series of massacres of Soviet and Polish forced laborers near Warstein, Germany, in March 1945.

LEFT, TOP 8. On May 5, 1945, a German mother covers the eyes of her son as they are made to walk past Soviet and Polish forced laborers who had been massacred in the forests near Warstein.

LEFT, BOTTOM 9. Female SS guards are forced by British soldiers to bury corpses after the liberation of Bergen-Belsen, April 1945..

10. Reunited: (front row, right to left) Susanne Vogel, an assimilated German Jew, who survived the war inside Germany thanks to her marriage to an "Aryan" husband, with her cousin Liselotte Dieckmann, who had managed to emigrate before the war, first to Turkey and then to the United States; (back row, left to right) Susanne's son-in-law, another cousin, and her husband; probably Kassel, Germany, 1969.

11. A still from the film *The Murderers Are Among Us* (1946), with Hildegard Knef and Ernst Wilhelm Borchert, which confronted audiences with German atrocities during the war. It was shown while the Nuremberg trials of war criminals were ongoing and watched by over 6 million Germans.

12. "When will you come back" reads a poster for the memorial week for POWs in 1953.

13. East Prussians fleeing from the advancing Red Army across the Vistula Spit and the Baltic in early 1945, trying to reach what was left of Nazi Germany. Some 12 million Germans fled or were expelled from their homelands in central and eastern Europe.

14. "Silesia appeals to the world": German Chancellor Konrad Adenauer addressing expellees at their "mass gathering" in 1959, in which they remembered their German homeland that had been given to Poland by the victorious Allies at the Potsdam Conference, August 1, 1945.

15. "Do not walk past! Help!": an appeal by the Inner Mission, 1950, one of the two main Protestant charities that provided vital aid to millions of Germans in the postwar years.

16. The iconic "hunger hand" of Bread for the World, 1959, one of the two largest aid agencies which mobilized Germans to give money to help the poor and starving in the world.

17. Young Germans tend war graves near Verdun, France, in 1966, as an act of remembrance and reconciliation. By 1970, volunteers were looking after 1.5 million war graves.

LEFT 18. East Germans throw rocks at Soviet tanks in the uprising of June 17, 1953, almost overthrowing the communist regime of the German Democratic Republic (GDR).

ABOVE 19. The People's Army: an East German soldier shows children around an army vehicle as part of the militarization of everyday life.

20. Erich Honecker (a member of the GDR politburo and future leader), Leonid Brezhnev (the Soviet leader), and Walter Ulbricht (the communist head of the GDR) cheering the parade at the VIIth conference of the German Socialist Unity Party (SED) in East Berlin in 1967.

21. German chancellor Willy Brandt falls to his knees on December 7, 1970, at the memorial to the heroes of the Warsaw Ghetto uprising.

22. Volunteers are sworn into West Germany's new army in 1955. The launch of the Bundeswehr, and conscription that followed, faced big protests and such ceremonies did not take place in public.

large groups. Germans cared little about Nazi victims to begin with, and in the process these groups were marginalized even further.

Two main divides cut across German society. One was between those who had lost their homes and those who had not. The other was between those who had lost their limbs or loved ones and those who had not.

Twelve million had been driven from former German provinces such as East and West Prussia; territories that had been annexed by the Nazis such as the Sudetenland; and other regions in central and eastern Europe where ethnic Germans had settled for centuries. (They posed an unprecedented challenge that we will examine later.) Then there were the many millions who had lost their homes in the bombings. There were tensions between these groups over who got access to the few apartments still standing. But they were united in demanding fair treatment from the rest of German society: the lucky ones whose homes had been spared were seen as having a duty to help all those unlucky ones who had lost theirs through no fault of their own. This moral imperative built on the Nazi *Volksgemeinschaft* and was an issue that would haunt postwar Germany.

In 1948, an emergency aid package was introduced, funded initially through a 2 percent tax on wealth, later raised to 3 percent. But the issue was only properly tackled in 1952 with an agreement to "equalize burdens" (*Lastenausgleich*). It was an explosive step, because people had radically different ideas about what fair equalization meant. For those who lobbied for compensation for their actual losses, it was impossible to get the ones who had caused the damage to pay up (be they Nazis or Allies), so the money would have to come from other Germans who still had some assets. The Central Union of Air-Raid Victims (Zentralverband der Fliegergeschädigten), for example, called for a tax on all those who had seen their wealth increase since 1935. As they explained their position in 1948, "The war has been lost by the entire German people. Accordingly, the burdens must also be borne by all citizens in proportion to their wealth." They would no longer be treated as "second-class citizens." Inaction, they warned, would be the "hour of death for private property in Germany," because frustrated victims would take measures into their own hands. If democracy was to have a chance, it needed to be put on "fair" foundations.[32]

The expellees were just as tired of waiting. Linus Kather, a Christian Democrat member of parliament, a refugee, and the head of the 1.5-million-member Central Union of German Expellees (Zentralverband der Vertriebenen Deutschen), rejected proposals for a long-term tax on wealth that would delay most compensation. The majority of expellees, he said in 1950, needed an immediate transfer of wealth and were "not helped by measures that only reached them in ten or more years." He wanted all those Germans who had more than 30,000 DM to hand over their second homes, branches of their firms, shares, and acres of their farmland. Half of all wealth should be transferred, he argued.[33] A year later, speaking to ten thousand expellees in Munich, he said the expellees would accept a graduated quota system in which those with little property got full compensation and those with enormous properties only a share of their losses. But they rejected outright the role of the beggar. All they wanted was recognition for what had been taken from them. With the "possessions and land they had left behind," the expellees had already "paid reparations for the entire nation."[34]

So many homes, farms, and firms had been lost in the war that full compensation was a fantasy. According to estimates at the time, the losses ran to 27 billion RM for bombing damage and 120 billion RM connected to the expulsions.[35] That was three times Germany's GDP in 1937. Compensation would have wrecked the economy and, with it, the prospect of reconstruction in the near future, and that would have been unfair to the next generation. It was unwise to rip off the head of the cow you want to milk, as a rural saying had it. In any case, modest Bavarian farmers had no interest in handing over some of their few cows and small fields to former big landowners from East Prussia. Family firms, too, opposed the proposals for burden sharing as the road to socialism.[36]

Some politicians proposed to restore the distribution of property as it had been before the war; this angered Social Democrats and progressive Christian Democrats. Those on the left preferred a collective approach, by which the yield from taxes would have funded public investment in homes and firms that would help people get back on their feet. This made economic sense but was also a political dead-end, because expellees did not want to just have a new start but also wanted to see their personal losses acknowledged. Then there were those who favored social equity. What was decisive in this moral calculus was not how much someone had lost but how vulnerable a person was.[37] Need trumped losses. It would be unfair to compensate an East Prussian count for his entire estate but give his poor servants only pennies for the few possessions they had left behind. Transfers also had to look fair to those who were being asked to hand over some of their wealth. In this "social" scheme, therefore, victims were asked to shoulder part of the burden themselves. Fairness here was not about making good past losses but about enabling future integration by promoting capital formation and economic recovery to help victims rebuild their lives.

The final policy, in 1952, was a compromise between the individual and social criteria of fairness. Compensation was graduated. Big losers got more than small ones in absolute terms, but less in relative terms. Someone who had lost possessions worth 10,000 DM in the bombings, for example, received 4,000 DM (40 percent), while someone who had lost a castle worth 1 million DM got 54,000 DM (5.4 percent). The sums were paid out in small chunks over thirty years. Some 57 million applications would be made in total. Linus Kather threatened to leave the Christian Democrats and take the other expellee MPs with him to the rival pressure group, the League of Expellees and Deprived of Rights (Bund der Heimatvertriebenen und Entrechteten), until Adenauer pledged an additional 850 million DM for immediate integration.

If the *Lastenausgleich* amounted to an unprecedented transfer of wealth, it fell short of the radical plans for full-scale compensation and redistribution, let alone confiscation. The funds were raised through a tax on capital returns, not on capital stock and assets themselves, and thus did not hurt capital accumulation.[38] Adenauer had managed to contain the anger of the expellees and bombed-out survivors; avoided a civil war between the propertied and the dispossessed; and found a way of giving some compensation for war losses without sacrificing his overall aim of reconstruction.

The second issue that divided Germans was pensions for victims of the war. Here, again, there was plenty of anger and pain after 1945—a colossal defeat, personal suffering, hurt pride, and a sense of entitlement made for an explosive mix. In November 1947, an outraged veteran who had left one leg behind on the battlefield wrote to the magazine *Der Spiegel*. A rumor had reached him that a woman had refused to give up her seat in the tram for a soldier, calling him a "war criminal." Returning soldiers, he insisted, deserved greater respect and at least as "fair" benefits as those returning from a concentration camp, many of whom, he added, were criminals.[39] The Association of the War-Disabled (Verein der Kriegsbeschädigten, or VdK), which in 1951 had 1.3 million members, directed most of its fire at privileged German pensioners. Its demands included giving brain-damaged soldiers the same pensions as those for the blind and providing better pensions for working-class widows and orphans. Their sense of injustice exploded at a conference in 1949. The press, delegates complained, always wrote about the many disabled people applying for benefits, but what about "the police general of the Nazi years who is paid a monthly pension of 1,100 DM by the state of Hesse or the childless widow of a senior civil servant who receives 4,800 DM a year?" People seemed to forget the "ethical and moral rights of the victims of the war," speakers said. "The disabled have sacrificed their health and their descendants their breadwinner . . . so that other men and women back home were able to acquire pension entitlements for themselves. How does anyone dare not grant the victims their right to a pension as well?"[40] Disabled soldiers and their suffering families were not only victims of the war; they were also victims of privileged Germans.

Disabled veterans, former prisoners of war, and the professional soldiers and civil servants who had their jobs and pensions taken away by the Allies all made the same, simple argument: they had done their duty and served the state, now it was time for the state to do its duty to them. Guilt and accountability toward Nazi victims was a subplot in this larger story of the state's responsibility toward Germans who had supported the war and lost their jobs during denazification.

In June 1950, returning POWs were awarded benefits, and relatives of remaining POWs maintenance support (*Unterhaltsbeihilfe*). A year later, the law that finally compensated Nazi victims who had been forced out of the civil service was passed on the very same day—May 11, 1951—as the historic Article 131, the law that allowed former Nazis to return to it.[41] The official recognition of the Nazis' victims was a political gesture; it would have been embarrassing to leave them out. But the government's main goal was the reintegration of those who had been implicated in their persecution. Compensation for Nazi victims was coupled with that for German war victims. In 1954, a law set out the terms for German POWs. Each was to receive 1 DM for every day of work in a Soviet prisoner-of-war camp. The German state took this on as its "own responsibility" (*eigene Schuld*). As the Liberal Margarete Hütter told parliament: "We all are in debt to the German prisoners of war" and hence it was "our duty to pay down part of our debt to these people."[42] This was *Wiedergutmachung*, too. It happened to be the same rate as that for survivors of Nazi concentration camps.

REMEMBRANCE REDEFINED

Memorialization moved in the same direction, with German soldiers and civilians being remembered alongside the Nazis' victims. On November 4, 1945, at 9 a.m., Harry Goldstein, one of the few Jews to have survived in Hamburg, spoke at the commemoration for the victims of Nazism at the city's crematorium in Ohlsdorf. The Jewish community, he began, had been so annihilated that there was not even a rabbi among them. Millions of Germans had also suffered death, but, he noted, "the families of the fallen soldiers could at least take some comfort from the fact that their loved ones had died in the course of fulfilling their duty to defend their homeland." Since many Germans knew that German soldiers had been involved in atrocities, Goldstein probably knew this, too. Still, he followed the capacious view of war victims decided on by the committee of former political prisoners. The Jews, he continued, did not even have that consolation. They were "silent heroes," driven to their death by their unmerciful tormentors. Where did their hatred come from, Goldstein asked? They were guilty because they had turned away from God and God had turned away from them. He appealed to all fathers and mothers to prevent similar hatred from spreading across the next generation. In his closing words, he bowed "in deepest respect before *all* victims of National Socialism." He wished their suffering and death had not been for nothing but would turn into a blessing for "our beloved *Heimat*" and for "the whole of humanity." Goldstein had united the dead in the hope of a common future for the living.[43]

Memorials create a community between the living and the dead. Just as important, they can provide a community among survivors. The memorial politics in West and East Germany were to diverge sharply in both respects. The GDR remembered not individual victims but the communist resistance as a collective. The memorial at Buchenwald in 1958 was a shrine to the eighteen nations from which prisoners had come—a communist international of death. West Germany, by contrast, stretched victimhood to make it inclusive of virtually all Germans who had died and suffered during the war except the Nazi leaders. In 1948, the SPD in Kassel proposed a memorial for the local victims of fascism, including the bombing victims, fallen soldiers, and refugees as well as inmates of the concentration camps.[44] The SPD's attention to dead soldiers was not surprising. Their families and surviving comrades made up lots of voters, and half the party's representatives in the Bundestag had themselves fought in the war.

As commemorations embraced German soldiers and civilians, Nazi victims were increasingly pushed to the sidelines. After the war, newly installed mayors in some towns presented returning political prisoners as the true heroes, to the anger of locals like the father of the missing pilot, for whom it was their soldier sons who cried out for recognition.[45] When Ernst Wiechert opened the commemoration at Dachau in May 1947, 1,500 former inmates were there, no other Germans. That year, the provincial governments gave the "victims of fascism" their own official memorial day: September 14. While a few Germans put up plaques in memory of their Jewish neighbors, the majority were conspicuous by their absence from memorial events such as the funerary speech at Munich's Prinzregententheatre.[46]

Political victim groups, too, were beginning to pull in different directions. In 1945, communists and Social Democrats had still honored each other as "comrades." The anti-fascist Vereinigung der Verfolgten des Naziregimes organized memorials in the big dockyards of Hamburg, in music halls and sports clubs. By 1947, the Social Democrats stopped attending such VVN events; so did officials. When the VVN opened an exhibition in 1946–47 called "Struggle and Victim," complete with instruments of torture from the local Neuengamme camp, most of the visitors were communist victims themselves. In 1949, Hamburg commemorated "the day of liberation." Communists wanted to have one urn for each nation of victims. The Social Democratic mayor, Max Brauer, instead chose the ashes of a prisoner from nearby Neuengamme. The dead ended up being remembered in two rival events, one mourning local victims, chaired by the Hamburg senate, the other honoring international communists, presided by the VVN.[47]

In April 1951, Bavaria held its annual hour of remembrance for the victims of Nazism. After a performance of Beethoven's *Fidelio* in the Munich state opera, the president of the Bavarian assembly, Georg Stang, began his speech in the customary style, honoring the racial, religious, and political victims of the Nazis, but then praised the fallen soldiers, bombing victims, and expellees, who, he said, were deserving of "the same high degree of care."[48]

A year earlier, the honorary president of the German war graves commission, Gustav Ahlhorn, had told the West German parliament that it was time to revive the *Volkstrauertag*, the national day of mourning, which had been introduced after the First World War. They needed to "overcome their timidity thinking about the millions of victims of our nation." In the Second World War, as in the First, the German soldier believed in "having to defend his beloved homeland." Soldiers died "a most honorable death," just like the fallen of other nations. Ahlhorn then reminded the audience of the millions of German refugees, POWs, and the disabled: "No nation had to make such grave sacrifices during the war as the German people!"[49]

The inclusion of German soldiers as victims alongside the few officers in the resistance became official. It fell to President Heuss, on the reinstituted national day of mourning two years later, to add a rare, critical afterthought. Yes, he said, the majority of soldiers felt they were defending their *Heimat*, but what kind of *Heimat* was it where "cynicism and sheer brutality had replaced honesty and law and hollowed out the inner meaning of 'the just war?' "[50]

Just as the burden of war was "equalized" among Germans, so was victimhood. Within just over five years, the Nazi *Volksgemeinschaft* had been converted into a West German *Schicksalsgemeinschaft*—a community of fate and suffering. The change was driven by a desire for integration and fear of a return to the antagonism and civil war that had destabilized the country after the First World War. Jews and other victims of the Nazis were pushed to the side in the process. Even for an understanding politician like the Liberal justice minister Thomas Dehler, whose wife was Jewish, *Wiedergutmachung* was ultimately for Germans as much as for Jews. "Everything that the German *Volk* did to the Jews," Dehler told a conference of Jewish lawyers in 1951, subsequently "happened to itself." Jews lost their freedom, Germans lost their freedom; Germans took property from the Jews, then had theirs taken by the war. "Germany will only see that made good again"—*wiedergutgemacht*—"by destiny, what it will do in amends to the Jews."[51]

Anti-communism rearranged the position of victims, opening the door to soldiers "defending" the *Heimat* against the Bolshevik enemy. In 1952, Hamburg unveiled its memorial to the many civilians killed in the bombing raids. For the speakers, the tragedy was a reminder of the importance of solidarity for the local community but also for the West more generally. It demonstrated, Mayor Brauer said, that in times of need the people of Hamburg pulled together. The bombing was not only a historic reminder of the Nazi years but also a general warning of the danger posed by today's dictators, he added, with a nod in the direction of the socialist East. Hermann Ehlers, the president of the Bundestag, spoke from personal experience of Operation Gomorrah; he had been in charge of an anti-aircraft-gun division at the time. They were prepared, he said, to defend their freedom against any threat from the East.[52]

The Nazi persecution of Jews was remembered, but that Jewish neighbors were also victims of the bombing, especially with air raid shelters closed to them, was forgotten. In 1957, Nuremberg followed with its own memorial to the victims of the bombing. Some of the stones for the memorial were taken from the rubble of the synagogue on Hans-Sachs Square that had been destroyed during Kristallnacht, after some discussion as to whether this might be seen as distasteful. Instead of an explanatory plaque on the memorial itself, the information was put *inside* the foundation stone. The fate of the Jews was literally buried in a monument to German victims.[53]

THE LIMITS OF REPARATION

On December 6, 1951, Chancellor Adenauer and Nahum Goldmann, the president of the World Jewish Congress and head of the JCC, met at Claridge's hotel in London. Adenauer was in town for a conference with the Allies to settle Germany's external debts, Goldmann in the hope of getting some reparations for the new state of Israel before Germany's coffers were emptied by its many prewar creditors. The two spoke in German. They had both been raised in the tradition of *Kultur* and patriotism of the educated bourgeoisie in the days of the German Empire. Goldmann had studied at Heidelberg and served in the Foreign Ministry during the First World War. Now, the mass murder of the Jews stood between the two men, though they nonetheless found time to converse about Bach and Goethe.[54] In his memoir, Goldmann recalled Adenauer saying that he felt the "wings of world history" beating in the room.[55] Goldmann decided to test Adenauer's commitment to reconciliation. To his amazement, Adenauer agreed to dictate a letter in which he recognized Germany's "moral obligation" to *Wiedergutmachung* in principle and in the amount of $1 billion, which had been the figure Jewish organizations had earlier put to the Allies and seen rejected. That was a big commitment, around one fifth of the federal budget.[56] That day at Claridge's laid the foundation of the Luxembourg Agreement between West Germany and Israel, which would be signed ten months later and in which West Germany pledged to pay 3 billion DM to Israel and another 450 million DM to the JCC to support Jewish refugees living outside Israel.

Wiedergutmachung was a central plank in Adenauer's strategy for reestablishing Germany's good name and position in the world. It typified the chancellor's ability to mix morality and realpolitik when it suited him. *Wiedergutmachung* was a "sacred duty" (*heilige Pflicht*), but it also served his overall goal of Western integration and German business interests in the Middle East; most of the payments to Israel would be paid in the form of German exports.[57] Adenauer was known as "the old fox," but his reputation for sober, cold reasoning should not be exaggerated. As his spontaneous decision at Claridge's shows, he could be impulsive, without thinking through all the implications. His finance minister, Fritz Schaeffer, was furious and tried to back away from the promises, but he was outmaneuvered. While Schaeffer was on an official visit in the United States, Adenauer arranged a decisive cabinet meeting to get his way. When Schaeffer found out about the meeting, he caught an earlier flight home but arrived too late to stop it. In parliament, Adenauer needed support from the opposition parties to get the agreement passed.

Adenauer ruled from 1949 to 1963. From the very beginning, his chancellorship was attacked as a "restoration." Already in 1950, commentators warned that a yearning for comfort was draining the courage needed for a new beginning.[58] When his last chancellorship was nearing its end, critics lamented the missed chances for reform. But these views came from contemporaries with their own axes to grind. Progressive conservatives such as Otto von der Gablentz had hoped for a rapprochement between East and West, socialism and capitalism, and were naturally disappointed when Adenauer turned to the West instead.[59] This is not the same as "restoration," however. Old civil servants were indeed reintegrated, but the price for their second chance was making peace with the new democratic order.

Adenauer oversaw an extraordinary transformation, in domestic as much as international policy. In the 1957 elections, he led the CDU and the CSU to a 50.2 percent majority. He fought the campaign under the motto "*Keine Experimente*"—"No Experiments." It remains one of the most famous slogans in German election history. It was also one of the most misleading. Adenauer pushed through one radical measure after another, steering the Federal Republic away from central Europe and reorienting it to the West, first joining France, Belgium, Italy, the Netherlands, and Luxembourg in a community of coal and steel in 1951, and then NATO in 1955. Domestically, he integrated groups in a new system of social solidarity. In his first few years in power, he supported an unprecedented public housing program and public assistance for the disabled and returning POWs. West Germany's public spending (as a share of GDP) was the highest anywhere in the West. The historic Luxembourg Agreement with Israel and the JCC, in September 1952, was followed, in 1953, by an equally unprecedented compensation package for many victims of the Nazis. These were huge commitments, and all taken before the economic boom would lift the Federal Republic and Western Europe to previously unknown heights of prosperity. To top things off, Adenauer pushed through radical pension reform, in January 1957, which raised workers' and clerks' pensions by two thirds. The elderly now shared in the improving fortune of the young. If there was one domain inspired by restoration, it was family policy, but even here patriarchal intentions were unable to stop change.

Adenauer had as little taste for unbridled capitalism as for socialism. As a devout Catholic, he believed that economic life involved responsibility as well as freedom. West Germany was a social market economy and its constitution recognized that private property came with public duties. Bismarck's social insurance system had been for the employed, leaving others in need at the mercy of discretionary benefits. From the mid-1950s, vulnerable people gained a right to social benefits, a radical change that would be sealed with the Federal Social Assistance Act of 1961 (Bundessozialhilfegesetz). By the time the Adenauer years came to an end, West Germany was unrecognizable. For the chancellor, social peace and international security were two sides of the same coin. Adenauer, like Bismarck, was a "white revolutionary," who understood that to conserve required radical change, not standing still.

In West Germany, almost all politicians rejected collective guilt but accepted moral responsibility. This did not mean that they automatically supported Adenauer's agreement with Israel. In the decisive vote, his coalition partners abstained. The CSU argued that the treaty with Israel would complicate compensation payments for individual victims, but was more concerned that the Arab League might boycott German exports as a result. Dehler, the Liberal justice minister, argued to his cabinet colleagues that moral claims were ultimately just that: moral, not material.[60] The nationalist Deutsche Partei wanted to see equal international recognition of the injustice done to the German expellees.[61] Ultimately, Adenauer needed the support of the Social Democrats, who believed that the crimes committed were such that Germany should pay up to the very limit of its ability.

At the same time, the chancellor and Germany's creditors were in agreement that the country's prewar debts had to be honored before it could enter into new commitments to Israel. How much Adenauer was under American pressure has been the subject of debate. At times, he warned his ministers that a breakdown of the negotiations with Israel would do irreparable damage to German-American relations, but that was Adenauer playing his trump card, not proof of external pressure. If anything, the United States was worried that payments to Israel might not leave enough for West Germany's rearmament, and that the bill for new German tanks might end up in Washington. When, in 1956, the U.S. did apply pressure on Adenauer to stop payments unless Israel withdrew from Sinai and the Gaza Strip, he refused.[62] The agreement with Israel served realpolitik, but it also rested on moral foundations.

Those foundations were missing in the GDR and also in the other country that had been part of Hitler's greater Germany: Austria. It brushed aside Israel's demands for reparations by saying it too had been a victim of Nazi "occupation." If Austrians had committed some crimes, they had done so as individuals or as obliged servants of the Third Reich. As a country, Austria owed Israel and Jewish victims nothing. Antisemitic charges of Jewish profiteering were never far from the surface. All Austria would provide, in 1955, was an "aid fund" for Nazi victims abroad, worth 550 million shillings, barely 2 percent of West Germany's compensation payments. Vienna also paid for the restoration of a few synagogues.[63]

West Germany's generosity had strict limits, too; the agreement with Israel and the JCC was atypical. In general, the Federal Republic refused to pay any reparation to countries that had suffered under Nazi occupation or to compensate their citizens. The London Debt Conference of 1952 focused on debts that had arisen before and after the war (such as the Marshall Plan), but excluded the costs of war itself. Their settlement was postponed until a "final" resolution was reached, which West Germany interpreted to mean a peace treaty. Such a neat distinction between military operations and persecution was artificial and defied the reality of a war of extermination. But, in the Cold War, it was an immensely powerful fiction that set the parameters for Germany's relations with its Eastern European neighbors until German reunification in 1990. By agreeing to pay prewar and postwar debts, West Germany got itself off the hook of paying reparations for the war itself.

In its approach to reparations for countries as in its approach to compensating individuals, Bonn got away with this by applying the territoriality principle to its moral obligations: German Jews and German emigrants were deserving victims; Jews from Kiev and forced laborers from Poland were not. Several occupied countries were, understandably, outraged. Greece, for example, submitted a claim worth $10 billion, but following the London Debt Agreement was told to agree to a share of a quota system or get nothing at all. Since the inter-Allied reparations agency in Brussels only worked with a total of $2–3 billion, it left very little for a small country like Greece. Eleven separate claims treaties were to follow between 1959 and 1964. Together these added only a further 876 million DM to be divided up among the victims. These global settlements were hugely favorable to West Germany, which confidentially calculated that private claims might be as high as twenty times that amount.

Some private companies were ordered to compensate forced laborers in exchange for future immunity. In 1951, for example, Norbert Wollheim, a former inmate of Auschwitz III, brought a civil suit for pain, suffering, and unpaid wages against IG Farben, whose top management had been found guilty in one of the Nuremberg successor trials. Wollheim, who had helped organize the *Kindertransport* to England, had been deported to Auschwitz in the spring of 1943 and was one of the forced laborers at the synthetic rubber plant at the Buna/Monowitz sub-camp; his wife and son were killed on arrival. In 1955, following a favorable decision for Wollheim and an appeal by the company, the parties reached a settlement: 5,855 Jewish forced laborers were to receive 5,000 DM each. In exchange, IG Farben and its successor firms could not be sued again in the future. Similar agreements by other companies followed. In the case of IG Farben, pressure by the International Auschwitz Committee eventually led to payments for Jewish survivors in Eastern Europe as well.[64] In general, though, such settlements made sure to exclude a whole series of Nazi victims: foreign and non-Jewish prisoners; forced laborers; Sinti and Roma; and the sterilized. They came to be known as "forgotten victims." In truth, they were deliberately excluded.

In the 1950s, France, Britain, and the Netherlands occasionally pushed for the inclusion of foreign resistance fighters and foreign victims of the camps in reparations, but in vain. West Germany stuck stubbornly to its position, in no small part thanks to the Cold War. The United States feared that an avalanche of claims would bury the Germany economy and pull down Western Europe with it. The territoriality principle had its downsides, but, from a Cold War perspective, it had the advantage of excluding the millions of foreign victims in the Eastern bloc.[65]

COMPENSATION—ON GERMAN TERMS

In 1956, West Germany passed its indemnity law (Bundesentschädigungsgesetz), which applied retroactively to 1953. In spirit, it was the twin of reparations and applied the same territorial limits to individual victims seeking compensation. Its principles followed the terms the Americans had laid down in their zone in the spring of 1949: victims of political, religious, and racial persecution by the Nazis qualified for compensation; all others did not. Victims could receive their pension anywhere—80 percent of all payments went abroad—once they documented that they had been German at the time of the persecution. A special category was created for Jews and other victims of the Nazis from areas of expulsion outside the Reich who, while not German nationals, could document their affinity to German language and culture.

For the next few decades, this law created two worlds of victims: those falling under its provisions, and those falling outside. From one perspective, the law stands out as a historic achievement. By the end of the twentieth century, West Germany had paid out 103 billion DM in compensation to survivors (159 billion euro in 2022 prices). This represented 70 percent of all types of *Wiedergutmachung* by West Germany. In the half century since 1953, 1 million victims received the same amount as the 20 million Germans who benefited from the "burden sharing" settlement; at its height, in the mid-1960s, compensation made up 2 percent of public spending. Never in the history of the world has a state been so generous to victims.

Yet, from another perspective, the vast majority of Nazi Germany's victims did not see a penny. The law was one-sided, discriminating against many victim groups. It only compensated German survivors for their pain and losses. It did not pay heirs awards for wrongful death, and it excluded the many foreign survivors.[66] The Social Democrat Hermann Brill presented a parliamentary committee in 1953 with the following memorable calculation. At the time of liberation, there were 35,000 prisoners in Buchenwald—Brill had been one of them—and the vast majority were Russians and Eastern Europeans. Only 1,800 were German, and the majority of those were "asocials" (which included Sinti and Roma), criminals, and homosexuals. Only 700 were German political prisoners. The new compensation law thus only reached one in fifty camp inmates.[67]

West German governments, courts, and businesses fought hard to preserve the line between the eligible and ineligible victims. In a typical case, the Federal Court of Justice in 1960 rejected the claim of a Polish forced laborer who had been deported to work in an armaments factory. He was not eligible for compensation, the judges ruled, because he was not a victim of racial or national persecution but had simply been called up as a skilled mechanic (*Schlosser*) to help with the war effort. Seven years later, a Polish woman who had been deported to a concentration camp had her case thrown out by a district court on similar grounds. She had been imprisoned for hiding a Jewish man, an act that the court explained was punished by the Nazi regime regardless of the race or nationality of the offender.[68]

In the early 1960s, in a bid to further Western integration, the Federal Republic paid several Western European countries 900 million DM (the equivalent of around $230 million at the time, or $2.3 billion in 2023) as a final settlement (*Globalabkommen*); this shielded German companies against all future claims from the West. In the early 1990s, with the Cold War at an end, reunified Germany signed similar agreements with Poland, Ukraine, Belarus, and the Russian Federation for a total of 1.5 billion DM ($1 billion). Those forced laborers who were still alive in 2000 received a one-time payment between 500 and 7,700 euros ($450 to $7,000 then), financed from a mix of federal and business funds.

For eligible survivors, the road to compensation was a steeplechase strewn with bureaucratic and legal hurdles, including insensitive caseworkers and the need for medical certificates. Seeking compensation required survivors to relive past pain and trauma. Many never submitted a claim. Others died while German courts were disputing how much (if any) of the damage to their organs was attributable to their treatment in the camps. The list of petty queries and heartless decisions is a long one, especially in the late 1950s and 1960s. A former civil servant who put in a claim for the restitution of his library was asked to provide title, price, and date of purchase for each of his nine hundred stolen books. In another case, a teenage girl, the only survivor in her family, was told that her tattoo was not sufficient evidence and that she needed to provide the names of two inmates who could testify to her time in the camp. Forced sterilization was routinely belittled—at a certain age, it was argued, all women became infertile anyway.[69]

Proving physical injury from Nazi persecution was difficult enough. Seeking compensation for psychological pain was even more so. A "Ms. B" had lived from birth until the age of four in several forced labor camps in Poland, before she was deported to the Warsaw Ghetto. Her father was murdered by the Nazis. From the age of thirteen she started having panic attacks whenever she saw a uniformed person, including the local postman. In 1974, officials in Hamburg rejected her compensation claim on the grounds that "someone who does not remember her childhood in a KZ cannot possibly have suffered from it."[70] Survivors like her found it all but impossible to have their psychological trauma certified before the 1970s.

The reasons for this failure have been the subject of debate. Some writers have pinned the blame on the survival of a Nazi mind-set among German doctors. A concentration camp, in this view, was like a POW camp, just with a crematorium added. The human organism was considered to be extremely flexible and the mind able to adjust and compensate for external stress. Distinguished professors pronounced on the impossibility of neurotic illness without bothering to examine the patient. Torture, witnessing atrocities, and the fear of death could not possibly lead to chronic stress, let alone trauma, most medical authorities said. Consequently, anxiety, panic attacks, or other psychological states could not have been caused by Nazi persecution but had to have their roots in some personal abnormality.[71]

Other historians have pointed out that the idea that people had extremely resilient, flexible willpower was nothing peculiarly German but the dominant medical opinion at the time, shared by doctors in the United States, including those who were sympathetic to victims. Psychological illness was said to be the result of physiological damage such as "famine dystrophia" observed among POWs. Émigré psychologists recognized that some victims suffered from a neurotic fear of persecution but, like their German colleagues, attributed this to physiological causes. Medical diagnosis, then, was not a simple cover for fascist habits of mind. The psychological problems of victims were attributed to their inability to cope with life in the present, not to their persecution in the past. Doctors and officials saw it as their job to separate the deserving from the undeserving victims. If they were too lax and generous, it would put the whole welfare system at risk.[72]

Under the aegis of the state, *Wiedergutmachung* was converted into a bureaucratic process. Victims did not meet their perpetrators face-to-face in a civil court, but dealt indirectly with the society of perpetrators via an administrative machine that assessed the victims' claims and certified or rejected them. Individual experiences of persecution were reduced to percentage points of disability and resulting benefits. The personal element of atonement all but disappeared in an impersonal process of public accountability. And the terms of *Wiedergutmachung* were set by the German state—victims either had to accept them or forgo compensation.

For all its flaws, however, the bureaucratic process had some benefits. Civil lawsuits would not have won survivors more compensation or expressions of remorse from their tormentors. Private efforts at restitution had proved to be extremely confrontational and disappointing in the late 1940s, and the sums they had yielded were tiny by comparison: the takeover by the state made at least greater financial compensation possible. Since persecution had involved theft and the loss of earnings and benefits, it was only reasonable that *Wiedergutmachung* tried to assess material damages and compensate victims for them.

How bureaucrats handled the process varied considerably across the country. In Cologne, for example, fewer than one in five claims for damaged health were rejected. In Düsseldorf, just a few miles down the Rhine, it was two in five. In Flensburg, in the north, it was four in five.[73] In total, some 40 percent of claims for *Wiedergutmachung* were successful, 30 percent were rejected, and 30 percent were "settled," often because people had passed away. Survivors stood a much higher chance of success if they had networks, resources, and lawyers; that was one reason only 15 percent of claims were rejected in metropolitan Berlin but 66 percent in provincial Baden-Württemberg, where the Jewish population had been less educated and professionalized. Former Nazi civil servants tended to have their pension claims processed more swiftly, but bureaucrats could also be unsympathetic to German applicants who did not strictly fit the criteria. Pastor Bernhard W., for example, had his claim returned because he had only spent four months in prison instead of the required minimum of six. Like many Jewish survivors who were turned down, he felt as if he was "punished for the second time" and protested against the "crying injustice."[74]

The problem was not only understaffed compensation bureaus, but also the staff they had. In Münster, the head of the *Wiedergutmachung* bureau had been in the resistance, but his dozen subordinates had all been Nazi Party members. Victims were often at the mercy of the same officials who had processed their exclusion from the *Volksgemeinschaft* in the first place. Not known for their flexibility or empathy at the best of times, German officials could be needlessly pedantic and coldhearted with survivors. In 1957, the compensation office in Essen, for example, asked the daughter of two German Jews murdered in Theresienstadt (Terezín) to provide proof that her parents had actually worn the yellow star between 1941 and 1943. Elsewhere, the claim on behalf of a child who had been forced to live in hiding for three years was rejected on the grounds that "primitive or poor living conditions are not beneath the dignity of man," even if the person had previously lived a better life.[75]

Not all officials were that insensitive. In Rheine (Westphalia), one caseworker went out of his way to help a Jewish woman get back on her feet. He went to the Labor Exchange to try and find her work, then to the German Red Cross, and, after that, to the local hospital—all in vain. No one wanted to hire a "Jewish" person.[76] In the light of so much hostility, what is striking about West Germany in the 1950s and 1960s is not so much that one third of all victim claims got rejected, but that the number was not higher.

For Adenauer, *Wiedergutmachung* was about accountability. Once old accounts had been settled, forgiveness could follow. This gave it a finite quality for many contemporaries, the famous *Schlussstrich*, the drawing of a line, once and for all. For the victims, by contrast, it was about guilt. Their wounds were open, and accepting compensation did not mean forgiving the perpetrators for what they had done.

Victims were split over whether to accept or reject compensation. For some, it was "blood money," impossible to accept. Others saw it as theirs by right—had the Nazis not taken away their property and health? Many families were divided. Albert Schäler and his sister Hannah grew up in Munich and survived persecution by joining their uncle in England. Their parents were killed in Auschwitz. After the war, Albert initially refused to pursue compensation: to him it was blood money. By November 1954, however, he was pleading with his sister to drop her own opposition. He was only taking "what is mine," he wrote to her. They could use the money to remember their parents or give it to a charity in their name. "The idea of negotiating with these bastards does not fill me with pleasure," he wrote, but he also felt that one needed to give the Germans "the chance to repent, even if they are only prepared to [do so to] a limited extent externally, and not at all on the inside." Schäler and his sister received 5,000 DM for their missed education—they had been banned from their local Munich school—and Albert received 1,226 DM damages for having to emigrate. For their parents, they received 5,100 DM for their imprisonment and the resulting damage to their liberty and professional career. For their parents' murder, however, they received nothing, since Albert and his sister were above the age of sixteen at the time.[77]

Compensation claims took many years. In the case of Marianne Ellenbogen (née Strauss), it was twenty.[78] In 1943, her parents were deported from Essen to Theresienstadt, where they were murdered. She survived in the underground. In 1946, she met a Jewish doctor working for the British army, married him, and left for Britain. The fate of her compensation claim is instructive for several reasons. She had the full support from other surviving family members, yet the pain of reliving the past made her repeatedly ignore her lawyers' letters. Before the war, her parents had owned several rental properties. The things most precious to her, however, were a painting and a Persian rug that had ended up with an old couple, Mr. and Mrs. Jürgens, who had brought her parents food before their deportation. For her, these were heirlooms and embodied the spirit of her parents. For the couple, however, they were presents given to them in exchange for what they considered their courageous help at a time of need. Marianne found it impossible to let go. It did not help that Mrs. Jürgens pointed out that the daughter could not have known of the gift since she was estranged from her parents at the time. One rug and a painting—not even oil, as Mrs. Jürgens noted—became spoils in a psychological war where compensation and memory were painfully entwined. Marianne Ellenbogen was not alone. In other cases, it was a grand piano or other objects that stood for a lost past. We can only properly understand *Wiedergutmachung* if we understand that possessions did not only carry monetary value but also in them "the material self" of their murdered owners.[79]

For many victims, the monthly check was more than welcome assistance in old age or poor health; it was also an official recognition of the wrong done to them and a vindication of the law. While it involved many bureaucratic hurdles, *Wiedergutmachung* was subject to law, and that made it possible for victims to complain and appeal. Letters were often written in a submissive tone, echoing the many years of persecution that had placed victims at the mercy of the state. Yet for those who had the strength to go through with it, the process marked at least a partial rehabilitation, giving them a sense of being treated as equals before the law. Fed up with delays, some victims wrote directly to the government. Such complaints were not only about frustration. They also signaled a new sense of recognition—of themselves, and of West Germany as a state that could be trusted. Edward Kossoy, a leading lawyer and himself a Nazi victim, noted how his clients began to distinguish between Germans then and Germans now. For several, it was the pursuit of their claim that made them set foot on German soil again for the first time.[80]

BEING JEWISH IN GERMANY

With *Wiedergutmachung*, the West German state relieved its citizens of the burden of confronting their personal responsibility. For most Germans, the

Luxembourg Agreement with Israel and the Claims Conference settled the issue once and for all, and appeared to be more than enough. That, in fact, it left behind a mountain of unresolved issues was barely noticed. Later negotiations with West European countries were diplomatic affairs, conducted behind closed doors. Most Germans adopted an attitude of indifference toward the victims of the Nazis. At the same time, Germany was home to a small community of Jewish survivors and displaced persons who were trying to find their feet in the land of the perpetrators. Their most immediate encounters were with small groups of Germans at opposite ends of the spectrum: one trying to drive them out with antisemitic attacks, the other wanting to embrace them with tolerance and atonement. It was in this triangle of relationships that we can observe the first signs of change in sensibility in West Germany in the 1950s and early 1960s, as well as their limits.

Could Germany after the genocide ever again be a home for Jews? For John McCloy, the U.S. high commissioner in Germany, the viability of West Germany hinged on that very question. For most international Jewish bodies, as for most survivors, the answer was a firm no. Unless disqualified by tuberculosis, the vast majority tried to leave for Israel or the United States, as did the Jews who had fled Eastern Europe after the war and were now sitting in DP camps. In 1947, when a new synagogue was consecrated in Darmstadt, all the speakers agreed that leaving for Palestine was the goal; only one of them spoke German.[81] It was mostly the sick and elderly who stayed behind. Jewish congregations had lost most of their members. In Hamburg, for example, nine thousand Jews had been murdered and fewer than seven hundred had survived. Several prominent German-Jewish thinkers and actors returned from exile and would leave their mark on cultural life in East as well as West Germany. The actors Ernst Deutsch and Curt Bois, who played the pickpocket in *Casablanca* (1942), returned from the United States to West Germany, as did the expressionist hero of the Weimar stage, Fritz Kortner—no one was able to bleed to death so convincingly, it was said. The philosopher Ernst Bloch arrived from America in East Germany in 1948 and stayed until the Berlin Wall went up in 1961. Theodor Adorno, the doyen of the Marxist Frankfurt School of critical theory, returned from California to West Germany in 1949. Their biographies, though, were entirely unrepresentative of their fellow émigrés. Of the half a million people who had fled Western Europe to escape the Nazis, only 5 percent came back in the late 1940s and 1950s. Return was the exception, not the norm, in Germany as in France and elsewhere. Just under fifteen thousand members of the Jewish community (*Glaubensjuden*) returned to Germany, plus another fifteen thousand Germans who had been persecuted for their Jewish descent.[82]

The encounter between Germans and Jews after 1945 took place in a number of sharply different settings. For Jews from Eastern Europe, it happened in and around one of the many camps for displaced persons. The barracks in Landsberg in Bavaria were home to some four thousand DPs, mainly Jews from Lithuania, Poland, and Romania. Immediately after the surrender of Nazi Germany, there had been a few instances of plunder. As elsewhere, DPs faced accusations of theft and profiteering; the black market, of course, would not have existed without many more complicit Germans. In Memmingen, in Bavaria, an antisemitic rumor of a ritual murder made the rounds in 1947. Overall, though, what is remarkable is not the friction between the communities but their relatively peaceful coexistence. Landsberg itself witnessed only one violent clash, in April 1946, when in a street fight a group of DPs attacked several Germans suspected of SS membership.[83] DP children attended local schools, and some young adults studied at universities. Jews got permission to open shops that had formerly belonged to Nazi Party members, and they hired locals to work for them. A few hundred lived in town with a German landlord. Locals did not go out of their way to help the DPs, but they tolerated them, and sometimes grew close to them. German and Jewish youth played football and danced together. After initial distrust, a young Jewish mother and her widowed German landlady decided to join forces: the mother had privileged rations; the widow knew how to get the best cuts from the local butcher and became fond of looking after the baby. An American doctor, in 1947, described how in the camps, "children have become a kind of religion, a symbol for the continued existence of a people." An old survivor from Buchenwald warned young Jews to resist the temptations of German maidens: "When our beloved Jewish girls were burned in the crematoria, their dresses were brought back to Germany, and perhaps these girls now wear their clothes and rings." Some listened, others did not. About a thousand Jews married Germans in the immediate postwar years, and some would stay behind for good.[84]

The situation was very different for the small number of German Jews who had managed to survive the Nazis inside Germany and now needed to decide whether to stay. One person in that situation was Harry Goldstein, who spoke at the commemoration of Nazi victims in Hamburg in 1945. His son Heinz had fled the city after Kristallnacht and settled in Sweden. When Heinz saw his father next, eight years later, he urged him to join him in Stockholm. He could not understand how his father could stay. He asked him, "Is it not difficult to live in a country where one does not know whether the postman, the local official, or one's neighbor is a murderer from Auschwitz?" His father refused to leave. He wanted to defy Hitler and prove that

Jewish life would continue. But he also wanted to prove himself right that not all Germans were Nazis. "God would not have destroyed Sodom," he told his son, "if only ten of the righteous had lived in that city." How could he possibly turn his back on his homeland? His entire life had been invested in Germany, and to leave now would mean to leave behind his self. In the First World War, Harry had fought for Germany in the 76th Infantry Regiment and was decorated with the Hanseatic Cross and the Iron Cross second class. Then, in the 1920s, he was active in the Imperial Federation of Jewish Front Soldiers (Reichsbund jüdischer Frontsoldaten), which combated antisemitic attacks. He was fired by his firm in 1934, but the following year he received the Honorary Cross for Front Soldiers in the name of the Führer. Into the late 1930s he was chairman of the sports group Schild (Shield) hoping to raise "strong, conscious German Jews." He survived the war thanks to being in a privileged mixed marriage. There had to be something in the Germany he loved that could be salvaged and rebuilt. On September 18, 1945, he was among the founders of the new German-Israelite congregation in Hamburg. As its chair, he oversaw the restoration of its cemetery and its synagogue and acted as a go-between for the Allied authorities and the victims of the Nuremberg laws.[85]

The few thousand Jews who had survived underground—the *U-Boote*—often felt a special obligation to their German helpers who had risked their own lives for theirs. One of them was the young Hans Rosenthal, a short man whose big jumps of joy in his quiz show *Dalli Dalli* would make him a darling of TV audiences in the 1970s. Rosenthal decided to stay in Berlin and work as a journalist to show that not all Germans were evil.[86]

For most Jews who survived in Germany, however, it was not idealism but a lack of options that made them stay. Unlike the emigrants, many of them were past the age of starting a new life. They were either married to an "Aryan" partner or had no family left. This spoke against a fresh start in a new country. Some turned to the new small Jewish congregations for support. Several survivors who had been in mixed marriages and converted to Christianity now reverted to Judaism. Contemporaries complained about so-called *Packetjuden*, who only reverted to get their hands on greater portions of rationed food. Such allegations were often unfair. One woman, for example, was forced into hiding when her Christian husband died in 1944. Earlier she had converted to Christianity on his urging. Now, after the war, she applied for readmission to the Jewish community "so that I once again know where I belong."[87]

In the early years after the war, new congregations were dominated by Eastern European Jews. In Munich, they outnumbered German Jews by three to one. Other communities were so small that they relied on Jewish volunteers from mixed marriages who had last seen the inside of a synagogue during their own bar mitzvah. By 1955, Jewish congregations had a mere fifteen thousand members in all of West Germany. By 1959, the number had risen to twenty-one thousand, partly in response to *Wiedergutmachung* and the government's efforts to encourage Jews to return from Israel.[88]

East Germany moved in the opposite direction. In the late 1940s, several Jewish intellectuals returned to East Berlin full of hope for a socialist future. One of them was the writer Alfred Kantorowicz, who had fought with the International Brigades against Franco in the Spanish civil war before emigrating to New York. He returned at the end of 1946. There was a "moral gain in Germany's defeat," he told radio audiences. Total destruction was a blessing in disguise, because they could build a new, peaceful society that did not carry the "deadly social disease" of Nazism.[89] He threw himself into the literary magazine *Ost und West* and was made a professor at Humboldt University in East Berlin. At a time of severe shortages, the regime even gave him a BMW to help him with his work as a publisher. (He had to learn to drive first.)

The honeymoon was short-lived. By 1950, the socialist regime had terminated his literary venture. At the university, free thought was being curtailed. Old comrades who had fought in Spain were silenced or removed by the party leaders. Stalinist purges, censorship, and corruption convinced Kantorowicz that the GDR was mutating into just another version of totalitarianism. The Soviet crackdown in Hungary in 1956 was the last straw. He fled to West Germany.[90] Even with some Nazis back at their desks, Adenauer's "chancellor democracy" was preferable to Ulbricht's dictatorship.

Antisemitism, anti-Zionism, and collectivization continued to prompt an exodus of Jews from East Germany. After 1965, the GDR did not have a single rabbi. When the Berlin Wall came down in November 1989, the Jewish community had shrunk to just 372 members. For East Germans, Jews had become an exotic species.[91]

Throughout Germany, the welcome for political exiles and returnees was halfhearted and conditional. Politicians pleaded with them to lend a hand in reconstruction. Their support would show the world that a new Germany was emerging from the ruins. At the same time, many Germans saw them as traitors who had abandoned their fatherland in its hour of need and had no right to lecture those who had loyally stayed behind. Many who came back encountered antisemitism. "Rootless" exiles were often automatically presumed to be Jews—including Thomas Mann, that most German and patrician of writers. Returnees were expected to chip in, not criticize. Many left disillusioned after a few years. Alfred Döblin, the author of *Berlin Alexanderplatz*, came back as "culture officer" in the French zone. By 1953, he had had enough. (Bertolt Brecht, the communist poet and playwright, tried to lure him to East Berlin. Döblin went back to Paris instead.)[92]

One area where returnees did play a critical role was the media. In the American zone, Hans Habe was the editor of the *Neue Zeitung*, which had an impressive circulation of 1.6 million. It was a democratic nursery for a whole new generation of writers, training more than forty future newspaper editors.[93] Radio Munich had Fritz Benscher, who had survived Auschwitz and Dachau. His postwar career illustrates how the Cold War and antisemitism were shrinking the space for outspoken returnees. Few survivors were able to match his guts or wit when it came to confronting Germans with their past. Benscher christened his dog "Führer" and would stun pedestrians by shouting out commands: "Führer, come; Führer, heel!" In 1947, he was producing radio programs on the liberation of the camps. Already a year later, though, his series *War, Never Again* was canceled by the Americans. Rearmament was the new imperative. Now working for Radio Bavaria, Benscher started to receive more and more antisemitic letters. And he was suspected of communism, although he was a Social Democrat. By 1950, he was subject to a formal ban on speaking (*Redeverbot*) for criticizing the Bavarian government on air; it showed how fragile freedom of speech still was in the young democracy. He eventually had a comeback in 1958, as the host of a TV quiz show.[94]

THE PERSISTENCE OF ANTISEMITISM

Antisemitism retreated only so far. In 1951, a survey asked West Germans whether it would be better if Jews emigrated. One quarter answered yes, one quarter disagreed, and the rest said they did not have a view one way or the other.[95] In the next decade, outspoken prejudice weakened but a hardcore minority remained. In 1952, 37 percent of West Germans felt it would be "better for Germany not to have Jews in the country." By 1963, this had fallen to 17 percent; still, that meant one in six Germans did not like having Jews in the country. Just as telling was the number who claimed indifference—more than 40 percent throughout the 1950s and 1960s—an attitude that would diminish only in the 1980s.[96]

Antisemitism was officially silenced, but it stuck around in many private corners, and some public ones, too. The government turned off its oxygen in political discourse relatively easily. In 1952, the Socialist Reichspartei

(SRP), a neofascist party that mocked the Holocaust as an Allied invention, was prohibited, but not before it had won several seats in state parliaments. Fascists were without a political home until 1964, when the NPD (Nationaldemokratische Partei Deutschlands) was founded.[97] Open rants against Jews became unacceptable. In December 1949, the national-conservative Deutsche Partei excluded their parliamentary member Wolfgang Hedler for repeatedly saying that people were entitled to disagree about whether gassing the Jews was the right method and that there might have been other ways to get rid of them. In Bonn, the president of the parliament banned Hedler from the assembly, before several Social Democrats literally pushed him out of the building.[98] Adenauer and Heuss invoked a shared Judeo-Christian tradition and condemned antisemitism.

Protestations in parliament did not automatically change behavior at the local level. In 1957, Ludwig Zind insulted the "half-Jewish" camp survivor Kurt Lieser in an inn in Offenburg, southwest Germany. Zind, who had been drinking heavily, shouted that Jews were to blame for Weimar's downfall and that the Nazis had been right to exterminate them. If only, he lamented, Lieser also "had gone up in the smoke." Zind was a senior teacher at the local high school and, thus, a civil servant, as well as a respected member of the community. What happened next demonstrates how thin the public veneer against antisemitism could be, and how critical pressure from media and civil society was to get the authorities to take action against it. Lieser complained first to school officials, who did nothing. He then turned to the state ministry of education, which likewise did nothing. It was only when *Der Spiegel* publicized the story that the authorities and courts took action. Zind was prosecuted for defamation. The reactions in the community were telling. Some pupils and parents had called for Zind's suspension the moment his outburst became known. Others, though, viewed him as the victim of a witch hunt. Was he a Nazi deep down or just someone who got carried away after having had a few drinks too many? In court, Zind made a point of repeating his opinions of the Jews and denied that he had been drunk, although in the course of the day he had managed to down ten glasses of beer, a bottle of sparkling wine, half a bottle of wine, and several shots of cognac and vodka. It was only once the national media turned its spotlight on the small city and the court found him guilty that the local community turned its back on him. The gymnasts' union, the hunting club, and the student corps—his social life outside the inn—all finally kicked him out. With all eyes on Offenburg, the local papers cast Zind as a deranged psychopath entirely unrepresentative of the community.[99] Zind had become an outcast, though less for his antisemitic opinions, which were well known, than because the widely publicized court case risked damaging the town's reputation.

What was sayable depended on where it was said and whether it was reported. Antisemitic prejudice continued to circulate in inns and living rooms. It became a problem only when it was exposed in the press or prosecuted in the courts. Zind was sentenced to one year in prison, but he absconded just in time and found exile in Libya.

Antisemitic attacks reached a peak over Christmas in 1959 when a number of synagogues and cemeteries were desecrated with swastikas and SS runes. Now it was not just Offenburg but West Germany as a whole that was put under the international spotlight. In Cologne, "Jews out" had been painted on the synagogue. Elsewhere, Jewish tombstones had been knocked over. In Scheinfeld, Lower Franconia, a carpenter admitted to having painted swastikas and "Down with the Jews" on the walls of the local court and sending a death threat to a Jewish pub owner.[100] The wave of vandalism threatened Adenauer's project of Western rehabilitation; that had been the intention of the KGB, the Soviet intelligence agency, which was behind several of the swastikas, as would be revealed many years later.[101] The chancellor denounced the events as a "disgrace and a crime" that would be punished with "all severity." At the same time, though, he belittled the perpetrators as stupid "louts" and declared that there was no place for antisemitism in German society.

In fact, the vandalism in 1959 was not as much of an aberration as often thought. Two years earlier, similar attacks had occurred in at least a dozen towns, and in 1950 in another eight.[102] Nor was East Germany immune—vandalism took place there, too. The difference was that for the anti-fascist GDR, antisemitism did not exist, an official myth that allowed a reservoir of racism to fill up. What the events in 1959 really showed—East and West—was that while antisemitism had been pushed underground for the most part, it proved a deep-rooted weed, and needed ongoing public and civil effort to keep it in check.

Jews continued to be stigmatized. There were small towns where only a single resident would talk to the one surviving Jew. Elsewhere, a woman had her concentration camp tattoo removed to avoid tactless remarks. Some survivors did not apply for *Wiedergutmachung* for fear of being ostracized. In Frankfurt, a survivor, with a job, committed suicide in 1953 out of despair after failing to get the local housing office to help him find a flat that would have enabled his Belgian partner and child to rejoin him.[103] In Cologne and Münster, the authorities used the public housing program to build flats for Jewish returnees, but in Düsseldorf, the city went back on its promises to do so. In 1956, the Jewish community complained about the antisemitic prejudice of the planners. New flats went disproportionately to German expellees. The twenty-eight families returning from Israel ended up in old sublets instead.[104]

Antisemitism continued to circulate in schools as well as at home. In West Berlin in 1958–59, school classes visited an exhibition on the resistance. Reporters were shocked by their ignorance. One pupil, egged on by his teacher and peers, interrupted the speaker to tell everyone that without Hitler Germany would have been overwhelmed by its enemies: the exhibition was all propaganda.[105] Several school directors said that it was too easy to blame just their parents for the antisemitic statements made by their pupils. Many denazified teachers were back at the lectern. A Berlin pastor who suffered a sleepless night after reading what pupils had written about the "Jewish Question" concluded that the country was "an infinity away from a genuine democracy."[106] We do not know what his high school students wrote, but we do know what three hundred thirteen- and fourteen-year-olds in lower Munich schools (*Volksschulen*) thought of Jews. A psychology student asked them to write an essay explaining Jewishness to an imaginary friend. In more than a third of the essays, Jews were said to be "deceitful" and "entrepreneurial." Two in three used other negative attributes and felt it would be okay if Germany stopped paying Israel compensation. Only every third student felt Jews were human like themselves. In response to the question of why Hitler had persecuted Jews, only seventeen wrote that Hitler had been wrong. On several occasions the researcher was insulted by teachers and forced to leave the classroom.[107]

East of the Elbe, the young were taught a rigorous anti-fascist curriculum, but this did not automatically translate into empathy with Jewish victims, let alone an understanding of German guilt. In 1961, a youth worker in a West German transit home for refugees reported on the reactions of teenagers who had fled East Germany and were watching the Eichmann trial on Western TV. Everything these boys and girls said, he noted, was "belittling Eichmann's crimes." He was merely following orders, they said. The youth worker pointed out that Eichmann had been at the center of the murder of the Jews and that he had volunteered for the SS. The teenagers responded that Eichmann could not have known that carrying out his orders would have these outcomes. Ultimately, they said, it was the Nazi rulers who were the responsible ones. The youth worker concluded that "the teenagers could not grasp Eichmann's guilt" and that their communist upbringing had left them unable to appreciate "the basic binding norm of the moral code that every human being has to answer for their actions."[108]

What was new in West Germany in the late 1950s and early 1960s was not the resurfacing of antisemitism but the determination of groups in civil society to fight back, educate, and commemorate. The government's center for political education distributed pamphlets on concentration camps in the 1950s and the media began to run programs on the Nazis, including a three-part series by the WDR (West German Radio) in 1957 devoted to antisemitism. A TV series on the Third Reich was watched by 15 million viewers in 1960–61.[109] Public broadcasting for schools had a series on Auschwitz. The main change, however, came from civic initiatives, community groups, and local schools. In 1957, Erich Lüth, whom we previously encountered in the boycott against the Nazi film director Veit Harlan, called on youth groups to join him in a pilgrimage to the Belsen camp. Several thousand accompanied him and laid flowers. One jazz club used all its assets to fund the trip for its young members.

The new engagement with the Nazi past is sometimes claimed for (and by) the student radicals of 1968, but it started earlier and was not the monopoly of either Marxists or hippies. In 1947, gravestones had been desecrated in the town of Salzgitter. Ten years later, a thousand youths marched with torches in protest against antisemitism. Later that year, on the anniversary of Kristallnacht, 2,500 young people joined a procession to Dachau. Organized by the trade unions, they included members of Protestant and Catholic youth groups as well as workers. These were coordinated events with institutional support, but they were complemented by a growing number of smaller grassroots initiatives. Some schools started history projects on the fate of the local Jewish community.[110] In the town of Bühl, in Baden, seventy pupils volunteered to restore the Jewish cemetery in 1958.[111]

It was these undercurrents that prepared the way for the public reaction against the antisemitic vandalism at the end of 1959. Instead of turning a blind eye or walking away in shame, youths now walked together in protest. Early in 1960, ten thousand of them marched in West Berlin with placards demanding, "*Nazis raus!*" ("Nazis out!"); they got their way with Oberländer, the minister for refugees and a former Nazi, who was forced to resign that summer, although Globke, who had drafted the race law of 1935, only left when Adenauer himself retired in 1963. In Berlin-Dahlem, the high school student committee stressed that they were no longer the Germans of 1933 and urged all pupils to inform themselves about the Nazi past, borrow books on the subject, and watch the antiwar film *The Bridge* (*Die Brücke*) and the French documentary on the camps, *Nacht und Nebel* (*Nuit et brouillard*; *Night and Fog*). The latter, directed by Alain Resnais, had caused an international scandal in 1956 when the German ambassador had asked for its withdrawal from the Cannes Film Festival because it hurt national feelings and endangered Franco-German amity. Public protests ensured that the film was shown outside the formal competition and in many German cinemas; the poet Paul Celan, whose family had been wiped out by the Nazis, was responsible for the German version of the text by Jean Cayrol, a French poet and survivor of the Mauthausen camp.

Nacht und Nebel was watched not only by radicals but also by young conservatives. In the small town of Ellwangen near Stuttgart, the Junge Union—the youth wing of Adenauer's Christian Democrats—chose it for their film evening in June 1961. A senior teacher explained that "the Jewish question became the engine of National Socialism." There were still reservations about addressing complicity directly. In a widespread formulation, the young viewers were told that few would have known nothing "of these things," but few would have known everything. At the same time, the local newspaper wrote that "when the bulldozer pushes the disfigured corpses into the ditch, then any thought of escaping from a shared responsibility vanishes." The Junge Union watched the horrific footage in West Berlin, too. Their invited speaker was Ferdinand Friedensburg, an MP and founding member of the CDU. While their own parents might have been misled by Hitler, he said, there were "tens of thousands of Germans who had actively participated in the atrocities." With a barely disguised nod in the direction of Globke in Bonn, Friedensburg added that "just because someone does not deserve to be in prison does not mean they should occupy a high office of state."[112]

RECONCILIATION AND ITS LIMITS

Slowly, the churches were also examining their position toward the Jews. In 1951, at a commemoration in Munich, the novelist Luise Rinser—who had been denounced and imprisoned for undermining military morale at the end of the war, which she recounted in her *Prison Journal* (1946)—had urged the churches to acknowledge their guilt for preaching revenge against the Jews for centuries.[113] At the time, her words fell on deaf ears. By 1960, however, in the wake of the desecration of Jewish cemeteries, the Protestant Church openly called on congregations to show solidarity with their Jewish neighbors. Some Protestants traced the roots of antisemitism to Christian anti-Judaism. Gas chambers and war crimes began to be mentioned in church newsletters. The Eichmann trial prompted a rethinking among Christians in East as well as West Germany. In the West, Catholic churches held prayer services for murdered Jews, civilians, and their perpetrators. The last now included all those who had been "complicit through their actions, inaction, or silence."[114] In 1962, 500 Catholic boy scouts visited the Ardeatine Caves outside Rome, where the Nazis had murdered 350 Italian civilians, and gave a confession "to the guilt arising from the German past." They left a sacrificial candle and wreath as signs of atonement. On Pentecost, in the ruins of the Colosseum, they added a commemoration for the victims of the Lidice massacre in Poland in 1942.[115] In both East and West, Protestants were asking themselves whether the mission of converting Jews to Christianity was any longer defensible after Germans had murdered 6 million of them.

In the GDR, the first commemoration of Kristallnacht took place in 1963—acknowledging "complicity through silence or toleration." In Halberstadt in the district of Magdeburg that year, the Good Friday prayers remembered the persecution of the Jews, and a group of Protestants made contact with survivors from Halberstadt now living in Israel. A few of the remaining Jews in East Germany began to give lectures to Christian congregations, but the space for such initiatives remained circumscribed by the GDR's official hostility to Israel. In 1982, Halberstadt erected a memorial for victims of the Nazis. It remembered both the Jews deported from the city and the civilians killed by Allied bombing. There was no Jewish congregation left to attend the ceremony.[116]

In West Germany, efforts at reconciliation between Germans and Jews were led by two bodies: the Society for Christian-Jewish Cooperation (Gesellschaft für Christlich-Jüdische Zusammenarbeit, GCJZ) and Aktion Sühnezeichen, an initiative for atonement; the latter also had an East German section. Taking its inspiration from the International Council of Christians and Jews, the GCJZ sought to promote greater tolerance through dialogue and awareness. From 1951 on, it organized an annual "week of brotherliness," with public speeches and events. By 1954, it counted two thousand members—Erich Lüth was one of them—and had branches across West Germany. In the small city of Kassel, the local branch organized fifty-five showings of *Nacht und Nebel* in 1958, watched by more than five thousand people. It worked with schools, and was among the first to invite survivors to speak publicly about their ordeals. On June 29, 1960, the camp survivor Werner Schnitzlein spoke to high school students in Charlottenburg in West Berlin. Local Jewish pupils were invited and sang songs in Hebrew. An elementary school in Berlin Neukölln heard accounts of Kristallnacht and life in the Riga Ghetto. During the week of brotherliness in 1961, pupils in Wilmersdorf read *Nathan der Weise* (1779), Gotthold Ephraim Lessing's play about religious toleration, and *The SS-State* (1946), the seminal account of the camp system by the Buchenwald survivor and Christian Socialist Eugen Kogon. They also went to an exhibition on the Nazi era. Next door, the high school in Charlottenburg extended the activities over forty weeks, with screenings of *Nacht und Nebel* and the twelve episodes on the Third Reich produced by Berlin's broadcaster RIAS.[117]

The spirit guiding these events was that of the Enlightenment, with its universal ideals of humanity and toleration. The Nazi past became a lesson to confront and overcome prejudice and racism in the present, at home and abroad. In the Spandau borough of West Berlin, a speaker reported on race problems in Ohio and ended by singing "a Negro song." How children of color were treated in Germany was identified to be the "touchstone of humanity." The GCJZ encouraged adoptions of mixed-race children and distributed booklets such as "Maxi, Our Negro-boy." These may fall well short of today's conversation about race, but at the time, they at least tried to solicit greater empathy, including for the children of African American GIs facing discrimination. There were also donation drives for the local elderly and for partner children in India. In the early 1970s, the GCJZ began to turn its attention to prejudice against the children of migrant "guest workers."[118]

Ultimately, these initiatives revealed just how difficult it was to rebuild bridges between Germans and Jews. In 1959, one teacher in Berlin took his pupils to a dialogue with their Jewish peers in the Jewish community hall. It did not go as planned. "The discussion was unsatisfactory," he noted afterward, "and the Jewish children were bitter and criticized the faults of the history lessons." In another school, a teacher was told by a student that *Wiedergutmachung* posed a threat to the Deutschmark. For the next lesson, the teacher returned with the original list of property confiscated by the Gestapo: "That's how the problem was solved," he assured like-minded colleagues. It is doubtful he was correct. In 1959, the GCJZ invited student editors of school newspapers to tea. The aspiring journalists confessed that they knew hardly anything about the society or its work. They also said that they "learned nothing from their teachers about the recent past." A film about the Nuremberg trials moved them, but they said they felt that "the Jewish dialogue is not so important right now. There are many more important things."[119]

The GCJZ protested against antisemitism and lenient sentences for perpetrators, but its battle against general indifference was an uphill struggle. In 1964, the Cologne section of the society looked back on its activities over the previous year and reached a sobering verdict. It relied almost entirely on a small core of committed members—forty-five of them traveled on a special trip to Israel that year. Overall, people in Cologne were "barely interested or not interested at all" in their work. The only popular events were those with a famous speaker. The dominant view was "I cannot change it anyway." "Self-righteousness, prejudice, and ignorance" were widespread, not only in society at large but also among their own members. For six years, they had worked hard to develop good relations with the local synagogue, but still only 10 percent of its congregation had joined their section.[120] By and large, the Jewish community and their fellow German citizens were keeping their distance from each other.

The stage provided the GCJZ with one way of bringing Germans and Jews together. The prize for the best new play in its competition in 1957 went to *Ein Rest Kehrt Um* (*A Few Turned Back*) by the actor Friedrich Kolander. In the play, the pianist Klimsch, a young SS guard in a concentration camp, stumbles upon a Jewish girl, Naemi, outside the camp. They begin to talk about good and evil, and guilt. The "pure, childlike, and devout" Naemi gives Klimsch the strength to follow his individual conscience instead of Nazi orders. She takes him to her family's secret hiding place. While her father, a rabbi, curses all Germans, Klimsch shares his bread with her brother. Naemi is killed by a Russian bullet. Her brother survives. After the war, the Jewish survivor and the former SS man meet again in a piano bar. Klimsch convinces the brother that Naemi did not die for nothing, bequeathing them the spirit of reconciliation. The play was shown in schools and army barracks as well as theaters, and also became a radio play. A theater agent summarized audience responses for the GCJZ: There was "contemplative quiet in the packed stalls. At the end, silence... and then hearty long applause." Some whispered during the play, "We have never seen anything like that before—how truthful it all is." After the show, members of the Jewish community thanked the author.[121]

Such reactions were not entirely surprising, for Jewish characters and their persecution were almost completely absent from German drama and literature after the war. A rare exception was *Ehe im Schatten* (*Marriage in the Shadows*), a film produced in the Soviet zone in 1947. Based on the true story of the actor Joachim Gottschalk and his Jewish wife, it recounted the tragic fate of a mixed marriage under the Nazis. Gottschalk had been a romantic lead on the silver screen until Goebbels heard of his marriage and ordered him to get a divorce. Gottschalk refused and asked to be deported together with his wife and their eight-year-old son to Theresienstadt. Goebbels gave him his marching orders to Russia instead. On November 6, 1941, with the Gestapo on its way, Gottschalk and his wife switched on the gas in the oven, killing themselves and their son.

The way the film told this tragic story was typical of how Germans after the war were ultimately searching for their own absolution rather than for empathy with their Jewish victims. Tellingly, the film was dedicated only to Gottschalk, and the main story is his path to suicide. It confirmed many Germans' wishful thinking that it was impossible to help Jews and that those who had tried ended up dead. Individual suicide was a popular motif in postwar movies and allowed viewers to close the chapter of their complicit past as if that subject had been done and dusted by 1945.[122]

One of the few books featuring Jewish characters was Heinrich Böll's early novel *Wo Warst Du, Adam?* (*And Where Were You, Adam?*) (1951). One of the characters is a tailor living in squalor surrounded by flies drowning in a greasy bowl of cucumber salad—an antisemitic image—the other, the pure maiden Ilona, who is befriended by the ordinary German soldier Feinhals. Ilona, although a Jew in Nazi eyes, is a devout Catholic, murdered by a deranged SS camp commandant when he hears her angelic voice. Feinhals manages to make his way home in the final stages of the war, only to be killed by a bomb on his own doorstep. Both are victims in a pointless war. In the following decades Böll would advance into the moral conscience of the new Germany and win the Nobel Prize for Literature. In the 1950s, however, *And Where Were You, Adam?* sold just a few hundred copies.[123]

While Böll at least mentioned the concentration camps, they featured as little more than a violent sideshow. In the following year, Erich Maria Remarque made the camp the center of his novel *Der Funke Leben* (*Spark of Life*). The main characters are political prisoners, but there are Jews as well; two are brutally strangled by an SS officer in the spring of 1945. Remarque had reached global fame with his antiwar novel *All Quiet on the Western Front* in 1929. He escaped the Nazis, first to Switzerland and then to the United States. His story of the camp was slammed by German reviewers. *Die Zeit* considered the book "irresponsible." *Der Spiegel* scorned it as a "portrait of the camps by someone-who-had-not-been-there for those-who-had-not-been-there: a stereotype out of a test tube"—the "there" referring not to the camps as such but to Germany as a whole, whose ordeal, it was said, émigré authors could not possibly understand. Only the weekly German-Jewish newspaper praised the book: Remarque was able to picture the camp, it said, precisely because he had not had to live through it. In Remarque's next book, his publisher cut out from the German edition those passages where German soldiers described themselves as murderers. As Remarque commented, Germans could be extremely generous, especially when it came to forgetting their own crimes.[124]

Remarque dedicated *Der Funke Leben* to his sister, who had been beheaded by the Nazis in December 1943 for declaring the war to be lost. Survivor literature took even longer to find readers in West Germany. In 1948, Paul Celan wrote a poetic monument to the murdered Jews with *Todesfuge* (*Death Fugue*). It includes the famous line "Death is a master from Germany, his eyes are blue." Celan was virtually unknown, and marginalized. When, in 1952, he read the poem to Gruppe 47, an influential literary circle, he was mocked for the unusual singsong of his recital. Celan would not return after that. While Gruppe 47 did include a few Jewish writers, several of its key figures, such as Walter Jens, had been members of the Nazi Party, and many had served in the war, including Günter Grass, who went to the Waffen-SS at the age of seventeen. There was little self-reflection among these writers about their own role in Nazi Germany and even less interest in hearing a Jewish author speak to them about German atrocities. For that, most German readers would have to wait until the 1960s. Primo Levi's *If This Is a Man*, for example, first published in 1947, would only be translated into German in 1961.[125]

A best seller on the camps did appear in East Germany: Bruno Apitz's *Nackt Unter Wölfen* (*Naked Among Wolves*), in 1958. In the next ten years, it went through fifty-eight editions and sold more than 1 million copies. It was compulsory reading in East German schools. From 1961 on, it was also available in West Germany. The film adaptation, directed by Frank Beyer in 1963, became a GDR classic. Supposedly based on real events, the story is set in the early spring of 1945 in Buchenwald, where Apitz himself had spent eight years as a communist prisoner. The arrival of a three-year-old Jewish child, smuggled inside a suitcase by a Jewish prisoner, confronts the communist prisoners with a moral dilemma: hide the boy and save his life but put their own at risk, or hand him over to the SS to protect their resistance network. They decide to save the boy. Not even torture makes the prisoners give up information about him or their comrades. As the Red Army is approaching, the prisoners liberate the camp from the inside with smuggled weapons and free the child and their fellow inmates.

Even in this story, though, the Jewish child is little more than a prop for good Germans. The boy has no agency and is treated more as a pet than a person by the prisoners "like a friendly puppy"; "like a beetle," "little maybug."

In 1963, it was sensationally discovered that the actual boy (Stefan Jerzy Zweig) had survived and was living as a student in Lyon. Zweig moved to the GDR the following year and was used by the regime as living proof of the Buchenwald story and the communist self-liberation from the fascists. It was a powerful foundation myth. The reality was more awkward. Zweig had not been secretly smuggled into the camp but had arrived in Buchenwald together with his Jewish father; his mother and sister had been murdered in Auschwitz. He survived, it was revealed later, thanks to being swapped by the prisoners with a Sinti boy who was sent to Auschwitz instead. Inside the camp, some Jewish prisoners actually suffered at the hands of communist inmates. And Buchenwald, in fact, was liberated by the U.S. 3rd Army.[126]

To get a sense of how West Germans in the 1950s were thinking about Jews and themselves, it is helpful to look beyond famous authors. In the archives of the Society for Christian-Jewish Cooperation, summaries survive for several unsuccessful plays that amateurs submitted to its 1957 competition. They make for troubling reading. One play carried the promising title *In the Name of Human Rights*. It turns out to be about an SS man who kills his officer to save a Jewish girl from death. He is sentenced to death in turn. She tries to free him with the help of partisans but he—a "model of integrity"—refuses, since he is a proper soldier and they are not. As he walks toward his execution, she runs up to him and joins him in death. The society's jury rejected the play as "naive" and "completely out of the question," but, clearly, this author thought he had captured the spirit of German-Jewish reconciliation. *The Wide Path*, another entry, is about a hate-filled Jew who is out to avenge the murder of his wife in a mass execution. In the course of his pursuit, he realizes that the SS man who had ordered the execution was not evil after all: he had saved the husband and later shot the camp commander and was "in reality a through-and-through noble character." In the end, the daughter of the Jew and the son of the SS man fall in love. The evil Jew was effectively saved by the good German. Guilt—ordering a mass shooting—was washed away by later good deeds. The play was written by a forty-nine-year-old teacher who would have been twenty-five when Hitler came to power. A local official from the same generation submitted his drama *The Angel of the Lord*, in which a young soldier in Russia has his conscience rebel when, after partisan attacks, his comrades begin to wipe out an entire village. On guard duty, he frees the surviving prisoners. Instead of fleeing himself, however, he insists on being put before a military court: his good deed would otherwise lose its ethical value.[127]

The GCJZ may have looked for inspiration to Lessing and the Enlightenment spirit of *Nathan der Weise*. But what these plays show is that for many contemporaries, right and wrong continued to be framed in terms of duty, not liberty and human dignity. These plays were, of course, fictional fantasies and far removed from the brutal reality of the war. But that is also what makes them so revealing. To their authors and their imagined audiences, they performed a moral cleansing that washed away anything bad Germans had done prior to the sudden awakening of their conscience in the face of love or barbarism. The encounter with a Jewish girl reveals the human heart beating inside the Nazi uniform. How a cultured pianist came to put on a SS uniform in the first place is not part of the story. The literary yearning to rehabilitate SS men and even camp guards manifested itself at the same time as lobbies of Waffen-SS veterans were pushing to be included alongside veterans of the regular army in the ever-longer list of victims of the war. These plays acknowledged evil, but mainly to highlight German virtue. Perpetrators turn into saviors. German soldiers die for Jews and civilians, following in the footsteps of Christ. The central motif of these plays was that Germans deserved to be forgiven. The works were not a search for reconciliation but rather the redemption of the German soul.

The play West Germans got to see more than any other was *The Diary of Anne Frank*, a dramatic rendering of her family's 761 days in hiding before their arrest on August 4, 1944; they would be deported to Auschwitz and Belsen, where Anne died in March 1945. Almost 2 million people saw the play in the late 1950s. Even those who missed it were able to quote Anne's famous last words of the play: "In spite of everything, I still believe that people are really good at heart." Together, the book and play made Anne Frank the human face of the Holocaust.

The first Dutch edition of her diary appeared in 1947, followed by a German translation in 1950. The Fischer paperback appeared in 1955; five years later it had sold 750,000 copies. There were public readings—Erich Lüth chaired them for the GCJZ in Hamburg—and high school students recommended the diary as essential reading to their peers. All these editions, however, were truncated, polished versions of the original diary, which Anne's father, Otto, who survived, had edited to remove sensitive passages he felt damaged Anne's memory and that of the family; a complete critical edition would only appear in 1986. Otto cut not only Anne's criticisms of her mother and her accounts of her own sexual awakening, but also her sense of betrayal by adults who had lost their moral authority yet kept preaching about right and wrong. Changes also minimized the collective role of the Germans. "The Germans" sometimes became "the occupying power." That her father had written German poems and Anne's mother had given her a German prayer book also disappeared from the published edition. To German readers, it obscured just how much Anne and her family had been one of them.[128]

The stage play went one step further and excised her knowledge of the deportations and the gas chambers. Audiences only saw Anne in the secret annex in Prinsengracht until the moment of her discovery and imminent arrest. They did not have to follow her to her death in Bergen-Belsen but could go home with the soothing sound of her final words. Her actual diary spoke of the evil in man as well. Hatred, violence, and aggression, she wrote, existed among ordinary people as well as political leaders and capitalists, and would continue unless humanity underwent a metamorphosis. Instead, it was Anne Frank who underwent a posthumous metamorphosis. Her darker thoughts and her fate as a Jewish victim easily vanished in her beatification as the universal victim with a universal message of hope.

The play's extraordinary success in the land of the perpetrators registered just how much Germans were looking to identify with Anne as a child and innocent victim, and, equally, how much they felt they should be forgiven. When, in the closing scene, Anne's voice was heard from the beyond expressing her faith in the good of humanity, what German audiences heard was that they, deep down, were good too. The play made it possible for them to engage with the Nazi past by focusing on the victims without having to look at the perpetrators or themselves; significantly, no German SS or police ever appear onstage. Newspapers saw in Anne Frank a "martyr for the love of mankind and charity." Teenagers put up Anne Frank's pictures in their bedrooms and wore Anne Frank blouses. "She has become a part of myself," one girl told a journalist, "I no longer know where I start and where Anne ends... I feel that God has created Anne for a purpose, and with her diary she walks like a guiding angel through my life and that of many others." Not everyone was swept away by the sensational success. One journalist observed that, in the end, all the play did was to arouse "anonymous compassion." It let people fall into a comfortable sentimentality instead of shaking them up to act. One lady in the stalls, he wrote, was "constantly sighing 'poor child, poor child' while simultaneously eating one praline after another."[129]

If East Germans had the Jewish child of Buchenwald for their myth of communist self-liberation, West Germans had Anne Frank with her apparent promise of universal humanity. Nonetheless, her *Diary* was an important step in confronting the Nazi past. The youth pilgrimages to Bergen-Belsen were a direct result of the play and public readings of the *Diary*. In 1957, Lüth called on the young who had traveled with him there to show more courage than their elders and overcome racial hatred. A seventeen-year-old German girl promised that her generation would reach out to Jewish youth. She was followed by a young Israeli who, quoting Anne Frank, urged them all to believe in "the good in people." The next speaker was a twenty-eight-year-old man who outed himself as a former Hitler Youth member who had been consumed by such shame that he moved to Israel in 1948, converted to Judaism, and worked on a kibbutz.[130] For others, though, Anne Frank pointed less to the Nazis than across the Iron Curtain as a warning against communists. In 1962, at Frankfurt University's annual Anne Frank commemoration,

Werner Hess, the head of the regional broadcaster, took listeners from the concentration camps and the German expellees straight to the Berlin Wall, erected the year before. "Once again," he told them, "the dead are hanging in barbed wire in Germany, the innocent, the unknown, people like you and me or Anne Frank." Anne Frank had become everyone.[131]

ATONEMENT

These were speeches, warnings, and declarations of faith. A more hands-on group was Aktion Sühnezeichen, which sent volunteers to work in Europe and Israel. Established in 1958 by the Protestant Church in East and West Germany, this organization today carries the formal English name Action Reconciliation Service for Peace. This clunky title does not quite capture its original mission. The founding fathers were, in the East, Lothar Kreyssig, a leading official of the Protestant Church in Magdeburg, and, in the West, Franz von Hammerstein, a pastor in West Berlin. Kreyssig was the one judge who had dared to stand up to the Nazis and challenge the killing of adults and children with intellectual disabilities. Perturbed by the sudden death of several of his wards, Kreyssig in 1940 filed a murder complaint against Philip Bouhler, the head of the euthanasia program. When Kreyssig refused to back down, he was sent into early retirement. In Hammerstein's case, his father had been the head of the German army command and the one senior officer to resign in protest of Hitler in 1934. Franz was confirmed by Martin Niemöller. Blind in one eye, von Hammerstein was exempt from military service, but two of his brothers were connected to the officers' resistance, and the family was arrested and imprisoned after the failed assassination attempt on Hitler's life on July 20, 1944.

In 1958, at their Synod, a kind of church parliament, where Protestants from both parts of the country still came together, Kreyssig in a call for action said that Germans had murdered millions of Jews and that the guilt extended to those who had been bystanders. It reopened the guilt question in the church. Peace, Kreyssig argued, would only come once Germans confronted their past. Reconciliation was the ultimate goal, but it was also a reciprocal act between the guilty and their victims. Since Germans were the guilty ones, it fell to them to show humility first. "*Sühne*" (atonement) had to come from the guilty. Sending a sign of atonement became the name and mission of Aktion Sühnezeichen. The establishment of the Aktion coincided with the Ulm trial of the Einsatzgruppen. For the founders, harsher sentences were important for confirming guilt, but not enough to promote reconciliation. Atonement went beyond the official policy of *Wiedergutmachung.* Whereas compensation payments appeared to pay down guilt, atonement assumed that humans were unable ever to relieve themselves of that burden. Ultimately, only God's grace could save them. All humans could do was work for peace and reconciliation, following in the footsteps of Christ.[132]

There had been isolated instances of atonement immediately after the Second World War that were often short-lived. In 1947, a group of Catholics erected a thirteen-foot-tall oak cross "in atonement for the murder of eighty foreign forced laborers" of the Warstein massacre we encountered previously. The cross was barely up when locals attacked it with axes and fire. Inhabitants felt the cross soiled the good name of their town and feared it might attract revenge. *They* had not murdered them, so why should they atone? Others went further: "Not eighty, but eight hundred Russians should have been killed." To save it, the cross had to be buried in a secret earth mound and would only be excavated in 1964, before finally being moved to the local church in 1981.[133]

The crosses in Aachen and Bühl fared better. These also called for repentance, but their guiding spirit was a general yearning for peace and less a specific confrontation with German guilt. In 1947, returning POWs carried a thirteen-foot-tall cross through bombed Krefeld and then on to Aachen, where more than 100,000 Catholics joined the procession. Three years later, the cross was blessed in Rome by Pope Pius XII. The cross in Bühl looked across the Rhine to Franco-German reconciliation. On the French side, it was sponsored by the bishop of Lourdes, Théas of Montauban, who had been in a concentration camp for speaking out against the deportation of the Jews. On the German side, support for reconciliation was linked to a campaign seeking the acquittal of a local soldier whose army unit had been collectively sentenced for the infamous massacre of civilians at Oradour-sur-Glane in June 1944; his advocates showed that he had been on leave at the time.[134]

At Bergen, a Catholic "church of atonement of the precious blood" was consecrated in 1961 as an "everlasting sacrifice to atone for all guilt, past, present, and future." We have earlier seen how Germans took on the mantle of victims. Now Nazi victims were enlisted in the Christian story of sacrifice and grace. The altar is shaped in the form of a grave, a reminder of the 100,000 corpses of Jews, POWs, and other prisoners confronting the arriving Allies in 1945. The artist who designed the bronze fourteen Stations of the Cross, Joseph Hauke, took inspiration from the pictures of dead camp prisoners. Their suffering, the bishop of Hildesheim preached at the foundation ceremony, was not "in vain." Had not Christ, a prisoner himself, atoned for our sins through his sacrifice? Over the tabernacle, a mosaic shows "the lamb of God" (Christ) with its blood flowing into the chalice. The ground plan of the church is that of a chalice opening toward the concentration camp. It is as if the victims murdered by the Nazis are called to follow the example set by Christ in the spirit of the *Imitatio Christi*. The living faithful are asked to atone for the sins of the perpetrators. The victims, however, like Christ, also appear to have to atone for sins, in this case those of the Germans.[135]

Aktion Sühnezeichen went beyond praying and pilgrimages. It put morality into practice. Its spiritual impulse was to do active service for the victims and the needy; to work together; to be humble, not self-righteous; to take others seriously; and to learn from dialogue. Reconciliation would happen through working and sweating together in building and restoration projects in countries that had suffered under Nazi Germany. In 1959, the first West German group left for the Netherlands and built a vacation camp for poor families from Rotterdam. Water irrigation systems in Crete, the site of mass executions, followed. In 1963, volunteers rebuilt a synagogue in Villeurbanne near Lyon in France, where they stayed with Jewish families. In the following year, the first groups went to Israel.

The Iron Curtain fenced in the eastern members of the organization and limited its operations. Atonement had no place in the official anti-fascist mind-set, which, after all, exonerated East Germany from any guilt. In the first few years, work camps were only tolerated on church premises, such as the clearing of rubble of the bombed churches in Magdeburg. Then, in 1965, Catholic chaplains took a group of teenagers to Auschwitz, where they worked to expose the foundations of the gas chambers. Within the GDR itself, Christian groups were only allowed to work at the Buchenwald site starting in 1979. As it happens, that was the same year when local authorities in the West, after years of resistance, permitted volunteers to do restoration work in the Dachau camp, near Munich.

Aktion Sühnezeichen was founded by devout Protestants who had lived and suffered under the Nazis. What, though, did atonement mean to the Germans who volunteered to do peace work in the 1960s but who were too young to have any memories of Hitler? In 1968, the Aktion had around six thousand members. The average age of the 256 volunteers who worked on projects in Czechoslavakia, Poland, and Israel was twenty-four, evenly made up of pupils, artisans, and clerks. Diaries, letters, and reports give us a glimpse of how they saw themselves. One young man described their visit to an exhibition about ghettos and concentration camps during their work in Israel in the autumn of 1964. The pictures and objects were "accusing us," he wrote. The photo of a small boy tortured by SS men caught his special attention. The resemblance with his own brother made him identify with the victims. It was at that moment, he wrote, that he grasped the "enormity of the destruction of people who could have been just as well one's brothers and sisters." "If I had not been so ashamed, I would have run out of the exhibition to tell the next Jew how much I regretted what had happened." He pondered: Was it even possible to atone for something in the past that had been so inhumane? Yes, he concluded, as long as one recognized the possibility of atonement as the enormous grace held out by God.[136]

A year later, two German boys and a girl were invited during their stay in Israel to the home of an Israeli professor. Earlier that day, after an "extraordinarily long" discussion about collective guilt, the group unanimously concluded that only atonement could pave the way to reconciliation. When their Israeli host wondered whether "we had the right to criticize our parents and accuse them," the young Germans told him they had not only the right but the duty to call guilt by its name.[137]

One volunteer in his early twenties was asked so many times in 1965 why he had come to Israel that he wrote an entire essay. "My answer is this: Why did my father fall in the Second World War?" His mother, he continued, told him about Hitler and "about Jews and concentration camps." In high school, he had learned about the Nazi period, began to read books about Jews and Israel, and decided to write his dissertation on Jews in modern Germany. The West German government, he acknowledged, paid *Wiedergutmachung*, but that did not cover even the material damage. Otherwise it followed realpolitik and forgot about the survivors. Still, he wrote,

> I am a German; I am implicated [*mitbetroffen*] in what grows out of the Germans; I am implicated by being part of German culture and ideas and sharing with them the same language, same origin, and same fate . . . I feel I have a share not only in what my contemporaries do but also in what has been handed down. I have to take on the guilt of the fathers. I accept complicity for the mental conditions of German life that made it possible to support such a regime.

Aktion Sühnezeichen enabled him to walk up to the victims, ask for "forgiveness," and promote "reconciliation." Günter Lorenz was another volunteer. For him, in Birkenau in October 1967, pulling out the weeds from the destroyed crematorium II was simultaneously tearing out the grass that had been allowed to grow over the Nazi past after 1945.[138]

Not everyone was so high-minded. In September 1968, two Aktion groups arrived in Auschwitz-Birkenau for a fortnight of work, mostly at the end of the "*Rampe*," the platform of arrival and selection where those deemed fit to work had been separated from those being sent to their deaths. The young Germans started their day by reading *The Investigation*, a play by Peter Weiss based on the Auschwitz trials in Frankfurt a few years earlier. Several of the boys and girls felt sick listening. Then, after breakfast, they worked for seven to thirteen hours, tackling weeds in the gas chambers of the crematoria II, III, and IV. They found buttons, dentures, children's shoes, and other personal items. In the evenings, topics of conversation ranged from Poland to the Vietnam War. The two weeks were not without problems, the group leader noted. "The work morale of some participants left much to be desired. Some clearly imagined they were on a study tour, mainly wanted to get to know Poles, and saw in their work in Auschwitz a somewhat annoying secondary matter." One young man, born in nearby Gliwice (Gleiwitz), announced one day that he "no longer felt like working" and instead went to the Upper Silesian town to take photographs of his father's former shop. He was evicted from the group. In general, the group leader concluded, "Participants found it difficult to understand that Auschwitz did not only pose a question about the guilt of our fathers but also came with a mission for us to take responsibility for what happens today and tomorrow and to fight the demon [*Ungeist*] which gave rise to Auschwitz and is still alive."[139]

The public reception of these exercises in atonement was decidedly mixed. The Eichmann trial in 1961 gave Aktion Sühnezeichen a fresh opportunity. Posters at subway stations confronted citizens: "The Eichmann trial is a warning! For how much longer will we not come to terms with the past? Action is our response." There were speeches at the Berlin congress center. The movement could count on support from the head of the trade unions and the senator for youth as well as from like-minded pastors. Some states urged schools to include the Aktion's work in their citizenship lessons. But there was resistance, too. Anonymous letters denounced them as "traitors."[140]

In November 1965, ten boys and girls returned from Dachau, where they had helped with the construction of the church of reconciliation (*Versöhnungskirche*). One boy summarized their experience: "All in all, the group met a unanimous rejection from the construction worker to the bishop... I think we must thoroughly reconsider on what sites we will be able to work in the next few years in Germany."[141] The following March, a group of twenty volunteers returned from Israel. In Ulm, in southern Germany, the local youth wanted to hear about their experiences and invited them to the *Donaukeller*, the Catholic youth's rustic wine cellar. The evening began in a "very cheerful and initially almost exuberant atmosphere." They soon realized "how far apart our members are from 'normal' youth." The young

Catholic chaplain took them aside and told them, "Your ideas are good. Your approach is right, but no one wants to hear it, no one wants to change, and no one wants to leave their comfort zone."[142] In 1967, Aktion volunteers returning from Israel talked to 3,800 pupils in vocational schools in their civics and religion classes. The "overwhelming majority" of the students were unconvinced by their work. An internal report summarized the negative responses: the students had "no relationship to the past, or its legacy; time heals everything; the guilt of the others; also pronounced resignation: What difference does your work make?"[143]

The idea behind Aktion Sühnezeichen was that the young generation carried a moral responsibility and needed to demonstrate their willingness to atone through service and sacrifice. But moral responsibility for what exactly? And work for what purpose? By the mid-1960s, the movement was split on these questions. Some wanted to keep the focus on the Nazis and on healing the wounds of the past. Others pushed for a more forward-looking approach.[144] Youth should not just be burdened with a sense of guilt for the crimes of their elders but be given a chance to create a culture of nonviolence for the future.

The Aktion was responding to growing competition for the attention of youth from groups who were discovering the "Third World," the Vietnam War, and peace politics. Confronting the past became increasingly linked to political responsibility and action in the present, with several significant consequences. One concerned the nature of volunteer work. Sweating on building sites increasingly gave way to caring for the vulnerable: for children, the elderly, disabled people, and drug addicts. Creating habits of empathy, tolerance, and nonviolence for disadvantaged groups in the present was seen as critical for peace as clearing the weeds from a violent past. The change in mission was reflected in the name of the organization: "Service for Peace" was added to "Reconciliation."

Dialogue with foreigners was a central aspect of the work camps, but letters and diaries show that working on oneself was at least as important. Volunteers had their conscience almost constantly tested by the question of what they would have done if they had stood on the *Rampe*. Here, the Eichmann trial was particularly important, because it served as a warning to the present, extending responsibility from perpetrators to the young. "What can I do to prevent today's German youth from consisting of lots of '*Eichmänner*'?" a volunteer working in Rotterdam in 1967 asked in his diary.[145] For many, the struggle began with themselves: they had to expel the "Hitler in us" and promote a peaceful personality.[146]

Aktion Sühnezeichen seminars traced the Holocaust back to the French

Revolution and stressed its modern, technological characteristics, but when it came to explaining why Auschwitz had happened in Germany, the answer swung to psychology, not history or sociology. "We believe," Aktion groups said at the annual meeting in 1967, "that the social system is a photograph of the mental-spiritual structure of the majority." Without the "fanatical fetishism and blind obedience" of the German mentality, "Auschwitz would have been unthinkable."[147] Their work in Auschwitz could not remain a quiet act of devotion for the victims of fascism but needed to be a psychological struggle to free themselves from oppressive patterns of thought. After hours of pulling weeds from its crematoria, volunteers in 1968 were reminded that Auschwitz, "far from belonging to the past," was "never a more burning" problem in a world consumed by "war, hatred, and genocide." In March that year, the Aktion called for demonstrations against the "genocide" in Vietnam. Their generation, they said, had their own Auschwitz with the atomic bomb and Vietnam.[148]

An initiative that had started out from a position of humility, with young Germans asking the victims of German crimes to allow them to perform acts of atonement in search of reconciliation, had ended up with self-assured Germans appropriating the Holocaust in order to purify themselves. The focus was not on the 6 million murdered Jews and the concrete situation of their suffering but on the human psyche now, and in general. As one of the new generation of Germans wrote, "Auschwitz is in me—in each of us. Auschwitz—that is our egotism, our indifference, our silence." More than a name, it was a "phenomenon" and it had happened in Mỹ Lai, Santiago de Chile, and many other places. It was not just something in the past, but their own reality.[149]

The rise of a psychological meaning of Auschwitz, rather than a historical one, had odd consequences. On the one hand, since the Holocaust was lurking everywhere, it made volunteering in the service for peace more urgent than ever. On the other hand, by making it everyone's business, it also threatened to lift it out of the specifically German context of guilt and atonement. In 1996, at an international seminar for volunteers organized by the Aktion, the question was "carefully" put whether making atonement the "exclusive right" of Germans was not itself another form of "fascism" by downgrading volunteers from other countries. Did German youth have more to atone for than their French, Polish, Hungarian, Norwegian, and Dutch peers, because via their nationality they had to "pay off" a guilt that their elders had committed thirty-five years before they were born? Some participants invoked universal rights and argued that as human beings they were entitled to do volunteer service anywhere in order to learn from the past. It was not a German monopoly. One volunteer even warned of the danger of continuing a "blood-and-race-ideology."[150] The seminar was held at Neuengamme, the site of the concentration camp outside Hamburg.

Wiedergutmachung changed the moral landscape of postwar Germany. The enormity of German crimes was such that compensation could never be more than a partial aspiration. That still left plenty to be decided: about the aims of compensation, its terms, and, above all, who was in charge of it. Each of these underwent a radical redefinition in the immediate postwar years. Early on, there were attempts at personal retribution: guilty Nazis should compensate their victims. This came closest to fusing a legal, financial, and moral settlement and promised victims the public satisfaction that their wrongdoers would be punished for crimes they had committed. However, the sheer scale of German crimes and complicity meant that personal reckoning was never a realistic method. Instead, in the early 1950s, *Wiedergutmachung* became a matter between Nazi victims and the West German state. This was also hedged with exclusions (nothing for non-German victims or war-related destruction), but camp survivors who had German roots were entitled to pensions and compensation What happened to morality in this transfer of accountability from individual guilt to public purse? It certainly got many guilty Germans off the hook personally and made it easy for the even larger number of bystanders to avoid uncomfortable questions about their own complicity, now that the state had taken over responsibility. Forced laborers, Sinti and Roma, and other victim groups were banished from the collective conscience. Socialist East Germany circumvented individual claims altogether and limited compensation to collective reparations to the Soviet Union.

The story is rich in failures, obstructions, and injustices. Still, it would be wrong to view it as one of complete amoralization. Few victims got the satisfaction of their tormentors showing remorse. Yet, compensation payments were not entirely anonymous transactions, either. Many victims saw compensation—however slow, partial, and painful the process—as an official recognition that they had been wronged and that justice was being restored. For the Federal Republic, in turn, *Wiedergutmachung* was a central piece of its newfound public morality. Morality and realpolitik have often been treated as enemies, but in the case of Adenauer's Germany they were symbiotic, both working to integrate the new country in the West. At home, *Wiedergutmachung* was part of a package of social integration that simultaneously rehabilitated denazified civil servants and compensated Germans for their losses in the war. Survivors received compensation, but only once Germans had recognized themselves as deserving victims. This has a sordid taste. From a political perspective, though, it is doubtful whether one would have happened without the other. By taking over their claims, the new state managed to pay Jewish survivors without punishing and alienating large numbers of former Nazis. At the time, many Germans hoped that public compensation would draw a line under guilt in their moral ledger, once and for all. In fact, over the next few decades, the opposite happened, and *Wiedergutmachung* deserves some of the credit for that. It was easier to confront the past and talk about guilt and reconciliation once the state had taken over public accountability for Nazi crimes, people had regained their footing in life, and the majority of Germans no longer had to worry about personal retribution.

What remained rare was atonement. As the Austrian-Jewish and Israeli philosopher Martin Buber wrote at the time, true atonement (*Sühne*) involved more than cleansing one's soul: it required a person to change their relationship to the world.[151] This was a journey that only a few Germans had begun.

PART TWO

ONE NATION, TWO STATES

1949-89

5

The House of Democracy: Liberal, Within Limits

Building a democratic country on the ruins of fascism was not easy. In July 1948, the Western Allies started the work by empowering the premiers in their occupied zones to call an assembly to work out a democratic constitution. With the resulting Basic Law (Grundgesetz) in 1949, West Germany laid strong foundations. The new constitution protected citizens against the state. "Human dignity shall be inviolable," announced the first sentence. Every person was guaranteed the right to the free development of their personality, freedom of expression, freedom of association, and equality before the law, including equal rights for men and women. These basic rights were declared to be inalienable and "directly applicable law" (Article 1/3). At the time, it was tempting to present these rights as a break with the constitution of the failed Weimar Republic, even though Weimar had already breathed legal and administrative force into several of these core freedoms and some jurists were invoking a "social constitutional state" (*sozialer Rechtsstaat*).[1] The decisive contrast with Weimar was that now the government was made fully dependent on parliament—in a crisis, power could not be delegated to a president or plebiscite. A federal structure of states (*Länder*) checked the concentration of power at the center. It was a "militant democracy" that would fight anyone wishing to destroy it.

Why this democratic structure is still standing depends on one's view of the foundations, the architects, and the builders—but also of the residents. Recent historians have stressed that quite a few Germans brought democratic skills with them to the task. Most of the constitutional "fathers" of 1948–49 had sat in Weimar's national or provincial assemblies and the four "mothers," who made "the actual implementation" of the equality of the sexes a duty of the new state (Basic Law 3/2), had already campaigned for women's rights in the 1920s. Before that, in imperial Germany, elected delegates had debated in the Reichstag. And before that, there were the constitutions of Westphalia (1807), Bavaria (1818), and other states during the Napoleonic period and in the abortive revolution of 1848. After unification, in 1871, the imperial Reichstag was directly elected by "one *man*, one vote"—one of the most progressive systems in Europe. Before the First World War, Germans were increasingly contesting elections and making noise about undue interference. There was a rich culture of clubs and associations. The historian Hedwig Richter has even suggested that "National Socialism grew out of a democracy and democratic traditions that were well over a hundred years old."[2]

That goes too far. The Nazis were enemies of democracy, and one reason they succeeded was that they had the support of old elites. That Germany was not destined to end up with Hitler does not mean it did not nurture powerful anti-democratic elements that, in a crisis, destabilized and destroyed the Weimar Republic. Imperial Germany had a strong state and monarch as well as a Reichstag, and it was the monarch who controlled the vital matter of war and peace. Authoritarian elites could exploit what the historian Heinrich August Winkler has called the "German *Ur-Angst* of chaos and civil war."[3] It was fed by the speed of industrialization, social change, and political unification in the late nineteenth century.[4] Rights and liberties became expendable for the sake of order and stability. Fear of unrest and division expressed low levels of trust between citizens. The German problem was not that there were no democrats but that there were plenty of others ready to overthrow them; together, communists and fascists won one third of the vote in the 1930 election and half in the elections of 1932.

To build a stable democratic home after the Second World War therefore required more than the repurposing of old building materials. The architects of the constitution recognized this when they discarded presidential powers and built in safeguards against wreckers. While built on strong foundations, however, the democracy they handed over to West Germans in 1949 was still little more than a shell. Turning it into a space of lived democracy depended on the residents as well as the builders, and came with the challenge of moral reorientation. Democratic culture depends on certain civic habits and ethical dispositions, including respect for others, living with difference, debate and persuasion, active participation, and a commitment to equality. These were not givens but had to be cultivated, and sometimes fought for.

MAKING DEMOCRATS

Neither the Allies nor the Germans had any illusions about the uphill struggle involved in making democrats out of a people who only a few years earlier had cheered Hitler. When it came to the word "democracy," Theodor Heuss said in 1946, "the Germans needed to go back to the first letter and learn how to spell it out."[5] Bishop Dibelius who had initially supported Hitler and was antisemitic but who later stood up for freedom of religion (although he was never active in the resistance), declared democracy to be an "alien ideology." Suspicion of it was widespread in the population. The twenty-one-year-old Gerhard Schulz, a young teacher and future historian, wrote in his diary in 1946 that "the word democracy is a lie": it always hid some other interest. For him, the essential German conflict was that between a Führer and "the mass." The solution was community (*Gemeinschaft*). Hitler's error, in his view, was that he made community an end in itself, at the expense of personality. The worst problem, he wrote a year later, was "the German Mensch": "It is so difficult to trust him."[6]

In autumn 1951, German pollsters asked people to pick the era during which they thought their country had been best off: 45 percent chose the years under the Kaiser before the First World War and 42 percent chose those under Hitler before the Second World War; only 2 percent chose the democratic present.[7] A year earlier, Americans found that 70 percent of German youth had no interest in politics; 40 percent did not know that Konrad Adenauer was chancellor. Their trust in democratic self-government was low, and most refused to take on any political responsibility. Asked to choose between economic security and personal liberties, most opted for the former; on this point, the young were even more emphatic than their parents. Many championed a single united youth movement as the best way to get heard (a quarter wanted it to be uniformed as well). Pluralism and democracy would only further complicate an already complicated situation: the monolithic will of the people would accomplish more. In a 1952 survey by the American High Commission, 72 percent of German adults said they could learn from other countries while 88 percent felt that foreign countries could also learn from Germany. Most wanted to learn about American science and technology, but only 17 percent were interested in U.S. politics. If democratic culture is about listening, learning from others, and getting engaged, there was a long way to go.[8]

Respect for personal liberties did not arise naturally after the Nazis were gone. Citizens denounced black-marketeering neighbors as "social parasites" (*Volksschädling*) and wanted a former camp prisoner thrown into a workhouse for sleeping with British soldiers.[9] In 1948, the occupation authorities studied police actions in a dozen cities in southwest Germany. In more than 90 percent of the cases, the police had searched people's homes without a warrant. When interviewed, police officers said they saw no problem with that: they were responsible for order, after all. Just as troublingly, many citizens agreed. They showed no sense that their rights had been infringed in any way. On the contrary, 40 percent said that under the Nazis, the police had guaranteed greater safety.[10]

Americans with a deep knowledge of Germany expressed their doubts about the country's democratic potential. The historian Carl Schorske, who had worked for American intelligence, thought the odds were stacked against it because of class conflict and late unification. Five years after the war, George Kennan, the father of containment strategy in the Cold War, warned that "the German people are still politically immature."[11] In the early 1950s, the U.S. high commissioner for Germany worried about authoritarian tendencies. Adenauer's Germany seemed to be a state of civil servants, without much of an opposition or a critical public sphere.

What these snapshots could not reveal was that underneath the apathy, the cultivation of democratic habits was underway. Schools and public meetings, the family, firms, and community centers acted as "nurseries of democracy"—in the felicitous phrase of the nineteenth-century thinker Alexis de Tocqueville—teaching Germans to debate, take on joint responsibility, and respect each other as partners.

"Talking is silver, silence is gold" emerged as a prominent motto in the nineteenth century. In 1947, ninth graders in Lower Saxony changed it in their school magazine to "Talking is silver, debating is gold."[12] Instead of evading disagreement by retreating into silence, the new ideal was to argue out differences and to criticize and persuade until the best, informed position was reached. This did not come easily. In 1947, a high school student lamented that their debates too often resembled "a wrestling match... where half those present vehemently try to hold on to their point of view" rather than engage with the other side.[13] American officials introduced town hall meetings, only to find that mayors and teachers would use them for long lectures to a captive audience; an observer called them "mutual admiration societies."[14] Still, there were those who felt it was worth persisting. The university student Hildegard Prinz watched an "English debate" in 1946 and compared it to "a kind of fencing with a blunt rapier." "They tackle serious topics lightly and solve problems with trust, and, yet, shed light on all the ideas from all possible angles: I think we can learn something from this custom." A seventeen-year-old girl in Lower Saxony initially refused to participate in a discussion group organized by the British because they had removed her father from his teaching post. She was stunned when her decision was met with tolerance instead of punishment. Within a year, she had become a regular debater and appreciated how everyone was treated as an equal.[15]

Public debates and press conferences taught people to share opinions more freely. Participants set up parent-teacher associations and civil rights committees. Starting in 1950, the Cologne train station hosted "Wednesday discussions" that attracted several hundred people each week. The Protestant academies of Bad Boll and Loccum added their own series of public conferences. The discussion culture benefited from official support via the Federal Center for Civic Education, which sponsored, among others, seminars for returning POWs to win them over to democratic reconstruction.[16] The undisputed star of the new debating culture was Werner Höfer, whose *Der Internationale Frühschoppen*, a German version of the American television program *Meet the Press*, first aired in 1952. His radio and TV show developed into a national ritual, followed by the Sunday roast. At its peak, one in five adults tuned in. Its extraordinary run came to a sudden end in 1987 when Höfer's past caught up with him: in 1943, he had written an article defending the execution of the pianist Karlrobert Kreiten for defeatist remarks.[17]

It is, perhaps, no coincidence that the concept of the "public sphere"—an arena where free discussion shapes public opinion—was popularized by a German intellectual: Jürgen Habermas. His life's work has been devoted to the idea of communicative action as a rational exchange that fosters social integration and mutual understanding. In 1953, the then-twenty-three-year-old student wrote a long letter to a weekly newspaper in which he championed open debate as the best way to select independent-minded democratic representatives.[18] By 1962, the year his *Transformation of the Public Sphere* was published, a more discursive approach had become a mainstream position and the young Conservative Helmut Kohl confronted the old Chancellor Adenauer to demand fewer speeches and more time for discussion at party conferences.[19]

Young Germans who had grown up under Hitler took away different lessons from the collapse of the Thousand-Year Reich. While some turned their back on all things political, others made democratic engagement their life's mission, including Heinrich Böll (born in 1917), Jürgen Habermas (1929, a *Jungvolkführer* and leader of a junior section of the Hitler Youth), the historians Martin Broszat (1926, Hitler Youth) and Hans-Ulrich Wehler (1931, also Hitler Youth). Reeducation camps and student exchange programs with the United States and Great Britain were important nurseries for this new democratic spirit. One of them was at Wilton Park, west of London. Initially set up for POWs, beginning in 1947 it offered seminars for select young students.

Many of its graduates would shape the Bonn Republic: the Social Democrat Hans-Jochen Vogel, a minister under Willy Brandt and Helmut Schmidt; the Christian Democrat Rainer Barzel, who lost the battle for the chancellorship to Brandt; and the Anglophile Liberal (later Lord) Ralf Dahrendorf. From the late 1940s, some 2,000 students went to the United States every year. Many returned as ambassadors of lived democracy and established debating clubs and student newspapers, and held elections for student representatives. By one estimate, each exchange student came into contact with 150 fellow Germans. Back from Michigan, a young man in the Ruhr organized seminars promoting German-American friendship and set up a discussion circle in a local school. It was called "Democracy in Action."[20]

There was an inverse relationship between this democratic energy and the style of politics. After Hitler, political parties and emotional appeals were viewed with deep suspicion. As one voter told an SPD official after the first general election in 1949, "I reject your party, because it is a party."[21] Nor could any of the mainstream parties in Germany build on the mythical aura of resistance that mobilized voters in Italy and France after the war. Notwithstanding forceful rhetoric, elections were fairly sober affairs where candidates avoided anything that smelled either of propaganda or Americanization. In post-fascist Italy, election campaigns were battled out in town squares. In post-fascist Germany, they were conducted indoors.[22] One communist was killed in the election of 1949, and here and there a few cars had their tires slashed in later ones, but this was a far cry from the political violence a generation earlier when on a single day in 1932 eighteen people had been killed in the city of Altona, Hamburg's western neighbor, alone. Facts and reason were taking the place of fists and pistols.

The more sober style was assisted by the erosion of the homogeneous milieus of the main parties as well as by the exclusion of extremist ones. On the Conservative side, the Allies prevented the Catholic Center Party from regaining its former strength, enabling the CDU to become a home for Protestants as well as Catholics. The working-class SPD gradually morphed into a people's party; already in the late 1940s, it began to absorb expellees and disillusioned members of the Hitler Youth. In the mining town of Kamen in North Rhine–Westphalia, for example, the SPD managed to recruit five times as many members in 1950 as it had in 1932.[23] Parties were opening up, and this encouraged a more open, tolerant style. The economic miracle and expansion of education, and the new professional and service jobs that came with them, completed this process.

Schools played a critical role in democratic education. There was a widespread view that the Germans' national cult of obedience had made them the submissive tools of the Nazis. This was a convenient fiction. Many people *chose* to vote for Hitler in 1930 and 1932 and become perpetrators. Still, it was a powerful myth, and the diagnosis of deference to authority as a peculiarly German disease demanded the disinfection of the classroom in which it was bred. In fact, German classrooms were probably no more or less authoritarian than French ones. In 1947, the Allies ruled that schools should teach "civic responsibility and a democratic way of life." School councils, student newspapers, and elections for student parliaments followed. Several states made it a constitutional requirement to teach citizenship. Not surprisingly, these initiatives were viewed with suspicion by old teachers and former Nazi party members who returned to their desks after the amnesty of 1951. Still, the momentum was with the civic side. A female teacher applied in her school in Berlin what she had observed in the United States: "Children must be taught to rely on themselves and form their own opinion."[24] Educational reformers took their inspiration from the American pragmatist philosopher John Dewey, for whom democratic habits were cultivated through learning by doing. Returning émigrés brought back adult education and civics lessons from Sweden. "Partnership," "tolerance," and "cooperation" were key words in the reformers' dictionary. A new course found its way into the curriculum: *Gemeinschaftskunde*, often rendered as "social science" but literally meaning "the study of community." The author of a school textbook in 1955 defined the goal of education as promoting "all the virtues of human togetherness and living for each other." This required teaching "respect for their fellow men . . . camaraderie, readiness to help, open exchange and compromise."[25]

In reality, citizenship in the 1950s came with only partial responsibility, not full rights and liberties. Pupils might organize festivals and ensure that classrooms were tidy, but the authorities decided what students were taught, although some student representatives did succeed in introducing lessons dedicated to public affairs.[26] Some schools gave pupils the chance to voice their concerns to teachers. The civic virtues preached were tolerance and self-discipline, not equal rights, let alone civil disobedience. Yet partial progress is still progress. By the early 1960s, there was broad agreement among headmasters and politicians that censorship of student newspapers was impermissible, and several states recognized the autonomy of student representatives.[27]

In the workplace, democracy's advance was limited. After the war, trade unions had pressed for a full-scale democratic overhaul of the economy to give equal rights to labor and capital and prevent the concentration of power in the hands of the few. A key demand was "codetermination" (*Mitbestimmung*), giving employees a say in how companies were run. In 1951, needing the unions' support for his Western integration into the European Coal and Steel Community, Adenauer granted them equal seats on the board of directors in those two industries. That was it, however. Other sectors did see work councils elected by the employees the following year, but they had no say over hiring and firing, investment, or management. The councils, nonetheless, performed an important function as intermediaries between employees and employers. Instead of class conflict, a culture of compromise and cooperation took root—the success of the "German model" or "Rhineland capitalism."

Harmony was the reward reaped from the economic miracle, the unique period of high growth between the early 1950s and early 1970s. In the course of the 1950s, the country's GDP tripled and exports more than quadrupled. Car production increased tenfold in the 1950s and 1960s. At Volkswagen, the number of workers rose from 25,000 in 1953 to 125,000 in 1970, at Daimler-Benz, from 35,000 to 100,000. It might be thought that the great demand for labor would have enabled trade unions to take on the bosses and threaten strikes, but the opposite was the case. Volkswagen and other big firms grew by absorbing expellees and people from the countryside who came from outside the world of organized labor. The boom turned people's eyes toward private comfort, away from collective struggle. If an extra shift paid good money, why abolish it? (In 1960, Volkswagen was partially privatized.)

The big unions opted for peace to let the economic cake grow so that everyone would enjoy a larger slice. Wildcat strikes in the 1950s were quickly shut down. Work councils, meanwhile, concerned themselves with vacation pay, company housing, bonuses for loyalty and extra hours, and the food in the canteen—here democratic participation took over areas that had previously been the gifts of paternalist bosses. Volkswagen introduced the five-day workweek in 1957, and the forty-hour workweek in 1966. A hard-fought expansion of codetermination came ten years later, when a law forced 480 big companies with more than 2,000 employees to elect new boards of directors and add worker representatives. This did not match the full parity of the coal and steel industries, since the bosses chose the chairman of the board who had the casting vote in case of a tie.[28]

The spirit behind codetermination left its mark on society more widely. Communities came to champion group work and self-governance in their leisure activities. Charitable centers had appeared in German cities, as elsewhere, in the late nineteenth century. The Nazis abolished them or took them over. After the war, so-called neighborhood homes (*Nachbarschaftsheime*) were reborn with the help of American and British Quakers. Mittelhof, in

West Berlin, had ten full-time staff and thirty-five volunteers. It attracted more than five thousand people every month, especially young folk. A hundred people came to "social lunch" every day. These homes offered libraries, sewing courses, and evening dances, and were a place to meet international students. Members would regularly get together to discuss the activities of their respective group. Each group elected its own leader. The federation of the neighborhood homes explained its philosophy of "democratic group management":

> The group program is being planned and designed by the group, and not the leader alone ... The leader is keen to make the group independent and to give each member an incentive to cultivate their abilities. Taking over responsibility is being practiced and encouraged ... That way, the leader helps the group member to gain a certain position and respect in the community he has chosen. The leader allows tensions and rivalries to be carried out in a fair manner ... he shows restraint with his own opinions.

In Berlin-Neukölln, locals and the YMCA built their community center out of an army barracks in Dahlem, which they dismantled and carried across town; they cleaned forty thousand bricks in the process. The center opened its doors in 1951. The budget came from self-generated income in addition to help from the city and foreign sponsors. It was home to sixty-four groups, from football and amateur theater to those visiting Frederick the Great's summer palace at Sanssouci in Potsdam. By 1958, it had a "Free Self-Help" committee that distributed secondhand clothing and a Rock 'n' Roll Club, where, for 20 pfennigs an evening, members could listen to records and their own skiffle band.[29]

Greater equality and respect were also the hallmark of new approaches to welfare. The Social Democratic Arbeiterwohlfahrt (AWO), a welfare association, started to hold seminars with the Community Services Society from New York City in 1949. Social workers felt uneasy about the labels "guardian" (*Betreuer*) and "person in need" (*Hilfsbedürftiger*). The "helping relationship" needed to become a "genuine partnership." A better term, they suggested, was "client" (*Klient*). From the first meeting, the client needed to be approached "on the same level, from human being to human being," and that was only possible "if we recognize that he has a right to help." In this way, "the client is being included in the process of assistance." Instead of over-identification, let alone pity, social workers needed to offer reciprocity. "Those searching for assistance will feel that we respect them as human beings, that we do not criticize or judge them for their difficulties, and that we trust them." In the words of one teacher and social worker, they were learning to "make our clients into our helpers."[30]

Respect extended to a plurality of values. At a conference in 1954, social pedagogues concluded that, since the war, values had "mostly been lost or become problematic." Instead of trying to restore them, they should recognize that "each individual has their own inner lawfulness" and should have "full freedom in deciding which values to adopt." It was misguided to try to steer an individual toward a fixed ideal. Instead, "the goal of education has to be to develop an individual's endowments and capabilities" so as to enable them to "grow" as a person and live with one another.[31] Young people did not only have a right to education—as they did during the Weimar years—but also had a right to being educated as citizens. For volunteers, helping others was a chance to "practice tolerance" and learn to "acknowledge the often contrary opinions and attitude of others."[32] AWO social workers used group work to help children develop "responsibility for their peers and the community" and turn them into "active and conscious citizens." By 1969, the homeless were included in "team talks" and had their own representatives.[33]

Social rights were anchored in law and policy. Benefits became entitlements to which citizens had a right, a paradigm shift that was sealed by the democratic spirit of the Federal Social Assistance Act of 1961 (Bundessozialhilfegesetz). While reforms had their antecedents in Weimar, it was the Basic Law of 1949 that put the force of the constitution behind them, with its emphasis on the fundamental right to life and dignity. The new right of citizens vis-à-vis the state was upheld in several test cases. In 1953, for example, Emma B. moved to a Catholic care home after a stroke. The local authorities wanted to put her in a cheaper home run by the state. The court in Hanover found in the widow's favor: to move her to a different home would be an interference in "the personal freedom of the person in need." Such cases had the backing of the free welfare associations and the organized religions, which had their own interests in protecting their homes and hospitals against the state. In a democratic state, people could not be shipped about "against their will like parcels in the mail," the head of the Protestant Inner Mission said. The state had to respect their human rights. In 1954, the highest administrative court (Bundesverwaltungsgericht) ruled that "while the individual was subject to public authority, it was as a citizen, not as a subject." A citizen could not be the "mere object of state action."

Instead, they had to be recognized as "an autonomous and ethically responsible personality and hence as a carrier of rights and duties."[34]

PATRIARCHY AND ITS LIMITS

The democratic challenge to authority in the public arena had its equivalent in the private sphere. The patriarchal father was the head of the family. For Catholics, his authority was even divinely ordained. Turning subjects into citizens began to shake at the self-understanding of power and subordination within the family.

The 1950s are often invoked as musty years of restoration, even reaction. For CDU Family Minister Franz-Josef Wuermeling, large families were bulwarks against communism, teaching sacrifice and discipline; he and his wife had five children themselves.[35] Beginning in 1954, families received benefits on the birth of their third child, although these were modest compared to pro-natalist France; second children brought benefits from 1961 on. A Protestant handbook warned in 1954 that single children suffered from their parents' excessive attention and ended up nervous, hypersensitive egotists. Children, it said, had a right to siblings. Plenty of children were also better for the mother because she then had no time to waste on her own beauty or other people: "Hysteria and neurasthenic conditions were an alien concept to her."[36]

Such voices, however, were countered by growing support for a more democratic family. Public commentators, family advisers, and, indeed, church leaders argued that democracy started at home. It was patriarchy and iron discipline that had turned children into concentration camp guards. Instead of being based on fear, paternal authority needed to be earned through trust. The heterosexual nuclear family remained the norm, but husband and wife were increasingly expected to be partners. Although the idea of woman's natural inferiority had not vanished, her contribution during the war and reconstruction made it more tenuous. At the Catholic conference in 1954, a leading priest said a woman should be a "comrade" and contribute her advice "in all matters."[37] Catholic newspapers called for "democratic fatherhood," movies idolized caring dads, and handbooks and advice columns told them to listen to their children, play with them, and even change their diapers.[38]

The family was in flux. A sociologist studied a thousand families in Darmstadt between 1949 and 1951. One quarter showed a "strong dominance of the man," but another quarter tended toward equality; the rest were in between. A growing number of children picked their profession themselves or in consultation with their parents. A young female student said she was raised with a "certain independence." Her father insisted that "she needs to make her own experiences. That way, she learns the most."[39] The student felt it impossible to say who in her family had the decisive word. Returning soldiers threw themselves into family life. Before the war, one former POW said, he had wanted his eldest son to be "as tough as leather and as hard as Krupp steel." But now, in 1951, he saw him as a "softer, dreamy, and musically gifted boy," and that was for the better. The man had grown close to his children and took an active interest in their talents and education. He treasured their joint excursions when the children pointed out to him each new flower and animal. In the family of an artisan, the child called his parents by their first name and was allowed to bring his friends home. The family "rejected any form of strict authority and blind obedience" and instead wanted to develop "the distinct... and independent personality of the child."[40] Spanking had not disappeared, but it was on the decline and more and more parents felt bad when administering it.

The advance of such democratic ideals stopped short of altering more deeply rooted gender roles. The discovery of the caring father did little for all the mothers who continued to do the bulk of housework and caregiving, looking after their frail parents as well as their own children. It was only in 1959 that the Constitutional Court took away from fathers the final say over their children's education. Many other inequalities persisted. Abortion was only allowed under certain circumstances and continued to be illegal in the Federal Republic after a reform effort failed in 1976, while the GDR had already relaxed it and (in 1972) legalized it.[41] Fathers were more likely to invest in their sons' education than their daughters', who were expected to marry a breadwinner. More women were going to work—4.8 million in 1950, 6.2 million by 1957—and by 1961 every third married woman had a paid job, though a lot of those were part-time jobs in shops and services.

In 1960, the women's magazine *Constanze* celebrated part-time work as the best way to stay young. If taking up a paid job had initially been motivated by need or the desire for a bit of discretionary income, women—including married women—saw it increasingly as a chance to get out into the world and develop their own personality.[42] In 1966, the government's official report on the condition of women still assumed that children and the household were female responsibilities. At the same time, it recognized the growing variety of women's roles and the appeal of professional work for "self-realization" and a "sense of performing a qualified piece of work"; it even quoted the French feminist Simone de Beauvoir in support of these notions. For a solution to these competing pressures, officials looked to a three-phase life cycle where women resumed their job after raising their little ones. This model was nothing peculiarly German but rather the international vogue, inspired by the Swedish and Austro-British social scientists Alva Myrdal and Viola Klein.[43]

There was greater tolerance toward unmarried couples and mothers with illegitimate children. The war left behind many widows and orphans. Unmarried partners in so-called uncle marriages defied the ideal of the "complete family" (*Vollfamilie*); tying the knot would have lost such couples one of their two pensions. The change in sexual practices was ongoing a decade before the birth control pill arrived in Germany in the early 1960s. (It was initially only prescribed to married women who already had several children.) When Adenauer attacked "Herr [Willy] Brandt alias Frahm" in the election campaign in 1961, the reference to the SPD politician's illegitimate birth backfired and ended up hurting the chancellor, not Brandt. Even in rural areas, people stopped following the Catholic teaching on sex as being all about procreation. "And if we love each other, what then?" a working-class woman asked a researcher in 1962. "It cannot be sin," her husband agreed. Women saw it as an "absolute impertinence" when priests approached mothers with a single child in the street, wanting to know, "When will you get a little sibling?" Catholic women stopped going to church, to avoid confession.[44]

For women, the advance toward greater equality at work and in the family was merely one step forward. In 1965, women made up only 7 percent of all delegates in parliament. That year, twice as many men said they would be displeased rather than happy if a woman became politically active; significantly, many women agreed.[45]

LIBERALISM AND ITS LIMITS

By the mid-1960s, West Germans had settled into democracy. The economic miracle helped. In 1963, 62 percent felt that the country's best time was the present, and only 10 percent and 16 percent were still nostalgic either for the years under Hitler before the war or for those under the Kaiser (42 percent and 45 percent in 1951). In 1967, 74 percent saw democracy as the best form of government, and only 4 percent thought another system might be better; 22 percent were undecided. Survey after survey showed that West Germans were becoming more interested and knowledgable about politics. Turnout in national elections reached 88 percent in the 1960s. When it came to raising children, independence and free will were considered more important than obedience and deference by the late 1950s. Social trust was rising, too, although from a very low base: in 1948 only 8 percent felt that most people could be trusted; in 1967 it was 26 percent.[46]

In 1947, two years before the Basic Law was enacted, Dolf Sternberger, a student of Karl Jaspers's and an influential political thinker and writer, wrote that the idea of a "fatherland only comes true in its free constitution—not only in the written but in the lived constitution which all citizens . . . share in daily and cultivate ourselves."[47] In the 1970s, this idea would become known as "constitutional patriotism." What filled most people with pride, however, was the strength of the Deutschmark, not the political system. Notwithstanding the many discussion clubs, Germans continued to struggle with the plurality of ideas and interests, at least when compared to Britons and Americans. In 1968, more than a quarter believed that a conflict between different groups hurt the public interest. In parliament, the opposition was meant to support the government, not criticize it, let alone bring it down. Police violence against demonstrators was condemned, more so than in Britain, France, or the United States. At the same time, Germans continued to find it difficult to live with difference and were comparatively more prepared to sacrifice freedom of speech if public order was at risk.[48] Almost one in three Germans thought that if there was a threat to public order, citizens should lose the right to strike and demonstrate.[49] In their essays, young sergeants in the Bundeswehr worried about the triumph of a "mass" mind unless democracy trained a new political elite.[50]

By the late 1960s, then, democracy demonstrated impressive stability. Hardly anyone wanted to tear it down. Parliament, parties, and elections were secure. However, not all democratic habits and values had been established. A considerable number of residents viewed diversity and critique with suspicion, and this, in turn, reflected a low view of the dignity, rights, and freedoms of their fellow citizens.

Two events in the late 1960s shine a disturbing light on the significant minority unmoved by the democratic spirit of the constitution. In 1969, a clerk in a small town was killed by several bullets. With little to go on except that the murderer probably wore a black anorak, the police turned to the public for help. More than seven hundred citizens obliged with their suspicions. They denounced a neighbor because he wore fashionable clothes and drank too much; a colleague who "asked four times for an advance because he was so wasteful"; a young man who played guitar in a "wild" band; and two "guys" who looked "like Italians or Spaniards" and had "the face of jailbirds." Others alerted the police to the local baker because he was a member of a shooting club; a teenager who had thrown bottles at their house seven years earlier; the assistant forester who had a communist uncle; a truck driver who skipped work and hence was a "type capable of anything"; people with dirty shoes or holes in their sweaters, and many others whose lifestyle deviated from the norms of decency and order. Apparently, it was a short step from expensive clothes, Mediterranean looks, and a lack of thrift to murder. Several of these people had to prove their innocence to the police.[51]

Two years later, in 1971, a sadist and serial killer who had abused and murdered four boys near Wuppertal, and who had been a minor when he committed the crimes, had his life sentence reduced to ten years in a psychiatric sanatorium. There was a public outcry. Hundreds of citizens wrote letters calling for the death sentence—which the Basic Law had abolished but which was in use in the GDR. The man should be "tied up... and tortured," one demanded. "Under Hitler, such things did not happen," another wrote.[52] Some called for the gas chamber, or at least a concentration camp. There was little respect for the rights of the murderer (despite his having been a minor), his mental state, or his traumatic upbringing—his foster parents had kept him behind bars in a basement room, fearful that he would otherwise learn he was not their biological child. At the original trial, experts had declared him to be *compos mentis*, and it needed a legal battle to establish his diminished responsibility. In the end, the convicted murderer, who married his nurse, died in 1976 of an anesthetic overdose in the course of surgical castration.

The Federal Republic was a liberal democracy with illiberal elements, no less so than older democracies like the United States and France.

TAKING ON THE STATE

"Jesus has risen, happiness and gratitude accompany this day; the revolution, the decisive revolution in the history of the world has taken place, the revolution of the world through all-transcending love."[53] The author of this diary entry on Easter 1963 was Rudi Dutschke, the leader of the 1968 student revolt in Germany. Born in 1940 and raised in East Germany, the pacifist Dutschke moved to West Berlin in August 1961, three days before the Wall went up. From 1965 onward he was organizing protests against the Vietnam War, imperialism, and the two-headed monster of capitalism-fascism. Following in the footsteps of Jesus, he wanted a revolution in this world, not the next. On April 11, 1968, Dutschke was shot in the head by a young casual laborer who was carrying a right-wing newspaper. Dutschke died eleven years later from damage to the brain, just thirty-nine years old. It was later revealed that the attacker had been in contact with neo-Nazis.

Nineteen sixty-eight was a transnational phenomenon. Everywhere students saw themselves as part of a global struggle against capitalism and colonialism. Germany had a sizable community of students from Iran, Egypt, and Angola who pulled their peers along in protests against foreign dictators, including Moise Tshombe from the Congo and the shah of Iran, during their visits to Bonn and West Berlin in the 1960s.[54] Vietnam was not some place far away; it was in Germany, too. Dutschke translated *Create Two, Three, Many Vietnams* (1966) by Ernesto "Che" Guevara, who at the time was training guerrilla fighters in the Congo. Yet Berlin was not Paris or Berkeley.[55]

As the words from Dutschke's diary make clear, Protestantism injected a special moral fervor into the students' struggle. Ulrike Meinhof, who in 1969 swapped her journalist pen for the bombs of the terrorist Red Army Faction (RAF), was remembered by a fellow student as a Protestant girl who played the recorder and said her prayers before lunch.[56] There was a deep belief in moral righteousness as well as a conviction that the emancipation of humanity was nigh and rested on one's own shoulders. The student radicals took over the politics of conscience developed in the peace movement—Meinhof started her career protesting against nuclear weapons—and pushed them to the extreme: to overcome violence in all its guises, violent resistance was necessary and justified. The attack on authority was total. The progressive Jürgen Habermas sensed "left fascism" and distanced himself from the radicals, while the conservative thinker Arnold Gehlen railed against their "hypermorality." Both had a point. Beyond the communist utopias of Karl Marx and Mao Zedong, the radicals should be placed in a longer tradition of Protestant fanatics in the sixteenth century and millenarians since then who believed they could rid *this* world of states and power and usher in the kingdom of God on earth.[57]

The idea of a generational conflict, on the other hand, needs to be taken with a large pinch of salt. The protestors were a tiny portion of their age cohort. The demonstration against the shah's visit to Berlin on June 2, 1967, a key event during which the student Benno Ohnesorg was shot dead by a policeman, involved a few thousand protestors. A year later, fifty thousand joined the central march on Bonn to protest against the imminent emergency law, which gave the state special powers to interfere in basic rights, such as privacy and the freedom to choose one's occupation, in an internal as well as external emergency. More Germans under the age of thirty supported the emergency law than opposed it. Three quarters of them saw politics as something negative, according to a major youth study in 1967. The

Catholic youth movement found their peers too "well behaved" and "virtually abstemious, politically and socially."[58]

Conversely, quite a few older Germans were sympathetic to at least some of the protestors' demands, such as reforming the universities. The radicals targeted old Nazis in the state, rarely their own fathers. Interviews then and since suggest that most families lived in harmony, not in a state of civil war. Many protestors could count on support from their parents, who had often been peace and leftist activists themselves. One of the students arrested for distributing flyers against the shah's impending visit was Judith Olek. Her father, a lifelong Social Democrat who had briefly been imprisoned in Belsen, went to the police and secured her release, and then had a doctor examine her bruises and hematomas, and encouraged her to press charges. Young radicals found sympathetic allies among an older generation of teachers and preachers; shortly before the attack on him, Dutschke had been staying with sixty-year-old Helmut Gollwitzer, the Protestant theologian and peace activist. Arguably, generational tensions were lower in 1968 than in 1948. One person who deserves credit for that is Adenauer, whose pension reform released the pressure between the young and the old "like a valve," in the words of the historian Christina von Hodenberg, as the elderly got to share in the growing prosperity and had their pensions upgraded and paid for by younger cohorts in work.[59]

By revolutionary standards, 1968 was a failure, and nowhere more so than in West Germany. Compared to the violent events in Paris, Berlin had a mild May. In France, 2 million people joined a wildcat general strike. The authority of the state was hanging by a thread, and Charles de Gaulle flew to West Germany to meet with French officers there to ensure that he had the support of the army. Nothing like this happened in West Germany. The attack on Dutschke turned out to be the end of a rebellious phase, not the catalyst of something bigger.

Part of the reason for that lies in the vision of the radicals. For them, everything was connected, as Dutschke explained in an article in 1967. The contradictions in the universities reflected larger contradictions in society, which, in turn, were linked to those in capitalism and global imperialism. The emancipatory struggle, consequently, had to stretch from the lecture halls of the Free University of Berlin to the villages of Vietnam and Bolivia and everywhere in between. Dutschke's list of anti-authoritarian measures was endless, ranging from tenant committees and counter-universities to shorter working hours, the takeover of the Springer media empire, the abolition of the police and state bureaucracy, all the way to local counseling centers that would sow "the seeds for the future self-organization of man."[60]

The all-encompassing vision made radicals feel they were at the center of a global struggle, but it did not exactly provide them with a clear target.

Radicals elsewhere, of course, struggled with similar problems in 1968. The weakness of West German protestors was also a reflection of the strength of the democratic state and its support across society. In France, students and workers marched shoulder to shoulder. In Germany, by contrast, the Federation of Trade Unions (DGB) was internally divided and, in 1966, voted against joining the congress of the Extra-Parliamentary Opposition (Ausserparlamentarische Opposition, APO) that challenged the emergency laws; only the metalworkers and chemical workers unions (IG Metal and IG Chemie) lent their support.[61] Many unions had developed good corporatist relations with the employers and had their eyes on better wages, not a general strike.

The late 1960s and early 1970s followed the opposite dynamic of the 1920s. Instead of an erosion of the middle and the growth of extremes, left and right, West Germany pulled together around the center. Significantly, neither the recession of 1966–67 nor the oil crisis of 1973 managed to reverse this consolidation. Instead, the threat of revolution and terror convinced conservative and nationalist skeptics to back the democratic regime. The clampdown on the Communist Party deprived student radicals of potential allies. The decisive factor, however, was that the state was more flexible than the student radicals were capable of seeing.

"Let us dare more democracy" was Brandt's famous motto on taking charge of a social-liberal government in 1969. A wave of reforms followed—eighteen-year-olds gained the vote, workers' delegates received greater rights, and housewives became equal partners in marriage; proposals for a no-fault divorce were introduced in 1970 and became effective in 1977. The momentum for change had already started during the previous government, a grand coalition of the CDU and the SPD under Kurt Georg Kiesinger (1966–69). When the emergency laws were passed in 1968, the SPD softened the more draconian measures. Homosexuality among adult men ceased to be a crime, in 1969 for those over the age of twenty-one, in 1973 for those over eighteen. It was a top-down reform rather than bottom-up. The state started to give up on moral policing. At the same time, it gave more money to the universities; one reason Dutschke was able to study at the Free University was that the number of student places tripled in the 1960s. In 1971, the Brandt government added free student grants for all. For crimes against humanity, the statute of limitations was lifted.

The rebels of 1968 liked to see themselves as harbingers of a new era that broke with the stuffy past. In truth, they were the products of a democratic fermentation that had begun in the mid-1950s. More democracy, less authority, open critique, and greater tolerance—these were increasingly mainstream ideas and enjoyed official approval. In 1967, the eighteen-year-old Karin Storch gave an end-of-school speech in which she reflected on the police murder of Benno Ohnesorg in June and called for civil disobedience to be made an integral part of democratic schooling. To avoid Weimar, she argued, Bonn needed to train "crisis-resistant democrats."[62] The city of Cologne agreed and distributed the speech to all pupils and teachers in its secondary schools. The following year, Storch was awarded the national prize for model democratic behavior and standing up for one's convictions (*Zivilcourage*) by the all-party Theodor Heuss Foundation. Student reformers were pushing at an open door in 1968.

It was the radical movement, not the state, that fell apart after 1968. The largest body—the New Left—flocked to the SPD: Why storm barricades if Brandt's social-liberal coalition government was listening? A second group tried to continue the revolution in everyday life. They moved into communes, experimented with sex, drugs, and rock 'n' roll, and set out on a never-ending quest for authentic experiences.[63] For all their creative energy, these subcultural groups never posed a political threat. They produced hedonists and organic bakers, not revolutionaries. Their private fantasies were co-opted by consumer culture, repackaged, and sold at a profit.

TERROR, RED AND BROWN

More dangerous were the anti-authoritarians who migrated to communist cells—so-called K-groups—and looked to Mao for guidance. They probably never exceeded more than thirty thousand people, but they carried anti-capitalist ideas into the alternative subculture and formed the vital hinterland for the Red Army Faction.[64] Like their Italian comrades in the Red Brigades, West German terrorists took from Mao the "urban guerrilla concept." Imperialists and reactionaries were nothing more than "paper tigers," they quoted the chairman.[65]

In two weeks in May 1972, the terrorists bombed the headquarters of the U.S. Army in Heidelberg, two police stations, the headquarters of the Springer publishing empire in Hamburg, and the car of a judge at the Federal Court of Justice. Four people were killed, many dozens wounded. After the leaders had been arrested, the rump turned its attention to their liberation with a spate of kidnappings. In 1975, the Helmut Schmidt government gave in to their demands and released a handful of terrorists in exchange for the CDU politician Peter Lorenz. The core group, however, remained in a high-security prison. Meinhof committed suicide in her cell on May 9, 1976. The following year, on September 5, the RAF kidnapped its most prominent victim: Hanns Martin Schleyer. An SS officer during the war who rose to the top of the employers' federation, he personified the link between Germany's fascist past and its capitalist present. This time, Schmidt and his ministers held their nerve. There would be no more negotiations with terrorists. The government stopped Schleyer's family from handing over 15 million Deutschmark in ransom money. On October 13, Palestinian terrorists hijacked a Lufthansa plane on its way from Palma de Mallorca to Frankfurt with ninety-one hostages on board and threatened to blow it up unless the prisoners were released. Shortly after midnight on October 18, an elite unit stormed the plane, freed the hostages, and shot three of the four hijackers. The same morning, the four RAF prisoners including the cofounder Andreas Baader, attempted collective suicide. Three succeeded, one survived. Schleyer was shot by their followers later that day.

Like the events of 1968, the terror acts had the opposite of the intended effect: it stabilized the young democracy. Whatever sympathy some sections of the population initially had for those challenging state authority was spent when innocent civilians, including many foreigners, became the target. Germans dreamed of flying to sunny beaches, not of being hijacked along the way. *Ostpolitik* (Brandt's treaties with Poland and the Soviet Union in 1970), social-liberal reforms, and the end of the Vietnam War in 1975 made the specter of a "fascist-capitalist-imperialist" state look further removed from reality than ever.

Red terror dominated the headlines, but there was also a series of right-wing attacks, although these have received less attention. The Federal Republic successfully kept neo-Nazis out of parliament, but this did not mean there were no militant neo-Nazis outside it. The attempted assassination of Dutschke was only one such instance. In the early 1970s, they seriously wounded a Soviet guard in Berlin at the border with East Germany. By the end of the decade, they turned on Jews and Americans. In February 1980, pipe bombs exploded at an Auschwitz exhibition in the town of Esslingen, near Stuttgart. In December that year, the German-Jewish publisher Shlomo Lewin and his partner were assassinated in their home in Erlangen. The murderer belonged to one of the fascist "military sports groups" that had sprung up. Other bombs targeted U.S. soldiers and German judges who had prosecuted neo-Nazis. The deadliest attack took place at the Oktoberfest in Munich in 1980, where thirteen people were killed and more than two hundred wounded. The motivation behind it remains unclear to this day; the assassin was among the dead. The public self-understanding of the Federal Republic as a democratic country that had overcome the fascist past and had arrived in the West encouraged a collective denial when it came to tackling right-wing terror.[66] In the investigation of Lewin's murder, police and media initially turned on the Jewish community, giving the neo-Nazi murderer a chance to flee; he committed suicide in Lebanon a year later. In 1986, West German intelligence knew of 1,460 active neo-Nazis—many times more than the Red Army Faction; eight of these were policemen and 124 civil servants.[67]

BODY POLITICS

There was one issue for which 1968 was lastingly important: female emancipation. For women, the student protests were a formative experience in political confidence building and action. Women made up a quarter of the Socialist German Student Body (SDS), but their voices were muffled by male leadership and behavior. Women's concerns, such as reproductive rights and the lack of day cares, were treated as private issues, subordinate to the politics that really mattered, and that happened to be in the hands of men. Feminists opened anti-authoritarian day cares (*Kinderläden*) and set up a council for the liberation of women. In 1968, the film student Helke Sander confronted the SDS head-on at their annual conference. She was tired of how certain spheres of life were labeled "private"; the private was political, too. In their separation of spheres—private belonging to women, public to men—the SDS was just as patriarchal as the establishment. Yet, she added, male comrades acted surprised when female students did not speak up and organize more.[68] There was no sudden awakening among male student leaders—out of frustration, a fellow student, Sigrid Rüger, threw tomatoes at them during the meeting. Women activists were divided over ideology and tactics. Was it better to tackle patriarchy or devote their energies to the overthrow of capitalism, the root cause of exploitation? Regardless, 1968 expanded the language and arena of politics to include sex, family, and marriage. The women's movement was reborn.

The issue of body politics that divided West Germany more than any other was abortion. In contrast to the liberal provisions in the GDR, West Germany treated abortion as a criminal offense. In 1971, the illustrated magazine *Stern* devoted its cover story to more than three hundred women who confessed, "We have aborted!," ranging from film stars such as Romy Schneider to ordinary women. The strategist behind the campaign was the feminist journalist Alice Schwarzer, who copied the idea from a similar manifesto in France. Five years of political and constitutional conflict followed.

In towns and churches, schools and firms, people were drawn into an ethical debate, weighing the respective rights of the mother and the embryo, and the question of life itself. Feminists defended women's rights over their own bodies, while for the Catholic Church all life was sacrosanct. In between were qualified supporters of abortion who accepted it in cases of rape or poverty. Others wanted a cutoff within three months of pregnancy, without limiting it to *Indikationen* ("specific justifications"). *Indikationen* divided the land.

The Nazi murder of disabled people gave the debate a particular charge. At a town hall meeting in Ostercappeln (Lower Saxony) in 1972, the legalization of abortion in cases with "eugenic grounds" triggered heated discussion. If it was permitted to kill a seriously disabled child in the mother's womb, then what would prevent its killing once it was born, especially in the case of misdiagnosis? "The door to euthanasia would no longer be barred," the meeting said in its petition to the minister of justice Gerhard Jahn against the reform. Signed by 637 local people, it noted, "it is barely necessary to point to our recent past." Critics feared that disabled people would only be devalued further. The remedy ought to be greater medical and social support for mother and child. Did the state not have a constitutional duty to protect all life? Others were more concerned about the survival of the *Volk*. Those shouting, "My belly belongs to me" were spoiled and self-indulgent, a member of the German YMCA told the minister: "We already have more than 2 million guest workers in our country, and it will inevitably have to go up further if we are lacking our own offspring."[69]

Protestant social workers and nurses were divided. Many accepted abortion where there were serious social and medical grounds, while a significant minority wanted to allow abortion as long as the mother saw a counselor first.[70] People were drawn into debates about what lay behind the rise in illegal abortions and precisely which indicators should be taken into consideration. At an evening school, young housewives with small children discussed the different proposals: six wanted to allow abortions but only subject to social and medical grounds, nine opted for complete liberalization, and twenty-five accepted all abortions regardless of "indication" as long as they took place in the first three months. Doctors in their majority opposed such a time limit and wanted an overall medical "indication" instead, with them in charge. Female trade unionists felt that adding a "social indication," such as poverty, did not go far enough. It "completely ignored," one woman wrote to the minister of justice, "that a woman in our society today must be given the right both to determine her own destiny and to avert hardship and suffering for her and her children, including unborn ones, when and where she wants."[71] After long debate, the German Housewives Federation agreed to support the legalization of abortion in the first three months of pregnancy. At the AEG-Telefunken electronics company, the majority of men as well as women supported abortion reform. The 200,000-strong rural women's association (LandFrauenverband), on the other hand, wanted to help women through greater awareness, family planning, and making men take up their joint responsibility: society needed to stop pushing the consequences of sex onto women. Conservative women and Catholic social workers similarly focused on social housing and assistance for families.

Young women picked up their pens to tell politicians about their constitutional rights. A seventeen-year-old pupil from Berlin wrote to parliamentary delegates in 1971. Since most of them were men, she said, they could not possibly know what it meant to be pregnant for nine months. She was a hardworking high-school student, not a "lazy bum," and she was tired of religious arguments. "Will you please leave it to each Christian whether they want to commit sin, or not. You do not prosecute someone for not practicing 'love thy neighbor' either." If a child was not wanted, its life would be "undignified." "Normally, I am a calm citizen. But when someone is trying to limit my very own personal rights, then I do become ferocious."[72] The female pupils of a trade school echoed this demand for autonomy: they wanted to be completely free to plan their family without "the mental burden" of having to visit a consultant first.

In 1974, Brandt's social-liberal coalition managed to squeeze a reform of the abortion Paragraph 218 through parliament. Abortion was no longer punishable if it took place within the first three months of pregnancy. The Christian Democrats immediately took their opposition to the Constitutional Court, which, a year later, struck down the reform for violating the state's duty to protect life, including unborn life. In accordance with the ruling, parliament, in 1976, tightened Paragraph 218. The three-month time limit was dropped. Abortion remained illegal but would not be punished if it was for one of the following *Indikationen*: rape; if the mother faced a desperate social situation; if pregnancy posed a risk to her own life; or in the case of a serious physical or mental disability of the fetus. In reality, doctors often refused to certify such *Indikationen*, especially in Catholic areas.

Reunification created the bizarre situation that abortion was lawful in the former East but punishable in the West. In 1995, parliament settled for a compromise, allowing all women to have an abortion as long as it was within the first twelve weeks of pregnancy and carried out by a doctor after a consultation. Whether with regard to their own bodies, family, work, or political representation, women were still not equal citizens.

GRASSROOTS

Less radical than the student protestors in 1968 but more profound for political culture was the rise of civic action groups in the ensuing two decades. In 1977, an estimated 1.5 million people belonged to tens of thousands of these *Bürgerinitiativen*, almost matching the 1.7 million in political parties.[73] These grassroots initiatives were fighting both *against* public projects, such as highways, nuclear reactors, and the destruction of historical neighborhoods, and *for* greater public services, especially schools and child care centers. Their rise was testimony to the extraordinary expansion of the West German economy and public spending since the mid-1950s, and an affluent lifestyle of comfort, convenience, and mobility. Not by accident were highways, power stations, and city centers the main zones of conflict; one of the first citizen initiatives was that in Eltville on the Rhine in 1958, which campaigned against a planned expressway along the banks of the river. Two decades later, when a highway threatened to slice Cologne in two, protestors invoked Goebbels's call for "total war," asking citizens, "Do you want total cement?"[74] Civic action groups arose at the local intersection of these two forces: state planning and consumer society.

Most initiatives came from single-issue groups who recruited people who were directly affected. They were overwhelmingly from the educated middle class, students, and people in their thirties and forties. At the time, the political scientist Claus Offe characterized these groups as "early-warning systems" for the state that conveniently identified the bumps in the road that needed fixing so late capitalism could race ahead. Contrary to their radical self-image, he said, they were a privileged "appendage" of the state.[75]

This was a somewhat uncharitable view. Notwithstanding their middle-class bias, these groups were an important conduit of civic participation for many locals who had previously been passive bystanders. In 1971, for example, residents in the Emsland near the Dutch border came together to protest against the nearby NATO bombing range, where the activity often shook them out of their sleep. The organizing committee included a manufacturer, a clerk, and a housewife. In 1973, four thousand local pupils went on strike, shouting, "The noise is my death." They were joined by dockworkers and local farmers on tractors, as well by a group of communists and anarchists hoping for their revolutionary moment. Housewives planted their picnic chairs outside the army gates. "Are we second-class citizens?" their flyer asked.

Campaigns also helped to redefine the public interest by pushing local issues higher up on the national political agenda. New environmental concerns, such as about nuclear power, were linked to older ones like noise and air pollution and the protection of local frogs and birds. Already in 1963, a few dozen people had come together to fight against the noise from aviation in the Rhine-Main area. Soon they had thirty thousand members and developed links with like-minded bodies elsewhere. One Protestant group wanted to show greater sympathy with all of God's creation. Others worried about polluted rivers, food safety, and nuclear radiation. In 1972, one thousand groups formed the National Federation for Environmental Protection (Bundesverband Bürgerinitiativen Umweltschutz).[76]

The citizen groups covered a vast spectrum of issues and ideas. At one end, they self-consciously carried on the "anti-capitalist resistance" of 1968. In 1969, several hundred pupils, students, and apprentices blockaded the tramlines in Hanover in protest of a 15 percent hike in ticket prices for public transport, even though student season tickets were to be frozen. There were clashes with the police and arrests. In an early form of ride sharing, students offered lifts in their cars. Their aim was to "break open hardened structures of communication" and, instead of retreating behind the walls of private comfort, to turn the street into an arena of public politics. The city council caved in, but the battle over public transportation flared up again and again in many cities in the course of the 1970s, including in Hanover. Students occupied flats earmarked for demolition and commercial development and campaigned for the preservation of historic districts. In Essen, in 1973, they occupied an empty house that belonged to the Ruhrkohle AG, the giant mining enterprise, demanding that it should be turned into a day care and youth center. It was eventually bought by the Protestant Church, which offered it to the students for community activities several days a week.[77]

At the other end of the spectrum were groups that were fighting to protect local traditions. They might be "new social movements" in style and organization but, in their outlook, civic initiatives often blended old and new. The years after 1945 saw a veritable cult of *Heimat*, as people looked to the medieval guilds of their cities for homegrown roots of democracy. The burghers of Cologne celebrated Carnival for its democratic, anti-Prussian tradition. In the Bavarian constitution, teaching pupils "love for the Bavarian *Heimat*" came immediately after educating them in the spirit of democracy.

This localism would form a natural reservoir of resistance against big infrastructure projects approved by state officials in an office far, far away, such as a six-lane expressway through the Neckar valley. After almost a decade of a local farmer protesting to the planners singlehandedly, he turned to his fellow citizens in 1978. He was joined by doctors who worried about the water, fellow farmers who feared for their harvest, and a student inspired by the farmer's courage in standing up to the state. What united them was a concern for their *Heimat*, its landscape and tradition, not the environment more broadly. Residents recalled the historic moment in 1791 when their ancestors had walked out of church in protest against the new Protestant hymnal. Their petitions against the road were accompanied by a local dance troupe and a band of alpine horns—and successful.[78]

Between these two poles lay a vibrant landscape of "autonomous" shops, community centers, and self-help groups. In West Berlin in the early 1980s, some fifteen thousand people were actively running such initiatives. Forty percent had something to do with the environment, urban planning, or public services. Seventeen percent worked in neighborhood theaters, galleries, and cultural projects; 21 percent ran artisanal cooperatives, feminist bookshops, "Third World" shops, and alternative travel bureaus; 5 percent were communal self-providers and experimented with solar and alternative energies. Not all citizen initiatives were progressive—there were also those who tried to keep out foreigners.[79]

This alternative economy gained in strength as the regular economy struggled in the early 1970s and again in the early 1980s, when unemployment reached 9 percent. More than a job, it promised liberation from the pressures of competition, consumption, and bureaucracy. Self-help, self-reliance, and self-discovery were the watchwords. Self-determination would replace distant authority, and autonomous living the seductive power of "false needs." In their critique of the democratic state with its distant members of parliament, these groups tapped into an older "republican" tradition of direct citizenship, except that many also wanted to get rid of its original foundation: private property. Alternative firms tried to be autonomous, cooperative, and self-administered. They started out paying uniform wages, rotated jobs, and discussed decisions until reaching a consensus. By the late 1980s, they had established themselves, but only by diluting their ideals. Specialization and differential wages were reincorporated. Those firms that survived often only did so because they were thrown a lifeline by wealthy parents or by the state.[80]

The 1970s also saw a boom in self-help groups, which numbered fifteen thousand by 1984. The movement was partly inspired by patient groups in the United States and ranged from self-help groups for disabled citizens to those for children suffering from allergies. It was often sympathetic doctors, social workers, and students who started them. The "Action Circle '71 for Social Psychiatry" spelled out why self-help in a group mattered. The social ills that produced mental illness could only be tackled by "a social group that was always open," fought "individualism and egotism," and put "the abilities of each member to social use." Through shared praxis and solidarity they would overcome the "alienation and misery in capitalism."[81]

Groups and communes wanted to rediscover an authentic self. Active citizenship would free the individual from external authority and consumerist temptations. Everything became a "workshop" (*Werkstatt*). There was a lively flow between groups that promoted self-determination, peacefulness, and anti-authoritarian education. In 1982, for example, the "peace workshop" in Rosengarten (Lower Saxony) morphed into a "life workshop" (*Lebenswerkstatt*). It aimed at nothing short of the "mental, physical, and spiritual healing of the individual as the precondition for sociopolitical work." Participants would rediscover their "inner harmony." The focus, consequently, was on their daily life, not on distant party politics. In Minden in North Rhine–Westphalia, pacifists worked together with a children's playgroup, a "Third World" shop, and a self-help project with the homeless; in 1978 they added a campaign against the planned parking garage in the old town. Provincial Germany had squatters and youth centers, too. For some, the "Provinz" and the "Third World" shared the same basic problem: they were left-behind victims of a metropolitan elite, which included the socialist avant-garde.[82] In the university town of Göttingen, a "grassroots workshop" attracted young people longing for autarchy; some installed solar-powered showers, others spun their own wool, modeling themselves on the Tvind School in Denmark, an alternative educational project where members built the world's largest wind turbine on an old farm. School committees, student politics, and anti-nuclear protests were stops on the way to these alternative communities. One former student arrived after a stay at the "Free Republic Wendland," an Asterix-style settlement of huts and tents that occupied a planned nuclear waste depot at Gorleben in Lower Saxony for one month in 1980 before it was cleared by the police; the facility would only open fifteen years later. The student had initially set out to become a pastor but found his true calling: baking organic bread.[83]

Social learning, emotional openness, and greater tolerance were core elements in the alternative curriculum. This made workshops attractive not only to their regular members but also to the growing number of social workers and therapists in the welfare state. One was Gudrun Libnau, a thirty-two-year-old married mother who was a social worker in a children's home. She spent her holidays at the "Summer School 80," which devoted itself to making self-determination a "concrete utopia." She was worried that her day job was taking over her life and that she was becoming a cog in the wheel of the welfare system. "I am afraid of losing my power of resistance," she wrote. "I want to change things and change myself and be strong enough to get up after each setback." She found that strength by living together with like-minded people in the summer school. Emotional learning created the solidarity needed to overcome their "fixation with authority." "It is very important for me to learn to take myself seriously and even more so others who do not have the same social and political ideas, with all their different needs, fears, and eccentricities." They all wanted to live "without oppression and exploitation." For her, the summer school meant "imagination, creativity, and sensitivity . . . : the joy of life."[84]

Others left the "concrete utopia" in despair. "Three disappointed" women wrote about their experiences that same year. They normally worked in a day care and a youth workshop in Munich. When they arrived, the summer school was barely habitable, with a small shed for building a solar power facility and a garden "covered in weeds." They had come to discuss social pedagogy. Instead, they found everyone making pottery. Talking was good, making something with their hands better, they were assured. There were teachers, students, social workers, and members of a woman's group. "Everyone was lounging about, three couples were ostentatiously cuddling each other, a woman was gently playing the guitar, and a few were singing along to the 'Che Guevara Song' "—"¡Hasta siempre, Comandante!" The group was happy and relaxed, but they only wanted to talk about utopias, not problems in everyday life. "If you talk about reality," the three women were told, "you are destroying our dreams." One of the new arrivals wanted to know why everyone was meant to make pottery or weave wool: back home, young people came to her workshop to fix cars. "That is a pedagogical issue," she was told: doing crafts taught people the value of work and enhanced their respect for workers. "Children," another chipped in, "should make their own cups instead of buying them and falling prey to consumerist shit." Karl Marx's idea of alienation found receptive soil in the German fondness for *basteln* ("making handicrafts"). Curiously, the visitors noted, "the workshop school did not contain a single handmade cup." The rebellion against bourgeois authority and search for subjectivity came with its own new norms and discipline. One man felt "alienated" because he was no good at pottery. After a couple of days, the three women left, exhausted.[85]

The demand for more self-determination was not limited to the counterculture but reached across society. The Liberals in 1971 campaigned for an open society and the reform of sex laws. There was no eternal truth, they argued, and hence no single right way of living, either. The "highest goal" was to "sustain and develop individuality... and the plurality of human coexistence."[86] The Junge Union, the youth section of the CDU, took on their conservative elders and pressed for more direct democracy at the local level, public consultations, and self-help. Not everyone was convinced. Young conservatives in Bavaria saw no need for more democracy in their schools. In Hamburg and Schleswig-Holstein, however, their peers were in favor, and demanded greater student representation, liberal teaching, and sex education, too. Hegel's classic separation of state and society had become obsolete argued Jürgen Echternach, the new leader of the Junge Union, in 1969. There was no separate system of needs: the social state existed within society. Subjects had to be lifted up and learn to walk as active citizens. Young Christian Democracts also protested against urban planners and speculators, and in some cities supported youth work with drug addicts. As the fastest growing political youth movement at the time and with an age limit of thirty-five—until 1970 it was the not-so-youthful forty—the Junge Union had a significant impact on their cohort. In 1972, young conservatives made up one third of all elected school representatives in the country.[87]

The confrontation between state and citizen initiatives should not be exaggerated. Some clashes resembled David fighting Goliath, as over the nuclear waste depot in Gorleben. In other cases, though, protest turned into dialogue. Not all protestors were opposed to nuclear power outright; some only wanted modifications to protect local jobs, rivers, and safety.[88] Several states responded to the demands for more democracy by giving citizens a greater say in local affairs. In the Rhineland-Palatinate, citizens in 1973 secured the right to have their petitions considered by the communal council (*Gemeinderat*) as long as they had the support of 2 to 5 percent of the local population, depending on the size of the town. In Bavaria, mayors were obliged to call a citizen assembly (*Bürgerversammlung*) to deliberate popular concerns.[89]

At the village level, ironically, it was the state that was mobilizing residents to be more engaged in the community with the campaign "Our Village Shall Become More Beautiful." The original idea harked back to Nazi visions of shaping the *Volk* by shaping the landscape. In the course of the 1960s, officials resigned themselves to the fact that the traditional farming village was gone for good. The new goal was to bring modern comfort and convenience to the countryside. Residents were urged to chip in and build new schools, roads, and village greens; in Altenburschla, a Hessian village of five hundred souls, locals in 1959 volunteered seventeen thousand hours to renovating houses and planting trees and roses. In the next two decades, more than forty thousand villages participated in these public competitions.[90]

Affluent Americans might increasingly be "bowling alone" from the mid-1960s on, in the memorable words of the political scientist Robert Putnam, but affluent Germans were big joiners.[91] Provincial associations were booming. In Steinhausen (Westphalia), the shooting club had 250 active members in 1950, 700 in 1981, and 1,006 in 1992, in a town of just over 3,000 souls. Across the country, shooting clubs had a million members. Small towns enjoyed their own conservative emancipation. Women in Strassdorf, east of Stuttgart, started the first ladies' shooting team in 1967. Protests elsewhere ensured that women at last gained a seat on committees and at the annual banquet. Social dances fell victim to television, but clubs compensated by broadening their repertoire to include foreign travel, music, and recycling. In Strassdorf, the great event in the 1960s was the annual pig-slaughter festival. By the 1980s, club members were busy collecting waste and traveling together to Antibes on the Côte d'Azur. Youth sections introduced the next generation to local songs and customs. There was no shortage of young men and women joining the volunteer fire brigades, which, in addition to putting out fires, were an example of self-administration in practice, involving themselves in everything from transporting sick patients to putting up Christmas lights.[92]

CHANGING VALUES

These civic initiatives simultaneously reflected and reinforced how individual citizens were expected to take their lives into their own hands. Instead of institutions telling individuals what to do, individuals were increasingly deciding for themselves how they wanted to live, work, and love. The key word, encountered again and again, was the "self": self-help, self-cultivation, and self-determination went hand in hand. This new orientation drew on a material transformation that touched almost all aspects of life. The 1960s and 1970s saw a simultaneous expansion of leisure time, education, flexible jobs, media, and mobility. The five-day workweek was introduced in 1967. By that time, every second household had a car, and virtually all had a television. The number of students at universities rose fourfold between 1960 and 1980, when it crossed the 1 million mark.[93] West Germany was an industrial society turning into a knowledge society.

That West Germany underwent "value change" in these years is beyond dispute. The big question concerns its nature and direction. For the American social scientist Ronald Inglehart, the 1960s saw a switch from "materialist" to "post-materialist" values as Western societies moved from scarcity to affluence, and the young turned toward green issues and greater freedoms. There are countless problems with this thesis. "Post-material" values are not the privilege of affluent societies. Environmentalism, for example, built on nature movements that were already a popular fixture in Germany and elsewhere a century earlier. Conversely, greater material comfort made some people prize material security more, not less. It is a mistake to view values as a zero-sum game and assume that "traditional" values were simply replaced by "post-material" ones. The 1960s and 1970s produced hedonists as well as critics of growth and consumption. The oft-lamented "decay in values" (*Werteverfall*) was in reality a reconfiguration, where some values disappeared and others survived in combination with new ones. Shifts in educational ideals are a case in point. In the decade after 1964, more and more parents aspired for their children to be independent and develop their own dreams and ambitions, and fewer looked to obedience and deference. At the same time, diligence and order were also finding growing support.

Germans longed for self-cultivation *and* duty. The young were in the vanguard, but the new pluralism of values reached older cohorts as well.[94]

If the change in values was ambivalent, so was its effect on democracy. Surveys show no expansion of post-materialist preferences in the 1970s and early 1980s. Support for participatory democracy did not translate into a declining respect for parliamentary democracy or the state. Calls for greater self-help and self-responsibility had to compete with an expanding welfare state that often followed the opposite logic. It is important to remember that citizen initiatives, notwithstanding their impressive numbers and worthy causes, were ultimately a minority affair. Grassroots activists would find a political home in the "post-materialist" Green Party, but most of their neighbors looked for material security and limited their political engagement to casting their vote in general elections.

"What is German today?" the family sociologist Helge Pross asked in 1982. She had been one of the young Germans who visited the United States after the war. Later she worked as an assistant to the former émigrés Max Horkheimer and Theodor Adorno in their Frankfurt Institute for Social Research. In 1981, she returned to America, lecturing college students on this very question. What Germans wanted more than anything else, she explained, was a life of peace and order. Order had taken the place of the nation and the church. It was a reaction partly to the war, and partly to the extensive health and welfare system that now existed, which coddled people in a culture of security. Democracy was a matter of convenience, not the heart. Distrust of conflicting interests remained strong and weakened genuine pluralism. "Ideas that transcend... private happiness... and ideas of solidarity that come at the expense of personal advantage," Pross said, "have no home in the Federal Republic." She warned against exaggerating the role of alternative movements, and likened them to religious sects that "presented their respective new faith as the only true blessing." Most Germans would have no truck with them. "Those who want to live a life of peace and quiet with their family, earn money, look after their homes, and spend their abundant free time in private... have little interest in an alternative existence." The sense of righteousness she diagnosed in the counterculture related to the limits of tolerance more generally. The high regard for one's own rights did not extend to an equal appreciation of the rights of others. Open violence toward minorities and nonconformists was rare and no longer considered acceptable. Still, this was a long way from recognizing difference as something positive in its own right. Active tolerance, she concluded, was "not a majority value."[95]

NEW HORIZONS

Citizen initiatives were nearsighted. They had their eyes on their neighborhood and nearby forests and rivers. Members wished to envision and manage their life and surroundings. This orientation was rarely insular, though, and was complemented by an openness to the world. There was a growing sense of global responsibility for distant others as well as those next door. In that sense, citizens were also becoming more farsighted. It was this bifocal lens that gave West Germans a new moral vision between the 1950s and 1970s. After conquest and catastrophe, Germans were trying to reposition themselves in the world. In the first place, this meant settling down in Europe. A second reorientation was more far-reaching: the discovery of the "Third World."

When it came to European integration, West Germany could not have hoped for a leader with better credentials. Cologne, Chancellor Adenauer's birthplace, fused the spirit of ancient Rome with that of Christianity. It was the center of his map of the world. In school, Adenauer learned Latin, Greek, and French—in that order—but no English. The countries he knew well were nearby: France, Belgium, Switzerland, and Italy. He looked to the United States as a spiritual offspring of the Christian West, but he was seventy-seven when he first visited it in 1953.[96] Adenauer's Europe was fundamentally different from the dream of a united Europe championed by

European Federalists in the postwar years. It was a little Europe—its western part only—part of an Atlantic alliance, not a separate "Third Force"; it saw integration as a means to regain national sovereignty, not to cede it to a supranational federation. In short, Adenauer's Eurocentric map was perfect for the Cold War.

European unity and peace had been the dream of Enlightenment thinkers such as the Abbé de Saint-Pierre, Jean-Jacques Rousseau, and Immanuel Kant. It needed the Second World War to persuade nation-states to turn some version of it into reality. The war left behind three favorable preconditions: it showed the need to channel and contain Germany's strength in the future; fear of communism made Western European countries pull together; and integration was shielded by a new superpower, the United States.

The first step was the European Coal and Steel Community (ECSC) in 1951, which was joined by Belgium, France, West Germany, Italy, Luxembourg, and the Netherlands. Six years later, "the six" formed the European Economic Community (EEC). The ECSC had its own "High Authority," made up of national representatives, which oversaw the pooling of coal and steel and removal of trade barriers. Governments do not usually like to give up national sovereignty. What made it suddenly so attractive was that a small transfer of national sovereignty promised to restore national strength. For Robert Schuman, the French foreign minister, who in 1950 envisaged the ECSC in a plan bearing his name, greater European unity and greater national power were two sides of the same coin. By gaining access to German coal, France would be able to rebuild its glory. The coal barons of the Ruhr, seen as the drivers behind German militarism, would be tamed by Europeanizing them. For Adenauer, the ECSC was a step on the road to establishing the Federal Republic as a fully independent state in the Western community. There was no loss of national sovereignty involved—to the contrary. The ECSC gave West Germany a seat at the table and did away with the veto the Allies had exercised over its coal and steel production under the International Authority for the Ruhr. By facilitating Franco-German understanding, it also eased the return of the industrial Saarland, after a plebiscite in 1955. With the Treaties of Rome in 1957, the EEC widened its ambition beyond coal and steel to a general common market and the free movement of not just goods but of labor, services, and capital.

We tend to speak of "the European Community." In reality, as the historian Kiran Patel reminds us, there were three communities to begin with—the ECSC, the EEC, and Euratom (the European Atomic Energy Community set up in 1957 to develop nuclear power for civilian use)—and they were not the only voices speaking for Europe.[97] There was competition from a series of overlapping bodies: the Organization for European Economic Co-operation (OEEC) in 1948, which arose from the American Marshall Plan and had sixteen members plus the Western zones of Germany; the Council of Europe, which produced the European Convention on Human Rights in 1950, became even larger; the Western European Union (1954), a military alliance between the United Kingdom, France, West Germany, Italy, and the Benelux countries; and the European Free Trade Association (1960) of the British and Nordic "outsiders." It was only in the years after 1965, when the ECSC, the EEC, and Euratom merged into a single set of institutions, that the European Community established itself as the undisputed center of gravity. In 1973, the original six took in Britain, Ireland, and Denmark; Greece would join in 1981, Spain and Portugal in 1986. The collapse of communism opened the door to East Germany as part of the reunified Germany, then to the neutral countries of Austria, Finland, and Sweden in 1995, and, in 2004, to seven countries of the former Eastern bloc, including Poland, the Czech Republic, and the Baltic States. It took until 1992, with the signing of the Maastricht Treaty, when the European Economic Community was rechristened the European Community, that it took the giant step to turn itself into a "European Union" with a common citizenship, foreign policy, and security policy. A single currency, the euro, had to wait until 2002.

Today, being a citizen of Europe is second nature to Germans. In the 1950s, however, they were deeply divided over the kind of Europe they wanted to live in. For the Social Democrats, the ECSC went too far, sacrificing national sovereignty and cementing the division of the country into East and West. For Federalists, it did not go far enough: they wanted a supranational Europe with its own parliament, army, and foreign policy. Adenauer ignored them both. That the ECSC was the brainchild of technocrats suited his own style of presidential politics—he barely kept the Bundestag informed about the progress of negotiations leading up to the Treaties of Rome in 1957. As its original name makes abundantly clear, the EEC was designed as an "Economic Community"—democracy, human rights, and defense were not yet central concerns and, indeed, had stronger advocates in the Council of Europe and the West European Union, which had their own parliamentary assemblies. Equally, supranational power was kept within limits. The High Authority of the ECSC was watched over by the Council of Ministers, made up of national delegates. The EEC would also get its own executive commission and even added a parliamentary assembly, but that was neither elected nor given any powers other than making recommendations. Charles de Gaulle's attacks on the "Frankenstein" monster—and, later, Margaret Thatcher's—vastly exaggerated the rather limited transfer of power to Brussels. When their national interests were at risk, governments imposed their own will.

In 1958, the ECSC was faced with a mountain of unused coal, following a drop in European demand and an influx of cheap gas and oil and even cheaper coal from the United States. Mines had to shut down, and there were strikes. The High Authority appealed to members to tackle the crisis together. Instead, the German government issued special discounts for its own coal and slapped tariffs on American imports. The Belgian vice president of the High Authority, Albert Coppé, accused Germany of "dumping." Whatever it was, it was certainly not in the spirit of the common market.[98] Nor did European law automatically apply at home. In 1974, the German Constitutional Court asserted its right to throw out provisions if they clashed with the Basic Law. It was only in 1986 that the court accepted that the European Court of Justice met German standards.

The growth of the European Community in these years was certainly extraordinary, especially with the Common Agricultural Policy, and the bigger the common market and the more freedom of movement, the more rules, regulations, and meetings. As the number of European committees multiplied, so did that of national experts and lobbyists sitting on them. State officials now had to learn to implement European directives at home. The result was thickening cooperation between Brussels and the member states, not a supranational empire. For a country like Germany with its own powerful tradition of the state, the effect was profound. Civil servants were Europeanized. By the early 1990s, every fifth civil servant in a federal ministry was also involved in an EU group. Thinking like a state now required them to see like a European as well as a German; whether citizens and politicians managed to do likewise in European crises only time would tell.[99]

Each step the Community took was a step away from the popular enthusiasm for a united Europe that had surged across the continent after the war. Prophets spoke in many tongues. In 1946, Winston Churchill called for a "United States of Europe," which mainly meant cooperation between countries and stopped short at the Channel; Britain, after all, still had its Empire. More numerous and ambitious were the Federalists who looked toward a genuine union without borders as the only guarantor of peace and democracy. Not surprisingly, it was anti-fascists who bore the scars of totalitarian state power who were in the vanguard of a movement striving to overcome the nation-state for good. The first president of the German section of the Union of European Federalists was Eugen Kogon, a survivor of Buchenwald.

Although polls in two West German towns in 1947 found that 96 percent of the residents were in favor of abolishing political and economic borders, federalism never became a mass movement. The German branches of the Federalists numbered ten thousand members in 1951, mainly from the educated middle classes. What it lacked in numbers, it made up in public outreach. There were rallies, films, and publicity stunts. In 1950, several hundred youths uprooted the border posts at a border crossing with France. Two years later, the traveling exhibition "Europe Calls" was seen by more than 1 million visitors. The Europe they dreamed of was democratic, unified, and big—some federalists looked all the way to the Urals. In other words, it was everything the emerging European Community was not. The ECSC and EEC were *for* the citizens, not *by* the citizens; the European parliament was not directly elected until 1979, and even then parliamentary powers over the executive remained limited.

Instead of nurturing a "Third Force" that would simultaneously offer salvation from communist Moscow and capitalist Washington, the Cold War deepened the divide across the continent. In 1952, the CIA, which had so far bankrolled European federalists, turned off the tap. Penniless, the German headquarters in Frankfurt even had its office furniture seized.

The federalists regrouped, but, tellingly, under the helm of a banker, Carl von Oppenheim. The European idea now circulated in chambers of commerce rather than in town squares, at least in Germany. German federalists would have nothing to do with the Italian Altiero Spinelli's plan of bypassing parliaments and mobilizing a People's Congress to demand a European constitution. It was pure self-deception, they argued: "a European-minded crowd [*Masse*] does not exist."[100] Popular outreach came to be limited to seminars for schoolteachers. Those who in the early 1950s had hoped that, somehow, the ECSC would be the start of greater union were largely disillusioned by the end of the decade. Franco-German reconciliation was no mean accomplishment, but the dream of closer union in foreign policy and security seemed more distant than ever; the proposed European Defense Community was killed by France in 1954. The engine of European integration had begun to stutter.

The European Community excited technocrats, steel magnates, and farmers. The general public barely took notice. In a poll in 1958, only every fourth West German knew that the Treaties of Rome had been signed. Every second one had at least heard of "the common market." Like their neighbors in the club of six, West Germans were generally in favor of "European integration." In 1962, roughly two in three supported the free movement of goods, labor, and business and also a common foreign policy—slightly ahead of the French, slightly behind the Dutch. At the very same time, most Germans (like most French) were unable to cite a single concrete accomplishment by the Community.[101] This was in spite of the fact that the export-oriented German economy was benefiting hugely from European integration and access to markets. In the late 1960s, only a third of Germans could name the six member states, at a time when virtually everyone would have known the names of the four Beatles.

For most citizens, travel and pop music shaped European understanding more than the common market in coal and steel. In the father's letters to his missing pilot son that were previously quoted, the father mentions the Schuman plan in passing, only to note that while some believe "it will make inner-European war impossible, it will probably only increase the tension between East and West." In the years to come, he would write about Germany's joining NATO, the Cuban Missile Crisis, and de Gaulle and Adenauer's mass for peace in Reims Cathedral in 1962, but never about the European Economic Community, and here was a man who took note of international affairs. Meanwhile, beginning in 1952, there is page after page about the annual holidays he and his wife took to Switzerland, Belgium, France, and, again and again, to Italy, with a steadily growing interest in foreign people and their customs as well as classical sites and architecture. "Time and again, we take pleasure from the friendly sociability of the Italian people, and their poverty and unpretentiousness, which is simply touching." In the summer of 1959, he drove with his Fiat a phenomenal 2,700 miles across the Dolomites, via Milan, Florence, and Rome, all the way to the bottom of the Italian boot and back to the Black Forest. He complained how his compatriots were taking over the *bel paese.* The Adriatic coast was so overrun by German tourists, he wrote, that "one virtually sees only German license plates . . . and in the cafés only hears the growling voices of compatriots, mostly coming from north of the Main."[102]

As it happened, the majority of his compatriots traveled to countries outside the EC, especially to Austria—the most popular destination into the 1980s—and to Spain, which attracted 12 percent of all German tourists by 1971, when Franco still ruled supreme. "Eviva España," the smash hit of the following year, shouted out, "The sun shines night and day."[103] A Eurovision song contest was launched in 1956 by the European Broadcasting Union, which copied the idea from the Italian Sanremo Festival. Independent-minded youth who did not want to join their parents on the Costa del Sol could travel extensively by Interrail, a cheap season pass introduced in 1972 by European railway companies, again, with no connection to the Community. Youth camps and town partnerships—which started in the wake of the First World War and really took off after the Second—similarly deepened contacts across Europe and, indeed, across the Iron Curtain.[104] Compared to these popular encounters with Europe, the European Community appeared a rather dull club of old men in gray suits. In 1968, as we have seen, German students had a long list of radical demands. European integration was not among them. A passionate rallying cry after the Second World War, it had slipped from the political imagination. Instead, all eyes were on Vietnam and the "Third World."

GLOBAL CONSCIENCE

When Adenauer looked at the world his eyes moved from West to East. European Christendom was the cradle of Western civilization threatened by a barbarian East. Asia triggered in his mind the Mongolian invasion of Europe in the thirteenth century. Russian, Chinese, and North Vietnamese delegates at the Geneva Conference in 1954 had the "physiognomy of a horde," he told his cabinet.[105] Decolonization in Africa would be a catastrophe for "the white race."[106] In the 1920s, he had briefly served as the deputy chair of the German Colonial Society, which mourned the loss of the country's colonies at Versailles.

While the chancellor's map was fixed, world politics in the 1950s and 1960s began to shift in a north/south direction. In 1952, the French demographer Alfred Sauby coined the term "the Third World" to convey that the global South was ignored just as the Third Estate had been in the run-up to the French Revolution. Barely ten years later, the situation was unrecognizable: "development" had advanced into a watchword of international politics and solidarity with the "Third World" was a central tenet across the West.

Four main factors were behind this change. There were, firstly, the newly independent countries that were asserting themselves against their former colonial masters in the "First World." In 1955, India, Pakistan, Indonesia, Egypt, North and South Vietnam, and several other countries came together at the Bandung Conference to promote Asian-African cooperation and oppose neocolonialism. The Non-Aligned Movement was born. Second, Western states feared the advance of communism. Third, international organizations shifted their attention from the humanitarian crisis in Europe after 1945 to the global South: 1959 was World Refugee Year, the following year the United Nations Food and Agriculture Organization called for "Freedom from Hunger," and the year after that the UN rang in the decade of development. Finally, there were church-based and secular aid organizations that were campaigning for greater global justice. In 1958, the Protestant

World Council of Churches passed a resolution that called on rich countries to give 1 percent of their GDP to development.[107] The churches and aid bodies gave rise to a new humanitarianism within Germany and played a central role in putting development into practice in Africa and Asia.

When it came to "development," West Germany was a latecomer. In 1956, the Foreign Ministry gave a mere 50 million DM (around $12 million at the time) for technical aid to promote markets for German business in Africa. The Ministry of Economic Cooperation was not set up until five years later, after pressure from Western allies for Germany to do its share.[108]

Development was another stage in the Cold War. West Germany followed the so-called Hallstein Doctrine (named after the diplomat Walter Hallstein), which punished any country that opened formal relations with the GDR by cutting off diplomatic relations in response. East Germany used medical and military aid for African states to break out of its international isolation. The GDR sent youth brigades to Algeria, built apartments and hospitals in Tanzania, and, in the 1970s, shipped military and technical support to Angola and Mozambique. Aid would demonstrate the superiority of the "better" Germany. Traveling exhibitions showcased socialist science and public health. At the World Agriculture Fair in New Delhi in 1959, Indian prime minister Jawaharlal Nehru marveled at Heidi, a transparent cow made of glass that could, among other things, speak Hindi.[109]

For East and West Germany alike, the governing principle was to foster self-help. Aid was given to help societies help themselves. Western experts would show them how to pull themselves up and become productive and self-reliant. The two German states were following the well-traveled path of "improvement." Protestants had preached for centuries that God helped those who helped themselves. In reality, before the First World War, Imperial Germany had combined its civilizing mission with extreme violence that climaxed in the genocide of the Herero and Namaqua in its colony in South West Africa (Namibia). Development took the principles of social work from European cities to the African village. Community development through voluntary labor entered British and French colonial policy in the interwar years, and the United Nations thereafter.

In fact, work was sometimes forced and, instead of fostering solidarity and self-reliance, many projects ended in rivalry and conflict. The two Germanies wanted experts to be broad-minded and cosmopolitan, but where to find them? Projects often attracted racists and careerists. In West Germany, the top civil servant in the responsible ministry was Gustav Sonnenhol, a former SS officer. Africans needed Europeans to lead them, he wrote in 1966. In 1958, the first West German–funded hospital in South Korea had to be closed down after the new head of internal medicine exposed chronic sexual abuse and beatings as well as mismanagement. The medical staff, he wrote, were "unreconstructed, dyed-in-the wool" Nazis.[110] The GDR had fewer Nazis but at least as many racists. In Cameroon, the GDR used prison labor. Brigades of the Freie Deutsche Jugend (FDJ, Free German Youth) went to Zanzibar in 1964 to teach the locals "diligence, hard work, and German quality labor." Multistory apartment blocks were to showcase socialist friendship and modernity. Instead, the building site degenerated into friction. The local youth organization used force to discipline its workers and disliked it when East Germans handed out clothes or cash as incentives. The foreigners, meanwhile, were reluctant to adapt their plans to local circumstances, let alone share the initiative with local experts. In 1971, they gave up and left, with the tower blocks and a supermarket unfinished.[111]

"Self-help," then, was rarely innocent. Still, to treat it as "old wine in new bottles" is doing it injustice.[112] Self-help underwent a fundamental change in churches and civil society between the 1950s and 1970s. The Good Samaritan appeal to assist those in need was joined by a structural understanding of global inequality in which the rich North not only had a moral duty to help the poor South but was partly responsible for its plight. The "Third World" held a mirror up to people in the "First World" to examine their own lifestyle and idea of "progress." Campaigns to help poor countries help themselves began to call for partnership, reciprocity, and mutual recognition between the global North and South, echoing similar views in social welfare, the peace movement, and citizen initiatives. If self-help required respect for difference, perhaps Germans could also learn one or two things from people in Ghana or Guatemala?

The initial concern was for victims of famine. In 1957, an ecumenical group in West Berlin came together to raise money for the world's hungry. Copying the British "Miss a Meal" idea, in the next year and a half they raised 300,000 DM from pupils, pensioners, and workers who donated the money saved from the meal they skipped; that was equal to the government's contribution to the UN for technical aid. The Catholic youth movement added its own fasting campaign in 1958. A newspaper in Fulda raised 500,000 DM for rice for Calcutta. Both major German Churches now seized the initiative and set up the two agencies that have dominated ever since: the Catholic Misereor (1958) and the Protestant Bread for the World (1959).[113] In their first year, together they raised 56 million DM; by 1980 it was 190 million DM.

Misereor took its name from the Latin and the New Testament where Christ says, "I have compassion for these people; they have already been with me three days and have nothing to eat" (Mark 8:2). Cardinal Josef Frings, who christened the organization, acknowledged that the colonial system was partly to blame for global injustice. Aid would restore the church's reputation overseas.[114] As much as concern for the starving poor in Asia and Africa, aid was about saving the souls of well-fed Germans. The cardinal hoped for a spiritual awakening: "As they will show compassion, so God will show them mercy." Frings was acutely aware of the growing influence of the state in social life. Adenauer's pension reform, he told the bishops, had helped people more than all the Catholic charities together. In the development field, though, the church wanted to retain its lead from missionary days. It needed to "appeal to the conscience" of those in power as well as their congregations. He called for a nationwide fast for 1959. If someone had a VW but was able to afford a Mercedes, he said, that person would be better off keeping his VW and giving the money he would have spent to feed the global poor instead.[115]

The aid campaigns merged older warnings against sinful luxury with memories of foreign help after the war and the new ethical responsibilities from living in a globalized world. "The German nation is well off," Catholic bishops said during the fasting action against world hunger in 1959. They were not asking for alms, but for "far-reaching sacrifice." "How will we face God's judgment one day, if we spend big sums . . . for excessive cosmetics . . . luxury goods and luxury clothes, luxury holidays and luxury cars" that could have saved others from their suffering? Collection boxes spelled out the gains from personal sacrifice: the pocket money that normally bought one chocolate bar could feed an entire family in Saigon for two days; a trip to the hairdresser for a "perm" was enough to protect 500 people in Africa against typhoid and death for an entire year. Active charity required a tangible sacrifice because the goal was "to overcome materialism," leaflets explained: "We are lazy for the misery of our fellow men, but insatiable and industrious to the point of nausea when it is about satisfying our own interests." Distance was no longer an excuse for doing nothing. Globalization had shrunk the circles of moral concern. "You can fly in three hours from Frankfurt to Tunis . . . and from there it is two hours by car to Le Kef. In this region, 130,000 people are living in holes in the ground," surviving on thirty-three pounds of wheat and a cup of oil a month. "Global aid today is nothing else than help thy neighbor."[116]

Initially, care for distant others was a repayment for the aid Germans themselves had received after the war. At its launch in 1959, the Protestant Bread for the World made a point of collecting donations in the foreign milk powder containers that had arrived just over a decade earlier. They remembered hunger, Misereor said, and thanked God with their sacrifice. Donors responded. A man who had arrived destitute from West Prussia wrote that he had "empathy with the need of the starving people" and happily donated to Misereor, regardless of being a Protestant himself. A widow from East Prussia had lost her homeland and her husband; she wished to thank God for sparing her only son. She scraped together 10 DM from her small pension.[117]

Some voices appealed to the guilt of the rich as well as the gratitude of the poor. Father Leppich, known as "God's machine gun" for his rousing (and amplified) sermons in factories and circus tents, returned from a tour of the world's slums in 1958 to castigate audiences back home: "All of us have profited from them, in Germany as much as in England... We have raised our standard of living on the back of coolies... If Europe is now offering Asia a helping hand, it is not an act of mercy but reparation."[118] Soul-searching over affluence began with sins of omission. Sermons in the 1960s reprimanded Germans for thoughtlessly throwing away bread while Indians were starving. While their shop windows were overflowing in the run-up to Christmas, the global poor went empty-handed.

By 1970, however, the diagnosis was that how the rich lived was responsible for the misery of the "Third World." Campaigns for global justice mirrored the new focus on "structural violence" noted earlier. Development was the new name for peace. Poverty in the South was blamed on tariffs, cartels, and selfish consumers in the North. Affluent shoppers feasted on cheap sugar and cocoa. In alerting consumers to their complicity, the campaigns replayed the boycotts against sugar harvested by enslaved people in the years around 1800, although now sugar and coffee producers were no longer enslaved but small farmers at the mercy of big corporations and commodity agreements that fixed prices.

There was pressure on the EEC to abolish its agricultural subsidies and open its markets. At the Lomé Convention in 1975, the Europeans agreed to give countries from the African, Caribbean, and Pacific Commonwealth (ACP) preferential access to the single market, with quotas for sugar and beef, and development aid. At the same time, Europe flooded the world market with its own subsidized beet sugar, undermining prices. Frustrated with international politics, "fair trade" bodies turned directly to European consumers. Taking their lead from Dutch campaigners, Germans opened "Third World" shops and sold sugar and coffee at fair prices directly procured from small farmers. Ethical consumption was taking the place of fasting.[119]

The shifting moral imperative of aid was reflected in the representation of the "Third World." Pictures of famine victims could pull at people's heartstrings. Yet campaigners were conscious that presenting one catastrophe after another also risked creating a sense that these distant societies were "basket cases." In 1962, Misereor's posters showed a starving child. It commissioned market psychologists to study its effect. Priests, active Catholics, and non-believers alike found the images "terrifying, terrible, uncanny, awful, horrible, horrifying, brutal, bloody, disgusting, alienating, repulsive, unimaginable." To be surrounded by such pictures, one person said, would make "living one's own life impossible." The child looked so close to death that others wondered whether it was even possible to save it. In 1964, Misereor replaced this poster with one of a well-proportioned child dressed in "clean clothes," a "human being where help still had a chance to succeed." Five years later, the motto of the donation drive was "Give every human being their chance."[120]

These years saw major campaigns for the victims of the Anatolian earthquake (1966), war-induced famine in Biafra (1968–70), flooding in Bangladesh (1973), and drought in Africa (1973). It is tempting to see here the triumph of a "catastrophic" approach to aid.[121] Arguably, the opposite was the case. The lion's share of the money collected went to structural development. In its first ten years, Misereor sponsored more than six thousand local projects with a total of 557 million DM; of this only 22 million DM was direct aid for catastrophes. The bulk supported public health initiatives and projects for farmers and artisans. Campaigns stressed that "aid for catastrophes is no solution for the problems of the future. Start-up aid is vital to create the conditions for a new, better life" (1966). To cut through the cycle of hunger and poverty required wells, tools for farmers, and schools such as the ones it supported in Uganda, Bolivia, and Guatemala. Bread for the World sponsored similar development projects. In West Berlin in 1973–74, more than eighty Protestant congregations were raising money for projects in Africa, Latin America, and Asia. They distributed almost half a million flyers, showed a dozen films, had market stands, street collections, brass bands, and a car convoy through the Tiergarten district of West Berlin, and raised an impressive 1.6 million DM. Schools held bazaars, flea markets, and cake sales. In 1978, in the small town of Borth-Wallach on the Rhine, the nine-year-old children of the local elementary school watched slides about the village of Gofa in Ethiopia. A girl wrote to Bread for the World, "The village is very poor and does not have a proper school. That is why we collected DM 50." She requested the money be used to support schools in Ethiopia. Not far from the North Sea, in the town of Bad Zwischenahn, a twelve-year-old enclosed 200 DM from her class to go to Bolivia. They asked for a report back on how it was used.[122]

Empathy was linked to greater respect for different cultures and, in turn, made Germans reflect on their own lifestyle and model of progress. A brief comparison of the campaigns in the mid-1960s with those ten years later illustrates the moral journey traveled. In 1966, Bread for the World got residents in Leverkusen to collect glass bottles, scrap metal, and rags and paper to fill twenty-five trucks with aid for India. A dozen beat bands raised 4,000 DM. A factory in Stuttgart worked overtime to add another 34,000 DM, and preschool teachers sacrificed the money they normally would have spent for their Sunday roasts. Articles explained that "our technical progress would not be possible without the raw materials from Africa and Asia." Aid ensured that Germans could export goods and enjoy a rich breakfast table. "If they do badly, then the white race will not do well in the long run either." Although there was a call to "shake off our Western arrogance and recognize colored people as partners and equals," it barely extended beyond a general spirit of cooperation.[123]

By the mid-1970s, campaigners tried to see the world through the eyes of the poor. The "recipient of aid should not be the object of our pity... he is a subject"—a reversal that mirrored that in social welfare at home.[124] Slide shows about the commodity chain of coffee no longer just asked for greater fairness for agrarian countries but for affluent Germans to rethink their idea of progress. In 1975, Bread for the World's seventeenth annual campaign was opened by Klaus von Bismarck, the head of West German Radio (WDR) and a devout Protestant. The person who "claims a right to irreplaceable resources," he said, "must put up with the follow-up question of how he justifies the right to steady growth of our consumer economy."[125] Posters displayed the disproportionate energy consumption of the rich global North as a "yardstick of misdevelopment": one U.S. citizen consumed as much as 2 Germans, 60 Indians, or 1,100 Rwandans.[126] The metropole and the slum now appeared in the same frame. "Live differently so others can live," was the motto of Catholic youth in the late 1970s.[127]

The poor were idealized as resourceful and "joyful" human beings who were demonstrating "day after day their sense of responsibility and ability to cope with life."[128] If Germans were more appreciative of other cultures they would begin to question their own consumerist mind-set. Sermons, games, and bazaars spelled out the implications: people should drive less and eat less meat. "A lentil stew with just a little salt meat" made for "a simple, hearty, and nutritious lunch."[129] Catholic youth cut out the meat altogether, and offered a vegetarian cookbook. In exchange for development aid, Kerala could teach them about taste and spices. In a colorful series of fairy tales, Bread for the World took children *Once to the Third World and Back* to imagine "what it would be like if Germany was a development country and the development countries were rich." Empathy was taught through role-play. Catholic congregations had meditations of "empty hands," where comfortable Germans were asked to switch into the position of a poor person unable to give anything back in return for aid. Intercultural "simulator games" made Germans play native people and international experts building a bridge together. In an activity for day cares, German children had a chance to meet "Juan and José—two Indios from the Andes" "to discover that other children live differently, dress differently, eat differently, look different, and speak differently."[130] The "Third World" could also teach grown-ups to be more tolerant toward each other in the "First World": what priests accomplished in the slums showed their German brethren how to work with groups at the margins of their own society (*Randgruppen*).[131]

These "Third World" campaigns might look naïve from today's vantage point, but the activists at the time were well aware of the obstacles in their path. Development was officially recognized as its own policy domain by the Brandt government in 1969, shepherded by Erhard Eppler, the minister of economic cooperation, a fervent missionary for global justice. There were commitments to cheaper credits, more aid, and technical experts. When the oil crisis hit in 1973, however, development aid was cut. German jobs took precedence over global justice.[132] Development once again became a servant of realpolitik and as such had to satisfy German industry's interest in cheap raw materials. At the United Nations Conference on Trade and Development (UNCTAD) in Nairobi in 1976, the Schmidt government opposed the demands by "Third World" countries for financial instruments to help them trade.

Solidarity and empathy with people in the global South never reached more than a minority in Germany. The aid campaigns look impressive next to other donation drives, much less so in terms of aggregate spending. On average, a West German in the 1970s only gave 73 pfennigs a year to development. The archives of the aid bodies are full of cynical remarks by members of the public. Africans were lazy, some said, and should take a lesson from Germans, who had pulled themselves up by their bootstraps after the war. The Africans would only buy guns, said others; send them money, and they would come and "slay" our children. Charity should start at home, with the local poor and those fleeing the GDR. When asked how to tackle world hunger, most answered: birth control.[133] Even among the active young Catholics, only half the regional sections held regular events on development issues.[134]

It would be equally wrong, though, to write off their influence. In addition to their own projects, the churches struck a deal with the state and served as intermediaries in the field of development, subject to the understanding that they did not use public funds for missionary purposes. In Germany as elsewhere in the West, development aid groups were increasingly working together with states.[135] Between 1962 and 1975, the Protestant Central Bureau for Development Aid (EZE) received federal funds worth 578 million DM. On top, in 1969, the Protestant Church decided to commit 2 percent of the revenue they received from church taxes to development projects. Development campaigns were not limited to a few idealists but reached the general public. Bowling clubs were "bowling for Biafra" in 1969. There were lively festivals and silent marches. By 1974, a thousand groups were selling tea, coffee, and handicrafts from small producers in the Aktion Third World Trade. Christian Democrats, who had a nose for spotting emerging trends and making them their own, embraced development in the course of the 1970s. The Konrad Adenauer Foundation sponsored projects by Christian Democratic groups in Latin America.[136] In 1981, the CDU adopted their youth section's motto "Live differently so others can live" in 1981. In the Saarland, members of the Junge Union went on a hunger march for the "Third World." In Baden-Württemberg, the rich state in the southwest and home of Mercedes, virtually every district section had a partnership project with the "Third World." The one in Ostalb set up Christmas stands, garden parties, and a secondhand shop to raise money for a power generator for a lepers' colony in Guatemala.[137] Even in the provinces, Germany was becoming less provincial.

Each year, Misereor devoted its fast to one country. In 1983, it was South Africa's turn. The campaign revealed the moral geography of West Germans before reunification. On Maundy Thursday, the day that commemorates the Last Supper, churches lit candles from Soweto. Towns organized street theater and marathon walks. No other fast generated so much debate. Was a Catholic body right to get involved in the bitter fight over apartheid? Franz Josef Strauss, the bullish Conservative overlord of Bavaria and friend of the P. W. Botha regime, then in charge in South Africa, attacked Misereor members as demagogues and fantasists who should leave politics to Christian realists like him. Strauss didn't just support regular German business with South Arica; he also, with Chancellor Kohl's knowledge, facilitated a contract for submarines, violating a UN weapons embargo that the country had signed on to in 1977. (Botha attended Strauss's funeral in 1988.) Some of Misereor's loyal donors were outraged that their organization was supporting the guerrilla South West Africa People's Organization (SWAPO). "We will give nothing!" one wrote in anger. People charged Misereor with supporting "communists" and "asylum-parasites" and endangering the "preservation of ethnic substance." This minority view was expressed in a quarter of the several hundred letters the organization received. Twice as many—young people, overwhelmingly—greeted the campaign with "enthusiastic support." The three biggest dioceses—Cologne, Freiburg, and Munich—alone raised 23 million DM. Most Misereor supporters had come to recognize that development aid was by its very nature political and that the churches needed to concern themselves with the causes of underdevelopment in order to lay the foundations for a dignified existence. Charity had widened into global justice. One donor thanked Misereor especially for choosing South Africa. He urged the organization not to be distracted by economic interests, and raised his usual donation.[138]

SECOND-CLASS CITIZENS

In its first three articles, the Basic Law laid down the fundamental rights and liberties that were the building blocks of a liberal democratic society. The problem was that, after 1949, they remained distant ideals for several groups.

West Germany was a republic with first- and second-class citizens. As we have seen, homosexuals and Sinti and Roma were excluded from *Wiedergutmachung* for the injustices they had suffered in the Third Reich. They continued to suffer discrimination and were targeted by the Federal Bureau of Investigation (Bundeskriminalamt), which was thick with old Nazis.[139]

In the 1950s and 1960s, some fifty thousand people were convicted under the notorious Section 175, which made consensual homosexuality between men a crime. Some gay men committed suicide. Petitioners turned to the Constitutional Court to defend their fundamental rights—to no avail. The Basic Law itself said that the right to the "free development of personality" was limited by "moral law" (*Sittengesetz*). Since homosexuals were said to suffer from a higher sex drive, frequent change of partners, and a tendency to commit crimes, the moral fabric of society was at risk. An architect saw it as his duty as a "responsible democratic citizen" to write to the court in 1957 that the country had to be saved from "the disease imported by ethically dubious non-Christian peoples"; it was the "one good thing" the Third Reich had accomplished.[140] Significantly, the European Commission for Human Rights, in 1955, found that states had the right to legislate against homosexuality in order to protect family life.

East Germany stopped punishing consenting gay adults from the late 1950s. West Germany, by contrast, maintained the Nazis' tougher version of Paragraph 175, which no longer required physical contact for punishment to be meted out. It made West Germany not only less liberal than contemporary France and Italy but also less than Weimar. After 1969, adult gay men were no longer criminalized, but they were hardly treated as equal citizens. Teachers who came out risked losing their jobs. In 1975, for example, a court upheld the dismissal of a gay teacher in Berlin, saying that he had no right to infringe the country's "unwritten laws of honor, convention, and decency." What he did in his private life was his business, the court said, but wearing nail polish in school made him an "agent of homosexuality who was, so to speak, sneaking into the teaching profession from behind." His behavior threatened to seduce his pupils to homosexual acts by removing their "psychological inhibitions."[141] Homosexuals themselves were conflicted and pulled between rebellion and respectability. Some embraced their difference and the new politics of "gay" liberation, while others continued to identify themselves as "homophile" to stress their "normality." Paragraph 175 would not be struck from the legal code until 1994.[142]

DEMOCRACY DISABLED

Another group that faced multiple barriers to liberty and fairness were people with disabilities. Looking at their ordeal is instructive in its own right, and holds up a mirror to the rest of society, revealing something about the limits of who was considered an equal citizen.

Postwar Germany was a nation of the disabled—4 million in West Germany alone in the early 1960s. At the same time, "the disabled" as a group did not exist. They were divided, first of all, by the cause of their impairment. The war wounded tried to keep their distance from those who were born with a disability or became blind or deaf later in life. When, in 1952, it was proposed to make it easier for civilian disabled people to enter the labor market, the Association of the War Disabled, a lobby with 1.5 million members, who already enjoyed that benefit, vehemently opposed it: "There is no getting away from the truth that one group of the nation did more and sacrificed more than the other."[143] In addition to patriotic sacrifice, distinct identities owed a good deal to the ethos informing the German insurance system since Bismarck. The deserving citizen was one who had made a contribution to society in the past for which they now received a pension in return. The hierarchy of claimants was based on the circumstances under which a fully functioning body was lost. A leg lost on the battlefield was not the same as a leg missing at birth. Disabled veterans had their own sports programs. They were "the elite among the disabled," one functionary reminded them at their annual competition in 1962, and should always act "in stark contrast to the miserable, dubious cripples who flaunt their disabled limbs and can be found as beggars on the street or as asocials at night outside the central station."[144]

Greater recognition and support for *all* disabled persons came slowly and partially. In 1957, a disability welfare law provided public help with education and retraining to those who were neither disabled by war nor covered by insurance. Four years later, the flagship Federal Social Assistance Act extended the right to personal aid to the blind and deaf, those with speech impediments, and those "with weak mental faculties." "Rehabilitation," not alms, was the goal, and this initially centered on work. As the director of the Federal Employment Agency explained, "Appropriate work gives people their personality and helps them cope with their fate." Unemployment, he said, would only add a "social deficit" to a person's existing "physical deficit."[145] The key word was "deficit." In this early phase, the job of rehabilitation was to repair "faulty" people.

By 1970, West Germany financed 170,000 rehabilitations a year. There were special schools with more than 300,000 places and a growing number of workshops where disabled people made brooms and brushes. Many problems remained. Many children continued to wait for a school that was equipped to address their particular needs. Genuine integration was (and remains) low compared to Nordic countries. Disability benefits were handed out by the welfare office (*Sozialamt*), which made them shameful to many recipients. Before 1975, only those doing sufficiently "valuable" work were included in a health insurance and pension program.

East Germany, too, focused on integration through work. When the Wall came down in November 1989, half of the 1.2 million officially registered disabled persons worked in the regular economy; that year, the GDR supported 40,000 rehabilitations. Leaving aside the long wait for orthopedic shoes and the appalling conditions in the few outdated institutions in the GDR, the big difference from West Germany lay in its approach to mentally disabled children. Whereas in West Germany they were taught reading and writing from the 1960s on, the East distinguished between those "capable" and those "not capable" of education, and condemned the latter to public neglect. In the GDR, mentally disabled people were considered to suffer from "damaged intelligence" (*Intelligenzschädigung*) and "mental deficiency" (*Schwachsinn*) and thus were consequently unfit for special education.[146]

The 1960s and 1970s brought a fundamental change, at least in West Germany. Instead of disabled people being "defective," they started to be seen as just different, and it was the rest of society that needed to adapt. This role reversal was part of the growing appreciation of pluralistic lifestyles. Disabled groups were both beneficiaries and drivers of this shift. The Council of Europe advocated rehabilitation regardless of the nature of disability or material benefit as early as 1950. Parents, doctors, and priests began to take inspiration from special schools and workshops in the United States, Britain, and Sweden. Better diagnostics, therapy, and education showed how it was possible to improve the lot of disabled people significantly. In the late 1950s, several thousand children were born without limbs because their mothers had been prescribed the popular tranquilizer thalidomide (Contergan) in pregnancy. A global medical scandal erupted in 1961. The plight of the children stirred public sympathy. Together with the growing number of people maimed in car accidents, they were seen as innocent victims rather than naturally "defective" people. Normality and disability were no longer separate states: it was possible to be both.

Greater equality of opportunities and Chancellor Brandt's call to "dare more democracy" opened the public sphere to marginalized groups. So did the fact that West Germany was increasingly becoming a consumer society. The narrow focus on rehabilitation for work widened to full participation in the life of the community, including leisure and travel. Buildings and transport needed to be accessible. In 1974, a new law gave every disabled person the right to get help with integration, irrespective of the cause of their impairment and past pension contributions. A lot of the pressure came from self-help organizations. In 1958, the Lebenshilfe ("help to live") association was set up by a group of doctors, lawyers, and parents fighting for the interests of mentally disabled people; half the founding members were not disabled. Ten years later, it had 38,000 members. In the 1970s, they were joined by so-called CeBeef Clubs ("Clubs for the Disabled and Their Friends") and radical "cripple groups." Slowly, disability began to lose some of its stigma. "Who of us is not disabled?" a Protestant group asked in 1975. Pastors invoked "the disabled Jesus" as a "thorn in the flesh of this world." Disabled persons were not "deficient" or "minus-humans" but the "conscience of the non-disabled."[147]

Instead of shutting disabled people away in institutions, church and youth groups began to include them in "open" programs of shared activities. The Catholic Scouts first took disabled members along on tours in 1965. Protestant youth followed with dance lessons and disco evenings. There were mixed apartment shares. Adult education centers introduced wheelchair classes to make people see and feel the obstacles disabled citizens faced day in and day out. When, in 1972, a church-based leisure center took a group to Lake Constance for a week of theater, games, and boating, they banned the term "disabled" and rechristened them "guests." In Essen, two youth centers organized joint holidays and leisure activities. They were sponsored by the city, congregations, and parents, and could count on three hundred local volunteers. In 1973, in Upper Franconia, disabled people were for the first time included in discussions of what working with them should be about. They told their carers they wanted to enjoy love and sex, to have problems and not be perfect, to have more space and pocket money, to be able to shape their home and place of work. As one participant summed it up, they wanted the "right and freedom to develop a personality" (as the Basic Law promised all citizens).[148]

Here was a major difference with East Germany. Without a civil society to support them, disabled people and their families were isolated. In Berlin-Mitte, parents of children considered "unfit for education" formed a support group and in 1969 voiced their frustration to the government by saying there was neither empathy nor help for them. Their children were treated as "damaged citizens" and ghettoized. Experts, the media, and everyone else ignored them. The waiting list for a wheelchair was four years.[149]

Greater public recognition did not automatically translate into lived citizenship for disabled people in West Germany. Many barriers remained, psychological as well as physical. Awareness was not the same as empathy. The Aktion Sorgenkind (Action "Problem Child") turned into the biggest TV lottery in the world. Between 1964 and 1989, it raised 1.5 billion DM for disabled children; one man raised 30,000 DM by doing 149 consecutive somersaults on his trampoline. On the one hand, it made people aware of the appalling conditions in overcrowded homes and helped fund better facilities. On the other, donations were a convenient way of appeasing the conscience and avoid thinking about what living together with disabled persons might require from oneself. There was pity and relief, as when a father generously gave 1,000 DM as thanks for the birth of his own healthy child.[150] For disability activists, the charity reinforced the idea of handicapped people as silent heroes who accepted their fate, gritted their teeth, and overcame obstacles, rather than as citizens who had a right to be included.[151]

The circle of compassion might have been expanding, but it remained strongest with the nearest and dearest. A public health study in the mid-1960s interviewed parents of children born without limbs, and, in some cases, without hearing or intestines. After the initial shock and a sense of guilt and rejection, parents pulled together around the children. Most fathers began to show "a lively interest in the future position of their child in society." "M. will go to elementary school," one father insisted, "even if I have to go to court." Husbands said that their disabled child had "only strengthened their union with their wife." Older siblings were caring; an army recruit requested a transfer to the local barracks so he would be able to visit his disabled sister on weekends. Neighbors, too, were mostly welcoming: "Don't hide your child, it belongs to us." "The child is the darling and center of the whole house."[152]

The problem was the general public. The greater the distance, the greater the prejudice. Parents were stopped with their children in the street by strangers who asked, "Did you take pills? Does it come from watching television? Is it the result of nuclear radiation?"[153] A survey in the early 1970s found that 70 percent of Germans felt disgust when facing a disabled person. Sixty-three percent thought such children would be best off living in an institution, out of sight, and 56 percent would rather not live in the same building with them. For every third person, physical disability implied a mental handicap as well. In devout communities, disability continued to be seen as God's punishment for the mother's sins. In-depth interviews revealed that many people continued to see euthanasia as the best solution: "Let's not bring up Hitler, but he did clean up in the homes and gave them a merciful injection."[154] Such opinions were not the preserve of old reactionaries. In 1973, sixteen young women who worked in a cornstarch factory gave their views about "crippled children": "The children should be killed: by a licensed doctor, immediately after birth." "[To] let them live is a sin against nature. Primitive races killed anyone unfit for life, and it was the same in the animal kingdom." "Pity was no help to them; they needed to be taken away at an early stage, so that they could be helped." "One cannot expect the other family members to live with disgusting cripples for the rest of their lives." Only one of the young women disagreed: these kids had a right to be raised, too, she said, adding that, one day, parents would have to answer for their neglect.[155]

Public authorities were slow to make living together easier. The Council of Europe declared that all public buildings should be accessible in 1959. It took West Germany until 1972 to introduce new norms for apartments, and even then most architects continued to design with a fictional "normal" person in mind. The brand-new, brutalist University of Bochum refused to make any of its flats accessible to wheelchair users, claiming a lack of demand. There were more than 300,000 disabled people in the state of Hesse, but only 20,000 of them lived in a suitable apartment, and those tended to be the more privileged war veterans.

Rehabilitation and work continued to be a football that official agencies and insurance bodies kicked back and forth between them. While everyone accepted that disabled workshops were a good thing in principle, the question was who should pay for them, and according to what criteria. For disability groups, doctors, and welfare organizations, the value of work lay in its positive effects on disabled people. For the Federal Employment Agency, what mattered was their productivity. The end of the economic boom in 1973 was followed by austerity measures. To qualify for assistance with integration in a workshop, a disabled person had to accomplish at least one third of what a non-disabled worker could do. Equal rights were competing with the German ideal of *Leistungsgesellschaft*, which tied fairness to merit and performance. A man from Augsburg suffering from cerebral palsy, for example, was the subject of a tug-of-war between the Social Welfare Court, which defended his job of putting plugs in a plastic bag for its social and psychological benefits, and the Employment Agency, for which its economic value was insufficient to justify further assistance; the person needed institutional care instead, according to the agency.

Discrimination continued in public life. A Hessian town banned mentally disabled children from its public swimming pool "for hygienic and other reasons"; a local Liberal explained that "a mentally disabled person is not a human being in a normal sense: he is merely a torso, eking out its existence." Further north, in Schleswig-Holstein, there were pastors who excluded disabled teenagers from confirmation. A young woman with cerebral palsy lamented that as a welfare recipient she was "condemned to a position of submissive gratitude." For twenty-four years, she had been made to feel "a disabled person first, and only then a human being."[156]

The United Nations made 1981 the year of disabled persons. The German run-up was not auspicious. In 1980, the district court in Frankfurt ruled in favor of a sixty-four-year-old woman who claimed that the value of her vacation had been diminished not only by defective air conditioning but also by the presence of disabled people in her Greek hotel; the tour operator had to reimburse her 750 DM. For the presiding judge, Dr. Otto Tempel, it was an "unmistakable" fact that disabled people "can impair the pleasure of a vacation for sensitive people," especially if it involved "deformed, mentally retarded people, who cannot speak ... giving off inarticulate screams in irregular rhythms and having occasional raving fits." Integrating people with disabilities might be a worthy goal, but a tour operator could "surely" not force it on its customers. "That there is suffering in the world cannot be changed; but one cannot refuse the plaintiff if she does not want to look at it during her vacation."[157]

Disability activists were outraged. A press conference by the court, which repeated these views, fanned the flames. The journalist Ernst Klee, who specialized in exposing discrimination against marginal groups, traveled to

Sweden to have a look at the people who had caused the German vacationer so much distress. It turned out that they were not mentally disabled at all. They had cerebral palsy. They had speech impediments and difficulty coordinating their movements but were calm, friendly, and alert. One of them was a law student. On May 8, 1980, several thousand disabled citizens and their friends converged on Frankfurt for their "Day of Liberation" to protest the verdict. Not only was the verdict upheld, the presiding judge successfully sued Klee for slander.

The following year, supporters of disabled people ran into opposition from the burghers of nearby Kirchhain. A resident had offered apartments to a citizen initiative that supported assisted living for disabled persons. Founded in 1973, the group already ran a workshop in town for mentally disabled people together with the Lebenshilfe. The mayor supported the project, as did a local judge. The locals, though, were up in arms. A citizen assembly unanimously vetoed the plan. They did not want integration; that would be letting loose "complete retards" on their community, one resident warned. Parents feared for their children. "Once they are here, they are here," one local person concluded, and "then the only way is to smoke them out."[158] A decade earlier, a new home for mentally disabled people had, in fact, gone up in smoke in lower Bavaria under mysterious circumstances—the innkeeper and head of the local CSU said that what citizens wanted was a "national park, not a park for idiots."[159]

The United Nations year was meant to open hearts. When the responsible Protestant bodies came together in 1982 to take stock, they reported instead "great resignation about the UN year among disabled and nondisabled alike."[160]

Anyone looking at democracy in West Germany in the 1980s could not but be impressed. The Federal Republic had a strong constitution, the rule of law, high voter turnout, democratic parties with mass membership, a culture of debate, and vibrant citizen groups. Extremists and terrorists had failed to pull it down. Adenauer was proved right: Bonn would not end like Weimar. It was an achievement few observers had thought possible after the war. Yet much remained undone to create a truly inclusive society.

6

A New Socialist People: The Many Moralities of the GDR

Prenzlauer Berg, the district in East Berlin with a little hill, might be no match for Mount Sinai, but it was here, at the Fifth Party Congress of the Socialist Unity Party of Germany (SED) on Thursday, July 10, 1958, that Walter Ulbricht, the communist leader, revealed the "Ten Commandments for the New Socialist Person" to the people of East Germany. They were:

> 1) You shall always work hard for the international solidarity of the working class and all workers and for the indestructible bond between all socialist countries.
> 2) You shall love your fatherland and always be ready to defend the workers' and peasants' power [*Arbeiter-und-Bauern-Macht*] with all your strength and ability.
> 3) You shall help to abolish the exploitation of man by man.
> 4) You shall do good deeds for socialism, because socialism leads to a better life for all workers.
> 5) You shall act in the spirit of mutual aid and comradely cooperation in building socialism, respect the collective, and heed its criticism.
> 6) You shall protect and increase state-owned property.
> 7) You shall always strive to improve your performance, be frugal, and strengthen socialist work discipline.
> 8) You shall raise your children in the spirit of peace and socialism to become well-rounded, principled, and physically hardened human beings.
> 9) You shall live a clean and respectable life and respect your family.
> 10) You shall show solidarity with the peoples fighting for their national liberation and with those defending their national independence.

Ulbricht's ruthlessness was matched only by his arrogance. He was known as "Germany's Lenin"—he copied the Soviet revolutionary leader's goatee and reminded people that he had met him before his death in 1924—and saw himself alongside Karl Marx and Friedrich Engels in the socialist pantheon. Ulbricht was convinced that the GDR—the first "workers-and-peasants state" in German history with a Marxist-Leninist party in command—was one step ahead in the evolution toward full communism, much to the irritation of "big brother" in Moscow. His exaggerated sense of self-importance would be his downfall in 1971.

It would be wrong, though, to belittle the socialist Ten Commandments. Their immediate purpose was to launch another attack in the ongoing battle with the churches, which, irritatingly, continued to attract many young hearts and minds away from the socialist project. Their ultimate ambition, however, was greater. As announced in the original title—which was subsequently changed to "Ten Commandments of Socialist Morality and Ethics"—it was to create a new type of human being. Comparing the two Germanies with regard to peace and aggression, nature and the environment, family and caring, and other topics is useful, but in many ways the GDR was one of a kind, with its own moral universe and its own dilemmas and faults, and it deserves separate consideration. The Ten Commandments are a reminder of the utopian zeal and emancipatory ambition that powered the regime: a better future was within reach. The GDR was a *Neues Deutschland*, a New Germany, as its official newspaper was called. Exploitation, hunger, and war would be things of the past. The aim was nothing short of comprehensive behavior change, having people learn to subordinate their private interests to that of the collective and walk arm-in-arm toward peace and harmony.

How much did the GDR change the moral lives of its citizens, and what happened to the moral project in the end?

MORALITY AND MATERIALISM

Moral crusades and socialism make an awkward couple. In Marxist theory, it is material relations that transform nature and society. Mind follows matter, not the other way around. As Marx famously put it in 1859, "It is not the consciousness of men that determines their existence [*Sein*], but their societal existence that determines their consciousness."[1] Consequently, socialists were meant to focus on seizing the means of production from the hands of the class enemy. There were no timeless moral truths, Engels proclaimed two decades later. "Consciously and unconsciously," he wrote, "men... derive their ethical ideas in the last resort from the practical relations on which their class position is based, that is, the economic relations in which they produce and exchange." A religious age produced religious morality, a bourgeois one its own bourgeois version. The future belonged to "proletarian morality," which, Engels believed, would usher in "truly human morality" because not only would it eliminate the antagonism between classes, it also would wipe its memory from the praxis of daily life. As private property vanished, so would the moral injunctions to defend it; "Thou shall not steal" would become meaningless.[2]

So much for the theory. In reality, the leaders and people of the GDR found themselves in a very different position. Marx and Engels might have been confident that each material stage of history gave rise to its own moral character, but at the time the socialist Ten Commandments were revealed, the GDR was in a transition between stages. Private property coexisted with collectivized industry. Socialism was still a building site—hence, the Fifth Commandment. Moral transformation could not wait for material transformation; it was needed to propel it. Moral policing therefore pursued two complementary goals. One was a kind of ethical catching up, bringing people's outdated ideals and actions into line with the new reality. Now that industry was owned by the state, people should learn to respect state-owned property (Commandment 6). The other looked to the future: by being productive, disciplined, comradely, and clean, and by educating their children to become mini-socialists, people would bring socialism within reach (Commandments 3–5 and 7–9). This view was closer to that of certain millenarians, who believed that good deeds could accelerate the Second Coming, than to Marx and Engels.

There was more common ground with Marx and Engels in treating morality as an outlook shared by an entire class. Antagonism between classes would give way to the rule of the proletariat, peace, and harmony. "Socialist morality" would bring the individual into unison with the collective. Since exploitation was over, how could conflicts possibly arise in the future?

What this view overlooked was that ideals themselves could be contradictory, pulling the same class, even the same person, in different directions. People might care a lot for others in their neighborhood but not much for their country, or vice versa. Someone might feel a great duty to their work, but not necessarily to their coworkers or trade union. Values can clash. What seems fair to one person might look unfair to another. Morality helps people decide between paths of actions, but people arrive at these crossroads with different road maps. Some socialist writers started to recognize these problems in the 1980s.[3] In the end, the socialist pursuit of harmony produced more moral dilemmas than it resolved.

In the years after German reunification in 1990, two polar opposite assessments of the GDR took hold. They can be summarized as the "Stasi" view and the "day care" view.[4] The first condemned the GDR as an "*Unrechtsstaat*," a dictatorship that violated basic human rights. The state intelligence service, the Stasi, with its unprecedented surveillance system, epitomized the spirit of a country where people spied on each other and were imprisoned behind a wall and shot if they tried to cross it. Significantly, "Thou shall not kill" did not make it into the socialist Ten Commandments, nor did "not bearing false witness." The opposite view held up the social accomplishments of the GDR: free child care, health clinics, cheap rents, and guaranteed jobs for all. The GDR took pride in its record of social and economic rights. The more that jobs were lost after reunification and the more people's lives were thrown into uncertainty, the rosier memories of the GDR became. *Ostalgia* took hold. Defending the positive bits of the GDR was simultaneously a way of defending the worth of one's own past. East Germans had led "normal" lives too, they insisted. They had had children and married (increasingly in this order), divorced, worked, read good literature, grown cucumbers in their allotments, and (with luck) spent summer vacation in a bungalow provided by the state trade union. What mattered to most people who held this view was this "normal" life, not the excesses of the Stasi.

Normality in the GDR, however, came with many not-so-normal moral dilemmas, trade-offs, and surrenders. To understand this, it's useful to look at people's lives from the perspective of society as well as from that of the individual, and to distinguish consequences from intentions. In his seminal essay "Power of the Powerless" (1978), the dissident Czech playwright and later president Václav Havel pondered why a greengrocer would put up a poster with the command "Workers in the world unite!" It was fair to assume, Havel wrote, that the shopkeeper did not really believe in the slogan. He did not dream of a world revolution. Nonetheless, by displaying the sign in his shop window, he sent an important message to the rest of the community. It signaled, wrote Havel, that "I, the greengrocer... behave in the manner expected of me... I am obedient and therefore have the right to be left in peace." The shopkeeper had been subordinated through fear and was powerless, and the poster was a simple way of suppressing this truth by going along. The grocer was, in Havel's words, "living a lie."[5]

The GDR was full of such grocers and posters. From the cradle to the grave, the majority of people passed through a web of socialist organizations, beginning with the "young pioneers" and the Freie Deutsche Jugend, across the state trade union and women's league, all the way to the National Front, a union of political parties and mass organizations dominated by the regime's SED, and the Volkssolidarität (People's Solidarity), which looked after some of the many vulnerable pensioners. A good school and a university place, a half-decent apartment, a vacation in a bungalow, a wheelchair—all of these and much else required collective engagement and at least outward conformity. In 1960, for example, three in four teachers held at least one position in the FDJ, the National Front, or one of the regime's other organizations.[6] Nursery schools took careful note of parents' socialist credentials when they enrolled their toddler. In school, children learned about Marx, Engels, and Lenin. At university, students began their academic year with a "red week" of Marxist-Leninist classes and FDJ assemblies and, in order to advance in their studies, had to pass written and oral tests in the associated foundation course.

The pursuit of a "normal" life fostered a habit of going along, suppressing doubts, and looking the other way.[7] And this left its mark on ethics. Individual conscience was muffled. The outward effects were just as significant. Demonstrations of solidarity with workers and peasants were accompanied by the discrimination and persecution of class enemies and other "misfits" for whom there was no place in the socialist community. At the same time as work brigades and housing collectives offered spaces for sociability, they disciplined those members who did not want to play by the rules. It is therefore wrong to treat the repressive apparatus and private life as opposites, or to try and minimize the former by idealizing the latter. Coercion and provision—the Stasi and the day care—did not so much coexist as condition each other. In the words of the historian Stefan Wolle, himself a child of the GDR, "the warmth of the community and collective control formed an indivisible unity."[8]

ARRIVAL IN SOCIALISM

The GDR was a socialist regime with German features. With the other members of the Soviet bloc, it shared faith in progress and the laws of history as revealed by Marx; promises of human emancipation through class struggle; centralization of power in the hands of a socialist party as the vanguard of the proletariat; collectivization of industry and agriculture; a planned economy; and censorship. Just as important was what it did not share. The GDR owed its existence entirely to the fact of Soviet occupation. Unlike, say, Poland or Hungary, it had no national soul and no historical memory. It had to build a collective identity to justify its existence. If that was not difficult enough, it had to do so while its sister, West Germany, moved in a very different direction.

These two facts would cast their shadow over the rest of the life of the GDR. Messianic faith in the future overcompensated for the absence of a national past. The GDR's national anthem opened with the words "Risen from the ruins, to the future turned." In the minds of activists of the regime's Socialist Unity Party, the SED, "utopia" was not "nowhere"—its literal meaning—but within their reach.[9] Initially, the country's chances of survival looked grim. The GDR was a provisional entity, at the mercy of the Soviet Union, and, internationally, did not exist as a state. Even its own anthem—composed by Hanns Eisler with lyrics by the regime's court poet, Johannes Becher—exhorted people to serve "Germany, our united fatherland." In 1952, Stalin offered the Western powers German reunification in exchange for neutrality and demilitarization. The GDR would have been snuffed out if the "Stalin Note" had not been rebuffed. It took another fifteen years for the GDR to introduce its own citizenship. Dependence on Moscow reduced the potential for reform and renewal. Czechoslovakia had a Prague Spring in 1968. East Germany knew only frost.

Finally, there was West Germany. The presence of an increasingly affluent, rival German neighbor presented the GDR with unique pressures but also unique opportunities. On the one hand, it established an unreachable yardstick. Poles and Hungarians marveled at how much better off people in the GDR were, but East Germans compared themselves to their cousins in Hamburg and West Berlin. On the other hand, West Germany was a safety valve that released some of the internal pressure. Before the Wall, critics and class "enemies" fled; after the Wall went up, West German television afforded at least mental escape. Poland had Solidarność, the GDR had *Dallas*. And, in the 1980s, the GDR had in West Germany its lender of last resort.

The life of the GDR consisted of two parts, before and after the Wall was built in 1961. The early life laid the foundations for socialism. The SED seized power. The party was "the mother of the masses" and "it was always right," in the words of its official song. By Soviet command, in 1948 private industry was turned into *Volkseigene Betriebe* (VEB; publicly owned enterprises). In the following ten years, agriculture was similarly collectivized. The first Five-Year Plan was launched in 1950 and set out to double industrial production. It exemplified the futurist vision and determination of the regime—with disastrous consequences. Frieda Hockauf, a fifty-year-old weaver in the textile VEB in Zittau, gave the plan its eventual motto: "The way we work today, we will live tomorrow." In reality, this translated into "Work harder and eat less." Resources were pumped into heavy industry, away from consumption. Shops cut prices in the early 1950s, but there were not enough foodstuffs and goods to go around—and those that were for sale (flour and oats) were hoarded. Most workers did not want to wait until tomorrow. The production "norms" required of workers were repeatedly raised. In the spring of 1953, rumors spread that wages might be cut by 20 percent. The mood on building sites and in many factories was volatile.

On March 5, 1953, Stalin, the "Father of Nations," died. Lavrentiy Beria, his short-term successor, was blunt. "We only need a peaceful Germany," he told the Soviet Council of Ministers. "Whether they have socialism there or not does not make a difference... The GDR? What is it worth, the GDR? It is not even a proper state. It is only kept alive by Soviet troops."[10] Ulbricht was summoned to Moscow and, on June 2, was told to put the brakes on industrialization and collectivization and boost consumption instead to contain tensions at home. It was a humiliation.

Nine days later, back in East Berlin, Ulbricht and the Politburo publicly acknowledged that they had made "a series of mistakes" and announced a "new course" (*neuer Kurs*) with a long list of concessions.[11] For many workers, the U-turn confirmed that the regime was politically bankrupt. Free elections and reunification were added to the demands for lower work "norms" and better living conditions.

On June 17, 1953, strikes spread to more than two hundred towns and communities. One million people joined the uprising, in a country of 18 million. They stormed town halls and freed political prisoners. The SED leadership had lost control. Soviet tanks crushed the uprising and restored order. At least fifty-five people were killed, more than ten thousand arrested.

The crackdown did not put a complete stop to strikes—smaller disputes erupted in 1956 and recurred in later years—but it provided rulers and ruled alike with an object lesson about the essence of power in the GDR. Neither group would forget it. To the people it made crystal clear that, notwithstanding its name, the German Democratic Republic was a dictatorship where the SED ruled in their name. It would not develop into rule by the people for the people. Any open attempts in that direction were futile and would be repelled, by force if necessary. To the SED leadership, it brought home just how precarious their hold on power was. Fear of another uprising like the one on June 17 effectively ruled out policies that involved cuts to the standard of living. That was the irony of June 17: people power was crushed, but the people won better living conditions. From now on, the regime operated with a more cautious stick-and-carrot policy. There would be future economic "plans" and attacks on remaining farmers, shopkeepers, and professionals. Food, housing, and other basic goods, though, were sacrosanct. Austerity was for capitalist countries. In the workers' republic, basic consumer goods would be kept cheap, at all costs.

The events of June 17 showed people's anger, but the young GDR was not without support. Peace, progress, and a better life were an attractive trinity, not least for the generation born before the First World War, who longed for stability above all else. They contrasted the GDR with their experiences of war and destruction, Nazi terror, and, before that, mass unemployment—not democracy and human rights. From that perspective, socialism looked appealing. The interwar crisis had made capitalism look bankrupt, and the quick succession of economic crises (1923, 1929–32) and the Nazi takeover lent some credence to the socialist claim that capitalism bred fascism.

Building socialism was also attractive for many members of the so-called *Flakhelfer* generation, the youngsters born in the late 1920s who were socialized under Hitler and just old enough to man anti-aircraft guns in the war. For them, defeat shook their faith in National Socialism. The new regime gave them a fresh start, in exchange for their loyalty, and opened the door to positions of authority.[12] The Free German Youth pledged to be "the architects of our new house of peaceful labor and fighting humanity! From the bottom of our hearts we greet our new shining future!"

Socialism hurt particular groups—factory owners, farmers, small businessmen, doctors, lawyers, and devout Christians, mainly Protestants in the GDR. It was these groups who led the flight to the West, especially in the late 1950s. As they were kicked down the social ladder, though, others were pulled up. Working-class people were catapulted into top positions in education and in the professions. Workers-and-peasants' faculties were set up. By 1954, more than half the seats in university lecture halls were filled by workers and farmers. Party membership was a ticket to social mobility; most students belonged to the FDJ.[13] While West Germany was rehabilitating Nazi judges, the GDR created a fast track for "people's judges." Here was a pool of many loyal functionaries serving the regime into the 1980s. Work in factories was not easy—adults worked a forty-eight-hour week, teenagers forty-two to forty-five hours—but under the Nazis it had been sixty, even seventy hours. And, in contrast to Weimar, there always was work.

The same could not be said of food. Ration cards were abolished in 1958, but this hurt poorer households, who had relied on cheap rationed goods. To soften the blow, the price for chocolate, watches, and other discretionary items was lowered. Less than a year later, shops were running low on meat, dairy products, and even apples and pears. Shortages remained endemic in the GDR.

The lure of a better world reached beyond the old socialist milieu. More than any other writer, the novelist Brigitte Reimann gave East German women a voice in their struggle for emancipation. She came from a petit-bourgeois background—her father was a bank clerk, and her mother's family had a small firm making gold cornices. For a moment, in 1957, she agreed to an overture from the Stasi to feed them information, before recanting. In her diary, she pondered her initial decision to accept. Her old ideals and religious faith had crumbled. She was not sure whether socialism had "a moral justification." "Only the future will show whether that system is good and right." Still, she was "certain that socialism with its original idea represents a higher stage of development and human progress when compared to capitalism."[14]

Reimann's 1961 novel, *Ankunft im Alltag* (*Arrival in Everyday Life*), echoed the regime's language of "arrival in socialism." It was set on an industrial site in Hoyerswerda, where Reimann had moved in 1960. Once a week, she put down her pen to lay pipes. The book tells the story of three high school graduates who are spending their year of national service before university helping to build the gargantuan lignite-fired power station "Schwarze Pumpe" (Black Pump): Recha, a half-Jewish girl whose mother had been divorced by her "Aryan" father and died in Ravensbrück; Nikolaus, a working-class boy and the first in his family to go to high school; and Curt, the spoiled brat of a communist functionary and resistance fighter. Recha is briefly charmed by Curt, who takes her dancing and drinking, but she comes to see that real life is more than the "high life." She switches to the sensitive and hardworking Nikolaus. Life at the power station is a daily struggle. Machines repeatedly break down, forcing overtime. Yet solidarity, mutual respect, and satisfaction in serving the public good more than repay the workers for their sacrifice. The FDJ gives young Erwin, who lives in an institution for problem children, a bicycle so he can join the others in extra shifts and still meet the closing hours of the home. "We have turned the country inside out," one worker announces, looking back on the last four years of building a coal briquette factory, and "we have turned ourselves inside out." Collective struggle repairs both faulty engines and individual souls.

In many ways, the book is a socialist successor to the bildungsroman, taking characters through trials and tribulations to reach their full character. Recha recognizes that the world is "not like it appears in most books and people are different from the newspapers." "But," she adds, "one must change it, and what is still mean and bad, we will make good, and what is good we will make better, and what the older generation no longer manages, we youth can accomplish." Life under socialism expands their personalities. In his spare time, Nikolaus is drawing sketches of "reading workers," while the leader of their brigade is taking the train to Dresden to admire paintings. Even Curt is transformed in the end. He realizes it is wrong to live the life of a social parasite and take advantage of his father's influence. Hoping to make amends, he arrives early to work one day but, unfortunately, directs the crane the wrong way and breaks the engine in half. Curt promises to pay for the damage out of his own pocket. It is not a question of money, the brigade leader explains; Curt had shown disrespect for the property of the working classes and the many hours they had sweated to produce these machines—failing the socialist Sixth Commandment. Ordered to the brigade meeting for public criticism, Curt flees (a breach of the Fifth Commandment). On the train home, his conscience and courage suddenly reawaken. He sees that he has to face the consequences of his actions. The moral education completed, the novel ends, Curt having arrived at socialism.[15]

Reimann's novel appeared in July 1961, one month before the Berlin Wall went up. It gave the name to an entire genre of writing: *Ankunftsliteratur* ("arrival literature"). Most people only felt they had arrived for good in the GDR after the Wall was constructed and they had to stay. This was in part because the ninety-six-mile-long cement wall, watch towers, and automated shooting ranges made flight impossible except for a courageous and determined few; in the year before the Wall, 200,000 had fled the GDR, a number that was rigorously brought down in the following three decades. People also felt that the GDR would be their permanent home because the Wall ushered in a new phase of stability that made it easier for people to accommodate themselves with socialism. What at first glance looked like a humiliating defeat turned into a "second birth."

The 1960s were the GDR's miracle years. In the five years after the Wall, wages rose by 15 percent. In 1966, the workweek was reduced to forty-five hours; the five-day workweek followed a year later. By the end of the decade, the majority of households had a television set and more than a quarter had a fridge and a washing machine. East Germans were showing signs of the diseases of affluence. Forty percent were overweight; people ate 50 percent more fat than advised, and washed it down with more beer and vodka.[16] Inside and outside the home, a new leisure culture was taking shape. An official study of apprentices and students in 1969 found that 68 percent owned a pair of skis, 66 percent a camera, 50 percent a portable radio, 30 percent a moped, and 17 percent a leather jacket. Sixteen percent had the item everyone was dreaming of for a sliver of freedom: a tent.[17] Pensioners, by contrast, were lucky to have a simple radio and a shared toilet in the stairwell. The big winners were men: their leisure time jumped from 37 to 48 hours a week; women had to make do with a meager additional hour, to reach 27 hours a week, as they continued to do most of the domestic chores.[18] Although it never was a golden cage, the GDR was certainly becoming more comfortable.

Internationally, the GDR finally emerged as a sovereign state. In 1967, it signed separate pacts with the socialist brother nations in Eastern Europe and was recognized by Cambodia, Egypt, and other "Third World" countries. The following year, it sent its own team to the Olympics in Mexico. Four years later, in the West German city of Munich, they entered with their own flag and hymn; from then on only the music of the hymn would be played, without the words extolling the united fatherland. In 1973, East and West Germany signed the Basic Treaty (Grundlagenvertrag), effectively treating each other as sovereign states. That same year, the two Germanies were admitted separately to the United Nations.

Struggle and love always beat together in the socialist heart. In its infancy, the East German regime had been obsessed with the class enemy on the outside. The Wall turned its gaze to the people on the inside. It was now that the SED became both caring mother and punishing father, and its "love" more coercive and invasive. And those in power had so much love to give! In the famous words of Erich Mielke, the recently resigned head of the Stasi, to the people's assembly in November 1989: "But I love all the people [*alle Menschen*]." The "children of the GDR," those born in the decade after 1945, grew up with more of the weight of that love on their shoulders than anyone else. For them, the SED's love was "simultaneously uplifting and oppressive," in the words of the historian Dorothee Wierling.[19] They had been chosen as the new socialist man and woman and at the same time were constantly reminded of their great debt to their anti-fascist parents and grandparents. The people more generally became objects of paternalism and surveillance, like children who are loved but not quite trusted. It was in the 1960s and 1970s that the Stasi expanded from a spy agency into a domestic surveillance leviathan, and that state child care and other welfare services were expanded. More than ever, people were looked after and looked at around the clock.

Although never renouncing physical force, the GDR developed and perfected other forms of discipline and power. The people were trained to walk on a leash that was gradually loosened while the regime watched to make sure the added bit of freedom was not abused. That little bit of extra room for leisure and pleasure came at a price: self-restraint.[20] In 1961, members of the FDJ had still climbed on rooftops to destroy antennas turned to the West. In the course of the 1970s, the regime resigned itself to the fact that people would find a way to watch West German TV regardless. It even allowed the production and sale of TVs fitted with the necessary PAL color encoding system. Similarly, youth clubs, rock music, and blue jeans were no longer attacked but tolerated—Levi's went on sale in November 1971 in East Berlin.

Such mini-liberalization, however, always had clear limits and only took place under the watchful eyes of the dictatorship. In the summer of 1973, the

GDR invited the youth of the world to East Berlin to the tenth World Festival. It wanted it to be a showcase of its openness. Long-haired young people were allowed to sit in the parks and play guitar. Western students distributed leaflets, and groups freely debated in front of crowds on Alexanderplatz. Officially, the festival was hailed a great success. No more than two dozen participants were arrested during the entire week. But that was only because the Stasi had swept through society with an enormous broom beforehand, removing any potential voices of disruption and dissent. In addition to their regular personnel in the capital, the Stasi enlisted more than 4,000 special staff and had 20,000 policemen, numerous helicopters, and the elite regiments of the army at their command. In dedicated camps, FDJ members were trained how to counter the arguments of the class enemy. When West German youth organizations performed, Stasi guards would don blue FDJ shirts and take up "strategic points" in the audience. In the six months leading up to the festival, 26,000 people were placed "under surveillance." Several thousands had their phones tapped. More than 1,800 were thrown in prison. A further 3,000 "asocials" were put in juvenile workhouses, special homes, and psychiatric asylums. The Stasi held "conversations" with another 20,000 people, to discourage them from even thinking of traveling to the capital.[21] The looser leash for the majority came at a terrible price for the minority, who were not trusted to walk nicely.

For all his flaws, Ulbricht clung to a utopian vision of socialism and showed some creativity. In 1963, he launched the "New Economic System" (Neue Ökonomische System, NÖS).[22] The aim was to catch up with the West in a technological spurt, and then leapfrog it. Centralized planning was relaxed and enterprises given greater say—among other things, they could keep some of their earnings to invest or pay staff, instead of handing it over to the state. Huge investment was channeled into research and development. The problem was that these new economic ideas clashed with the regime's political reality at every level. Internationally, the East German economy was coupled to that of the Soviet Union, which limited the room for flexibility and restructuring. Domestically, it was difficult to promote competition without differential rewards and incentives. Prioritizing research and technology for the future came at the expense of consumption now. Above all, by empowering economists and engineers, the NÖS challenged the power of party functionaries.

On January 21, 1971, Erich Honecker and a dozen other members of the Politburo turned secretly to Moscow. Ulbricht, they told Leonid Brezhnev, was a technocrat and out of touch with reality; they also reminded him that he was rude and arrogant. They knew what lessons to draw from the protests in Prague in 1968 and strikes in Poland. Ulbricht was replaced by Honecker, who proclaimed the "unity of economic and social policy." The NÖS was buried, and with it the socialist Ten Commandments. There would be no more visionary experiments. What mattered was the nation's performance in the present. Ulbricht died during the tenth World Festival two years later, barely noticed; Honecker saw to it that his memory was erased.

"Security" was the brace that held East German society together. If the State Security Agency represented one side—the "shield" of the party—social and material security was the other, providing people with a sense of *Geborgenheit*, the feeling of being safe, snug, and cared for. Instead of utopia and adventure, the 1970s and 1980s prized certainty and comfort. In the course of these two decades, the GDR built more than 2 million new apartments. When Honecker took power, every third home had its own toilet, bath or shower, and warm water; ten years later, two thirds did. The average income climbed from 755 GDR Marks in 1970 to more than 1,000 Marks in 1980. That same year, more than one in three households had a car, and virtually all had a TV and a fridge. At the same time, the price for housing, water, gas, and electricity was kept artificially low. Already in 1960, households spent merely 4 percent of their income on rent; in the 1980s it dropped to 2 percent. New day care centers mushroomed. Child benefits were raised, and paid pregnancy leave was extended; from 1976, a "baby year" allowed new mothers 80 percent of their salary, initially for six months, later for twelve.[23]

There was one hitch: Honecker's GDR was living beyond its means. It spent more than it earned, and what started as a gap widened into an unbridgeable chasm. Shortages remained endemic. In its early years, the GDR's productivity was already poor compared to West Germany's, and in the 1970s and 1980s it dropped further (one reason the GDR needed more women in the workforce). Its investment and earnings from exports fell, too. Honecker brushed experts aside when they pointed this out in the 1970s. What people wanted, he said, was a decent apartment, a steady job, and bread on the table. As long as ministers provided those, he said, the regime was safe.[24] A higher standard of living, he believed, would make people work harder for socialism. Stalin had had the same idea in the mid-1930s when he proclaimed, "Life has become better, comrades." What neither Honecker nor Stalin grasped was that people's expectations expanded with rising comfort. Citizens were steadily raising their demands on the state. Moreover, wages were too similar to give people incentives. Instead of becoming more industrious on the shop floor, East Germans beavered away at home and in their dachas (the small GDR led the world with more than 3 million of these cabins). It was a vicious cycle: more public spending on consumption starved investment, which translated into lower productivity and fewer export earnings, which resulted in a deficit and required international loans to maintain spending on consumption, which left less for investment, and so forth, all over again. As if things were not bad enough, the oil crises of the 1970s put an end to artificially cheap crude oil from the Soviet Union, much of which the GDR had refined and sold to the West for hard currency. In order not to lose that lucrative business entirely, the country began to limit oil consumption and burn even more of its own dirty lignite coal.

The GDR thus faced the political imperative of maintaining the standard of living, the economic one of raising investment, and the international one of keeping the creditors at bay. In the form of subsidized housing, health care, and child care, the regime was handing people a "second pay packet" that was getting fatter and fatter; between 1986 and 1988, it grew by 7 percent a year, almost twice as fast as the economy.[25]

To survive, the GDR turned into a credit junkie, sinking deeper and deeper into foreign debt. In 1970, the GDR owed 12 billion Marks, ten years later 43 billion, and by 1988 123 billion, making it the world champion of debt. In 1983–84, West Germany bailed it out with a loan worth 2 billion DM (around $700 million). (At the time, 1 Deutschmark was worth 8 GDR Mark on the black market.) More lucrative and heinous was the discreet sale of 33,755 political prisoners to the West between 1964 and 1989 in exchange for 3.4 billion DM. These payments put the later costs of reunification (2 trillion euros) into perspective: the "social transfers" from West to East were not a new departure but a continuation of decades of subsidies.

In October 1989, an internal analysis for the Politburo estimated that to pay existing interest and stop sinking deeper into debt, the GDR would have needed to cut the standard of living by 25 to 30 percent.[26] It just so happened that 25 percent of public spending went to subsidize food, rent, transport, energy, and children's clothes. (In 1970 it had been 19 percent.)[27] Clearly, the GDR deserves less credit for cheap housing and child care than it is often given. These were effectively paid for by foreign creditors—increasingly, West Germany. The GDR was close to bankruptcy in the autumn of 1989.

SURVEILLANCE AND REPRESSION

The GDR operated a finely tuned system of formal and informal repression. In the course of its life, the GDR incarcerated 231,000 political prisoners, who suffered depression, stress, sleeplessness, and other long-term consequences. It killed between 270 and 1,900 people trying to flee. Most of them were shot, some blown up by mines, others drowned or were shot down in their balloons and light aircraft; the figures vary depending on whether one includes heart attacks after arrest, suicides, and other deaths following kidnapping and a forced return.[28] Those who applied for permission to leave faced the loss of their job and life as outcasts—their number rose from 5,400 in 1978 to 57,600 in 1984; roughly half were eventually allowed to move to the West.

It was surveillance, however, that provided the GDR with its own pervasive system of control. Its heart was the Ministry for State Security (Stasi), its veins and arteries the official and unofficial members (IMs, *inoffizielle Mitarbeiter*), who signed written contracts to report to the Stasi as directed. These connected with many smaller capillaries that reached almost every part of the social body. Firms, schools, town halls, and even hospitals—they all had willing collaborators who spied on their colleagues and fellow citizens and filed reports with the Stasi. So did neighbors who, for example, denounced young women who were changing their partners too often for their own taste. Many thousands of innocent and entirely healthy women were arrested and detained in institutions that nominally existed to cure venereal disease but in reality were about correcting flaws in the socialist personality, such as "asocial behaviour" and "hanging around." Inmates were "taught" the Seventh and Ninth Commandments: socialist work discipline and cleanliness.[29]

The growth of surveillance was phenomenal. In the mid-1950s, there were around 30,000 IMs. By 1989, there were 189,000, including over a thousand who operated in West Germany. There was one IM for every eighty-nine citizens. At one stage or another, more than 600,000 people spied for the Stasi.[30] In addition, the Stasi had 91,000 full-time officials. In total, it kept files on 4 million East Germans and opened more than 90,000 letters a day. The Stasi's paper files alone extend for seventy-four miles. By comparison, the Gestapo, with its staff of 31,000, was tiny, although, of course, members of the SA and neighbors also spied under the Nazis. Surveillance and denunciations touched all spheres of life.[31]

The Stasi reached deep into East German society but was not identical to it. The "firm" recruited its full-time staff mainly from within official cadres: the SED, the police, the army, and the Stasi itself. "Like father, like son" applied to many officials. For the full-timers, the Stasi resembled a company town, with its own vacation camps and doctors, and even a savings bank that reprimanded them when they were in debt.[32]

The motivations behind becoming an informal assistant were more varied. An internal study in 1967 found that most signed up because they "recognized the pressing societal demand" or felt "a sense of ethical duty and moral compulsion." A good quarter, though, were lured by "personal advantages" and the promise of travel and other privileges.[33] A typical case of such opportunistic motives was the informal assistant Lorac, who over the years secured for himself visits to spas, a professorship, and a job for his future sister-in-law.[34] For 12 percent, spying was an "end in itself," with its allure of secrecy and adventure and the power to exact revenge. Only a quarter said they had been coerced. Although these figures need to be treated with caution since the survey, after all, was conducted by the Stasi itself, the importance of believing one was "doing the right thing" and defending or even reforming socialism is borne out by later interviews with former IMs. Johannes Diba, for example, was born in 1948 and grew up a communist. In 1965, his love of rock music landed him in prison, but that experience did not shake his commitment to advance real socialism. In 1981, now at Dresden University, he was easily recruited by the Stasi. For him, the political imperatives of the Cold War trumped any moral unease. Tanja X. was a teacher who was recruited after her marriage to a Tanzanian man in the late 1970s. "I was not in a criminal organization: I wanted a better society," she recalled. It was only in 1988 that she realized the regime was beyond reform. As far she was concerned, it was she who was betrayed by the GDR, not the people she reported on. Georg Brühl was attracted by the idea of gaining some influence over events and felt he owed the regime for enabling him to go to university. In a society of subordination, working for the Stasi conferred a sense of power many like him found irresistible.[35]

It was only in the mid-1980s that recruitment ran into difficulties and the number of discharges exceeded that of new collaborators; the Stasi now met resistance even from members of the FDJ. Informers became less reliable: by 1986, dishonesty and the deliberate blowing of one's own cover (*Dekonspiration*) made up one third of all cases where contracts were torn up.[36]

Clearly, there were plenty of ideals as well as weaknesses for Stasi officers to exploit. The regime's control of education, careers, and freedom of movement provided it with added leverage. Being an upright person is difficult enough, but in a dictatorship it is especially so. The case of "G." stands for many others. In 1977, the young man submitted his formal application to be allowed to leave the GDR. After three years of waiting and being treated as an outcast, he withdrew the request and gave in to pressure to work as an IM. True to its motto—"Who helps us, we help in return"—he was given his dream job at the DEFA film studio. "On the first day, I felt terribly dirty—almost threw up when looking in the mirror—because I had always been so opposed to it—and now I myself... I felt like the greatest brownnose. Did not last very long, though, that feeling."[37]

Once a person had signed up to spy for the Stasi and started to betray acquaintances, it was easier to keep going than to stop. Gerd S. had the courage to turn around. In 1982, he was asked to sign an arrest warrant for a fellow pupil from his schooldays. Here, for the first time, was a victim he knew well. His conscience rebelled. The man was a show-off, he knew, but he was not a criminal enemy of socialism. Gerd refused to sign the warrant. He had crossed a line, and soon after resigned. No enterprise would hire him. In May 1983, he was picked up at his home and taken to the Hohenschönhausen prison for one month.

For family members, turning against a partner in the Stasi was akin to trying to leave the Cosa Nostra. One nurse who married in 1970 enjoyed all sorts of privileges: a large flat, two cars, a dacha by a lake, a motorboat, a university place to study medicine. A few years into the marriage, she figured out that both her husband and her father-in-law were Stasi officers. In 1979, when she threatened to flee to the West with her children, her husband pointed his pistol at her. She filed for divorce. From one day to the next, her car was gone and the Stasi had emptied her flat. Her official complaints about her treatment remained unanswered. She lost her job as a nurse. Her new partner was demoted and then committed suicide. Her daughter could not find an apprenticeship, in spite of top grades. She herself spent time in a psychiatric hospital. In 1983, the Stasi tried to recruit her as a form of "reparation." She refused. After ten days in custody, she signed the usual code of silence (*Schweigeverpflichtung*), promising not to reveal anything about the encounter.[38]

The roles of spy and suspect were not fixed. The Stasi recruited among its victims and targeted its unofficial collaborators. The celebrated chemist Robert Havemann was an example of the latter. Although a convinced communist, Havemann survived the Nazis with a death sentence hanging over his head because his expertise was considered indispensable for developing chemical weapons. After the war, he provided intelligence to his saviors, the Soviets. In 1953, he was recruited by the Stasi as a "secret informer" (*Geheimer Informator*, GI). For the next ten years, he passed on information about Western scientists and also reported on colleagues back home who were ambivalent about the GDR or considered fleeing the country. The trouble with Havemann was not that he was not a productive informer. Rather, he was increasingly straying from the official script. Nikita Khrushchev's revelation of Stalin's crimes in 1956 shattered Havemann's blind faith in the wisdom of the party. A headstrong man, he began to pursue his own course toward a more humane socialism and to defend freedom of expression. His Stasi minders were put on their guard by the "opportunistic and revisionist views" he expressed to colleagues and students at Humboldt University. He was developing "unclear philosophical ideas," they concluded, "oriented in a one-sided way toward the need of studying Hegel's philosophy."[39] Since the truth could only be found in the works of Hegel's disciple, Marx, Havemann was clearly heading in the wrong direction. When the Stasi formally broke off their "operational contact" with him in November 1963, they had already been tapping his phone for four years. In March 1964, he was excluded from the party. The Ideological Commission of the Politburo explained the fundamentals at stake: "Havemann turned the motto of freedom against the GDR, against our party and the workers-and-peasants state." With "his talk . . . of 'freedom for all' . . . he put grist in the mills of all those who want to strangle the GDR 'in the name of freedom.' "[40] The following year he was banned from his profession. House searches and surveillance followed. From 1976 to 1979, Havemann lived under house arrest. A lodestar for dissidents and peace activists, he died in 1982.

Full-time Stasi officials were expected to report on their family. Among unofficial collaborators, spying on relatives was rare, although when it did happen the emotional pain was particularly acute. A notorious case was that of Vera Lengsfeld, a peace activist in the 1980s, who, after reunification, discovered that her husband had spied on her and divorced him. Most IMs were more likely to report on those one or two steps removed from their intimate circle: neighbors, colleagues at work, or people who had a summer cottage nearby.

One strategy the Stasi perfected was that of *zersetzen*, that is, breaking up "subversive" groups by sowing suspicion and amplifying tension. It was a form of psychological warfare used against a wide range of real or potential "enemies," from dissidents to nonpolitical youth groups. The dissident writer Jürgen Fuchs called it the "quiet form of terror." Fuchs and his family lived in Havemann's garden house in 1975–76, before Fuchs was arrested and, after 281 days in a Stasi prison, expelled to West Berlin with his wife. The Stasi taught "operative psychology" at its university in Potsdam-Eiche. Proven techniques for *zersetzen* were, in the Stasi's own words, the "systematic discrediting of people's public reputation and prestige" by mixing "untrue, believable, or non-verifiable" statements with true, verifiable, and discrediting ones; the "systematic organization of professional and social failure to undermine individuals' self-confidence"; "the determined erosion of convictions . . . [and] ideals and the creation of doubts about their personal perspective"; "the sowing of distrust and suspicion . . . and creation or amplification of rivalries within groups"; "making groups preoccupied with internal problems . . . e.g., by assigning members to jobs far away from each other."[41]

In practice, this meant, for example, running anonymous letter campaigns that slandered one leading member of a student group and glorified another. To raise suspicions further, the Stasi placed apparently genuine advertisements in local newspapers that offered a target's personal items for sale, suggesting that the person was thinking of fleeing. A popular technique was to sow jealousy with gossip about extramarital affairs; this was one of the measures used against Havemann after his house arrest in 1976.[42] *Zersetzen* was routinely used against church and peace circles in the following years. Zittau, near the Czech and Polish border, for example, had one of the "tearooms" sponsored by the churches that sprang up across the country in the early 1980s. It became a magnet for young men who considered becoming conscientious objectors. The IM "Tina Tom" was given the job of splitting up the group. Its most influential member was immediately called up to do his mandatory military service. She persuaded another to serve in Erfurt, far away from the others. Step by step, the local pastor's influence was undermined and the group broken up. Soon young people stopped going to the *Teestube.* Two years after it had opened, the pastor agreed to shut it down. "Tina Tom" had accomplished her mission.[43]

Since one of the IMs' primary aims was to sow distrust, they occupied a special position in settings that had trust at their center: religion, medicine, and law. Eight percent of the clergy served as an IM, and so did many doctors. For lawyers, socialist justice gave a particular twist to professional ethics. On the one hand, the GDR was emphatic that it, unlike the Nazis, followed legal norms—it was this that made the later charge of having been an unjust "lawless state" (*Unrechtsstaat*) so galling for many East Germans. On the other hand, in the GDR *Justitia* was not meant to be blind. Judges and lawyers were tasked to defend "socialist justice." In liberal legal systems, the confidentiality between lawyer and client is not absolute either, but in the GDR these exceptions went much further. Lawyers had a duty to bring charges against anyone planning to commit a crime and report on their clients' secrets more generally. Since it was illegal to flee the country, a client who was pondering escape was left in an impossible situation. If he or she sought advice from a lawyer, the lawyer was expected to pass on that confidential information, and many did. In addition, after 1979, any lawyer working with a client applying for official permission to leave the GDR was disbarred.

IM lawyers were torn between professional ethics and political imperatives. Their recruitment followed the generational patterns of support characteristic of the GDR more generally. For the older cohort of die-hard communists, working for the Stasi raised no ethical qualms: after all, they had fought and sometimes killed the enemy in the Weimar years. It was for the murder of two policemen in 1931 that Erich Mielke, the head of the Stasi, would be convicted six decades later, after reunification. For those with a Nazi past, the Stasi represented a second chance. Clemens de Maizière, the father of the last prime minister of the GDR, Lothar, had been an active member of the SA and a somewhat less active, mediocre student of law. In 1948, he lost his license. Signing up as an IM was a step on the road to professional rehabilitation. (Opportunism made such men susceptible to blackmail.) De Maizière became the lawyer for the Protestant Church and betrayed many of his clients. The next generation were grateful to the GDR for a university place and social advancement. The most controversial figure in this cohort remains Gregor Gysi, the charismatic leader of the PDS (Party of Democratic Socialism)—the successor to the SED—in the 1990s and, at the time of writing, a member of parliament for Die Linke, the Left party. In the 1970s and 1980s, he represented several dissidents, including Havemann. In 1998, the German parliament concluded that all evidence pointed to Gysi as the IM with the codename "Notar" (Advocate), a conclusion Gysi has vehemently denied ever since.[44]

Having a Stasi lawyer sometimes had its uses and could provide a go-between to extract better conditions from the regime. In the main, though, it stacked the law against those it should have protected. In the 1970s, justice morphed into fast-track injustice, with cases for permission to leave decided in little over an hour. IM lawyers reported on fellow lawyers and judges as well as their clients. In political cases or those involving soldiers, they were effectively the mouthpiece of the Stasi against their clients. The IM Wolfgang Schnur incriminated, among others, the writer Freya Klier for having a manuscript critical of the GDR in her attic and pressed her to accept expulsion in 1988. A decade later, he would be sentenced to one year on probation. In other cases, defendants were left without an advocate altogether. In 1984, a drunk man walked to the West German Permanent Mission in East Berlin and, when told to go home by the East German guards, clung to the rails. He was arrested and sentenced by the court entirely on the basis of the Stasi report, without a lawyer present to stress his diminished capacity.

How people responded to being trapped in the Stasi web had a lot to do with their families, the shock absorbers of the dictatorship, and ways of looking at the world passed down the generations. The encounter with the regime, therefore, was highly subjective, and their particular understanding of it would color how victims experienced the "*Wende*," the transition after reunification.

The historian Babette Bauer interviewed thirty men and women from the Chemnitz area born between 1933 and 1968 who had been targeted by the

Stasi. She identified five types of responses, ranging from rejection and flight to hope and accommodation. Frau Rose exemplified the first. Born in 1937, her parents were liberal-minded Catholics who transferred their suspicion of the Nazis to the new regime. Raising her own children after the Wall went up burdened her with a feeling of complicity. What kind of life was she preparing her children for? She herself always felt on the outside of life in the GDR. When her colleagues went to official meetings, she went home. Instead of collective belonging, she only knew collective distrust. When her mother died, the Stasi watched the funeral, hoping to pick up her father, who had fled to West Berlin. People such as Frau Rose gradually edged closer toward a complete break with the regime. For them, the only viable moral option was exit. The last straw came in 1970, when the regime denied her permission to visit her brother-in-law in the West on his deathbed. In 1973, she tried to flee. She was caught and spent nine years in jail. Her children were first detained in a special prison (*Kinderzuchthaus*), then moved to a state home before they were ultimately handed over to her parents-in-law.

A rather different type of family learned to live a dual life. The children of farmers or artisans had often witnessed firsthand how their parents were pressed to give up their independence and join the collective. Instead of taking the risky flight to freedom, they took refuge in the cocoon of their private lives and capitulated at least in the sense of showing the occasional sign of conformity in public.

A third group were people who had been raised in apolitical families and started out as fellow travelers, joined the FDJ, and initially conformed with the regime. Their shock came when they suddenly found themselves interrogated by the Stasi because of gossip or critical statements made by friends or partners. From one day to the next, their seemingly well-ordered life fell to pieces, with problems at work, university, and home. Their dominant feelings were fear and powerlessness.

This was in marked contrast to families that were able to fall back on either their religious or their socialist faith. For the former, the church was an anchor as well as a hope that dialogue might be possible. The latter saw themselves as builders of socialism. Their socialist upbringing enabled them to compartmentalize and justify their own painful encounters with the regime. The problem, as they saw it, lay with Honecker and certain officials, not with socialism as such. They clung to a belief that the GDR could be reformed.[45]

Few people had higher hopes for the GDR than the singer-songwriter Wolf Biermann. Born in Hamburg in 1936, he was raised in a communist working-class family. His Jewish father was active in the resistance and was murdered in Auschwitz. Mother and son survived the firestorm of Operation Gomorrah by jumping into a canal. In 1953, the young pupil left West Germany for the East to build the socialist future. A gifted musician with a sharp tongue, he, like a jester, exposed the flaws of the ruling elite, and soon became a thorn in the side of the authorities. In 1965, he was blacklisted and banned from performing. The SED was trying to get rid of him. The problem was that, unlike thousands of other citizens, Biermann did not want to leave. The GDR was the fatherland he had been waiting for all his life, and he believed that with songs, debate, and teasing he could help reform it from within. The SED could ban Biermann from the stage but could not silence him. Stasi surveillance did not stop him from recording an album in his apartment in East Berlin in 1968 with the help of a tape recorder smuggled in from the West. His living room became a socialist salon for authors and radicals from West and East, from the Swiss novelist Max Frisch and the West Berlin student radical Rudi Dutschke to the American folk singer Joan Baez. In 1976, the SED finally succeeded by laying a trap. After having been refused travel permits previously, Biermann was granted one to perform in West Germany. A few critical comments at the Cologne concert were sufficient pretext for Honecker to strip him of his citizenship. Now Biermann could not come back. Prominent writers and artists came out in protest. It signaled that the regime was not reformable. In West Germany, Biermann then joined the peace and anti-nuclear movement.[46]

COLLECTIVE AND COERCIVE

"My work-place is my place of battle for peace" was the motto chosen by the *Brigade* (a team of coworkers) of the planning department of the VEB Automobilwerk, the state-owned car company in Eisenach in Thuringia. People had yearned for peace since the beginning of time, they explained in 1987, but recent history demonstrated that only "with the strengthening of a socialist order is it possible to translate people's longing for peace into action." Current international tensions showed that it was not enough to talk of peace: "One must fight for peace." It required everyone to be productive and strengthen socialism. "Every member of the collective will thus be included in a form of Marxist-Leninist training." The diary of the brigade, which recorded their achievements and problems, pictured individual workers as branches of a tree.[47] How much did these bodies succeed in instilling a new sense of socialist duty toward the collective, and how much did they operate through discipline and conformity?

Near the end of the GDR, more than 5 million employees belonged to a brigade like the one in Eisenach—roughly two thirds of the working population. They were the team unit in almost all publicly owned enterprises. The first brigades were formed in the 1950s, but it was in the following decades that they expanded in number and ambition. By 1970, they had 2.5 million members. Their original goal, as under their creator Stalin, was to raise work spirit and reduce tensions. With time, the brigades developed into a second, collective family that looked after their members and relatives in other spheres of their lives, from school days through marriage and into retirement. The brigade was a microcosm of life in the GDR, with its idealistic pursuit of collective harmony, by coercion if necessary.

In Radebeul, on the outskirts of Dresden, the Karl Liebknecht brigade of the local machine tool factory maintained a mentor arrangement with the fifth grade of the local school. Workers attended when school certificates were handed out. In return, pupils visited the shop floor. Like brigades elsewhere, they signed a mentor contract that listed various pledges, from sending factory representatives to parent-teacher evenings and teaching the children traffic safety to sending delegates along on joint hiking trips and tramway rides to Dresden. Brigades helped children recycle old bottles and paper to raise money for Mozambique and other "solidarity" campaigns. In exchange, the pupils contributed to cultural activities and designed posters pinned to the wall (*Wandzeitung*) for official anniversaries—May 1, May 8 (liberation from fascism), and days of the party's congresses. In 1981, the brigade also finished building a four-person bungalow at Knappensee, an artificial lake known as the "little Baltic," created by the unplanned flooding of an open-pit lignite mine not far from the massive power station where Reimann had set her novel about arriving in socialism. The bungalow provided seventy-four families with a vacation each year. There was also a factory-owned camper van.[48]

That the collective workplace played an important role in holidays and leisure is beyond doubt—in 1967, 18 percent of all trips were organized through firms and another 26 percent through the general trade union, FDGB.[49] How successful the brigades were in cultivating a collective spirit is another question. An internal survey of employees in 1975 found that the majority did not know what their own collective's targets were. Over a third were unhappy with their working conditions and felt that their suggestions were ignored. Outside a brigade, however, satisfaction and productivity were found to be even lower.[50] The brigades were run by a small minority of enthusiasts. Just as small was the number of "refuseniks." It was the collegiality—the "good collective relationships," to use GDR vocabulary—that members cherished most. In theory and by law, brigades also had a duty to look after the social and cultural well-being of retired coworkers. Some enterprises had dedicated "pensioner brigades" that helped build child care centers. For the vast majority, though, retirement meant the end of any contact.[51]

Instead of the biblical "Thou shall not steal," the socialist commandment was to honor and increase public property (Commandment 6). In the words of a National Front functionary in 1961, they had to overcome "the old, individualist, egocentric separation of one individual from another . . . this bourgeois world which called out from the embroidered wall-hanging . . . 'Klein aber mein.'" ("Home, sweet home," or literally, "Small, but mine.")[52] In real life, state socialism had the opposite effect. In a world of shortages and hoarding, people got into the habit of helping themselves to publicly owned machinery, cement, and other material to build their private cabins and redecorate their homes. A local tribunal in Brandenburg in 1974 reported on the never-ending battle with "petit-bourgeois individualism" and pointed the finger at enterprises for tolerating these transgressions. "Time and again, this is confirmed by citizens who had committed a criminal offense and give statements such as 'Well, it was just lying there.'"[53] An internal survey in 1975 revealed that one third of employees felt that the "*Kollektiv*" should not necessarily interfere if a comrade helped himself to public property.[54] What was so bad about taking home some drills or paint, or dodging the tram fare? After all, one did not steal from another person! In one case, in 1975, a car mechanic was found to have taken 300,000 Marks' worth of tools and supplies from his enterprise to carry out jobs after hours. Tellingly, judges routinely took a softer line with citizens who stole from the state than with those who stole from each other.

Instead of feeling pride in joint ownership, the GDR ended up with a mentality that public goods did not belong to anyone. Public property was devalued, morally as well as materially.[55]

Power, then, was not completely top-down in the workers' and peasants' state. In addition to bungalows and parties, brigades and trade unions provided workers with some collective voice and solidarity. Brigades defended their bonus pay, and trade unions intervened with local authorities to secure better living conditions for their members, as well as to protect health and safety. In 1967, for example, a delegate complained on behalf of a married couple to local officials. Both colleagues were hardworking and indispensable. Unfortunately, six of their seven children were of school age and assigned to four different schools, turning drop-offs and pickups into a logistical nightmare. For such parents, it was the *Kollektiv* that intervened on their behalf.[56]

In return, however, the brigade disciplined members, in more or less subtle ways. Brigades reprimanded workers for slacking, falling behind at work, and not contributing to the collective cause. Members were expected to "volunteer" their weekends to build bungalows and child care centers or help farmers during the harvest. The craftsmen of the VEB *Getreidewirtschaft* ("grain processing") in Angermünde north of Berlin rose at 4 a.m. to harvest sugar beets in twelve- to fourteen-hour shifts. Between semesters, students were expected to commit some time "*in Produktion*"; failure to do so resulted in a loss of their university stipend.

The brigade Frieden ("Peace") was made up of silk weavers from Zittau. In 1967, it stipulated that all members pledge to give an additional 10 percent of their monthly trade union contribution in solidarity with Vietnam. In February 1968, after a discussion of the new "socialist constitution" of the GDR, the eighteen members present turned on the one colleague who had not bought the solidarity stamps "for the fighting people of Vietnam." She was warned to do her duty in the future. Two months later, and "after repeated arguments," the woman still refused, "on religious grounds." She was formally expelled from the brigade. It did not matter that the new constitution recognized the right of each citizen to follow their religious faith (Article 39).

Together with their partner schools, brigades also set norms of socialist behavior for the young pioneers fighting alongside the workers. In Frankfurt (Oder), in 1986, children were made to write down their good intentions. Christiane, Sven, and Sylvie promised to "improve our tone with each other"; Sylvio and Jan that they would be tidier. Others pledged that they would join the next wreath-laying for the victims of fascism.[57]

As a collective family, the brigade watched over the private family. It was expected to support members in their domestic struggles and help them overcome marital tensions. As early as 1955, the GDR allowed for a "no guilt" divorce on the grounds of irretrievable breakdown. In the 1960s and 1970s, however, the two parties in a crisis were often made to feel precisely that: guilt. The brigade was partly acting in its own interests: when a couple broke up, the group risked losing a coworker who would look for a fresh start elsewhere. Partly, it supported the regime's ambition to create the socialist personality. In 1960, a judge learned that dockworkers were treating affairs and divorces as a private matter. She organized a seminar for two dozen shift workers on "socialist morality and ethics" to instruct them in their collective responsibility for private happiness.[58]

The 1960s saw a growing clash between those collective expectations and a sense of individual entitlement, well captured in one of the dozen films that fell victim to the censors in 1966: *Jahrgang 45* (*Born in '45*). The film follows young Alfred, a car mechanic, through East Berlin on his few days off. "Al" loves motorcycles and allows himself to drift. He has become estranged from his wife Li, a nurse, and decides to initiate divorce proceedings. His brigade leader calls him in for a chat. Does he not have everything: a job, an apartment, and a motorbike? Al responds, "It is not what I do have, but what I don't have." Marriage, the brigade leader reminds him, is about making compromises. "What if I do not want to make any compromises?" asks Al. The film ends with Al and Li lying in the grass and looking out over the new block of apartments rising on the horizon. That the ending held out the possibility of a reunion was not enough to appease the censors: Al's attitude was "practically asocial," and the film "untrue" in its portrayal of socialist reality.[59]

In real life, 14 percent of all divorce proceedings were temporarily suspended (*ausgesetzt*) by courts in the hope that a couple might reconcile. Family courts saw their main function as turning the warring parties back into socialist citizens who worked for the collective good. Domestic abuse was minimized as something that happened in capitalist societies. Women who were beaten by their drunken partners were told to give them another chance. Estranged husbands were made to feel the social pressure. "I wanted to divorce my wife," one man said in 1972, "but the entire *Kollektiv* was against it. They kept talking to me until I changed my mind." As late as 1976, the collective was represented in 15 percent of all divorce proceedings. It was only after that that marriage and divorce were respected as a private matter.[60]

The GDR is remembered as a nation of grumblers and moaners. Just as formidable were the efforts devoted to resolving conflicts. One fed the other. The GDR operated an extraordinary two-track system for individual complaints and societal conflict resolution. One encouraged citizens to address their personal problems to party leaders and other authorities via individual "petitions" (*Eingaben*). The other concerned tensions and transgressions at the workplace and in the community, which were handled by *Konfliktkommissionen*, "conflict tribunals." The main motivation behind these tribunals was to resolve disagreements between the parties, making it unnecessary to involve the courts. They were among the more democratic institutions in the GDR, and their delegates were elected by secret vote. By 1968, East Germany was home to almost thirty thousand *Konfliktkommissionen* and *Schiedskommissionen* ("arbitration tribunals") with a quarter of a million arbitrators.[61] That year, the law of societal tribunals removed the "violation of morals" from their remit. Political cases such as attempted border crossings or slander against the state were also dropped. Their main proceedings came to concern troubles at the workplace. Since work was a socialist duty as well as a right, however, there was an inevitable spillover from problems in other spheres of life that had repercussions for work, from irritations about deviant youths to complaints about "irresponsible" single mothers and annoying neighbors.

The tribunals were a microcosm of the GDR, with its faith in cultivating a socialist personality and its compulsion toward harmony and conformity. Moral policing was an essential part of their job. They were the choke collar for those citizens who proved troublesome walking on the leash and needed some correction to their behavior. An internal review of four hundred *Schiedskommissionen* in the Potsdam district in 1968 gives a sense of the breadth of their purview. There were a lot of denunciations for idleness and dawdling at the workplace (*Arbeitsbummelei*). In Luckenwalde, south of Berlin, the tribunal wanted to send the "endangered children of an asocial family" to a home.

The new constitution of 1968 would supersede the formally more liberal one of 1949 and bring it into line with the country's progress toward communism. The draft constitution was submitted to wide public debate before it was passed by a plebiscite with 95 percent of the votes. Basic rights were now openly tied to corresponding duties. "Freedom and equality" were promised, but several tribunals were unsure of what that meant. In the town of Königs Wusterhausen, delegates wondered whether freedom included the right to import Western magazines. Those in Brandenburg wanted courts to make it a crime to listen to Western broadcasts, which they saw as the "cause behind criminal deeds." Others wanted the tribunals to have greater powers to punish transgressors with tougher fines, such as by docking the pay of drunk husbands. In Warsow just south of Berlin, citizens went to the tribunal unhappy because the local court had punished a milkmaid who had repeatedly committed theft with "only" a year and a half of prison.[62]

Georg Winter was sixteen when he was called to appear before the tribunal in Wustermark, a small municipality just west of Berlin, in May 1969. A month earlier, the young apprentice blacksmith had been arrested for petty theft. With the stolen money, he had bought himself a camera and got drunk. He had started out as a good apprentice, his master told the commission, but then started smoking, drinking, and becoming undisciplined. The next time he caused difficulties, the master would fire him. The parents testified that they were begging Georg to pull himself together. He was threatened by the tribunal with detention in a juvenile workhouse unless his attitude improved. (Around two thousand "difficult" youths were sent to these institutions each year to learn the meaning of socialist discipline and cleanliness.) In such a difficult situation it was wise to show remorse and volunteer one's time in a socialist spirit. Georg thought of joining the local fire brigade.

Why had he not done so earlier? the tribunal wanted to know. "What more do you want?" he pleaded. He paid back the 230 Marks he had stolen and added another 150 for good measure. The tribunal was still not satisfied. Georg promised not to go to the pub so often, and his mother said that she would supervise his progress. Nudged by his mother, Georg threw in that he would also single-handedly harvest half an acre of sugar beets. He even took up the tribunal's suggestion to help with building a new path in town. Whether Georg emerged from all this a reformed, socialist man is unknown, but at least he evaded the brutal conditions of the workhouse.[63]

Not everyone bowed their heads. Socialist conformity and discipline was powerful, but transgression was possible. The same month, two other youths were arrested for breaking into a cabin and taking a clock and an old radio. They showed "no remorse" and simply laughed when one of the fathers reminded them of their socialist responsibility. They were ordered to apologize, pay a fine, and paint the fence of the local parking lot.

Public remorse was an integral feature of socialist morals and conflict resolution, and while the GDR never reached the excesses of public shaming of Mao's China, tribunals made sure that apologies and pledges were posted on bulletin boards at work and in hallways at home. Single mothers found themselves in an especially vulnerable situation. Poor "work ethic" (*Arbeitsmoral*) reflected badly on their socialist personality and ability to raise their children. This created particular tensions in the 1960s and 1970s when day cares were scarce. Even anti-fascist heroes had to justify themselves in front of tribunals. Frau Vollmer was a recognized victim of the Nazi regime (*Verfolgter des Naziregimes*, VdN) whose "lifestyle" attracted complaints in 1967. "She rarely works, neglects the children and much else." She would pursue a proper job, she responded, once there was finally a day care for her child. The VdN committee found her a place and swore it would look after her better. In exchange, she had to promise that from now on she would "try her hardest to live in an orderly manner" and agree to "ongoing checks."[64]

In the case of Vollmer, the complaints against her came from her neighbors in her *Hausgemeinschaft*. These tenant bodies formed the final piece in the network of collectives that were designed to join individuals together in socialist harmony. Most blocks of apartments had such a house collective. In the words of one functionary in 1961, they were "a mirror image of our new socialist life in our homes . . . [and] proof of the political-moral unity of our population. Capitalism does not know anything like it."[65]

Hausgemeinschaften had practical, social, and ideological functions. Members committed to clean the stairs, shovel snow, and do repairs. In some cases, these were major jobs. In one apartment block in Prenzlauer Berg, in East Berlin, for example, members installed the hot-water system and restored the courtyard in 1957, insulated the attic the following year, and cleaned the facade and painted the interior a few years later. Elsewhere, *Hausgemeinschaften* helped with the construction of schools and child care centers; in 1961, a collective in Dresden convinced all tenants to chip in instead of leaving it up to those with children. For a regime that faced a constant shortage of skilled craftsmen and that prioritized new cement blocks over the restoration of old housing stock, this kind of self-help brought huge savings. With their own treasurer, collectives also offered a convenient method of rent collection. In return, the house collectives earned premiums, that they could spend on communal pleasures, social events, or to convert basements into club rooms.

A stone's throw from the Reichstag, in Marienstrasse, forty tenants came together in 1957. None of them belonged to the party, and half were pensioners. Over the next four years, they committed twenty thousand hours of work to their building. With the savings they earned, they turned one apartment that proved difficult to rent into a club room with a television and its own "house bar." In addition, they acquired a shared library, a washing machine, and a vacuum cleaner and installed "a communal bath." In 1959, they entered the TV competition "10 Jahre DDR" (10 years GDR) and went home with a record player and "precious records." In the capital, they won top prize for the best house collective: a new paddleboat for their communal cabin at Lake Zernsdorf. Each member had their role. Seven were "officers on duty" in charge of the television, another six served on the internal "Cultural Commission." They worked out a social timetable for the club room with sessions for the card, chess, and film fans, and readings with authors. The propagandist TV series *Der schwarze Kanal* (*The Black Channel*) would be followed by discussion. They organized mutual aid, with rounds for helping the elderly and sick neighbors. And they collected the scrap metal in their neighborhood together with the young pioneers of the local elementary school.[66]

Few house collectives rose to such levels of hyperactivity. For many people in the GDR, the *Hausgemeinschaft* involved little more than the occasional round of sweeping and cleaning, watching a little TV together, and, perhaps, entertaining visiting students from Vietnam over tea from the collective samovar. Borrowing books and records tended to be more popular than sitting through a lecture on one of the regime's many anniversary days. In a house with twenty units in Karl-Marx-Stadt (now Chemnitz), only three tenants showed up in 1976 for a slide show on the centenary of the birth of Wilhelm Pieck, the first president of the GDR.[67]

"*Hausklubs*" mushroomed in the 1970s and 1980s, and were particularly important in the new concrete jungles at the outskirts of cities, such as Dresden-Prohlis, with its seventeen-story prefab blocks. Except for two schools and the club of the philanthropic Volkssolidarität, this suburb had nothing to offer, not even a pub.[68] Even in these clubs, though, politics was never far away. *Hausklubs* were consciously promoted by the regime as spaces to "shape socialist morality and ethics." For the National Front, which operated at the neighborhood level, the clubs' job was to teach a "communist attitude to work and to public property, cultivate a socialist behavior toward fellow citizens, promote socialist consciousness and socialist personality, and implement socialist norms of living together."[69]

Of course, there is nothing wrong with promoting good neighborly relations. House collectives helped elderly neighbors who faced isolation as well as deprivation. In addition to sociability, they provided a space to share dreams and frustrations. At the same time, the collectives could generate an atmosphere of conformity that tended to snuff out personal freedom and made help perfunctory.

The diary of a *Hausgemeinschaft* in Berlin Friedrichshain from 1959 to 1962 shows how emancipatory ideals and social pressure sat side by side. In this house, the main activists were women. They produced the occasional newsletter and took the regime at its word about making greater equality for women a reality. "Are women capable of logical thinking?" one female tenant asked sarcastically. They were stuck in lower-paid positions instead of being given better education and greater authority so they would enjoy work and help build socialism. Others complained about shortages and poor customer service. Since it tended to be women who did the shopping, working women were especially hard hit when, at the end of a long working day, shopkeepers told them, "We have run out." To change this, they wrote, women needed to become functionaries.

The problem was that not everyone in their building saw it like that. Frau Müller, for example, did not go out to work, and neither she nor her husband wanted to change that. The activists wanted to reeducate her.

Women who held official positions did not find it easy to juggle three jobs: worker, mother, and functionary. Frau Mehner headed a section in the NDPD (the National Democratic Party of Germany, which had been founded in 1948 to absorb former Nazi Party members), was a member of the National Front, served on the local school committee, and attended night school. She also was a secretary, a mother, and a wife. When her neighbors came to her in August 1960 to organize a collection in solidarity with the people of Congo, she said she did not have time. The delegates of the house collective could not sway her. In a signed letter, the activists let everyone in the building know that if her husband helped more, surely Frau Mehner would have time to take charge of the collection drive. They reminded everyone which duties should take priority: "We believe that everyone should ask themselves whether they have the right attitude to the cause of solidarity and are prepared to act on it financially and ideologically by subordinating their own personal affairs."[70]

Until the end of the GDR, refusal to join in communal activity could land a tenant in difficulties. In 1988, a house collective in Eisenhüttenstadt, on the border with Poland, went to the local tribunal with two charges against a neighbor. In addition to not doing her bit sweeping the courtyard, the woman had repeatedly said that she "does not care about the problems of the *Hausgemeinschaft* and wants to be left in peace." The woman was reminded of her duties and urged "to reconsider" her position. Luckily for her, the Wall came down a year later, and with it the power of the collectives.[71]

Collectives and commissions sought to create harmony and steer laggards toward a socialist personality. Tribunals sometimes managed to reach genuine compromise between the bickering parties, and members would make house visits to ensure that the pact was honored. At the same time, proceedings reveal plenty of stubborness and a fixation on "what is mine" that was the very opposite of the socialist commandments. Tenants went head-to-head over issues ranging from access to common areas to verbal and physical assault. In Luckenwalde in Brandenburg during 1970 conflicts between neighbors made up the bulk of the tribunal's work. It tried hard to get the parties to accept a "minimum of decency and cooperation according to the principles of peaceful coexistence" but had to concede that "in most cases, this did not succeed." People were "pigheaded" and refused to make concessions, even after a second or third hearing. The elderly, landlords, and tenants who liked their drink proved especially stubborn. "Educating or reeducating people rarely succeeds." In nearby Königs Wusterhausen, a quarter of all cases ended up in court in 1983.[72]

Collective pressure at the workplace was one thing, conflict resolution in the private sphere another. The regime was fighting two wars, neither of which it managed to win. By approaching conflicts as manifestations of an underdeveloped socialist morality ("petty-bourgeois individualism"), it turned them into individual failings waiting to be corrected. This was what gave the regime its moralistic drive and made youth a particular target. There were youth welfare commissions, staffed with no fewer than 25,000 volunteers whose job was to teach "difficult" youth how to behave in a manner according to the norms of socialist life (*normgerechtes Verhalten*), such as regular attendance at work or school, contribution to collective life, and "above all regular personal hygiene," to quote a report from 1984; failing these put a person in the "criminally at risk" category.[73] Yet these were often the result of life under socialism, with its many structural problems. Poor work discipline, for example, was partly a response to shortages, shift work, long commutes, and inadequate services. When divorced couples fell out with each other, it hardly helped that in many cases the estranged parties were obliged to still live under the same roof, sometimes with their in-laws, because there were not enough small apartments available to move to.

The second battlefront arose from East Germans' retreat into their own private cocoon, a process actively fostered by Honecker's reckless pursuit of a higher standard of living. Instead of fading into a distant memory of the petit-bourgeois past, "home, sweet home" became sweeter than ever. Apartments were converted into private, personal temples, filled with knick-knacks and redecorated according to one's own taste, do-it-yourself ability, and access to tools and materials; like its socialist neighbors, the GDR spawned a vibrant interior design culture. The irony of socialism was that its economy of shortage increased the value of private goods and the status derived from them, creating new fault lines of inequality in turn. In 1970, a mother went to a tribunal because her neighbor refused to give her and her three small children access to the toilet on their shared corridor; he had built a door from his bedroom, turning it into an en suite toilet, and claimed it was now his alone and that he had the landlord's permission. The tribunal failed to get either party to compromise.

Bungalows and dachas made for particularly sensitive battlegrounds. In 1983, a tribunal in Brandenburg heard the case of two squabbling neighbors, one denying the other access to her plot, which happened to be where the electric meters were installed. The aggrieved neighbor was also blocked from getting to the landing stage on the local lake, even though he was a member of the boating association. The complainant further took offense at the smoke from the neighbor's chimney—the chimney, it turned out, had been added without planning permission and was ordered removed. A fire-place was one private addition too far.[74]

IT'S NOT FAIR!

As mentioned earlier, from its birth, the GDR gave its citizens the constitutional right to submit *Eingaben* ("petitions") to party leaders and state ministries with their complaints or suggestions. In the 1980s, more than 100,000 people exercised this right every year. Two thirds of all households sent off such a formal letter at one time or another. Housing conditions, shortages of goods, waiting lists for telephones and cars, pensions, and working conditions were most often cited. They were joined, in the 1980s, by requests for permission to visit the West.

For the regime, the *Eingaben* system served as a mass survey that alerted it to emerging concerns and enabled it to contain individual dissatisfaction. For citizens, petitions provided an opportunity to express their frustrations and, perhaps, a means for redress. Some scholars have found in them evidence of popular participation in the GDR and of a shared conviction among citizens and functionaries that socialism could be made to work, or at least be made to work better. In the late 1960s, for example, working women used petitions to assert their right to an abortion under the democratic principles of the constitution, leading first to the relaxation of restrictions and, in 1972, to its legalization.[75] From that perspective, the petitions were "system sustaining," rather than repressive.[76] Others have pointed to the cynicism with which the powerless tried to play the same game as the powerful, mimicking and mocking the overblown language of their socialist masters, although one should not exaggerate the capacity for irony among Germans, a notoriously sincere people.

Of course, many petitioners hoped their letter might move them up the line for a modern apartment or a telephone, and it is equally true that at least some functionaries genuinely tried to help. Still, the overwhelming tone was one of deep frustration. In the petitions, citizens not only recorded what was wrong but also articulated reasons for their complaint, giving moral justifications for material demands. They often made people reflect on what was wrong with their lives and why, and evaluate the regime's performance according to their sense of right and wrong. Like all morality, that sense fed off social norms, including ideals held up by the party itself. However, these could be used to interrogate and challenge the principles by which the dictatorship ruled their lives. To expect collective protest would be naive. The logic of the petitioning system was to fragment criticism. Still, the disillusionment with the regime was palpable.

One frequent tactic was to take the regime at its own word and find it falling short of its socialist principles. The petitions to Paul Verner, a powerful hard-liner in the Politburo, offer a good illustration. Verner was immortalized in song by Wolf Biermann in 1974, after another arrest, as a "birdbrain with a lion's mouth."[77] A woman from Zwickau who wrote to Verner in 1986, after praising the eleventh party congress and its "successful economic policy," turned to what was on her mind. She was a single mother who worked in the medical care department of a publicly owned enterprise and, in addition to many night shifts, was often sent to training camps for students and young recruits in the army. She wanted at least to be able to telephone her fifteen-year-old son at home when necessary to make sure he was all right. For ten years, she had been waiting for a telephone connection. All she got was "heartless" bureaucratic responses telling her that "it was impossible." As a "citizen, who has always done my duty, I am no longer able to understand this process. My principle has always been that who gives something to our society has a moral right to get something back from society."[78]

Here was socialist fairness in a nutshell, as many of her contemporaries understood it. Socialism, in this view, meant just deserts. It was a reciprocal arrangement between the regime and its supporters that ought to reward activists and workers before anyone else, and, if necessary, at the expense of anyone else.

This version of fairness resonated particularly with the elderly, whose meager pensions meant that their standard of living was falling behind that of the rest of their society as well as of their cousins in West Germany. The regime was treating their contribution to the building of a socialist society with contempt, a female pensioner complained to Ulbricht's wife in 1966. At the time, pensioners received a mere quarter of the average wage.[79] Minimum pensions were raised in 1968, but this did not stop the elderly from continuing to fall behind young wage earners. "It hurts," a retired engineer wrote in 1971, "having to recognize in old age that in spite of all my efforts and accomplishments for the collective good, there is no reward in return." It was "unfair." A seventy-year-old woman who had worked for thirty-four years, clearing rubble and loading coal in snow and ice, losing two fingers in the process, put it more bluntly: "Respect for the old, bullshit!" She did not even have running water in her room and there were holes in the wall. She threatened to reveal the truth to visiting foreign socialists. The local office responded by ordering basic renovations.[80] A man from Magdeburg recited his long communist career. He had joined the young Spartacus League in 1925, distributed communist leaflets after 1933, and, after 1945, rallied to build socialism, first in local government, then in the army, and later working for the railways. (He conveniently omitted his time as a clerk in Hitler's army during the war.) As an "old comrade" with more than forty years of service, he felt he was entitled to a higher pension. His petition was unsuccessful. It was pointed out to him that pensions were based on employment contributions, not years of party membership.[81]

Whereas Adenauer's reform tied pensions to rising prosperity and created a contract between the generations in West Germany, the East turned old against young. For many poor pensioners, the regime's special benefits for young couples and large families were a betrayal of basic principles of fairness.[82]

Chronic problems with housing made people link their personal problems to structural ones. Siegrid B. was a physiotherapist, her husband a manager at the state-owned retail organization (HO). Both belonged to the SED. They had two small children. She wrote to Verner in 1973. For three years they had lived "in truly primitive conditions" in Friedrichshain in Berlin in a one-and-a-half-room apartment, consisting of a living room with a kitchenette plus a separate "half-room" (between 19 and 32 square feet). Their building had been earmarked for demolition, which was repeatedly postponed. She enclosed a supporting letter from a physician who felt that the children's frequent bronchitis might well be related to the unhealthy conditions in the flat. As if things were not hard enough, she had to take her children to two separate day cares far away, which meant that she was only able to work part-time. In the evenings, her husband was trying to study for his correspondence course in their cramped surroundings. "Difficulties are appearing in our marriage," she wrote, "and I see their causes in the conditions under which we live."

This was a two-way critique of a regime that prided itself on overcoming the conflicts between private and public interests under capitalism. Socialism made the family more (not less) important as the smallest "cell" of the new society, a vision enshrined in the Law of Unified Education in 1965.[83] The woman's complaint was not only that poor social conditions were destroying her private happiness but also that they prevented her family from playing its socialist part as the nucleus of moral education. The district mayor with whom the inquiry ended up noted that, unfortunately, he was deluged by letters from people in the same situation, some indeed from neighbors in the same building. Within a year, the marriage had broken down.[84]

A man from an old communist family pointed out that his children were living "in exactly the same bad housing conditions" in 1971 as when he was growing up in the 1930s. Their apartment was damp and his pregnant eighteen-year-old daughter had to share the one tiny bedroom with his three boys. His application for a better flat had been sitting in a line for three years. He had lost faith in the local authorities. Of course, this father was writing to a bigwig in the hope that he might do something for him. At the same time, he wondered what he, as a socialist, had worked for all his life. After more than two decades the regime had still not managed to provide him with what he considered a basic right: a dry apartment.[85]

In their letters, many citizens tried to put in words the growing dissonance between socialist ideals and reality. Everyday life felt out of joint. A printer in Zwickau put it bluntly in 1977: Were the local authorities "taking the piss"? It had been five years since he first applied for one of the newly built two-and-a-half-room apartments for himself, his wife, and his widowed mother. When the blocks were finished, he was ignored. To stand a chance, he was told, he would have needed children, "as if a two-and-a-half-room flat is dependent on children and not on the number of people in a household." When his mother died in 1975, he followed official advice and put in a new application for a two-room apartment. He was overlooked again. Why did the regime not tell him straight out, "There is no apartment for you, you ugly mug, you can stay in your hole"? At least he would know where he stood. Here was someone who had worked for the people's printing press for almost three decades, with a long commute and many years of overtime on Sundays and early-morning shift work. He had been a party member for more than twenty-five years, an "*Aktivist*," and a recognized "champion worker" (*Bestarbeiter*) with certificates in bronze, silver, and gold, plus the "Banner of Labor." "Nice words," this veteran said, were no substitute for a decent apartment. And he was wondering about the meaning behind those words. When he was setting into print official slogans that called on everyone to "increase the productivity of labor to ensure the unity of economic and social policy that will benefit individuals and society," he felt that the state was "making fun of him."

As far as the local authorities were concerned, the printer did not suffer from "overcrowding," and his case was not urgent. What his letter did produce was a visit from a local party official, who in a typical heart-to-heart talk (*Aussprache*) explained to him that his "charges against the organs of the state were untenable."[86]

This and similar complaints were in a different register from grumbling in the Nazi era, when people routinely imagined that "if only Hitler knew," their problems would be resolved. In the GDR, many petitioners wrote after years of frustration with their local authorities. Their gripe was not with corrupt or incompetent individuals but with the apparatus of the state. It was about the system, not personalities, and articulated a clash between rival principles of social justice. The printer left no doubt what the overarching rule was when he quoted back the official slogans: "As we work today, so we will live tomorrow. The worker is the central figure!... Who contributes to society, gets something from society in return."[87] This was the principle of equivalence that had guided the 1950s and 1960s. By contrast, in the 1970s the regime did everything it could to boost the number of children and of women at work, channeling funds to child care, maternity leave, and interest-free loans to young married couples. That followed the opposite principle: people were rewarded not for what they had done in the past but for what they might do in the future. The conflicts over housing expressed the deeper clash between these competing ideas of fairness. By turning to the young, the regime was losing the old. The frustrations from old workers and communists who had devoted their life to building the GDR should therefore not come as a surprise. They had invested in a project in good faith and felt the time for payback had come. When they were overlooked, they felt cheated.

Unequal access to consumer goods added another layer of unfairness. Precious Western goods were visible markers of inequality, especially in the last two decades of the GDR, when the regime actively promoted their sale in order to attract hard currency. Alongside Intershops and Interhotels, where East Germans could buy Western products for West Deutschmark, the Genex company enabled their West German cousins to order them televisions, cars, and bungalows. "Each according to his ability" was replaced by "Each according to the residence of his aunt," as a popular saying put it. On a recent trip to East Berlin, a man from Brandenburg had seen a VW Golf C with GDR plates several times, he told the Council of Ministers in 1986. He worked very hard and wanted one too.

Regional pride reinforced the sense of injustice only further. A petitioner from Bautzen was angry that the people in the capital had privileged access to VWs and Mazdas while he and people elsewhere had to wait forever; did the constitution not declare all citizens equal? He was fifty-eight and had worked forty years to build the country. "Is that not long enough to have finally a claim to a second, new car?"[88]

In fact, people in the capital were just as consumed by a sense of unfairness. By the summer of 1989, an East Berliner had already been waiting patiently for twelve years for a camper when he stumbled across a depot with several models of the Queck 325. He could take one home right away, he was told, if he put 7,200 West DM on the table. He used to have "a good attitude to our state," he wrote, "but... in the last five years, I have been asking myself the same question over and over again: What is the point of all the hard work and all the overtime my wife and I have put in if we then cannot fulfil our modest desires, or only with foreign currency?" Unfairness hurt his sense of self and his moral authority as a father. "How am I meant to explain to my children that a neighbor immediately gets his car, a caravan, and much else because he has relatives in West Germany while I have to wait twelve or fourteen years for these things?"[89]

The roots of unfairness lay at home, in the GDR's endemic shortages.

Rationing and waiting lists produced constant examples and gossip about people who jumped the line or managed to lay their hands on something thanks to "connections" (*Beziehungen*, dubbed the essential "vitamin B"). Citizens were trapped in a hall of mirrors. Turning one way, they looked at a shining rights culture, crowned by the new Civil Code of 1975; turning the other way, they saw a shadow economy that taught them to bend the rules and tell white lies. The distinction between right and wrong became distorted. Was it a crime to barter with rationed products or, perhaps, a sign of mutual help?

Citizens looked in vain to the party for answers. In 1976, a man from Erfurt sent the party's Central Committee a dozen clippings from local newspapers where people openly advertised boilers and radiators in exchange for a Wartburg, the three-cylinder, medium-sized car one step up from the Trabant. At the time, the official waiting list for the car was fourteen years. "Something surely is not right here," the man concluded.[90] In addition to unfair access, it meant that new buildings could not be finished. He was wrong, the party assured him: there was nothing illegal about the barter arrangements as such, although, unfortunately, profiteering sometimes did happen. Those without radiators to offer jostled for position on the waiting list. A man from Karl-Marx-Stadt wrote to the Council of Ministers in 1986 wanting his nine-year-old reservation for a Wartburg to be fast-tracked in the same way it had been done for a family friend; he was not so lucky.[91]

Trying to keep up with Honecker's promises of the good life, factories rolled out appliances ever faster, which then broke down just as fast. A lack of spare parts and poor service exacerbated existing shortcomings. By the late 1970s, the problem was no longer getting one's hands on a washing machine but getting it fixed when, after barely a year, the heating coil stopped working. The Ministry for Machine Construction alone received fifty-eight thousand petitions in 1977. More than half concerned problems with obtaining spare parts. The defects were putting "a serious strain" on citizens' confidence in the regime, the ministry warned in its internal report.[92]

The shortage of goods compounded the shortage of time. People were provided with a workplace, a home (however decrepit), cheap bread, and (from the 1970s) a place in a day care for their young children. The problem was that for many, each of these was in a completely different place, requiring long commutes, school runs, and expeditions to the shops. It was women who ended up making most of these journeys, and they already had their hands more than full with a job and housework. Trying to get a fridge repaired or locating a pair of children's shoes could be the straw that broke the camel's back. A petitioner from Dresden, who preferred to remain anonymous, wrote to Günter Mittag, the secretary for the economy in the Central Committee of the SED, in 1981. No doubt, socialism was morally superior, the letter began. Still, all the shortages took a toll on female workers, who ended up having to use their vacations to track down scarce goods and services. This was not only a waste of time and hurt productivity, it also caused "moral damage."[93]

It would be a mistake to assume that all petitioners were freedom-loving liberals. In 1979, a man from Dessau sent his *Eingabe* to Verner. In April, his son had bought himself a moped with his hard-earned savings. Two months later, it was stolen. It was his "duty as a citizen" to point to the rise in crime. "It is not acceptable that the many months of hard work by a conscientious citizen are wiped out by a criminal (who only needs seconds for his 'reward'); it ruined the young psyche of a properly raised child." He insisted that the state pay compensation because it had "neglected its duty to fight crime in a timely and effective manner." He himself had foreseen the danger the moment groups of teenagers attached American symbols to their clothes and became "walking billboards of imperialism in our Republic." There was too much "touchy-feely humanitarianism" (*Humanduselei*). The state needed to crack down on such people.[94]

From the 1970s on, a growing number of petitioners invoked their rights and, in particular, the freedom of movement. In 1975, the GDR signed the Helsinki Accords for greater security and cooperation in Europe. This agreement included a guarantee to act in accordance with both the charter of the United Nations and the Universal Declaration of Human Rights (1948), which, alongside the right to life, liberty, and security, and freedom of speech and religion, specifically listed a person's "right to leave any country, including his own, and to return to his country" (Article 13). The GDR's support of the Helsinki pact might appear cynical, but it is important to remember that the regime believed it was charting its own historic course where social, economic, and human rights were becoming one.[95]

Petitioners invoked an internal rights culture, pointing to the GDR constitution, as well as international conventions. Anita E. lived in a small village in Saxony, her mother in West Germany. She had requested permission to visit her mother on her seventieth, seventy-fifth, and seventy-sixth birthdays and had been refused each time. She hadn't seen her mother for nine years. "Why do I not have the same rights as other citizens of our GDR?" she asked.[96] The Department for Security dutifully answered: she had been turned down because she did not participate in the elections and her sons refused to do regular military service. On this occasion, though, the officials granted her a one-week visit. Her point of reference was national rights. Others went further and invoked universal human rights, sometimes quoting directly from the Universal Declaration. A family from Berlin wrote to Verner in 1978, their twentieth petition. They reminded him of his recent speech in defense of human rights in order to stress that "the right to decide whether one wants to live in this state at all should be second to none." They wanted to leave for political reasons and raise their children how they saw fit. The government could take their house. The GDR, they wrote, was a "feudal state," which exploited workers' labor and deprived them of the freedom to choose where to live. That was why only pensioners were allowed to leave. "We do not understand what this state hopes to accomplish by keeping us here by force."[97]

If the 1970s had been marked by a "standstill agreement" between the rulers and the ruled, in the words of the East German novelist Günter de Bruyn,[98] the 1980s saw a breakdown of trust. Instead of quietly accepting the rules of the dictatorship, ordinary people began to speak out or opt out. A widow from Zwickau complained to Verner, the number-one candidate on the electoral list for the People's Assembly in her hometown, in 1981. The GDR put its faith in the young, she said, but for the elderly like her, all that was left was "distrust." One of her sisters lived in Cologne. The woman's application to visit her had been repeatedly rejected, even though she posed no flight risk—in Zwickau, she had an older sister to care for, as well as her own son. For her, a line had been crossed: "My government does not trust an old woman like me, yet at the same time expects me to go to the ballot box to put my trust in a candidate."[99] She was sure he did not need her vote to win. She was right about that.

More troublesome was the estrangement among activists and party members. The years leading up to 1989 saw an exodus from the SED and other organizations. There was growing disagreement about the country's economic direction, and declining confidence in the leadership, which, it seemed, had lost touch with reality.[100] For some it was a profoundly personal step. A pensioner in Berlin had joined the communists as a young man in 1931. In 1983, he "no longer" understood "the party," with all its handouts to the young "even though they don't deserve it."[101] The young generation was not won over either. Instead of anti-fascism and a utopian faith in building a new society, those born after the Wall went up grew up with a sense of no future.

In 1977, Bernhard T. complained about the confiscation of his personal mail, from West Germany. Customs had opened the packet and removed two books seen to agitate against the GDR and a beach ball "with conspicuous advertising." The books in question were an illustrated two-volume coffee table book about the Montreal Olympics in 1976 by a West German sports journalist. At the Games, the GDR had won forty gold medals, four times as many as West Germany and second only to the Soviet Union. Regardless, Customs saw the books as dangerous examples of "the political claim by West Germany to be the sole representative of the nation." The petitioner talked to coworkers at their publicly owned enterprise (VEB) about the incident. They were "disappointed that simple workers were not given any rights." They could not understand the decision: the books were about sports, not "crime, sex, or militarism." At least, the authorities should have the "decency" to return them to him. Until now, Bernhard T. wrote, he had been a good citizen, and he would continue to stand by his state. But, "on serious reflection," he had reached the decision that he would resign from the Conflict Commission. "I do not want to administer justice, if I myself am given only duties and no rights."[102]

FANTASIES OF A GOOD LIFE

On September 18, 1985, the newly qualified teacher Bärbel Spengler arrived at her high school in Magdeburg and was asked to take over the ninth grade from a sick colleague. On the spot, she came up with an original assignment: "What do I imagine (my) life will look like in the year 2010?" In their answers, the fourteen- and fifteen-year-old pupils, with one exception, articulated their vision of the future and a good life, however fantastical in parts. (One punk, loyal to the slogan "No future," boycotted the exercise.)[103]

These were Honecker's children, born in the year he seized power. Like a litmus test, the essays reveal which socialist ideals had left a mark on these young minds. The closest trace of official culture was their faith in technological progress. The students imagined a world where factory workers and, indeed, teachers would be replaced by robots and computers, allowing people to sleep in and enjoy a life without toil, or the need to learn Russian. (At the time, the GDR was trying desperately to produce a microchip in an abortive effort to catch up with the West.) A couple of pupils expressed fears of nuclear war and environmental pollution. Overall, though, there was hope for world peace and clean rivers. In stark contrast to their restricted lives behind the Wall, the students saw themselves whizzing about in the world—the boys tended to fly to Mars in spaceships, the girls to New York and Paris in winged automobiles. For both, a private automobile was a given: "One can drive to wherever one wants to," and "everyone has a nice car"; several specified a Mercedes.

Only Heiko M. looked forward to a world where "everything should be as under socialism": "the capitalists are dead, and there is no more oppression or greed... and no racial discrimination, poverty, or hunger."

For the other students, international peace—the existential promise of the GDR—came with a yearning for private consumption: a house of their own, a garden with a dog, a car, fashionable jewelry, and foreign vacations. Instead of sticking to the future tense, several students spelled out how life ought to be. "Everything should be affordable," wrote Jana. "One should be able to go to the department store and buy the most beautiful things for little money," added Grit. The pupils fantasized about vacations in Paris, New York, and "Ulu Ulu" (possibly meaning Honolulu). For the girls, the ideal was a married life with one or two children, and a weekly visit from their siblings and parents. Evelyn was certain that her parents "will be happy, too, that I have made such a good choice": she would be a hairdresser married to the director of a bank. Mandy saw her future as a seamstress working from home, with a garden big enough for the dog to romp about, while her husband drove off to his office in a Mercedes: "We will all be happy because my husband earns enough money to look after us." If a job was the unquestioned norm for women in the GDR, the girls instinctively accepted that it would be one in a subordinate position. "I can already see myself sitting behind a large desk," Peggy wrote, "working for a multimillionaire, as his secretary." It was her husband who would have a "large car company." They would own a "large house and travel to Brazil each year" in the summer and escape to the mountains in the winter.

Happiness was a private world of material comfort. Far from being evil, luxury and riches were a good thing. There was no *Kollektiv*, no good deeds for socialism, and no state-owned property, either. If in 1985 the GDR still existed in the present, it had lost its claim on the future.[104] The project of instilling a new socialist morality had failed.

7

Searching for *Heimat*: East and West

In 1950, a curious text was circulating among the Sudeten Germans who had been driven out of Czechoslovakia after the war: *Der blinde Jüngling*, or *The Prophecies of the Blind Youth.* A blind young man met Charles IV, the Holy Roman Emperor and king of Bohemia, in Prague in 1356 and shared with him a vision of the future as terrifying as it was accurate. When one foreign ruler will have been "Lord over Bohemia for more than sixty years," he predicted, "a great war will be triggered by the assassination of a prince." Was this not precisely what happened in 1914, when the Emperor Francis Joseph I had reigned for sixty-five years and his nephew, Archduke Franz Ferdinand, was shot in Sarajevo? Two national groups would live alongside each other in Bohemia, the prophecy continued. Once the Bohemian lion had risen up, the one in power would take away the other's liberties, until a powerful master arrived on the scene. A new war would break out "among all the nations of the earth. Germany will be a great heap of rubble... The great war will come to an end, when the cherry trees blossom." It was incredible, the blind youth had again been right, this time about the discrimination suffered by the Sudeten Germans, the coming of Hitler, and the Second World War, which ended in May, the very time when cherry trees start to bloom. "As long as the cherries ripen," the blind youth warned, "I would not want to be a German. But after the second harvest, I would not want to be a Czech." The first time, only as many Germans would stay behind as "fit under one oak tree." But then "a new war will break out, and it will be the shortest." This time, "only as many Czechs will remain as would fit into one hand." Peace would not return until Prague, too, was "a heap of rubble." "A sun will fall, and the earth will tremble." The second time the cherries will blossom, "the sorrowful expellees from Bohemia will return to their masters, their looms and fields." They would only be a few, but they would enter a new "golden age."[1]

From the assassination of Franz Ferdinand and the two world wars to the foreboding of a nuclear bomb ("a sun will fall..."), *The Prophecies* seemed extraordinary. Their almost apocalyptic vision of the twentieth century struck a chord with German refugees like the Sudeten, who copied the text and passed it from hand to hand, until it found its way into print in a slim book of the same title. Here was a prophecy that simultaneously foresaw the fate of the expellees and promised them revenge. There would be a third world war, and the survivors among them would return and reclaim their land.

The Prophecies was a clever fake. Manuscripts bearing the same title had been circulating in Bohemia since the seventeenth century, and the genre, with its evocative language about cherries and war, would have been familiar to people from that region. The visions of twentieth-century catastrophes, however, were the creation of Max Erbstein, a fellow refugee writing under the name of "M. Gunter." There was an appetite for paranormal visions and sightings at the time. Elsewhere, ethnic Germans from Hungary and Romania reported Marian apparitions in which former partisans suddenly suffered epileptic fits or saw their shooting hand turn lame as punishment for having murdered Germans.[2]

The Sudeten Germans were among the 12 million Germans who fled or were expelled between 1944 and 1950 in what was the largest forced population transfer in European history. When they arrived, they called themselves "refugees" or "expellees," but what their official status should be soon became a matter of major contention. Together, they embodied centuries of German history and its unresolved patchwork between state and people. The expelled included Germans whose families had lived for centuries in a German state (East Prussia had been a state of the Teutonic Order since the Middle Ages and, since 1701, the Kingdom of Prussia), in regions that had been German provinces until the end of the First World War (Posen and West Prussia, largely ceded to Poland, or the Sudeten region to Czechoslovakia), as well as those who spoke dialects of German but had not lived under German authority for centuries, the so-called *Ostsiedler*. These last were the descendants of German migrants who in the Middle Ages and early modern period had formed settlements in the Baltic region, Romania, Serbia, and Hungary (the Banat-Germans and Danube Swabians), and later, under Catharine the Great, in Russia. The 12 million also included "*Volksdeutsche*," people with some ethnic German ancestry who were registered by the Nazis in the occupied territories but who often had been assimilated and could not speak German.

The expulsions were one of the tragic ironies of history. Hitler had called on all Germans to come "*Heim ins Reich*" ("back home to the Reich"). It was his defeat that accomplished it. Instead of a greater Germany, they found themselves driven into a smaller one, a country amputated and divided.

Expellees would sometimes compare their camps and death marches with those the Jews had had to endure. The expulsions, it needs be stressed, were not genocidal, and cannot be equated with mass extermination under the Nazis. There was no plan to exterminate the German people as a whole. It was, however, a form of ethnic cleansing, and torture, murder, and forced labor were certainly tolerated. The Cold War gave their suffering special resonance, and their deaths were creatively added up in a moral ledger presented to rival those of the Nazis' victims in central and Eastern Europe. The official figure gave 2 million dead during the flight, and this was the number expellee lobbies continued to use. The true number was closer to half a million—as calculated by the churches' tracing service already in 1965 and confirmed by recent historians.[3]

The expulsions left Germans with a moral challenge that was radically different from that of confronting Nazi crimes. "Forgive and forget" was easily said when others were the victims. The expellees found this more difficult. After all, they had been uprooted against their will. Their homeland and livelihood had been taken from them. How should or could that wrong be repaired? When it came to dealing with the victims of the Nazis, the leitmotif was reparation and reconciliation. For German refugees, by contrast, these had to compete with righteousness and revenge, as *The Prophecies* made clear.

There was a danger that expellees might get sucked into a persistent hatred of their enemies, what Friedrich Nietzsche, that great critic of modern morality, called "*ressentiment.*" In *On the Genealogy of Morals* (1887), Nietzsche pointed out how the oppressed, by investing themselves too much in their own suffering and hatred, locked themselves into the position of victims who directed their anger at an "evil" enemy. Instead of overcoming injustice, the victims' *ressentiment* recycled the roles of oppressed and oppressor.[4] It produced the opposite disposition from that so celebrated by Adam Smith. Instead of an "impartial spectator" capable of empathy, we get an "angry spectator" who wants revenge. As the writer Ian Buruma has warned more recently, when remembrance of suffering becomes obsessive, it can spell myopia and vendetta.[5]

The changing relationship between the hosts and their co-national newcomers in the following decades says a lot about the moral landscape in the two Germanies. In 1949, Heinrich Albertz, the future mayor of Berlin, called the refugee crisis "the top problem of our current German destiny." "If we pass by its reality, we will be standing outside life in Germany."[6] A pastor and Social Democrat, Albertz knew what he was talking about. He was himself a refugee from Breslau (Wrocław) in the Prussian province of Silesia that was now in Poland, and had firsthand experience of the tensions between locals and newcomers in Celle in the British zone, where he served as refugee commissioner.

Being uprooted and putting down new roots triggered fundamental questions over identity. Where was "home" and what was "Germany"? There was a clash between customs, confessions, and dialects, down to basic disagreements about "good" and "bad" behavior. Contemporaries worried that uprootedness might create millions of chronically "asocial" people: nihilistic, irresponsible, and "crazy," who "do not belong anywhere," to quote the Westphalian Synod in 1948.[7] Such a type would be dangerous for society because it was susceptible to totalitarian ideas. The host communities, too, came under scrutiny. While the expellees arrived with little or nothing, many locals still had their farms, shops, and homes—but did they also have the moral capital to help? What would "Love thy neighbor" mean in practice when there were suddenly so many new neighbors?

EXPULSION AND FLIGHT

One of the 12 million was Martha Zollinger, who recorded her flight in her diary. Zollinger's life was framed by the two world wars. She was born in East Prussia, the most northeastern tip of the German empire, on November 4, 1914. The fortress of Insterburg (Chernyakhovsk), her hometown, had served the medieval Teutonic knights as a base for colonizing Lithuania with the cross and the sword. Thirty years later, in October 1944, with the Soviet troops advancing, she fled with her seven-year-old boy. Their first stop was Ellerbruch (Olszówka) in West Prussia, her husband's parents' home. On January 23, 1945, she, her son, and her in-laws moved further west, to Stolp (Słupsk) in Pomerania (northern Poland). The Red Army had cut off East Prussia, and it was closing in on them. On March 7, a day before the Red Army occupied Stolp, the Zollinger family tried to reach the Baltic coast on foot via side roads. The port of Danzig, annexed by Hitler at the start of the war, was still in the hands of the Wehrmacht. After a few days, they were overtaken by Soviet troops near the small town of Glowitz (Glowczyce). A Russian officer pulled his pistol and took her to a room. "There he raped me," she wrote, "with the pistol in his hand." Zollinger and the others were able to reach the next village, where for one month they were left in peace. On April 5, the Red Army returned. She was raped again by another officer; "kicking up a row," she managed to repel the unarmed soldier who assaulted her next. Her son got measles, and when summer came, she came down with typhoid. "Everything lost—and now also the homeland [*Heimat*]. What is going to happen? A life under the Poles—it is frightful." They lived off stolen apples and potatoes and were begging for food.

On October 5, 1945, she and her boy managed to get on a train from Stolp to Berlin—the journey of roughly 250 miles took a week—and from there on to Schwerin. In nearby Crivitz, in Mecklenburg-Vorpommern, the mayor parceled out the new arrivals among the neighboring villages. She was now in the Soviet zone and for the first time in months sleeping in a bed. By early November, there were about eight hundred refugees like her in the village, and she began to worry about the approaching winter. "When I think of the future, my mind stops. How will I see my relatives again? I am longing for my husband so much . . . I know nothing about him, not even whether he is still alive." The Red Cross tracing service was unable to help. She tried to get across to the British zone, but was stopped at the border and turned back. By early May 1946, she was in despair: "I so much want to die, so that this misery will finally come to an end." A couple of weeks later, she wrote, "We no longer have anything to eat." "We cannot stay here, where no one is sharing even a potato with us."

On May 22, 1946, with the help of a train attendant, she and her son escaped the Soviet zone on a hospital train, hiding in the brake compartment. In the transit camp she was de-liced and then moved to a former barracks in Kiel. A month later, she received her permit to move in with relatives in Bielefeld, in Westphalia. Almost two years after she had left East Prussia, her flight had come to an end. The diary breaks off in 1947, and we do not know her husband's fate. She would not see her homeland again. Martha Zollinger died in Bielefeld in 1952, at only thirty-seven years old.[8]

Martha Zollinger's odyssey is a reminder that flight and expulsion were drawn-out processes that involved multiple stages, attempted border crossings, and a succession of villages and camps, until the prospect of a new home finally opened up. Although she did not have long to live, Zollinger and her son were among the lucky ones. Tens of thousands of fellow East Prussians did not survive—Nazi fanatics dreaming of a final victory left communities hopelessly unprepared. The dead included more than eight thousand refugees on the transport ship *Wilhelm Gustloff*, which was sunk by Soviet torpedos in the Baltic Sea on January 30, 1945. Other Germans from the east were deported to Siberia and the Urals. Which of these fates awaited a refugee depended in no small part on location and timing. More than 3 million, like Zollinger, were driven out before the German surrender on May 8, 1945. At the Potsdam Conference in August 1945, the Allies sealed the fate of the remaining German populations in Poland, Czechoslovakia, and Hungary by approving population transfers by force. In the next five years, a further 7.4 million Germans would be swept up by them.

These expulsions were only the latest in a series of forced population transfers in Europe since the late nineteenth century, most notably the expulsion and mass murder of the Armenians from Turkey in 1915, and the compulsory exchange of almost 2 million Greek and Turkish minorities decreed by the Lausanne Conference in 1923.[9] Following the Hitler-Stalin pact of 1939, some 250,000 Germans were moved out of eastern Poland, Estonia, Moldova (Bessarabia), and Bukovina. The Nazis, in turn, drove 400,000 Poles from the Warthegau into the occupied *Generalgouvernement* to make room for German settlers. Their vision was to resettle 20 million ethnic Germans eventually. For some refugees, the post-1945 expulsions were a second or even a third round of migration.

An engineer who first fled in 1940 to Upper Silesia when Stalin took Bessarabia, and eventually ended up in Stuttgart, pointed his finger at the Nazis and their racial ideology when explaining the refugee crisis to the Catholic Church in the summer of 1945.[10] Acknowledgment of that longer history, however, was the exception. Most expellees' private and public memories began in 1944–46 with their own tragedy. The reception awaiting them in what was left of Germany also came with a prehistory. Many of the refugee camps that received them had housed forced laborers from the East and prisoners of war. To local residents, the German expellees appeared as just the latest wave of arrivals from the East.

Population movements did not come to a sudden stop with the end of the expulsions in 1950. Germans would later have a troubled relationship with foreign guest workers and asylum seekers. And there were the almost 3 million Germans who fled the GDR until the Berlin Wall went up in 1961, the 250,000 who managed to escape afterward, and the half a million who left legally.

At Potsdam, in August 1945, the Allies had agreed that any transfer "should be effected in an orderly and humane manner" and that the Czech, Polish, and Hungarian governments should "suspend further expulsions" in the meantime. Reality was the brutal opposite. The initial transfers in the spring and summer of 1945 came to be known as "wild expulsions," as if bottled-up vengeance among the local Czech and Polish populations spontaneously exploded at the Nazi fifth columnists in their midst. In truth, the transfers were an "eruption of a massive state-sponsored carnival of violence," in the words of the historian R. M. Douglas.[11] It was mainly the police and paramilitary troops that carried out the expulsions with the full support of the Czechoslovak and Polish governments and passive approval of the Allies. Anger at Nazi crimes and local collaborators—understandable in its own terms—was used to justify the program of ethnic cleansing to create "pure" states. Ethnic Germans were rounded up and put on overcrowded trains that could take two weeks to reach Berlin, without food and water. In September 1945, the German churches and the Red Cross presented the Allies with a list of horrors, including a trek of 2,400 people from Troppau in the Sudetenland. After six weeks, only 1,400 were still alive.[12] In Teplice nad Metují (Wekelsdorf), two dozen women, elderly, and children were marched to the Polish border. When the Poles refused to let them in, the Czech officer took them into the nearest forest and shot them.[13]

German communities did include many who had cheered Hitler, but the expulsions targeted all Germans alike, even those who had joined the resistance, those who had fought against Hitler, or Jews who survived Nazi occupation but happened to be registered as German. Anti-Nazis were told to pack up as well. Having German roots, not Nazi sympathies, was the critical test. Czech and Polish collaborators were not expelled. Unlike their nationalist leaders, Czech and Polish residents often did not want their German neighbors to be taken away: moral issues aside, how would they be able to bring in the harvest or run the local factory without them? In 1945, it was not rare for expellees to turn around immediately, trying to get back to their homes in the Sudetenland or Pomerania. The German churches pleaded with the Allies to let them back in time for the harvest. Instead, the transfers were turning vibrant borderlands into barren ghost zones.

For thousands, Potsdam's promised "order" meant the order of the camps. The motto greeting German detainees at the Linzer Vorstadt camp in southern Bohemia was "An eye for an eye, a tooth for a tooth" ("*oko za oko, zub za zub*"). At Bolesławiec (Bunzlau), more than a thousand boys became forced laborers. Torture, rape, and malnutrition were routine. In September 1946, the British Labour MP Richard Stokes gained access to several Czech camps. He returned with a harrowing account. Inmates received "750 calories a day, which is below the Belsen level," he noted, a comparison that ignored the 50,000 who had died there because of hunger, thirst, and disease.[14]

After December 1945, the expulsions became more "organized." People received advance notice of their transfer and a luggage allowance—roughly 110 pounds per person, thanks to Soviet pressure on the Czechoslovak government. Inevitably, the trains attracted many "unofficial" passengers who were not on the list but for whom they were the only alternative to starvation. The authorities detained "official" expellees, especially young men, for use as forced labor. Those on the trains suffered frostbite and hunger. It was only in the winter of 1946–47 that Britain and the United States turned against the expulsions they had helped unleash. The U-turn came partly in response to the growing number of outspoken voices, such as Stokes, who complained about human rights abuses, and partly because the flood of starving and sick expellees eventually swamped their own occupation zones in Germany. The international window for large-scale expulsions was closing. It was too late for Hungary, which had only managed to drive out a quarter of the roughly half a million ethnic Germans. It was the only central European country where the majority of Germans were not uprooted.

"STRANGE AND ALIEN ELEMENTS"

Compared to the flood of Germans from the East, the numbers of refugees trying to reach Europe in more recent memory has been a mere trickle. In 1950, every sixth person living in West Germany was an expellee; in the smaller East Germany, it was one in five. If anything, such averages underestimate the humanitarian crisis facing the regions that took in the greatest numbers—the East and West Prussians who had walked across the frozen Baltic ended up primarily in Schleswig-Holstein (British zone) and Mecklenburg-Vorpommern (Soviet zone) and made up 33 percent and 43 percent of the population respectively in 1949; the Sudeten Germans crossed the border into Bavaria (American zone; 21 percent). The French zone, further to the west, tried to block the refugees, who made up a mere 5 percent of the population.[15]

The refugee commissioner of the Evangelisches Hilfswerk, the main Protestant aid agency, toured camps across West Germany in 1946 and 1947. His reports give a picture both of the gravity of the situation and of the variety of local conditions and responses. Thousands were arriving each day at a Bavarian camp across the Czechoslovak border. There were not enough beds, and a bucket behind a curtain served as the toilet. The local authorities, he felt, were looking the other way, hoping the problem would disappear. The mayor of Furth im Wald told him, "I sh[it] . . . on the whole refugee stuff." A Catholic Caritas officer reported a similar lack of compassion. Trains arrived crowded with refugees from the East, some "half mad from hunger and . . . crawling on all fours across the tracks begging for food." Yet some locals responded, "It would be better if they stayed at home, even if the [Soviet] occupation is so hard... our own need is so great... why do they have to come to us?"[16]

In East Frisia and Oldenburg in the north, the welcome was no warmer. In Campen, the elderly and infants were put in Nissen huts (semicircular cabins made of sheets of metal). There were not enough beds, and many had to sleep on heaps of straw on a cement floor. The local farmer had removed the electric lighting and used the wiring for his farm buildings instead. No one brought them peat to heat and stay warm. "The farmer even refuses them drinking water, so they have to fetch water from a ditch." The same farmer, the refugee commissioner noted, also happened to be the head of the local Protestant congregation. In Oldenburg, in Lower Saxony, the expellees were put up in a camp that until recently had housed members of the Reichsarbeitsdienst, the Nazi Labor Service. The food was "bad and expensive," and all the beds had been "stolen by the farmers." In Altena, a small town with a picturesque medieval castle in Westphalia, the sixty refugees preferred to stay in a camp because the locals only offered them empty rooms in their homes, without any furniture.[17]

The situation the commissioner found in the Rhineland was more encouraging. In Hilden, the town hall showed "goodwill." There were five camps for three hundred people "in good condition." The rooms were heated, and there was a public canteen. In Solingen, the camp was home to ninety-six adults and fifty-four children. The hall was cold, but two ovens mitigated it and the communal meals were "good and free." Shoes and clothes from foreign donations were distributed. The children received milk from Quakers abroad. There was even a day care.[18]

Admittedly, North Rhine–Westphalia only had to accommodate a fraction of the 3 million people from the East flooding into Lower Saxony and Schleswig-Holstein. On the other hand, this more industrial and urbanized region had also suffered far more severe war damage. People here had much less to give than the farmers in the north, whose homes and farms had barely been scratched. Germans who had themselves been bombed out showed greater empathy with the expellees than those whose houses were still standing. Bombed-out residents had also been displaced. In addition, the region had been home to coal miners from Poland since the late nineteenth century. Living with migrants had been fairly normal. Some camps in the Rhineland had already been set up for evacuees from nearby cities. In such places, the expellees from the East stepped into existing local networks of charity—the local Catholic youth even put on social evenings at the camp in Dülken. Giessen was a transit camp for refugees before they were sent to private homes across the district. It was run by the Hilfswerk with plenty of volunteers. Its heart and soul was the wife of Pastor Scriba, a mother of ten children, who herself had been bombed out.[19]

In the Soviet sector, the situation in the camps was no better. Right along the Polish border lay Görlitz. An official visitation of the camp there in January 1946 found toilets but little else. At night, 4,300 people had to make do with 600 straw sacks to sleep on. They needed one hundred tons of coal a month to heat the camp but only got thirty-nine. Adults received the same amount of food as one-year-olds: roughly three quarters of a quart of warm soup per day. New arrivals with anti-fascist credentials were somewhat luckier. Those in Pirna were moved to the "model camp" Sonnenstein in November 1946. It had kitchens, washrooms, and a special sick bay. All camps across Saxony, though, suffered from the same problem, according to the official report: "Care and welfare were completely unsatisfactory, from local authorities and mayors to the women's committee and the resettlement commission."[20] In September 1948, Saxony-Anhalt still estimated a shortage of 292,000 straw sacks; people were sleeping on plain straw.[21]

The welcome was often a virtual slap in the face, especially in relatively closed rural communities. For many locals, the expellees were not only outsiders but aliens. An Allied observer noted in 1948 how in Bavaria, the pejorative "*Saupreusse*" ("Prussian pig") had been replaced by "*Sauflüchtling*" ("refugee pig"). In Saxony, in the Soviet zone, the preferred term of abuse was "*Umsiedlerschwein*" ("resettler pig"), and farmers were found treating their fellow citizens like the "*Ostarbeiter*," the forced laborers from Poland and the Ukraine, making them work from 5 a.m. to 7 p.m.; after that, they could sleep on the floor.[22] "*Polacke*" was another widespread label. Near Hanover, in the British zone, a poem was circulating that portrayed them as "the gypsies from the East / who pollute our land / live at our expense" and prayed to God that "He may liberate us from the burden of the evil star."[23]

Such views were not confined to extremists. Ernst Martens was a Liberal member of the coalition government in Lower Saxony. In May 1947, he wrote to the regional prime minister about his impressions from a recent visit to Oldenburg. The expellees in the town, he said, were lazy and preferred the black market to honest work; they had brought these shady dealings with them from the East. They were the "trendsetters for amoral and asocial forces," and the only solution was to toss them back to where they came from.[24] In nearby Eversen, the pastor doubted whether the expellees were of "pure" German blood and worried that the German people would lose their "authentic quality" if they mixed with such "strange and alien elements." For a fellow pastor, the refugee crisis was an Allied plot to dissolve the German *Volk*.[25]

Such suspicion and hostility showed how thin and brittle the *Volk* and national identity were for many Germans. For years, the Nazis had invoked a racial empire uniting all Germans. Now locals spat at the Sudeten Germans, denounced ethnic Germans from the Baltics to Romania as "Also-Germans," and gave the cold shoulder to people from East Prussia, which had been united with Brandenburg since 1618 and was the birthplace of Immanuel Kant and part of Bismarck's unified Germany. Defeated and divided, Germans turned inward to their community and region for their identity. The sudden influx of Germans from the East with their own customs, dialects, and interests destroyed ultranationalism.

Not surprisingly, the biggest source of conflict was housing. In the Soviet and Western zones, it tended to be the communities with the most to spare who shared the least. In Joachimsthal, north of Berlin, not a single house had been damaged in the war, but there was no compassion for the refugees. In Saxony, one of them who was a recognized victim of fascism complained in January 1947 that he had been promised a roof over his head, but the town officials preferred not to antagonize their local friends who sat comfortably in their large apartments. One month later, in Leipzig, a group of fifty protested that they had been put in damaged apartments while "the Nazis still owned their large and good ones." In Pirna, living conditions for the newcomers were unacceptable, but the director of the local steel plant had a 2,150-square-foot apartment to himself, his wife, and one child. There were constant complaints about mayors dragging their feet. The small town of Stolpen, just east of Dresden, had a socialist mayor. When twenty-three families arrived, he gave them a list of addresses and told them to organize their own accommodation. They met with "general rejection by the population." A mother with children went back to the mayor and said she would rather hang herself than move into "that hole" she was being offered. He told her he would gladly give her the rope—"then, thank God, he would have one resettler less in the community."[26]

In the British zone, Celle had, similarly, escaped the worst of the war. Here, too, residents were more likely to shut their doors in the face of refugees than throw them open. When a mother with a two-year-old toddler was sent to live with a pastor, his sister locked the door and refused them entry—the police had to be called.[27] As long as locals greeted the newcomers with an ax, one contemporary noted, it was difficult to establish trust and neighborly relationships.

In East as in West Germany, it was a widespread practice for residents to move furniture temporarily to the attic or circulate it among family members rather than give it to those who had nothing. Farmers would suddenly give their servants individual bedrooms in order to keep out the newcomers. In Hersfeld (Hesse), a farmer was sentenced to three months in prison after first prohibiting one of the refugees housed with him from taking water from the tap and then beating him unconscious when he caught him helping himself to water in the horse barn.[28]

HELPING HANDS

Animosity and meanness were widespread, but they were never universal. Complaints inevitably leave a bigger paper trail than simple acts of kindness. Interviews at the time and the records of charities and welfare organizations tell a more nuanced story. In one village near Celle, a farmer and former mayor praised the expellees. "They are very hardworking, clean people, and one never hears any complaint from them." An elderly woman added, "I mean, it is our moral duty to help them, but they are also morally obliged to recognize that. My refugees are always there when I need them." For a high school student, seeing the refugees and their privations taught him "respect for our fellow men who, in spite of all their losses and worries, never gave up but courageously and energetically built a new life."[29]

The humanitarian crisis prompted a powerful call for aid. The United Nations Relief and Rehabilitation Agency (UNRRA) helped DPs and the victims of the Nazis, not Germans. Into the breach stepped foreign churches and donors. Swedes, the Swiss, and American Quakers were particularly generous. Many German children survived thanks to the free milk and medicine they provided. Donations went initially to both East and West Germany. To give a sense of proportion, in 1948 Lutheran congregations from the United States and Canada sent enough food to feed 120,000 children in the Soviet zone for three months. Of the 100 million CARE packages the Cooperative for American Remittances sent to Europe, 10 million reached West German families. A typical packet contained four pounds of meat (beef, liver, and bacon), several pounds of margarine, sugar, raisins, egg powder, and, that most precious item, coffee. In popular memory, the CARE package came to symbolize the relief effort. In fact, a lot of foreign aid came in the form of money, medicine, and clothes as well as raw materials, such as cotton, which was turned into bed linen and underwear in Germany. Between 1945 and 1955, a formidable 253 million pounds of foreign aid reached West Germany. The peak was in 1948 (119 million pounds), but as late as 1954 it was still 22 million.[30]

Just as vital was self-help. Churches and welfare organizations within Germany distributed CARE packages and fed children while also soliciting donations directly from fellow Germans, which were considerable. In November 1946, for example, when Württemberg received 573,000 pounds of food and almost 350,000 pounds of clothes from abroad, the Protestant Hilfswerk collected 5.7 million pounds of food and 500,000 items of clothing, shoes, and furniture locally. The food alone was enough to fill 130 train cars. Germans would not have survived without foreign aid, nor would they have survived without self-help.[31]

What was self-help in West Germany was called solidarity in the East. In the Soviet zone, the socialist agency Volkssolidarität took the place of the fascist winter aid. Its goal was not only to clear the physical rubble, it was explained at a meeting in 1946, but also to clear the "mental rubble" and cultivate the spirit of mutual aid necessary for peace and reconstruction. The organization ran hundreds of child care centers and sewing circles and mobilized volunteers to give millions of hours of free labor to rebuild schools, roads, and farm buildings. In 1949, miners worked extra shifts to raise more than 11 million pounds of briquettes for pensioners.[32] Above all, it led donation drives. In Saxony, between autumn 1945 and autumn 1946, it collected and distributed almost 18 million pounds of food, 2.8 million items of clothing, and 109,000 pieces of furniture. Children received a million toys, and housewives 1.4 million household appliances—an impressive amount that simultaneously showed a degree of generosity and how well stocked German homes still were at the end of the war compared to the neighboring countries they had ransacked.[33]

Need, unfortunately, was on an even bigger scale. According to one survey, by September 1947, 17 percent of newcomers in the eastern zone still did not have a bed and 57 percent lacked pots and pans to cook their food. That month, Anna Thiem appealed to the district administrator in the town of Havelberg near the river Elbe: "We have lost everything, as refugees. We do not own bedding, just a thin blanket, and sleep on the floor; no table, nothing. My son, my provider, cannot go to work. He has no clothes." She asked for a pair of work shoes and clothes for her son. Why, she wanted to know, were "some people" treated so badly here? "It is the complete truth. There is only unfairness, otherwise nothing, one sees a lot that ought not to be."[34] She received a wardrobe and a pillow case.

"Resettler weeks" sought to drum up donations and raise awareness that the newcomers were there to stay. Their motto was "New homeland, new life." "No one must stand aloof," posters urged. "Give furniture and household effects for the new settlers and the bombed-out!" "Everyone who still has his possessions should see it as their duty and honor to help as much as he can. Everyone needs to put himself in the position of those who have lost everything."[35]

The response was mixed. Some small towns put on a big show. In Buckow, east of Berlin, at the end of October 1947, the market square was decorated, children sang, and, after the mayor's speech, there was a special screening of *The Big Number* (*Die grosse Nummer*), a dramatic circus romance of love and lions. The film was shot under the Nazis in 1942. During the week, there was dancing in restaurants and the hotel. Some small communities gave generously. In Thuringia, the few hundred villagers of Effelder, for example, donated 104 pieces of furniture and 700 Reichsmark for their ninety-nine new neighbors—the Reichsmark remained the currency in the Soviet as well as the Western zones until the summer of 1948. Overall, though, the population showed a "lack of interest," according to an official report. In Erfurt, the provincial capital, not even the halls were made to look festive. A comprehensive assessment a few months later found progress in some places like Apolda but plenty of unused furniture and spare rooms in Erfurt and elsewhere. Saxony-Anhalt estimated that newcomers there needed a total of half a million suits and dresses—of which it managed to collect 1 percent. This was after more than two thousand resident assemblies and promotional entertainment in cinemas and social evenings. The socialist authorities had succeeded in moving almost all refugees out of camps, but most of their new homes were barren.[36]

The appeal to solidarity faced moral as well as material limits. In reality, donations were not entirely voluntary. Going from door to door, the collectors noted who gave and who did not. In Havelberg, five households in Domherrstrasse gave 10 Marks; Frau Erika Zimmermann even scraped together two small plates, four pots, three spoons, and a towel rack. But in one of the houses, the occupants "gave nothing!"[37] Thuringia and Saxony-Anhalt introduced emergency powers that enabled them to confiscate unused furniture standing in lofts and cellars, although the new rulers abstained from heavy-handed use for fear of antagonizing residents. Instead, helpers were told to stress that donations were voluntary but to "hint that a regulation existed that would probably be applied if the yield of the collection was disappointing... In negative cases, a follow-up visit might be necessary."[38]

The problem was that, two years after the war, many communities either would not or could not give any more. In Brandenburg, the minister in charge found that many mayors were completely inactive and "the resettler committees only existed on paper."[39] Hermersdorf publicized its meeting for Sunday, October 26, 1947, but only eleven people showed up. Schoolchildren and socialist youth (FDJ) were more easily mobilized and managed to drum up 655 RM, but the final ceremony was again "rather sparsely attended." In nearby Lebus, several residents spoke out against a new collection drive: "The general view was that it was for the government to help." In addition to the war and reparations, these communities had been hit by a flood in 1947. The few spare beds and tables they had to begin with had already been donated or loaned to the "resettlers" when they first arrived.[40]

SOLIDARITY OF SUFFERING

In West Germany, the relief effort brought back to life the charitable networks that had distributed aid and alms before the Nazis took centralized control: the Red Cross, the social democratic Workers' Welfare (Arbeiterwohlfahrt, AWO), the Catholic Caritas, and the Protestant Inner Mission. The end of the war added one major new body: the Protestant aid agency Evangelisches Hilfswerk. It was these bodies with their many volunteers that ran many of the camps, distributed food and foreign aid, and offered care and comfort to the expellees. The German Red Cross, for example, looked after 1,293 refugee camps and handed out 40 million meals between 1946 and 1949. Caritas distributed almost 500 million DM of foreign aid in the first decade after the war. Following the efforts of the Hilfswerk can demonstrate what this new spirit of charity meant in practice.

Although its official birth was not until August 1945, the Evangelisches Hilfswerk was conceived by Eugen Gerstenmaier behind the bars of his Nazi prison cell in the final stages of the war. Gerstenmaier was a theologian who worked in the culture department of the Foreign Ministry and was a member of the Kreisau resistance circle. On July 20, 1944, he sat with pocket Bible and pistol in Berlin waiting to seize power with the other conspirators upon the news of Hitler's death. He was one of the few members of the resistance who escaped execution. He was freed from prison by the Americans in April 1945. The first plans for postwar aid had already been laid, in 1942, before the defeat at Stalingrad, by the ecumenical council of churches in Geneva. By 1944, it seemed clear to Gerstenmaier and several bishops that the approaching collapse of Nazi Germany would be so total that only the churches would be left to pick up the pieces.[41]

Like much of West German relief, the Evangelisches Hilfswerk was founded on the principle of "self-help." This made obvious practical sense.

In 1945, Germans were excluded from international aid, and, after that, foreign donors were more likely to help a nation that was helping itself. Spiritual and political reasons were just as important. The postwar crisis was the hour of the churches and the Good Samaritan. For a nationalist churchman such as Wilhelm Pressel in Württemberg, the Hilfswerk inherited the hopes he had invested in Hitler, with the difference that now it was charity, and no longer Nazism, that would liberate Germans from materialism and lead them back to the faith. For Gerstenmaier, a Christian Democrat with a social heart, the aid agency's mission went much further. Karl Marx, he said in a lecture in 1947, had a point when he criticized the Protestant ethic. Protestants needed to act, not just preach, and concern themselves more with the material problems of people's lives. This did not mean the churches should try to take the place of political parties or the state. But they needed to cultivate a political conscience—that was the lesson of the Nazi period. Theirs had to be a struggle for the whole person. The Hilfswerk, in short, needed to be much more than an ambulance rushing from one emergency to the next. Charity was not enough, Gerstenmaier stressed: they needed to integrate those without a "home."

As in the Soviet sector, the refugee crisis was thus a chance to cultivate social solidarity. Where socialists looked to the future, however, Gerstenmaier pointed to the present "solidarity of suffering" (*Solidarität des Elends*) between refugees and locals. He connected the Christian embrace of suffering as teaching love and sacrifice with a political acknowledgment that all Germans were in the same boat. "All of Germany has lost the war," Gerstenmaier stressed. "Not only the Silesians and East Prussians. And, unfortunately, not only the NSDAP!" They all needed to share the burden.[42]

The language of self-help was so powerful because it spoke to Germans both as victims and as actors who shared responsibility for the situation they found themselves in. "We know it is God's will," Gerstenmaier told a public meeting in December 1947, "that we must walk through a valley of penance and reflection." "We have been cheated, but to the rest of the world we cannot act as if we had just been innocently taken in. We ourselves need to take responsibility for having ended up in the situation in which we find ourselves today."[43]

Over the next few years, the Hilfswerk grew into a vast charitable enterprise. In the summer of 1945, it set up milk kitchens for the thousands of mothers and babies passing through Hof, near the Czechoslovak border, and built homes for children and the elderly. That autumn, Protestant churches in Württemberg collected 1 million RM in offerings from their flocks. In November, the Hilfswerk there sent twenty wagons of potatoes to Berlin.

In Hessen-Nassau, a region with 1.6 million inhabitants, the harvest festival in 1948 brought in 176,000 pounds of food. Even inhabitants of Schleswig-Holstein, often seen to be cold-hearted, donated 860,000 pounds of potatoes and 11,000 loaves of bread that autumn. Across the country, the aid agency collected 180 million RM in the first three years after the war; in 1948–49, the first year after the currency reform, donations reached 15 million Deutschmark. By 1948, the Hilfswerk had 1,500 full-time refugee counselors and many thousands of volunteers. As late as 1955, it ran three thousand camps for a quarter of a million refugees, including those from the GDR. In 1957, it fused with the Inner Mission and, as the Diakonisches Werk (the Protestant social welfare organization), became a pillar of the mixed welfare system in West Germany.[44]

In many rural areas, the Hilfswerk was the expellees' lifeline. The town of Schorndorf in Württemberg, for example, had 13,000 inhabitants and took in almost 8,000 newcomers. Betweeen 1946 and 1949, the Hilfswerk carried out 10,000 individual care visits and distributed 10,000 meals and more than 13,000 pounds of clothes and bedding. Some of the food came from foreign donations, but 48,000 pounds were given by locals in harvest festivals.[45]

From the churches' point of view, the donations were also lessons in charity for their hosts. As *Pfennighelfer* ("penny helpers"), children were taught the joy of making a personal sacrifice for the sake of others. In Kassel, for example, when a pastor started his group in 1947, those who did not have a pfennig to spare could leave candy. Some girls donated their dolls. The group even adopted a child care center in Pomerania. Caritas allowed poor girls to keep 5 to 10 percent of what they collected for their effort (in Catholic areas, the helpers tended to be girls). In Kurhessen-Waldeck, a region with around 300,000 Protestant families, children asked their parents for a pfennig each week. In addition, they went from house to house to collect from regular 10-pfennig and 20-pfennig "customers." Between 1949 and 1952, the children collected more than 30 million pfennigs. The Hilfswerk monthly newsletter said, "The children are raised to have an open eye and open heart for the need of their neighbor." The collections were known as the "Olympics of love," and participation was mandatory for those preparing to be confirmed. In the Nazis' winter aid campaign, it had been the donors who received badges; now it was the collectors. A *Pfennighelfer* received a copper-colored pin after six months, a silver one after one year, and a gold one after three.[46]

Aid depended on tens of thousands of charitable workers and volunteers, who handed out food, collected old clothes and furniture, administered medicine, and provided words of spiritual comfort. In the pages of history, volunteers tend to be an anonymous regiment of foot soldiers. Fortunately, letters and reports in the archives of the Evangelisches Hilfswerk allow us in this case to give them a face.

People found their way to the Hilfswerk via three main routes. One group experienced a spiritual awakening in the final stages of the war. Karl-August Stuckenberg had fought in Africa and Sicily, where, he said, God "put His protective hand over me." Then, in the final battle for Berlin, he found himself in a hopeless position under enemy fire. "Like a miracle, God led me safely out of the collapsing ruins" and "mercifully protected my wife and my children during the terrible flight from the East." By taking away his possessions, the Lord showed him "only more radiantly his great charity, love, and mercy" (*verzeihende Liebe*). "Should I not thank Him with my life?" He joined the Hilfswerk and looked after refugees in East Holstein, near the Baltic coast. Elizabeth Schellenberg's husband was not as fortunate. He was killed by a grenade in his home in southern Germany in the final days of the war, leaving behind six children. The widow was in despair until she heard a pastor from the Hilfswerk speak about the plight of the refugees from the East. She was won over and began to care for blind refugees and returning POWs. Their courage, she said, comforted her in her own despair.[47]

These were new recruits. Just as important were their veteran brothers and sisters. The Hilfswerk was able to draw on charitable habits that reached back to the Weimar years. Charlotte Berling had been trained as a social worker in the Protestant women's seminar in Berlin in the late 1920s. In the Nazi years, she visited prisons. In 1948, she was helping expellees stranded in the moors near Hanover. Marga Burrlein, a widow with six small children, took in an elderly couple as well as two teenage girls whose parents were missing. She had been trained as a preschool teacher and worked in youth welfare. Her eldest daughter, who was twelve years old, also helped. Their family motto was "Always prepared."[48]

Finally, refugee aid meant in the most literal sense "self-help." In many camps and communities, it was the expellees themselves who provided the volunteers. In Quedlinburg, at the edge of the Harz Mountains in the Soviet zone, a priest observed in 1948 that the Hilfswerk had effectively been unknown until the refugees began to volunteer.[49] Marianne Hamm von Sahr had been driven out of Saxony in November 1945 and ended up in Württemberg in the West. In her old homeland, she had been the regional head of the Protestant Service of Women (Christlicher Frauendienst), and she put that knowledge to immediate use in her new surroundings. She paired refugees with local helpers and young refugees preparing for confirmation with local mentors.

Recipients often turned into givers of charity. Annemarie Hörich lost everything in February 1945 when she fled East Brandenburg (now Poland) together with her mother and her three-year-old son. A year later, they ended up in the Odenwald, near Frankfurt. She found a room and some profitable handiwork to do at home. The few clothes they had were thanks to the Hilfswerk. Within half a year, she repaid her debts by helping the local priest. There was nothing more beautiful than helping those in need, she said.[50]

Self-help was a matter of pride and recognition for the expellees—they wanted to demonstrate their worth and independence, not be treated as passive recipients of alms. "After all," a Caritas organizer explained, "it is about togetherness in the fight against need, and less about looking after the needy." The refugees had a "special right" to put their resources to use, not least to demonstrate that they had overcome their "personal great suffering." And who was better placed to understand their fellow migrants?[51]

Charity has traditionally been cast as a female calling, so it is important to note that men were helpers too. In the city of Kaiserslautern, in the Palatinate, near the French border, 220 volunteers were active in 1947. The group included "men who after a day's work in the office or in the factory made themselves available, or pensioners who want to give their life a new purpose." One of them, a civil servant, wrote that he and his family had been loyal to the church and its charities for "many years prior to the Second World War": "We always collected old clothes... and donations" for the church "and we continued doing so under the Nazis." A disabled man volunteered together with his fifty-nine-year-old wife, his daughter (who had lost her husband in Russia in 1943), and his grandchildren. Their "greatest happiness" was to help a "poor and worthy family that faced nothing."[52]

The softening of masculinity, arguably, was well underway before the 1960s. Catholic and Protestant charities alike called on men to lift up their downtrodden brothers instead of passing them by. Posters and stamps echoed the iconography of the Good Samaritan used in charity drives between the wars and evoked the soldierly ideal of brothers-in-arms giving each other support.[53]

Charity can make the heart glow, but it is not be romanticized. For every example of compassion and generosity, there is one involving indifference or discrimination. Charity was rarely blind. The distribution of food and clothes gave priests and aid workers the power to rank different groups in need and reward the "deserving" poor. The Burzlaff family was from Western Pomerania (northern Poland) and now lived in a former army barracks in Schleswig-Holstein. They worked hard to survive by making slippers. In recognition, they received a wool blanket and some donated

"South African leather scraps." Down the road, by contrast, the Fritz family lived in a 172-square-foot old barn where, according to the Hilfswerk visitor, "one sees mice and rats running about. There was no wardrobe, yet a rather large radio"—no doubt "acquired in a shady manner." The wife "has a very bad reputation, is clumsy and rather sloppy. She had seven children, of whom none survived"—as if that must have been her fault. In fact, the family showed a charitable spirit and asked to adopt a girl whose mother was among the many thousands missing. The Hilfswerk visitor denied them any aid and recommended that the "uneconomical and untidy" woman was unfit to adopt.[54]

Nor did the charitable impulse travel smoothly from activists to the rest of the community. A Hilfswerk worker reached a sober assessment of the situation in Hesse in December 1947. While they had been able to extend the circle of volunteers, they came disproportionately from the social elite; only one fifth were workers. There was a growing feeling of exhaustion, partly in the face of their own personal worries, partly because of the "paralyzing feeling of not being able to help as much as necessary." They were completely overwhelmed. The community was "sharply divided into two parts: the old residents and the new. A world stands between them." Disabled refugees received no sympathy at all. As aid workers, he concluded, they might be able to "soften these opposites in individual cases," but ultimately it needed the state.[55] A refugee welfare officer organized women's circles to raise awareness about the suffering of the expellees. Come Sunday, even old residents who attended these meetings would not honor the newcomers "with a single word... or a glance in church, nor greet them afterward." Even women who know of "Christian love and compassion" cannot get themselves to show kindness to "such 'vagabonds.'"[56]

In West as East Germany, collection fatigue set in. Many parishes were unhappy that the bulk of special collections went to the Hilfswerk instead of staying in their own community. Some accused the aid agency of being centralized, anonymous, and unbiblical, and even of using Nazi methods.[57] In August 1949, a priest wrote to Gerstenmaier, "If one wants to make sure that a collection turns out badly, one just needs to make it out 'for the refugees.'"[58]

At the time, Germans spoke of charitable donations as *Liebesgaben* ("gifts of love"), a literal expression of Christian *caritas*. According to this tradition, their true value lay in their moral as much as their material contribution, warming the heart of donor and recipient alike and creating a bond between them. This was not always the case. In 1947, representatives of the International Red Cross visited Potsdam. In one school, they found flowers on the tables, and "the children, when asked, knew where the donations had come from and assured us that they were well fed." But at another school down the road, the kitchen feeding almost four hundred children was "not clean." Their mothers complained that the food was sometimes watered down and left uneaten. "Not one mother offered a word of thanks or recognition of the donor." The Red Cross visitors pointed out that the mothers were free to gain some control by volunteering with the cooking and feeding, which put an end to the complaining.[59]

That their recent enemies had it in them to send Germans food and clothes rather than see them freeze and starve triggered a range of moral reactions. CARE packages from the Allies eroded Germans' mistrust. When a pastor was handing out milk and bread to children near bombed-out Kassel, one mother initially expressed doubts that the white flour was a gift of the Americans: "It is all a lie . . . fraud and propaganda." The pastor took her aside and showed her the label, which read, in English, "In the name of Christ." The American bread, he told her, was like the olive branch carried by the dove after the flood. Elsewhere, children drew pictures of the dove and the cross as thanks for the donors. At the University of Mainz, foreign donations fed seven hundred students every day in spring 1948. "It proved the best medicine against nihilism," the university pastor wrote to foreign donors. It had encouraged students "to trust themselves and others more." Bitterness was now rare, and students were meeting with foreign visitors more frequently. Again and again, students came to the pastor to ask who was sending them these gifts and why.[60]

A gift calls for thanks. Thank-you letters provided an opportunity for the recipients to reflect on how they had ended up in a situation where they needed foreign aid to survive. For one young man who had been taken prisoner by the Americans, the donation was "a claim, even a judgment," and a "constant question to ourselves, what we were and are doing." Every gift that reached them was rebuilding a connection they themselves had cut, he wrote. Everywhere "we can see the consequences of our actions." The fact that others offered help rather than revenge was an act of forgiveness. "And it was often only this forgiveness that points to guilt."[61] The donations were a call for atonement.

This young German, though, was a theology student and hardly typical. Many others took the donations as recognition that they were deserving, innocent victims and used the thank-you letters to foreign donors to testify to their suffering. In December 1946, a pastor in Marburg wrote to his Christian brothers and sisters in the United States. Since 1933, he wrote, the German people had been kept in fear by a regime of terror. "Can you imagine, how much we, who abhorred the regime, who longed for its collapse, had to suffer and nonetheless had to send our sons into battle?" Now, Germany was "one big concentration camp." The American donations were greatly appreciated by a "horribly seduced and brutally abused people." Another man asked his priest to thank "the generous donors in America" for helping to diminish their "misery that was through no fault of their own."

In the advancing Cold War, having recently fought the Soviets and communist partisans became a distinction. An East Prussian freely shared with his donors in 1949 that he "participated in the fighting against the partisans" in Croatia and fought "the Russians" until the bitter end. He spent four years in Leningrad and on a collective farm as a POW. He was grateful, he said, that the donations reached those "who have been hardest hit by the war and its consequences"—like himself.[62]

It is still sometimes assumed that rape was the great secret that was suppressed in the postwar years. In fact, in their letters to foreign charities, many women mentioned being raped. A family in a refugee camp in the British zone thanked their "friendly donors" in Canada in September 1946. "At home, in Silesia we had everything we needed . . . now we have been driven out of our homeland and are poor like beggars." How they were treated by "the Russians" almost defied description. "The worst were the rapes of the young girls and women."[63] Then the Poles drove them with truncheons into a ghetto, beat them, and made them do hard labor. A female teacher wrote an eyewitness report for the Hilfswerk of events in Parchim (Mecklenburg), north of Berlin, between 1945 and 1947.[64] When the Soviets occupied the town, "Frau Sch., in our house, was raped in the presence of her husband and children." Herta, a twelve-year-old girl, "was raped twice over New Year's Eve." Ursel, an eleven-year-old pupil, died of the consequence of rape in April 1947. In Husum, on the North Sea, expellees were inspired to send their Swedish donors a poem with illustrations. The East was a wonderful place, it began, civilized by the industrious Germans. Unfortunately, "the demon of power . . . drove the faithful unknowingly to the machines of death." Then the Russians came and brought "destruction and no mercy . . . Each female being; innocent child; breastfeeding mother . . . they were spared as little as the old in their pious dignity."[65]

The rape of German womanhood came to embody the barbarian rape of the German East; rapes also happened in the Western zones but were less widespread and symbolic. Catholic churches and, in the 1950s, the West German government were gathering testimony of rape and violence; the book *Der grosse Treck* (*The Big Trek*) offered a popular synthesis in 1958.[66] A recommended outline for a Catholic sermon from 1946 told congregations "that what German women and girls had suffered through rape exceeded the powers of the imagination. Day and night one heard their screams."[67]

The donations had various effects. Some recipients were moved to think of the needs of others, near and far. In medieval Ulm, on the Danube, one woman who had received several CARE packages was moved by the "human greatness" of the distant donors. "Have I ever sent a package to strangers in China or Arabia... of whose plight I heard?" she asked in 1951. "Never."[68] In return, she started a local initiative where those who had received help from America in exchange gave of their own free time to do the laundry for overburdened mothers and help build a sports field for a school. There were donation drives for refugees from the GDR and later arrivals of ethnic Germans across the 1950s. By the end of the decade, compassion was also flowing outward across borders. Advent collections were made for starving populations in Palestine, Syria, and Hong Kong, as well as for rebuilding German churches behind the Iron Curtain. It was part of the new global sense of ethical responsibility behind the discovery of the "Third World," as we saw earlier.[69]

In Bavaria, the main charities launched a joint campaign, "Children Help Children," in 1956. A few years earlier, UNICEF had sent Bavarian children 235,000 pairs of stockings, 58,000 pairs of shoes, and 41,000 suits and dresses. Instead of simple letters of thanks or money, the charities now asked Bavarian children to return the favor by sending "useful and pretty gifts" to children in need in Egypt. They wanted to "finally make visible our people's readiness to help in view of the major states of emergency in the world." Getting people to give for those close by was hard enough, they acknowledged, but they also needed to "develop a global conscience from that charity that draws its power from the finest sources of Christianity and humanism." In Munich, one hundred schools participated. The student committee explained that with giving, as with faith, the thought had to come from the heart. Hence, it was vital that helpers "concern themselves in depth with the personality of the recipient, so... the gift and aid do not turn into injury." Children saw documentaries on the agrarian lives of *fellahin* peers in Egypt and collected shorts, soaps, and school supplies; many decided that the rural poor also needed pocket mirrors. Girls sewed little bags for the items and embroidered them with alpine flowers. An exhibition showcased the results, complete with a drawing of the Sphinx at the feet of the twin towers of the Frauenkirche, the landmark Munich cathedral, and a performance of folk songs. A local paper hailed the "Bavarian shorts for Egyptian boys," seeing it as a way for Germans to pay off some of the debt they themselves had received as aid. Some 100,000 children contributed altogether—impressive but hardly a universal success in a state with twenty times that number. Several schools refused to be part of the initiative because it was not official and because their children were already overloaded with schoolwork and donation drives for youth hostels, animal shelters, and other domestic causes. Some directors told the organizers that "the needs of children in our own country should be eliminated first."[70]

GOODBYE GDR

The exodus from the GDR added to the pressure. Between 1949 and 1961, when the Berlin Wall went up, 2.7 million people fled to the West. In many ways, they followed in the footsteps of the expellees and were greeted by a similar mix of charity and hostility. The divided city of Berlin was at the center of the storm. Catholics launched a special relief effort (Katholisches Notwerk Berlin). In May 1953, it estimated that there were a quarter of a million Catholic refugees from the "Soviet Occupied Zone," as West Germans called the GDR. It sent 112 wagons of donated clothes, shoes, bedding, and food to West Berlin; American Catholics added another 1,100 tons of provisions, worth $15 million.[71] The Evangelisches Hilfswerk, the Red Cross, and other charities organized similar aid packages.

Some voices embraced these new refugees as allies in the battle with communism. In the population at large, however, the welcome was muted: how could one be sure they were not communist infiltrators? In 1950, a survey asked people whether "Germans who find living in the Soviet sector unbearable... be welcomed in West Germany, or whether all those should be sent back who cannot clearly document that they have been politically persecuted?" Only 45 percent chose the first option, 35 percent preferred deportation, and the rest were undecided.[72]

In fact, most were fleeing the worsening work and living conditions that would trigger the uprising of June 17, 1953. That year, the number of refugees reached a record 331,000. A few months later, Caritas organized a conference with refugees. It was "astonished" when none of those present talked of either political or religious convictions as a reason for their flight. They also heard how, after an initial welcome, the local population had become "distant, even spiteful."[73] Charity workers were alarmed by the many young girls arriving with sexual diseases and loose morals, although they acknowledged that their Western sisters were not much better. The Hilfswerk assessed the character of several thousand refugees. Many had left for work-related reasons. Half of them were eighteen to twenty-one years of age, 20 percent under eighteen. Two thirds showed "good" conduct: the rest had a "bad" or "questionable" character. The trouble with that difficult minority, according to the charity, was "their mentality": they had been "progressively uprooted," were "unsteady," and "often lacked a work ethic." In a society where work defined character, this was a damning report card.[74]

The government released special funds for housing, training, and integration. By the late 1950s, more refugees arrived with skills and their *Abitur* (the rough equivalent of an American high school diploma), which eased the situation. Still, for many companies they were cheap labor. They were given extra shifts and put up in garages or temporary shelters, for which they were charged excessive rent. A youth worker in Cologne noted in 1961 how they were treated just as badly as the Italian and Spanish guest workers who had recently arrived. Young refugees ended up in shelters with old, divorced, and unstable residents where "drinking and fighting at night are routine."[75]

In 1955, every second young refugee went through a youth home run by charitable institutions and increasingly subsidized by the government. These were closed institutions not dissimilar from army barracks. At 7 a.m., it was time to get up and have breakfast. Then came a daily regime of work. In the evening there were lectures or games. By 10 p.m., it was lights out. Infractions or refusal to work were punished with the loss of pocket money or eviction. These institutions gave instructions in work and discipline, including the virtue of saving and frugality. Eventually, the youths were placed with firms and farms. The majority appeared happy enough with the arrangement, though the system was open to abuse. An unskilled refugee who worked on a farm in eastern Westphalia in 1955 said, "The farmers in this region are very bad, for one is treated here like a slave . . . They think just because we come from the eastern zone, they can do whatever they want." Many experienced the welcome as unfair and paternalistic, robbing them of their independence and equality. The young democracy had some way to go.[76]

Around 400,000 were so disillusioned with the capitalist West that they returned to the GDR. They were joined by a smaller wave of 200,000 West Germans who tend to be forgotten, and who chose to move *to* the GDR. Only a few were dedicated communists. Most were looking for work, housing, or love. They soon found out that while the GDR had little problem giving them the first, the housing situation was even more catastrophic than in the West. And overcrowding and having to live with one's future parents-in-law took its toll on romance.

If integration was difficult in the Federal Republic, in the GDR it was doubly so. Neighbors and workers viewed arrivals from the West with suspicion and confusion: even if they were not spies, they were competitors for housing and clothes that were already scarce enough. A girl who moved with her family to East Berlin in 1960 recalled how her teacher greeted her on her first day in a socialist school: "How can anyone be so stupid to move from the West to the East!"[77] Many did not stay long. The transit camp Friedland in the West conducted a study of these returnees to West Germany in 1960. The vast majority had no stable family home in the West; many had fled as orphans. Most of them could not cope with how life was politicized in the GDR or were unhappy about their job and housing. Two thirds had lasted only a few months there. Michaela Heyden moved to East Berlin in May 1959 to be with her fiancé. On arrival, the Stasi tried to recruit her, unsuccessfully. A trained laboratory assistant, she managed to enroll in a university. After three months, she was sent to work in a factory to prove her socialist credentials. On February 2, 1960, she fled back to West Berlin.[78]

NEUE HEIMAT

Aid was vital but ultimately short term. The expellees and refugees needed to put down their roots somewhere. How they would be integrated was decided by the authorities, not charities. East and West Germany pursued radically different approaches that were reflected in the collective names given to the newcomers. In the Soviet zone, they were officially known as "resettlers" (*Umsiedler*), a term that made their migration sound voluntary and foreclosed any critique of the socialist brother countries that had forced them out. In 1947, a group from Poland, who included recognized victims of fascism, met to demand better housing and work. When a speaker addressed them as "*Umsiedler*," there were protests from the floor: "We are only poor refugees… we are expellees, those without a homeland." The following day, the organizers were arrested and the body was dissolved.[79] The GDR was barely born when it declared integration to be complete. "Resettlers" were renamed "new citizens" (*Neubürger*).

In West Germany, by contrast, in 1953 they were officially recognized as "expellees" (*Vertriebene*)—literally, those who had been driven from their homeland against their will; the term even extended to their children born after the expulsion. "Refugees" now stood for people fleeing the GDR. While the East quickly dissolved resettler committees, the West gave the expellees their own department of state and lamented the loss of their "*Heimat*," a term that invoked emotional and territorial roots, a sense of belonging and safety, as well as one's *patria*: the place where one felt at home.

West Germany pursued a double game. Domestically, politicians left and right played to the sense of grievance among the expellees and kept alive their dream of a return to their homeland while, in foreign policy, they respected the new borders. East Germany was more honest and administered the bitter medicine more quickly: the "resettlers" were told to abandon such dreams, accept that there was no chance that the Soviet Union or Poland would hand back their former homelands, and make their new home in the GDR. Such realism robbed these groups of their voice and identity.

In both societies, integration was piecemeal and incomplete, but for different reasons. The GDR managed to move its migrants quickly out of camps, leaving most of them to fend for themselves. Support was limited to emergency aid, interest-free loans, and land reform. The first tided people over with the bare necessities. The second offered 1,000 Marks to help them furnish their new homes with a bedroom or sofa. This held little appeal for the many "resettlers" who had neither job nor property or who subsisted on a meager pension and saw no prospect of repaying the loan. Land reform carved up big estates into lots of little farms. For socialists, it had a mythical aura. Reality was harsher. Only one in twelve resettlers got a farm, and the only knowledge many of those had of agrarian life came from novels. They did not belong to local networks, either. The result was that the new arrivals often ended up with the worst soil and a weak mare. For many, early frost, a dead animal, or a sick family member spelled the end of their farming career. Their housing situation was no more inviting. One of the new farmers complained in 1952 that he could not understand how seven years after the war, the five-year plan that was meant to modernize homes built them "such dog kennels" instead. Quite a few packed up a second time and fled to the West.[80]

Those who stayed behind faced a variety of disadvantages. In 1953, "new citizens" enjoyed thirteen square feet of living space while old residents had thirty-five. With collectivization the artisans and small traders among them lost their independence. "New citizens" were also less likely to join the official party. The patchy evidence suggests that newcomers—like the Catholic Silesians in the Protestant regions of Mecklenburg—often lived at the margins of established communities and were not fully integrated into local life until the 1970s. Some tried to maintain their old networks in the guise of alumni school trips with meetings in zoos and other places, under the watchful eye of the Stasi.[81]

Speaking of the expellees' suffering was not completely taboo in East Germany, as is sometimes assumed. In 1947, Peter Huchel's poem "Der Vertriebene" ("The Expelled") captured their despair, sitting in "the dust of the wagons," their canvas covers pierced by "thorns and branches": "What does the bird lament at night?"[82] A few years later, Anna Seghers, a celebrated communist author who had moved from West to East Berlin in 1950, wrote stories about their fate and how they fled "ragged, dirty, and with broken shoes and bleeding feet, poisoned on the inside by fear, despair, and lies." One character makes it known that, three years after leaving Poland, "she was just as bad off [in the GDR] as on the first day." Twenty years after that, in 1968, a TV series followed their *Paths Across the Land.* In Christa Wolf's *Patterns of Childhood* (1976), by contrast, the pain of uprooting is presented as just punishment. In official explanations, their expulsion was the boomerang of Nazi aggression. The anti-fascist GDR offered rehabilitation, a new home built on peaceful foundations.

Underneath the official veneer, many "new citizens" clung to the old *Heimat.* Twenty years after the war, an internal GDR survey found that every third refugee wanted a return to the 1937 borders—reclaiming East Prussia, Pomerania, and Silesia.[83] That was not so different from their cousins in West Germany. What was different was that in East Germany there were no public outlets for such nostalgia. The "new citizens" were like everyone else; they withdrew into their private cocoon.

In West Germany, integration was more drawn out and contested. From the outset, the authorities committed considerable resources. In Hesse, in 1949, for example, 85 percent of all welfare benefits came directly from that state, and only 15 percent from charities. That year, Bavaria spent 6 percent of its entire revenue on the expellees, for camps, benefits, and pensions. In Schleswig-Holstein, it was 12 percent. In 1947–48, the state of Hesse gathered 118,000 pairs of shoes, 100,000 shirts and dresses, 300,000 pieces of cutlery, 85,000 stoves and ovens, and 60,000 mattresses and straw sacks. "Burden sharing," as we have seen earlier, compensated expellees for some of their losses. And, yet, in 1954, more than 300,000 of them were still in camps.[84]

The mood among the expellees was fickle and explosive. The primary question was whether they should fight to reclaim their old *Heimat* or settle down in their new one. Until 1948, refugee organizations with a political agenda were prohibited, but that did not prevent people from speaking their mind. The refugee adviser to the Zonal Advisory Council in the British zone argued in September 1946 that just as Germany could not live without the industrial Ruhr, so it needed the East to feed the nation. In Berlin, the head of the eastern branch of the Christian Democrats, the Ost-CDU, said that, regardless of the Potsdam agreement, the eastern question was not settled, and that "the Poles did not need that space." Expellees signed petitions demanding the return of German "*Kulturland*," the land their forefathers had "civilized." Such calls tapped into anti-communism as well as Nazi fears about Asian "hordes." "Europe will never find peace as long as Asia's border has been moved to the Elbe," Christian Democrats on refugee committees warned in 1948. "Turning East German and Sudeten-German regions into a desert" threatened the survival of Western civilization. It would either make West Germany an expensive burden on the Allies or spread hunger, making it ripe for a communist takeover. The only way out was for the expellees to move back home.[85]

From the churches came a range of voices. Catholics could look to Pope Pius XII, who had condemned the expulsion as a great injustice as early as November 1945. A crime could not be punished with a new one, and the sin of one people did not give another the right to commit new sins. But what did this mean in practice for the future? For Emmanuel Reichenberger, a Catholic priest from the Sudetenland who was heralded as the "father of the expellees," it was crucial to preserve the will to return. The Allies, he said, needed to be "de-Potsdamized." The expulsions were the worst crime in human history, he told fellow expellees: "If it was a crime—and there can be no doubt about it—to exterminate hundreds of thousands of Jews... then it is also a crime to exterminate millions of German people"; such an equivalence and distortion of numbers was not uncommon at the time.

The expulsions were widely seen to be an offense not only against human rights but also against the divine right to *Heimat.* The first lesson Catholic youth circles learned about "*die Heimat*," in 1950, explained that since one's homeland was a gift of God, anyone taking it away was committing a sacrilege and would provoke the wrath of God. "To repair the injustice of the theft of the *Heimat* before God was the only duty with which the Christian West can justify its continued existence."[86] Here was fertile soil for the *Prophecies of the Blind Youth.*

The impulse behind such "revisionism" is easy to understand, but ultimately it was realism that gained the upper hand. Pastoral letters urged their flock to embrace their suffering and its divine redemptive purpose. In this view, even innocent Germans had to confront their collective responsibility, and the expellees were bearing God's judgment on behalf of the entire German people. By following in the footsteps of Christ, they were moving closer to God. Tens of thousands went on pilgrimages for spiritual comfort and guidance. One of them was to Schwäbisch Gmünd, outside Stuttgart, on October 15, 1947, the saint's day of Hedwig (1174–1243), duchess of Silesia, when eight thousand people came to hear Paulus Sladek, an Augustian priest from the Sudetenland. They would not forget the crimes of the Nazis, he told them, and they knew that they, as a nation, had to pay for them. That did not, however, justify the new crimes against humanity they had suffered. They needed to be realistic, though. In the near future, a return to the East was "hopeless." Their "*Heimat* lay far behind them" and they needed to "make a new *Heimat* for themselves."[87]

Protestant clergymen sent similar messages to their scattered flock. In his circular letters to his congregation, a pastor from East Prussia urged them to accept their suffering as a divine judgment for the lack of faith that had existed in Germany well before the Nazis. Ultimately God would show them mercy. The only way forward, the Gospel taught, was through reconciliation, not hatred. Many expellees he had talked with, he wrote in 1950, agreed that "notwithstanding all human malice and violence, the way out of the *Heimat* is God's command, and consequently must be a blessing." He warned his flock against those who only raised "false hopes."[88]

These voices shifted the focus back from the Poles and the Allies to the relationship between the newcomers and their settled neighbors. God had called them to their new home. What they now needed was to get their German hosts to accept them as equal citizens and help them find their feet. Their solidarity in suffering had to become a community of mutual aid for all Germans. In the process, the question of guilt was transformed. Instead of asking "Who is guilty?," the head of the Evangelisches Hilfswerk in Württemberg said they should ask, "What do we owe each other as Christians?"[89]

On August 5, 1950, five years after the Potsdam agreement, the various homeland associations signed the "Charter of the German Expellees."[90] It asserted the right to *Heimat* as a fundamental human right given by God that had been taken from them. Although not giving up the claim to their old lands, they renounced "revenge and retribution" and pledged to work to unite Europe and reconstruct Germany. In exchange, they wanted equal treatment as citizens in daily life, a fair sharing of the costs of war across all groups, and the integration of all their occupational groups in the new *Heimat*. It was a compromise that was capacious enough for most, those who accepted that the eastern territories were lost for good and those who clung to the idea that Silesia and East Prussia remained German by right.

As for their new *Heimat*, geographic fate meant that the greatest numbers had reached either Schleswig-Holstein in the north or Bavaria in the south. These were mostly rural regions. Hundred of thousands were stuck there, in part because West Germany was a system of federal states and many refused to share the burden, feeling they had enough on their hands with their own bombed cities—first new buildings, then new people, was their argument.

In the winter of 1951–52, a quarter of a million expellees sat in camps or temporary housing in Schleswig-Holstein, and many had had enough. The federal ministry had made a lot of promises but only managed to resettle twenty thousand of the expellees in the previous year. Those who were fed up threatened to march together in a "trek" southward unless the government came to their aid. "We are like streams," one poem warned: unstoppable and ready to "swamp your order."[91] By spring, more than thirty thousand had come aboard and local farmers were volunteering carts and horses. These were people who had made it across the frozen Baltic, so a second trek to southern Germany must have looked like a walk in the park.

The despair was palpable in the many letters asking to join the trek. Richard Rohde had lost one leg in the war and was stranded on the North Sea coast near Husum. "I often stand on the mud flats and shout out my misery, but no one is helping."[92] He was from East Prussia. His wife had been in an internment camp before ending up in Lüdenscheid, 310 miles south of where he was. His twelve-year-old son had been deported to Russia at the end of the war and returned in 1949 but he could only find work as an unskilled laborer on a boat. Only his fourteen-year-old daughter was still with him. All he wanted was to have a regular family life, and for that he needed a regular home. If necessary, he would walk on crutches. Others complained of being housed "in a basement that had not seen a single ray of sunshine" and of the local "fog climate" that made their asthma and rheumatism unbearable. Above all, it was the hopelessness of being stuck in the middle of nowhere with no jobs, no future, and no permission to move elsewhere. It was as if they were buried alive. "We are not so familiar with agriculture," one family wrote. They were paid a pittance and wanted to move to the urban Ruhr or Westphalia, "before we go to the dogs." The elderly, invalids, and widows with children were especially hard hit. A war-disabled father felt completely ignored by the authorities: by banishing parents like him to remote villages, they were making it impossible for their talented children to attend high school. It was all so unjust. A clerk pleaded that all he wanted was to be sent to a small town so he could be independent and no longer a burden on the state.

The resettler commissions sent delegates from the other states to Schleswig-Holstein to pick the young with the greatest work potential. The "social baggage" of the old, disabled mothers and ill got left behind. A local mayor compared the situation to "slave markets."[93]

In the end the great *Treck* stalled. Under pressure, the federal government sped up its resettlement program, built more new homes, and made states take in pensioners and the less employable. By the end of 1952, half a million people had been resettled, the following year another quarter of a million.[94]

Expellees faced multiple disadvantages, especially in rural areas. In Bavaria, many who came from towns and cities in Bohemia ended up in small rural communities. Most of them were unhappy and wanted to move to a city. Twenty percent were unemployed, compared to 6 percent of the old residents. Suicide rates were high. Only a quarter had their own flat, and barely more had a kitchen. In West Germany as a whole, 67 percent of the expellees lived in a sublet; among the old inhabitants it was 27 percent. In the words of one contemporary researcher, "The family no longer gathers around a lively fire." Artisans and members of the professions found their way back to their old job most easily. Farmers and merchants, on the other hand, ended up as farmhands or unskilled workers, or unemployed. In Schleswig-Holstein, by 1953 every second local was back in the job they had had before the war. Among the expellees, it was only one in four.[95]

The cultural gulf between the two communities was often as vast as the material one. Provincial towns and rural villages were monocultures. They were transformed by the arrival of the expellees in ways at least as significant as the "boom" of the 1960s that has excited social scientists. The newcomers opened up these provincial islands by introducing different beliefs, tastes, and customs.

In Bavaria, before the war, there had been 1,400 municipalities where all residents shared the same faith. By 1950, there were none. Across Germany, Catholic communities suddenly had Protestants from the East in their midst, Protestant ones were confronted with Catholics from Silesia, and sober Protestant burghers of the Reformed faith of Zwingli and Calvin had to come to terms with the more joyful Lutherans from East Prussia and Pomerania.

Mardorf was a solidly Catholic small town north of Frankfurt. Wartime evacuees from the Rhine and Ruhr were still with them when the first families from East Prussia arrived in spring 1945. The expellees were put up in the community hall, which, until 1942, had been the home of Jakob and Rosa Maas, members of Mardorf's small Jewish community, before the two were deported and murdered in Sachsenhausen and Auschwitz. By 1949, there were 351 expellees, a quarter of the town's population, many of them Protestant. Children threw stones at the door of their own church when the newcomers held their service inside. Elsewhere, expellees were forced to bury their dead outside the cemetery walls. In some places, they walked miles to hear a Lutheran pastor from the East (*Ostpfarrer*) rather than attend the local Reformed church.[96]

To add to the tension, national identity had a different meaning for communities that had been inside the German nation-state since the days of Bismarck and the German diaspora outside it. The Hessian town of Allendorf, except for a handful of Jewish families and the Protestant locksmith, had been solidly Catholic before the war. Religion was their core identity. For the Protestant Sudeten, being a minority in Czechoslovakia had meant that nationality was key. "How backward you are," an expellee from Prague told the old inhabitants. "You act as if you are still in the Middle Ages, fighting the wars of religion."[97]

A little further to the east lay rural Gersdorf, a village with 176 inhabitants. The soil here was poor and the village too small to attract traders and artisans. Life was defined by modesty, work, and self-sufficiency. The people here had been raised in the sober spirit of the Reformed Church. "Simplicity and earnestness" were their distinctive feature, according to an ethnographer at the time. Women over the age of forty wore "plain clothes in gray, brown, or black." Meals had to be "good and hearty." Their homes were "without any luxury" and even the church was unadorned. They were a "taciturn" lot. "Showing feelings is seen as a weakness, as a lack of self-control." They had a "peculiar sense of honor." The smallest provocation would estrange families for generations. Similarly, they would not accept gifts without immediately giving a gift in return. Children who "accepted food from other families are reprimanded and even punished." The result was that Gersdorf had hardly any communal life.

One hundred and twenty-eight expellees from the Moravian town of Znaim (Znojmo) arrived in Gersdorf after the war. The war had already shaken up the village by exposing its young soldiers to the outside world, but the expellees represented a genuine culture shock. Not only did they speak in Moravian-Austrian dialect, but they came from a thriving town with a medieval castle, church, and frescoes. Their soil was rich, and so were their artisans. Theirs was a commercial culture where money was spent on fine food and fine clothes. They enjoyed life as well as work. They were well educated. And they were Catholic. In their festive procession for Corpus Christi, they shook noisy rattles. It was as if color and sound had suddenly been introduced into a black-and-white silent movie.

The expellees were relatively fortunate in being allowed to bring 220 pounds of luggage with them, including bedding. Accommodation was tight, but they were spared the camps. There was very little for them to do. Four of them helped the local farmers, and a few of the women spun jute. Most artisans, however, were dependent on benefits, and as 10 percent of the funds came directly from the village, it added to the tensions. For the locals, the newcomers' openness was a sign of empty chatter, their taste for modest luxuries waste, and their open religiosity hypocrisy.[98]

THE POLITICS OF NOSTALGIA

Similar scenes played themselves out across provincial Germany. The expellees brought with them a breath of fresh air and modernized rural regions, helping to turn Bavaria into the industrial powerhouse it is today. Local costume gave way to urban suits and dresses. The integration of the expellees is often celebrated as one of the success stories of West Germany. But how successful was it exactly, and for whom?

Together, the expellees were 12 million strong, divided by background and identity. There were twenty-one distinct homeland associations alone. A league (*Block*) tried to mobilize them into a single political voice in the 1950s. In regional elections, where particular groups had a concentrated presence, this federation was quite successful—it secured 23 percent of the vote in Schleswig-Holstein in 1950 and still 9 percent in Bavaria in 1958. At the national level, though, voters from the Bukovina (Romania and Ukraine) and East Prussia (Poland and Soviet Union) had as little in common with each other as with all the other Germans. In 1953, the *Block* made it into the Bundestag—just—and joined Adenauer's coalition government. Four years later, it failed to cross the 5 percent threshold of votes required to win a seat. Expellees, surveys found, were mostly suspicious of these lobbies. More important than these negative factors, though, were public and private efforts at assimilation.

In 1995, on the fiftieth anniversary of the expulsions, the head of the Federation of Expellees (Bund der Vertriebenen) looked back and lamented how little public attention their fate had received.[99] That was a lie. In the first two decades after the war, there was a deluge of books, films, and memorials dedicated to the loss of the old *Heimat.* In the 1950s, most newspapers carried special supplements for the expellees; in addition, they had 350 newspapers of their own. Newspapers carried articles about the tragic sinking of ships, and novels shared graphic scenes of violence. Ernst Wiechert's last book, *Missa Sine Nomine* (*Tidings*), sees children drowned in a cesspit and a priest nailed to the church door. In *The Gallows in the Vineyard* (*Der Galgen im Weinberg,* 1951), Josef Mühlberger narrated the fate of (non-Jewish) Germans in Theresienstadt (Terezín) after the camp was liberated. In the process one German boy is trampled to death by a raving Czech; the author used Albrecht Dürer's woodcut *Fratricide* as a metaphor to trace the origins back to Cain and Abel. The best seller was Jürgen Thorwald's *Es begann an der Weichsel* (*It Started on the Vistula*, 1950), a mix of fact and fiction that went through fifty editions. Artists made woodcuts of deported girls and statues of mothers during their flight. In Berlin, the House of Pedagogy and Art curated an exhibition by refugee children with colorful drawings of the many-headed hydra of Bolshevism.[100]

Films about the *Heimat* were big at the box office. This genre is now often remembered as nostalgic kitsch—and a lot of it was. In the 1951 hit *The Heath Is Green* (*Grün ist die Heide*), the beautiful expellee heroine falls in love with a dashing young gamekeeper, uniting the old and the new *Heimat*. The film did not suggest that all journeys ended so happily. Notwithstanding her father's warm welcome at an uncle's estate on the Lüneberg Heath, he is so tormented by the loss of his homeland that he turns to poaching for escape: "One is no longer allowed to be a man," he tells his daughter. "Only when I am out in the forest do I forget all my misery."[101] Others had become circus performers and dreamed of emigrating to America. The screenwriter was Bobby Lüthge, who built a career from military comedies and the early Nazi propaganda film *Hitlerjunge Quex* (1933), about a Nazi youth from a leftist family who is murdered by the communists. Himself a Silesian, Lüthge consciously added the "Song of the Giant Mountains" ("Riesengebirgslied") toward the end of the film—"Blue mountains, green valleys / and in their midst a sweet little home... Giant Mountains, German mountains / My beloved homeland, you!" Audiences were in tears. This Silesian anthem only dated back to the First World War and shows how quickly nationalist traditions were adopted. Not surprisingly, Czechoslovakia took offense at the reference to "German mountains," and the song was prohibited in the GDR.

In the West, the expellees could count on public support from the federal government, regional states, towns, and cities. Recognition of their cultural heritage was as important for their peaceful integration as bricks and mortar, and money. Their biographies, customs, and history, it signaled, were a valued part of German culture. Here was a major difference with the more condescending treatment East Germans would receive after reunification in 1990. Bavaria embraced the Sudeten as the "fourth tribe" come home, rejoining Franks, Swabians, and old Bavarians; and St. Hedwig, the patron of Silesia, had been a Bavarian countess, ministers pointed out. In the context of the Cold War, arrivals from the East were embraced as experienced "defenders of the frontier of Western civilization," in the words of the Liberal deputy Kurt Weidner.[102] The Bavarian government urged schools to preserve the heritage of the Sudeten and Silesians, and, from 1951, subsidized their sports and folklore. Bayerischer Rundfunk, the Bavarian radio station, broadcast a weekly series on their customs. Turning the dial, listeners had a chance to tune in to the Silesian choir that had regrouped in Regensburg and the Eghalanda Gmoi band from Bohemia.

In 1953, the federal parliament included a special paragraph in the expellee law that recognized their right to a distinct culture and government support for it. Lessons about the East (*Ostkunde*) were part of the school curriculum, and the Ministry for the Expellees distributed maps and films about the former homelands. Towns and regions in the West assumed mentor roles for "lost" areas in the East. Bavaria took the entire Sudeten region under its wing; Schleswig-Holstein took Pomerania. Hundreds of small homeland museums (*Heimatstuben*) sprung up, with collections of regional art, handicrafts, and other memorabilia. Across the country, signposts indicated the distance to Danzig, Breslau, and Königsberg, and were more or less explicit about their orientation. "Silesia remains German," read the one in Giessen, erected in 1956.

The expulsions were memorialized in churches, too. St. Nikolai in Kiel had been destroyed by Allied bombing, just like Jakob's Church in Stettin (Szczecin). When St. Nikolai was rebuilt, a Pomeranian chapel was added, with the seals of its eastern cities on the floor and windows with Christ on the cross watching over a line of suffering women, children, and elderly people fleeing their homeland. When more than a thousand church bells that had been taken down by the Nazis for their copper and tin were discovered in Hamburg a few years after the war, those from the East were distributed to communities with large numbers of expellees so they would hear "a living voice of the *Heimat*." Elsewhere, people from Silesia and East Prussia donated church bells that carried the inscription "I call the *Heimat*." The names of those who died in the expulsions started to appear in memorials and tablets alongside the local dead of the two world wars.[103]

There was no taboo on mourning. More than a thousand rocks, towers, and groves commemorated the old *Heimat*. The rocks and crosses evoked romantic and nationalist symbols of German loyalty and Christian mission in the East. One of the biggest was the eighty-two-foot-tall cross towering on the cliffs of the Harz Mountains above Bad Harzburg, within shouting range of the GDR. The initiator was a former tank major who had fled the Soviet zone, and the architect and the builder were from Silesia and the Warthegau (western Poland). The "Cross of the German East" took its inspiration from the cross inside the giant Tannenberg memorial in Hohenstein (Olsztyn, Poland), dedicated, in 1927, to General Paul von Hindenburg's rout of the Russian army there in August 1914, which had "avenged" the defeat of the Teutonic knights by Poles and Lithuanians five hundred years earlier. It was unveiled on June 24, 1950, amid a mix of Christian, nationalist, and *völkisch* rituals, with twenty thousand people watching from their beer tents. Opening speeches by clergymen from Protestant and Catholic churches and arias by Bach and Händel were followed by a celebration of the summer solstice. A small black shrine filled with soil from the old *Heimat* was sealed inside the pedestal. Then women placed wooden plaques with the coats of arms from the eastern provinces around it.

The cross expressed several meanings. There was the Christ-like suffering of the expellees and the promise of resurrection; Germany's historic mission as Teutonic crusaders and bulwark of Western civilization against the barbaric "Slavs" from the East; and, finally, a more personal memorial to dead loved ones left behind in cemeteries in the old homeland and makeshift graves along the flight. The cross itself was inscribed with the years 1945 and 1950, but kept a spot vacant for the year when the German lands would be reunited. The minister of the expellees, Hans Lukaschek, a Silesian Catholic, assured the assembled that "the federal government will never renounce" their eastern homelands "as long as there are Germans." With amazing views of up to more than sixty miles, the cliff top became a popular tourist destination in the summer months. Brightly illuminated at night, the cross sent a signal to their brothers and sisters across the border in the GDR.[104]

In 1956, the expellees gained their own official holiday, the Tag der Heimat (Homeland Day), on the second Sunday in September. The biggest public festivities, though, were the annual gatherings of the various homeland associations. The tenth Sudeten Day, in 1959, for example, attracted 350,000 people. For political parties, these were opportunities to signal their commitment to the right of *Heimat.* Chancellor Adenauer, in 1953, told the Silesians that he was "deeply convinced . . . that the day will also come for you when you will return home."[105] A few years later, Willy Brandt, the popular Social Democratic mayor of Berlin, stressed that Silesia "remains in our mind a German land." In 1963, the SPD leadership put it even more strongly: "Renunciation is betrayal."[106]

Such professions were surrounded with qualifications about the need for peace, reconciliation, and European unity instead of aggression and revenge. Still, they explain the shock among the organized expellees when in 1970 Brandt, now chancellor, fell to his knees at the monument to the Warsaw Ghetto uprising and then signed a treaty with Poland accepting the postwar borders. In the thaw created by Brandt's *Ostpolitik*, the expellee lobby found itself out in the cold. It was this sudden role reversal that created the idée fixe that their suffering had always been ignored, a view that gained greater strength as Jews and other victim groups were beginning to win public attention.

Cultural recognition worked as a form of political containment. Instead of forced assimilation, as in the GDR, the expellees were granted a dual identity in West Germany. Preserving their customs and costumes made political sense. Many politicians did not want expellees to assimilate too quickly in the hope of an eventual return and change of borders. Previous decades had shown how suddenly population movements could reverse. In the meantime, nostalgia absorbed and tamed revanchist energies. By the end of the 1950s, the Federation of Expellees was down to 2 million members, a third of its strength at the beginning of the decade. Some homeland associations retained a political wing. For the majority of expellees, though, *Heimat* ceased to be a territorial ambition and lived on as a place of memory. When, in 1955, the publisher Brentano advertised a competition for stories and poems from expellees, it was deluged with twelve thousand entries. Hardly any were motivated by revenge. The published collection bore the telling title *Aber das Herz hängt daran—But the Heart Clings to It.*[107]

LOVE, WORK, AND RABBITS

The real test for integration came in daily life. Its relative success depended most of all on work, marriage, and clubs.

Notwithstanding the expellees many struggles, they also had precious assets that set them apart from most migrants before and after. They were highly educated, spoke German, and were citizens, with rights that included the vote. And they arrived at a favorable moment. Nazi Germany had relied on millions of forced laborers, who, if they had not been killed, mostly left after the war. The expellees offered a pool of skilled, flexible labor. The American Marshall Plan made cheap credit available in the late 1940s. When the Korean War broke out in 1950, it provided German industry with a golden opportunity. With their competitors at war, German firms could export and expand. It was the start of the *Wirtschaftswunder*, the economic boom that happened across Europe but in West Germany was "miraculous." It would have been far less miraculous without the 12 million expellees. The expansion of the service sector in the 1960s would, similarly, have been inconceivable without the many educated women among the expellees. In addition, they reestablished firms and industries for which they had been famous in the East, such as the glass industry of Gablonz (Jablonec), which found a new home in Neugablonz in Bavaria, or the stocking manufacturer Kunert, which likewise hailed from Bohemia.

With economic recovery came a sea change. Once seen as a burden, the expellees were now valued as a human resource. Federal and state governments played a major role in this transition. From the start, their motto was "*Arbeit schafft Heimat*" ("Work creates the homeland"). Quotas were introduced in 1947—one job for an expellee for every four going to locals. Firms could get start-up loans underwritten by the state. Hesse came up with its own plan and moved the newcomers from the north of the state to its industrial south, where firms in Darmstadt and Offenbach were hungry for skilled labor. Work was a great unifier, partly because it expressed a shared value system that glorified industriousness. The technical director of a clothing factory, himself an expellee, told a researcher in 1949 that there were no separate cliques on the shop floor. Old and new residents were "organically connected" because they depended on each other. "All I care about is performance."[108]

Civil servants, teachers, journalists, and other professionals found their way back into their old jobs most quickly. By 1952, children of expellees were already as likely to attend high school and university as those of old residents. Even for farmers and others who lost their old job for good, the new life was not all bad—a farmer who used to work more than seventy hours a week now only worked forty-five as a laborer. The objective decline in status was sometimes softened by subjective satisfaction in a new position, as in the case of an independent salesman who found work as a courier for a doctor and enjoyed the respect he earned from patients. In the late 1950s, the gap between the new and the old inhabitants was still visible in their possessions—12 percent of the expellees had a car and 18 percent a fridge, compared to 18 percent and 27 percent among the established residents—but it was narrowing.[109]

In 1957, West Germany reached full employment. The following year, a pastor from Nordenburg, near Königsberg in East Prussia (Kaliningrad, Soviet Union), sent his regular update to the surviving members of his congregation, who had been scattered across Lower Saxony and the Ruhr; he himself ended up in Duisburg. It captured the remarkable transformation in their lives. Fritz Behrendt had found a job as a machine minder in an engine factory. Fritz Kullik was in his fourth year at AEG, the appliance manufacturer, with a job for life. Both sons of the Geyer family were studying in Göttingen. Such letters recorded the pride with which men were finding their way back into jobs and authority, but they also noted how much women still had to do. The Beuters, both hairdressers back home, for example, had settled in Oldenburg, but he was a disabled veteran and it was she who opened a "good salon" there. The pastor ended with a round of good news from his own family: his eldest son had passed his law exams and was now training at the district court; the middle one was on his way to becoming a meteorologist; and the youngest was studying theology. His daughter, he proudly noted, had married a pastor with a secure position.[110]

Love (or at least marriage) was the second path to integration. The rise in intermarriage was extraordinary and shows how quickly the two communities were becoming one. In 1952, 72 percent of all expellees marrying in Bavaria tied the knot with a local. In Upper Franconia it was 80 percent, something contemporaries attributed to the more lively, open-minded character of the Franks. Yet even among the uptight, thrifty Swabians it was 68 percent.

These figures put prejudice and antagonism in perspective. For every cold shoulder, there was a warm bed. They are a reminder how unique the experience of German expellees was compared to later migrants from Italy, Greece, and Turkey, who were not citizens and rarely made close friends with Germans (or vice versa), let alone married one. Even in Mardorf, where locals still wore their traditional costumes and the priest warned of their village turning into a "diaspora," newcomers and old residents married each other. It was just that marriage was rarely between equals, at least by their past status. The new arrivals tended to marry downward, and locals upward. In Mardorf, for example, former traders and salesmen from the East married single poor local women.[111]

Initially, regional customs could reinforce segregation, especially where expellees lived in their own settlements at the outskirts of a town. Kaufbeuren-Neugablonz, in southern Bavaria, was home to nine thousand inhabitants in 1956. Ninety percent of them came from the Iser Mountains (Jizera/Czech Republic today). Their homeland association celebrated the summer solstice with torches and a marching band, ending in a great bonfire where people threw wreaths into the fire shouting, "Flame arise!" to keep alive the hope of a return to the old *Heimat.* They had their own Sudeten song circle and a gymnastics club whose coach pledged to defend folk dance and regional costumes against foreign jazz and chewing gum. "The Sudeten-German gymnast," he said, "must not be a sports expert in the materialist current of the times but a fighter for *Heimat* in the spirit of the [nationalist] father of gymnastics Jahn." People began to adopt more of a dialect, not less. In such an introverted setting, moving on was not so easy. In 1950, there was a performance of *Iserine*, a "romantic play" written by a fellow Sudeten German. It turned out to be not so romantic. Iserine is the daughter of a German count and is raped by the Bohemian landowner Drahomir. When the curtain fell, there were loud calls of "*Heimat!*"

Yet, even here, old and new ways started to merge. Children began to copy the local kids' lantern processions. Their parents stopped having wedding celebrations over several days and, instead, smashed old dishes in one big party the evening before, just as the locals did. In this and similar settlements, the homeland associations were losing members. Expellees continued to reassure each other that the *Heimat* was "irreplacable," but by the late 1950s, it was little more than a formulaic lament.[112]

In the big cities, the vibrant mix of commerce and culture made it easier for the newcomers to fit in. In 1950, a Hamburg newspaper observed that so many of them already identified as "Hamburger" that there was little interest in the weeklong *Heimat* celebrations.[113]

Provincial Germany was a different world. There, it was clubs that were the door to communal life. Unfortunately, little of this world shows up in mainstream histories, which tend to focus on cities rather than the provinces, which can appear stifling, conservative, and petit-bourgeois—what Germans call "*spiessig*." But this is where a large segment of the population continued to live. For hundreds of thousands of expellees, it was the shooting or rabbit-breeding club that really mattered and that turned outsiders into insiders. For men, these places were hugely consequential because, at least until the 1960s, clubs were a male preserve where friendships and networks were formed. Unless one was a member of a local club, one did not really count.

Club doors opened slowly. In the rural village of Körle, south of Kassel in northern Hesse, for the first seven years the local farmers routinely denied the expellees planning permission to build their own homes and kept them out of their clubs. The Sudeten were a soccer-playing folk. The locals played handball and would not let them join their sports club. Eventually, the expellees set up their own—the locals called it "the communist club." In Greene, in Lower Saxony, a Silesian boy of sixteen was luckier. After he arrived in 1946, he told an ethnologist twenty-five years later, "the first thing I did was to join the sport club. They all played handball then . . . Later I also played [soccer] . . . All the friends I have today I got to know through the sports club." In Stadthagen, a town with fifteen thousand inhabitants a little farther north, it took expellees on average seven years before they joined a club; one third had still not become a member after ten years. Fittingly, integration was quickest where people had to be quick: in the voluntary fire brigade. It was the rabbit-breeding club, though, which by 1955 could claim the greatest number of members.[114]

The provincial turn after the war reoriented people's minds from a greater Germany toward the local *Heimat.* Perhaps paradoxically, this also eased the assimilation of those who had lost their homeland. For *Heimat* culture was not always something that was already there. It often had to be constructed, and those looking to put down roots could chip in. In Bavarian Ichenhausen, for example, the "Forest Boys" (D'Waldbuam) *Heimat* and folk costume club was initiated in 1947 not by a local, but by a bombed-out evacuee from nearby Augsburg; it is active to this day, with thirty-five members, and meets every Friday. Refugees brought with them an experience of associational life and self-organization that could be precious in more isolated communities. And clubs had festivals, partnerships, and exchanges that brought everyone together. There might be prejudice, but who among the old residents of Mering in Bavaria could resist the tasty goulash the *Donauschwaben* from Hungary have served up at their annual party every Shrove Saturday since 1955?[115]

LETTING GO

In the debate between return and reconciliation, the ground began to shift in the mid-1960s. Already, five years before Brandt fell to his knees in Warsaw in 1970, the Protestant Church published a long memorandum that, while recognizing the expellees' suffering, urged people and politicians to abandon their stubborn fixation on restoring the 1937 border and recognize the territorial rights of the Polish population living beyond the Oder-Neisse line. Dialogue, it stressed, was only possible if each side recognized that the other also had a rightful claim.[116] The mailboxes of bishops and pastors overflowed with complaints.

Some expellee groups continued to campaign openly for a return of the eastern territories. The Ostpolitischer deutscher Studentenverband, a student association, rejected Brandt's treaty with Poland as a breach of the constitution. The Silesian Youth defended the continued existence of Germany in its 1937 borders. So did the Bund Heimattreuer Jugend (BHJ), which honored the dead of the expulsions and organized autumn camps with hiking and campfires. Their call to the East mixed nationalist ecology with a critique of modern civilization. German youth needed to escape the cold cement of urban tower blocks and return to nature. Why else were drugs and depression on the rise? East Prussia and Pomerania were held up as the spiritual as well as physical granary of the German nation.[117]

By the 1970s, these groupings were minority affairs, attracting a few right-wing voices but falling on deaf ears with the teenage children of expellees. The Silesian Youth had fewer than twenty thousand members, and, tellingly, by the late 1960s, the BHJ's leader came from Braunschweig, in Lower Saxony, and had no family connection to the East.

The Deutsche Jugend des Ostens (German Youth of the East) was larger. Founded in 1951, its original aim was to keep alive the will to resettle the East. In 1974, it changed its name and mission to Deutsche Jugend in Europa, seeking reconciliation with its European neighbors instead. By then, it had around 160,000 members, but only a minority still had a direct experience of the expulsions. "German politics" for them was no longer about territory and borders but about culture and integration. Most of their parents and grandparents, too, came to accept the loss of their *Heimat*—in a 1992 survey, only 30 percent of the expellees were still insisting on an official acknowledgment of the injustice done to them, and even fewer demanded some form of compensation.

Hildegard Kroepelin was seventy-three when, in 1997, she looked back on her life for an oral history project. Born in Insterburg in East Prussia (Tschernjachowsk, now in Russia) in 1924, she had spent her youth as a *Führerin* of the Bund deutscher Mädel, the sister organization of the Hitler Youth. On one of their tours to Danzig, she saw Adolf Hitler. She never screamed so much in her life, she told the interviewer. Then, in early 1945, she and her mother fled to Verden in Lower Saxony, where she worked as a nanny for an English family. At first, she did not want to work for the enemy, but "all the food and marmalade in the kitchen" made it difficult to refuse, and the "dirty children" turned out to be quite "sweet" after a proper German scrub. The English mother even gave her some food to take to her SS uncle in an internment camp. In 1951, she married a local man from nearby Hamburg. Their daughter was born the following year. Her husband built them a nice big house. Their life was good. The two never talked about her lost *Heimat*—until one day in the late 1950s. It was a Sunday, she recalled, and they were sitting around the dinner table, when their daughter suddenly turned to her husband and said, "Papi, you know, don't you, once the Russians are gone, then we will go home." Her husband almost fell off his chair. When the mother was alone with her daughter, she had constantly fantasized about her *Heimat*. Another forty years in Hamburg did not end her feeling like a stranger. "I am still an East Prussian," she said. It was only after the fall of the Wall that Hildegard Kroepelin would see her homeland again.[118] This case of repressed nostalgia serves as a reminder that integration is not an event but a journey. Some refugees completed it more quickly than others. Others never arrived.

Integration was relative as well as gradual, and for every success story it is possible to find a not-so-successful one. Bente Hagen was from West Prussia and seven years old when her family fled. They first lived in camps near Lübeck. Although refugees and the local homeless lived in separate quarters, the children played with each other. It was her mother and father who impressed on her that they were different. Even after they had left the camps, her parents only maintained social contacts with other expellees.[119]

Families developed split identities. An East Prussian man born in 1932 fled with his family first to the Soviet zone, and then to the Lüneburg Heath, the site of *The Heath Is Green.* He trained as an upholsterer before moving to Hamburg, where he joined the police. He saved with a building society, married a woman from northern Germany, and built a house. In many ways, his life seems to be a success story of integration. At the same time, he headed the local branch of the East Prussian Homeland Association. Now that Poland was applying to join the European Union, he suggested to an interviewer in 1997, perhaps the time had come to demand something back in return: "Of course, it does not need to be a claim to get the land back or that we want to Germanize it." He was just sad, he said, to see their former fields uncultivated. His children—born in the 1960s—had no connection at all to the old *Heimat.* While he continued to speak of East Prussia, they called it Poland.[120] A study of more than two hundred similar interviews conducted in 1992 revealed the spectrum of loyalties: 40 percent of the expellees identified as citizens of the Federal Republic of Germany; 39 percent had a dual identity, shared between their old and new *Heimat*; 21 percent still clung to their old *Heimat.*[121]

The decline of revanchist feeling reflected the advance of integration and generational change, but it also resulted from the growing confrontation with the Nazi past that recast flight and expulsion as a consequence of a German war of aggression. The "boomerang," sighted in the GDR long ago, finally also hit West German minds. For many expellees it shook the moral foundations of their own biography: instead of pointing to the guilt of others, their victimhood now pointed back to German guilt. Personal innocence was entangled in historical complicity. It was this reorientation that broke the vicious cycle of *ressentiment* of which Nietzsche had warned.

Often it was their children who helped them see their past in a new light;

the whole heritage industry ensured that the old *Heimat* was rarely a taboo topic in families. Ulla Dammert was born in Breslau (Wrocław, Poland) in 1921. She owed her flat in West Germany to the interventions of the Silesian Club (*Schlesierverein*). Fifty years after the war, she was still sad about the loss of her homeland, and took the first opportunity that presented itself to return on a visit in 1989. By then, however, she no longer felt that her *Heimat* had been wrongly taken from her. She used to rail about the subject until her daughter told her, "*Mutti*, stop it, for goodness' sake—it is sad that you lost your *Heimat*... but you cannot blame others for it and say they do not belong there." It was her daughter, she told an interviewer in 1997, who "straightened me out." Her daughter was right when she said, "This is the price you had to pay for all the wrong Germany had done."[122]

Mrs. Dammert was not alone. In 1990, the year of German reunification, when the GDR joined the Federal Republic, the Bund der Vertriebenen launched a petition for a plebiscite to see whether Silesia should not rejoin Germany as well. It attracted only 200,000 signatures and was politely ignored by Chancellor Helmut Kohl.[123] The blind youth was a false prophet.

8

War and Peace: The Dilemma of Arms

World War II ended in Europe on May 8, 1945, but war continued to define the lives of Germans for a long time after. They were surrounded by the legacies of physical and psychological destruction, from the rubble and the disabled soldiers to the many millions dead or missing, and the weight of their own crimes. Even as the dust of their defeat began to settle, the mushroom cloud of Hiroshima lingered in the air.

West Germany is remembered as a success story characterized by an economic miracle and stable parliamentary democracy. It was also, though, "a republic of fear," in the words of the historian Frank Biess.[1] From birth, in 1949, to reunification, in 1990, and beyond, the country was haunted by the specter of war, even though not a single German soldier fired a bullet in action (that would change in 1993, when two destroyers were dispatched to the Adriatic under NATO command, and in earnest in 1999, with the participation of the German air force and ground troops in the Kosovo War. Adenauer's formation of a new army (the Bundeswehr) in 1955, conscription in 1956, and a commitment to nuclear weapons in 1958 ignited strikes and mass protests. They were followed by Easter Marches for disarmament in the 1960s and even more massive demonstrations after NATO's decision to deploy cruise missiles in 1979. If the peace movement of these years was transnational, the arms race had a particular salience in the country that had launched the last world war and found itself at the potential epicenter of a next one.

East Germany, too, rearmed, but with far fewer qualms. (Its very uniforms resembled those of the Wehrmacht.) Socialism had its own theory of a "just war" against the imperialist class enemy. Peace, in this view, required violent struggle, and the regime successfully remilitarized society with little resistance until the late 1970s. West Germany did not travel on a straight path of demilitarization either. Children in Munich and Cologne did not learn to throw hand grenades as they did in Leipzig and Dresden, but, in addition to the millions of regular recruits, more young West Germans volunteered to train as officers than became conscientious objectors. West Germany was divided not only between supporters and critics of the army. There were also clashes within each camp about the true ethos of the military and the nature of peace.

Honor and conscience were the principal battlegrounds in this struggle. Did one have a duty to comrades, family, and nation, or to oneself, the weak, humanity, and, perhaps, God? Seven years before military service was made compulsory, the Federal Republic had pledged in its constitution that no one could be forced against their conscience to take up arms (1949, Article 4-3). In the past, it had been the churches that provided moral guidance with the idea of a "just war"—"*Gott mit uns*" ("God with us") was the battle cry of the Prussian soldiers fighting Napoleon and was engraved on the buckles of the Wehrmacht in the Second World War. In 1958, the Protestant Church, trying to avoid a split, retreated to a position of neutrality: peace, it ruled, could be served with or without weapons. It was up to the individual to decide what was right or wrong. Soon thereafter, the Catholic Church began to voice its own doubts whether a "just war" was possible at a time when nuclear weapons would annihilate friend and foe alike. As never before, moral reasoning and action were to invade the public ethic of responsibility, to the alarm of politicians who saw themselves as the custodians of the latter. It is over war and peace, then, more than any other subject, where the Germans' changing conscience at work can be seen.

DUTY UNTIL DEATH

Modern Germany was known as a "nation in barracks."[2] From Frederick the Great onward, military life held a central position in culture and society, with officers enjoying high status and soldiers taking pride in how service for the fatherland set them above ordinary civilians. Honor, courage, camaraderie, and selfless sacrifice were noble virtues.

Nineteen forty-five was a blow to the heart of that military culture. Defeat was too comprehensive to allow for the myth that a valiant army had been stabbed in the back, so powerful after 1918. German soldiers had failed to protect their families and their homeland. Their generals were executed for war crimes or sat in prison. Professional soldiers found themselves without guns or pensions, and often interned. Once a source of pride, Prussianism was vilified by the Allies as the handmaiden of Nazism: the cult of blind obedience had turned would-be knights into murderers. In the brutal final phase of the war, German soldiers had executed their own comrades and civilians who refused to fight to the bitter end for being "deserters" and "defeatists." The tradition of the German army had died, Theodor Heuss wrote in September 1945: the long line from August von Gneisenau, the Prussian field marshal who reformed the army and, with Wellington, defeated Napoleon at Waterloo, to Alfred von Schlieffen, the chief of the German general staff under Wilhelm II, had "ended and disappeared, unraveled and distorted, in complete intellectual and moral inadequacy."[3]

Never before had being a soldier been so unpopular. A survey in 1950 found that three quarters of Germans did not want to see their sons or husbands become soldiers. God had struck the gun from their hands, not once but twice, Protestant delegates told the synod that year: it was time for Germans to accept 1945 as a divine judgment and never pick up arms again. Disabled veterans warned that rearmament would inevitably lead to war and opposed it in any form. In May 1952, some 2 million workers joined strikes and demonstrations against rearmament. In Munich, they carried a big black cross with an American helmet and a sign saying "U.S. Adenauer." The leading Social Democrat Carlo Schmid hoped that, without arms, Germany might "exercise a moral pull on the rest of the world."[4]

And yet Germany rearmed. In 1950, Adenauer began to prepare for a new army as part of a West European alliance. Five years later, the first volunteers were sworn into the Bundeswehr. Conscription followed in 1956; military service was initially for twelve months, rising to eighteen months in 1963. In 1957, the chancellor told a press conference that his government was also committed to nuclear weapons, presenting them as "nothing more than a continuation of the artillery." In fact, the United States had stationed "Atomic Annie" cannons in West Germany since 1953.[5] The revelation sparked a mass campaign: the "Fight Against Nuclear Death" (Kampf dem Atomtod). Again, it was disarmament that lost. Why?

Adenauer's tactical skill is part of the answer. The "chancellor's democracy" operated without much regard for public opinion. In this case, there was a concerted crackdown. In 1951, police arrested seven thousand demonstrators and put a thousand on trial.[6] The following year, thirty-one people were killed by the police. One of them was Philipp Müller, a twenty-one-year-old communist worker who had traveled to Essen to protest against rearmament. The state minister withheld permission for the rally. When several thousand demonstrators refused to disband, the police gave the order to shoot. Two shots were fired, the second of which hit his heart. The Constitutional Court provided a second line of defense. The city-states of Hamburg and Bremen pressed for a plebiscite against nuclear arms; so did

Frankfurt. The court rejected the idea as violating the principles of parliamentary democracy.

The decisive factor, however, was that the opponents of rearmament were as divided among themselves as they were opposed to Adenauer. The "Without Me" movement against conscription encompassed pacifists, communists, and militant nationalists who were itching to resume the fight against the Soviets but loathed the idea of serving under a European command while some of their old comrades sat in prison as war criminals. The Protestant Church was split between pacifists, nationalists, and anti-communists. To the theologian Martin Niemöller, Adenauer's army destroyed the chance of reuniting the country; it also sold the German soul to American "plenty." His old adversary Hans Asmussen, by contrast, defended nuclear weapons as "God's punitive rod" that protected the Christian West against godless communists.[7] The Korean War and the Soviet tanks that crushed the uprising in the GDR in 1953 and in Hungary in 1956 convinced many contemporaries that he was right. Pope Pius XII and his bishops endorsed rearmament against the communist enemy, marginalizing the few Catholic youth circles that campaigned for a neutral Germany in a united Europe.[8]

The Social Democrats initially provided the ramshackle movement with leadership. After losing hands down to Adenauer in the 1957 general election—with 31.8 percent of the vote to the CDU's 50.2 percent—it repositioned itself. The SPD wanted power, and for that it needed to win over the center and lose its negative image of being in bed with the communists and always saying no. The party cut its ties with the peace movement and accepted NATO and the stationing of nuclear weapons, as long they were not built by Germany.

Rearmament also gained from the momentum for "moral rearmament," as the former Wehrmacht General Johannes Friessner called it in 1951 in an address to the Federation of German Soldiers.[9] He had to resign as chairman later that year after defending the invasion of Poland as a legitimate measure to protect ethnic Germans. The object of that moral repair was the German soldier. Privately, Adenauer had no illusions that the army—not just the SS—had committed war crimes, but he also knew that the Allies would not be impressed if he sent them new divisions led by eighteen-year-old generals, as he put it. He needed at least some of the old guard back. It was this that gave the veterans their leverage, in addition to their numbers as voters. They demanded the restoration of their pension rights, the release from prison of their comrades (the "so-called war criminals," as they referred to them), and public recognition that they had fought honorably. Adenauer obliged. In the spring of 1951, he promised to do everything possible to facilitate the prisoners' early release and said the number of those guilty of war crimes was so "extraordinarily small" that the "honor" of the Wehrmacht was intact; old soldiers would suffer no discrimination in a new army. On December 3, 1952, he added a formal declaration of honor in parliament, testifying that "the good reputation and great accomplishments of the German soldier... were still alive among our people." The task now was to merge the "ethical values of German soldiery with that of democracy."[10]

In 1970, the sociologist Peter Berger claimed that "honor occupies about the same place in contemporary usage as chastity."[11] The 1950s and 1960s, however, showed that it was not extinct, because there was a renaissance of honor in West Germany. This can be seen as tactical: protestations of honor after the war deflected from crimes committed during it. More was involved, though. For veterans it was a way to regain social standing and construct a stable sense of personality.

The nineteenth-century philosopher Arthur Schopenhauer, who railed against the stupidity of the duel, distinguished between outer and inner honor. The first concerns other people's opinion of what we are worth. The second is our fear of that opinion. In contrast to the inner orientation of one's conscience, honor was outward facing. A soldier found his inner worth in fighting and, if necessary, dying for the fatherland. "National honor" (*Nationalehre*), as Germans had started to call it in the nineteenth century, reflected back on personal honor. The genius of honor was that it persuaded the individual to see its defense not as something externally imposed but as his own natural self-interest.[12]

Honor was simultaneously inclusive and exclusive. Soldiers had fought, suffered, and died for the whole nation, veterans insisted. At the same time, public duty, courage, and honor also elevated a soldier to a higher plane than the ordinary civilian concerned with their private interests. At stake was their "*Standesehre*," their professional honor, as well as their individual one.

Across Europe, there were efforts to restore masculinity after the war but nowhere more so than in Germany, where soldiers had first been defeated on the battlefield and then, as they saw it, dishonored by the Allies and their own compatriots. France and Italy had resistance heroes to identify with. The German troops, by contrast, had almost to a man gone down fighting for Hitler. This is what made the Federal Republic's official attempts to build its moral legitimacy on the few aristocratic officers who were executed after their failed plot to assassinate Hitler such a divisive issue. If Count von Stauffenberg and his allies had acted ethically on July 20, 1944, what did this say about all the millions of soldiers and officers who had continued to obey the Führer? In 1952, Otto Ernst Remer, the officer who had helped foil "Operation Valkyrie"—and was duly promoted by Hitler—publicly denounced the plotters as "traitors"; he was sentenced to three months in prison, but instead fled to Egypt, where he became a military advisor to President Nasser. (In the 1980s Remer was back in Germany organizing small but vocal neo-Nazi groups and was sentenced for hate speech but, again, escaped, this time to Spain, where he died in 1997.)

After bitter infighting, the head of the Federation of German Soldiers, former Admiral Gottfried Hansen, produced in 1951 a convenient formula that recognized the honor of those who had placed their loyalty to the *Volk* above the sanctity of their oath ("to render unconditional obedience to the Führer") as well as those who had remained loyal to it. This moral equivalence would be the midwife of the Bundeswehr. Importantly, Hansen granted only the plotters some knowledge of the "course of events," as he euphemistically called war crimes, that justified their decision to break their oath. By implication, everyone else was doing their duty in the genuine belief that they were fighting for a good cause. Only the few comrades who had acted out of self-interest and without "honorable motives" were to be criticized.[13]

In their defense, army veterans stressed that the Allies had found the High Command of the Wehrmacht not guilty at Nuremberg. The Waffen-SS was not so fortunate, and this made it shout even louder about its honor. General Felix Steiner, the last commander of the "Germanic SS-Panzerkorps" (a tank regiment mainly recruited from ethnic Germans in Romania), addressed one thousand Waffen-SS veterans at the first of their annual Nordmark gatherings in 1954. With a silent march through Rendsburg in the north they paid their respects to their 350,000 comrades who had fallen in the "fight against Bolshevism." Steiner summarized what would become their lobby's mantra for years to come. The "collective sentence" passed on them was an unprecedented historic injustice, he said. They had dutifully fought for their fatherland, indeed they were the pioneers of the European community: "In the Waffen-SS we experienced Europe, not as a political aim or vision, but as a human community." They were a purely military formation and had been wrongly associated with the SS proper. This was a fiction, since thousands of men moved from the first to the second and served as concentration camp guards, too. Raised in the "tradition of the best soldierly values," they could be proud of their accomplishments. Their "ethical concepts" were the trinity of "courage, love, and death. The courage of the heart, which is a manly feature, love of all that has created us, and love of family, *Heimat*, and our country. Death is not the decisive factor. Courage and love are stronger!"[14] They were the natural candidates for a new army,

Steiner stressed, and they stood ready to serve the new democratic state, but they could only do so when their last comrade had been released from prison. Although the veterans of the Waffen-SS never gained the full equality they hankered for, they did get some of their benefits restored. And they were allowed into the Bundeswehr—initially only the lower ranks, but from 1961 senior officers and generals, too.

In the 1950s, West Germany was home to some two thousand veteran associations. Many of these were small affairs. The Infantry Regiment 77, for example, had its own newsletter, which went out to 665 of their known surviving comrades. It had a regular monthly gathering in an inn in Bonn, collected information for a regimental history, and assisted widows with their pension applications. Caring for survivors and the war-disabled made regiments a second family to some, and expressed the "softer" virtues of comradeship. The popularity of veteran clubs should not be exaggerated—by 1959, the organizers of the Infantry Regiment 77 association complained that only 13 percent of their comrades responded to their mailings[15]—but it should not be underestimated, either. In the 1970s, they still claimed 2 million members. Their meetings combined sociability and the search for comrades missing in action—as late as 1977, there were still 1.7 million active searches—with a reassurance that they had fought a "good" war.

In September 1956, eighteen thousand men of the former Deutsches Afrika Korps descended on Düsseldorf. The corps had been led by Erwin Rommel, the "Desert Fox," whose spirit was present in the form of his widow. (Rommel had been pushed to commit suicide in October 1944 to avoid the disgrace of execution, after being charged with conspiracy for supporting the officers of the July 20, 1944, plot.) Their old jeeps motored through the streets. A few protestors threw stink bombs and painted "War: Never Again" on the monument there to the fallen heroes. They were drowned out by Lale Andersen singing "Lili Marleen" to the crowds. It was almost like the old days, except for being on the Rhine instead of in the African desert. A crucial sign of the "restoration" of honor was the presence of Allied brass, in this case General Richard Gale of the British Rhine Army. To be fair, Rommel's troops were not the SS, but they were not all knights, either; they, too, had been involved in poisoning civilian wells and stood ready to round up Jews.[16] In 1976, the "desert foxes" celebrated their twenty-fifth anniversary with a grand gala. Speeches about their "knightly" war were followed by the *Nabucco* prisoner choir ("Va, pensiero") and the "Panzerlied" ("tank song"). The veterans were diplomatic enough to opt for an orchestral version of that Nazi favorite, although everyone present probably remembered the lyrics of this attack song, which ended with a heroic death inside the tank.

Affluence and respectability had blown away postwar uncertainty. There was ballroom dancing before the long evening reached its finale with a "surprise polonaise" and a tombola of prizes.[17]

Prussia, too, was rehabilitated. The military march "Prussia's Glory," which celebrated Germany's defeat of France in 1871, was another favorite with the "desert foxes" and similar reunions. Hitler, veteran associations said, had perverted its noble ideals with his cult of unconditional obedience. True Prussian obedience was a voluntary act and gave officers the freedom and responsibility to consider an order's intention. An episode widely cited by veterans occurred in the Seven Years' War, during the battle of Zorndorf in 1758, when Friedrich Wilhelm von Seydlitz refused to carry out Frederick II's order for an immediate cavalry attack on the Russians because it would be suicidal and counterproductive.[18] When Frederick threatened that he would pay for the outcome of the battle with his head, von Seydlitz supposedly replied, "Tell the king that after the battle my head will be at his disposal, but for the duration of the battle he might allow me to make use of it in his service." The decision earned the Prussians victory over the Russian troops, although with horrendous losses on both sides.

Unfortunately, this appreciation of an officer's traditional capacity for critical reflection did little for his direct descendant, General Walther von Seydlitz, who, after surrendering at Stalingrad, had tried to convince fellow officers that to continue the war was futile and self-destructive. When the POW returned to his hometown of Verden in 1955, he was greeted with signs of "Traitor, go home." His family was ostracized. His wife was unable to understand how her husband could have broken his oath of allegiance.[19] By contrast, convicted war criminals such as Kurt "Panzer" Meyer, the Nazi commander of the 12th SS Tank Division "Hitler Youth," were greeted with garlands and brass bands on their release from prison; he had been sentenced for executing Canadian POWs, although his crimes had begun immediately after the invasion of Poland with the murder of Jews.[20]

The change in atmosphere was tangible in literature, film, and culture at large. In the late 1940s, antiwar themes had been in the ascendant. The undisputed best seller was Theodor Plievier's *Stalingrad*, a novel based on more than a hundred interviews he had conducted with POWs in Soviet camps. Published in 1945, the book sold 2 million copies in East and West Germany, was serialized for radio, and was put on stage. Plievier was a larger-than-life character who, after a childhood in the poor Berlin district of Wedding, had traveled the world as sailor, anarchist, and bartender. First and foremost, he was an anti-militarist.

Stalingrad was a moral novel that took readers through the dehumanizing effect of war toward the prospect of human liberation. Plievier exploded camaraderie, duty, and heroic sacrifice as myths. The generals go on a hunt while their men pee and shit blood. "I am not a hero, I am hungry," one soldier protests. "We are objects," another complains. The reader wades knee deep in dismembered bodies, blood, and bones. The dead have their skulls hacked open and their brains sucked out and eaten: "This is the consequence of the doctrine of the superior race!" the main character named Colonel Vilshofen explains to a soldier. The war is exposed as a brutal war of aggression. "'They died so that Germany can live!': "What a lie." "The fatherland had no border to defend at the Volga." The soldiers were betrayed not only by Hitler but also by their generals, and by themselves. Soldiers recall the murder of villagers and children and reflect on their guilt. One looks at his broken bones as proper punishment for "all the misery we have brought into this land." "Yes," Vilshofen notes, "we have committed crimes."

In the book, the colonel stands for the conscience that slowly rises up and dares to protest to the generals, "The battle is being continued with half-dead and dying men! And to what end? Only to drift into hopeless chaos. It is against conscience... against honor, also against a soldier's honor, what is demanded and ordered here." Stalingrad, Plievier told readers, was the "deepest moral and political fall of the German people" as well as a military catastrophe. The final pages offer a sliver of hope and redemption. Vilshofen surrenders to the Red Army. He has been thinking not only about their defeat, he tells a soldier from a penal battalion, but also about their guilt toward their own misled and vulnerable people: "Here repair is needed!" Side by side, officer and soldier are walking in the snow, united in the hope of a better, peaceful Germany.[21]

In 1947, Plievier left the Soviet zone, disillusioned by the hardening of communist rule. Six years later, he also had enough of West Germany and its Cold War mind-set and moved to Switzerland. His departure did not mark the end of the antiwar genre. The following years saw, notably, *Die Brücke* (*The Bridge*, 1959), a popular movie that exposed the fanaticism that made a group of high school boys try to defend their local bridge against the U.S. Army in the final days of the war; by its end, only one of them is left alive. The conflict between conscience and blind obedience was the central theme of *Unruhige Nacht* (*Restless Night*, 1958), which followed a deserter on the Eastern Front during his last hours before his execution; the film was based on a 1950 book by Albrecht Goes, who had observed several such executions as a military priest.[22]

Such works, however, now had competition. There was an avalanche of militarist memoirs, novels, and penny booklets. Their unifying theme was

"Lost Victories" ("Verlorene Siege"), to borrow the title of Erich von Manstein's memoirs of 1955. In this view, the German army had fought heroically and honorably and might have won had it not been for Hitler. The good Wehrmacht was separated from the criminal SS. Where crimes against Jews and civilians were mentioned—as in Peter Bamm's novel about the war in the East, *Die unsichtbare Flagge* (*The Invisible Flag*), which sold almost half a million copies between 1952 and 1961—they seemed to happen without the army's knowledge. In Heinz Konsalik's best seller *Der Arzt von Stalingrad* (*The Doctor of Stalingrad*, 1958), brutal Russians faced heroic Germans, and a Jew featured as a "filthy bug."[23]

For young readers there was the *Landser*, a weekly magazine launched in 1957, packed with battle action, military know-how, and short biographies of Iron Cross daredevils. Sold at kiosks for 60 pfennigs, its circulation reached around half a million copies each month, and still sold a quarter of a million a month in the 1970s. Only briefly, in 1959 and 1960, a few issues were banned for endangering youth.[24] The magazine turned the Second World War into a serial adventure, told from the perspective of the regular soldier (*Landser*). Reading these stories now, one sometimes has to remind oneself that the German army actually lost the war. This was precisely their point: Hitler lost the war, but the German soldier fought valiantly and even in military defeat emerged the moral victor. Unlike "cowardly" partisans who relied on ambushes, German soldiers were "real men" (*ganze Kerle*) who confronted the enemy. They fought hard but always clean and fair. They were "fighters who overcame themselves because they knew they had a duty to fulfill." In a story about the defense of Brest in Brittany in 1944, for example, the fictional paratrooper Bolle sneaks up on two Americans. He briefly considers throwing a hand grenade their way before "shaking his head in disgust. That would be murder, naked murder, my dear Bolle, and would be thoroughly mean and vile [*grenzenlose Schweinerei*]! To kill harmless GIs in their sleep. French partisans might do that. But he, Hänschen Bolle, was a paratrooper!"[25]

The result of all this was what the Israeli writer Amos Elon described as "moral schizophrenia" after his travels across Germany in 1965. Publicly, the war was condemned as a bad war, but when individuals talked about it, it turned into their own good war. Germans began to learn about the Holocaust but clung to the memory of their own heroic father or grandfather. It was the myth of the "clean" army that prevented the one from spilling over into the other, and that explains the furious reaction as late as 1995 to a traveling exhibition that put the Wehrmacht's crimes on public display.[26]

There were limits, though, to how unapologetic old soldiers could be. The changing fortunes of General Albert Kesselring's reputation is a good illustration. Kesselring had been commander of Army Group C in Italy. In 1947, a British military court sentenced him to death for allowing the execution of hostages and for his orders to show no restraint in the fight against partisans, including women and children. The following year, the sentence was commuted to life in prison. He was one of the "so-called war criminals" whom veterans wanted to see freed. Citizens volunteered to take Kesselring's place and spend Christmas in his cell. The field marshal used the proceedings in and outside the court to present himself as an innocent model officer. He had a "duty" to fight the charges, he said, not just to restore his own honor but to defend the "high moral ethos" of all German soldiers and to prove "to the mourning mothers, women, and children that their loved ones' sacrifice had not been for nothing." "Perhaps it will also make international understanding easier," he added diplomatically.[27] In 1952, Kesselring was released early, on health grounds. He left prison a popular hero, and immediately became the honorary president of three veteran associations, including the Stahlhelm. That December, Adenauer received him to discuss the situation of the remaining prisoners.

The apotheosis was short-lived. His memoirs in 1953 and subsequent speeches caused a public storm. Kesselring had the nerve to tell the Italians that, instead of pursuing him for war crimes, they ought to build him a monument for saving Rome. In a widely reported interview with the BBC he explained that, with better preparation, the invasion of England would have succeeded and meant a shorter war for all. Anti-Bolshevism was one thing, but Kesselring's suggestion that West Germany would, of course, recruit SS veterans—"the best blood of Germany"—went one step too far. "Might have, might have, might have," one newspaper entitled its article on Kesselring's counterfactual replay of the war, which failed to grasp that it had always been an ideological, not a conventional, one. Even newspapers that praised his military talent found his fiction of the apolitical soldier impossible to stomach. Kesselring's fantasy that a "final victory" (*Endsieg*) might have been possible ignored the many German soldiers who died pointlessly. Papers wanted to know why Kesselring continued to obey Hitler until the end; where was his conscience and concern for his men? Von Seydlitz had shown "true virtue" when he stood up to Frederick II. Kesselring lacked it, and was thus unfit to defend Western civilization against a totalitarian threat. Politicians distanced themselves from the field marshal, including vocal champions of rearmament such as Adenauer's bullish Bavarian ally Franz Josef Strauss, soon to become his minister of defense; Strauss had been lucky to escape the hell of Stalingrad when he was sent home with frostbite on both his feet. "Never again," Strauss told party delegates, would "people like him hold a position of influence." If they had all followed orders in those days, Strauss said, many more people would have died needlessly. He urged the general who had supported the "brown scoundrels" to show some remorse.

Kesselring's appearance as witness in several trials about "end phase" crimes destroyed what was left of the field marshal's mystique. He defended the officers who had strung up "deserters" and executed civilians for refusing to blow up their village in April 1945. They had acted in a "considerate" manner, he said. Resistance to the last man was justifiable. His words sparked furious letters. The chairman of the war-disabled association told Kesselring to show some respect in light of such "terrible murder." Another veteran told the general to shut up given his "enormous shared responsibility for this criminal period."[28].

One of the men Kesselring defended was General Ferdinand Schörner ("Bloody Ferdinand"), who had ordered several executions in the final phase of the war and was sentenced to four years in prison for second-degree murder. Schörner was among the last ten thousand POWs who returned from the Soviet Union in 1955. Their homecoming added a new dimension to the moral rearmament of the nation. For Adenauer, who had gone to Moscow to negotiate their release, it was a triumph. For their families and society at large, it meant coming face-to-face with war criminals and unreconstructed militarists, on one end, and with broken men, on the other. Neither was an easy fit with the ideal of the good soldier.

HOMECOMING

The fate of the German POWs was the subject of intense hope and despair. Five years after the unconditional surrender, rumors spread that perhaps as many as 1.5 million men missing in action might still be alive. The German Red Cross and charities began to channel thousands of letters from Soviet camps to relatives. In 1952, Adenauer lowered expectations to 100,000 survivors. The following year, the Verband der Heimkehrer (Association of Returnees, VdH) organized ten thousand demonstrations. Seven million West German citizens signed a petition calling for the release of the prisoners, which was deposited in a shrine of honor. People put candles in their windows to show their support. Waiting wives received flowers and donations. The VdH erected memorials and recruited schools and companies to send relief packets to POWs in Soviet camps. Each Sunday afternoon, the radio broadcast a song chosen by a relative, a ritual that kept alive the wartime *Wunschkonzert,* when soldiers had sent in their requests—"Prisoners' Chorus" from Verdi's *Nabucco* was a favorite. The POWs were seen to follow in the passion of Christ, suffering for the nation at home. Schoolchildren sent them handmade gifts for Christmas: "I don't know you, and you suffer for me. You don't know me, and I draw for you."[29]

Honor and comradeship were central planks of the VdH, which formally excluded men from membership who had abused or committed crimes against their brothers-in-arms. This did not stop concentration camp guards from applying to join; they were rejected out of fear that members who had been inmates would resign in protest. Internal communication shows that the leaders were quite aware that soldiers had not always fought a "clean" war.[30]

The Soviet Union's release of the final ten thousand prisoners in 1955 followed a West German initiative; the GDR had no interest in welcoming a group that included many Nazis and war criminals. Geographic fate, however, meant that the trains needed to pass through East Germany on their way from Russia to the West. Veteran associations were prohibited in the GDR; police reports of the public reaction to the trains offer a rare snapshot of how regular East Germans saw these men. Some hundred people gathered every day in October 1955 along the train line near Ziegelrode, west of Leipzig, to cheer the returnees as their trains stopped there briefly. The police were unable to stop the spectators from reaching the cars. At the outskirts of Berlin, in Königs Wusterhausen, people defied orders and handed the passengers food and cigarettes. A Red Cross nurse passed them buckets of coffee and water and told the overwhelmed policemen, "You should be ashamed to wear this uniform and betray the fatherland."

Across East Germany, there were lively debates about the POWs' ordeal and amnesty. Were all these people really war criminals, as the authorities had it? Workers in Magdeburg were outraged that those released included fanatical Nazis such as Rudolf Jordan, who had ruled over their city, but they wanted to see an exception made for sixteen- and seventeen-year-olds because they had "acted either under pressure or through blindness." Elsewhere, people went further. A factory worker in nearby Halberstadt told his coworkers that "these people are not war criminals, they only did their duty." That the released also included women was taken as proof of this. The dominant view was that these soldiers had fought the Soviet Union and were consequently POWs, not war criminals. Some drew a line between innocent soldiers and guilty officers. The real culprits, a man in Torgau (Saxony) said, were the Nazis, not the soldiers. All they had done was to carry out orders;

if they had not done so, they would have been shot. This was the same myth that circulated in West Germany.[31]

What made the homecoming such a sensitive issue was that it concerned not only soldiers who had committed crimes during the war but also several thousand civilians detained for crimes committed *after* the war. The latter group had been sentenced by military tribunals and were either in prison in the GDR or in camps in the Soviet Union, sometimes for little more than uttering an ill-advised word against the new regime. Amnesty for war criminals was therefore entangled with questions over socialist justice. In a power station in Saxony, workers led "heated discussions": "They cannot understand that such criminals, who had thousands of murders on their conscience, are released while people who committed crimes in the GDR that bear no resemblance to war crimes have to spend several years in prison." Near Leipzig, in the coal-mining Kombinat Espenhain, a female worker confronted the police. One of the "war criminals" happened to be a local young man who had been deported after making some drunken "enemy remarks" in 1948 at a football match. "The people," she said, did not agree with such harsh punishment, because he was young and careless, and had his family life destroyed by the affair, when his wife got pregnant by another man. We do not know what happened to this young man. One of the lucky ones who did make it back was Gerhard Leipold. In 1951, when he was a student, he had been sentenced to five years in prison for "espionage" and deported to the Soviet Union. In 1955, he was pardoned. A hundred people welcomed him back home with cheers and flowers.[32]

In 1955, the trains traveled straight on to West Germany, but earlier trains, in 1953–54, had dropped several thousand returning prisoners in East Germany. The authorities watched them closely. They "would be pronounced idiots," one of them said, if they "ever touched a gun again" after what they had been through. Many more, though, took away the opposite lesson. Attempts to try to argue with the men and persuade them to stay backfired. Former SS men declared that "it was over with their friendship with the Soviet Union." They would not turn a finger to help build a socialist state, nor would they accept the new border with Poland—"Germans have to think of their living space [*Lebensraum*], after all." "I will never pick up a gun," a man from Aachen said, "except one more time in a fight with the Soviet Union to get revenge, and then I will kill anyone who gets in my way."[33] Almost all of them decided to move to the Federal Republic.

The returnees reached West Germany in various states of ill health. Doctors reported a rise in impotence and marital problems; every third marriage ended in divorce. Some of the former prisoners were psychological wrecks. The glorification of self-sacrifice could trigger an unbearable sense of failure and guilt for those who had survived while their comrades had not. The young soldier Dietmar F., for example, was haunted by a recurring nightmare in which he had to carry fifteen dead comrades on his shoulders to their grave.[34]

Those who had helped POWs and refugees received a bronze medal from the VdH with the words "Light, Life, Love" and "Loyalty for Loyalty." The medal bore an image of the *Madonna of Stalingrad*, a drawing by Kurt Reuber, a military surgeon and pastor, that had been shipped out on one of the last departing transport flights. Reuber surrendered with the remnants of the 6th Army in January 1943 and died of typhoid in a POW camp in Tatarstan a year later.

A few had discovered Christ in a Soviet POW camp. Many others, though, returned with their earlier worldview, only hardened.[35] Former POWs professed their innocence but sometimes only to show how little the experience of the Soviet camps had altered their fascist views of right and wrong. In 1956–57, the Frankfurt Institute of Social Research conducted focus group interviews with nearly four hundred returnees. They revealed totalitarian tendencies, a denial of Nazi crimes, and a desire for a German nation, although more than a third were fearful of being used as fodder in another war and were opposed to rearmament. The VdH lobby was not pleased by these findings and withdrew their support for the study. It was biased and unrepresentative, they said.[36] In fact, when returnees sent the VdH their personal recollections, they were even more outspoken. One man devoted a hundred pages to the injustices he had suffered at the hands of the Soviets. He had been the subject of misidentification and maltreatment, he wrote. He went on a hunger strike and raised a formal complaint with the camp authorities about the unacceptable sanitary conditions; he had no toilet in his cell and had to use a bucket. By comparison with the "arbitrary" conditions in the Soviet camp, he wrote, "Hitler's extermination policy was humane." "Hitler was at least honest: the Jews are a destructive element and, hence, have to be destroyed; the Slavs are spreading too quickly and have to be exterminated to restore a European balance." He saw so many Jews in Russia that he doubted that "the few existing ovens" could possibly have killed 6 million. When, in 1956, he read in his trusted newspaper for the returnees (*Der Heimkehrer*) that perhaps as many as 4 million might have been murdered, he felt "ashamed": "I did not imagine the whole thing to be quite so bad," as if a smaller number would have made it all right.[37]

By the mid-1950s, such views were no longer acceptable in public, as we have seen. Whatever their personal views, the returnees and their experiences were turned into a lesson that had to fit the needs of West Germany as it navigated its way through the Cold War and the economic miracle. The returnees became the subject of a traveling exhibition "Wir Mahnen" ("Our Warning"). It had a million visitors, including many school classes. In some small towns, half the inhabitants went to see it.

When the exhibition was launched in 1951, the focus was on the suffering in the camps. By the end of the decade, this was no longer considered appropriate. Visitors should take away practical insights from the past for the present. The exhibition needed to "confront the Zeitgeist." The space devoted to suffering was reduced; that for lessons learned was expanded. The aim, the planners explained, was to show how "out of the experience itself a new task [*Aufgabe*] emerges that... succeeds in applying the insights gained in daily life for the benefit of all as well as for oneself." On entering, visitors were greeted by the motto "We were unfree, with no rights, and our world collapsed, but we developed powers we did not know we had." The exhibition showcased everything from poems and handcrafted wooden spoons and chess sets to clothes stitched together from sugar sacks as evidence of how the German POWs were able to master and overcome "material... and spiritual suffering through creative activities." The old virtues were as important as ever. The most "precious treasure we returnees brought home with us," one of them wrote to the *Frankfurter Allgemeine Zeitung*, was "our unbroken spiritual values." "No *Volk* and especially no democratic state can exist in the long term if concepts like honor and loyalty are broken."[38]

What the exhibition did not show was that, by 1953, charities were receiving ever-longer wish lists from POWs—for wristwatches, musical instruments, sneakers, and other little luxuries. Mental illness was on the rise, too.[39] The exhibition, by contrast, showed the prisoners as undamaged by the camp experience. From victims in need of compassion, the returnees had been turned into role models deserving respect and admiration. And their redemption was not only directed against Moscow. At a time of growing affluence, the resilient POWs also offered reassurance to those worried that American "mass" consumption might corrupt the German soul.

This was the view of the curators and sponsors. As for West Germans, as luck would have it, a bundle of visitor comments from 1957 survives in the Federal Archives. Some were perplexed by the displays—"Why don't we say: we no longer want war?" one visitor wanted to know. Two teenagers in Frankfurt wondered whether the exhibition was trying to dissuade them from enlisting in the army. For Bundeswehr units, by contrast, it was welcome proof "why we need an army again." Most responses, though, were about spiritual resilience. Through their personal struggle and "composure" (*Haltung*), the POWs were shining a "radiant light" in "hectic times that are oppressing our inner humanity," one visitor wrote. The objects on display were not seen as signs of a material self but as their very opposite: reminders of the fleeting insignificance of things for the human soul. For one pupil from Tübingen, the exhibition showed how "all things retreat that are not essential, and only the inner life is important." Plato, the Christian fathers, and German Romantics would have nodded approvingly. The comment neatly expressed the moral ambivalence and denial Germans continued to feel toward the world of stuff, even as (or, perhaps, because) they were making themselves more and more comfortable within it. "Misery destroys material life," another student wrote, "but the spiritual life is enriched, if man is strong enough to bear the misery." The POW experience, in this view, was a test of soul and character that Germans had passed heroically.[40]

CONTESTED MOURNING

The returnees' passage led them from the Soviet Union to Friedland, a village in Lower Saxony that carried the name of a medieval fortress and stood, literally, for "pacified land." This was the site of a central transit camp, first for the expellees, and then for refugees from the GDR and "late repatriates" (*Spätaussiedler*) from the Eastern bloc. By the time the Berlin Wall stemmed the flow in 1961, some 2 million people had passed through it. From 1949, a bell was rung to welcome the new arrivals. In public ceremonies during the Cold War, returning POWs walked alongside political refugees on a joint "path to freedom."

In 1963, the bell of the Friedland camp went on a tour across West Germany, ringing the sound of freedom, with dedicated stops near the East German border. The small town of Schöppenstedt welcomed it on June 22. After special services in both the Protestant and Catholic churches and a concert by the police music corps in the market square, sirens announced the arrival of the bell. The mayor formally received it, accompanied by the deputy of the Federation of Returnees and delegates from local schools, clubs, and other organizations. A pupil read a veteran's poem—"Ring bell, ring the faith, which neither tyrant nor border can steal. Deeds pass, but hearts last, and our hearts are stronger than walls." After further speeches, flowers, and the national anthem, the bell continued on its way.

In Friedland itself, four massive "gateways to freedom" were erected three years later, a ninety-one-foot-high monument tall enough to be visible from East Germany. Each block carried tablets with the number of dead German soldiers, prisoners of war, and expellees. In the words of the document that was placed in the foundation stone, it was a "memorial to the sacrifice [*Opfergang*] of the German *Volk* and their sons."[41]

Germans were increasingly divided about what their fallen sons were to be commemorated for. Since 1952, the national day of mourning was officially intended to be for dead soldiers of both wars as well as for the victims of the Nazis. That year, President Heuss declared the time for "heroification" to be over: all that was left was "infinite suffering." At the same time, the German War Graves Commission (Volksbund Deutsche Kriegsgräberfürsorge) advised local communities to prepare speeches that praised soldiers' "love and loyalty for Germany . . . their death-defying courage . . . and loyal camaraderie," and how they had "fulfilled their hard service at the front in silent obedience . . . as part of their nature."[42]

Public attitudes began to pull in opposite directions. In 1956, the official speech on the day of mourning was given by the writer Manfred Hausmann, who himself had been a fellow traveler during the Nazi years. He urged Germans to remember not only their own soldiers and victims of the bombing but also all those "who because of their . . . noble convictions, their faith, their deep humanity, their politics, or their birth were deliberately tortured, beaten, shot, decapitated, hanged, and suffocated in gas chambers."[43] Four years later, President Heinrich Lübke said soldiers had suffered a "tragic conflict" between their own good faith and their creeping awareness that they were no longer fighting in a "just war"; in order not to despair, they had lied to their own conscience.

The Ministry of the Interior, meanwhile, was trying to revert to the traditional view of war graves as reserved for fallen heroes. Groups of Nazi victims were outraged. The Second World War, they stressed, was not a traditional war.

By and large, however, local commemorations followed the formula adopted by the veterans: the Nazis' war was evil, but the soldiers fighting it were not, and those who died were heroes. A favorite song at local days of mourning continued to be the "Good Comrade"—"A bullet came a-flying / Is it my turn or yours? / He was swept away . . . / You stay my good comrade / In eternal life."[44]

A few raised protests. In 1958, Heinrich Böll, a veteran himself, wanted soldiers' heroic deaths to be exposed as "counterfeit money" (*Falschgeld*). Real heroes, he said, acted out of their own volition and died for something, calling to posterity: "Freedom." The dead German soldiers were different, he said: they had performed "not action, but passion." Mothers should claim back their sons from official commemorations and mourn their death in private. Ten years later, during a church service on the day of mourning in Wolfenbüttel, Lower Saxony, two students of theology unrolled banners that declared, "War is among us" and "This is the spirit of Hitler." Those sitting in the first row seized the young men and beat them up. The following week, one of the men returned with an ax and chipped away at the memorial plaque for the heroes of the First World War—this type of Christianity had made Auschwitz possible, he said. Tellingly, it was the young protestors, not their attackers, who found themselves in front of a judge, who reprimanded them for not showing the past sufficient respect.

In the early 1970s, activists spray-painted across the inscription "They died so that Germany can live" on the monument for the 76th Infantry Regiment in Hamburg (erected in 1936), and, here and elsewhere, initiatives sprang up to remove such monuments. They were defeated. A veteran of the First World War and father of a soldier killed in the Second told the local newspaper that he would be a coward if he did not defend the monument. For others, the fallen were heroes who had saved them from having Russians on the Rhine. Letters to newspapers showed that love of the fatherland and respect for soldiers remained inseparable for many citizens: to chisel away at the memorials was to chisel away at patriotism.[45]

The guardian of the day of mourning and German war graves abroad was the Volksbund Deutsche Kriegsgräberfürsorge. Founded after the First World War, it regrouped after the Second and grew into one of the largest humanitarian organizations in the country. By 1970, it had 700,000 members organized into 12,000 district groups, including schools and companies. With the help of thousands of volunteers, it looked after 1.5 million war graves.

Critics attacked the Volksbund as a "Trojan horse of militarism,"[46] and it is easy to see why. In 1970, for example, there were speakers who praised the "personal integrity, courage, and untouched honor" of German soldiers, while the *Volksbund* magazine urged people to remember the "immensity of their final sacrifice, the death-defying examples of camaradarie in battle... and their knightly actions," and to thank them for "fulfilling their duty out of love for their *Heimat*." Neofascist groups used the day of mourning to meet with Flemish nationalists to commemorate the Waffen-SS.[47]

Alongside such protestations, however, commemoration was changing, and nowhere more so than among the young volunteers who traveled to Belgium and France to tend to cemeteries there. In 1954, a pupil still wrote that the soldiers had died "so we can live," echoing the standard phrase. Care for their graves united the dead and the living of the German nation. "Take the dead into your circle—as silent comrades," the Volksbund told youth groups, "who live on in you and your works."[48] In the following years, the dead were increasingly seen as speaking to humanity and reconciliation. Groups started to combine their trips to war graves with a visit to the Bergen-Belsen concentration camp—the young did not shoulder the guilt of their fathers, they said, but they did have a duty to recognize "the horror" and reflect on its causes. In 1961–62, some fifteen thousand youths were applying to join the youth camps, more than twice the number of places available. For some, it was a cheap chance to travel. For many, though, it was an opportunity to heal wounds. One young man whose father had died in Russia wrote that the work had taught him to have not just "sentimental piety" but also "respect for life and to help stop people's mania for extermination." Another returned from a cemetery in France proud of having done a service not only to the German dead but also "to the dead of a nation with which we did not manage to live in peace in the past."[49]

Christiane Pahl was fifteen when she set off for her first Volksbund youth camp in Veslud, in northern France, in the summer of 1962. She recorded her experiences in a school essay. Her grandfather had died in the First World War, an uncle in the Second. Her group came from a range of backgrounds and included pupils, university students, and army recruits; she herself attended a middle school (*Realschule*). They were seen off by a Hamburg senator. The dead, he told them, would rise up and ask them: "Was our sacrifice for nothing?" Their work would be their answer, an "act of peace and reconciliation" that demonstrated respect for others, truth, and justice. It would be a "purification for themselves and humanity." With pickax and shovel, Christiane arrived at the war cemetery to clear the weeds from graves. One grave she cleaned was that of a German soldier killed in 1917. "Did he leave behind wife and children?" she wondered. She put some flowers on his grave. In the village of Laon, they were surprised by the warm welcome from the mayor, who had been in a concentration camp and was said to be a "German hater." Each of them received a bottle of wine as a gift. She danced with the local boys. In Paris, she marveled at the pissoirs and Versailles. It was her first trip abroad and made her reflect on cultural differences. "The Frenchman . . . is a revolutionary," she wrote. "By our standard, he has little taste." "He is untidy as well . . . stockings and dirty clothes lie in every corner." Yet she had also acquired a fondness for the culture and its people. When Charles de Gaulle visited Hamburg that September, she cheered: "*Vive de Gaulle, vive la France!*" Her report carried the dedication "Long live Franco-German friendship!"[50]

The cult of death, violence, and sacrifice was starting to give way to international peace and reconciliation. By the 1980s, the Volksbund was teaching peace in elementary schools. A puppet play had Monsieur Dupont and Herr Meier live happily as neighbors across the border from each other until the dark clouds of war tore them apart. One loses a leg, the other his two sons. Then one day they happen to walk out into their garden at the same hour, greet each other, and shake hands, with tears in their eyes. At that moment, a new tree shoots out from the old trunk: the "tree of Europe" (*Europabaum*). *Peace—A Child's Play?* used roleplay to teach children how to "turn toward the other... take on shared responsibility... and join in cooperation." The goal was to make war graves "memorials for peaceful action in the present."[51]

BARRACKS DIVIDED

The German army is reputed to be a fierce fighting machine. However much that might have been deserved in earlier eras, it certainly did not apply to the new federal army. The Bundeswehr was a mess. It suffered from low levels of education in general and a chronic shortage of sergeants in particular. Young officers who had been fast-tracked by Hitler had received little or no strategic training. Troops struggled with new technologies such as the supersonic Starfighter, of which nearly three hundred crashed in the 1960s, with many fatalities. In 1962, *Der Spiegel* leaked a damning report after NATO exercises which found the army's capacity for defense to be "limited."[52] This sparked a political scandal that began with the illegal search of the magazine's offices—the editor was wrongfully thrown in prison for treason for 103 days—and ended with the resignation of Franz Josef Strauss, the defense minister. Disciplinary breaches in the young army were on the rise. The public was shocked by several cases of routine brutality. In 1957, fifteen soldiers died when their sergeant ordered them to ford the cold and raging River Iller in full battle gear; senior officers had not objected to the practice. Parachutists were made to jump and squawk like frogs, others had to do push-ups over knives. In 1963, a parachutist died after he collapsed on an extreme march and an officer had beaten him trying to make him continue.[53] The incident led to the dissolution of the training company 6/9, an unprecedented step in the annals of the German military.

Above all, the Bundeswehr suffered from an identity crisis. Was it a newborn servant of democracy or a proud upholder of military tradition?

The confusion extended to the most basic detail of correct behavior. Some insisted that soldiers salute all superior officers; others wanted to see such respect reserved for commanding officers only. The result was confusion and embarrassment. When the German navy visited the Netherlands in 1959, the men saluted neither their Dutch allies nor other German officers, to the bewilderment of both.[54] In the past, military ritual had been a source of public pride. The Bundeswehr's first hundred volunteers, by contrast, were sworn in inside a vehicle shed behind a barrack fence. It was as if the young army was trying to hide from public view.

Recruitment mirrored these tensions. Vocal antisemites were rejected, but, overall, interviewers cared more about battle experience than attitudes. In the first two years, the Bundeswehr accepted 125,000 veteran soldiers and 37,000 officers. Thirty-one of thirty-eight of its generals had served on Hitler's general staff. Eighty percent of all commanding officers in 1961 had been decorated with the Iron Cross first class, and they carried forward ideas as well as medals. The leadership academy (*Führungsakademie*) of the new army was modeled on the training for the general staff designed in 1936.[55]

Yet a new spirit was trying to assert itself. Its champion was Wolf Count von Baudissin. Born into an old noble family in Saxony, Baudissin joined the army in the Weimar years. He was one of Rommel's men, serving on the general staff of the Afrika Korps, and was captured in 1941. He spent the next six years in a POW camp in Australia. When he was back in West Germany, he developed the concept of "*Innere Führung*" ("leading in a civic spirit"), which sought to put the army on democratic foundations. Soldiers were to see themselves as "citizens in uniform" rather than as a separate caste of warriors. There could be no unconditional obedience, as under Hitler. Bundeswehr soldiers pledged "to defend the rights and freedom of the German *Volk*."[56] Criminal orders had to be resisted. The officers who had plotted to assassinate Hitler became the official touchstone for that democratic self-understanding.

Baudissin, unfortunately, was surrounded by a tight-knit group of decorated officers who had a low opinion of him as a soldier and took their inspiration from the past instead. One of them was his deputy, Heinz Karst. Before fighting under Hitler, many officers had served in Weimar's Reichswehr, some even under the Kaiser. Breaking the oath of allegiance went against the core of their military ethos. When in 1957 a chapel was consecrated for the two Stauffenberg brothers, Claus and Berthold, near the family castle, officers were conspicuous by their absence. In 1969, the General of the Mountain Infantry Hellmut Grashey earned applause from fellow officers when he declared that the men of July 20 had no honor. That a soldier did not question orders remained the mantra at the very top in the Bundeswehr. Duty was fundamental for Ulrich de Maizière, who as general inspector was the highest ranking officer (he was the brother of Clemens, the Stasi lawyer in the GDR mentioned earlier). In his view, it was impossible for a soldier to have a conflict of conscience.[57] In brief, the Bundeswehr had a clear view of what they were fighting against—the communist threat—far less than what they were fighting for.

In 1969, the traditionalists went on the offensive with an explosive memorandum. Defense took priority over democratic values, they wrote. Civilian values had been allowed to dangerously soften the military spirit. A soldier was first and foremost a fighter. To restore discipline, they wanted separate military justice. The Federal Republic rebuffed the challenge to its democratic authority. Karst chose early retirement. The showdown brought to light how far the army still was from embracing democratic values, but also that West German democracy was robust enough to prevent the Bundeswehr from becoming a state within a state.

Tradition and ritual were the flashpoints in these battles over the soul of the new army. For elite troops especially, their regiments' past accomplishments were a core part of their identity. Given the army's involvement in war crimes, tradition was a sensitive issue. Tank troops, for example, adored General Heinz Guderian for his Blitzkrieg strategy, but he also ordered the shooting of prisoners and civilians. Fifteen years after the war, *Panzer* magazine quoted approvingly from the final Wehrmacht communiqué of May 9, 1945, with its call for unconditional loyalty to the end. In its search for an appropriate tradition, the young Bundeswehr was pulled back and forth. Some wanted to see soldiers put their hands flat against the seam of their trousers when they stood at attention, as in the past, while others preferred to see a closed fist as a sign of change. Officers were allowed to wear their old medals as long as the swastika was removed; it was often replaced with a cross. The officer training center displayed flags from East and West Prussian regiments. In 1958, the "Panzerlied" fell foul of the *Innere Führung* for glorifying military attack and was removed from the army songbook, though soldiers were not forbidden to sing it. Five years later, the song was back, shorn of the final stanza where a deadly bullet turns the tank into a grave; the song would be banned again in 2017 in a renewed effort to root out right-wing elements.

There *were* winds of change. Soldiers got their own trade union, to the dismay of old-school officers. There was greater respect for the private sphere. From 1970 onward, after a series of protests from recruits, soldiers no longer had to submit a written declaration that their bride had an "unchallenged reputation" and came from "an honorable family," only that they intended to marry. Recruits arrived with mop tops, and Allied troops joked about the "German Hair Force." In 1971, the army tried to accommodate them with an ordinance for olive-green hairnets. A year later, a more practical regulation took effect: hair could not touch the collar of the uniform.[58]

In 1965, a general decree on tradition was passed, an acrobatic balancing act between new democratic commitment and old military values. Its author was Defense Minister Kai-Uwe von Hassel, a Christian Democrat. Born in German East Africa to an officer of the brutal colonial troops, he served as an interpreter in Admiral Wilhelm Canaris's military secret service during the Second World War, earning an Iron Cross second class. Tradition, the decree began, was the "record of a valid heritage" and enabled a soldier "to understand and fulfill the commands dictated by the present." It required respect for both the "accomplishments and suffering of the past." Soldiers needed to fulfill their "duties conscientiously for the sake of a rational command." However, an officer who broke his oath ("to defend the right and freedom of the German people") could be disobeyed. The Bundeswehr, in this view, resumed the principle of "freedom in obedience," a German military tradition until the Nazis. Here were direct nods to the men of July 20 and to General von Seydlitz under Frederick II. The soldier had to be a "politically thinking and acting citizen," echoing Baudissin's ideal. At the same time, the decree praised knightly conduct and loyalty. The basic attitudes that mattered included tolerance, justice, and respect for the dignity of man, but equally "courage and sacrifice… restraint in appearance and lifestyle, [and] self-discipline in mind, body, and language." Soldiers were urged to cultivate relations with all their former comrades; no club of the former Wehrmacht was to be excluded. "The veterans should see that the Bundeswehr appreciates their soldierly achievement and sacrifice."[59]

The decree put politics into the Bundeswehr and took it out of the Wehrmacht. It tried to have respect for both democracy and Hitler's soldiers. It was only in 1982 that a new decree would acknowledge that parts of the army had been "entangled in guilt"; even then, though, military customs continued to be treated as separate from the Wehrmacht's crimes, and its helmets could be found in regiments' "memorabilia rooms." Barracks bore the names not only of Stauffenberg but also of Nazi generals and war criminals, such as General Eduard Dietl, whose mountain corps executed slave labor and penal soldiers in Norway and Finland; the barracks were renamed "Allgäu-Kaserne" after its Swabian home in 1995, following a decade of protests. The fighter pilot Werner Mölders, the first to be honored by Hitler with the Knight's Cross of the Iron Cross with Oak Leaves, Swords, and Diamonds, had a destroyer and an entire fighter wing named after him.[60]

BETWEEN DISCIPLINE AND DEMOCRACY

So much for the view from the top. But what did being a soldier mean to the rank and file of the Bundeswehr? In 1961, some fifty NCOs wrote an essay as part of their seminars on *Innere Führung*: "How has the position of the soldier in the German *Volk* changed in the last fifty years?" Most of these men had signed up for a number of years and were on their way to becoming sergeants. Their answers capture the range of military ideals considered valid then. Some respected the men of July 20—at the time, one wrote, the "conscience of many Germans... only belonged to one party and its ideology" and the resisters were "damned and cursed," but now it was clear that they had grasped their oath in "its highest and purest form." They gave West Germany "the moral right" to have an army, said another, echoing the official view.

Many, though, reached different conclusions. Hitler might have waged an unjust war, but the soldier's values lived on: "courage, obedience, loyalty, a sense of duty, and camaraderie." In the Second World War, their actions had been "clean," and all Germans, including conscientious objectors, should feel pride in how they had "resisted the large enemy so courageously."[61] One Bundeswehr soldier's favorite book was a war novel about a group of fighter pilots. What he liked about it, he explained, was that the men knew "that they were serving a cause that was condemned to fail" but nonetheless kept fighting. Their sense of "honor and shame" gave them "composure" (*Haltung*) and made them the "inner victors."[62] The tough, selfless soldier was needed more than ever to save civilization from the avalanche building in the East because the middle classes were too well fed, "degenerate," and "remote-controlled" by various interests—a classic antisemitic trope. One soldier concluded his essay with a personal poem:

> Be proud of the deeds of your fathers,
> Who faithfully fulfilled their duties,
> And stood for Germany as soldiers,
> Do not think of glory and advantage...
> Protect the country, protect your loved ones,
> Think of the Suffering of the German East,

Help all who have been driven out by force:
Then you will be Germany's loyal son![63]

The "best" essays selected for publication in 1962 covered topics from the United Nations to the future of engine power. The opening article, though, was about marriage and came from a thirty-three-year-old sergeant who belonged to the generation that had manned anti-aircraft guns in the final stages of the Second World War. For him, the soldier was the vital antidote to a "modern worldview" that promoted a mass culture of "inwardly uniformed people . . . who dance around the Golden Calf." A soldier, by contrast, won his "inner freedom" through the "courage of obedience." Affluence was like a cancer eating away at the "cell" of society: the family. As a father and creator of the community, the soldier had a special duty to ensure that marriage and family stayed "clean." Before tying the knot, a soldier and his bride needed to make sure they met the "physical, psychological, . . . and moral and social requirements." The sergeant suggested that it might be helpful to set a minimum age or military rank, or give the commanding officer veto power.[64]

The civil ethos of *Innere Führung* might be an ideal, one soldier wrote in 1961, but in reality the soldier's first duty was to the German *Volk*. They were not regular citizens, others added. "Being a soldier is not a job but a quality [*Eigenschaft*]," another said, and that set them above ordinary civilians. A "soldier has to be trained to be hard." For most recruits, *Innere Führung* meant comradeship, not citizenship.[65] Officers believed that it would take another fifty years to reach that civic ideal. It remains a work in progress to this day.[66]

The German soldier was changing, but not in one direction. On the one hand, there were unreconstructed militarists. For one lieutenant colonel, a soldier should always and only be guided by what was best "for my men, my unit, my fatherland." When an officer took hostages and had them executed in reprisal against partisan attacks, he wrote, this was entirely justified because inaction would have weakened the fighting strength of his troops and made him "a murderer of his own men." The battlefield was no place for law or human rights. On the other hand, there were those for whom individual conscience, law, and respect for human life were what made a true soldier. The humane treatment of prisoners and civilians was a critical test of their ethics, one soldier wrote. For other recruits, moral action arose from religious conscience. It was conscience alone, one soldier explained, that showed man where to find "the good" by freeing him from all earthly ties. Communism with its materialist worldview was so dangerous because its fixation on the "here and now" turned off that divine inner voice.

The soldiers in between these two poles tried to graft new ideals onto old ones. In 1963, sergeants were asked to critically compare Ernst Jünger's *Storm of Steel* (*In Stahlgewittern*, 1920), a classic portrayal of brave and brutal combat in the First World War, with Pierre Henri Simon's recent *Portrait of an Officer* (1961), which followed a French officer's moral conflicts through the Second World War and Indochina. Soldier No. 265's solution was to take elements from both: from Jünger, courage and sacrifice; from Simon, conscience as a guide to action. The problem of inner conflict would disappear, he wrote, once politicians and generals stopped giving "unlawful and unworthy" orders.[67]

In 1963, young recruits were asked about their role models. Among public figures, the humanitarian doctor and critic of the nuclear bomb Albert Schweitzer led with 27 percent. He was ahead of Rommel (18 percent), who was admired for his willpower, skill, and "courageous" death. Stauffenberg ranked well below, at 2 percent, tied with Kirk Douglas; the politicians Adenauer and Brandt scored 4 percent. When it came to social roles, fathers routinely trumped sports and film stars as well as teachers and military superiors. A role model was expected to care as well as lead—"he should love his fellow man . . . and possess authority," one soldier said. The ideal was the "whole man," someone who was father, friend, and comrade in one.[68]

Many of the Bundeswehr's first generation arrived as soldiers hardened by the Second World War. Others were novices who grudgingly accepted military service or had their ideals quashed by it. It was "shocking," a young man who had signed up to train as a reserve officer confided to his diary in 1963, how in the space of six months, his "interest in the place has radically faded and the last bit of idealism has been killed completely." It was "pointless nonsense," with "barely any space for personal initiative." The one thing he learned about was being bullied. When he left in 1964, he felt two years had been "stolen" from him.[69]

There were also, however, civilians who were turned into professional soldiers by the Bundeswehr. Erich Hinkel was seventeen when he signed up for twelve years of service in 1956. He did not have any military ideals when he arrived at the barracks gate. For him, the army was a gateway to a better life. He had left school at thirteen to work in a shoe factory where he earned 35 DM a week, part of which he gave to his parents. In the Bundeswehr, he would earn 120 DM a week and enjoy free food and lodging. In addition, the seminars for sergeants promised him education. Most of his family and coworkers thought he was "crazy." His family had been bombed out, and his grandfather and great-uncle had lost their lives in the war. Only his father, who had fought on the Eastern Front and returned as a POW in 1949, approved. Hinkel left the army in 1969, a sergeant. He had learned to carry out all functions in the motorized infantry, was decorated with the golden marksmanship award, and could shoot with everything from a pistol to a bazooka; he was also qualified to lead the unit assigned for defense against "ABC" weapons: atomic, biological, and chemical. He wore his uniform with pride and was married in it.[70]

In his recollections, he took stock of his experiences in the late 1950s and 1960s. While old war songs were prohibited, fascist songs from the Spanish civil war remained common. So was the Silesian nationalist hymn. Other men, however, sang along to the "Moorsoldaten," a marching song written by communist concentration camp prisoners in 1933. To keep a sense of greater Germany alive, his first commanding officer ordered each company to adopt a region from the lost territories—Hinkel ended up with East Prussia—and they decorated their walls with pictures of Königsberg and the Tannenberg monument. He and his comrades also went to see the antiwar movie *The Bridge*. Tradition was a good thing, he concluded, as long as it served a just purpose. Personally he wanted to see greater recognition for the leaders of the Peasants' War (1524–25) such as Florian Geyer, a noble knight (he was one of Hitler's favorites, too). Hinkel was among the few who did not see the men of July 20 as traitors. A military leader was not always right, and the Wehrmacht had not been completely "clean," he noted. The Bundeswehr, he felt, needed to show "moral courage" and learn from mistakes. Most men in his regiment saw conscientious objectors as shirkers, although they agreed that a democracy needed to make allowances for them. "Courage without justice is the lever of evil," he quoted Thomas Aquinas, the medieval philosopher.[71]

He went along with the *Innere Führung*, up to a point. Their task was to defend justice and freedom, not blindly follow any military offensive. Nonetheless, it was impossible to have a truly democratic army, he felt, because an army needed order and discipline. The soldier was a citizen with a special duty and mission that included the ultimate sacrifice. He preferred to translate *Innere Führung* as "inner mission" and "inner decency." Beatings with a belt went "too far," but forcing a recruit with a casual attitude to "cleanliness" into a cold shower was a "well-proven educational measure." Discipline and respect placed limits on individual rights and freedoms.

In 1968, he was assigned a long-haired driver. He ordered him to take a shower and get his hair cut. The driver refused, on the grounds that the order had no official rationale and violated the free development of his personality; the latter point echoed Article 2 of the constitution. Hinkel complained to his superior, who told him to relax. After sleeping it over, he went to the company commander. He told him that he could not be expected to sit next to an "unwashed and uncombed" soldier and would refuse, if necessary; his own "human dignity" counted more than the right to develop one's personality. After short deliberation, he was assigned a new driver.[72]

Sergeant Hinkel left the Bundeswehr in 1969, in what would turn into one of its most tumultuous years. First came the traditionalist assault by Generals Heinz Karst and Albert Schnez. Then, in the spring of 1970, there was a counteroffensive by a group of young lieutenants whose "Nine Theses" articulated the new democratic spirit: "I want to be an officer," their fourth thesis read, "who can question the conduct of a superior and allows his own conduct to be the subject of critique by a subordinate or anyone else." Officers should "not only maintain peace but help create it"; the best Bundeswehr was one "that never stops asking when it will dissolve itself" (the seventh thesis). Widely discussed on television, in newspapers, and inside barracks, the theses of the so-called Leutnant 70 wanted all soldiers to learn about conflict resolution without the use of military force.

Their commanding officer at the academy, General Hans Hinrichs, was outraged. "Natural authority" was crucial for an officer, he told journalists. Angry veterans sensed a collapse of discipline and order. By contrast, Minister of Defense Helmut Schmidt, who had served as a lieutenant with a tank regiment on the Eastern Front, welcomed the "Nine Theses," believing they showed how well the army had become integrated into democratic society. The spokesman of the democratic lieutenants, Anton Uthemann, finished at the top of his class in the officers' academy. It fell to the traditionalist Schnez, as chief of staff, to congratulate him and present him with the customary gold watch. Tradition had some benefits, after all.[73]

Soldiering became task oriented and, as such, no different from a civilian job in engineering or management. Loyalty and duty were toward a rational goal, no longer to a person only because of their rank. Where a ritual had lost its purpose, it needed to go. What was the point, the young lieutenants asked, of making a tank soldier present a rifle on parade if in battle he did not have one? The Leutnant 70 struck a chord because they chimed with modernizing ideas circulating at the time. In "Soldier for Peace," Baudissin spelled out the skills for these new times: thinking and acting in a changing division of labor. Instead of a top-down hierarchy of command, decisions were shared horizontally. "Teamwork" entered the German vocabulary.[74] In its "White Book" on the army in 1970, the key document on national security, Brandt's social-liberal coalition confirmed the verdict of the military commissioner (*Wehrbeauftragter*), a kind of parliamentary ombudsman for the Bundeswehr: "Cooperation and coordination come before automatic obedience." The troops of the past were giving way to "soldiers as specialists," who worked together in "different teams." Camaraderie was joined by "partnership."[75]

There was a whiff of 1968 here, with the critique of authority and its embrace of group discussion. Mainly, though, the army was marching in step with the advanced industrial society West Germany was turning into. In an era of technocrats and managers, the traditional officer was giving way to the military expert. What mattered were skills and merit, not birth and seniority. Ironically, the democratic Federal Republic reaped the benefits of Hitler's social revolution, which had broken the old elite's hold on the officer corps. Before Hitler, aristocrats had made up 25 percent of the German officer corps. By 1944, the number had fallen to 7 percent as the Führer promoted new men on the basis of fighting spirit and fanaticism. By 1964, it had sunk to 3 percent.[76] It was clerks, not aristocrats, who now became lieutenants. Being an officer ceased to be a family calling and became a job.

Social mobility was aided by the modernization of officer training. Schmidt and General Inspector de Maizière founded dedicated army universities where aspiring officers learned about economics and international relations as well as strategy, supported by generous stipends.[77] The number of students with an *Abitur* who signed up for twelve years shot up instantly. For the first time, the Bundeswehr went on a publicity campaign. In 1974, "open days" attracted more than a million visitors to barracks, and soldiers gave three thousand lectures to public audiences. Thousands of schools were visited by "youth officers" (*Jugendoffiziere*).[78] The rebranding and growing popularity of the army was remarkable, though the peace movement was very much in evidence.

At best tolerated, at worst hated, in its early years, by 1977 the Bundeswehr was considered "important" or "very important" by 79 percent of the population surveyed.[79]

REACTION

A not-insignificant minority felt estranged or, worse, betrayed by the army's new democratic spirit. Neo-Nazis in Germany failed to attract the electoral support necessary to cross the 5 percent threshold to gain a seat in the federal parliament—the closest they came was 4.3 percent in 1969. But, to be sure, there were rumblings in the undergrowth of local politics. Today's populism taps into older frustrations with the shift in values. The election of the fascist National Democratic Party (NPD) to regional assemblies, the fall in voter participation in national elections—1972: 91 percent; 1987: 84 percent—and the breakaway of the right-wing Republicans from the Bavarian CSU in 1983 hinted at the existence of this hinterland.

In 1965, a group of young people in Kiel challenged Waffen-SS veterans to a public debate over their annual silent march for their dead comrades. For those young people, remembrance of the war was a "moral question" and they wanted the veterans to show their historical responsibility by instead joining a march for the victims in a spirit of atonement. This was not the moral conclusion drawn by everyone. An architect who had lost his son in the war thanked the veterans for their "heroic and knightly" fight against Bolshevism. At least, a young man added, the veterans had an ideal they were fighting for, unlike his own generation.[80]

In towns and cities in the 1970s, Christian Democrats and many Liberal Partys fought tooth and nail against initiatives that sought to alter or remove war memorials. Even in Social Democratic Hamburg, a counter-memorial would only be unveiled in 1985, and even that was not strictly for the victims of Nazism, but represented locals who had died in the firestorm as well as camp inmates who died when the *Cap Arcona* was erroneously sunk by the British in the final week of the war (the Nazis had moved the prisoners to the ship hoping to eliminate evidence of the camps, and there were plans to blow them up). The following year, young Christian Democrats in Bremen called the idea of a monument for executed "deserters" a "mockery of all those who had fallen in the war."[81]

The last head of state of the Third Reich, Admiral Karl Dönitz, Hitler's brief successor, died on Christmas Eve in 1980. A convicted war criminal, he was released in 1956 and retired to Aumühle, at the outskirts of Hamburg, close to where Bismarck had lived out his final years. In 1963, in one of his rare public appearances, Dönitz gave a personal history lesson to a high school in Geesthacht in northern Germany. Teachers, students, and locals found nothing wrong with it. It was only when *Le Monde* and national magazines seized on the event as typifying the fascist mind-set in a provincial town that it turned into a scandal; the school director, who had not invited the admiral but had given his permission, committed suicide after an article unfairly portrayed him as a Nazi.[82]

When Admiral Erich Raeder, a fellow war criminal, died in 1960, a *Bundeswehr* vice admiral, Friedrich Ruge, spoke at the funeral. Ruge, remarkably, had served continuously in the German navy since joining as a cadet under the Kaiser in April 1914. By the time of Dönitz's funeral on January 6, 1981, West Germany was in many ways a changed society. For the first time, the Ministry of Defense was headed by someone who had not served in the war, Hans Apel, a Social Democrat who announced that Dönitz would be buried without the military honors normally accorded to holders of the Knight's Cross. Soldiers of the Bundeswehr were forbidden from attending in uniform. The official line was that ordinary men might say they had been deceived by Hitler, but not a supreme commander.[83]

The official rebuke did not stop five thousand people from flocking to Aumühle to pay their last respects. They included old comrades, a general and rear admiral of the Bundeswehr in civilian dress, and a couple of officers in uniform who were disciplined afterward. The student president who had invited Dönitz to speak at his school seventeen years earlier, Uwe Barschel, was by then minister of the interior in Schleswig-Holstein and, allegedly, appeared incognito with top hat and false beard. Outraged citizens vented their anger at the "shameful" and "undignified" snub of Dönitz in letters to the press and to the head of state, President Karl Carstens. Sympathizers wanted to believe that Dönitz had saved many thousands of civilians in the spring of 1945—expellees from East Prussia awarded the admiral their highest honor, the Prussian Shield. It has since been shown that, if anything, Dönitz obstructed the rescue operation across the Baltic by prioritizing fuel to fight on in the West.[84] The reactions of those who were upset ranged from a defense of military values and a denial of war guilt to a wider sense of moral crisis. How could Carstens attend the funeral of the Yugoslav dictator and "mass murderer" Josip Tito the previous year yet stay away from that of Dönitz, a loyal patriot and his predecessor? Others blamed the war on Britain and "world Jewry." If Dönitz and Hitler were war criminals, what about Winston Churchill? "In the whole world former soldiers are honored," a woman wrote, "except in Germany, which is shameful"; her brother had died in the submarine war. The "defamation of all soldiers" had to stop. Had the Bundeswehr not happily taken on many veterans? A man who had fought four years on the Eastern Front said he was "ashamed to be a German today."

History and commemoration were proxy wars in a battle over moral change. Duty, loyalty, and respect were under threat. "What kind of state has this become!" Edith H. lamented in her letter of complaint. "I recognize authority because I respect the constitution," but all she saw around her was "alcohol, drugs, abortion, porn, kidnapping, terrorism, in short, a general state of immorality!" Why did everything that made "our *Volk* great" always need to be dragged into the gutter? "I also see a deadly danger in being swamped by foreigners [*Überfremdung*]." Others said that legal toleration of abortion and homosexuality had made them "disillusioned with the state [*staatsverdrossen*]." Not all of these voices came from unreconstructed veterans or pensioners. A thirty-year-old truck driver wrote that he had done his military service with pride in the early 1970s but now felt "disappointment, shame, and anger," which had freed him, as he put it, from "democratic thinking." "This state is dead to me. In future, I would rather get arrested than pick up a gun for this rundown club, let alone use it." He would have loved to throw his military passport in Apel's face in person but, unable to do that, was returning it by mail.[85]

RED PRUSSIA

The GDR had no such qualms about the military. In a socialist country, soldier and nation were one and indivisible. It was an honor as well as a duty to defend the achievements of workers and peasants. Militarism pervaded society. While West Germany was trying to make the soldier a citizen, East Germany was turning its citizens into fighters, with workers' battle regiments and military exercises for schoolchildren. The calendar for pioneers reminded six- to fourteen-year-olds in 1973 that "fighting is good."[86] More than any other institution it was the army that provided the GDR with its heroes, including the peasant leader Thomas Müntzer in 1525; the Prussian reformer Gerhard von Scharnhorst, who introduced general conscription during the Napoleonic wars; the Baden revolutionaries in 1848; the sailors in the mutiny of 1917; the "Communist Bandit" Max Hoelz with his combat groups in an uprising in 1920.[87] When the GDR prepared for the possibility of a war in 1968, it minted fresh medals in advance and named them after Gebhard von Blücher,[88] the Prussian field marshal who fought Napoleon in the wars of liberation. Hitler's Wehrmacht was seen as a short-lived aberration. Honor, duty, sacrifice, and obedience were dusted off and given a new lease on life in the service of class struggle. Fittingly, the Nationale Volksarmee (NVA, National People's Army) was known as "Red Prussians."

The NVA was not launched until 1956, in response to the Bundeswehr, with conscription following six years later, after the Berlin Wall went up. Remilitarization, though, got underway the moment the war was over. The Soviet authorities established a "People's Police" in the summer of 1945. Five years later, there were some 100,000 armed police in barracks, ten times that in West Germany. The bulk of them were returning POWs, targeted for their war experience and often pressed into service.[89] The leadership of the East German army proper, however, marked a break with the past. In stark contrast with the Bundeswehr, only 3 percent of NVA officers had served in the Wehrmacht, and even fewer in Weimar's Reichswehr.[90] While the navy and air force were popular, promising adventure and skills, in the late 1970s and 1980s the NVA found it increasingly hard to convince young men to swap a civilian career for ten years' service in the army.

Alongside the army, there were the Combat Groups of the Working Class (Kampfgruppen der Arbeiterklasse). They were set up after the uprising in 1953 as a military reserve to defend enterprises and guard border regions against the class enemy. Hungary and Czechoslovakia, the other two countries where the socialist rulers were almost overthrown, had similar paramilitary bodies. Initially, discipline was poor—in 1958, half the "fighters" did not show up for exercises. While a few thousand guarded the Wall as it went up, a few hundred used the chance to flee.[91] Discipline stepped up after the Wall. The Kampfgruppen were trained to shoot with machine guns and air defense weapons, and had their own medals and ceremonies. Some saw service as their socialist duty; for others it was an obligation sweetened by a bit of manly sociability. The 200,000 "fighters" more than matched the strength of the NVA under Erich Honecker. Whether their fighting ability came close is more doubtful.

Rearmament triggered some resistance. In the mid-1950s, some workers refused to join the Kampfgruppen. In Thuringia, youth damaged an official shooting range. When young men were pressed to volunteer for military service in 1961, a group of pupils in Anklam, near the Baltic coast, appeared in school dressed in black to show they were carrying their future to the grave. Their entire class was expelled, the ringleader sentenced to three years in prison, and several teachers were fired.[92] In the following two years, some three thousand young men refused to do their military service, at the risk of a prison sentence. In 1964, the government stopped criminalizing conscientious objectors as long as they agreed to serve in a noncombat role, as so-called *Bausoldaten* ("construction soldiers"). Overall, however, the GDR lacked the civil society space necessary for any sustained opposition to militarism, until the peace movement of the early 1980s.

The state militarized more and more spheres of social life. The Society for Sport and Technology (Gesellschaft für Sport und Technik) was founded in 1952. Beneath its innocent name lurked a mass paramilitary body. It started out as a voluntary affair to prepare young workers for military defense, but that changed after the Prague uprising of 1968. For apprentices and students with an *Abitur*, training became obligatory. NVA General Lieutenant Günther Teller was put in charge of the society. The industrial-technological revolution, he explained, made it more important than ever that military training start well before the army. What was needed was greater discipline, better qualified teachers, and, especially, the "political-moral education of the next generation of professional soldiers."[93] In practice, this meant more lessons and exercises. The society became a recruiting ground for the army proper. In 1977, premilitary training consisted of sixty hours of drill practice, shooting, crossing terrain, and bandaging wounds. Those who had signed up for officer training had another fifty-six hours to complete that included diving and parachuting. The society had more than half a million members, its own guns, trucks, motorboats, and gliders. (Several courageous souls put their knowledge of lift and thermals to unexpected use and flew into exile across the border to the West.)

In a handbook, the army explained *The Meaning of Being a Soldier* to each new crop of recruits and their families. They could be proud of being "the first German army in the service of the people." Instead of carrying arms for big business and feudal Junkers, they, the sons of workers and peasants, enjoyed the constitutional right to defend their own interests. "Orders had to be executed unreservedly," and "there cannot be any discussion, no ifs or buts." This was different, though, from the "blind obedience" of the fascist and imperialist enemy. Since socialism had supposedly put an end to exploitation, obedience was an expression of freedom. "Our obedience arises from the mutual interests of the free citizens in our state."

The socialist army was by definition a defender of the peace. It was inconceivable that an officer would ever order his men to fight in a war of conquest; it was simply "incompatible" with their class position. This defensive philosophy was silent about weapons of mass destruction, which would kill far more than the class enemy. In exercises in the early 1980s officers had to swear to use nuclear weapons if necessary, and tactical atomic weapons were part of the GDR's strategic plan to break through enemy lines.[94]

The orders directed against citizens inside the GDR went unmentioned. "Who does not respect our border, will get to feel the bullet," as Heinz Hoffmann, the minister of defense, put it. Hoffmann was the personification of the GDR's militarist ethos. In 1933, a communist machine fitter, he first went underground and then to the Soviet Union. He returned to East Germany after the war a trained officer. It was Hoffmann who was charged with the development of the armed police in the early years of the GDR, and who headed the Ministry of Defense under both Ulbricht and Honecker; his death in 1985 saved him from prosecution for his order to shoot-to-kill wall jumpers. "Never forget where you belong," he told pupils at a coming-of-age ceremony in Brandenburg in 1972, "and never lose sight of who is your friend and who is your foe!" He wanted young people to remember their precious peaceful childhood: "None ever heard from their mother's mouth the anxious question: Will we survive this bombing attack?" They only knew peace and security. Those who dreamed of fashionable clothes or a television were miserable human beings. Was it not far nobler to know that their help with the harvest and recycling improved "all our lives and will soon bring peace to the children in Vietnam!"[95]

"Struggle" occupied a central place in the socialist lexicon. The step-up in the militarization of society in the 1970s was a reaction partly to the protests in Prague, partly to the diminishing hold of the *Feindbild* ("image of the enemy") at home. Justifying a potential fight against their German brothers across the border had always required ideological acrobatics. "Our enemy is imperialism," the NVA explained, and this included West Germany, which continued in the fascist and militarist footsteps of the earlier world wars. The enemy were not merely capitalists and generals but also regular Bundeswehr soldiers, who had been injected with the poison of imperialism. "We are therefore not fighting against 'Germans,'" the NVA said, but "against mercenaries of imperialism." Taken together, the attempts to ease tensions between the United States and the Soviet Union (known as détente), Willy Brandt's acceptance of the Oder-Neisse line as the eastern border with Poland, the Helsinki Accords of 1975, and Western peace movements meant that the fascist enemy was starting to look less terrifying. Young men accepted premilitary training, the head of the Society for Sport and Technology told the Ministry of Defense in 1979, but their image of the enemy was "not clearly enough defined in terms of class... Hatred of the enemy is poorly developed." Almost half of them thought that a military confrontation with West Germany was "not likely." Others felt that the Soviet Union offered sufficient protection and that they could do more for socialism by following a civilian career.[96] The vast majority of pupils agreed that peace required military defense. However, those who said they were prepared to sign up as an officer dropped from 37 percent in sixth grade to 7 percent in the tenth. And those tended to be students at the bottom of the class.[97]

From preschool to high school, there was a militarist campaign. Nursery school children got toy soldiers and visited real ones in their barracks. In one game, children sat in a circle and, one after the other, moved to the center, singing, "When I am big... I will drive a tank, *ra-ta-ta, ra-ta-ta*... when I am big, I will load the cannon, *rum-bum-bum*," and so forth. In their advice columns, women's magazines told mothers to familiarize their children with the army to help them develop a "picture of friend versus foe." "Already the preschool child knows that soldiers protect our homeland." West German veterans had the "Song of the Old Comrade," young pioneers in East Germany that of the "Little Trumpeter," an original tune from the First World

War to which socialists added a stanza that the soldier's death in battle had not been in vain: socialist youth completed his task. In the children's magazine *Bummi*, the cuddly bear told stories about how the soldiers of the NVA were watching over them so they could sleep in peace. There were dolls in uniform, coloring books like *Daddy Is a Soldier* (1976), and books about tank commanders. Young pioneers who were really keen could climb into a Schützenpanzer SPW 152 and drive about in the half-sized armored vehicle during May Day demonstrations.[98]

Militarization reached its climax in 1978 with a directive that made military lessons a compulsory part of the school curriculum. In ninth grade, all fourteen- and fifteen-year-olds received eight hours of military education a year. In addition, boys had to attend a twelve-day-long military camp, girls one for civil defense. Three days of military preparedness (*Wehrbereitschaft*) followed in tenth grade. Some pastors and parents saw it as a radical step, but military education had been expanding across the Eastern bloc in the preceding decade. Poland and Czechoslovakia started their lessons even earlier, in sixth and seventh grade, and Bulgarian children spent twice as long as their East German peers in military training.[99] In the GDR, premilitary competitions had already been introduced in high schools in 1967. In these "Hans-Beimler Wettkämpfe," named after a communist who died in the Spanish civil war, children shot with air rifles and small-bore weapons and threw practice hand grenades. A ten-kilometer endurance march was added in the early 1970s.

Against the background of this steady buildup, the sudden protests in 1978 against the new military lessons took the authorities by surprise. There was grumbling at parents' evenings in schools and in churches, and a rise in formal complaints, sometimes signed by an entire congregation. In church services across the land, letters critical of the new directive were read out. In Frankfurt (Oder), the head of the church urged his flock not to submit. In Mecklenburg, congregations sang the third verse of an old church song: "Even if the enemy is pressing us, we will not succumb to fear."[100]

These critical voices gained strength from three sources. The first was the new "rights talk" triggered by the GDR constitution of 1968, which explicitly defended freedom of conscience and religion. How could a socialist state possibly force military training on all pupils, regardless of their beliefs? Second, there were the Helsinki Accords, which the GDR had signed to much fanfare. The new directive put them in an impossible situation, church leaders told the minister for church affairs. How, wondered Bishop Albrecht Schönherr, the head of the Protestant Church in the GDR, could he continue to assure churches abroad that "the GDR is not preparing for war" if aggression and hatred were preached in its classrooms? The churches supported national defense, he said. However, the new lessons were a "militarization of thought." Young minds might end up "glorifying everything military." It also made it harder for the bishops to quiet the young hotspurs among their priests.[101] Finally, the potential of nuclear weapons for mass destruction undermined the socialist defense of "just war." "In a world full of weapons," the Protestant Churches said in their official guidance in 1978, "force as a means of conflict resolution is self-destructive." Military security called instead for mutual trust. "Thinking in clichés of 'friend' and 'foe' makes one incapable of recognizing the shared responsibility of all for the world of tomorrow."[102]

Here were the first signs of the peace circles that would help bring down communism a decade later. In 1978, however, the regime was still firmly in the saddle and saw no need to recall the directive. If the affair brought to light critical voices, it also showed how marginal and easily contained they still were. At a parents' evening in a school in Saalfeld, Thuringia, for example, the Protestant bishop and his wife criticized the military lessons as "a slap in the face" of their children. The chair of the parents' committee and the school director quickly silenced them.[103] The matter was closed. In the small town of Neschwitz, in Saxony, the local pastor, the organist, and a theology student decided to send a joint letter to Honecker. They asked him to reconsider whether the new military lessons were "really necessary" and look into prohibiting toy tanks and soldiers instead. Their suggestion earned them a long lecture by the local party bosses, who clarified for them the nature of the "international class struggle and the role of the GDR as an agent of peace in Europe." The three expressed their "gratitude" for the exposition, although the officials doubted that they were genuinely persuaded.[104]

Christianity had steadily lost its influence in East Germany, and in the few places where the churches continued to matter, the SED was able to count on support from their leaders. There were only so many outspoken young pastors, and those were monitored closely. The authorities received no more than 2,500 letters about military education—a tiny fraction compared to complaints about poor housing. In one school in the district of Freiberg (Saxony), the entire tenth grade stood united and refused to take part in the military lessons.[105] Such open defiance, however, was extremely rare. Official visitations found good discipline in almost all schools. In the entire district of Karl-Marx-Stadt—a region with almost 2 million inhabitants—only fifty-nine pupils refused to participate in the lessons.[106] Most skeptical parents and pupils would not risk losing a university place or a decent apprenticeship.

THE KEY TO HELL

In May 1958, a delegation of the city of Frankfurt returned from a two-week trip to Hiroshima. City councilors were accompanied by public figures such as Eugen Kogon. Brochures produced by the German city showed harrowing pictures of deformed heads and young girls dying of their burns. Locals' experience of wartime bombing was nothing compared to it, they explained. A single nuclear bomb like the one dropped on the Japanese city would wipe out all of Frankfurt and its 700,000 inhabitants in one stroke. The brochure carried the title "Your Life Is at Stake."[107]

Frankfurt's campaign was part of the nationwide "Fight Against Nuclear Death," which was a big wave in the rising sea of antiwar demonstrations that swept across Europe and North America between the 1950s and the 1980s. The peace movement had been a pioneer of global civil society in the nineteenth century, and German activists continued to draw strength from international connections. The chair of the West German section of War Resisters International in the 1950s was Theodor Michaltscheff, an émigré who had refused to do his military service in Bulgaria in 1920, and who looked to Leo Tolstoy, Mahatma Gandhi, and the British anarchist William Godwin for inspiration. In the 1960s, German protestors, like their peers elsewhere, walked in annual marches for peace over Easter weekend, quoted Martin Luther King Jr., and protested against the Vietnam War.

What gave these international influences such powerful resonance in West Germany—by 1980, its peace movement would be the largest in Europe—was their interplay with national concerns. Nuclear warheads felt more threatening in the geographical center of the Cold War than on its margins. Concern for world peace also drew on anti-Americanism and nationalist worries about the survival of the *Volk*.[108] For many Germans, opposition to weapons was a test of how far they had moved on after Hitler and were willing to take responsibility into their own hands and confront the state. As the meaning of peace broadened from the absence of war into peacefulness, people were asking themselves what they were doing to foster mutual trust in order to eliminate the causes of conflict. Private conscience invaded public politics.

Hiroshima was kept constantly in sight in postwar German cities. "Remember Hiroshima and Nagasaki" signs urged citizens in the "Fight

Against Nuclear Death" in the late 1950s. Hiroshima was included in local commemorations of aerial bombing. In Darmstadt, in 1958, speeches on the anniversary of the bombing of the Hessian city in September 1944 ended with a reminder of the fate of the Japanese city, while banners at a mass demonstration in Hamburg invoked the firestorm of 1943 and warned against "Hamburg's second Hiroshima."

Hiroshima was recognized not just as a fellow victim of the recent war but also as the human face of the possible nuclear death to come. Pictures and eyewitness accounts played a major part in the campaign. In 1955, the documentary *Hiroshima* was shown at the Berlinale film festival. A few years later came *Key to Hell* (*Schlüssel zur Hölle*). An art exhibition showed photos of the victims. In a lecture tour across West Germany, Professor Yasushi Nishiwaki from Osaka told audiences how the radiation from tests with hydrogen bombs in the Pacific had damaged fishermen's health and reproductive organs. The German section of the International Women's League for Peace and Freedom published children's eyewitness accounts of the atomic bomb, and women's circles gave lectures on the birth defects in children born nine years later. The popular futurologist Robert Jungk, who spent several weeks in Hiroshima, reported how he had seen people who looked healthy one day spit blood the next. On August 6, 1960, the anniversary of the bombing, protestors in Mannheim erected a sixteen-foot-tall tower covered on each side with pictures and articles about Hiroshima.[109]

Nonviolence provided a second international source of inspiration. In Hamburg, in 1958, pacifists held a vigil for fourteen days and nights in the city square, where they were joined by the seamstress Yoshiko Murato and Hayao Shimizu, a student union leader who carried scars from the explosion. It was organized by Konrad Tempel, a young Quaker and primary school teacher. Two years earlier, he had corresponded with Gene Sharp, an American pacifist and Gandhi follower who had protested against conscription during the Korean War and edited *Peace News* in London. Together with his future wife, Helga, Tempel produced German editions of classic texts on nonviolence by Sharp, Henry David Thoreau, and others. At the vigil, Tempel was joined by Bayard Rustin, an ally of Martin Luther King Jr., and April Carter, from the British group that organized the first Easter March against atomic weapons that year. Two years later, in 1960, one thousand Germans followed Tempel on their own Easter March—Fasia Jansen, who was half-Liberian, half-German, and had her own experience with racial discrimination, sang the American civil rights anthem "We Shall Overcome." The second march attracted nine thousand people. One hundred thousand people would join on Easter 1964.

The Nazi years were a common point of reference. A student pastor reminded Easter Marchers that not so long ago the state had turned into a "mass murderer." The father of Hans and Sophie Scholl, the White Rose students who had been executed by the Nazis, invoked their memory in the fight against nuclear weapons. Campaigners in Hamburg put it simply: "Who says nothing becomes complicit."[110] The destination of the first Easter March in 1960 was Bergen-Hohne, where NATO had recently stationed "Honest John" rockets (surface-to-surface missiles capable of carrying a nuclear warheard), not far from Bergen-Belsen concentration camp.

TESTING CONSCIENCE

Few campaigners were strict pacifists like Tempel, and most endorsed nuclear power for peaceful use. What was more widely shared was the belief that, in a nuclear age, survival was the responsibility of each and every citizen: "Who accepts the atomic bomb will die from the atomic bomb," as a placard seen at the vigil put it. In a democracy, Tempel said, "the highest authority is conscience, and not a parliamentary majority."[111] University students reached a similar conclusion. When a state included mass destruction in its political concept, students in Heidelberg said, it threatened its citizens' freedom of conscience and shook at the "ethical foundations of society." Protestors liked to quote the dramatist Gerhard Hauptmann: "The only man is the ethical man."

Freedom of conscience was one of the basic laws in the constitution, but in contrast to the other freedoms, it was unclear what precisely it was that was so important to defend. Conscience, the lawyer turned sociologist Niklas Luhmann pointed out in 1965, was treated as something "inner," highly personal, even secret, which only articulated itself in action. Since it was no longer limited to religious conscience either—as it had been in the Weimar years—its essence was so subjective that it proved difficult to pin down. If the principle was "to each their own conscience," why not simply leave the conscience to itself? Luhmann's solution was to turn the problem inside out. Conscience, he argued, "is not a voice, but a function." It worked as a shock absorber that enabled an individual to navigate the complexities of modern society and still maintain a personal identity across time. In this way, society could run smoothly even as it pressed people into different social roles. Conscience was the psychological pursuit of a "life formula" that linked past, present, and future. Its role, however, was steadily shrinking in modern times, according to Luhmann, first because truth was divided up between law, science, and religion, and second because more and more concerns were delegated to other rules and institutions. The salesperson no longer felt personally responsible for selling something to someone who could not afford it. With delegation came exculpation. That was why so many Nazis were able to murder so many people in a routine manner, Luhmann said. Except for a few atomic physicists, he wrote, most people were able to arrange themselves in ways that did not trouble their conscience. Life would be chaos if individuals began to put the consequences of their actions on their own conscience.[112]

Yet this was precisely what a growing number of Germans did. They reached the conclusion that peace and the survival of the human race depended on them personally. Private conscience expanded to take responsibility for global consequences. One thing that lay behind this remarkable advance was that religion and science experienced their own crisis of moral authority. Instead of providing moral guidance for troubled souls, bishops, like scientists, were having their own doubts about nuclear arms. Delegation stalled and reversed.

Carl Friedrich von Weizsäcker had worked on the military potential of nuclear fission during the war. After it, he emerged as the preeminent physicist leading the challenge against nuclear armament. He accepted conventional weapons but believed that atomic weapons represented something fundamentally different, not merely some kind of continuation (as they were for Adenauer). Humans risked ending up the slaves of technology, he warned. If it was wrongheaded to get rid of technology, Weizsäcker told students, it was just as wrong to try to do everything that was technically possible. Fear of nuclear escalation drew on a more general unease with Americanization and modernity that was particularly acute in the German peace movement. Weizsäcker stressed that he was not passing judgment on the American scientists behind the first bomb—they had been fighting for freedom. But he did criticize Americans for always wanting to take what looked like the easiest route. In addition to a halt to atomic tests, Weizsäcker called for a new "ethic in a technological age." People needed to "learn to remain human, and in crucial points learn to become human," he said. By 1970, after playing through a number of military scenarios, Weizsäcker warned that one could no longer count on deterrence to prevent war. Citizens, as well as scientists, needed to take responsibility. A nuclear war was hanging over their heads, like the sword of Damocles, he wrote. Whether it was hanging by a thin thread or a strong rope would depend on people's political consciousness and actions.[113]

Since Martin Luther, the Protestant Church had been an obedient supporter of the state. Christians had to live with conflict and accept the authority of the state and its monopoly of violence, where necessary. Nuclear arms shattered the neat division between private conscience and public duty. Some Protestants insisted that atomic weapons were legitimate means of deterring (or even fighting) an enemy—a "just war." What mattered, they said, was not peace at any price but "peace in freedom," and nuclear weapons helped secure that by keeping communism in check. "Better dead than red," or, as the more cultured liked to say, quoting Friedrich Schiller, "Life is not the good supreme."[114]

Others, however, condemned nuclear weapons as sin and incompatible with the Christian ethic of war. The idea of a defensive or preventative war was meaningless in a system of counterstrikes; it was collective suicide. Atomic weapons made murderers of them all, the theologian Helmut Gollwitzer said, because it needed a "murderous ethic" to produce them. All life belonged to God, Niemöller told audiences, and it was therefore blasphemy for people to claim the right to decide about the life and death of the human race. Hitler was "a little beginner compared to his successors" who had atomic weapons. Those who quoted Schiller, he added for good measure, should do so in full: "The greatest ill of all is guilt." Not to speak out against nuclear arms would make them complicit in mass murder.

In the face of these polar extremes, church leaders threw up their hands and opted for unity over consistency. The stationing of (American) nuclear weapons in West Germany counted as a Christian pursuit of peace, the synod ruled in 1958, but so, too, did the renunciation of arms. As the Protestant Churches put it in a memorable formula a decade later, they stood by those "serving peace with and without weapons." Pastors offered counsel to both soldiers and conscientious objectors. Ultimately, it was for each individual to decide in which direction their own conscience was pointing them.[115]

Anti-communism made the Catholic Church initially a strong supporter of rearmament. But here, too, nuclear weapons prompted a reconsideration of age-old teachings. In 1963, in response to the Cuban missile crisis, Pope John XXIII wrote the encyclical "Pacem in terris" ("Peace on Earth"), which called for an end to the arms race. In the course of the Second Vatican Council, the critique led to a wider reappraisal of the nature of peace. Completed by his successor Pope Paul VI in 1965, "Gaudium et spes" ("Joy and Hope") defined peace no longer negatively, as the absence of war, but positively, as the promotion of peacefulness and harmony. Military conflicts were ripples on the surface. Their fundamental causes lay beneath, in poverty, underdevelopment, and hatred—"structural violence," as it came to be known in the following decade.[116] Peace came to stand for human flourishing and was soon extended to all sentient beings.[117] The pursuit of peace could no longer be delegated to governments and armies. Peace expressed love of "one's neighbors" and the ability to solve problems without violence. From there peacefulness radiated out into society and the world at large.

Minimizing conflict thus became everyone's business. By 1966, German Catholics had their own progressive think tank, the Bensberger Circle, which, like their Protestant cousins, offered advice to conscientious objectors. A new ethic of personal responsibility was taking root.[118]

BETTER ACTIVE THAN RADIOACTIVE

The peace movement is often grouped under the label "new social movements," alongside feminists, ecologists, and gay rights activists, who gained prominence in the late 1960s, triggering images of long-haired students and creative, young professionals of the new middle classes. In fact, what gave it its strength was its ability to appeal to old and new alike. Already in the 1950s, when the movement was led by the SPD and trade unions, its base went well beyond the working-class milieu. The fight against rearmament had support from housewives and pensioners, doctors and actors, as well as working-class youths in the socialist Falken (Falcons) and Naturfreunde (Friends of Nature). In Frankfurt, in May 1957, a decorator collected more than three thousand signatures against nuclear weapons from housewives, artisans, teachers, and students. In addition to radical youths, there were the respectable matrons of the West German Women's Peace Movement (WFFB), founded in 1951—a princess, Olga zur Lippe, became their honorary president.

After the SPD distanced itself from the protests in 1959 to escape the image of working with Moscow's fifth column, the peace movement grew into the Extra-Parliamentary Opposition (Ausserparlamentarische Opposition, APO) and turned to the left. The Easter Marchers were not exclusively young radicals. In 1963, for example, they included a seventy-year-old grandmother and Quaker, booksellers, postal workers, and clerks. Entire families marched along.[119] The father of the missing fighter pilot, whom we met earlier, a retired doctor, joined an anti–nuclear weapons group in 1966.[120] The following year, the campaign for disarmament could count on lawyers, priests, and engineers as well as university teachers, students, and trade unionists. Supporters included Heinrich Böll, Martin Niemöller, and Jürgen Habermas, but also artists such as the composer Hans-Joachim Wunderlich and Lil Dagover, the star of the German silver screen. Dagover had been cast in the silent classic *The Cabinet of Dr. Caligari* in 1920 and continued to be in high demand under the Nazis. In 1943, she entertained troops on the Eastern Front. Twenty-five years later, Dagover appeared alongside Niemöller speaking on a charity "single" of Vietnamese folk songs raising money for hospitals and aid for North Vietnam.[121]

The arms race divided generations among themselves as well as from each other. In 1965, a young leftist man went from door to door in his lower-middle-class neighborhood in Hamburg to collect signatures in support of disarmament. He reported back on his difficulties to the Easter March committee. Some people called him a "communist pig" and slammed the door in his face. Others threatened to call the police. At the local pub, he reminded everyone of the bombing raids in 1943. "That was twenty years ago!" young men shouted back. When he sought to explain to them that they needed to campaign against the Vietnam War to prevent a recurrence, the "rowdies" (*Halbstarken*) responded that "the biggest murderers" were living in the GDR. One of them grabbed him by his jacket and tried to hit him in the face. He ran out, shattering the glass door, with two of the "gangsters" in hot pursuit. He was saved by someone in a passing car.[122]

The Easter Marches were a historic bridge between the anti-nuclear protests of the 1950s and the peace movement of the 1970s and 1980s. Some of the later activists had been taken on their first protest by their parents in the 1960s. What was new about the Easter Marches was their grassroots philosophy. The slogan of the first march was "Have faith in the power of the individual." It was a bottom-up movement, without members, elected officials, or party programs. Groups debated until they reached a consensus.[123]

The open atmosphere invited protestors to be creative. Politics was injected with a splash of color and fun, closer to a carnival than the staid world of party conferences. In addition to music, marches, and catchy slogans—"Better active today than radioactive tomorrow!"—there was street theater and gallows humor. In Hesse, in 1965, campaigners organized the "Aktion People's Coffin," which satirized a new law for civil defense and fallout shelters. With leaflets and posters, they advertised a supposed new federal law that guaranteed "a coffin for each citizen." In the sleepy town of Oberursel (Hesse), they exhibited Models I, II, and III of the "People's Coffin," made from cardboard and painted black. People who preferred cremation were presented with alternative options. Worried about missing out, some residents tried to order their coffin straightaway. Were the coffins covered by social benefits? they wanted to know.[124]

The Easter Marchers had no unifying political vision. What they shared was fear, which was their strength and also their weakness. Fear of nuclear war gained in intensity from three mutually reinforcing sources. There was, first, the fear of an authoritarian, even neofascist, revival. Emergency laws were a constant topic of debate from 1958 onward and eventually passed in 1968, after Kurt Kiesinger of the CDU had formed a grand coalition with Brandt's SPD. The laws gave the government wide-ranging powers in an emergency, from civilian defense and censorship to arrest without cause and restricting a person's freedom to choose their occupation (which violated the constitution). That authoritarianism bred war was an old staple of radical thought. "Our no to the bomb is a yes for democracy" was the number-one slogan of the Easter Marchers.[125]

Second, there was Vietnam. The harrowing images of U.S. aggression undercut the sense of a Soviet threat, which had been used to justify nuclear deterrence. In 1962, 63 percent of Germans thought the communist threat was very great; by 1971, it was only 39 percent.[126] If Vietnam provided peace movements across Europe with a shared cause, it carried a special meaning in the country responsible for the Holocaust. American forces began to bomb North Vietnam in 1964 just as the Auschwitz trial of twenty-two mid- and low-level officials in that extermination camp was underway in Frankfurt. (Six were sentenced to life for murder; ten to three to fourteen years in prison for being an accessory.) For protestors, it was self-evident that Auschwitz and Vietnam were two of a kind. Pictures of the two routinely appeared next to each other, and American presidents were shown with a swastika. "Who today identifies with Vietnam might just as well identify with Auschwitz," the youth secretary of a trade union said at a demonstration in 1967.[127] For a local newspaper, the Vietnam War was a dangerous sign of a "moral perversion" that showed how easy it was for people to treat others as "unworthy of life" (*lebensunwert*), placing the war in the tradition of Nazi eugenics and genocide. Easter Marchers held demonstrations and solidarity bazaars. Children initiated collections of toys and coloring pens for children in North Vietnam. Two girls who had survived the notorious U.S. massacre in the village of Mỹ Lai in South Vietnam visited Germany on their European tour in February 1970.[128]

Finally, there was violence more generally. The urgency of peace expanded along with the understanding of violence. The new papal definition of peace was part of a wider reassessment that traced violence beyond its physical manifestation to its social, economic, and psychological forms. A Protestant advocate of peace camps explained the new, broader vision in 1970. Peace, he said, was the highest form of being human. Reaching it required internal as well as international change. People needed to learn to practice justice and reconciliation in their own lives, but to do so they also had to confront the structural sources of violence. Industrial society was marked by "latent aggression." The West suffered from "secret existential angst" that sprang from a deep unease about technology and progress and the erosion of family and community. The signs of aggression were everywhere: riots, police brutality, sport, film—even aggressive driving on the Autobahn. Other contemporaries added sexual violence, violence in schools and families, and the supposedly coercive stranglehold of advertising and shopping (*Konsumterror*).[129]

Attempts to turn the APO into a force inside parliament failed miserably. In the 1969 elections, the German Peace Union entered into an alliance with the Communist Party and received just 0.6 percent of the vote. Willy Brandt was the winner that year and formed a coalition government with the Liberals. Nor did it stop the nuclear arms race; the number of warheads only dropped in the late 1980s when Mikhail Gorbachev led the Soviet Union.

The peace movement's long-term impact on political culture, however, was profound, and not only for the future Green Party. Civic mentality and activism were transformed, as the next great agitation would show—the mass demonstrations against the stationing of NATO's nuclear-armed cruise missiles and intermediate range Pershing II rockets in the early 1980s. In 1980, a forum in Krefeld in North Rhine–Westphalia issued an appeal urging the federal government to retract its support for cruise missiles and press for disarmament instead. The appeal warned of "nuclear death," echoing the slogan of earlier protests, and the convenors included the veteran campaigner Niemöller as well as the young Petra Kelly, who had helped found the Green Party earlier that year. By 1983, more than 4 million citizens had signed the appeal. Several hundred thousand joined hands in a human chain of sixty-seven miles from Stuttgart to Neu-Ulm. Cities and companies adopted peace initiatives. Districts declared themselves nuclear-free zones. Catholic youths held vigils in front of the American and Soviet embassies calling for disarmament. In provincial Uelzen, in Lower Saxony, hippies and other citizens watched films about Nagasaki together. In nearby Tostedt, the inhabitants of the small town organized a peace week and collected 1,425 DM for a development project in Somalia—200 DM more than Bonn spent on defense each second, they pointed out.

Ironically, it was the churches, which officially continued to adhere to a "yes and no" position, that ended up the great winners from the new politics of conscience. After decades of losing members, millions flocked to the chuches' peace circles and tearooms looking for answers from the Lord of

Peace. Church congresses attracted more people than the Rolling Stones. For Catholic as for Protestant youths, peace was now firmly linked to justice, in their own lives and in the world at large.[130]

THE ETHICS OF RESPONSIBILITY

Political leaders were especially irritated by the many Christians who were turning to the Sermon on the Mount for political guidance—"Blessed are the peacemakers, for they will be called children of God . . . If anyone strikes you on the right cheek, turn the other also . . . Love your enemies . . . Do unto others as you would have them do unto you" (Matthew 5:1 and 5:9). On April 19, 1981, during the official reopening of Bremen's St. Petri Cathedral, President Karl Carstens criticized priests for abusing their spiritual position for political purposes; Carstens had served as dean of that cathedral after the war. A devout Protestant, he vehemently rejected the notion that the government's policy of nuclear deterrence was a violation of the Sermon on the Mount. Quite the opposite, ministers were performing their public responsibility by shielding citizens from danger, he said.[131] The chancellor, Helmut Schmidt, joined the fray. To apply Jesus to foreign policy would be utterly naive, he said; it would have meant the Soviets standing at the Rhine and on Crete, not just at the Elbe. In 1958, as a young member of parliament, he had warned in a rather different tone that the adoption of nuclear arms would one day be remembered as being as fateful as the Enabling Act of 1933, which gave Hitler the power to pass laws at will. Now, Schmidt invoked Max Weber to draw a sharp line between a private ethic of conviction and a public ethic of responsibility. Believers should stick to the former and leave the latter to politicians.[132]

The two statements unleashed a storm of protest. This was how dictators talked, wrote Heinrich Albertz, a popular pastor and the former mayor of Berlin. The Sermon on the Mount was not just a "rule of life for nutcases and dreamers." The spiritual call for peace would lose its credibility if confined to private life. Christian groups wrote open letters to the chancellor defending the Sermon on the Mount as a realistic basis of political action and promising to resist armament.[133] Following their conscience did not make them enemies of the constitution, they said. In Wolfsburg (Lower Saxony), a group of Protestants published a booklet called "No to 'Rearmament.'" Such was the popular demand that by the end of the year they had printed 100,000 copies. They attacked the government for trying to monopolize the defense question and stigmatizing critics as "the communists." "Not so long ago," they warned, "Germans had carried out a witch hunt against 'the Jews,' 'the communists,' 'the Gypsies' that ended in the gas chambers." Christian ethics, they said, were not private. They could not be divided into churchgoer on one side and citizen on the other. They, too, cited Weber, but argued that an ethic of conscience and an ethic of responsibility were "not absolute contrasts, but complements that only together made the true man." It seemed to them that "the people in the peace movement had thought more about their responsibilities and the consequences of their actions than those in 'responsible' positions of power who are meant to care for our survival." The Sermon on the Mount was realpolitik because, by inviting people to take the first step, it freed them of hatred and promoted trust.[134] In their pastoral letter in 1983, Catholic bishops similarly urged that Jesus' words be applied to society and politics. The motto of their conference was "Justice creates peace."[135] Several hundred thousand readers turned to *Frieden ist möglich* (*Peace Is Possible*), the best-selling book describing a personal journey to the Sermon on the Mount by the journalist Franz Alt, a Catholic member of the CDU.

It lies in the nature of protests that they challenge power but do not hold it. Helmut Kohl toppled Schmidt in 1982 in a vote of confidence and, a year later, won the election for the CDU/CSU with 49 percent of the vote. Many hundred thousand Germans might have held hands for disarmament, but even more citizens voted for Kohl and, by extension, for cruise missiles. Kohl liked to quote Bismarck's line that it was not possible to govern with the Sermon on the Mount. There was a fast-growing conservative youth movement as well as an alternative one, and, in no small part, it was this wave that carried Kohl to power. The Junge Union set up school clubs and doubled its membership in the decade after 1968; by the time Kohl took office, it had a quarter of a million members, unrivaled in Europe. Young conservatives began to call for solidarity with the "Third World" and question unlimited growth, as we have seen, but in matters of defense Christian solidarity translated into support for NATO's stationing of middle-range missiles in Germany to restore the nuclear balance of power and push the Soviet Union to disarm.

Catholic pacifists were greeted with suspicion and outright opposition. On the idyllic shores of the Bavarian Ammersee, high school students wanted to organize a peace fast together with Pax Christi, the international Catholic peace movement. The local church told them that the community center was off-limits, except for meditation. In Rheinberg, on the lower

Rhine, the Easter Marchers in 1985 ended up literally standing before closed doors. The deacon found them too anti-American and withdrew the use of the parish center. Rheinberg had a U.S. Army base, and his congregation, he said, appreciated their defense of "our freedom." He quoted Mao to the pacifists: "All politics comes from the barrel of a gun."[136]

The CDU could count, too, on many women who feared communists more than rockets; the long-term memory of the mass rapes by Soviet soldiers in 1945 cannot be discounted. In a short story written for women's clubs in 1983, the member of parliament Ursula Benedix-Engler imagined a cookout that turns into a debate about peace. Several guests wear peace stickers and assure each other of the need for peace at any price, until "Frau Klar" arrives and tells them of her personal experience with "brown" and "red" dictatorships. She knows how precious freedom is not only for them but also for all those in the gulag who were putting their faith in the West. The United States, Frau Klar continues, never started a war of conquest, only the Soviet Union did. History had shown pacifism to be a failure. Her friend and host "Sabine" wants to know: How can she say such things as a Christian who believes in the Sermon on the Mount? She is indeed a Christian, Frau Klar explains, but that is her private faith and does not apply to matters where we have responsibility for others. The peace movement is full of communist wire-pullers, she warns the guests. The story gained credibility from Benedix-Engler's experience as a young anti-aircraft gunner in Bohemia in March 1945 and her flight two years later from the Soviet zone to the West.[137]

This fictional exchange was a world apart from the scenes that took place in Mutlangen, east of Stuttgart, on the morning of September 1, 1983—the anniversary of the German attack on Poland—when a thousand people gathered outside an army depot awaiting the arrival of Pershing II rockets. In rotating six-hour shifts, they sat down in front of the entrance for three days. They would be charged with *Nötigung* ("coercion").

The nonviolent blockade was a culmination of the earlier peace campaigns, their ideas, actions, and luminaries. In addition to Albertz, Kelly, and the ill Böll, now a Nobel Prize winner for literature, there was Inge Aicher-Scholl, the older sister of Hans and Sophie of the White Rose resistance group. The lead organizer was Klaus Vack, whose opposition to nuclear weapons had taken him from the SPD and trade unions in the 1950s to the Easter Marchers and the APO in the 1960s. Like him, his wife, Hanne, a secretary, came from a working-class background and had been a member of the youth section of the socialist Naturfreunde. As she told the court during the trials in 1984, where she and others were prosecuted for coercion, films on Hiroshima and the concentration camps (*Night and Fog*) had left a deep impression on her. She had visited Auschwitz with her youth group. In the 1960s, she and her husband blockaded the Soviet embassy in protest against nuclear tests and stopped traffic in a vigil for Vietnam. She quoted Gandhi to the judge: "There is no path to peace—peace is the path." She practiced it in her own family: she never beat her children; problems were always solved "amicably and consensually."

Hanne Vack, born in 1940, belonged to the new generation that grew up after Hitler. For Meta Lambertz, four years older, peace was a learning process and came late in life. She belonged to an older generation of teachers, she confessed to the court, for whom it was natural to resort to "the occasional slap in the face." "I am an apolitical person who tends to trust blindly in authority." It was the declaration of the ecumenical Council of Churches in 1981 and the arms race that woke her up. She felt she needed to do something, especially in light of people's complicity in the Nazi era. She joined the boycotts against South African products. She also realized that, as a taxpayer, she was implicated in the arms buildup: "I *cannot* leave these things to the politicians; I must involve myself." She began by taking 5.72 DM off her automobile tax—1 pfennig per Pershing II or cruise missile.

Günter Fuchs was a nurse, born in 1960. Armament had to be seen in relation to global poverty, he told the court. With West Germany's economic policy and arms exports, he said, "we help stabilize exploitative regimes that treat humanity with contempt." Even if no Pershing was fired, it was already killing the poor. Posters at the time showed rockets next to baby bottles: "Armaments kill—every day."

The blockade also attracted older cohorts such as Helga Einselne, a retired senior civil servant. She was thirteen when Hitler came to power. "I belong to the generation that never came to terms with the fact that they did not sit down on the tracks when the [troop] trains began to roll into the Rhineland in 1934, Austria in 1938, and Poland in 1939." The oldest defendant was Fritz Hartnagel, born in 1917. He had been Sophie Scholl's fiancé and, after the war, married her sister Elisabeth. Stalingrad had turned the young officer into a fervent supporter of war resisters. As it happened, he was also a recently retired judge and outraged by the criminalization of nonviolent protest.

Between 1983 and 1985, more than a thousand protestors received a criminal record (*Vorstrafe*); judges and prosecutors who lent public support to the protests faced disciplinary action. There was a bitter irony here. For a generation, the peace movement had broadened the definition of violence.

Now the state used it against them. The rulings would be overturned by the Constitutional Court in 1995.[138]

"SWORDS INTO PLOWSHARES"

In West Germany, the peace movement was stigmatized as a communist Trojan horse. History, however, moved in the opposite direction: the peace movement helped bring about the downfall of the GDR.

On January 28, 1982, just a year after the Krefeld Appeal for nuclear disarmament, Pastor Rainer Eppelmann and the dissident Robert Havemann followed with theirs from East Berlin. The Berlin Appeal echoed many of the same concerns. To stand a chance of survival, it argued, Europe needed to become a nuclear-free zone. Money would be better spent feeding the hungry in the "Third World" than on missiles. The state should allow for a social peace service as an alternative to military service. It also cited Jesus' Sermon on the Mount.

The big difference was that in East Germany such ideas struck at one of the key self-sustaining myths of the socialist regime. As we have seen, for the rulers only the SED (Socialist Unity Party) could guarantee peace, by establishing socialism and shielding the country against the capitalist-imperialist enemy. Now some pastors and dissidents were saying the SED's defense policy could lead to mass suicide and advocating "making peace without weapons." Nuclear weapons, they argued, made thinking in terms of "friend versus foe" obsolete. Dialogue needed to take the place of hatred and antagonism. Like their Western cousins, they called for tolerance, freedom of expression, and "spontaneous declarations of the will to peace." They wanted to demilitarize everyday life, ban toy soldiers, and end military education in schools. They turned to "the public" for support: "Blessed are the peacemakers."[139]

The churches in the GDR had challenged the "friend/foe" thinking in a nuclear age once before, in 1965, in an internal leaflet, where they held up those who refused to bear arms as giving a clearer testimony of the Lord's offer of peace than those who carried a gun. At that time, church leaders quickly caved under pressure from the regime. The situation in the early 1980s was more favorable because two factors were coming together: a surge of youth peace circles at home and ecumenical support from abroad. The idea for a "peace decade" originated with the Ecumenical Youth Council in Europe in 1979—"decade" referred to the ten days before the Day of Prayer and Repentance in November. The following year it was adopted by the

Protestant youth organizations in the GDR and developed a momentum of its own.

What the peace symbol was to campaigners against nuclear disarmament in the West, "swords into plowshares" became in the GDR. The words came from the Old Testament (Micah 4:3) and surrounded an image of a man beating a sword into a plowshare, based on the sculpture by Yevgeny Vuchetich the Soviet Union had given to the United Nations in 1959. The symbol was the choice of the youth pastor for Saxony. He had 100,000 printed as bookmarks by a local textile printing firm, and since they were printed on fleece, not paper, no license was required. Creative youths cut them out and wore them as badges on their coats. A second print run of patches followed suit. By the time the Stasi paid a visit to the printing firm in spring 1982 and confiscated the mold, the patch had spread into a visible public marker. In Frankfurt (Oder), some fifty pupils showed up at school wearing one. Half took theirs off after pressure, the other half refused. Police removed offending teenagers from soccer stadiums and, in some cases, arrested them. In Dresden, one of the hotbeds of dissent, almost three hundred pupils continued to wear the patch in defiance of school directors and the FDJ. Others took theirs off under threat of expulsion, only to put white spots in their place.

In a report, the district official responsible for church matters, and himself a pastor, pointed out to ministers the dangers of heavy-handed intimidation. At parents' evenings, he noted, teachers were criticized for threatening the children instead of reasoning with them. Worse, the regime lost the little trust it had left with students, who suddenly found themselves lumped together with enemies of the state. The result was hypocrisy and fear. The official cited the case of two teenagers who were humiliated by their school director until they also removed their white dots. Ultimately, "this kind of education" was counterproductive. The two boys "left feeling like winners . . . and the school director as the moral and pedagogical loser—and I have to agree with them."[140]

Nor were these young East Germans just the children of a few pastors. In the late 1970s, "open youth" programs took off and made churches one of the few safe spaces for atheists and Christians alike to express their hopes and fears. The evangelical youth weeks in Potsdam in 1979 attracted four thousand people. Peace circles grew into a substitute public sphere that served as an umbrella for environmentalists and other dissidents. East German citizens also signed their own private nonaggression pacts with their West German peers.

The main hubs of this network were in the big cities. In the spring of 1982, for example, the church in Alt-Pankow in East Berlin hosted a youth night. It began at 10 p.m. with an hour of songs and was followed by a sermon, a candle procession at midnight, extensive group discussion, and, finally, rock music. The Stasi watched and listened. In the course of the night, peace and rearmament became connected to Wolf Biermann's expulsion, the repression of the Solidarność trade union movement in Poland a few months earlier, and the suppression of youth more generally. Similar events took place that night in several other churches. The Zionskirche in East Berlin had its own underground library and mimeographed leaflets. The offshoots, though, reached all the way into the provinces, where youth groups attracted apprentices and young farmers as well as students. The village of Grosshennersdorf, near the Czech and Polish borders, had its own peace circle and organized three days of "peace fasting" in the summer of 1983 in memory of Hiroshima. The Stasi sabotaged these activities, but it could not stop them.[141]

Being in a minority was a source of strength for these groups. They took pride in having seen through the dominant consumerist mind-set and its disregard for the environment. Many hoped to reform socialism, not to bury it. Still, by advocating self-determination and raising awareness of social problems, this view of peace challenged the foundations of the SED dictatorship. "What does peace mean to us?" the peace community in Jena asked. "Living in free responsibility in community with each other." Where was the party in this vision? Nonviolent conflict resolution would bring justice and restore harmony with the natural world. Support for peace involved "actively confronting personal and social situations," entering into dialogue, and being open to new ways of feeling and thinking. Peace groups performed Micah's prophecy in puppet shows and cared for the disabled. Peace was not abstract talk, the Dresden peace week reminded participants in 1981. It involved helping people who were suffering from illness and isolation, by cleaning their stoves and repairing their roofs. They were to understand such needs and problems. New solutions would only emerge through dialogue.[142] It was another way of saying that the SED did not always know best.

Not surprisingly, the regime did not like it. Right up to the fall of the Wall, dialogue was denounced as a plot by the imperialist enemy. The Combat Groups of the Working Class were taught to separate the "reactionary circles of the church" from the hard core of troublemakers in order to stop them from mobilizing the "negative enemy forces, criminals, decadents, and socially uprooted groups," as they were called in language reminiscent of the Nazis.[143] It was not the peace movement that toppled the regime in 1989, but it did carve out an alternative space and style of politics that made it possible to do so.

SOLDIERS WITH SPADES

One of the deepest spheres of conflict between individual conscience and public obligation in the modern era has been military service. The tension is the inevitable result of the parallel expansion of conscription, on the one hand, and of freedom of conscience, on the other. Should people have a right to refuse to bear arms and opt out of national defense? If yes, on what grounds? And how does one separate the saints from the cowards?

While all modern societies have had to confront these questions, their answers have varied enormously. Religious sects such as the Quakers and the Mennonites were already granted exemptions from military duty by some countries in the eighteenth century. It was total war and the compulsory military service that came with it that made conscientious objectors an issue of national significance. Britain recognized the right to refuse to bear arms when it introduced conscription in 1916, as did the Netherlands the following year. In the next decade, all the Nordic countries allowed for some form of civilian service. France, however, only legalized conscientious objection in 1963, Italy and Spain in 1972 and 1976, and Switzerland not until 1996. Socialist countries defined their military service as peace service and consequently could not recognize it. In world politics, the subject has remained contentious. The Universal Declaration of Human Rights, created in 1948, included "the right to freedom of thought, conscience and religion" (Article 18), but whether this included a right to conscientious objection was only settled in 1993, when the UN's Human Rights Committee explicitly said it did. At the time of writing, China does not accept such a right, nor do Turkey and Israel.[144]

Refusal to do military service acquired disproportionate significance in Germany, although in radically different forms in East and West. The GDR celebrated the armed liberation from the Nazis and had little sympathy with those who refused violence outright.

West Germany lacked this progressive lineage of violence. Guns and bullets stood for the Nazis, conquest, and war crimes, not liberty and freedom. Conscientious objectors here had fewer moral rivals to contend with. Still, the right to conscientious objection was not a foregone conclusion. In the late 1940s, it had democratic as well as reactionary critics. For the

Liberal Theodor Heuss—soon to become the country's first president—conscription was the "legitimate child of democracy"; national liberals had long looked back nostalgically to the Prussian reforms during the Napoleonic era when (supposedly) militias and political reforms marched hand in hand. Heuss had no problem with a refusal to bear arms on an individual basis, but he was opposed to making it a constitutional right. Democracy came with duties, and military service was an essential, even existential, one. "A completely general formula for conscience," he felt, "turns conscience into a product of irresponsibility."[145] The critics lost. Bavaria, Hessen, and Berlin included conscientious objection in their constitutions in 1947–48. The following year, the federal Basic Law was unequivocal: "No person shall be compelled against his conscience to render military service involving the use of arms" (Article 4/3).

The GDR did not formally recognize conscientious objection but, in contrast to its socialist allies, in 1964 reached a compromise creating special construction units (*Bausoldaten*) for those who refused to bear arms. Initially a few hundred each year, their number exceeded a thousand by the end of the GDR.[146] Jehovah's Witnesses and anyone else who refused either option ended up in prison for eighteen months; so-called total objectors shared a similar fate in the West.

For the regime, as for most objectors, the arrangement was a moral fudge. *Bausoldaten* were exempt from shooting, but they remained part of the army. Instead of the typical oath to the flag (*Fahneneid*), they had to give a special pledge (*Gelöbnis*) promising to defend the Warsaw Pact and to be "sincere, courageous, disciplined" and give "unconditional obedience."[147] In the early years, refusal to give the pledge could spell prison. By the early 1970s, some officers grudgingly accepted silence. To offer objectors purely civilian functions, however, was out of the question. Military service embodied a "high political and moral obligation toward the state." As the deputy minister of defense, Admiral Waldemar Verner, the younger brother of Paul, who sat on the Politburo, put it in 1969, the GDR was reaching out to the *Bausoldaten* who "have so far not grasped that in our socialist state armed service is peace service."[148] Work on military installations made conflict of conscience inevitable. Pulling weeds was one thing, carrying munition something else. Objectors petitioned for work that had no "killing potential." The furthest the regime would go was to assign them to build military airports and maintain the barracks' heating systems.

A contemporary account of forty-eight *Bausoldaten* in the Ore Mountains in Saxony in the mid-1960s gives a snapshot of this group of men. The majority were in their mid-twenties and married. Overwhelmingly they were pacifists for religious reasons. Half of them were Lutherans or Calvinists, a few others Adventists and Jehovah's Witnesses. Half were workers, the rest artisans, farmers, or members of the "intelligentsia." All of them felt their conscience tested by military orders, but they varied in their responses. Some took part in strategic training while others refused—without consequence. Elsewhere one *Bausoldat* was sent to prison for refusing to build a shooting range, as were the Adventists in the Ore Mountains who would not honor official state holidays. Church services, while not allowed officially, were tolerated, and some of the *Bausoldaten* sang in choirs in churches nearby. Their own joint Bible hours, though, gradually unraveled. Some "resigned themselves," others "arranged themselves," and then there were those who "remained worried" and felt morally compromised: "We have done something that we should not have done."[149] A few demonstrated their commitment to social service by working with mentally handicapped people on the weekends and some even volunteered a month for Aktion Sühnezeichen after completing their eighteen months in the army. This was hardly typical, though. As a report on the next group concluded in 1969, for most the service was "a personal matter and rarely a social commitment."[150]

In spite of the discrimination they faced, most of these "soldiers with a spade" saw themselves as part of a socialist community, not outside it. They organized collections for North Vietnam and freedom movements in Africa. When Ho Chi Minh died in 1969, eight *Bausoldaten* on the island of Rügen sent their condolences to the ambassador of North Vietnam. They expressed their "sincere sympathy with the pain of the Vietnamese people" and condemned the "American campaign of extermination." "We like you want peace: we just have different views about how to reach it." These people may have been physically behind the Wall, but intellectually they, too, were part of the international peace movement. They talked about Martin Luther King Jr. as well as Martin Niemöller and sang "We Shall Overcome" in honor of Angela Davis, the American civil rights activist, feted in the GDR. They discussed texts on the arms race by Weizsäcker and the American Linus Pauling, who had the unique distinction of winning two Nobel Prizes, one for chemistry and the other for peace, for his campaign against nuclear arms.[151]

The *Bausoldaten* were fewer than 1 percent of regular recruits, but their influence far outweighed their number. Their work in churches and youth groups made them amplifiers of a counter-public that nourished the peace movement in the 1980s. Prior to becoming a dissident pastor in East Berlin, Rainer Eppelmann was a conscientious objector; in 1966, he spent eight months in prison for refusing to take the pledge of obedience. (He could hardly have imagined that, in 1990, he would be in charge of winding down the East German army as minister of disarmament and defense in the last government before reunification.) Hansjörg Weigel was born in Chemnitz in 1943. His rebellion against his Nazi father made him initially a model socialist. He even volunteered to be a border guard. Religious conversion made him lay down his gun in 1963. In 1970, he was elected to the church council of the small Saxon town of Königswalde. Four years later, he took charge of youth work there and launched the first of many peace seminars.[152]

It was a short step from the *Bausoldaten*'s critique of militarism to a demand for democratic rights. The very concept of serving "with a gun in one's hand" became meaningless in an age of nuclear weapons, a group argued in an anonymous protest letter in 1985. They demanded full equality between civilian and military service, including the "increasing democratization of the command principle." They wanted their own elected delegates to represent their interests in the army. Ultimately, military service should be voluntary, leaving it up to citizens how they wanted to serve their country.[153] That choice would come, but not until the GDR itself was gone.

I REFUSE!

In West Germany in the 1960s and 1970s, the question of conscience and alternative service became the testing ground for the moral direction of society at large. Civilian service began to stand for self-development, social caring, and lived democracy. The number of "*Zivis*"—*Zivildienstleistende*, objectors doing their civilian service—took off, and the sixteen to twenty months of alternative service developed into a life stage for a new generation of West Germans, one that made citizens out of them just as the army had been said to "make a man" out of its recruits. The 500,000th conscientious objector was recognized in 1982.

The constitution was clear that citizens could not be compelled against their conscience to use arms, but it did not say what that conscience was or how it would be tested. For the next four decades, the conscience was the subject of a tug-of-war between the state, courts, churches, and social movements.

One disagreement concerned its depth. Should the use of arms plunge a person into a crisis of conscience at all times (the "universal" position) or was it sufficient to be troubled by the prospect of a particular war, such as a nuclear conflict, or having to aim a gun at one's cousins in East Germany (a "concrete" position)? The Army Law in 1956 (Paragraph 25) took the former view. The latter "concrete" view, though, was not without support, and not only from war resisters. A young Christian Democrat, Heiner Geissler, wrote his law PhD on the subject in 1960 and would rise to be a combative party secretary of the CDU in the 1980s before he came to be known in his old age as "Yoda," for his looks and his wisdom. Geissler defended conscientious objection as a source of strength for a democratic state and argued that the constitution covered concrete and absolute resisters alike. Both reached the same conclusion for the same reason: "Thou shalt not kill," in this particular situation. That was all that mattered. And if there was no difference between the two groups, they needed to be treated alike: the Army Law thus violated the constitution.

This was also the conclusion reached by perhaps the most eminent jurist of his generation, Ernst-Wolfgang Böckenförde, who was both a Social Democrat and, as a pupil of Carl Schmitt, a firm defender of the state. In this view, following Hegel, the state was upheld by the ethics and morality of its citizens, who, in turn, recognized the state as the guarantor of their freedom. To reject particular objections as irrelevant downgraded certain types of conscience and, thus, undermined the integrity of the state itself. By 1985, Böckenförde sat on the Constitutional Court. The constitution, he said, defended freedom of conscience in general, regardless of the form it took. Moreover, what was to be tested was not conscience in the abstract but conscientious *objection*, that is, a decision deriving from it, and a decision was, by definition, taken in a concrete situation. His fellow judges were not swayed by his view, but his minority opinion put a significant dent in the orthodoxy.[154]

The search for "absolute" criteria had profound consequences. Fourteen days prior to their inspection for military service, conscientious objectors were required to submit a written justification of their reasons, which formed the basis for an oral examination in front of a tribunal, chaired by a representative of the Ministry of Defense. The final decision rested with the lay assessors who carried out the examination. Inevitably, the process was likened to the Spanish Inquisition. That was an exaggeration, but it contained a kernel of truth. To grant certification, the tribunal had to be convinced of the depth and sincerity of a candidate's ethical principles. Long-standing membership in a church, sect, or pacifist body served them well. A sudden conversion or break in someone's career, on the other hand, could just as easily be held against a candidate. In the case of a car mechanic who became a social worker, the change in jobs was seen not as proof of his sincerity but of his "imbalance" (*Unausgeglichenheit*). Others had their application rejected because they belonged to a shooting club. Some tribunals expected objectors to be dogmatic; others saw this as proof that they were schematic and, hence, artificial.[155]

The conscience had to be performed as a part of the self in a way that was coherent and convincing. The inner voice had to speak out, which required an emotional as well as an intellectual response. Recent writers have noted how suffering has become an increasingly important litmus test in asylum and welfare policies in many parts of the world in recent years.[156] The politics of emotion, though, did not start with our own neoliberal times. The fascination with sympathy reaches back to the Enlightenment. Earlier, we have seen repeatedly how expressions of suffering played a critical role after the war, for the expellees in particular.

The tribunals for conscientious objectors created a new platform for emotional reason. If carrying a gun caused someone an existential crisis, even if their own country was under attack, then the depth of that concern should be palpable—coercion would need to damage his "ethical self" (*sittliche Person*), in the words of the Bundesverwaltungsgericht, the highest administrative court. Tribunals argued that in Germany it was "natural" to have inhibitions against killing, but that these could be overcome through willpower. "Natural" conscientious objectors interjected at this point: "In spite of Auschwitz?"[157] Self-help groups advised candidates what to expect and how to prepare for the tribunal: be punctual and appear confident, "one must have internalized one's attitude"; "a bit of acting does not hurt—let the emotions flow a little." Candidates could turn to sample questions and model statements. "What would you feel when you have fatally wounded the attacker?" Another frequent question concerned tyrannicide: "Would you support the murder of a dangerous dictator such as Hitler or, perhaps… even carry it out yourself?"[158]

Given the still widespread idea that the 1960s were all about generational conflict, it is worth stressing that many resisters had the support of their fathers. A young printer in Munich—the first in his firm to register as an objector in 1961—chose his father as a witness to testify to his integrity; the father had lost both brothers in the war and agreed that any war was a crime and the sheer existence of an army preparation for it. A decade later, a high school student who had been politicized by the war in Vietnam thanked his father, who had served in the war, for raising him to be an antimilitarist; he was also grateful to his teachers, former POWs, for making him aware of the bloody side of war. In general, parents and peers were more important guides on the path to conscientious objection than the APO.[159]

Support groups advised candidates to write their own case against war by weaving together personal tragedy, convictions, and emotions into a single moral autobiography. A sample letter from 1976 offered a blueprint. It came from an objector born in 1955. The pain of war was part of his biography from earliest childhood. His uncles had died fighting in Russia and France, his father returned from a POW camp. "This fact," the letter spelled out, "made the idea of war terrible to me, because war killed people whom I would have loved to have as uncles." When he told his father he was thinking of applying for conscientious objection, his father "suddenly began to cry—the first time I have seen him like that. Never before had I been so close to him." The father told him that he was proud of him. Nonviolence, the son added, had been part of his upbringing. Even when he was attacked by thugs on a trip to England he did not fight back; initial hatred turned into pity for the attackers. Reading aloud antiwar poems by Kurt Tucholsky made him cry in front of his girlfriend. ("And if they come and threaten you with pistols! Don't go . . . No conscription! No soldiers! . . . You are the future! Yours is the land! Shake off the shackles of serfdom. If only you want, you will be free," from 1922.) The letter ended by documenting his social commitment. He volunteered in the local youth center—"We see ourselves as the alternative to the pricey and stupid discos and bars." He saw his future as a social worker and had already completed an internship in a hospital that brought him face-to-face with people's suffering: "I often felt so low." This was how one bared one's sensitive soul to the tribunal.[160]

Of course, communicating emotions was not everyone's strength, nor were all candidates able to draw on dead uncles and weeping fathers. The rate of rejections was high—in 1969, tribunals rejected half the candidates in the first round. Candidates could appeal, but this cost time and money. The process tended to favor privileged students over their less educated, poorer peers, and that put it at odds with the normative principle of equality that underpinned all constitutional rights.

The churches were increasingly uneasy about the procedure. Candidates were expected to prove that they were opposed to war at all times and, effectively, greater "ethical purists" than the Catholic and Protestant Churches themselves, which, after all, had distinguished between "just" and "unjust" wars for centuries. Spiritual counselors found themselves in an awkward position, worrying that the test of conscience encouraged dissimulation and alienated young citizens from the state.

By 1970, deep divisions were running through both churches. On one side, the Protestant military bishop Hermann Kunst and the Catholic bishop Franz Hengsbach diagnosed objectors as "the disease of society." Kunst was convinced that only every third candidate had "genuine reasons of conscience"; the others were hoping to evade service altogether. The tribunals therefore played a vital role in sifting the authentic objectors from the shirkers. On the others side, a growing number of Christians came to demand an end to the tribunals.[161]

In 1977, Helmut Schmidt's social-liberal coalition scrapped the tribunals and replaced them with a simple postcard that young adults could send in to indicate their refusal, without having to give a reason. The Christian Democrats were up in arms and appealed to the Constitutional Court, which ruled the postcards a breach of the Basic Law. The right to refuse specifically said that people could not be forced to use arms "against their conscience," not that they could choose between military and civilian service as they pleased; the conscience needed to be checked somehow. In 1983, a compromise was reached. The oral examination was dropped, but the written justification was kept; only objectors who were already in the army had to submit to both.

The sharp rise in the number of conscientious objectors—from 6,000 applications in 1967 to 27,000 in 1971 and 70,000 in 1977—raised another thorny question: Was civilian service becoming so attractive because it was a "soft" option? By law, the two types of service were meant to be equivalent. Some Christian Democrats proposed moving all objectors into barracks, others wanted them to chop trees and clear swamps—such forest work had, in fact, been the norm for their peers in Norway, Britain, and the United States, but its association with the Nazi labor service made it a political dead letter. Extending the length of civilian service appealed as a way of sorting the genuine objectors from the shirkers, especially once the verbal examination was gone. In 1984, the Kohl government made civilian service five months longer than the fifteen months required in the army. On the Constitutional Court, it was, again, Böckenförde who opposed this on grounds of equality; making conscientious objectors serve longer risked marking them out as cowards or less worthy citizens. The principle of equivalence also came under attack from conscientious objectors and their friends in the churches. There was a world of difference between serving in an army with nuclear weapons and serving in a care home. The latter worked to reduce conflict and build trust, while the former did the opposite. To treat the two as equal and complementary was obscuring their fundamental difference, a

Catholic action group said. The deepening of peace placed civilian service on a higher moral plane.[162]

"PEACE, BALANCE, AND TENDERNESS"

In the first decade after conscription, the number of those who applied for conscientious objection was small and never more than 5,000 out of the 400,000 men who were called up each year, of whom 3,000 were granted the requested status.[163] Since it was also possible to avoid the draft by moving to West Berlin, these official figures need to be treated with caution. Still, in the early years of West Germany its ratio was comparable to that for the first generation of war resisters in Britain during the First World War. It was from the late 1960s that West German numbers multiplied, until, by the early 1980s, 12 percent of young men applied and by 1990 even 25 percent. There was nothing typical about this boom; in Denmark, in contrast, the number of objectors was falling in the 1970s.

What came together in the person of the conscientious objector were fundamental shifts in the way West Germans began to see themselves, their society, and their place in the world. Until the mid-1960s, Quakers and war resisters were small groups with limited reach. When they were invited to speak in schools, they were stunned by how few pupils were aware of their constitutional rights. Some believed objectors had to work for ten years, others that they faced execution.[164] The Auschwitz trial (1963–65), the Vietnam War (1955–75), and the Second Vatican Council (1962–65) brought a change in atmosphere. Advice bureaus multiplied, and Catholics added their support to that of Protestants. Schools began to debate the issue, and leaflets found their way into the barracks. For soldiers who already had doubts, nuclear weapons made it even harder to justify their service on conventional grounds of defense; from 1968 onward, a couple thousand would apply for conscientious objection every year. Simultaneously, the turn to active peacefulness raised the status of civilian service. Instead of standing for a negative act of refusal, it made conscientious objectors positive contributors to trust, reconciliation, and social healing. In the process, conscience was transformed from a repressive into an emancipatory force that, according to progressive Catholics, "shows itself in the course of social goals, political planning, and communicative action": "a force of mutual action for peace."[165]

By 1972, it was possible to hear on radio programs that the *Zivi* was a more valuable member of society than the regular soldier because not only had he inspected his conscience, he was also helping those whom society had failed.

Civilian service was a service for peace, the Protestant delegate for conscientious objectors in Hesse explained that year, because working with vulnerable groups and minorities confronted them with "entirely new learning experiences" and made them "reflect on their sociopolitical significance."[166]

Caring for others was not automatically selfless. On the contrary, it inspired a new care for the self. Social service called for empathy, which, in turn, required one to look deep into one's own soul. Fear of nuclear technology and growing doubts about state planning found their outlet in a new romanticism—not for nothing did the German prog-rock band Novalis call itself after an ethereal romantic poet. Shedding tears was the sign of a new, sensitive manliness. If the army repressed the self, civilian service liberated it.

These cultural shifts, of course, swept across the West. What made them so resonant for objectors in West Germany were the peculiar nature of the welfare state and the Nazi shadow that hung over authority. Many hospitals and care homes were in the hands of the churches and independent welfare bodies. Civilian service was thus easily embraced as anti-state, a step toward autonomy and freedom that would shed the authoritarian elements of the fascist personality. One *Zivi* who worked with cancer patients in a center for alternative medicine, for example, understood his civilian service as a form of "direct action." Society, he wrote in 1966, had become too bureaucratic: "The life course is fully planned, and there is a ministry, committee, and official for everything." For him, civilian service was a chance to practice "social self-responsibility" by becoming aware of his duty toward the ill and helping those who had been failed by society and its institutions. Civilian service was giving him "peace, balance, and tenderness"; he called it a "way of life."[167]

When some *Zivis* were put in barracks on army grounds with guard towers in 1969, it immediately led to comparisons with Auschwitz and triggered strikes. There lay a deep irony in this anti-statist thrust. For not only was this generation the beneficiary of an unprecedented and publicly funded widening of access to schools and universities, which made it possible to pursue a career as a social worker or psychologist; the expansion of welfare services, too, was ultimately underwritten by the state, even if a lot of those services were delivered by the churches. In short, the rise of conscientious objectors would have been inconceivable without the rise of the social state.

Until the mid-1960s, objections were mainly made on religious grounds. By 1968, however, humanitarian ethical reasons (49 percent) had beaten religious ones (23 percent) into second place; social and political grounds made up the rest.[168] Mahatma Gandhi and Martin Luther King Jr. leapfrogged

Jesus Christ. Objectors were increasingly drawing on an alternative milieu that stretched from peace weeks and Aktion Sühnezeichen to "open" youth work and "Third World" shops. Dutch activists were important contacts, as were British and American pacifists.[169]

Instead of hierarchy and submission, social service promised equality and freedom. A *Zivi* in the 1970s explained that he enjoyed his work in a psychiatric hospital near Munich because there he was recognized as a member of a "team." Everyone chipped in to the discussion. "I have the same rights as the educators." Another objector wrote of his time in a school for disabled children. The food was often awful, he admitted, but at least he had his own room and anyone could stay over, in stark contrast with life in the barracks: "I can come and go as I please." Not everyone was that fortunate. In the Ruhr region, the government concentrated one hundred *Zivis* in a former boarding house for coal miners and guest workers. By 1975, however, every second objector had their own private quarters. Most found their work through their own efforts—or their mother's; only 15 percent of places were arranged through the churches.[170]

Freedom and recognition were hard won. In the early 1960s, it was normal for conscientious objectors to be treated as "malingerers or a necessary evil" by the main Protestant charity.[171] Catholic homes for children and the elderly were almost exclusively staffed by women, and young men were often turned away lest they bring a "certain disturbance" with them, as a Caritas offical put it in 1970. Those who took them on were mostly satisfied, although there were repeated complaints about "poor punctuality, diligence, irresponsible handling of disabled children, disruption of peaceful work relations, and undermining of work ethic." Some *Zivis* brought female nurses back to their rooms, in which they had hung pictures of Chairman Mao; it was not clear which was the worse offense. *Zivis* with an *Abitur* were singled out as lacking the "necessary service ethos and proper inner disposition." Catholic institutions had better experiences with religious than with political objectors.

What added to the tensions was a clash of expectations. Objectors wanted to do hands-on peace service, to heal the sick and feed the old. Many institutions, by contrast, saw them as a cheap pair of hands for the kitchen. A Catholic children's sanatorium in southern Germany relied on three objectors in 1963. One worked as a porter; a second was used as a handyman (the "excessive electricity consumption caused by his playing cards at night" was a constant source of complaint); and a third was assigned to peel potatoes and feed the pigs (how he could refuse to do so on holidays and was "repeatedly found sleeping in the hay" instead was beyond his superiors).[172]

Work with patients, disabled persons, and vulnerable groups expanded in the 1970s and 1980s. More than anything else, it was the rise in outpatient treatment (*ambulante Pflege*) that gave the *Zivis* a new public face. The unpatriotic coward and malingerer from yesteryear turned into the nice young man who was bringing the elderly their lunch or pushing a wheelchair in the park. Employers began to appreciate the flexibility and independence that former *Zivis* brought with them. By the 1980s, social service was considered as important as military service by most of the population. For a growing number it was even the more valuable of the two.[173]

The mainstreaming of social service was not without its own dilemmas. For "total objectors," civilian, like military, service was an unacceptable imposition by the state. Civilian life, they argued, was being subordinated to military logic, and, in an emergency, objectors could be deployed for civilian defense. (In 1983, total objectors were estimated to number between ten thousand and thirty thousand, either in prison or living in the safe haven of West Berlin, where there was no conscription.) One did not have to be a fundamentalist to express doubts about the direction civilian service was taking. In 1978, mentors in churches reported how recent cohorts were increasingly "searching for their own individual happiness." "The anti-militarist elements that they partly still had when applying as conscientious objectors are barely left in their consciousness."[174] The picture of life in a rural commune was as clear to them as the political vision of peace service had become hazy.

Even for those with the best intentions, peacefulness was a path strewn with doubts and obstacles. It was in the nature of "structural violence" that its causes lay deeper than what individuals could hope to fix themselves. One young man doing his service in a psychiatric hospital wondered whether social service was a cure or whether it simply recycled systemic problems. Many patients, he felt, were wrecks because of their parents and the society around them. It made him "part of a repair workshop for the substandard goods produced by society." The best he could do was to help them live an "inconspicuous life."[175]

"SOLDIERS ARE MURDERERS"

In 1981, a printer in Schleswig-Holstein was told by his boss to produce advertisements for a series of books with accounts from German combat soldiers during the Second World War. The printer said he could not reconcile it with his conscience to print material that glorified war, and refused. He was fired. Three years later, in a public meeting in a school in Frankfurt, a doctor told an army youth officer that "every soldier is a potential murderer—you too." The officer sued him for defamation.

Similar cases kept German courts busy over the next few years. They illustrate how far Germany had come since 1945 but also how polarized the country remained. These years are often summed up under the label of *Vergangenheitsbewältigung* and *Aufarbeitung*—that is, learning to confront and work through the past. The Second World War was center stage in that confrontation, but people took different moral lessons from the past. Instead of leading to resolution or closure, the process produced new divides.

The printer, who happened to be a recognized conscientious objector and a supporter of the victims of fascism (VVN), had his claim for unfair dismissal rejected first by the local and then by the regional labor court on the grounds that he seemed to have a problem only with fascist violence and not with the communist kind. His refusal therefore expressed his politics, not his conscience. The books were not illegal. The court wished he had shown more flexibility. It took another appeal before the federal labor court eventually overruled the decision. Not only did it agree with the printer that the books glorified the war, it also came to the rescue of his conscience. It was precisely because he had a conscience—"a genuinely palpable mental phenomenon"—that he could not possibly be receptive to "reasonable" arguments and reach a compromise with his employer.[176]

The Frankfurt doctor had served in the army ambulance unit before joining the campaign for nuclear disarmament. His case went through five courts before, in 1992, it was eventually discontinued for involving "negligible guilt" only.[177]

The slogan "Soldiers are murderers," meanwhile, sparked heated debates in town squares and barracks across the country. It had a politically charged history. The words were from a 1931 article by the antiwar writer Kurt Tucholsky. The editor responsible for printing it, Carl von Ossietzky, was prosecuted for defamation of the Reichswehr. Ossietzky was already in prison for treason—he had revealed the secret buildup of the German air force, which circumvented the Versailles Treaty—but was found not guilty of defamation, and released in a Christmas amnesty. In 1933, he was among the first to be thrown in a concentration camp by the Nazis, and neither an international campaign for his release nor the Nobel Peace Prize in 1936 was enough to save him. He died in 1938, in a Berlin hospital under Gestapo surveillance, of tuberculosis and torture.

Fifty years later, a couple of pacifists in Osnabrück, in northern Germany, had their banners and flyers with the same slogan seized by the police for obstructing a navy recruitment stand. A different group of soldiers took out an advertisement and wrote to MPs saying they agreed with the statement: nuclear deterrence created a crisis of conscience for them, because its failure would enlist them in "indiscriminate mass murder." One major was disciplined and demoted to captain as a consequence, a decision that would be overruled by the Constitutional Court. The Federal Administrative Court ultimately recognized his motivations as of a "high ethical standard" but fined him 500 DM regardless.[178]

Christoph Hiller did not get away so cheaply. In February 1991, the thirty-one-year-old social worker put three stickers on his car: "Swords into Plowshares"; "Soldiers Are Murderers," and a picture of a dying soldier based on Robert Capa's iconic photograph from the Spanish civil war. A month earlier, the United States had launched Operation Desert Storm against the Iraqi invasion of Kuwait. The campaign exposed the sore spot of postwar Germany's self-image as a post-militarist nation. The consensus was that the Bundeswehr existed for national defense only; missions abroad had been limited to humanitarian aid. The idea of sending troops not only into battle but even outside NATO's area set off popular and constitutional alarm bells. The Kohl government turned down the Americans' request for direct involvement but nonetheless dispatched a fighter bomber squadron to Turkey and mine sweepers to the Persian Gulf in support of Germany's NATO partners; he also wrote a check worth 17 billion DM ($10 billion at the time). When a first lieutenant of the reserve stumbled across Hiller's car and sticker, he sued him for "incitement" (*Volksverhetzung*). A local court duly fined him 8,400 DM—four months' salary. Hiller appealed and invoked his freedom of conscience and opinion. The officer responded by adding a claim for compensation (*Schmerzensgeld*). Hiller had his salary attached to cover the fine, including court costs, until the Constitutional Court in August 1994 came to his rescue and overruled the decision: the stickers expressed a general opinion and had not defamed Bundeswehr soldiers specifically.[179]

This was not how a considerable section of the German public understood the slogan. The verdict set off a public storm. Only a month earlier, the Constitutional Court had found that German troops could legitimately be sent "out of area" as long as parliament supported it. The ruling validated the historic decision by the Kohl government, in 1993, to dispatch planes to the war zone in Bosnia. For the first time since 1945, German soldiers were now engaged in combat. Against this background, newspapers denounced the "Soldiers are murderers" verdict as an "intolerable impertinence": the constitutional right to freedom of expression was damaged if it was used as a protective shield to discriminate against entire groups.[180] The Bundeswehr was not Hitler's army. It was a defensive force of peace and humanitarianism whose soldiers had flown through hails of bullets to feed the starving in Sarajevo. Their job was to stop Bosnian-Serbian planes from bombing and violating the UN no-fly zone. They deserved the nation's thanks and protection.

That was also the view of Evelyn Haas, the one dissenting judge on the Constitutional Court. A state that made it a duty for men to serve in the army, she wrote, also had a duty to protect them from defamation. The "reciprocal relationship between protection and obedience" was a "fundamental principle of the legal system."[181] The newspaper *Die Welt* spelled out the moral lesson that it wanted to be drawn from the Nazi past: concentration camp victims had been saved by "soldiers with tanks and guns, not by peace protestors." The same Heiner Geissler who as a young law student had written a broad-minded defense of conscientious objection now warned of the "total degeneration [*Verwilderung*] of political debate." In parliament, the Liberal Hans-Dietrich Genscher, the veteran former foreign secretary, called it a scandal that robbed soldiers and their families of their first right under the constitution—the protection of their human dignity. For Chancellor Kohl, the attack was personal—both his sons had signed up for two years of military service.[182]

The mailbags of newspapers were bursting with letters expressing a mix of anger and sympathy. Some readers suggested placing limits on freedom of expression where it undermined the public interest. Officers wanted recognition for their contribution to "the longest period of peace in German history": "Do we active and former soldiers of the Bundeswehr have no honor?" Others were troubled by the disproportionate reaction to an antiwar slogan at a time when neo-Nazis were given suspended sentences because courts found that their denial of the Holocaust did not disturb the public peace. Like the rest of German society, war veterans were increasingly divided. The slogan was entirely correct, one veteran wrote in 1995: "We were murderers." He doubted it would be any different for Bundeswehr soldiers now. "Are there still people who do not understand that those who reach for the sword will also die by the sword?"[183]

9

Strangers at Home: The Difficulties of Difference

On the eve of reunification, in 1989, West Germany was home to 5 million foreigners. Most of them were so-called *Gastarbeiter,* guest workers from Italy, Spain, Portugal, Greece, Yugoslavia, and, especially, Turkey who had started to come during the economic boom and ended up staying for good, bringing their families and children. Together, they made up 8 percent of the population. Across the Wall, in East Germany, lived some 160,000 foreigners, mainly contract laborers from socialist Vietnam, Poland, and Mozambique, plus a sprinkling of foreign students—around 1 percent of the GDR's population, not counting the twice as many Soviet soldiers stationed there.

"Germany is not a country of immigration [*Einwanderungsland*]" was the gospel of West German leaders. In truth, migration had long shaped Germany. In the nineteenth century, it had been Germans who emigrated to the New World. From the 1890s, the flow was also in the other direction, with Polish laborers going down the coal mines of the Ruhr. Smaller colonies of Italian workers and Ottoman Jews sprang up, too. During the First World War, almost 2 million POWs were put to work. The Nazis transported 8 million civilians from Eastern Europe to the Reich, forcing them to work in armament factories, on farms, and in private homes.

Foreigners, in other words, had been a regular sight in German society, and German industry had long been powered by their sweat and muscle. The new arrivals from the Mediterranean were often called by the same name that had been in use during the Nazi years for forced workers from central and Eastern Europe: *Fremdarbeiter* ("alien workers").[1]

The new term that would gain currency—*Gastarbeiter*—signaled one fundamental difference between the migrants from the South and their immediate predecessors from the East: they had come voluntarily and were free to return home whenever they chose. That was, in fact, what the majority did. The label "guest workers" was not completely wrong. Eleven million people who came to work in West Germany during the boom returned to their home country. But then there were the 3 million who decided to stay.

That migration on this scale would confront the host society with challenges was apparent from the start. In 1963, the permanent committee on labor questions—a joint body of the Federal Labor Office, the welfare organizations, and the social security offices of the states—met in Frankfurt. Although some 800,000 foreign workers were by now living in West Germany and some had brought their families, the committee found that it was still "unclear whether foreigners should be integrated, who should be integrated, and under what conditions and in what form." Officials seemed to have no idea "where all of this will lead."[2] Time would tell.

What did "more democracy," partnership, compassion, and respect for others mean when distant strangers became local neighbors, and when, in the West, boom turned to bust? In the GDR, where foreign laborers were less numerous, their presence presented its own type of challenge—a society where calls for solidarity with socialist brothers and sisters was matched by a shortage of goods. How the hosts treated their guests can tell us a lot about what living with difference meant in the two Germanies.

IN DENIAL

West Germany signed its first recruitment deal with Italy in 1955. Spain and Greece followed in 1960. A massive increase in foreign labor came after 1961, when the Wall closed off the influx of cheap labor made up of Germans fleeing the GDR. To plug the gap, West Germany concluded treaties with Turkey (1961, 1964), Portugal (1964), and Yugoslavia (1968). South Korea (1963) sent much-needed nurses.

The agreements served the overlapping interests of all parties. West Germany was booming and had lots of machines, southern Europe had lots of idle hands. In Germany, the unemployment rate fell below 2 percent in 1960, and migrant workers could expect to earn four times what they made back home. For the Federal Republic, the guest worker program was a huge "win-win." The migrants stoked the engine of growth and took over the hardest jobs in coal, steel, and textiles, thereby enabling local workers to switch to better jobs and rise up the social ladder. The mostly young and healthy foreigners helped fund the welfare state with their taxes without making any demands on it themselves. Greater movement of labor served European integration and the government's foreign policy interests. Officials hoped that on their eventual return to their homes, guest workers would become ambassadors of the reformed Germany, a not unimportant consideration in the case of Greece and Yugoslavia, which had suffered heavily under the Nazis. "The Turk," meanwhile, "would change into a European person thanks to his encounter with Germans," reasoned an official at the Federal Labor Office who was one of the champions of that agreement.[3]

For the Mediterranean countries, in turn, emigration relieved demographic pressure and promised valuable Deutschmark in remittances. For Turkey, which had joined NATO in 1952, labor recruitment was another bridge to the West. In addition, there was the hope that migrants would return with skills and savings to help develop the mother country. As members of the European Economic Community, Italians enjoyed free movement as early as 1961, although countries retained the right to reserve key jobs in hard times. After 1968, Italians (and other citizens from the EEC) could stay, even after finishing their job. Turkish workers had their work permits initially limited to two years, but the time limit was lifted in 1964 after protests that workers from Spain and Greece (neither of which was yet in the EEC) were allowed to bring their families with them. Sending and receiving countries both proceeded on the assumption that eventually the guest workers would return home. Most did, but millions stayed. It was a textbook illustration of how economic interests can distort understanding of the real world, ignoring how people actually live their lives.

On Monday, September 7, 1964, the thirty-eight-year-old carpenter Armando Rodrigues de Sá boarded a train at Canas de Senhorim in Portugal. When he arrived in Cologne three days later, he was ceremoniously welcomed as the millionth guest worker. The event became an iconic moment, remembered for his perplexed look at the many photographers and the Zündapp moped he received as a gift. Forgotten was the revealing answer he gave when asked how long he intended to stay. He was unsure, he said, but what he did know was that he was planning for his wife and two children to join him.[4] It signaled the state of affairs to come.

If migration followed the logic of the labor market at the start of the 1960s, it was doing less and less so by the end. Between 1964 and 1972, some 400,000 workers were returning to their home country each year, but they were outnumbered by new arrivals in Germany. For a growing number of migrants, West Germany was becoming a country to settle in. There were plenty of indicators of this change, for anyone who wanted to see them. Official figures in 1973 showed that 19 percent of foreigners had been in the country for four to six years, and 16 percent for ten years or longer.[5] Fifty-six percent of married workers were already living together with their families. And the national composition of the migrant community was changing: Turkish citizens were now the dominant group. In stark contrast to Italian guest workers, who (as members of the EEC) could draw unemployment benefits back home and whose wives and children stayed behind in the Mezzogiorno, where they received family allowances from the Federal Republic, Turkish parents were increasingly bringing their children to live with them in Germany. Many were still dreaming of an eventual return, but as the last group to arrive en masse, they also tended to have the fewest savings to do that.

The German government made the decision as to whether they would stay or leave for them. In November 1973, in the wake of the oil crisis, rising unemployment, and concerns over the resulting demands on state coffers, it decided to stop all foreign recruitment, hoping to drive down the number of migrants. The effect was the opposite. Not only were there few prospects in Turkey to lure them, but now traveling home would mean the loss of residence status and any chance to reenter West Germany. Instead of leaving, the "guests" decided to bring their families and put down roots. For many, the moment they came to accept that they would be in Germany for good was the day their children entered a German school. The "stop" of foreign recruitment simultaneously managed to reduce the number of foreigners in paid work paying taxes and increase the number of children, dependents, and those out of work calling on the state for assistance. The military coup in Turkey in 1980 and the mass arrests and persecution that followed added a wave of refugees. In 1973, 900,000 Turks lived in the Federal Republic; by 1981, it was more than 1.5 million. The total number of foreigners had risen to 4.6 million by then. As the historian Peter Gatrell has observed, "Migration was not a tap that could be turned on and off at a moment's notice."[6]

The mantra that "Germany is not a country of immigration" was a fateful self-deception that incapacitated successive governments and let down citizens and migrants alike. Instead of a policy, there was the Hellas-Istanbul Express, which delivered migrants who had signed up with German firms to Munich and Dortmund. Inaction was, in part, a convenient response to an irreconcilable conflict of interests. West Germany was trying to have its cake and eat it, too. The Labor Office and Foreign Ministry wanted as much free movement of labor with as few strings attached as possible—that was best for German business and European integration. The Ministry of the Interior, on the other hand, wanted national security and limited work permits to keep out "undesirable elements" and foreign communists and prevent militants from continuing their struggle on German soil—in 1962, right-wing Croatian separatists had bombed the Yugoslavian Trade Mission in Bonn-Mehlem.

The new Aliens Law of 1965 offered a pragmatic compromise. For their residence permits, foreigners were at the mercy of five hundred local Aliens Offices that decided whether their presence was "in the interests of Germany." These offices had wide powers and could reject applications for family reunion and withdraw permits for infractions, leading to deportation. Political activity was explicitly forbidden in a clause that was also used against strikers.

The root of the problem, though, was German citizenship. Attempts to control migration have been widespread across the modern world. What set West Germany apart was its citizenship law and the rigid mind-set that came with it. It assumed that only people with shared descent were fit to be citizens. This was not a deep tradition, as is sometimes believed. Before unification in 1871, it was common for citizenship to be awarded on the basis of domicile, not blood.[7] The latter basis (*ius sanguinis*) only became the norm in 1913. Nazi rule left behind a country that was not only truncated and divided but also ethnically more homogenous than before, and it was against this background that politicians viewed the influx of foreigners. It made for a radically different legal constellation to that in the United States or, say, in Britain, where for two decades after the war migrants from former colonies arrived as Commonwealth citizens with the right to work and stay, before immigration was restricted in 1968 and 1971. In West Germany, guest workers were outside the mental as well as legal pale of citizenship, in addition to speaking a different language. There was broad consensus across the political spectrum that one was either born a German citizen or one was not. Citizenship was not something one could grow into. To try to assimilate the guest workers would only damage them, the leading Social Democrat, Carlo Schmid, one of the constitutional fathers, explained in 1971: it would cut off the "root base that made them grow and from which they drew the juices and salts without which there can be no spiritual and mental growth."[8]

There was nothing inevitable about this dogmatic course. The Netherlands was also hit by the oil crisis, yet kept its doors open and promoted family reunion. Sweden, like Germany, had citizenship by descent, but in 1975 embraced multiculturalism, eased naturalization, and gave foreigners the right to vote in local elections. It recognized migrants' equal rights to welfare and left it up to them to decide whether they wanted to assimilate or preserve their native culture.[9] The German "stop" was not followed by mass deportations. Guest workers could not suddenly be chucked out, Chancellor Brandt insisted: to treat them as an "industrial reserve army" would be "asocial . . . inhumane," and, he added, "uneconomical";[10] firms did not want to start recruiting and training all over again once the economy picked up. Still, Willy Brandt was not Olof Palme. His motto "Dare more democracy" was for German ears only. Foreigners would have to wait until 2000 for citizenship to be liberalized.

Being "guests," not citizens, had fundamental consequences for how hosts and migrants engaged with each other. On the one hand, West Germany was spared racist riots such as those in Notting Hill in 1958, when several hundred white Londoners attacked their neighbors from the West Indies. Since foreigners were "guests" only, they appeared more of a temporary nuisance than a permanent threat to native jobs, housing, and identity. Discrimination and individual assaults were plentiful, but they did not coalesce into collective violence. Being at the mercy of the Aliens Office and imagining a return also made migrants less prone to direct their frustrations at their host society. When violence erupted, it was over the future of their homelands and targeted their fellow countrymen, as in fights between nationalist Croats and supporters of Tito's Yugoslavia, the Greek left and the Greek right after the military coup in 1967, and attacks by the militant Kurdish PKK on Turkish facilities in Germany and elsewhere in Western Europe.

On the other hand, the lack of rights and the mutually shared illusion of an eventual departure left migrants with little stake in the country they lived in and with no say over its future. Naturalization was possible after ten years of residence and proof of assimilation, but it was the extreme exception to the rule and strongly discouraged by the authorities. Insufficient income, problems with alcohol, and even car accidents were sufficient grounds for rejection. No provision for dual citizenship was a further obstacle, since many migrants did not want to cut their ties to their home country completely. Between 1973 and 1986, 900,000 Turkish residents became eligible for naturalization: barely 8,000 applied.[11] Yugoslav migrants were three times as likely to naturalize in Belgium than in Germany.[12] Children born to migrants settled in Germany were born and remained foreigners, as did their children in turn.

The Federal Republic has been widely heralded as a *demokratischer Rechts- und Sozialstaat* ("democratic welfare state based on the rule of law"). For guest workers it was neither democratic nor particularly social. In the 1960s, taxes on their wages and consumption raised ten times as much public revenue as the state spent on them. Italian and Turkish workers, in other words, not only built Volkswagen Beetles and shoveled coal, they also paid for German schools and pensions. The city of Munich estimated that its foreign residents contributed one quarter of all the pension benefits it paid out in 1970.[13] When it came to their own needs, migrants found themselves at the bottom of the food chain. Precious public housing and day care spots went to Germans first.

By the early 1980s, many German cities paid lip service to integration. Yet, when they were asked to support a "week of friendship" or free up the local football pitch for a couple of hours, there was suddenly no money or space available.[14] The contrast with the treatment of the 3 million ethnic German emigrants (*Aussiedler*) who arrived from Eastern Europe in the 1980s and 1990s was stark. Before 1989, most came from Poland, thereafter from the former Soviet Union. As citizens, they were greeted by a well-oiled machine of state officials and social workers who picked them up at the train station, set up intensive language courses, handed them a generous start-up package, obtained furniture, and found them work. They even managed to locate places in day cares that were officially full.[15]

"WE ASKED FOR WORKERS, AND PEOPLE CAME INSTEAD"

The "guests" had many faces. They were doctors from Istanbul, peasants from Calabria, artisans from Portugal, and students from Iran. The label "guest worker" stuck in media and daily speech and reflected and reinforced a perception of migrants as a homogeneous group. Their diverse biographies and experiences were ignored. In 1965, for example, 36 percent of all Greek migrants were women, but only 13 percent of those coming from Turkey. A couple of years later, in Cologne, 56 percent of all married Greek men were living with their wives, but only 13 percent of Turkish men were.[16] Those who crossed the Bosporus included Alevites and Kurds as well as ethnic Turks. Contrary to a widespread idea, the first groups of Turkish migrants were the most (not least) qualified of all groups, with better education and skills than Italians and Spaniards, who tended to be from rural areas. Many Turkish migrants were artisans, tailors, and skilled miners. The women were educated and would work in electronics and textile factories. Some were doctors, such as Dr. Pala, who bought herself a Volkswagen Beetle from her first salary and drove from Hamburg to the Alps to go skiing. A male colleague belonged to the local sailing club and had his own boat.

In these first few years, the majority of Turkish migrants came from Istanbul and the surrounding Marmara region. They were urban, educated, and secular. Germany enjoyed a positive reputation, thanks in part to having fought alongside the Ottoman Empire in the First World War. Some Turks had learned German in school. Looking back on their arrival in the mid-1960s, a Turkish doctor and his wife said that "actually, there was nothing that felt strange or unusual to us... well, we were amazed by the many motorways... the orderliness, and that the water was always running. But otherwise, nothing. No problems."[17] It was only in the late 1960s that the balance shifted toward migrants from rural Anatolia, who were more religious and had little or no schooling, giving rise to the German stereotype of "the Turk."

Then there were foreign students, who made up 10 percent at major universities and who mainly came from Iran, Greece, and Egypt. One of them was Bahman Taghizadeh, who arrived in 1958 from Tehran to study civil engineering and stayed on working for the railway operator in that capacity. He was one of the few foreigners who naturalized, after the demonstrations against the shah and threats on a visit back home. German citizenship required a recognized first name. In 1988, "Bahman" became "John"—he had always had a soft spot for John Wayne.[18]

Labor migrants arrived via government recruitment programs (Turkey and Greece, especially), a personal job offer, and a consular stamp, or, illegally, by entering the country on a holiday visa and staying on to work (there were some 100,000 of these overstayers in the early 1970s, according to trade union estimates). Most jobs were in coal and steel, car manufacturing, and construction.

An orientation booklet from 1966 told new recruits what to expect in Germany, in their native languages. *Hallo Mustafa!/Hallo Mario!/Hallo Jose!/Hallo Spiros!:* "We want to be good friends. We are fellow citizens, not just in the whole wide world but in this little Europe, which we want to reconstruct together in peace, simply because we belong together." "You are a foreigner, but not alien. We are all sitting in the same boat." The booklet held out the prospect of a long-term future. With tenacity and a little flexibility, the new arrivals were certain to succeed and "not remain a foreigner or guest forever," but be accepted as "an equal and esteemed coworker."[19] The lead author was not a German but Giacomo Maturi, a young lawyer from northern Italy who worked with migrants, first for the Catholic organization Caritas and later for German companies, and who gave advice to many thousands of his countrymen in a dedicated program on West German Radio.

Reality proved somewhat different. Guest workers were handed the dirtiest, most dangerous, and worst paid tasks. Incidents of discrimination are too long to list. "Four days training period, and then assembly line, carrying rocks, and hauling heavy loads," a study for the city of Cologne in 1967 summed up the general approach. "Germans," it continued, "let them do the heavy work, such as digging out a big pipe... while they watch and smoke a cigarette—at the end, they tighten a few screws, barely lifting a finger."[20]

There were some signs of growing appreciation. Initially worried about protecting their members' jobs, the trade unions came round to accepting foreigners as indispensable for growth and prosperity. The guest worker was "a good, diligent, proper worker," several locals told the researchers of the Cologne study—no small praise in a society where diligence (*Fleiss*) came next to tidiness in importance. Still, it was the hosts who dictated the terms. A Turkish worker remembered his foreman telling him, "What a German tells you, you have to do."[21] Training and promotions tended to go to the natives. "The harder I toiled, the quicker I was thrown away like a squeezed lemon," was how Cemal Tümtürk remembered the 1970s. German colleagues hated him for outperforming them. Instead of rewarding him, his boss moved him to the dust-filled stone mill, the most dangerous place around.[22]

Quite a few migrants were recruited for their skills but never given a chance to use them. Several thousand nurses arrived from South Korea and the Philippines in the late 1960s and early 1970s. They had college degrees and were often more qualified than their German peers. A third ended up doing nothing but cleaning hospital floors. "I am sometimes confused," one of them said, "because I do not know whether I am a cleaning lady or a kitchen help... I remember my time in Korea where I administered medication and injections."[23] At a meeting with them in 1975, German mother superiors concurred: the Korean nurses were routinely discriminated against by their German colleagues, assigned the lowest and dirtiest tasks, had their days off canceled without notice, and after six months were still paid on the lowest grade, as if they were untrained. There was a spate of suicides. It was "no surprise," social workers said, that in such a "foreign and frequently cold environment" many were suffering mental illness.[24]

Wildcat strikes erupted repeatedly. The largest took place in the steel and automobile industries in the early 1970s. There were plenty of grievances, from poor pay and unsafe working conditions to employers refusing to give them unpaid holidays so they could go on longer visits back home. Workers were often recruited without receiving clear information about their wages and deductions. At the Hella automobile plant in Lippstadt (North Rhine–Westphalia), guest workers went on strike because as unskilled laborers they were excluded from the pay raises given to their skilled German coworkers. Employers tried to play the two sides off against each other, but this increasingly backfired, as more and more foreigners joined unions. By 1972, almost four thousand of them served on work councils. During the Mannesmann steel strike in spring 1973, foreign and local workers came out together and won a raise for all. At the Pierburg auto parts plant, it was foreign women who took the lead—many were stuck in the lowest pay grade even though they had worked there for five years. The police arrested several women strikers, but, in the end, the workers carried the day, and the lowest wage category was abolished.[25]

The strikes made plain that the "guests" saw their future in Germany. At the same time, they highlighted their vulnerability as aliens. In 1975, for example, more than a hundred Korean miners demanded the reinstatement of their countrymen who had been fired for skipping work—a serious offense, because dismissal, like political activism, meant the withdrawal of a residence permit. One of the workers was actually recovering from an accident at work, while others were tending to sick family members. The bosses took back four of the men needed in deep mining. The others were notified by the Aliens Office to leave the country voluntarily or face removal.[26]

The other major flashpoint was housing. With little prospect of social housing, guest workers faced a harsh choice between either living in temporary barracks or searching for overpriced accommodation on the private market. The first left them at the mercy of their bosses, the second at that of rent sharks. In North Rhine–Westphalia, the industrial heart of the country, a quarter of foreign workers still lived in barracks in 1971, half of which breached the federal requirement of roughly sixty-five square feet per person. The dormitory in Eschweiler had cramped four-bed rooms and one shower for 150 residents.[27] Other barracks had a common room with neither table nor chairs. On their return from a night shift, workers were greeted by guard dogs. Many barracks were fenced in—to protect the residents and keep prostitutes out, employers said. Inside, there was a strict regime. Strangers and women were not allowed. Where a common room had a television set, its control lay with the warden, who fined residents for not keeping floors clean and other infringements. The house rules of the barracks for Italian workers at the MAN engine corporation listed "*non è permesso*" and "*è proibito*" ninety-seven times: it was not allowed to hang any pictures on the walls or cupboards; it was not allowed to lie in bed with your clothes on; before switching on the lights, residents "had to" open the curtains.[28]

In 1970, churches and civil society groups in Hesse organized an early "Day of of the Foreign Fellow-Citizen." When church leaders and Italian delegates tried to enter the barracks of the Holzmann construction firm outside Frankfurt, they were blocked. The firm charged its workers 396 DM a month for sharing a 129-square-foot room with five others—roughly the same a tenant paid for an entire apartment in public housing. "Housed Like Under Hitler," one newspaper headline read. Others spoke of slavery and serfdom. An article commissioned by German churches and charities concluded that "they were integrated into the economy, but as human beings they are left outside... They are fellow citizens only when it comes to paying taxes... [otherwise] their fundamental rights are restricted."[29]

In the small private housing market (still recovering from war damage), guest workers were greeted either by advertisements specifying "no foreigners" or by profiteers. In Frankfurt, 60 percent of migrants already rented privately by 1964. Their lodgings were overpriced, unmodernized, and often damp. A court in Stuttgart fined one landlord 100,000 DM for overcharging his foreign tenants; the sentence included the "loss of honor" (*Ehrverlust*), which involved the loss of civic rights.[30]

Frankfurt and other cities were fully aware of the appalling housing conditions but did not want to renovate for fear of attracting more migrants. Run-down houses were earmarked for demolition to build profitable high-rises instead. In the early 1970s, foreign residents and German students in Frankfurt's "Westend" joined forces in a rent strike and occupied several houses. Overwhelmingly, the courts found against the tenants. The city eventually promised to rehouse the foreigners elsewhere. Migrants who happened to be citizens were in an altogether different situation. In 1979, the state of Hesse built 1,360 flats for 4,200 ethnic Germans. For its half-million foreigners, it managed ninety-one.[31]

Here, then, was the dark side of affluence. In large part, segregation was the result of discrimination. In the early 1970s, cities introduced zoning laws that blocked migrants from moving into "overburdened" areas where foreigners exceeded 12 percent of the population; the rule did not apply to Italians and other citizens from the EEC. It was billed as an anti-ghetto strategy, but its goal was to prevent Turkish men from bringing their wives and children to Germany. By the end of the decade, courts declared such statutes to be unconstitutional, but by then the damage had been done. Turkish families had become the scapegoats for the crunch on child benefits, social housing, and other public services in hard times.

There was nothing inevitable about the emergence of parallel societies. True, the early years were not free from prejudice and hostility. At Volkswagen, there were fistfights in 1962 when Italian workers started dancing with German women. Six years later, after a shooting outside a bar in Augsburg in which one Italian man died, many restaurants put up signs saying

"No guest workers." The practice was upheld as lawful by the highest court in Bavaria on the grounds that guest workers were not a genuine part of the population and that the rule did not apply to other foreigners.[32]

In hindsight, it is striking how much interaction and goodwill there was between hosts and guests in the early years. Alongside patronizing kindness and curiosity were efforts at inclusion. Newspapers praised Italian migrants for bringing a bit of color, temperament, and *la dolce vita* to the gray atmosphere of German cities; some also portrayed them as hardworking, sensitive, and imaginative. The head of the Caritas counseling service compared their warmth to a violin, with its rich register ranging across "dramatic, tragic, jubilant, [and] crying" sounds. In Hamburg, the municipal electricity provider organized a cooking club with students from the developing world to build bridges to other cultures.[33] When Farkhondeh Taghizadeh arrived in the provincial city of Oldenburg from Iran in 1962, her elderly landlady would take her to enjoy coffee and cake and play cards with her friends.[34] Evser Y., a Turkish woman who arrived in Germany four years later, remembered how her female coworkers immediately came up to her in the company canteen. They "showed us everything." "After a month, they invited us to their homes, every weekend." "Perhaps," she wondered, "it was because we were the first Turks."[35]

Opinions were always divided but suggest that attitudes were becoming more welcoming and understanding in the years before recruitment was banned in 1973. In 1964, Germans were almost equally split between those who felt that it "was going fairly well" with the guest workers (36 percent), those who saw a "serious problem" (32 percent), and those who were undecided (32 percent). By 1972, the positive view had gone up to 46 percent. In all key categories—being diligent, helpful, friendly, polite, and thrifty—Germans had a more positive image of their foreign neighbors in 1972 than eight years before, in spite of their growing numbers.[36] Even in a small working-class town like Greene in Lower Saxony, only 9 percent felt that the migrants should leave Germany. Two thirds favored integration, although only as long as foreigners lived like the locals. Half the inhabitants never exchanged a word with their Portuguese, Italian, and Turkish neighbors.[37] And their frugality prevented many migrants from participating in everyday life and leisure.

At the same time that the state closed the gates, a new vision was opening up in civil society: multiculturalism. The churches and welfare bodies, in particular, recognized early on that a new, multiethnic Germany was emerging. In the mining sector, firms introduced prayer rooms for their Muslim workers and sent greetings on their religious holidays; Deutsche Bahn

(German Rail) introduced mobile prayer vans. In 1965, Cologne Cathedral opened its doors to Turkish residents to celebrate Ramadan.[38]

Few words have been more widely quoted in debates over migration than those of the Swiss writer Max Frisch: "We called for workers, and people came instead." He wrote these words in a preface to a 1965 book about Italian workers in Switzerland, which relied on a strict rotation system. Virtually the same line was already circulating on both sides of the Rhine in the Catholic Caritas and Protestant welfare organizations a couple of years earlier.[39]

Foreigners were standing out, Caritas said, because German society stood "like a wall in front of them." They, too, were people with human needs and desires. The distant neighbor now "lived and worked among us." That they were "voluntary" was an "empty phrase, unless filled with human spirit."[40] It was shocking, a speaker said at a meeting of the ecumenical council of churches in 1963, that Greeks were still called "*Fremdarbeiter*," with all its echoes of the Nazi past. He called on congregations to show some interest in Greek culture and to remember the "monstrous things" Germans had done in Greece during the occupation. He was similarly unhappy with the term "*Betreuung*," which placed the foreign workers in the role of objects under supervised "care"—after all, "even the Gestapo said it *betreute* [looked after] the Jews." Instead, congregations should treat them as "partners": "Their difference should be recognized and given a space, even if that requires us to adapt a bit."[41] Greater mutual understanding and respect would benefit both sides, helping the new arrivals to settle in and expanding Germans' horizons and sympathy for others.

Some might return, Caritas told the Federal Ministry of Labor in 1966, but "many" would stay. Their "eventual naturalization" needed to be considered.[42] Caritas reminded its helpers of Leviticus 19:34: "The foreigner residing among you must be treated as your native-born. Love them as yourself, for you were foreigners in Egypt." They should be treated as "fellow citizens," not "guest workers."[43]

LIVING TOGETHER, LIVING APART

In 1970, the Society for Christian-Jewish Cooperation devoted its "week of brotherliness" to the foreigners in their midst, with language courses, excursions, and social events. Schools put on folklore evenings where girls from Greece and Morocco sang songs from their homelands. Turkish parents served Turkish *moka*, a "gesture that made a big impression on German parents," as did their hand-tailored costumes. The following year, children from schools across Berlin sent in their suggestions of how to help their foreign classmates. "Do not push them away—take care of them," a third-grader wrote. Others added: play with them, visit them in the hospital, help them with their homework, give them your cast-off clothes. Some suggested assigning school buddies. Not everyone thought so positively, however. A twelve-year-old girl wished there was a separate "home where all foreign children live, especially Turks and others who do not have our skin color," complete with its own school. "Then, no one can speak badly about them because they won't be as much together with the Germans... The children could then move more freely and no one would make fun of them anymore."[44]

In 1971, the Social Democratic welfare body (AWO) concluded that the idea that Germany was not a country of immigration "is no longer tenable."[45] In Frankfurt, the main Protestant charity, Diakonisches Werk, developed with Greek immigrants the concept of "partial integration," living together with the right to be different, and keeping open the option of return. In the same year, the Council of German Protestant Churches (EKD) said the encounter with strangers was an "enrichment" for the country.[46] It accepted the ban on foreign recruitment two years later but in exchange wanted more support for those who decided to stay, including the unlimited right to remain after five years.

German women who were married to foreigners organized legal aid and protested at the routine discrimination they received at the hands of officials and landlords, from not being able to find a day care spot for their "foreign" child to the removal of their husbands. One wife went to the Aliens Office to ask why her Iranian husband was given such a short residence permit. The civil servant burst out, "First you get involved with such a guy, and then, on top of that, you want to have it certified." Another woman recounted her difficulties applying for a passport for her child. The official told her, "Marrying a Frenchman or an Englishman I might have understood, but a Spaniard!... that goes too far."[47]

For the welfare bodies, the primary aim was to reunite families, the family being the basic unit of society in Catholic thought. Half the migrants were Catholics and arrived alone. In 1962, the congress of cities stressed that "it was irresponsible from a human and moral point to separate married men from their families for years."[48] The churches reactivated their counseling centers for foreign workers, which reached back to the years before the First World War—Catholic charities looked after Italians and Spaniards, Protestant ones after Greeks, and the AWO after Turkish migrants. By 1965, there were close to two hundred of them. The charities searched for apartments and acted as intermediaries with the local authorities. As social workers complained time and again, officials did not blink an eye when migrant workers were stacked in overcrowded dormitories, but when they wanted to bring their families, a one-bedroom apartment was suddenly considered too small and breached official standards.

There were plenty of noble arguments made for family reunion, including better health and well-being and a stable environment for the children. A steady home, the charities argued, would also make migrants better workers and save them money because their wives were better shoppers and cooks. Just as important were fears of loose sexual morals and a resulting collapse of social order. In 1962, a Catholic social worker complained about the "prostitute-like lifestyle" of some of the young Spanish women working in industries and inns near Hanover. One had just given birth to an illegitimate child. Two others had fallen under the influence of young men "of ill repute" and were expecting. Their counselors would have preferred them to be in the safe hands of a Catholic hostel. The offer was rejected "with the argument that they were anyhow planning to convert to the Protestant faith of the [local] men." Loss of virginity was topped by loss of faith. In other cases, Spanish women were said to have "forced themselves into German marriages in the most outrageous manner."[49]

In the late 1960s, a series of sexual assaults and offenses by migrants made front-page news. In 1966, Cologne was shaken by nineteen instances of violent crime. Were the guest workers turning the city into "Chicago on the Rhine"? Newspapers pinned the blame on their sex drive and barbaric customs—"They keep their women like camels," one headline declared.[50] In the hands of the media, the once hardworking, soulful southerner morphed into a sex-obsessed, knife-wielding criminal. These tropes would cast a long shadow.

In Cologne, Turkish and Italian men did commit more violent crimes than their German peers; Greeks and Spaniards committed fewer. (When it came to fraud and damage to property, it was Germans who topped the list.) Data was biased, however, because young Turks were more likely to be suspected, searched, and arrested by the police. In a study commissioned by the Social Security Office in Cologne in 1968, social psychologists concluded that nowhere, including in public offices, had they encountered "so many prejudices, stereotypes, and maladjustment than with regard to the Turks." For the authors, the charge that guest workers were "untidy, dirty, and take our money" was a way of repressing the subject of forced labor under the Nazis and turning a prejudice into a seemingly rational opinion.[51] Comparisons with young Germans were not very meaningful because most criminal migrants were already broken individuals when they left their home country, the study found—that was one reason they emigrated. On arrival, they were isolated. It was not a recipe for healthy socialization.

The physical segregation in out-of-town barracks added to the tensions. At Volkswagen, several thousand foreign men lived in wooden barracks on the outskirts of Wolfsburg in Lower Saxony. Bars and dance halls were closed to them, and before 1978 there were no female foreign workers, either. In the early 1970s, local women campaigned for the city to confront the "expanding problem of repressed sexuality of these . . . fiery southerners" and recognize that "they are people of flesh and blood and cannot live by work and bread alone." They wanted the city to set up a brothel for them.[52]

For many families, migration was not a one-way street but a long commute. Livia Martino was born in Sicily and first came to the Rhineland when she was five, in 1958. For the next five years, she shuttled between Düsseldorf and Italy.[53] Finally she settled in Germany. The thirty-four-year-old Abdullah D. A. from Turkey started working as a miner in Gelsenkirchen in 1969. The following year, he was joined by his wife and their two boys and little daughter, aged eight, six, and two. In 1972, a year after his wife gave birth to their second daughter, she joined Siemens as a machine operator. Between 1974 and 1980, she took all her children back with her to Turkey, one after the other. In 1982, she returned with the two youngest before moving permanently back to Turkey in 1984. The last to return to their homeland was the father, in 1985.[54]

Such back and forth left its mark on people's lives, not least by disrupting education. Education was in the hands of the regional states. Only after 1962 did they begin to make schooling compulsory for foreign children, a full seven years after the first recruitment deal with Italy. For the next decade, attendance was abysmal. As late as 1970, in North Rhine–Westphalia, most migrant children still did not go to elementary school. States and cities saw little need to devote resources to a group that were expected to leave, not assimilate. Many migrants who planned to return thought likewise. Their lives were complicated enough without having to struggle with a foreign school on top. Those planning to stay, however, often could not find a school place for their children. For migrant families with two earners, the dearth of preschool spots posed just as pressing a problem. In Munich, only 10 percent of foreign children went to preschool in 1970. More day care places was one of the demands in the strikes in the early 1970s.[55]

A mishmash of educational programs made a bad situation worse. Some states offered optional classes in the foreigners' native tongue in addition to the regular curriculum, while others left language classes up to the respective home countries, which assigned their own "consular teachers." North Rhine–Westphalia and Hesse introduced separate "national classes" with the aim of preparing migrants for their return and teaching them just enough to help them get by in the meantime. They failed them in both. Researchers in 1976 found that they were neither integrated in their German cohort nor sufficiently prepared for life in their home country. Only one in five foreign children belonged to a German friendship group. German children rarely visited them at home. Two in three children of "guest workers" in the early 1970s left school without the most basic degree (*Hauptschulabschluss*) needed to help them start an apprenticeship. The dominant view was that school was not worth it, with high rates of absences and dropouts. All that schools did, in the words of the researchers, was to "produce a Germanized sub-proletariat."[56]

Things improved slightly over the next decade. By 1980, 92 percent of all children in migrant families attended school. The problem was that when they left it, almost half still did not have a basic degree, and only every fifth teenager secured an apprenticeship; these figures include children born in Germany to migrant parents. That year, 80 percent of all three-to-six-year-old German children attended preschool (*Vorschule*), but only 47 percent of foreign children did, and only 15 percent of those who were Turkish. Migrant children commonly ended up in "special schools" (*Sonderschulen*).[57]

IN OR OUT

By the late 1970s, public policy was pulling in opposite directions. At the federal level, the government clung to the idea that Germany was "not a land of immigration." At the regional level, by contrast, the demands for housing and education forced states and cities to accept that they had become just that. Duisburg, in the industrial Ruhr region, abandoned the two-track education model. The city-state of Hamburg, in 1975, declared that willing foreigners should be integrated and advocated dual citizenship and more rights for noncitizens. In the port district of St. Pauli, where the Beatles shot to fame, every fifth resident was a foreigner by that point. A democratic society could not exclude people from political participation just because they were foreigners, the ruling Social Democrats argued. The mayor of the other city-state, Bremen, agreed: all the talk of being a "no-immigration country" was an illusion and excuse for doing nothing.[58]

In 1978, Bonn decided to act. Chancellor Schmidt appointed the first federal commissioner for foreigner affairs, Heinz Kühn, to work out a plan. The memorandum he came back with nine months later was nothing short of a bombshell. Kühn demanded a "recognition of de facto immigration." There was to be full integration, including Turkish and Greek languages in regular school lessons.[59] The second and third generations were to be entitled to citizenship from the age of eighteen. Older foreigners who had been in the country for eight years were to gain local voting rights. The entire logic of naturalization was turned around. Instead of foreigners having to show that they were good Germans before they could apply for citizenship, they were to receive rights first to ease their integration. None of the proposals were adopted. By 1980, Kühn was gone.

Such ideas fell on more receptive ears with the churches and welfare bodies, which acted as the main intermediaries between migrants and local authorities. Integration, the AWO stressed, had to move in both directions: Germans needed to learn to understand migrants' views and customs as well as vice versa. Native language classes only led to long-term separation—Bavaria was a case in point. Instead, their languages needed to become part of regular classes. "All solutions," it said, "must start from the assumption that the teenagers will stay for the long term." As taxpayers, foreigners had a right to be heard in decisions about public services and infrastructure.[60]

Making integration a reality without federal support was easier said than done. There were only so many social workers and volunteers. Dortmund, the coal and steel metropolis in the Ruhr, was home to 22,000 Turks and 7,000 Yugoslavians. The welfare bodies' advice bureaus were overwhelmed with requests for the translation of official documents, leaving little time for other pressing needs. Starting in 1981, eighty-three Turkish children in one district received after-school help with their homework. For sixteen- and seventeen-year-old late arrivals, there were fifteen intensive German courses. In a city with more than ten thousand foreign children, it was clearly insufficient. In the Mengede district, the elementary school took its pupils on an excursion to a local game park and hosted a joint German-Turkish music band. A German-Turkish circle started to meet in 1980 to counter prejudice. Its motto was "Living together in the same district." Of its fifteen members, only two were German—a housewife and an educator. After the summer holidays in 1981, the circle was suspended because of a "lack of interest among the participants." In Dortmund-Derne, social counselors offered seminars on parenting, school, and housing. Only Turkish families attended. Integration was at least as much a German problem as a Turkish one.[61]

Enterprising migrants faced official hurdles. In addition to residence permits, the Aliens Offices controlled permits to start a business. Together with the local authorities, they conducted a *Bedürfnisprüfung*, a test to establish whether there was "need" for, say, a Turkish shop or a Greek restaurant. For officials, that need was primarily ethnic. They had no problem with a Croat wishing to open a Balkan restaurant in an area with many residents from Yugoslavia. If the same person, however, wanted to open a pub for drinkers of all nations, he was turned down. Greek food was for Greeks. In 1980, almost half of all business applications from non-EEC foreigners were rejected; only Switzerland and Austria were more restrictive.

From 1978 on, foreigners were exempt from the "needs test" if they were either married to a German or had lived in the country for at least eight years. For the lucky ones, ethnic food shops, restaurants, and travel bureaus were a step up on the ladder of social mobility. In 1973, 2 percent of Greeks had their own business. Ten years later it would be 11 percent. Like their owners, the shops often grew out of a shuttle between the old and the new homeland, as in the case of Neci Caiskans, who first came to Berlin in 1973 at the age of twelve, later ran a restaurant in Izmir, and then returned to Berlin-Charlottenburg to open a deli there.

Ethnic cuisine in Germany was not something completely new in the 1980s. It could build on earlier Polish eateries, Balkan grills, and Italian ice cream parlors. The first Chinese restaurant opened in Berlin in 1923 and served Germans customers as well as Chinese students.[62] Still, instead of facilitating cultural exchange, the public check of "needs" left behind a landscape of discrete ethnic islands. Should one go to "the Turk" or "the Greek" or "the Italian" for a bite to eat? That in some Italian restaurants it happened to be the German wife who stood in the kitchen was carefully concealed. The cultural encounter rarely extended beyond the order of a *döner kebab*, which was adapted to suit the German palate, with chicken smothered in garlic mayonnaise rather than lamb with a hint of mutton and hot peppers.

The 1970s and 1980s were marked by deepening polarization. On one side stood the champions of multiculturalism. Local initiatives sprung up to facilitate mutual understanding and help foreigners with their daily problems. In Munich, one such group started in 1971. Ten years later, it could draw on 260 helpers, mainly housewives, students, and pensioners. They accompanied foreigners to the doctor, filled in official forms, and helped the children with their homework. In a special week of events in 1973, German children performed a "folklore" dance on Tuesday evening. On Thursday, their Greek peers followed with a play. On Sunday, there was a quiz in six languages. Starting in 1975, , the churches were organizing a nationwide "Day of the Foreign Fellow-Citizen" to show how migrants and their heritage were an asset to German culture. Cities put on community festivals—the one in Gostenhof, a district in Nuremberg, drew a thousand participants. Even here, though, racial stereotypes did not vanish. A musical game taught children the song "In Hong Kong lives Tsching-Tschong Li, his beard hangs all the way to his knee," and a German teacher showed them the "features and typical customs of the Chinese."[63]

On the other side, there were those who saw an unbridgeable civilizational divide between Germans and Turks. The percentage of Germans who believed that guest workers should go home rose from 39 percent in 1979 to 60 percent in 1982. In Berlin, ominous graffiti appeared on walls: "What the Jews already have behind them, the Turks still have ahead of them."[64] These were the years after the boom, when the unemployment rate climbed to 9 percent. Although it tended to be foreigners who got fired first, that did not minimize anxieties in the host population.

Politicians made guest workers the scapegoats for the hard times and the crunch in public services. Their chief crusader was the interior minister, Friedrich Zimmermann, a right-wing Catholic with a checkered past; he had been entangled in a bribery scandal over casinos and sentenced for perjury in the first instance. In 1984, he pushed to limit future family reunions to children under the age of six. Older children, he argued, would never integrate and were just a pretense for drawing benefits and a drain on an already struggling economy. His Liberal colleague Hans-Dietrich Genscher, the foreign secretary, killed the proposal by threatening to resign.

Chancellor Kohl, who had pledged to halve the foreign population, tried to solve the issue with a golden handshake. Those who had been laid off were given the opportunity to apply, until June 30, 1984, for public assistance with their return home, worth 10,500 DM plus 1,500 DM for each child, which together amounted to almost a third of the average annual income at the time. For those who accepted the offer, the lump sum was a bird in the hand that enabled them to set themselves up in business or buy some land back home. The state's short-term generosity hid its long-term interests: every returnee saved public coffers unemployment and other benefits now and huge pension claims later—returnees only got back what they had paid in, without interest; the employers' contribution stayed in Germany. In the end, only 150,000 took the cash and left.[65] In a foreign population close to 5 million, the measure barely made a dent.

Ultimately, the issue was not about money, but identity. For Zimmermann and like-minded Conservatives, welcoming migrants would mean giving up the German nation that was built on a shared history, language, and culture underpinned by Christianity. Mosques and Koran schools were alien invaders. The first mosque in Duisburg opened in 1974, just as German churches were emptying. Although 85 percent of the population were still registered as Catholic or Protestant by the mid-1980s (compared to 97 percent in 1961), the majority now only found their way to church for Christmas or weddings.[66] This may explain why the loudest warnings against Islam came from politicians in what remained one of the most devout Christian heartlands: Bavaria. Ministers (on both the left and the right) received plenty of letters from citizens who wanted "Germany for the Germans." Pensioners and the unemployed protested against foreigners, as did a group of right-wing professors who warned that migration was destroying the ethnic substance of the German *Volk*.[67]

There were limits to multiculturalism on the left, too. In the 1970s, progressives still pointed to social factors to explain the predicaments faced by Turkish women in Germany, such as isolation and language barriers. By the early 1980s, the blame was pinned on "traditional" customs. German feminists wrote about "brides for sale" to expose the oppression of Turkish women. The headscarf came to be the visible symbol of all that separated the backward *Orient* from the enlightened *Occident*. Guest workers needed to shed their customs, with the help of their Western sisters. It was the latest installment in a long line of civilizing missions driven by good intentions yet marred by ignorance and condescension. It overlooked the central role of the family for Turkish women as well as their own strategies of resistance. German progressives and feminists had marched against racism in America, but when it came to the guest workers in their own country, if they saw them at all, it was only to find signs of backwardness that reinforced their pride in their own emancipation.[68]

GERMANY, "BITTER HOMELAND"

Just how "traditional" Turkish families actually were is debatable. As noted earlier, the majority who came in the 1960s were urban, educated, and Westernized. From the late 1960s, a growing number were working women. This left a mark on gender relations, especially when it was the male breadwinner who was hit by unemployment in the 1970s. Hyllal Belim was sixteen when she arrived in Germany in 1970 to work at a company producing technical drawing tools. In 1978, she went back to Turkey to marry. Three years later, she returned to Hamburg, initially to her old job, then as a caregiver for old people. When her husband gained permission to join her, it was she who was earning a salary and had learned German, helped by her coworkers and a neighbor. He only managed to find odd jobs, doing a bit of wallpapering here and there. As she summed it up: "I was the man."[69] The new roles could lead to conflict, but employment also brought greater confidence and freedom—sometimes only the wife had a driver's license.[70] Elders faced similar challenges to their authority over children.

From the late 1960s on, Turkish migrants came more and more from rural areas, bringing village customs to German cities. An anthropologist followed families from Anatolia to Germany in the 1970s and early 1980s. For several, work in Istanbul was an important stage in that journey, and it was there that they (and not the larger family) chose their spouse. Fatma Eren was twenty-two when she left Turkey in 1972. Her husband joined her the following year. In Berlin, the village norms of right and wrong, honor and shame, progressively softened as neighbors came and went, and social control was much weaker than where they had grown up. In their marriage, new forms of conflict resolution took root. When there was a quarrel, the woman would fall silent for a day rather than an entire week. Living in a strange environment made partners more dependent on each other. Leisure and excursions began to be appreciated as shared activities. When it came to laundry and cleaning, Turkish women continued to do the bulk, as did women the world over. Still, the roles in the household were no longer those of the village, either: if her husband asked her for tea, Ms. Eren told him to get it himself. A saying captured the new sense of freedom: "*Burası Almanya*"—"This is Germany."[71]

Migrants were occasionally invited to weddings by their German coworkers, and there were some signs of solidarity with hunger strikers after the 1980 coup in Turkey. At that time, every second foreigner had "some contact" with Germans in their leisure time; among Turkish women it was every third. It was largely, though, a relationship at arm's length. Only one in twenty Turks had "close contact" with Germans, and three out of four had never set foot in a German home.

Migrants had plenty of positive things to say about Germany: it was clean and correct, there was law and order, and one could rely on being paid at the end of the month. Their expectations of friendliness, however, were very modest and often meant little more than Germans giving them directions when asked.[72] Concetta arrived with her children from Italy in 1966. During her first Christmas, she rang her neighbors' bell to give them a poinsettia plant and a bottle of wine, and to invite them over, "if you feel like having a coffee sometime." Seven years later, she was still waiting for a response. Exchange was limited to a short, formal "'Good day,' as if they are afraid to meet me," she said.[73] The cold atmosphere was especially painful for migrants who had left their family behind, as captured in a song at the time:

"*Deutschland*, bitter homeland / never smiles at a person / I still do not know it / Some never return..."[74]

Those lucky to receive a helping hand were likely to run into a wall of prejudice elsewhere. Thanks to the intervention of a local Social Democrat, a Turkish worker managed to secure an apartment in a German neighborhood, only to find himself shunned by his new neighbors and told to leave the local pub. He eventually moved back into a Turkish neighborhood.[75]

A Turkish teacher recounted her life in Hamburg in the 1970s in a detailed autobiography. In her first six years in the country she noted only three encounters with Germans: her foreman at work, the doctor who delivered her baby, and the woman from the Aliens Office. This changed in 1978, when she started teaching Turkish children in an elementary school. When one of her sons died of leukemia, her fellow teachers were compassionate. There was little empathy, though, for the concerns of most Turkish parents and their children. Her other son was told he was incapable of grasping German grammar because he was Turkish, even though his Turkish father taught German. Ignored by the teachers' union, she organized her own group.[76]

It was around this time that doctors began diagnosing "guest worker stomach ulcers," which they traced to daily worries about the future. When children fell ill, they tried to hide it for fear their mothers might lose their jobs if they stayed home and they would end up having to leave the country.[77] Nine-year-old Pina recalled how at pickup time at her day care German mothers would separate and reprimand their children in front of everyone else: had they not told them to stop playing with these "shitty foreigners" (*Scheiss Ausländer*)? In 1982, one of the few Turks who went to university concluded that in Germany there was hardly "any space for universal concepts like goodwill, love, friendship, and brotherliness." Germans worked, he said, came home, ate, watched TV, went to bed, and got up to go to work again. He did not see that these were the very same years when millions of Germans marched for peace or donated to the "Third World." They were living parallel lives. The worker Ayse Tümen sensed "an emptiness in the life of Germans."[78]

SOCIALIST SERFS

East Germany had its own program for recruiting foreign workers, signing an agreement with Poland in 1965, followed by those with Hungary (1967), Cuba (1975), Mozambique (1979), and Vietnam (1980). In the final years of the regime, their numbers rose fourfold, from 24,000 in 1981 to 94,000 in 1989.

Over the course of its short life, the GDR was a temporary home to 100,000 Vietnamese and 22,000 "Madgermanes," as Mozambicans were called. It was a far smaller guest worker population than that across the Wall, but this did not make the encounter with strangers any less problematic.

Official propaganda hailed the agreements as proof of the international friendship among socialist peoples. The foreigners were students and apprentices who the GDR was taking under its wing to help develop their young socialist motherlands now that they had thrown off the yoke of imperialism. Mozambique gained independence from Portugal in 1975, the same year the Vietnam War came to an end. A couple thousand Vietnamese were trained in electronics in the early 1970s; the main interest, though, lay elsewhere. For the GDR, the contract workers eased its chronic labor shortage—Hungarians sweated in the coal mines, and Mozambicans worked in factories and slaughterhouses—and they were a payment in kind for the money it was owed by its poorer socialist cousins. The GDR had sent guns to Mozambique and goods to Vietnam, and since neither of the two countries had much of value to send in return, they sent people instead. The GDR paid the minimum wage, but the foreign workers only saw a fraction of it. The rest was transferred to their home governments, which only paid out part of it on their return; Vietnamese workers had 15 percent of their wage deducted, those from Mozambique initially 25 percent, and after 1986 60 percent. The maximum stay was five years. As in West Germany, foreigners in the East ended up with the dirtiest jobs. Existing skills received little recognition: the nurses scrubbing hospital floors in Leipzig were from Mali, instead of from South Korea as in Cologne.[79]

There was one crucial difference: foreign workers in the GDR were completely tied to government contracts. A worker from Hanoi or Maputo was not free to resign and move jobs. Protests, failure to fulfill work norms, sickness, and, notoriously, pregnancy, ended in instant dismissal and removal. They were in the GDR to work, not to have babies and start new lives—the respective governments were in agreement on this point; only Polish women had the right to remain if they became pregnant. There was no provision for family reunion, and marriage with a local was strongly discouraged.

The threat of removal was a mighty disciplinary stick, the carrot was the "separation bonus," which gave foreigners at the end of their contracted stay a few additional Marks for each day they had fulfilled their quota. These did not stop grumbling and resistance. In 1975, several thousand Mozambicans went on strike over their working conditions. The following year, six hundred Algerians downed tools in protest at being used as cheap labor instead of receiving the training they had been promised. In Zittau, on the border with Poland and Czechoslovakia, Vietnamese apprentices rebelled at the food in the canteen of their truck factory and went on hunger strike; they wanted rice. A dozen of them were put on a plane back to Hanoi. In 1987, thirty-nine Cubans went on strike in Leipzig when a quarter of their first paycheck had been deducted; according to the agreement made in 1975, this would be paid in pesos on their return. Their firm—which made insulation for nuclear power stations—failed to resolve the situation and placed them under surveillance in their dormitory. Two of the "troublemakers" were immediately sent home; others faced disciplinary measures and the loss of their separation bonus. A year earlier, the East German authorities had sent back one thousand Cubans after a series of violent clashes with the locals. In 1988, Fidel Castro canceled the agreement.[80]

The years after reunification were blemished by violent attacks on foreigners. This gives the issue of how foreigners were treated before, in the old GDR, special importance. In 1993, Wolfgang Thierse, a Social Democrat and future president of the federal parliament, who grew up in Thuringia, in the East, said real socialism had created "its own type of apartheid."[81] Contract workers had restricted rights and were housed in separate dormitories, as were foreign students. Barracks were ruled out because they were reminders of forced labor under the Nazis. Visits were possible before 10 p.m. but only in a special visiting room and after prior notification and approval by the porter. In reality, though, the sheer rise in numbers in the final years of the regime made strict control of the overcrowded dormitories impossible. Some Mozambicans started relationships with local women, and Vietnamese turned their rooms into workshops to make jeans and jackets.

Outside the dorms, there were two radically different worlds. The majority of East Germans had no contact with foreigners. Those who worked in firms that relied on contract laborers had constant contact with them, since "brigades" were mixed. Two thirds of foreigners described their relationships at work as "rather collegial," according to an official survey taken in December 1990, immediately after reunification. Only 15 percent felt they were "rather negative." Two thirds also had "frequent" contact with German colleagues after work. A quarter even spent their leisure time "mainly" with them. This did not necessarily mean that relationships were reciprocal. Frankfurt (Oder), for example, relied on a contingent of Polish workers who commuted across the nearby border. The regime sponsored sports and cultural events to cement socialist friendship. The result was uneven. While almost half the Poles had contact with their coworkers, the vast majority of Germans had none with them. They had not picked up a single word of Polish, except for the occasional swear word.[82]

Foreign workers were incentivized to work extra shifts, which did not endear them to locals, who preferred a slower pace. The official trade union (FDGB) noted in 1981 that in the entire year not one of the sixty-two Vietnamese workers in a glass factory had missed a single shift. Foreign workers were diligent, the union said, but they were "coming under the influence of the partly negative level of discipline among East German workers."[83]

Officially, racism did not exist. So contract workers who complained about discrimination were sent home. Mozambicans were frequently criticized for being lazy or drunk, at a time when East Germans had a serious drinking problem of their own. If a Mozambican lost a thumb in a machine, it was attributed to his carelessness, never to the faulty machine. Internal reports suggest that racism was a frequent presence on the shop floor. At a vehicle factory in Suhl, in Thuringia, in 1984, it was said to be "not rare" to hear that "you Blacks are here only to work. If you don't do that, then go back to where you came from."[84] As it happened, that was precisely what many foreign laborers did—in some years, a quarter of the contracts were terminated early, either because workers found the work too hard and the living conditions and diet unbearable, or because of illness, accidents, and disciplinary problems.

There were some signs of solidarity. In Rostock, on the Baltic coast, German workers chipped in with extra shifts to help a Vietnamese colleague get extra pay as well. Such sympathy, however, tended to depend on the locals being in charge. The moment the racial hierarchy came under threat, solidarity disappeared. When a foreigner made it to the level of foreman in Rostock, German workers refused to take his orders: "What, a Vietnamese, a *Fidschi* ["gook"]? And he is meant to give me orders? Where are we? I won't do it."[85]

The GDR was a regime of shortages—one long line, and it mattered where foreigners entered it. Poles, in particular, were seen to be cutting in. When the "friendship border" between the two countries was opened in 1972, 9 million Poles visited the GDR and bought up women's shoes, underwear, and chewing gum. Their footfall in the shops reinforced preexisting xenophobic stereotypes. "The Polacks are a swarm of locusts," people said. In mining districts, locals complained that Polish contract workers got new apartments and drove a moped while they had to wait for both. In 1989, petitions borrowed antisemitic images and urged the authorities to keep them out: "The Poles are a trading people, they cannot resist it."[86]

In a society suffering from a shortage of textiles and domestic appliances, it is not surprising that the packages foreign workers took back home with them attracted envy and gossip. The labor agreements included special shopping conditions and allowed workers to send six parcels a year plus a two-cubic-meter crate on their return, tax free. Over the course of five years, a Vietnamese worker could ship up to 2 mopeds, 5 bicycles, 2 sewing machines, 150 meters of cloth, 50 rolls of film and 100 kilos of sugar. Rumor had it that foreign workers were paid in hard West German Deutschmark and could travel to the West; in truth, they had to hand over their passports the moment they stepped off the plane in Berlin-Schönefeld in the East.

At the same time, Vietnamese workers offered the locals a way out of the line. Many of the workers were married women whose extra earnings were sent to the family back home—a typical migrant practice. In their dormitories, they produced fashionable clothes and copied Western music tapes that were hard to get in the East. The small town of Gröditz attracted customers from all over Saxony yearning for a pair of stylish corduroy pants, which the Vietnamese turned out when they were not working at the local steel mill; the Stasi reckoned that every second laborer worked on the side. Moonlighting was tolerated as long as the workers did their day job.[87]

The greatest foreign presence were the 300,000 Soviet soldiers stationed in the GDR. Soviet-German friendship was a centerpiece of official propaganda, from children's stories to public parades. In everyday life, it barely registered. For the troops, sealed off in their barracks, human encounters were rare. When the regime organized "friendship meetings" with Soviet soldiers, most locals stayed away. In 1969, an internal survey found that two thirds of young people had never attended these gatherings; 16 percent had been once, and only 19 percent "several" times.[88] Tensions between Soviet soldiers and the local population were never recognized officially; neither were the many rapes at the end of the Second World War.

Foreign students were a smaller contingent—some 75,000 altogether in the GDR's forty-year existence—hailing from India, Zambia, and Chile as well as the Soviet bloc. Especially in the 1960s, when East Germans were not even able to travel to Poland or Hungary, they brought a breath of fresh air into the staid provincial atmosphere. The regime tried to keep a tight watch on them and prevent all unregulated contact with the locals. The Herder Institute in charge of them had the motto "Where we are not, there is the enemy." And the enemy lurked everywhere: in bars, nightclubs, and wherever their foreign charges might come under the influence of "people with a petit-bourgeois mind-set." The visitors were housed in separate dormitories in two or three bedrooms; only one in six lived with German students. For the authorities, friendship translated into paternalism. When on the "Day of the Foreign Student" several complained about the monotonous diet, they were told to get used to the German menu. Vegetarian students from India had to eat German pork. More generally, the GDR had a duty to civilize them and break the habit of "dawdling away the time and taking unhealthy long naps," in the words of the director of the Herder Institute. The ideal of "rational leisure" had emerged in the nineteenth century as a bourgeois mission to "civilize" workers. Now the dictatorship of the working class took over the job to reform "backward" foreigners.

Unfortunately, the GDR also suffered from a scarcity of organized leisure. It meant foreign students made their own contacts with the locals in their free time. In 1961, an Indian graduate who had studied in Leipzig and Dresden moved to West Germany, where he denounced the GDR as a Nazi state. He nonetheless recalled how "whenever we were seen in the street, on buses, or in restaurants we were immediately approached and often invited along to people's homes. Above all, they wanted to hear from us about life in our countries and in the West."[89]

States can block marriages, but they cannot stop sex and procreation. One thousand babies were born to Mozambican fathers, but the regime permitted only three marriages. Several children from mixed relationships were sent to special homes. Vietnamese-German couples were more successful, with 323 marriages, although the authorities fought against them fiercely. "Five and a half years we battled until we got permission to marry," a Vietnamese man recalled. "We lived constantly... in a state of uncertainty, worry, and fear." Vietnamese women were forced to have an abortion unless they wanted to be sent back. The GDR was more generous with Hungarian partners, but fellow Europeans did not escape discrimination either. A pregnant German woman who was married to a Polish man wanted to leave the country because they were treated "like the scum of the earth."[90] In 1980, foreigners gained residence rights on marrying a German, but plenty of other hurdles remained. Students and apprentices, for example, had to pay back 27,000 or 12,000 GDR Marks if they did not return to their home country—even an unskilled laborer, who did not benefit from years of training, faced a bill of 8,000 Marks.

SOCIALISM, RACISM

Amina Selemane was from Mozambique and lived through the final years of the GDR, working as an electronics technician. In the entire time, "I did not encounter racism," she later told East German researchers seeking to defend the GDR against an all-around negative portrayal. After work, "I was able to move freely in pubs and discos without any problem." She took the train and black-market taxis at night, she said, "and I was never afraid." As far as she was concerned, the problems only started after 1989.[91]

Not everyone was so lucky. In 1964, two Syrian students were beaten up by East Germans, another from Malawi by three students, and a Moroccan man almost died from knife wounds inflicted by a local. The year ended with a New Year's Eve party in a bar where the East German girlfriends of Black South African students were abused as "Negro whores": "In Hitler's days, we would have shorn off their hair."[92]

If not universal, racism was certainly a widespread fixture of everyday life. A visiting professor from Colombia noted that whenever he sat down in a restaurant, GDR citizens tended to get up and leave. In Leipzig, taxis refused to drive Black Africans who were accompanied by German women. Citizens wanted to know whether back home Black Africans were cannibals and "still live in trees." At the synod in 1978, a pastor confessed that fellow East Germans needed to face up to the fact that racism was not just something west of the Elbe. His list of concerns ranged from discrimination toward "Polacks" to talk of Algerians as "camel drivers" and Jews as "crooks."[93] The following year, two Cubans were killed as they tried to flee their attackers after a brawl in Merseburg.

The situation worsened in 1987 when foreigners began to be attacked in the open. That October, a group of skinheads was arrested after terrorizing foreigners for a month. The following year, authorities registered five hundred attacks a month. There were clashes outside youth clubs as East Germans tried to deny foreigners entry. In April, five young German men were convicted for beating up a Mozambican man. In Berlin, a group from Yemen were attacked in a public park, Poles on a campsite, and Mozambicans in broad daylight on the central Alexanderplatz.[94] Worse was to come.

In the late 1980s, the Stasi counted six thousand neo-Nazis in the GDR. West Germany, as we have seen, was not as free from right-wing violence as it liked to believe. Still, adjusted by population, there may have been sixteen times as many neo-Nazis active in East Germany; direct comparisons are complicated by the fact that the Stasi was arguably more meticulous than their West German colleagues. The GDR's problem with right-wing extremism was largely homegrown—Western neo-Nazis had little influence before 1990—and the result of mutually reinforcing factors: the anti-fascist credo of the regime, the estrangement of East German youth from the socialist project, and the absence of civil society.

Anti-fascism was the legitimating foundation of the socialist dictatorship. This made it impossible to acknowledge and confront homegrown right-wing violence. For the regime, this would have been like sawing at the branch on which it sat. In 1988, the Stasi launched a project to investigate the right-wing scene. When it became clear that those cheering Hitler were not "rowdies" manipulated by Western agents but good students and steady workers who often came from card-carrying families, the project was promptly shut down.

That same year, the Leipzig Institute of Youth found that 2 percent of fourteen-year-old East Germans openly identified as skinheads and a further 12 percent thought that fascism had had its good sides—and these were only those who did not censor their answers for the official investigators. The socialist utopia had lost its magic spell for this generation of teenagers. Disoriented and disillusioned, their motto was "No future." Fascist slogans were an attractive way of defying the rulers. The crisis of legitimacy was for everyone to see, and hear. At the soccer cup final in 1988, Erich Mielke, the head of the Stasi, was greeted with old Nazi marching songs. A few neo-Nazis were thrown in prison, but this bestowed only greater kudos on brown networks. Fascist ideas also circulated in the army and the police.[95] In a country in which the exclusion of "asocials" and sects was the norm, it was a small step to target foreigners.

Counterefforts for inclusion and diversity were few and far between. So were the spaces for migrants to organize themselves. The absence of a civil society meant that foreigners in the GDR lacked the support of charities and associations that, in the West, stood up for their right to be different. A few churches offered bilingual prayer services, but when a pastor invited Mozambicans to his house in Suhl in 1982, locals were stunned that he allowed them to wipe their hands on the towels, and they called his wife a "slut." The Protestant Mission introduced monthly meetings with foreigners in Leipzig in 1986, but in the face of stiff opposition from both church and state. It was only in the penultimate year of the GDR's existence that a community center (*Cabana*, "little hut") opened its doors in East Berlin to show that solidarity was not only something for those living abroad.[96]

A DIFFICULT PLACE OF REFUGE

While guaranteed in international law, the right to asylum is inherently political. Refugees need to show that they have been the subject of persecution or are at risk of it. But what counts as persecution and who is entitled to protection from it are contested. One person's place of refuge is another person's home. Asylum seekers need to be housed and fed—especially if they are not allowed to work—and they include "bogus" claimants hoping for a better life as well as "genuine" refugees. How they are treated and who is considered deserving of sanctuary is therefore a litmus test for the range and depth of compassion in a society. It tells us how a country views its responsibilities toward vulnerable others vis-à-vis its own citizens. Societies across Europe have wrestled with these issues, but none more so than Germany. On the eve of the fall of the Berlin Wall, no single issue divided Germans more than that of asylum.

The refugee regime that emerged after 1945 was a direct response to the millions who had fled totalitarian rule and were now displaced across Europe. A refugee, according to the United Nations Convention of 1951, was someone who was unable or unwilling to return to their country "owing to a well-founded fear of being persecuted for reasons of race, religion, nationality, membership of a particular social group or political opinion."[97] Such a person must not be returned "in any manner whatsoever" to a country where they face threats to their life or freedom—the principle of "non-refoulement." They are also entitled to a range of social and economic rights, while their host state has a duty to facilitate their "assimilation" and naturalization. The original concern was exclusively with postwar Europe, and persecution had to be the result of events that had occurred before January 1, 1951.

West Germany was among the many signatories of the convention. Unique in the world, it also anchored asylum in its constitution: "The politically persecuted shall enjoy the right of asylum" (Article 16/2 then; Article 16a/1 today). The GDR did not sign the convention and limited the right to communist freedom fighters: foreigners could not be removed "if they were persecuted abroad for fighting for the principles laid down in this constitution" (Article 10/2).

How Germany would apply these principles was far less clear. In West Germany, the debate leading up to the constitution signaled a clash of opinions. Some politicians had themselves enjoyed exile. For them, the tragic fate of Jews who had been denied a safe haven from Hitler as well as their own experience made it imperative that the new country be generous to all refugees. Others wanted the right limited to fellow Germans; there was a fear that in the case of an uprising in the East, the Western Allies might deport fleeing Germans back to the Soviet-occupied zone (the issue became moot when the constitution extended citizenship to all Germans).[98] Initially, the constitutional right was irrelevant and almost forgotten, because the operative asylum decree (*Asylverordnung*) took its cue only from the 1951 Geneva Convention; reference to the constitution would only be added in 1965. A progressive judge later lambasted the omission as a foundational error that "blocked the interpretation of asylum law in line with the constitution."[99]

In practice, asylum seekers were judged by Cold War politics instead of universal principles. The typical asylum seeker in the 1950s and 1960s was someone fleeing communist Hungary, Czechoslovakia, or Yugoslavia; there were also a few Nazi collaborators and SS soldiers from France and the Netherlands.[100] Total numbers were small—between two thousand and three thousand a year—and those being granted asylum even smaller, around 25 percent. However, there was a tacit understanding that those from the communist bloc who were denied would be "tolerated" and not deported. Citizens from Tito's breakaway Yugoslavia were not so lucky.

When it came to victims of its Western partners, by contrast, the Federal Republic shut its doors. Several thousand Algerians fled across the Rhine during the Algerian war of independence (1954–62). In 1959, some were the victims of French state-sponsored attacks and assassination attempts on German soil. The German authorities freely shared details about the Algerian asylum seekers with their French colleagues on the suspicion that they must all be Arab "terrorists"—a clear violation of the Geneva Convention, which only excludes individuals when there is good reason to believe that they have committed crimes against humanity or other serious crimes. After the Palestinian terrorist attacks at the Munich Olympics in 1972, Arab and North African students as well as asylum seekers were placed under surveillance or had their residence permits taken away.[101] In the 1980s, the West German authorities exchanged information about Kurdish asylum seekers with their NATO ally Turkey. Interests of state trumped the protection of refugees.

In 1956, there was a warm welcome to fifteen thousand Hungarians and again, in 1968, to five thousand Czechoslovakians after their respective uprisings. It showed that the West German population and authorities alike were capable of opening their hearts (and pockets) to refugees when the conditions were right. Importantly, they were fleeing the communist enemy. In 1956, there were mass demonstrations in their support, and Adenauer ensured that they were able to enter without the normal procedures; to meet the 1951 cutoff of the Geneva Convention, their flight was treated as a long-term effect of the regime change in 1948–49.

Such compassion was exceptional. In general, West German authorities worked on the basis that their country could not possibly take in more refugees, as it told the UN High Commissioner for Refugees time and again. Even small numbers were rejected; the space was reserved for the millions of German expellees and those fleeing the GDR.

In the GDR, too, protection served Cold War interests. Barely born, the new state took in more than a thousand Greek orphans of communists killed

LEFT 23. Fight Nuclear Death: one of many mass demonstrations against nuclear weapons, this one in Hamburg's central square in 1958

ABOVE 24. Pacifist campaign against toy tanks for children, Christmas 1965, targeting militarist values in daily life.

25. The Circle for Non-Violence in 1960, with the initiators of the Easter Marches for peace in Germany. The Quaker activists Konrad Tempel and Helga Stolle (bottom right).

NIE WIEDER!
DESHALB:
KRIEGSDIENST
VERWEIGERN!!
WARUM? WIE? Darüber gibt diese Broschüre der
Selbstorganisation der Zivildienstleistenden
(SOd L) Mü hen Auskunft.

26. "Never Again!—therefore: refuse military service!!": a pamphlet with advice for the growing number of conscientious objectors in the 1970s. In 1982, the 500,000th conscientious objector would be recognized in West Germany.

27. A protest march by disabled citizens and their supporters in Frankfurt in 1980, with the disability rights campaigner Gusti Steiner (right) wearing a yellow badge evoking the star Jews were forced to wear in Nazi Germany.

28. "Live differently so that others can live," the motto of young Catholics campaigning for global solidarity and development in 1977. The rich lifestyle of the West was seen as responsible for poverty in the "Third World."

29. Comfort, color, and affluence: a family home in West Germany, 1960s.

30. Socialist modern: fashion models at the Leipzig fair in East Germany, 1972.

31. The virtue of saving, according to a fourteen-year-old girl's drawing for "savings week" in 1956. Saving was glorified to raise funds for industrial reconstruction but also to teach discipline, sacrifice, and thrift. For this West German girl, however, it meant the promise of a fur coat.

32. The one millionth "guest worker," Armando Rodrigues de Sá from Portugal, is given a moped on his arrival in Cologne in 1964. Several million migrants from southern Europe and Turkey came to work and live in West Germany, but their hosts clung to the idea that Germany was "not a country of immigration."

33. Women migrant workers demanding equal pay in one of many wildcat strikes in 1973, this one at the automotive supplier Pierburg in Neuss, North Rhine–Westphalia. Their protests signaled that they were there to stay.

34. At the Brandenburg Gate, November 10, 1989, the day after the fall of the Berlin Wall.

35. The border opening at Bornholmer Strasse on November 11, 1989. Eleven months later, the two Germanies were reunited.

36. A refugee holding up a picture of Chancellor Angela Merkel on arrival at the Munich train station in September 2015. Merkel had kept the borders open, allowing almost one million asylum seekers to enter the country that year.

DER STORCH BRINGT DIE KINDER
DER KRANICH NIMMT SIE WIEDER WEG
...obwohl es sich kaum für ihn lohnt:Der Lufthansa- Konzern erledigt einen relativ geringen Teil des Abschiebungsgeschäfts. Der Umsatz durch Abschiebungen entspricht nur einem winzigen Bruchteil des Gesamtumsatzes.
Wenn Sie Zeuge einer Abschiebung werden, schreiten Sie ein. Weigern Sie sich vor dem Start des Flugzeugs, Platz zu nehmen. Behindern sie die rassistische Politik der BRD.
Lufthansa DeportationServices

37. "The stork delivers the children, the crane takes them away again"—a poster by the campaign group Kein Mensch ist Illegal (No Person Is Illegal) targeting deportations of rejected asylum seekers on Lufthansa flights, 2000. Many thousands were deported that year.

38. "Today we are tolerant, tomorrow strangers in our homeland": protestors on a march against refugees in Freilassing, Bavaria, January 2016.

39. November 8, 2011, Chancellor Merkel and Russia's president Dmitry Medvedev open the Nord Stream pipeline, meant to bring cheap gas from Russia to German homes and factories and tie Russia to Europe, flanked by (left to right): François Fillon (France's prime minister), Mark Rutte (the Netherlands' prime minister), Günther Oettinger (EU commissioner for energy), and Erwin Sellering, (premier of the German state of Mecklenburg-Vorpommern). On the far left is ex-chancellor Gerhard Schröder.

ABOVE, LEFT 40. One of many brown coal or lignite mines in Germany, this one in Spreewald, East Germany, 1959. Brown coal is a poor source of energy and a big contributor to pollution and climate change. It was East Germany's principal fuel.

ABOVE, RIGHT 41. Relics of progress: nuclear power stations on Delft-like porcelain wall plates, designed in 2015, four years after the decision to phase out nuclear power. Here Isar II in Bavaria is shown, one of three nuclear reactors that, after the Russian invasion of Ukraine, had its life extended until April 2023.

RIGHT 42. Ende Gelände, grassroot activists for climate justice and against capitalism, 2022. Their protests, civil disobedience, and occupations of coal mines have attracted many supporters—but failed to stop the opening of a new lignite mine in 2022–23.

in the Greek civil war. In a dedicated home in Radebeul on the outskirts of Dresden, they were taught in Greek and German to prepare them for their ultimate return. Most were apprenticed as skilled workers; a few made it to university. The problems started when they began to mix with their German peers. They were in the GDR to steel themselves for the anti-fascist struggle, not make love to local teenagers. A little samba and rock 'n' roll landed a dozen Greek refugees in trouble after a New Year's Eve party in 1957. Eight lost their status as recognized "victims of fascism" and the extra benefits that came with it. Five were sent back to Greece.

The GDR also provided a sanctuary for veterans of the Spanish Civil War. In the late 1950s, they were joined by several hundred Algerians and Moroccans. For officials, their lifestyle posed a particular danger to good morals and the purity of German womanhood—a sign that old prejudices did not stop at the border. Were they even "genuine" communists? officials wondered. Solidarity did not mean supporting their "adventurism or love of travel."[102] In one factory, fistfights broke out when the Algerians refused to stick to "their" seats in the canteen. The refugees, in turn, protested about too much pork and too little training. Several threatened to go back to the West: after all, what was Zwickau (Saxony) compared to Paris?

In 1973, the military coup in Chile drove 200,000 Chileans into exile. Two thousand made the GDR their second home, especially members of the intelligentsia such as the leading functionary Carlos Altamirano and the poet Gonzalo Rojas. Rojas landed a teaching job at the University of Rostock. Most of his countrymen, though, were put to work in car factories and concentrated in newly built apartment blocks in Zwickau. While this made their surveillance easier, it inevitably produced tensions. Former students wanted to sit in lecture halls, not lie underneath the chassis of a Trabant car. When some went on strike, the Stasi threatened to withdraw their "guest" status. To help them settle in, the Chileans received cash and interest-free loans as well as keys to a modern apartment. What irked East Germans more than the money was their freedom to travel to the West to meet with fellow Chileans in exile.[103]

EMPATHY FLOWS AND EBBS

By the mid-1960s, the European postwar crisis of the wandering refugee was over. Most "displaced persons" had been repatriated or had emigrated to Israel and the United States. There were still thousands of DPs in West Germany, including 35,000 Russians and Ukrainians, but the camps were shutting down. Bavaria closed its final "foreigner camp" in 1964. Outside Europe, decolonization, famine, and civil war brought new refugee crises. In 1967, a new Protocol to the Refugee Convention scrapped its geographic and time limits. Refugees now had rights regardless of where and when in the world they faced persecution. When West Germany signed the 1967 Protocol, its asylum system was designed to deal with a few thousand refugees a year from communist Eastern Europe. In 1970, the largest number of asylum seekers by far were 5,272 Czechoslovakians, followed by 2,000 from Hungary, Yugoslavia, Poland, and Romania combined. Between 1976 and 1979, however, some 40,000 refugees reached the country, from Pakistan, India, Lebanon, Ghana, Bangladesh, and elsewhere. The military coup in Turkey in 1980 added another 58,000. That year, the number of asylum seekers for the first time crossed 100,000 (107,818).[104]

The West German response was one of widening extremes, with rising waves of humanitarianism on one side and higher walls to keep out asylum seekers on the other. Importantly, these extremes cut across society and the state as well as between them. Municipalities and regions, which had responsibility for asylum seekers, pulled in the opposite direction from the federal government. In 1975, for example, two years after the "stop" on recruiting foreign workers, asylum seekers were given the right to work—a sensible step for them and local authorities, which saved on benefits, but something that flew in the face of the federal policy of reserving work for Germans.

The oscillation between welcome and deterrence reached a crescendo in 1979–80 when the rescue operation for the Vietnamese "boat people" coincided with a new regime of defensive measures against asylum seekers.

In November 1978, the world watched as a damaged freighter carrying more than 2,000 desperate Vietnamese, including many children, was denied permission to land in Malaysia after two weeks at sea; that country was not a signatory to the UN Refugee Convention. They were part of the 800,000 so-called boat people who fled oppression by communist Vietnam; ethnic Chinese were especially targeted by the regime. Canada instantly offered to take several tens of thousands. The United States would take more than 400,000. Britain raised its quota to 10,000. West Germany initially tried to limit its share to 1,300 and pay its way out of international responsibility by offering money to aid organizations.

Bonn was outflanked by the governor of Lower Saxony, Ernst Albrecht. The ambitious Christian Democrat pledged to fly 1,000 boat people from Malaysia to his state. The initiative set in motion an unprecedented humanitarian response. Cities began to compete for their share of the Vietnamese refugees, newspapers started their own donation drives, and Bundesliga clubs auctioned off soccer balls with their stars' autographs. Soon, the federal government was promising to take 30,000 boat people. Citizens played an active role in the rescue operation. The broadcaster Rupert Neudeck and his wife, Christel, chartered the freighter *Cap Anamur*. With a team of doctors and nurses, they provided medical aid to 35,000 people over the next three years and rescued another 10,000; Neudeck took the idea from a similar French project. Within a few months, donations to their ship topped 6 million DM.[105]

The plight of the Vietnamese pulled at particular German heartstrings. That defenseless people in their rickety boats were shot at on the South China Sea reminded many of the fate of their German brothers trying to cross the Berlin Wall. Both were victims of communism. Collective memory also made aid a form of atonement for Nazi crimes. We have already seen how the peace movement invoked the past to awaken moral responsibility in the present: those who did nothing were accused of being complicit bystanders, as under the Nazis. Public acknowledgment of victims as well as perpetrators reached new heights with the screening of the American TV series *Holocaust* in January 1979. In the words of the historian Frank Bösch, support for the boat people "almost worked like a compensation for the mass murder of the Jews."[106]

It was also an affirmation for the German expellees. Neudeck himself was a child refugee from Danzig (Gdansk) and had fled within a few days of the sinking of the *Wilhelm Gustloff* by Soviet torpedoes in January 1945. Countess Marion Dönhoff, the journalist who led the donation drive of the weekly *Die Zeit*, had been driven out of the family castle outside Königsberg (Kaliningrad) on the Baltic coast. In parliament and town halls, expellees reminded the public of their own tragic flight. Not all expellees were compassionate to other refugees, but memory culture inserted a competitive edge. As more attention was finally devoted to the victims of the Holocaust, German expellees wanted to make sure that they did not lose their place in collective memory. The boat people upgraded the expellees' role in the national past and present: they had been through a similar ordeal and could now act as ambassadors of empathy. It was at this moment that a series of children's books appeared written by authors who recalled their own expulsions from the Sudetenland and East Prussia.[107]

The welcome of the Vietnamese built on private ethics of civic action cultivated in the peace and "Third World" movements. Citizens, in this view, had a personal responsibility to do something to minimize violence, misery, and hunger in the world. Not surprisingly, Cap Anamur had the fervent support of Heinrich Böll, Franz Alt, Klaus von Bismarck, and many others. The main difference was that earlier campaigns required only limited, mainly indirect support for strangers. Donations were sent to Biafra, and development aid to Latin America. Now, people in distress came to Germany and Germans pulled refugees from the open sea. Cap Anamur raised the bar for direct humanitarian action.

Once in Germany, the Vietnamese boat people were overwhelmed by public sympathy and support. There was remarkable, unbureaucratic coordination between state and civil society. The 250 refugees who arrived in Frankfurt in January 1979, for example, were greeted at the airport by the German Red Cross, which liaised with the local hospitals. The city took care of legal issues and organized their accommodation in a holiday camp. Charities and the city joined forces in a donation drive. Firms offered them jobs, landlords vacant flats, and the Society for Human Rights care and support.[108] More Germans wanted to be a "godfather" (*Pate*) or mentor than there were refugees. They offered to teach them German, help them interact with the authorities, and go shopping with them. One counselor complained how "our Vietnamese children are constantly invited by bowling clubs, *Stammtischen*, choirs, and sports clubs. Even the bishop invited them! One day I said, 'That's enough now.'" When asked what impressed him most about the refugees, one mentor said it was "their patience and the calmness with which they bear the wave of German helpfulness that rolls over them."[109]

Not everyone was happy about so much help. Direct humanitarianism trespassed on affairs of state. It also stepped on the toes of the classic aid agencies. The general secretary of the German Red Cross accused Cap Anamur of giving "bogus" asylum seekers a free ride to Germany. Some who had marched for Ho Chi Minh derided the middle-class refugees as profiteers and American collaborators. Most of the Vietnamese had fled expropriation and economic collapse and did not fit the narrow constitutional definition of the "political refugee." They were accepted as "quota refugees," and only four thousand would submit an asylum application in Germany.

The public mood, too, was brittle. Behind the wave of sympathy lurked prejudice and self-interest. The state of Rhineland-Palatinate was initially trying to cherry-pick men who were young, fit, and skilled. Members of German Youth Europe (formerly the expellee body "Young Germans of the East") conducted a series of interviews in a shopping street in Paderborn a year after the arrival of the first boat people. "I do not have anything against them," one person told them, "but let's not overdo it." Another wished "they'd go back to where they came from, and as quickly as possible."

"I really feel sorry for the Vietnamese," one citizen said. "But that is not our problem... I have seen some in the department store—in a fur coat. Until recently, my wife could not afford a fur coat. It was the ones with money who first climbed on board *Cap Anamur*." In all the interviews, only one elderly man was "benevolent and positive without limitations."[110]

Citizens who volunteered to take in unaccompanied minors were overwhelmingly in their forties and had at least one child themselves. For the majority, foster care was a new chapter in their lives; only 20 percent had had previous experience. They were comfortable middle-class families, but they were not necessarily all members of a cosmopolitan multicultural tribe. In Baden, two thirds of the helpers lived in rural villages and small towns. Food and fashion were the main sources of tension—some children nagged their foster mothers to buy them expensive shoes and bell-bottom jeans; social workers blamed the initial avalanche of gifts for spoiling them. Overall, though, most families stressed the trust and harmony they developed at home and at school. They said they would do it again. One parent spoke for many: "I had the feeling I was needed."[111]

The integration of older cohorts proved more difficult. Looking back in 1982, a Caritas official said she was stunned how people imagined integration would be "almost child's play." The unbureaucratic welcome translated into a range of different conditions. Some refugees lived in centralized hostels, others in decentralized accommodation or with families. For this official, the key to success was "respect for their difference, their religious values, and their independence." Excessive care had to be avoided at all costs.[112]

The boat people found themselves in a different psychological as well as legal situation from that of political refugees, such as the Chileans; departing from its previous anti-communist bias, West Germany also gave refuge to Chileans fleeing the military dictatorship of General Augusto Pinochet after 1973. Chileans, social workers found, adapted more easily because they had strong group solidarity and shared a hope of return. The Vietnamese, by contrast, were a heterogenous group with a range of motives and little prospect of return. When social workers interviewed a group in a temporary shelter in 1979, only 7 percent mentioned "political persecution." Many dreamed of "the golden West." Two years after their arrival, one third were unemployed and another third worked as casual laborers. Large families had sometimes left children behind. Depression and suicidal thoughts were widespread.[113]

The wave of empathy petered out as quickly as it had arisen. In early 1981, several German states refused to take in any more boat people. The recession of the early 1980s—when unemployment doubled, reaching 8 percent in 1983—dampened the welcome. It would be too simple to blame the economy, though. Fear over jobs and benefits reinforced existing xenophobia, it did not cause it. Already on July 30, 1980, a pipe bomb exploded in the federal asylum processing camp at Zirndorf near Nuremberg. Two weeks later, another hit a home for Ethiopian refugees in Lörrach across the border from Switzerland. Outside Stuttgart, there was an arson attack on a hotel housing asylum seekers. Shortly after midnight on August 22, 1980, three Molotov cocktails set another provisional accommodation center on fire in Hamburg. Two refugees died. On the wall, graffiti demanded "Foreigners out." Behind the terror attack was a group of neo-Nazis: a plumber, a doctor, and a disbarred lawyer. The following year saw attacks on Turkish residents and flyers threatening "Turkish pigs to concentration camps." In 1982, two Black Americans and an Egyptian were shot in a discotheque in Nuremberg.[114]

THE BOAT IS FULL

Refugees became the scapegoats for the pent-up antipathy toward the guest workers. West Germany was a signatory to the Refugee Convention, but that did not mean that people and politicians had a clear understanding of refugees and their rights. In the earlier-mentioned interviews in the shopping street, respondents did not distinguish between asylum seekers and guest workers: "Foreigner equals foreigner," as one citizen put it.[115]

By 1982, no one was talking about German expellees after 1945 anymore, a Caritas official observed, let alone the 50 million refugees across the world. The metrics had changed. Now a few thousand refugees set off alarm bells of *Überfremdung* ("being swamped by foreigners") even while Germans still made up 93 percent of the population. The Federal Republic had 62 million inhabitants and had absorbed 12 million expellees after the war, German Youth Europa pointed out; how can the boat now possibly be too full to take in 30,000 Vietnamese? There was so little empathy toward refugees that this association developed a board game in order to teach it: "Flight and Expulsion Across the World." A player who landed on square B9 was moved into a refugee camp in Hesse, where he got ill from the "unfamiliar food, not being allowed to work, lack of contact with the outside world, and worry about the family back home." The player had to miss one turn. "Before you can resume the game, you must imagine how you would feel in such a situation."[116]

This board game would have made little sense a few years earlier. The imagined scene was part of a new regime of deterrence and surveillance that was introduced in 1980. Step by step, asylum seekers had their little support and freedoms taken away from them, at a time when their applications and appeals regularly took several years. They lost the right to work while waiting for a decision and for another two years after being recognized (five years beginning in 1986). Refugees from Eastern Europe were initially exempted. Instead, asylum seekers could be ordered to do community work at 1 DM an hour, a tenth of what a German worker earned at the time. Language courses were abolished. Parents lost their child benefits while other benefits were replaced by services in kind. They were prohibited from cooking their own food and had to eat what was on the menu at dedicated hours in the canteen, regardless of whether it happened to be pork or was Ramadan. To accelerate decisions, a single judge took over from a tribunal panel and the number of appeals was reduced. Legal aid was virtually nonexistent, and lawyers who tried to offer pro bono advice were threatened with fines by the bar association. Finally, barely fifteen years after proudly closing the foreigner camps, ministers opened new regional camps with just as much pride.

All asylum seekers were now gathered in camps, including those who had successfully found private quarters. Indeed, even people who, after years, had been granted refugee status had to move back into these camps if they wanted to be together with their wives and children, regardless of the fact that the family members had come to join the refugee, not to claim asylum. Arrivals from Afghanistan, Sri Lanka, and other non-European countries now needed a prior visa, and airlines were penalized for carrying anyone without one (even if a traveler was later granted asylum), something that became a widespread European practice. For a few years, East Berlin served as a back door. The GDR ran a lucrative asylum-tourism venture in the divided city, letting Africans and Asians land at its Schönefeld airport and then walk into the Western sector, where they would claim asylum. The threat of economic sanctions closed that remaining gap in 1986.[117]

Asylum policy was turned into a weapon against economic migrants. Since the barring of guest workers had failed, ministers now at least wanted to block asylum seekers. Morally, this was a slippery slope, for in the hands of politicians and the media there lurked behind almost every refugee the figure of the scheming migrant who came to Germany to help himself to a slice of its wealth and welfare. Ministers were blunt about their motivations. In July 1980, the governor of Baden-Württemberg, Lothar Späth—the same Christian Democrat who had campaigned for solidarity with the "Third World" and taken in boat people—told the Federal Council of Ministers (Bundesrat) how his strategy had paid off: taking away the permission to work had lowered the number of asylum seekers in his state from 5,000 to 1,400. Concentrating them in a camp would lower it further. "The reason is simple," he explained. "The Turks no longer come to Baden-Württemberg, because they no longer receive permission to work and can no longer approach their contacts and instead have to go to an assembly camp [*Sammellager*]."[118]

Of course, not all asylum seekers qualified as refugees. The majority had always been refused—forty-seven thousand between 1976 and 1980. Almost half of those left voluntarily; two thousand were deported. A large number went underground—44 percent in Bavaria in 1989. The problem was that by deterring "bogus" refugees, the new regime was also failing "genuine" ones. A victim of persecution was unlikely to walk into a German embassy in broad view of their tormentors to ask for help. And of those who made it to Germany, refugees were hit harder by the dehumanizing conditions in the centers than economic migrants. The latter could go home, the former could not.

The head of the Europe section of the UN Office of the High Commissioner for Refugees visited several refugee centers in 1983. She had received reports from their Bonn office, but "it was difficult to imagine how bad the conditions actually are... without actually seeing them." Hirsemühle was a pretty, old converted school in Hesse but typical in all other respects: it was "miles from the nearest village... totally isolated, no local transport... broken furniture." She was struck by the "state of total dejection" of the Afghans and Eritreans she met there. In the entire time they had been there, they had been visited only once, by a priest. Otherwise they had no contact with the outside world. She listened to "their misery and panic over their future" and worried about "the danger for their mental health and decreasing ability to integrate into a society that they have learned to fear and distrust, as it has rejected them and destroyed their dignity as human beings, but in which they must remain, as they have nowhere else to go." As she pointed out, the restrictions on their freedom of movement were probably a violation of both the Universal Declaration and the European Convention on Human Rights, as was compulsory community work. France and Switzerland, she noted, had a higher share of foreigners in their population and comparable or higher numbers of asylum seekers but nonetheless offered language courses and allowed them to work.[119] It was a scathing report. The minister of the interior responded swiftly by canceling his scheduled meeting with the high commissioner. A subsequent UNHCR inspection of the centers arranged by the German authorities was no less damning.

Deterrence would prove a shortsighted policy, for refugees and locals alike. Segregated and with nothing to do, refugees drifted into depression and crime and turned on each other. The local population, in turn, became more fearful and hostile, more convinced than ever that asylum seekers were lazy, living at their expense, and a danger to the safety of their women. For the integration of those who after years of waiting finally received recognition as refugees, as well as for the many who were denied but "tolerated" and not removed, it was a preprogrammed disaster.

Deterrence went hand in hand with a more restrictive approach by the courts. What counted as "political" and "persecution"? The Federal Administrative Court tightened persecution to mean politically motivated by an organized state.[120] Tamils fleeing violence in Sri Lanka were denied asylum on the grounds that "civil war conditions" did not constitute "political persecution." Ahmadis who had suffered a pogrom in Pakistan in 1974 and feared repression as a religious minority were also denied—in this case because they supposedly faced only legal and economic discrimination on return. For a constitutional expert, the criteria were becoming so restrictive that "probably ... not even the Jews in the Warsaw Ghetto uprising would have a chance to get asylum with us."[121] It needed the Constitutional Court to point out that religious discrimination could be political persecution.[122]

From 1986 on, German courts also disregarded grounds that arose after the original flight unless there was a continuation of earlier acts of opposition. This, again, was in direct conflict with the Geneva Convention, which protected people who might, for example, have arrived as economic migrants but then became refugees while in the host country ("*sur place*") because of a subsequent regime change in their home country. Sometimes asylum seekers became politically active after their flight to produce the precious evidence their host country demanded of refugees; others did so to create a risk of persecution where none had existed. Whatever their motivation, the crucial test in international law was whether or not they had a "well-founded fear of persecution" on return. German courts made it a test of good character, instead.

Kurds and others tortured by the Turkish military regime were denied because torture was "normal" in Turkey and their scars had not necessarily been inflicted for political motives. Victims of communist states did not need such proof. For information about the local situation, the courts tended to rely on the Foreign Ministry, which in turn took at face value what its NATO ally said about its respect for law and order. Instead of proceeding from the interests of the individual refugee (as both the German constitution and the Geneva Convention did), the courts looked at asylum from the view of the state—with tragic consequences. In 1983, faced with the threat of deportation, Cemal Kemal Altun, a critic of the Turkish regime, jumped from the sixth floor of the Higher Administrative Court in Berlin to his death.

That year, the number of asylum seekers fell below twenty thousand. How much credit the accommodation centers deserve is debatable; after all, numbers fell by half across Europe in the early 1980s. Asylum politics, however, had come to stay. Pictures in the news of people fleeing global crises cut both ways. They triggered empathy but also stoked fears that West Germany would be "swamped" by foreigners. Each European country convinced itself that its welfare system made it the chosen land for the world's downtrodden. In reality, most refugees ended up displaced in neighboring countries in Africa and Asia. In the hands of sensationalist media and populist politicians, however, Germany was on the verge of becoming a modern-day Noah's ark for the rest of the world.

What was at stake was no longer the "bogus" asylum seeker but the very right to asylum. As numbers began to rise again—seventy-four thousand in 1985—the Christian Democratic leaders of Bavaria, Berlin, and Baden-Württemberg painted apocalyptic scenarios: the country would be "flooded" by millions unless the right to asylum was restricted. The former president of the Constitutional Court warned that "1 billion Chinese" would need to be admitted if the forced one-child policy in China qualified as persecution.[123] In 1985, the three states went on the offensive: they proposed implementing *Asyl auf Zeit* ("time-limited asylum")—with two checks after two years each to ensure that requirements were still met—and stretching the terms of "manifestly unfounded" applications to cases where people had fled military conflicts or general crises. The Liberals in Kohl's coalition initially balked, but with the federal election in 1987 around the corner eventually abandoned their opposition. There would be no *Asyl auf Zeit*, but the other provisions found their way into a new law. Rising anti-foreigner sentiment cut across party lines. The interior minister of Hesse, a Social Democrat, rejected any tinkering with the constitutional right to asylum as "inhumane" and "blind to history." It did not stop him and colleagues in Hamburg and North Rhine–Westphalia from agreeing with CDU ministers that Poles who had been denied asylum or had not applied for it should be removed—if Turks were sent back, why not Poles as well?[124] Both big parties were shaking a pillar of the postwar asylum regime, which had guaranteed émigrés from communist countries that their stay would be tolerated. Only the Green Party wanted to offer sanctuary to refugees fleeing humanitarian crises.

The crumbling of the Soviet bloc released two fresh waves of migrants into West Germany. One was of Polish and Yugoslavian asylum seekers—in

1988 and 1989, a total of almost 100,000, twice as many as those from Turkey, Iran, and Sri Lanka combined. The second wave was of people with German roots from the Soviet Union, Romania, and Poland. In 1988, 200,000 of these so-called *Aussiedler* arrived in West Germany. Their number would peak at 400,000 two years later.

As ethnic Germans, the *Aussiedler* were citizens and had an automatic right to stay. Still, they, too, were unable to escape the xenophobic backlash as each party played off their "good" migrants against the others' "bad" ones. Christian Democrats defended the *Aussiedlers'* privileged status; Greens and the SPD challenged it. The SPD's Oskar Lafontaine, the red "Napoleon of the Saar," who would lose to Kohl in the 1990 election, dared to ask whether the "existential need of a stranger" should not take precedence over the fact that someone "had a German-speaking ancestor umpteen generations ago."[125] Even among old expellees, compassion had limits. "Why do we need to take in so many, anyhow?" asked a sixty-two-year-old woman who herself had been driven out of Silesia at the end of the Second World War. That they had one German grandfather did not make them "real" Germans, in her view. First they had robbed the Germans, and now they came to Germany looking for more? "Frankly speaking, I have no sympathy for these people, and none at all if they are real Poles."[126] In people's minds, the refugee, migrant, and ethnic German blended into "the foreigner," regardless of legal and social distinctions.[127]

A deep fault line ran across society. Whether refugees were taken in or not was no longer a question of life and death only for them; it developed into an existential crisis for their hosts, the German nation, as well. For some, the absolute right to asylum was the hallmark of the new Germany after Hitler; without it, the Federal Republic lost its moral right to exist. For others, it spelled national suicide: a state had to serve the interests of its own people first, before giving asylum to strangers.

The Conservative mayor of the idyllic town of Vilshofen on the Danube spoke for many angry local politicians. He wanted refugees to be separated by ethnic group and detained in camps the moment they crossed the nearby border with Austria and Czechoslovakia. Everything else was "exaggerated humanitarianism" and hurt the "interests of the German *Volk*." "Today we are given the asylum seekers bicycles, tomorrow some of our daughters."[128] Towns introduced new bus lines so their children no longer had to walk past the asylum center. In the village of Neureut, at the edge of the Bavarian Forest, residents blocked asylum seekers from reaching the vacant inn that had been earmarked as their temporary shelter.

Roughly 125 miles to the west, in the old Bavarian city of Augsburg, it was a very different scene. In October 1989, the Lutheran St. Johannes Church gave "church asylum" to seven young men who had fled the military regime in Bangladesh. Their asylum claims had been rejected by the courts as "manifestly unfounded" and they were now facing deportation. The Foreign Ministry considered the situation to be calm, even though the embassy in Dhaka reported hundreds of deaths in violent clashes and warned German students against travel. The men were put in touch with the church through a "Third World" partnership group. Some members of the congregation had been active in support groups for asylum seekers since their student days in the late 1970s, when they had organized Christian-Muslim-Hindu prayers. A national umbrella organization (PRO ASYL) would be founded in 1986.

The case galvanized support from across the community. Volunteers taught German to the refugees, who cooked for them in return. For a middle-aged German housewife and her husband, a civil servant, the case changed their lives: "Once apolitical churchgoers, we turned into critical, thinking citizens." A female carpenter recalled how she used to try hard not to look at "dark men" in the public square because she did not know how to encounter strangers. Getting to know these refugees taught her to see the individual in the mass. A pensioner was reminded of his youth as a soldier and POW and his own powerlessness then. For him, the idea that people fled to Germany to take away its wealth was utter nonsense. If anything, affluence had made his fellow citizens too materialistic. A tax consultant and his wife felt they would have become "complicit" had they ignored the plight of the seven. An insurance saleswoman said she could not look away, because "their problems with hunger and social injustice are, after all, caused by us and by the unfair distribution of goods on our planet." "Not only do the strangers need us," she stressed, "we also need the strangers." As they became friends, she learned to be more tolerant.

Eight thousand signatures, support from the bishop, and a debate in the Bavarian assembly were not enough, however, to make the authorities change their mind. Their deportation imminent, the seven fled north to Lower Saxony, to a church in Hildesheim, in August 1990. The local pastor there had lived in South Africa and seen apartheid with his own eyes. Another nine months of sanctuary bought them and their supporters the time they needed to get recognized as refugees in Germany, where they continue to live.[129]

Both German societies struggled with living with difference. Neither country saw itself as a melting pot. Migrants and refugees were subject to racism and attacks in the West as well as the East. There were, however, profound contrasts. Millions of migrants did make West Germany their home—in a liberal society, ending recruitment of foreign labor was not an impediment to families joining workers already in the country. Discrimination was widespread, but foreigners lived amid native Germans and transformed neighborhoods. They could move jobs and homes. The mantra that Germany was "not a country of immigration" began to be challenged by those supporting multiculturalism and assimilation.

In East Germany, by contrast, migration was tiny, and the contract laborers and students who did come were separated as far as possible from the local population and could not settle or bring their families. There was little or no encounter with foreigners and high degrees of prejudice and xenophobia.

The different way each of the two Germanies lived with the strangers in their midst also increased their estrangement from each other. When the Wall came down, East Germans began to chant, "We are one people." Who would be included in that category remained to be seen.

PART THREE

AFTER THE WALL

1989–2022

10

United and Divided: The Cost of Freedom

When the Berlin Wall fell on November 9, 1989, not only did it bury the GDR, it also toppled the postwar international order and shook the foundations on which the other Germany had built its identity. In the Cold War, each side knew where they stood. There was stability in fear. With reunification in 1990, Germany entered a period of turbulence. The collapse of the Eastern bloc put a big unified country back at the center of Europe. What would be its new role in the world?

For East Germans, reunification quickly turned from hope into shock. For many, it spelled the end of life as they knew it, and they lost their jobs. Almost 2 million of them packed up and moved West, especially young women. Birth rates plummeted—a quarter fewer children were conceived in the decade after the *Wende*—the "turn," used to describe the period around reunification—than in the one before. West Germans did not experience such dislocation, but they, too, saw old certainties tumbling thick and fast. In 1993, the right to asylum was restricted in a historic change to the constitution. Six years later, Germany took part in its first combat mission since the Second World War, sending Tornado fighter jets to Kosovo in a NATO operation. In 2000, citizenship was finally liberalized to include children born on German soil to foreign parents. The Deutschmark—the symbol of stability—was replaced by the euro in 2002. The next year brought the overhaul of the welfare system, with deep cuts to unemployment benefits.

Since it was reunited, the country has been convulsed by an identity crisis. In part, this was because westerners seized control of the process of reunification, with little regard for their fellow citizens in the east. But disquiet about relations within Germany was matched by unease about Germany's relationship with the rest of the world. Globalization made it harder for the nation to come together. Chancellor Angela Merkel's decision to keep the borders open for more than 800,000 refugees in 2015 laid bare the deep divides cutting across the country. Was Germany showing the global West much-needed moral leadership or was it committing national suicide? Public life became morally supercharged and confrontational. While millions of volunteers welcomed the refugees, other citizens threw firebombs at them. In the general election of 2017, 12.6 percent voted for the populist Alternative für Deutschland party (Alternative for Germany, AfD). For the first time since the 1950s, the far right sat again in the federal parliament.[1]

Each of these convulsions has its own history, but they are all connected. Reunification started a domino effect. Kohl gave up the Deutschmark, for example, in exchange for French president François Mitterrand's support for reunification. In turn, there was a rush to a common currency, the euro, before a fiscal union was in place to agree on spending and taxes. This left the European Union unable to deal swiftly with the worldwide financial crash in 2008 and the Eurozone crisis that followed. Reunification also generated its own domestic momentum. Its costs were far higher than expected and paid for through additional pension and social insurance contributions, but these raised the cost of labor, which hurt sales and caused unemployment, only adding to the burden on the state. To stop this vicious cycle and boost exports, Helmut Kohl's successor, the Social Democrat Gerhard Schröder, cut unemployment benefits and introduced low-paid "mini-jobs" as part of a neoliberal reform of the welfare system. Germany began a stubborn pursuit of zero public debt, which it also imposed on the European stage, almost killing the European project in the process. No sphere was immune from the austerity campaign. In 2000, the Bundeswehr had 320,000 soldiers. Twenty years later, it had just over half that; military conscription was suspended in 2011. It was a telling illustration of the unresolved contradictions of the new, bigger Germany searching for its place in the world.

Three leaders steered Germany through these storms, their political styles as different as their personalities: Helmut Kohl (CDU, chancellor 1982–98), Gerhard Schröder (SPD, 1998–2005), and Angela Merkel (CDU, 2005–21). Kohl, the "chancellor of unity," was a federal Europeanist by conviction and literally a colossus at six foot four, with a large waistband and love for haggis (*Saumagen*) from his homeland, the Palatinate. Inside the fairly ordinary man ticked a feudal lord who, over the years, built up a vast network of loyal knights and supporters. A corruption scandal would cast a dark shadow over his final years. The sudden events of 1989–90 would catapult this provincial man to the center stage of world politics.

Schröder was a horse of a different color. A self-made man from lowly origins, he rose to be Germany's first media-friendly chancellor, attracting attention for his shiny hair, fourth wife, Cohiba cigars, and Italian suits—in spite of having come of age in the 1960s, he did not own a single pair of jeans. The charismatic Schröder inherited not only the costs of reunification but also its opportunities. The people, he declared in his first address as chancellor in 1998, had authorized him and his SPD-Green coalition government "to lead Germany into the next millennium." The time had come for Germany to act with the "self-confidence of a mature nation."[2]

Merkel had neither Schröder's charisma nor the feudal instincts of her patron, Kohl. A pastor's daughter and trained physicist, she grew up inside the GDR. When she entered politics in 1989, she was already thirty-five years old. Within a decade, she had climbed to the top of the CDU, a meteoric rise without parallel. What Merkel did have in abundance was composure. With her analytical mind, she cut through the most complex problems and carefully weighed the options until the least bad solution revealed itself. What appeared to be cautious and wise to some was dithering to others, adding a new word to the German language: "to *merkeln*." It was another irony of history that, time and again, it was the risk-averse, unpretentious Merkel who found herself in the eye of a storm where energetic leadership and speedy action were called for, as in the global financial and Eurozone crises and the pandemic. The two times she acted swiftly she made dramatic, still-controversial U-turns that put Germany on a separate track from the rest of Europe—phasing out nuclear power after the disaster in Fukushima in 2011, and keeping the borders open to refugees in 2015.

THE PEOPLE'S REVOLUTION

The GDR at the beginning of 1989 resembled a snow-covered mountain after rain. Outwardly, the snow-packed slope looked secure. The regime was in control, enjoyed international recognition, and was getting ready to celebrate its fortieth anniversary on October 7. The few thousand people in the peace and civil rights circles hardly posed an existential threat and were closely watched by the Stasi. Underneath the surface, however, perestroika—reconstruction—by the new Soviet leader, Mikhail Gorbachev, was melting the snow. The thousands of East Germans who sought refuge in the West German embassies in Prague and Budapest in the summer of 1989 were the avalanche that would sweep aside the GDR.

Perestroika and "greater openness" (glasnost) began in 1985 as an attempt to reform the Soviet economy and save communism, but ended with elections in the spring of 1989 and the breakup of the Soviet Union. Gorbachev emboldened reformers across the Eastern bloc. Their strengths vis-à-vis the regimes they lived under, however, differed markedly. Before 1989, the GDR had neither a mass movement such as Solidarność in Poland nor a civil society on the scale of Czechoslovakia, with its Charter 77. When its dissidents became too troublesome, they were deported to West Germany.

Arguably, it was the very absence of a critical mass of opponents that gave SED leaders their fatally false sense of security. Whereas Hungary introduced reforms from above, they dug in their heels. As the SED chief ideologist Kurt Hager explained in 1987, "Just because your neighbor happens to change his wallpaper, do you feel obliged to repaper your own apartment as well?"[3] The analogy had one flaw. The Soviet Union was not just any neighbor but the housekeeper and the security guard as well. In the past, it had rushed to prop up neighbors when things were breaking down—the Brezhnev doctrine of military intervention. Gorbachev posted new house rules: from now on, neighbors were on their own. Unlike in 1953, there would be no Soviet tanks rolling down the streets to save the GDR.[4]

In 1988, 30,000 East German citizens were given permission to move to the West. In addition, 10,000 crossed the border illegally—double those of the previous year. By July 1989, some 133,000 exit-visa applications were pending. In the past, the regime had used exile as a safety valve to release pent-up pressure. For Erich Honecker, people who stomped on "our moral values," and excluded themselves from the socialist community, were "not worth shedding a tear over."[5] The problem was their growing number, assertiveness, and expertise. Each person who exited left behind a gap that reminded everyone else of the hopelessness of their lives—yet another doctor's practice closed and butcher shop boarded up. Those waiting for their permit no longer retreated into private despair but were meeting up in town squares and tying white flags to their cars. Since 1982, the medieval St. Nicholas Church in Leipzig had held a small prayer for peace every Monday, followed by a walk through the old town. By March 1989, the small group of civil rights activists were joined by several hundred exit-visa applicants.

The possibility of driving to Czechoslovakia without a visa (since 1972) or to Hungary with a simple travel permit (*Reiseanlage*) created fresh opportunities. By July 1989, a first group of GDR citizens sought refuge in the West German embassy in Budapest. On September 11, Hungary broke rank. Instead of stopping people at the border with Austria and returning them to the GDR, it allowed them to travel onward to a country of their choice. Within days, some 18,000 were on their way. West German embassies and communist border crossings turned into gateways to freedom. More and more East Germans decided that it was "now or never." By the time the GDR suspended its travel permits, thousands had left. At the end of September, the embassy in Prague was bursting with more than 3,000 East German refugees inside and several thousand more camping on the grounds. Under Soviet pressure, Honecker gave in and, on October 1, allowed them to leave for the West.

To get there, however, the GDR insisted that the trains had to pass through its territory, a demonstration of national sovereignty that backfired. Stasi officers, soldiers, and police tried to seal off the train stations to which people now flocked. In the district of Karl-Marx-Stadt, more than 3,000 desperate people tried to jump onto the special trains making their way from Prague to Hof in Bavaria. In the first nine months of 1989, 102,000 East Germans left the GDR, two thirds via the Hungarian route. It was just the beginning.

The exodus shook the aging regime's self-belief. The GDR was a dictatorship with political prisons and secret police, but it did not rule through terror and coercion alone. It also relied on public demonstrations of support. Not for nothing did it call itself a "democratic" republic. Of course, the SED guarded its monopoly on power, but it also saw itself as the voice of the people. A first crack in that facade of legitimacy appeared in May 1989. That elections were manipulated was common knowledge. What was new was that citizens now recorded major irregularities in communal elections and called the authorities to account; in Leipzig and Dresden, observers watched almost every polling station. The mass flight widened the crack into a chasm. People had visibly given up on the regime. The novelist Jurek Becker, who had moved from East to West Berlin a decade earlier, traced it to a "loss of hope": young people were afraid of ending up like their parents, who had tried to wait out the problems only to end up disillusioned because nothing ever changed.[6]

Secret reports between July and September 1989 noted people's growing anger at distant functionaries who would not or could not see their daily frustrations. The complaints were about more than a lack of bananas and fancy products. The Stasi itemized shortages including pots and pans, bread, milk, and underwear. In provincial Saxony, citizens began to speak out openly against the regime, causing "veritable turmoil" in one market hall. In Karl-Marx-Stadt, graffiti called for "freedom" and urged, "Erich, hand over the keys." A growing number of cars sported GDR country code stickers with the West German flag.[7]

The population showed overwhelming sympathy with those who fled. At the turbine manufacturer Bergmann-Borsig in Berlin, trade unionists wrote an open letter criticizing the media portrayal of the flights as the work of the class enemy; officials needed to acknowledge and address the underlying political and economic problems that were driving people away.[8] Formerly loyal party members lost faith in their leaders and resigned.

It took less than a month after Hungary opened the border on September 11 for the exodus to produce a revolutionary situation on the streets. Its beating heart was Leipzig, where the ritual of weekly peace prayers and walks across town provided the space for a mass movement to coalesce. On the 11th, more than a thousand people found their way to St. Nicholas Church. Outside, chants of "We want to get out" were now joined by "We will stay here." The latter contained its own threat to the regime by making loyalty conditional on reforms. A day earlier, peace, human rights, and women activists had founded the Neues Forum (New Forum) to enter into dialogue with the regime. They were soon outpaced by the thousands of citizens who swelled the demonstrations and drove them forward. By and large, the activists had lived in their own "ghetto," as the artist Bärbel Bohley, one of the founders of the Neues Forum, would acknowledge a few years later.[9] Their names were known to the Stasi but virtually no one else. Citizens who tried to sign up in support of the movement could not even find its address. East Germany produced no charismatic leader such as Lech Wałęsa in Poland or Václav Havel in Czechoslovakia. The revolution was made by the people.

The breakthrough came between the 7th and 9th of October 1989. On the 7th, while the regime celebrated its fortieth anniversary, already in the morning some five hundred protestors were gathering around St. Nicholas Church. For the first time, the police confronted protestors with truncheons and water cannons. The crowd had barely been disbanded when more people arrived. By the afternoon, they numbered seven thousand people. The fact that it was market day made it easy to slip back and forth between the demonstration and the market stalls, evading capture. At 5 p.m., the police advanced toward the crowd, beating their shields with their truncheons. Demonstrators chanted, "No violence," "Stasi out," and "Neues Forum"; a few sang "The Internationale." A Combat Group of the Working Class (*Kampfgruppe*) and a dog unit were sent to the central station. More than two hundred people were seized and detained in a horse barn.

The big question on everyone's mind was what would happen on October 9, at the next Monday's peace prayer. Local officers prepared for an expected fifty thousand protestors in Leipzig. By the early afternoon, two thousand incognito Stasi officers and party members had poured into St. Nicolas, taking up the entire central nave; another five thousand occupied the square outside. By 6 p.m., they were outnumbered by the seventy thousand people who began their march, chanting, "No violence," "We are the People," and "Democracy, now or never."[10] Regiments of soldiers and armed police were standing ready but, awaiting their orders, let them pass. Not a shot was fired. Just before 9 p.m., the crowds returned to Karl Marx Square and dispersed peacefully. Leipzig had become the "city of heroes."

Lech Wałęsa would later play down the heroism of those autumn days in Germany.[11] The East German people, he said, had it easy: they were jumping on a train that Polish workers had got rolling at the risk of their lives. There is some truth to that; forty-one strikers were killed in Gdansk in December 1970 alone. Still, it took considerable courage for the people in Leipzig to face the troops and march peacefully on that historic October 9—and for the troops not to fire.

The events are now remembered as a peaceful revolution, but at the time a scent of violence was hanging in the air. The troops were armed, and it was far from clear that the day would not end as Bloody Monday. The previous Monday, protestors had clashed with the police and cars were set on fire. In Dresden, on October 4–5, troops had used truncheons and dogs against demonstrators who were trying to storm the train station, filmed by an American TV crew. People threw stones in response and piled chairs and tables into barricades. The main station was reduced to a hall of broken glass. People chanted, "String up the communists" as well as calling for "Gorbi."[12] The Tiananmen Square massacre had only happened four months earlier and was on everyone's mind. Egon Krenz, the SED leader-in-waiting, had sent the Chinese government congratulations on the brutal crackdown. Honecker used the welcome of the Chinese delegation at the fortieth-anniversary celebrations to declare that the strict adherence to socialist principles was the "fundamental lesson from the counterrevolutionary turmoil."[13] China was "not as far away as it might appear geographically," one minister warned church leaders.[14]

Why was there no "Chinese solution" in the GDR? Unlike the predominantly student protests in Beijing, the demonstrations in East Germany were diffuse, socially and geographically. There were parents with children and senior citizens as well as young activists. Some shared cars to Leipzig from the countryside. Protests were erupting across the region. All this made it far harder to portray them as "rowdies" and drill a "counterrevolutionary enemy" picture into troops. Several members of the working-class combat troops lowered their weapons or stayed home; they wanted nothing to do with fighting their neighbors, especially as the protestors appeared to be peaceful. Nonviolence was the big gift the small peace circles gave to the revolution. In the 1980s, physical violence in general was arguably more unacceptable in East Germany than in China, where millions had died in the recent Cultural Revolution (1966–76). The GDR prided itself on being a champion of human rights. That the October demonstrations coincided with the regime's fortieth anniversary further raised the threshold for a bloody crackdown. The world was watching. Honecker did consider sending tanks to Leipzig as a deterrent in October but was dissuaded. Shooting with tanks was out of the question, the Stasi chief Erich Mielke told him. Nor were the troops battle-hardened. In Leipzig, the general in charge told the head of police that his young sergeants barely knew how to use their truncheons.[15]

The decisive factor, though, was the breakdown at the center of power. In July Honecker had his gall bladder and part of his colon removed; that the cancer had spread to his kidney was kept from him. He returned to the Politburo in September, a ghost of his former self. While the demonstrations swelled in Leipzig, the struggle for succession got underway in East Berlin. It was in this power vacuum that the Leipzig conductor Kurt Masur managed to meet with the local party leaders and extract from them a public pledge that they would support peaceful dialogue, calling on everyone to show "calm" (*Besonnenheit*). As the demonstrators began to march, the local commanders were waiting for instructions from Berlin: Did the original order to stop the crowds with force if necessary still stand? There was no answer. Egon Krenz, the crown prince, was busy removing Honecker and did not want to stain his hands with blood. The commanders decided to follow the lead of the local party bosses and deescalate the situation. By the time Krenz called back at 7:30 p.m., the crowds had been around the old town and passed the Stasi building. Nonviolence had won.

Krenz replaced Honecker on October 18, 1989, but the regime never recovered its authority. The SED was as moribund as Honecker himself. The events that autumn laid bare a degree of disorientation and failure of nerve not seen since the uprising in 1953. This time, though, the Soviet Union did not lift a finger. Soviet tanks stayed in their barracks. For the GDR, it was the point of no return.

The momentum was now with the people. Emboldened, the demonstrations got bigger and bigger. On the last Monday of October, some 300,000 people joined the protests in Leipzig, a city with barely twice that many inhabitants. In Dresden and Karl-Marx-Stadt, a quarter of the population was in the streets in early November. Prayer meetings, petitions, and silent marches spread across the region. Outside the church in Zwickau (population: 100,000), 10,000 people rallied in support of democracy, reunification, and the Neues Forum.[16]

For some dissidents, this was too much people power. They wanted the people to go home so they could enter into dialogue with the SED and reform socialism on their behalf before the situation got out of hand or ended up in the hands of Western capitalists. The Neues Forum itself was divided. In Berlin, Bärbel Bohley was happy to leave the SED in the driver's seat as long as it took more people on board. In Saxony, by contrast, the grassroots had no interest in a reformed SED.

Krenz promised a *Wende* with economic reforms, a constitutional court, and recognition of conscientious objectors—with the SED at the helm. Shaken, the party agreed to a hundred local dialogues, which only confirmed the suspicion that the SED was trying to cling to power by any means available.

Suddenly emerging critical newspapers and public readings by arrested protestors about their mistreatment deepened distrust further. That a twelve-year-old girl had "odor samples" taken for the future use of sniffer dogs smacked of the very Nazi methods against which the anti-fascist GDR had defined itself.[17] Civil rights activists and writers continued to agitate for a reformed socialist republic. The novelist Stefan Heym derided those fleeing the GDR as consumerist "philistines" (*Spiessbürger*) with a primitive view of democracy.[18] The dissidents had their "own wall in their heads," Bohley self-critically noted later: "We could only see up to the Wall and not beyond it."[19] More and more people did just that. In October, only a few demonstrators here and there had waved the West German flag or burned that of the GDR.[20] By early November, calls for an end to the Stasi and SED rule were being joined by those for reunification.

The regime was paralyzed. On November 1, Krenz flew to Moscow and confessed to Gorbachev that the GDR was effectively bankrupt. Back home, the people kept up the pressure. That week, more than a million people were in the streets calling on the leaders to resign. On November 4, 1989, between a quarter and half a million people gathered in Berlin's Alexanderplatz at a demonstration that, uniquely, had been given official permission and was shown live on state television. Prominent actors called on the SED to give up its monopoly on power, and were cheered. The former head of the Stasi, Markus Wolf, was among the official speakers and was booed.

The hemorrhage of people fleeing to West Germany via Czechoslovakia continued. Gorbachev told Krenz to open the borders to let off steam and prevent an explosion. On November 6, the Politburo released a new travel law that promised thirty-day visas to be issued within thirty days. Only a couple of months earlier, this would have been received as a miracle. Now, however, it met with public outrage. People complained about the many clauses, arbitrary loopholes, and (in their view) excessive processing time. Those without family connections and western Deutschmark were annoyed that the law said nothing about foreign currency. SED leaders were perplexed by the angry reaction. To make things worse, Czechoslovakia threatened to close its border to the GDR to stop being overrun. The regime hit on a new idea: What if they gave exit-visa applicants permission to cross directly into West Germany, without the Czech detour? It would save precious fuel! The problem was that citizens who wanted to go on a quick visit to see the West might end up applying for an exit visa and never come back.

On November 9, 1989, the SED Central Committee met and, among other business, amended the travel rules. Applications for permanent emigration would be processed without delay. In addition, trips to the West could take place at short notice and without having to document family connections. That evening, while the amendment was still awaiting formal approval by the Council of Ministers, Politburo member Günter Schabowski gave a press conference. Toward the end of it, he read out the amendment. At 6:57 p.m., a journalist asked him when the new resolution would come into effect. Having missed the earlier discussion of the new rules, Schabowski hesitated, before declaring, "Immediately." Whether he was poorly briefed or staged his confusion is a matter of dispute.[21]

Thousands took him at his word and rushed to the border crossings in Berlin. Many more switched on West German television and learned from the evening news that the border was open. A stream turned into a flood. That the new rules still required bureaucratic checks and a visa got lost in the frenzy. Having been kept in the dark, the border guards were overwhelmed. No one, including the leaders, wanted to take responsibility for a bloodbath. Just before 11 p.m., the commanding officer at the border crossing at Bornholmer Strasse opened the checkpoint, and with it the floodgates. A planned amendment to travel policy had turned into an open border. Within little more than a few hours, the Berlin Wall, the seemingly indestructible bulwark between East and West for twenty-eight years, had fallen.

"WE ARE ~~THE~~ ONE PEOPLE"

The events of November 9 had elements of farce. They nonetheless revealed two serious facts: that the SED had lost control of the GDR, and that the

Soviet Union was no longer in control either. Together, that meant what was at stake was not just the future of the SED but the very existence of a separate East Germany. Reunification had moved into the realm of the possible.

Millions of East Germans now flocked to the West, where they collected their "welcome money"—100 DM a person plus another 40 DM in some states—and spent it on consumer goods familiar from Western magazines and television. On November 17 alone, more than 3 million people drove across the border. A week later, the East German writer Christa Wolf and reform-minded artists issued an appeal "for our country." They warned of "selling out our material and moral values" and urged their fellow citizens to stay and build an alternative to West Germany that would guarantee "peace and social justice, the freedom of the individual... and the preservation of the environment."[22] It happened to be precisely what the heroine had done in her novel *Divided Heaven* (*Der geteilte Himmel*) twenty-five years earlier: instead of following her lover to the West, she stayed to make socialism better. Two hundred thousand people signed in support.

For far larger numbers, however, the sellout had already taken place. Dissidents' critique of capitalist consumer society fell on deaf ears in a socialist society of shortages. This did not mean that people had only shopping on their mind, as some intellectuals liked to lament, in both East and West. Crucially, the people kept up the pressure on the regime by continuing to protest, and not only in Leipzig, where hundreds of thousands marched in support of a united Germany by the end of November. In the small city of Plauen, for example, there were weekly demonstrations from October 7, 1989, all the way to the GDR's first (and last) democratic election on March 18, 1990. Unlike in Berlin, the Neues Forum here supported reunification. In Leipzig, on November 13, protestors began to sing, "Germany, United Fatherland!," the original words of the East German anthem, not heard since the 1960s. "We are the people" became "We are one people"—the slogan first appeared on banners in early December 1989. That same month, local firms staged a warning strike for a referendum on unification. The following month, some eighty thousand people came together for a "suitcase demonstration" in the Eichsfeld district (Thuringia): "If the SED returns to power and might, we will leave that very same night."[23]

The opening of the Berlin Wall took West Germans and their Western allies by surprise as much as it did Gorbachev and the East German people. In June 1989, Gorbachev had visited Bonn. In a joint declaration, the Soviet Union pledged to respect the self-determination of all nations, including the right to free elections. His advisers immediately clarified that this did not mean reunification was on the table. West German politicians were sharply divided. On the one hand, the restoration of national unity was enshrined in the constitution. In July 1989, the finance minister and head of the Bavarian CSU, Theo Waigel, went so far as to include East Prussia (which had been lost to Poland and the Soviet Union in 1945). On the other hand, surveys revealed a dwindling sense of shared nationhood, especially among the generations born after the war. More than a third of West Germans looked at the GDR as a foreign country.

After forty years, the Federal Republic had developed its own identity, one that rested on its commitment to the West and an acceptance of its responsibility for the Second World War and the Holocaust. On May 8, 1985, President Richard von Weizsäcker characterized in a historic speech in parliament the end of the Second World War as a "day of liberation." This was not altogether a new idea, and had been gaining ground since the 1960s. What gave these words special weight now was that they were uttered not only by the head of state but by someone who had dutifully fought in Hitler's army from the moment of the attack on Poland in 1939 to the end and who, after the war, had defended his diplomat father at the Nuremberg trial against charges of cooperating in the deportation of French Jews to Auschwitz, unsuccessfully—Ernst von Weizsäcker was sentenced to seven years in prison. In his speech, the president moved beyond Germans' fixation with their own suffering to commemorate all the victims of Nazi Germany. When it came to German guilt, however, he halted. The perpetration of the genocide, he said, was "in the hands of a few people." He criticized the majority, including his own generation, for "not burdening one's conscience, of shunning responsibility, looking away, keeping mum," only to add that guilt was individual, never collective. The perpetrators remained nebulous, and in his memoirs he continued to invoke "the demonic force of evil," so popular after the war.[24]

A year later, a public storm erupted—the so-called *Historikerstreit*—when the philosopher-historian Ernst Nolte tried to present Hitler as merely mimicking Stalin's gulag. Recognition of the singularity of the Holocaust and the country's democratic stability were two sides of the same coin. To relativize the former was automatically a nationalist threat to the latter. "The only patriotism that does not estrange us from the West," Jürgen Habermas said, "is a constitutional patriotism."[25] From that perspective, the partition of the country was an unambiguous history lesson: the nation-state was evil.

Shouldering the responsibility for the genocide gave Germans a special mission. It made them "downright predestined to take over the driving role in . . . the supranational unification of Europe," Oscar Lafontaine, the deputy leader of the SPD, declared in 1988. Lafontaine was one year old when the war ended. In contrast to Willy Brandt (born in 1913), the national question was a red flag for him and the postwar generation of Social Democrats. In September 1989, the chair of the party council, Norbert Gansel (born in 1940), declared that reunification stood "no chance" and that the Germans in the GDR ought to be given their own "historic chance of freedom." Two months later, Lafontaine mooted the idea of stopping the millions driving across the border; it had to be pointed out to him that the constitution made East Germans natural citizens who had a right to come and stay in West Germany. The strongest opponents of reunification were the Greens. Pacifism, environmentalism, and the hope for a "third way" between capitalism and socialism made them the natural allies of the dissidents in the East. To react with panic to "everything national" forty-five years after Auschwitz, the Green leader Joschka Fischer said, was "no cause for shame but a vital duty for all democrats for at least another forty-five years."[26]

It was Chancellor Kohl who seized the national question and ran with it. The immediate response was mixed. When he addressed the crowds outside the Schöneberg city hall in West Berlin the day after the fall of the Wall, he was booed. Kohl called on everyone to keep a cool head and promised East Germans, "We stand by your side!" At the same time, he reminded the crowd that global and European as well as German interests were at stake. He ended with a call for a "free, united Europe" and a "free German fatherland." The word *Wiedervereinigung*—reunification—did not cross his lips. His speech was directed at the nervous Allies as much as the East German people. It fell to Brandt to declare that "now grows together, what belongs together," echoing what he had said as mayor of West Berlin twenty-five years earlier. On November 28, Kohl threw caution to the wind. Without giving the Allies advance notice, he set out a ten-point plan to parliament. In addition to promising the GDR help in exchange for reforms, it proposed a confederation between the two states. What precisely a reunified Germany would look like, Kohl said, no one knew, but he was certain it would come, "if the people in Germany want it." All parties supported the plan, except the Greens.[27]

The all-German train had started to roll, and it took on speed as popular pressure stoked the engine. Emboldened by Kohl, the calls for reunification became overwhelming. By early December, Krenz and the old guard of the SED had abdicated. Having lost its monopoly on power, the reformed SED joined a roundtable with civil rights activists. Both sides hoped to retain a separate East Germany, but they also agreed to hold free elections in the spring of 1990. Kohl first set foot in the GDR on December 19, visiting Dresden. Unlike in Berlin, he received a hero's welcome. Thousands greeted him at the airport, waving the West German flag. "My goal, if this historic hour allows it," he declared later that day, "remains the unity of our nation." The crowds erupted, chanting, "Deutschland, Deutschland" and "Helmut, Helmut."[28] Long after midnight, back in his hotel, Kohl, visibly moved, reviewed the day with his staff: "I think we can get unity. It is rolling... it cannot be stopped, the people want it."[29]

The chancellor threw his weight behind his party's eastern partner (CDU-East) which campaigned alongside the new smaller Deutsche Soziale Union (DSU) and the civil rights group Demokratischer Aufbruch ("Democratic Awakening"). In the election on March 18, 1990, their "Alliance for Germany" won 48 percent of the vote (41 percent for the CDU-East), well ahead of the SPD (22 percent). The parties holding out for a separate East Germany—the Partei des Demokratischen Sozialismus (PDS, the rebranded SED) and the Bündnis 90, an umbrella group of civil rights and green activists—managed a mere 16.4 percent and 2.9 percent, respectively. It was an overwhelming vote for reunification.

But there were obstacles. Kohl's ten points set off alarm bells in Moscow, Paris, and London—only U.S. president George Bush pledged his full support. Mitterrand had nightmares of 1914, while British prime minister Margaret Thatcher carried in her handbag a map of the greater Germany in 1937 as a warning about where unification would lead.

Mitterrand had the answer as to how the Germans could be kept in check: take away their mighty Deutschmark and embed them more deeply in Europe. It meant leapfrogging the agreed stages of European integration. The 1992 Maastricht Treaty fast-tracked a currency union before a political union was in place. For Kohl, it was a price worth paying. For the rest of Europe, the haste would have painful consequences, as the euro crisis would show, when several Mediterranean countries and their banks were caught in a prolonged debt crisis. The Soviet Union was in no position to bail out East Germany; perestroika had only deepened its own economic crisis. Kohl's offer of generous aid to Moscow helped bring Gorbachev around to the point that he even accepted a unified Germany that would be in NATO.

In September 1990, the former Allies and West and East Germany signed the Treaty on the Final Settlement with Respect to Germany (the Two-Plus-Four Agreement). The so-called Four Powers—Britain, the U.S., France, and the Soviet Union—renounced the rights they had held since 1945 and handed full sovereignty back to Germany. Germany, in turn, recognized the current border with Poland and gave up its claims to lost territories east of the Oder-Neisse line. On October 3, 1990, less than a year after the fall of the Berlin Wall, Germany was reunited.[30]

"NO WORK, NO LOVE, NO *HEIMAT*"

Seven years later, anonymous flyers appeared under the windshield wipers of cars parked in Hof, the Bavarian town just across the old border from Thuringia, which had welcomed East Germans—Ossis—fleeing on the trains from Prague in October 1989. *"Hallo Ossis!"* they read:

> It is high time to tell you what the Wessis [Germans on the western side] think of you... Keep your mouth shut and be grateful for all the support you are given. It would be better if you worked your way out of your own mess... Or do you think that our prosperity in the West landed in our lap... You were probably busy spying on other people... You should be ashamed of the pigsty you left behind. No wonder that a Wall was put up around it... if you did not like it, why did you not protest?... [Once the border opened] you behaved like the Huns, completely inconsiderate, just to get your hands on DM 100 Welcome Money. Then the Ossis came to take away the Wessis' jobs... That Germany is now stuck in a financial crisis is entirely your fault... It would be a good idea to put up the Wall again and add 10 meters on top—there would be plenty of volunteers—so that you arrogant Ossis stay among yourselves.

A few days later, a counter-flyer made the rounds: "*Hallo Wessis!!!*... Who do you inbred monkeys think you are!!!" While East Germans suffered under the Russians and were "performing superhuman tasks to keep the state alive... the Ami [United States] was spoiling you rotten... and built up your state with billions!!! And because you are the laziest assholes since time immemorial, you brought loads of foreigners into the country to do the dirty work for you."[31]

The two flyers showed how far apart the two populations could be in the newly united country, and the prejudice, distrust, and blame each side heaped on the other. It was one thing to fuse the two territories politically, quite another to unify the hearts and minds of the people living in them. The very terms chosen to define the process divided the new country. Was it a democratic "accession" (*Beitritt*), according to Article 23 of the constitution, a neoliberal "takeover" (*Übernahme*), or even "colonialism"—"*Ko(h) lonialism*," as some spelled it? "Inner reunification," as the Germans call it, has been a slow, painful process that remains fragile and unfinished to this day. Freedom came with immense costs—mental as much as material—that were unevenly shared and linked to rival views about entitlements and appropriate behavior, as the two flyers illustrate.

Winding up the GDR was a moral, judicial, and economic undertaking. Amid closures and mass unemployment, the GDR was subjected to a public autopsy. Was it an "unlawful state" (*Unrechtsstaat*) or a "caring dictatorship"? Collective verdicts about the GDR inevitably raised moral questions about the lives people had lived in it. Furthermore, as the second flyer recognized, reunification was never a purely German affair; it also affected the millions of foreigners in the land. Unity was so fractured that the great achievement of the people's revolution was all but forgotten.

In 1990, Kohl promised East Germans "blossoming landscapes." It turned out to be as misleading as Honecker's portrayal of the GDR as one of the top industrial nations in the world. Three months before reunification proper, a currency, economic, and social union went into effect. Adults could exchange up to 4,000 GDR Marks for 4,000 Deutschmark; pensioners a bit more, children a bit less. Salaries, pensions, and rents were similarly converted one to one. Equivalence had been the demand of the last prime minister of the GDR, Lothar de Maizière (CDU). It was five times what Western experts saw as a realistic value of East German products and labor. For Kohl, politics trumped economics. He wanted to be reelected and remembered as the "chancellor of unity," not for introducing a two-class system.

The East German economy went into free fall. Hugely overpriced exports crashed instantly. That the Poles and Czechs chose to devalue their currency only made things worse. A "trust agency" (*Treuhand*) was set up to oversee the privatization of all state-owned enterprises; the decision was one of the last made by the reformed GDR parliament. While it prevented the old elite from seizing the crown jewels, as happened in Russia and elsewhere, the privatization drive ended up shutting down almost as many enterprises as it saved. Consolidating Carl Zeiss Jena, the world-renowned optics manufacturer, was one thing. Finding buyers for run-down, unproductive plants was another. In four years, one third of the twelve thousand enterprises had been liquidated. Two out of three industrial workers had been laid off. In the summer of 1993, workers in Bischofferode (Thuringia) went on a hunger strike, desperate to avert the closure of their potash mine—to no avail. Elsewhere, West German buyers took precious patents and machinery and then mothballed plants, feeding rumors that western takeovers were really a cunning way to destroy the competition; a generation later, there were still calls for a truth commission.[32]

The *Treuhand* had promised up to 600 billion DM profit. When it was wound up in 1994, its balance sheet showed a loss of 270 billion DM instead (around $170 billion). Privatization was in part a political calculation: by leaving things up to the market, the Kohl government washed its hands of responsibility. Compared to other post-communist countries, Germany pursued a particularly dogmatic course. Unlike in Poland, the government refused to take over key industries or provide a temporary cushion. The many smaller family firms that had miraculously survived collectivization were similarly left to fend for themselves. The fundamental source of the malaise, though, was not the *Treuhand* but the GDR and the disastrous state in which it had left the economy. Toward its end, 39 percent of enterprises had been on the brink of bankruptcy.[33]

Almost overnight, a republic of workers turned into a society on the dole. In 1994, unemployment in the former East reached 15 percent; ten years later, it was 20 percent. In addition, nearly 2 million people ended up in early retirement or on retraining courses. Sooner or later, unemployment left its mark on the biography of most East Germans. Researchers in Leipzig had begun to study fourteen-year-olds in 1987. When they revisited them in 1996, half of their subjects had been unemployed at least once; by 2009 it was almost three quarters. Hardest hit were women, who were out of work for twenty-four months on average, compared to fifteen months among the men. Not surprisingly, many suffered from depression and poor health.[34]

Katja Kramer was thirty-six when her country disappeared. She was a model of the professional woman in the GDR: a single mother, she was also a trained engineer and, in 1987, joined a group working on computer technology. Chips that were cutting-edge under socialism, unfortunately, turned out to be worthless on the world market. The ink had barely dried on the treaty for the currency union when she was informed that job cuts were imminent. By September 1990, she was sitting at the unemployment office, out of work and humiliated. In her diary, she recorded how the new reality devalued everything she had accomplished in her life. The very forms she had to fill in were based on a West German lifestyle. She was asked whether she had attended a *Gymnasium*—a selective type of school that did not exist in the GDR—and "whether I have studied outside the Federal Republic." "They want to extinguish us completely," she wrote. "I attended a polytechnic secondary school (POS) and an extended secondary school (EOS) in the GDR, and I see no reason to hide that; I am proud of it. Why do they refuse to recognize that? It makes me want to throw up." She and her colleagues had been "such a good team." Now their "life support" had been taken from them. In a few months, the "joy of November" and "feeling of community and confidence" had given way to a sense of "anger and powerlessness." For her, 1990 was "a nosedive" that ended with the "haggling for our souls." October 2, the last day of the GDR, was "one of the blackest days of my life." She felt "like a convict awaiting execution... expelled, a stranger in my own country... unspeakably sad. No work, no love, no *Heimat*, no happiness." Just before midnight, she put on the national anthem to thank her fatherland for "all that was good and beautiful in the last thirty-six years." "It is like a funeral."[35]

Life in the GDR had been no picnic for women. They had to juggle three shifts—work, household, and collective responsibilities. At the same time, work bestowed a sense of pride, equality, and independence. "Respect as a woman *and* human being, and not being treated as a second-class citizen as a single mother," were essential values for a Ms. Kramer. Unemployment devalued her entire biography. Retraining, drawing benefits, settling for temporary jobs, and having to adapt to West German superiors left a "callus on one's soul," as another woman put it. She was fifty when the Wall came down, a horticulturalist who belonged to the generation that had enjoyed upward social mobility in the GDR. This made the fall after reunification only the greater. By 1995, she had found an ecological post through a job creation program. Her new boss was a West German, twenty-five years her junior, who had studied law and did not know much about the environment. He reprimanded her publicly when she acted on her own initiative. The competitive, dog-eat-dog atmosphere depressed her: "Everyone only sees the mistakes of the other, and no longer their qualities and good sides."[36]

Professionals who did manage to hang on to their jobs had their qualifications questioned or were downgraded. Privatization taught a radiology assistant vital things about credit and debt but also took away her vacation allowance and Christmas bonus and erased her twenty-five years of loyal service in the collective health system. Here was someone who, objectively, had done well out of reunification: she owned her flat, had a weekend house, life insurance, color TV, VCR, and fridge-freezer. The uncertainties at work, the pushy commercials on TV, and the shift to private pension contributions, however, made her feel "like a beggar" at the mercy of others.[37]

Those without qualifications faced a different kind of ordeal. A fifty-year-old mother who had worked all her life in the collective bakery ended up selling tickets in a movie theater. She had never had much—no color TV, let alone a car—but now the advertisements for fancy new brands rubbed it in: she was a loser. Although never a party member, she now identified with the old GDR, an underdog like her, overwhelmed by the West. By the end of 1994, she noted doing things that she would have considered "amoral" only a few years earlier. At work, she was helping herself to sandwiches and cake, and even smuggled cold cuts back home, without paying for them. The new world had upset her sense of right and wrong: "Since it is not my enterprise, and I am underpaid and have to put up with psycho-terror, I must compensate myself somehow."[38]

Not everything was bleak. Pensioners were big winners from the social union, and the early 1990s saw a boom in start-ups. Overall, though, the East was a place to move away from, not move to. Those with initiative tended to take it with them to the West. The Faber family was among them. The husband was invigorated by the sense that he was finally taking his life in his own hands. He landed an engineering job near Lake Constance. His wife followed and started work in a small electronics firm. What the West did not have was child care centers with long hours. Her son's "day" care had a two-hour-long lunch break, and she had to pick him up promptly at 11:30. Overall, though, she counted herself among the winners of reunification. "I have learned a lot," she said. When their second child arrived, she abandoned the idea that she could "bring up children on the side"; her old friends pitied her as a "western housewife." Return visits were increasingly "a shock," she wrote in 1997: "The discrepancy between East and West only seems to get worse."[39]

In the twenty years after reunification, the East lost 10 percent of its population. Talk of a "Kohl Plantation" was understandable but, unlike in slave-based empires, East Germans were citizens and the West German core not only extracted wealth from its eastern periphery, it also poured vast resources into it. The transfers were enormous: an estimated 1.6 to 2 trillion euros in the twenty-five years since unity, roughly 3 percent of GDP each year.[40] In 2014, the transfers were the equivalent of 20 percent of everything made in East Germany. The burden fell mainly on West Germans who were working and better off, in the form of higher pension and social insurance contributions, and, after 1991, a "solidarity surcharge" on income tax (a supplement that would only be abolished thirty years later, and then only for the majority of taxpayers).

If West Germany had preexisting problems with its welfare system and public finances, reunification magnified them into a crisis.[41] By 1994, national debt had doubled. The West now had its own vicious circle to deal with. Higher taxes and contributions raised costs, which hurt exports and investment, which meant job losses and more people on welfare, which added to the burden on the state, and so forth. Here was the backdrop to the flyer by the angry Wessi complaining about the lazy Ossis.

The transfers created a moral economy that set Germany apart from all the other post-communist states: East Germans were reduced to recipients of West German generosity. A good bit of the mutual misunderstanding and paternalist condescension had its roots in this unequal setup. The fact that East Germans were not all "takers"—those paying income tax also contributed to the solidarity fund—tended to be forgotten.

TRANSITIONAL JUSTICE REVISITED

What to call the GDR was a bone of contention. In 1992, the federal parliament set up a commission devoted to "work through the history and consequences of the SED-dictatorship." For the PDS (the SED successor), that title put it uncomfortably close to the Nazi dictatorship. It preferred the neutral term "power relations." Echoing postwar language, it denounced the commission as victor's justice and worried that the West was putting all East Germans on trial. That the GDR was not genocidal, President Roman Herzog stressed, did not mean there were not important lessons to be learned from looking at the two dictatorships side by side. For one thing, both had ruled with open terror from the start.[42]

Yet 1990 was not 1945. There was no total defeat, and the whole country did not lie in ruins. Only one part of the country had lost, while the other had the political and economic resources needed to absorb it. Unlike in 1945, Germans (not the Allies) sat in judgment over other Germans. And there were plenty of Germans in the West with democratic credentials ready to fill vacated posts.

The greatest clearout took place in the courts and in the army. By 1996, only every sixth judge in the East had worked in the GDR. When the NVA was fused with the federal army, half the officers were discharged, especially senior ones. Of 8,180 lieutenant colonels, only 612 were kept on. To some extent, the shrinkage was inevitable. The GDR had been a hugely overblown state; in a population of 16 million, more than 2 million people had a job in the army, administration, or postal service, double the ratio in the West. It was the way personnel changes were rolled out that left behind bad blood. For GDR generals, it was a humiliation that they were discharged by a secretary of state, not by the head of state, while decommissioned officers lost the right to use their former rank. Those who were kept on were often demoted and received only 60 percent of the pay of their western peers. Western soldiers, meanwhile, received a bonus for working in the East—popular references to this as "bush money" only deepened grievances. In Berlin, policemen in the western part of the city refused to go on the beat with their colleagues from the East. Professors lost their chairs and institutes. Some judgeships could have been filled by East German lawyers but went to underqualified westerners instead. Not surprisingly, many easterners felt bitter and alienated from their new country and retreated into nostalgia and support for the PDS.[43]

The noisy gripe of the losers can easily distract from the bigger picture of remarkable continuity. The Stasi was terminated, but there was no "de-Stasification" along the lines of denazification. Dismissals were selective and required proof of individual guilt. Many functionaries found a new home in the *Treuhand*, although in subordinate positions. The various federal ministries (including Justice and Defense) took over almost 19,000 officials as civil servants; only 1,300 were discharged. In the entire police force, only 7 percent were dismissed. Almost everywhere, teachers stayed in their posts. The few who did lose their jobs did so mainly because they lacked teaching qualifications, not because they had been Stasi informers. In 1996, out of 1,200 school principals in the East only 8 were from the West. In Saxony, the minister even proposed giving those with links to the Stasi a fresh start after five years. The federal Constitutional Court applied fine distinctions. In a case of three lawyers—all members of the Stasi—it found only one of them guilty of violating the human rights of a client.[44]

Nor were criminal prosecutions simply brought by the West against the East. The first step was taken before reunification by the state prosecutor of the GDR, who charged sixty SED bosses with electoral fraud, economic corruption, and abuse of office.[45] In the years after reunification, prosecutors initiated a total of 75,000 investigations. They led to only 1,021 prosecutions of 1,737 defendants, of whom just over half (54 percent) were convicted. One hundred and sixty-five got off with a fine, chiefly for doping in sports and economic crimes, but several for mistreating prisoners. Only 580 people went to prison—266 for violent crimes at the border, 169 for perverting the course of justice, and 38 for Stasi crimes, the remaining for denunciation, maltreatment of prisoners, corruption, or doping. The vast majority (90 percent) were out of prison in less than a year. In addition, 7,099 people were investigated for spying—a tiny fraction of the Stasi empire—and one third of them were West German citizens. Hardly any of them were convicted. Only a dozen spies received prison sentences longer than two years.[46]

While the GDR was publicly branded an "unlawful state," the courts ended up punishing only a few hundred criminals. The crucial factor in explaining this paradox was that the courts judged what East German officials, soldiers, and spies did by the legal codes by which they were bound at the time. The united Germany was careful not to repeat the rollercoaster of collective denazification followed by mass amnesty, which had cast a brown shadow over the Adenauer years. Simply "drawing a line" (*Schlussstrich*) under the GDR would have let down its victims and deprived society of a vital lesson in democracy, namely that "state power, too, has its limits and is tied to fundamental principles of law and morality," as a law professor explained to the parliamentary commission.[47] There would be no amnesty after 1990—politicians and judges were united on this point.

In practice, however, criminal law ended up granting just that. All but an unlucky few got off scot-free. All the law cared about was individual crime, not the collective guilt of the regime in which it took place. This was why so few Stasi members were convicted. Listening in on phone calls or opening private letters was not a criminal offense in the GDR. Constant surveillance might have ruined a victim's life, but broken down into discrete acts it involved at best a minor crime, such as unlawful entry, little worse than shoplifting. The spy chief Markus Wolf was sentenced not for spying but for unlawful detention and inflicting bodily harm. Denunciation, threats, and official harassment were, similarly, rarely crimes. Victims were at a loss as to the lack of severe punishment, including the chair of the commission, Rainer Eppelmann, a dissident turned MP for the CDU. He reminded his fellow members that Stasi officers had considered exterminating him: "We are dealing with violence, blackmail, coercion, and much else, which had been ordered by the state or at least willed by it, and not by [private persons like] Kutte, Luise, or Fritz. I cannot understand that these are the same things and are treated alike."[48]

The test case for this individual approach to justice were the shootings at the Berlin Wall. Over a hundred people were killed in their attempt to cross it. One of them was Michael Schmidt. On December 1, 1984, shortly after midnight, the twenty-year-old carpenter picked up a hidden ladder from a building near the border and climbed across the first warning fence. Two guards spotted him from their watchtower and began to fire. Schmidt managed to reach the final barrier, only to be struck down by further shots hitting his back and leg. He died later that morning in a police hospital in the East.[49]

The guards said they were not legally responsible for his death, pointing to their orders and Section 27 of the border law. In this case, however, the law at the time offered no place to hide. Their shots violated the International

Covenant on Civil and Political Rights, which the GDR had signed up to in 1966, the Federal Court of Justice ruled; this both prohibited the arbitrary deprivation of life and protected the right to leave one's own country. The two young guards who had shot Schmidt eventually received eighteen and twenty-one months suspended sentences; one was twenty at the time of the crime. The Youth Court took into consideration that the two men had grown up after the Wall, had been subject to indoctrination, and had served at the bottom of the military hierarchy. In a way, the Court ruled, they were "victims" (*Opfer*) too. Still, the Court concluded, even to them the "elementary" principle "do not kill" should have been obvious.[50]

In 1992, the courts extended their reach to the "perpetrators behind the perpetrators." While the regime could not be charged collectively, those who had signed the shoot-to-kill order could. That included Honecker and Heinz Kessler, the minister of defense, among others. Cancer of the liver saved the former. The court suspended proceedings against him in view of his ill health in January 1993, and he would die in exile in Chile a year later. Kessler, however, was sentenced to seven years in prison. Of the 132 charged with murder or homicide in Berlin and Potsdam, ten were SED leaders and forty-two were senior officers. The widespread notion that the "little people" got punished while the "big fish" were let off the hook was proved at least partly wrong.[51]

In its approach to transitional justice, Germany was hardly exceptional. Reconciliation, not revenge, was the preferred path in virtually all successor states in the Eastern bloc. The presumed continuity of law under communism shielded functionaries almost everywhere; only Albania put its leaders in prison. The true exception was Czechoslovakia, which passed two laws in 1991 and 1993 that designated the Communist Party a criminal organization and condemned the regime for violating national law as well as human rights and destroying the values of European civilization across its forty-year existence. Here, victims were given the right to moral reparation.[52] In Germany, by contrast, it was only with regard to the shootings at the Wall that the criminal nature of the regime was formally recognized.

For the many victims, this was far too little. "We wanted justice and got the rule of law instead," Bärbel Bohley lamented.[53] It was, of course, difficult to have the former in the absence of the latter, but its presence did not automatically guarantee it either. Victims were looking for moral recognition and material compensation in addition to legal rehabilitation. As in the 1950s, the law was imperfectly equipped to give them all three. Former political prisoners received 550 DM in compensation for each month spent in prison. Documenting how persecution had damaged mind and body proved much harder, and most victims shied away from the intrusive procedures of documenting their pain. A victims lobby found that of the 100,000 political prisoners who were rehabilitated between 1991 and 1994, only 5 percent had been certified as suffering from psychological consequences and only 2 percent received a pension for damage to their health. In Cottbus, in Brandenburg, 20 percent of claimants under the prisoner aid law (*Häftlingshilfegesetz*) died before a decision was reached.

It might be assumed that the earlier experience with camp survivors would have given unified Germany a head start with diagnosing victims of the GDR. The opposite was the case. A study of psychiatric hospitals in Berlin found that most doctors continued to be ignorant of the international criteria for the diagnosis of post-traumatic stress syndrome. Rehabilitation payments, moreover, were meant to be a little help in hard times or to fill gaps in pensions, not full compensation. There was no compensation for the loss of earnings, nor for the damage to someone's career. Poverty was thus widespread. The families left behind by those killed at the Wall did not receive a penny. Even though many victims had their pensions raised—the state of Saxony paid out 109 million DM between 1990 and 1996—the underlying sense of injustice remained. That key officials of the dictatorship received generous pensions did not help. The parliamentary commission heard of a case of a young man who in the 1960s had spent seven weeks in prison for allegedly tearing down the GDR flag—he denied it—and now had his rehabilitation application rejected by the state prosecutor on the grounds that a regime had the right to protect its symbols from being insulted. Another victim found his case reviewed by the same person who had sent him to the Bautzen prison in the first place; only in Berlin were GDR judges not allowed to sit in rehabilitation hearings. Finally, there were all those people who had suffered under the regime but not in ways that the law recognized or redressed: couples whose marriage was ruined by Stasi subversion; Christians and punks who were blocked from going to university; people who refused to conform and sacrificed a career; and many others.[54]

Leaving the reckoning with the GDR to criminal courts was meant to take the politics out of it. In reality, it created a difficult political legacy because everyone felt treated unjustly: members of the regime, their victims, and the majority of East Germans who were neither. Only a minority had been in the SED. The GDR ran on outward conformity. It did not co-opt people to commit crimes on the scale of the Nazis. The sharp divide between the Stasi state and its victims that came to dominate public discourse left space neither for the heroes of 1989 nor for people's ordinary lives in the GDR—marriage and divorce, raising a family, the work collective, and harvesting cucumbers on weekends at the dacha. Instead of facing up to how everyday life was entangled with the regime, people became resentful and withdrew.

At the beginning of the revolution, in the autumn of 1989, uncomfortable questions about complicity were raised. Ten days before the fall of the Wall, Christa Wolf published an article about a public reading she had recently given. A doctor called on the audience to give their honest opinion and not be intimidated. A woman said "quietly and sadly" that she could not suddenly articulate an opinion since she did not even know what her own opinion was. From childhood, she had been obliged to conform and give the answer expected of her. A "chronic schizophrenia" had hollowed out her personality. For Wolf, who wanted to rescue socialism from itself, it was a "damning but not surprising finding." The only way forward was to confront the truth that "our children have been raised to untruthfulness" and left "deformed, discouraged, and disenfranchised." Many citizens, Wolf concluded, were now in the process of "squeezing the slave out of themselves," and not in drops, as Anton Chekhov's original metaphor had it, but gallon after gallon.

Her article caused a storm. A fifty-year-old woman, an economist, found it "liberating": "I am so happy to see this day when such frank words are printed." She had been a party member for thirty years. They needed to look for the responsibility for the country's "desolate state" within themselves, not just blame others: "In a way we were all corrupted and comfortable." Some readers expressed a sense of shame: by living a lie, they had betrayed themselves as much as the socialist project. For others, however, it was a blow below the belt. To question the GDR was to question their lives in it. A fifty-seven-year-old woman was "appalled." She sold newspapers and was a "simple person," but she remembered the war. Wolf's article was a "slap in the face of all those people who had survived the horrible war, lost relatives, or seen their homeland devastated." Her children and grandchildren had turned out decent people with decent jobs and did not betray their republic. They had been blessed with a long era of peace. She was proud of the GDR just as she was proud of them.[55]

In December 1990, two months after reunification, one of the few teachers who had been fired bared his soul to his diary. He had been a loyal local SED party secretary and felt like a coward for giving in to pressure and forcing students to leave the church. He criticized himself for years of self-deception. However much he wanted to believe that the Prague spring in 1968 was a counterrevolutionary uprising, he now acknowledged that murder remained murder. Above all, he blamed himself for telling his pupils lies about the Wall. "The dead at the Wall will stay with me until the end of my life." None of this diminished his praise for the GDR's many accomplishments. The vision of a better world continued to give him strength; now he sat in the local assembly for the PDS.

INVENTING A BETTER YESTERDAY

In the storm that followed reunification, most East Germans were struggling to keep their heads above water, not pondering questions of complicity with a regime that had gone under. The darker the economic clouds on the horizon, the brighter their memories of the GDR became. "*Ostalgie*" was born, a nostalgic yearning for eastern sweets, songs, and sweaters from bygone times. The term was coined by the Dresden comedian Uwe Steimle in 1992. Going to a retro-party featuring a Honecker lookalike did not mean people wanted the real one back. Rather, East Germans were reclaiming things of the socialist past as a way of asserting their distinct identity in a present dominated by stars and products from the West. The advertisement for the revived Club-Cola spelled it out: "Hurray, I am still alive!"[56]

The positive makeover of the GDR reached children born after its demise. A study of five thousand high school students conducted between 2005 and 2007 found remarkable differences between the former East and West. Two in three children in the West felt that before 1989 the Federal Republic was better than the GDR, but only one in three in the East. The majority of eastern schoolchildren did not think that the GDR was a dictatorship; indeed, a quarter felt that some repression was justified and that those who had been shot trying to escape had only themselves to blame. Most shifted responsibility for the Wall to the Soviet Union. None knew about the death penalty, and they saw the Stasi as an ordinary secret service. The researchers were stunned by the "naïveté," myths, and ignorance they encountered. To the post-1989 generation, the GDR appeared to be a social paradise, blessed not only with child care centers everywhere (true in the 1980s) but also with more generous pensions and university places than the West (both wrong). The SED regime had undergone a "moral-political exoneration." The teaching material was "grim," researchers noted, but, in the final analysis, they blamed the pupils' families for spreading these distorted ideas. Teachers reported a backlash from parents and grandparents whenever they tried to introduce a more critical picture of the GDR. A decade of unemployment, uncertainty, and disorientation had made many forget just how unbearable they had found the GDR in 1989.[57]

The other victims in these memory wars were the people who had brought it down. After two failures (1848 and 1918), Germany finally got a successful revolution in 1989. Several dissidents rose to prominent public positions—Eppelmann chaired the parliamentary commission that investigated the SED dictatorship, and Marianne Birthler was the federal commissioner in charge of the Stasi records (2000–11). The people in the street, though, all but faded from public memory.

There was little space to begin with for German heroes in a "negative memory" culture that since the 1980s has concentrated on remembering the victims of German aggression.[58] And the little there was was squeezed further by the polarized picture of the GDR as either Stasi prison or social paradise. Museums devoted themselves either to spy technologies and damp prison cells or to the "thousand little things" of everyday life. There were wreaths for those who had died at the Wall, not statues for those who toppled it.

In 1998, nine years following the fall of the Wall and shortly after the second competition for the monument for the murdered Jews, Lothar de Maizière, the last prime minister of the GDR and a Kohl ally, launched a campaign to erect a "citizen monument" (*Bürgerdenkmal*) to German unity on the base of the National Kaiser Wilhelm monument, which the SED had pulled down after the war. It was to honor the people who had dared to challenge the regime. When the proposal first reached parliament, it was rejected by the cultural committee. In 2007, it was approved, but ten years later parliament's budget committee again tried to cancel the project; a colony of bats would have to be moved, making the costs unacceptable. The committee eventually relented and found some money but wanted it to go to restore the Kaiser Wilhelm statue instead. Former dissident MPs were furious at the backroom maneuver and, after lobbying, saved the original winning design—an interactive 164-foot-long kinetic bowl that will move gently as visitors walk on top of it. The "unity-seesaw" will carry the slogan "We are the people. We are one people." Critics have objected that the monument rolls freedom and unity into one, as if all revolutionaries were automatically in favor of reunification. Construction finally began in 2020 and has been held back this time not by bats but by a shortage of steel and labor.[59] In Leipzig, the "city of heroes," a 2011 initiative for a monument to the peaceful revolution came to naught. Bärbel Bohley did have a street named after her in Berlin in 2016, six years after her death from cancer.

UNFINISHED BUSINESS

Each year, the German government produces a bulky report on the state of reunification. In 2020, it glowed with indicators of all that has been accomplished in the thirty years since 1990. For East Germans, GDP per person had quadrupled. The demographic exodus stopped in 2014 and the pension gap had narrowed, too. By 2018, easterners' household income had reached 88 percent of westerners'. In booming Leipzig and Dresden it was virtually identical. Historic city centers shine once again, although the shiniest pieces now belong to westerners. Nonetheless, the government had to acknowledge that "the process of inner unity is not completely finished."[60]

In fact, the main shrinking of the gap between East and West had already taken place by the mid-1990s. There has been little progress since then. In 2019, GDP per capita in Saxony was two thirds of that in Bavaria, almost exactly what it was in 1996. In 2019, a worker in the West still produced 20 euros more per hour than their peer in the East, the same as twenty years earlier.[61] At the current snail's pace, it will take at least another fifty years before parity is reached.

The West also has structurally weak regions such as the Saarland, the Ruhr, and Bremen, but these are islands in a sea of wealth. In the East, it is the reverse: with the exception of Leipzig, Dresden, and Erfurt, the entire region suffers from structural problems, in particular lower productivity and less research and development. It is a region with small firms and little big industry. That an East German, Merkel, occupied the chancellery for sixteen years is little consolation when out of the top five hundred firms only thirty-four have their headquarter east of the Elbe. By the end of 2020, only two East Germans among the two hundred directors sitting on the boards of the firms listed on the German stock market index (DAX).[62] Research centers are more likely to have a foreigner than an East German at the helm. East Germany has only two teams in the top flight of the soccer Bundesliga, and, tellingly, only one is a traditional club (Union Berlin) while the other (Red Bull Leipzig) is a recent venture of an Austrian energy drinks company.

The fundamental problem is not regional difference as such. The gap in wealth between Milan and Sicily or between the northeast and the southeast of England is infinitely larger. Rather, it lies with the assumption that the East should be like the West—another version of the difficulty of living with difference noted earlier in relation to migrants, disabled people, and others. In 1994, the constitution made the "equivalence of living conditions" (*Gleichwertigkeit*) an explicit goal; previously it had been their "uniformity" (*Einheitlichkeit*). The West continues to be the yardstick against which the East is measured. When it fails to follow the western model of big industrial firms, it is consequently seen to fall short. The East is viewed not as different but as deficient. The data thus ends up confirming the lack of recognition East Germans have experienced in other spheres of life. In the 1960s and 1970s, as we have seen, some West Germans were developing an interest in other cultures, from "Third World" countries to alternative lifestyles at home. When it came to their own new fellow citizens after 1990, there was little of that empathy. Transfers, however generous, could not compensate for the lack of respect.

In all the talk about the gap between the two, it is easy to lose sight of the values that East and West Germans shared, especially the importance attributed to family life, duty, and hard work. Hedonism was rising on both sides of the Wall before it came down.[63] Social security in the two states were variations on the same theme. In the wake of reunification, anthropologists observed life in two small towns in the Vogtland region that had been cut in half by the border. In both towns people prized diligence, moderation, and, above all, community (*Gemeinschaft*). They were "respectable people," their feet firmly on the ground, who owned their homes, belonged to local clubs, and were suspicious of outsiders and change. The mental divide was not between East and West—the proverbial "Wall in the head"—but between an idealized protective community and the alien, dangerous world outside. For those ready to help themselves there was mutual help. People on welfare and others who did not conform to the local moral script were stigmatized and excluded. When cars with Polish or Czechoslovak license plates passed through, people in both towns were quick to shut their doors and windows.[64]

Nonetheless, thirty years after reunification the divergence in lives and mentalities remains striking. The convergence of women entering the labor force is the exception to the rule. West Germans are more likely to own their home, while easterners rent. The gap in life expectancy has narrowed for women, but eastern men still die more than a year earlier on average than those in the West. The former GDR has fewer migrants and more racists. While most West Germans believe that it is irrelevant which side of the Wall someone grew up on, most East Germans think it makes all the difference. Easterners remember the end of the GDR as their achievement, westerners as the inevitable failure of socialism. Few in the East want the GDR back, but support for representative democracy remains lukewarm—78 percent see it as the system best suited for the country, compared to 91 percent in the West. Among eighteen-to-thirty-four-year-old East Germans, 56 percent see themselves as second-class citizens.[65] For them, genuine unification has not moved closer but become an ever more distant dream. In 1990, East German teenagers hoped that "inner unity" would be reached in 1998. By 1996 they had pushed it back to 2019, by 2013 a further twenty-five years, to 2038.[66]

WHO ARE "THE PEOPLE"?

The year 1990 solved the German question that had defeated liberal nationalists since the abortive revolution of 1848: it won liberty in unity. But whose country was the reunified Germany? As Nietzsche had wisely noted a century earlier, it was typical of his countrymen that the question "What is German?" never died away.[67] When the government monitors the progress of "inner unity," it treats it almost exclusively as a family affair among ethnic Germans. However, as we have seen, the old Federal Republic was home to 5 million "guest workers" and foreigners. The sudden incorporation of 15 million East Germans changed the balance of their lives overnight.

"I was raised here" in West Berlin, a Turkish student said on the first anniversary of the fall of the Wall, "but never before have felt such a stranger."[68] Friends who strayed into East Berlin found themselves attacked by local skinheads. As the migration expert Haci-Halil Uslucan put it in a radio interview, the "first place had always been taken by the West Germans . . . but now the battle was on for the second place."[69] In that competition, qualifying as a "proper" German acquired new currency.

The years after 1990 followed a zigzag course. In 2000, Schröder's SPD-Green coalition government introduced a new nationality law that extended citizenship to children born in Germany to foreign parents if one parent had lived there for eight years. Initially they had to choose between German citizenship and that of their parents on reaching adulthood. In 2014, they were allowed to retain both.

There was an immediate backlash. Now that "blood" was no longer required by law, conservatives turned to national culture to separate "genuine Germans" from "passport Germans." Multiculturalism, they argued, had failed. It was imperative that migrants subscribe to a (West) German "core culture" (*Leitkultur*). Anything else would bring social chaos and national decay. Some argued that constitutional patriotism, as championed by Jürgen Habermas, was too weak to hold a reunified country together in an age of globalization. Others pointed to the terror attacks of 9/11 and the threat of fundamentalism. The question was what that presumed "core" consisted of in a society with a plurality of tastes, lifestyles, and communities.

For the second and third generation of Turkish migrants, the new Germany was a challenging environment. There are some signs of improvement.

Migrant children today, for example, are more likely to go to a preschool and finish school. Uğur Şahin, the chair of BioNTech and father of the German COVID-19 vaccine, was the first child of guest workers in Cologne to pass the *Abitur*; his wife and the cofounder of BioNTech, Özlem Türeci, was the daughter of a surgeon and a biologist—a reminder that not all Turkish "guest workers" were peasants. Cem Özdemir, whose father came from a provincial town in Turkey to work in a German textile factory, rose to become joint leader of the Green Party in 2008 and, in 2021, the minister of agriculture, the first cabinet member with Turkish parents.

Such success stories, however, remain the exception. Every third person in Mönchengladbach in the Rhine-Ruhr region, for example, had a migration background but not a single one of the sixty-six councilors in that city in 2009 did; elsewhere they made up between 1 and 5 percent of representatives.[70] To this day, the educational gap remains huge—only 15 percent of students of Turkish descent graduate with an *Abitur* compared to 45 percent of native Germans. Indeed, in preschool the gap has widened.[71] Turkish-Germans continue to find it more difficult to secure an apprenticeship and are more than twice as likely to be unemployed.

Discrimination remains a fixture in public and private life. Women who wear a headscarf find it harder to find a job and get support from social workers, and young men of Turkish descent are routinely barred from discotheques and fitness studios. Housing conditions have improved, but, when house-hunting, it is not unknown to read "German-Turkish families not wanted; pets no problem," to quote a recent federal report on discrimination.[72]

Xenophobia, of course, is not peculiar to Germans. A survey in 1997 asked citizens of the European Union whether an ethnically mixed society was "a bad thing." Germans came out in the middle: less open to it than the Dutch and British but more tolerant than Greeks and Belgians. Where Germans were in the lead (with 79 percent, alongside Greeks and Belgians) was in agreeing that their "country has reached its limits" and could not take more foreigners. While the gap in unemployment between migrants and natives might be smaller in Britain and Italy, it is even higher in Belgium and Norway.[73]

The new citizenship law in 2000 was a step in the right direction but came too late to fix decades of missed integration. A study in 2014 found that only one in five Turks living in Germany had become a citizen.[74] Many were happy to live there, but half felt unrecognized. For dual citizenship, no solid figures exist, but surveys suggest that it is primarily Russian and Polish migrants who have obtained a second passport.

Ironically, for many the sense of belonging has become more conflicted in the years after citizenship reform, not less. Turkey has launched its own diaspora politics to remind them of their roots.[75] The Turkish-Islamic Union (DTIB) has one thousand branches in Germany today and sends imams direct from Turkey. In 2014, Turkey changed its laws to give Turks living abroad the right to vote in presidential elections. Four years later, more than 600,000, almost half of those eligible in Germany, went to the polls. (Two thirds cast their vote for Recep Erdoğan.) In 2000, every third Turk felt that their roots were in Turkey (*Heimatverbundenheit*); by 2017, it was every second. Those who saw Germany as their exclusive homeland declined from 22 percent to 17 percent; those who identified with both from 42 percent to 30 percent. Young people of Turkish origin mingled more freely with German peers than their parents had, but at a time when ethnic intermarriage was on the rise in the United States and other countries, in Germany women of Turkish descent almost exclusively married men who were also of Turkish descent. Interfaith marriages between Muslim men and Christian women have declined.[76]

After decades of being in denial, in 2005 an official statistical category was introduced for people "with a migrant background." Overnight, Germany gained 11 million people with migrant roots. The intention was to give them greater recognition. Instead, by lumping together all foreign-born individuals with anyone who had a foreign-born parent, it ended up obscuring the huge differences between the lives of refugees, ethnic Germans from Russia, professionals from the EU, children of German-American parents, and children of Turkish guest workers.

The state of North Rhine–Westphalia—home to 2 million foreigners—launched "integration through sports" in 1989. Over the next two decades, Oldenburg and other cities introduced soccer teams for migrant girls. At the 2010 World Cup, the German soccer association celebrated the national team with players hailing from eight countries as a showcase of newfound tolerance: diversity was "an opportunity and an advantage." (Germany made it to the semifinals, where they lost to Spain.)[77]

One of the poster boys of diversity was Mesut Özil, born and raised in Gelsenkirchen, in the country's rust belt. In 2010, he received the Bambi media award for successful integration. Two years later, at the European championships, the greatest player of his generation was attacked on Twitter as a "false German." Özil pressed charges. On the eve of the 2018 World Cup in Russia, the gifted midfielder posed for photographs with Erdoğan, alongside his teammate İlkay Gündoğan. Their home country erupted. The two players were accused of lacking loyalty to Germany and attacked for endorsing a human rights abuser. No one had blinked an eye when the veteran player Lothar Matthäus had met with Vladimir Putin, the Russian dictator, who had annexed Crimea four years earlier. There was clearly a double standard. As one journalist commented, "Who is German is German forever, who has become German is so on probation only."[78] When the team crashed out in the first round, an unprecedented debacle, more fingers were pointed at Özil. Instead of rallying to his support, the soccer association left him out in the cold. For Özil, it was the last straw. He had merely wanted to show his respect to the president of his family's homeland, he said. He had had enough of racism at the top of the soccer association. For them he was "a German when we win and an immigrant when we lose." He resigned from the national team.[79]

German history and memory reinforced a sense that migrants were second-class citizens at best. By the 1990s, German responsibility for the Holocaust had become a civil religion that defined national identity. Peter Eisenman's memorial to the murdered Jews of Europe, with its 2,711 concrete stelae next to the Brandenburg Gate, was completed in 2004.

The singularity of the Holocaust did not automatically prevent attention to other genocides, as is sometimes claimed.[80] Arguably, Auschwitz has at times been rather too freely invoked, from analogies with the Vietnam War in the 1960s to the war in Kosovo in the late 1990s. In other cases, it invited overdue comparison. The historian Taner Akçam, for example, was an asylum seeker in Germany when he began to write about the Armenian genocide in the 1990s.[81] In 2015, President Joachim Gauck acknowledged the country's complicity in the atrocities, and the following year, the German parliament added its official recognition to that of France, Canada, and Russia. Five years later, the government asked for forgiveness for the genocide of the Herero and Nama people in the former German colony of South-West Africa (Namibia). There can be no doubt that colonial crimes deserve greater attention, and whether a billion euros for development projects are sufficient compensation is debatable—the two tribes demand a direct apology and reparations to them. Still, compared to Britain, which has simply deleted from its official history for new citizens the millions of enslaved people who died on British ships and later victims of imperial violence, Holocaust awareness has helped Germany to at least take a step in the right direction.[82]

Recognition of a collective responsibility for the Holocaust, however, did have a paradoxical side effect. As members of a *Schicksalsgemeinschaft* ("community of fate"), ethnic Germans occupied an exclusive moral position unreachable for recent arrivals, albeit a penitent one.[83] While the legal reform of citizenship made blood less relevant, public memory made it more so. The sins of their fathers gave ethnic Germans a monopoly on the national past and made them gatekeepers of collective memory. Champions of a "core culture" expected anyone wanting to become a citizen to subscribe to this history.[84] A Turkish-German journalist, born in Flensburg in 1977, recalled her schooldays: "German history is free of Turks." She was left with the role of an "onlooker" reading about the Second World War, "without a granddad in the Wehrmacht."[85] A Conservative Bavarian MP put it bluntly in 2015: There was no need for students from Muslim or refugee backgrounds to visit concentration camps, because they "do not have any connection to the history of German National Socialism. And this should remain so."[86] The Holocaust was in German hands.

In truth, history was not that clear-cut—Turkish Jews had lived in interwar Berlin and were among the Nazis' victims, too.[87] Germany has tried but struggled to include migrants and refugees in public memory. In museums and visits to camps, they have been expected to show empathy with Jewish victims, and not speak of their own fears that they might be next. To bring up neo-Nazi attacks in Berlin or Israeli human rights abuses against Palestinians violated the moral script, since they appeared to be competing with the victims of the Holocaust.[88]

11

In the Wide World: Germany at Its Limits

As if the challenges at home were not big enough, reunified Germany had to find its place in a dramatically changing world. The ruling mantra since Konrad Adenauer's days had been restraint and nonintervention, shielded by NATO. Now the country was confronted with a new era of globalization, the expansion of the European Union, wars in the Balkans and the Middle East, financial crises, the rise of China, and the Russian invasion of Crimea and Ukraine.

Contrary to Margaret Thatcher's fears, Germany did not relapse into a great power addicted to territorial conquest. The role it did adopt has been more difficult to define. Its actions (and inaction) have defied the familiar categories of empire, hegemon, or superpower. Analysts have had to invent new hybrids such as "semi-hegemon" and "civilian power."[1] One of the most perceptive, Hans Kundnani, has diagnosed a "German paradox," a country that is just as economically "assertive" within Europe as it is "unassertive" beyond it.[2] Germany might be the world champion of exports, but it has none of the geopolitical ambition of Britain or France. Its military spending has been closer to that of Switzerland, until the war in Ukraine in 2022 led the government to commit 100 billion euros in additional funding for the Bundeswehr; how much of this will find its way into tanks and guns remains to be seen.

Actually, there is no paradox. Germany has been able to sell its wares to the world (including arms) while others (first and foremost the United States) have paid for its security. It has behaved as a "free rider." Since 2018, however, globalization has gone into reverse, with the flow of goods and capital slowing down and the United States and China embroiled in a trade war. Deglobalization, the pandemic, and the war in Ukraine have exposed the costs of Germany's strategy: military and economic vulnerability thanks to simultaneous dependence on American military power and on a few foreign markets, suppliers, and energy sources.

Military intervention proceeded with one step forward and one step back. In 1994, the Constitutional Court ruled that the Bundeswehr could engage in military and humanitarian action outside NATO territory as long as it had a UN mandate. A year earlier, Chancellor Kohl had sent surveillance planes to Bosnia. The Kosovo war in 1999 raised the stakes. In their coalition agreement, the new Social Democrat–Green government had declared that "German foreign policy is peace policy." Now Joschka Fischer, the invincible Green foreign secretary in Gerhard Schröder's government, pleaded with his party to support a NATO intervention to stop the Serbian killings of Albanians in Kosovo, regardless of the lack of a UN mandate. "Never again war! Never again Auschwitz," he told delegates; the two went hand in hand for him. Established morality was turned upside down: the argument against taking up arms was now used for it. Germany sent fighter planes.

That Fischer used moral principles to win over his party and the public, did not mean they also were the driving force behind the intervention. A few months later, Fischer told the German Society for Foreign Affairs (DGAP) that it was not "only about moral values but about interests," primarily stability in southeast Europe; Germany's recognition of Slovenia and Croatia in 1992 had done its bit for the nationalist breakup of Yugoslavia that set off a wave of migrants to Germany. Kosovo, he stressed, was neither a "precedent" for unilateral intervention nor a turning point in German foreign policy. He advocated continued self-restraint, multilateralism, and further European integration—not so different from Kohl's rule book. Fischer said no to humanitarian interventionism across the world. Indeed, according to him, Germany's "European preference" arose naturally from "its history as a non-maritime and non-colonial power," exhibiting a curious amnesia about Germany's short but brutal time as a colonial power.[3]

Chancellor Schröder had in fact already pledged U.S. president Bill Clinton his support before moving into the chancellery. But Germany was not merely doing its loyal duty toward its American ally, as the German public was told. Originally it had been the German Foreign Ministry that, in May 1998, urged NATO to build up a military threat and plan for ground operations as well as aerial strikes. It is hard to know what the public reaction would have been if German soldiers had been deployed on the ground, as was contemplated by NATO. In the end, Serbia accepted an international peace plan in June 1999. For all the heated argument, Germany's actual military involvement was extremely limited, contributing no more than 3 percent of all air strikes.[4]

After the terror attacks of 9/11, the Schröder government immediately rallied to the support of the United States. German soldiers were dispatched to Afghanistan before the end of 2001. There were clear limits to multilateralism and military intervention, however. In 2002, Schröder assured German voters that he would not support further American adventures, and it won him the election. Fighting terrorists was one thing, regime change something else. He would follow "the German way," not "the American way," he said, and that was a policy of peace. Already before the UN Security Council met (on which Germany had a non-veto seat at the time), the chancellor announced that he would not support the American invasion of Iraq.[5] Germany was saved from isolation by subsequent backing from Russia and France.

Schröder's public assertiveness vis-à-vis the United States would have been unthinkable during the Cold War. Earlier chancellors, though, had not exactly been Washington's poodles. Germany's peace policy used moral principles to advance national interests, as the former editor of the weekly magazine *Die Zeit*, Josef Joffe, has recently reminded us, although one can quibble whether this makes it a "moral superpower."[6] When Willy Brandt fell to his knees in Warsaw, he signaled atonement and simultaneously unlocked the eastern door for West German relations with Moscow and Warsaw. European integration similarly clothed national interests in the mantle of peace. It was Helmut Schmidt, Brandt's successor, who pushed for the first world economic summit in 1975, together with French president Valéry Giscard d'Estaing. Schmidt went along with the Americans in boycotting the Moscow Olympics in response to the Soviet invasion of Afghanistan in 1979, but not with economic sanctions. A big gas pipeline deal with the Soviet Union went ahead. As Schmidt put it enigmatically to industrialists: "The normal business with the Soviet Union should continue, it just cannot be business as usual."[7] Significantly, it was the architect of Brandt's *Ostpolitik*, Egon Bahr, who, after reunification, insisted that the country had the same right to pursue its own foreign policy as any other. Instead of a special path (*Sonderweg*), Germany had its own "normal" path; the crimes of the past should not be a roadblock to the future.[8]

In truth, Germany's newfound military engagement was anything but "normal." War remained a dirty word in the German lexicon. Schröder preferred to speak of a "fight against terrorism." His defense secretary, Rudolf Scharping, insisted that the country was not at war, merely conducting a "police action with military means."[9] The campaign was presented as a humanitarian mission to stabilize Afghanistan.

Such wishful thinking exploded on the night of September 4, 2009, when, under Chancellor Merkel, German troops called in a U.S. fighter plane for a preemptive strike against two tankers stolen by insurgents in Kunduz province. It also killed a hundred civilians nearby. The chief of staff and the defense secretary responsible at the time both had to resign after initially downplaying the possibility that civilians had been killed. It was only now that Chancellor Merkel openly referred to a "combat mission." Soldiers who previously had simply "died" were now recognized as "fallen."

Kunduz revealed not only the bloody reality of war but also the systemic contradiction at the heart of German policy. Until a year earlier, its soldiers had been equipped to build roads and preserve the peace, not to fight, unless under attack. Preemptive strikes were ruled out as counterproductive to the stabilizing mission. Instead, German troops sat in their barracks and left the fighting to their allies. They did not even have their own helicopters. The Taliban exploited the freedom they were given with a northern offensive. The spread of the insurgency to villages took the German troops by surprise. It was only in 2008 that commanders sent them out into the streets on patrol with Afghan partners and gave them the green light to fight.

The Afghan mission was a victim of the irreconcilable interests of Berlin, the Bundeswehr, and the public; Merkel's government did not want to lose face with its allies, but it equally risked losing the public if it turned the army into an actual fighting force. The result was understaffed, underequipped troops without a clear strategic mission. Combat troops had been whittled down to seventeen operational infantry battalions, and security forces had to be scrambled together from other units. Within these constraints, a low-risk, networked, civilian-military approach to stabilization made good sense to German generals and defense officials. It just happened to be out of touch with the local theater of war. After Kunduz, not even a quarter of Germans wanted their soldiers to continue to be involved in the International Security Assistance Force, and only 15 percent thought that the mission in Afghanistan contributed to national security.[10]

By the time of the allies' humiliating departure in 2021, some 160,000 German soldiers had served in Afghanistan at some stage or other. It was the Americans, though, who, after the Afghans, paid the greatest price: 2,442 American soldiers died in Afghanistan compared to fifty-eight from the Bundeswehr, fewer than the number of journalists killed. Washington spent seventy times as much as Berlin. Talk of a "German Vietnam" only shows how peculiarly distorted the country's sense of war remains.

Soldiers could count on some public recognition for their bravery and sacrifice—Ralf Rönckendorf was blinded in the course of saving the life of a comrade and honored with a Bambi media award in 2011—but it continues to be a far cry from what is "normal" elsewhere. While the United States, Britain, and France remember their fallen "heroes" with massive monuments in their capitals, one of the two memorials for Bundeswehr soldiers is on the grounds of the Ministry of Defense while the other is tucked away in a "forest of remembrance" on the grounds of a barracks outside Potsdam.[11]

THE CALL OF THE EAST

Reunification was followed by global reorientation. Whereas the old Federal Republic reached out across the Atlantic, the new one increasingly looked east, to markets in Eastern Europe, Russia, and China. The transatlantic alliance was loosening long before Donald Trump called it "obsolete" in 2017, because with the shared enemy—the Soviet Union—gone, Germany and the United States seemed to need each other less.

A good bit of Germany's newfound global fortune was sheer luck. The revolutions across Eastern Europe in 1989–90 opened access to both new markets and cheap skilled labor; Volkswagen bought Czech Škoda in 1991. The undervalued euro gave German exports a competitive edge, contrary to what Deutschmark defenders had feared. Above all, the Chinese economic miracle created millions of new middle-class customers hungry for German cars and products. More than ever, Germany lived off its exports. By 2010, exports accounted for half its GDP; ten years earlier, it had been a third. If anything, trade statistics downplay just how dependent on foreign markets the country has become, because they ignore the growing number of factories that moved abroad. "Made in Germany" was increasingly supplemented by German products "made in China." In 2017, Mercedes for the first time built more of its cars abroad than at home.

To cash in on globalization, though, also required bold steps. That fell to the Social Democrat Schröder, who rolled out the greatest package of social reforms since Adenauer. In the late 1990s, Germany inherited the nickname of "the sick man of Europe" previously given to Great Britain. It was stunted by low growth, high unemployment, and ever higher wages and taxes, struggling to bear the costs of reunification. Unemployment crossed the 4 million mark and 10 percent in 1996. Schröder made it the test of his chancellorship to bring it down. Distracted by foreign affairs in his first term (1998–2002), he devoted his second (2002–05) to the "Agenda 2010," which aimed to create a more flexible (and cheaper) labor market. Its centerpiece was the "Hartz reforms," named after the head of human resources at Volkswagen, Peter Hartz, an old friend of Schröder's from his time as premier of Lower Saxony, the home of Volkswagen. Hartz had dared to dream of the four-day workweek, which the carmaker trialed for two years in 1993–95. It became easier to fire people and to hire them for low-paying part-time jobs; social security contributions were eliminated for those earning less than 400 euros a month. Above all, generous unemployment benefits were drastically cut and fused with basic social benefits. If an unemployed person refused a job, it was possible to withhold benefits, regardless of how low paid it was or the fact that it required a new skill set. The official motto was "support and demand" (*Fördern und Fordern*).

A traffic jam of overdue reforms had been piling up under Kohl. Why would a Social Democrat, of all people, force them through? There are few instances where politics and personality have been so remarkably aligned. Inspired by Tony Blair in Britain and Dutch reformers, Schröder followed the "Third Way" in the belief that the only way to save the social state was by liberalizing it. Personal responsibility needed to take over from redistributive social justice. Unlike the middle-class Blair, Schröder had had to pull himself up by his own bootstraps. The Third Way was as much part of his personal biography as a political philosophy. Barely six months old when his father died at the front in Romania in 1944, Schröder grew up in poverty and left school at the age of fourteen, to work first as an apprentice in a hardware store, then in a small-town shop. He is probably the only living leader who knows how to decorate a shop window. He had to go to evening classes to acquire the *Abitur* credential needed to study law. His career was a testimony to the virtues of personal responsibility, iron discipline, and creative flexibility. "There is no such thing as a right to be lazy in our society," he told the tabloid *Bild* in 2001. He defended the introduction of low-paid "mini-jobs" from personal experience; without the odd cleaning job, he said, his mother would never have been able to raise her children.[12]

Outside his cabinet, Schröder faced powerful opposition from the rank-and-file of his party, the trade unions, and the Young Socialists, whom he had led in the late 1970s. He needed the support of the opposition to pass the reforms. For not a few Social Democrats, he had single-handedly killed a century-long tradition of social justice. Workers felt betrayed by the cuts to unemployment benefits, the unemployed humiliated by the threat of sanctions. Business, however, was jubilant. By 2007, unemployment had fallen below 10 percent, four years later below 7 percent.

What Germans took to be just rewards was to others the result of unfair "dumping." Together with the cheap euro, the reforms made German labor the cheapest in the European Union. In 2008, non-wage labor costs (especially contributions to social security and holiday pay) were more than a quarter below those in Spain and Greece, and even ten years later, after the Eurozone crisis and ensuing cuts, they were still 10 percent below.[13]

Schröder had to watch the turnaround from outside the chancellery. In the process of saving the German economy, he split the SPD. In the 2005 election, Schröder managed a tie with Angela Merkel, but had to leave the field to her because there was no chance of a coalition with the breakaway left. Merkel formed her first grand coalition with the SPD as junior partner. Votes for the SPD tumbled from 39 percent in 2002 to 23 percent in 2009 and have never fully recovered (25.7 percent in 2021).

The result of the economic reawakening was a growing asymmetry between the country's commercial interests, which were turning east, and its security and moral principles, grounded in the West. The surplus of its current account not only caused problems with its European partners but also widened the divide at home, since the East had less industry and wealth, and fewer exports. At the same time, business was booming with the authoritarian regimes in China and Russia. Schröder preferred to "go east" and leave trips across the Atlantic to his foreign secretary, Fischer. He visited the Middle Kingdom six times in as many years. Kohl had visited five times in his sixteen years as chancellor, Schmidt once in 1975. These years have become known as the heyday of neoliberalism. In truth, German success was as much a child of mercantilism. In 1999, Schröder clinched a 6 billion DM contract for a high-speed train from Beijing to Shanghai, but only after throwing in a German subsidy to lower the price. On future trips, Schröder took along his tennis partner, Heinrich von Pierer, the head of Siemens.[14]

In Russia, Schröder immediately hit it off with Vladimir Putin. Both came from poor backgrounds, both had studied law, and both were alpha males. In January 2001, he took his wife on a private visit to Moscow to celebrate Orthodox Christmas together with the Putins. The product of their partnership manifested itself in October 2005, ten days before national elections, when the German government underwrote an agreement for a gigantic pipeline across the Baltic—Nord Stream 1—to bring Russian gas directly to Germany. Having lost the election, Schröder became chairman of its board. A second pipeline, Nord Stream 2, was added by Angela Merkel.

From the outset, these projects were embroiled in controversy. For their supporters, they were an essential source of cheap, secure energy that would tie Russia to Europe. For critics, they were a costly diversion from renewables and one that sacrificed Poland and Ukraine to Putin. The second pipeline was agreed on in June 2015, one year and four months after Russia's invasion of Crimea, and threatened to cut off Ukraine from Russian gas. Digging began in 2018. On February 22, 2022, the new coalition government under Social Democrat Olaf Scholz suspended certification of Nord Stream 2 in response to Putin's recognition of Russian separatist people's republics in the Donbas region of Ukraine. It was too late. Two days later, the Russian invasion of Ukraine began in earnest. Turning the gas on and off with Nord Stream 1, Putin held Germany ransom. The critics were proved right.

Business with authoritarian regimes was done under the official mantle of "change through trade" (*Wandel durch Handel*). The idea behind it has a formidable history. It reaches back to Montesquieu and other Enlightenment thinkers who believed in the "*douceur*" of commerce, which with its gentle, civilizing touch would reduce aggression and foster understanding. Schröder and Merkel, though, were realists, not idealists. Both trusted the "visible hand," with big business deals underwritten by the state. Schröder told President George W. Bush in 2005 that he was "convinced that Putin really wants democratization"; he just needed to erect a strong state first on the ruins of communism.[15] Turkey's Erdoğan was similarly presented as a democrat-in-the-making. When dealing with China, German governments accepted the "one China" policy and, instead of raising human rights issues, preferred to focus on the commercial rights of their firms and their patents.

Wandel durch Handel naively assumed that authoritarian regimes would somehow become more like their trading partner, Germany, but after two decades of greater trade and investment, Putin and China are more authoritarian and aggressive instead—and Schröder became a lobbyist for Putin, serving from 2017 through May 2022 as the chair of the board of Rosneft, the energy company controlled by the Russian government. Not even the invasion of Ukraine in February 2022 made him distance himself from his Russian friend. In May that year, parliament canceled his privileges as former chancellor and the German Soccer Association (Deutscher Fussball-Bund) his honorary membership. Schröder handed back his honorary citizenship of Hanover before his hometown could take it from him. He retains his honorary doctorate from St. Petersburg University.

German foreign policy since reunification has been playing on a loop. Every few years, a leading politician calls on the country to grow up and stand up for its moral principles. Then comes a reaction by those urging restraint and caution, followed by another wake-up call. In 1999, President Horst Köhler said the country could no longer simply demand human rights, it had to fight for them. What followed was "change through trade." Merkel's Liberal foreign secretary, Guido Westerwelle, spoke out in 2012 against "neo-bellicism" and surgical strikes that risked killing civilians. Two years later, in Merkel's second grand coalition, his successor (and predecessor), Frank-Walter Steinmeier, a Social Democrat, announced that it was time for Germany to play a greater role in crisis management: restraint should not mean watching passively from the sidelines. President Joachim

Gauck was even more outspoken. The time for restraint was up, the country had to fight for democracy and against dictators, and, if necessary, "take up arms."[16]

The call fell on deaf ears. Foreign engagement has remained tiny by any historical standard. In 2015, the Bundeswehr trained Kurdish troops in northern Iraq, and, the following year, sent 650 soldiers to Mali to relieve French troops in the fight against the Islamic State. While there, one of their four "Tiger" combat helicopters crashed. Back home, all submarines were sitting in their docks waiting for repairs and the vast majority of fighter planes were grounded. The many nonoperational planes and assault rifles that did not shoot straight probably reflected both incompetence and convenience. In 2019, defense spending was a mere 1.1 percent of GDP, below France (1.7 percent), Italy (1.3 percent), and even Denmark (1.2 percent), and a long way from America's and NATO's demand for 2 percent. In 2020, it was raised to 1.5 percent, although at this point "significant reductions" were already planned for 2023–25.

It needed Russia's invasion of Ukraine to get the Scholz government to commit to an upgrade of its armed forces, but even now Germany continues to fall short of NATO's 2 percent target. To put current defense spending in historical perspective: in the Adenauer years it had been over 4 percent and under Brandt 3.5 percent. After initial hesitation, by August 2022 Germany had sent Ukraine ten self-propelled howitzers (Panzerhaubitze 2000), 14,900 antitank mines, and 3,000 antitank weapons (Panzerfaust 3) as well as tents, helmets, and ready-meals. They were only joined by Leopard 2 battle tanks in January 2023. How much more military support the country is prepared to give, and for how long, is still to be seen. Only the right-wing populist party Alternative für Deutschland (AfD) wants to bring back conscription. Generals and ministers alike have ruled it out.[17]

Sanctions have followed a similar pendulum. Schröder called on the EU to abolish the remaining sanctions on arms exports that had been imposed on China after the Tiananmen Square massacre in 1989. In 2014, Merkel put European security above national economic interests when she supported sanctions against Russia after it annexed the Crimea. While arms exports to Russia were stopped, however, she simultaneously opposed an American plan for military assistance from NATO. Each of these cases can be viewed on its own merits, but they follow a pattern. When moral principles served German interests, they were flaunted; when they stood in the way, they were ignored. After the violent coup in Myanmar, in spring 2021, Germany and the EU quickly imposed sanctions. When China cracked down on Hong Kong, they did not. In spring 2022, Germany joined the sanctions against

Russia but at the same time kept buying its gas. Half a year into the war, Germans were equally divided between those prepared to bear the costs of sanctions and those calling for their end.[18]

Relations with Israel are an exception. When Merkel told the Knesset in 2008 that Israel's security would never be negotiable, she was following in the footsteps of Adenauer and Kohl. The roots of Germany's unwavering support for Israel are obvious. But this unique commitment demands its own moral compromises. Whether sending Israel a nuclear submarine squares with Germany's "peace policy" is debatable. In 2021, the Foreign Ministry challenged the right of the International Court of Justice to investigate war crimes in the Palestinian territories, and was promptly criticized for sacrificing Germany's commitment to universal human rights.[19]

TOUGH LOVE

The reunited Germany makes up a fifth of the population in the European Union and a quarter of its economy. It is too small to lead on its own yet too big to be brushed aside. A common European army and foreign policy would have been the obvious way out of this impasse, but the unity required for such geopolitical ambition was sacrificed on the altar of austerity in the financial and Eurozone crisis of 2007–15. With its disciplinarian crisis management, Germany acted like a centrifuge. Instead of pulling closer together, the European Union was pulled apart and almost broke up. Some of the responsibility rests with Angela Merkel. Her cautious, procrastinating leadership style was ill-suited to a crisis that cried out for speedy action.

Deep down, Merkel was an Atlanticist—as a teenager in the GDR she dreamed of visiting the United States, and when the Wall came down, one of the first things she did was travel to California with her husband.[20] Understandably, for someone who had grown up behind the Wall, European integration was never the matter of the heart it had been for Kohl. Instead of an ever closer union with a federal center, Merkel was keen to preserve the power of national governments—and did so with the Lisbon Treaty of 2007, which made the European Council the voice of their representatives. If Kohl was the driver of the European train, Merkel put on the brakes.

To reduce it to a matter of personality, however, would be too simple. In her approach to the crisis, Merkel articulated norms and interests that were widely shared across Germany, in the media, among experts, and in the population at large, in her cabinet and in parliament. They reveal a distinctive German understanding of the world of finance and the virtue of good housekeeping. A global crisis of liquidity and debt became a morality play. Rescue packages were not only about rescuing others but about defending the German way and the country's image of itself.

The 2007–08 financial crisis was triggered by a subprime mortgage crisis in the United States. The root cause, however, was global. Banks everywhere had overlent and interbank credit collapsed. When Merkel, on October 7, 2008, briefed parliament on the crisis, however, she traced it to the "greed, irresponsible speculation, and mismanagement in the financial sector" and ended by praising the country's social market economy as "the best economic and social model" around.[21] Her government rushed to bail out the Munich-based Hypo Real Estate bank, but cast the blame on "bad" American banks whose irresponsible practices had infected otherwise "solid" German ones. Christian Democrats hailed the sound investment of family firms (*Mittelstand*), Social Democrats the many local savings banks and public *Landesbanken* (regional banks backed by the taxpayer) as an alternative to Anglo-American casino capitalism. In contrast to the speculative anarchy across the Atlantic, the German state, in this view, guaranteed stability and order.[22]

What all this ignored was that German governments, too, had deregulated capital markets after 1990. German banks no longer just provided a few local businessmen with credit. They had joined the world of high-risk trading and were deeply entangled in global securitization. And none more so than Deutsche Bank, which survived thanks to the largesse of the U.S. Federal Reserve; it had sold more mortgage-backed securities to the Fed under quantitative easing than any American bank.[23] Savings banks (*Sparkassen*) were not much better. Newspapers reported how a Frankfurt woman had been persuaded by her local *Sparkasse* to buy Lehman Brothers certificates as a safe way to supplement her pension plan; she lost 20,000 euros overnight.

In the German mind, bankers were not profit-seeking investors but service providers who gave credit to worthy customers. The reputable *Frankfurter Allgemeine Zeitung* distinguished "real money" (book money) from the "virtual money" of derivates markets.[24] Such idyllic views might have fit life in a provincial German town a century earlier, but were completely out of touch with the world of capitalism since the 1970s. Germans might be export world champions, but when it came to finance, they were effectively illiterate.

While the U.S. Federal Reserve took on the role of the global lender of last resort, the Europeans bickered. On October 5, 2008, Merkel went on TV with her finance minister, Peer Steinbrück, to assure citizens that their savings were safe, taking her European partners by surprise and panicking markets instead of calming them. Each government now put together its own guarantees and funds for capitalization. Germany vetoed a "transfer union" and burden sharing. After national bailouts came austerity. Instead of putting out the fire, it blew it across the Eurozone. As a liquidity crisis morphed into a national debt crisis, the cast of villains switched from "irresponsible" bankers to "extravagant" governments—first Greece, in 2010, then Portugal, Italy, and Spain (the so-called PIGS). It was not until 2012 that the European Central Bank came to administer the Fed's medicine when its president, Mario Draghi, pledged to "do whatever it takes to preserve the euro."[25]

Economically, Greece was peripheral, its GDP not even a tenth of Germany's. Politically, though, it became the central test case for the rules governing the Eurozone. In the late 1990s, EU countries agreed to keep their budget deficits below 3 percent and their debt below 60 percent of GDP. The first to breach the agreement were Germany and France, in 2003. They got away with a slap on the wrist. Greece would not be so lucky. In October 2009, it revealed that its deficit had climbed above 12 percent and its total debt burden had reached 115 percent of GDP—and it was insolvent. To survive, its debt needed to be restructured, with the help of its European partners. The richer northern countries—the Netherlands, Finland, and, first and foremost, Germany—wanted to be sure that they were not throwing good money after bad and being taken for a ride by profligate southerners. Without promises to reform, Greece might set a dangerous precedent. In early 2010, Finance Minister Wolfgang Schäuble floated the idea of a federal European fund modeled on the International Monetary Fund. Merkel shot it down—she had no interest in moving fiscal control from Berlin to Brussels.

What followed were five years of acrimony and pain, with one European rescue package after another subjecting Greece to deep cuts in public spending and social benefits. A democratic member state was left at the mercy of the European Commission, an unelected body. The repeated bloodletting meant a collapse of demand and a rise in unemployment (25 percent by 2015), poverty, and rage. The other Mediterranean high-debt countries faced similar austerity measures, although here the operation was conducted in a less aggressive manner. There was a resurgence of nationalist prejudice and hostility toward Germany not seen since the 1950s. Instead of an ambassador of peace and democracy, the European Union appeared to be the velvet glove hiding the iron fist of the Fourth Reich. Germany's brutal wartime occupation of Greece had not been forgotten. In Athens, placards depicted Merkel with a Hitler mustache; in Lisbon, she was greeted with

"Hitler go home." Was the European dream turning into an anti-democratic nightmare? Jürgen Habermas, Germany's most influential living thinker, lamented that Greece had been reduced to a "protectorate."[26]

Why was Germany so obstinate, almost destroying the European house it had so carefully built? "No deficits" and "no inflation" turned stability into a secular religion that ruled out more interventionist or Keynesian measures that could have saved young Greeks and Spaniards years of pain. Nobel Prize–winning economists and international organizations such as the IMF shook their heads in despair. There were, however, interlocking reasons German politicians and the public stuck to their home remedy.

For one, the country fared quite well with it. It recovered quickly from the 2008 world recession. The following year, a "debt brake" was written into the constitution to balance the federal budget. While a storm swept across the Mediterranean, Germany enjoyed solid growth, sound finance, and close to full employment. Why change what was working? Instead, sickly neighbors were to be given a dose of German medicine. In self-defense against its many foreign critics, the Finance Ministry in 2017 stressed that greater public investment would only have had a marginal effect on current accounts, and that far from being stingy, fiscal stability had enabled the government to increase public investment by 4.5 percent a year since 2015.[27] The officials must never have traveled by train or stepped inside a school. Delayed trains, missing power lines, neither laptops nor Wi-Fi, and broken toilets were just some of the results of years of underinvestment; public investment has grown but only because the whole economy has grown.

Fiscal discipline, secondly, expressed a peculiar economic philosophy that came to dominate West Germany after the Second World War: "ordoliberalism." A healthy economy, in this view, required strict rules and order. Break the rules, and mayhem follows.[28] Greece had to be taught a lesson and feel the pain in order to change its behavior. In 2014, Schäuble proudly announced that beginning with the following year federal deficits would be a thing of the past. "We do not want to be model pupils," he explained in good ordoliberal spirit, "but we think it is not bad if everyone in Europe sticks to the rules. We do not expect anything from others that we do not perform ourselves."[29] If rules were agreed to only to be broken, all trust would dissolve. What this view ignored was that the rules were not being applied on a level playing field—they were in Germany's favor, thanks to the cheap euro, which gave it an edge over its neighbors and a big trade surplus. For Greece, Italy, or Spain, the euro and balanced budgets were a straitjacket, which in a downturn prevented them from lowering interest rates, increasing public spending, or devaluing their currency to boost their economy.[30]

Domestic politics, moreover, militated against bending the rules in Europe. Since Germans had had their own benefits cut in the Hartz reforms, they were disinclined to be generous to their Greek and Italian neighbors. In fact, the European crisis was discussed in the same language as the earlier reforms at home. Schäuble invoked "help to help yourself." On July 17, 2015—her birthday—Merkel justified to MPs the latest European loan to Greece, worth 86 billion euros. Aid, she stressed, came with conditions and checks and was only given on a "quid pro quo" basis. Its principles were "consideration for good performance—self-responsibility and solidarity." It was the international equivalent of "support and demand" for the unemployed at home. "In the long run," she said, "Germany will only be doing well if the rest of Europe is also doing well." Whether the reverse was equally true was another question.[31]

What ultimately held these various arguments together and made them so impregnable was the simple moral conviction that a nation's economic success mirrored the virtues of its citizens. When the Greek prime minister George Papandreou visited Merkel in Berlin on March 5, 2010, he was greeted by an open letter in the tabloid *Bild*, telling him that he was entering a country where people worked until the age of sixty-seven, "gas stations have cash registers, taxi drivers give receipts, and farmers don't swindle the EU out of subsidies for millions of nonexistent olive trees." Germans also had debts, but they managed to settle them "because we get up early and work all day... and always put aside a penny for a rainy day."[32] To anyone who has ever stood outside a German office closed for one of the seemingly innumerable "coffee breaks," this was a bizarre statement. Germans enjoyed more holidays than Greeks and most other mortals, and they retired on average a few months short of sixty-two years of age, just as ordinary Greeks did; Greek pensions appeared so large because there were few other benefits.

The most insensitive remark was that Germans always settled their debts. It was a myth that not only downplayed growing problems with private indebtedness but was also a remarkable form of collective amnesia—when it came to defaulting, it was Germany that had been the greatest sinner in the twentieth century. At the London debt conference, in 1953, West Germany had half its debt written off, enabling it to take off on its economic miracle with 15 billion DM less hanging around its neck. Greece could expect no such generosity. On the contrary, Germany fought tooth and nail against Greek attempts to recover the debts and costs of its wartime occupation. In 2016, Greece estimated German debts at 270 billion euros—roughly 10 percent of the total costs of reunification. The German government rebuffed these demands, pointing to the "global agreements" reached in the 1960s, when they paid Greece the equivalent of 60 million euros, mainly compensation for the murder of Greek Jews. In recent years, relatives of adults and children murdered by the SS in 1944 have launched their own civil claims, and an Italian court seized assets held by the Deutsche Bahn, the national railway company. In all these cases, Germany has continued to invoke state immunity (which under international law protects one state from being sued in the courts of another) regardless of the crimes against humanity involved.[33]

Merkel held up the well-run household as a microcosm of a strong economy. It was "really quite simple" why financial markets stood on the brink of collapse, the chancellor told her party delegates in Stuttgart in 2008. A "Swabian housewife" would have reminded them of the simple worldly wisdom that "it is not possible to live beyond one's means. That is the crisis in a nutshell... [Applause]."[34] For anyone with a basic knowledge of economics or history, this is like saying the world is flat—Britain's national debt was always above 100 percent of GDP between 1750 and 1850, a century in which it became the world's superpower. The national economy is not like a household. States can print money and pump it into the economy. As the Nobel Prize–winning economist Joseph Stiglitz has pointed out, when the Swabian housewife tightens her belt, her husband does not lose his job, but when the entire nation does ("austerity"), many people will.[35] The simple moral truism has another flaw. Virtuous private behavior does not necessarily produce public benefits, as Bernard Mandeville pointed out a long time ago in his *Fable of the Bees* (1714). Instead it is often "private vices" such as luxury and vanity that turn the wheels of commerce.

Across Europe austerity policies apportioned moral blame, but nowhere more so than in Germany. That the euro favored Germany at the expense of Greece was not mentioned, and a sense that the stronger ought to help the weaker disappeared. What was needed instead was "tough love." Among newspapers, the high-brow *Handelsblatt* was alone in favoring a bailout and restructuring of debt. Three in four Germans held the Greek government, not the global financial crisis, responsible for the country's problems, according to a survey in spring 2010; in Britain, France, and Italy it was only every other person. Only a quarter of Germans were prepared to support Greece; 55 percent felt that they themselves were above the whole crisis and safe; only 36 percent of their European neighbors were that confident (or naive). In 2015, when the third rescue package was strung together, most Germans wanted Greece to remain in the EU, but half thought that "Grexit" would have no effect on the group.[36] Their main concern was what these packages did not to the Greeks but to themselves—"honest" hardworking Germans who lived according to the virtues of "self-responsibility" and were no burden on the state. Only Finns took a tougher view in the Eurozone crisis, but their loans to Greece made up 10 percent of their national budget and they had been through a devastating recession in the early 1990s.

Germans saw themselves as paymasters of Europe, never its beneficiaries. In the words of *Bild*, "Yet again, we are the fools of Europe!" In 2017, the former head economist of the Deutsche Bank—the very bank that had been rescued by the United States just eight years earlier—warned that "we will pay forever for Greece," as if the European loans were gifts by the German taxpayer.[37] Perversely, Germany, in fact, benefited from the Greek tragedy to the tune of 100 billion euros; investors looking for a safe haven flocked to *Bunds* (debt securities issued by the German government) and, in the process, drove down interest payments.[38]

Germans pride themselves on being "good Europeans," and they are less Euro-skeptic than their neighbors. But what kind of Europe do they want? In autumn 2018, the Social Democratic Friedrich Ebert Foundation investigated expectations of the European Union. For a quarter of respondents, the advantages of EU membership outweighed its disadvantages; for another quarter, it was the reverse; and the rest were undecided. Older and low-income groups were especially skeptical of the EU. For most Germans, the EU was about peace, democracy, human rights, and economic success. Solidarity and tolerance came well down the list. Ideally, the EU should look after the environment, crime, and security but leave pensions, welfare, education, health, and debt to each nation-state. More than half saw the EU as a body run by bankers for bankers. Two thirds felt that European policies "do not care about people like me."[39] Opposition to debt relief was as strong as support for a European carbon tax and minimum wage. A few commentators have aspired for their country to take on the role of "friendly hegemon" and act as "the Americans of Europe," a little bit like the United States with its Marshall Plan after the war.[40] That was precisely what most Germans did not want. To them, Europe was not about solidarity. There was little appetite for burden sharing.

"WE CAN DO THIS"

On August 31, 2015, outside a refugee camp near Dresden, Chancellor Merkel told a press conference, "We have managed such a lot—we can do this."[41] They would become the defining words of her sixteen years in office. Four days later, together with Austria, she threw the border open to the thousands of refugees who had trekked from Syria, Albania, and Afghanistan across the Balkans and Hungary. By the end of the year, 890,000 people had made their way to Germany, many but not all of them refugees. Another 310,000 followed in 2016. By the end of 2017, Germany had become a safe haven to 1 million refugees; another 300,000 people were given limited permission to stay or were waiting for an asylum decision. Compared to Turkey and Lebanon, these were not particularly large numbers—relative to their population, these countries hosted four and ten times as many refugees, respectively.[42] Within Europe, however, they were extraordinary—only Sweden came close.

Merkel's call on her European partners to share the burden fell on deaf ears. The limited solidarity in the financial crisis came back as a boomerang in the refugee crisis. Just as Germany had blocked a "transfer union" for debt, the rest of the EU now torpedoed plans to transfer people seeking protection. Germany was on its own.

Merkel's decision sharply divided opinion. For many refugees, foreign journalists, and humanitarians at home, it made her a saint. Germany, it seemed, had completed its metamorphosis and, through confronting its dark past, reemerged as the moral beacon for the world. "When it comes to helping others, we are the world champions," the head of the Green Party, Katrin Göring-Eckardt, told parliament with pride in September 2015.[43] For others, it was reckless, a threat to national integrity, law, and order. The chancellor was a selfish agent of "moral imperialism," in the words of Hungarian prime minister Viktor Orbán. It was as if the sins of their fathers made Germans think they owned morality. Were they really "better" than other Europeans?[44] At home, critics, mostly on the right, blamed Merkel for the state's "loss of control" (*Kontrollverlust*). These extreme views articulated strong opinions, but they do not especially make for convincing history. Each distorts more than it explains. To take the last charge first, arguably the state lost control in August 1992 when police and politicians stood by as a right-wing mob in Rostock attacked asylum seekers with rocks and Molotov cocktails, to the applause of thousands of onlookers.

What made Merkel take the historic step? It was not the result of a deep-seated humanitarianism. Just a year before, she had addressed the congregation in the church where she had been confirmed, the Mary Magdalene Church in Templin, about the ethics of being chancellor. She talked about military intervention, assisted suicide, and whether the leader of one country had the right to criticize the head of another. Afterward, members pressed her on the government's then-restrictive policy toward refugees.

The removal of refugees to safe countries, she replied, might not look Christian at first glance, "but it would perhaps be even less Christian if we took in too many, and then find no space for those who really are persecuted."[45] It was a version of the old "the boat is full" mind-set, with a curious twist of ethical discounting that refused help to people in distress now on the grounds that other more deserving people might need help in the future. It was a far cry from the biblical story of the Good Samaritan that Merkel would have heard in her childhood.

Her decision in September 2015 was primarily about managing an increasingly chaotic situation. Thousands were already marching on highways toward Germany. The choice was between letting them in or beating them back and causing a humanitarian crisis and potential violence on the nation's doorstep, which would have carried its own political costs. Merkel chose the former as the least bad option, a classic demonstration of her style of crisis management. As in the financial meltdown, she reacted to events rather than trying to preempt them with strategic leadership.

The refugee "crisis" had been long in the making, but Germany, sheltered in the center of Europe, tried to wash its hands of it. Following the hard-fought "asylum compromise" of 1993, refugees who arrived from another EU country could no longer claim asylum in Germany; that effectively left only the short coastline or arriving by plane as a means of entry. Ten years later, the Dublin Regulation routinely made refugees the problem of the state where they first entered the European Union, such as Greece; the European core had outsourced the problem to the periphery. Cutting the Greek state to the bone financially probably did not help it cope with rising numbers. It was only when the problem hit home that Germany woke up to the idea of a joint European quota system—it would take the EU until 2023 to take the first modest steps in that direction. When Merkel proclaimed "We can do this," the other Europeans counted themselves out.

Who were the "we" and what exactly was it that they were meant to accomplish? Opening the border was a gamble, but it was thinkable and manageable because Merkel could count on vital support from two sources: needy business and civil society.

The events of that autumn are now remembered for giving birth to a "welcome culture" (*Willkommenskultur*), with thousands of Germans flocking to train stations to greet refugees with blankets, food, and toys. In fact, the term predated these events. It was officially coined three years earlier as the last in a long series of attempts to attract skilled foreigners. The halting of recruitment in 1973 hung like a millstone around the economy's neck. Chancellor Schröder tried to lessen the weight with a work visa for "computer

Indians" in 2000. Merkel followed with a new immigration act and more liberal rights of residence in 2005 and 2007. They barely made a difference. Fewer than 20,000 IT specialists came. Many more were deterred by the remaining red tape, rules against self-employment, and the lack of a right to work for their spouses. To make things worse, German professionals were seeking their fortune elsewhere—between 2003 and 2009, almost 200,000 left the country. Mathematicians, scientists, and technicians were especially in short supply. Thousands of apprenticeships stood vacant. The Employers' Federation predicted a shortfall of 4 million skilled workers by 2035.

To plug the gap, German corporations discovered diversity. In 2006, Daimler (Mercedes), Deutsche Bank, and Telekom signed a "charter of diversity" (*Charta der Vielfalt*), pledging to create a workplace where all employees were respected regardless of ethnicity, sex, age, or religion. By 2013, more than a thousand firms had joined. The newfound tolerance was hard-nosed business: "To recognize and promote these manifold potentials creates economic advantages," in the words of the charter.[46] Together, globalization and the skills shortage revalued migrants, old and new. Instead of being cheap stopgaps, migrants came to be seen as valuable assets who brought fresh air, mobility, and "intercultural competence" to a company and could open doors to new markets. Deutsche Telekom, for example, introduced international menus and "buddies" for foreign staff, and Ford set up Turkish networks to attract more Turkish-German customers to the brand.

On June 11, 2013, over two hundred companies and organizations held their first "diversity day," where their staff could "for one day slip into the role of a refugee," giving them "a shift in perspective to see their environment in a new light and become aware of prejudices and challenges."[47] Santander Bank gave paid leave to employees who volunteered to help refugees. Here was the backdrop to the warm welcome refugees got from business in autumn 2015, when the head of Daimler, Dieter Zetsche, dreamed of the "next German economic miracle." The country, he said, could not afford to turn away such "highly motivated" people.[48] That many Syrians arrived with academic qualifications only added to the optimism; that those were not exactly the skills needed by business, and that many Afghans had none at all, soon complicated the picture.[49]

The welcome, secondly, could tap into the growing concern for refugees in churches and civil society. In 1997, a group of Benedictine nuns sat down in front of a police car in Dinklage (Lower Saxony), preventing the removal of a Ukrainian asylum seeker.[50] By 2012, some fifty churches were providing church asylum. Two years later, Catholic churches in Cologne launched a "campaign new neighbor" in aid of refugees. Congregations opened cafés in temporary hostels.

For other volunteers, the springboard was family care and politics. After retirement, "Herr E." initially looked after his mother-in-law, who suffered from Alzheimer's disease, before switching to help refugees. "Frau H.," a fifty-three-year-old teacher, offered free German lessons—she had been active in the AWO, the Social Democratic welfare body. "Herr I.," an educator, had worked with young people and the elderly. It was the violence in Rostock in 1992 that convinced him it was important to show one's support for asylum seekers. He joined a silent march and began looking after a recognized refugee from Africa.[51] New grassroots initiatives sprang up. In Potsdam, citizens initiated a "dinner for all" in 2002. In Dresden, they started women's circles and cycling courses. In Berlin, a young couple founded a humanitarian-style Airbnb for refugees in 2014; the project has since spread to other countries. "A Stage for Human Rights," a Berlin club, performed "asylum monologues" in eighty cities across the country. Sports clubs were opening their doors to refugees; the SGV Freiberg soccer club (near Stuttgart) could count on the traveling support of their four loyal drumming fans from Gambia.[52]

Deportations became the target of nonviolent protests after the tragic death of Aamir Ageeb, a Sudanese man who suffocated while being restrained aboard a Lufthansa plane in 1999. The two border police officers responsible received a suspended nine-month sentence. "No person is illegal" emerged as the motto of demonstrations. German activists creatively adapted a recent Dutch campaign and took on their own national airline, causing confusion at airports and travel agencies. Pretending to conduct a survey for an advertising agency, they asked Lufthansa passengers waiting to board if a 30 percent discount and extra luggage allowance tempted them to book a seat in "deportation class," traveling alongside a rejected asylum seeker? "If it is cheaper, why not?" many replied. Clever posters shamed the airline by mocking its logo: "The stork brings the children . . . the crane takes them away again."[53] Trying to limit the damage to their brand, Lufthansa temporarily suspended deportation flights, forcing the city of Hamburg to hire a charter plane to remove a Turkish family.

The popular response to the refugee "crisis" built on these longer trends and raised them to new heights. Between the autumn of 2015 and spring of 2017, 55 percent of the population helped refugees in one way or another. Many donated money, food, and clothes; others wrote letters to the press or gathered signatures in their support. A quarter of the population were "active helpers" who accompanied refugees to doctors and the authorities, taught them German, helped with the shopping, or took them along to the local sports club. They devoted five and a half hours a week, on average. Eleven percent of the active helpers (so-called *Paten*, "godparents") took individual refugees under their wing, and 6 percent invited them to stay with them for a while. These are impressive figures historically.

The majority of volunteers were novices who had had no previous contact with refugees or been involved in other charitable activities. For this cohort, the refugee crisis opened the door to volunteering. By 2017, half of these first helpers had moved on to other social causes. Just as important, however, was the experienced core of active helpers. Most of them had worked as a volunteer or organized donations for other causes in the past. And one in four were themselves from a migrant background, a far higher share than in other civic initiatives. It was often previous migrants who piloted refugees through the Kafkaesque labyrinth of German bureaucracy that they themselves had once navigated.[54]

The moral impulse built on a politics of conscience that had made it important to stand up against right-wing tendencies, but it was not primarily an urge to atone for Nazi crimes. The vast majority were concerned about social solidarity and justice now. Interestingly, only a quarter of the volunteers cited the plight of the refugees themselves as their central motivation. For twice as many it was about the future of their community and country; integration, they said, needed their help.[55]

A lot of volunteering developed through informal circles and began with a private encounter with refugees in the neighborhood, at work, or in sports clubs. In Potsdam, for example, the soccer club SV Babelsberg 03 started a new team: "Welcome United 03." Churches and welfare bodies were of secondary importance. A major difference from former charitable campaigns was that the welcome sometimes responded to preexisting local needs. Germany suffered from a shortage not only of skilled workers but also of schoolchildren, soccer players, and much else. The coach of KSV Lützkendorf had been recruiting refugees since 2011 to have enough players on the pitch. In Golzow (Brandenburg), the mayor persuaded the locals to take in three refugee families to prevent the closure of the undersubscribed village school. In the small city of Erkrath (North Rhine–Westphalia), annual community action days gave local firms and civic initiatives a ready platform to work with refugees. In Schwäbisch-Gmünd, in southern Germany, a retired engineer, who had previously worked with disadvantaged youths, set up a tool workshop and with nine like-minded pensioners trained more than three hundred refugees.[56]

"*We* can do this" thus primarily meant local communities, not the state, and certainly not other countries. That was a strength but also a weakness. Volunteering could accomplish only so much. The tool workshop, for example, lapsed when the founder was unable to get official support to hire a full-time master mechanic. In Golzow, the villagers were prepared to take in three refugee families, not more. Local authorities would probably have struggled with the arrival of 1 million people under any circumstances. Years of underfunding, however, ensured that the situation was more chaotic than it might have been. The obsession with cutting public debt had human costs. On the eve of the refugee crisis, the Netherlands, for example, had one decision-maker for every thirty asylum seekers; Germany had one for every four hundred. In Berlin, the municipal Office for Health and Social Affairs, which registered refugees, had complained about personnel cuts and impossible working hours for years. Now, in 2015, it was asked to register one thousand arrivals a day. One of them was Anis Amri, a Tunisian man who had previously been sentenced for arson and other crimes. He slipped through with a fake name that translated as both "cockroach" and "little dove." A year and a half later, he drove a truck into a Christmas market, killing a dozen people.[57]

The welcome always had its limits. In 2015, there were more than one thousand attacks on refugee homes. Hate crimes and right-wing terror were on the rise across Europe—how much as a result of better recordkeeping is a subject of debate. Comparison is complicated by the fact that, other than Germany, only Greece, Finland, and the Netherlands record hate crimes that specifically target asylum seekers. Whichever way they are looked at, the figures make for depressing reading. In Germany, attacks on asylum centers increased fivefold in 2015 and were increasingly violent, including against children and women. In 2014–15, there were 157 arson attacks and 195 cases of assault; much smaller Finland saw 47 attacks on asylum centers. The greatest number of incidents happened in Saxony, in the former GDR. There were also attacks in the western part of the country, especially in North Rhine–Westphalia, but, adjusted by population, violence was most pronounced in the eastern part; one district on the Czech border was the site of five instances of arson and thirty-one assaults and other attacks in 2014–15.[58]

Like the welcome, the violent backlash did not come out of nowhere. Right-wing crimes had been rising steadily in Germany, from 14,725 in 2001 to 23,555 in 2016. The majority were incitement to hatred (*Volksverhetzung*). Anarchist and left-wing crimes were smaller and stable in this period. In the thirty years after reunification, more than two hundred people were killed by racists. Right-wing murders happened in the west as well as the east—in

May 1993, for example, three girls and two women of Turkish descent died when a group of skinheads set fire to their house in Solingen, in the Rhineland (West). In 2013, some two thousand people took to the street against refugees in Schneeberg, a Saxon town with fifteen thousand inhabitants in the east, attracting neo-Nazis with torches shouting, "We are one people." In many places, refugees had to be led to their asylum center under police guard.

When it came to right-wing violence and terror, Germany towered above the European average. The police were often blind to the right-wing motivation behind crimes and looked for the perpetrators in the wrong place, as happened in Sweden, too. When a Turkish shop owner in Nuremberg was shot in broad daylight in 2000, it was suspected to be the work of foreign organized crime. This allowed the National Socialist Underground (NSU) to kill another nine ethnic Turks and Greeks and a police officer over the next five years. On February 19, 2020, a right-wing extremist killed eleven people in two "shisha" (hookah) bars in Hanau (West). Official figures recorded a rise in the number of skinheads, but, in fact, perpetrators were often well-integrated members of their local community. One of the three extremists who threw a Molotov cocktail at the refugee center in Salzhemmendorf, in Lower Saxony, in the West, on the night of August 28, 2015, was a twenty-four-year-old member of the local fire brigade.[59]

The state itself was Janus-faced. More migrants were allowed in, but more were also kicked out again. In 2015, 21,000 people were deported, more than twice as many as in 2014; in 2018, it was 26,000. Numbers would have been higher had it not been for rejected asylum seekers being ill or going underground. Germany also started to push refugees back to the European country they came from, carrying out 9,200 so-called Dublin transfers in 2018. There were police raids with dogs, and pregnant women were handcuffed. Again, these numbers would have been even higher had Greece not rejected virtually all "take-back" requests.[60] Unable to get her European colleagues to share the burden, Merkel and the EU in 2016 turned to Turkey to stem the tide of illegal migrants in exchange for several billion euros and visa-free travel for Turkish citizens.

Within Germany, the government ran a two-class system: one for recognized refugees, a second for the rest. Recognized refugees enjoyed liberal access to jobs and education. Even asylum seekers still waiting for their decision could work after three months. Observers heaped praise on the country for its newly discovered vision of quickly integrating refugees into the labor market. (In France, asylum seekers had to wait nine months, while in the United Kingdom they have no effective right to work at all.) By autumn 2016, every tenth refugee of working age who had arrived a year earlier had a job, and every third refugee who had come in 2013.[61] Not everything was rosy, though. The right to education only reached to the age of sixteen. Since asylum seekers only received a residence permit for six months at a time, employers were wary of giving them an apprenticeship that took three years. As long as they were housed in one of the reception centers, moreover, they were not allowed to work at all—Bavaria and Saxony had the power to stretch that period to twenty-four months. Even the lucky ones with liberal access to language and integration courses often ended up in low-skilled cheap jobs propped up by benefits.[62]

Other migrants found themselves in second class. A growing number were granted "subsidiary protection" instead of refugee status. This entitled them to stay in Germany. However, the "Asylum Package II" in spring 2016 stopped their families from joining them. In 2016–17, half the Syrians ended up in that category; in 2018, the number of family visas was capped at one thousand a month. Those who had fled Afghanistan were even worse off. Many were denied subsidiary protection and put on deportation flights because officials considered Kabul and Panjshir province safe enough for young men fit to work—a fiction decision-makers stubbornly clung to until days before the capital fell to the Taliban in August 2021.[63]

For many volunteers, the Asylum Package II was a slap in the face. They had given months to Afghans, Syrians, and Albanians in need and, in the process, gotten to know them, their pain and hope. They took "We can do *this*" to mean helping them to rebuild their lives in Germany. Now the state suspended family reunion for many, took away language classes, and started to remove others who had just settled into school or an apprenticeship. Tensions ran especially high in Bavaria, where Merkel's ally, the ruling CSU, fueled anti-refugee rhetoric and introduced various cuts and restrictive measures. When the populist Hungarian prime minister Orbán attacked Merkel for her "moral imperialism," he was speaking in Bavaria, not Budapest. Many of the volunteers learned to see their state a little bit with the eyes of a refugee. There were protests against the criminalization of refugees. In Landsberg, integration helpers organized a twenty-four-hour strike. Elsewhere, they went to court to challenge the extra fees asylum seekers were expected to pay for their accommodation.[64]

The grassroots circles that had mushroomed in 2015 did not suddenly disappear. By 2017, however, they had lost many members who were angered or disillusioned by the state seizing back control. Particularly controversial were the deportations to Afghanistan, a country at war, with thousands of civilian casualties. High school students petitioned to save their classmates, and employers demanded to keep their apprentices. Deportation flights were sabotaged by passengers who refused to sit down and pilots who would not take off. In 2017, pilots stopped more than two hundred expulsions to Afghanistan, most of them on Lufthansa flights.[65]

During the New Year's Eve celebrations in Cologne in 2015, over six hundred women were sexually assaulted, mostly by young North African men. Right-wing populists were quick to seize on the incidents as proof of the danger migrants posed to the German *Volk*, and its women in particular. Contrary to media headlines, however, there is little evidence that the events marked a sharp mood swing from a welcome to an unwelcome culture. Indeed, surveys suggest that the number of active helpers continued to grow during 2016.[66] In light of the huge challenges involved, popular attitudes were remarkably stable. In 2018, 53 percent of Germans said it made them happy if migrants felt at home in their country while 19 percent did not, the same as before the refugee "crisis" (55 percent versus 19 percent in 2014).[67] Three years after the borders were thrown open, only one in four Germans thought that the country had taken on more than it could handle and that it should take in fewer people fleeing conflict in the future.[68]

Throughout these years, German society was torn between humanitarian sentiment on the one side, fear and hostility on the other, and a pragmatic welcome in between—a range that was obscured by the initially one-sided glowing media coverage. Germans were not saints. They felt just as negatively toward Muslims and immigrants from outside the EU as their neighbors did (around 53 percent), according to a Eurobarometer survey in 2016. Where Germans stood out (together with Swedes) was that only one in ten were against offering support to refugees; in the rest of Europe, it was almost three times as many.[69] There were wide differences of opinion, though, about the kind of support they deserved. At the end of 2018, 45 percent thought the government was doing too much for refugees, 17 percent too little, and the remainder about the right amount.

There were similar divides about what individuals could be expected to do. At the Christian aid organization Bread for the World, the head of the human rights department insisted that Christians needed to side with the weakest, even if that meant challenging the state. Conservative theologians agreed that charity was a Christian duty, but believed that individuals could not possibly be responsible for people the whole world over—that was best left to states.[70] In late 2017, Lutheran Bishop Heinrich Bedford-Strohm acknowledged that many citizens had felt pressured by the constant appeals to "love thy neighbor." The church, he said, should resist such moralism just as it resisted demands for an upper limit for strangers in need.[71]

With the refugees, the world might have arrived in their community, but most citizens viewed the situation from their local perspective. For the majority, asylum and the right to stay were not entirely matters of humanitarian principle. Three quarters believed that those who were integrated and had a job or an apprenticeship should be allowed to stay, regardless of whether they were recognized refugees or not. The right to remain was seen in relation to a migrant's prospect of making a contribution to their community.[72] The test was not the persecution suffered by the individual but their fit with the host society. In sum, it was a conditional welcome.

THE PERSISTENCE OF VIOLENCE

From the attacks on foreigners to the gallows "reserved" for Merkel and her ministers, right-wing populism has promoted an increasingly violent style of politics. On June 2, 2019, the administrative head of the Kassel district, Walter Lübcke, a Christian Democrat known for his support of asylum seekers, was assassinated by a neo-Nazi. Political violence is not unique to Germany, of course, but its return came as a particular shock in a society that prided itself on its successful metamorphosis from militarism to peace after 1945. That self-image was not without basis, but it easily obscured how other types of violence have plagued the Federal Republic. In 1952, German police shot more than thirty people, as mentioned earlier. Numbers since then have fallen and are low by comparison with France (where several hundred Algerian demonstrators were killed by the police in Paris in a single day in 1961) or the United Kingdom (where British troops killed fourteen people on a civil rights march in Derry on January 30, 1972, "Bloody Sunday"). Police violence has not vanished completely, though. In recent times, there have been around two thousand investigations a year, only a few dozen of which have led to prosecutions. Unofficial estimates are considerably higher. Only one in ten protestors, for example, reported when they had been kicked or hit by the police during a demonstration, including some with broken bones.[73]

Within civil society, the classroom, and the family, physical violence was first stigmatized and then outlawed altogether, but it was not a linear success story. Already in the 1950s, pedagogues, advice columnists, and social workers urged parents to replace the belt and the rod with love and understanding. In 1954, the Federal Court of Justice ruled beatings in school illegal. Three years later, however, the decision was overturned, and it was not until the 1970s that states again banished corporal punishment from their classrooms.

It was symptomatic of the uneven and incomplete advance of peacefulness. Rather than being in the vanguard of liberalization, West Germany was lagging behind the Nordic countries. Sweden had already outlawed corporal punishment in secondary schools in the 1920s, extending it to younger pupils in 1957 and prohibiting it in the family in 1979. It took Germany until 2000 to take that last step. Rape in marriage had only become a criminal offense three years earlier. Victims of domestic violence have received greater protection since 2002, when the police gained the power to ban a perpetrator from the home; previously, it was their victims who often had to flee to shelters. If these reforms helped to delegitimate violence, they obviously did not eradicate it. While serious spanking is rare today, about a third of German parents still resort to the occasional "mild slap" in the face or on the bottom—more than in Sweden, though fewer than in France. The number of children who survived serious abuse doubled between 1995 and 2010. While the number of robberies has fallen since the early 2000s, cases of dangerous and serious bodily harm have not (140,000 in 2018). There were as many homicides and child murders (*Kindestötung*) in Germany in 2018 as in 1938, although, of course, state violence then toward racial, political, and social enemies was on another scale.

Violence against women has declined but has hardly been eradicated. An EU study in 2014 put German women in the middle of the spectrum. Women in their twenties were safer than their mothers and grandmothers had been, but one in five was still a victim of violence. Every fifth relationship involved violence against women. Lesbian, bisexual, and transgender women were routinely attacked in public. Violence was psychological and structural as well as physical, a linkage that legal reforms failed to address. And the laws that did exist were rarely enforced. In 2010, the Federal Ministry for Family Affairs reported that the police only took photos of injuries from domestic violence in 2 percent of cases. Three quarters of legal proceedings were suspended or discontinued, often because judges and prosecutors considered them not to be sufficiently in the public interest. Women who had suffered domestic abuse were told to pursue a private lawsuit instead. Their perpetrators (often their partners) had little to fear—half of them did not even complete the "offender programs" the state had set up for them.[74]

Physical violence remains a routine part of growing up in the western as well as the eastern part of the country. The town of Nordenham is one example. Located at the mouth of the Weser River on the North Sea, the town makes fuselage shells for airplanes and boasts a sea park for tourists and their canine friends. In 2017, its high schools were the subject of an in-depth investigation. Every third pupil in seventh to tenth grade reported that they had been the victim of physical violence, assault the most common type. While most enjoyed parental affection at home, every fourth teenager had been slapped by their parents or had objects thrown at them, and every fifth had been beaten, kicked, or worse. One in six admitted having committed an act of violence themselves. Twelve percent believed that one should use "targeted force against the oppression by the state and the police."[75]

Nordenham was Germany in miniature when it came to the link between intolerance and violence. In schools in the eastern city of Rostock, every fifth pupil self-identified as xenophobic and approved of violence.[76] In 2016, during the height of the refugee crisis and populist attacks, every fifth German in both west and east alike said they were "quite prepared to use physical violence to enforce their interests." The figure has declined in the latest survey (2020), but even now one in six said that, although they themselves would never use force, they thought it was "good that there are people around who let their fists do the talking when other methods fail."[77]

POPULISM WITH GERMAN CHARACTERISTICS

The general election of 2017 was an earthquake in German politics: the far-right AfD took 12.6 percent of the vote. Four years earlier, it had failed by a few thousand votes to cross the necessary 5 percent threshold to enter the Bundestag. Now, it was the third-largest party, with ninety-four delegates, behind only the CDU and SPD and ahead of the Liberals, the Left, and the Greens. The 2021 election showed that it was there to stay; although its share of the vote fell slightly, it remained above 10 percent. What was happening to German democracy?

The answer depends on one's point of reference. For those looking back to Weimar and Hitler, the result set off alarm bells. Perhaps the coming to terms with the past had been less profound than thought. To those looking across Europe and the Atlantic, Germany was simply being swept by the same wave of populism that had risen elsewhere in the world; in France, after all, the National Front had been a fixture of political life for three decades, Italy had the Lega Nord, Hungary Fidesz, and even generally moderate Britain succumbed to the Brexit variant of the disease.[78]

Certainly, the AfD echoes right-wing parties in other places: it is against "the establishment," the European Union, foreigners, and Islam, and for strong leaders, "traditional" values, and the glorious national past. It mocks parliamentary democracy and sees direct referenda as the only way to stop the "authoritarian and partly totalitarian behavior" of elected officials, to quote its 2021 manifesto.[79] Its heartland is in the east, which has seen an exodus of people and industry. Yet, in just as many ways it is abnormal—it has been pro-market as well as anti-foreigner, and its supporters are not mainly the unemployed or uneducated.

Right-wing populism did not come out of nowhere. It had raised its head repeatedly before. The "Republikaner," a breakaway faction from the Bavarian CSU, scored around 10 percent in a series of regional and European elections in the late 1980s and early 1990s. Its motto was "Yes to Europe—No to this European Community."[80] The German nation, it warned, was being swamped by foreigners. Refugees were fraudsters who came to the country to have their teeth fixed at the expense of the taxpayer. In Hamburg, Roland Schill, popularly known as "judge merciless" for his tough verdicts, established his own law-and-order party in 2000 to clean the city of criminal foreigners and protect the "little man" against "big business" (*Grosskapital*) and political nepotism.[81] He blamed the euro for inflation and wanted the Deutschmark back. In the city elections, Schill received 19 percent of the vote—in districts with many migrants almost double that—and joined a coalition government with the Liberals and the Christian Democrats. These right-wing surges, though, failed to break through at the federal level. Without a party base, their fortunes fell as quickly as they had risen. After less than two years in office, Schill was fired, and then expelled from his own party; when he resurfaced in the national media, he was snorting cocaine in Brazil.

The AfD was a different operation. It was founded in 2013 as a fundamentalist liberal challenge to Merkel and the euro. The party name was a riposte to the chancellor's declaration that there was "no alternative" to the rescue packages. The AfD has had its own share of infighting—in 2015, extreme nationalists drove out the economic liberal founding fathers. But it also developed a party structure, put down roots in towns and companies, and, importantly, was quicker than the established parties to realize the power of social media in mobilizing support.

While the refugee crisis presented the AfD with a golden opportunity, the party tapped into a reservoir that was already there. Voters with far-right leanings were at last offered a respectable face. Unlike the jackbooted hooligans of the fascist fringe, AfD leaders have been professors, business consultants, and journalists in tweed jackets and neckties sporting cute Labrador retrievers. Overwhelmingly, their success in 2017 was due to their ability to attract conservatives who felt abandoned by the CDU and nonvoters who felt abandoned by the political system in general. By pulling the Christian Democrats toward the center, Merkel inevitably sacrificed previously sacrosanct ground on the right, even if she herself voted against same-sex marriage in 2017. The AfD provided a home for homeless conservatives.

In other words, the rise of the populists did not reflect a general rise in right-wing attitudes. Quite the opposite. Surveys show that during the Merkel years Germans as a whole were becoming more tolerant toward foreigners, disabled persons, gay people, and many others; xenophobic attitudes were less than half as widespread in 2016 as a decade earlier.[82] The AfD captured a shrinking group who felt increasingly belittled and marginalized as the rest of society moved toward more liberal attitudes—not so different from Donald Trump in the United States.[83] It was this feeling of being under siege and of seeing one's once respectable views treated as backward that triggered the backlash against the political elite, the media, and virtuous "good people" (*Gutmenschen*), as they cynically came to be called.

The political momentum behind the rise of the far right in today's Federal Republic was the very opposite of what had brought down the Weimar Republic. Instead of an erosion of the middle, the center held firm. A one-sided focus on right-wing populists tends to distract from that countervailing trend. Party loyalties have weakened. Still, the majority of Germans continue to cast their votes somewhere in the middle—they simply switched from the CDU to the SPD, the Greens, and the Liberals, as happened in 2021 when the Christian Democrats suffered their worst election result ever (24 percent, down from 33 percent in 2017 and 42 percent in 2013). In contrast to Weimar, extremists have not been eating up the middle from both sides. In fact, Germany has all but lost a radical left; in the 2021 election, Die Linke did not even reach 5 percent and scraped through by the skin of their teeth thanks to a constitutional provision that rewards a party that manages to win at least three direct mandates (Die Linke won the minimum). The Greens, meanwhile, have morphed from the anti-state and anti-business party of their early years into trustworthy partners of the establishment.

Populism is often said to be a rebellion by the losers of globalization. However much this may be true for supporters of Trump or Marine Le Pen, it does not explain the AfD. Unlike for many Americans, French, and Italians, the 2010s were good times for Germans. Growth was solid, unemployment low, and inequality stable. AfD supporters are mainly middle-aged men with a decent job or their own small business. To actual losers of globalization, the AfD has very little to offer. The unemployed have voted SPD and Green as much as AfD. In 2016, its rightist leader in Thuringia, Björn Höcke, said that the problem was no longer about the distribution of wealth from top to bottom; the "new social question of the twenty-first century is about its distribution between the inside and the outside."[84] Social imperialists in 1900 had similar ideas. What was new about the AfD was that it was just as liberal on the inside as it was restrictive on the outside. Social imperialists wanted external barriers partly to fund social reforms. Not so the AfD. It believes in rolling back the state and in incentivizing people on benefits to take up poorly paid jobs; welfare "parasites" come right after migrants in the list of enemies. A rare exception is its "welcome culture for children": to reverse the demographic decline, parents would receive 20,000 euros on the birth of a child.

The AfD's main constituency has been skilled workers, artisans, and the lower middle class, especially in the east, whose personal situation is not bad but who believe the world around them is out of control. A huge gap has opened up between perception and reality; many, for example, thought unemployment stood at 20 percent in 2016, more than four times what it actually was.[85] That many of them were not losers of globalization did not stop them from worrying that they might soon be. It was that fear of decline that the AfD stoked with its doomsday vision of foreign invaders coming to take away jobs and benefits and destroying social peace and public morals.

These voters' sense of insecurity is not altogether unfounded, however. It arises from the erosion of the communities they live in, with young people (and women especially) moving to the cities and local shops and train stations closing.[86] Here is the main source for the AfD's phenomenal appeal in the former GDR. In Saxony and Thuringia, it received 24 percent of the vote in 2021, making it the strongest party; in Brandenburg and Mecklenburg-Vorpommern, 18 percent. In the few thriving eastern cities, such as Leipzig, it did less well. In the western states, the party only managed 5 to 9 percent. Depopulation has spread a sense of being left behind, cementing a collective identity of easterners as victims of a western takeover. In truth, villages and small towns were already shrinking in Erich Honecker's GDR.[87] The emptying out of regions was nothing unique to East Germany. It has been a fate shared by aging communities including southern Italy, Latvia, and rural Japan. A crucial difference is that West German politicians had vowed to reverse it. Thirty years after the fall of the Wall, the "blossoming landscapes" Helmut Kohl promised had not materialized. The irony was that the regions that most needed to attract newcomers to survive were also the ones most determined to keep them out.

The sense of being "left behind" and forgotten by the metropolitan "establishment" created a fertile ground for populists. Eastern women were hardest hit by reunification, but they were also the ones ready to take risks, pack up, and seek their fortune elsewhere. Eastern men tended to be less flexible. It made those who stayed behind all the more determined to defend what was left of their male authority against gender equality, alternative sexual identities and family structures, and attempts to make the German language gender neutral—what populists vilify as "gender madness" (*Genderwahn*). In Thuringia, people's occupational status had been improving in the two decades before the AfD took off; it was the demographic balance that had deteriorated.[88]

The "country versus city" divide is more than a physical one. It does not need an actual village to develop a siege mentality. Urban segregation can create a threatened village in one's head. That is why the AfD also did exceptionally well in several suburban housing developments and urban quarters in the west where old inhabitants and recent migrants effectively lived in separate villages, such as Pforzheim-Haidach (43 percent in 2017) and Mannheim-Schönau (21 percent), both in Baden-Württemberg, in the southwest. In Schönau, inhabitants had attacked refugees as early as 1992. Populism built on long-standing battles of "us versus them."[89]

The AfD's defense of the Christian family, authority, and the nation has resonated well with ethnic Germans from the former Soviet Union who felt abandoned by Merkel; the "Young Alternatives" were official partners of United Russia, Putin's youth organization. The original founder of the AfD, the economist Bernd Lucke, is a devout Protestant. The publisher Götz Kubitschek, the cofounder of the German Identitarian movement and the brains behind the current far-right leadership, is an outspoken Catholic, with a biological-racist bent. God, he believes, created man according to nations, such as the German *Volk*. Mass migration is consequently a defiance of divine will.[90] Beyond ethnic German *Aussiedler* and small circles of Christian fundamentalists, however, Christianity has played little role in German populism, in contrast to the United States. The AfD's heartland, the former GDR, is virtually de-Christianized, and so are the vast majority of its supporters.

More importantly, the GDR left behind strong xenophobia and a weak civil society that was drained further by austerity programs in the 2000s. Populists were able to take over public spaces with little resistance. On October 20, 2014, three hundred people gathered in the center of Dresden to warn against Islamic fundamentalism. Only a handful of Muslims lived in the Saxon capital. The only mosque residents had ever passed was an old cigarette factory built to look like one. It did not stop the protestors from being alarmed by local plans to house more asylum seekers and news stories that Islamic terror might spread to German soil. By January 2015, their weekly Monday protest "strolls" (*Spaziergänge*) had swelled to 25,000 people, many coming from the provincial hinterland. PEGIDA (Patriotic Europeans Against the Islamicization of the Occident) failed to live up to the territorial ambition of its name. It sparked no European movement, other than a guest appearance by the Dutch populist Geert Wilders. In Saxony, however, it spread like wildfire for a good year—at the end of 2015, there were still three thousand people "strolling" through Dresden each Monday evening.

It was a populist déjà vu of the Monday walks that culminated in the peaceful revolution of 1989. "We are the people" was back, only with a different enemy. Instead of an unaccountable socialist elite, now it was a democratic elite that flooded the country with migrants, against the popular will, as they saw it (and continue to see it). High levels of xenophobia and distrust of representative democracy made for a toxic mix, and nowhere more so than in Saxony in the east, where people prided themselves on resisting outsiders, be they from Berlin or Damascus. The Monday marches provided a ready ritual of people power. Their chants were primarily directed at the German establishment, not foreign Muslims: "the lying press," "traitors to the people," and "Merkel must go." In western cities, PEGIDA was almost immediately snuffed out by local opposition. In Saxony, by contrast, the local ruling CDU tolerated right-wing excesses and allowed them to spread. None of the western democratic parties had managed to put down strong roots in the state.[91]

The man behind PEGIDA was Lutz Bachmann, who ran a small advertising agency in Dresden and who had previously served three years in prison for burglary and assault. He had acquired vital organizing skills as a volunteer in the aid effort during the great flood of 2013, for which he received a medal. All he needed to get PEGIDA started was a Facebook page. It would be his downfall, too, when postings appeared in which he referred to asylum seekers as "filth" (*Dreckspack*) and a photograph began to circulate in which he posed with a Hitler mustache. Bachmann stepped down as chair, at least officially.

What made people follow this Pied Piper became a subject of heated controversy. Organizers presented their followers as ordinary citizens who were simply exercising their democratic right to protest. They were regular, concerned people, not racists, one of them assured the nation on a prime-time TV talk show. True, most PEGIDA supporters were not Nazis, but that did not make them average citizens, either. As with the AfD, most of them were middle-aged men with a decent income. University graduates and small businessmen were overrepresented. They did not behave as typical protestors—in contrast to other social movements, most refused to talk to researchers or abused them; this is why surveys need to be read with care. The "strolls" were accompanied by racist chants and nationalist slogans. Some members formed militias to keep out refugees, others smashed the windows of their political opponents. Xenophobia ran deep and was not just a problem of a few rotten apples. One researcher found that PEGIDA supporters were three times as likely to classify themselves as "right wing" and vote for the AfD as the rest of the population.[92] Sociologically, they might come from the middle of society, but ideologically they were on the extreme right.

In 1986, Chancellor Kohl declared that his fellow citizens, and especially the young generation, were "immune" to antisemitism. It was merely an isolated slip of the tongue when the mayor of the small town of Korschenbroich on the Lower Rhine, Graf von Spee-Mirbach, said that, to fix the hole in the local budget, it might be necessary to "kill a few rich Jews."[93] But Kohl, like Adenauer before him, made a naive and dangerous misjudgment. Antisemitism might be officially taboo, but it was not like polio, a disease that had been virtually wiped out and could be contained by swift action against occasional outbreaks. Rather, it flourished on the inside of society, drawing on a reservoir of prejudice and hatred that Holocaust memorials and history lessons failed to dry up.[94]

The reservoir replenished itself in the western as well as eastern half of the country. A sociological study in the early 1980s came to the conclusion that one in five West Germans was antisemitic (Kohl rejected these findings as "absurd"). According to some surveys, anti-Jewish sentiment was higher in western Germany than in the east into the mid-1990s, and it was only the subsequent decline in the former that has made the latter stand out. In 2018, 35 percent of easterners agreed strongly or partly that "even today Jews have too much influence"; among westerners, it was 30 percent.[95] In the schools in Nordenham on the North Sea (West), every sixth pupil believed there was "worthy and unworthy life." One in eight agreed that "Jews have too much influence in this world" and that Hitler and the Nazis had their "good sides," too. Five percent of the teenagers had themselves committed a right-wing crime, such as spraying a swastika on a house wall or "foreigners out" in a public toilet.[96]

Officially, the AfD defends Jewish life and even has a small Jewish section, although that is little more than a fig leaf. Its leaders have repeatedly belittled the Holocaust. In 2017, Höcke complained that Germans were the only nation that planted "a monument of shame" in its heart—the memorial for the murder of the Jews, in Berlin. Activists hit back and planted two dozen copies of the memorial's concrete slabs outside his home in Thuringia. The following year, after right-wing excesses in Chemnitz, Alexander Gauland, the party leader with a Labrador necktie, declared that the Nazi years were no more than a single "bird shit" in a thousand years of glorious German history. A few moderate voices notwithstanding, antisemitism is widespread among the AfD rank-and-file. Remembrance of the liberation of Auschwitz in January 2020 sparked comments on the party's Facebook page that "the Holocaust did not really happen." Fifteen percent of AfD voters consider it Allied propaganda. More than half the AfD voters agree that "Jews have too much influence in the world"—roughly three times as many as among other voters.[97]

Antisemitism has mutated, not disappeared, from German society. Religious motifs—such as the murder of Christ—and biological racism have retreated, but prejudice has recycled many other anti-Jewish stereotypes and conspiracy theories, including being the wire-pullers of global finance and profiteers of Holocaust memory. Jews everywhere are held accountable for Israel's policies. In 2020, 34 percent of Germans in the east and 29 percent of those in the west felt strongly that Israeli policy in Palestine was just as evil as that of the Nazis in the Second World War. More than 40 percent believed that reparations were driven by a "Holocaust industry of canny lawyers." Every fourth German in the west and every third in the east agreed that "the Jews just have something peculiar about them and do not quite fit in with us." For only a third did Jews belong to the German population as "a matter of course."[98]

On October 9, 2019, a twenty-seven-year-old extremist tried to kill Jews inside a synagogue in the eastern city of Halle on Yom Kippur. Only a heavy wooden door prevented the Day of Atonement from turning into a massacre. Two locals were shot outside. In 2016, 644 antisemitic crimes were registered in the country; the actual figure is estimated to be many times that, because crimes without an identified perpetrator were generically classified under the broad label "right wing," while less violent crimes were often not reported at all. Four years later, the authorities counted 2,351 antisemitic hate crimes alone.[99] The majority happened in the East, but not all. Rhineland-Palatinate—Kohl's homeland—has counted around thirty antisemitic incidents every year since 2014. They have included antisemitic slogans featured during right-wing demonstrations, the burning of Israel's flag, graffiti threatening to send Jews and leading politicians "to the gas"—and physical assault.[100]

In the wake of the refugee crisis, the rise in incidents was often treated as a foreign import, blamed on migrants from Islamic countries with little knowledge of the Holocaust. In truth, a lot of the problem has been homegrown. In Rhineland-Palatinate, virtually all the crimes were committed by right-wing natives; in the country as a whole, the authorities similarly classified 95 percent as right wing.[101]

Rhineland-Palatinate was the first state, in 2017, to appoint a special representative for Jewish life and issues concerning antisemitism. Other states and the federal government followed. New synagogues have opened in both the east and the west, in Cottbus and Schwerin as well as Mainz and Constance. Jewish congregations have grown and now claim 100,000 members. They face open antisemitism, from antisemitic web pages to concerts by "hatecore" rock bands such as Racial Purity and White Resistance.[102] "*Scheissjude*" and "you Jewish bitch" are common terms of abuse in schoolyards. Old stereotypes about greed and diabolical powers find resonance among left-wing enemies of globalization as well as right-wing nationalists. Myths have resurfaced in attacks on Jews as "child murderers." German teachers have at times been found either to be tone deaf to such tropes or to slip from criticizing Israel's human rights abuses in the occupied territories to holding Jews collectively responsible for them.[103]

From a liberal-democratic perspective, there is good news and bad news. The good news is that, compared to France, Italy, or Trump's America, right-wing populism in Germany has been limited, its rise halted. Nationally, the AfD stood at 10 percent at the beginning of 2022. In February 2023, one year into the war in Ukraine, polls showed it at around 16 percent, but even then it was isolated. A strong democracy should be able to live with that. Time and again, populists have found themselves outnumbered by the tens of thousands of citizens who joined candlelit processions, demonstrations, and music festivals against racism—"We are more," they rightly claimed. The bad news is that populism has put down extensive roots, especially in the former GDR, where a right-wing party regularly receives up to one quarter of the vote. In the spring of 2023, polls gave it even 30 percent in Saxony and Thuringia, ahead of all other parties (in Bavaria it was 10 percent, in North Rhine–Westphalia it was 14 percent). Populism has deepened the divide between east and west, reinforcing a sense of deprivation and alienation among millions who feel overlooked. Racism, intolerance, and disrespect for representative institutions have secured a foothold.

PART FOUR

TRYING TO BE GOOD

1950s to the Present

12

Money Matters: Thrifty, Wealthy, and Unequal

In 1956, two women passed each other on a shopping street in a provincial town. "But Frau Müller, how did you manage to afford a fur coat?" one of them asked. "Well, Frau Meyer," the other explained, "I have been saving every penny" (see insert fig. 31). The scene was one of the entries children submitted to the savings week competition that year, and illustrated what the virtue of saving meant to a fourteen-year-old girl. Thrift is often equated with modesty. Here it was the path to luxury. What is more, the young artist placed the two women in front of a shop window filled with fashionable dresses and run by Neckermann, one of the new mail-order companies that offered installment credit (see illustration).[1]

Saving stands at the center of a myth about Germans—that they are frugal, disciplined, and restrained, ready to resist temptations now for the sake of security and satisfaction later. Unlike spendthrift Anglo-Americans who cannot resist instant gratification and live beyond their means, it is said, thrifty Teutons worship at the altar of stability. Many still do not have a credit card, but savings banks are everywhere—about four hundred of them with more than twelve thousand branches. They are commercial enterprises, but cities and charities are their main shareholders and they operate under a public mandate to serve their communities. Other nations have their Queen and their Statue of Liberty; Germans had their Deutschmark, a tangible icon of the economic miracle. They were "DM patriots."[2] A recent exhibition typically held up thrift as a distinct "German virtue" that ran so deep it was "self-evident."[3] Well, it clearly was not to the German teenager to whom it appeared in the shape of an extravagant coat, nor to some of her peers who eulogized their grandparents as model savers who happened to build their solid existence with the help of mortgages (the opposite of saving).[4] Nor was saving anything unique to Germans. In the 1950s and 1960s, Americans, Italians, and Japanese put aside a greater share of their earnings.

What needs explaining is why a people who recently had their hard-earned savings wiped out not once but twice—in the hyperinflation of 1923 and the currency conversion after the Second World War—nonetheless started to save again and then kept at it while from the 1980s on almost everyone else did so less and less. The German household saving rate rose from 3 percent in 1951 to 10 percent in 1964 and has hovered around that figure ever since; the only major country with a similarly high constant rate in recent decades is France.[5]

The cult of stability was the product of politics and interests. It articulated a particular vision of fairness based on merit: success would go to those who worked hard and lived in moderation. That was the ideal. In reality, such virtues were put under serious strain, most dramatically by the economic miracle and the rise in leisure and consumption beginning in the mid-1950s, and unemployment, poverty, and growing inequality since the early 1990s. The cult of stability produced losers as well as winners.

THE GOSPEL OF THRIFT

In our own era of easy credit, thrift can appear traditional and antiquated. But in fact saving was a modern invention, as revolutionary as the steam engine and the airplane. "If you would be wealthy... think of Saving as well as Getting," Benjamin Franklin advised American colonists in the mid-eighteenth century. In the next century, thrift became the mantra of bourgeois liberals and social reformers: it would free people from slavish dependence on their creditors and teach them self-reliance instead, inoculating them against socialists and revolutionaries. Postal and national savings banks spread across Europe, America, and Japan, for workers and farmers, Catholics and Protestants. Children began to receive pocket money and schools started their own savings funds. By teaching children self-control at a young age, thrift was thought to build character as well as capital. Housewives were expected to be domestic managers whose rational housekeeping would keep their families out of poverty. The First and Second World Wars were fought with savings bonds as well as tanks.[6]

Germans emerged from the Second World War with little appetite for saving. The Nazis had used people's savings accounts to finance their enormous war debt. At the same time, they printed lots of Reichsmark. The result was rampant inflation amid rationing and black markets. In 1948, the Western Allies carried out a currency reform in their zones to pave the way for a free market economy. The Deutschmark replaced the Reichsmark.

(The bills were printed in the United States and shipped in wooden trunks to Germany.) Each inhabitant received 60 DM cash for 60 RM. All balances above that were converted 1 to 10. The conversion was great news for anyone in debt or with a mortgage, since they could write off 90 percent at a stroke. For savers, it was a disaster: a savings book with 1,000 Reichsmark one day showed a mere 100 Deutschmark the next. People who owned real estate or fixed assets were more fortunate. Prices shot up dramatically, as did unemployment, leading to demands for a U-turn, fresh controls, and nationalization. Ludwig Erhard, the director of economic affairs in the Western zones, held off. Prices began to settle down, and the economy turned the corner.

The introduction of the Deutschmark is now remembered for launching the economic miracle, but that was in the future. All contemporaries knew was their ruinous past and insecure present. More than half of those who participated in a survey at the time said they would not save in the future or were unsure if they would do so.[7] The Korean War in 1950 added new jitters. Why risk losing savings again? Have fun now! Churches and banks—the twin guardians of moral economy—were in despair. A year after the currency reform, Archbishop of Cologne Josef Frings lambasted the high living, gambling, and excessive partying that "endanger our youth, ruin marriage and family, weaken our manpower, and cripple our will to save."[8] People were deceiving themselves, savings banks in Hesse said in 1950. "We keep pretending that we did not lose a war. In reality we are destitute. The self-delusion is the result of us consuming our entire income—to some extent, even going into debt."[9]

Ten years after the war, researchers asked manual and clerical workers whether they thought it made sense to plan ahead. "*Nein*," one told them, "the state has cheated us often enough . . . two currency reforms, bad social insurance." "My parents had twice made provision," another said, "and both times it went kaput."[10] One in three were deeply skeptical. Even among those who took a more cautious view, only a tiny fraction had a savings account. The fact that banks in these years reported a sudden surge in deposits during popular campaigns, such as World Saving Day (October 30), suggests that many people were hoarding cash at home.[11]

Hyperinflation does not automatically convert people to the idea of saving for the sake of stability. Hungary, in 1946, and Yugoslavia, in 1994, suffered extreme cases, but people there did not become committed savers, while in countries that went through long periods of high inflation such as Argentina (1974–91) and Brazil (1980–95), saving fluctuated greatly.[12]

Saving had to be taught, promoted, and internalized. Savings banks had a marketing blitz and lured new customers with "prize" and "premium" accounts that promised cash awards and made it easier to plan for bigger purchases such as furniture, sometimes with credit thrown in. Up and down the land, children were targeted in school competitions. In 1958, more than 300,000 children took part in the small state of Hesse. Along with crayons and calendars, every single new pupil received a savings coupon.[13]

Crucially, thrift had powerful friends in politics and finance. President Theodor Heuss addressed the public on World Saving Day in 1952, explaining that saving combined the private with the public interest. "By thinking of himself, the saver helps others."[14] Self-reliance meant he was no burden on society. Saving was about more than a few marks and pfennigs: it set people free. And it gave them an interest in stability and order, unlike people who followed adventurers. Such views were not new, but they carried extra weight in a young democracy after years of Nazi dictatorship.

They were also the imperative of economic recovery. Germany, like Japan and Italy, was desperate for capital to rebuild its industries. People needed to save, not spend, so banks could then lend the money to industry. The government prodded them with a range of incentives, large and small, from generous tax benefits to savings vouchers for newborns, which banks handed out to newlyweds in registry offices.[15] Unlike Japan, Germany received American Marshall Plan funds, but savings banks warned that this must not be allowed to paralyze the "will to self-help" and leave the country dependent on the "changeable will of a foreign people." Unless Germans wanted to end up like "helots" (Sparta's slaves), they needed to rediscover thrift. "A healthy people help themselves," the savings banks in Hesse said (which happened to also be the slogan of the Nazi winter relief aid).[16]

Finally, there was the central bank, the Bundesbank, the monetary high priest of moderation. Its fight against inflation made it the natural ally of the saver. That was not its primary motive, though. At a time when exchange rates were fixed and trade barriers no option, keeping prices and wages in check was a way of giving German exports a leg up over their competitors—a form of "monetary mercantilism."[17] The Deutschmark was not as stable as often imagined. In the first two decades of the Federal Republic, it lost one third of its value. But it was stronger than the British pound and the French franc, which lost almost half their value in those years. That price gap explains part of the economic miracle. For a foreign buyer, a Volkswagen Beetle became progressively cheaper than a Morris Minor or Citroën 2CV.

The Bundesbank's power was literally the stuff of legend. The Allies were keen to have an independent central bank, while Konrad Adenauer wanted it to be an arm of his government. It was one of the few battles the chancellor lost. Whenever possible, the Bank of German States and the Bundesbank that succeeded it in 1957 would invoke the ghost of inflation to defend its autonomy. There could be only one lesson from hyperinflation in 1923, with its terrifying specter of people rolling wheelbarrows full of devalued notes through the street to pay for a loaf of bread. To be able to resist short-term opportunism, a central bank needed to be independent. In an early form of public relations, the Bundesbank hired its own journalist to proselytize this story.[18] Its version of the past was more myth than history. In 1923, the Reichsbank had been independent of the government, but that had guaranteed neither economic nor political stability; the final crisis-ridden years of Weimar that led to Hitler were hardly an advertisement.

Ultimately, the Bundesbank's strength derived from the relative weakness of the young democratic state. Adenauer attacked the central bank for being accountable to neither parliament nor government. That was precisely the point. It presented itself as the servant of the public interest against all the sectional interests that were only thinking of themselves. "We do not serve the [sic] industry," the first president of the Bank of German States, Wilhelm Vocke, explained in 1955, "nor do we serve the workers, or agriculture, or any other group ... Even the largest groups are minorities when compared to the grand total of our nation, whom we serve undividedly; this total includes the housewives ... the officials, the pensioners, and, last but not least, the savers." It was important to nip inflation in the bud, as he had done by raising interest rates. A "hard currency" could not be defended with "soft measures."[19] Only an independent central bank was able to safeguard the nation against extravagant spending plans, right or left. When independence came up for renewal in 1957, the central bankers could count on Erhard, now Adenauer's economics minister, to whom a dependent bank meant inflation.

The key word in these years was therefore *masshalten* ("moderation") with regard to earnings as well as spending. Business, unions, and consumers all needed to show restraint. It was a cultural as much as an economic concern. Vocke's successor, Karl Blessing, worried that "dancing around the golden calf" would upend the values of the *Bürgertum*. Was technological progress "a blessing or a curse?" he asked in a public lecture in the midst of the boom, in 1962. As long as it assisted "cultural development [*Bildung*] and ethical improvement," it was to be welcomed. "But the through-and-through consumer who cannot get enough is not a pleasing sight." Fortunately, he concluded, there were signs that "respect for eternal ethical-moral values" was on the rebound.[20]

How successful was the Bundesbank in implanting its ideals in the hearts and minds at home? Jacques Delors, the president of the European Commission, was sure. "Not all Germans believe in God," he said in 1992, "but they all believe in the Bundesbank."[21]

In truth, German attitudes were more conflicted and changeable than the bankers cared to admit. In 1963, at the height of the Cold War, Germans told pollsters that inflation terrified them even more than the end of the world. Seven years later, by contrast, with unemployment on the rise, more than twice as many respondents wanted the state to spend and create jobs as wanted it to save and keep prices down.[22] It would be a similar story in recessions to come in the mid-1970s, 1986, and the late 1990s. Nor were all savers convinced that the Bundesbank defended their interests, or that the Deutschmark was as steady in its value as it was made out to be. In 1968, the central bank was attacked for its "crimes against savers," robbing them of 50 percent of their purchasing power.[23] In 1990, only 30 percent of Germans even knew that the Bundesbank was independent. As many credited the stable DM to industry as to the central bank. More people felt that it was a servant to other banks, not to the public interest. In the late 1990s, most Germans wanted the European central bank to be subject to the European parliament, not independent like their own.[24]

Whether Germans are particularly averse to inflation is debatable. In 1976, surveys began to ask Europeans what they saw as the most important task of their respective state: political stability, fighting inflation, or protecting freedom of speech. During the next two decades, 41 percent of Belgians and 31 percent of French respondents put price stability at the top. Among Germans, it was only 19 percent, and the trend was downward. Not surprisingly, perhaps, countries with low inflation like Germany and Denmark tended to care less about price stability—until prices shot up.

It is easy to assume that Germans know more about money than they actually do. Barely a quarter were able to give the rough rate of inflation, according to an investigation by banks in 2011; among young adults, it was a stunning 6 percent.[25] All this does not mean that Germans do not worry about rising prices, merely that price stability is not as much of a fetish as it is often presumed to be.

In East Germany, saving was no less an official mantra, albeit with a socialist tenor. The Soviets closed all banks in their zone but in autumn 1945 reopened communal savings banks to promote thrift. When East Germany got its own currency reform in 1948, it hurt savers less than in the West—a savings bank in Dresden (East) was left with 25 percent of its deposits, compared to 5 percent in Würzburg (West). For Karl Marx, savings banks were "the golden chain" by which capitalist regimes controlled the working class. By providing housing, health, and security in old age, socialism would liberate thrift. Instead of having to save for a rainy day, people could put aside a little for something special. That was the ideal. In reality, shortages made savings a national necessity to generate much-needed capital for firms. In the 1960s, a quarter of total investment came from savings. And since there were few things to buy, savings deposits absorbed the excess liquidity when wages were raised.

Like its western neighbor, the GDR had savings promotions for parents and schoolchildren with vouchers and lottery prizes; teenagers in the socialist youth body (FDJ) saved for their excursions while parents blessed with a fifth child received an "honorary godparent gift" from the president worth 500 Marks, which had to be deposited until school age. Unlike in West Germany, saving was not altogether voluntary but rather a socialist duty. Starting in 1951, firms pressed workers to commit 3 percent of their wages to a national fund for reconstruction—in exchange, they received a lottery ticket for one of the modern apartments on the capital's monumental new boulevard, the Stalin-Allee (today's Karl-Marx-Allee).

Credit, too, was a servant of socialist planning. From 1971 on, young couples on low incomes could apply for up to 5,000 Marks of interest-free credit to furnish their home—each newborn reduced their obligation, until the third child, when it was completely written off. (The policy was copied from the Nazis.) By the time the Wall came down, almost 3 million citizens had availed themselves of these cheap loans. In other areas, however, incentives fell flat. The GDR sponsored deposits with building societies even more than the West, offering workers interest-free credit for the bulk of their construction costs. There was so little subscription that the program was shelved in 1970. What good was a building society plan without building materials for sale?

Overall, East Germans saved less than their cousins in the West, and they saved differently. When their wages declined—as happened in 1962 and 1980—they did not tighten their belts but dipped into their savings instead. Saving was part of the waiting game for the moment scarce goods came up for sale. The regime tried to make the best of it by introducing special purchase plans for unwanted record players and models of furniture that were acquiring dust in the warehouse—with limited success. Instead, most people preferred to keep a few thousand Marks under their mattress.[26]

FAMILY VALUES

In modern societies, money is a symbolic marker of people's lives, recording their ambitions and accomplishments. Do you spend what you earn and live in the moment, save, or buy now and pay later because you are banking on making big strides in the future? Economists view saving as a rational response to financial opportunities (such as high or low interest rates) and the ups and downs of life, as the prudential foresight of middle age gives way to old age, where one empties the coffers ("dissaving"). What this ignores is that people can have radically different ideas about what is rational in the same situation. And diverging money cultures are the result of upbringing, memory (and amnesia), and ideas of character as well as markets.

In 1996, a group of sociologists interviewed more than a hundred Germans from three generations. The earliest were born around 1900 and experienced the hyperinflation of 1923, their children lived through the currency conversion of 1948 and the economic miracle, and their grandchildren grew up in the 1960s and witnessed the fall of the Wall. Half of the first generation said they did not draw any lessons from their savings being wiped out in 1923, and only a quarter tried to drum advice into their children. Many considered it a "stroke of fate," beyond their comprehension, let alone their control. "See how you get through it and make the best out of this whole story," were the only words of wisdom one man received from his grandfather.

Families that did take lessons from their losses reached diametrically opposite conclusions. Herr Sittler (born in 1908) had only one motto for his wife: "Buy! Buy!... I do not want to pile up money... I want to convert it so that we get something out of it." Their daughter and granddaughter agreed, although the latter also paid into a pension plan and took out life insurance. Several families adopted a "fairly positive" view of credit.

In stark contrast, every blow to the family finances made Frau Möller only thriftier. Her father lost his small haulage firm in 1924, her husband his shop in 1948. "*Nein, nein, nein*," she told the researchers, what would the world come to if, instead of saving, people were just spending or, worse, taking out credit? "Morally, that would be terrible, because the others would suffer... one would be taking things away from them, *nein*, to me it is fraud." The currency conversion wiped out a bricklayer's savings but did not make a dent in the values he had been raised with: "Prussian values... loyal, good, sincere, a sense of duty." Frau Menne lost not only her husband in the war but also 10,000 Reichsmark in the currency conversion of 1948. Her thrift remained unshaken, and helped her persevere with the porcelain shop she was now running by herself. Saving in these cases was a psychological survival strategy more than a financial risk assessment. Thrift helped maintain values of right and wrong in a chaotic world that had lost its moral compass and gave people the feeling they had some control over their lives. It restored a sense of pride. Frau Menne said she managed "because we did not make any big claims on life . . . always content with what we had . . . honesty is the best policy."[27]

In practice, however, saving and credit were not necessarily mutually exclusive. They increasingly complemented each other as the economic miracle got underway in West Germany. While wages were slow to rise, shop windows were bursting with goods. Installment credit and loans from parents bridged the gap. At the end of 1952, almost every fourth family wore shirts and dresses they had bought on installment plans—it was such a lucrative market that the savings banks began offering credit, for example, to buy furniture. The following year, 15 percent of all retail sales were financed with credit—only half as many as in the United States but far from insignificant.[28] And the bigger the item, the more important credit became. How did you pay for your most expensive acquisition last year? a survey asked people in 1957. Thirty-one percent had put aside money, 27 percent bought theirs in installments.[29]

A young printer in Munich told of his money woes in 1961. Hans G. had recently gotten engaged and finally had the prospect of an apartment. Barely twenty-two, he did not have enough for either the deposit or the furniture. Housekeeping for this young couple was a formidable juggling act, with all available instruments: savings and credit, gifts and spending. Hans first turned to his mother-in-law, but in vain. A widowed expellee, she had spent all she had received from "burden sharing" on her children, a new sewing machine, and "a very expensive accordion." He had more luck with the local cooperative bank, which lent him 2,000 DM. After paying several months' rent in advance, this left him with only 25 DM ($6 at the time), with which he bought an electric iron—the "ironing board will come later." The landlord provided a stove, his fiancée bed linen, and his mother-in-law a stereo for which she had no need, now that she had an accordion.

Every week, the couple went to the shops to compare prices. He wrote "long lists" of what they needed, divided into "absolutely necessary, necessary and, if need be, later." A colleague's wife worked in a furniture store and sold them a table and four chairs at half price—it was still twice as much as they had budgeted for, but since they would last, they would "rather do without a fridge."

For their wedding, coworkers gave them cash, which Hans used to pay for the photographer and the black Mercedes and Chevrolet Impala he had hired for the day. Storing food was a problem, because their cellar was too warm to serve as a larder. If only they had waited with the furniture! The cheapest fridge cost 475 DM. His wife wanted to buy it immediately on installment, but he would not have it. After all, he still had to pay back the 2,000 DM they had borrowed, and he was unsure how much overtime there would be in the near future. What his wife earned as a shop assistant barely covered the rent and her cosmetics and trips to the hairdresser. Ritual gift-giving meant, annoyingly, that they had to start saving for Christmas in August. "If I add it all up, I always end up spending more than I had planned. I get stuff that I do not absolutely need, and then don't have the money for what I actually do need." Trying to find suitable gifts at a price he could afford tired him out—except when shopping for his wife, who loved Chanel N° 5. In February, his mood lifted and he took his wife on a one-week skiing holiday to Austria.

For this young couple, thrift, prudential planning, and a sense of "essential needs" coexisted with little luxuries, impulse purchases, and the pursuit of "wants."[30] Hans hardly lacked courage; he was among the first conscientious objectors and joined the Easter Marches for peace. But he found it embarrassing to ask the personnel department for the certificate of employment he needed to be able to apply for credit with the bank: "It sucks; now all the women up there know that I need money and don't have it."[31]

In this regard, West Germany was behind the United States, where consumer credit had come to be accepted as a sign of the up-and-coming man and woman. Installment buying continued to be known as "the dowry of the little man." Still, in Germany, the character of credit was in flux, too, as can be seen from the advice column in *Hörzu*, the TV and radio magazine read by millions every week. A wife's purchase of a fur coat in installments sparked a heated debate in 1959. One reader warned of "American conditions" and a revolution of the sexes: to pay for such luxuries, housewives would have to swap their aprons for a paying job. Others defended credit as a spur to self-improvement—an argument American prophets of abundance had made after 1900. "Frau Irene," the paper's popular advice columnist (in real life, "she" was Walther von Hollander, a writer who had already in the Weimar years favored marriage as a partnership between equals; his nom de plume was the most guarded secret in German publishing), took a more liberal view. Young people's "iron saving is very laudable," Frau Irene told readers in 1959, but if "the times of deprivation last too long, they get weary." To save every penny until there was enough to set up a comfortable home together meant sacrificing many years of happiness. Irene told a nineteen-year-old housemaid that, contrary to her parents' wishes, she was quite right to do with her pay as she pleased rather than sending it home to be saved; some might consider it "reckless," but in money as in life, "everyone should be free to pursue their own happiness," as long as they did not become a burden on their parents.[32] That well-known motto had been coined by Frederick the Great in support of religious toleration. A more easygoing attitude to money now cited "Prussian values," too.

SAVE YOURSELF RICH!

Savings campaigners were in despair about the moral decline they saw all around them. A study for the Federation of Savings Banks in 1961 found that, in addition to their pocket money, most children were spoiled by their parents and grandparents with additional cash to buy "sweets, ice cream, books, records, bicycle parts, excursions, perfume, and stockings." The worst were children with two working parents. Instead of sending them to school with a homemade sandwich, they let them buy cake! "Standards have mostly been lost," the author sighed. A secondary school in Cologne confronted parents with two hundred items their youngsters had abandoned, including brand-new sneakers. Two thirds of eighth graders regularly went to the movies to watch films released for adults. "Do the parents know what they are doing to their children?" They were creating a "soft" generation. Showing off, extravagance, and a lack of self-control were the inevitable side effects of this "wrong appreciation of money." Only saving could teach them the healthy middle way between the extremes of wastefulness and stinginess.[33]

In fact, West German savings banks played an active role in the shift toward a more hedonist and materialist attitude. Instead of preaching thrift as a sign of virtue and precaution, they began to promote saving as the road to riches. The slogans of the savings campaigns in these years tell the story: "Be thrifty and help yourself" (1954); "Who saves gets ahead" (1961); and "Wealth starts with saving" (1965). By the early 1970s, savings banks were targeting young families as "the rich of tomorrow." The savings book had morphed into a "book of wishes."[34]

Two developments fostered the idea of "Save yourself rich." One was the expansion of personal banking. Beginning in the mid-1950s, wages were increasingly paid directly into "saver-giro" accounts, which included a current account and offered easy payment and "credit for everyone," advertisements explained.[35] New "contract" and "target" savings accounts automatically deducted a specified amount each month. Saving here ceased to be a function of willpower and habit: once set up, it became a standing order. The second and decisive boost came from the government. In the early 1950s, all parties, including the Liberals and the Christian Democrats, promoted the coownership of firms as a way of giving citizens a share in wealth creation. The firms, understandably, were not keen, nor were many unions. Special tax exemptions for savers offered an alternative route to creating assets; deposits with building societies—credit unions—had enjoyed tax privileges since 1934. From the late 1950s, a series of policies encouraged people to save for a home or to build up future wealth; shares in Volkswagen became available in 1960. Employees could ask their firm for up to 312 DM of their monthly wages to be paid into a savings bank or building society, without having social insurance deducted from it; the amount was doubled in 1970. Building one's own home was subsidized. In total, these programs generated 128 billion DM for "Save to build" (*Bau-Sparen*) between 1950 and 1974, at a cost to the state of 37 billion DM.[36]

Why would a state not known for its generosity be handing out so much money so liberally? Promoting saving was, partly, about attracting capital for industry. It was also about a particular ideal of a good society where fairness was based on merit. Adenauer laid out the principle when he took power in 1949: "Giving the diligent and hardworking every opportunity to advance" was an "essential condition" of social peace.[37]

The German "social state" (*Sozialstaat*) was a hybrid creature, and it might be better to speak of it as a fiscal-social state. While one hand helped the poor and vulnerable, the other promoted the wealth of the middle classes.[38] The bonuses to savers rewarded those who wanted to "get ahead," stand on their own feet and sit in their own home. The goal was a republic of property-owning citizens. For Christian Democrats, the saving and building programs were a counterweight to socialism: they promised people greater wealth without redistribution. "Wealth for all" was Erhard's famous slogan, but the industrious in particular deserved a better life. Privileging saving and homeownership was the fiscal equivalent of Adenauer's pension reform: reward was tied to "performance" (*Leistung*).

In reality, rewards were increasingly propped up by the state, including pensions, the state chipping in with special grants (*Sonderzuschuss*) that reached the equivalent of 26 billion euros a year by the time of reunification and ballooned thereafter. By 1969, more than a third of all households had a savings account that offered tax advantages, and almost a quarter had a "building-savings" account. The better-off took the greatest advantage—44 percent of civil servants put money into "building-savings" but only 20 percent of manual workers.[39] Tax policy encouraged those with high incomes to buy real estate.

Clearly, not all savers were the same. There was an emerging divide between old-fashioned prudential savers and the new breed who were accumulating wealth. The first deposited their money into a basic interest-bearing account while inflation was eating away at it; the second put theirs in land, a home, and, beginning in the 1970s, securities, and saw theirs grow. The belief in the virtue of saving thus disguised its role in widening inequality.

THE ANXIETIES OF AFFLUENCE

Appeals to thrift drew on deeper fears of materialism. Compared to neighboring commercial empires like Britain and the Netherlands, Germany had been slow to embrace the world of goods in the early modern period. Guilds and churches were powerful bastions against fashion and novelties that threatened to undermine the rule of men and the word of God—women sporting colorful cotton scarves from India were fined or thrown in prison in Württemberg in the eighteenth century.[40]

To critics, Americanization in the 1950s and 1960s was simply the latest guise of their old enemy Mammon. Suspicion of consumer culture was one thing that united churches, conservatives, and the 68ers on the left. The economic miracle simultaneously threatened Christianity, *Kultur*, and the authentic self. Christ's sacrifice faced unprecedented competition with consumer desires, the outgoing head of the Protestant aid agency Evangelisches Hilfswerk warned in 1964. The more people desired, the less they thought of their Savior. The challenge was getting bigger by the day, because "with the help of billions and the cleverest brains," capitalism was "artificially keeping alive the insatiable human demand for goods." People were losing the ability to make sacrifices as installment credit tempted them to buy more than they could afford. They were entering a lonely, mechanized world in which everything was for sale.[41] That same year, a brochure promoting volunteering warned of the dangers of materialism. What was called "progress," young readers were told, was really the "production of affluence . . . a tyrant to which all thinking and planning is directed and which relentlessly swings its whip over the mass of consumers." The authors hoped that the young would rebel against that "soulless dictatorship" and seek their true self in the family. Only "sacrifice, suffering, and compassion" made life worth living.[42] These views had the support of the Federal Ministry for the Family and Youth as well as the churches.

Substitute free love for early marriage, add a few references to Marx, Freud, and the Nazis, and this was not so different from what young radicals were preaching in their communes and "happenings." Consumerism brainwashed individuals and alienated them from their true selves and from each other. In 1963, a group of "subversive" antiauthoritarian artists attacked "high-industrial consumer society as a perfectly internalized fascist system which understands birth as the beginning of conditioning through the hypnoidal state of trance"; the hypnoid state was a condition for hysteria caused by sexual daydreams, according to the founding fathers of psychoanalysis, Josef Breuer and his protégé Sigmund Freud. People were "conditioned through advertising." A year later, flyers targeted the "masseurs of the soul" who were planting needs that people did not have.[43]

These texts took their cue from the situationist Guy Debord and the neo-Marxist Herbert Marcuse, who extended Marx's analysis of commodification from work to consumer culture to show how alienation had become all-pervasive. People were slaves to television, Marcuse wrote, and so hooked on the satisfaction of their needs that they were easily controlled and repressed. His Frankfurt School colleagues Theodor Adorno and Max Horkheimer had already warned in 1944 from their American exile that the "culture industry" of radio and movies was grooming its audience through "retroactive needs" into a state of passive conformity.[44] These ideas attracted an international audience, but the supposed affinity between consumerism and a fascist personality struck a particular chord with the young in the land of the perpetrators. Marcuse's *One-Dimensional Man* was an instant best seller when it appeared in German in 1967.

Anti-consumerism began with a playful mockery of advertisements and a call for boycotts. The "Subversive Aktion" updated the biblical story of Christmas to read: "And it came to pass in the days of the economic miracle, that everyone was classified as a consumer." "Today, love is born as a commodity which means *Gleichschaltung* [the Nazis' total coordination of society] and exploitation." People were urged to "extinguish the candles" at Christmas, "think of the misery" of their lives, and "unite in resistance" against such consumerist rituals.[45]

Direct action soon took a violent turn. The radical artist Dieter Kunzelmann became the chief provocateur of the first commune in Berlin. The son of a savings bank director, Kunzelmann knew the weak spots of bourgeois society. One was sex, the other commerce. In 1962, he and fellow artists in the situationist group Spur ("Trace") were convicted for blasphemy and pornography. In 1968, one year after three hundred people died in an accidental fire in a department store in Brussels, the Kommune I asked, "When will the Berlin department stores burn?" Firebombs were exploded in a Frankfurt department store, though no one was hurt. Among those arrested were Andreas Baader and Gudrun Ensslin, who would found the terrorist Red Army Faction. "Consumerism terrorizes you, we terrorize the goods," was their justification.[46] The war against "*Konsumterror*" and American imperialism embraced violent antisemitism. On November 9, 1969—the anniversary of Kristallnacht—a timed bomb was set to blow up the Jewish community center in Berlin. Hundreds of deaths were prevented thanks to an outdated detonator. The group that claimed responsibility for the attack were the "Black Rats." Its leader was Kunzelmann. The attack did not result in a persecution. The following year, however, Kunzelmann was sentenced to three years in prison after a Molotov attack on the villa of a Berlin journalist.

Affluence troubled more than extremists. A sensitive high school student in the town of Osnabrück kept a diary in 1962, half a year after the Berlin Wall had gone up. "Our political mentality is being dissolved by the terrible fight over the golden calf," he wrote. In an approaching war with "the Reds," what "use is all the technological progress, if we spiritually rot away? Ours is an age of excess."[47] Nine years later, a school magazine in nearby Bielefeld showed on its cover a naked man tied to a TV next to a boy carrying a submachine gun. Its title was "*Konsum KZ* [concentration camp], profit from manipulating leisure." Inside, articles criticized profit-driven pop music and the manipulative fashion industry. Reports on the "Third World" and the words of Che Guevara put affluence at home in perspective.[48] Young reform-minded Christian Democrats warned that hyperconsumption was polluting the air and destroying cities with private cars and shopping malls. Advertising was all about the image, not the product. Their list of guilty parties ("*Schuld*") was long and headed by the Wertheim department store and its food hall that overflowed with eight thousand items.[49] Such jeremiads would receive a fresh boost from the Club of Rome's report on the "limits of growth" in 1972, which happened to coincide with the opening of the first McDonald's in West Germany, in Munich.

Anxieties about affluence did not mean that people were consuming less—to the contrary. Educated, better-off contemporaries condemned the materialist "masses" but rarely turned their critique on themselves. When hoi polloi spread their towels on the Costa Brava, it was consumerism. When cultivated *Bürger* or radical students drove to Italy in a gas-guzzling Mercedes, it was *Kultur* and self-discovery. By focusing on the aesthetic disposition of the individual, the elites simultaneously asserted their distinction from "the masses" and airbrushed out their own material appetite. Discerning taste came with more cars, more flights, and bigger homes. In 1971, for example, senior managers and civil servants took twice as many holiday trips as workers.[50] Those attacking *Konsumterror* were equally inconsistent. The terrorist Baader loved fast cars, and was eventually arrested behind the wheel of an exclusive Iso Rivolta. Moving into a commune did not automatically mean sharing more and consuming less. A study in 1974 found that communes had more televisions, stereos, and washers and dryers than other households—one had three private cars parked outside.[51] Germany might have had a bad conscience, but it was still very much a consumer society.

In the economic miracle, real wages were lagging behind growth, but they were rising swiftly nonetheless, and this expanded the demand for everything from automobiles and television sets to lipstick and liquor. The savings rate only rose to 12 percent, and this left plenty to spend. "Not so long ago, sparkling wine was good enough," one young sergeant wrote, "today it has to be champagne." No one, he complained in 1963, made birthday presents by hand anymore.[52]

Such nostalgia conveniently ignored long-term trends. Consumer culture was not a sudden American invasion in a land of modest, self-sufficient burghers. Imperial Germany had department stores. Before that, drapers' shops offered sales and discounts. Leisure and entertainment were sources of self-fulfillment well before the 1960s, women's diaries show.[53] The much idealized work ethic was an ideal, no more. Already in 1929, a study of young workers found that half of them viewed work as "coercion" (*Zwang*) and another quarter merely as a means "to get ahead." Twenty-four years later, with the economic miracle barely begun, another survey concluded that "the joy of work or the meaning of life as a motive for working, separate from making money and living in comfort, does not appear in the responses at all."[54] One reason the tsunami of goods that followed swept so easily across the land was that the moral defenses had already been largely washed away.

In the course of the 1960s, spending on cosmetics increased more than threefold, and by the end of the decade women in Munich and Frankfurt were using as much lipstick and eyeliner as their counterparts in Paris and London. German "teenagers" followed on the heels of their American cousins, with their own distinctive music and fashion. A "teenage fair" in Düsseldorf in 1969 attracted 300,000 of them in just over a week—German singers now shared the stage with the Small Faces; two months later, Pink Floyd and Fleetwood Mac rocked in Essen.[55] Counter to the neo-Marxist dystopia of ever greater uniformity and inauthenticity, consumer culture diversified into subcultures that offered new identities and experiences. A fixation with the alienation of labor made Marxists blind to the liberating use of things in self-fashioning.

The Greens added a new environmental critique, but hardly curbed the craving for more. Between 1965 and 1975, car ownership doubled from 10 to 20 million vehicles; by 1989, it reached 31 million, almost one car for every two people. The dip in the sale of new cars in the wake of the oil crisis of 1973 was short-lived. Car-free Sundays, first introduced in November of that year, proved so unpopular that the umbrella organization of environmental groups (Deutscher Naturschutzring) changed its strategy and appealed to drivers' self-interest as consumers: taking their foot off the gas and switching to a bicycle now and then would save them cash at the fuel pump that they then could "spend on other things!" Its new motto in 1981 was "*Optimismus*."[56]

By funding satellite towns, public housing, and transport and energy infrastructure, the state actively promoted a new culture of mobility and comfort. It was after the first oil crisis that most Germans began to shower and bathe more than once a week. Municipal energy providers had dedicated advertising campaigns to rebrand daily hot showers as "fun!" and "wonderful" to overcome the suspicion that frequent bathing was "thinning out the skin."[57] The hot water—and the gas, oil, and (coal-powered) electricity needed to fire the boilers—was consumption, too.

By the mid-1970s, most Germans were not only consuming more but also feeling good about it. A study in 1975 found 64 percent of Italians and 52 percent of the French to be skeptical of or hostile toward consumer society. Among Germans it was 39 percent.[58] The "Revolutionary Cells" carried on the fight against *Konsumterror* in the late 1980s with attacks on the International Monetary Fund and Siemens as well as department stores—the term retains its appeal with some anti-globalization activists to this day. In general, however, critical groups increasingly made their peace with the world of goods.

The battle *against* consumption turned into one *for* more ethical consumption. Campaigns for a "fair" price for small producers had a long history that reached back to the boycotts of slave-grown sugar in the years around 1800. The trade justice movement that emerged in the 1960s and 1970s drew its strength from three sources: missionary networks, Catholic and Protestant concern for the global poor, and student solidarity with colonial struggles. The "Third World" shops that opened in Germany in the early 1970s took their inspiration from a Dutch precursor. Initially, underdevelopment in the global South and affluence in the rich North appeared to be opposite sides of the same coin. As the group Kritischer Konsum ("Critical Consumption") explained in the run-up to Christmas in 1970, Germans were able to enjoy lots of cheap chocolate only "because the farmer in Cameroon or Ghana is paid a famine wage."[59] To help the global poor demanded simple living at home in addition to a "fair" price overseas. Students and church groups believed that they could learn a sense of balance and humility from the "Third World," as we have seen.[60]

The initial "Third World" shops saw themselves as schools of a more responsible, alternative lifestyle. By the 1990s, however, they were overtaken by a certified "fair trade" label that went mainstream. Fair trade mutated into a brand. Fair trade coffee, chocolate, and bananas appeared in supermarkets next to candy and soft drinks by global corporations. Saarbrücken became the first fair trade town in Germany, in 2009—today, it is joined by 1,400 other towns and fair trade schools. There are now almost 8,000 fair trade products on sale. In their defense, supporters can point to the rise in sales following the move from dingy, alternative shops into the aisles of big, bright supermarkets and the signing up of coffee giants such as Tchibo and Darboven. Their turnover has shot up from 190 million euros in 2003 to 2 billion euros in 2019. Still, all those purchases take up a tiny corner in people's shopping baskets. On average, a German shopper spends a mere 22 euros (about $20) on fair trade products in an entire year (2019), slightly more than the French and Italians though less than the Irish and Swedes and, especially, the Swiss (80 euros). Whichever scale we apply, economic or ethical, 22 euros a year is a drop in the ocean.[61]

The growing moral value of money was not limited to consumer spending. It advanced across society. Immanuel Kant, the father of German philosophy, had drawn a sharp line between money and dignity. "In the kingdom of ends," he wrote in the late eighteenth century, "everything has either a price or a dignity."[62] Something with a price tag could be replaced by something equivalent. Human dignity was above money. The German Civil Code, which took effect in 1900, devoted a single article to compensation for immaterial damage (such as to health or reputation), and that was unsympathetic. As a popular saying at the time had it: A person did not have much honor to lose if they hoped to repair it by suing for money.

The wind began to blow in a new direction in the 1960s. In 1961, Soraya, the ex-wife of the shah of Iran, sued a German tabloid magazine for printing a fake interview with her. A district court awarded her 15,000 DM in damages ($3,700 at the time). The landmark ruling was later confirmed by the Constitutional Court. It was just the beginning. Caroline of Monaco, in 1996, received 180,000 DM for a fabricated announcement of her wedding in the illustrated magazine *Bunte.* With the civil law no use, judges turned to the constitutional principles of "inalienable" human dignity and the right to develop one's personality to justify damages. Financial compensation was intended to give satisfaction and to deter similar intrusion. By British and American standards, the amounts were modest—the actress Koo Stark received £300,000 from one British newspaper for a made-up story about rekindling an affair with Prince Andrew, and Elke Sommer, a German teenage beauty turned Hollywood actress, a phenomenal $3.3 million by a Los Angeles court when her glamorous costar Zsa Zsa Gabor publicly denigrated her in German magazines as being so poor that she had to sell hand-knitted sweaters. (Admittedly, virtually everyone was poor compared with Gabor, who lived in a nine-thousand-square-foot mansion in Bel Air.) Still, the floodgates had opened. In 2015, a meteorologist received a record 635,000 euros from a tabloid in compensation for false rape accusations. The following year, ex-chancellor Kohl sued his former ghostwriter for 5 million euros for violating his right to personality by publishing more than a hundred quotations attributed to him; one of them was that Angela Merkel did not know how to eat with a knife and fork. Kohl died in 2017, before he could collect the 1 million euros he was awarded; his widow kept up the fight, but such awards could not be inherited.[63]

Kant had been turned on his head. Not only was dignity no longer considered priceless, in the interests of deterrence (aimed at the media) immaterial damage came to carry a higher price tag than physical harm. A sixteen-year-old pregnant girl, who had been repeatedly raped and threatened in the seventy-two hours she was under the control of her tormentor, was awarded only 50,000 euros in 2013 for her ordeal and the scars it left behind—and that was double the amount of similar previous cases. When a mentally and physically disabled woman was raped and impregnated by her father, the court ruled that she was due only a fraction of that amount since she was unable to obtain "satisfaction" from damages. In 2007, the record sum for the "complete destruction" of personality ran to 620,000 euros, and was awarded to a child who had ten years earlier suffered serious brain damage at birth due to malpractice.[64]

THE HAVES AND THE HAVE-NOTS

In 2010, the Bundesbank began to carry out triennial surveys of the wealth of the nation. The first findings were jaw-dropping. In 2013, the richest 10 percent owned 60 percent of all net wealth, while the bottom 9 percent had no wealth at all or were in debt. Among the poorest 25 percent, the average household had assets and savings worth only 5,400 euros, down from

6,600 euros four years earlier. The Gini coefficient, which measures inequality, stood at 76 percent, well above the European average (63 percent). If we draw a line between the richest and the poorest half in Europe, the household at the median line had total assets worth 140,000 euros. In Germany, it was only 51,400 euros (around $68,000 at the time). One of the richest countries in Europe was also one of the most unequal.[65]

Measuring inequality is hugely complicated because it comes in many forms—wealth, wages, health, education, and opportunities—and these do not all point in the same direction. The German health system, for example, provides high-quality and affordable health care regardless of income. The school system, by contrast, continues to let down the children and grandchildren of "guest workers," as we have seen. When it comes to economic inequality, Germany has been part of a broad trend of widening extremes across the West since the 1970s, caused by globalization, the deregulation of labor and financial markets, and an exodus of good jobs.[66] Income inequality in Germany rose dramatically after reunification along with unemployment; workers' share of gross income fell from 55 percent to 48 percent between 1992 and 2007. According to a recent estimate, incomes under Merkel were as unequal as under the Kaiser a century earlier.[67]

Income inequality stopped growing after 2008. What has entrenched inequality since has been the ever more uneven distribution of wealth, the result of inheritance and tax benefits for the rich; the richest 10 percent received half of all inheritances in 2005–20.[68] Statistics can produce an exaggerated picture, however, because the data does not include Germans' pension wealth, which is considerable, and the country today includes many recent refugees (who tend to be poorer).[69]

From the outside, German worries about inequality can appear inflated. The country continues to have one of the most generous health and welfare systems in the world. In 2019, on the eve of the coronavirus pandemic, it devoted 30 percent of its GDP to social benefits, more than in the 1990s (27 percent), 1980s (25 percent), or 1970s (23 percent).[70] Theaters and concert halls receive generous public subsidies and offer cheap tickets for the poor, students, and the elderly. If such benefits and transfers were taken into account, income inequality (which looks at wages and salaries) would look less pronounced.

On the inside, however, signs of inequality are eating away at Germany's self-image as a just society. For a long time, the country had been in denial of inequality.[71] Extremes were meant to be an Anglo-American disease. Now, Germany, too, had ever richer heirs and CEOs with huge salaries at one end, and low-paid workers and pensioners who went to food banks on the other. Inequality, like poverty, is relative as well as absolute. The European Union considers people to live at "risk of poverty" when they earn less than 60 percent of the median income in their country. In 2020, that was almost every fourth German (23 percent) but only every eighth Czech (12 percent); the EU average was 22 percent.[72] It might be said that a German who had 2,000 euros a month ($2,300) was not really poor and would be considered well off in the Czech Republic, but people consider themselves poor in relation to their fellow citizens, not to distant strangers, let alone to those suffering absolute poverty in the global South.

The simultaneous expansion of riches and poverty during a period of growth and (from 2006) falling unemployment brought into collision the two core principles of the "social market economy": to reward success and enterprise, and at the same time to guarantee equal opportunities and a basic minimum for all. What happened to merit and fairness, if a growing chunk of wealth was passed on by parents to their children, who had never lifted a finger? This is what made the widening extremes of wealth (rather than income) such a sensitive issue.

THE BURDEN OF DEBT

Inequality had particular features in Germany, notably a deep conviction that debtors ought to be punished; a high regard for family firms and the consolidation of family wealth; the suspension of a wealth tax, in 1997; a big rental market and small homeownership; little accumulated wealth in the former GDR; and a widespread fear of risk. Let us start at the bottom, with those who have had less than nothing.

In public morals as in law, the sinful debtor has been the reverse of the virtuous saver. "*Man macht keine Schulden*" was a widespread saying: Going into debt is not done. Debtors had to be punished for their irresponsibility, otherwise others would be encouraged to live beyond their means. Until 1999, an insolvent person in the Federal Republic was treated the same way as in the days of Kaiser Wilhelm I. Under the bankruptcy law (*Konkursordnung*) of 1877, debtors had to service their creditors' claims for up to thirty years. Even after reforms in 1999 and 2013, a debtor in Germany had to be "upright" (*redlich*) and demonstrate their "good behavior" (*Wohlverhalten*) for six years before they were cleared of residual debt. Debt relief had to be earned.

At the time of the Kaiser, this punitive approach to moral hazard was the international norm. A century later, however, Germany's position had become exceptional as more and more countries warmed to liberal credit and giving debtors a second chance. The United States introduced a "fresh start" as early as 1898; Denmark switched to a speedy reintegration of debtors in 1984; Sweden tested a person's "uprightness" separately, and France (since 2003) allowed even the most hopeless cases to get back on their feet after two years. While other countries came around to providing relief to debtors, Germany continued to stigmatize them. The priority was to protect creditors, and if that meant excluding "failed" citizens from social and commercial life, it was a price worth paying. The six years of "good behavior" were a modern version of the medieval debtors' tower.[73]

History has yet to produce a single "good" system of getting and spending. For all its advantages, easy credit has caused plenty of problems, as millions of Americans discovered in the subprime mortgage crisis after 2007. But so, too, has the German demonization of debt. Under the Kaiser, bankruptcy primarily befell businessmen. By the time of Helmut Kohl it was a nightmare for millions of consumers. In the 1980s and 1990s, there was an explosion of citizens unable to repay their debts. When the first debt counseling centers opened in the 1970s, they were for former prisoners and marginalized groups. As the century drew to a close, more than a thousand such centers were advising broad sections of society. In 1999, almost 3 million households (7 percent of the population) were unable to service their outstanding obligations—they carried an average debt of 40,000 DM in the West and 20,000 DM in the East. By 2017, it would be 3.4 million households, with some 7 million people, notwithstanding almost a decade of growth and falling unemployment.[74]

Contrary to their public image, most debtors were not in trouble because they were reckless or extravagant. Countless studies show that shopping sprees were the problem of a small minority—one in nine debtors, according to the National Statistical Office in 2015–16. The majority were struggling to pay their mortgage or outstanding taxes; debts to mail-order companies were a pittance by comparison.[75] The main cause was a sudden drop in income following unemployment, illness, divorce, or the death of a partner—factors often beyond the control of the individual. Single parents were particularly vulnerable, since they tended to have more precarious, low-income jobs, especially women who, in addition, sometimes inherited part of their ex-husbands' debt after a divorce. East Germans, who had few assets, were easily pushed over the edge by unemployment. By the 2010s, debt was beginning to eat its way into the middle classes, following the rise of freelance and part-time work.

The moral stigma attached to debt came at a human cost: people felt shame and withdrew from friends and society, only to sink deeper into debt. In Saxony, this was true for every third debtor. "I was ashamed and for that reason did not want to ask for help," one man told official researchers.[76] Two in three skipped going to the doctor rather than ask friends to lend them the 10 euro copay, according to welfare bodies. Debt led to depression and loneliness, and alcohol and gambling were often its consequence, not its cause. Middle-class families who were no longer able to pay the bills found it hard to give up "normal" life. Mothers worried that their children would be separated and stigmatized if they took them out of the tennis club or a private school. Instead of downscaling or seeking help, couples took on second jobs.[77] Even those who sought advice found it difficult to break out of the vicious cycle of debt, dependence, and stigmatization. In 2008, an official study found that after eight months of help, only a minority had managed to reduce their obligations and only 10 percent had found a job. Most pinned their hope on eventually being recognized as insolvent and having the millstone of residual debt lifted. In the interim, they were condemned to live at a subsistence level. Four out of ten felt excluded from society.[78]

The moral calculus also had costs for the country at large. Creditors rarely saw a penny during the six years of "good behavior," the economy lost potential start-ups, and the state lost precious taxes. In 1999 and 2013, the government took the first steps toward liberating debtors by making it easier to write off residual debt. Debtors could now buy their way to a fresh start in three years, but only by paying their creditors a third of what they owed. These reforms, however, were mainly for insolvent entrepreneurs, to give them a fresh chance in business. Politicians were afraid of giving carte blanche to all debtors. For the unemployed, people on benefits, single mothers, and many others it made little difference, regardless of how frugal they were; they did not even have the money to pay the court fees involved. In 2017, 7 million people were still unable to service their debts, and 600,000 were waiting to have their residual debt written off.[79] It was the European Union that ultimately came to their rescue, with guidelines for consumers as well as businessmen. In 2020, Germany followed and declared that all honorable debtors would be free of their obligations after three years, even if they had not made a single repayment.[80]

It's difficult to say whether Germans are more responsible with money than other Europeans because credit can be a step toward a brighter future and need not end in bankruptcy; that countries define over-indebtedness in different ways complicates things further. As many commentators have noted, Germans remain wary of credit cards. To this day, many restaurants and retailers decline "plastic." Even when the pandemic boosted online sales in 2020, 32 percent of payments were made by invoice, another 18 percent by debit card, and 20 percent via PayPal (which is often linked to a debit card).[81]

Germans just do credit differently. In the 1970s and 1980s, consumer credit as a share of disposable income doubled, from 15 percent to 28 percent, and in the 1990s it doubled yet again, reaching 432 billion DM in 2000. The savings rate fell to 9 percent in 1999.[82] The big item was the car. By 2000, every fourth German bought their new car on a credit plan. Civil servants, those traditional advocates of thrift, took out the largest amount of consumer credit, just as better-off citizens did elsewhere.[83] In 2009, outstanding consumer credit made up 14 percent of Germans' disposable income, exactly the average in the European Union, slightly more than in France and Italy, and well below Britain and Hungary. "Thrifty Teutons" were just as likely to be behind in payments (6 percent in 2007) as supposedly profligate Britons, although much less so than Poles or Hungarians. In 2008, one in ten Germans had arrears or outstanding debts worth more than 100 percent of their disposable income, roughly the same as in Britain, while it was only one in fifty Danes and French people.[84] Single parents in Germany found it especially hard to make ends meet.

What set Germany apart was that debt was so demonized that people were badly prepared for the financial world—one reformer lambasted the "anti-credit education in schools."[85] The biggest difference, though, was that fewer Germans bought their homes. Mortgages amounted to only 47 percent of a household's disposable income, whereas a boom in house prices made it climb to 135 percent in Britain and to 243 percent in Denmark; the EU average was 68 percent.[86]

Here was the crux: housing wealth and other assets were in fewer hands in Germany than in the rest of Europe. In part, this was a legacy of the war. Affordable and subsidized rental apartments rose up out of the ruins. Nowhere else in the European Union do so few people own their home as in Germany. It was 51 percent in 2019; the European average is 70 percent.[87] When real estate prices began to rise in Germany after 2009, inequality naturally rose with them.[88]

Inequality was made worse by the ruling mantra of stability and thrift and the zero-risk behavior it encouraged. Germans fell into three groups: non-savers, "stupid" savers, and savvy, wealth-oriented savers. The first group either had no money to save or decided that, in light of inflation and low interest rates, it was better to spend it—19 percent of people in a study carried out in 1980. The second group, the largest (43 percent), put money aside every month but were so cautious that they only got back what they had put in, if they were lucky. They considered shares to be something for the rich and were terrified of the word "credit." It was the third group of savers who reaped the benefits from the rising share and property prices: the professional classes, property owners, higher earners, and family heirs.

The study found an overwhelming sense of "insecurity and fear."[89] Two in three Germans at the time wanted to avoid risk at all costs. Few people changed their financial behavior when interest rates went up or down; the Bundesbank noted that in the twenty-five years since reunification, rate changes had a "rather insignificant" effect.[90] A banking survey in 2015 found that a savings account was still the preferred form of investment (31 percent), well ahead of real estate (18 percent), shares (17 percent), and gold (6 percent).[91] This was at a time when savers earned less than 1 percent on their deposits and the stock market had been rising by leaps and bounds for six years. Strikingly, shares made up a smaller percentage of Germans' financial assets in 2015 than in the mid-1990s. In a period of mild inflation, twice as much money lay in savings accounts that earned no interest as in shares on the German stock exchange.[92] Growing inequality was the flip side of a public policy that promised the people an impossible world of stability without risk.

A NATION OF HEIRS

The extremes between rich and poor were widened by the privileged treatment of heirs. In 2019, a phenomenal 31 percent of all wealth in Germany was inherited—in France, it was 23 percent and in the United States and Belgium only around 15 percent.[93] "Every man is the architect of his own fortune" was increasingly turning into "Every man is the product of his family's fortune."

In the last generation, many countries have reduced their taxes on assets for fear of losing investors to tax havens in the Caribbean and elsewhere. Germany took an extreme approach and suspended its wealth tax altogether at the end of 1996. The previous year, the Constitutional Court had ruled that treating other assets (such as shares, gold, and cars) worse than real estate violated the principle of equality. This was a major turn away from the earlier understanding of fairness, which had honored *Leistung* and taxed effortless wealth. Inheritance tax also declined, to 1.7 percent in 2010, half its level in the 1960s. Furthermore, property tax is tiny in Germany. The very rich have been able to lower their tax burden by moving assets into their firms and family trusts. What all this added up to was that by 2018, only 2.6 percent of the country's total revenue came from wealth-related taxes, compared to 11 percent in the United States, 10 percent in the United Kingdom, and 9 percent in France.[94] Meanwhile, more and more tax was raised by VAT—a regressive tax that hits everyone. The same country that prided itself on avoiding Anglo-American extremes was the one that taxed its rich the least. It was not so different from the unequal tax regime that favored the landed elite in eighteenth-century England.

That the suspension of the wealth tax enjoyed overwhelming political support tells us something about the moral compass of contemporary Germany. Only the hard-left Die Linke and the Greens put up serious opposition—the Greens proposed a 15 percent wealth tax to be paid in installments over ten years. The eminent jurist Ernst-Wolfgang Böckenförde warned that there came a point when inequality turned into unfreedom, but his was a minority view. Otto Schily—who started his career as a defense counsel to terrorists, was a cofounder of the Greens, and ended as an SPD minister under Gerhard Schröder—denounced the wealth tax as "asocial, unfair, and hostile to medium-sized firms."[95] That bringing it back might kill the family firm—the golden goose of the German economy—was a scenario that filled almost everyone with horror, from sections of the SPD across Liberals and Christian Democrats all the way to the Alternative für Deutschland. Entrepreneurs' effort and success should be rewarded; they should be able to pass on their wealth to their children. Individual merit morphed into family entitlement. When the new SPD-Green-Liberal coalition government led by Olaf Scholz was formed at the end of 2021, it agreed that there would still be no wealth tax. In sharp contrast to the immediate postwar years, there was little support for calling on the wealthy to "share burdens."

There was nothing natural about the sanctity of family fortunes. The United States might celebrate self-made millionaires, but it also taxes wealth to safeguard democracy against powerful lobbies, although implementation is far from perfect.[96] In Germany, by contrast, inequality widened as a byproduct of an economic model centered on mid-sized family firms, the so-called *Mittelstand.* Their tax privileges were the other side of the coin to the cuts in benefits in the reform of the labor market. "The *Mittelstand* is and remains the engine of growth," Chancellor Schröder stressed in the parliamentary debate of his welfare reforms, to applause from both Greens and Christian Democrats. ("Where he is right, he is right.")[97] Their contributions to social security consequently needed to be reduced and their taxes simplified.

In reality, the "middle" stretched from the local father-and-son plumbing business all the way to the discounter colossus Aldi, owned by the billionaire Albrecht family. The system was self-perpetuating: family firms were given tax incentives to invest in their enterprise, which made them grow, which, in turn, added to their existing wealth. In 2012, big family firms invested almost twice as much of their turnover in research and development as other enterprises.[98] Success was rewarded with success. For new entrants and start-ups, Germany was a less auspicious place.

JUST DESERTS

This model was not only defended by the lucky few who benefited from it. Taxing wealth was unpopular with the many, too. In surveys in 2013 and 2015, two in three Germans considered inheritance tax to be unfair, at a time when it only affected a small elite (2 percent of the population) and the first 2 million euros were tax-free. People were opposed to raising it because they feared there would be capital flight to the Bahamas; the state would simply waste the extra revenue; a higher inheritance tax would discriminate against savers and reward those who lived the high life now in order not to pay taxes later. Above all, what right did the state have to the hard-earned money people were planning to pass on to their children and grandchildren?[99]

Moral convictions and hopes trumped financial realities. Inherited wealth enjoyed the greatest approval from those with the lowest level of education.[100] People were imagining that they, too, might have a legacy to give away. Adam Smith had noted two centuries earlier how the poor person was "enchanted with the distant idea of his felicity."[101] It was one reason the poor did not cut the throat of the rich: deep down, the desire to better their condition made them admire and imitate the wealthy, however corrupt and despicable they might be. Family fortunes were also read as an index of virtue across generations. When the journalist Julia Friedrichs in 2015 published a book critical of heirs, her mailbox overflowed with angry letters, many of which said that just because she and her parents had failed to get anything profitable done in their lives did not give her the right to take away a well-earned inheritance from anyone else. Again and again, she was told, "You are just driven by envy!"[102]

We know a lot about German attitudes to the poor but surprisingly little about those toward the rich. In a rare study in 2018, pollsters tested social envy in four countries. One question was whether people were in favor of reducing managers' salaries and sharing the cut among the staff, even if it only meant a few dollars extra each. Forty-six percent of the Germans interviewed agreed, slightly fewer than the French (54 percent) but considerably more than Americans (31 percent) and Britons (29 percent). Overall, the poll found social envy to be more widespread in France and Germany than in Britain and the United States.[103]

That does not necessarily mean that greater inequality in recent years has made Germans more envious. Envy needs a voice and justification as well as a target—it is, after all, one of the "deadly sins" that made Cain slay his brother Abel, and one we have been urged for millennia to resist. In Weimar, in the 1920s, the Left wanted to expropriate land and money from princely families and was accused of appealing to base motives by the bourgeois parties. The Nazis overcame such disquiet by blaming the victim. When "Aryan" Germans helped themselves to the firms, apartments, and fur coats of Jews, it was said, they were simply defending themselves against alien "parasites." After the war, envy subsided, as the miracle years made everyone a winner, although some more than others. In the words of the historian Ute Frevert, "In a land of affluence marked by a new awakening and optimism about the future there was little room for envy."[104]

For West Germans, those golden years have remained the benchmark and reinforced a general faith in merit. For many East Germans, by contrast, their struggles in the 1990s were proof that success was determined by the side of the border one grew up on, not hard work and initiative. From their vantage point, other people's riches looked less deserved. Not surprisingly, then, wealth taxes have been more popular in the East. This also means, however, that, by themselves, West Germans are perhaps not that far apart from Americans and Britons after all.

Another reason for the relative lack of resentment in Germany is that the rich have tended to maintain a low profile, some to signal their responsible wealth via a commitment to the local community, others to avoid public vilification for their forebears' profiteering during the Nazi years. German multimillionaires are more likely to be found sailing the Baltic in a classic wooden boat than cruising the Mediterranean in a mega-yacht; Oliver Berking, whose family has made its fortune from silver cutlery ever since the days of Bismarck, devoted fifteen thousand hours to the restoration of his old, sixty-six-foot boat. In the south, the family head of the Trumpf machine tool maker, Nicola Leibinger-Kammüller, is venerated as the "Madonna from Swabia" for her concern for her workers—including introducing flexible hours and arranging for a stroller for a pregnant cleaner. (Two billion euros' turnover a year certainly left enough change for a baby buggy.)[105]

If most Germans today are conflicted about inequality, their faith in just deserts helps them live with it. Two in three view their own income as fair—the same as in the 1980s—but worry that society as a whole is no longer so. Gone are the days when everyone knew what a "fair" wage was because trade unions said so in nationwide agreements. Today, fairness stands on more slippery ground because the justification for big bonuses on the one hand and "one-euro jobs" on the other is less clear. (The subsidized mini-jobs that paid 1–2 euros per hour were introduced in 2005 to help the unemployed reenter the workforce.)[106]

People's assessments of their own situation and of the society around them are increasingly pulling in opposite directions. When an official survey in 2015 asked people about the sources of wealth, more attributed it to an advantageous starting point and the right connections than to hard work. There was widespread concern that extremes hurt democracy. At the same time, eight out of ten agreed that it was "good that everyone is free to get rich" and that it was "fair that one can keep what one has earned through one's work, even if that means that some are richer than others." Two in three felt themselves to be "a little richer" than the rest of the population. The structural causes behind one's own success and, even more so, behind the failure of others, were ignored. The most widely cited reason for people being poor was their "bad handling of money" (67 percent), followed by the need to care for children or others (65 percent), "too much honesty" (56 percent), and not enough support from family and friends in times of need (42 percent)—in other words, private virtues and vices or family circumstances. Only 15 percent linked poverty to an unfair economic system. The higher their own education, the more respondents blamed the poor.[107]

NEW POOR LAW

Manja Weissler, a twenty-eight-year-old mother of two children, lived in the Rhineland. Her first child arrived while she was completing her *Abitur*. She abandoned her plans to become a teacher and trained as a media and information specialist instead. A few years later, she separated from her abusive husband. In 2012, when she told her story to official researchers, she was working twenty hours a week as a maternity leave replacement and commuted daily to Bonn. She took home 760 euros and received 500 euros in child benefits plus some extra welfare benefits for her two sons; this included "alimony advance" (*Unterhaltsvorschuss*), which the German state pays to single parents who do not receive support from the other parent.

"It sounds like a lot of money," she said, "but it is never enough." She still had to pay back part of her student loan. She began cleaning the floors in her building to earn a little extra money. She was so exhausted from work, commuting, child care, the household, and the second job that she often did not have the strength to fill in all the necessary forms for the welfare office. She tried hard to do everyone justice, but some bills just had to wait. Every year, she started well in advance to save a little in order to give her children a birthday party. "I never know whether it will be enough: I feel like a bad mother [*Rabenmutter*]." They only had warm meals on weekends. She worried about ending up with a miserly pension and she was afraid of sinking into depression. She felt like "an octopus who twists and turns to get a little money from here and there. I barely do anything any longer for myself. It is terrifying how one's self shrinks." Manja was poor, and she and her children depended on the basic support from the state known as Hartz IV.[108]

"The poor you will always have with you," Jesus said (Matthew 26:11). In the 1960s, on the back of the economic miracle, West Germans came close to believing that the poor had vanished forever. The end of full employment, though, meant the return of poverty. In 1972, some 800,000 people depended on basic social aid (*Sozialhilfe*). By 1984, it was 1.8 million, and on the eve of reunification (1990) almost 2.8 million.[109] And the face of poverty was changing. Whereas in the past destitution had been synonymous with old age, now it touched the young. By 1990, children were twice as likely to be welfare recipients as the rest of the population, migrants (old and young) four times as much.

That year, the Catholic welfare organization Caritas launched an investigation among the many thousands who turned to one of its centers for help. The "Poor Among Us" painted a shocking picture. Two thirds of their clients were unemployed, but one third had a job. Half of them were in debt and lived in an apartment that had no indoor toilet or bath. A quarter spent more than 40 percent of their income on rent. Five percent were homeless; in 1988, half a million people lost their homes. The one bright finding was that being poor did not mean people had no social networks.[110]

Schröder's Hartz reforms (2003–05) reversed the downward spiral of unemployment but not the overall trends. The poor were increasingly children, single mothers, young workers, and migrants. Part-time jobs deepened the malaise: more and more people were poor in spite of working. By 2014, almost 8 million people were in "mini" or "midi" jobs, which suited some (pensioners and the mothers of young children) more than others. The working poor made up 10 percent of all employees, double that of ten years earlier and more than in Britain, France, and the Netherlands. Only 20 percent of Hartz recipients were unemployed; the rest worked (40 percent full-time) but were poorly paid.

The year 2014 brought a minimum wage and an overall rise in wages, followed by a string of reforms. Single parents who were waiting for their alimony could claim part of it from the state. Mothers were gifted a year of pension contributions in recognition of their work as caregivers. Disabled persons benefited from a greater allowance.

Some of these benefits met long-standing demands by Caritas and other welfare bodies. Overall, however, their effect has been limited, because the root problem of new poverty did not lie so much in the welfare state as in the changing reality of work. A mini-job was better than no job, but it rarely was a stepping stone to a good job, which depended more and more on human capital and education. For the long-term unemployed, the gulf became unbridgeable. Work was also increasingly precarious. In Germany, this hit young people especially hard; older workers were more likely to be in jobs that were still protected by trade union rules, in contrast to Britain. Since young people had fewer reserves and pension claims, they were at higher risk of poverty.[111] For the growing army of the working poor, the supposed reward for *Leistung* rings hollow. It needed the pandemic to remind citizens how much their lives depended on low-paid caregivers, cleaners, and cashiers.

RIGHTS AND SANCTIONS

In the days of the economic miracle, it was easy to believe in both personal merit and social benefits. With mass unemployment, debates about fairness returned with a vengeance. The question was, fair to whom—the welfare recipient or the taxpayer? Was it right to expect the cashier in a supermarket to work long hours so that others could live off generous benefits? There was outrage at "asocials" and "social parasites" (*Sozial-Schmarotzer*), terms with Nazi echoes. "Florida-Rolf" gave them a face. He was a chronically ill man who had fallen on hard times and depended on benefits: he also happened to live in Miami, near the beach. In 2003, a German court ruled that, like any other welfare recipient, he was entitled to six months of rent support while looking for a cheaper home. The case became a cause célèbre, seized by the tabloid *Bild* ("He is laughing at us") and then making the rounds of TV talk shows all the way to parliament.[112] When Schröder insisted that there was no right to laziness, he was tapping into a widespread sentiment. The Hartz reforms put an end to such privileges. "Florida-Rolf" had to move back to the fatherland and make do with "basic social security" (*Grundsicherung*).

How "basic" such support should be was a thorny question. Set it too low, and it violated the principle of dignity and solidarity; too high, and it sabotaged that of merit. For Christian Democrats, there was no question that work had to pay off: someone who got up in the morning to go to work needed to know that when they returned home in the evening they would have more money in their pocket than a neighbor who did not work. The cuts to unemployment support triggered widespread protests—at their peak, in August 2004, some 200,000 people were marching in the streets. For many, the old arrangement under which an unemployed worker continued to receive 60 percent of their earlier wage was an entitlement they had earned through years of contributions, not a benefit. The groups that were most vocal were those who stood to lose the most. Those previously on social assistance (*Sozialhilfe*) benefited from the reforms because they were now covered by health insurance.

In 2010, a year after the global financial crisis, the Constitutional Court ruled that the rates on which benefits were calculated were so low that they violated the constitutional right to a life in dignity (Article 1/1) and the principle of the social state (Article 20/1). The Liberal leader Guido Westerwelle warned that the country was on the verge of "late Roman decadence," where soon no one would go to work.[113] For others, the relevant history lesson was more recent: the bailout of the banks. Oliver Küster was fifty-seven and single and received the new type of unemployment benefit. After paying his bills, the trained mechanic had 320 euros left to live on each month—"not a lot," he said, but at least he had a roof over his head and did not have to turn to crime to survive. Like many in his position, he took on a part-time job that paid 1.50 euros an hour—he hoped to buy a scooter with it to win back his mobility. He was grateful the *Sozialstaat* existed. What angered him was the double standard by which the state handed out money. When big banks failed, they were rescued with billions of euros, "but when the little Hartz IV recipient is meant to get 10 euros extra, it is a huge drama. I don't get it. One should speak up and fight back."[114]

The battle turned on sanctions. These existed before the Hartz reforms, but (compared to Britain or Denmark) they were used only as a last resort; a fifty-year-old woman, for example, had her benefits suspended when she first considered it unacceptable, for a woman, to go to a job interview at 7 a.m., and then rejected a job offer to help the elderly with their shopping because, in her view, it would be irresponsible since she had no experience in the care sector.[115]

The Hartz reforms followed the broader European push to "activate" benefit claimants into job seekers. Instead of a safety net, the welfare system was to be a springboard. Tax incentives and retraining would help people to jump higher and households were urged to launch start-ups and turn themselves into a *Familien-AG* ("family firm"), a mini-version of the *Mittelstand.* Sanctions were to keep them on their toes, their "dosage" adjusted like pills. Even then, Germany was not particularly harsh. In 2016, 134,000 people were sanctioned, not even one in thirty Hartz recipients. Britain punished three times that many people, and Portugal, Croatia, and Estonia were tougher as well. Most sanctions were mild (on average, 108 euros a month), only 8 percent of which were for refusing to take a job. Still, repeat offenders could have their benefits cut by up to 60 percent.[116]

That was the fate that befell an unemployed man in Thuringia when, in 2014, he turned down a job offer in a warehouse, even though he had been trained in storage and logistics; he wanted to work in sales instead. The job center cut his benefits, first by 30 percent, then by another 30 percent. The man sued, arguing that the cuts were a breach of the Constitution. The social court in Gotha (Thuringia) passed the case on to the Constitutional Court.

The state argued that the man's personal interests had to be weighed against those of the general public, which paid for his benefits: the man had a duty to take a job even if it was not in his preferred line of work. The plaintiff and the judge invoked the basic rights enshrined in the Constitution. One was the right to choose one's occupation (Article 12/1); the others were the guarantee of "human dignity" (Article 1/1), "the right to life and physical liberty" (Article 2/2), and the principle that Germany was a "social state" (Article 20/1). Together, the Gotha judge argued, these meant that every citizen had a right to "the minimum necessary for a dignified life" (*menschenwürdiges Existensminimum*), and that included their social and cultural existence as well as their physical subsistence. When the job center slashed the man's basic security, first from 391 to 274 euros and then to a mere 157 euros a month ($170), it was depriving him of that bare minimum. Defenders of sanctions argued that without them people would not seek the help they needed to get back on their feet. The judge found that their threat only made claimants more vulnerable. There were cases where sanctioned people had committed suicide, died from malnutrition, or been driven to prostitution. The objection that sanctions were needed to protect the existential minimum of the tax-paying public was brushed aside as out of touch with the country's riches. In any case, it was inadmissible to play off one human dignity against another.[117]

In 2019, the Constitutional Court finally ruled on the matter. On the one hand, the court accepted the broad view of the existential minimum and struck down a 60 percent cut as unconstitutional. "Human dignity . . . cannot be lost even on grounds of supposedly "undignified" behavior." On the other, it defended a 30 percent cut. As long as sanctions were limited, they were lawful. A citizen had the right to receive enough benefits to participate in life, but the state also had a right to expect them to help overcome their own need.[118]

That was the law. That people had a right to social support had been the ruling orthodoxy ever since the mid-1950s and was codified in the Bundessozialhilfegesetz, the landmark welfare law of 1961. Workhouses for "asocial" youths, vagrants, and "loose" women were declared unconstitutional in West Germany shortly thereafter. East Germany continued to apply the criminal code that dated back to 1872 (STGB Article 42) and rounded them up. Having a right and making use of it, however, are not the same thing. Merit continued to cast a powerful shadow over people's right to assistance. According to estimates, in the late 1990s every third and perhaps even every second citizen did not claim the *Sozialhilfe* they were entitled to.[119] In other words, 2 million citizens (and half a million foreigners) lived below the official welfare threshold.

The low uptake was in part the result of ignorance. Caritas found that two thirds of its clients at the time wrongly believed that they would have to pay back *Sozialhilfe* from later earnings, half did not know that they could receive it in addition to their wages, and one in five assumed they would have to use up all their savings first. It was also to do with shame. In 1979, more than two thirds did not want their family, neighbors, and friends to know they were receiving benefits. The notion of the "deserving poor" lived on, and not just among market liberals. It was a Social Democrat and minister of labor in Merkel's first grand coalition, Franz Müntefering, who justified the benefits reforms with the New Testament: "If a man would not work, neither should he eat" (2 Thessalonians 3:10).[120]

One of the ambitions of the Hartz reforms was to tackle "hidden poverty." Those on small pensions, the long-term unemployed, and children would receive a basic social security payment, *Grundsicherung*, and thus would be spared a separate, humiliating trip to the *Sozialhilfe*, and their family members helping support them. In 2007, the national household survey revealed a depressing fact. Of the 1 million elderly who qualified for basic support, only a third took it. Among those under the age of sixty-five, it was still only 61 percent.[121]

Shame has never entirely disappeared, but there is some indication that the stigma attached to benefits has declined since the 1970s. By the early 1990s, almost every second person said it did not bother them that people knew they were on benefits. Now "only" 11 percent worried about being "found out" by their children and 44 percent by their friends and neighbors.[122] Most people living in hidden poverty had as much a sense of their rights as did those who claimed their benefits. Their biggest fear was that their children (or parents) would eventually have to pay back their benefits. By law, children were responsible for their elderly parents and the cost of their care home, even if they themselves had been neglected by them in their childhood.[123] In practice, though, this was rarely enforced, and the state paid the lion's share (98 percent).

Contrary to the widespread image of the welfare scrounger, the poor often shared the ideal of merit, performance, and independence. One of them was Marianne Hauser, who mainly lived off her husband's small pension. Others might apply for "*Fürsorge*," the eighty-year-old widow told official researchers, tellingly using the older, more shameful term for public assistance in the interwar years. She had managed her entire life without it and would not start now. "For me, the most important thing is that I do not need to rely on any state agency." They would just harass her and ask why she had worked so few years. "No... I won't go begging."[124] Such pride in independence has an admirable side to it. But in the case of Frau Hauser, the unwillingness to turn to the state for what was hers by right condemned her to loneliness. After rent and electricity, she had only 450 euros a month left. Her husband's funeral cost 6,000 euros, and then the washing machine broke. She stopped going to the theater, no longer took any trips, and very rarely visited her sister and cousin, because the bus ride involved complicated changes and a taxi was too expensive. Her philosophy was that she "did not want to be a burden."

Those who did brave the trip to the welfare office often returned humiliated. In 2018, a part-time dental technician characterized the routine appointments as a psychological striptease.[125] She had written 180 job applications and needed to provide officials with proof of everything from her heating bill to health insurance. When she was in the hospital, her support was cut by the number of meals she had there, and the little money her fifteen-year-old son brought home from odd jobs was treated as household income, not pocket money, and similarly deducted. Older unemployed Hartz recipients found the endless job applications they were required to send off pointless and little more than a form of window dressing by the state. An unemployed mother with two children compiled six ring binders in as many months to document her expenses. For her, "it was a circle of misery." "Each visit to the authorities involved shame, and I got whacked... Everyday life with the children I could always manage, but I simply failed with the authorities." "Poverty knows no evening, weekend, or holiday," said a fifty-two-year-old social education worker who had retired early with a chronic illness. She was unable to participate in society and felt trapped in "spiritual poverty": "I have the feeling that slowly my own personality is dissolving."

These life stories were collected not by radicals but by the Ministry of Work and Social Affairs in North Rhine–Westphalia in the course of official investigations in 2012 and 2016. The Hartz regime, they concluded, provided "no support for the diversity of life situations." Its standard rates were too rigid and blind to the fact that social contact, such as a visit to a café or a concert or walking the dog, cost money too. People were assigned to tasks without considering their suitability, "on the premise that any work is better than none." They lost their self-esteem, and when poverty was joined by illness, daily life became all but unmanageable. The reports spoke of "segregation." The aim of the reforms—to "support" people (*fördern*)—got lost in their implementation. Instead, they left behind "rage, powerlessness, and frustration." Social courts were flooded with nearly 150,000 claims a year that challenged everything from sanctions to insufficient rent support—half of them were decided in favor of Hartz recipients.[126]

In towns and cities, food banks gave social deprivation unprecedented visibility. In German, they called themselves "*Tafeln*" (tables) and offered social inclusion as well as food. The first three dozen were born out of the fight against food waste, in the early 1990s. By 2000, they had mushroomed to a thousand; a decade later there were two thousand, and their main function had become helping those in need. In 2014, over a million people went regularly to a *Tafel.* The coffee chain Tchibo dedicated a special chocolate bar (also called *Tafel*) in their support, and at the discount supermarket Lidl, shoppers could donate their deposit for returnable bottles to food banks. In contrast to North America, most of the food comes from small retailers in the neighborhood—a kind of alternative local economy, supported by donations in money and kind.

The spectacular rise of food banks did not follow from neoliberal austerity, at least not in Germany. Paradoxically, it happened alongside greater public assistance and, as we just saw, an official recognition that people did not live by bread alone. The people who turned to the *Tafeln* were not the ones who needed them most; the homeless made up only 1 percent of their clients. In Baden-Württemberg, the *Tafeln* reached only 8 percent of the poor. The largest group were unemployed recipients of Hartz, followed by asylum seekers and poor pensioners. It was not so much that the poor were getting poorer, but that more of their fellow citizens took note of them. In fact, the greatest number of food banks were in the richest parts of the country: Bavaria and Baden-Württemberg.

Just under half the *Tafeln* were voluntary associations; the others operated under the umbrella of the independent welfare bodies. Only in a few rare cases were they sponsored by a city, as in Magdeburg. Across the country, food banks attracted sixty thousand volunteers. Helpers wanted to include those who had been excluded or overlooked by the state; bringing migrants and native Germans together was part of that social mission. Along with the cans of food, they were handing out social recognition. Several centers offered child care and other services in addition to a warm meal. In many countries, neoliberal reforms asked claimants to display both their worth and their pain to the authorities.[127] At the food banks, however, help and compassion were not conditional on demonstrating "worthiness." In 2017, the food banks joined the main welfare bodies in a call for a "dignified life," with better jobs, fairer taxes, and greater benefits. People who had worked all their life should not have to live in poverty. Caregivers deserved basic pensions in recognition of raising children.[128]

The Hartz system also had liberal critics. In 2006, Germany spent 700 billion euros on social benefits, or 8,500 euros (equivalent to $11,000 at the time) per person. That year, the prime minister of Thuringia, Dieter Althaus, a Christian Democrat, proposed that the government stop such transfers and instead hand all adults a "citizen income" of 800 euros a month, regardless of their situation; each child would receive 500 euros.

The idea of a universal basic income reaches back to radicals in Britain and France in the 1790s who looked to greater social equality.[129] Its reception in Germany in the past generation tells us a lot about the ethos of fairness that continues to dominate there. Proponents of a universal basic income have been mainly antistatist libertarians. Their aim has been to roll back the state as much as to free claimants from the stigma of welfare. The late drugstore chain tycoon Götz Werner likened the Hartz system to an "open prison"; he took his inspiration from Rudolf Steiner's anthroposophy and ethical individualism. A citizen income would give people enough of a cushion to make them take greater risks, and at the same time reward caregivers for looking after their children or elderly parents. A proposed low uniform income tax of 25 percent would lift the tax burden from the shoulders of the enterprising many. Universal basic income also attracted some support from

Catholic theologians, who saw it as a source of dignity, and from the liberal-radical Pirate Party, which adopted it in the election in 2013.[130]

Overwhelmingly, though, the idea was greeted with suspicion, if not outright rejection. (The Pirate Party won only 2 percent of the vote.) The unions and young Social Democrats feared that firms would treat it as a subsidy for cheap labor. If doing no work was suddenly equal to doing paid work, why invest in education and specialization? And who would protect wages and working conditions? Others worried that the most vulnerable would be left even further behind, because towns and communities might stop helping them altogether.

Above all, the debate highlights the central importance of work and performance. The social state offered a safety net but for exceptional circumstances, and claimants had to have grounds for assistance. Citizens were expected to stand on their own two feet. Solidarity rested on self-responsibility. "Universal basic income" sounded less alarming in countries (like the United States and Britain) where social security systems were less tied to past performance. In Germany, by contrast, it sounded dangerously egalitarian, threatening to upset the fine balance between rights and duties that hinged on individual performance (*Leistungsprinzip*). As one angry citizen put it bluntly to a magazine, sure, every person had the right to do nothing, but that did not mean the state and those who went to work and paid taxes had a duty to support them in their idleness.[131]

In 2022, the Scholz government followed through on its promise to reform the benefits system. For the Social Democrats, it was a long-awaited chance to repair their reputation by burying the measures associated with mean-spiritedness and punitive sanctions that their last chancellor, Gerhard Schröder, had introduced two decades earlier. In 2022, close to 4 million people received "Unemployment Benefits II" (Hartz IV). The much-maligned Hartz benefits were to be replaced by a "citizen's income" (*Bürgergeld*). The radical reform of the social state soon ran into difficulties. In opinion polls in November, most citizens felt that even a modest rise in benefits from 449 euros a month to 502 euros ($472) went too far, because it would eliminate the incentive to look for work. The Bundesrat, where the Christian Democrats controlled the majority, blocked the initiative. In the end, a compromise was reached. In the future, those on benefits would receive 502 euros a month—hardly a big jump at a time of inflation—but sanctions remain in place for those who do not seek work or do not show up for appointments. The original idea of "trusting" a newly unemployed person for the first six months was abolished. The grace period, in which a person's wealth and home cannot be touched, was reduced from two years, as originally envisaged by the government, to one, and the protected assets from 60,000 to 40,000 euros. There is more support for retraining. The divisive name "Hartz" might have been buried, but its spirit remains alive, if on slightly more generous terms. Whether the new "citizen's income" will be enough to silence debates about poverty and the right to a dignified existence is another matter. What it showed clearly was how broad the consensus remains behind the principle that work should be rewarded.

The cult of stability, thrift, and performance that helped make Germany an economic powerhouse came at a price. Its champions promised that, with restraint and perseverance, anyone could prosper. In reality, the rich got richer and left the poor further behind. Ideals of hard work and saving entrenched inequalities. Not everyone would or could save, and many others who did were so risk averse that they got back less than they put in. By making thrift a test of character, it ended up stigmatizing those who failed to make ends meet, often for reasons beyond their control.

13

The Circles of Care: Family, Community, and State

In liberal hands, modern history can read like a forward march of rights, from the right to vote to social and economic rights all the way to the right to identify one's own gender. The "neoliberal" era since the 1970s can appear as the culmination of a "me culture" grounded in notions of individual rights. The problems with this grand narrative are apparent from a global perspective. China started with economic rights and has yet to reach political ones. In parts of the West, social and economic rights are perpetually deferred. In India, Mahatma Gandhi said that "true" civilization lay in the performance of duty—rights were merely its result.[1]

A sole focus on rights would also give a distorted picture of Germany. In its constitution, rights are paired with duties. Parents have duties to their children as well as rights (Article 6/2), and vice versa. "Property entails obligations" and "shall serve the public good" (Article 14/2). Citizens have a right to a dignified existence and the state a duty to respect and protect it (Article 1), but when they hit hard times, they are expected to help themselves and turn to their families before turning to the state. Germany is a *Sozialstaat*, a social state, that guarantees social security, but it also is a caring society with millions looking after their loved ones at home, and countless volunteers.

Conservatives and feminists might not see eye-to-eye on much. When it comes to caring, though, they agree about its central role for human flourishing. Caregiving is morality in action and articulates fundamental values about the social order. By looking after vulnerable individuals, caring nurtures sympathy and, from a young age, teaches children about right and wrong. It creates the social bonds necessary for humans to live in a community. Caregiving regimes reflect a society's core ideas about what we owe each other and what states expect of citizens, and vice versa. Where conservatives and feminists differ is whether caregiving should be seen as a "labor of love" or recognized as "work," with profound implications for gender roles. Notwithstanding equal rights, care continues to be disproportionately the duty of women and is poorly paid or not paid at all, in no small part thanks to the peculiar evolution of welfare in Germany.

SUBSIDIUM (LATIN), NOUN: HELP, SUPPORT, RELIEF

The Federal Republic's welfare system is an amalgam of three components: a statutory contributory insurance system, which people pay into to protect themselves against the risks of illness and old age; state benefits for special groups, such as war widows and civil servants, in recognition of their service to the nation (so-called *Versorgungsleistungen*); and, finally, social aid (*Sozialhilfe*) to assist people in times of need and in special circumstances, such as pregnancy, disability, or loss of income.[2]

The first is the best known and remains the basis of the German pension system, although the state has increasingly been forced to add on to private contributions. It was founded by Otto von Bismarck, in the 1880s, on a simple idea: by sharing risk, the insured joined a community built on solidarity, a *Solidargemeinschaft.* Next to the Iron Chancellor, however, towers a second figure: the pope. In 1931, in his encyclical "Quadragesimo anno" ("In the Fortieth Year"), Pius XI looked to self-determination as the bedrock of community and justice. It was unjust as well as unnatural for the state to take away from individuals what they could accomplish with their own powers. He called it the "principle of subsidiarity" (*subsidiarii officii principio*). As it happens, the encyclical was co-drafted by a German Jesuit, Oswald von Nell-Breuning, who would be a major influence on Christian Democrats from the postwar years all the way through to the Helmut Kohl era; he died in 1991.[3]

It was Konrad Adenauer who put subsidiarity at the center of the German welfare system, where it has stayed ever since. This gave it a distinct Christian Democratic flavor, unique among welfare states. In essence, social policy was the counterpart of the ordoliberal approach to the economy that we encountered earlier. The state, in this view, should not steer but merely create the underlying order that allows people to act on their own initiative. At the end of the war, millions of people were disabled, bombed out, or expelled, through what they considered to be no fault of their own. This produced a more inclusive sense of welfare. In addition, the new democratic order created a community of citizens, with rights as well as duties. The right to social assistance became irresistible and, after being endorsed by various courts in the 1950s, was enshrined in the Federal Social Assistance Act in 1961. In 1955, Adenauer called in four experts on welfare and ethics to advise him on the future social order. Their "Rothenfels Memorandum" spelled out the dual logic of subsidiarity. It meant, first of all, "drawing a boundary" to protect individuals and the "smaller circles of life" against the "totalizing claims" of the bigger social structures surrounding them.[4] Aid should always proceed from the smaller circles to the larger ones, with people first trying to help themselves, then turning to their family and their community, before approaching independent welfare bodies and the state. State assistance was a last resort and only to be given to help people get back on their feet—a little bit like "help for self-help" for developing nations. People in difficulty should be offered support but without undermining their autonomy. The right to social assistance followed from the duty of self-reliance and mutual aid.

Subsidiarity promised to combine more rights with little state, offering Christian Democrats a third way between free market and state socialism. It drew strength from three sources: alarm at how Nazis and communists had invaded the sacred sphere of the family; a democratic spirit; and Catholic social thought.

One of the brains behind the "Rothenfels Memo" was Joseph Höffner, the future bishop of Münster and, later, of Cologne, a man who had the rare distinction of holding four doctoral degrees—in philosophy, political science, and theology (twice)—and who had been the dissertation supervisor of Adenauer's son. Democracy, Höffner argued in 1954, was a new order, in which citizens were responsible for the political community and for general well-being. In the past, he said, Germans had been too happy to give up their freedom in exchange for promises of security. Contemporaries worried that welfare reforms would unleash a "pension psychosis," in which people looked to an omnipotent provider-state to feed and support them—a "*Versorgungsstaat.*" Subsidiarity aimed to prevent this by coupling social security with self-help. To Höffner, its basic unit was the family, "the bulwark against mass society and the collective." Catholic bishops saw it as "the natural order of aid." It was here that its members learned to love and support each other and to work together, in the process weaving and mending the ties that made up the social fabric.[5]

The delivery of social aid raised fundamental questions about the relationship between state and churches. Unlike many other European countries, Germany did not have a state church, and this had encouraged rival religious subcultures of care; only equally divided Belgium came close in that respect.[6] The Social Democrats and their allies in the Workers' Welfare Organization (Arbeiterwohlfahrt, AWO) wanted local authorities to take charge and represent the public interest. For the Catholic Caritas and the

Protestant Inner Mission and Hilfswerk, such a transfer posed an existential threat. Their own hospitals and nursing homes would lose out to the state, while their clients risked finding themselves in a home run by members of a different faith or even by atheists. The democratic right to social aid, they insisted, entailed the freedom to choose a nursing home run by one's own denomination.

The battle was about more than institutional survival. For Christians, and Catholics in particular, charity was as essential for human existence as self-responsibility, and it was this combination that set them apart from secular traditions. For Plato and the ancients, the good citizen was self-sufficient, but it followed that compassion was for the weak. The Stoics and Nietzsche believed that it was better to be tough and accept one's fate than end up dependent on others. Pity merely stoked the lust for revenge. Kant had more to say for compassion, but for him it was a rational duty.[7] For Thomas Aquinas, by contrast, charity was an expression of love, the literal meaning of *caritas*.

For Catholics since, it has been a matter of the heart, not the mind, a passion that springs from man made in the image of Christ the Redeemer. In the battle over the future of welfare in the 1950s, they quoted from Matthew 25:40, where Christ tells his disciplines, "Whatever you did for one of the least of these brothers and sisters of mine, you did for me."[8] Charity, in this view, manifested the small piece of Christ humans had inside them. An anonymous benefits check was no substitute for personal aid that sprang from the heart. On their own, coins were cold, the influential German priest Romano Guardini said.[9] It needed a personal touch to lift people up. Protestants expressed their similar ideal of service with the Greek "*Diakonie*." What would happen to social cohesion if people no longer felt a sense of duty and gratitude toward each other? Both the giver and the recipient of charity would be diminished. The exercise of charity was also said to bring helpers one step closer to happiness in the next world.

The recognition of recipients as citizens with rights meant that paternalist alms and appeals to good works for God's sake became less frequent in the 1950s and 60s.[10] Still, charity continued to be about the dignity of suffering as much as about the human dignity protected by the constitution. All humans were vulnerable and needed God's help.

When the new social aid system was finally unveiled in 1961, it had a distinctly Christian Democratic look. Its aim was to allow people in need to lead a dignified life by providing them with a basic level of subsistence. Social aid targeted those unable to support themselves, who received ongoing subsistence support (*laufende Hilfe zum Lebensunterhalt*), while people in special circumstances, such as pregnant mothers, tuberculosis sufferers, or disabled persons, received a temporary helping hand (*Hilfe in besonderen Lebenslagen*).

Legally, social aid ceased to be charity and became a right, but the old independent charities were the ones in charge of handing it out. Subsidiarity guaranteed them precedence over the state. Social aid was only state welfare in the sense that the state was the paymaster, much to the irritation of town governments and communities that had to foot the bill for nursing homes run by religious and other "free" welfare bodies. Social Democrats complained of a betrayal of democracy, with Christians being allowed to impose their vision on the rest of society, as if the municipalities did not represent the interests of all citizens. Adenauer's Christian Democrats would have none of it. In the cold modern world, the Protestant Ernst von Bodelschwingh told parliament in 1961, the "powers of faith, of love, and of hope" had to be kept alive;[11] he was the grandson of the founder of Bethel, a pioneering institution for disabled people. To find courage and get their lives back in order, recipients had to feel that they were not alone. Aid had to reach the soul, not just the pocket.

The personal touch not only survived but expanded, as help in special circumstances ballooned in the next two decades; by 1981, it reached more than a million people and cost 10 billion DM—three quarters of all spending on social aid.[12] Nonetheless, social aid remained a last resort. Recipients had to demonstrate their need and that they had exhausted their personal income, family support, and search for a job first.

Subsidiarity has had admirers elsewhere, and the European Union has made it a principle of governance. Nowhere, though, has it shaped the entire welfare system like in Germany. Fewer and fewer Germans went to church in these years, but when they were ill or frail they more and more found themselves looked after in a hospital or care home run by the Catholic Caritas or the Protestant Diakonie, which fused the Inner Mission and Hilfswerk in 1975.[13]

The revival of the faith-based welfare providers after the Nazi years and their growth in an era associated with secularization was nothing short of phenomenal. Their hospitals, nursing homes, and day cares grew enormously. In 1990, Caritas ran 1,500 nursing homes for the elderly, with 103,000 places. Even after the entry of private competitors since then, Caritas and Diakonie managed half of all 15,400 in-patient and part-time nursing homes in 2019, looking after half a million people. Every third day care is owned or run by one of the churches. In 1950, Caritas had 100,000 people working for it. In 2020, it was almost 700,000, a figure that does not include several hundred thousand volunteers. In Germany, every fifth employed caregiver comes from a church organization; in Norway, it is one in twenty-five, in Holland one in fifty. Together, Diakonie and Caritas today employ more than three times as many people as Volkswagen.[14]

These were the providers. People's opinions varied hugely on what to make of their new right to social aid. Self-reliance and subsidiarity appeared far less natural than the many proclamations by its advocates might suggest. In 1958, blue- and white-collar workers were asked who should help if someone, through no fault of their own, ended up in difficulties. Only a quarter replied "the family." Half looked immediately to the state.

The courts were kept busy by citizens who felt entitled to much more than the state and the law were prepared to give them. Theo S. was a pensioner in Berlin Steglitz who received a small disability pension. In 1959, he had his request for additional social assistance refused on the grounds that he had not made use of his own "small circle" of family support; his second wife, who had received daily sickness benefits, was expected to return to work and help make ends meet. The man sued the local authorities, all the way to the Federal Administrative Court. His case, he said, was of "fundamental importance because to call on his wife to make such a contribution to his upkeep violated morals and the law." He lost. Two years earlier, another pensioner had his application for two weeks of social support for himself and his wife rejected, even though they had "nothing edible left at the moment," he wrote. The husband was a recognized disabled war veteran with brain injuries who, in addition to his own small employee pension, received a veteran's pension plus a care allowance. He had already collected an advance on his pension but had spent most of it on a pair of secondhand shoes, a dress for his wife, paying off some debts, and moving out of his apartment, which he could no longer afford. This left him with only 40 DM, he said. The dormitory charged him 5.50 DM a night and did not have a kitchen. He and his wife consequently had no choice but to eat out and "even for the dog he had to buy boiled potatoes in pubs." The court rejected his claim. If he had not bought the dress and had delayed repaying his debts, he would not have found himself in distress. Only those in genuine need had a right to assistance.[15]

On the other end of the spectrum were people who qualified for social aid but either thought they had no right to it or were ashamed to ask, as we have seen. The stigma attached to alms and poverty relief persisted regardless of the new focus on special circumstances that could hit anyone. For most people, an official in Cologne said in 1964, social aid remained "the stuff of poor people ... like having lice and scabies."[16] The prewar obligation to pay back assistance later cast a dark shadow over social aid long after most officials dropped it in the early 1950s; by the end of the decade, such reimbursements made up a tiny contribution to welfare budgets.[17] What remained in force, however, was the rule that individuals only had a right to assistance once their families had exhausted their own resources. Many old people did not want to go to the "*Sozi*" because they were afraid of becoming a burden on their children.

Since social aid was designed as temporary help to help oneself, it involved regular checks. The state retained the power to reduce support if people were wasteful or refused work. The well-intentioned focus on special needs and personal advice created its own new form of surveillance and discipline. In 1960, a year before the federal law was passed, the senator in charge of social assistance in Berlin had a staff of fifty special auditors whose exclusive job it was to examine applications based on special life circumstances.[18] People were forced to open up their books and lives to show they were really in need and trying to better themselves, not shirkers buying boiled potatoes for their dogs.

Social aid spending was meant to be a temporary measure for people experiencing "special circumstances" and as a last resort for the few not covered by the other branches of social insurance. It was soon overwhelmed. Between 1970 and 1990, demands on its budget multiplied tenfold. By 1980, more than 2 million people relied on social aid, and a decade later almost 4 million. The two largest groups were disabled persons receiving help with integration and the growing number of penniless elderly people in care homes.

Conceived for "special" circumstances, social aid became a normal part of life for elderly people in need of long-term care who were poor and without a family to support them. This was in part because the population was aging, in part because medical advances made it possible to offer more care. The main reason, though, was that subsidiarity assumed that care would be provided by the family in the first instance, not paid for by the social insurance system (as was the case, for example, in Sweden). Germans had insurance for medical treatment but not for care, with profound consequences. A person who, after a stroke, was treated in a university hospital was lucky because their health insurance picked up the bill and left their wealth and pension untouched. If the same person, by contrast, was moved to a nursing home, their health insurance paid nothing. Social aid, designed as the last resort, required them to use up their own assets first, and given the cost of a nursing home, that did not take long—in 1992, the day rate for around-the-clock care (*Schwerpflegebedürftige*) was 156 DM, or 4,680 DM a month, ten times a widow's pension at the time and four times what the average employee took home. In just a few months, institutional care turned previously independent citizens with a little nest egg into dependent paupers. Once they had spent their wealth, the authorities pursued their family members for contributions, although many elderly no longer had a partner or children who earned enough to qualify; in 13 percent of cases, dependents did have to chip in.[19] The country eventually introduced care insurance in 1995.

Over time, subsidiarity and *Leistung* (performance), the twins of the social system, entrenched class and gender inequalities. The city of Cologne found in 1988 that retired manual workers were 50 percent more likely to be in need of care than former civil servants or the self-employed.[20] Above all, the system deepened the divide between the male breadwinner and the female caregiver. Contributory pensions rewarded those with a long record of paid work—that is, mainly men. Since women had shorter and disrupted careers, they got tiny or no pensions. By 1981, almost a third of social aid for subsistence went to elderly citizens in that precarious position.[21] Caring might be repaid by God in the next world, but in this world it punished women twice over: as unpaid caregivers, they were more likely to have little savings in old age, and if it came to the point where they needed institutional care themselves, the absence of insurance made them destitute.[22] In 1986, mothers and caregivers born after 1921 were given one additional pension year in recognition of their service. Even that was only partial compensation—single women who were caregiving and working ended up 10 percent worse off in old age than their peers who did not shoulder a dual burden.[23]

MORE WORK FOR MOTHER

"Marriage and family are the natural and ethical foundations of human community and stand under the special protection of the state," declared the Bavarian constitution in 1946, the first of many such official paeans in the postwar years.[24] Marriage was a divine institution and one of the seven sacraments. The family was the "primordial cell" (*Urzelle*) of society, coming before the state and other collective organizations. Defending society against the totalitarian incursion of Nazism and communism therefore meant defending the family; the Federal Constitution (Basic Law) guaranteed it special protection in Article 6. Christian Democrats, in particular, believed that it was in the bosom of the family where individuals learned to be human and to cooperate, preparing them to live and work together in larger social groups.

The "normal" family was more of an ideal than a reality. The war had blown many marriages to bits, and often survivors were living together without tying the knot. Contemporaries were divided on whether they were "living in sin," as they were about sex itself. The film *The Sinner* (*Die Sünderin*) dropped a moral bombshell on audiences in 1951. Not only did it show the heroine (Hildegard Knef) nude; worse, she was a former prostitute who resumed her old trade in order to raise money for brain surgery for her lover, a failed artist, before easing his own death with pills and committing suicide herself. Not surprisingly, the Catholic Church and Catholic youth were up in arms and tried to prohibit this sympathetic portrayal of prostitution and euthanasia. Just as revealing, though, was the support the movie attracted. In ultra-Catholic Regensburg, seven thousand citizens marched against a boycott, and the town's parliament eventually allowed it to be screened. Across the country, an estimated 5 million Catholics saw the film.[25]

In Germany as elsewhere, the postwar decades saw heated battles over the precise meaning of equal rights for husband and wife, such as in the historic decision to give mothers equal say over their children's education mentioned previously. None of these changes managed to undermine the fundamental position assigned to the nuclear family as such, and the role of the mother in particular. "Without the family, society will lose its cohesion," proclaimed the CDU in 1979. If society could no longer do without the "professional woman," it still needed the "family woman" (*Familienfrau*). It was the mother and housewife who, through her love, care, and self-sacrifice, nurtured the "consciousness of mutually supportive action... She gives help to self-help."[26]

None of the postwar policies were able to halt, let alone reverse, the long-term rise in female employment, divorce, and premarital sex, or the decline in the birthrate. The baby boom from the late 1950s to the mid 1960s merely interrupted this trend. In this respect Germany was fairly typical. This does not mean, however, that the family ideal was inconsequential—far from it. Instead, West Germany is a good illustration of how moral norms continued to weigh on social practices, even as these were changing, diverting the direction they would otherwise have taken.

Child support, like other welfare provision, was linked to performance. While republican France championed lots of babies for everyone, in Adenauer's Germany child support favored the middle classes and was paid for by their employers. Large families deserved help—support started with the third child in 1954, before being extended to the second child in 1961—but only for those who were already standing on their own feet. Otherwise child support might turn into a "social wage" (*Soziallohn*) and create an underclass dependent on the state. It was only ten years later that the state took over paying child benefits. Even then, it was complemented by a tax credit that favored higher earners. Families with a higher standard of living were expected to have greater needs. Fairness for Christian Democrats meant reducing the inequality between households with children and those without them, not between classes. Helmut Schmidt and his Social Democrats briefly suspended the tax credit in 1975. Kohl duly put it back in 1983.[27] Families were thus entitled to their own type of "burden sharing" (*Lastenausgleich*), similar to that for the expellees and those bombed out after the war.

None of this stopped women from joining the workforce, although for some child benefits and tax credits were an incentive to stay home and look after their children. Work was increasingly accepted as a source of self-realization, but it still had to be in sync with the imperatives of child care. The number of child care centers for toddlers and preschool children was small and shrinking. In Bavaria, for example, roughly every third child under the age of six went to a day care in 1954. Fifteen years later, it was down to every sixth. Perversely, as more women went to work, more care moved back into the family. In 1954, 49 percent of preschool children were looked after by family members. In 1969, it was 80 percent—not something that is usually associated with this supposedly liberating decade.[28] Since most preschools were only open for part of the day and most schools sent their pupils home by lunchtime, West German mothers with little children either switched to part-time work or stopped working altogether. By the early 1970s, 40 percent of all mothers worked part-time.

Their children's care and education were "the natural rights . . . and duties" of parents, according to the constitution (Article 6). In the absence of alternative care norms and policies to support them, traditional maternal ideals continued to flourish in the Federal Republic far longer than elsewhere in Western Europe or in the GDR. In the mid-1980s, 80 percent of German men believed that children should be raised by their mother at home until they reached the age of ten. That fathers were now more likely to be present at birth did not mean that they took on more child care or housework—in contrast to men elsewhere in the European Union in the 1970s and 1980s. In 1986, "maternity leave" was rechristened "child-rearing leave" (*Erziehungsurlaub*), and father and mother could swap it within the first ten months. In reality, it continued to be the mother who took time out. The sense of being the natural caregiver left working mothers feeling guilty and inadequate. In 1992, a majority of women as well as men believed that putting a child under the age of three in a day care would harm its development. Handing a child to its grandmother was one thing, but to a complete stranger? West Germans were far more skeptical and hostile than their British, French, and Nordic neighbors.[29]

Separation and divorce exacerbated this inequality. Attitudes to marriage were becoming more relaxed in the postwar decades—by 1979, half of young Germans agreed that it should be easy to dissolve a marriage; in 1953, it had been only 15 percent.[30] If breaking up was easy, getting child support from the biological father was not. Mothers of children born out of wedlock were especially shortchanged. In Dortmund in 1964, barely every third identified father paid regular child support.[31] Divorced and separated mothers were only slightly better off.

No-fault divorce was introduced in West Germany in 1976 but greeted with widespread suspicion. Half of those interviewed in a survey in 1980 were opposed to the idea of men paying alimony if the woman had left the marriage. That year, "parental care" replaced "parental authority" (*Gewalt*) in family law, and in 1982, the Constitutional Court ruled that custody could also be split. Many single mothers nonetheless found themselves and their children condemned to poverty. Among Caritas clients in 1991, 99 percent of divorced mothers had a legal claim to alimony for their children, yet 39 percent received nothing at all; among single mothers and those living in separation the figure was 45 percent each. Some fathers were unable to pay, but, at least in this sample, just as many simply refused.[32]

CARE AND NEGLECT IN THE GDR

The GDR took a socialist turn on the Bismarckian road to welfare. Social and health insurance remained mandatory and universal, except now the state trade union took over the contributions previously paid by capitalist bosses. The constitution guaranteed the right to work and social security. Not everyone was equal, however. East Germany retained special pension and insurance classes for privileged groups, such as doctors and artists as well as army officers and party and Stasi officials after twenty-five years of service. In 1960, the average pension of a regular citizen was one quarter of a worker's wages; by 1980, it had risen to one third. By contrast, a member of the intelligentsia retired with 90 percent of their salary.[33]

The historian Konrad Jarausch has christened the GDR a "*Fürsorgediktatur*," a regime that simultaneously cared for its citizens and coerced them. Against crude black-and-white pictures of the GDR as either horribly totalitarian or basically "normal," the term has the advantage of capturing the regime's contradictory soul.[34]

When it came to actual welfare, though, reality fell far short of the paternalist ideal. To recruit women into the workforce but still encourage them to have more babies—three children was the socialist ideal—the regime gave women its particular attention, expanding day cares and extending paid maternity leave in the 1970s. Still, it is wrong to think of the GDR as a powerful father figure that might be strict but, in the end, looked after everyone. For many of its most vulnerable citizens, it did not care at all.

In East Germany, work set the parameters for care. Women were expected to go to work, no matter how young their children. When the Wall came down, three quarters of mothers with infants (children under the age of three) were employed in the East; in the West, it was just over a third. Ninety-two percent of all women between the ages of twenty-five and sixty were working in the GDR, compared to only 60 percent in the West. Early-childhood care, therefore, was critical. By 1989, *Krippen* (day cares) offered free places for 54 percent of all children under the age of three; in West Germany, the average was 2 percent, and only West Berlin managed as much as 18 percent. For three- to six-year-olds, the gap in coverage was narrower but still significant: 94 percent in the East compared to 68 percent in the West.[35]

Even day cares were not a simple success story. They only became widespread in the last two decades of the GDR. For the earlier generation, working while caregiving was a daily struggle, often unwinnable. In 1961, the party's official paper, *Neues Deutschland*, carried an article entitled "Emancipation for Women—But Without Children?" by a woman who worked in a Berlin coat factory. Mothers, she wrote, often searched in vain for a place in a day care, and when their children fell ill, they had little choice but to stop work in order to look after them. The inevitable result, the author pointed out, was that women rarely moved up the career ladder—in textile factories, women made up 85 percent of the workforce but only 7 percent of the supervisors (*Meister*). "We are facing momentous obstacles in making emancipation a reality," the article concluded.[36] Twenty-five years and many day cares later the situation had not fundamentally changed—three in four women were in low-skilled positions earning no more than 600 to 700 Marks a month in 1990.[37]

Employment was an important source of independence and respect, but it barely changed traditional gender roles. Men began to chip in a little more at home than in the West, but women still did the bulk of cooking, cleaning, and child care. In 1965, women in the East devoted thirty-one hours each week to housework, exactly as many as their sisters in the West. In 1991, it still stood at twenty-seven hours (compared to thirty-two hours in the West; men contributed sixteen and thirteen hours respectively).[38]

Throughout the 1960s, absenteeism was a chronic problem. A Berlin factory with 158 single women routinely lost seventy hours a month because mothers stayed home to look after sick children. The Democratic Women's League (Demokratischer Frauenbund Deutschlands, DFD) appealed to "grannies" (*Omis*) to volunteer. Here and there, veterans were darning stockings and helping with the laundry. A Leipzig cotton factory had a "pensioner working group" (*Rentner-AG*) that came to the rescue. By and large, officials acknowledged, such initiatives "proved a failure."

In 1961, the regime's trade union (FDGB) reached an agreement with the People's Solidarity (Volkssolidarität), a kind of socialist Caritas, to sponsor paid home help for mothers with sick children. For some it was a lifesaver. "I really appreciate the help," one mother from Plauen said. She left the house at 8 a.m. and when she returned at 4 p.m., she found the apartment cleaned, the shopping done, and her child fed and looked after. Her coworkers in the clothing factory were not convinced. "I won't let a stranger into my apartment" was a widespread view.[39] Above all, there was the cost, which was split with the mother. Yes, a mother complained in 1965, she could call up the Volkssolidarität to send someone to look after her twins when they fell ill. In the past, when she stayed home, she lost 113 Marks in earnings. But the home help cost her 104.50 Marks for ten hours—"not a financial incentive, really," as she pointed out. In fact, few were even aware of the program's existence. A women's delegate of the national assembly visited four firms in Magdeburg in 1965 where the workforce was overwhelmingly female: not a single women's committee had heard of home aid. At the Schwarze Pumpe power station, it was the same story. By 1969, the loss of working hours had reached such proportion that the women's commission at the Politburo called on firms to set up wards for sick children.[40]

Here was the rationale for the dramatic expansion of child care centers in the following decade. Where needed, they offered nighttime and weeklong care (*Wochenkrippen*). In Eisenhüttenstadt shift workers often did not get to see their children for four or five days at a time.

Under Erich Honecker, working mothers gained one year of maternity leave and up to thirteen weeks of paid leave to look after sick children. If it was a big help at the time, it did little for equality. One of the last reports produced for the official gender equality commissioner before the GDR was wound up concluded that the "baby year" had brought no relief for mothers.[41] It might even have reinforced the idea that family and household were women's natural responsibilities. Shift work ruled in the GDR. When mothers returned to work and asked for a day shift, they were often unable to get their old jobs back. "Skilled cadres were offered day shifts as cleaners and kitchen helpers," an investigation in Halle noted.[42] In the nineteenth century, women's role in society came to be summed up as "*Kinder, Küche, Kirche*" (children, kitchen, church). The GDR successfully did away with the last of the "three *K*s." The other two it largely left intact.

Divorce was a double-edged sword. East Germany made it easier to dissolve a broken marriage in 1955, a generation before comparable reforms in the West. At the same time, it abolished the maintenance obligation between estranged spouses. The right to divorce and the duty to work went hand in hand. The fact that a man left his wife for another woman, the magazine *Die Frau von Heute* ("Today's Woman") explained to its half-million female readers, did nothing to diminish the abandoned woman's duty to build socialism and join the workforce.[43]

The elderly were largely left to fend for themselves. Shortages in the care sector in the West pale against the crisis of neglect in the East. An official from the district of Leipzig let off steam in 1971: "Nowhere was there a concrete idea on how to help these people." Local councils did not even know how many pensioners lived in their midst, let alone what their needs were. A year earlier, the Council of Ministers had called for a national survey of care needs—most towns did not bother to fill in their form.[44] In 1974, East Berlin counted a quarter of a million pensioners, but there were only five thousand beds in hospitals and retirement homes. At least 2,600 people who were in serious need of care did not receive any at all, according to the Department of Health. Single rooms were a rarity and respect for human dignity a fiction, the report conceded; homes typically had twenty or twenty-four beds per room. For disabled senior citizens, bathing facilities were "virtually nonexistent."[45] Not only was the food bad and linen and cutlery scarce in homes, but the elderly suffered social and cultural exclusion as well.

The GDR almost doubled the number of places in care homes in its last twenty years, and the Volksolidarität visited more pensioners at home, too. The regime swallowed its anticlerical prejudice and tolerated the hospitals and care homes run by what remained of Caritas and Diakonie east of the Elbe. Still, in an aging society with plenty of vulnerable senior citizens this only went so far. In 1980, the district of Potsdam was home to 194,000 pensioners. Only 1 percent lived in an age-appropriate apartment. Officials estimated that every eighth old person was in need of care, but nursing homes were only able to look after a third of them. Neighborhood help and warm meals reached only 0.2 percent. Social isolation was widespread.[46] The Volksolidarität had twenty-eight caregivers for every thousand pensioners.

When the Wall came down, the GDR had the nineteenth-lowest life expectancy in all of Europe—seventy years for men and seventy-six for women, one year ahead of Albania.

For the disabled, there were just nine thousand places in homes or apartments in the entire GDR, with long waiting lists for specially equipped vehicles. Wheelchairs faced barriers virtually everywhere, including at the entrance to doctors' practices.[47] A study of fourteen psychiatric care homes found that only three had a specialist doctor. In the vast majority of cases, patients were sedated with psychotropic drugs and effectively warehoused; on a lower scale, West Germany was not exempt from such abuse, and forcible confinement and harmful drugs have continued to scar institutional care, in spite of legal protections passed in 1992.[48]

"A CALM HAND AND A GOOD HEART"

With reunification, East Germans were absorbed into the social insurance system of the West. In 1995, after a decade of debate, a new pillar was added at last: care insurance, split between employee and employer, with an initial contribution of 1 percent of gross salary; by 2022, it had risen to 3 percent for adults with children and 3.4 percent for those without children.

If its introduction was long overdue, it did not fix the chronic problem of care. Coverage was only partial and still founded on the principle of subsidiarity. Those receiving care (and their families) continued to be expected to contribute to its costs, just a little less than before—on average, 1,800 euros a month ($1,900) for living in a nursing home. Those unable to do so still became dependent on social aid. The well-off, by contrast, were able to stay well-off, thanks to the partial coverage. Care insurance thus stayed loyal to the overall design of the German social state, which has favored the middle classes.

One major change was that it created a market for care. In the 1950s, charitable providers had defended the democratic right of citizens to choose their nursing home. At that time, it meant a choice between a Catholic, Protestant, and municipal home. The reforms in 1995 added commercial rivals. By 2015, 42 percent of nursing homes and 65 percent of all outpatient services were in private hands. The fresh money from insurance did pay for a doubling of nursing care staff. Even that, however, was not enough in an aging society. (By 2019, there was a shortage of 36,000 skilled personnel.)[49] Notwithstanding a minimum care wage (2010) when it came to pay, training, and recognition, professional care lagged behind other Western countries.

Low skills and low wages were the other side of the coin of the voluntary Christian ideal of caring as a labor of love. "In order to feed an eighty-year-old woman, you do not need six semesters of psychology," said the father of care insurance, Christian Democrat Norbert Blüm: "What you need is a calm hand and a good heart."[50] Blüm had learned about the trinity of German welfare from the Jesuit Nell-Breuning: subsidiarity, solidarity, and charity.

The lopsided architecture of German welfare left its mark. Nursing homes are popular nowhere, but having to sink so much of their savings into them meant elderly Germans and their families viewed them with particular horror. In 1990, 1.6 million people in Germany were in "significant need of care" (*erheblicher Pflegebedarf*). Three quarters were looked after in their own homes, and one fifth of them lived alone. Six hundred and fifty thousand people needed daily or around-the-clock care. Only a third had support from professional care services, again partly deterred by their cost. Apartments often did not have appropriate beds, washrooms, and other facilities. In brief, many families were overwhelmed, and many elderly people did not receive the care they needed.[51] Rather than impoverishing the whole family, wives, daughters, and daughters-in-law took on caregiving at home; in 1991, only every sixth primary caregiver was a man, a proportion that would go up to one in four after care insurance and care money were introduced in 1995.[52] Institutional care was underfunded, and there was a chronic shortage of staff and places.

Adult children have continued to take responsibility for their elderly parents. German law recognizes "parental support" (*Elternunterhalt*), an obligation abolished or unknown elsewhere in Europe. It is one of the distinctive features of the subsidiary care system. When it comes to filial duties, the German family is closer to those in India and Singapore than in Britain or the Netherlands. Above a certain threshold for their own needs, children are obliged to support their parents in poverty and old age.

What that threshold should be has been the subject of ongoing debate. In 1996, the authorities in Duisburg went after a fifty-seven-year-old woman to reclaim the costs for the four years her mother had spent in a nursing home until her recent death: 123,000 DM ($82,000 at the time). The daughter had just lost her part-time job that had brought in 1,100 DM a month. She also, however, owned half of a house with four apartments, where she herself lived, in separation from her estranged, retired husband. Surely, the officials said, she could easily pay by taking out a mortgage. The district court agreed. The daughter objected, all the way to the Constitutional Court, which, in 2005, ruled in her favor. Yes, children were responsible for caring for their parents if the need arose—unless that need was the result of alcohol, drugs, or gambling—but this could not be at the expense of their own maintenance and provision for old age. And her property was her pension.[53]

That still left adult children with considerable responsibility. By 2022, a single person was entitled to no more than 2,000 euros a month for themselves (after allowances for housing, pension, and education). Savings were exempt but only up to 5,000 euros ($5,400). Importantly, the filial duty also applied to children who themselves had been treated badly by their parents and become estranged from them. Between 2006 and 2008, a middle-aged man with a decent salary repeatedly refused to contribute to the cost of his mother's care home. In his childhood, his mother, who suffered from schizophrenia, had shredded his clothes and locked him out on several occasions and he had suffered from obsessive-compulsive disorder (OCD) ever since. For thirty years, he had had no contact with her, except for the occasional encounter at a family gathering. The Federal Court of Justice—the supreme court for civil law—ruled in 2010 that his childhood pain and subsequent estrangement did not absolve him of his duty to pay parental support.[54]

Gender equality exists nowhere on earth, but some places come closer to it than others. In terms of work, pay, and care responsibilities, the gap between women and men in Germany today is narrower than in eastern and southern Europe but wider than in the Nordic countries and the Netherlands. Preschools have shot up—one of the few things the West took from the East; subsidies for early-childhood places were doubled in 2013. And more women went to work, too. None of this has changed the fact that women continue to do most of the housework and caregiving. Seventy-three percent of German women go to work today, but half of them work part-time; in Sweden, Italy, and France, it is only one in three. German men continue to be the main breadwinners, and women the principal caregivers, who interrupt or stop their careers. In 1992, 83 percent of all principal caregivers were women, mainly wives and daughters. Almost half did not work when they took over caregiving, while another quarter either cut back in their paying jobs or stopped work altogether—leading to smaller pensions and greater dependence in their own old age. The pay and pension gap remains vast. In 2016, the government's "7th Report on Old Age" noted that women typically received half a man's pension, virtually the same as in the 1960s. Fifteen years after parental allowance (*Elterngeld*) was introduced in 2007, only one in ten fathers claims more than two months (the maximum is twenty-four months) and half do not use it all.[55]

According to the International Labor Office, the value of unpaid care work performed by German women is equivalent to 15 percent of GDP

(2011), almost twice as much as that for men, the largest share in Europe and globally only exceeded by Australia and New Zealand (in poorer countries, women's work carries lower value). When it comes to unpaid domestic work as a whole, the gulf has slightly narrowed, but that is mainly because women do a bit less, not because men do a lot more. German men, in fact, helped eleven minutes less in the household in 2012 than they had in 1997; French men cut back even more. On average, German women do an hour and a half more unpaid caregiving than men each day. At the current snail's pace, it will take another century for the gender gap to close.[56]

Women with children and elderly parents to look after continue to find themselves in an especially precarious situation. Of the 4.1 million people in need of care in Germany today, fewer than a million are in a nursing home. Eighty percent (3.3 million) are looked after at home. Family care has grown faster than institutional care. This trend has been facilitated by the small care allowance paid out by care insurance, which has made more families turn to additional help from professional outpatient services and to migrant workers from eastern Europe; there are an estimated 100,000 to 300,000 "transnational" caregivers in this poorly regulated shadow economy, often overworked and underpaid.[57] Nonetheless, in 2019, every second person in need of care was looked after exclusively by a family member. Husbands and sons today are helping more than they did a generation ago. When it comes to serious cases, however, two in three caregivers are wives and daughters.[58]

In southeastern and eastern Europe where social spending is low, the family is naturally the last resort. In Germany, by contrast, social spending is as high as in the Nordic countries and the Netherlands and yet it clings to family care as the natural norm. In a European survey, 19 percent of people in Helsinki and 24 percent in Amsterdam expressed a preference for family care. In Berlin, it was 43 percent.[59] Compared to the Nordic countries, Germany spends less on professional services and relies more on women working part-time. The family has been a crucial shock absorber in the German system of welfare. Fear of immiseration reinforced the fear of neglect. Rather than give up the little wealth they had built up to pay for institutional care, families opted to provide "free" unpaid care at home as long as possible.

Today, families in Germany devote far more time to care than they did in the 1950s. The bulk, to be precise, is women's time, often in addition to a job, and continues to be taken for granted; a principal caregiver typically devotes almost eight hours a day to it, according to a detailed recent study—this includes basic care, running the household, washing, and feeding, in that order, and rises dramatically if dementia takes hold.[60] Looking after a partner or parent can, of course, be fulfilling. While media and public discourse have plenty to say about abuse in nursing homes, the side effects of caring at home get little mention—illness, depression, loneliness, even violence.

A NATION OF VOLUNTEERS

Heinrich Lübke was the Federal Republic's second president, and his career straddled four Germanies. In the First World War, Lübke fought valiantly for the Kaiser (Iron Cross first and second class); in the Second World War he worked for Albert Speer and expanded the test center for the air force in Peenemünde on the Baltic, with the help of concentration camp prisoners. Lübke was also a Catholic who had sat in the Prussian parliament for the Center party during Weimar's last year. He had served twenty months of prison under the Nazis, for alleged corruption in 1933–34. These were his ticket to a career with the new Christian Democratic Union, which he joined in 1945. Lübke became Adenauer's minister of agriculture and was the chancellor's choice to succeed Theodor Heuss in 1959.

The German president's job is mainly ceremonial, but its incumbents do pick public causes close to their heart. A few weeks before Christmas 1961, Lübke announced his: greater respect for the elderly. He said youth was overvalued and old age undervalued. The country was failing to take advantage of their life experience—this echoed the discovery of senior citizens as "national assets" and "active aging" in the United States ten years earlier.[61] Lübke launched a campaign for their social inclusion. Its motto was "The elderly must not be left on the sidelines." A foundation, Deutsche Altenhilfe, was set up to combat their isolation, recruit young people as their sponsors (*Paten*), and organize help in their neighborhoods. It received proceeds from a television lottery ("with each other—for each other"). The crucial watchword was "community spirit" (*Aktion Gemeinsinn*), and that meant volunteers.

The campaign started with a test run in three cities in the first ten months of 1962 and could barely have gone worse. Cologne, a city with 85,000 elderly inhabitants, at least mobilized ten brass bands and carnival clubs and a few school classes; Mannheim, with 30,000 senior citizens, produced fewer than 500 helpers; West Berlin, with 400,000 old inhabitants, barely 900. The organizers reached the depressing verdict that it was "getting more and more difficult to win over people for active volunteer work."[62]

They could not have been more wrong. Instead of being snuffed out by self-centered consumerism and an expanding welfare state, volunteering has boomed in the half century since. German society would unravel without it—from those children who collected pennies for the German expellees to the young adults who fasted for the "Third World," to those looking after war graves in France or spending their holiday working in Auschwitz and Israel, and millions welcoming refugees in 2015. In the early 1960s, there were an estimated 2.5 million volunteers (*Ehrenamtliche*); thirty years later, there were 12 million; in 2019, 29 million—that is, 45 percent of adults in the former West and 37 percent in the former East.[63]

Volunteering is as diverse as it is vast. Its study is consequently fraught with problems. In 1996, research across ten European countries put Germany at the bottom, causing panic in a land proud of its *Vereine* (clubs). Subsequent investigations, by contrast, have placed the country toward the top. A Eurostat survey in 2011 found that every fifth German volunteered on a regular basis; in the rest of the European Union it was only every ninth person. Only the Dutch and the Danes were more committed. The German figures are so large partly because the country is home to a vast network of sports clubs and other associations, which are run by their members. Today, some 8 million people belong to 92,000 clubs. One million are active in the voluntary fire brigades alone. Of course, there is a world of difference between a person who helps out each Sunday in a nursing home and someone who organizes the Christmas raffle for their club or congregation. Time commitments vary greatly. The typical German spends no more than seven minutes a day on volunteering. To put this in perspective, child care takes up only six minutes more. Active participants, meanwhile, spend two hours and thirty-two minutes each day. More than fifty thousand people today are enrolled in a "voluntary social year"—in practice, its duration ranges from six to eighteen months. Finally, it needs to be noted that voluntary work is not always free—while many helpers are unsalaried, they often receive some compensation in the form of social insurance, travel money, or a small honorarium for their time.[64]

A milestone was the Diakonisches Jahr ("year of service") launched by the Protestant bishop of Bavaria, Hermann Dietzfelbinger, in 1954. The volunteer would be like Christ in the community. By sharing in the suffering of the less fortunate and helping to carry their burden, the young would be trained in the art of solidarity and sacrifice. The first three helpers to sign up were two office clerks and a seamstress, all young women. The Caritas followed suit and hoped that volunteering would nurture maternal instincts in girls whose own mothers had been corrupted by Nazism and materialism. The Catholic bishop of Essen assured parents that "your daughters will return to you with open-minded understanding and useful know-how for the many hardships of sickness and old age. They will be better equipped as future wives and mothers to fulfill their innate task of selfless help for family, nation (*Volk*), and church."[65] The steadily declining number of deaconesses added to the urgency to find helpers for church-based hospitals and nursing homes.

In 1961, the "voluntary social year" was launched, soon extending to secular bodies such as the AWO, the Workers' Welfare Organization. Three years later, the government gave these initiatives its legal blessing and put them on a par with apprenticeships, which meant that parents could continue to claim child and tax benefits. The Federal Youth Plan paid for social insurance and a little pocket money. The Netherlands and Finland followed with their own program a few years later. By 1990, more than 100,000 West Germans had completed a voluntary social year.[66]

Far greater (and often forgotten) was the number of teenagers who sacrificed their weekends for others. The AWO introduced "social service in your free time" (*Freizeitdienste*) in 1962. In Kassel, that year, 150 high school girls went to nursing homes each weekend to feed the elderly. In Essen, an entire vocational school gave up their Sunday mornings to help out in the local hospital. By 1968, there were tens of thousands of such short-term or "Sunday helpers."[67]

At the start, nine out of ten who committed an entire year were young women; men had to do compulsory military service (or civilian service if conscientious objectors) until 2011, although a significant minority escaped as "unfit." Most volunteers were between eighteen and twenty-five years old. On the Protestant side, the largest group had worked in offices before and a quarter stayed on in the care sector afterward. In the Caritas, half the volunteers in 1963 were office clerks, another third artisans. At the end of their social year, almost every second volunteer continued in a social or care profession.

One of the attractions of the voluntary year was that it offered a way out of an unloved job or a stepping stone toward a desired one. The internship was especially attractive for girls who wanted to train as nurses but had not reached the required minimum age of eighteen. An electrician, one of the few men, joined the AWO for a year because he found his true calling in social work.[68] Parents were a major obstacle, often unconvinced by such career switches or wanting their daughters to start earning or enrolling in an apprenticeship right away. "Time and again, we observe that 50–60 percent have had to overcome major resistance from their parents," a female vicar noted in the Rhineland. A twenty-one-year-old recalled how her mother would not shake hands with her when she left home to take up her post as volunteer.[69]

The story of volunteering since reflects the changing realities of education and the labor market. By the early 1970s, the majority were recent school graduates, not office workers. As unemployment soared in the late 1970s, so did the appeal of a "bridge year" between school and job. By 1996, almost two in three volunteers had their *Abitur*. More young men were joining the program, although they still only accounted for a quarter. Since 2000, volunteering has once again attracted more young people with lower secondary education. It is they who predominantly feed and clean the elderly, while their academic peers tend to prefer ecological and cultural projects.[70]

It is tempting to read these changes as a shift from tradition to postmodernity, with other-regarding charity giving way to self-interest and CV-padding. Roswitha from the Rhineland was frank about her motives. "For me," she told the Diakonisches Werk, the Protestant umbrella welfare body, "the point of the voluntary social year lies in purely personal, almost egotistical reasons." It gave her "considerably more freedom in terms of time and money than under the watchful eye of my parents." It was a convenient "compromise between my thirst for adventure, my wish to be independent, and their worries." She was able to enjoy "a relatively carefree life" and escape the "pressure to perform" in the job market, at least for a while. And it broadened her "geographic and mental horizon, because one gets to know other people and other spheres of life," which, she hoped, would give her "a fresh impetus for planning the future and a career." Volunteering made her more "mature" and gave her "confidence." It tested her "entire personality."[71] She wrote this in 1971, at the height of industrial modernity and social democracy, not in the postmodern, neoliberal 1990s.

In truth, self-interest and compassion were always intermingled. What changed was their particular form. From the outset, volunteers were promised self-discovery and satisfaction. "The pleasure you give to others will find its way back to your own heart," Catholics in Aachen promised in the 1960s. Caritas urged the young to think of helping others as "a present to oneself."[72] After all, mercy and charity brought a person one step closer to God. Such transcendental goals were complemented with practical steps in personal development. In "Letters from Rich Girls," a promotional booklet from 1964, for example, interns talked about how they had matured and learned patience, self-discipline, and a better understanding of human nature.[73] Helping others was probably never selfless, but from the late 1960s on it became more explicitly tied to helping oneself. As one organizer put it, there were fewer "angels" and "more sober realists" who expected to learn from their experience and get a taste of "real life."[74] While volunteering was increasingly meant to be "fun," it continued to be about self-discovery and a sense of duty toward others. Indeed, the national volunteering survey (2009) pointed to a "renaissance" of duty. In the first decade of the twenty-first century, the share of young volunteers (fourteen- to thirty-year-olds) who said that their prime motivation was "the common good" (*Gemeinwohl*) rose from 18 percent to 30 percent, ahead of gaining new personal experiences and insights into a job.[75]

In the nineteenth century, voluntary associations came to be recognized for nurturing democratic talents by teaching members the art of self-governance. In Weimar Germany, however, a flourishing landscape of clubs undermined a weak democratic system further by pitting groups against one another. In the 1960s, the "social state" and rights to welfare revived the appreciation of the democratic qualities of the volunteer. In 1966, for example, the historian Percy Ernst Schramm gave speeches in which he argued that "everyone had the duty to sacrifice part of their labor power for the common good—voluntarily, because the community provided the preconditions for their own existence."[76] The social state made volunteers more, not less important. By guaranteeing all citizens a basic standard of living, the *Sozialstaat* enabled individuals to devote their attention to others. Time, rather than money, became the most precious donation. Catholic youth in the late 1960s stressed how a voluntary social year empowered participants "to think and act responsibly."[77] For the umbrella body of the independent welfare organizations (Deutscher Paritätischer Wohlfahrtsverband, DPWV), the greater use of volunteers pursued "in the first place a social-political and socio-pedagogical aim": "to create a training ground for democratic virtues and behaviors that awaken and strengthen the public spirit and individuals' sense of responsibility for the weaker members of society."[78]

In the mid-1960s, and again in the mid-1990s, a few toyed with the idea of making the social year mandatory for girls to alleviate the crisis in the care sector. The proposal was killed off by twin concerns over democracy and subsidiarity as well as echoes of Hitler's Reich Labor Service. For the churches and welfare bodies, volunteers were not there to plug the gaps in the care sector. Their contribution lay in practicing solidarity, respect, and self-determination. By giving their own time freely, they were respecting those in need as "partners." To make social service compulsory would take away such respect. Full-time care workers were not excited by the prospect of cheap competition, either. A compulsory year for girls also threatened to entrench traditional gender roles, with women as natural caregivers and men as warriors. Above all, there was a fear that it would stifle civic responsibility, giving people the dangerous idea that the state would automatically take care of everything. To be free, a democratic society needed volunteers. Without them, citizens would be at the mercy of a faceless, bureaucratic state.[79] Volunteers were a major element of the social contract that underpinned democracy.

The AWO collected feedback from its first cohorts in the late 1960s that gives a glimpse of how close to the ideals the voluntary social year came in reality. The majority worked in children's or care homes. Several spent the first few months cooking and cleaning rather than caring, as they had hoped. One of them was Brigitte H. For her, the year was "a stopgap" because she was too young to train as a nurse. She started in a nursing home, where she spent the first half year "almost exclusively in the kitchen." Things picked up when she was reassigned to a children's recreation home on the island of Sylt. When the day care teachers were busy, she was able to take charge of the children. She had "a lot of fun," she said. Another eighteen-year-old wrote, "I have become more independent and confident." She learned a lot from the day-to-day interaction with colleagues: "I can pull myself together and at the same time speak up when necessary." A few felt that their superiors could have entrusted them with more responsibility and interfered less in their private lives. Overall, though, the responses were positive. The sense of being needed and making a difference were ample rewards. Even those who in the course of the year changed their future plans from nursing to banking had no regrets.[80]

At the same time, professionalization and the recognition of clients as equals created new pressures. Formerly paternalistic (and overconfident) helpers were now often anxious or lost. The Social Service of Catholic Men had been active in Kempen-Krefeld, a textile region with a quarter-million inhabitants, since the 1920s. In 1973, the full-time social workers noted problems with their local volunteers. "They shy away from taking on tasks because they feel overtaxed. Again and again they express their fear of failing. 'Am I being accepted—is my help appreciated?' are frequently recurring questions." Volunteers were increasingly leaving tasks to the social worker as "the 'expert who, after all, had the training.'"[81] A few years later, a group of students who volunteered in an autonomous therapeutic housing project near Marburg opened up about their problems. While their hearts beat for psychiatry, they found it hard to "take any pleasure from the necessary organization of everyday life," such as doing the shopping or planning leisure activities. They confessed to "anxiety and insecurity," and often left group meetings feeling "dejected and frustrated." It was only in the course of meetings with supervisors that they overcame their "shame" and admitted to feeling that they were "helpless helpers." Part of the problem was their competitiveness: "Who is the best volunteer; who is most loved by the members of the housing group?"[82]

The surge of volunteers was partly a recovery from the decline during the Nazi years. Catholics had already organized young volunteers in the countryside in the years before Hitler. In 1962, the Social Service of Catholic Men (Sozialdienst Katholischer Männer) equaled their number; they worked especially with orphans and the unemployed. The Catholic mission at train stations, founded in 1895, was looking after 2 million people and handing out half a million meals in 1950. New groups were also replacing old. The number of organized volunteers who helped the elderly in their congregations (*Pfarrercaritas*) fell from 750,000 in 1949 to half that number in 1962. Caritas, Diakonie, and the Red Cross took their place and more. In 1975, the half-million full-time staff in the various independent welfare bodies could count on the support of 4.5 million volunteers. More state spending on welfare came with more volunteers, another reflection of the mixed nature of the German welfare system.

Across the border, in the GDR, a paternalist state set out to look after its citizens all by itself and abolished subsidiarity. This did not mean the end of the volunteer, however. Rather, the place of bourgeois and church-based charities was taken by the "People's Solidarity." Although the Volkssolidarität never reached the size of the independent welfare bodies in the West, it was not inconsequential. In the immediate postwar years, it mobilized more than 2 million "reconstruction helpers" (*Aufbauhelfer*) who cleared bombed cities of rubble and built new roads, apartments, and schools. The lives of German expellees and refugees from Greece and Korea were hard but would have been even harder had it not been for the Volkssolidarität's volunteers, who solicited donations and gave them clothes and food.[83]

In the 1950s, the regime turned the Volkssolidarität into a mass organization, partly to marginalize the churches. Its main focus of attention now became the elderly—both as helpers and recipients. The Volkssolidarität ran a socialist version of "meals on wheels." *Veteranenklubs* offered sociability, games, and the occasional party and excursion. Volunteers helped senior citizens with household chores—the helpers were often women who themselves were in their sixties and seventies. In 1970, home helpers and "pensioner brigades" gave 11 million hours of their time.

In a dictatorship, "voluntary" aid was never altogether free. The Volkssolidarität was subordinated to the regime and its auxiliary parties (*Blockparteien*). Still, while key officials might be loyal supporters of the regime, local groups attracted plenty of people who were not party members. In 1960, there were 7,400 local groups with more than 1 million paying members; 103,000 were active volunteers, so-called people's helpers (*Volkshelfer*). By 1988, their number had doubled. For the overall care needs of the elderly, this was little more than a band-aid, as we have seen. In the district of Cottbus, volunteers delivered two thousand meals six or seven days a week—in a region that was home to almost 1 million people.[84] For the helpers, though, the local clubs and cultural events, the pensioner brigades, and "Join In" (*Mach mit*) campaigns to beautify neighborhoods were important parts of their identity. They released energies typical of voluntary associations elsewhere but with fewer outlets in a dictatorship, mixing a sense of doing good with an opportunity to shape one's community in one's own image.

The fall of the Wall spelled the end for the Volkssolidarität's privileged niche. After 1990, membership collapsed. By 2000, the number of volunteers had fallen to 36,000. Two of the few groups that were growing were its sports and hiking clubs. The Volkssolidarität now had to compete with western welfare bodies in providing social services. Meeting places for the elderly and lunch and home help—its bread and butter—were not reimbursed by the western social security system, accelerating the decline. Caritas, Diakonie, and the Red Cross were just as much beneficiaries of the western takeover of the East as western elites and investors. By 2014, the Volkssolidarität looked after fewer than 34,000 people in nursing homes and outpatient centers.[85]

THE FUTURE OF CARING

Germany today is more than ever a nation of volunteers. In the past two decades, the number of volunteers aged sixty-five or older has almost doubled. People in the West with high levels of education and no migrant background tend to volunteer most. Sports, culture, and education continue to attract the greatest numbers. Still, for caregiving, volunteers also remain crucial. The Diakonie picked 2011 as its "year of the volunteer." At that point, its staff of 450,000 were assisted by 700,000 volunteers. Half of them were engaged in the care of the elderly; the rest worked with disabled people, children, the sick, and addicts.

The degree of commitment, of course, varied. Across the country, the majority gave two hours a week of their time. In the Diakonie, one in three volunteers gave between eleven and twenty hours a week, and one in ten more than forty hours. Most said they volunteered because they wanted to do something "meaningful" and "have fun," others cited sociability, religious conviction, and the opportunity to learn. Half the helpers had their expenses paid, and a third received a small allowance. The typical volunteer was a woman, over the age of sixty, who devoted ten hours per week.[86]

The coronavirus pandemic lockdown hit the voluntary sector hard. Although it is too early to tell what the long-term legacy will be, a study sponsored by several states in 2020 pointed to troubling divides. Thanks to their regular members and steady fees, clubs were least affected. By contrast, youth and cultural centers, self-help groups, and religious centers that relied on donations or income from cafés and events suffered disproportionately—this was true for Protestant, Catholic, and Islamic associations alike. New activities emerged—such as sending emails to lonely people—or were rediscovered, such as helping neighbors with their shopping. At the same time, restrictions and fear of physical contact disproportionately hurt those most in need of it: the elderly, refugees, addicts, and the dying. Established charities were relatively well cushioned, as were young people enrolled in the official voluntary social year who qualified for furlough (temporary paid leave). Those who ran a local food bank or meeting place, meanwhile, faced bankruptcy. The pandemic highlighted the central role of the volunteer as a societal lifesaver in times of crisis but those on the front line and spontaneous helpers felt overlooked and undervalued by politicians. "Public policy makers," the study concluded, "have failed to recognize civil society as a partner."[87]

Subsidiarity has proved a remarkably strong pillar of the country's welfare system. In the past seventy years, it has survived the rise of divorce, more women in the workplace, new family arrangements, affluence, higher life expectancy, mass unemployment, and reunification. In Germany, neoliberal reforms, with their emphasis on self-responsibility, were less a break with the postwar social order than a continuation, building on the ideal of self-help in the family and community. The big question is how much such "bottom-up" care will be able to deliver in the future when the number of people in need of care is growing while the number of families is shrinking.

In particular areas, the principle has already been in retreat. In the 1980s and 1990s, the Constitutional Court rallied to help families with children; parents had some of their caregiving recognized, and, from 1998, tax exemptions covered the costs of education as well as basic subsistence.[88] Subsidiarity was diluted by a cross-generational idea of fairness: society, not just parents, should contribute to the cost of raising children, because it was the new generation that guaranteed society's future. Traditionally, the disabled, too, had to use up almost all their wealth before they were able to claim social benefits. In 2011, they won a major victory when the courts granted them (and their parents) the right to renounce an inheritance so it did not eat up their parents' wealth.[89] Once vilified as an unethical attempt to get out of one's obligations, such "wills for the disabled" are now the norm. Elderly people also have become increasingly vocal, refusing to hand over their hard-earned wealth to pay for a nursing home, keeping the social courts busy. Personal initiative and self-reliance might be idealized for most of one's life but lose their shine when one is in need of care oneself.

The pandemic highlighted just how "systemically relevant" caregivers are. In the summer of 2021, parliament passed a fresh reform package that raised the support both for outpatient and institutional care. The longer a person stays in a nursing home, the lower the share of their own contribution; in the first year, they will receive a subsidy of 5 percent, after twenty-four months 45 percent. There have been repeated efforts to boost the number of caregivers and nurses—personnel has almost doubled in the twenty years since 1999.[90] According to one of the major insurance providers, however, this will not be enough. In 2021, 4.5 million people were in need of care, within their own four walls or in a nursing home. By 2030, the provider forecasts that number to reach 6 million, resulting in a potential shortage of 182,000 full-time professional caregivers.[91]

The German medical system has many positives, but staffing is not one of them. Caregiving is officially considered a critical "bottleneck" profession. To reach the current level of care in Norway or Denmark, German hospitals would need to hire an additional 270,000 doctors and nurses; to match American hospitals, it would need 146,000.[92] Whether wives, their daughters, and, occasionally, their sons will be able or prepared to shoulder the burden of caregiving in the future is doubtful.

14

Mother Nature: Loving and Trashing

Germans believe themselves to be great lovers of nature. Their forests and birds, "Father Rhine" and the Bavarian Alps—they all form a central part of national identity, as do the song and verse about them. Generations have been moved by the Romantic poet Novalis (Friedrich von Hardenberg, 1772–1801):

> The fields were clad in tints of green,
> The hedgerows deck'd with leaves were seen,
> Fresh flowers unfolded to my sight,
> The air was mild, the heavens bright;
> I knew not what the change might be,
> Nor what had wrought this change in me.[1]

Nature has inspired awe and activism in Germany. Founded in 1899, the Nature Conservation Union (Naturschutzbund) has almost 1 million members today. The Greens launched their party in 1980. Barely five years later, they were sharing power at the regional level. By 1998, they were part of Gerhard Schröder's coalition government, something ecologists in other big countries could only dream of. In 2010–11, Germany made itself the global vanguard of an "*Energie-wende*," a turn toward wind and solar power, and the OECD, the club of rich nations, has hailed it for "leading the way" to "green growth."[2]

At the same time, Germans are also carmakers and car owners whose intensive consumer lifestyle is contributing to the destruction of the planet. Their warm homes and auto mobility continue to rely almost entirely on gas and oil. Coal might no longer be king, but it is still a formidable presence. In 2018, Germany mined and burned more lignite, a moist brown coal that produces little heat but plenty of carbon dioxide (CO_2) and sulphur dioxide (SO_2), than any other country; lignite generated one third of the nation's electricity, as much as wind and solar combined. That year, 166 million tons of *Braunkohle* were extracted, and even more soil was removed—the equivalent of digging out the entire Suez Canal fifteen times over. Germany shut down its last hard coal (*Steinkohle*) mine in 2018 but continued to import it, primarily from Russia—part of its continuing fossil fuel dependence laid bare when Vladimir Putin attacked Ukraine in February 2022.[3]

All of this has serious consequences. Although the country has lowered its greenhouse gas emissions by almost 40 percent since 1990, a German on average still produced 8.5 tons of CO_2 in 2019, a ton more than the average European, and a long way from the 2 tons that the Paris climate agreement finds necessary by 2030 to keep the rise in temperature under 1.5°C by 2050. In 2021, German emissions went up, not down, as the country powered out of the coronavirus pandemic. The picture gets even bleaker once Germans' appetite for foreign goods and resources is considered—and the damage their extraction, production, and transportation ("spillovers") leave behind for water, air, and species; on the eve of the pandemic, Germany imported more gas, oil, and coal than in any year since reunification. The Global Commons Stewardship Index puts the country near the bottom internationally for its "very high" impact on the environment.[4]

THE GREENING OF (WEST) GERMANY

Humans have always interacted with nature, but it was only after the Second World War that they discovered "the environment." It was then that previous concerns about local pollution, rivers, and wildlife expanded into an all-encompassing vision of planet earth and its interconnected systems of oceans, soil, and atmosphere. In that transition, nature shifted from a conservative to a progressive cause.

The initial momentum came from the United States, where scientists warned of scarcity, overpopulation, and pesticides' destruction of entire ecosystems, and activists formed the first environmental NGOs, such as Friends of the Earth, in 1969. That same year, Congress passed the National Environmental Policy Act, which created the Environmental Protection Agency.[5] Germans followed the American lead. Early in 1970, West German Minister of the Interior Hans-Dietrich Genscher set up a section for "*Umwelt*" (a literal translation of "environment"); the GDR introduced an entire ministry in 1972.

By the early 1980s, West Germany had the largest anti-nuclear movement in the world, a Green Party in the Bundestag, a collective psychosis about its apparently dying forests, and was promoting energy saving. Germany had begun to set the international environmental agenda.

The ecological turn had deep roots. The doctor and zoologist Ernst Haeckel already coined the word "*Ökologie*" in the late nineteenth century to describe how plants and animals interacted with their surrounding habitat, with their "friends and enemies, their symbiotic partners and parasites."[6] Concerned citizens tried to save the white egret and bird of paradise whose feathers were ending up on ladies' hats. Above all, and in contrast to campaigners elsewhere in Europe, German conservationists found an ally in the state. In 1906, Prussia pledged to look after its "natural monuments" (*Naturdenkmalpflege*). In 1935, the Nazis instituted a groundbreaking law for the protection of nature. After the war, conservationists liked to remember it as their finest hour, in the category of "some good things happened under Hitler, too, at least in the beginning." In reality, rearmament and the war made the law a dead letter and wetlands, trees and birds gave way to dams, highways, and industry.[7] In nature protection, as elsewhere, denazification was limited in the young Federal Republic, and with the continuity in personnel came a continuity in mentality and tactics. Conservationists were civil servants, sometimes retired and often unpaid, who sought to protect nature by working with the state. Their energies were focused on local planners, not on winning over the general public.[8]

Nature protection after the war began with fairly isolated local protests. In 1953, people mobilized to save the Wutachschlucht, a whitewater canyon in the Black Forest, from a dam designed to generate power for peak hours; the authorities eventually gave in. A year later, a bird lover sounded the alarm when he found thousands of dead ducks near their resting area of Knechtsand, a sandbank in the mudflats of Lower Saxony that the Royal Air Force was using for bombing exercises. Protestors took journalists to the sandbank in fishing boats and demanded that it be declared a conservation zone; in 1958, the British government agreed to suspend its military use. On the outskirts of Cologne, concerned citizens forced the coal industry to scale back a planned expansion of lignite mining that would have cleared several hundred hectares of forest. (One hectare is two and a half acres.) Inhabitants of the Saar region were less fortunate: the coal mines in neighboring Lorraine were pumping out so much water from their fields and ponds that several towns were left with a chronic shortage of water and deep cracks in the ground. The fish in the Rossel River were killed by pollution. Several thousand homeowners and small farmers joined forces, to no avail. Farther south, in Bavaria, it was funiculars and ski lifts that divided communities. Were bigger ski resorts gold mines or reckless gambles? In several places, critics pointed out, the investment in cable cars had failed to pay off. The Naturfreunde, the "Friends of Nature," a socialist youth movement, championed hiking and was initially opposed to funiculars.

Alongside these local battles, there were two larger causes sponsored by the elite: the campaign for national parks by the rich merchant Alfred Toepfer, which led to the creation of sixty-two such parks, and the "Green Charter of Mainau" (1961), a manifesto initiated by Count Bernadotte on his private island in Lake Constance that declared healthy nature a fundamental human right.[9]

The umbrella organization of nature lovers was the German Naturschutzring. Founded in 1950, it was an example of the top-down origins of nature conservation, initiated by the head of the state's section for the preservation of natural monuments, Hans Klose, who only a few years earlier had worked for the Nazis. By the late 1960s, it had 2 million members and ran annual photo competitions with the popular magazine *GONG*: "Save the German Landscape!" The entries ranged from a "giant tree on a rock—under nature conservation!" to the "trunk of a beech tree with carved initials." There was awe of natural wonder but also a touch of anthropomorphism. One of the few female participants sent in a picture of the "Burning Mountain" near Dudweiler, where a coal seam had been on fire for more than two centuries, sharing Goethe's amazement at the spectacle in 1770. An apothecary submitted photos of a moor and its diverse flora he had saved from drainage. Others selected images of spruce with trunks shaped like human feet. A teacher was in "awe" of a thousand-year-old linden tree, held up like a dying old man (*Baumgreis*). There were photos of castle ruins, churches, and new suburbs as well as of car wrecks abandoned in the middle of a cornfield as "an impressive memorial to human tastelessness."[10]

Conservationists were almost exclusively educated, middle-class men, and mostly conservative. Nature, for them, was an "oasis of peace" away from the hustle and bustle of the modern world, a kind of temple where the individual could sense the work of God and undergo spiritual renewal. They were romantic paternalists whose sensibility, habitus, and knowledge of birdsong made them nature's elect missionaries. Above all, nature was about identity. Protecting nature was protecting one's homeland. The protestors against the planned open-cast mine outside Cologne, in the early 1960s, for example, were defending not just any group of trees but "a piece of *Heimat*."[11] Elsewhere, people rallied to "their" rocks and caves. If, after Hitler, it was difficult to champion the *Volk*, one could still rally to the *Heimat*.

In reality, there was very little authentic nature left in Germany, since the human hand had corrected God's creation by draining moors and straightening rivers and so much more. There was little pursuit of wilderness—what today is called "deep ecology"—at least at home; that was left for the screen and Bernhard Grzimek's Oscar-winning film, *Serengeti Shall Not Die* (1959) and his popular TV series on endangered wildlife in Africa. For the anti-coal protestors and the Friends of Nature, forests and mountains were places for a day out or a group excursion; Toepfer had joined the Wandervogel ("young ramblers") before the First World War. More leisure time and more cars fueled tourism in the "miracle years." The top prizes of the photo competition were holidays in the Luneburg Heath, the Bavarian National Park, and the High Tatras in Slovakia. Antimodernism had limits. The "Green Charter," for example, sought to secure a "balance between technology, economy, and nature."[12] Quite a few conservationists saw their job as saving nature by "improving" it. A dam that was designed to fit in its surroundings beautified the landscape "as wonderfully as a scar that heals over in the gifted hands of a skilled surgeon," in the words of a Bavarian official.[13]

It was in the 1970s that these diverse elements coalesced into a popular environmental front. The first action came from the state. Social Democrat Willy Brandt had already called for blue skies over the Ruhr in 1961. It was the Liberals, though, who were the first party to capitalize on green issues. When the two joined power, in 1969, environmental problems were earmarked as a priority. The Liberal minister Hans-Dietrich Genscher presented the government's program in 1971. Unlike in earlier campaigns for local flora and fauna, the focus was now on systemic threats to citizens' well-being. "Every citizen," Genscher told parliament, "is entitled to clean water and healthy air for himself and his children, not to be troubled by noise, and not to have to worry about toxins and harmful substances in their products and food." The time for cosmetic measures, he said, was over. The threat to the environment was not a passing one but "the basic problem of our industrial culture" and showed that "man was reaching its limits." His alarm was part of a growing diagnosis that, a year later, would gain international fame with a report by the Club of Rome, a group of business leaders and thinkers, about *The Limits to Growth*, a groundbreaking use of computer simulation that predicted a dramatic fall in population and industrial activity unless things changed. The state, Genscher said, had a duty to secure the future. "Eco-friendliness has to become a natural yardstick for all our actions, for the state, for industry, and for citizens in their consumption." He outlined the government's priorities: long-term planning of the environment and land use; making the polluter pay; environmentally friendly technologies; greater public awareness; and international collaboration. A series of laws were passed to tackle waste and emissions and prohibit the use of DDT.[14]

The government got the ball rolling, but soon it lost control. Notwithstanding its attention to "limits," Genscher's program was ultimately a child of the modernizing optimism of the 1960s, with its faith in planning. In 1971, the economy was growing by more than 3 percent and nuclear technology promised a new golden age. Only two years later, the first oil crisis hit. By 1975, the economy was in recession, and in 1979, the Three-Mile Island reactor in Pennsylvania suffered a partial meltdown. While the government switched its attention from saving nature to saving jobs, the opposition to nuclear power gathered momentum. Planning and big technology, once the magic solution, came to be viewed as part of the problem.

NUCLEAR POWER: FROM "*JA, BITTE!*" TO "NO THANKS!"

In the 1950s and 1960s, nuclear power arrived on a wave of euphoria, in Germany no less than elsewhere. It promised a perpetual source of cheap energy. People were marching against nuclear weapons, not nuclear reactors. In 1955, on Mother's Day, a rally of one thousand women in Duisburg urged the "so-called civilized" big states to share the gift of atomic power with "backward" countries. Actresses and sports stars voiced their support. Heinz Fütterer, the European champion sprinter, said that only crazy people wanted atomic weapons but nuclear power offered "undreamed-of possibilities for humanity."[15] Not everyone was convinced. The Friends of Nature warned that radioactive substances were not sufficiently understood to rule out grave dangers even from their peaceful use. Some doctors traced the rise in cancer and birth defects to the fallout from nuclear tests, and a concerned citizen went to the length of sending the Constitutional Court a tulip bulb as proof of the high level of radiation, which she blamed for her burning throat and irritated thyroid.[16] Such fears, however, had no political home as of yet and subsided once the Soviets and Americans agreed to stop nuclear tests in 1963.

A first research reactor was switched on in Garching near Munich in 1957. Three small, so-called demonstration power stations followed in the early 1960s. Conservationists had no problem with Germany's first commercial nuclear power station (Kahl in northern Bavaria), which started up in 1961, as long as a few bushes were planted around it.[17] In 1974, in the wake of the oil crisis, the social-liberal government planned to build enough commercial nuclear plants to produce 45 percent of the country's electricity in ten years' time. One that was awaiting official approval that year was to be built along the Rhine in Wyhl in the southwest.

In the next few years, the idyllic small town gave birth to a new environmental politics. Wyhl was not the first site of protest; in 1971, Fessenheim, just across the border in Alsace, France, was. Wyhl, however, built a popular alliance that ranged from local farmers to students from nearby Freiburg and beyond. Students feared radiation; farmers were more worried about damage to their microclimate. Wyhl lay at the foot of the Kaiserstuhl, which, with its volcanic hills, was one of the warmest as well as one of the most humid regions in the country, renowned for its *Spätburgunder* wines. The steam the cooling towers would release threatened to block out the sun and turn fine pinot noir into cheap plonk, as well as causing fungal diseases and hail. A tobacco farmer put his protest in plain words: "Nuclear power station—an existential threat for me."[18] Residents felt steamrolled by the planning process. The first they heard about the decision to build a nuclear reactor in their town was in 1973, on the radio. A year later, they were given only one month to register any objections. The authorities, who appeared to be in the hands of a nuclear lobby unaccountable to the people, were flooded with tens of thousands of letters. Close ties with their French and Swiss neighbors across the Rhine provided the protestors with a special regional identity that gave the fight an Asterix quality, with proud Alemanni fighting powerful outsiders. Even the local priest and Christian Democrats joined the protests.

When construction began in Wyhl, in February 1975, citizens climbed across the fence and occupied the building site. Two years later, a court in Freiburg ruled in their favor: while it was highly unlikely that the reactor would blow up, the planners had not made sufficient efforts to mitigate potential damage. The verdict was later overruled, but politically the project was dead. Its start was repeatedly postponed, before, in 1994, it was abandoned altogether.

As this case shows, it is unhelpful to reduce environmentalism to a shift from "material" to "post-material values," as some social scientists have done.[19] Nineteenth-century Romantics were hardly materialists. Nor was there anything new about better-educated social groups such as students rallying to the defense of nature—so had the Wandervogel in 1900. In any case, what could be more "material" than concerns about agriculture, health, and survival?

The more interesting question is what was special about Germany. Nuclear power came to be controversial everywhere but in different ways and with different results.[20] At one extreme were Austria and Italy, which terminated it completely after referenda in 1978 and 1987, at the other Britain and especially France, which relied on it more and more. Germany reached a compromise: while it stopped building new reactors—the last one was at Neckarwestheim (Baden-Württemberg) in 1982—it kept many existing ones running. For more than a decade after the Chernobyl disaster in 1986, when the reactor in the Ukrainian power plant exploded, releasing radiation into the air, Germans continued to get 25 to 35 percent of their electricity from nuclear power. In 2000, Gerhard Schröder's Social Democrat–Green coalition decided to end the use of nuclear power. In 2010, Angela Merkel initially extended the remaining lifetime of nuclear plants, but after the Fukushima disaster in March 2011 she decided to phase out all remaining nuclear power stations by 2022. As late as 2021, nuclear still generated 12 percent of the country's electricity. The war in Ukraine and fear of shortages led Olaf Scholz's government in 2022 to keep the three newest reactors running for another four months.[21]

The historic contribution of the anti-nuclear protests, however, is their mass following, their grassroots politics, and their clash with the state. In 1979, some 100,000 anti-nuclear protestors marched in Hanover, a number unmatched elsewhere. In contrast to the Adenauer years, when environmental protestors tended to go on excursions and sing folk songs, they now confronted the state head-on. In 1980, activists set up a "Free Republic Wendland," a protest camp in Lower Saxony, complete with its own flag and passports, to stop nuclear waste from being deposited in a salt mine in the community of Gorleben there. Demonstrations in solidarity were held in eighty cities, and twenty churches were occupied. In Hamburg, demonstrators blocked street traffic dressed as corpses of radiation victims. Mass demonstrations and police attempts to stop them produced increasingly violent clashes, notably in Brokdorf in 1981 at the building site of a power station, and five years later in Wackersdorf, the Bavarian town earmarked for a nuclear fuel reprocessing plant, where several hundred protestors and police officers were injured; one demonstrator died from an asthma attack caused by tear gas. Unlike Wyhl, Brokdorf went ahead, and its nuclear power plant was built; in 2005, it was the world's biggest reactor and was only switched off on December 31, 2021.[22]

The initial anti-nuclear movement had been led by feminists, pacifists, and anarchists, but it also had a wing on the far right. The physician Bodo Manstein, who had joined the Nazi Party early on, led a group worried about the eugenic damage from radiation. The blockade at Brokdorf was supported by the German Citizens Action Group (Deutsche Bürgerinitiative) around Manfred Roeder, a right-wing terrorist who had briefly served as Rudolf Hess's lawyer before declaring himself the "lawful" successor to

Admiral Dönitz. The group was out to defend blood and soil against alien technology and big capital—an old antisemitic trope. One of the cofounders of the Greens in Schleswig-Holstein was the father of "bio-regionalism," Baldur Springmann, an ecological farmer who had signed up to the "World Union for the Protection of Life," a fascist body founded in Austria in 1960. In addition to leukemia and malformed babies, he worried about the "alienation" (*Entfremdung*) of coastal areas by nuclear plants and foreign workers.[23]

On the left, too, nuclear power stations were about much more than atomic energy. The link between military annihilation and environmental destruction was self-evident—"fast reactors" could create the plutonium on which atomic bombs depended—and campaigners drew on earlier associations between industrial capitalism, imperialism, and pollution. As the Friends of Nature put it during an exhibition on the "endangered environment" in 1971, only fools could pretend that "Vietnam . . . has nothing to do with the sky over the Ruhr."[24]

That Germany found itself at the center of the Cold War understandably heightened the sense of apocalypse. The determination not to be a passive bystander to a nuclear "holocaust" had particular moral force in the land of the perpetrators and linked the protestors of the 1970s with those in the 1950s. For the novelist Günter Grass and many others, anti-fascism and anti-nuclear were two sides of the same coin. *The Cloud*, Gudrun Pausewang's prizewinning children's book about a teenage girl in a nuclear accident, published a year after the accident at Chernobyl, carried the subtitle "Now We Can No Longer Say We Did Not Know."[25] Just as a new generation was coming to terms with the guilt of their fathers, campaigners argued, atomic energy threatened to reinstall authoritarianism. Since nuclear power stations were never completely safe, they inevitably needed special security measures. The use of paramilitary police at Wyhl and elsewhere was ample warning, said the national umbrella organization of environmental citizen groups (Bundesverband Bürgerinitiativen Umweltschutz, BBU) in 1977: "The tendency toward a totalitarian police state is preordained with the introduction of nuclear power."[26] There was widespread fear of an "atomic state," the title of a popular book by the futurologist Robert Jungk. During the war, Jungk had alerted Swiss newspapers to the Nazi murder of the Jews—in vain—and in 1959 he traveled to Hiroshima to report on the suffering of survivors there, as we have seen.[27]

If big technology went hand in hand with a big state, then the future of democracy lay with local, decentralized energy systems such as solar panels and windmills, grassroots politics, and a simple lifestyle: "Small is beautiful." The synod of Baden called on congregations to consume less, "with a view to future generations."[28] A fair in Hamburg's old market hall in 1977 gave a glimpse of what an alternative future could look like, with stalls for renewable technologies, communal living on the land, "bio" bakeries, and homespun wool. In their first election program, in 1980, the Greens campaigned for energy saving, car-free city centers, and a ban on new highways and airports.

Not all was doom and gloom. Apocalyptic fear prompted an almost messianic faith that it was possible to change the course of history and build an entirely new type of society, here and now. The Greens' 1983 manifesto called for a great "conversion" (*Umkehr*), beginning with disarmament and an end to exploitative, mind-numbing jobs and extending to solidarity with the "Third World." Instead of looking for technological fixes, they sounded a wake-up call: "We must change our lives fundamentally, we must redesign our civilization, if we want to live in dignity in the future or survive at all."[29] It won them 5.6 percent of the vote—4 percent more than in 1980 but 94 percent less than the parties committed to industrial civilization.

The discovery of "the environment" marked a paradigm shift in science, but one reason for the strength of the anti-nuclear movement was that it managed to win over old nature groups as well as new ecologists. German boy scouts, for example, set up a summer camp in the small town of Gartow next door to the planned nuclear waste depot in Gorleben in 1977. The four hundred young people learned about the dangers of nuclear power, helped local farmers with their harvest, and played football against the locals. "I came to Gartow without really knowing what a reprocessing plant is," one participant confessed a year later. "I decided to join because I had not made any plans." He left appreciating much more than the risks of nuclear technology. One day, cycling to town for some bread, "I was riding past the meadows, where horses were grazing, and right in front of me swallows were darting across the street. I was amazed—I have never seen swallows fly so low; but then I thought, how often have you actually seen swallows. It was so beautiful, I felt: you must not forget it." He was seduced by "the beauty and peace of the landscape"—feelings not so different from those expressed by earlier Romantics. The summer camp also introduced him to biogas facilities. For this young man, producing alternative energy was an "important part of resistance against nuclear facilities... a practical demonstration that one can get by without industrial electricity, that one can take matters into one's own hands."[30]

Nuclear energy had friends as well as enemies, and the friends were in the majority well into the 1980s. A power station promised jobs, not just risks. Even in Wyhl, 55 percent of inhabitants voted in favor of selling the site to the power company. In Biblis (Hesse), a restaurant carried the sticker "Yes to nuclear power" and the local priest railed against protestors as Moscow's fifth column.[31] In the Rhineland, citizens felt that they and their villages were being sacrificed to expanding coalfields because "fanatics" elsewhere blocked an environmentally friendlier alternative. There were good reasons the government was taken so by surprise by the wave of opposition. In 1975, an officially commissioned study examined thousands of newspaper articles and found barely any that were critical of nuclear reactors. Where citizens' groups featured at all, they were cast as image-hungry egotists and criticized for their "unrealistic attitude."[32] Not a single article called into question the faith in economic growth. That year, open house days at the Wackersdorf nuclear plant in Bavaria were so popular that the energy company organized four bus trips a day for curious visitors. The Brunsbüttel plant at the mouth of the Elbe ran bimonthly photo competitions to win over the locals and show them that technology and landscape could coexist—a first prize pictured power lines across the fields of rural Dithmarschen.[33]

Young Christian Democrats also discovered the environment in the 1970s. They wanted more recycling now and zero-emission cars by 2000. They created a working group that examined the planned obsolescence of consumer goods and urged the CDU to pass a law establishing a lifetime guarantee that would make their producers cover the cost of all repairs. But they also wanted to build reactors. With renewables in their infancy, nuclear power appeared to them to be the best available option for the environment and the economy. They, too, had the interests of future generations in mind. Not having nuclear reactors, they argued, would cause other risks: energy shortages, less competitive industry, unemployment, and social meltdown. No nuclear power meant no growth, which would leave the next generation with a dismal future. The problem for either side in the debate, of course, was (and remains) that it is impossible to know what a future generation will value. Even after Chernobyl, Christian Democrats, young and old, did not waver—until Merkel in 2011. In 1991, at a nuclear forum in Hesse, young Christian Democrats were three to one in favor of nuclear power.[34]

In contrast to Britain, where anti-nuclear campaigners had a foothold in the Labour Party, in Germany they faced a pro-nuclear consensus across the political parties; the Social Democrats only called for phasing out nuclear power in August 1986, after Chernobyl. This made for a more confrontational encounter between protestors and the "the atomic state." Without a political ally, ecological groups turned to grassroot activism almost by default. Here the ground had been prepared by the peace movement, the Extra-Parliamentary Opposition (APO) of the late 1960s and the many citizen groups (*Bürgerinitiativen*). The federal system gave them a tactical advantage because it fragmented the planning process. Since power stations were a matter for regional states, each with their own politics and law courts, activists could attack on multiple fronts.

The fact that Germany remained a coal country—much more so than France, which had less coal to begin with, or Britain, where Thatcher closed down the mines to break the trade unions—ironically proved an aid to the anti-nuclear activists. German governments instead pursued a slow, piecemeal decline of coal mining, cushioned by subsidies. The biggest power company, the Rheinisch-Westfälisches Elektrizitätswerk (RWE), sat on mountains of coal. Nuclear power stations might be cheap in the long term but were hugely expensive to build. Why take the risk of protests, blockades, and legal injunctions? In addition, the energy forecasts that had been used to justify building reactors turned out to be vastly inflated—electricity demand no longer doubled every ten years but was almost flat in the late 1970s. If there was an "atomic state," it was France, which had the bomb but little fossil fuel of its own, which together made developing nuclear power a national mission. In Germany, where nuclear energy had domestic competitors, the fact that no new nuclear power stations were built after 1982 had as much to do with the coal lobby as with the Greens. The environmental movement was lent a helping hand by the greatest polluter around.[35]

In hindsight, the early 1980s were a turning point for nuclear power. The Green Party entered the Bundestag in 1983. Since reactors do not last forever, unless new ones are added their numbers will naturally decline as old ones die off. All that Merkel did after Fukushima was to put a date on their tombstone.

That was in the future, however. People at the time had to live with nuclear power and the risk of apocalypse. Transnational networks of skeptical "counter-experts" raised awareness of the risks. In September 1979, the BBU published the government's confidential reports, which showed that there had been a malfunction or accident every three days on average.[36] A few months earlier the Three-Mile Island reactor had suffered a meltdown. Seven years later, after the Chernobyl accident, the Green MP Hannegret Hönes castigated the world's nuclear reactors as a "declaration of war on all humans." She demanded an immediate switch-off, "here and now."[37] At the time, this was a minority voice. Christian Democrats rallied to the defense of nuclear energy, the Liberals urged greater safety, and even the increasingly skeptical Social Democrats only wanted a gradual phaseout.

In the population at large, Chernobyl prompted a sharp swing in opinion. In 1981, two years after Three-Mile Island, 29 percent of Germans still favored building more nuclear power stations, according to surveys, and only 12 percent wanted to shut them down; the other 45 percent preferred to keep existing ones running. The German anti-nuclear movement might be the largest and most confrontational in Europe, but that also earned it a higher rate of popular disapproval than in Italy, Belgium, Denmark, and the Netherlands, according to a large survey.[38] By May 1986, a month after Chernobyl, the tables had turned: now 69 percent were for abandoning nuclear power. Still, public opinion has proved to be changeable. Only five years later, 61 percent wanted at least existing nuclear plants to continue to operate. By 1997, it was 81 percent. Arguably, Christian Democrats had their fingers on the people's pulse at least as much as the Greens did.[39]

THE GERMAN FOREST

If splitting the atom divided Germans, the threat to their forests united them all. In 1980, a scientist rang the alarm bell when he said acid rain was wiping out *the* German forest. Within a decade it might be gone completely. In the next few years, a public panic took hold about *Waldsterben* ("forest dieback"). It was "five minutes to twelve," the party secretary of the CDU, Heiner Geissler, said. The magazine *Der Spiegel* warned of an "ecological Hiroshima"; the Federation for the Environment and Nature Conservation (BUND), an environmental NGO, feared an "ecological holocaust."[40]

It was not the smoke itself that was new. Pollution was a natural child of the industrial revolution, and that sulfur dioxide damaged plants had been known for a century. What was new in the 1980s was the nerve it touched and the reaction it triggered. The traditional response had been to build higher chimneys and compensate forest owners for their losses.[41] Two thirds of all SO_2 was emitted by coal power stations. The government had passed a regulation in 1981 with stiffer standards, but flue gas desulfurization "scrubbers" were astronomically expensive, and several power plants were given exemptions. Scientists were alarmed that spruces appeared to be losing their needles across many areas, not just in the vicinity of a polluter.

Waldsterben was a uniquely German nightmare; similar findings were reported across the border in France and other countries without causing much of a stir. The panic partly expressed political interests. For the officials in the environment section in the Ministry of the Interior, the specter of dying trees gave the political clout to push for the anti-emission measures they had been working on. Forest scientists lapped up the media attention and, finally, felt heard. For the Greens, it was proof of just how precarious the ecological equilibrium was. It was seen as an existential crisis: the fate of the forest foreshadowed the fate of humanity. "If the forest dies, so does man," as one headline put it. Fir trees were described as "cripples" or "corpses," as if they were people, not plants.

Crucially, nature and nation were inseparable, and the commotion was about *the* German forest, not separate forests with their own characteristics. Hubert Weinzierl, the head of BUND, called the situation a "*nationale Kultur-Katastrophe.*" Helmut Kohl explained that Germans had a unique emotional relationship with their forest, which made its survival a matter of national fate. Why else, he asked, did Germans rally to its defense and the French did not?—a statement that, however logically flawed, played successfully to national stereotypes of the soulful German versus the abstract Frenchman and the money-grubbing Englishman. Several newspapers quoted Joseph von Eichendorff's "Farewell" (1810):

> O broad valleys, o heights
> O beautiful green forest
> Devoted place
> Of my desire and sorrow!

In 1983, activists of the environmental group Robin Wood climbed up Neuschwanstein, the fantastical castle of Ludwig II, and unrolled their banner: "Save the *Heimat.*"[42]

It was a false alarm. Spruce and fir were, after all, not like humans on their deathbed, and many made a remarkable recovery. What exactly had caused them to lose their needles has been a subject of scientific controversy ever since. Before the forest "dieback" was proved to be an illusion, however, it had stirred profound feelings in a generation of Germans. Among them was the young Krems family. The father, Burkhardt Krems, taught public administration at a polytechnic; his wife, Bettina, was a housewife and doctoral student in history. Their two daughters were three and ten, their youngest child a five-month-old boy. In the summer of 1983, they petitioned the Constitutional Court to protect their right to nature. In June, the parents had been driving from their home near Cologne to the annual church congress in Hanover. Crossing the hilly Sauerland, they were shaken by the sight of "dying forests and trees falling down." How could they possibly justify leaving behind such a world to their children? On their return, the couple worked day and night and gathered material about smoke pollution. Professor Dr. Krems was a Social Democrat. Disappointingly, he found that most of his comrades were only paying lip service to the environment out of fear of the Greens and, in the end, put "workplace ahead of a place to live." The couple put together their own network. They discovered a self-help group of parents with children whose larynges had been damaged by emissions from nearby industry, so-called pseudo-Krupp children. They won over aristocratic forest owners, the environmental delegates of several regional churches, and the popular animal filmmaker Bernhard Grzimek.[43]

Their case for the right to clean air is fascinating on several levels. For one, it put the blame squarely on big industry and government; that year, a group of "critical shareholders" attacked the coal and electricity giant RWE as the "final forest terminator." That the Krems, like millions of fellow drivers, were not entirely innocent disappeared from sight. They pressed for catalytic converters and cleaner gas stations, but, still, they drove their car and did not take the train. Their legal justification reveals the range of ideas feeding environmentalism in these years: citizenship, Christianity, and fear of complicity. The Krems argued that the smoke and sulfur violated their "right to life and physical integrity" and the "free development of their personality" (Article 2). They tried to hold the state to account for not enforcing its own emission rules and becoming complicit in a "chemical war" by failing to perform its duty. They defended the rights of children to grow up and breathe clean air—anticipating later arguments for generational justice. They also invoked Christian and romantic ideals. The "experience of nature" (*Naturerlebnis*) was a constitutional right, they argued, since the Basic Law had its roots in Christianity and Western civilization. The ability "to experience in nature the work of the Creator" arose logically from freedom of faith. Their rights as parents gave them a duty to raise their children "to respect living nature." They defended their "right to hear the lark sing and the frog croak, even if they had no immediate economic value." The Constitutional Court politely told them to take their case to a lower court first. Bettina Krems-Hemesath joined the Greens, berated the government for obstructing higher European emission standards, and continued her fight for an ecological rule of law in the public sphere; in 1986, she left the regional party executive because, she felt, for most Greens the environment was no longer a priority; women and asylum issues were.[44]

By the mid-1980s, environmentalism stood out in Germany, in that it had the largest base, the Green Party in parliament, and lots of vocal protestors.[45] What about the population at large? Surveys in 1982 urge caution in assuming Germans were "greener" than their neighbors. "The environment" was a growing concern across Europe, but societies had different worries. Germans were more troubled by air pollution than the Dutch and the Danish, although even among Germans it was only one in three. Britons, Danes, and Italians worried more about the depletion of world forest resources. Germans and Italians expressed more concern about "the possible damage to the atmosphere" from the carbon dioxide released by burning coal and oil than did the French and Belgians. Interestingly, "damage done to the landscape" troubled few Germans and Europeans—so much for the paeans to *Landschaft*. Germans and Italians were marginally readier than the British and the French to protect the environment "even at the risk of holding back . . . economic growth," but less committed than the Danes.[46]

These were the views of adults. German children started to find ecology on their timetable. The 1970s saw school projects for which pupils took samples of chlorite and measured oxygen levels in nearby rivers. In Clausthal-Zellerfeld, an old iron ore mining town in the Harz mountains, the secondary school introduced a course on environmental problems in 1974. They took their motto from American environmentalists: "Think globally, act locally." The students produced their own ecological newsletter, talked to local politicians, and, with the help of a Berlin firm, had a water meter with a timer installed in the school toilets to reduce water consumption. They hoped that cities and big users elsewhere would follow their example, "so that we do not have to worry about our ponds in the upper Harz."[47]

At this point, however, these initiatives were the exceptions. In classrooms across the country, biology stood for "lofty expressions . . . of nature philosophy as well as dogmas of a Christian worldview," an investigation concluded in 1975. How, the author asked, could they have "awe" of nature amid its destruction? Teaching pupils to love nature was no longer good enough. Lessons needed to link ecology to responsible action.[48]

UNESCO launched its program for environmental education the following year. The 1980s saw the comeback of the "school garden"; in densely populated industrial North Rhine–Westphalia, every second school had one by the end of the decade. Rather than ensuring that children got enough vitamins—such gardens' raison d'être after the Second World War—their main purpose now was to teach the young to live in greater harmony with nature. Schools worked with conservation and garden centers and with the World Wildlife Fund. In day cares, small children made a weather calendar for Easter, planted seeds, and observed the coming of spring. By the time they reached seventh grade, children advanced to "godparents" of the local pond. Older pupils studied forest ecology, and, in history, the impact of mining on water systems in the industrial era. Schools set up "biotopes" (habitats for plants and animals) and compost heaps and raised awareness about resources. Preschool children, for example, took apart a table to find out where wood, screws, and glue were coming from and where the pieces might end up: as bulky waste by the side of the road, as compost, or burned, as an example of waste turned into energy. The lesson started with a visit to a carpenter and ended with a trip to the incinerator.

The environment minister in North Rhine–Westphalia sponsored a children's book, complete with games, to teach the young to conserve resources. It pitted the "environmental angel" against "the wasteful sluggard" (*Müllimuff*). This bad creature, it explained, lived in the back of people's minds: "When you produce dirt and rubbish, it is happy." The "environmental angel" learned to recognize its mocking laughter and fight dirt and waste. The story had a whiff of the "coal thief" (*Kohlenklau*), the evil cartoon creature designed by the Nazis in their battle against energy waste. As then, children were told to be detectives at home and check on their parents, although now the mission was on behalf of Mother Nature, not the fatherland. They were urged to hunt down old batteries and collect single-use soda cans. Chemical detergents had to be banished before they ended up in their local pond. "In the evening, the children are scolding Mom and Dad" and tell them to reuse glass bottles, recycle batteries, and clean their dishes with lemon water.[49] It was in schools that the greening of Germany went mainstream.

DARK SKIES OVER EAST GERMANY

Across the border, East Germany traveled in the reverse direction. In the 1950s, the GDR was in many respects in the vanguard of environmentalism. Its forest faculty at Tharandt, in Saxony, was a world-leading center of research and pioneered a system of "landscape diagnostics" that enabled it to chart the damage from smoke and sulfur across the country.[50] It was the second country in Europe to appoint a minister for the environment, in 1972, just behind the British. By the end of its life, the GDR was an environmental disaster zone. More sulfur from the GDR rained down on Norwegians than from within their own country.[51] The situation was so bad that, in 1982, the East German regime decided to make environmental data a state secret.

The GDR started out with the best of intentions. From Marx and Engels, it inherited a utopian faith that communism would bring man and nature into eternal harmony. Capitalism was said to treat the natural world as it did labor, exploiting it and spitting it out once it no longer made a profit, without caring about the consequences. Waste would disappear under communism as resources were being channeled back into production—what later came to be known as a "circular economy." In the East German lexicon, old glass bottles and newspapers were "valuable material" (*Wertstoffe*), not "waste" as in the West.

To reach the communist utopia, however, required growth and development, which meant more industry, energy, and extraction. Had not Lenin wisely said that "communism equals Soviet power plus electrification"? It filled SED leaders with pride that their country used more electricity (per capita) than West Germany, one of the few indicators where the GDR came out ahead. Unfortunately, that electricity was generated by one of the few fossil fuels that geological fate had buried between the Elbe and the Oder: lignite, or brown coal, an extremely damaging fossil fuel extracted from vast open-pit mines. The environment in East Germany bore the scars of this contradiction between the utopia of a circular economy and the reality of material plunder.

As in the West, flora and fauna had plenty of friends in the East. From the birth of the GDR, districts got their own nature conservation delegates. The Kulturbund, a mass organization to promote socialist culture, provided "friends of nature and *Heimat*" with a new home. In 1957, for example, it rallied to the defense of the beaver in the middle section of the Elbe, while in the mining district of Leipzig it criticized the reckless removal of soil (overburden) in open-face mining, which left behind wastelands and ruined rivers: "People, like plants and animals, are finding themselves in many places in a tough fight for air, water, and soil!"[52] An annual nature conservation week was launched that same year. Two years later, residents in Bautzen could admire a dozen types of birds in an aviary, in Bernburg (Halle) they went on a guided ornithological tour, and in the small town of Bad Dürrenberg five hundred people watched the film *Black Bird.* By the late 1960s, such events were popular fixtures in the local calendar. The district of Cottbus, in 1968, organized several hundred nature excursions, lectures, and film showings and six exhibitions. In the town of Lübben, teenagers helped maintain hiking paths and local parks and put up nesting boxes and feeding troughs. There were "Rhododendron Clubs" and, in 1970, the "Friends of Cacti" held their first meeting.[53]

In the 1960s and 1970s, a series of campaigns mobilized citizens to pick up their rakes and improve their local environment. There were initiatives with the slogans "More beautiful our villages and communities" ("*Schöner unsere Dörfer und Gemeinden*"), "More beautiful our cities, join in!" ("*Schöner unsere Städte, Mach mit!*"), "Clean up parks and gardens" ("*Parkaktiv*"), and "socialist national culture weeks." As in the West, the protection of birds and forests drew on a provincial pride in *Heimat*; the district conservationist was not infrequently also the head of the local *Heimat* museum. Volunteers were not necessarily driven by a concern for the environment—some just wanted to beautify their own village or, for that matter, their own house. Nor was help always voluntary. In the town of Sonneberg (Thuringia), local activists had to have a "discussion" (*Aussprache*) with every single household in one neighborhood to get them to "join in." The widespread engagement in these years was impressive nonetheless. Some forty thousand villages participated. In 1972, the villagers of Garbow pledged to plant 2,300 shrubs. In Calbe, on the Saale River, near Magdeburg, members of the angling club together with teams (*Brigaden*) from local enterprises volunteered four thousand hours to turn a former landfill site into a local recreation area. Schoolchildren progressed through a nature syllabus. Young pioneers (six- to ten-year-olds) collected stamps of protected plants and animals, the Thälmann pioneers (ten- to thirteen-year-olds) planted trees and collected acorns and chestnuts for boar and deer, and, once children reached the eighth grade, they learned about the importance of clean air and soil for human health.[54]

Nature was not exactly blooming in the 1960s—industry, agriculture, and tourism, were leaving their footprints—but it had its defenders, and there was hope that wise planning might lead to a cleaner socialist future. By the late 1960s, the GDR had more than six hundred nature reserves. At landscape congresses, delegates openly talked about the challenges facing nature conservation.[55] Researchers produced detailed data on smoke pollution, which led the Council of Ministers to introduce emissions ceilings. By favoring greater efficiency and less waste, Ulbricht's "new economic system" contained elements of a circular economy. No part of the planning system was to produce at the expense of another. While there was no carbon pricing, this principle assigned nature some value and offered compensation. In 1966, a state forest sent the nearby state-owned electrochemical enterprise in Bitterfeld a bill of 7 million Marks for damage to its trees; the calculation was provided by the Institute of Plant Chemistry with explicit reference to the "new economic system."[56]

The film produced for "the socialist week of national culture" in 1972 carried the title *We and Our Environment*. By the time it was shown, the atmosphere had fundamentally changed. In May 1971, Erich Honecker had replaced Walter Ulbricht, and for the environment, as for everything else in the GDR, it would prove a turning point. Honecker scrapped "the system" and made a higher standard of living the new telos. Better homes, more cars, and more chicken on the plate translated into concrete suburbs, asphalt roads, and industrial farming. Where nature happened to be in the way, it was steamrolled.

In the late 1960s, Ulbricht benefited from artificially cheap Soviet oil, a fossil fuel that, though far from clean, was less dirty and more efficient than domestic brown coal. It also gave the GDR a chance to earn precious hard currency by refining Soviet crude into petrol and heating oil and selling it for a profit, including to West Germany. That luck ran out under Honecker, because a higher material lifestyle required more energy at the very moment energy costs were escalating. In 1975, the GDR experienced its own oil crisis when the Soviet Union began to raise the price for its black gold. By 1980, a barrel of Soviet crude cost the GDR three times as much as it had ten years earlier. The regime had promised more goods and comforts when oil was still cheap. Unable to pay for foreign fuel, the GDR became a prisoner of its geological destiny, and that meant lignite—when the Wall came down, 83 percent of all East German electricity came from brown coal (in West Germany, hard and brown coal together made up 48 percent). The GDR had great hopes for nuclear power but only managed to build two reactors.[57] It is an irony of history that Angela Merkel, the chancellor at the helm between 2005 and 2021 when Germany tied itself ever more to Russian gas, oil, and coal, had herself lived through the Honecker years and seen how quickly fuel from the Soviet Union could turn from a blessing into a curse.

Environmentalism went up in smoke. Less oil meant digging deeper for coal. Oil imports fell by two thirds between 1970 and the mid-1980s, while consumption of lignite rose by a quarter.[58] The vast open-cast mines of Espenhain were carving their way toward Leipzig, while those in Lusatia were closing in on the town of Zittau, on the Polish-Czech border. A dozen smaller towns were swallowed up. In the 1980s, residents in Leipzig were breathing in five times as much SO_2 as those in the Ruhr, the industrial cockpit of West Germany. In brief, the GDR had its own energy transition, from one bad fossil fuel to an even worse one.[59]

KEEPING THE LIGHTS ON

East Germany was almost constantly on the brink of an energy shortage. To narrow the gap between electricity supply and demand, countries have three main choices: they can produce energy more efficiently; they can save it; or they can try to spread its use across day and night to lower demand during peak hours. The GDR failed in all three. If the Soviet dismantling of machinery for reparations after the war and shortages of material and skilled staff had caused difficulties from the outset, the lure of cheap oil amplified them. The GDR allowed its existing coal mines and power plants to run down. When the flow of oil dried up, the country had to fall back on rickety old plants that struggled from one breakdown to the next: *Havarie* ("accident") is a key word in official records. In 1985, the majority of power plants were at least fifteen years old and produced more smoke and less electricity than new ones; they used one third more brown coal for each kilowatt-hour generated than an up-to-date power plant in the West.[60]

Energy saving was constrained by political imperatives. Rolling blackouts had been one of the grievances that brought out the people against the regime in 1953. With the "new course," the leaders committed themselves to try everything to keep the lights on, although the evening peak problem sometimes made cutoffs inevitable.[61] There would be appeals to save electricity—a "100 watt" campaign urged people to use no more than that, and party youth attacked the *Wattfrass* ("watt glutton").[62] Their effect was limited. Not only were there few low-wattage light bulbs around; energy (like housing and water) was treated as a basic right, and hence so cheap that households had little incentive to save. (In 1976, the price for electricity was raised, but only for industry.) In Berlin, in 1957, a woman activist put up posters in the entrance to buildings urging housewives to switch off their irons and heaters in the evening. When she later talked to them, she found that "all the women said that they never paid attention to these peak hours."[63]

The construction of modern high-rise blocks in the 1970s delivered some savings. Even here, though, there was plenty of leakage. Thermostats were far from universal, and to regulate the room temperature many residents simply opened their windows. In 1983, new flats were found to use 37 to 60 percent more heat than planned. Infrared tests revealed cracks in the cement, drafty windows, and defective insulation. That same year, the regime decided to crack down on electric space heaters and ordered everyone to hand them in. Twelve months later, many thousands of users had been granted permission to hang on to them.[64]

If households could not be made to save, this left industry as a target. In 1952, the regime appointed "energy delegates" to promote energy saving in enterprises, complete with ranks and a gray-blue uniform. Most enterprises were not impressed. A few introduced meters, insulated pipes, or whitened walls and ceilings to save electric light. Many more, however, did not even have an energy plan or, where they did, simply ignored their allocated quotas (*Normen*). When scarce materials finally showed up, enterprises went into overdrive to make up for lost hours, especially when it concerned the production of vital exports, regardless of whether they were breaching their electric quotas. A small fine or slap on the wrist was a price worth paying for fulfilling their part of "the plan." The regime tried to move more production into nighttime, when families were asleep and electricity was ample—again with limited success. For understandable reasons, night shifts were not very popular, in spite of the nighttime child care set up to help working mothers.[65]

Harsh winters put this shaky system to an existential stress test. Brown coal had a high water content and easily froze in the ground. Mines installed heating sheds to prevent it from freezing again in the wagons. The harsh winters of 1962–63, 1968–69, and 1978–79 led to so-called winter battles where the regime mobilized students, soldiers, and supporters to fight to keep the lights on. In Erfurt, in January 1963, more than a thousand activists of the National Front delivered scarce coal to vulnerable households. If ever there was a good time to start saving energy, it was then. This was not, though, how most people saw it. Internal reports recorded the mood on the street. "Twenty-one years GDR and still not enough electricity," the hairdressers in the "Figaro" brigade in Suhl complained. "Why haven't more power plants been built?" others wanted to know.[66] To a farmer from a collective, "It is all the fault of socialism."[67]

These views rested on a simple assumption that energy was meant to be plentiful. They had been promised that by their socialist leaders. The situation was therefore the regime's fault; citizens ignored their own role as increasingly hungry energy consumers. In Rostock, shops disobeyed orders and kept selling hot water boilers. The FDJ, the party youth, launched a campaign on January 29, 1963, urging people to dim their lights and switch off appliances. Thanks to German bureaucracy and attention to detail, we know exactly how the citizens of Erfurt and Gotha responded. There was an immediate saving of 8 percent and 5 percent compared to the electricity used the week before. Only twenty-four hours later, the lights and appliances were back on.[68]

For the environment, the GDR's energy regime was catastrophic. A confidential report, in 1981, briefed the Council of Ministers on the scale of the problem.[69] While it had been possible to reduce air pollution in Cottbus and Halle since the mid-1970s, it had worsened in Berlin, Leipzig, and Dresden. Industrial water use was down, but the recultivation of lignite fields had been a failure. Above all, SO_2 emissions continued to rise, in Dresden by 40 percent in five years. Ninety-five percent of the residents of East Berlin suffered excessive exposure. Just to the east of the capital, in Rüdersdorf, the local cement works emitted lime dust twenty times the official limit. In the district of Halle, a quarter of all woodlands, including recreation areas, were damaged by smoke pollution—in the Ore Mountains near the border with Czechoslovakia, it was even worse. The report noted the growing number of petitions by concerned citizens. The regime adopted a strategy of containment. The limited resources for environmental protection were prioritized for the big cities. An official Society for Nature and Environment (Gesellschaft für Natur und Umwelt) was set up to control and isolate critical voices.

Ecological critics found themselves at the fringes and never posed a systemic threat to the regime. Unlike elsewhere in the Eastern bloc or in the West, they failed to attract scientists to lend them weight. The petitioning system helped to defuse the situation. In 1981, for example, a woman from the Ore Mountains wrote to the Ministry of Environment Protection to express her opposition to the pesticide DDT, citing the concerns of the World Health Organization. She wanted to know when the pollution would stop in her region. She duly received an official answer: not before the new millennium because of the current fuel situation. The matter was closed.[70] In the course of 1988, a man in Zittau wrote to his district council, the national council of ministers, and the SED Central Committee. The moment he opened the windows in his flat, he said, dust and ash from the heating plant of the textile factory next door would cover his carpet and curtains. Two years earlier during the election, residents had been assured that a dust-removing installation was imminent. Now he was told to wait until the year 2000. What use, he asked, were child benefits when his daughter's airways were damaged by pollution? He was happy to forgo the benefits. In these and similar cases, the regime risked losing the trust of individual supporters, but it was a long way from having to face a collective opposition.[71]

Environmental groups—to call the seventy or so groups a "movement" would go too far—formed alongside the peace circles under the protection of the churches. In Wittenberg, where Martin Luther had sparked the Reformation with his Ninety-Five Theses, an ecological seminar began to meet at a Protestant study center in 1976. Its traveling exhibition on damage to nature was seen by twenty thousand people. In Wismar, a group protested against the planned motorway. Several parishes started their own environmental libraries and shared information via mimeographed leaflets. By and large, their ethical concerns echoed those that had gained ground in the West in the previous decade: humans carried a responsibility for God's Creation and there was a link between environmental destruction, the arms race, and poverty in the "Third World." Less money spent on weapons would mean more money could be used to save the planet, a Dresden memorandum explained in 1983. The ecological crisis in the GDR and poverty in the global South were by-products of their own wasteful lifestyle.[72]

Global concerns remained anchored in a local-spiritual *Heimat.* In the Zittau Mountains, Christian groups held an "acid rain weekend" in 1988. Horrified by the industrial conquest of nature, of "animal factories" and an "agrarian steppe," they wanted to preserve "our *Heimat*": "the little garden that has room for the blackcap bird and hedgehog, . . . the village lime tree . . . and the scent of lilac."[73] Invoking Kant, the Protestant churches said that to stop the ecological crisis they had to free themselves from their "self-inflicted immaturity."[74] They urged people to switch to a bicycle, do their laundry at a lower temperature, and forgo cold cuts once a week and the Sunday roast once a month.[75] People wasted electricity, these circles pointed out, because 1 kilowatt-hour cost only 8 pfennigs: "the rest of the bill is paid by our forest."[76] Eco groups urged people to be "mobile without a car," sponsored cycling tours, and planted trees. When local firms in Espenhain said they had no money to install filters, environmentalists raised 100,000 Marks to send the children of the town on a clean air holiday.

Overall, these groups looked to individual lifestyle change. Leaflets gave practical tips on how to avoid pollution and conserve resources: avoid busy roads and buy a stroller with a seat higher than the exhaust of cars; collect paper, instead of burning it; separate plastic, aluminum, steel, and old camera film; keep the room temperature to 64–66°F and put on a cardigan if cold; use a solar water heater and put the right-sized lids on cooking pots to save energy; clean your windows with an onion instead of using chemical detergents.[77] These calls were, in essence, not so different from what champions of "simple living" have preached before and since. They displayed a Protestant ethic or, in the taxonomy of the regime, a "bourgeois" mind-set with a focus on private virtue and motivation instead of the material structure of society. The crucial difference was that the GDR was a society of shortages and pent-up demand. Ecologists in the East copied the slogan of the Greens in the West and urged citizens to "turn around" and "win through sacrifice."[78] In a society where people had to wait many years to get their own private car, such calls fell on deaf ears.

ENERGIEWENDE

If there is one German term that took off internationally in recent years it is "*Energiewende*," a turn away from fossil fuels to renewable energy from wind, sun, soil, and water. It was a cornerstone of Merkel's second cabinet (in coalition with the Liberals) and announced in September 2010. Initially, it was complemented by extending the lifetime of nuclear power stations. The following spring, as mentioned earlier, the Fukushima disaster added a complete nuclear phaseout by 2022 to the agenda. From President Barack Obama to environmentalists across the world, Germany was held up as a shining example of how to save the planet from climate change. How much of the praise is deserved?

Coal, gas, and oil had long played a crucial role in modern industrial societies, but it was only after the 1960s that they were bundled together as "energy" and moved to the center of politics. The push came from two seismic forces: the oil crises of the 1970s and climate change, caused in large part by burning fossil fuels. Power, economic life, and the future of the planet were now inextricably connected. Merkel's policy was, in fact, the country's second stab at energy transition. Germany had its original *Energiewende* in the late 1970s and early 1980s, when Social Democrats first coined the term.

When the first oil crisis hit in 1973, the Federal Republic was in a precarious position. Oil made up 55 percent of its primary energy consumption; ten years earlier it had been 33 percent. The fate of hard coal was almost exactly the reverse, down from 51 percent to 22 percent; natural gas was at 10 percent in 1973, lignite 9 percent, and nuclear power and hydropower at 1 and 2 percent respectively.[79] Willy Brandt and his ministers were not completely taken by surprise by the crisis; fear of shortages had already prompted a strategy review in 1970. The chancellor brushed aside American critics and conservatives at home who warned against a growing dependence on the communist enemy. That same year, West Germany signed its first pipeline deal with the Soviet Union. What had started out as part of Brandt's Ostpolitik to normalize relations with the Eastern bloc became a cornerstone of national energy security.[80]

To the public, Brandt presented the energy crisis as an opportunity: by giving the young generation their own first experience of scarcity, it would remind all citizens that society was founded on mutual aid. In the end, the government asked for minimal sacrifices. A speed limit on highways was lifted after barely six months. There were four car-free Sundays at the end of 1973; after that, the government would only appeal for voluntary action. Devotees continued to join bicycle demonstrations on Sundays, but their numbers were dwindling. In 1981, fewer than one hundred cyclists came together in Frankfurt, while across town the International Automobile Show attracted its 1 millionth visitor. Düsseldorf's "Kö" (the Königsallee) celebrated its neighborhood festival with eight hundred cyclists; far more visitors came by car. In Hamburg, traffic in the tunnel under the Elbe was even busier than normal on the voluntary car-free days. The national automobile club demanded "a free ride for free citizens." The conservative *Frankfurter Allgemeine Zeitung* and the tabloid *Bild* did not agree on much, but they shared in the vilification of these appeals to voluntary sacrifice that, to them, resembled earlier Nazi drives for simple "Sunday stews" to save on imports.[81]

How did West Germany maneuver itself out of this tight corner? Partly with the help of nuclear power, at least initially. By 1985, it contributed 11 percent of total energy, while reliance on oil had fallen to 41 percent. Since no new power stations were being built, however, this only offered so much relief. The new Green Party called for lifestyle change as well as an end to nuclear power. They got neither. Their influence was more indirect, pushing ecological topics up the agenda.

Among the Social Democrats, the trailblazer was Erhard Eppler, a left-leaning Protestant who until 1974 was in charge of development aid. He supported the peace movement and, in 1982, helped bring down Schmidt over the stationing of nuclear warheads on German soil. Especially for younger members, he was the conscience of the party. Eppler drew a simple conclusion from the Club of Rome's report on the limits of growth: the age of affluence had to give way to an age where people understood what was superfluous. It was Eppler who imported "quality of life" into public discourse. In 1975, he wrote a book with the alarmist title *Ende oder Wende*: either the end or a turn to a less wasteful use of resources.[82]

Here was the second answer to Germany's energy dilemma. What nuclear power was to France, and North Sea oil for Britain and Norway, energy conservation came to be for West Germany.[83] If fuel was used more sparingly, then it was possible for an industrial country to grow without having to build more nuclear power stations. If the pioneer of this sea change was California, Germany was a close second. In 1976–77, the country introduced energy standards for appliances and more efficient building codes. In towns, district heating networks pumped waste heat from power stations burning coal, biomass, or trash straight into people's homes. By the end of the decade, the old paradigm of steadily rising energy use lay in tatters. It now seemed possible to "decouple" economic growth from energy growth.

It would prove a decisive shift. "Environmental protection," Eppler said, was "not a quirk of the bored middle classes."[84] It created much-needed jobs. His fellow Social Democrat, the new minister for technology, Volker Hauff, picked up the baton in 1980. At party conferences, Social Democrats might express doubts about progress and consumption. In practice, however, they showed faith in ecological modernization, very different from the Greens' uneasiness with modernity. Economic growth, industrial work, and private comfort all seemed possible again, as long as there was double-glazing and more efficient machinery. Why worry about lifestyle change? Technology would fix it.

There was one problem. Hauff and Eppler were early supporters of decentralized renewables, such as wind turbines, but they were also realistic enough to appreciate that their future was yet to come. In the 1980s, their contribution to Germany's energy mix was tiny. With nuclear on the way out, this left coal, which, with its powerful unions, happened to be a SPD stronghold. When Hauff wrote a book immediately after Chernobyl he gave it the title *Energiewende.* Today, we tend to equate *Energiewende* with decarbonization, but in its early phase it was primarily anti-nuclear, and dirty coal was still very much part of it—in the 1980s, West Germany mined more lignite than in the 1950s or the 1960s, and it halted the decline of hard coal. The hope was that modern plants, filters, and combined heat and power would help coal to clean up its act. In 2011, after a long period in political exile, Hauff would reemerge as a member of the Ethics Commission for Secure Energy Provision, appointed by Merkel.

In Germany, two pioneering champions of "decoupling" were Werner Müller and Bernd Stoy at the energy giant RWE, where one worked as an economist and the other as a technical director. Their 1978 book *Entkopplung* (*Decoupling*) reveals the remarkable optimism behind green growth, and its blind spots. New technologies made it possible to enjoy growth without burning through more resources, they argued, with the help of markets and human nature. The two authors took their inspiration from Adam Smith, the Scottish moral philosopher and author of *The Wealth of Nations*, and Hermann Heinrich Gossen, a mid-nineteenth-century Prussian official and economic writer. Market forces were much better than the state in fostering cleaner energy systems, they argued. Similarly, people could be trusted to consume less because, according to Gossen's "first law" of diminishing marginal utility, the more someone consumes of the same good, the smaller the pleasure derived from it. The first slice of pizza is heaven, the twentieth hell. "Today's consumer," they wrote, "is starting to feel that their purely material consumption is reaching the limits of additional pleasure." "Slowly but surely they will shift their consumption to immaterial elements: quality, longevity, services, a holiday in natural surroundings, meaningful leisure." In rich societies, material growth was reaching its limits "all by itself." "Softer" energies would be accompanied by softer lifestyles. Müller and Stoy were proved right with their forecasts about the relative decline of energy use. They were just as wrong about lifestyles, which have continued to be materially more intense than ever before.

Decoupling economic growth from energy consumption was a significant step, although the statistics can make it look more impressive than it really was. At the end of the 1980s, West Germany consumed no more energy than it had at the beginning of the decade. Greater efficiency in the metal industries and better-insulated buildings played a role, but so did sluggish growth and the departure of shipbuilding. Statistics for the years immediately after reunification in 1990 show a drop in energy consumption. When broken down, however, it is clear that the decline happened in the East and resulted from the collapse of industry there. In the West, energy use was rising, although more slowly than economic growth. Rather than reducing their consumption, German companies were offshoring production to central Europe and, later, to China.[85]

Renewables took off with the new millennium. Helmut Kohl's government was the first, in 1990, to pay anyone generating electricity from solar panels, although the reward was tiny. In 2000, Gerhard Schröder's coalition raised the feed-in tariff to 50 cents per kilowatt-hour. From one day to the next, solar became lucrative. The Renewable Energy Law set off a boom in solar panels and was copied in many countries. In 2003, electricity from photovoltaics doubled. Other measures were more contradictory and revealed the conflicting interests in Germany's energy transition and Schröder's coalition. An eco-tax was levied but only on oil, not on coal—and companies only had to pay half of what consumers did. After the Fukushima disaster and Merkel's U-turn on nuclear power, wind and solar were once again in high demand and expected to pick up the slack.

For all the hype it has attracted, the *Energiewende* should more appropriately be called an "electricity Wende." By 2021, renewables provided 43 percent of Germany's electricity consumption; thirty years earlier, it had been 4 percent. Unfortunately, electricity covers only one fifth of the country's energy use. Cars, homes, and industry are overwhelmingly powered by fossil fuels; in 2021, renewables only contributed 16 percent to the total energy mix, behind coal's 18 percent and well behind gas (27 percent) and oil (32 percent). The dramatic takeoff of renewables in the 2000s was followed by just as dramatic a slowdown in the 2010s; in 2012 and 2018, it even went into reverse.[86] At the grassroots, NIMBYism ("Not in My Backyard") now often trumped environmentalism. In 2021, a single new windmill went up in Saxony.

The energy transition was riddled with problems. The hoped-for technological spillovers failed to materialize. The producers of solar panels and the farmers and people who put them up cashed in on the subsidy. Then the technology migrated to China. The cost of the feed-in tariff disproportionately fell on poor households, while industrial users were partly exempted to keep their competitive edge. Wind turbines went up in the windy north, but there was no electric highway to take the power to factories in the south, an embarrassing oversight in a country that prided itself on its engineers and motorways. When the wind blew too much, existing lines had to be switched off to prevent overload. When it blew too little, nuclear electricity was allowed in from France. Wind and solar have dominated the headlines, but the unsung hero has been biomass, which accounted for 44 percent of all renewable energy in 2020—a situation that is far from ideal, because there is only so much space, and every acre given over to rape, corn, or wood for energy is a loss for food production. In 2018, the World Economic Forum ranked Germany seventeenth in their energy transition index, behind the Nordic countries, Austria, France, the United Kingdom, and several others.[87]

Why the energy transition stalled is a highly complex question, but the short answer can be expressed as the four Cs: coal, cars, chemicals, and consumers. Each carries its share of responsibility. Energy was not a level playing field. Fossil fuels enjoyed generous state support. In contrast to Greece and the United Kingdom, coal in Germany was allowed a gentle decline. And when domestic mines did close, the iron and steel industries switched to Russian coal rather than change their production methods. Carmakers formed a united front defending their conventional petrol and diesel vehicles. In 2013, Merkel blocked plans by the European Union to raise fuel economy standards for cars. BASF, the world's biggest chemical company, could not resist the temptation of bigger profits from gas and oil from Russia, even after Putin annexed the Crimea in 2014.

Bad enough in itself, dependence on fossil fuels increasingly meant dependence on Russia. By 2020, it was supplying 55 percent of Germany's gas, 34 percent of its oil, and 57 percent of its hard coal. For comparison, the GDR at its peak imported 30 percent of its energy, most of it from the Soviet Union.[88] Putin's invasion of Ukraine brutally exposed the hidden costs of these flows. Germany was a carbon democracy that had left itself at the mercy of a foreign dictator.

There was no shortage of warnings, and not only from the United States. In 2011, the government's own Ethics Council (Ethikrat) warned against entering "into one-sided dependence." The World Economic Forum and McKinsey ranked Germany 110th out of 114 countries for the poor structure of its energy system; it scored 87th for its high imports. A year before the Russian invasion of Ukraine, the International Energy Agency stressed that it was "increasingly important" for Germany to "diversify its gas supply options, including through the import of liquefied natural gas." Pipelines to Russia distracted from the need to build LNG terminals and storage tanks.

Those pipelines and the "debt brake" withheld much-needed investment for renewables such as electrical highways.[89] Gas, the supposed "bridge" to a carbon-neutral future, turned out to be a bridge to nowhere.

Throughout these years, governments defended the *Energiewende* for ensuring that energy would be secure, affordable, and "cleaner." It failed on all three counts. Not only was the country left dangerously dependent on one foreign autocrat, its electricity prices were the highest in Europe, and it continued to be its main polluter; Russian gas was not especially cheap, either.[90]

The days when concern for the environment belonged to a counterculture are long over. The mantra of "sustainability" (*Nachhaltigkeit*) illustrates its migration to the center of power. The term can claim German ancestry and was first used by Carl von Carlowitz (1645–1714), who oversaw mining in Saxony and pioneered the sustainable use and replanting of forests, although he only once explicitly used "*nachhaltend*," and more often referred to "careful," "continuous," "permanent," and "conserving" use.[91] By the late nineteenth century, sustainability had advanced into a quantifiable formula in forestry. It was still equated with a steady state and sufficiency by the authors of *Limits to Growth* (1972).[92] In the following decades, a more expansive vision took hold in which sustainability came to stand for the use of social and economic as well as natural resources that met "the needs of the present without compromising the ability of future generations to meet their own needs," in the words of the UN (Brundtland) Commission on Environment and Development in 1987. People in the present no longer needed to cut back. Innovation and management would make it possible to reconcile their needs with those of later generations. The future was once again bright: Brundtland looked forward to a "new era of economic growth."[93]

Baden-Württemberg, home to Riesling wine and Mercedes limousines, was the first state in the country to introduce a "sustainability strategy," in 2007—five years before the UN launched its Sustainable Development Goals. There has been no shortage of goodwill. By 2017, its annual sustainability days attracted nearly two thousand activities across the state. Making sustainability a reality has proved more difficult. The latest "indicator report" (2019) gives a snapshot of successes and failures. In the previous decade, Baden-Württemberg managed to lower its energy consumption by 12 percent while raising its productivity by 19 percent. At the same time, though, energy use for transport went up. In this sunny region, solar power met only 1.7 percent of primary energy consumption. The combined result was that the state was missing its targets for lowering energy use and greenhouse gas emissions. Ecological farming was up, but so was car use and car ownership. Most birds were doing better, but the skylark and tree sparrow were doing worse. The picture was just as mixed when it came to social needs and development. Fewer people smoked, but more were obese. More people were at risk of poverty, especially migrants, and the number of disabled residents in work had fallen.[94]

An international peer review of the country's sustainability strategy as a whole reached a similarly mixed verdict in 2018. It found many strengths: technology, institutions, social cohesion, and economic resources. Yet it also noted how biodiversity was being lost, groundwater exceeded nitrate threshold levels, and the carbon footprint of transport was not getting smaller. It called on all parties to show more ambition to phase out fossil fuels, promote a circular economy, and change the dairy and meat industry—and diets, with it. And it urged both industry and individuals to take greater ownership.[95]

EMISSIONS AND OMISSIONS

Carbon's staying power had to do with politics and morality as much as economics and infrastructure. Renewables advanced along the path of least resistance. Where they made uncomfortable demands on companies or consumers, they made little progress. Wind turbines on the horizon and solar panels on the roofs distracted from the fact that the German people continued to rely on gas and oil to heat their homes and drive their cars. As consumers, they were complicit beneficiaries of fossil fuel from Russia.

Thirty-nine percent of all energy in Germany today is used by households. Close to two thirds of them heat with gas or oil and virtually all fill up the tank of their car with petrol or diesel. When it comes to renewable heating, Germany lags behind the rest of Europe—15 percent compared to 23 percent; in 2020, every third new home was still designed to be heated with gas. Transport is little better. In 1998, there were 36 million cars on German roads. In 2021, it was 48 million, of which not even 3 percent were hybrid or electric. While industries and buildings might conserve more energy, private consumption remains high. Solo living and bigger apartments, with the thermostat set to 72°F, have effectively wiped out any gains from better insulation in the past thirty years; 41 percent of households today are single ones.[96]

Greater mobility, too, has driven up energy consumption. Not only have Germans' once-compact cars expanded into SUVs, but the people behind the wheel are increasingly driving to leisure activities, shops, and restaurants as well as commuting to work—the average length traveled each day by a city dweller went up from nineteen miles to twenty-two miles in the last two decades, and for those in the countryside from twenty-three miles to twenty-seven miles. Cycling may be more popular again, but it has mainly replaced walking, not driving. While Germans shop more online, they are also more likely to take the car when they physically visit the shops.[97] German airports went from one record year to the next, until the pandemic hit. In 2019, three times as many passengers took to the skies as twenty years earlier. For a long weekend, flying became normal. The increased use of energy that has come with this lifestyle reaches so deep into everyday life that it is barely noticed anymore. More frequent hot showers are one example. The growing popularity of the barbecue another. To have a German grill party, you need not only beer and sausages—which carry their own environmental costs—but charcoal. In 2018, Germany imported 234,000 tons of it—50 percent more than ten years earlier. The bulk comes from Poland, Ukraine, and Paraguay, often from endangered forests.[98]

Germans, of course, are not the only hyper-consumers on the planet. The difference is that the *Energiewende* has been a balm to their conscience, making them feel like ecological trailblazers, or at least creating the comfortable illusion that wind and solar will fix the problem, without change in their own lives. It has focused attention on how energy is generated rather than what it is used for, that is, the daily things we do that create the demand for it in the first place. Technology is, of course, important, but if the twentieth century has one lesson for us, it is that technological progress and greater efficiency have not been nearly enough to halt the growing appetite for material resources.[99]

Since coal, oil, and gas are the prime culprits of greenhouse gas emissions, Germany's halfhearted energy transition inevitably slowed down the fight against climate change, too. In 2010, Merkel pledged to lower greenhouse gases by 2050 between 80 percent and 95 percent. By 2018, the country was 12 percent below targets. On the basis of the limited progress made until then, Germany would only reach the goals it had set itself for 2030 in 2075. This dark forecast came not from some eco-rebels but the climate expert at the government's Environment Agency.[100] By the end of 2020, Germany had managed to lower emissions by 41 percent from 1990 and reach its target, but that was thanks to the pandemic. When the economy picked up steam in 2021, it quickly wiped out recent gains—emissions, in fact, rose by 5 percent that year. The country will need to triple its efforts in the 2020s to reach its Paris target in 2030, a Herculean task that, in addition to phasing out coal, would require four times the photovoltaic capacity currently installed and tens of billions of euros each year to insulate and upgrade buildings.[101]

Germany externalized its shared responsibility for the climate in part by doing little now and leaving more for later. By 2020, this tactic came under attack from Fridays for Future, the international movement launched by Greta Thunberg. Luisa Neubauer and fellow activists in that group, including individuals from Bangladesh and Nepal, took the government to court for "the persistent failure... to take suitable and prospectively sufficient measures to stay within the remaining national CO_2 budget" that put their lives and freedom at risk. A year later, in a landmark decision, the Constitutional Court largely found in their favor and ordered the government to tighten up its provisions, especially with regard to adjustments beyond 2030.[102]

The second mode of externalizing was across space. Environmental flows do not stop at national borders. An honest accounting would need to include the environmental costs of all goods and activities, including those embedded in imports. Steaks and avocados, sneakers and sweaters have to be produced somewhere, after all. Twenty-nine percent of all the greenhouse gas emissions caused by German consumers can be traced to imports; food is a major item in that regard.[103] In national accounts and climate goals, these magically disappear. By contrast, Sweden deserves credit for including imports in its pledge to become climate neutral.

Once again, that leads back to the attraction of Russian fossil fuels. Gas from Russia promised that it was possible to have it all: "cleaner" energy to power German industry and keep homes warm, to switch off risky nuclear power plants, and to phase out dirtier coal. This rosy picture conveniently ignored the true environmental as well as strategic costs. More methane (CH_4) is released during the extraction and transport of Russian gas than when it is eventually burned in Germany.[104] The running of gas compression stations adds CO_2 emissions. Put simply, Germany took the gas and left most of the emissions behind. It was an environmental version of the solipsism we have encountered elsewhere, a desire to be good that was ultimately self-regarding and could not (or would not) see the consequences for others. With hard coal from Russia, it was a similar story.

Once these "leakages" and "spillovers" are taken into account, a somber picture gets even darker. In 2019, Germans were responsible for 9.8 tons per head of domestic greenhouse gas emissions (GHG), over a ton more than the average European. Add the spillovers from imports, and emissions almost double—by 7.9 tons GHG, per capita; in the EU, it was "only" 6.3 tons. Officials trumpet the nation's success in lowering its domestic emissions by 40 percent between 1990 and 2020; a large part of that came from cleaning up the former GDR. For the planet, however, the emissions it has been causing elsewhere are just as consequential. That is why the country lands near the bottom of the Global Commons Stewardship Index.[105]

Sweeping these spillovers under the carpet is one reason constituencies tied to carbon have been so distrustful of the *Energiewende*. In Lusatia, near the border with Poland, coal miners went from hero to zero after reunification. They literally became the dirty face of climate change. In 2020, Berlin decided that it would close down remaining mines and plants and exit coal, step by step, by 2038. To the locals, it was a slap in the face. Lignite was not only their bread and butter, it was their *Heimat*, their past and their future. That foreign coal and electricity generated from it continued to be imported made the whole energy transition appear suspect. "What good is it," one miner wondered, "if an old coal power plant in Romania keeps running while we are closing down our own new one?... It looks hypocritical and dishonest to me."[106]

To climate activists, the *Energiewende* looked no less hypocritical. The very moment the government announced the exit from coal, in spring 2020, the hard coal power station Datteln 4 was switched on. From the start of its construction in 2007, it became a symbol of the fight against all fossil fuels, homegrown and imported; the bulk of its hard coal has come from Russia and Colombia—what activists call "blood coal." That year, a climate justice movement came together at the G8 summit of the world's most powerful leaders in the seaside resort of Heiligendamm on the German Baltic, and developed links with anti-globalization and ecological anarchists. Its aim has been to decentralize and democratize energy by taking it out of the hands of big corporations and putting it back under municipal control. The movement has also pressed for immediate decarbonization, including lifestyle change.

In 2012, climate activists occupied part of the Hambach forest, a 1,235-acre area outside Cologne that the energy giant RWE had in its sight for its rich lignite deposits. Plans to clear the forest had attracted protests from church and environmental groups since the late 1970s; it was home to the rare Bechstein's bat. The occupation sharpened the conflict. There were violent clashes with the police and RWE employees. Stones and Molotov cocktails were thrown, machinery blocked, and power lines attacked. Several groups formed Ende Gelände ("here and no further"), which since 2014 has organized civil disobedience protests against coal mines and pipelines.

These protests have recycled the grassroots politics of earlier movements. What is new is the radical link the climate justice movement has drawn between carbon, capitalism, and colonialism. RWE is not only attacked as a profiteering corporation, but with its emissions, it is said to be responsible for the climate crisis and the many people dying or fleeing rising temperatures and sea levels. While the global vision of the Ende Gelände network is impressive, its support on the ground so far has been modest, at least when compared to the tens of thousands of people who occupied the building sites of various nuclear power stations and processing plants in the 1970s and 1980s. Ende Gelände has around fifty groups and mobilized four thousand people to blockade the coal plant Schwarze Pumpe for two days in May 2016.[107]

A far larger phenomenon is the German wing of Fridays for Future. Across the country, more than 1 million people joined the second global climate strike protests on September 20, 2019; 300,000 people were in the streets in Berlin alone, more than in New York or anywhere elsewhere in Europe. Initially attracting fourteen-to-nineteen-year-old young women, the movement has begun to attract older cohorts as well—in September 2019, three quarters of the participants were women older than twenty-five. Senior citizens have started "Grannies for Future." Participants told researchers they felt they had a moral obligation to protest. Surveys taken in several European cities suggest that German protestors had pronounced but hardly exceptional views. Participants in Florence put greater emphasis on voluntary lifestyle change than those in Berlin, but people in Helsinki and Oslo even less. Protestors in Berlin and Chemnitz had less faith in government than those in Stockholm or Gothenburg. On the other hand, teenagers and adults in Germany and Sweden believed strongly that protecting the environment took priority over growth and jobs, and that governments needed to follow scientific advice even if the majority of citizens disagreed.[108] How many of their own material habits they are prepared to change remains to be seen.

If the war in Ukraine exposed the shortcomings of Germany's energy transition, it has not (so far) led to a reversal of its underlying principles. Green growth remains the mantra, and the country continues to pursue a dual-track policy of renewables plus carbon. In April 2022, Robert Habeck, the

Green minister for economic affairs and climate action, pledged to accelerate the installation of wind farms and solar plants so they will supply 80 percent of electricity by 2030—up from the previous target of 65 percent.[109] At the same time, there was silence about cars and housing. Less gas will come from Russia, but more from Qatar and in liquefied form, and there are plans to drill for oil in the North Sea. Months before Putin's invasion of Ukraine, the Red-Green-Liberal coalition led by Olaf Scholz had reached a carefully worded compromise which promised that all coal plants would "ideally" be closed by 2030, eight years sooner than previously fixed. What the reality of war will do to such ideals is an open question. In June 2022, Habeck, despite being a Green minister, decided to restart mothballed coal plants to free up gas. And instead of being decommissioned, the three last nuclear power stations had their life extended by four months.

Climate activists have demanded an immediate end to the use of Russian gas and, with a sit-down strike, blocked the biggest power station in Berlin, the hard coal plant Reuter West. The environmental NGO BUND said it was "deeply ashamed" that the government continued to finance Russia's war by importing its gas and oil, and called for a ban on short flights, energy saving, a speed limit, and massive investments in clean energies and greener homes.[110]

The one demand the government granted was a cheaper ticket for public transport. At the same time, it compensated car drivers for rising prices with a discount at the fuel pump (*Tankrabatt*) worth 33 cents per liter of gasoline (17 cents for diesel). Italy was quick to limit cooling and heating in public buildings—people had to choose between peace in Ukraine and air conditioning, Italian prime minister Mario Draghi said. Japan had taken these and additional steps after the Fukushima disaster. It took the German government six months into the Ukraine war to decide that they would lower the heat in public buildings to 66°F from September 2022 onward. (Spain extended such temperature restrictions to commercial spaces such as supermarkets and shopping malls.) The government would not even apply the few measures Brandt had introduced during the first oil crisis, such as car-free Sundays. There would be no speed limit on highways, either—a measure urged by the International Energy Agency.[111] People's lifestyles were untouchable.

Speed limits and less heating would not have fixed the country's energy problem or stopped Putin, but they certainly would have helped the climate and reduced Germans' entanglement with an aggressive regime. That at a time of an international war and a climate crisis a country that has repeatedly presented itself as a moral leader has (so far) not been able to take these steps is telling.

FELLOW CREATURES

On Sunday morning, November 27, 1955, while other residents were asleep or on their way to church in the leafy Hamburg suburb of Blankenese, "Schiko" ran off in search of the opposite sex. When he reemerged from the local woods, he was shot. He was "moaning for another three minutes," witnesses reported, "and making pained sounds" before another shot put him out of his misery. Schiko was a four-year-old Chow Chow with a champion pedigree. He was the joy of the neighborhood, his owner said, and had never hurt anyone or anything. Now "he was no more. An unfortunate hand had taken from his master and all the little children their dear and loyal friend." The owner complained to the local police, the animal protection association, and the local Chow Chow Club.

Opinion was divided. For the local newspaper, Schiko was a "victim of passion," although, in the end, it granted that he had strayed into the woods where hunting was allowed. The senior game warden saw it differently. Far from being a victim, Schiko was a perpetrator whose hunting instinct had made him a menace for rabbits, and he was shot not by a random hunter but by a game warden, whose job it was to protect rabbits, pheasants, and the occasional deer. How many songbirds were routinely killed by crows and cats in the area? He had had many letters from residents who wanted such predators shot. Just the other day, he noted, an Alsatian had chased a rabbit until it had it cornered, and then tore it to pieces "before the eyes of a number of appalled viewers." If they did not protect their wildlife, "the generation after next will only know it from a museum." Schiko's owner went to the district court, to no avail. Recent legislation was very clear that game wardens had a right to shoot dogs to protect game. In the end, the hunting zone was reduced to protect children and pets running about.[112]

Schiko met his fate at a moment when Germans' interaction with animals began to polarize sharply. The postwar years saw the triumph of the pet. Instead of doing physical work, such as herding sheep or guarding the home, dogs now performed emotional labor, providing company, cuddles, and entertainment as "man's best friend." By 1990, only 6 percent of all dogs in Hesse were working as guard dogs, serving as guide dogs, or in breeding, while 94 percent were domestic pets.[113] These same years also brought the breakthrough of factory farming. While dogs and cats moved into the bedroom, chickens, pigs, and cows were taken from the fields and concentrated in industrial-scale barns and batteries, out of sight and touch, from which they returned as anonymous portions on the plate. The embrace of some creatures thus coincided with a growing distance from others. Both of these trends have longer roots—people kept dogs as pets in ancient Egypt and Rome, and the scientific breeding of sheep and cattle for better fleeces and more meat was pioneered in eighteenth-century England. Mass consumption in the second half of the twentieth century propelled them to new extremes, raising thorny questions about the rights of animals and how we treat our fellow sentient beings.

Overall, Adenauer's Germany had fewer cats and dogs than Britain or France. In cities, though, life was beginning to get more crowded. In Hamburg, for example, one in thirty-three residents had a dog in 1959, almost twice as many as before the war.[114] This placed a strain on urban parks, waste management, and civic nerves. A leash law tried to control the dogs (and their owners). In the city's central park, a small area was fenced in for a dog run. Overall, though, such special enclaves were rejected for inserting alien elements into the urban landscape. Dogs thus spilled over into parks and paddling pools, just as people were enjoying more leisure time. Parks became battlegrounds. The city's three dozen volunteer "pensioner custodians" were overwhelmed. During one police raid in a local park, more than a hundred dog owners were fined in a single hour for not having their pooch on a leash.[115] Attempts to ban dogs from public lawns met with resistance. Her "Snoopy" would continue to go on the lawn, one owner declared, even if she had to go to prison: did she not pay dog tax, after all?[116] (There was no cat tax.) Restrictions were deeply unfair, animal protection groups argued, because the rich had their private gardens while the poor only had public parks. Several thousand joined a street protest. "Yes, indeed, dogs mean more to us than children," one man explained: "the children destroy everything."[117]

On the other side were citizens who saw all these paws stepping on their human rights. Poop in parks and on pavements was a major source of irritation—the average dog left behind roughly 120 pounds of it a year. Since owners paid dog tax, quite a few of them saw it as the city's business to pick it up. Other citizens were outraged by such an attitude. A woman in Hamburg complained to the city government how she and other "ordinary mortals" were routinely expected to put up with this nuisance. "Who protects our children from rolling in dog poop?" For her, animal lovers came right after terrorists and motorcycle gangs. She did not want a nation of informers, but, equally, she did not want a bloody nose from confronting wrongdoers herself. Her proposal was to fine irresponsible owners, stop renting to people with dogs, and ban advertisements for dogs needing a home. Instead, "as in the old days, when a dog is not picked up from a shelter within ten days, put it to sleep." The official response was that she should confront difficult neighbors directly since, in a democracy, the active engagement of each citizen was better than "active bureaucracy."[118]

Pets joined their masters in consumer society. "Waldi," the first Olympic mascot, was designed for the Munich Games in 1972, and appeared on key chains, pillows, puzzles, and as a toy, in wood, stuffed, and inflatable. Waldi was modeled on a wire-haired dachshund or *Dackel*, the most popular breed in Germany at the time, ahead of Alsatians and poodles. The lead in breeding and dog shows had been taken by Victorian Britain. Germany followed. Into the 1930s, though, the bulk of breeding was in the hands of hunters and small farmers who did not sell for gain, although a growing number of Alsatians and terriers were exported for profit. Police, the army, and security companies were the main customers. By the 1970s, breeding, selling, and feeding had become big business. A young dachshund now fetched up to 200 DM, about half a woman's monthly wages. The mail-order company Quelle offered puppies in their catalog and delivered them by train in a special container.[119] Customs seized cocker spaniels smuggled across the border with fake pedigrees.

Between 1970 and 1990, the number of registered dogs in Germany rose from 2.4 million to 3.5 million, and their actual number was estimated to be around 5 million, alongside 6 million cats and 5 million birds. Instead of scraps and leftovers, cats and dogs were increasingly fed processed food; the annual value of such ready meals crossed 500 million DM in 1972. As the chair of the Dortmund canine club put it, a dog "is no garbage can."[120] Soon, West Germans were spending more on pet food than on baby food, and there was greater variety, too; in East Germany, processed pet food was rare. In 1985, the Futterkiste ("Food Box") opened in Munich, the first restaurant for dogs in Europe. A few years later, an enterprising ice cream vendor was selling "Pfiffi" ice to his customers' four-legged friends. The deeper emotional and commercial investment reached across this life and beyond. As consumers, pets, too, leave a footprint with the meat and imported soy in their food, and with higher indoor comfort; one driver behind more cooling and heating at home, studies suggest, is that owners worry about their pets' comfort level.[121] In the 1980s, insurance companies added health and life insurance for cats and dogs. At this point, Germany had none of the pet cemeteries for which France has been famous. Dead pets were either buried in the wild or mixed together with other killed animals and processed into soap or "meat meal" and then fed to pigs or chicken—a form of an animal circular economy. The first pet crematorium in Germany opened in 1996.[122]

What could (and could not) be done to dogs in particular has remained the subject of debate, and reflects what it means to be human. In 1930, in the middle of the world depression, every third dog killed in Hamburg was put to death because their owners were unable to pay their outstanding taxes and the animal had been confiscated. The local newspaper was outraged: to kill an animal—"man's special friend"—because the owner had fallen on hard times "does not exactly fit a civilized people." It was "cruel and medieval." Especially for a person in need, a dog was a source of comfort: how often did his eyes not give such a person "the strength and courage to defy fate?"[123] The Club of Animal Friends publicized that the unemployed and disadvantaged could pay in installments, without added interest. A few cities introduced a dog tax amnesty. Six decades later, in 1996, the interest group "Dog Friends" (IG Hundefreunde) challenged the tax in court: technically, it was a duty on things, whereas a dog, it was argued, was "a fellow creature of man."[124] Shortly after reunification, dogs got their day in parliament: they were now protected in the civil code (BGB) and could no longer be repossessed by the authorities. The court, however, defended the dog tax as lawful: communities had the right to tax things that were not essential to life, and the public was more affected by dogs than by other animals.

In the late 1980s, Europe was gripped by a panic about gangs and other owners of fighting dogs that had mauled children, in some cases with fatal consequences. Some cities required a license for their breeders and owners and levied a stiff tax on pit bulls and Rottweilers. Others, however, withdrew such measures after protests. Leash laws, too, were unevenly enforced. Investigations found that the number of biting incidents was much smaller than the media panic suggested—a total of ten cases in all of North Rhine–Westphalia (a state with 18 million people) in 1990—and those had been mainly committed by Alsatians, the quintessential German sheepdog, not imported beasts from the Bronx. To ban an entire breed was unscientific, the eminent German Animal Welfare Federation (Deutscher Tierschutzbund), founded in 1881, argued, since the root problem was the irresponsible owner, not the dog. Unlike the United States or France, Germany did not permit the state to put down dangerous dogs.[125]

If dogs and cats enjoyed a broadening of their social, economic, and emotional identity, pigs, chickens, and cows saw theirs reduced to a simple function, that of the food machine: predictable, productive, and profitable. The postwar decades saw the rapid ascent of factory farming, in East as in West Germany. Instead of strolling across the yard in little flocks picking corn, hens were locked up in cages less than one and a half feet tall, three to four on top of each other, in gigantic halls, and fed vitamins under infrared heat lamps to stimulate egg production. In 1968, a chicken farm in Rheine (West Germany) held half a million hens. In Thuringia (East Germany) a single worker was in charge of fifteen thousand hens. Pigs and cows underwent a similar process of concentration and control, with artificial insemination, specialist breeding, antibiotics, continuous feeding with concentrated fodder (*Kraftfutter*, a mix of grains, soy, and sunflower seeds), and mechanized milking—the GDR, in 1969, introduced a milking carousel so that a worker could attach the milking machine to their udders in rotation. Such industrial-style operations fundamentally altered the relationship between man and beast.

The core principles of this type of agriculture were those of Fordist mass production in industry: standardization, division of labor, and productivity. Cows were now bred and kept for either milk or meat, chickens to be egg-laying hens or broilers. Earlier conditions were not exactly a Romantic idyll—little piglets were often squashed by their mother sow, and pneumonia and intestinal diseases were widespread. In the postwar decades, factory methods transformed the lives of animals and their keepers beyond recognition. In 1950, a cow gave 528 gallons of milk a year; by 1990, it was double that. Chicken laid twice as many eggs. The population of cows, chickens, and pigs shot up—the number of pigs doubled to 23 million in West Germany and 12 million in East Germany, while the number of farms and farmworkers steadily shrunk—in 1950, one in five people still worked in agriculture in West Germany; forty years later it was one in thirty. Never before had there been so few keepers looking after so many animals.[126]

Intensive animal farming was an international phenomenon. West Germans learned a lot during study tours to poultry farms in America in the 1950s. The national context gave it a special significance. The productivity drive was able to build on the Nazis' campaign for greater efficiency in husbandry. In the barn, the Nazis wanted to eliminate the useless "feeders" (*Fresser*), such as the weaker pigs that did not make it to the front of the trough, echoing how they sought to eradicate the disabled, the "asocial," and other "unproductive" elements from "the people's community." In the 1950s and 1960s, *Leistung*—"high performance," the core ideal of the boom years—came to apply to pigs, chickens, and cows at least as much as to their masters. The intense rivalry between the two German states meant that the GDR did everything possible to match the rise in grilled meats and sausages across the border—cheap mass-produced grilled chicken (broilers) compensated for fewer eggs and less beef. The two regimes traveled in the same direction, but the East used planning and the West used subsidies by the European Economic Community to promote bigger farms. In both societies, the reality of factory farming jarred with the idyll of an unchanging *Heimat* of rolling hills and small farmsteads with animals ranging freely, and the oversized American incursions were hidden away.

One difference was that the democratic West had a space for critical voices who challenged the extremes of the productive calculus. One such moment came in the early 1970s, when a new method to make the most of a heifer and its unborn calf was being showcased in Bavaria. Young cows carried a high risk of dying in the process of giving birth for the first time. A professor came up with a surgical solution. Shortly before giving birth, the cow would be killed by an expert butcher who then, with a few expert slices, would cut the unborn calf from the body of the dead mother; after a few months the calf would be butchered, too. Several farmers were outraged. How could humans, "the crown of creation," dream up such barbaric things? Factory farming was one thing; these were "cruel acts" and immoral. There were still some ethical limits to how much money could be made from fellow creatures. The accepted solution was to allow the heifer to give birth and suckle its calf, before both were butchered.[127]

From the mid-1950s onward, Germans' waistlines were steadily expanding, in both East and West. The hunger of the postwar years gave way to obesity, high cholesterol, and cardiovascular disease. In 1971, an investigation in the GDR found that people ate 50 percent more fat than recommended and 40 percent were overweight.[128] The rise in meat consumption was dramatic, and outpaced only by China's in the last two generations. In 1950, a West German on average ate 66 pounds of meat, and an East German 48 pounds—in 1935, it had been 116 pounds. When the Wall came down, in 1989, they each consumed 220 pounds a year. This was partly because people became more productive and could afford it, especially in the West. It was facilitated, however, by the sharp fall in the price of food, resulting from globalization and factory farming. In 1954, West Germans still spent 40 percent of their income on food; by 1980, it was down to 20 percent; by the end of the century, it had fallen to 13 percent, where it stayed until the pandemic drove up prices in 2020. People were able to enjoy more space and mobility for themselves, in part, because chickens, cows, and pigs lost theirs. Cheaper eggs, milk, and cutlets freed up money for the home, car, and leisure.[129]

The fixation with the usefulness of animals has proved remarkably robust, notwithstanding repeated attempts to improve their lot. The modern origins of animal protection reach back to the nineteenth century. England was the first to outlaw dogfights and cruelty to horses, and have campaigns against testing on animals. The initial concern was with civilizing man as much as saving animals. Animals were largely cast as the passive victims of barbaric people. A person who was cruel to dogs or horses was a potential danger to society at large.

In Germany, the Nazis put animal protection on the statute book. Heinrich Himmler and Rudolf Hess were strict vegetarians; Hitler was not and made concessions for his favorite liver dumplings. In April 1933, three months after seizing power, the Nazis outlawed the slaughter of animals without stunning them first; Jews slit the throat of the animal with one big cut, a practice known as "*shechita*" or "*Schächten*," believed to give animals the fastest and least painful death. The Nazis were motivated by racial hatred as much as a love of animals, with Jewish butchers and traders in their sight. Later that year, an animal protection law (*Tierschutzgesetz*) punished cruelty to animals and required a permit for animal testing, although it continued in racial and military research.

After the war, the Allies allowed *Schächten* once again, and the provisions of the animal protection law stayed on the books in both German states. When in West Germany plans for a new slaughterhouse for dogs were raised in the mid-1950s—dog meat was considered a cure against tuberculosis in some areas, and only completely prohibited in 1986—there was an outcry from animal protection groups. Tellingly, for the Ministry of Agriculture the case did not fall under the rubric of animal protection. Rather, it argued, such slaughter should be prohibited because it "violated human and ethical sentiment."[130]

In the West, the law was subjected to a first ethical overhaul in 1972. Protection now included "animal well-being" and "species-appropriate" treatment. What that meant precisely, however, was left to veterinary and agricultural experts to decide, and they could not agree. Courts continued to rule that usefulness and profit could be "reasonable grounds" for causing animal suffering.[131] The following year, the wildlife filmmaker Bernhard Grzimek used his popular TV show to bring the plight of battery cage chickens into people's living rooms. Viewers were shocked. The farming lobby was unable to stop Grzimek from speaking of "concentration camp husbandry," but it succeeded in blocking material change. In the GDR, the Nazi animal protection law remained in place without amendment, although in reality safeguarding animals took a back seat to maximizing their output, and many veterinarians were not even aware of the law's existence.[132] Only in 1999 would the Constitutional Court rule that small cages violated the animal protection law. The lobby's response was to add a couple of inches. In 2015, the Bundesrat finally decided to stop all small cages by 2025.

In 1993, just over a decade after it started in America, People for the Ethical Treatment of Animals (PETA) arrived in Germany. They have been challenging the very notion that animals exist to be used by us. Whether on the plate or as a coat, in zoos, circuses, or laboratories, animal use is wrong, they argue, regardless of how well they may be treated. They have extended the battle for equality to the animal kingdom, challenging "speciesism" in the same way as racism and sexism. In the words of one activist, "Speciesism is when you are petting a dog while eating a pig." All animals deserve equal respect and a life free from suffering.[133]

In 2002, Germany became the first country in Europe to enshrine the rights of animals in its constitution. "Mindful also of its responsibility toward future generations," the amendment says, "the state shall protect the natural foundations of life and animals" (Article 20a). The change came in the wake of a major decision by the Constitutional Court defending the slaughter of animals without prior stunning if it was mandated by a religious community. After the Allies left, some German states (*Länder*) formally permitted *Schächten*, while others merely tolerated it. When in 1986 the new animal protection law absorbed the law on slaughter, it carried a general prohibition of slaughter without stunning that was immediately followed by a clause creating exemptions on grounds of religion. In practice, German states recognized such exemptions for Jews but not always for Muslims. In 1990, a Sunni Muslim Turk, who had lived in the state of Hesse for twenty years, took over the family's butcher shop and was granted the necessary exemption. In 1995, when it came up for renewal, the exemption was withheld. His appeal made it all the way to the Constitutional Court. Its decision, which balanced animal protection with religious freedom, tried to settle a controversy that had been running for decades.[134]

A constitutional amendment required a two thirds majority in parliament. The Greens were performing a balancing act—they had long called for a constitutional recognition of animal rights but equally for greater rights for "guest workers." In public, the campaign against *Schächten* had been taken over by right-wing groups who attacked it as un-German and uncivilized. The Greens voted for the amendment, distancing themselves from such xenophobic groups, trusting that a recognition of animal rights would still allow Jewish and Muslim communities to continue to practice slaughter without stunning. It helped that there were scientific doubts about whether stunning animals before slaughtering them actually eliminated pain and was necessarily humane. The opposition Christian Democrats, who represented farmers, came around in response to the growing support for animal rights among voters and to the public outcry against the recent mass cull of cows afflicted by mad cow disease.[135]

Legally and ethically, the admission of animals into the constitution was a big step. Animals no longer just deserved human pity. Now they had natural rights. To their lives on the farm, it made little difference. Animal protection today sets out to secure their "well-being" (*Wohlbefinden*), but there are major differences of opinion about what that consists of; the Ministry of Agriculture is looking for ways to monitor and measure it. Whereas consumers might imagine happy pigs, for many farmers it stands for basic health, not more. In court cases, experts have been known to argue that laying lots of eggs was proof enough a hen was feeling well. What does "species-appropriate" (*artgemäss*) treatment mean for animals that have been bred and raised for human consumption for centuries? Consumer groups have complained that currently any type of husbandry and farming qualifies as species-appropriate, and that, unless they violate regulations, farmers can promote their meat for its "well-being" qualities. Prosecution of animal cruelty in farming has proved notoriously difficult. A dog owner who left her pet locked in a car in the summer heat would face a serious fine, whereas factory farmers routinely got off scot-free when hundreds of their pigs died from suffocation or other preventable causes, citing ignorance or lack of intent. In tight cages, pigs bite each others' tails, a form of cannibalism. The European Union prohibited amputations in 1994, but the tail docking of piglets with pliers and without anesthesia continued to be common practice in Germany as well as Denmark twenty-five years later.

Change has been mainly entrusted to information, labels, and the farmers and retailers. In 2001, the government introduced a "bio" label for products from certified organic farms that worked without antibiotics, pesticides, and artificial fertilizers and gave their animals more space. Even here a "bio" chicken might have to share a cage of thirty-nine square inches with five other hens in a barn that held up to three thousand—better than the dozen chickens crowded together in the same space in a factory farm, but hardly roomy. In 2021, there were 22 million pigs in Germany, 99 percent of them on conventional farms. Only 5 percent of chickens and 8 percent of cows lived on "organic" farms.[136] "Bio" farms in 2021 remained a niche, covering no more than 10 percent of the 42 million acres in the country. In surveys, consumers speak highly of ecologically farmed food. When it comes to the point of purchase, however, "bio" food still accounted for only 7 percent of all sales—at a time when food was cheaper than ever before. In Denmark, it was twice that portion.[137] In 2021, a group of discounters and supermarkets pledged that they would gradually phase out selling meat from animals kept in such restricted conditions, until, by 2030, they would sell only cutlets from a pig that enjoyed one square meter in a cage instead of .75 of a square meter; and had a ball of straw to play with, instead of a piece of wood dangling from a chain.

Factory farming has come under fire from several directions and for a number of reasons: health, environment, and ethics. In 2015, the dozen scientists advising the Ministry of Nutrition and Agriculture released a blistering report. It stated that animal well-being was compromised, emissions dangerously high, and public health at risk from antibiotics and too much meat on the plate. The way most animals were currently kept, the scientists concluded, was "not sustainable."[138] Vegans and radical activists agreed and went one step further, urging an end to the farming of animals altogether.

According to official statistics, Germans ate less meat in 2020 than two decades earlier, down from 220 pounds to 187 pounds a year (for comparison, Americans consume about 270 pounds of meat today). Even that would still add up to a thousand animals in the course of a human life.[139] Women are just within recommended health guidelines, eating only half as much meat as men, who are off the charts. People began to eat less pork in those twenty years—down from 121 pounds to 95 pounds a person. They ate more chicken—up from 42 to 48 pounds. Beef was steady at 29 pounds a person.[140]

These figures, however, give an overly optimistic view. Official figures count what is eaten at home but ignore the grilled sausages, burgers, and kebabs consumed at fast food stands and restaurants. The population also had a different makeup in 2021 than in earlier decades, in terms of age, ethnicity, and food culture. It was getting older, and old people generally eat less. And it included more than 2 million new arrivals from Syria, Afghanistan, Iraq, and Pakistan—many of them Muslims, who traditionally eat little meat.

The real test would be whether the *same* people were eating less meat. The data is inconclusive. Some studies initially examined children with German citizenship only and added migrants later; others traced households, which shrank in size.[141] A recent opinion poll suggested that Germans have become Europe's leading vegetarians and vegans (with 7 percent and 3 percent of the population respectively in 2021), but that recorded aspirations, not necessarily what people ate.[142] The most robust study, which followed the diet of a representative sample of fifteen thousand people in 2008, found that only 2.5 percent were not eating any meat and 87 percent fell short of the nutritional guideline for 400 grams of vegetables a day. Young men were the biggest carnivores, consuming 120 grams a day, the equivalent of two sausages. When the researchers revisited the participants five years later, they found no change.[143] Food habits, tastes, and identities have proved to be sticky. It may be possible to take the German out of the sausage, but more difficult to take the sausage out of the German.[144]

FUTURE PRESENT

The reckoning with its dark past has left Germany with a distinct orientation toward the future. Collective memory of Nazi crimes thwarts the nostalgia for a "glorious" past open to other countries. The past, instead, is meant to provide lessons to avoid a relapse. Talk of the future is ubiquitous in German life, and it goes well beyond the "fear of the future" (*Zukunftsangst*) that is sometimes treated as a national character trait. In 2011, Angela Merkel launched a "*Zukunftsdialog*," which brought citizens and experts, young and old, together in town hall meetings to talk about their hopes and fears. Ten years later, her successor, Olaf Scholz, rode to victory with the slogan "Courage to advance" ("*Mut zum Vorsprung*"). His coalition treaty with the Greens and the Liberals duly followed with a pledge to "Dare more progress," a political version of the carmaker Audi's slogan "*Vorsprung durch Technik*." Standing still was not an option, let alone turning back. When it comes to science and public education, the Deutsche Museum has produced visionary exhibitions on the Anthropocene and on energy transitions that have traveled the world. In 2019, the Futurium, an exhibition, lab, and event space, opened in Berlin, a stone's throw from the Reichstag. It aims to give citizens a glimpse of the future.

For their road map to a better tomorrow, many towns and cities have turned to the seventeen Sustainability Development Goals. Adopted by the United Nations Member States in 2015, they include ending poverty and promoting peace as well as making cities sustainable and consumption responsible. In the autumn of 2019, the southern town of Dornstadt sponsored a series of events in support of sustainability with the slogan "Live well!" Over a space of two months, the eight thousand inhabitants had a chance to eat a vegan brunch in the community center, watch a puppet show about peace and development, learn about sustainable fashion, and exchange secondhand strollers and children's clothes. Animal rights groups talked about the benefits of plant-based milk, and the curious could visit the two-year-old soy-planting experiment on the bridge across the A8 highway. Dornstadt had a citizen energy project that put solar panels on the roofs of the local schools and day care. Schools appointed "climate ambassadors" and pupils have planted some two thousand trees since 2012. The town gave its inhabitants monthly tips on using fair trade products and how to reuse wrapping paper at Christmas time. And it supported climate action with an official electric car and two e-bicycles.

Similar activities took place across the country in communities trying to give their citizens a better future. Ettlingen, near the French border, won a European "climate star" award in 2018 for its energy-saving boxes that provided two hundred households with a meter, LED lamp, and thermometer for the fridge (at a discounted price). It also introduced twenty electric charging points for e-cars. Its "Masterplan 2021" looked toward more car sharing and rental bikes. The cathedral and university town of Münster built cycling paths and subsidized cloth diapers. Gelsenkirchen, a former mining town in the Ruhr that was reinventing itself with the help of solar technology and red pandas in its zoo, was awarded a UNESCO Learning City Award in 2017 for its vision of giving "residents a new idea of the future." It sponsored cooking courses on "wholesome nutrition" and workshops on recycling but also a "smart parking" app that enabled drivers to park their cars without having to search for coins.

However well intentioned, most of these initiatives shared the same shortcoming: their primary focus was on the supply side and technological innovation. Bathrooms would get water-saving showerheads, kitchens smart meters, and cars would be powered by battery. The future was bright because it was more efficient. As far as daily life was concerned, it was more of the same. In the "future dialogues" initiated by Chancellor Merkel, citizens wanted to see more community spirit and less crime, and a running theme was how to perfect the country's industrial model through innovation and learning. There was little room for alternative "utopias."[145]

A more efficient use of resources is a good thing but can only deliver so much. At the end of the day, driving an e-car is still driving. To unclog cities would require changing mobility itself. The difficulties were starkly illustrated in Essen, next door to Gelsenkirchen, and home to the industrial powerhouses of RWE and ThyssenKrupp. Essen was the only city in Germany that adopted binding targets to promote public transport in 2014 and, three years later, won the European capital award. It set itself the target of having an equal 25 percent share of walking, cycling, public transport, and car use by 2035. Unfortunately, the use of cars in Essen was up from 54 percent in 2011 to 55 percent in 2019, as was car ownership.[146] Barcelona and Zurich succeeded in lowering car use to 25 percent, with the help of speed limits, dedicated bus lanes, pedestrian zones, and stiff parking fees. Paris introduced a low emission zone and restricted cars in its historic center.

German cities, by and large, have been slow to take such steps. They have found it easier to put electric buses on the roads than to take private cars off them. According to mobility experts, change will be modest unless innovation is matched by "exnovation."[147]

The modern era has unleashed fantastical futures—think of Jules Verne, the Futurist artists after 1900, or science fiction. Germans today prefer their tomorrow to be a better version of the present, a view promoted and reinforced by the dominant discourse of green growth and "sustainability." Since energy can be abstract, the German government in 2018 had the good idea of bringing citizens together with artists to put their "visions of a successful energy transition" on canvas. The result was paintings with wind farms, solar panels, and digital technologies. People were more "flexible," with the help of apps that switched on their washing machines when electricity was cheap and abundant, but ultimately their daily lives were not all that different. They just had e-cars and smart meters. "*Energiewende* made in Germany," read one painting: "intelligent—clean—secure—affordable." For this artist the key words were "Export, Intelligence, Energy." The Futurists wanted to clear the decks so they could build a radically new world. Germans today are trying to hang on to as much of the present as possible. One of the artists involved concluded pessimistically that the road to utopia was currently closed because of a lack of public and political interest.[148]

In 2020, the Futurium in Berlin held a "future workshop" to explore what life might look like in 2050. Wind and solar power had become part of the landscape. All homes would have heat pumps, and planes were propelled by hydrogen. To get about, people boarded high-speed trains and booked driverless cars. They still ate meat but only in a healthy and sustainable manner. Children were playing in a virtual reality room while their parents did the shopping online. They lived in networked homes, fully insulated, with smart meters and electricity from hydrogen. On their roofs, they grew lettuce ("sky farming").

At first sight, this version of a "smart city" sparkles with change. Thanks to basic income, people would work less and devote more time to gardening and repairing instead. A circular economy would eliminate waste. A closer look at the workshop's vision reveals how a lot of the future, in fact, recycles today's normality. Apartments are naturally given their own washing machines and modern eat-in kitchens. Far from immutable, though, such arrangements have been the product of major changes in the past. Laundry was a communal activity before the advent of the private washing machine in the 1960s. The Futurium exhibition asks visitors, "How can we satisfy our needs in the future without destroying nature even further?" as if "our needs" are somehow given.[149] But human needs have changed dramatically over the course of history, and especially so in the last century. Why not reimagine and change "our needs" for the future?

In the "technology first" approach, people's lives tend to follow the path set by innovation. Earlier energy transitions show that this is far too simple—people often resisted new fuels and technologies or modified them to suit their habits.[150] Social norms and practices shape demand and infrastructures as well as respond to them. One transformation that participants of the "future workshop" dared imagine was "No expensive long-distance trips as long as Cologne is green and the air is clean"—a curious view of travel and leisure, as if people since the 1970s have been flying to Mallorca and New York to escape smog at home.[151] In many of these visions, it is as if the future jumps straight from the drawing board of an engineer, full of shiny technology but somewhat dull and conventional when it comes to everyday life.

There are, however, pockets of greater creativity. In Wuppertal (North Rhine–Westphalia), for example, a defunct train station has been converted into a "utopian city" where one hundred people combine urban gardening and digital repairing with poetry and film. The self-declared "utopians" champion local skills and resources, open data, and "post-growth"—they did not dump the car completely, but at least they shared it freely.[152] In Augsburg, a vacant shop in a housing bloc became a "utopian living lab" in 2014. With the help of volunteers, it offers a meeting place for lonely seniors, and holds dance sessions and repair demonstrations in a "bike kitchen"—"commonism" instead of communism, as the members put it. For those who like haiku, every third Monday offers the chance to practice the art form with a Japanese expert. Once a month, the "electronics whisperers" make an appearance to save defective appliances from the trash can.

The utopian space was one of a small group of initiatives that had initially been kickstarted by the official agenda for sustainability before taking its own creative turn. Augsburg recognized it with a "Future Award."[153] In 2012, the foundation *FuturZwei* ("FutureTwo") set out to challenge the "business as usual" mind-set with dreams and experiments of lifestyles fit for our grandchildren. Renewable technologies were not enough. What was needed was both social and ecological transformation. Its *Almanacs of the Future* have gathered practical examples, from alternative housing projects and the pleasure of taking a night train to insulating walls with seagrass. An exhibition in Hamburg in 2019 invited visitors to look back at their present lives from the perspective of the year 3050 with the help of archaeological finds gathered in a "lost property office of the future." A former fodder silo was transformed into a teahouse with space for meditation.[154]

For all their creativity, so far these voices have been drowned out by the broad chorus extolling a future that is a more efficient version of the present. The German future has been drained of some of its color, not only when compared with the nuclear utopias of the 1950s and 1960s or the enthusiasm for alternative living in the 1970s and 1980s but also with what is happening in other parts of Europe today. The transition town movement (community projects seeking to mitigate the climate crisis through more local farming and self-sufficiency) is stronger in Britain, France, and Belgium. The pandemic offered a missed opportunity to redesign everyday life. In some ways, united Germany has gone the way East Germany did under Honecker: the horizon of the future has been shrinking.

The technological optimism about green growth has been one factor, but so has disillusionment with utopias. While in France and America thinkers and architects marveled at the sun rising over postmodernity, Germany's public intellectual number one, Jürgen Habermas, sank into gloom. The welfare state had reached an impasse, he wrote in 1985, and with it the modern project itself. The utopian energies invested in a laboring society had "exhausted" themselves. All that was left was "banality" and neoconservatism.[155] As far as Habermas was concerned, the future had entered a downward spiral of a nuclear arms race, unemployment, inequality, global poverty, and environmental catastrophes. It was a rather German view that reduced modernity to industry, welfare, and social democracy, ignoring commerce, empire, race, and gender. The potential of computers and globalization left him cold.

The Greens, meanwhile, began to shed their own emancipatory vision of alternative lifestyles and, after the electoral debacle in 1990 (when they sank from 8.3 percent to 3.8 percent of the vote), warmed to a "cleaner" version of industrial consumer society, with recycling, renewables, and "green jobs." This facilitated alliances with ecological modernizers in the SPD and also made the Green Party more attractive to conservative voters who wanted to protect their *Heimat* without sacrificing their own comfort.

Few embody this conservative-liberal-green symbiosis better than Winfried Kretschmann. A Catholic with Maoist leanings in his student days, Kretschmann was one of the Green Party's cofounders in the state of Baden-Württemberg in 1980. Sustainable, he argued in a recent book, was the "new conservative": love of nature, *Heimat*, tolerance, and growth. His goal was a "win-win" situation, good for the climate and for the local car industry. "The emission-free car of the future must roll off the assembly line in Untertürkheim and not in Fremont or Wuhan." He called the new conservatism the "politics of And."[156] Far from being in contradiction with each other, ecology and economy could be brought into harmony. It was a winning formula, at least at the polls. In 2011, Kretschmann was elected the first Green head of a German state. He has been at the helm of Baden-Württemberg ever since.

There is much to admire about Germans' concern for the natural world and their many efforts to save it. The country's rivers and air today are much cleaner than they were fifty or even thirty years ago, and, for all its limitations, energy saving has been a remarkable success story. At the same time, Germans carry a more than average responsibility for the climate crisis, pumping out more carbon dioxide than most other Europeans. Sustainable development is, of course, an international mantra, but it has been central in a country that continues to define itself as an industrial society that wants to produce and consume as well as be good. With energy saving and the *Energiewende*, earlier green doubts about technological systems (even capitalism) gave way to a technological environmentalism. In the process, the social imagination of an alternative future shrunk. There are still appeals to individuals to do "the right thing," by recycling, buying "bio" food, using smart meters, or switching to an electric car. But these involve changes between products, not in ways of living. They make few demands and tend to disguise Germans' complicity in the climate crisis. It is hoped that new technological systems will, somehow, save us from the approaching doom.

Epilogue: What Is Germany For?

Over the course of the past eighty years, Germany has gone through a remarkable moral and material regeneration. The two have pulled the country in opposite directions. Growth, prosperity, and comfort have been powered by exports, much more so than in neighboring countries. In material terms, Germany today is more deeply entangled with the world than ever before. Germans' moral reorientation, meanwhile, has been mainly inward looking, first preoccupied with their own suffering, later with their role as perpetrators and collaborators. There were, of course, moments when some groups looked outward—young Europeanists, Christians fasting for the starving poor in the "Third World," volunteers working for reconciliation in Israel and Greece, students marching arm in arm with peers from Iran and Congo in protest against foreign dictators. As a whole, though, the field of vision has been provincial, preoccupied with rebuilding the country and coming to terms with the Nazi past.

Moving out of the darkness absorbed enormous energy. Reconstruction, the renunciation of revanchism, and the reintegration of millions of citizens after 1945 and, again, after 1990, were historic achievements. In the process, Germans developed many noble ideals: democracy and solidarity, hard work and self-reliance. And, against considerable internal resistance, they learned to take responsibility for the Second World War, the Holocaust, and crimes against humanity.

But this has favored introspection. The long and bitter conflict over guilt and memory eventually provided Germans with a new identity and self-assurance, giving them a sense of pride in not being proud that, at times, turned into self-satisfaction. In exchange, the rest of the world often disappeared from sight, even where it had become a visible presence. West Germany clung to the image of being "not a land of immigration," notwithstanding the fact that several million migrant workers and their families had decided to stay. East Germany celebrated Soviet friendship and colonial freedom fighters, but in their private lives most of its citizens were no less provincial and kept their distance from Russian soldiers and foreign workers alike. The lesson of history was that Germans could not be trusted with power and better stay clear of international conflict.

However sensible in a particular situation, the culture of restraint has come at a price, leaving Europe with a vacuum of leadership at its center. What Germans want from the world has been clear—that it buys their cars and chemicals—what they think they owe the world far less so. Learning to take responsibility for past crimes made Germans forget to take responsibility for living in an interconnected world in the present. The country reaped the benefits of a global order—and never more so than when markets opened up in Eastern Europe and China in the 1990s and 2000s—but it did not contribute much to its upkeep. No European country slashed its army as ruthlessly as reunited Germany after the Cold War; in 1989, West Germany had 2,000 Leopard battle tanks, but by 2016 the number was down to 244, and half of those were not operational.[1] Weapons exports, meanwhile, were flourishing. The economic giant was a strategic dwarf, with no sense that its high share of international trade carried great risks as well as great benefits. Strikingly, when the trade war between America and China erupted in 2015, COVID-19 disrupted supply lines in 2020, and Russia invaded Ukraine in 2022, Germany had no national security strategy, let alone a security council.

The geopolitical denial is about much more than a lack of strategic experts. Whether through exports or consumption, the life of effectively everyone in Germany is tied to the fate of the world. Yet when it came to the environment and human rights, Germany was often similarly inward looking, building wind turbines and shutting down its hard coal mines and nuclear power stations while importing more fossil fuels and nuclear electricity.[2] Most of the coal and gas was from Russia, and a growing share of trade and investment was with China, even while human rights standards in these countries plummeted.

Remembrance of the past cannot avoid responsibility in the present. After decades of knowing what they are against—"never again" Hitler and Auschwitz—Germans need to figure out what they are for.

Putin's attack on Ukraine on February 24, 2022, made this question impossible to avoid. In a historic speech to parliament three days later, Chancellor Scholz pronounced the invasion a *Zeitenwende*, a "new era."[3] The botched career of the term *Wende* should have put a damper on anyone hoping for a decisive switch from traditional restraint to assertive leadership. Chancellor Kohl had been longing for a conservative *geistig-moralische Wende* ("intellectual and moral renewal") in the early 1980s, and did not get it. The peaceful revolution in East Germany in 1989–90 is now remembered as "*die Wende*," but its original champion was Egon Krenz, Honecker's successor, hoping to save the moribund GDR. The much-hyped *Energiewende* stalled halfway.

A nautical term, "*Wende*" means tacking, changing course by moving the bow of the boat through the wind. Scholz announced the maneuver with the release of an extra 100 billion euros for the Bundeswehr. Turning money into munition has proved more difficult. By the end of 2022, troops still only had enough bullets for two days of fighting.[4] Germany ordered three dozen F-35 fighter jets from the United States, but they will not fly before 2028. When it came to military support of Ukraine, Germany in 2022 resembled a boat standing in the wind with its sails flapping. Helmets, medicine, and defensive weapons were sent but the call for battle tanks was resisted until pressure from its NATO allies became overwhelming at the start of 2023.

Putin's war marked a "*Zeitenwende*," Scholz said, because "the world is no longer like the world before."[5] This is true in many ways, although it ignores Russia's previous invasion of Georgia (2008) and Crimea (2014) and its bombing in Syria since 2015. To make sense of Germany in the new era, we must place it in a broader context. Germany did not suddenly awake from its inward-looking slumber in 2022. You can try to limit foreign engagement, but in a globalized world you cannot stop the world from coming to you, as the nearly 1 million refugees heading for Germany in 2015 showed so dramatically. The complacency of the Federal Republic has been shaken by several forces: migration; the socioeconomic fallout of globalization; the challenge to historical memory from greater attention to racism and colonial violence; and the climate crisis.

In 2022, Germany was the country hosting the third-largest number of refugees in the world (after Turkey and Colombia): 2.2 million people.[6] The so-called refugee crisis in 2015 cannot be treated as a one-off. If anything, conflict and climate change can be expected to drive more people from their homes. Germans are deeply divided on how to respond. On the one hand, German volunteers are out in the Mediterranean risking arrest for rescuing migrants, and Angela Merkel is collecting international prizes for her "welcome policy," including from the UN High Commissioner of Refugees. On the other, the Scholz government has announced plans to broker deals with countries in Africa and in the Arab world for them to screen and process refugees and to take back the migrants Germany does not want in exchange for letting in the ones it does. Experts caution that such ideas are out of touch with reality—why would unwanted migrants no longer try to reach Germany, and how would their weak states stop them?[7] The fact that

Germany has established a special representative for migration is a recognition that the issue is here to stay.

In terms of national wealth, Germany has been one of the great winners from globalization. The country has also weathered the storm of the pandemic much better than most; its economy shrank by merely 3.7 percent in 2020 (UK, –11 percent; Italy, –9 percent; France, –7.8 percent; USA, –2.8 percent).[8] People temporarily out of work received up to 80 percent of their wages from the government for up to twenty-eight months, a scheme unrivaled in the world. Welfare benefits and public services, while slimmed down, remain comparatively generous.

You would not know this from the complaints about social injustice and fear of decline inside Germany. In addition to high expectations (not a bad thing in themselves), popular anger is fed by a feeling that globalization disproportionately benefits the few. In fact, income inequality has not worsened since 2010 and is the same as in France and much less pronounced than in Italy, Great Britain, and the United States. What gives globalization a bad name is the marked rise of a low-wage sector. Having to turn to welfare benefits and food banks in spite of having a job is completely at odds with the national mantra that performance pays. Whether the increase in the minimum wage from 9.82 euros to 12 euros per hour in 2022 (12.42 euros from 2024) will be enough to restore a sense of fairness at a time of inflation is debatable. All the talk of German virtues during the global financial and European debt crises has made many citizens more convinced than ever that they are the paymasters of the European Union, a far cry from the enormous benefits they actually reap from the internal market. If the country wants to step up and play more of a global role, it will need to confront those myths and anxieties, be more outward facing, and explain why cooperation and exchange are good.

The reckoning with race, slavery, and empire reached Germany later than America, Britain, and France, but when it did it carried a particular sting. By working through the past and commemorating the Holocaust, many Germans came to believe that they had successfully confronted racism. In the years after 2000, a series of campaigns began to draw attention to the suppressed legacy of colonialism and to Germany's short but brutal colonial past, a dark chapter missing from its history books and public discourse. There were calls to rename streets that carried racist images and honored colonial administrators, return Benin bronzes (initially looted by the British) to Nigeria, and recognize as genocide the murder of 100,000 Herero and Nama in German Southwest Africa (today Namibia) before the

First World War, most of which the German government eventually did. Some writers claimed that the discourse of the singularity of the Holocaust was a clever ploy by German, American, and Israeli "elites" to obscure the West's own racist violence, by silencing the victims of other genocides.[9]

As history, this is plain wrong. The Holocaust moved to the center of German national identity in large part thanks to civic pressure from below. The murder of the Jews had distinctive qualities in that the Nazis wanted to wipe Jews off the face of the earth, including those from their own midst, and they drew on antisemitic ideas that had deep roots in Christianity. Recognizing and commemorating those features does not mean being blind to other mass murders—in fact, civil rights activists and critics of empire reflected on the murder of the Jews in the 1950s, comparative genocide studies have thrived since the Srebrenica massacre in 1995, and many scholars have explored links and parallels between colonial violence and the Nazi empire.[10]

What made the arrival of postcolonialism so explosive was politics. Recognition of the singularity of the Holocaust has been inseparably tied to Germany's unquestionable solidarity with Israel, and this made critique of its treatment of Palestinians in the occupied territories an extremely sensitive matter; in 2019 the Bundestag condemned the Boycott, Divestment, Sanctions (BDS) movement as antisemitic, a decision that sparked widespread criticism. The memory wars touched an additional nerve because West and East Germans carried with them rather different historical memories. While the Holocaust became a cornerstone of West German identity in the 1980s, the Nazis' killing of Soviet soldiers and civilians had pride of place in the GDR. After reunification, the house of memory, like so much else, would bear the imprint of the West. Suddenly colonial, Soviet, and other victims were knocking at its doors. Why, some were asking, did the Herero only get development aid and not compensation like the Jews, and the Greeks get nothing? There were worries that the Holocaust could be relativized by a postcolonial left as well as a populist right, ending up as just another genocide in a global history of violence. At a time of violent antisemitic attacks, such fears took on a sense of urgency.

The recent German past shows that justice for victims need not be a zero-sum game. Public memory does not have a fixed, limited number of places. Commemoration of the Holocaust opened the door in the 1980s for recognition of the genocide of the Sinti and Roma and in 2016 for that of the Armenians. The house of memory, like any other house, sometimes requires renovation. It no longer belongs to ethnic Germans alone. In addition to Black Germans, there are millions of people with a migrant background and refugees who all come with their own memory, pain, and prejudice: the

Holocaust needs to speak to them even though they do not carry the mark of Cain. Soon there will be no survivors left, and no perpetrators either. Memorial sites have been reaching out to a diverse population, but more will need to be done to make the Nazi past their public memory, too.

The final shock to complacency has been delivered by the climate crisis. In itself, the link between environmental and international justice is nothing new—the Greens in 1980 campaigned for partnership with the global South. At that time, though, their principal enemy was nuclear power, and they called for the more efficient use of fossil fuels as well as energy saving and "softer" technologies such as wind and biomass. Since then, global warming has stretched responsibility across time and space by showing how carbon dioxide emissions damage the planet as a whole. Digging up and burning coal from a mine near Cologne is no longer seen just to darken the skies over Rhine and Ruhr but to endanger people around the world now and in the future.

History hands German environmentalists powerful assets. They can build on the politics of conscience nourished by the large peace and anti-nuclear movements, and the confrontation with the Nazi past has meant that inaction is recognized as complicity. At the same time, they face formidable obstacles. By trying to shut down coal, gas, and oil, climate justice activists are simultaneously challenging the model of growth and the generational compact that has buttressed the Federal Republic since the 1950s.

Carbon is so deeply embedded in people's lives that an appeal to individual conscience may not be enough to undo underlying norms and habits. So far, people—including politicians—have shown little interest in interfering with lifestyles. If anything, the war in Ukraine deepened the problem of complicity, for at the same time as supporting Kyiv, Germany paid Russia handsomely for its fossil fuels during the first nine months of the war. Environmentalists have not quite reached the point where socialists were in 1900, split between revolutionaries and reformists. But they are now divided between a new generation of radicals committed to blocking mines and traffic and a Green Party that sits in government and tries to keep the lights on by all possible means, including domestic brown coal and fracking gas from America. The war in Ukraine has had the perverse effect of simultaneously giving a fresh boost to wind and solar power and making Germany scour the earth for fossil fuels.

Germany may be polarized, but it is also resilient, much more so than those predicting economic collapse and social conflict in 2022 gave it credit for. The specter of the Weimar Republic feeds fears that a recession would lead to disaster. Keeping those fears alive does its own bit to defuse the situation. Still, the Federal Republic has come through many previous storms without serious damage. If any of the earlier panics about deindustrialization and disintegration had come even half true, the country would have long since disappeared. German democracy has proved remarkably robust. The country managed the much-feared autumn and winter of 2022 without serious shortages or unrest.

What is revealing is the course it took. "Never alone" was Germany's mantra, but it played it in a different key to its citizens than to the international community. While in military affairs solidarity with its partners was said to prevent Germany from taking the lead, in energy and fiscal matters solidarity was sacrificed for domestic interests. The government handed companies and consumers, rich and poor, 200 billion euros to help them with higher energy prices, putting the stimulus program during the pandemic into the shade. What appeared to be a helping hand in Berlin looked like an unfair advantage in Brussels, violating the level playing field of Europe's internal market. For those hoping for a more powerful, united Europe it is not a good omen.

No other European country has been as conflicted about the war in Ukraine as Germany. The issue of military support has challenged deeply held beliefs about what the country stands for and the lessons to take from its past. It has been highly personal. For many citizens, the earlier mass movements for peace and against nuclear weapons had been a formative experience, and so were the debates about collective responsibility for the Holocaust. Opinion has been so passionate that it sometimes appeared as if Germany itself was under attack. Three camps are discernible: (1) a significant and vocal minority that demanded negotiations and to withhold heavy weapons from Ukraine; (2) those who believed that Germany must do everything in its power to help Ukraine win; (3) those for whom it is enough that Ukraine not lose.

What set these camps against each other was more than rival strategies. They occupy different moral-political time zones. The first camp is strongest where leftist and populist sympathies with Putin are strongest: in the former GDR.[11] Memories of the pain of reunification remain formidable. Unemployment, uncertainty, breakups, and breakdowns have left deep scars, and there was fear that losing Russian gas would finish off the few industries that had managed to stay alive east of the Elbe. People in the East worried that they are being asked to make another existential sacrifice, after barely having managed to put their lives back together. Opposition to the weapons, however, also draws on a Western mentality of the 1980s, marked by an oppressive fear of nuclear war, suspicion of U.S.-Western imperialism, and an instinctive distrust of foreign intervention as carrying within it the seed of German aggression. This can produce a self-centered view, more concerned with what the war might do to Germans than what it has already done to Ukrainians. In this, it is drawing on Germans' fixation with their own suffering that continued long after the Second World War; Ukrainian victims of the Nazis were a footnote in West German memory. In addition to nuclear annihilation, many fear that an escalation would undo the civilizing work that turned militant Nazis into peace-abiding Germans, the life project for a generation of progressive politicians, writers, and thinkers, some of whom had grown up under Hitler or fought in the Second World War.

The second group sees the war through a different lens. For many Greens and conscientious objectors, new genocides since the 1990s turned "never again" into a justification for foreign engagement. For younger generations, the sins of the fathers are now the sins of the great-grandfathers, and with many added years of democracy, the fear of slipping back into Nazism looks surreal. They have grown up in a globally connected age, marked by a new humanitarianism and empathy for the suffering of distant others that make foreign policy personal. Theirs is a compassionate politics that commands the defense of liberal values and human rights, by foreign intervention if necessary.

The war in Ukraine has revealed and sharpened the tensions between these rival mind-sets, but it is only one piece in the bigger geopolitical dilemma that confronts Germany today: in a world of growing conflict, its economic interests are increasingly at odds with its values and national security.

Trade with authoritarian regimes is nothing new; West German firms did good business with military dictatorships in Chile, Brazil, and Argentina from the 1960s to the 1980s. Two things have changed since then. Germans today are more sensitive about human rights abuses, partly because they eventually learned to confront their own past crimes. The carmaker BMW slowly began to examine its role in the Third Reich in the 1980s and by 1999 had joined the foundation that would offer forced laborers long-overdue compensation. Twenty years later, Volkswagen agreed to pay workers in its Brazilian factory compensation to atone for their persecution during Brazil's dictatorship. At the same time, Germany's economy is more heavily invested in nonliberal regions of the world than ever before. China has become Germany's biggest trading partner. In the first half of 2022, 7 percent of Germany's exports went to the Middle Kingdom and 12 percent of its imports came from there; twenty years earlier, it was 2 percent and 4 percent respectively.

The country's vulnerability should not be exaggerated—a trade war would probably knock 3 percent off GDP—but it should not be belittled, either.[12] China is a core market for German cars, chemicals, and machine tools, and, in reverse, batteries, solar panels, and much else rely on its silver and rare earth metals. Paradoxically, when Germany got a wake-up call about its dependence on Russia, it responded by deepening ties with China. In 2022, German firms invested more in China than ever before, and in October of that year the chancellor brushed aside critics and handed a Chinese shipping corporation a stake in the port of Hamburg, which is the country's largest. With surging tensions over Taiwan and human rights, steering between economic interests and values-oriented policy will be more challenging than ever.

Since the Second World War, Germany has accumulated formidable moral capital. The country's future will be shaped by whether that will be strong enough to reorient the country's economic capital. Sacrifices will be necessary. Reconstruction, reunification, and taking in 2 million refugees show they are possible.

List of Archives

ADCV	Archiv Deutscher Caritasverband, Freiburg
ADE	Archiv für Diakonie und Entwicklung, Berlin
AdsD	Archiv der sozialen Demokratie, Friedrich-Ebert-Stiftung, Bonn
AWO	Arbeiterwohlfahrt, AdsD, Friedrich-Ebert-Stiftung, Bonn
BArch Berlin	Bundesarchiv Berlin-Lichterfelde
BArch Freiburg	Bundesarchiv Freiburg
BArch Koblenz	Bundesarchiv Koblenz
BLHA	Brandenburgisches Landeshauptarchiv, Potsdam-Golm
DOMiD	Dokumentationszentrum und Museum über die Migration in Deutschland, Köln
DTA	Deutsches Tagebuch Archiv, Emmendingen
Eco-Archiv	Eco-Archiv, AdsD, Friedrich-Ebert-Stiftung, Bonn
FZH	Forschungsstelle für Zeitgeschichte in Hamburg
GCJZ	Gesellschaft für Christlich-Jüdische Zusammenarbeit
GIZ	Stiftung GIZ, Genossenschaftliches Informationszentrum, Berlin
HIS	Hamburger Institut für Sozialforschung
IfS	Institut für Stadtgeschichte/Stadtarchiv, Frankfurt
IfZ	Institut für Zeitgeschichte, München
JHD	Jugendhaus Düsseldorf, Bundeszentrale für katholische Jugendarbeit
KAS	Konrad-Adenauer-Stiftung e.V., Sankt Augustin
LAB	Landesarchiv Berlin
LKAN	Landeskirchliches Archiv der Ev.-Luth. Kirche in Norddeutschland, Hamburg-Harburg
MAA	Misereor-Archiv Aachen
StAHH	Staatsarchiv der Freien und Hansestadt Hamburg
TNA	The National Archives, London, Kew
UBG	Umweltbibliothek Grosshennersdorf
VDK	Volksbund Deutsche Kriegsgräberfürsorge, Kassel
Wende	Wende Museum, Culver City, California

Notes

INTRODUCTION

1. See www.bundestag.de/dokumente/textarchiv/2022/kw08-sondersitzung-882198.

2. 28 April 2022, www.emma.de.artikel/offener-brief-bundeskanzler-scholz-339463; see also the talk show *Anne Will* (ARD), 8 May 2022, "Mehr Waffen für die Ukraine," www.ardmediathek.de.

3. 31 August 2022, www.bundesregierung.de/breg-en/news/military-support-ukraine-2054992.

4. For overviews and further literature, see Ulrich Herbert, *A History of Twentieth-Century Germany* (Oxford, 2019; German edn., 2014); Richard Evans, *The Third Reich in Power* (London, 2005) and *The Third Reich at War* (London, 2008); Ian Kershaw, *Hitler 1889–1936* (London, 1998) and *Hitler 1936–45* (London, 2000); Jane Caplan, *Nazi Germany* (Oxford, 2008); Norbert Frei, ed., *Wie bürgerlich war der Nationalsozialismus?* (Göttingen, 2018); Andreas Wirsching, *Deutsche Geschichte im 20. Jahrhundert* (Munich, 2001).

5. Figures from the U.S. Holocaust Memorial Museum, www.encyclopedia.ushmm.org.

6. Bulletin der Bundesregierung, no. 13/2, 27 January 2015, p. 9.

7. "*Sündenstolz*," as the philosopher Hermann Lübbe called it, in *Neue Gesellschaft/Frankfurter Hefte* 36 (May 1989): 412. Neil MacGregor, *Germany: Memories of a Nation* (London, 2014).

8. Theodor Adorno, "Was Bedeutet: Aufarbeitung der Vergangenheit," in Adorno, *Eingriffe* (Frankfurt, 1963); Charles Maier, *The Unmasterable Past* (Cambridge, MA, 1988); Aleida Assmann and Ute Frevert, *Geschichtsvergessenheit—Geschichtsversessenheit* (Stuttgart, 1999); Torben Fischer and Matthias Lorenz, eds., *Lexikon der "Vergangenheitsbewältigung" in Deutschland* (Bielefeld, 3rd edn. 2015); Susan Neiman, *Learning from the Germans* (London, 2019).

9. Henryk Broder, "Im Chor der Gutmenschen," *Der Spiegel*, 24 September 1995.

10. David Hume, *A Treatise of Human Nature* (1739); Adam Smith, *The Theory of Moral Sentiments* (1759); Martha Nussbaum, *Upheavals of Thought* (Cambridge, 2001); Peter Singer, *The Expanding Circle* (Princeton, NJ, 2011); Richard Wrangham, *The Goodness Paradox* (London, 2018); D. Birnbacher and N. Hoerster, eds., *Texte zur Ethik* (Munich, 1980); Stanford Encyclopedia of Philosophy, at www.plato.stanford.edu.

11. Derek Parfit, *On What Matters*, vol. I (Oxford, 2011), p. 26.

12. For a (consequentialist) philosopher's history of mass murder, see Jonathan Glover, *Humanity* (London, 1999). Whether historians do and should pass judgment is the theme of Donald Bloxham, *History and Morality* (Oxford, 2020).

13. Michael Kretschmer, in *Die Zeit*, 27 July 2022.

14. Max Weber, "Politik als Beruf" (1919), in *Gesammelte Politische Schriften* (Tübingen, 1988), pp. 505–60. N. Gane, "Max Weber on the Ethical Irrationality of Political Leadership," *Sociology* 31, no. 3 (1997): 549–64; N. O'Donovan, "Causes and Consequences," *Polity* 43, no. 1 (2011): 84–105; S. Satkunanandan, "Max Weber and the Ethos of Politics Beyond Calculation," *American Political Science Review* 108, no. 1 (2014): 169–81. Older views: Karl Löwith, *Karl Marx and Max Weber* (London, 1982); Michael Walzer, "Political Action: The Problem of Dirty Hands," *Philosophy and Public Affairs* 2, no. 2 (1973): 160–80.

15. Henry Chadwick, "Gewissen," in *Reallexikon für Antike und Christentum* (Stuttgart, 1978), part 10, pp. 1025–1107; M. Breitenstein and J. Sonntag, "Das Gewissen und das Spiel," *Denkströme* 17 (2017): 96–133; Heinz D. Kittsteiner, *Die Entstehung des modernen Gewissens* (Frankfurt, 1991).

16. Nussbaum, *Upheavals of Thought*, quoted at pp. 319 and 392 (below). Arthur Schopenhauer, *Über die Grundlage der Moral* (1840).

17. Christopher Kutz, *Complicity* (Cambridge, 2000). Such a view remains controversial, especially with regard to the notion of "joint enterprise" in murder and felony.

18. Max Horkheimer, "Materialismus und Moral," in *Zeitschrift für Sozialforschung*, II (1933); and "Egoismus und Freiheitsbewegung," in ibid., V (1936).

19. Leon Trotsky, "Their Moral and Ours," *The New International* VI, no. 6 (1938): 163–73.

20. Émile Durkheim, *The Division of Labour in Society* (1893).

21. Émile Durkheim, "The Determination of Moral Facts" (1906), in Durkheim, *Sociology and Philosophy* (London, 2009; 1st French edn. 1951).

22. Ritchie Robertson, *The Enlightenment* (London, 2021); John Brewer, *The Pleasures of the Imagination* (New York, 1997); K. Eichhorn and L. Van Laak, eds., *Kulturen der Moral* (Hamburg, 2021).

23. H.-U. Winkler, *Der lange Weg nach Westen*, 2 vols. (Munich, 2000); A. Schildt, *Ankunft im Westen* (Frankfurt, 1999); K. Jarausch, *After Hitler* (New York, 2006); U. Herbert, ed., *Wandlungsprozesse in Westdeutschland* (Göttingen, 2002); A. Doering-Manteuffel, *Wie westlich sind die Deutschen?* (Göttingen, 1999); E. Wolfrum, *Die geglückte Demokratie* (Stuttgart, 2006); H.-U. Wehler, *Deutsche Gesellschaftsgeschichte*, V (Munich, 2008). Cf. F. Bajohr et al., eds., *Mehr als eine Erzählung* (Göttingen, 2016); F. Biess, *Republik der Angst* (Reinbek, 2019); S. Levsen and C. Torp, eds., *Wo liegt die Bundesrepublik?* (Göttingen, 2016); F. Biess and A. Eckert, "Why Do We Need New Narratives for the History of the Federal Republic?," *Central European History* 52 (2019): 1–18.

24. C. Kleßmann, *Zwei Staaten, eine Nation* (Göttingen, 1997); F. Bösch, ed., *A History Shared and Divided* (New York, 2018).

25. Arnold Gehlen, *Moral und Hypermoral* (Frankfurt, 1969).

26. Ronald Inglehart, "The Silent Revolution in Europe," *American Political Science Review* 65 (1971): 991–1017, and *The Silent Revolution* (Princeton, NJ, 1977). Cf. the special issue *Comparative Political Studies* 17 (1985); H. Klages, *Wertorientierungen im Wandel* (Frankfurt, 1984); G. Datler et al., "Two Theories on the Test Bench," in *Social Science Research* 42, no. 3 (2013): 906–25; *European Value Studies* book series (Leiden: 2007–present).

27. B. Dietz et al., eds., *Gab es den Wertewandel?* (Berlin, 2014); Ute Frevert, *Mächtige Gefühle* (Frankfurt, 2020); Biess, *Republik der Angst*; William Reddy, *The Navigation of Feeling* (Cambridge, 2001); Martha Nussbaum, "Morality and Emotions," in *Routledge Encyclopedia of Philosophy* (London, 1998); H. Knoch and B. Möckel, "Moral History," *Zeithistorische Forschungen* 14 (2017): 93–111.

28. Charles Taylor, *Sources of the Self* (Cambridge, MA, 1989); Hans Joas, *Die Entstehung der Werte* (Frankfurt, 1999).

29. J. Laidlaw, "For an Anthropology of Ethics and Freedom," *Journal of the Royal Anthropological Institute* 8 (2002): 311–32; D. Fassin, "Beyond Good and Evil?," *Anthropological Theory* 8, no. 4 (2008): 333–44; J. Cassaniti and J. Hickman, "New Directions in the Anthropology of Morality," *Anthropological Theory* 14, no. 3 (2014): 251–62; S. Hitlin and S. Vaisey, "The New Sociology of Morality," *Annual Review of Sociology* 39 (2013): 51–68; M. Fourcade and K. Healy, "Moral Views of Market Society," *Annual Review of Sociology* 33 (2007): 285–311.

30. Didier Fassin, *Humanitarian Reason* (Berkeley, CA, 2012).

1 PARZIVAL AT WAR

1. IfZ: MS 2019, "An Patroklos . . . Brieftagebuch eines Kriegsfreiwilligen," 13 February 1943, name anonymized; he joined Grenadierregiment (mot.) 8.

2. Ibid., 6 August 1943.

3. Ibid., 15 June 1943.

4. Grenadierregiment (mot.) 92.

5. "An Patroklos," 7 and 13 January 1944.
6. Ibid., 13 January 1944.
7. Ibid., 17 January 1944.
8. Ibid., 20 April 1943.
9. Ben Shepherd, *Hitler's Soldiers* (New Haven, CT, 2016), quoted at p. 56.
10. "Richtlinien für das Verhalten der Truppe," quoted in ibid., p. 127. Felix Römer, *Der Kommissarbefehl* (Paderborn, 2008).
11. Ben Shepherd, *Terror in the Balkans* (Cambridge, MA, 2012), pp. 207–208.
12. "An Patroklos," 17 September 1943.
13. Ibid., H. letter, 3 October 1943; Richard Wagner, *Parsifal*, Act 1, Scene 2.
14. "An Patroklos," 26 September 1943.
15. Ibid., 23 June 1943.
16. The Petri congregration in Bielefeld. Mebus and his youth group had tried to force their way into the community center blocked by the German Christians. See Bernd Hey, "Zum Kirchenkampf im Raum Bielefeld," in *69. Jahresbericht des Historischen Vereins für die Grafschaft Ravensberg* (1974), pp. 105–22.
17. "An Patroklos," 28 June 1943.
18. Ibid., 19 and 20 January 1944.
19. Ibid., 5 February 1944.
20. Ibid., 8 February 1944.
21. Ibid., 5 February 1944.
22. Ibid., 21 May 1944.
23. It was, perhaps, no coincidence that he had chosen to address his letters to Patroclus. In the *Iliad*, Patroclus wore Achilles' armor and beat back the Trojans in that disguise, but he then also defied Achilles' order to return.
24. "An Patroklos," 21 May 1944.
25. Ibid., 10 January 1945.
26. J. W. v. Goethe, *Ganymed* (1774), transl. E. G. Bowring (1853).

2 THE WAGES OF SIN

1. Numbers have been subject to debate. I follow Rüdiger Overmans, *Deutsche militärische Verluste im Zweiten Weltkrieg* (Munich, 1999); Richard Overy, *The Bombing War* (London, 2013).
2. Michael Wildt, *Hitler's Volksgemeinschaft and the Dynamics of Racial Exclusion* (New York, 2012; 1st German edn. 2007); Jane Caplan, *Nazi Germany* (Oxford, 2008); Frank Bajohr, "'Consensual Dictatorship' (Zustimmungsdiktatur) and 'Community of the People' (Volksgemeinschaft)," *Politeja* 14 (2010): 521–26; Janosch Steuwer, *A Third Reich as I See It* (Bloomington, IN, 2023).
3. For the following, see Ben Shepherd, *Hitler's Soldiers* (New Haven, CT, 2016), pp. 256–73.
4. T. Diedrich and J. Ebert, eds., *Nach Stalingrad: Walter von Seydlitz' Feldpostbriefe und Kriegsgefangenenpost* (Göttingen, 2018), pp. 371–77.
5. Bruno Kaliga, age unknown, private, 31 December 1942, reprinted in *Feldpostbriefe aus Stalingrad*, ed. J. Ebert (Göttingen, 2003), pp. 241–42.
6. Henry Picker, *Hitler's Tischgespräche im Führerhauptquartier* (Stuttgart, 1976), p. 32.
7. Felix Römer, *Die narzisstische Volksgemeinschaft* (Frankfurt, 2017), pp. 183–208.
8. I have adapted the English translation from the *Bulletin of International News* 20, no. 3 (6 February 1943), pp. 100–104.
9. Römer, *Die narzisstische Volksgemeinschaft*, 31 January 1943, p. 314; 14 June 1943, quoted at pp. 202–203, 315.
10. H. Boberach, ed., *Meldungen aus dem Reich: Die geheimen Lageberichte des Sicherheitsdienstes der SS, 1938–45*, XII, 4 February 1943, (4751).
11. Ursula von Kardorff, 31 January 1943, quoted in Walter Kempowski, *Das Echolot: Ein kollektives Tagebuch*, II, 18–31 January 1943 (Munich, 1993, 4th edn.), p. 651. From *St. Matthew Passion*—the

original words are "Hier zittert das gequälte Herz." See also Klemens von Klemperer, *Voyage Through the Twentieth Century* (New York, 2009), p. 18; Axel Schildt, *Medien-Intellektuelle in der Bundesrepublik* (Göttingen, 2020), pp. 82–83; M. Föllmer, "Was Nazism Collectivist?," *Journal of Modern History* 82, no. 1 (2010): 94–95.

12. Hans Woller, *Gesellschaft und Politik in der amerikanischen Besatzungszone* (Munich, 1986), p. 43; Götz Aly, *Volkes Stimme* (Frankfurt, 2006), pp. 107–109.

13. H.-P. Klausch, ed., *Oldenburg im Zweiten Weltkrieg: Das Kriegstagebuch des Mittelschullehrers Rudolf Tjaden*, 15 August 1941 (Oldenburg, 2010), p. 84.

14. Ibid., pp. 132–38.

15. Ibid., p. 138.

16. Ibid., 30 January 1943, p. 138; 1 and 13 February 1943, p. 139; 25 September 1944, p. 202.

17. Ibid., 13 May 1943, p. 151.

18. Printed versions of the speech were cleaned up, see Helmut Heiber (ed.), *Goebbels-Reden* (Dusseldorf, 1971), II, pp. 177, 183, and Nicholas Stargardt, *The German War* (London, 2015), p. 362.

19. Nathan Stoltzfus, *Resistance of the Heart* (New Brunswick, NJ, 1996).

20. Eisenhower Presidential Library, "Report on Atrocities Committed by the Germans Against the Civilian Population of Belgium," February 1945, witness statement by Adolf Singer, an Austrian-Jewish doctor in the camp, Appendix G, pp. 33–34.

21. See Stargardt, *The German War*, esp. p. 362, and Thomas Kühne, *Belonging and Genocide* (New Haven, CT, 2010).

22. Quoted in *Frankfurter Allgemeine Zeitung*, 18 April 1996, no. 91, pp. 13–14; see also Frank Biess, *Homecomings* (Princeton, NJ, 2006), pp. 32–33.

23. Gisela Diewald-Kerkmann, *Politische Denuziation im NS-Regime* (Bonn, 1995), p. 116.

24. Robert Gellately, "The Gestapo and German Society," *Journal of Modern History* 60, no. 4 (1988): 654–94; P. Gerhard and K.-M. Mallman, eds., *Die Gestapo im Zweiten Weltkrieg* (Darmstadt, 2020).

25. Martin Broszat, "Politische Denunziationen in der NS-Zeit," *Archivalische Zeitschrift* 73 (1977): 221–38. For the following, see Diewald-Kerkmann, *Politische Denuziation.*

26. See Overy, *The Bombing War.*

27. U. Büttner, "Gomorrha," in *Hamburg im Dritten Reich*, ed. Forschungsstelle für Zeitgeschichte Hamburg (2005), pp. 614–17.

28. FZH: Coll. Hamburg Bombenkrieg 292-8, Bock diary, 28 July 1943.

29. Mr. Boje, 2 September 1943, quoted in Erhard Klöss, ed., *Der Luftkrieg über Deutschland 1939–45* (Munich, 1963), pp. 75–76.

30. Report of R.-Owt. K.Z., in ibid., p. 108.

31. *Meldungen aus dem Reich*, 15 July 1943, p. 5475.

32. Ibid., 20 December 1943, p. 6172.

33. Feldpostbriefsammlung, http://www.museumsstiftung.de/briefsammlung/feldpost-zweiter-weltkrieg/.

34. IfZ: MS 311/2, Heinrich Voigtel diary, 12 July 1944.

35. The influential view of W. G. Sebald, *On the Natural History of Destruction* (London, 2003; German edn. 1999); see also Volker Hage, *Zeugen der Zerstörung* (Frankfurt, 2003).

36. Malte Thiessen, *Eingebrannt ins Gedächtnis: Hamburgs Gedenken an Luftkrieg und Kriegsende 1943 bis 2005* (Munich, 2007), quoted at pp. 63, 65.

37. *Meldungen aus dem Reich*, XIV, 2 July 1943, p. 5432.

38. O. D. Kulka and E. Jäckel, eds., *Die Juden in den geheimen NS-Stimmungsberichten 1933–45* (Düsseldorf, 2004), p. 515 (Bad Brückenau; Nuremberg), p. 528 (Würzburg).

39. Peter Longerich, *"Davon haben wir nichts gewusst!"* (Munich, 2006), pp. 281–90; Nicholas Stargardt, "Opfer der Bomben und der Vergeltung," in *Ein Volk von Opfern?*, ed. L. Kettenacker (Berlin, 2003), pp. 67–68; teacher Ludwig Klahold to Goebbels, 15 April 1944, in *Die Verfolgung und Ermordung der europäischen Juden durch das nationalsozialistische Deutschland 1933–45*, XI: *Deutsches Reich und Protektorat Böhmen und Mähren, April 1943–45*, ed. Susanne Heim et al. (Berlin, 2020), doc. 128, p. 391.

40. Dietmar Suess, *Tod aus der Luft* (Munich, 2011), p. 110.

41. Kulka and Jäckel, *Die Juden in den geheimen NS-Stimmungsberichten*, quoted at p. 527.

42. Lothar de La Camp, quoted in Longerich, *"Davon haben wir,"* pp. 285–86; Frank Bajohr and Dieter Pohl, *Massenmord* (Frankfurt, 2nd edn. 2014; original edn. 2008), pp. 65–83, 100ff.

43. Ruth Andreas-Friedrich, *Der Schattenmann: Tagebuchaufzeichnungen 1938–45* (Berlin, 1986, 1st edn. 1947), 2 March 1943, p. 103.

44. April 1944, SD Bad Brückenau, quoted in Kulka and Jäckel, *Die Juden in den geheimen NS-Stimmungsberichten*, p. 540.

45. Frank Bajohr and Dieter Pohl, *Der Holocaust als offenes Geheimnis* (2006), quoted at p. 67. See also the intelligence reports in Appendix F in S. Schrafstetter and A. Steinweis, eds., *The Germans and the Holocaust* (New York, 2016).

46. 22 October 1943, in Kulka and Jäckel, *Die Juden in den geheimen NS-Stimmungsberichten*, p. 532.

47. 19 May 1943 (Berlin); 22 May 1943 (Halle); 10 June 1943 (Augsburg), in ibid., pp. 516–22; Heim et al., *Verfolgung und Ermordung der europäischen Juden*, XI, doc. 23, SD informer, Warthegau, May 1943, p. 158.

48. 6 November 1944, in Kulka and Jäckel, *Die Juden in den geheimen NS-Stimmungsberichten*, p. 546.

49. The Confessing Church formed in opposition to attempts to merge all Protestant Churches into one pro-Nazi Evangelical body.

50. Uwe Kaminsky, "Integration der Fremden," in *Auf dem Weg in "dynamische Zeiten,"* ed. T. Jähnichen et al. (Münster, 2007).

51. Reprinted in G. Schäfer and R. Fischer, eds., *Landesbischof Wurm und der nationalsozialistische Staat 1940–1945* (Stuttgart, 1968), p. 312.

52. Irena Ostmeyer, *Zwischen Schuld und Sühne: Evangelische Kirche und Juden in SBZ und DDR 1945–1990* (Berlin, 2002), quoted at p. 37.

53. Quoted in Thiessen, *Eingebrannt*, pp. 73, 77.

54. LKAN: NL Sammet, Nr. 6 Predigten Schöffel, 10 April 1944.

55. LKAN: NL Sammet, Nr. 6 Predigten Schöffel, 4 February 1945. See Rainer Hering, *Die Bischöfe Simon Schöffel & Franz Tügel* (Hamburg, 1995).

56. See Herwart Vorländer, "NS-Volkswohlfahrt und Winterhilfswerk des deutschen Volkes," *Vierteljahrshefte für Zeitgeschichte* 34, no. 3 (1986): 341–80; F. Tennstedt, "Wohltat und Interesse," *Geschichte und Gesellschaft* 13 (1987): 157–80; Richard Evans, *The Third Reich in Power* (London, 2005), pp. 484–90.

57. Gertrud Bäumer, "Nächstenliebe und Fernstenliebe," *Die Frau* (December 1938).

58. Landesarchiv Saarland, MZG-Ld 144, 1944, "Opfer von Lohn und Gehalt," *Meldungen aus dem Reich*, XIII, 18 March 1943, p. 4976.

59. Suess, *Tod aus der Luft*, pp. 179–237.

60. *Meldungen aus dem Reich*, XV, p. 6030; demonstration in Witten on 11 August 1943.

61. Ibid., 18 November 1943, p. 6029.

62. Ibid., 15 July 1943, p. 5478.

63. Ibid., 10 August 1943, pp. 5643, 5645.

64. Feldpostbriefsammlung, parents to Helmut Schneiss, 7 May 1943.

65. Feldpostbriefsammlung, Martin Meier to his wife, 17 August 1943.

66. C. F. Rüter, ed., *Justiz und NS-Verbrechen*, 49 vols. (Amsterdam, 1968–2012), XI, pp. 381–85.

67. Ibid., pp. 381–95.

68. U.S. National Archives and Records Administration (NARA) (College Park, MD), RG 165, Entry 179, 17 August 1944; with special thanks to Felix Römer for sharing with me copies of records for twenty-nine prisoners. Römer, *Comrades: The Wehrmacht from Within* (Oxford, 2019; German edn., *Kameraden*, 2012).

69. DTA: 1828, Hugo Manz, "Briefe an einen vermissten Sohn."

70. Goebbels, Tagebuch, 2 March 1943. Elke Frölich, ed., *Die Tagebücher von Joseph Goebbels* (Munich, 1993).

71. Figures vary, especially for Soviet civilians. The ones cited here are those of the "Holocaust Encyclopedia" by the U.S. Holocaust Memorial Museum. The latest survey by Alex Kay, *Empire of Destruction* (New Haven, CT, 2021), gives a lower figure of 13 to 14 million; see also Dieter Pohl, *Verfolgung und Massenmord in der NS-Zeit 1933–45* (Darmstadt, 2011, 3rd edn.); Wolfgang Benz, ed., *Dimension des Völkermords* (Berlin, 2014). See further: Raul Hilberg, *The Destruction*

of the European Jews (New York, 1985; 1st ed. 1961); Saul Friedländer, *The Years of Extermination: Nazi Germany and the Jews, 1939–1945* (New York, 2007); David Cesarani, *Final Solution* (London, 2015); Dan Stone, *The Holocaust* (London, 2023).

72. Kay, *Empire of Destruction*, ch. 1.

73. Christian Gerlach, *Kalkulierte Morde* (Hamburg, 1998).

74. *Verhandlungsbericht der medizinischen Gesellschaft Freiburg*, 12/19 (13 May 1933), p. 768.

75. For this and the following, see IfZ: MS 796, Susanne Vogel to Liselotte Dieckmann, 28 March 1947. For Anne Herrnstadt, see www.ushmm.org. I am greatly indebted to Agnes Stieda, Neisser's granddaughter, for several conversations in 2016–17 and additional letters, and also to Richard Brook for further information on the Pauly family.

76. Marion Kaplan, *Between Dignity and Despair: Jewish Life in Nazi Germany* (Oxford, 1999); C. Goeschel, "Suicides of German Jews in the Third Reich," *German History* 25, no. 1 (2007): 24–45.

77. For the following, see Kulka and Jäckel, *Die Juden in den geheimen NS-Stimmungsberichten*, pp. 642–45.

78. Mathilde Bing to Gerhard and Heinz Bing, 27 June 1943, in Heim et al., *Die Verfolgung und Ermordung*, XI, doc. 46, pp. 203–204.

79. Leopold to Johanna and Victor Mayer, September 1944, in ibid., doc. 278, pp. 725–26.

80. Victor Klemperer, *Ich will Zeugnis ablegen bis zum letzten: Tagebücher 1942–45* (Berlin, 1995, 4th edn.), 27 January 1943, p. 318.

81. Ibid., 17 August 1943, p. 420.

82. Ibid., 5 May 1943, p. 372.

83. FZH: 11S/13, Solmitz diaries, 28 February 1941. See also Evans, *Third Reich at War*, pp. 555–56.

84. For 1938, see Wolfgang Benz, *Gewalt im November 1938* (Berlin, 2018) and the eyewitness accounts in U. Gerhardt and T. Karlauf, eds., *The Night of Broken Glass* (Cambridge, 2012; German edn. 2009).

85. Bajohr and Pohl, *Holocaust als offenes Geheimnis*, quoted at p. 49. Wolf Gruner, "Indifference?," in Schrafstetter and Steinweis, *The Germans and the Holocaust*, ch. 3. Wolfgang Dreßen, *Betrifft: "Aktion 3"* (Berlin, 1998); Aly, *Hitler's Volkstaat* (Frankfurt, 2005), pp. 139–50.

86. *The Von Hassell Diaries, 1938–44* (1971), 1 November 1941 (Ebenhausen); see also 8 April 1941 and 31 December 1942.

87. Feldpostbriefsammlung, Anton Böhrer to his sister and father, 16 November 1941.

88. Feldpostbriefsammlung, Hans Albring to Eugen Altrogge, 21 March 1942; Altrogge to Albring, 24 March 1942, quoted.

89. Bajohr and Pohl, *Holocaust als offenes Geheimnis*, quoted at pp. 60–61. See also Sönke Neitzel and Harald Welzer, *Soldaten* (Frankfurt, 2011), pp. 119–20, 145–66.

90. Andreas-Friedrich, *Schattenmann*, 2 December 1942, p. 96.

91. KZ Gedenkstätte Buchenwald, exhibition "Ausgrenzung und Gewalt" (opened April 2016), www.buchenwald.de.

92. Andreas-Friedrich, *Schattenmann*, 19 September 1941.

93. Gedenkstätte Deutscher Widerstand, Berlin. In English, see A. Lloyd, ed., *Defying Hitler: The White Rose Pamphlets* (Oxford, 2022).

94. Neitzel and Welzer, *Soldaten*, pp. 156–66.

95. NARA: RG 165, Entry 179, Box 515/1, independent room conversation, 13 June 1943.

96. NARA: RG 165, Entry 179, conversation between Breitlich and Hanelt, 4 April 1945; Mewes in conversation with Siegfried Käss, 30 April 1945. See also Horst Krapoth, 12 January 1945.

97. IfZ: MS 311/2, Voigtel diary, 29 October 1944; he was near Poggio.

98. Rüter, *Justiz und NS-Verbrechen*, VIII, no. 276, pp. 364–71. The initial trial took place in 1951, with a verdict for twelve and fifteen years in prison. The sentence was revised in 1953. For the change in law, see pp. 140–42 in this volume.

99. Claudia Schoppmann, "Rettung von Juden," in *Überleben im Untergrund*, ed. B. Kosmala and C. Schoppmann (Berlin, 2002), p. 114.

100. Andreas-Friedrich, *Schattenmann*, 18 March 1945.

101. Kristen Renwick Monroe, *The Hand of Compassion: Portraits of Moral Choice During the Holocaust* (Princeton, NJ, 2004), p. 260.

102. Susanna Schrafstetter, *Flucht und Versteck* (Göttingen, 2015), pp. 89, 155.
103. Dr. Sophie Mayer, statement to Spruchkammer, reprinted in Schrafstetter and Steinweis, *Germans and the Holocaust*, Appendix H, p. 169.
104. Bajohr and Pohl, *Massenmord.*
105. Johannes Hürter, *Hitlers Heerführer* (Munich, 2007), p. 558.
106. Hans Mommsen, "Der Nationalsozialismus: Kumulative Radikalisierung und Selbstzerstörung des Regimes," in *Meyers Enzyklopädisches Lexikon*, XVI (Munich, 1976), pp. 785–90; Ian Kershaw, "Working Towards the Führer," in *Contemporary European History* 2, no. 2 (1993): 103–18.
107. Peter Longerich, *Heinrich Himmler* (Oxford, 2012), pp. 657–72.
108. Himmler, speech at Posen, 4 October 1943; see https://www.1000dokumente.de/pdf/dok_0008_pos_de.pdf.
109. Karin Orth, *Die Konzentrationslager-SS* (Göttingen, 2000), pp. 208–209.
110. See further Claudia Koonz, *The Nazi Conscience* (Cambridge, MA, 2005); Evans, *Third Reich at War*, ch. 6; and W. Bialas and L. Fritze, eds., *Ideologie und Moral im Nationalsozialismus* (Göttingen, 2014).
111. The case of Untersturmbannführer Max Täubner; see Ernst Klee et al., *Schöne Zeiten: Judenmord aus der Sicht der Täter und Gaffer* (Munich, 1988), pp. 184–90.
112. Hannah Arendt, *Eichmann in Jerusalem* (New York, 1963).
113. Quoted from Bettina Stangneth, *Eichmann vor Jerusalem* (Zurich, 2011), p. 258, pp. 392–93.
114. For this and the following, see Ulrich Herbert, *Best: Biographische Studien über Radikalismus, Weltanschauung und Vernunft, 1903–89* (Bonn, 1996). See also Michael Wildt, *Generation des Unbedingten* (Hamburg, 2002).
115. Herbert, *Best*, quoted at p. 94.
116. J. Hürter, ed., *Notizen aus dem Vernichtungskrieg: Die Ostfront 1941/42 in den Aufzeichnungen des Generals Heinrici* (Darmstadt, 2016).
117. Oliver von Wrochem, *Erich von Manstein* (Paderborn, 2006); see also W. Petter, "Wehrmacht und Judenverfolgung," in *Die Deutschen und die Judenverfolgung*, ed. U. Büttner (Hamburg, 1992). In the murder of the Kiev Jews in September 1941, the army moved more than thirty thousand Jews to the Babi Yar ravine, where they were shot by the Sonderkommando 4a with support from the police regiment South.
118. Felix Römer, *Der Kommissarbefehl* (Paderborn, 2008), esp. p. 565.
119. Shepherd, *Hitler's Soldiers*, pp. 376–77.
120. For Stülpnagel, see Herbert, *Geschichte Deutschlands im 20. Jahrhundert*, pp. 371–72. See also Peter Lieb, *Konventioneller Krieg oder NS-Weltanschauungskrieg* (Munich, 2007).
121. J. Hürter, "Auf dem Weg zur Militäropposition," *Vierteljahresheft für Zeitgeschichte* 52, no. 3 (2004): 527–62, and the debate in *VfZ* 54 (2006). Other members in the resistance implicated in NS crimes were Stülpnagel and Speidel.
122. Hellmuth Stieff to his wife, 10 January 1942, in *Briefe*, ed. H. Mühleisen (Berlin, 1991), pp. 138–42.
123. Speidel, quoted in Shepherd, *Hitler's Soldiers*, p. 351.
124. Daniel Goldhagen, *Hitler's Willing Executioners* (New York, 1996); Christopher Browning, *Ordinary Men* (New York, 1992).
125. H. F. Meyer, *Blutiges Edelweiss* (Berlin, 2008), pp. 212–38.
126. Shepherd, *Hitler's Soldiers*, pp. 411–14.
127. Römer, *Kameraden*; Römer, *Narzistische Volksgemeinschaft*; Hürter, *Notizen aus dem Vernichtungskrieg.* For greater stress on situational factors, see Neitzel and Welzer, *Soldaten.*
128. See, for example, the case of Swoboda, who did not see himself as a criminal and felt that the killing of civilians and defenseless American POWs was justified; Römer, *Kameraden*, pp. 405–408. See also Jan Philipp Reemtsma, "Tötungslegitimationen," in *Bruchlinien: Tendenzen der Holocaustforschung*, ed. G. Koch (Cologne, 1999), pp. 85–103.
129. C. Blair, *The Hunted, 1942–5* (New York, 1998), pp. 53–62.
130. Mark Mazower, *Inside Hitler's Greece* (New Haven, CT, 1993), pp. 253–54.
131. Meyer, *Blutiges Edelweiss*, p. 187.
132. In 1981, Battel was recognized as Righteous Among the Nations, see www.righteous.yadvashem.org.

133. David H. Kitterman, "Those Who Said 'No!,'" *German Studies Review* 11, no. 2 (1988): 241–54. See also Herbert Jäger, *Verbrechen unter totalitärer Herrschaft* (Olten, 1967).

134. Nikolaus Wachsmann, *KL: A History of the Nazi Concentration Camps* (New York, 2015); Ulrich Herbert et al., *Die nationalsozialistischen Konzentrationslager*, 2 vols. (Göttingen 1998).

135. Rüter, *Justiz und NS-Verbrechen*, XI, Schwurgericht Bremen, 1952–3. Mirbeth had two years discounted for custody and would already be released at the end of 1956. He died in Munich in 1975. For the postwar trial, see pp. 145–46 in this volume.

136. Quoted in Karin Hartewig, "Rote Kapos in Buchenwald," in *Abgeleitete Macht—Funktionshäftlinge zwischen Widerstand und Kollaboration*, ed. KZ-Gedenkstätte Neuengamme (Bremen, 1998), p. 120. See also Herbert et al., *Die nationalsozialistischen Konzentrationslager*, II, pp. 946–47; Lutz Niethammer, ed., *Der "gesäuberte" Antifaschismus: Die SED und die roten Kapos von Buchenwald* (Berlin, 1994).

137. Yveline Pendaries, *Les procès de Rastatt, 1946–1954* (Bern, 1995); Annette Neumann, "Funktionshäftlinge in Ravensbrück," in *Bulletin für Faschismus- und Weltkriegsforschung*, Beiheft 1 (Berlin 2001), pp. 44–48; Katharina von Kellenbach, *The Mark of Cain* (Oxford, 2013), pp. 98–104.

138. M. Sporrer and H. Steiner, eds., *Rosa Jochmann* (Vienna, 1987); Neumann, "Funktionshäftlinge."

139. Primo Levi, *Survival in Auschwitz* (New York, 1976; 1st edn. 1947), p. 92. On Levi's Hobbesian view, see Frederic D. Homer, *Primo Levi and the Politics of Survival* (Columbia, MO, 2001), ch. 5.

140. Quoted in Tzetan Todorov, *Facing the Extreme: Moral Life in the Concentration Camps* (London, 1999; 1st French edn. 1991), p. 31.

141. Primo Levi, *Moments of Reprieve* (New York 1986; 1st edn. 1981), pp. 150–54.

142. See Todorov, *Facing the Extreme.*

143. Quoted in Sporrer and Steiner, *Rosa Jochmann*, p. 84.

144. As reported by Erich Kästner, *Notabene 45: Ein Tagebuch* (Berlin, 1961).

145. Draft declaration of the Beck/Goerdeler government, summer 1944, quoted from the reconstructed text, Gedenkstätte Deutscher Widerstand, Berlin; the original has been lost. C. Dipper, "Der Widerstand und die Juden," in *Der Widerstand gegen den Nationalsozialismus*, ed. J. Schmädecke and P. Steinbach (Munich, 1985), pp. 598–616.

146. 4 July 1944. Peter Hoffmann, *Stauffenberg* (Montreal, 2003, 2nd edn.), pp. 244–45 and Appendix; cf. Thomas Karlauff, *Stauffenberg* (Munich, 2019).

147. Herbert, *Geschichte Deutschlands im 20. Jahrhundert*, p. 529.

148. Feldpostbriefsammlung, Günter Wolf to his wife, 24 July 1944. Ian Kershaw, *The End* (London, 2011), pp. 30–35.

149. Kershaw, *The Hitler-Myth* (Oxford, 1987), pp. 214–17.

150. Kershaw, *The End*, p. 220.

151. Bernd Wegner, "Hitler, der Zweite Weltkrieg und die Choreographie des Untergangs," *Geschichte und Gesellschaft* 26, no. 3 (2000): 493–518; Michael Geyer, "'There Is a Land Where Everything Is Pure: Its Name is Land of Death,'" in *Sacrifice and National Belonging in Twentieth-Century Germany*, ed. G. Eghigian and M. Berg (Arlington, 2002).

152. Andreas Kunz, *Wehrmacht und Niederlage* (Munich, 2014, 2nd edn.), pp. 230–51. Stargardt, *German War.*

153. NARA, RG 165, Entry 179, Box 514, Matzdorf in Schreiner file, 19 December 1944.

154. Feldpostbriefsammlung, Hans-Joachim S. to his wife, 16 October 1944.

155. Jörg Echternkamp, *Soldaten im Nachkrieg* (Munich, 2014), p. 106.

156. LKAN: NL Sammet, Nr. 1, Schneider, "Auffindung des Kreuzes," no date, c. 1942–44.

157. Römer, *Kameraden*, p. 241 and ch. 10 for the following.

158. DTA: 3916, Inge and Heinz Zabel, Briefe, December 17, 1944. See also Benjamin Möckel, *Erfahrungsbruch und Generationsbehauptung* (Göttingen, 2004), p. 128.

159. Willy Peter Reese, *Mir selber seltsam fremd* (Munich, 2003), quoted at pp. 136, 145, 147, 182, 244–47.

160. Giesen diary, 12 March 1944 and 24 August 1944, quoted from K.-T. Schleicher, ed., *Aus Feldpostbriefen junger Christen, 1939–45* (Stuttgart, 2005), pp. 306, 327–28.

161. DTA: 150, Eva Schwedhelm, Kriegsjahre i. Köln.

162. IfZ: MS 311/2 Voigtel diary, 17 March 1945.

163. DTA: 1828, Manz letters, 25 March 1945.

164. NARA: RG 165, Entry 179, Box 492, Käss to Mewes, 30 April 1945; and H. Müller, 2 March 1945. Translator: Käss war Hauptmann.
165. Klemperer, *Zeugnis*, in Unterbernbach, 23 April 1945, p. 754.
166. Kershaw, *The End.*
167. Rüter, *Justiz und NS-Verbrechen*, I, no. 23, pp. 521–28.
168. Unterbernbach, 21 April 1945, Klemperer, *Zeugnis*, pp. 750–51.
169. DTA: 168, Ronke diary, 26 March, 25 April, and 19 May 1945.
170. Dwight D. Eisenhower Presidential Library (Abilene, KS), U.S. Army Unit Records Box 1182, G-5 reports, 4 May 1945, HQ of 95th Infantry Division, Charles McDaniel, Major CE, to commanding general, 9th U.S. Army (report on 3 May), quoted; and reports by McDaniel, 5–8 May 1945. See further: *Der Spiegel*, 11 December 1957, pp. 32–35; Peter Bürger et al., "'Zwischen Jerusalem und Meschede'"—daunlots: Internetbeiträge des christine-koch-mundtarchivs am museum eslohe, no. 76 (2015); and pp. 151 and 205 in this volume.
171. "An Patroklos," 1 April 1945.
172. "An Patroklos," 8–21 May 1945.
173. FZH: Coll. Bombenkrieg 292-8, A-F, Bock diary, 3 May 1945, emphasis in original.

3 THE MURDERERS ARE AMONG US

1. IfZ: MS 796, Susanne Vogel to Liselotte Dieckmann, 28 March 1947 and 6th letter, spring 1947.
2. IfZ: MS 796, Vogel to Dieckmann, 6th letter, spring 1947.
3. Ibid.
4. IfZ: MS 796, Vogel to Dieckmann, 28 March 1947.
5. Ibid.
6. Ibid.; Luke 6:27, Revelation 21:5.
7. Bertold Brecht, *Die Dreigroschenoper* (1928), 2nd act. Alexander and Margarete Mitscherlich, *Die Unfähigkeit zu Trauern* (Munich, 1967); Aleida Assmann in Aleida Assmann and Ute Frevert, *Geschichtsvergessenheit—Geschichtsversessenheit* (Stuttgart, 1999), pp. 112–23; Alexander Gauland in *Die Russen sind da*, ed. P. Böthig and P. Walther (Berlin, 2011), p. 483.
8. On the confusion of therapy and social policy in Mitscherlich's approach, see Tilman Moser, *Vorsicht Berührung* (Frankfurt, 1992), pp. 203–20. For collective guilt, see Aleida Assmann, "Ein deutsches Trauma?," *Merkur* 608 (1999): 1142–54, but cf. Norbert Frei, "Von deutscher Erfindungskraft," *Rechtsthistorisches Journal* 16 (1997): 621–34, and Barbara Wolbring, "Nationales Stigma und persönliche Schuld," *Historische Zeitschrift* 289 (2009): 325–64, and p. 104 in this volume.
9. Hannah Arendt, "The Aftermath of Nazi Rule," *Commentary* X, no. 10 (1950), reprinted in *Essays in Understanding, 1930–54* (New York, 1994; 1st edn. 1954), pp. 248–69, quoted at p. 249.
10. James Stern, *The Hidden Damage* (London, 1990, 1st edn. 1947), pp. 128, 276, 278.
11. UNRRA looked after 9.6 million DPs and refugees in Germany at the end of the war; H. Harmsen, *Die Integration heimatloser Ausländer* (Augsburg, 1958), pp. 13–16.
12. IfS: V5a/17, 20 Jahre VdK (Verein der Kriegsversehrten, 1966); EHW camp figures reprinted in ADCV: 379.056 Fasz. 01, Caritas Lagerdienst, 11 November 1954.
13. Ernest Landau, "Die ersten Tage in Freiheit," reprinted in Michael Brenner, *Nach dem Holocaust* (Munich, 1995), p. 119.
14. Stefan Schröder, *Displaced Persons im Landkreis und in der Stadt Münster 1945–1951* (Münster, 2005), pp. 215, 220ff. For German fears, see now F. Biess, *Republik der Angst* (Reinbek, 2019), esp. pp. 57–64.
15. There was some plunder immediately on liberation—e.g., in nearby villages of the Neuengamme camp complex, see K. Hertz-Eichenrode, ed., *Ein KZ wird geräumt* (Bremen, 2000), p. 301—but, overall, crime was limited, see Wolfgang Jacobmeyer, *Vom Zwangsarbeiter zum Heimatlosen Ausländer* (Göttingen, 1985).
16. Quoted in Juliane Wetzel, "Die Überlebenden des Holocausts," in *Von Stalingrad zur Währungsreform*, ed. M. Broszat et al. (Munich, 1988), p. 342.

17. See Atina Grossmann, *Juden, Deutsche, Alliierte* (Göttingen, 2012; English orignal 2007), quoted at p. 366.
18. Julius Posener, *In Deutschland: 1945 bis 1946* (Berlin, 2001; 1st edn. Jerusalem 1947), pp. 138–39; Constantin Goschler, *Schuld und Schulden* (Göttingen, 2005), p. 69.
19. HIS: SBe 562-G1, Albin Stobwasser, "Die den Roten Winkel trugen" (1983); Julia Volmer-Naumann, *Bürokratische Bewältigung* (Essen, 2012), pp. 34–35.
20. Constantin Goschler, "Der Fall Philipp Auerbach," in *Wiedergutmachung in der Bundesrepublik Deutschland*, ed. L. Herbst and C. Goschler (Munich, 1988), pp. 77–98; Tobias Winstel, *Verhandelte Gerechtigkeit* (Munich, 2006).
21. Henning Fischer, *Überlebende als Akteurinnen: Die Frauen der Lagergemeinschaft Ravensbrück* (Konstanz, 2018), pp. 108–109; Insa Eschebach, *Öffentliches Gedenken* (Frankfurt, 2005), pp. 111–12.
22. Hertz-Eichenrode, *Ein KZ wird geräumt*, quoted at p. 332.
23. Marieluise Scheibner, "Das Massengrab im Langenbachtal: Erinnerungen einer damals Dreizehnjährigen," in *Sauerland* 2 (1995): 44–45. See the documentary footage of German civilians walking past the corpses, 3 May 1945, U.S. Holocaust Memorial Museum, Steven Spielberg Film and Video Archive, www.collections.ushmm.org, Film Accession Number: 1994.119.1, RG Number: RG-60.2339. For the Warstein massacre, see p. 109 in this volume.
24. FZH: Coll. 292-8 Hamburg Bombenkrieg, Bock diary, 20 and 24 May 1945.
25. Stephen Spender, *Deutschland in Ruinen* (Heidelberg, 1995), pp. 31–32.
26. Bischof Halfmann, 13 May 1945, quoted in Stephan Linck, *Neue Anfänge: Der Umgang der evangelischen Kirche mit der NS-Vergangenheit und ihr Verhältnis zum Judentum*, I: 1945–65 (Kiel, 2013), p. 100.
27. Quoted in Fischer, *Überlebende*, p. 109.
28. DTA: 5, Walter to Elli S., 4 July 1945.
29. 1 June 1945; Habbo Knoch, *Die Tat als Bild* (Hamburg, 2001), quoted at p. 171.
30. DTA: 2764, Erich Schmalenberg diaries.
31. Stern, *Hidden Damage*, pp. 80–81; Knoch, *Die Tat als Bild*, p. 136.
32. Truman papers, No. 1384, Communiqué, 2 August 1945, https://history.state.gov/historicaldocuments/frus1945Berlinv02/d1384.
33. Feldpostbriefsammlung, Heinz Sartorio to his sister Elly, 21 June 1943.
34. See Ulrike Weckel, *Beschämende Bilder* (Stuttgart, 2012), esp. ch. 3.
35. TNA: FO 939/72, Commandant 305 POW Camp to PID Mission GHW, 19 July 1945.
36. TNA: FO 939/371, "Reactions of German Prisoners of War to Concentration Camp Atrocity Film" (confidential), summary of reports from camp commandants.
37. TNA: FO 939/72, "Report on Individual PW's reaction to Concentration Camp Film," 3 September 1945, and "Excerpts from Ps/W letters showing the reaction to … Film shown from 9–16 July 1945," in Colonel Thornhill to Minister Resident, 13 August 1945.
38. TNA: FO 939/72.
39. TNA: FO 939/72, Gef. Marquard.
40. TNA: FO 939/72, 30 July 1945, for a copy of the introductory remarks.
41. TNA: FO 939/72, for this and the following.
42. Quoted in Weckel, *Beschämende Bilder*, p. 414.
43. *Der Tagesspiegel*, 17 April 1946, quoted from ibid., p. 466, and p. 484 for the survey from Eichstätt.
44. Bernard Williams, *Shame and Necessity* (Berkeley, CA, 1993). See also Ute Frevert, *The Politics of Humiliation* (Oxford, 2020).
45. What Krista Thomason calls "self-conception"; see her "Shame, Violence and Morality," *Philosophy and Phenomenological Research* 91, no. 1 (2015): 1–24.
46. DTA: 168, Christa Ronke diary, 3 November 1945.
47. TNA: FO 939/72.
48. Reported by *Der Tagesspiegel*, 17 April 1946; see Weckel, *Beschämende Bilder*, p. 466.
49. TNA: FO 939/72.
50. Theodor Heuss, "In Memoriam," 25 November 1945, in Heuss, *An und über Juden* (Dusseldorf, 1964), quoted at p. 100.
51. IfZ: MS 796, Vogel to Dieckmann, 28 March 1947.

52. Ernst Wiechert, *Der Totenwald* (Zürich, 1946), p. 117.
53. Ernst Wiechert, "Rede an die deutsche Jugend," 11 November 1945, reprinted in Wiechert, *An die deutsche Jugend* (Luton, 1946), published for the YMCA in aid of POWs, quoted at pp. 59, 75.
54. Ibid., pp. 70, 74.
55. Points of entry into this large literature: Ian Kershaw, *The Nazi Dictatorship* (London, 1993, 3rd edn.); Herbert, *History of Twentieth-Century Germany*; Caplan, *Nazi Germany*.
56. Baeck to Heuss, 26 September 1951, quoted in H.-E. Volkmann, "Deutsche Historiker im Banne des Nationalsozialismus," in *Verwandlungspolitik*, ed. W. Loth and B.-A. Rusinek (Frankfurt, 1998), p. 305. Friedrich Meinecke, *Die deutsche Katastrophe* (Wiesbaden, 1946).
57. Wiechert, "Rede an die deutsche Jugend," pp. 56, 61, 68–69, 81. See also Edson M. Chick, "Ernst Wiechert and the Problem of Evil," *Monatshefte* 46, no. 4 (1954): 181–91.
58. ADCV: 374.065 Fasz 00, Pater Marius Stark, "Liebe Mitbrüder," pamphlet, October 1947.
59. Dan Diner, ed., *Zivilisationsbruch: Denken nach Auschwitz* (Frankfurt, 1988).
60. *Die Zeit*, 24 June 1948. Erwin Reisner, *Der Dämon und sein Bild* (Berlin, 1947).
61. G. Baumert, *Deutsche Familien nach dem Kriege* (Darmstadt, 1954), p. 195.
62. National Archives, Washington, DC, Collection JFK-22, Samuel H. Beer Personal Papers, 1945–62, Beer interview of Dr. Kuper, 28 July 1945.
63. Barth interview with *Die Weltwoche*, 15 September 1945, reprinted in *Die Schuld der Kirche: Dokumente*, ed. M. Greschat (Munich, 1982), p. 83, also for the following. See Gerhard Ritter, *Europe and the German Question* (Munich, 1948).
64. "Rede anläesslich der Gedächtnisfeier für die Opfer des Faschismus," Rendsburg, November 1945, in Theodor Steltzer, *Reden, Ansprachen, Gedanken 1945–47*, ed. K. Jürgensen (Neumünster, 1986), quoted at pp. 31–32.
65. April 1946; Werner Blessing, "Deutschland in Not," in Broszat et al., *Von Stalingrad zur Währungsreform*, p. 63.
66. Greschat, *Schuld der Kirche*, p. 102.
67. Niemöller, speech at the church assembly at Treysa, 28 August 1945, in ibid., pp. 79–81.
68. In Nordelbien (Northern Germany), the British only investigated twenty-one pastors during denazification; Linck, *Neue Anfänge*. On the American zone, see Clemens Vollnhals, "Die Evangelische Kirche," in Broszat et al., *Von Stalingrad zur Währungsreform*, p. 142. Luke Fenwick, "The Protestant Churches in Saxony-Anhalt in the Shadow of the German Christian Movement and National Socialism, 1945–49," *Church History* 82, no. 4 (2013): 877–903.
69. Rheinische Provinzialsynode, 20 September 1946, and Pfarrer Klose (Bochum) to Asmussen, 25 February 1946, in Greschat, *Schuld der Kirche*, pp. 265, 257.
70. Letter to Asmussen, 29 October 1945; and Thielicke, 8 November 1945, both in ibid., pp. 168–71.
71. Präses Halfmann, 28 October 1945; Greschat, *Schuld der Kirche*, p. 228.
72. Kirchenleitung Sachsen to Bruderrat EKD, 9 Februrary 1946; Greschat, *Schuld der Kirche*, p. 239.
73. Asmussen, Kommentar, 6 December 1945, in Greschat, *Schuld der Kirche*, pp. 135–41.
74. Niemöller, Neustädter Kirche, Erlangen, 22 January 1946, reprinted in Greschat, *Schuld der Kirche*, p. 190. For the mixed reactions among audiences, see Posener, *In Deutschland*, pp. 30–32. See now Benjamin Ziemann, *Martin Niemöller* (Munich, 2019), chs. 13–14.
75. See B. Ziemann, "Martin Niemöllers Antisemitismus und die Frage der Schuld nach 1945," in *Martin Niemöller und seine internationale Rezeption*, ed. L. Bormann and M. Heymel (Göttingen, 2023).
76. Greschat, *Schuld der Kirche*, pp. 171, 222, 255.
77. Vollnhals, "Die Evangelische Kirche," quoted at p. 134.
78. Letter to Wurm, 15 February 1946, in Greschat, *Schuld der Kirche*, pp. 147–48.
79. Greschat, *Schuld der Kirche*, pp. 289–95.
80. Hannah Arendt, "Karl Jaspers: A Laudatio" (1958), in Arendt, *Men in Dark Times* (New York, 1970), p. 77.
81. Karl Jaspers, *Die Schuldfrage* (Zurich, 1946; 1979 edn.), p. 69; here he was quoting the liberal Wilhelm Roepke.
82. Ibid., p. 57.

83. Willy Brandt, *Verbrecher und andere Deutsche: Ein Bericht aus Deutschland 1946* (Bonn, 2007), published in Norway and Sweden at the time.

84. Jaspers to Arendt, 18 September 1946, in Hannah Arendt and Karl Jaspers, *Briefwechsel 1926–69*, ed. L. Köhler and H. Saner (Munich, 1985), p. 95.

85. Arendt to Jaspers, 17 August 1946, in Arendt and Jaspers, *Briefwechsel*, pp. 89f.

86. Heinrich Blücher to Hannah Arendt, 15 July 1946, in Arendt und Blücher, *Briefe 1936–68* (Munich, 1996), pp. 146–48.

87. Thomas Mann, *Essays, II: Politik*, ed. H. Kurzke (Frankfurt, 1977), p. 299.

88. Walter von Molo, the president of the Poetry Section in the Prussian Academy, in an open letter to the *Berliner Allgemeine Zeitung*, 8 August 1945.

89. *Münchner Zeitung*, 18 August 1945; Thiess was the author of popular historical novels. See J. F. G. Grosser, *Die grosse Kontroverse* (Hamburg, 1963), and Detlef Haberland, ed., *Ästhetik und Ideologie* (Munich, 2017).

90. Quoted in Christof Schneider, *Nationalsozialismus als Thema im Programm des Nordwestdeutschen Rundfunks: 1945–48* (Potsdam, 1999), pp. 144–47.

91. See now Ziemann, *Niemöller*, ch. 15.

92. Anna M. Parkinson, *An Emotional State* (Ann Arbor, MI, 2014), pp. 56–67, quoted at p. 59.

93. 4 March 1946, in Ernst Wiechert, *Sämtliche Werke* (Munich, 1957), p. 638.

94. Ernst Wiechert, "Abschied von der Zeit" (1946), in Wiechert, *Der Totenwald... Tagebuchnotizen* (Munich, 1979), pp. 197–202.

95. *Passauer Neue Presse*, 20 May 1947.

96. Ernst Wiechert, *Missa Sine Nomine* (Munich, 1950), quoted at pp. 314, 419.

97. Alexander Parlach (Erich Kuby), "Die erste und einzige Rede deutscher Jugend an ihren Dichter," *Der Ruf* (May 1947): 10; Kuby was thirty-seven at the time. See also anon., "500. Rede an die deutsche Jugend... frei nach Ernst Wiechert," *Der Ruf* (August 1946).

98. *Rhein-Neckar-Zeitung*, 15 February 1947.

99. *The Murderers Are Among Us*, at 00:51 min.

100. Cf. Ursula Bessen, *Nachkriegszeit und Fünfziger Jahre auf Zeulluloid* (Bochum, 1989); Lukas Bartholomei, *Bilder von Schuld und Unschuld* (Münster, 2015).

101. Wolfdietrich Schnurre in *Deutsche Film-Rundschau* (1946), quoted in Bartholomei, *Bilder von Schuld und Unschuld*, at p. 104.

102. DTA: MS 2176, Manz letters, 20 October 1946.

103. In 1946, see Alexander Brochhagen, *Nach Nürnberg* (Hamburg, 1994), p. 35.

104. One hundred and twenty mayors (94 percent) and 71 officials (56 percent); see John Gimbel, *The American Occupation of Germany* (Stanford, CA, 1968), p. 142.

105. February 1946, quoted in Frank Bösch, "Politische Sammlungen," in *Der lange Abschied vom Agrarland*, ed. D. Münkel (Göttingen, 2000), p. 241.

106. Bernd Mayer and Helmut Paulus, *Eine Stadt wird entnazifiziert* (Bayreuth, 2008), p. 41.

107. Hans Woller, *Gesellschaft und Politik in der amerikanischen Besatzungszone: Die Region Ansbach und Fürth* (Munich, 1986), p. 146.

108. Carl Zuckmayer, *Deutschlandbericht für das Kriegsministerium der Vereinigten Staaten von Amerika* [1947], ed. G. Nickel et al. (Göttingen, 2004).

109. Dr. Ziegler, zweiter Landrat, see Mayer and Paulus, *Eine Stadt wird entnazifiziert*, p. 131.

110. Woller, *Gesellschaft und Politik*, pp. 158–59.

111. IfZ: MS 2018, Hansjörg Maurer letters and diary, 1947–48.

112. DTA: MS 2176, Manz letters, 17 November 1946 and 9 May 1948.

113. Dietmar von Reeken, *Lokale Strukturen im gesellschaftlichen und politischen Umbruch* (Hildesheim, 1990), pp. 273ff.

114. AdsD: 4/awoA003284, "Pläne und Tatsachenmaterial." Cf. Lutz Niethammer, *Die Mitläuferfabrik* (Bonn, 1982).

115. Gimbel, *American Occupation*, p. 144.

116. Konrad Adenauer to Pastor Custodis, 23 February 1946, in Adenauer, *Briefe über Deutschland*, ed. H. P. Mensing (Berlin, 1986), p. 33.

117. Quoted from Jessica Erdelmann, *"Persilscheine" aus der Druckerpresse?* (Hamburg, 2016), p. 73.

118. BArch Berlin: DY 30/68800, Arbeitstagung Volkssolidarität, Leipzig, 1–3 October 1946.

119. In the Soviet zone, 60 percent were kept on in public jobs, in the American zone 54 percent; Olaf Kappelt, *Die Entnazifizierung in der SBZ* (Hamburg, 1997), p. 251.
120. Andrew Port, *Conflict and Stability in the German Democratic Republic* (Cambridge, 2007), pp. 26–27.
121. Alexander Sperk, *Entnazifizierung und Personalpolitik in der Sowjetischen Besatzungszone Köthen/Anhalt* (Dössel, 2003).
122. Just over one third in Brandenburg; see Julie Deering-Kraft, "Transitions from Nazism to Socialism: Grassroots Responses to Punitive and Rehabilitative Measures in Brandenburg, 1945–52" (unpublished PhD thesis, UCL 2013), pp. 146–63.
123. Damian van Melis, *Entnazifizierung in Mecklenburg-Vorpommern* (Munich, 1999), pp. 263–64.
124. Norbert Frei, *Vergangenheitspolitik: Die Anfänge der Bundesrepublik und die NS-Vergangenheit* (Munich, 1996); Christian Meyer-Seitz, *Die Verfolgung von NS-Straftaten in der SBZ* (Berlin, 1998), pp. 214–27; Mary Fulbrook, *Reckonings* (Oxford, 2018), ch. 9
125. December 1946; Torben Fischer and Matthias N. Lorenz, eds., *Lexikon der "Vergangenheitsbewältigung" in Deutschland* (Bielefeld, 2015, 3rd rev. edn.), p. 117.
126. Manfred Haussmann, "Jugend zwischen gestern und morgen," *Aufbau* 7 (1946), quoted at p. 669; Wolfdietrich Schnurre, "Offener Brief an Manfred Haussmann," *Horizont* 24 (27 October 1946).
127. Wolfgang Borchert, "Draussen vor der Tür," *Das Gesamtwerk* (Hamburg, 2015, 4th edn.), pp. 192, 191, 154, 153.
128. "Generation ohne Abschied," 22 June 1947, in ibid., p. 67.
129. Arbeitskreis Schulen; Friedhelm Boll, *Auf der Suche nach Demokratie: Britische und deutsche Jugendinitiativen in Niedersachsen nach 1945* (Bonn, 1995), quoted at p. 199.
130. Ulrike Weckel, "Spielarten der Vergangenheitsbewältigung," *Tel Aviver Jahrbuch für deutsche Geschichte* 31 (2003): 140–41.
131. BArch Freiburg: B/438/204, *Der Freiwillige* (November 1974), p. 22.
132. Barbara Fait, "Die Kreisleiter der NSDAP—nach 1945," in Broszat et al., *Von Stalingrad zur Währungsreform*, pp. 247–55, 292–96. See also the case of Mayor Richard Hänel in Ansbach; Woller, *Gesellschaft und Politik*, pp. 164–65.
133. Wilhelm Noske, quoted from Wolfgang Kraushaar, *Die Protest-Chronik, 1949–1959* (Hamburg, 1996), I, pp. 495–96, and www.jüdische-gemeinden.de for the following.
134. E. L. from Berlin, *Allgemeine Wochenzeitung der Juden in Deutschland*, 1 February 1952.
135. Carl Zuckmayer, *Des Teufels General*, Act I. In total, it had a run of eight thousand performances, see *Zuckmayer Jahrbuch*, IV, 2001.
136. Zuckmayer, *Deutschlandbericht*, pp. 120–24.
137. *Mittelbayerische Zeitung*, 12 October 1948.
138. "Inventur," in Günter Eich, *Inventur: Ein Lesebuch* (Frankfurt, 2002 edn.).
139. Günter Eich, "Fränkisch-tibetischer Kirschgarten," in Eich, *Botschaften des Regens* (Frankfurt, 1955).
140. Heinrich Vormweg, "Literatur," in *Die Bundesrepublik*, ed. W. Benz, IV: Kultur (Frankfurt, 1983), p. 53.
141. Guenter Lewy, *Perpetrators* (Oxford, 2017); Andreas Eichmüller, "Die Strafverfolgung von NS-Verbrechen durch westdeutsche Justizbehörden seit 1945," *Vierteljahreshefte für Zeitgeschichte* 56, no. 4 (2008): 621–40.
142. Frei, *Vergangenheitspolitik*; H.-C. Jasch and W. Kaiser, *Der Holocaust vor deutschen Gerichten* (Ditzingen, 2017); J. Osterloh and C. Vollnhals, eds., *NS-Prozesse und deutsche Öffentlichkeit* (Göttingen, 2011); Oliver von Wrochem, *Erich von Manstein* (Paderborn, 2006), p. 121.
143. The Federal Court of Justice then overturned the decision, but Peters was again sentenced in 1953 by the jury court (*Schwurgericht*) in Wiesbaden, this time for six years. He would eventually be acquitted, in 1955, by the jury court of the Frankfurt district court, which ignored evidence of shipments of the gas to the gas chambers. LG Frankfurt/M., 27 May 1955, see C. F. Rüter, ed., *Justiz und NS-Verbrechen*, 49 vols. (Amsterdam, 1968–2012), XIII, pp. 105ff.
144. Meyer-Seitz, *Die Verfolgung von NS-Straftaten in der SBZ*, pp. 143–263.
145. Ibid., pp. 277–78.
146. Heiner Wember, *Umerziehung im Lager* (Essen, 1991), pp. 318–21.

147. Ibid., p. 302.
148. LG Frankfurt/M, 3 March 1951, Rüter, *Justiz und NS-Verbrechen*, VIII, pp. 269–70.
149. Maria Nothaft, 6 September 1947, quoted by Edith Raim, "NS-Prozesse und Öffentlichkeit," in Osterloh and Vollnhals, *NS-Prozesse und deutsche Öffentlichkeit*, p. 41.
150. In 1949; Meyer-Seitz, *Die Verfolgung von NS-Straftaten in der SBZ*, p. 147.
151. Wember, *Umerziehung*, p. 303.
152. OLG Tübingen, 20 January 1948, Rüter, *Justiz und NS-Verbrechen*, I, p. 502.
153. The reservation was only withdrawn on 1 October 2001; see Council of Europe, Treaty Office, "Reservations and Declarations for Germany," ETS No. 005. See also Habbo Knoch, *Im Namen der Würde* (Munich, 2023).
154. Frei, *Vergangenheitspolitik*, p. 129.
155. BGH, 8 November 1956, Rüter, *Justiz und NS-Verbrechen*, XIV, pp. 228–34.
156. *Hamburger Abendblatt*, 23–24 August 1958, and *Süddeutsche Zeitung*, 30–31 August 1958; on the growing public critique after 1955 and the Ulm trials, see Andreas Eichmüller, *Keine Generalamnestie* (Munich, 2012), pp. 135–222.
157. Jürgen Bevers, *Der Mann hinter Adenauer* (Berlin, 2009); Klaus Bästlein, *Der Fall Globke* (Berlin, 2018).
158. Press conference on 27 December 1950, quoted in Bert-Oliver Manig, *Die Politik der Ehre: Die Rehabilitierung der Berufssoldaten in der frühen Bundesrepublik* (Göttingen, 2004), p. 254. For Russell, see Von Wrochem, *Manstein*, p. 157.
159. Hubert Rottleuthner, *Karrieren und Kontinuitäten deutscher Justizjuristen vor und nach 1945* (Berlin, 2010). Gerald Hacke, "Der Dresdner Juristenprozess 1947," in Osterloh and Vollnhals, *NS-Prozesse und deutsche Öffentlichkeit*, pp. 167–88. On Melsheimer and Grossmann, see Kappelt, *Entnazifizierung in der SBZ*, pp. 95, 125–26.
160. Christoph Schneider, *Diener des Rechts und der Vernichtung* (Frankfurt, 2017), p. 217, and for the following; Irmtrud Wojak, *Fritz Bauer 1903–1968* (Munich, 2009).
161. Peter Reichel, *Vergangenheitsbewältigung in Deutschland* (Munich, 2001), p. 152.
162. Felix Bohr, *Die Kriegsverbrecherlobby* (Berlin, 2018).
163. LG Bremen, 27 November 1953, Rüter, *Justiz und NS-Verbrechen*, XI, quoted at pp. 587–89, 639–40.
164. LG Bremen, 27 November 1953, Rüter, *Justiz und NS-Verbrechen*, XI, p. 655.
165. Jasch and Kaiser, *Der Holocaust vor deutschen Gerichten*.
166. See Christina Ullrich, *"Ich fühl' mich nicht als Mörder": Die Integration von NS-Tätern in die Nachkriegsgesellschaft* (Darmstadt, 2011), quoted at p. 225 (8 August 1961).
167. Heuss to Gottfried Traub, 8 November 1954, and to James Conant, 25 August 1955, in Theodor Heuss, *Der Bundespräsident: Briefe 1949–1954*, ed. E. W. Becker (Berlin, 2013). See also Joachim Radkau, *Theodor Heuss* (Munich, 2013).
168. Frei, *Vergangenheitspolitik*, pp. 299–300.
169. Martin Heidegger, "Aus der Erfahrung des Denkens" (1947), *Gesamtausgabe*, XIII (Frankfurt 1983), p. 81.
170. August Hä., Franz H., and Walter He., in Ullrich, *"Ich fühl' mich nicht als Mörder,"* pp. 179, 181, 193.
171. Kraushaar, *Protest-Chronik*, I, p. 177.
172. Lüth, 20 September 1950, see https://www.hausderpressefreiheit.de/Präzedenzfälle/Der-Fall-Erich-Lüth.html.
173. Bundesverfassungsgericht (BVerfG): Erster Senat, 15 January 1958, 1 BvR 400/51—Rn. (1-75).
174. *Hamburger Abendblatt*, 20 November 1950, 9 January and 21 and 27 February 1951.
175. *Hamburger Abendblatt*, 12 May 1951 and 2 August 1952; Kraushaar, *Protest-Chronik*.
176. *Hamburger Abendblatt*, 3 January 1958.
177. C. Vollnhals, "Zwischen Verdrängung und Aufklärung," in *Die Deutschen und die Judenverfolgung*, ed. U. Büttner (Hamburg, 1992), p. 368.
178. *Westfälische Rundschau*, 3 December 1957; *Die Zeit*, 12 December 1957; *Der Spiegel*, 11 December 1957.
179. See Claudia Fröhlich, "Der 'Ulmer Einsatzgruppen-Prozess' 1958" and Anette Weinke,

"'Bleiben die Mörder unter uns?,'" in Osterloh and Vollnhals, *NS-Prozesse und deutsche Öffentlichkeit*, pp. 233–62, 263–82.

180. *Die Welt*, 11–12 June 1960.

181. 2 April 1952, in: Konrad Adenauer, *Teegespräche 1950–54*, ed. H. J. Küsters (Berlin, 1984), p. 245.

182. Erich Gniffke, May 1946; van Melis, *Entnazifizierung in Mecklenburg-Vorpommern*, p. 175.

183. Fulbrook, *Reckonings*.

184. Jon Elster, *Closing the Books: Transitional Justice in Historical Perspective* (Cambridge, 2004), pp. 56–59; see also Susanne Buckley-Zistel et al., eds., *Transitional Justice Theories* (New York, 2014); Nico Wouters, ed., *Transitional Justice and Memory in Europe, 1945–2013* (Cambridge, 2014).

185. Between 1996 and 2000, see www.justice.gov.za/trc/amntrans/index.htm. Elster, *Closing the Books*, p. 72; Priscilla B. Hayner, "Fifteen Truth Commissions—1974–94," *Human Rights Quarterly* 16, no. 4 (1994): 597–655.

186. Manfred Kittel, *Nach Nürnberg und Tokio* (Munich, 2004), chs. 6 and 7.

4 MAKING (SOME) AMENDS

1. *1. Deutscher Bundestag: Stenographisches Protokoll der 5. Sitzung* (Bonn, 1949), pp. 22–30.

2. *Allgemeine Wochenzeitung der Juden in Deutschland*, 25 November 1949, p. 1.

3. The term is Jeffrey K. Olick's. See his *The Sins of the Fathers* (Chicago, 2016), esp. pp. 122–60.

4. Tobias Winstel, *Verhandelte Gerechtigkeit* (Munich, 2006), pp. 36–39; Julia Volmer-Naumann, *Bürokratische Bewältigung* (Essen, 2012), pp. 24–51.

5. IfS: Verfolgtenbetreuungsstelle, 18 Bl./S. 204 Bll., Frankfurt, Versammlung der Wohnungssuchenden Nazi Opfer, 2 November 1948, report.

6. IfS: Verfolgtenbetreuungsstelle, 78 Bl./S. 403 Bll., Oberbürgermeister, Frankfurt, 24 October 1945.

7. IfS: Verfolgtenbetreuungsstelle, 78 Bl./S. 403 Bll., Hanau, Oberbürgermeister, 25 October 1945.

8. Heiko Scharffenberg, "Die Wiedergutmachung nationalsozialistischen Unrechts in Schleswig-Holstein dargestellt an Flensburger Fallbeispielen" (unpublished PhD thesis, Flensburg, 2000).

9. IfS: Verfolgtenbetreuungsstelle, 31 Bl./S. 484 Bll.: "H."

10. IfS: Verfolgtenbetreuungsstelle, 31 Bl./S. 484 Bll., 4 July and 25 October 1947.

11. In the SBZ, the VVN provided 17 ministers, 50 mayors, 230 party and trade union leaders, and almost 10 percent of the police force; Constantin Goschler, *Schuld und Schulden* (Göttingen, 2005), p. 83.

12. Henning Fischer, *Überlebende als Akteurinnen: Die Frauen der Lagergemeinschaft Ravensbrück* (Konstanz, 2018), pp. 285–88.

13. Goschler, *Schuld und Schulden*, p. 385, and part VI on the GDR.

14. Kristina Meyer, "Verfolgung, Verdrängung, Vermittlung," in *Praxis der Wiedergutmachung*, ed. Norbert Frei et al. (Göttingen, 2009), pp. 179–80.

15. Ibid., pp. 159–202. For a different view, see Jeffrey Herf, *Divided Memory* (Cambridge, MA, 1997).

16. Winstel, *Verhandelte Gerechtigkeit*, p. 192.

17. Constantin Goschler and Jürgen Lillteicher, eds., *"Arisierung" und Restitution* (Göttingen, 2002). Significantly, additional payments (*Nachzahlungen*) in the process of restitution were subject to the 10:1 exchange rate under the currency reform of 1948, in contrast to the payments to the Claims Conference after 1953.

18. Open letter, 25 January 1951; C. Goschler, "Die Politik der Rückerstattung in Westdeutschland," in Goschler and Lillteicher, *"Arisierung" und Restitution*, p. 111.

19. Winstel, *Verhandelte Gerechtigkeit*, p. 368.

20. Neil Gregor, *Haunted City: Nuremberg and the Nazi Past* (New Haven, CT, 2009), p. 113.

21. Constantin Goschler, 'Der Fall Philipp Auerbach' in: *Wiedergutmachung*, eds. Herbst and Goschler.

22. Winstel, *Verhandelte Gerechtigkeit*, p. 359.
23. 20 November 1949; ibid., pp. 346–47.
24. Jürgen Lillteicher, *Raub, Recht und Restitution* (Göttingen, 2007), pp. 180–98. For Rosenthal's international success in the 1950s, see now Suzanne Marchand, *Porcelain* (Princeton, NJ, 2020).
25. July 1945; Jan Philipp Spannuth, "Rückerstattung Ost" (PhD thesis, Freiburg, 2001), pp. 188–89, and ch. 3 for Thuringia.
26. Götz Berger, May 1948; Goschler, *Schuld und Schulden*, p. 116.
27. Spannuth, "Rückerstattung Ost."
28. Judith Butler, "Can One Lead a Good Life in a Bad Life: Adorno Prize Lecture," *Radical Philosophy* 176 (2012): 10–18, quoted at p. 16. For a different view, see Barbara Honig, *Antigone Interrupted* (Cambridge, 2013). Hannah Arendt, by contrast, traced action to natality and being born into the political sphere.
29. Elisabeth Noelle and Erich Peter Neumann, eds., *Jahrbuch der Öffentlichen Meinung 1947–55* (Allensbach, 1956), p. 130 (August 1949); *Trends in German Public Opinion*, report no. 32 (10 December 1946), cited in Jörg Echternkamp, *Soldaten im Nachkrieg* (Munich, 2014), p. 163.
30. October 1951, survey by the U.S. High Commission for Germany (HICOG); Herbst and Goschler, *Wiedergutmachung*, pp. 212–13.
31. HIS: BdD 502, Bund der Deutschen, "Ratgeber für Kriegsversehrte" (1955), pp. 71–73.
32. ADE: ZB 847, Lastenausgleich, Zentralverband der Fliegergeschädigten, "Proklamation," 25 May 1948.
33. Kather quoted in *Der Spiegel*, 21 November 1950.
34. *Passauer Neue Presse*, 22 May 1951, p. 2.
35. Friedrich Käss, *10 Jahre Lastenausgleich* (Bad Homburg, 1959), p. 60.
36. *Passauer Neue Presse*, 22 May 1951, Oberpfalz.
37. ADE: ZB 847, Prof. (Ulrich) Scheuner, "Probleme des Lastenausgleichs," 13 August 1948.
38. Michael L. Hughes, *Shouldering the Burdens of Defeat* (Chapel Hill, NC, 1999); Lukas Haffert, "War Mobilization or War Destruction?," *Review of International Organizations* 14, no. 1 (2019): 59–82.
39. *Der Spiegel*, 22 November 1947.
40. IfS: V 5a1, VdK, Erster Landesverbandstag, 7–10 April 1949.
41. Herbst and Goschler, *Wiedergutmachung*, pp. 234–41.
42. Deutscher Bundtestag 1WP, 233. Sitzung, 9 October 1952, 10674. Those still in POW camps after 1949 received 2 DM per day; BGBl, part 1, 2 February 1954, pp. 5–9.
43. FZH: Coll. 1.1.11/G8, Harry and Heinz Goldstein papers, emphasis in original. For the committee's approach, see Thiessen, *Eingebrannt*, pp. 109–110.
44. Jörg Arnold, *The Allied Air War and Urban Memory* (Cambridge, 2011), p. 107.
45. DTA: 1828, Manz letters, 19 August 1945. The Landrat in Esslingen (Fritz Landenberger, a Liberal) had called the returning KZ inmates the "true bearers of the Iron Cross."
46. *Passauer Neue Presse*, 20 May 1947.
47. Thiessen, *Eingebrannt*, pp. 113–26.
48. Quoted in Herbst and Goschler, *Wiedergutmachung*, p. 219.
49. VDK: C1-15, Sammlung von Reden zum Volkstrauertag (1979), Ahlhorn, 5 March 1950, Plenarsaal, Bundeshaus, Bonn.
50. 16 November 1952; VDK: C1-15, Sammlung von Reden zum Volkstrauertag (1979).
51. 17 December 1951; Herbst and Goschler, *Wiedergutmachung*, p. 203.
52. Thiessen, *Eingebrannt*, pp. 148–52.
53. Gregor, *Haunted City*, pp. 177–78; see also Robert Moeller, *War Stories* (Berkeley, CA, 2001).
54. Goschler, *Schuld und Schulden*, p. 145.
55. *The Autobiography of Nahum Goldmann* (New York, 1969), p. 260.
56. Adenauer's note to Goldmann is included in the draft of the agreement sent to the president of the Bundestag, in Deutscher Bundestag, 1. Wahlperiode, 1949, Drucksache Nr. 4141, 28 February 1953. See also Henning Köhler, *Adenauer* (Frankfurt, 1994), pp. 702ff.
57. Daniel Marwecki, *Germany and Israel* (London, 2020), part 1.
58. Walter Dirks, "Der restaurative Charakter der Epoche," *Frankfurter Hefte* 5, no. 9 (1950): 942–54.

59. Otto Heinrich von der Gablentz, *Die versäumte Reform* (Cologne, 1960).
60. In the cabinet meeting of 20 May 1952, as noted by Otto Lenz, *Im Zentrum der Macht: Das Tagebuch von Staatssekretär Lenz 1951–3* (Dusseldorf, 1989), p. 340. For the CSU abstention, see the declaration by F. J. Strauß, Deutscher Bundestag, 255. Sitzung, 19 March 1953, 12362.
61. Von Merkatz (DP) in Deutscher Bundestag, 254. Sitzung, 18 March 1953, pp. 80–81.
62. Michael Wolffsohn, "Das deutsch-israelische Wiedergutmachungsabkommen von 1952 im internationalen Zusammenhang," *Vierteljahreshefte für Zeitgeschichte* 36 (1988): 691–732.
63. Ibid., pp. 721ff., quoted at p. 724.
64. Katharina Stengel, "Competition for Scant Funds" (2010) at www.wollheim-memorial.de.
65. Hockerts, "Entschädigung"; Ulrich Herbert, "Nicht entschädigungsfähig?," Wolfgang Benz, "Der Wollheim-Prozess," and Arnold Spitta, "Entschädigung für Zigeuner," all in: Herbst and Goschler, eds., *Wiedergutmachung.*
66. Unlike other European legal systems, German law did not grant compensation for the immaterial damage caused by the death of a relative. This only changed in 2017, after a copilot deliberately crashed German Wings Flight 9525 in the French Alps.
67. Goschler, *Schuld und Schulden*, p. 316.
68. Herbert, "Nicht entschädigungsfähig?," pp. 297–99.
69. Christian Pross, *Wiedergutmachung* (Frankfurt, 1988).
70. Ibid., pp. 226–27.
71. Ibid., pp. 149–56.
72. Svenja Goltermann, "Kausalitätsfragen: Psychisches Leid und psychiatrisches Wissen in der Entschädigung," in Frei et al., *Praxis der Wiedergutmachung*, pp. 427–51.
73. Kristina Meyer and Boris Spernol, "Wiedergutmachung in Düsseldorf," in Frei et al., *Praxis der Wiedergutmachung*, pp. 690–727.
74. In 1950, Bernard W. to Minister for Social Affairs, North Rhine–Westphalia; Volmer-Naumann, *Bürokratische Bewältigung*, p. 156.
75. Susanna Schrafstetter, *Flucht und Versteck: Untergetauchte Juden in München* (Göttingen, 2015), p. 263. For the previous case, see Mark Roseman, "'It Went On for Years and Years,'" in Frei et al., *Praxis der Wiedergutmachung*, p. 66.
76. 1950; Volmer-Naumann, *Bürokratische Bewältigung*, p. 91.
77. See Winstel, *Verhandelte Gerechtigkeit*, p. 271.
78. For the following, see Roseman, "'It Went On for Years and Years,'" pp. 51–78.
79. The term is William James's; see Frank Trentmann, *Empire of Things: How We Became a World of Consumers, from the Fifteenth Century to the Twenty-first* (New York, 2016), p. 233; for Max F.'s pursuit of their stolen Bechstein grand piano in 1960, see Winstel, *Verhandelte Gerechtigkeit*, p. 285.
80. Winstel, *Verhandelte Gerechtigkeit*, p. 209.
81. IfZ: ED 141/3 Tagebuch (Prof. Dr.) Ludwig Bergsträsser, 29 July 1947.
82. Jan Foitzik, "Die Rückkehr aus dem Exil," in *Die Erfahrung der Fremde*, ed. W. Briegel and W. Frühwald (Weinheim, 1988), pp. 255–56; Marita Kraus, "Jewish Remigration," *Leo Baeck Institute Year Book* 49 (2004): 107–19.
83. Angelika Eder, *Flüchtige Heimat: Jüdische Displaced Persons in Landsberg am Lech 1945 bis 1950* (Munich, 1998).
84. Grossmann, *Juden, Deutsche, Allierte* (Göttingen, 2012), pp. 316–17, 350–51, 367.
85. FZH: 1.1.11/G8, Harry and Heinz Goldstein papers; Heinz Goldstein, "Wiederaufbau der jüdischen Gemeinde."
86. Schrafstetter, *Flucht und Versteck*, p. 205.
87. Grossmann, *Juden, Deutsche, Allierte*, p. 167.
88. Wolfgang Benz, *Zwischen Hitler und Adenauer* (Frankfurt, 1991), ch. 4; Julius H. Schoeps, ed., *Leben im Land der Täter* (Berlin, 2001).
89. Radio Bremen, January 1947, in Alfred Kantorowicz, *Vom Moralischen Gewinn der Niederlage* (Berlin, 1949), quoted at p. 341.
90. Alfred Kantorowicz, *Deutsches Tagebuch*, 2 parts (Munich, 1959–61).
91. Joachim Käppner, *Erstarrte Geschichte* (Hamburg, 1999); Irena Ostmeyer, *Zwischen Schuld und Sühne: Evangelische Kirche und Juden in SBZ und DDR 1945–1990* (Berlin, 2002).

92. Irmela von der Lühe et al., eds., *"Auch in Deutschland waren wir nicht wirklich zu Hause": Jüdische Remigration nach 1945* (Göttingen, 2008); Emnid-Institut, *Zum Problem des Antisemitismus im Bundesgebiet* (Emnid, 1954). Alfred Döblin, "Abschied und Wiederkehr," in *Autobiografische Schriften und letzte Aufzeichnungen*, ed. E. Pässler (Freiburg, 1980).

93. Marita Kraus, "Deutsch-amerikanische Presse- und Kulturoffiziere als Teil der Besatzungsbehörden," in *Demokratiewunder*, ed. A. Bauerkämper et al. (Göttingen, 2005), pp. 129–55.

94. Beate Meyer, *Fritz Benscher* (Göttingen, 2017).

95. HICOG survey, cit., Richard Merritt, "Digesting the Past," *Societas* 7 (1977): 102.

96. Institut für Demoskopie, *Deutsche und Juden—vier Jahrzehnte danach* (Allensbach, 1986), table 13; *Jahrbuch der öffentlich Meinung*, II (1957), p. 126, and later yearbooks.

97. In the 1950s, the Deutsche Reichspartei tried to keep Jews out of top positions in the country but only once managed to enter a regional assembly, in 1959, when it won 5.1 percent of the vote in the Rhineland-Palatinate.

98. Frei, *Vergangenheitspolitik*, pp. 309–25.

99. "Israel wird ausradiert," *Der Spiegel*, 18 December 1957; Andreas Lörcher, "Antisemitismus in der öffentlichen Debatte der späten fünfziger Jahre" (PhD thesis, Freiburg, 2008).

100. See Wolfgang Kraushaar, *Die Protest-Chronik, 1949–1959* (Hamburg 1996), pp. 2146, 2347, 2350.

101. James Loeffler, *Rooted Cosmopolitans: Jews and Human Rights in the Twentieth Century* (New Haven, CT, 2018), pp. 238–39.

102. See the map in Kraushaar, *Protest-Chronik*, p. 2489.

103. Peter Miska, "Sind wir schon wieder so weit," *Frankfurter Rundschau*, 13 March 1954.

104. Georg Wagner-Kyora, "Lastenausgleich und Sozialer Wohnungsbau," in *Rechnung für Hitlers Krieg*, ed. P. Erker (Heidelberg 2004), pp. 185–216.

105. LAB: B Rep. 232-35: Gesellschaft für Christlich-Jüdische Zusammenarbeit, Nr. 60: GCJZ with Schülerzeitungen, 1958–61, *Berliner Allgemeine*, 16 January 1959: "Was denkt die Jugend?"

106. LAB: B Rep. 232-35, Nr. 60, Conference with 50 school directors, report, 15 December 1959.

107. HIS: *Informationen*, Monatszeitschrift für Kriegsdienstverweiger, August 1960.

108. AdsD: 4/AWOA000521, Betreuung der Flüchtlingsjugend, Rundbrief, 31 August 1961, Jugendbetreuungsstelle Waldbröl.

109. C. Vollnhals, "Zwischen Verdrängung und Aufklärung," in *Die Deutschen und die Judenverfolgung*, ed. U. Büttner (Hamburg, 1992), pp. 377–79.

110. 17 March 1957; Kraushaar, *Protest-Chronik*, , p. 1597; Gregor, *Haunted City*, pp. 236ff.

111. 6 May 1958; Kraushaar, *Protest-Chronik*, , p. 1879.

112. KAS: Junge Union, IV-007, 191/1. Ewout van der Knaap, ed., *Uncovering the Holocaust: The International Reception of "Night and Fog"* (London, 2006).

113. 11 November 1951, Bayrischer Landtag—the memorial was organized by the Lessing Society; Kraushaar, *Protest-Chronik*, I, p. 501.

114. K. Richter, ed., *Die katholische Kirche und das Judentum: Dokumente von 1945–1982* (Freiburg, 1982), document 4.

115. JHD: A 0202, BDKJ Informationsdienst 1962, p. 99.

116. Ostmeyer, *Zwischen Schuld und Sühne*, ch. 3.

117. LAB: GCJZ, Nr. 61, WdB 1961, Erfahrungsberichte der Schulen, WdB 1961; Kassel cited in Vollnhals, "Zwischen Verdrängung und Aufklärung," p. 364.

118. LAB: GCJZ, Nr. 394: WdB 1954; Nr. 61, Erfahrungsberichte, WdB 1961; Nr. 60, Schülerzeitungen, 1958–61; Nr. 366: WdB 1971.

119. LAB: GCJZ, Nr. 60: Schülerzeitungen, report of conference with 50 school directors, 15 December 1959, and Aktennotiz, Tee Empfang für Schülerredakteure, 17 February 1959.

120. LAB: GCJZ, Nr. 124: Tätigkeitsberichte, Cologne report on 1963.

121. LAB: GCJZ, Nr. 471: Amateur play summaries; Erika Sterz to Käthe Reinholz (GCJZ), 5 March 1958.

122. DEFA, *Ehe im Shatten* (1947), director Kurt Maetzig; Daniel Jonah Wolpert, "Opfer der Zeit," in *Reflexionen des beschädigten Lebens? Nachkriegskino in Deutschland zwischen 1945 und 1962*, ed. B. Blachut et al. (Munich, 2016), pp. 57–73.

123. Heinrich Böll, *Wo Warst Du, Adam?* (Opladen, 1951). See further Ernestine Schlant, *The Language of Silence* (New York, 1999), ch. 1.

124. Volker Hage, *Zeugen der Zerstörung* (Frankfurt, 2003), pp. 40–43, 62–63.

125. On Gruppe 47 and antisemitism, see Klaus Briegleb, *Missachtung und Tabu* (Berlin, 2002).

126. Bruno Apitz, *Nackt unter Wölfen* (Halle, 1958); Bill Niven, *The Buchenwald Child* (Woodbridge, 2007).

127. LAB: GCJZ, Nr. 471.

128. Hanno Loewy, "Das gerettete Kind," in *Deutsche Nachkriegsliteratur und der Holocaust*, ed. S. Braese et al. (Frankfurt, 1998); Vollnhals, "Zwischen Verdrängung und Aufklärung," pp. 376–77. Th. Heuss to Toni Stolper, 28 October 1956, in Heuss, *Der Bundespräsident: Briefe 1949–1954*, ed. E. W. Becker (Berlin, 2013).

129. *Schwetzinger Zeitung*, 6 October 1956; *Die Welt*, 10 October 1956 (teenagers); *Westdeutsches Tageblatt*, 8 November 1956; see Katja Heimsath, *"Trotz allem glaube ich an das Gute im Menschen": Das Tagebuch der Anne Frank und seine Rezeption in der Bundesrepublik Deutschland* (Hamburg, 2013), pp. 245, 249, 255.

130. Hans Horwitz, 17 March 1957; Kraushaar, *Protest-Chronik*, III, p. 1598.

131. Loewy, "Das gerettete Kind," p. 34.

132. Lothar Kreyssig, "Bewältigung und Versöhnung," *Kommunitat* (January 1959). Gabriele Kammerer, *Aktion Sühnezeichen Friedensdienste* (Göttingen, 2008).

133. Bürger et al., "Zwischen Jerusalem und Meschede," quoted at pp. 60, 71.

134. Jan Kirschbaum, *Mahnmal als Zeichen* (Bielefeld, 2020), pp. 66–68; Kurt Oser, *Die Geschichte des Bühler Friedenskreuz* (Bühl, 1983).

135. Insa Eschebach, *Öffentliches Gedenken* (Frankfurt, 2005), pp. 169–70; www.Suehnekirche-Bergen.de.

136. ADE: Allg. Slg. 906, Aktion Sühnezeichen; Israel Gruppe IV, diary, 23 October 1964.

137. Ibid., 4 August 1965, Israel Gruppe V.

138. Ibid., 2 February 1965, Israel Gruppe IV ADE: Allg. Slg. 903, Aktion Sühnezeichen, Bericht vom ersten Arbeitstag in Auschwitz!, 16 October 1967.

139. ADE: Allg. Slg. 905, Aktion Sühnezeichen, 1968–69, Volker von Törne, Sühnezeichen in Polen—Auschwitz 1968, 29 September 1968.

140. Kammerer, *Aktion Sühnezeichen*, p. 103.

141. ADE: Allg. Slg. 903, Aktion Sühnezeichen, Bericht meiner Reisen nach Dachau, 11 November 1965.

142. ADE: Allg. Slg. 903, Aktion Sühnezeichen, Bericht von der Dienstreise nach Ulm, 29 March 1966.

143. ADE: Allg. Slg. 903, Aktion Sühnezeichen, Bericht von der Schulwoche im Kreis Biedenkopf, 24–28 April 1967.

144. E.g., Gollwitzer to Bischop Kurt Scharf, 12 August 1966, ADE: Allg. Slg. 903, Aktion Sühnezeichen.

145. ADE: Allg. Slg. 908, Aktion Sühnezeichen, 1966, diary Gruppe Holland III/3 Rotterdam, 23–29 January 1967.

146. Already in 1946, the Swiss writer Max Picard had written a book with a similar title (*Hitler in uns selbst*), but his diagnosis concerned the disconnected nature of the modern world and the confusions it had left in people's minds, leaving them susceptible to Hitler; Picard was a friend and influence on Ernst Wiechert.

147. ADE: Allg. Slg. 904, Aktion Sühnezeichen, 1967–68, Ergebnisse der Gruppenarbeit, annual meeting, 28–30 December 1967.

148. ADE: Allg. Slg. 905, Sühnezeichen in Polen—Auschwitz 1968, 29 September 1968.

149. Detlef Garbe, "Auschwitz," *Zeichen* 1 (1975), quoted in Kammerer, *Aktion Sühnezeichen*, p. 171.

150. Kammerer, *Aktion Sühnezeichen*, quoted at p. 246; see also *Zeichen* 2 (2003): 13.

151. Martin Buber, "Schuld und Schuldgefühle," in Buber, *Werke*, I (Munich, 1962).

5 THE HOUSE OF DEMOCRACY

1. See Gerhard Anschütz, *Die Verfassung des Deutschen Reiches vom 11. August 1919*, 14th rev. edn. (Berlin 1933), pt. 2, pp. 505–750; Hermann Heller, *Rechtsstaat oder Diktatur?* (1930) in C. Müller et al., *Ges. Schriften* (Tübingen, 1992).

2. Hedwig Richter, *Demokratie* (Munich, 2020), pp. 325–26. See also Margaret L. Anderson, *Practicing Democracy* (Princeton, NJ, 2000) and Sheri Berman, "Civil Society and the Collapse of the Weimar Republic," *World Politics* 49, no. 3 (1997): 401–29.

3. Heinrich August Winkler, *Wie wir wurden, was wir sind* (Munich, 2020), p. 81.

4. See Herbert, *History of 20th-Century Germany*.

5. Till van Rahden, *Demokratie* (Frankfurt, 2019), quoted at p. 30.

6. Gerhard Schulz, *Mitteldeutsches Tagebuch* (Munich, 2009), 16 February 1946.

7. Institut für Demoskopie, *Jahrbuch der öffentlichen Meinung*, V (Allensbach, 1974), p. 223, tables for 1951, 1959, 1963, and 1970.

8. Karl-Heinz Füssl, *Die Umerziehung der Deutschen* (Paderborn, 1994), pp. 165–80. Jarausch, *After Hitler*

9. April 1947; Stephanie Abke, *Sichtbare Zeichen unsichtbarer Kräfte: Denunziationsmuster und Denunziationsverhalten 1933–1949* (Tübingen, 2003), pp. 224, 259.

10. R. Lammersdorf, "'Das Volk ist streng demokratisch,'" in *Demokratiewunder*, ed. A. Bauerkämper et al. (Göttingen, 2005), pp. 90–91.

11. Hermann-Josef Rupieper, *Die Wurzeln der westdeutschen Nachkriegsdemokratie* (Opladen, 1993), quoted at p. 21.

12. Boll, *Suche nach Demokratie*, p. 209.

13. HIS: III 4 E ab, "Xenophon spricht," Schülerzeitung des Landgraf Ludwig Gynasiums, Giessen, 10 March 1947.

14. Gimbel, *American Occupation*, p. 196.

15. Boll, *Suche nach Demokratie*, pp. 50–51.

16. Bundeszentrale für Heimatdienst; from 1963: für Politische Bildung; see Gudrun Hentges, *Staat und politische Bildung* (Berlin, 2013).

17. Axel Schildt and Detlef Siegfried, *Deutsche Kulturgeschichte* (Munich, 2009), pp. 151–52; Nina Verheyen, *Diskussionslust* (Göttingen, 2010), ch. 2.

18. *Der Fortschritt* (March 1954), see Stefan Müller-Doohm, *Habermas* (Cambridge, 2016), p. 67; Jürgen Habermas, *The Structural Transformation of the Public Sphere* (Cambridge, MA, 1989; German edn. 1962) and *Theorie des kommunikativen Handelns* (Frankfurt, 1981). Feminists and historians since have pointed out that the public sphere was neither always inclusive nor rational, see C. Calhoun, ed., *Habermas and the Public Sphere* (Cambridge, MA, 1992).

19. Frank Bösch, "Politik als kommunikativer Akt," in *Sehnsucht nach Nähe*, ed. M. Föllmer (Stuttgart, 2004), pp. 210–11.

20. Brian M. Puaca, "Missionaries of Goodwill," in Bauerkämper et al., *Demokratiewunder*, pp. 305–31; Richard Mayne, *In Victory, Magnanimity—In Peace, Goodwill: A History of Wilton Park* (London, 2003); Christina von Hodenberg, *Konsens und Krise* (Göttingen, 2006), ch. 4; Schildt, *Medien-Intellektuelle*, pp. 348–59.

21. Quoted in Claudia C. Gatzka, "'Demokratisierung' in Italien und der Bundesrepublik," in *Wo liegt die Bundesrepublik?*, ed. S. Levsen und C. Torp (Göttingen, 2016), p. 156.

22. Thomas Mergel, *Propaganda nach Hitler* (Göttingen, 2010); Claudia C. Gatzka, *Die Demokratie der Wähler* (Düsseldorf, 2019).

23. Everhard Holtmann, "Die neuen Lassalleaner," in *Von Stalingrad zur Währungsreform*, pp. 169–210.

24. Quoted in Puaca, "Missionaries of Goodwill," p. 318.

25. Philip Wagner, "Das Mitbürgerliche und das Staatsbürgerliche," in *Bürgertum*, ed. M. Hettling and R. Pohle (Göttingen, 2019), quoted at pp. 272, 280.

26. "Schwarz auf Weiss," Schülerzeitung, Gummersbach (where Habermas and Wehler went to school), 1952–53, p. 15, www.lindengymnasium.de/media/schwarz_auf_weiss/1952c.pdf; with thanks to Till van Rahden for pointing me to this source.

27. Sonja Levsen, "Authority and Democracy in Postwar France and West Germany, 1945–1968," *Journal of Modern History* 89, no. 4 (2017): 812–50.

28. Dimitrij Owetschkin, *Vom Verteilen zum Gestalten: Geschichte der betrieblichen Mitbestimmung in der westdeutschen Automobilindustrie nach 1945* (Bielefeld, 2016), ch. 3; Leo Kißler et al., *Die Mitbestimmung in der Bundesrepublik Deutschland* (Wiesbaden, 2011); Fritz Vilmar, *Mitbestimmung am Arbeitsplatz* (Neuwied, 1971). See further Bernhard Dietz, *Der Aufstieg der Manager* (Berlin, 2020).

29. ADE: Allg. Slg. 679, Verband deutscher Nachbarschaftshilfe, "Unsere Nachbarschaftsheime," 1963–64.

30. AdsD: 4/AWOA002998, "Verstehen um zu Helfen," 1953.

31. AdsD: 4/AWOA003284, "Bericht über Tagung," 4–6 January 1954.

32. AdsD: 4/AWOA000331, "Selbstdarstellung der Arbeiterwohlfahrt."

33. AdsD: 4/AWOA002549, Praxisheft, Bonn, c. 1965; 4/AWOA003020, "Interner Bericht... sozialen Rehabilitation... Obdachlose," c. 1970.

34. BVerwGE 1, 159–163 (24 June 1954); ADE: DEVA 33, Informationen no. 74 (October 1959), and Dephul to IM Schleswig-Holstein, 18 May 1955 (parcels). The Bavarian constitution of 1949 already stipulated a right to welfare (Article 168/3). I am grateful to Helge Pösche for discussion; see his "Gesetz und Moral: Konflikte um das Recht auf Sozialhilfe, c. 1945–65" (MA diss., Humboldt-Universität, 2017) and now his "Soziale Rechte einklagen: Gerichte im (west) deutschen Wohlfahrtsstaat des 20. Jahrhunderts" (PhD diss., Humboldt University) 2023.

35. Christiane Kuller, *Familienpolitik* (Munich, 2004); Astrid Joosten, *Die Frau, das "Segenspendende Herz der Familie"* (Pfaffenweiler, 1990).

36. "Kinderreich," in *Evangelisches Soziallexikon* (Stuttgart, 1954), p. 586.

37. Diözesanpräses Pfarrer Rath; see Lukas Rölli-Alkemper, *Familie im Wiederaufbau* (Paderborn, 2000), pp. 98–103, 146–52, quoted at p. 101.

38. See van Rahden, *Demokratie*, ch. 3.

39. G. Baumert, *Deutsche Familien nach dem Kriege* (Darmstadt, 1954), p. 136; the qualitative study by Gerhard Wurzbacher, *Leitbilder gegenwärtigen deutschen Familienlebens* (Dortmund, 1951), found an even higher egalitarian share.

40. Wurzbacher, *Leitbilder*, pp. 196, 205.

41. Donna Harsch, "Society, the State, and Abortion in East Germany, 1950–72," *American Historical Review* 102, no. 1 (1997): 53–84.

42. Kuller, *Familienpolitik*; Christine von Oertzen, *The Pleasure of a Surplus Income: Part-Time Work, Gender Politics, and Social Change in West Germany, 1955–69* (New York, 2007).

43. See Elisabeth Zellmer, *Töchter der Revolte?* (Munich, 2011), pp. 9–40.

44. Osmund Schreuder, *Kirche im Vorort* (Freiburg, 1962), quoted at pp. 417, 427, 432. See further Thomas Grossbölting, *Der verlorene Himmel: Glaube in Deutschland seit 1945* (Göttingen, 2013).

45. David Conradt, "Changing German Political Culture," in *Civic Culture Revisited*, ed. G. Almond and S. Verba (Boston, 1980), table 22.

46. Ibid., esp. tables VII, 2, 9, 18, 19.

47. Dolf Sternberger, "Begriff des Vaterlandes," *Die Wandlung* 2, no. 6 (August 1947): 494–511, at p. 502. See further J.-W. Müller, *Constitutional Patriotism* (Princeton, NJ, 2007).

48. Oscar W. Gabriel, ed., *Die EG-Staaten im Vergleich* (Bonn, 1992), pp. 107ff.; Oscar W. Gabriel, *Politische Kultur, Postmaterialismus und Materialismus in der Bundesrepublik Deutschland* (Opladen, 1987); Conradt, "Changing German Political Culture"; Habbo Knoch, ed., *Bürgersinn mit Weltgefühl* (Göttingen, 2007).

49. Gabriel, *Politische Kultur*, p. 286, table 4-19.

50. BArch Freiburg: BW 6/51, nos. 0578, 0604, 0636, and 0637.

51. "Die Bevölkerung als Mitfahnder," *Die Zeit*, 19 September 1969, pp. 13–14.

52. Kerstin Brückweh, "Bedenkliche Einzelerscheinungen oder antiliberale Gesinnung des Durchschnittsbürgers?," in *Mit dem Wandel Leben*, ed. F. Kiessling and B. Rieger (Cologne, 2011), pp. 79–106.

53. Quoted in Gretchen Dutschke, *Rudi Dutschke* (Cologne, 1996), p. 45; see further Angela Hager, "Westdeutscher Protestantismus und Studentenbewegung," in *Umbrüche*, ed. S. Hermle et al. (Göttingen, 2007), pp. 111–30.

54. Quinn Slobodian, *Foreign Front: Third World Politics in Sixties West Germany* (Durham, NC, 2012).

55. From the large literature, see Detlef Siegfried, *1968* (Ditzingen, 2018); Christina von Hodenberg, *Das andere Achtundsechzig* (Munich, 2018); Wolfgang Kraushaar, *Achtundsechzig* (Berlin, 2008); Götz Aly, *Unser Kampf 1968* (Frankfurt, 2008); Gerd Koenen, *Das rote Jahrzehnt* (Cologne, 2001); Ingrid Gilcher-Holthey, ed., *1968* (Göttingen, 1998). Herbert, *Geschichte Deutschlands*, pp. 855–59, 923–29.

56. Karin Bauer, "From Protest to Resistance: Ulrike Meinhof and the Transatlantic Movement of Ideas," in *Changing the World, Changing Oneself*, ed. Belinda Davis et al. (New York, 2010), pp. 171–88, esp. p. 175.

57. Dominique Colas, *Civil Society and Fanaticism* (Stanford, CA, 1997); Arnold Gehlen, *Moral und Hypermoral* (Frankfurt, 1969); Heidrun Kämper, *Aspekte des Demokratiediskurses der späten 1960er Jahre* (Berlin 2012), pp. 84–98.

58. JHD: A 0908, Protokoll, 15 December 1967; Shell Jugendstudie, 1967.

59. Hodenberg, *Das andere Achtundsechzig*, p. 56 (Olek), quoted at p. 86. For pension reform, see Hans Günter Hockerts, *Sozialpolitische Entscheidungen im Nachkriegsdeutschland* (Stuttgart, 1980); Cornelius Torp, "The Adenauer Government's Pension Reform of 1957," *German History* 34, no. 2 (2016): 237–57.

60. HIS: SBe 692-G3, Dutschke, in "Oberbaumblatt," no. 5, 12 June 1967, reprinted in "Strategie und Organizationsfrage in der antiautoritären Bewegung: Eine Documentation," ed. H. Martin, mimeo, 1970.

61. Michael Schneider, *Demokratie in Gefahr?* (Bonn, 1986).

62. Karin Storch, "Erziehung zum Ungehorsam als Aufgabe einer demokratischen Schule" (1967), at www.imge.info/extdownloads/Arbeitsgrundlagen/AbiturredeKarinStorch.pdf; see also www.theodor-heuss-stiftung.de/thp/1967-2/.

63. Sven Reichardt, *Authentizität und Gemeinschaft* (Berlin, 2014).

64. See Detlef Siegfried, "K-Gruppen, Kommunen und Kellerclubs," *Mittelweg* 36, no. 3 (2014): 99–114.

65. Koenen, *Das rote Jahrzehnt*; Julia Lovell, *Maoism* (London, 2019), pp. 292–99.

66. See Barbara Manthe, "Ziele des Westdeutschen Rechtsterrorismus vor 1990" (2019), www.idz-jena.de/wsd6-4/.

67. IfZ: ED 716/15, Verfassungsschutzbericht 1986, no. 290, 15 June 1986.

68. Heike Sander, speech at the 23rd conference of the SDS, 13 September 1968, at www.1000dokumente.de/pdf/dok_0022_san.pdf. See also Ute Kätzel, ed., *Die 68erinnen* (Königstein, 2008); Hodenberg, *Das andere Achtundsechzig*, chs. 5 and 6.

69. BArch Koblenz: B 141/26715, Bd. 2, Josef D. to Jahn, February 1972; Leonard A. to Jahn, 25 October 1971.

70. ADE: HGSt 3961, Die diakonische Schwester, 68/2 (February 1972); "Erklärung des Rates der EKD," 5 April 1973.

71. BArch Koblenz: B 141/26715, Bd. 2, Anneliese Girnatis-Holtz (DGB) to Jahn, 1 February 1972.

72. BArch Koblenz: B 141/26715, Bd. 2, Klasse Z01 to Jahn, 25 January 1972; Ellen C. to MPs, 30 July 1971.

73. Estimates for their number vary from ten thousand to fifty thousand at the time; Uwe Thaysen, "Bürgerinitiativen, Parlamente und Parteien in der Bundesrepublik," *Zeitschrift für Parlamentsfragen* 9, no. 1 (March 1978): 87–103.

74. HIS: III 4 E a/b, "Kölner Maulwurf," no. 1, 1977.

75. Claus Offe, "Bürgerinitiativen und Reproduktion der Arbeitskraft im Spätkapitalismus," in *Bürgerinitiativen*, ed. H. Grossmann (Frankfurt, 1971), pp. 152–62.

76. Sabine Eckstein, *Nordhorn-Range* (Frankfurt, 1974); HIS: SBe 590-G1, Kurt Oeser, "Evangelische Kirche und Bürgerinitiativen" (1978).

77. HIS: SBe 591-G1/4, SDS, "Agitation, Trikont Verlagskooperative—Strassenbahnaktionen '69"; HIS: III 4 E a/b, "Tatsachen," Schüler und Lehrlingspresse NRW, no 1. September 1973. See further Alexander Sedlmaier, *Consumption and Violence* (Ann Arbor, MI, 2014), ch. 4.

78. B. J. Warneken, ed., "*Niemals sechsspurig durchs Neckartal!*" (Vereinigung für Volkskunde,

1982); Bavarian constitution, Art. 131, Para. 3; Jeremy DeWaal, "*Heimat* as a Geography of Postwar Renewal," *German History* 36, no. 2 (June 2018): 229–51.

79. *Frankfurter Rundschau*, 31 January 1984; Peter de Gijsel, ed., *Schattenwirtschaft und alternative Ökonomie* (Regensburg, 1984); Karin Hunn, *"Nächstes Jahr kehren wir zurück": Die Geschichte der türkischen "Gastarbeiter" in der Bundesrepublik* (Göttingen, 2005), pp. 492–93.

80. See Reichardt, *Authenzität und Gemeinschaft*, ch. 4, esp. pp. 336–50.

81. ADE: HGSt 1958, DASHG, "Selbsthilfegruppen info, July 1978," Informationen des Aktionskreis 71 (11 June 1976).

82. Bloech, *Tagebuch eines Friedensarbeiters* (Minden, 1983); DTA: T Otto 1, Martin Otto, "Wiederaufstieg" (Rosengarten); Julia Paulus, ed., *"Bewegte Dörfer"* (Paderborn, 2018).

83. FZH: A11, "Grasswurzelrevolution," October 1984, no. 88, 8/84.

84. HIS: SBe 692.G5, "Sommerschule '80," p. 2.

85. HIS: SBe 692.G5, "Ein Erlebnisbericht von Drei Enttäuschten," in "Sommerschule '80," pp. 32–34.

86. FDP, Freiburger Thesen (1971), These 1; www.freiheit.org/de/grundsatzprogram-und-dokumente.

87. KAS, and 106/2, JU 21. Landestag Rheinland-Pfalz; KAS: 04-007-001/4, "Für eine humane Gesellschaft" (Grundsatzprogramm, JU 1972); KAS: Add 192/2, *Hamburger Monatsblatt* 12 (1969) (Echternach). FZH: JU 771-65, Schülerunion Hamburg, 21 June 1968. See now also Anna von der Goltz, *The Other '68ers* (Oxford, 2021).

88. Bundesminister für Forschung und Technologie, ed., *Bürgerinitiativen im Bereich von Kernkraftwerken* (Bonn, 1975), report by the Battelle Institute, pp. 163ff.

89. Ulrich Scheuner et al., *Bürgerinitiativen* (Hanover, 1978), pp. 16–17.

90. Sebastian Strube, *Euer Dorf soll schöner werden* (Göttingen, 2013).

91. Robert D. Putnam, *Bowling Alone* (New York, 2000). Other data shows the United States still well ahead in 1974, with 32 percent of Americans active in a community action organization, compared to 18 percent in Germany, 15 percent in the Netherlands, and 11 percent in Japan; Almond and Verba, *Civic Culture Revisited*, table VII.16, p. 249.

92. Richard Stratmann, *Steinhausen und sein Schützenwesen* (Steinhausen, 1998); Gerd Noetzel, *100 Jahre Schützenverein in Straßdorf: 1897–1997* (Schwäbisch-Gmünd, 1997); E. Trox and J. E. Behrendt, *"Schützen-Welten"* (Lüdenscheid, 2006); a few clubs had female shooting sections as early as the 1930s, see Hansjörg Pötzsch, *Das Braunschweiger Schützenwesen: 450 Jahre* (Braunschweig, 1995).

93. See www.datenportal.bmbf.de/portal/Tabelle-2.5.23.html.

94. Ronald Inglehart, *The Silent Revolution in Europe* (Princeton, NJ, 1977). Helmut Klages, *Wertorientierungen im Wandel* (Frankfurt, 1985); Klages "Werte und Wertewandel," in *Handwörterbuch zur Gesellschaft Deutschlands*, ed. B. Schaefers and W. Zapf (Opladen, 2001, 2nd edn.), fig. 1, p. 730; Dietz et al., eds., *Gab es den Wertewandel?* (Berlin, 2014).

95. Helge Pross, *Was ist heute deutsch?* (Reinbek, 1982), quoted at pp. 123, 125, 135, 138–39.

96. Hans-Peter Schwarz, "Die Welt des Bundeskanzlers," in *Die Herausforderung des Globalen in der Ära Adenauer*, ed. E. Conze (Bonn, 2010), pp. 16–34.

97. Kiran Patel, *Project Europe* (Cambridge, 2020), and for the following. Wilfried Loth, *Building Europe* (Berlin, 2015); Ian Kershaw, *Roller-Coaster: Europe, 1950–2017* (London, 2018), pp. 153–67.

98. Dirk Spierenburg and Raymond Poidevin, *The History of the High Authority of the European Coal and Steel Community* (London, 1994), pp. 395–404.

99. Wolfgang Wessels, *Die Öffnung des Staates* (Wiesbaden, 2000), pp. 197–258.

100. Vanessa Conze, *Das Europa der Deutschen* (Munich, 2005), pp. 292–384, quoted at p. 345 (1955). Frank Niess, *Die europäische Idee—aus dem Geist des Widerstands* (Frankfurt, 2001).

101. Patel, *Project Europe*, pp. 134–40.

102. DTA: 1828, Manz letters, 23 March 1951 and 28 June 1959.

103. Sina Fabian, *Boom in der Krise* (Göttingen, 2016), pp. 170–83. See https://www.youtube.com/watch?v=-Q6kodMOorY.

104. Corine Defrance et al., eds., *Städtepartnerschaften in Europa im 20. Jahrhundert* (Göttingen, 2020); N. Papadogiannis, "Political Travel Across the 'Iron Curtain,'" *European Review of History* 23, no. 3 (2016): 526–53; Richard Jobs, *How Youth Travel Integrated Europe* (Chicago, 2017).

105. Alexander Troche, *"Berlin wird am Mekong verteidigt": Die Ostasienpolitik der Bundesrepublik in China, Taiwan und Süd-Vietnam* (Düsseldorf, 2001), p. 60.
106. Schwarz, "Die Welt des Bundeskanzlers," quoted at p. 30.
107. At the time of writing, Germany spends 0.6 percent, slightly more than the European average; only Sweden and Norway meet the target; see www.oecd.org/dac.
108. Bastian Hein, *Die Westdeutschen und die Dritte Welt* (Munich, 2006), esp. pp. 28–92.
109. Young-sun Hong, *Cold War Germany, the Third World, and the Global Humanitarian Regime* (Cambridge, 2015).
110. Ibid., quoted at p. 102; Hubertus Büschel, *Hilfe zur Selbsthilfe* (Frankfurt, 2014), pp. 234–77.
111. Büschel, *Hilfe zur Selbsthilfe*, pp. 324 (quoted), 462–81.
112. Ibid., p. 519.
113. Joseph Kardinal Frings, "Abenteuer im Heiligen Geist," founding speech, Misereor (August 1958), www.misereor.de/fileadmin/publikationen/rede-misereor-gruendung-frings_1958; Bernhard Ohse, "Einmal kein Mahl," in *Ökumenische Diakonie*, ed. C. Berg (Berlin, 1959), pp. 185–94.
114. Dirk van Laak, "Entwicklungspolitik," in Conze, *Herausforderung des Globalen*, p. 164.
115. Frings, "Abenteuer."
116. MAA: Misereor Materialien für Allgemeinheit und Zielgruppen 1959, "Bischofswort zur Fastenaktion: Gegen Hunger und Krankheit in der Welt" (1959); Materialien 1960, Fastenopferbüchse; Materialien 1961, Priester und Mission, Heft 1/1961, and Arbeitsmaterial zur Fastenaktion, 5 February 1961, Materialien 1962, *Hunger.*
117. ADE: BfdW-S 9, Achte Aktion, 1966, Brot für die Welt, Nachrichten; C. Berg, ed., *Brot für die Welt: Dokumente* (Stuttgart 1962), p. 21. MAA: Materialien 1960, "Briefe, die uns erreichten" (1959).
118. MAA: Materialien 1960, Pater Leppich in *Hunger.*
119. Trentmann, *Empire of Things*, pp. 573–77; and see pp. 562–63 in this volume.
120. MAA: Interne Papiere, "Ergebnisse einer psychologischen Untersuchung," 11 November 1965; Materialien 1969, Misereor, 1/March 1969.
121. Andreas Eckert, "Westdeutsche Entwicklungszusammenarbeit mit Afrika," in *Deutsche Zeitgeschichte—Transnational*, ed. A. Gallus et al. (Göttingen, 2015), pp. 27–44.
122. MAA: Materialien 1969, Misereor 1/March 1969; Materialien 1966, Misereor '66. ADE: HGSt 3310, Bericht über die XV Aktion BfW 1973/74 in Berlin-West; HGSt 3311: 20. Aktion, 1978.
123. ADE: BfdW-S 9BfW, Information 10/1966 and BfM, Materialsammlung 5 (1966).
124. Hans Otto Hahn, director of the EKD ecumenical department, at the first joint conference Misereor and BfW, 1971, in *"Gemeinsam Handeln,"* ed. S. Baumgartner and H. Falkenstörfer (Misereor, 1971), p. 16.
125. ADE: BfdW-30, 18. Aktion, K. von Bismarck, "Hilfe zum Leben," 27 November 1975.
126. ADE: BfdW-S 33, "Energieverbrauch als Massstab von Fehlentwicklung," 1977–78.
127. JHD: 02/015-050, Jugendaktion, "Anders leben damit andere überleben," 1977.
128. ADE: BfdW-S 31, 18. Aktion, Hilfe zum Leben, October 1976.
129. ADE: BfdW-S 3; and JHD: 02/015-050, Jugendaktion, 1977.
130. Jugendaktion '79, Arbeitsmappe Misereor/BdkJ: "Anders leben: Teilen Lernen" (ADCV library); ADE: BfdW-S 33: Arbeitshilfe BfW, "Juan und Jose—zwei Indios aus den Anden," 1977; the story of Severino was adapted from a book by the Brazilian poet João Cabral.
131. Baumgartner and Falkenstörfer, *"Gemeinsam Handeln,"* p. 13.
132. Hein, *Die Westdeutschen und die Dritte Welt*, sections IV and V.
133. ADE: HGSt 3310, 1974 Vorurteile gegen BfW; HGSt 3348, "Meinungsumfrage—Aktion Hunger," 1969; MAA: Interne Papiere, "Ergebnisse einer psychologischen Untersuchung," 1965, p. 45.
134. JHD: 02/015-034, EPA—Umfrage entwicklungspolitisches Engagement, BDKJ, 1972.
135. Michael Barnett, "Evolution Without Progress?: Humanitarianism in a World of Hurt," *International Organization* 63, no. 4 (2009): 621–63; Manfred Glagow, "Zwischen Markt und Staat," in Glagow, ed., *Deutsche und internationale Entwicklungspolitik* (Opladen, 1990); Heike Wieters, *The NGO CARE and Food Aid from America, 1945–80* (Manchester, 2017).
136. Martin Rempe, "Ambivalenzen allerorten," *Archiv für Sozialgeschichte* 58 (2018): 331–52.

137. KAS: 04-047-009/2, Spendenaktion Zimbabwe; JU Hessen, 53. Landestag, September 1981; "Zur Aktion Dritte Welt."

138. MAA: Misereor im Widerstreit der Meinungen: Informationsschwerpunkt Südafrika, N. Herkenrath et al. (1984). *Passauer Neue Presse*, 24 February 1983 (Strauss). *Der Spiegel*, 3 July 1988, and Claudius Wenzel, *Südafrika-Politik der Bundesrepublik Deutschland 1982–92* (Wiesbaden, 1994), pp. 172–87.

139. Sonja Begalke et al., eds., *Der halbierte Rechtsstaat* (Baden-Baden, 2015).

140. BArch Koblenz: B 237/89767, petitions and expert advice; H. W. T. to First Senate, 15 May 1957.

141. P. Hedenström, *Schwule, sich emanzipieren lernen: Materialien* (Berlin, 1976), quoted at p. 16.

142. Craig Griffiths, *The Ambivalence of Gay Liberation* (Oxford, 2021).

143. Jan Stoll, *Behinderte Anerkennung?* (Frankfurt, 2017), p. 57.

144. Sebastian Schlund, *"Behinderung" überwinden?* (Frankfurt, 2017), p. 149.

145. Manfred Hofrichter in Valentin Siebrecht, ed., *Rehabilitation von Behinderten in Deutschland* (Dt. Verein f. Öffntl. u. Priv. Fürsorge, 1966), p. 93.

146. Elsbeth Bösl, *Politiken der Normalisierung: Zur Geschichte der Behindertenpolitik in der Bundesrepublik Deutschland* (Bielefeld, 2009); Sebastian Barsch, *Geistig behinderte Menschen in der DDR* (Oberhausen, 2007).

147. ADE: Allg. Slg., 1066, Arbeitskreis "Hilfe für Behinderte," Anleitung, 11/1975; Allg. Slg., 1036, Pfarrer Helbich, "Der behinderte Christus"; Allg. Slg., 1035, Theodor Schober, "Behinderungen—unser gemeinsames Schicksal" (1981). Peter Runde and Rolf G. Heinze, *Chancengleichheit für Behinderte* (Neuwied, 1979).

148. ADE: Allg. Slg., 1035, "Der Behinderte Mensch in der Gemeinde," 1973 (Freizeit Degersheim); Allg. Slg., 1066, Hannelore Schlenger, "Essener Freizeitprojekte"; Allg. Slg., 1044, Urlaubsgemeinschaft, "Zum leiblichen, geistigen und seelischen Wohl des Behinderten," report, 18 September 1973.

149. ADE Lib: Eltern Helfen Eltern, "Streiflichter aus der Arbeit für Familien mit Behinderten," 8 July 2000.

150. ADE: Allg. Slg., 656, Aktion Sorgenkind, *Eine Idee setzt sich durch* (1989); Deutsche Behindertenhilfe, "Aktion Sorgenkind: Dokumentation" (1987).

151. See the critical voices in ADE: Allg. Slg., 1066, "Behinderte und Freizeit."

152. Wilhelm Bläsig and Eberhard Schomburg, *Das Dysmelie-Kind* (Stuttgart, 1966), pp. 11, 15, 43.

153. Ibid., p. 16.

154. ADE: Allg. Slg., 1035, "Der Behinderte Mensch in der Gemeinde," quoted at p. 8; Gerd Jansen, *Einstellung der Gesellschaft zu Körperbehinderten* (Neuburgweier, 1974, 2nd edn.).

155. ADCV: 319.4 F08/03, Fasz. 1, "Bericht über die Situation der Arbeitnehmerinnen in den Maizenawerken, Delmenhorst," n.d., c. 1973.

156. ADE: Allg. Slg., 1035, Christa Schlett "... Krüppel sein dagagen sehr—Lebensbericht," in "Der Behinderte Mensch in der Gemeinde," 1973. ADE: Allg. Slg., 1048, Otto Speck, "Möglichkeiten und Grenzen für Werkstatt für Behinderte aus der Sicht unterschiedlicher Lösungen," 1986 (Augsburg). Ernst Klee, *Behinderten-Report* (Frankfurt, 1977, rev. edn.), p. 13 (Bochum); Ernst Klee, *Behinderte im Urlaub? Das Frankfurter Urteil: Eine Dokumentation* (Frankfurt, 1980), p. 11.

157. Klee, *Behinderte im Urlaub?*; "8. Mai 1980: Erinnerung an Demo gegen Frankfurter Reiseurteil," *kobinet-nachrichten*, 8 May 2020, https://kbnt.org/sefijny.

158. ADE: HGSt 1947, local press reports.

159. Hans Bachl, quoted in Klee, *Behinderte im Urlaub?*, p. 9.

160. ADE: HGSt 1852, Konferenz Diakonischer Behindertenhilfe, 16–17 February 1982.

6 A NEW SOCIALIST PEOPLE

1. Karl Marx, preface to *A Contribution to the Critique of Political Economy* (1859); *Marx-Engels Werke* (*MEW*), XIII, p. 9 (Vorwort) (Berlin-Ost, 1971, 7th edn.).

2. Friedrich Engels, "Herrn Eugen Dühring's Umwälzung der Wissenschaft" (Anti-Dühring, 1887), in *MEW*, XX, pp. 32–135, quoted at pp. 87–88.

3. Reinhold Miller and Akademie für Gesellschaftswissenschaften beim ZK der SED, eds., *Sozialismus und Ethik* (Berlin-Ost, 1984), pp. 46–53.

4. Deutscher Bundestag, ed., *Materialien der Enquete-Kommission "Überwindung der Folgen der SED-Diktatur im Prozess der deutschen Einheit"* (Baden-Baden, 1999), cf. vol. 1 (Debatten) and vol. 2 (Victims) with vol. 5 (Everyday Life). See further Jürgen Kocka and Martin Sabrow, eds., *Die DDR als Geschichte* (Berlin, 1994); Hartmut Kaelble et al., eds., *Sozialgeschichte der DDR* (Stuttgart, 1994); Mary Fulbrook, *Anatomy of a Dictatorship* (Oxford, 1995) and *The People's State* (New Haven, CT, 2005); Konrad H. Jarausch, ed., *Dictatorship as Experience* (New York, 1999); Stefan Wolle, *Der grosse Plan* (Berlin, 2013), *Aufbruch nach Utopia* (Berlin, 2011), and *Die heile Welt der Diktatur* (Berlin, 2009, 3rd rev. edn.; original 1998).

5. Václav Havel, "The Power of the Powerless" (1978), pp. 5–8.

6. Fulbrook, *People's State*, pp. 237–38.

7. Lothar Fritze, *Täter mit gutem Gewissen* (Cologne, 1998).

8. Stefan Wolle, *The Ideal World of Dictatorship* (Berlin, 2019), p. 14; Wolle, *Die heile Welt*, p. 18.

9. See Martin Sabrow, "Sozialismus," in Sabrow, ed., *Erinnerungsorte der DDR* (Munich, 2009), pp. 188–204.

10. As remembered by Andrej Gromyko, quoted in W. Subok and K. Pleschakow, *Der Kreml im Kalten Krieg* (Hildesheim, 1997), p. 230.

11. *Neues Deutschland*, 11 June 1953, p. 1.

12. See Dorothee Wierling, *Geboren im Jahr Eins: Der Jahrgang 1949 in der DDR* (Berlin, 2002), and her contribution to *Enquete-Kommission*, vol. V, pp. 343–51; M. Fulbrook, *Dissonant Lives* (Oxford, 2011).

13. Wolle, *Der grosse Plan*, pp. 169–75.

14. Brigitte Reimann, *Ich bedaure nichts: Tagebücher 1955–1963* (Berlin, 1997; 2nd edn.), p. 74, 28 September 1957.

15. Brigitte Reimann, *Ankunft im Alltag* (1961), pp. 71, 168–69.

16. BArch Berlin: DL 102/543, "Zur Entwicklung sozialistischer Verbrauchs- und Lebensgewohnheiten," 30 June 1971.

17. BArch Berlin: Library, FDJ/6147, Zentralinstitut für Jugendforschung, Freizeit 69, Abschlussreport, confidential, esp. XI/13 and XI/17.

18. BArch Berlin: DL 102/543, "Entwicklung sozialistischer Lebensgewohnheiten," pp. 4–5.

19. Wierling, in *Enquete-Kommission*, vol. V, p. 347.

20. Learning to walk on the leash went further than the "dressage" of daily routines that Henri Lefebvre found in modern societies or the "governmentality" stressed by Foucauldians. The end of the leash was held by formal powers of discipline and repression: prisons, the Wall, sharpshooters. Lefebvre, *Rhythmanalysis* (London, 2004; French edn. 1992).

21. Wolle, *Die heile Welt*, pp. 214–17.

22. André Steiner, *The Plans That Failed* (New York, 2010); see also the NÖS economist Helmut Koziolek, "Hatte das Neue Ökonomische System eine Chance?," *Sitzungsberichte der Leibniz-Sozietät* 10 (1996), 1/2: 129–53.

23. Overviews in Herbert, *Geschichte Deutschlands*, ch. 19; Wolle, *Die heile Welt*, pp. 234–59.

24. In 1979, remembered by Gerhard Schürer, see Steiner, *Plans*, p. 160.

25. BArch Berlin: DY 30/J IV 2/2A/3252, Gerhard Schürer et al., "Analyse der ökonomischen Lage der DDR," 30 October 1989, p. 5; accessible at file: www.bpb.de/system/files/dokument_pdf/w5.grenze.1989_10_30_PB_Vorlage_Schuerers_Krisen_Analyse_BArch_DY_30_J_IV_2_2A_3252. See further Steiner, *Plans*; Charles S. Maier, *Dissolution: The Crisis of Communism and the End of East Germany* (Princeton, NJ, 1999), ch. 2.

26. Schürer, "Analyse," p. 9.

27. André Steiner: "Zwischen Konsumversprechen und Innovationszwang," in *Weg in den Untergang*, ed. K. Jarausch and M. Sabrow (Göttingen, 1999), p. 163.

28. The lower figure is the official one by Berlin state prosecutors, the higher one by the Arbeitsgemeinschaft, 13. August; see "1900 Opfer—keine Endbilanz," press release, August 2018, www.mauermuseum.de/wp-content/uploads/2018/12/13.-August_Pressemitteilung-2018.pdf.

29. See Florian Steger and Maximilian Schochow, *Traumatisierung durch politisierte Medizin* (Berlin, 2016). In 1968, 2,763 individuals were subject to compulsory hospitalization; only 28 percent were diagnosed with venereal disease.

30. See the figures at www.bstu.de/mfs-lexikon/detail/inoffizieller-mitarbeiter-im/. Jens Gieseke, *The History of the Stasi* (New York, 2014), gives 1:77.

31. Anita Krätzner, ed., *Hinter vorgehaltener Hand: Studien zur historischen Denunziationsforschung* (Göttingen, 2015).

32. Ilko-Sascha Kowalczuk, *Stasi konkret* (Munich, 2013).

33. Gieseke, *History of the Stasi*, pp. 90–91.

34. Clemens Vollnhals, "Denunziation," in *Der Schein der Normalitaet*, ed. C. Vollnhals and J. Weber (Munich, 2002), p. 133.

35. Christhard Läpple, *Verrat verjährt nicht* (Hamburg, 2008), quoted at p. 62.

36. Gieseke, *History of the Stasi*, p. 95.

37. Martin Ahrends, ed., *Verführung, Kontrolle, Verrat—Das MfS und die Familie: Zeitzeugen berichten* (Berlin, 2015), p. 101.

38. See ibid.

39. MfS Auskunftsbericht zu Prof. Havemann, 8 April 1963, quoted in Arno Polzin, "Der Wandel Robert Havemanns vom Inoffiziellen Mitarbeiter zum Dissidenten im Spiegel der MfS-Akten" (BF informiert 26/2005), at p. 12, and for the above.

40. The words were Kurt Hager's, quoted in Polzin, "Wandel Havemanns," pp. 45–46.

41. Jürgen Fuchs, "Unter Nutzung der Angst: Die 'leise Form' des Terrors," in BF informiert 2/94; reprint BStU (Berlin 2017), quoted at pp. 9–10.

42. MfS, "Plan zu Massnahmen der Zersetzung… von Robert Havemann," 31 January 1978, at www.stasi-mediathek.de/fileadmin/pdf/dok1117.pdf.

43. UBG: 63-2, Zittau OPK, "Treffpunkt," 22 June 1983.

44. Christian Booß, *Im goldenen Käfig* (Göttingen, 2017), pp. 557–76 and 640ff. for the following.

45. Babett Bauer, *Kontrolle und Repression: Individuelle Erfahrungen in der DDR 1971–89* (Göttingen, 2006); I have changed her sequence for stylistic reasons.

46. See the edited documents by the BStU, "Staatsbürgerliche Pflichten grob verletzt" (Berlin, 2016); Wolf Biermann, *Warte nicht auf bessre Zeiten!* (Berlin, 2016).

47. Wende, 2010.890.001: 1987 Brigade Organisationsprojektierung, VEB Automobilwerk Eisenach.

48. Wende, 2010.425.001: Brigade "Karl Liebknecht," Werkzeugfabrik Radebeul.

49. BArch Berlin: DL 102/44, "Tendenzen der Freizeitgestaltung," 1967, p. 3.

50. Thomas Reichel, *"Sozialistisch arbeiten, lernen und leben," die Brigadebewegung in der DDR, 1959–89* (Cologne, 2011), pp. 279–80.

51. Figures varied. According to data from 1967, a mere 10 percent of pensioners had contact with their former workplace; Philipp Springer, *Da konnt' Ich mich dann so'n bisschen entfalten: Die Volkssolidarität in der SBZ/DDR 1945–69* (Frankfurt, 1999), p. 102. In the small town of Pölzig, in Thuringia, the figure was 50 percent, but that was still considered an outrage by an activist, see BArch Berlin: DY 67/26, Kreissekretär Gera, 30 June 1970.

52. BArch Berlin: NY 4301/17, Nachlass Horst Brasch. "Die Rolle der Nationalen Front," March 1961.

53. BLHA: Rep. 481/121, Rechenschaftsbericht, SK Wustermark, 12 June 1974.

54. Reichel, *"Sozialistisch arbeiten,"* p. 281.

55. Inga Markovits, *Gerechtigkeit in Lüritz* (Munich, 2006), esp. pp. 51–60.

56. BLHA: Rep. 451/109, Vors. der BGL to Rat der Stadt, Beschwerde, 28 August 64. See further Fulbrook, *People's State*, pp. 223–29.

57. Wende, 2009.900.906: Kollektiv der Betriebshandwerker, Angermünde; 2010.176.001: Tagebuch, Brigade Frieden, Zittau; 2010.097.001: Brigadebuch, Kollektiv Fuhrpark 34 (Frankfurt/Oder).

58. Markovits, *Gerechtigkeit in Lüritz*, p. 99.

59. *Jahrgang 45*, 1966, dir. Jürgen Böttcher. Franz Jahrwow (HV Film), quoted in *Apropos Film: DEFA Jahrbuch*, ed. R. Schenk and E. Richter (Berlin, 2000), p. 22.

60. Markovits, *Gerechtigkeit in Lüritz*, p. 100. In 1989, the share of divorce proceedings that were

suspended was down to 4 percent, and to 6 percent when the *Kollektiv* was present. Jane Freedland, "Morals on Trial," *Perspectives on Europe* 44, no. 1 (2014): 55–60, and see now Jane Freedland, *Feminist Transformations and Domestic Violence Activism in Divided Berlin, 1968–2002* (Oxford, 2022).

61. Wolfhard Kohte, "Konfliktkommissionen," in *Der Schein der Stabilität: DDR-Betriebsalltag in der Ära Honecker*, ed. R. Hürtgen and T. Reichel (Berlin, 2001), pp. 251ff.

62. BLHA: Rep. 401/7328, Bezirksgericht Potsdam to Ministerrat DDR, 4 March 1968.

63. BLHA: Rep. 481/121, Protokoll, 9 April and 6 May 1969; name anonymized.

64. BLHA: Rep. 601/24957, Protokoll, 15 January 1967; and for the two youths: Rep. 481/121, 5 May 1969; name anonymized.

65. BArch Berlin: DY 6/2118, "Erfahrungsaustausch mit Vertretern von Hausgemeinschaften," Leipzig, 14 July 1961, Bolduan; and for the following cases.

66. BArch Berlin: DY 6/2118, "Erfahrungsaustausch."

67. BArch Berlin: DY 6/3028, Jahresbericht, HG Wartburgstr., 1975.

68. BArch Berlin: DY 6/1067, "Abt. Kultur, Erfahrungsaustausch," 1 December 1981.

69. BArch Berlin: DY 6/1067, "Abt. Kultur, Rahmenkonzeption," n.d., c. 1979.

70. BArch Berlin: DY 6/2494, "Von Tür zu Tür"—Mitteilungsblatt, I/3 (December 1959), II/4 (March 1960), II/15 (August 1960); Reportage, 8 March 1962.

71. BLHA: Rep. 681, Kreisgericht Eisenhüttenstadt, Schiedskommission.

72. BLHA: Rep. 481, Kreisgericht Luckenwalde, 10 July 1970, "Einschätzung der Tätigkeit"; Schiedskommission IV, Bericht, 10 January 1971.

73. See C. Bernhardt and G. Kuhn, *Keiner darf zurückgelassen werden! Aspekte der Jugendhilfepraxis in der DDR 1959–89* (Münster, 1998), quoted at p. 158.

74. BLHA: Rep. 481/76. See further Paul Betts, *Within Walls: Private Life in the German Democratic Republic* (Oxford, 2010).

75. Harsch, "Society, the State, and Abortion."

76. Fulbrook, *People's State*, p. 284 and ch. 13. Cf. Felix Mühlberg, *Bürger, Bitten und Behörden* (Berlin, 2004); Jochen Staadt, *Eingaben* (Berlin, 1996); Ina Merkel, ed., *Wir sind doch nicht die Meckerecke der Nation!* (Cologne, 1998).

77. Wolf Biermann, "Die populär-Ballade."

78. BArch Berlin: DY 30/69937, Heidemarie D. to Verner, 21 May 1986.

79. E.g., anon. to Lotte Ulbricht, 30 September 1966, in *Volkes Stimmen, "Ehrlich, aber deutlich"—Privatbriefe an die DDR-Regierung*, ed. S. Suckut (Munich, 2016), pp. 139–40.

80. BArch Berlin: DY 30/69944, Johannes S. to Verner, 9 October 1971; Martha S. to Verner, 13 August 1975.

81. BArch Berlin: DY 30/69937, Werner D. to/from Verner, 14 August and 20 October 1971.

82. See further Johannes Frerich and Martin Frey, *Handbuch der Geschichte der Sozialpolitik in Deutschland, II: Sozialpolitik in der DDR* (Munich, 1996).

83. *Unser Bildungssystem . . . Materialien der 12. Sitzung der Volkskammer* (1965), p. 29.

84. BArch Berlin: DY 30/IV 2/2.036, Siegrid B. to Verner, 14 March 1973.

85. BArch Berlin: DY 30/69938, Harry G. to Verner, 12 October 1971.

86. BArch Berlin: DY 30/69937, Manfred E. to Verner, 16 October 1977; SED Zwickau to Verner, 30 December 1977.

87. BArch Berlin: DY 30/69937, Manfred E. to Verner, 16 October 1977.

88. BArch Berlin: DG 7/1769, Johannes K. to Ministerrat, 26 September 1986.

89. BArch Berlin: DY 30/IV, 2/2.039/154, Bernt M. to Krenz, 1 August 1989.

90. BArch Berlin: DY 30/3261, Franz A. to ZK SED, 14 September 1976.

91. BArch Berlin: DG 7/1769, R. Leiste to Ministerrat, 16 November 1986.

92. BArch Berlin: DG 7/2012, "Bericht über die Eingabenarbeit," 13 March 1978.

93. BArch Berlin: DY 30/3261, anon. to ZK SED, 23 February 1981.

94. BArch Berlin: DY 30/69939, Bernd H. to Verner, 14 July 1979.

95. See Paul Betts, "Socialism, Social Rights, and Human Rights: The Case of East Germany," *Humanity* III, no. 3 (June 2014).

96. BArch Berlin: DY 30/69937, Anita E. to Verner, 14 January 1984.

97. BArch Berlin: DY 30/69939, Familie H. to Verner, 19 November 1978; see also Karl H. to Verner, 12 September 1979, and DY 30/69942, Marianne and Horst M. to Verner, 12 May 1983.
98. Günter de Bruyn, *Vierzig Jahre* (Frankfurt, 1996), p. 186.
99. BArch Berlin: DY 30/69942, Irma M. to Verner, 4 June 1981.
100. See the internal Stasi analysis from 11 September 1989 quoted in Wolle, *Die heile Welt*, pp. 428–30.
101. BArch Berlin: DY 30/69942, Paul M. to Verner, 3 October 1983.
102. BArch Berlin: DY 30/69946, Zoll to ZK SED, 9 November 1977, Bernhard T. to Verner, 8 December 1977.
103. See also BStU, MfS, BV Erfurt, KD Apolda, "Ausgewählte Leitpsprüche von Punkern" (1986).
104. I am grateful to Bärbel Spengler and the filmmaker Gunther Scholz for further information and a full set of transcripts; a few of the original essays are in the collection of the Museum in der Kulturbrauerei, Berlin. See further Scholz's documentary *Heute war damals Zukunft* (2010).

7 SEARCHING FOR *HEIMAT*

1. Max Gunter [Max Erbstein], *Der blinde Jüngling* (Munich, 1950).
2. Ibid. For comparison with earlier versions, see Alexander Gann, *Zukunft des Abendlandes* (Salzburg, 1986), pp. 104–17. See also Tobias Weger, "Die Katholische Rhetorik bei den vertriebenen Sudetendeutschen," *Bohemia* 45, no. 2 (2004): 466–68, and Monica Black, *A Demon-Haunted Land* (New York, 2020).
3. Theodor Schieder, ed., *Dokumentation der Vertreibung der Deutschen aus Ostmitteleuropa*, 5 vols. (Bonn, 1953–61). Cf. Ingo Haar, "Die deutschen 'Vertreibungsverluste,'" in *Ursprünge, Arten und Folgen des Konstrukts "Bevölkerung,"* ed. R. Mackensen et al. (Wiesbaden, 2009), pp. 363–82; Mathias Beer, "Im Spannungsfeld von Politik und Zeitgeschichte," *Vierteljahresheft für Zeitgeschichte* 46 (1998): 345–89; Moeller, *War Stories*, ch. 3.
4. Friedrich Nietzsche, *On the Genealogy of Morals* (Cambridge, 2006; 1st German edn. 1887). See also Wendy Brown, *States of Injury* (Princeton, NJ, 1995).
5. Ian Buruma, "The Joys and Perils of Victimhood," *New York Review of Books*, 8 April 1999, pp. 4–9. See further Tony Judt, *Postwar* (London, 2005), chs. 1 and 2. Roger Petersen, *Understanding Ethnic Violence* (Cambridge, 2012); Pieter Lagrou, *The Legacy of Nazi Occupation* (Cambridge, 1999).
6. Heinrich Albertz in 1949, quoted in *Zwischen Heimat und Zuhause: Deutsche Flüchtlinge und Vertriebene in (West) Deutschland 1945–2000*, ed. Rainer Schulze (Osnabrück, 2001), p. 7.
7. Westfälische Landessynode (November 1948), quoted in L. Albertin, "Flüchtlinge," in *Flüchtlinge und Vertriebene in der westdeutschen Nachkriegsgeschichte*, ed. R. Schulze et al. (Hildesheim, 1987), p. 301.
8. DTA: 2368, Martha Zollinger diary.
9. See Donald Bloxham, "The Great Unweaving," and Ronald Grigor Suny, "Explaining Genocide," in *Removing People*, ed. R. Bessel and C. Haake (Oxford, 2011), chs. 8 and 9.
10. BArch Koblenz: Z 18/134 (Kirchliche Hilfsstelle), Denkschrift by Dipl. Ing. Rüb, 28 July 1945.
11. R. M. Douglas, *Orderly and Humane: The Expulsion of Germans after the Second World War* (New Haven, CT, 2012), p. 129, and for the following.
12. BArch Koblenz: Z 18/134, Vertreter der evang. und kath. Kirche und des Roten Kreuzes an den alliierten Kontrollrat, 4 September 1945.
13. Douglas, *Orderly and Humane*, pp. 119–20.
14. Quoted in ibid., p. 151–52.
15. BArch Koblenz: BD 28/10, "Was geschah für Heimatvertriebene?" (Bonn, 1953), Anlage 6/1; Elisabeth Pfeil and Ernst W. Buchholz, *Eingliederungschancen und Eingliederungserfolge* (Bad Godesberg, 1958), table 12. Heike Amos, *Die Vertriebenenpolitik der SED 1949 bis 1990* (Munich, 2009).
16. ADE: ZB 894, Reiseberichte des Flüchtlingskommisars West/Evang. Hilfswerk, von

Freyberg, "Bericht über eine Informationsfahrt," 14–23 March 1946; ADCV: 329.1+374, Fasz. 01, C. Denis, "Unsere Brüder und Schwestern aus dem Osten," 1946.

17. ADE: ZB 894, von Freyberg, "Bericht... V. Informationsfahrt," 30 August–12 September 1946.

18. ADE: ZB 894, von Freyberg, "Bericht... VII. Informationsfahrt," 13–30 November 1946.

19. ADE: ZB 894, von Freyberg, "Bericht... III. Informationsfahrt," 4–20 May 1946. See also Alexander von Plato, "Skizze aus dem Revier," in Albertin, *Flüchtlinge und Vertriebene*, pp. 264–69.

20. BArch Berlin: DO 2/41-44, Zentralverwaltung für deutsche Umsiedler, Bericht über Land Sachsen, 21 November 1946.

21. BArch Berlin: DO 2/68, Landesregierung Sachsen-Anhalt, 10 September 1948.

22. BArch Berlin: DO 2/41-44, Chwalczyk, Besprechung mit SED, 20 February 1947. For "Sauflüchtling," see C. A. MacCartney's report for OMGUS, "Das Flüchtlingsproblem in der amerikanischen Zone Deutschlands," 28 June 1948, copy in ADCV: 374, Fasz. 01.

23. Martina Krug and Karin Mundhenke, *Flüchtlinge im Raum Hannover und in der Stadt Hameln 1945–1952* (Hildesheim, 1988), pp. 47–48.

24. Dieter Brosius and Angelika Hohenstein, *Flüchtlinge im nordöstlichen Niedersachsen* (Hildesheim, 1985), quoted at p. 53 and p. 101.

25. Quoted in Schulze, *Zwischen Heimat und Zuhause*, p. 44.

26. BArch Berlin: DO 2/41, letter by Alfred Weiss, 28 January 1947; Versammlung antifaschistischer Umsiedler in Leipzig, 22 February 1947; Fischbech, Nachtrag, 15 February 1947 (on Pirna); Chwalczyk, Besprechung, 20 February 1947 (on Stolpen, quoted). For Joachimsthal, see Arnd Bauerkämper, "Scharfe Konflikte und 'feine Unterschiede,'" in *Vertreibung, Neuanfang, Integration*, ed. C. Kleßmann et al. (Potsdam, 2001), pp. 123–50.

27. Albrecht Lehmann, *Im Fremden ungewollt zuhaus* (Munich, 1991), p. 33. Andreas Kossert, *Kalte Heimat* (Berlin, 2008).

28. IfS: Ausgleichsamt III/9-96/147, Staatsbeauftragte für das Flüchtlingswesen, Hessen, report, 1 December 1949, p. 11.

29. Schulze, *Zwischen Heimat und Zuhause*, pp. 83, 93–94.

30. Zentralbüro des Hilfswerks, ed., *Dank und Verpflichtung: 10 Jahre Hilfswerk* (Stuttgart, 1955), pp. 164–73; *Mitteilungen aus dem Hilfswerk der evangelischen Kirchen in Deutschland* 89 (August 1954), p. 17. For the international humanitarian effort, see Johannes-Dieter Steinert, *Nach Holocaust und Zwangsarbeit* (Osnabrück, 2007), and Jessica Reinisch, *The Perils of Peace* (Oxford, 2013).

31. Zentralbüro des Hilfswerks, *Dank und Verpflichtung*; Dietmar Merz, *Das Evangelische Hilfswerk in Württemberg von 1945 bis 1950* (Epfendorf, 2002), pp. 41–42, 62–64; J. M. Wischnath, *Kirche in Aktion: Das Evangelische Hilfswerk 1945–57* (Göttingen, 1986).

32. AdsD: 4/AWOA003416, "Rechenschaftsbericht des Zentralausschusses der VS," October 1945–October 1955.

33. BArch Berlin: DY 30/68800, Arbeitstagung, VS, Leipzig, 1–3 October 1946.

34. BLHA: Rep. 8 Havelberg, nr. 1790, Umsiedlerwoche, 25 October–2 November 1947, Anna Thiem to Landrat, 28 September 1947.

35. BLHA: Rep. 250 Lebus, nr. 360.

36. BArch Berlin: DO 2/68, "Umsiedlerwoche: Ergebnisse im Land Brandenburg," 22 August 1948, and Land Thüringen, Bericht, 10 February 1948; DO 2/43, "Die Wohn- und Lebensverhältnisse der Umsiedler," Bericht, n.d., January 1949.

37. BLHA: Rep. 8 Havelberg, nr. 1790, Sammelliste no. 36.

38. BArch Berlin: DO 2/68, Provinzialreg. Sachsen-Anhalt, 28 January 1947.

39. BLHA: Rep. 250 Lebus, nr. 360, Friedrichs to Rat des Kreises, 7 April 1948.

40. BLHA: Rep. 250 Lebus, nr. 360, Rat Kreis Lebus, Erfahrungsbericht, 28 January 1948.

41. Wischnath, *Kirche in Aktion.*

42. *Mitteilungen aus dem Hilfswerk*, no. 5 (August 1947), p. 72 (23–24 June 1947, Stuttgart).

43. *Mitteilungen aus dem Hilfswerk*, no. 9 (December 1947), p. 132 (Westphalia). For Pressel, see Merz, *Evangelische Hilfswerk.*

44. ADE: Allg. Slg. 504, "Die Stadt Hof berichtet ihre Sorgen," B4-53; Allg. Slg. 503, "Was tun die Deutschen?," n.d., 1949. Zentralbüro des Hilfswerks, *Dank und Verpflichtung.*

45. Merz, *Evangelische Hilfswerk*, p. 51.

46. ADE: Allg. Slg. 503, "Was tun die Deutschen?" *Mitteilungen aus dem Hilfswerk*, no. 72 (March 1953), p. 7, and no. 31 (15 April 1958), "Die Pfennighilfe der Jugend," by Pfarrer Carl Eichenberg, Kassel.
47. ADE: Allg. Slg. 507, Laienarbeit, Stuckenberg, December 1947; Schellenberg, September 1947.
48. ADE: Allg. Slg. 507, Laienarbeit, Berling, January 1948; Burrlein, n.d., 1947.
49. ADE: Allg. Slg. 507, Dr. Sprengel, 19 February 1948.
50. ADE: Allg. Slg. 504, "Wer mit ganzer Kraft hilft, weckt Hundertfache Hilfe"; Allg. Slg. 507, Hoerich (January 1948).
51. ADCV: 329.1+374, Fasz. 01, C. Denis, "Caritas und Ost-Flüchtlinge." For Protestant teams, see, e.g., ADE: Allg. Slg. 507, Seehausen, 3 January 1948. The AWO similarly attracted many expellees.
52. ADE: Allg. Slg. 507, Paula Brünings, Evang. Gemeindedienst Kaiserslautern, 22 December 1947.
53. E.g., compare insert fig. 15 in this volume with Hans Franke's woodcut *Barmherzige Samariter*, which featured on cards by Caritas in the 1930s.
54. ADE: Allg. Slg. 503, reports on visits, 27–30 July 1948.
55. ADE: Allg. Slg. 507, G. Blähser, Oberliederbach, 19 December 1947.
56. ADE: Allg. Slg. 507, Friedel Kayser, Heidelberg, Flüchlingsfürsorgerin, 19 December 1947.
57. ADE: Allg. Slg. 375, Pfarrer Dyroff, at conference on "Das Sammlungswesen," June 1952.
58. ADE: ZB 869, Flüchtlingshilfe, 1949, Pfarrer Berg to Gerstenmaier and others, 15 August 1949.
59. BLHA: DO 2/90, Kinderspeisung, "Bericht über eine Kontrollfahrt nach Potsdam," 20 September 1947.
60. ADE: Allg. Slg. 503, "Bericht aus einer Gemeinde des Kreises Ziegenhain, Bz. Kassel," 11 December 1946; ADE: Allg. Slg. 509, Dankbriefe, Christian Semler, Studentenpfarrer, Mainz, 16 June 1948.
61. ADE: Allg. Slg. 509, Dankbriefe, Ulrich Finckh, 28 March 1948.
62. ADE: Allg. Slg. 503, Dr. Karl Bernhard Ritter, Kirchenrat, Marburg, 1 December 1946; A. Gercke Landau/Waldeck, 8 August 1946; ADE: Allg. Slg. 510, Dankberichte, Erich Hopp, Wetzhausen, 3 May 1949.
63. ADE: Allg. Slg. 513, Erlebnisberichte Familie Hillmann, Brake, 20 September 1946.
64. ADE: Allg. Slg. 503, Bericht einer evakuierten Lehrerin. Günter Karweina, *Der grosse Treck* (Stuttgart, 1958, 3rd edn.).
65. ADE: Allg. Slg. 502, Berichte, "Die Deutsche Not."
66. Schieder, *Dokumentation*, e.g., I/1, pp. 100–101; Karweina, *Der grosse Treck*, pp. 79–80, 182.
67. BArch Koblenz: Z 18/101, Kirchl. Hilfsstelle, Predigtskizzen.
68. ADE: Allg. Slg. 503, Ulmer Monatsspiegel (Volkshochschule), May 1951.
69. ADE: Allg. Slg. 376, Adventsammlung, 29 November–12 December 1957, and see Lora Wildenthal, *The Language of Human Rights in West Germany* (Philadelphia, 2012).
70. AdsD: 4/AWOA003347, Bericht über eine Hilfsaktion, "Kinder helfen Kindern," 26 November 1956; *Der Helfer* (August 1956): 3.
71. ADCV: 374.059, Fasz. 02, "Kirchliche Hilfe für neue Flüchtlinge," 6–7 May 1953.
72. Helmut R. Külz, *Die Flüchtlinge aus der sowjetischen Besatzungszone* (Frankfurt, 1950), p. 30.
73. ADCV: 319.4 BII, 10, Fasz. 02, SBZ Flüchtlinge, "Bericht über erste Tagung," 16–18 September 1953.
74. ADCV: 376, Fasz. 01, Evang. Hilfswerk, "Rechtsstellung und soziale Lage der illegalen Sowjetzonenflüchtlinge," summer 1952.
75. AdsD: 4/AWOA000522, Betreuung der Flüchtlingsjugend, 27 September 1960.
76. Frank Hoffmann, *Junge Zuwanderer in Westdeutschland* (Frankfurt, 1999), quoted at p. 486.
77. Andrea Schmelz, "West-Ost Migranten," in *50 Jahre Bundesrepublik, 50 Jahre Einwanderung*, ed. J. Motte et al. (Frankfurt, 1999), p. 93.
78. ADCV: 374, Fasz. 02, Auswertung der Angaben von 151 "Rückkehrern," 20 April 1960.
79. Michael Schwartz, *Vertriebene und "Umsiedlerpolitik"* (Munich, 2004), quoted at p. 485.

80. Cf. Schwartz, *Vertriebene* (quoted at p. 892), with the more positive picture in Philipp Ther, *Deutsche und polnische Vertriebene* (Göttingen, 1998).

81. Heike Amos, *Die Vertriebenenpolitik der SED 1949 bis 1990* (Munich, 2009), pp. 32–42; Jan Palmowski, *Inventing a Socialist Nation* (Cambridge, 2009), pp. 35ff.; Leonore Scholze-Irrlitz, "Umsiedler im Landkreis Beeskow/Storkw," in *Alltagskultur im Umbruch*, ed. W. Kaschuba et al. (Weimar, 1996), pp. 135–49.

82. Peter Huchel, *Die Sternenreuse* (Munich, 1967), p. 90; Anna Seghers, *Der Bienenstock* (Berlin, 1953), pp. 171–80. Christa Wolf, *Kindheitsmuster* (Berlin, 1976); Louis Ferdinand Helbig, *Der ungeheure Verlust* (Wiesbaden, 1996).

83. Amos, *Vertriebenenpolitik der SED*, p. 228.

84. IfS: Ausgleichsamt III/9-96/147, Staatsbeauftragte für das Flüchtlingswesen, ed., *Hessen und das Flüchtlingsproblem* (1949); Zentralbüro des Hilfswerks, *Dank und Verpflichtung*, p. 171.

85. Landesrat E. Andrée, *Neue Illustrierte Zeitung*, Cologne, 5 September 1946; Jakob Kaiser (Ost-CDU), *Die Neue Zeitung*, 20 September 1946; ADE: ZB 859, Flüchtlingshilfe 1946–47, "Ostpreussen, Ostdeutsche—Heimatlose," flyer, January 1947; ADCV: 374.065, Fasz. 00, Tagung, CDU/CSU delegates of Landesflüchtlingsausschüsse, 27–29 April 1948.

86. Weger, "Die katholische Rhetorik," quoted at p. 454; Emmanuel Reichenberger, *Ostdeutsche Passion* (Dusseldorf, 1948). ADCV: 374.065, Fasz. 00, Ostdeutsche Jugendstunde, Arbeitsmaterial, Folge 1: Die Heimat, n.d., c. 1950.

87. ADCV: 374.065, Fasz. 00, Briefe an die Weggefährten (c. December 1947).

88. IfZ: MS 747, Paul Terpitz, Rundbriefe eines ostpreussischen Flüchtlingspfarrers, 6 January 1950.

89. ADCV: 374.065, Fasz. 00, Oberkirchenrat W. Pressel, lecture at Bad Boll, February 1950.

90. See https://www.bund-der-vertriebenen.de/charta.

91. BArch Koblenz: B 125/5, fol. 1, Treck-Vereinigung, "Flüchtlinge kommen."

92. BArch Koblenz: B 125/5, fol. 1, *Die Zeit*, 22 November 1951, and *Neue Illustrierte*, 12 December 1951, p. 3.

93. Letters from BArch Koblenz: B 125/3, fol. 1, 22 January and 4 July 1952; B 125/1, fol. 1, 2 January and 4 July 1952; B 125/2, fol. 1, 28 May 1952; Mayor Ehler (Süderbrarup), *Nordpress-Standard*, 13 November 1951, and *Die Zeit*, 24 April 1952.

94. BArch Koblenz: B 125/15, fol. 1, Bericht des Bundesministers für Vertriebene, *Vertriebene, Flüchtlinge, Kriegsgefangene, Heimatlose Ausländer 1949–52* (Bonn, 1953).

95. Elisabeth Pfeil, *Fünf Jahre später: Die Eingliederung der Heimatvertriebenen in Bayern* (Frankfurt, 1951), quoted at p. 60; Else Bohnsack, *Flüchtlinge und Einheimische in Schleswig-Holstein* (Kiel, 1956); Eugen Lemberg, *Die Vertriebenen in Westdeutschland*, I (Kiel, 1959).

96. Karl Apel, "Mardorf," in *Die Entstehung eines neuen Volkes aus Binnendeutschen und Ostvertriebenen*, ed. E. Lemberg and L. Krecker (Marburg, 1950). Friedrich Prinz, "Integration von Vertriebenen und Flüchtlingen," in Prinz, *Flüchtlinge und Vertriebene*, pp. 252–63. Plaque, "Gemeenshaus," Mardorf.

97. Kurt Völk, "Allendorf, Kreis Marburg," in *Entstehung eines neuen Volkes*, p. 140.

98. Karl Kurz, "Der Wandel des Dorfes Gersdorf, Kreis Hersfeld," in Apel, *Entstehung eines neuen Volkes*, pp. 33–42.

99. Rudolf Wollner, Paulskirche, 28 May 1995, in *1945–1995, 50 Jahre Flucht, Deportation, Vertreibung* (Bonn, 1995); see similarly Kossert, *Kalte Heimat*, p. 325.

100. ADCV: 374.065, Fasz. 00, Komitee Flüchtlingsdank, Eine Chronik, Berlin 1954, "Flüchtlingskinder Malen," Haus der Kunstpädagogik. Wiechert, *Missa Sine Nomine*, pp. 131–32. See, e.g., the sculptures of the refugee mother by Annemarie Suckow von Heydendorff and of the deported girl by Joachim Utech. See further K. H. Gehrmann, "Versuche der literarischen Bewältigung," and Karl O. Kurth, "Presse, Film und Rundfunk," both in *Entstehung eines neuen Volkes*, III. On Thorwald, see David Oels, "'Dieses Buch ist kein Roman,'" *Zeithistorische Forschungen* VI, no. 3 (2009): 367–90.

101. *Grün ist die Heide* (1951), dir. Hans Deppe, Lüdersen quoted at 13 min.; see also Katrin Steffen, "Funktionalisierung des Verlustes," in *Praktiken der Differenz*, ed. M. Rürup (Göttingen, 2009), pp. 148–71.

102. Karin Pohl, *Zwischen Integration und Isolation* (Munich, 2009), p. 70.

103. Ibid.; Kurth, "Presse, Film und Rundfunk," pp. 419–21; Jeffrey Luppes, "To Our Dead: Local Expellee Monuments and the Contestation of German Postwar Memory" (PhD thesis, University of Michigan, 2010), table on p. 12, p. 230 (Kiel); for signposts and bells, see the database at http://www.bund-der-vertriebenen.de/fileadmin/programmierung/bilder/mahnmale, e.g., for Giessen and Felsberg (Hesse), and Stephan Scholz, *Vertriebenendenkmäler* (Oldenburg, 2015), quoted at p. 147, for Hamburg; Cornelia Eisler, *Verwaltete Erinnerung, symbolische Politik* (Munich, 2015).

104. H.-W. Retterath, "Das Kreuz des deutschen Ostens bei Bad Harzburg," *Acta Ethnologica Danubiana* (2011); Scholz, *Vertriebenendenkmäler*.

105. Adenauer, in Cologne, see www.youtube.com/watch?v+ZhwsBsvbB8w.

106. Brandt, Schlesiertreffen, 12 June 1961, quoted in Bohr, *Die Kriegsverbrecherlobby*, p. 160; SPD telegram to Schlesiertreffen, 1963, in Kossert, *Kalte Heimat*, p. 165. See also Pertti Ahonen, *After the Expulsion* (Oxford, 2003).

107. Hans Lipinsky-Gottersdorf, ed., *Aber das Herz hängt daran* (Stuttgart, 1955).

108. Günter Jäger, "Der Wandel Rotenburgs an der Fulda," in *Entstehung eines neuen Volkes*, pp. 109–10.

109. IfS: Ausgleichsamt, III/4-88/32, Ministerium des Inneren, Hessenplan, 13 September 1950. Pfeil, *Fünf Jahre später*; Pfeil and Buchholz, *Eingliederungschancen*; Rudolf Endres, ed., *Bayerns vierter Stamm* (Cologne, 1998); Bohnsack, *Flüchtlinge*, pp. 167–70.

110. IfZ: MS 747, Paul Terpitz, August 1958, Rundbrief. See also Vera Neumann, *Nicht der Rede wert* (Münster, 1999).

111. Pfeil and Buchholz, *Eingliederungschancen*, pp. 178–79; Apel, "Mardorf."

112. Hermann Bausinger et al., *Neue Siedlungen* (Stuttgart, 1959), quoted at pp. 30–31, 158–59.

113. Lehmann, *Im Fremden ungewollt zuhaus*, p. 48.

114. Karl Wagner, *Leben auf dem Lande im Wandel der Industrialisierung* (Frankfurt, 1986); Annett Schulze, *Vereine in Stadthagen 1945–1970* (Bielefeld, 2004); Albrecht Lehmann, *Das Leben in einem Arbeiterdorf* (Stuttgart, 1976), quoted at p. 74.

115. Astrid Pellengahr and Helge Gerndt, *Vereinswesen als Integrationsfaktor* (Munich, 2005); https://gauverband.info/index.php/das-gaugebiet-2/bezirk-burgau/ichenhausen.

116. EKD, "Die Lage der Vertriebenen und das Verhältnis des deutschen Volkes zu seinen östlichen Nachbarn" (Hanover, 1965), see www.archiv.ekd.de/EKD-Texte/4592.html.

117. IfZ: Dq 232.002-1985 BHJ—"Na klar," Jugendzeitschrift für Umwelt, Mitwelt, Heimat, no. 32, 31 December 1985; Dq 231.101-1983/88, Schlesische Jugend i.d. DJO.

118. FZH: WdE 512, Hildegard Kroepelin, interviewed 27 October 1997.

119. FZH: WdE 527, Bente Hagen.

120. FZH: WdE 519, Gerd Selle, interviewed 15 December 1997.

121. Michael von Engelhardt, "Die Bewältigung von Flucht und Vertreibung," in Endres, *Bayerns vierter Stamm*, pp. 236–46.

122. FZH: WdE 517, Ulla Dammert, interviewed 2 December 1997.

123. There were around 350,000 Upper Silesians (*Oberschlesier*) living in Poland at the time. For the petition, see Oliver Dix, "Die Vertriebenenpolitik von Herbert Czaja," in *Herbert Czaja*, ed. C. M. Czaja (Bonn, 2003), p. 93.

8 WAR AND PEACE

1. Biess, *Angst*.

2. Ute Frevert, *A Nation in Barracks* (Oxford, 2004; German edn. 2001).

3. Ulrich Baumgärtner, *Reden nach Hitler: Theodor Heuss, die Auseinandersetzung mit dem Nationalsozialismus* (Stuttgart, 2001), p. 267.

4. *Süddeutsche Zeitung*, 16 January 1950 (Emnid survey); IfS: Va/16 VdK FaM, VdK Protestkundgebung, 1 July 1951; Eckart Dietzfelbinger, *Die westdeutsche Friedensbewegung 1948 bis 1955* (Cologne, 1984), p. 131; Carlo Schmid, 5 April 1946, quoted from Patrick Bernhard, *Zivildienst zwischen Reform und Revolte* (Munich, 2005), p. 18.

5. In reality, Adenauer kept well informed. See Hans-Peter Schwarz, "Adenauer und die Kernwaffen," *Vierteljahreshefte für Zeitgeschichte* 37, no. 4 (1989): 567–93, quoted at p. 569.

6. Helga Anna Meyer, "Women's Campaigns Against West German Rearmament, 1949–55" (unpubl. PhD thesis, Colorado, 1989), pp. 62–63.

7. *Christ und Welt*, 27 November 1958. Ziemann, *Niemöller*, pp. 435–41.

8. Anselm Doering-Manteuffel, *Katholizismus und Wiederbewaffnung* (Mainz, 1981); Hendrik Meyer-Magister, "Individualisierung als Nebenfolge," in *Teilnehmende Zeitgenossenschaft*, ed. C. Albrecht und R. Anselm (Tübingen, 2015) pp. 341–44.

9. BArch Freiburg: MSG 194/454, Frießner, speech to Verband deutscher Soldaten, 19 October 1951.

10. Bundestag, 240. Sitzung, 3 December 1952, 1141; see further Frei, *Vergangenheitspolitik*, ch. 3.

11. Peter Berger, "On the Obsolescence of the Concept of Honor," *European Journal of Sociology* 11 (1970): 339–47, at p. 339. For recent reappraisals, see Dan Demetriou and Laurie Johnson, eds., *Honor in the Modern World* (Lexington, 2016).

12. Arthur Schopenhauer, *Aphorismen zur Lebensweisheit* (Leipzig, 1913; 1st edn. 1851), ch. IV; see also Georg Simmel, *Soziologie* (Leipzig, 1908), pp. 532–36.

13. See Helmut R. Hammerich, ed., *Militärische Aufbaugenerationen der Bundeswehr 1955 bis 1970* (Munich, 2011), p. 193; Manig, *Politik der Ehre.*

14. BArch Freiburg: HIAG Waffen-SS, B 438/191, Nordmarktreffen 1954–5; *Rendsburger Tageblatt*, 20 September 1954, 12 September 1955, quoted.

15. BArch Freiburg: MSG 194/454, Kameradschaftliche Vereinigung des ehem. Inf. Rgt. 77, Nachrichtenblatt Nr. 2/59; see further Thomas Kühne, "Kameradschaft," *Geschichte und Gesellschaft* 22, no. 4 (1996): 504–29.

16. Klaus-Michael Mallmann and Martin Cüppers, *Halbmond und Hakenkreuz* (Darmstadt, 2006).

17. BArch Freiburg: B 438/390, Festabend, 25 Jahre Wüstenfüchse Köln, 11 December 1976. For the meeting in Dusseldorf, see Kraushaar, *Protest-Chronik*, II: 1452–54 (28 September 1956).

18. BArch: MSG 194/454, *Der Soldat* 1, no. 1 (2 October 1952).

19. T. Diedrich and J. Ebert, eds., *Nach Stalingrad: Walther von Seydltitz' Feldpostbriefe und Kriegsgefangenenpost: 1939–1955* (Göttingen, 2018), p. 12.

20. Heinz Brüdigam, *Der Schoss ist fruchtbar noch* (Frankfurt, 1965, 2nd edn.), p. 119. Patrick Brode, *Casual Slaughters and Accidental Judgments: Canadian War Crimes Prosecutions, 1944–1948* (Toronto, 1997).

21. Theodor Plievier, *Stalingrad* (Berlin [West], 1961 edn.), pp. 249, 591.

22. Paul Cooke and Marc Silberman, eds., *Screening War* (Rochester, NY, 2010), pp. 22–23, 43–44, 71–74, 112–13. H. J. Wulff, "Bundesdeutsche Kriegs- und Militärfilme der 1950er Jahre," *Medienwissenschaft* 132 (2012).

23. Von Wrochem, *Manstein.* Heinz G. Konsalik, *Der Arzt von Stalingrad* (Munich, 1956).

24. In 1954, a Federal Inspection Agency (*Bundesprüfstelle*) was set up to protect youth against crime and sex in media.

25. Landser-Grossband Nr. 36, quoted in Walter Nutz, "Der Krieg als Abenteuer und Idylle," in *Gegenwartsliteratur und Drittes Reich*, ed. H. Wagener (Stuttgart, 1977), p. 269. See also *Der Spiegel*, 20 October 1959; Matías Martínez, "Der trivialisierte Krieg," in *"So war der deutsche Landser,"* ed. Jens Westemeier (Paderborn, 2019), pp. 101–22; Jörg Echternkamp, *Soldaten im Nachkrieg* (Munich, 2014); M. Greven und O. von Wrochem, eds., *Der Krieg in der Nachkriegszeit* (Opladen, 2000).

26. Amos Elon, *Journey Through a Haunted Land* (London, 1967; German edn. 1966), p. 20; see also H. Welzer, "Kumulative Heroisierung," *Mittelweg 36* 10, no. 2 (2001): 57–73; Hamburger Institut für Sozialforschung, ed., *Vernichtungskrieg: Verbrechen der Wehrmacht 1941 bis 1944* (Exhibition Catalogue, 1996) and *Eine Ausstellung und ihre Folgen* (Hamburg, 1999).

27. FZH: 1.1.12K, *Hamburger Allgemeine Zeitung*, 11 August 1950.

28. "Hätte, hätte, hätte," *Der Mittag*, 25 September 1955; *Allgemeine Zeitung*, Mainz, 16 June 1955; *Nürnberger Nachrichten*, 26 November 1953; Strauss quoted in *Frankfurter Allgemeine Zeitung*, 30 November 1953. Kerstin von Lingen, *Kesselrings letzte Schlacht* (Paderborn, 2004), pp. 327–46.

29. BArch Freiburg: MSG 194/451, Weihnachtsbescherung für die Kriegsgefangenen, 6 December 1952.

30. Cf. Birgit Schwelling, *Heimkehr—Erinnerung—Integration* (Paderborn, 2010), and Frank Biess, *Homecomings* (Princeton, NJ, 2006).

31. BArch Berlin: DO 1/8.01/30801, pt. 1, all 1955: 18 October, Bitterfeld/Ziegelrode; 15 October, Königs Wusterhausen; 21 October, Magdeburg; 14 October, Halberstadt; 24 October, Torgau.

32. BArch Berlin: DO 1/8.01/30801, pt. 1, 20 December 1955; 19 October 1955.

33. BArch Berlin: DO 1/8666, Stimmungsberichte, 12 October 1953.

34. Svenja Goltermann, *Die Gesellschaft der Überlebenden* (Munich, 2009), p. 59; Robert G. Moeller, "'The Last Soldiers of the Great War' and Tales of Family Reunions in the Federal Republic of Germany," *Signs* 24, no. 11 (1998): 129–45.

35. See Biess, *Homecomings*, pp. 106–109.

36. D. Braunstein and F. Link, "Die 'Heimkehrerstudien' des Instituts für Sozialforschung und ihr politisches Scheitern," *Zyklos* 5 (2019): 433–47.

37. BArch Freiburg: B 433/133, "Rückblicke," October 1956.

38. BArch Freiburg: B 433/124, Plan, 24 January 1957; "Neufassung der Ausstellung," June 1959; "Kriegsgefangenen-Ausstellung Wir Mahnen" (1957). BArch Freiburg: MSG 194/461, "Zum geistig-seelischen Problem des Heimkehrers"; *Frankfurter Allgemeine Zeitung*, 8 January 1957.

39. BArch Freiburg: MSG 194/461, "Material zur Arbeitstagung am 2./3.V.1955 über Kriegsgefangene in der S. U."

40. BArch Freiburg: B 433/124, 1956–57.

41. BArch Freiburg: B 433/210, 1963 Friedlandglockenfeier; BArch Freiburg: B 433/204, Grundsteinlegung, 15 May 1966.

42. VDK: C1-15, Heuss, 16 November 1952, in *Eine Sammlung von Reden zum Volkstrauertag* (1979), p. 19; C.1–2, Handreichung zum Volkstrauertag, 1952.

43. VDK: C1-15, *Reden zum Volkstrauertag*, pp. 33, 38.

44. VDK: C1-5, Mitteilungen der Hilfsstelle für Rasseverfolgte, Mitteilung XII/62. In Heidelberg, for example, the song was discontinued only in 1989; see *Rhein-Neckar Zeitung*, 18 October 1989.

45. "Heldengedenktag," in Heinrich Böll, *Werke, 1957–59* (Cologne, 2005), X, p. 515. VDK: A.100-213, *Saarbrücker Zeitung*, 25 March 1969; see also *Der Spiegel*, 2 December 1968. *Hamburger Abendblatt*, 26 January 1972.

46. FZH: 075 IDK, IDK Dokumentation: Volksbund deutsche Kriegsgräberfürsorge (1971).

47. *Stimme und Weg* 8, no. 29 (November 1970): 6; Elisabeth Guenther in Detmold, Volkstrauertag 1970, *Kriegsgräberfürsorge* 47, no. 4 (May 1971): 80–81. IfZ: Dq 237.003-1968/72, Wikinger 3/69 (Antwerpen).

48. VDK: A.100-844, 1954–5.

49. VDK: D-197, "Versöhnung über Gräbern: 10 Jahre Jugendarbeit" (Kassel, 1962), quoted at p. 104.

50. VDK: D-197, Erinnerungen der Christiane Pahl an Jugendlager in Frankreich, 1962.

51. Eva Köberle, *Der Europabaum: Nicht nur ein Märchen für Kinder* (VDK: Kassel 1987); Volksbund, "Frieden—ein Kinderspiel?" (1987), handout accompanying the film, pp. 2–3.

52. *Der Spiegel*, 10 October 1962.

53. Helmut Hammerich et al., *Das Heer 1950 bis 1970* (Munich, 2006).

54. Frank Pauli, *Wehrmachtsoffiziere in der Bundeswehr* (Paderborn, 2010), p. 179.

55. Detlef Bald et al., eds., *Zurückgestutzt, sinnentleert, unverstanden: Die Innere Führung der Bundeswehr* (Baden-Baden, 2008), p. 53; Pauli, *Wehrmachtsoffiziere*, p. 23.

56. In a country that was divided and had lost territories, this reference to the *Volk* was host to competing interpretations. See further R. J. Schlaffer and W. Schmidt, eds., *Wolf Graf von Baudissin 1907 bis 1993* (Munich, 2007).

57. John Zimmermann, "Der Prototyp: General Ulrich de Maizière," and Elke Horn, "Die militärische Aufbaugeneration der Bundeswehr," both in Hammerich, *Militärische Aufbaugenerationen*, pp. 409–36, 437–68. On Grashey, see Detlef Bald, "Restaurativer Traditionalismus," in *Was ist aus der Inneren Führung geworden*, ed. D. Bald et al. (Hamburg, 2007), p. 14. Cf. now Sönke Neitzel, *Deutsche Krieger* (Berlin, 2020), pp. 265–318.

58. Hammerich, *Das Heer*; Frank Nägler, *Der gewollte Soldat und sein Wandel* (Munich, 2009); Rudolf J. Schlaffer, *Der Wehrbeauftragte 1951 bis 1985* (Munich, 2006), pp. 230–34, 294.

59. Bundesminister der Verteidigung, "Bundeswehr und Tradition," Bonn, 1 July 1965 (Fü B I 4-Az 35-08-07).

60. Detlef Bald et al., eds., *Mythos Wehrmacht* (Berlin, 2001); Martin Rink, *Die Bundeswehr 1950/55–89* (Berlin, 2015).

61. BArch Freiburg: BW 6/416, nos. 89, 9, 155, 113, 47, 179, 0338.

62. BArch Freiburg: BW 6/412, no. 268 (1906–61), the novel was *Die sterbende Jagd* (1953) by Gerd Gaiser, a Nazi pilot.

63. BArch Freiburg: BW 6/416, no. 265 and no. 195, 296, and 53 for the above.

64. Heinrich Stanger, "Soldatenberuf—Ehe und Familie," in *Unteroffiziere Heute* (Boppard, 1962), pp. 11–26.

65. BArch Freiburg: BW 6/416, nos. 240 and 0340.

66. Pauli, *Wehrmachtsoffiziere*, p. 8.

67. BArch Freiburg: BW 6/424, nos. 51 and 0230; BW 6/481, no. 265.

68. BArch Freiburg: BW 6/469, no. 0035. Although not statistically representative, these internal surveys echoed earlier ones by the Emnid Institute in 1955.

69. DTA: 36-2 (32-2), diary, 26 April and 24 October 1963, 15 March 1964.

70. DTA: 2044, Erich Hinkel, *Erinnerungen*, 1957–69; this has now been published by the author as a book on demand: *Bundeswehrsoldat der ersten Stunde* (2020).

71. Hinkel, *Erinnerungen.*

72. Ibid.

73. IfZ: ED 447/29: Bernd Hesslein, "Leutnant 70" papers; *Die Welt*, 3 February 1970 (Hinrichs); *Frankfurter Rundschau*, 28 January 1970 (Schmidt).

74. Wolf Graf von Baudissin, *Soldat für den Frieden* (Munich, 1969), pp. 137–61.

75. *Weißbuch 1970: Zur Sicherheit der Bundesrepublik Deutschland und zur Lage der Bundeswehr* (Bonn, 1970), p. 126 (point 162).

76. Detlef Bald, "Soziale Herkunft und soziale Mobilität des deutschen Offizierkorps 1900–78," in *Wie integriert ist die Bundeswehr?*, ed. Ralf Zoll (Munich, 1979), cit. at p. 186.

77. Mathias Jopp, *Militär und Gesellschaft in der Bundesrepublik Deutschland* (Frankfurt, 1983).

78. *Weissbuch 1973/1974* (Bonn, 1974); Jopp, *Militär und Gesellschaft*, p. 102; HIS: SBe 544-G8, Nrs. 13/14, "Der Frieden ist der Weg," Material etc. (1981).

79. Zoll, *Wie Integriert ist die Bundeswehr?*, p. 48.

80. BArch Freiburg: B 438/196, HIAG meeting with Rendsburg youth, 1965.

81. HIS: SBe540-G5, "Ein Desertoer [sic] berichtet: Dokumentation" (Heidelberg, 1989), and "Reservisten verweigern sich: Dokumentation" (Bremen, 1987).

82. See the documentation by the *Abitur* class (13a) of the Otto-Hahn-Gymnasium Geesthacht in 2010–11, "Der Grossadmiral und die kleine Stadt," at https://www.ohg-geesthacht.de/images/stories/Aktuelles/2010-11/Doenitz-Affaere/2011_02_28_OHG_13a_Doenitz-Affaere.pdf. See further M. Hettling and J. Echternkamp, eds., *Bedingt erinnerungsbereit: Soldatengedenken in der Bundesrepublik* (Göttingen, 2008).

83. BArch Koblenz: B 122/27998, Bundesminister der Verteidigung, statement, 20 January 1981.

84. Dieter Hartwig, *Großadmiral Karl Dönitz* (Paderborn, 2010).

85. BAarch Koblenz: B 122/27998, Eingaben, Joachim A., 15 January 1981; Johannes D., 7 February 1981; Erna K., 9 January 1981; Martin H., 29 December 1980; F.R. H., 27 December 1980; Edith H., 30 December 1980; Johannes D., 7 February 1981; Wolfgang M., 24 February 1981.

86. Jürgen Hartwig and Albert Wimmel, *Wehrerziehung und vormilitärische Ausbildung der Kinder und Jugendlichen in der DDR* (Stuttgart, 1979), p. 123.

87. Wende, NVA, *Vom Sinn des Soldatenseins* (Leipzig, 1979), pp. 23–25.

88. Wende, 2010.063.001, Gebhard von Blücher, Orden in Gold.

89. Biess, *Homecomings*, pp. 146–47.

90. Stephan Fingerle, *Waffen in Arbeiterhand?* (Berlin, 2001).

91. Volker Koop, *Armee oder Freizeitclub? Die Kampfgruppen der Arbeiterklasse in der DDR* (Bonn, 1997), esp. pp. 83–109.

92. Patrik von zur Muehlen, "Der Eisenberger Kreis," and Rainer Penzel, "Der Fall Anklam," both in *Protestierende Jugend*, ed. U. Herrmann (Munich, 2002). Port, *Conflict and Stability*, p. 130.

93. BArch: DVW 1/55614, Ministerium für nationale Verteidigung, Sekretariat des Ministers, Kollegiumsprotokoll, no. 13/79, Teller, "Stand und Wirksamkeit der wehrpolitischen Bildung und Erziehung in der GST," 29 October 1979.

94. NVA, *Vom Sinn des Soldatseins*, pp. 19, 79, 82. Udo Baron, *Die Wehrideologie der Nationalen Volksarmee der DDR* (Bochum, 1993), Appendix 6f for the planned use of tactical atomic weapons.

95. Hoffmann in the NVA-Film *5. Jahrestag des Mauerbaus* (1966), AFS 8/66, http://www.youtube.com/watch?v=TqMoyTg_Yns. Hoffmann, "Damit Euer Leben einen tiefen Sinn erhält!," Festrede zur Jugendweihe, 1 April 1972, in Hoffmann, *Sozialistische Landesverteidigung* (Berlin/Ost, 1974), pp. 313–19.

96. BArch: DVW 1/55614, Teller, "Stand und Wirksamkeit," 29 October 1979; for the previous quotes, NVA, *Vom Sinn des Soldatseins*, pp. 46, 49.

97. Bernd Pröll, *Vormilitärische Erziehung in beiden deutschen Staaten* (Frankfurt, 1981), p. 31.

98. Quoted in ibid., p. 7; Hartwig and Wimmel, *Wehrerziehung*, p. 51; "Wenn ich gross bin," words and melody by Günther Preissler. A model of the SPW 152 from Halle from the 1970s now stands in the August Horch Museum, Zwickau. See also www.puppenhausmuseum.de/ddr-militaerspielzeug-1.html.

99. BArch Berlin: DO 4/771, Bd. 1, Argumentation: Politische Hauptverwaltung der NVA, 7/78. Michael Koch, "Der Wehrunterricht in den Ländern des Warschauer Paktes" (unpubl. PhD thesis, University of Jena, 2006); Baron, *Wehrideologie.*

100. BArch Berlin: DY 30/95208, Kirchenfragen Rat des Bezirkes Rostock, 26 June 1978. The song was "Zieh an die Macht, du Arm des Herrn" ("Take Power, You Arm of the Lord").

101. BArch Berlin: DO 4/575, Bd. 3, Gespräch, 1 June 1978.

102. "Orientierungshilfe," quoted in BArch Berlin: DY 30/95208, Bericht.

103. BArch Berlin: DY 30/95208, 2. Sek. SED, Kreisleitung Saalfeld, 6 June 1978.

104. BArch Berlin: DY 30/95208, Bezirksleitung Dresden, Aktennotiz, 12 February 1980.

105. BArch Berlin: DO 4/575, Bd. 3, S. Hoyer to Gen. Arnold, 1 November 1979—the POS in Niederbobritzsch. Thomas Widera, "Bausoldaten in der DDR," in Widera, ed., *Pazifisten in Uniform* (Göttingen, 2004), pp. 177–80.

106. Rat des Bezirks an Ministerium für Volksbildung, 22 May 1981, in *Streng vertraulich! Die Volksbildung der DDR in Dokumenten*, ed. Gert Geißler et al. (Berlin 1996), doc. 304, p. 496.

107. FZH: Ordner 468, vol. II: Aktion Kampf dem Atomtod, *Es geht um Dein Leben* (Magistrat der Stadt Frankfurt, 1958).

108. See B. Ziemann, "A Quantum of Solace?: European Peace Movements During the Cold War and Their Elective Affinities," *Archiv für Sozialgeschichte* 49 (2009): 351–89, esp. pp. 377–78. See further Holger Nehring, *Politics of Security: British and West German Protest Movements and the Early Cold War, 1945–1970* (Oxford, 2013).

109. IfZ: ED 716/130, Hirsch papers, *Aktion* (1958) ("Remember"). FZH: Ordner 468, contact sheets of 1958 Hamburg demonstrations, and for *Hiroshima* film; FZH: 107 DFG-IdK, 236 (Autokorso), 9 August 1959; FZH: 468, press cuttings, 5 December 1958 ("Schlüssel zur Hölle"). FZH: A1, Michelsen papers, Professor Nishiwaki, "Die Folgen," 17 September 1954. Internationale Frauenliga für Frieden und Freiheit, *Kindererinnerungen aus Hiroschima*; HIS: TEM 100, 01 and 02a, Tempel papers, Mahnwache, and *Informationen: Monatszeitschrift für Kriegsdienstverweigerer* 10 (1960): 77 (Mannheim). IfZ: ED 716/130, incl. *Darmstädter Echo*, 28 June 1958 (birth defects). FZH: Ordner 468, vol. II, "Kampf dem Atomtod," brochure, 1958, quoting Jungk at pp. 38–39. For Y. Nishiwaki, see *Chugoku Shimbun*, 9 November 2015. Thanks to Benjamin Ziemann for sharing a copy of the film *Schlüssel zur Hölle*, and see his "The Code of Protest," *Contemporary European History* 17, no. 2 (2008): 237–61.

110. FZH: 468, vol. II, Kampf dem Atomtod (Hamburg); similarly, Hessische Naturfreundejugend, 26 September 1959; Kraushaar, *Protest-Chronik*, III, p. 2279. And for the above, HIS: SBe 541/542, "Gelsenkirchener Protokoll . . . Und Du?" (1958) and Westdt. Friedenskommittee, *Die öffentliche Meinung* (1955).

111. HIS: TEM 100, 01, Tempel, "AK Gewaltosigkeit," n.d.

112. Niklas Luhmann, "Die Gewissensfreiheit und das Gewissen," *Archiv des öffentlichen Rechts* 90 (1965), pp. 257–86, quoted at pp. 285–86.

113. "Die Verantwortung der Wissenschaft im Atomzeitalter," 29 April 1957, reprinted in *Junge Kirche*, 9–10 May 1957. Carl Friedrich von Weizsäcker, ed., *Kriegsfolgen und Kriegsverhütung* (Munich, 1971, 2nd edn.).

114. Aufruf des evang. AK CDU, June 1958, in Uli Jaeger, *"Wir werden nicht Ruhe geben"* (Tübingen 1982); BArch Freiburg: BW 6/424, no. 20 (1960).

115. Hellmut Gollwitzer, "Die Christen und die Atomwaffen" (January 1958), reprinted in *Atomwaffen und Ethik*, ed. C. Walter (Munich, 1981), p. 53—see also Jugendausschuss der evang-ref. Landeskirche Nordwestdeutschland, "Wort an die wehrpflichtigen Jugendlichen," (1961), ibid., p. 149. *Martin Niemöller zur atomaren Rüstung* (Darmstadt, 1959), pp. 27–28. EKD, Kirchentag Hannover, 1967.

116. The term was coined by Johan Galtung, "Violence, Peace, and Peace Research," *Journal of Peace Research* 6, no. 3 (1969): 167–91. Galtung was the world's first Professor for Peace and Conflict Research, appointed by the Norwegian government.

117. FZH: IDK 88, Gewaltfreie Aktion, 3–9 January 1977.

118. "Pacem in terris," "Gaudium et spes," see www.vatican.va/archive. BArch Koblenz: B 122/21396, Bensberger Kreis, "Die katholische Kirche . . . und Kriegsdienstverweigerung," March 1974; the circle was cofounded by Kogon.

119. HIS: *Informationen*, 4/1963. *Blaubuch: Dokumentation über den Widerstand gegen die atomare Aufrüstung der Bundesrepublik* (1958, 2nd edn.), p. 118, for a decorator's campaign in Frankfurt; FZH: A4, *Frau und Frieden* 13, no. 9 (September 1964). FZH: 230, DFG, letter by Gerda S., 26 March 1966. Nehring, *Politics of Security*, ch. 2.

120. DTA: MS 2176, Manz letters, 1 January 1966.

121. *Helft Vietnam! Aufruf zur Tat* (1968); FZH: A4, *Frau und Frieden* 13, no. 9 (September 1964): 26, 33. FZH: DFG 212 and 230, Ostermarsch Aufruf, Offenbach, 16 February 1967.

122. FZH, 230: DFG, Herbert R. to Kampagne für Abrüstung, 23 November 1965.

123. HIS: TEM 100, 04, flyer, 1960. FZH: A3, interview with Horst Bethge, 15 November 1981; FZH: 468, Kampf dem Atomkrieg.

124. FZH: DFG 230, Kampagne für Abrüstung, "Bericht über die 'Aktion Volkssarg,'" 21 July 1965; FZH: A1 for the flyer.

125. FZH: A1, "Slogans für den Ostermarsch 63."

126. Detlef Bald, *Militär und Gesellschaft* (Baden-Baden, 1994), p. 129.

127. Hinrich Oetjen of the IG Chemie, at a rally at the Rheinhalle, *Neue Rhein-Zeitung*, 13 February 1967.

128. AdsD: Eco-Archiv 01/2007, IIVS, Vietnam Hearings Solidaritätswoche, November 1970.

129. Wolfghang von Eichborn, *Freiwillige für den Frieden* (Stuttgart 1970), pp. 24–26, and see p. 559 in this volume.

130. JHD: 02/010-029, Mahnwache in Bonn, 1983; *Der Spiegel*, 15 June 1981 (Tostedt); FZH: "Neue Sammlung Friedensbewegung," Uelzen, 8 and 11 August 1983; FZH: A11, Deutsche Friedens Union, "Lasst Hamburg in Frieden!," brochure, 1983; EAK, "Wenn Christen den Kriegsdienst verweigern" (1981).

131. Karl Carstens, *Reden und Interviews*, II (Bonn, 1981), pp. 186–87.

132. Schmidt in *Evangelische Kommentare* 14 (1981): 209–16; Bundestag, 20. Sitzung, 22 March 1958, p. 1041.

133. FZH: B1, Dokumentation, Evang. Pressedienst, 18 May 1981, Kirchliche Bruderschaft im Rheinland to H. Schmidt. Albertz in *Die Zeit*, 10 April 1981.

134. HIS: SBe 544-G8, Arbeitskreis kirchlicher Mitarbeiter, Wolfsburg, "Nein zur 'Nachrüstung,' eine Argumentationshilfe" (September 1983, 8th edn.), quoted at pp. 48, 61.

135. *Gerechtigkeit schafft Frieden: Wort der Deutschen Bischofskonferenz zum Frieden* (Bonn, 1983).

136. JHD: 03/008-015, Hans H. to Arno K., 18 March 1985, quoted. UBG: Nachlass Alisch, 1–7, Robert F., December 1984 (Inning, Ammersee).

137. KAS: And 017/3, U. Benedix Engler, "Sabines Wochenendbesuch bei ihrer Freundin" (September 1983), mimeo. Benedix-Engler, "Ich habe immer versucht, mich als Christenmensch zu entscheiden," in *Mut zur Verantwortung*, ed. B. Neuss and H. Neubert (Cologne, 2013), pp. 33–43.

138. Hanne und Klaus Vack, eds., *Mutlangen—unser Mut wird langen! Elf Verteidigungsreden wegen "Nötigung"* (Sensbachtal, 1986), pp. 22, 43–44, 48–49, 54.

139. "Frieden schaffen ohne Waffen," 25 January 1982, see www.jugendopposition.de/node/150380.
140. BArch Berlin: DO 4/771, Bd. 2, Lewerenz, Rat des Bezirks Dresden, Kirchenfragen, 7 April 1982.
141. BArch Berlin: DO 4/771, Bd. 2, "Information über eine Kontrolle," 11 April 1982; UBG: Nachlass Alisch, 1-7: Weihnachtsbriefaktion; UBG: 79-90, photo collection.
142. UBG: 80-143, Markus- und Petrigemeinde Dresden, 8–15 November 1981; UBG, 80-201 "Konzeption der Friedensgemeinschaft Jena," March 1983.
143. UBG: 80-105, Zentralschule für Kampfgruppen, "Ernst Thälmann," Lesematerial, December 1988.
144. War Resisters' International, "World Survey of Conscription and Conscientious Objection to Military Service," https://wri-irg.org/en/co/rtba/index.html. The Russian Federation introduced the right in the 1993 constitution. Israel limits it to women and religious grounds.
145. Heuss to Paul Helbeck, 21 December 1948, repr. in *Theodor Heuss: Erzieher zur Demokratie; Briefe 1945–9*, ed. E. Becker (Munich, 2007), p. 447.
146. Bernd Eisenfeld, *Kriegsdienstverweigerung in der DDR, ein Friedensdienst?* (Frankfurt, 1978); Widera, *Pazifisten in Uniform.*
147. Eisenfeld, *Kriegsdienstverweigerung in der DDR*, doc. 11.
148. Admiral Verner to Bausoldat, 4 March 1969, in Eisenfeld, *Kriegsdienstverweigerung in der DDR*, doc. 34; and doc. 18 for the previous (Sekretariat des Pres. VK der DDR, 4 November 1966).
149. UBG: 39-2, "Bärenstein I, Durchgang November 1964 bis April 1966; 80-160, anon. to *Nationale Verteidigungsrat der DDR,* 27 January 1970.
150. UBG: 39-2, "Bärenstein III, Durchgang November 1967 bis April 1969."
151. UBG: 80-159, 8 Bausoldaten from Prora to Nguyen Viet Dung, 8 September 1969; UBG: 39-2, Bärenstein I.
152. Matthias Kluge, "'Bausoldat ist man lebenslänglich,'" in Widera, *Pazifisten in Uniform.*
153. UBG: 80-160, anon., "Bausoldaten über die Möglichkeit ihres Friedensengagements," September 1985.
154. Heiner Geißler, *Das Recht der Kriegsdienstverweigerung nach Art. 4 Abs. III des Grundgesetzes* (PhD dissertation, Tübingen, Reutlingen, 1960); E.-W. Böckenförde, "Das Grundrecht der Gewissensfreiheit," in Böckenförde, *Staat, Gesellschaft, Freiheit* (1976); BVerfG: 69; Judge Mahrenholz also supported the minority view.
155. BArch Koblenz: B 122/21396, EAK and KAK, "Wenn ein Kriegsdienstverweigerer anerkannt werden will... Dokumentierte Erfahrungen," 2 April 1974.
156. Didier Fassin, *Humanitarian Reason* (Berkeley, CA, 2012).
157. BArch Koblenz: B 122/21396, EAK and KAK, "Wenn ein Kriegsdienstverweigerer," p. 27.
158. FZH: A11, SODZL, "Nie Wieder!" (Eigenverlag), quoted at pp. 19–20, 27.
159. Bernhard, *Zivildienst*; DTA: 2079.2, Der Tanzkurs (Munich); Michael Hepp, ed., *Soldaten sind Mörder: Dokumentation* (Berlin, 1996), p. 283 (Borchert).
160. FZH: A11, SODZL, "Nie Wieder!," personal statement, 14 October 1976; Kurt Tucholsky, "Drei Minuten Gehör" (1922), in: Tucholsky, *Drei Minuten Gehör* (Reinbek, 1987 edn).
161. ADE: HGSt 8414, "Entwurf des Ausschusses der EKD für Fragen der KDV," and HGSt 8432, Gespräch mit Iven, 1 July 1970 (Kunst); FZH: B1, Diskofo no. 34, 1979 (Hengsbach).
162. ADCV: 258.030, Kath AG für KDV (KAK), annual meeting, 1 October 1971, with thanks to Patrick Bernhard for his generous help. Hans Iven, the government representative for conscientious objectors, wanted them in barracks and work in civil defense, *Die Welt*, 2 December 1977.
163. See Bernhard, *Zivildienst*, tables 3 and 4.
164. HIS: *Informationen*, 1/1961, p. 5; Albert Krölls, *Kriegsdienstverweigerung* (Frankfurt, 1980).
165. BArch Koblenz: B 122/21396, Bensberger Kreis, "Die katholische Kirche... und die Kriegsdienstverweigerung," March 1974.
166. HIS: SBe 540 G2, Evang Akademie Arnoldshain et al., eds., *Militärpolitik Dokumentation* (Stuttgart 1977), pp. 63–64, and Fritz Deppert, "Verweigerung," Hörspiel (1973).
167. HIS: *Informationen*, 1/1966, Bad Boll.
168. BArch Koblenz: B 122/14316, Statistische Kurzinformation B.M. Verteidigung, Karl N. to Heinemann, 23 December 1970.

169. E.g., Falk Bloech, *Tagebuch eines Friedensarbeiters, 1978–83* (Minden, 1983).

170. FZH: A11, SODZL, "Nie Wieder!," pp. 36, 39; FZH: WdE 1979, Hans Walden, interviewed October 2011–February 2012. ADE: HGSt 8415, "Ergebnis der Erhebung 1975."

171. Das Diakonische Werk, 1963, quoted in Bernhard, *Zivildienst*, p. 80.

172. ADCV: 258.028 Fasz. 2, "Auswertung," 19 September 1969; 258.030 Fasz. 2, Kinderheilstätte, Caritas, Buchau, Dr. W., 14 July 1964.

173. Bernhard, *Zivildienst*, ch. 7.

174. ADE: HGSt 8432, "Vermerk über die Tagung," 12–13 March 1978.

175. FZH: A11, SODZL, "Nie Wieder!," p. 39.

176. BAG 2. Senat, 20 December 1984, 2 AZR 436/83; Arbeitsgericht Elmshorn, 11 May 1982: 3 a Ca 2075/81; Landesarbeitsgericht Schleswig-Holstein, 6 January 1983: 2 (3) SA 353/82.

177. Hepp, *Soldaten sind Mörder*, pp. 95–98, 122–29.

178. Ibid., pp. 96–97.

179. Ibid., pp. 125–36.

180. *Hamburger Abendblatt*, 20 September 1994.

181. BVerfG 93, 266, Abweichende Meinung, Haas, 10 October 1995.

182. Hepp, *Soldaten sind Mörder*, pp. 145–72.

183. Franz Wellschmidt, *Badische Zeitung*, 29 January 1995, and, for the previous quote, Klaus-Dieter Schlottau, *Cellesche Zeitung*, 27 September 1994, reprinted in Hepp, *Soldaten sind Mörder*, pp. 199, 206. Werner Hill, "Tucholskys Schuh—Anmerkungen zum Soldatenurteil," *Deutsche Richterzeitung*, 1994, p. 458.

9 STRANGERS AT HOME

1. Overviews: Klaus Bade, *Vom Auswanderungsland zum Einwanderungsland?* (Berlin, 1983); Ulrich Herbert, *Geschichte der Ausländerpolitik in Deutschland* (Munich, 2001); Maren Möhring, "Mobility and Migration in Divided Germany," in *Shared and Divided*, ed. F. Bösch (Oxford, 2018), pp. 447–500; Jan Plamper, *Das neue Wir* (Frankfurt, 2019); Peter Gatrell, *The Unsettling of Europe* (London, 2020).

2. ADE: HGSt 2955, Bericht, February 28, 1963.

3. Karin Hunn, *"Nächstes Jahr kehren wir zurück . . .": Die Geschichte der türkischen "Gastarbeiter" in der Bundesrepublik* (Göttingen, 2005), quoted at p. 58 (Dreyer), and for the following.

4. *Frankfurter Allgemeine Zeitung*, 11 September 1964. Tragically, he never did bring his family. In 1970, on one of his many visits back home, he was diagnosed with cancer, stayed, and died in Portugal a few years later.

5. Statistisches Bundesamt, *Ausgewählte Strukturdaten für Ausländer* (Stuttgart, 1973), p. 15. For the following figure, see C. Bals and F. Böltken, "Zur Lebenssituation der Ausländer," *Informationen zur Raumentwicklung* 6 (1985): 451–52.

6. Gatrell, *Unsettling of Europe*, p. 201.

7. Andreas Fahrmeir, *Citizens and Aliens* (New York, 2000).

8. For these years, see Karen Schönwälder, *Einwanderung und ethnische Pluralität* (Essen, 1995), quoted at p. 526.

9. See Tomas Hammar, ed., *European Immigration Policy* (Cambridge, 1985).

10. Schönwälder, *Einwanderung*, p. 562.

11. See *Die Zeit*, 24 March 1989, for one journey to obtain a German passport.

12. Jenny Pleinen, *Die Migrationsregime Belgiens und der Bundesrepublik seit dem Zweiten Weltkrieg* (Göttingen, 2012), p. 229.

13. ADE: HGSt 3128, Landeshauptstadt München, "Kommunalpolitische Aspekte des wachsenden ausländischen Bevölkerungsanteils," 1972, p. 89.

14. AdsD: 4/AWOA001419, Nuri Musluoglu (AWO) in *Heilbronner Stimme*, 24 October 1981; Ali Oezarpat, *Hanauer Zeitung*, 10 March 1982.

15. AdsD: 4/AWOA002178, Koblenz, spring 1985.

16. Karl Bingemer et al., *Leben als Gastarbeiter* (Cologne, 1970), p. 59.

17. Lisa Peppler, *Medizin und Migration* (Göttingen, 2016), p. 124 quoted, and for the above.
18. Interview by the author, 24 August 2019.
19. DOMiD: OS 0019, Giacomo Maturi et al., "Hallo Mustafa!" (1966), pp. 4–6.
20. ADE: HGSt 3078, E. Meistermann et al., "Die Integration der ausländischen Arbeitnehmer in Köln," 1967, Zwischenbericht, p. 22.
21. Mathilde Jamin, "Aus Interviews," in *Fremde Heimat*, ed. A. Eryilmaz and M. Jamin (Essen, 1998), p. 222; for the previous, Meistermann et al., "Die Integration," p. 54.
22. Dursun Akçam, ed., *Alaman Ocagi: Türkler Almanları anlatıyor—Deutsches Heim-Glück allein wie Türken Deutsche sehen* (Bornheim-Merten, 1982), pp. 38–42.
23. Quoted in Young-Sun Hong, "Entwicklungsutopien und globale Identitäten," in *Entwicklungswelten*, ed. H. Büschel and D. Speich (Frankfurt, 2009), p. 230.
24. ADE: HGSt 3180, "Uri-Schinbo: Eine koreanische Zeitung," no. 8, 20 January 1975; Koreanischer Sozialdienst, Stuttgart, Bericht, 7 January 1975.
25. Jennifer A. Miller, "Her Fight Is Your Fight," *International Labor and Working-Class History* 84 (2013): 226–47, and Jennifer A. Miller, "Postwar Negotiations: The First Generation of Turkish 'Guest Workers' in West Germany, 1961–1973" (PhD diss., Rutgers University, 2008); Simon Goeke, *"Wir sind alle Fremdarbeiter!"* (Paderborn, 2020).
26. ADE: HGSt 3174, Resolution, 18/19 October 1975.
27. Hunn, *"Nächstes Jahr,"* p. 223.
28. Franziska Dunkel and Gabriella Stramaglia-Faggion, *"Für 50 Mark"* (Munich, 2000), pp. 170–71.
29. ADE: HGSt 2976, *Die Tat*, 19 December 1970, and "Tag des ausländischen Mitbürgers," 1970; the author of the latter was Ernst Klee; see pp. 567–68 in this volume for his advocacy for disability rights.
30. *Stuttgarter Nachrichten*, 25 October 1965, and for the following, Goeke, *"Wir sind alle Fremdarbeiter!,"* pp. 330ff.
31. ADE: HGSt 1970, Hessen, Sozialbericht 1979, pp. 23, 110.
32. Dunkel and Stramaglia-Faggion, *"Für 50 Mark,"* p. 214; Schönwälder, *Einwanderung*, p. 176.
33. Vattenfall/HEW archive, HEW Sammelschiene, 4/1961, pp. 18–20; Yvonne Rieker, *"Ein Stück Heimat findet man ja immer": Die italienische Einwanderung in die Bundesrepublik* (Essen, 2003), quoted at p. 58.
34. Farkhondeh Taghizadeh, interview by the author, 24 August 2019.
35. Dunkel and Stramaglia-Faggion, *"Für 50 Mark,"* p. 211.
36. ADE: HGSt 2996, AG der DT Familienorganizationen, March 1966, no. 12; "Laut und sparsam," Allensbacher Berichte, 1/1972: 23–24.
37. Albrecht Lehmann, *Das Leben in einem Arbeiterdorf* (Stuttgart, 1976), pp. 55, 89.
38. Hunn, *"Nächstes Jahr,"* pp. 107–37.
39. ADCV: 319.4 C03/01 Fasz. 1, Protokoll, Grundsatzkonferenz, "Betreuung der ausl. Arbeitskräfte," 15 May 1961, Dortmund, Msgr. Kewitsch quoting the chair of Caritas, Ernst Schnydrid: "Wir wollten Arbeitskräfte importieren, und es kamen Menschen"; ADE: HGSt 2996, "Es kamen Menschen," Das Diakonische Werk, March 1963, p.1. Max Frisch's preface appeared in *Siamo italiani—die Italiener*, ed. A. Seiler (Zurich, 1965).
40. ADCV: 319.4 C03/01 Fasz. 1, G. Maturi, "Zur Frage ausländischer Arbeiter," 1961; ADE: HGSt 2996, D. Pilgarm to Pastor Suhr, 12 December 1963.
41. ADE: HGSt 2955, Conference, Ökumenischer Rat der Kirchen, Gerhard Möckel, "Die Herausforderung zum Engagement der Ortsgemeinde," 1 June 1963.
42. Prälat Albert Stehlin (Caritas) in *Magnet Bundesrepublik*, ed. Deutsche Arbeitgeberverbände, Informationstagung (Cologne, 1966), p. 34; Schönwälder, *Einwanderung*, quoted at p. 289 (1962).
43. ADCV: 319.4 C03/01 Fasz. 1, Arbeitsblätter für den Helfer, 30 June 1966.
44. LAB: B Rep. 232-35, Nr. 366, Kurt-Tucholsky Grundschule to GCJZ, 7 July 1971, and report on school responses, 1971.
45. AWO, Jahrbuch 1971.
46. ADE: HGSt 3933, EKD, November 1971; for the below, see EKD, 1975 and 1978.
47. BArch Koblenz: B 122/7099, Eingaben der Interessengemeinschaft der mit Ausländern verheirateten deutschen Frauen (IAF), 1973.

48. ADE: HGSt 2955, Bericht, 28 February 1963, Ständige Ausschuss, Appendix 5.
49. ADCV: 319.4 C03/01 Fasz. 1, Kath. Fürsorgeverein, Göttingen to Zentrale KFSV Dortmund, 5/1/1962.
50. *Bild*, 27 January 1967.
51. Bingemer, *Leben als Gastarbeiter*, pp. 57, 110.
52. Anne von Oswald, "Volkswagen, Wolfsburg und die italienischen 'Gastarbeiter,' 1962–75," *Archiv für Sozialgeschichte* 42 (2002): 76.
53. Rieker, *"Ein Stück Heimat,"* p. 142.
54. Lutz Raphael, "Türkische Bergmannsfamilien," in *Lebensläufe im 20. Jahrhundert*, eds. J. Später and T. Zimmer (Göttingen, 2019), pp. 312–14.
55. ADE: HGSt 3128, München, "Kommunalpolitische Aspekte," 1972, pp. 151–55.
56. Achim Schrader et al., *Die zweite Generation* (Kronberg, 1976), p. 203.
57. BArch Koblenz: B 122/23880, Information des Bundespräsidenten... Förderung der Rückkehr ausländischer Arbeitnehmer, incl. Bundesminister für Arbeit, 20 April 1982, Antwort auf grosse Anfrage, p. 21; ADE: HGSt 3933, Kommission für Ausländerfragen, EKD, "Zur gemeinsamen Erziehung," 25 August 1981.
58. Koschnick in 1977, see Hunn, *"Nächstes Jahr,"* p. 385. FZH: Nachlass Michelsen, 16-5, vol. 1, Senat, Leitlinien für die hamburgische Ausländerpolitik, 2 November 1976; Brian van Wyck, "Guest Workers in the School?," *Geschichte und Gesellschaft* 43 (2017): 466–491.
59. H. Kühn, "Stand und Weiterentwicklung der Integration" (Bonn, 1979), https://www.germanhistory-intersections.org/de/migration/ghis:document-125; English précis in Deniz Göktürk et al., eds., *Germany in Transit* (Berkeley, CA 2007), p. 248.
60. AdsD: 4/AWOA001073, Grundsatzpapier, "Integration," November 1979.
61. AdsD: 4/AWOA001419, Bericht Kreisverband Dortmund, 1981.
62. Maren Möhring, *Fremdes Essen* (Munich, 2012).
63. IfZ: ED 894/22, "Eisbrecher," October 1981; see also Internationaler Arbeitskreis Sendling, Heft 1 (1982).
64. H.-G. Kleff, *Vom Bauern zum Industriearbeiter* (Mainz, 1985, 2nd edn.), p. 294.
65. Rita Chin, *The Guest Worker Question in Postwar Germany* (Cambridge, 2007), pp. 194–200.
66. In 1986, only 30 percent of Catholics and Protestants went to church at least once a month, 26 percent a few times a year, and 44 percent more rarely or never; www.fowid.de/meldung/kirchenhaeufigkeit-deutschland-1986-2016. In the 1970s and 1980s, the number leaving the churches exceeded 200,000 each year.
67. Rainer Guski, *Deutsche Briefe über Ausländer* (Bern, 1986). The professors' Heidelberg Manifesto of 17 June 1981 can be found at www.apabiz.de/archiv/material/Profile/Heidelberger percent20Kreis.htm.
68. Rita Chin, "Turkish Women, West German Feminists, and the Gendered Discourse on Muslim Cultural Difference," *Public Culture* 22 (2010): 557–81, and Chin, *Guest Worker Question.*
69. FZH/WdE 580: Hyllal Belim, interview 18 September 1998.
70. Hannes Straube, *Türkisches Leben in der Bundesrepublik* (Frankfurt, 1987), pp. 314–18.
71. Werner Schiffauer, *Die Migranten aus Subay* (Stuttgart 1991), esp. pp. 232ff.
72. Ursula Mehrländer, *Situation der ausländischen Arbeitnehmer* (Bonn, 1981), p. 519; Straube, *Türkisches Leben*; FZH/WdE 1804: Lale Alkan.
73. Rieker, *"Ein Stück Heimat,"* at p. 88.
74. Haydar Gedikoğlu, in Aralik Arkadas, *Deutschland, bittere Heimat*, transl. Carl Koß (1985), pp. 12–13.
75. *Türkler Almanları anlatıyor—Deutsches Heim-Glück allein*, pp. 38–42.
76. Nebahat S. Ercan, *Mein Leiben als türkische Lehrerin in Deutschland* (Norderstedt, 2005).
77. Kleff, *Vom Bauern*, pp. 231–32.
78. *Türkler Almanları anlatıyor—Deutsches Heim-Glück allein*, pp. 14, 49, 146.
79. Oliver Raendchen, "Vietnamesen in der DDR," in Hinz (ed.), *Zuwanderungen*, Berlin, 2001), pp. 78–101; Ann-Judith Rabenschlag, *Völkerfreundschaft nach Bedarf* (Stockholm, 2014); Eva-Maria and Lothar Elsner, *Zwischen Nationalismus und Internationalismus: Über Ausländer und Ausländerpolitik in der DDR 1949–90* (Rostock, 1994); Young-sun Hong, *Cold War Germany, the Third World, and the Global Humanitarian Regime* (Berlin, 2015).

80. Sandra Grunder-Domic, "Beschäftigung statt Ausbildung," in *50 Jahre Bundesrepublik, 50 Jahre Einwanderung*, pp. 215–42; Mike Dennis and Norman LaPorte, *State and Minorities in Communist East Germany* (New York, 2011), p. 90; and the interviews at www.bruderland.de/episodes/werktaetige/.

81. Wolfgang Thierse, "Ausländerfeindlichkeit im vereinten Deutschland," at a conference at the Friedrich-Ebert-Stiftung, 8 June 1993, www.library.fes.de/fulltext/asfo/00228001.htm#LOCE9E2.

82. Study by Bundesminister für Arbeit, cit. in Elsner and Elsner, *Zwischen Nationalismus und Internationalismus*, p. 61. Rita Röhr, *Hoffnung, Hilfe, Heuchelei: Geschichte des Einsatzes polnischer Arbeitskräfte in Betrieben des DDR-Grenzbezirks Frankfurt/Oder 1966–91* (Berlin, 2001), pp. 128–32.

83. Elsner and Elsner, *Zwischen Nationalismus und Internationalismus*, p. 56.

84. Quoted in Rabenschlag, *Völkerfreundschaft*, p. 143.

85. Britta Müller, *Ausländer im Osten Deutschlands* (Cologne, 1996), p. 47.

86. Jonathan Zatlin, "'Polnische Wirtschaft'—'Deutsche Ordnung'?," in *Ankunft-Alltag-Ausreise*, ed. C. T. Müller and P. G. Poutrus (Cologne, 2005), p. 302; Rabenschlag, *Völkerfreundschaft*, p. 209; Marianne Krüger-Potratz, *Anderssein gab es nicht* (Münster, 1991), pp. 50–51.

87. Dennis and LaPorte, *State and Minorities*, pp. 100–101.

88. Christian Müller, "'O' Sowjetmensch!,'" in Müller and Poutrus, *Ankunft-Alltag-Ausreise*, pp. 131–32.

89. Vijoy Batra in 1963, quoted in D. Mac Con Uladh, "Studium bei Freunden," in Müller and Poutrus, *Ankunft-Alltag-Ausreise*, p. 205, and p. 197 for the above.

90. Krüger-Potratz, *Anderssein gab es nicht*, pp. 108 and 182.

91. Ulrich van der Heyden et al., eds., *Mosambikanische Vertragsarbeiter in der DDR-Wirtschaft* (Münster, 2014), p. 240.

92. Mac Con Uladh, "Studium bei Freunden," pp. 210–11.

93. Ludwig Große, superintendent in Saalfeld, an early advocate of the peace and ecological circles, quoted from Krüger-Potratz, *Anderssein gab es nicht*, p. 109.

94. Bernd Wagner, "Vertuschte Gefahr," at www.bpb.de/geschichte/deutsche-geschichte/stasi/218421/neonazis.

95. Bernd Wagner, *Rechtsradikalismus in der Spät-DDR* (Berlin, 2014); Wagner worked on the Stasi project in 1988 as a criminologist.

96. Dennis and LaPorte, *State and Minorities*, p. 113; Krüger-Potratz, *Anderssein gab es nicht*, pp. 111–13.

97. UNHCR, "Convention and Protocol Relating to the Status of Refugees," www.unhcr.org/.

98. Patrice G. Poutrus, *Umkämpftes Asyl* (Berlin, 2019), ch. 1.

99. Fritz Franz, "Politisches Asyl in der Bundesrepublik Deutschland zwischen Grundrecht und Verwaltungspraxis," in *Praxisprobleme im Asylverfahren*, ed. U. O. Sievering (Frankfurt, 1982), p. 23.

100. See Michael Mayer, "Demokratie verwalten lernen: Die Entstehung einer Asylpraxis," *Heuss-Forum* 6 (2019): 1–7.

101. Patrice G. Poutrus, "Zuflucht im Nachkriegsdeutschland," *Geschichte und Gesellschaft* 35, no. 1 (2009): 135–71.

102. 1960, Patrice G. Poutrus, "'Teure Genossen,'" in Müller and Poutrus, *Ankunft-Alltag-Ausreise*, at p. 250.

103. Jost Maurin, "Die DDR als Asylland," *Zeitschrift für Geschichtswissenschaft* 51 (2003): 814–31.

104. UNHCR, "Asylum Applications in Industrialized Countries: 1980–99" (November 2001), tables I.7, VI.19, VI.12, pp. 7, 177, 184; www.unhcr.org.

105. Frank Bösch, *Zeitenwende 1979* (Munich, 2020), ch. 5.

106. Ibid., p. 199.

107. E.g., Annelies Schwarz, *Wir werden uns wiederfinden* (DTV Junior, 1981), and Arno Surminski, *Kudenow oder An fremden Wassern weinen* (Rowohlt, 1978).

108. IfS: Ausgleichsamt 127 Bl/S.193 Bl., Oberbürgermeister, 3 March 1979, and *Frankfurter Stadt-Rundschau*, 18 January 1979.

109. AdsD: 4/AWOA001293, N. Huppertz et al., "Soziale Integration von Flüchtlingen aus Südostasien," AWO, BZK Baden, 1982, quoted at pp. 115, 280.

110. IfZ: DJO-Deutsche Jugend in Europa, "Flucht und Vertreibung—Weltweit" (1981/2); on the German Red Cross, *Der Spiegel*, 31 May 1981.
111. Huppertz et al., "Soziale Integration."
112. IfZ: DJO, "Flucht und Vertreibung," Mathilde Lang (Caritas).
113. AdsD: 4/AWOA001293, final reports 1983 by AWO Beratungsstellen Stuttgart, Hamburg, and Lahr.
114. *Der Spiegel*, 10 January 1982; Barbara Manthe, "Ziele des Westdeutschen Rechtsterrorismus vor 1990," www.idz-jena.de/wsd6-4/.
115. IfZ: DJO, "Flucht und Vertreibung," p. 15.
116. IfZ: DJO, "Flucht und Vertreibung—Weltweit" (1982).
117. Ursula Münch, *Asylpolitik in der Bundesrepublik Deutschland* (Opladen, 1993), ch. 3.
118. Bundesrat, 491. Sitzung, 18 Juli 1980, p. 361.
119. UNHCR, "Memorandum on Mission to the Federal Republic of Germany," by Candida Toscani, 1 July 1983, UNHCR Fonds 11 Series 2, 600-GFR, "Protection and General Legal Matters—Federal Republic of Germany," vol. 13, 1983, Folio 388A, reprinted in *Refugee Survey Quarterly* XXVII, no. 1 (2008): 150–63.
120. For the following, see Reinhard Marx et al., *Asylverfahrensgesetz: Kommentar* (Frankfurt, 1987, 2nd edn.); Münch, *Asylpolitik*; Franz Nuscheler, *Internationale Migration* (Wiesbaden, 2004, 2nd edn.).
121. Manfred Zuleeg, quoted in *Der Spiegel*, 27 July 1986.
122. BVerfGE: 54, 341 (2 July 1980).
123. Wolfgang Zeidler, 1985, quoted in Münch, *Asylpolitik*, p. 106. Herbert, *Geschichte der Ausländerpolitik*, pp. 263ff.
124. Horst Winterstein, quoted in *Der Spiegel*, 17 February 1985.
125. Quoted in *Der Spiegel*, 6 November 1988.
126. Quoted in Albrecht Lehmann, *Im Fremden ungewollt zu Haus* (Munich, 1991), p. 177.
127. See further, Regina Römhild, "Fremdzuschreibungen—Selbstpositionierungen," in *Ethnizität und Migration*, ed. B. Schmidt-Lauber (Berlin, 2007), pp. 157–78.
128. Rainer Kiewitz (CSU), quoted in *Der Spiegel*, 27 July 1986.
129. IfZ: ED 935/33, Waltraud Wirtgen collection, "Dulden statt abschieben! Die Dokumentation des Augsburger Kirchenasyls"; see also *Die Zeit*, 27 July 1990, and "Kirchenasyl in Deutschland," Deutschlandfunk Kultur, 29 December 2014.

10 UNITED AND DIVIDED

1. In the federal election of 1949, the DKP-DRP (Deutsche Konservative Partei–Deutsche Rechtspartei) won only 1.8 percent of the vote but nonetheless crossed the 5 percent hurdle and earned five seats, thanks to securing 8 percent in Lower Saxony. The right-wing DP (Deutsche Partei) had three delegates until 1957.
2. Gregor Schöllgen, *Gerhard Schröder* (Munich, 2015), quoted at pp. 393–94.
3. The interview was with the West German magazine *Stern* on 9 April 1987, and reprinted the following day in the SED's *Neues Deutschland.*
4. See the instant histories by Hartmut Zwahr, *Ende einer Selbstzerstörung* (Göttingen, 1993); Konrad Jarausch, *Die unverhoffte Einheit 1989–90* (Frankfurt, 1995); and Charles Maier, *Dissolution*; as well as more recent overviews by Ilko-Sascha Kowalczuk, *Endspiel* (Munich, 2009), and Andreas Rödder, *Deutschland einig Vaterland* (Munich, 2009). How sensitive the subject remains was shown by the heated reactions to two recent books: Dirk Oschmann, *Der Osten: eine westdeutsche Erfindung* (Munich, 2023) and Katja Hoyer, *Beyond the Wall* (London 2023).
5. *Neues Deutschland*, 2 October 1989.
6. Jurek Becker interview with *taz*, 25 September 1989.
7. Michael Richter, *Die Friedliche Revolution: Aufbruch zur Demokratie in Sachsen 1989/90* (Göttingen, 2nd rev. edn. 2010), pp. 180–94.
8. *taz*, 29 September 1989.

9. *Der Spiegel*, 7 November 1994, p. 40.
10. Richter, *Friedliche Revolution*, pp. 372–84.
11. Lech Wałęsa interview in *Der Spiegel*, 8 November 2009.
12. Richter, *Friedliche Revolution*, p. 277.
13. *Neues Deutschland*, 9 June and 10 October 1989.
14. Secretary for Church Affairs Kurt Löffler, as remembered by Pastor Martin Lange and *Oberkirchenrat* Martin Ziegler, interview 3 April 1990, quoted in H. Herles and E. Rose, eds., *Vom Runden Tisch zum Parlament* (Bonn, 1990), p. 335.
15. See Martin Sabrow, ed., *1989 und die Rolle der Gewalt* (Göttingen, 2019), and Richter, *Friedliche Revolution*, esp. p. 372.
16. Richter, *Friedliche Revolution*, pp. 509–51.
17. *taz*, 30 October 1989.
18. *Deutsches Allgemeine Sonntagsblatt*, 25 August 1989.
19. *Der Spiegel*, 7 November 1994, p. 40.
20. E.g., in Plauen on 7 October 1989, see Thomas Küttler, "Die Wende in Plauen," in *Die politische "Wende" 1989/90 in Sachsen*, ed. A. Fischer and G. Heydemann (Weimar, 1995), pp. 147–55.
21. The full press conference is at www.youtube.com/watch?v=F65XKAc4BrA (quote begins at 1:01:53).
22. "Für unser Land," 26 November 1989, reprinted in *taz*, "DDR: Journal zur Novemberrevolution" (1989), p. 154.
23. Hartmut Zwahr, "Die Revolution in der DDR 1989/90," in *Die politische "Wende,"* esp. pp. 217–29; Küttler, "Die Wende in Plauen."
24. See https://www.bundespraesident.de/SharedDocs/Downloads/DE/Reden/2015/02/150202-RvW-Rede-8-Mai-1985-englisch.pdf?__blob=publicationFile; Richard von Weizsäcker, *Vier Zeiten* (Berlin, 1997), pp. 63–64. A. Wirsching, "Primärerfahrung und kulturelles Gedächtnis," in *Mehr als eine Erzählung*, ed. F. Bajohr et al. (Göttingen, 2016), pp. 113–28.
25. Jürgen Habermas, "Eine Art Schadensabwicklung," *Die Zeit*, 11 July 1986. On the *Historikerstreit*, see Maier, *Unmasterable Past;* and Richard J. Evans, *In Hitler's Shadow* (New York, 1989).
26. See Heinrich August Winkler, *Der lange Weg nach Westen*, II (Munich, 2000), pp. 476–521 (Lafontaine, p. 477; Gansel, p. 497; Fischer, 16 November 1989, p. 521).
27. Winkler, *Lange Weg nach Westen*, II, pp. 518–24.
28. See www.bundesregierung.de/breg-de/themen/deutsche-einheit.
29. Helmut Kohl, *Erinnerungen 1982–1990* (Munich, 2005), p. 1028.
30. See further Hans Kundnani, *The Paradox of German Power* (London, 2014), chs. 2 and 3.
31. Deutscher Bundestag, ed., *Materialien der Enquete-Kommission "Überwindung der Folgen der SED-Diktatur im Prozess der deutschen Einheit"* (Baden-Baden, 1999), V, pp. 511–12.
32. Petra Köpping, *Integriert doch erst mal uns!* (Berlin, 2018).
33. Marcus Böick, *Die Treuhand* (Göttingen, 2018). See also www.ifz-muenchen.de/aktuelles/themen/geschichte-der-treuhandanstalt, and Dierk Hoffmann, "Von der Plan- zur Marktwirtschaft," in *Jahrbuch Deutsche Einheit 2020*, ed. M. Böick et al. (Berlin, 2020), pp. 187–205. For Eastern Europe, see Philip Ther, *Die neue Ordnung auf dem alten Kontinent* (Berlin, 2016).
34. H. Berth et al., "Arbeitslosigkeit und Gesundheit," in *Erwerbslosigkeit*, ed. S. Mühlpfordt et al. (Lengerich, 2011), pp. 35–53; H. Berth et al., *30 Jahre ostdeutsche Transformation: Sozialwissenschaftliche Ergebnisse und Perspektiven der Sächsischen Längsschnittstudie* (Giessen, 2020).
35. DTA: 1350-143, Katja Kramer, 31 August, 11 and 17 September, 2 October 1990. We owe these *Wende* diaries to a timely project initiated by Professor Irene Dölling at Potsdam University; see further I. Dölling, "Weibliche Wendeerfahrungen 'oben' und 'unten,'" in *Soziale Ungleichheit und Geschlechterverhältnisse*, ed. P. Frerichs and M. Steinrücke (Opladen, 1993), pp. 101–16.
36. DTA: 1350-152, Brauer, 7 June 1995.
37. DTA: 1350-123, Ziemler, 12 September 1994.
38. DTA: 1350-150, Tarnow, December 1994.
39. DTA: 1350-89, Faber, Nachschrift 1991 and 1997.
40. For different estimates, see Joachim Ragnitz, "Die Kosten der Einheit," 9 May 2014, at www.wirtschaftlichefreiheit.de.
41. Gerhard A. Ritter, *Der Preis der deutschen Einheit* (Munich, 2007).

42. *Enquete-Kommission "Überwindung,"* I, pp. 117–19, 858–61.

43. Volker Koop, "Die Nationale Volksarmee," and Hans Hubertus v. Roenne, "Die Praxis der Entscheidung über die Übernahme von Personal in den öffentlichen Dienst," in *Enquete-Kommission "Überwindung,"* II, pp. 508–43, 611.

44. V. Roenne, "Praxis der Entscheidung," and Udo Scheer, "Verbleib von Nomenklaturkadern," in *Enquete-Kommission "Überwindung,"* II, pp. 544–649, 755ff.

45. Klaus Marxen et al., *Die Strafverfolgung von DDR-Unrecht* (Berlin, 2007).

46. Marxen et al., *Strafverfolgung*, pp. 49–53.

47. Udo Ebert, "Erfolge, Defizite und Möglichkeiten strafrechtlicher Aufarbeitung von SED-Unrecht," in *Enquete-Kommission "Überwindung,"* II, pt. 2, p. 1387.

48. Rainer Eppelmann in *Enquete-Kommission "Überwindung,"* II, pt. 1, pp. 74–75.

49. See https://www.chronik-der-mauer.de/todesopfer/171322/schmidt-michael.

50. See https://www.ohchr.org/en/professionalinterest/pages/ccpr.aspx, Art. 12/2 and 6/1. Bundesgerichtshof, 3 Nov. 1992 (5 StR 370/92), BGHSt 39, 1.

51. BGHSt 40, 218—Mittelbare Täterschaft hoher DDR-Funktionäre, verdict of 26 July 1994.

52. Georg Brunner, "Justitielle Aufarbeitung in Ost- und Mitteleuropa," in *Enquete-Kommission "Überwindung,"* pp. 1798–1849.

53. 9 July 1991, cited in *Frankfurter Allgemeine Zeitung*, 9 November 1991.

54. Stefan Priebe and Doris Denis, "Folgeschäden politischer Verfolgung," in *Enquete-Kommission "Überwindung,"* II, pt. 2, esp. pp. 321–28, and also pp. 13, 93, 340–66; C. Vollnhals, "Rehabilitierung und Entschädigung der Opfer der SED-Diktatur," in *Nach den Diktaturen*, ed. G. Heydemann and C. Vollnhals (Göttingen, 2015), pp. 127–55.

55. Christa Wolf, "Das haben wir nicht gelernt," *Wochenpost* 43 (1989), reprinted in *taz*, 31 October 1989; readers' letters in *Wochenpost*, 17 November 1989.

56. Thomas Ahbe, *Ostalgie* (Erfurt, 2016); Jonathan Bach, "'The Taste Remains,'" *Public Culture* 14, no. 3 (2002): 545–56; Daphne Berdahl, "'(N)Ostalgie' for the present," *Ethnos* 64, no. 2 (1999): 192–211.

57. Monika Deutz-Schroeder and Klaus Schroeder, *Soziales Paradies oder Stasi-Staat?* (Munich, 2008), quoted at pp. 600, 604.

58. See Martin Schönfeld, "Ein erinnerungspolitischer Gegenpol," *Zeithistorische Forschungen* 6, no. 1 (2009): 129–39; Volkhard Knigge, "Zur Zukunft der Erinnerung," *Aus Politik und Zeitgeschichte* 25–26 (2010).

59. BPA, Pressemitteilung 174, 19 May 2020.

60. *Jahresbericht der Bundesregierung zum Stand der Deutschen Einheit, 2020* (Berlin, 2020), p. 49.

61. Ibid., pp. 114, 156–57.

62. *Handelsblatt*, 3 October 2020; Torsten Jeworrek at Munich Re, and Hiltrud Werner, the head of compliance at Volkswagen.

63. See Helmut Klages in *Enquete-Kommission "Überwindung,"* V, pp. 459–78; Thomas Gensicke, *Mentalitätsentwicklungen im Osten Deutschlands seit den 70er Jahren* (Speyer, 1992).

64. W. Gebhardt and G. Kamphausen, *Zwei Dörfer in Deutschland* (Opladen, 1994).

65. Berliner-Institut für Bevölkerung und Entwicklung, ed., *Vielfalt der Einheit* (Berlin, 2020); Berth et al., *30 Jahre ostdeutsche Transformation.*

66. H. Berth, "Generation Wende," *nitro* 3 (2014): 42–45.

67. Nietzsche, *Beyond Good and Evil*, no. 244 (1886).

68. *Taz*, 13 November 1990 (Dilek).

69. BR24, 3 October 2020.

70. Karen Schönwälder et al., *Vielfalt sucht Rat* (Berlin, 2011).

71. Antidiskriminierungsstelle des Bundes, *Diskriminierung im Bildungsbereich und im Arbeitsleben*, 2nd report (Berlin, 2013), p. 341; between 2008 and 2012, day care attendance among children under three with a migration background rose from 9 percent to 16 percent, but for other Germans it climbed from 22 percent to 33 percent.

72. Antidiskriminierungsstelle des Bundes, *Diskriminierung im Bildungsbereich und im Arbeitsleben*, 3rd report (Berlin, 2017), quoted at p. 103.

73. Eurobarometer Opinion Poll 47.1, "Racism and Xenophobia in Europe," 1997. European

Commission, DG Migration & Home Affairs, "Labour Market Integration of Third-Country Nationals in EU Member States," 2019.

74. Franziska Woellert and Reiner Klingholz, "Neue Potenziale: Zur Lage der Integration," Berlin-Institut für Bevölkerung und Entwicklung, 2014.

75. Sezer İdİl Göğüş, "Die neue Diasporapolitik der Türkei und Türkeistämmige in Deutschland," *Aus Politik und Zeitgeschichte* 48 (2018). Sonja Haug, "Interethnische Kontakte, Freundschaften, Partnerschaften und Ehen von Migranten in Deutschland" (BAMF, 2010).

76. Martina Sauer, "Identifikation und politische Partizipation türkeistämmiger Zugewanderter in Nordrhein-Westfalen und in Deutschland," Stiftung Zentrum für Türkeistudien und Integration (2018), pp. 129–30.

77. DOMiD Lib.: DFB, "Tor! Integration fängt bei mir an" (2011).

78. Jörg Häntschel, *Süddeutsche Zeitung*, 28–29 July 2018. Cf. *Neon*, 23 July 2018; *Frankfurter Allgemeine Zeitung*, 23 July 2018.

79. 22 July 2018 @MesutOzil1088.

80. In 2021, Dirk Moses sparked controversy by claiming that Germans see comparison as "a heresy, an apostasy from the right faith"; Moses, "The German Catechism," 23 May 2021, https://geschichtedergegenwart.ch.

81. Taner Akçam, *Armenien und der Völkermord* (Hamburg, 1996).

82. Frank Trentmann, "How Not to Be an Alien," *Times Literary Supplement*, 4 September 2020.

83. Dan Diner, "Nation, Migration, and Memory," *Constellations* 4, no. 3 (1998): 293–306.

84. E.g., the head of the CDU parliamentary group Volker Kauder to the *Frankfurter Allgemeine Zeitung*, 16 July 2006.

85. Özlem Topçu, in Alice Bota, Khuê Pham, and Topçu, *Wir neuen Deutschen* (Bonn, 2012), pp. 44–45.

86. Kurt Steiner (CSU); see Esra Oeszyürek, "Rethinking Empathy: Emotions Triggered by the Holocaust Among Muslim-Minority in Germany," *Anthropological Theory* 18, no. 4 (2018): 456–477, quoted at p. 457.

87. Marc David Baer, "Turk and Jew in Berlin," *Comparative Studies in Society and History* 55, no. 2 (2013): 330–55.

88. Michael Rothberg and Yasemin Yildiz, "Memory Citizenship," *Parallax* 17, no. 4 (2011): 32–48; Oeszyürek, "Rethinking Empathy."

11 IN THE WIDE WORLD

1. Hanns W. Maull, "Germany and Japan: The New Civilian Powers," *Foreign Affairs* 69, no. 5: 91–106.

2. Hans Kundnani, *The Paradox of German Power* (London, 2014), p. 6.

3. Speech at DGAP, 24 November 1999, www.glasnost.de/db/DokZeit/99fischer,html.

4. Hans-Peter Kriemann, *Der Kosovokrieg 1999* (Ditzingen, 2019).

5. Schöllgen, *Schröder*, Kundnani, *Paradox of German Power*, ch. 4.

6. Josef Joffe, *Der gute Deutsche: Die Karriere einer moralischen Supermacht* (Munich, 2018), and chs. 6 and 7 for the following.

7. Quoted in Frank Bösch, *Zeitenwende 1979* (Munich, 2020), p. 245. See further Werner Link, "Gemeinsame Führung und die Kultur der Zurückhaltung in der deutschen Außenpolitik," *Zeitschrift für Außen- und Sicherheitspolitik* 8, no. 1 (2015): 289–312.

8. Egon Bahr, *Der deutsche Weg: Selbstverständlich und normal* (Munich, 2003).

9. Quoted in M. Nonhoff und F. A. Stengel, "Poststrukturalistische Diskurstheorie und Außenpolitikanalyse," in *Diskursforschung in den Internationalen Beziehungen*, ed. E. Herschinger and J. Renner (Baden-Baden, 2014), pp. 37–74, at pp. 61–62.

10. Timo Noetzel, "The German Politics of War: Kunduz and the War in Afghanistan," *International Affairs* 87, no. 2 (2011): 397–417; for the "civil-military gap," see Klaus Naumann, "Eine

Rechnung mit vielen Unbekannten," in *Einsatz ohne Krieg?*, ed. J. Maurer und M. Rink (Göttingen, 2021), pp. 129–49.

11. See www.bundeswehr.de/de/ueber-die-bundeswehr/gedenken-tote-bundeswehr/wald-der-erinnerung; Bundesministerium der Verteidigung, *Das Ehrenmal der Bundeswehr* (2014). Helen McCartney, "Hero, Victim or Villain?," *Defense and Security Analysis* 27 (2011): 43–54; Heiner Möller, ed., *Sonderfall Bundeswehr?* (Munich, 2014).

12. See Schöllgen, *Schröder*.

13. BMF-Monatsbericht March 2017, "Der deutsche Leistungsbilanzsaldo," pp. 5–6, at www.bundesfinanzministerium.de/Monatsberichte.

14. Schöllgen, *Schröder*, pp. 478–81.

15. In Mainz on 23 February 2005, quoted in ibid., p. 770.

16. Link, "Gemeinsame Führung," quoted at p. 297.

17. Eurostat, general government expenditure by function (COFOG), web.archive.org/web/20220313133646/ https://www.bmvg.de/de/themen/verteidigungshaushalt/faq; Bundeswehr-Generalinspekteur Eberhard Zorn, in *Focus*, 22 August 2022. List of military support as of 31 August 2022: www.bundesregierung.de/breg-en/news/military-support-ukraine-2054992.

18. *Stern*, 20 August 2022 (Forsa-Blitzumfrage); cf. slightly higher support in July: Tagesschau, ARD-DeutschlandTrend, 22 July 2022.

19. *Guardian*, 31 May 2021; Omri Boehm, "Die universalen Menschenrechte und die Fallen der Realpolitik," *Die Zeit*, 12 August 2021, p. 46.

20. Stefan Kornelius, *Angela Merkel* (Hamburg, 2013), p. 121.

21. Regierungserklärung, Merkel, Bulletin der Bundesregierung Nr. 104-1 (7 October 2008).

22. See Sascha Münnich, "Readjusting Imagined Markets," *Socio-Economic Review* 14, no. 2 (2016): 288–307.

23. Adam Tooze, *Crashed* (London, 2018), pp. 210, 217.

24. See Sascha Münnich, "Thieves, Fools, Fraudsters, and Gamblers?," *European Journal of Sociology* 56, no. 1 (2015): 93–118.

25. For this and the following, see Tooze, *Crashed*, part III.

26. Quoted in *Der Tagesspiegel*, 28 July 2015. On Portugal: *Der Spiegel*, 12 November 2012.

27. BMF, Monatsbericht March 2017, p. 5.

28. See Claus Offe, "Narratives of Responsibility: German Politics in the Greek Debt Crisis," in Offe, *Staatskapazität und Europäische Integration* (Wiesbaden, 2018), pp. 365–88.

29. 8 April 2014, at www.wolfgang-schaeuble.de/bundeshaushalt-ohne-neuverschuldung-soll-neue-normalitaet-werden.

30. See Joseph Stiglitz, *The Euro* (London, 2016).

31. Deutscher Bundestag, 18. Wahlperiode, 117. Sitzung, 17 Juli 2015, p. 11354.

32. *Bild*, 5 March 2010.

33. See International Court of Justice, judgment of 3 February 2012, *Jurisdictional Immunities of the State (Germany v. Italy: Greece intervening)*, at https://www.icj-cij.org/en/case/143; G. Heinecke, "Nicht verjährt, nicht entschädigt, nicht vergessen," in *Grundrechte Report 2020*, ed. M. Armbruster et al. (Frankfurt, 2020), pp. 181–85.

34. Bericht der Vorsitzenden der CDU Deutschlands, 22. Parteitag, 1 December 2008, p. 8, at www.kas.de: CDU, Protokolle.

35. Stiglitz, *The Euro*, p. 133.

36. IFOP survey, March 2010, cit. in C. Schneider and B. Slanchev, "The Domestic Politics of International Cooperation," *International Organization* 72, no. 1 (2018); "Fünf Jahre Griechenland-Krise—so denken die Deutschen über Griechenland," *Bild*, 28 June 2015. K. Otto and A. Köhler, "Die Berichterstattung deutscher Medien in der griechischen Staatsschuldenkrise" (2016), https://www.boeckler.de/pdf/p_imk_study_45_2016.pdf.

37. Thomas Mayer quoted in *Bild*, 26 April 2017; *Bild*, 10 May 2010.

38. Leibniz Institute for Economic Research, "Germany's Benefit from the Greek Crisis," 2015.

39. Martha Posthofen and Frieder Schmid, "Gerechter. Sozialer. Weniger ungleich. Was die Deutschen von Europa erwarten" (FES, 2018), p. 17.

40. The sociologist Heinz Bude in *Luzerner Zeitung*, 6 September 2013, and *Die Zeit*, 3 September 2015, p. 5.
41. *Frankfurter Allgemeine Zeitung*, 31 August 2015.
42. Rosa-Luxemburg-Stiftung, ed., *Atlas der Migration* (Berlin, 2019).
43. Bundestag, 9 September 2015.
44. Viktor Orbán, quoted in *Deutsche Welle*, 23 September 2015. See also *Die Zeit*, 4 April 2016 and 1 September 2016 (Ulrich Greiner), p. 2.
45. Quoted in Robin Alexander, *Die Getriebenen* (Munich, 2017), pp. 29f.
46. DOMiD Lib.: Bundesvereinigung der Deutschen Arbeitgeberverbände (BDA), "Willkommenskultur—ein Leitfaden für Unternehmen" (2013). "Charta der Vielfalt," https://www.charta-der-vielfalt.de/ueber-uns/ueber-die-initiative/die-urkunde-im-wortlaut/.
47. "1. Deutscher Diversity-Tag 2013," www.charta-der-vielfalt.de.
48. *Frankfurter Allgemeine Zeitung*, 15 September 2015.
49. Barbara Heß, "Volljährige Asylerstantragsteller in Deutschland im ersten Halbjahr 2018," BAMF-Kurzanalyse 03/2019.
50. DOMiD: E 0981,0324.
51. Peter Kühne and Harald Rüßler, *Die Lebensverhältnisse der Flüchtlinge in Deutschland* (Frankfurt, 2000), pp. 189–95.
52. DOMiD Lib.: PRO ASYL, "Refugees Welcome," 2013; www.zusammenleben-wilkommen.de.
53. DOMiD: PS0007, "Kein Mensch ist illegal," 2000, and E 0991,0629.
54. Bundesministerium für Familie, Senioren, Frauen und Jugend (BMFSFJ), "Engagement in der Flüchtlingshelfe—Ergebnisbericht einer Untersuchung des Instituts für Demoskopie Allensbach," 2017.
55. Ibid.
56. Werner Schiffauer et al., eds., *So schaffen wir das* (Bielefeld, 2017).
57. *Der Tagesspiegel*, 9 August 2015; *Die Zeit*, 14 June 2018, p. 16. Deutscher Bundestag, Beschlussempfehlung und Bericht, 19/30800, 21 June 2021.
58. European Union Agency for Fundamental Rights (FRA), *Current Migration Situation in the EU: Hate Crime* (Luxembourg, November 2016); D. Benček and J. Strasheim, "Refugees Welcome?: A Dataset on Anti-refugee Violence in Germany," *Research and Politics* (October–December 2016): 1–11.
59. Statistics vary between official figures, which require clear evidence of right-wing motivation, and investigations by NGOs. The introduction of a new police metric in 2001 makes long-term comparisons with earlier periods impossible. The total figure for right-wing crimes cited follows the Home Office (PMK). The number of murdered follows the data gathered by the Amadeu Antonio Foundation, www.amadeu-antonio-stiftung.de. See further Amadeu Antonio Foundation and PRO ASYL, eds., *Die Brandstifter* (Cottbus, 2014).
60. AIDA and ECRE (Asylum Information Database and European Council on Refugees and Exiles), *Country Report: Germany* (2018), pp. 34–39.
61. Herbert Brücker et al., "Arbeitsmarktintegration von Geflüchteten in Deutschland," Institut für Arbeitsmarkt- und Berufsforschung (IAB), 4/2017.
62. AIDA and ECRE, *Country Report: Germany* (2018), pp. 84–86; IAB, Kurzbericht 25/2020.
63. AIDA and ECRE, *Country Report: Germany* (2018), pp. 65–66, 117.
64. Schiffauer, *So schaffen wir das*, pp. 22–23. Jost Herrmann, "5 Jahre 'Asyl im Oberland,'" at www.asylimoberland.de; Julia Poweleit, "Zivilgesellschaft in der Migrationsgesellschaft," in *Zivilgesellschaft in der Bundesrepublik Deutschland*, ed. B. Grande et al. (Bielefeld, 2021), pp. 113–18.
65. In the first nine months, 222 stopped flights, according to government figures, see *Deutsche Welle*, 7 December 2017. See further Deutscher Bundestag, 18/4025, 16 February 2015, "Antwort der Bundesregierung auf die Kleine Anfrage der Abgeordneten Ulla Jelpke, Dr. André Hahn, Gökay Akbulut, weiterer Abgeordneter und der Fraktion Die Linke. Abschiebungen im Jahr 2014."
66. Study by the EKD (Protestant Churches) in 2017, cit. in Serhat Karakayali, "Ehrenamtliches Engagement für Geflüchtete in Deutschland," state-of-research paper 09, IMIS/BICC (2018).

67. Andreas Zick and Madlen Preuß, “Einstellungen zur Integration,” 2019, p. 13, www.stiftung-mercator.de/content/uploads/2020/12/ZugleichIII_Stiftung_Mercator_Langfassung.pdf.

68. Bertelsmann Stiftung, ed., “Willkommenskultur im Stresstest,” 2017, and “Willkommenskultur zwischen Skepsis und Pragmatik,” 2019, pp. 16–17.

69. “Integration of Refugees in Austria, Germany and Sweden,” study for the EMPL Committee, European Parliament, 2017, pp. 24–25. See http://www.europarl.europa.eu/RegData/etudes/STUD/2018/614200/IPOL_STU(2018)614200_EN.pdf.

70. See the exchange between Julia Duchrow (Brot für die Welt) and Gerhard Arnold (CSU) in *welt-sichten* (October 2017): 10.

71. *Süddeutsche Zeitung*, 13 November 2017, p. 6.

72. Rainer Faus and Simon Starks, “Das pragmatische Einwanderungsland, 2019, p. 19, a study by the Friedrich Ebert Foundation based on representative surveys in November and December 2018.

73. L. Abdul-Rahman et al., “Körperverletzung im Amt durch Polizeibeamt*innen,” Zwischenbericht 2020, p. 13.

74. BMFSFJ, “Gemeinsam gegen häusliche Gewalt” (2010) and “Lebenssituation, Sicherheit und Gesundheit von Frauen in Deutschland” (2004). FRA (European Union Agency for Fundamental Rights), “Violence Against Women: An EU-wide Survey” (2014). K. D. Bussmann, “Auswirkungen des Gesetzes zur Ächtung der Gewalt in der Erziehung für das Bundesministerium der Justiz” (MS 2005); C. Pfeiffer,”The Abolition of the Parental Right to Corporal Punishment in Sweden, Germany and other European Countries,” KFN report no. 128 (2015); Forsa, “Gewalt in der Erziehung” (2011) survey; M. Tsokos et al., “Kindliche Gewaltopfer,” *Rechtsmedizin* 25 (2015): 227–31; BKA, Polizeiliche Kriminalstatistik, PKS-Kompakt 2018, pp. 7–9, and “Geschichtliche Entwicklung PKS 2018” (2019), p. 3; LesMigraS, “. . . nicht so greifbar und doch real . . .” (2012). D. Schumann, “Legislation and Liberalization: The Debate About Corporal Punishment in Schools in Postwar West Germany, 1945–75,” *German History* 25 (2007): 192–218; *Zeithistorische Forschungen* 2/2018, special issue: “Gewaltabkehr.”

75. Laura Beckmann et al., “Sicherheit, Toleranz und Gewalt in Nordenham,” Kriminologisches Forschungsinstitut Niedersachsen, Forschungsbericht no. 146 (2019). In Berlin, one in six pupils in seventh grade admitted having committed assault in 2014, Berliner Forum Gewaltpräventation, Abschlussbericht no. 64/2 (2018).

76. Uwe Dörmann, “Das ganze Ausmass rechter Gewalt” in BKA: Polizei und Forschung, vol. 21: *Ehrengabe für Leo Schuster* (Neuwied, 2003), pp. 41–54.

77. See O. Decker et al., “Die Leipziger Autoritarismus Studie 2020,” in *Autoritäre Dynamiken*, ed. O. Decker and E. Brähler (Gießen, 2020), pp. 67–69.

78. See Lars Rensmann, “Radical Right-Wing Populists in Parliament,” in *German Politics and Society* 36, no. 3 (2018): 41–73; Ofra Klein and Jasper Muis, “Online Discontent: Comparing Western European Far-Right Groups on Facebook,” *European Societies* 21, no. 4 (2019): 540–62; Ruth Breeze, “Positioning ‘the People’ and Its Enemies,” *Javnost—The Public* 26, no. 1 (2019): 89–104; Jan-Werner Müller, *What Is Populism?* (Philadelphia, 2016).

79. AfD, “Deutschland. Aber normal,” Programm 2021, p. 12.

80. Thomas Assheuer and Hans Sarkowicz, *Rechtsradikale in Deutschland* (Munich, 1992).

81. FZH: 782-5, PRO, Schill Partei, flyers, and FZH Library., Roland Barnabas Schill, Programm, Partei Rechtstaatlicher Offensive (2000).

82. Andreas Zick et al., *Gespaltene Mitte* (Bonn, 2016), pp. 50–51.

83. See Pippa Norris and Ronald Inglehart, *Cultural Backlash* (Cambridge, 2019).

84. Facebook, 1 May 2016, quoted in K. Priester, “Die Alternative für Deutschland,” *Vierteljahreshefte für Zeitgeschichte* 67, no. 3 (2019): 443–53, at p. 443.

85. Michael Hüther and Matthias Diermeier, “Perception and Reality—Economic Inequality as a Driver of Populism?,” *Analyse & Kritik* 41, no. 2 (2019): 337–57, p. 351; Thomas Fricke, “Angst im Aufschwung,” *Wirtschaftsdienst* 99, no. 12 (2019): 849–54.

86. Larissa Deppisch, “Wo sich Menschen auf dem Land abgehängt fühlen, hat der Populismus freie Bahn,” Thünen Working Paper no. 119 (2019).

87. In the GDR, the rural population declined by half a million between 1972 and 1983. See

Kurt Krambach, *Wie lebt Man auf dem Dorf?* (Berlin/East, 1985), pp. 68–71, and Nicole Hördler, *Prettin liegt in Deutschland* (Berlin, 2015), pp. 263–72.

88. On Thuringia, see Kaja Salomo, "The Residential Context as Source of Deprivation," *Political Geography* 69 (2019): 103–17.

89. Maximilian Förtner et al., "Stadt, Land, AfD," *sub/urban* 7 (2019): 23–44, www.zeitschrift-suburban.de/sys/index.php/suburban/article/view/483/689.

90. 3sat, "Kulturzeit," March 2016.

91. Oliver Nachtwey, "PEGIDA, politische Gelegenheitsstrukturen und der neue Autoritarismus," in *Pegida*, ed. K.-S. Rehberg et al. (Bielefeld, 2016), pp. 299–312.

92. See esp. the chapters by Piotr Kocyba and Dieter Rucht in Rehberg et al., *Pegida*, pp. 147–64, 189–205. For different views, see Werner Patzelt and Joachim Klose, *Pegida* (Dresden, 2016), and Hans Vorländer et al., *Pegida* (Wiesbaden, 2016).

93. Werner Germann, *Antisemitismus in öffentlichen Konflikten* (Frankfurt, 1997), esp. pp. 440–53; *Frankfurter Rundschau*, 27 February 1986; *Der Spiegel*, 2 March 1986.

94. I borrow the concept of the reservoir from my colleague David Feldman; see D. Feldman et al., "Labour and Antisemitism," *Political Quarterly* 91, no. 2 (2000): 413–21.

95. Oliver Decker et al., "Die Leipziger Autoritarismus-Studie 2018," in *Flucht ins Autoritäre*, ed. O. Decker and E. Brähler (Gießen, 2018), p. 78.

96. Laura Beckmann et al., "Sicherheit, Toleranz und Gewalt in Nordenham."

97. Ntv, 1 February 2020, according to an RTL-ntv survey of 2,500 voters in November 2019, and for the Facebook quote.

98. Decker and Brähler, *Autoritäre Dynamiken*, p. 225, pp. 211–48. See also Wolfgang Benz, *Was ist Anti-Semitismus?* (Munich, 2004), and Peter Longerich, *Antisemitismus* (Munich, 2021), pp. 392–451.

99. Bundeskriminalamt (BKA), "Politisch motivierte Kriminalität im Jahr 2020," 4 May 2021, p. 7.

100. Amadeu Antonio Stiftung, ed., *Zivilgesellschaftliches Lagebild Antisemitismus, Rheinland-Pfalz* (Berlin, 2019).

101. BKA, "Politisch motivierte Kriminalität," p. 8.

102. With an estimated one thousand internet pages across the country and thirty bands alone in Saxony, see Landesamt für Verfassungsschutz Sachsen, *Jugend im Fokus von Rechtsextremisten* (Dresden, 2010).

103. Julia Bernstein, *Antisemitismus an Schulen in Deutschland* (Weinheim, 2020).

12 MONEY MATTERS

1. Genossenschaftliches Archiv, Hanstedt, Sparwoche Egestorf, 1956.

2. See Harold James, "Die D-Mark," in *Deutsche Erinnerungsorte*, ed. É. François and H. Schulze, vol. II (Munich, 2001), pp. 434–49.

3. Deutsches Historisches Museum, Berlin, 2018, "Sparen: Geschichte einer Deutschen Tugend."

4. GIZ: BISP.06.04, and Genossenschaftliches Archiv Hanstedt, essay by Christa B., 8th grade, 29 October 1951.

5. OECD, www.data.oecd.org/hha/household-savings.htm. The German household savings rate appears high, in part, because official statistics include contributions to company pensions but not to mandatory public pensions, which are more widespread in several European countries. The fall in the savings rate in the United States in the 1990s was partly the result of the tax on stock market holding gains, which depressed the measured rate of personal saving.

6. Sheldon Garon, *Beyond Our Means* (Princeton, NJ, 2012); Sandra Maas, *Kinderstube des Kapitalismus?* (Berlin, 2017). Benjamin Franklin, *Poor Richard Improved* (Philadelphia, 1758).

7. The polls were taken in July 1948, cit. in *Allensbach Jahrbuch* (1956), p. 153.

8. Quoted in Clemens Vollnhals, "Die Evangelische Kirche," in *Von Stalingrad zur Währungsreform*, ed. M. Broszat et al. (Munich, 1988), p. 152; for entertainment, see Harald Jähner, *Wolfszeit* (Hamburg, 2020).

9. GIZ: Raiffeisenverband Kurhessen, Jahresbericht 1948–50, p. 6.
10. Ludwig Friedeburg and Friedrich Weltz, *Altersbild und Altersvorsorge der Arbeiter und Angestellten* (Frankfurt, 1958), p. 51.
11. Rebecca Belvederesi-Koch, "Weltsparmarketing im 'Wirtschaftswunder,'" *Vierteljahresschrift für Sozial- und Wirtschaftsgeschichte* 97, no. 3 (2010): 283–309, esp. 293–95.
12. Hanno Beck and Urban Bacher, *Inflation* (Frankfurt, 2017).
13. GIZ: Raiffeisenverband Kurhessen, Jahresbericht 1959, p. 63.
14. Quoted in Belvederesi-Koch, "Weltsparmarketing," p. 298.
15. GIZ: Raiffeisenverband Kurhessen, Jahresbericht 1959, pp. 62–65.
16. GIZ: Raiffeisenverband Kurhessen, Jahresbericht 1948–50, p. 3.
17. As Carl-Ludwig Holtfrerich has called it, "Monetary Policy in Germany Since 1948," in *Central Banks as Economic Institutions*, ed. J.-P. Touffut (Cheltenham, 2008), pp. 22–51.
18. Volkmar Muthesius. See further Simon Mee, "Monetary Mythology: The West German Central Bank and Historical Narratives, 1948–78" (Oxford, DPhil, 2016), published since as *Central Bank Independence and the Legacy of the German Past* (Oxford, 2019).
19. Wilhelm Vocke at Übersee-Club, Hamburg, 7 November 1955, reprinted in *Monthly Report of the Bank Deutscher Länder* (October 1955), pp. 2–3, at www.bundesbank.de/resource.
20. "Technik—Segen oder Fluch?," in Karl Blessing, *Im Kampf um gutes Geld* (Frankfurt, 1966), p. 113.
21. Quoted in "Different Views on the Deutsches Bundesbank," www.bundesbank.de.
22. E. Noelle-Neumann, "Geldwert und öffentliche Meinung," in *Geldtheorie und Geldpolitik*, ed. C. A. Andreae et al. (Berlin, 1968), pp. 41–42.
23. Mee, "Monetary Mythology," p. 299.
24. See the chapters by Bernd Hayo, "Inflationseinstellungen," and Dieter Lindenlaub, "Deutsches Stabilitätsbewusstsein," in *Die kulturelle Seite der Währung*, ed. B. Löffler (Munich, 2010), esp. pp. 52, 84.
25. Bundesverband Deutscher Banken, ed., "Finanzwissen und Finanzplanungskompetenz der Deuschen" (2011) and "Jugendstudie 2012."
26. Josef Wysocki and Hans-Georg Günther, *Geschichte der Sparkassen in der DDR, 1945–90* (Stuttgart, 1998).
27. Tilman Heisterhagen and Rainer-W. Hoffmann, *Lehrmeister Währungskrise?!: Drei Familien-Generationen zwischen Gold, Mark und Euro* (Wiesbaden, 2003).
28. Jan Logemann, "Different Paths to Mass Consumption," *Journal of Social History*, 41, no. 3 (2008): 525–59.
29. Michael Wildt, *Am Beginn der "Konsumgesellschaft"* (Hamburg, 1994), p. 63.
30. DTA: 2079.2, Der Tanzkurs.
31. Ibid.
32. *Hörzu*, 25–31 January 1959, p. 45; 1–7 March 1959, pp. 28–29; 22–28 March 1959, p. 33. See further Trentmann, *Empire of Things*, pp. 153–54, ch. 9.
33. AdsD: 4/AWOA003404, Werner Höcker, "Erhalten unsere Kinder zuviel Taschengeld?," Deutscher Sparkassen and Giroverband, 1961.
34. Belvederesi-Koch, "Weltsparmarketing"; Norbert Emmerich, *Geschichte der deutschen Sparkassenwerbung, 1750–1995* (Stuttgart, 1995).
35. Emmerich, *Sparkassenwerbung*, ch. 7.
36. Twelve billion DM in lost tax revenue and 25 billion DM for the bonuses to savers; R. Dittmar, "Ein Vierteljahrhundert vermögenspolitische Bestrebungen," *Sozialer Fortschritt* 26, no. 1 (1977): 1–7.
37. 1. Deutscher Bundestag, Stenographisches Protokoll der 5. Sitzung, 20 September 1949, p. 26.
38. Dagmar Hilpert, *Wohlfahrtsstaat der Mittelschichten?* (Göttingen, 2012).
39. Yorck Dietrich, "Vermögenspolitik," in *Geschichte der Sozialpolitik in Deutschland seit 1945, Vol. IV (1957–66)*, ed. M. Ruck and M. Boldorf (Baden-Baden, 2007), pp. 795–817.
40. Trentmann, *Empire of Things*, pp. 39–43.
41. ADE: HGSt, Allg. Slg. 308, Pfarrer Preuss memo, 5 February 1964.

42. ADE: HGSt, Allg. Slg. 679, AG für Jugendpflege, ed., "Das Freiwillige Soziale Jahr," 1965.
43. HIS: SBe 692-G3, "Unverbindliche Richtlinien," no. 2, December 1963, in H. Martin, ed., "Strategie und Organizationsfrage in der antiautoritären Bewegung: Eine Dokumentation," mimeo, 1970, pp. 17–18; IfZ: ED 750/4, APO Archiv/Heinz Koderer, "Subversive Aktion," flyer, May 1964.
44. Herbert Marcuse, *One-Dimensional Man* (London, 1964); Max Horkheimer and Theodor Adorno, *Dialektik der Aufklärung* (Amsterdam, 1947); Vincent Kaufmann, *Guy Debord* (Berlin, 2004).
45. IfZ: ED 750/29, Subversive Aktion, "Weihnachtsevangelium," December 1964.
46. Trentmann, *Empire of Things*, pp. 321–23; A. Sedlmaier, *Consumption and Violence* (Ann Arbor, MI, 2014), ch. 3.
47. DTA: 36-1, 20 January, 4 February 1962.
48. HIS: III 4 E a and b, "Kritik," issue 4/71.
49. FZH: 771-60, Bd 1: Junge Union, J/Info, Extra II, Städtebau, 1973; KAS: 106/2, JU, Rheinland-Pfalz, "Verschleissproduktion, Verschwendung, Wachstumsproblematik," 1974.
50. Sina Fabian, *Boom in der Krise* (Göttingen, 2016), p. 163, table 5.
51. Trentmann, *Empire of Things*, pp. 322–23.
52. BArch Freiburg: BW 6/51, 0575. See further: Reinhild Kreis, *Selbermachen* (Frankfurt, 2020).
53. Peter-Paul Bänziger, "'Materialism Is a Very Comfortable Thing,'" in *Wertewandel in der Wirtschaft und Arbeitswelt*, ed. B. Dietz and J. Neuheiser (Munich, 2017), pp. 55–72.
54. Helmut Schelsky, ed., *Arbeiterjugend gestern und heute* (Heidelberg, 1955), quoted at p. 295; Rudolf Regnet, *Das Arbeitserlebnis des jugendlichen Werktätigen in der industriellen Großstadt* (Leipzig, 1931).
55. Axel Schildt and Detlef Siegfried, *Deutsche Kulturgeschichte* (Munich, 2009), pp. 260–66, and at www.pinkfloydarchives.com/posters.
56. AdsD: Eco-Archiv 12/2006, Aktionswoche Verkehr und Umwelt, DNR, Aktionsausschuss Auto und Umwelt, 1984.
57. HEW *Sammelschiene*, 4/1972, p. 19.
58. Detlef Siegfried, "Prosperität und Krisenangst," in *Mit dem Wandel Leben*, ed. F. Kiessling and B. Rieger (Cologne, 2011), p. 71.
59. Quoted in W. Balsen and K. Rössel, *Hoch die internationale Solidarität* (Cologne, 1986), p. 284.
60. See pp. 552–60 in this volume.
61. Fairtrade Deutschland, "Jahres- und Wirkungsbericht 2019/20" (Cologne, 2020); www.swissfairtrade.ch; see further Trentmann, *Empire of Things*, pp. 562–80; Ruben Quaas, *Fair Trade* (Cologne, 2015); Benjamin Möckel, "Postkolonialwaren," *Zeithistorische Forschungen* 17 (2020): 503–29.
62. Immanuel Kant, *Grundlegung zur Metaphysik der Sitten* (Leipzig, 1906, 3rd edn.; original 1785), 2. Abschnitt, p. 60.
63. OLG Köln, Az.15U 193/14 (for Kohl), and *Frankfurter Allgemeine Zeitung*, 29 November 2021; BG, *NJW*, 1996: 1128ff. (Caroline); BVerfG: *NJW*, 1973: 1221ff. (Soraya). *Los Angeles Times*, 9 December 1993 (Sommer). Christian v. Bar, "Schmerzensgeld und gesellschaftliche Stellung des Opfers bei Verletzungen des allgemeinen Persönlichkeitsrechtes," *Neue Juristische Wochenschrift* (*NJW*) 32 (1980): 1724–29; Johannes Ady, *Ersatzansprüche wegen immaterieller Einbußen* (Tübingen, 2004).
64. OLG Zweibrücken, 22 April 2008 (5 U 6/07); Andreas Slizyk, *Beck'sche Schmerzensgeld-tabelle* (Munich, 2018, 14th rev. edn.), esp. pp. 183ff.
65. Bundesbank, "Haushaltsstudie," 2014, and "Studie zur wirtschaftlichen Lage privater Haushalte." Average net wealth was 195,200 euros in Germany and 245,400 in the eurozone. See also E. Sierminska and M. Medgyesi, "The Distribution of Wealth Between Households," European Commission Research Note, 11/2013. In the EU-15, only Austria was marginally more unequal.
66. Thomas Piketty, *Capital in the Twenty-first Century* (Cambridge, MA, 2013).
67. C. Bartels, "Einkommensverteilung in Deutschland von 1871 bis 2013," *DIW Wochenbericht* 3 (2018); S. Bach et al., "Einkommens- und Vermögensteilung—zu ungleich?," *Wirtschaftsdienst* 94, no. 10 (2014): 691–712; Thomas Piketty, *Capital and Ideology* (Cambridge, MA, 2020), esp. pp. 419–23.

68. K. Baresel et al., "Hälfte aller Erbschaften," *DIW Wochenbericht* 5 (2021).

69. If pension wealth is included, the Gini coefficient falls from 0.77 to 0.51 in Germany, and from 0.89 to 0.70 in the United States; Timm Bönke et al., "A Head-to-Head Comparison of Augmented Wealth in Germany and the United States," SOEP 2017, no. 899. See further Eric Seils and Jutta Höhne, "Einkommensarmut in Deutschland," WSI Policy Brief, no. 26 (08/2018); Judith Niehues, "Einkommensentwicklung, Ungleichheit und Armut," in IW-Trends 3/2017: 117–35, and Georg Cremer, *Deutschland ist gerechter als wir meinen* (Munich, 2018), esp. chs. 4 and 7. The base year chosen makes a further difference. If it is 1991—the year after reunification—the real income of the poorest 10 percent takes a dramatic fall in the next two decades. But, then, the early 1990s were years of steep unemployment in the East. Pick 1994, and although income distribution still widens, the poorest decile now earns a few euros more in 2014.

70. Bundesministerium für Arbeit und Soziales (BMAS): Sozialbudget 2019, www.bmas.de.

71. One reason Germany has been lagging behind in its statistics on inequality. Lifting the tax on wealth in 1997 has left us with poor knowledge about the rich. For the absence of a multiple deprivation index, see Felix Römer in *Die Zeit*, 3 March 2021.

72. Eurostat, "Living Conditions in Europe—Poverty and Social Exclusion," October 2021.

73. G. Lechner and W. Backert, *Dynamik des Verbraucherinsolvenzverfahrens* (Berlin, Bundesministerium für Familie, Senioren, Frauen und Jugend, 2005); V. Hottenrott, "Überschuldung privater Haushalte in Deutschland" (PhD thesis, Heidelberg, 2002).

74. *SchuldnerAtlas Deutschland* (2017).

75. Destatis, https://www-genesis.destatis.de/genesis/online/, Code 63511, Überschuldungsstatistik 2016; M. Bock, "Das 'unwirtschaftliche Handeln' als Gegenstand interdisziplinärer geisteswissenschaftlicher Forschung?," and C. Hergenröder, "(Un-)Wirtschaftliches Haushalten im Angesicht der Statistik," in *(Un)wirtschaftliche Haushaltsführung*, ed. C. Hergenröder (Wiesbaden, 2015), pp. 17–32, 81–102. Similar earlier findings in the Caritas study by G. Zimmermann, *Überschuldung privater Haushalte* (Karlsruhe, 1998).

76. Staatsministerium für Soziales und Verbraucherschutz des Freistaats Sachsen, *Geld, Finanzen, Schulden* (Dresden, 2015), p. 23.

77. *SchuldnerAtlas Deutschland* (2017). An official study of more than 12,000 people seeking debt counseling in Rhineland-Palatinate in 2012 found that average debts were mostly to banks—144,000 euros, of which 114,000 euros were for mortgages—followed by 20,000 euros in unpaid taxes and 10,000 euros in outstanding maintenance payments; mail-order debts amounted to only 1,800 euros; Karla Darlatt, "Statistik der Schuldnerberatung in Rheinland-Pfalz im Jahr 2012," in Hergenröder, *(Un)wirtschaftliche Haushaltsführung*, pp. 76–77.

78. BMFSFJ, *Lebenslagen von Familien und Kindern: Überschuldung* (Berlin, 2008), p. 50.

79. Institut für Finanzdienstleistungen (Iff), *Überschuldungsreport 2017*.

80. It was five years for people who had been cleared of their debts once before. Deliberately wasteful or other "*unredliche*" debtors were excluded.

81. "Overview of the Retail Sector in Germany," 2021, www.centurionlgplus.com/retail-sector-germany. Other data shows as the most popular online payment: PayPal (75 percent), invoice (64 percent), debit card (56 percent), and credit card (40 percent), www.emerchantpay.com/insights/online-payments-germany/, 2021.

82. Dieter Korczak, *Überschuldung in Deutschland: Gutachten für BMFSFJ* (Stuttgart, 2001).

83. Statistisches Bundesamt, "Wirtschaftsrechnungen, Einkommens- und Verbrauchsstichprobe Geld- und Immobilienvermögen sowie Schulden privater Haushalte," Fachserie 15 (Wiesbaden, 2014), p. 28.

84. EU-SILC, Social Europe, research note 4/2010: Over-indebtedness.

85. Udo Reifner, "Mythos Jugendverschuldung," 2006, https://www.schuldeninfo.ch, p. 15.

86. EU-SILC, Social Europe, research note 4/2010.

87. Eurostat, "Distribution of Population by Tenure Status," online data: ILC_LVHO02, 2 December 2021. In addition to few flexible mortgages and relatively high taxes and fees on the purchase of a home, Germany in 1987 abolished deductions from income tax for the financing and depreciation of owner-occupied housing, while deductions stayed for rental housing.

88. Half the households who owned their home gained 34,000 euros between 2010 and 2014,

while those who rented were not even 1,000 euros better off, according to the Bundesbank; Bundesbank, "Haushaltstudie," p. 66.

89. Spiegel, ed., *Soll und Haben* (Hamburg, 1982), p. 85.

90. Deutsche Bundesbank, "Das Spar- und Anlageverhalten Privater Haushalte," Monatsbericht, October 2015, p. 28.

91. Bundesverband deutscher Banken, "Geldanlage 2014/15" and "Geldanlage 2015/16," Berlin, 2014 and 2015.

92. Bundesbank, "Das Spar- und Anlageverhalten," and www.dasinvestment.com. In 2018, only a quarter of savers made use of the benefits from capital accumulation funds supported by employers (such as a *Bausparvertrag* or *Fondsparplan*); among those with a net income below 1,000 euros it was a mere 8 percent; Deutscher Sparkassen- und Giroverband, "Die Deutschen und ihr Geld," 2018, p. 10.

93. A German who had between 500,000 and 1 million euro had typically inherited 39 percent of that. Deutsche Bank, Monatsbericht 4/2019, and G. Corneo et al., "Erbschaft und Eigenleistung im Vermögen der Deutschen," *Perspektiven der Wirtschaftspolitik* 17, no. 1 (2016): 35–53; their figures revise the estimates by T. Piketty and G. Zucman, "Wealth and Inheritance in the Long Run," in *Handbook of Income Distribution*, ed. A. B. Atkinson and F. Bourguignon, vol. 2 (Amsterdam, 2014), ch. 15.

94. Deutscher Bundestag, 19. Wahlperiode, 7. Sitzung, 18 January 2018, p. 563 (Klaus Ernst, Die Linke); Stiftung Familienunternehmen, *Die Entwicklung der Vermögenssteuer im internationalen Vergleich* (2017), p. 10.

95. Otto Schily in *Die Zeit*, 24 October 2019.

96. Jens Beckert, *Unverdientes Vermögen* (Frankfurt, 2004). See now also Ronny Grundig, *Vermögen vererben* (Göttingen, 2022).

97. Bundestag, Plenarprotokoll 15/32, 14 March 2003, p. 2486.

98. Friederike Welter and Jutta Gröschl, "Unternehmer und Unternehmerinnen in Deutschland," *Aus Politik und Zeitgeschichte* 66, nos. 16–17 (2016), p. 8.

99. J. Beckert, H. Lukas, and R. Arndt, "Verdient—Unverdient: Der öffentliche Diskurs um die Erbschaftssteuer in Deutschland und Österreich," *Berliner Journal für Soziologie* 27, no. 2 (2017): 271–91.

100. Fifty-two percent of *Volksschule* and *Hauptschule* leavers, and only 38 percent from those with *Fachschulreife* or *Hochschulreife*, the equivalent of a high school degree in the United States; BMAS, ed., *Lebenslagen in Deutschland: Wahrnehmung von Armut und Reichtum* (Berlin, 2015), p. 71.

101. Adam Smith, *Theory of Moral Sentiment* (1759), IV.1.7.

102. Julia Friedrichs, 11 April 2017, https://oxiblog.de/deutsche-erben-haben-es-gut/; Julia Friedrichs, *Wir Erben* (Berlin, 2015). See also https://www.spiegel.de/forum/wirtschaft/vermoegensverteilung-deutschland-viele-erben-fuehlen-sich-schuldig-thread-255893-14.html.

103. Rainer Zitelmann, "Upward Classism," *Economic Affairs* 40, no. 2 (2020): 162–79; Rainer Zitelmann, *The Rich in Public Opinion* (Washington, DC, 2020).

104. Ute Frevert, *Mächtige Gefühle* (Frankfurt, 2020), pp. 229–50, quoted at p. 240.

105. Christian Rickens, *Ganz Oben* (Cologne, 2011), pp. 67–80; *Frankfurter Rundschau*, 6 July 2017. For earlier periods, see now Eva Gajek et al., eds., *Reichtum in Deutschland* (Göttingen, 2019).

106. A point made by Stefan Liebig (DWI), *Die Zeit*, 25 January 2018.

107. BMAS, *Lebenslagen in Deutschland*, pp. 39–70.

108. *Sozialbericht NRW 2012: Armuts- und Reichtumsbericht*, pp. 342–45.

109. This figure includes only those who received constant support for subsistence (*laufende Hilfe zum Lebensunterhalt*). Those in receipt of *Sozialhilfe* for special circumstances (*besondere Lebenslagen*) climbed from 1 million people (1973) to 1.5 million (1990).

110. Richard Hauser and Werner Hübinger, *Arme unter uns* (Freiburg, 1993), 2 vols—the estimated number who lost their homes did not include ethnic German migrants and foreigners. Since German poverty statistics are based on household questionnaires, they do not capture groups who do not live in regular households, such as the homeless, refugees, and people in care homes.

111. A. Haupt and G. Nollmann, "Warum werden immer mehr Haushalte von Armut

gefährdet?," *Kölner Zeitschrift für Soziologie und Sozialpsychologie* 66, no. 4 (2014): 603–27; Cremer, *Deutschland ist gerechter*, chs. 6 and 7. See further: Lutz Raphael, *Jenseits von Kohle und Stahl* (Berlin, 2019), esp. ch. 4.

112. *Bild*, 13 August 2003, p. 1. See now: B. Rieger, "Florida-Rolf lässt grüssen" in: *Vierteljahrshefte für Zeitgeschichte* 70 (2022): 361–389.

113. *Der Spiegel*, 11 February 2010 (Westerwelle); the point about the CDU paraphrases the prime minister of Baden-Württemberg, Stefan Mappus, also quoted here.

114. *Sozialbericht NRW 2012*, p. 331.

115. Sozialgericht Berlin, 20 October 2003: S 70 AL 5274/02. The *Landessozialgericht* in Berlin-Brandenburg upheld the decision.

116. European Commission, European Semester Thematic Factsheet: Unemployment Benefits (2014), chart 8, p. 11; National Audit Office, Benefit sanctions (29 November 2016); Tina Hofmann, "Arbeitslosigkeit und Armut," in *Menschenwürde ist Menschenrecht*, ed. Der Paritätische Gesamtverband (2017), pp. 42–43; *Die Zeit*, 22 June 2017.

117. Sozialgericht Gotha, 2 August 2016, Az.: S 15 AS 5157/14.

118. BVerfG: Urteil des Ersten Senats, 5 November 2019, 1 BvL 7/16-, Rn. 1-225.

119. Irene Becker, "Verdeckte Armut in Deutschland," in FES Fachforum no. 2 (2007).

120. SPD Bundestagsfraktion, 9 May 2006, quoted in *taz*, 11 May 2006.

121. From the Socio-Economic Panel (SOEP), a longitudinal survey of more than ten thousand households. For this and the following, see Irene Becker, "Finanzielle Mindestsicherung und Bedürftigkeit im Alter," *Zeitschrift für Sozialreform* 2 (2012); cf. Tatjana Mika, "Informationsdefizite und Schonung Angehöriger," *Informationsdienst Soziale Indikatoren* 35 (2006): 7–10.

122. Caritas, *Arme unter uns*, pp. 122–29.

123. Bundesgerichtshof, 15 September 2010, XII ZR 148/09. Since 2020, adult children earning less than 100,000 euros (pre-tax) a year have been exempt.

124. *Sozialbericht NRW 2012*, p. 339.

125. See https://www.deutschlandfunkkultur.de/hartz-iv-sozialhilfe-grundsicherung-ueberleben-in-der-100.html.

126. *Sozialbericht NRW 2012*, pp. 329, 346; *Sozialbericht NRW 2016*, p. 552.

127. Didier Fassin, *Humanitarian Reason* (Berkeley, CA, 2012).

128. H. Hoffman and A. Hendel-Kramer, "Angebot zur Würde," in *Transformation der Tafeln in Deutschland*, ed. S. Selke and K. Maar (Wiesbaden, 2011), pp. 123–36; H.-J. Benedict, "Die Ausgegrenzten," *Zeitschrift für Evangelische Ethik* 59 (2015): 17–29, M. Oechler and M. Schwellwat, "Alternative Formen der Armutsbekämpfung: Die neue Mitleidsökonomie," *Soziale Passagen* 7 (2015).

129. Philippe van Parijs and Yannick Vanderborgth, *Basic Income* (Cambridge, MA, 2017).

130. See www.d-althaus.de/22.0html; Joachim Bischoff, *Allgemeines Grundeinkommen* (Hamburg, 2007); Dominik H. Enste, "Bedingungsloses Grundeinkommen," Roman Herzog Institut, Informationen no. 5 (2008); Thomas Straubhaar, *Wirtschaftsdienst* 9 (2013): 583–605; Straubhaar et al., "Unconditional Basic Income," *CESifo Forum* 19, no. 3 (2018).

131. Letter to *Nitro* magazine, 21 June 2018, with thanks to Bettina Schellong-Lammel. 21 June 2018. Jusos National Congress, 25–27 November 2016, https://jusos.de/wp-content/uploads/2021/06/Beschlussbuch-Buko-2019-Schwerin.pdf. Silke Bothfeld, "Das bedingungslose Grundeinkommen zwischen Utopie und sozialstaatlicher Wirklichkeit," *Leviathan* 46, no. 1 (2018): 81–108; Guido Raddatz, "Das bedingungslose Grundeinkommen," *Argumente zu Marktwirtschaft und Politik* 123 (2013); Franz-Xaver Kaufmann, "Sicherheit," in *Wohlfahrtsstaatliche Grundbegriffe*, ed. S. Lessenich (Frankfurt, 2003), pp. 73–104.

13 THE CIRCLES OF CARE

1. M. Gandhi, *Hind Swaraj or Indian Home Rule* (1909), ch. 13.

2. Bundesministerium für Arbeit und Sozialordnung, *Grundlagen der Sozialpolitik, vol. I, Geschichte der Sozialpolitik in Deutschland Seit 1945* (Baden-Baden, 2001); H. G. Hockerts, ed., *Drei Wege deutscher Sozialstaatlichkeit* (Munich, 1998).

3. Heribert Klein, ed., *Oswald von Nell-Breuning* (Freiburg, 1989), pp. 36–43.
4. H. Achinger, J. Höffner, H. Muthesius, and L. Neundörfer, *Neuordnung der sozialen Leistungen* (Cologne, 1955), pp. 22–23.
5. Joseph Höffner, "Eigenverantwortung und Wohlfahrtsstaat" (1952), in Joseph Höffner, *Ausgewählte Schriften*, V (Paderborn, 2014), p. 53. Lukas Roelli-Alkemper, *Familie im Wiederaufbau* (Paderborn, 2000), quoted at p. 499.
6. See B. Fix and E. Fix, *Kirche und Wohlfahrtsstaat* (Freiburg, 2005).
7. Nussbaum, *Upheavals of Thought.*
8. "Kirchliche Caritas und Staatliche Wohlfahrtspflege," *caritas* 56 (1955), H.1.
9. Romano Guardini, *Der Dienst am Nächsten in Gefahr* (Würzburg, 1956).
10. A. Henkelmann, "'Der Dienst am Nächsten in Gefahr'?" in *Auf dem Weg in "dynamische Zeiten"*, pp. 127–73.
11. Von Bodelschwingh, Deutscher Bundestag, 157. Sitzung, 3 May 1961, Stenog. Berichte vol. 49, p. 9026.
12. W. Adamy et al., "Sozialstaat oder Armenhaus?," *Sozialer Fortschritt* 32, no. 9 (1983): 193–200.
13. Expansion and professionalization came with their own challenges, not least the the loss of autonomy and the growing number of staff who were no longer devout Christians; by the 1980s, the Diakonie depended on the state and the statutory health insurances for three quarters of its funds; H. Seibert, "Finanzierung der Diakonie," at www.diakonie.de/finanzierung.
14. H. H. Bühler, "Die katholischen sozialen Einrichtungen der Caritas," *caritas* 92: 319–36; Ursula Röper and Carola Jüllig, eds., *Die Macht der Nächstenliebe* (Berlin, 1998); "Millionenfache Hilfe—Die Caritas in Zahlen," at www.caritas.de. Destatis, *Pflegestatistik 2019* (2020). Fix and Fix, *Kirche und Wohlfahrtsstaat*, p. 176.
15. LAB, B Rep. 074 Nr. 8766, VG XIV A 14/59, 20 August 1959; B Rep. 074 Nr. 8774,VG XIV A 694/56, 25 June 1957.
16. U. Brisch, in *Vier Jahre Bundessozialhilfegesetz* (Frankfurt, 1966), p. 537.
17. In 1957, 0.6 percent in Regensburg and 3.8 percent in Bochum, see Friederike Föcking, *Fürsorge im Wirtschaftsboom* (Munich, 2007), p. 228.
18. ADE: Allg. Slg. 705, Senator für Arbeit und Sozialwesen, Berlin, "Bericht über den Fürsorgerischen Dienst" (March 1960). F. Barabas and C. Sachße, "Bundessozialhilfegesetz," *Kritische Justiz* 9, no. 4 (1976): 359–76.
19. See C. Barkholdt and G. Naegele, "Armut durch Pflegebedürftigkeit," in *Sozialpolitische Strategien gegen Armut*, ed. W. Hanesch (Opladen, 1995), pp. 404–28; ADE: Allg. Slg. 688, Armin Clauss (Minister for Social Affairs, Hesse), "Pflegeversicherung," June 1984.
20. Stadt Köln, "Senioren in Köln," *Kölner Statistische Nachrichten* 5 (1989).
21. Adamy et al., "Sozialstaat oder Armenhaus?"
22. M. Dieck, "Interessengegensätze zwischen der Wohlfahrtspflege und den betroffenen Leistungsempfängern," *Theorie und Praxis der sozialen Arbeit* 6 (1992).
23. Barkholdt und Naegele, "Armut durch Pflegebedürftigkeit," pp. 410–15.
24. Verfassung des Freistaates Bayern vom 2. Dezember 1946, Art. 124.
25. Christian Kuchler, *Kirche und Kino* (Paderborn, 2006), pp. 151–74.
26. KAS: 04-070/008/3, Frauen Union, 1979–80.
27. Christiane Kuller, *Familienpolitik im föderativen Sozialstaat* (Munich, 2004); Jan Künzler et al., "Gender Division of Labor in Unified Germany," WORC Report 2011, pp. 19–21.
28. Christiane Kuller, "'Stiefkind der Gesellschaft' oder 'Trägerin der Erneuerung'?" in *Gesellschaft im Wandel, 1949–73*, ed. Th. Schlemmer and H. Woller (Munich, 2002), p. 297.
29. Wiebke Kolbe, *Elternschaft im Wohlfahrtsstaat: Schweden und die Bundesrepublik im Vergleich 1945–2000* (Frankfurt, 2002), pp. 414–18.
30. Peter Kielmansegg, *Nach der Katastrophe* (Berlin, 2000), p. 403.
31. Elisabeth Zillken, "Zur Reform des Rechts des unehelichen Kindes," *Jugendwohl* 11 (November 1964): 390–96.
32. R. Hauser and W. Hübinger, *Arme unter uns*, I (Caritas, 1991), pp. 204–14.
33. Manfred G. Schmidt, "Grundlagen der Sozialpolitik in der DDR," in *Grundlagen*, I, pp. 685–798.

34. See Konrad H. Jarausch, "Care and Coercion," in *Dictatorship as Experience*, ed. Jarausch (New York, 1999); Konrad Jarausch, "Fürsorgediktatur," in Docupedia-Zeitgeschichte (2010), http://docupedia.de/zg/Fürsorgediktatur.

35. J. Künzler et al., "Gender Division of Labour in Unified Germany", WORC Report (Tilburg, 2001), table 3, Appendix table A, 13–16.

36. BArch Berlin: DY 34/14921, Nachbarschaftshilfe; *Neues Deutschland*, 22 January and 18 February 1961.

37. G. Winkler, ed., *Frauenreport '90*, for the Beauftrage des Ministerrates für die Gleichstellung von Frauen und Männern (Berlin, 1990), pp. 88–89.

38. Künzler et al., "Gender Division," fig. 14.

39. BArch Berlin: DY 34/14921, Bericht, 26 April 1961.

40. BArch Berlin: DY 34/2940, FDGB, Beratung, 30 April 1969.

41. *Frauenreport '90*, p. 81; Anna Kaminsky, *Frauen in der DDR* (Berlin, 2016), pp. 139–40.

42. BArch Berlin: DY 30/36878, "Information über Probleme," 4 October 1982.

43. 1955, cit. in Kaminsky, *Frauen in der DDR*.

44. BArch Berlin: DY 67/26, Volkssolidarität, vol. II, Bezirk Leipzig, 1971.

45. LAB: C Rep 118/652, Information, 28 August 1974.

46. BLHA: 401 RdB/Pdm/23992/2, Analyse, 30 May 1969.

47. BLHA: Rep. 401, no. 20144, Analyse . . . Kreis Gransee 1988, 4 January 1989.

48. K.-P. Schwitzer, "'Senioren' and 'Behinderte,'" in *Sozialpolitik in der DDR*, ed. G. Manz et al. (Berlin, 2001). BMFSFJ, *Siebter Bericht zur Lage der älteren Generation in der Bundesrepublik Deutschland* (Berlin, 2016), pp. 184–85.

49. *Das Parlament*, 12 November 2018, p. 3. Destatis, *Pflegestatistik 2017*; BGW Forschung, "Altenpflege in Deutschland" (2015). For comparatively low pay, see ILO, *Care Work and Care Jobs* (Geneva, 2018), p. 224.

50. Norbert Blüm, speech to CDU New Year reception, Bremen, cit. in *taz*, 22 January 1998.

51. Infratest 1992, cit. by Barkholdt and Naegele, "Armut durch Pflegebedürftigkeit"; one hour of help per day added up to 1,200 DM a month at the time.

52. Germans also relied far less on outpatient social services—in 2013, only 3 percent of Germans over sixty-five years old used mobile services that came to their home, compared to 12 percent in Sweden. Institutional care, too, was small and chronically underfunded; Sweden spent three times as much on it; Diana Auth, *Wandel von Care-Regimen in Grossbritannien, Schweden und Deutschland* (Münster, 2017), esp. pp. 401–17.

53. BVerfG: 1 BvR 1508/96, 7 June 2005.

54. BGH: XII ZR 148/09, 15 September 2010.

55. U. Brehm, M. Huebener, and S. Schmitz, "15 Jahre Elterngeld," *Bevölkerungsforschung Aktuell* 6 (2022).

56. ILO, *Care Work and Care Jobs*, fig. 2.4, value of unpaid care work as a percentage of GDP. BMFSFJ, *Siebter Altenreport*, pp. 84–88; European Commission, *Report on Equality Between Women and Men in Europe* (2018).

57. *Migrantinnen aus Osteuropa in Privathaushalten*, ver.di (Berlin, 2014), p. 6.

58. H. Engstler and C. Tesch-Römer, "Zeitverwendung von Erwachsenen, die ein Haushaltsmitglied pflegen," in "Wie die Zeit vergeht'" (Destatis, 2017), pp. 232–37. BMFSJ, *Siebter Altenbericht*; Destatis, *Pflegestatistik 2019*; in nursing homes, more than 80 percent of caregivers are women.

59. B. Blinkert, *Chancen und Herausforderungen des demografischen Wandels* (Berlin, 2013), pp. 176–78.

60. V. Hielscher et al., "Pflege in den eigenen vier Wänden," Hans Böckler Stiftung, Study no. 363 (June 2017), pp. 54–61.

61. Trentmann, *Empire of Things*, pp. 500–506.

62. ADE: DEVA 296, Aktion, "Das Alter darf nicht abseits stehen," 1961–63.

63. BMFSFJ, *Freiwilliges Engagement in Deutschland* (FWS, 2019), Outline 31b; Freiwilligensurvey 2004. See also A. Hacket and G. Mutz, "Empirische Befunde zum bürgerschaftlichen Engagement," *Aus Politik und Zeitgeschichte* 9 (2002): 39–46.

64. K. Gaskin et al., *Ein neues bürgerschaftliches Europa* (Freiburg, 1996). Eurobarometer, "Volunteering and Intergenerational Solidarity" (2011); Destatis, *Statistisches Jahrbuch 2016*, p. 175.

65. JHD: 021043-010 [RR296], "Ein Jahr für die Kirche" (Essen, 1960). ADCV: 329.1. 058, Fasz. 01, Elisabeth Denis, "Mädchenschutzarbeit" (c. 1951).

66. JHD: Informationsdienst BDKJ, 31 August 1989, p. 185; JHD: RR296, *Das Freiwillige Soziale Jahr: Ein dokumentarischer Bericht*, ed. Arbeitskreis FSD (1973).

67. AWO, 4/AWOA000331, "Freiwillige soziale Dienste," 20 March 1966; BDKJ, Informationsdienst, 6 December 1963.

68. ADCV: 921.9+339, Freiwilliges soziales Jahr, 15 March 1966; AWO, 4/AWOA000331, letters 1968.

69. ADE: HGSt, Allg. Slg. 308, Mitteilung no. 31, 15 April 1958.

70. JHD: *Das Freiwillige Soziale Jahr*; C. Jax, *Von der Pflicht zur Freiwilligkeit* (Berlin, 2006), pp. 81–82.

71. JHD: *Das Freiwillige Soziale Jahr*, p. 30, cit. from a survey by Das Diakonische Werk, 1971.

72. BDKJ, 021043-010 [RR296], Aachen; Informationsdienst, 9 April 1959.

73. ADE: HGSt, Allg. Slg. 308, "Briefe reicher Mädchen," 1964.

74. ADE: HGSt, Allg. Slg. 308, Erfahrungsausstausch, 9–10 February 1967.

75. BMFSFJ, Hauptbericht des Freiwilligensurveys 2009 (Berlin, 2010), pp. 124–25.

76. At Forum '66, Wiesbaden, cit. in ADCV: 319.5/6, "Gesellschaftliche Hilfe."

77. JHD: 02/010-059, RR 332, BDKJ, "Dienste auf Zeit," 1969–70; Marianne Puender, "Die Funktion der ehrenamtlichen Arbeit in einer Demokratie," *caritas* (May 1972), p. 129.

78. DPWV-Nachrichten, 9/1966, p. 132, and L. Moll, "Der ehrenamtliche Mitarbeiter," *Blätter der Wohlfahrtspflege* 3 (1965): 93. See also KAS: CDU, "Die Frau in der Gesellschaft," 2 September 1977.

79. JHD: *Freiwillige Soziale Jahr*; *BDKJ Journal*, 5 December 1995, pp. 9–12. Puender, "Funktion der ehrenamtlichen Arbeit in einer Demokratie."

80. AWO: 4/AWOA000331, Stellungnahmen 1968–69; letter, 28 March 1968.

81. ADCV: 319.5/3 M 305 Fasz. 01,1 September 1973, Anlage.

82. ADE: HGSt 1947, Tätigkeitsbericht 1978.

83. AWO, 4/AWOA003416 "Rechenschaftsbericht des Zentralausschusses der VS," Oct. 1945–Oct 1955. See pp. 523–24 in this volume.

84. BLHA, Rep 955/11578, Plan-Ist-Vergleich 1986, 9 Feb. 1987.

85. Gunnar Winkler, "Zur Geschichte der Volkssolidarität" (2015, MS), pp. 29–39; Springer, *Da konnt' Ich mich dann so'n bisschen entfalten*; S. Angerhausen et al., *Überholen ohne einzuholen: Freie Wohlfahrtspflege in Ostdeutschland* (Opladen, 1998).

86. ADE, Allg Slg 1718, Diakonie "Repräsentative Stichprobe," 2011.

87. H. Krimmer et al., "Lokal kreativ, finanziell unter Druck, digital herausgefordert" (Ziviz, 2020), p. 9; the study was supported by Bavaria, Rhineland-Palatinate, Berlin, and Mecklenburg-Vorpommern.

88. BMFSFJ, ed., *Gerechtigkeit für Familien* (Stuttgart, 2001).

89. BGH: IV ZR 7/10, 19 January 2011.

90. Destatis, *Pflegestatistik 2019*; www.bundesgesundheitsministerium.de/themen/pflege/pflegekraefte.

91. Bifg, *Barmer Pflegereport 2021*. Bundesagentur für Arbeit, Arbeitsmarktsituation im Pflegebereich (May 2021).

92. Hans Böckler Stiftung, "Arbeitsbedingungen in der Pflege," 11 November 2021.

14 MOTHER NATURE

1. Novalis, transl. *The Eclectic Magazine of Foreign Literature, Science and Art*, 1849, p. 245 (from *Bentley's* magazine).

2. OECD Environment Director Simon Upton, 31 May 2012, www.oecd.org/newsroom/environmentgermanyalaboratoryforgreengrowth.htm.

3. Destatis, *Datenreport 2021*, ch. 13, esp. pp. 431ff.; Umweltbundesamt, *Daten und Fakten zu Braun- und Steinkohlen* (Texte 28/2021); International Energy Agency, *Coal 2020* (December 2020). In his day job, the poet Novalis helped develop the lignite fields for the local salt works in Thuringia.

4. BMUV, *Klimaschutz in Zahlen* (2021), p. 15. In 2021, Germany emitted 33 million more tons of greenhouse gases than in 2020, according to UBA president Dirk Messner, 15 March 2022, www.umweltbundesamt.de. SDSN, Yale Center for Environmental Law & Policy, and Center for Global Commons at the University of Tokyo, *Global Commons Stewardship Index 2021* (2021), pp. 146–47.

5. Paul Warde et al., *The Environment: A History of the Idea* (Baltimore, 2021); Joachim Radkau, *The Age of Ecology* (Cambridge, 2014).

6. Ernst Haeckel, *Aus Insulinde* (Bonn, 1901), p. 75.

7. David Blackbourn, *The Conquest of Nature* (London, 2006), pp. 266–80; Frank Uekoetter, *The Green and the Brown* (Cambridge, 2006).

8. Jens Ivo Engels, *Naturpolitik in der Bundesrepublik* (Paderborn, 2006).

9. Landesarchiv Saarland, HBL 39, Interessengemeinschaft der HBL-Geschädigten, *Saarbrücker Allgemeine Zeitung*, 5 August 1958; HBL 45, Mitteilungsblatt des Verbandes der Berggeschädigten im Saarland, "Bergbau und Grundbesitz," no. 11 (November 1958); HBL 69: "Hilfe! Wasser! Alarmschrei aus Grossrosseln," 22 February 1958; Frank Uekötter, *Naturschutz im Aufbruch* (Frankfurt, 2004), pp. 57–80; Frank Uekötter, *Deutschland in Grün* (Göttingen, 2015) pp. 83–90; Ute Hasenöhrl, *Zivilgesellschaft und Protest* (Göttingen, 2011); Engels, *Naturpolitik*, pp. 97–148.

10. Eco-Archiv 12/2006, Fotowettbewerb ENJ, 1970.

11. Uekötter, *Naturschutz*, p. 67.

12. See www.mainau.de/grune-charta.html.

13. Hasenöhrl, *Zivilgesellschaft*, quoted at p. 160.

14. Deutscher Bundestag, 6. Wahlperiode, 155. Sitzung, 3 December 1971: 8914–15. Dennis Meadows et al., *The Limits to Growth* (New York, 1972); P. Kupper, "Die '1970er Diagnose,'" *Archiv für Sozialgeschichte* 43 (2003): 325–48.

15. Westdeutches Friedenskommitee, "Die öffentliche Meinung in der Bundesrepublik gegen die Vorbereitung des Atomkrieges" (1955), pp. 17, 27; Naturfreundejugend, 20 April 1958, Hannover, cit. in *"Wir werden nicht Ruhe geben,"* ed. Uli Jäger (Tübingen, 1982), p. 20.

16. BArch Koblenz: B 237/97207, Frau K., 4 June 1958. See Caitlin Murdock, "Public Health in a Radioactive Age," *Central European History* 52, no. 1 (March 2019): 45–64.

17. Hasenöhrl, *Zivilgesellschaft*, pp. 210–11.

18. See Stephen Milder, *Greening Democracy* (Cambridge, 2017), quoted at p. 40.

19. Inglehart, *Silent Revolution* and *Modernization and Postmodernization* (Princeton, NJ, 1997).

20. See the group "History of Nuclear Energy and Society," cordis.europa.eu/project/id/662268.

21. See www.ag-energiebilanzen.de, "Stromerzeugung nach Energieträgern," 26 April 2022; the figures of Destatis are less comprehensive and, e.g., do not include industry's own power stations. The figure cited here concerns the relative share of different types of energy in gross electricity generation. See also W. Kramer and U. Maaßen, "Das Bruttoprinzip ist europäische Vorgabe," *Energiewirtschaftliche Tagesfragen* 72, no. 4 (2022): 45–47. With thanks to H. G. Buttermann (EEFA) of the AG Energiebilanzen for helpful information.

22. HIS SBe 730, G7, Republik Freies Wendland, *Gorleben* (Selbstverlag, 1980); Die Tageszeitung, ed., *Gorleben: Dokumentation* (1981); D. Halbach, ed., *Gorleben ist überall* (1979). BMWE, Energiedaten (2021), table 23.

23. HIS SBe 576-G2, Das Junge Wort, "Rechtsradikale im grünen Gewande," 10 July 1980. Bodo Manstein, *Im Würgegriff des Fortschritts* (Frankfurt, 1964); E.-O. Cohrs and W. Knigge, *Atomenergie* (Weltbund zum Schutz des Lebens, 1978).

24. Eco-Archiv 01/2007, NF Ausstellungen, Bedrohte Umwelt (1971).

25. Gudrun Pausewang, *Die Wolke: Jetzt werden wir nicht mehr sagen können, wir hätten von nichts gewusst* (Ravensburg, 1987).

26. HIS SBe 730-G5, BBU, Informationen zur Kernenergie, no. K10.

27. Robert Jungk, *Der Atomstaat* (Munich, 1977), and *Trotzdem: Mein Leben für die Zukunft* (Munich, 1993); and see p. 395 in this volume.

28. HIS SBe 590-G1, Kurt Oeser, "Evangelische Kirche und Bürgerinitiativen" (1978), p. 11; for the following: *Die Zeit*, 6 October 1978.

29. Die Grünen, "Diesmal die Grünen Warum?" (January 1983), p. 3.

30. HIS SBe 730-G7, Bund Dt. Pfadfinder, ed., "Nirgends, nie woll'n wir sie die Atommülldeponie" (1978), p. 37.
31. Julia Paulus, ed., *Bewegte Dörfer* (Paderborn, 2018), p. 231.
32. Batelle-Institut, *Bürgerinitiativen im Bereich von Kernkraftwerken* (Munich, 1975), p. 99.
33. HEW Archive, *Sammelschiene*, June 1972.
34. KAS: 106/2, Junge Union Rheinland-Pfalz, "Verschleissproduktion, Verschwendung, Wachstumsproblematik" (1974); 04-007-460/2, Junge Union, Bezirksverband Unterfranken, "Positionspapier zur Energiepolitik' (1979); ASM 06-059-079/1, Weissbuch Energie (1979–80). *Süddeutsche Zeitung*, 6 September 1971.
35. Joachim Radkau, "Das RWE zwischen Braunkohle und Atomeuphorie 1945–68," in *RWE*, ed. D. Schweer (Wiesbaden, 1998), pp. 173–96; Hendrik Ehrhardt, "Energiebedarfsprognosen," in *Energie in der modernen Gesellschaft*, ed. H. Ehrhardt and Th. Kroll (Göttingen, 2012), pp. 193–222.
36. HIS Sbe 730-G5, BBU, "Unfälle in deutschen Kernkraftwerken" (September 1979).
37. Henning Türk, *Treibstoff der Systeme* (Berlin, 2021), pp. 85–97, quoted at p. 89.
38. Eurobarometer 17, "Energy and the Future," April 1982, J.-R Rabier, H. Fiffault, and R. Inglehart, Q.216A.
39. N. Dube, *Die öffentliche Meinung zur Kernenergie in der Bundesrepublik Deutschland, 1955–86: Eine Dokumentation* (Berlin, 1988), esp. pp. 16–17. For polls in the 1990s, see World Nuclear Association, "Nuclear Power in Germany" (January 2022).
40. *Der Spiegel*, 13 February 1983.
41. K. Anders and F. Uekötter, "Viel Lärm ums stille Sterben," in *Wird Kassandra heiser?*, ed. Uekötter and J. Hohensee (Stuttgart, 2004), pp. 112–38.
42. Roderich von Detten, ed., *Das Waldsterben* (Munich, 2013); Birgit Metzger, *"Erst stirbt der Wald, dann du!"* (Frankfurt, 2015).
43. Eco-Archiv, 12/2006, B. and B. Krems, Neunkirchener Aufruf, 26 June 1983; Prof. Krems to Erhard Eppler, 26 June 1983; Prof. Krems, statement and Presserklärung, 4 and 21 July 1983.
44. Eco-Archiv 12/2006, Krems 1983, 4f. *Der Spiegel*, 26 February 1984, 5 October 1986; BUND, Arbeitskreis Immissionsschutz, "Programm für saubere Luft" (1987); B. Krems-Hemesath, *Bundesdeutsches Umweltrecht* (Oldenburg, 1990).
45. Dieter Rucht, *Modernisierung und soziale Bewegungen* (Frankfurt, 1994), pp. 248–90, 458–59.
46. ICPSR 9057, Eurobarometer 18: Ecological Issues (October 1982), J.-R. Rabier, H. Riffault, R. Inglehart. The age group was fifteen to sixty-five-plus. Critical: R. Graf, "Verhaltenssteuerung jenseits von Markt und Moral," *Vierteljahreshefte für Zeitgeschichte* 66 (2018): 435–62.
47. UBG: Ministerium für Bildung und Wissenschaft, Modelle zur Umwelterziehung in der Bundesrepublik Deutschland (1989), II, pp. 52–53.
48. UBG: Lothar Staeck, Synopse der Richtlinien und Lehrpläne für Biologie, IPN Arbeitsbericht no. 11 (Kiel, 1975), p. 20.
49. *Süddeutsche Zeitung*, 24 March 1971, Realgymnasium Voelklingen, prize in biology. UBG: Modelle zur Umwelterziehung (1989); Minister für Umwelt, NRW, "Wir und unsere Umwelt: Einfälle statt Abfälle" (1990), quoted.
50. Tobias Huff, *Natur und Industrie im Sozialismus* (Göttingen, 2015), ch. 1.
51. Ibid., p. 303.
52. BArch Berlin: DY 27/7550, Kulturbund Denkschrift, 1957.
53. BArch Berlin: DY 27/10913, "Kurzbericht über die Naturschutzwoche 1959 im Kreise Bautzen"; ditto "1959 im Bezirk Halle"; DY 27/10455, "Einschätzung der Naturschutzwoche," Cottbus, 9 August 1968; DY 27/10656, Dresden (Rhododendron); DY 27/7396 Merseburg (Kakteenfreunde).
54. BArch Berlin: DY 27/7399, Saalfeld; DY 27/10660, Suhl, 1972; DY 27/10454, Guido Thoms, 27 April 1973; DY 6/1855, Nationale Front, Suhl, "Informationen ... 'Mach-mit!,'" 13 April 1978. Sebastian Strube, *Euer Dorf soll schöner werden* (Göttingen, 2013).
55. H. Behrens, "Landschaftstage in der DDR," in *Natur- und Umweltschutz nach 1945*, ed. F.-J. Brüggemeier and J. I. Engels (Frankfurt, 2005).
56. Huff, *Natur und Industrie*, p. 138, and for the above.

57. Friedrich-Ebert-Stiftung, *Die Energiepolitik der DDR* (Bonn, 1988); Türk, *Treibstoff der Systeme.* André Steiner, "'Common Sense Is Necessary': East German Reactions to the Oil Crises of the 1970s," *Historical Social Research* 39, no. 4 (2014): 231–50.

58. AG Energiebilanzen, "Primärenergieverbrauch—Neue Bundesländer." In actual tons of lignite mined, the GDR raised 258 million in 1980 and 319 million in 1987; *Statistisches Jahrbuch der DDR 1979* etc.

59. Lignite's share in the GDR's primary energy consumption rose from 63 percent in 1980 to 72 percent in 1985—and that for generating electricity from 73 percent to 83 percent—while the share of oil fell from 17 percent to 11 percent; natural gas (also mainly from the USSR) increased from 9 percent to only 10 percent in these years.

60. M. Jänicke et al., *Alternative Energiepolitik in der DDR und in West-Berlin... Gutachten im Auftrag der Alternativen Liste* (1987), pp. 12–14.

61. BArch Berlin: DC 16/21, Staatssekretariat für Energie, "Stromversorgung der Bevölkerung," 14 August 1953; Minister für Hüttenwesen to Grotewohl, 20 August 1953.

62. LAB: C Rep 135-01, no. 253, Protokoll Kohle- und Energiekonferenz, 6 February 1958.

63. LAB: C Rep 902, no. 139, SED Konferenz, Energieprogramm in Berlin, 31 October 1957.

64. BArch Berlin: DC 20/27420, AG Rationelle Energieanwendung beim Ministerrat, Stand der Ablösung der elekt. Raumheizung, 10 February 1984. BEWAG Archive (Berlin): A/26434, Kombinatsdirektor, Entwicklung des Energieverbrauchs, 1983.

65. See H. Shin and F. Trentmann, "Energy Shortages and the Politics of Time," in *Scarcity in the Modern World*, ed. F. Albritton Jonsson et al. (London, 2019), ch. 15.

66. BArch Berlin: DY 6/4990, Nationale Front, report, Suhl, 11 January 1971.

67. BArch Berlin: DY 6/4678, Nationale Front, report, Rostock, January 1963.

68. BArch Berlin: DY 6/4903, Nationale Front, report, Erfurt, 31 January 1963.

69. UBG: Ministerrat der DDR, Ministerium für Umweltschutz, Bericht 1976–80 (1981, vertrauliche Verschlusssache).

70. BArch Berlin: DK 5/69, I. M. to Vorsitzenden, Ministerium für Umweltschutz, 3 June 1981.

71. UBG: 9-1, R. E. to Ministerrat, 16 November 1988.

72. BArch Berlin: DO 4/1445, Bund der evang. Kirchen in der DDR, Energie und Umwelt (1988); Hans-Peter Gensichen, "Wie man in den Wald russt," 5 June 1985; Gensichen, "Briefe zur Orientierung im Konflikt Mensch-Erde, no. 15 (April 1987). DO 4/805, Bd.1, Mecklenburgische Kirchenzeitung, 3 February 1985. UBG: Nachlass Umweltgruppe Görlitz, 69-2, "Dresdner Denkschrift," July 1983. UBG: Lausitzbote no. 1 (February 1989), editorial Informationspapier (IP).

73. UBG: 59-1, UWG Zittau, "Erklärung von Oybin," 28 May 1988.

74. BArch Berlin: DO 4/1445, Bund der evang. Kirchen in der DDR, Energie und Umwelt (1988).

75. UBG: 59-1, Fernkurs 1983/84, "Leben lernen für morgen."

76. UBG: Lausitzbote no. 1 (February 1989).

77. UBG: 59-1, Ökologischer Arbeitskreis der Dresdner Kirchenbezirke, Material für die Gemeindearbeit (c. 1988); 45-1, AG Umweltschutz Leipzig, "Umweltschutz im Haushalt"; 69-2, "An alle Gemeinden und Jungen Gemeinden der Stadt Görlitz" (February 1989); 62–78, UWG Zittau flyer, "Mobil ohne Auto."

78. UBG: 45-1, AG Umweltschutz Leipzig, "Umweltschutz im Haushalt."

79. "Primärenergieverbrauch, alte Bundesländer, 1950–94," www.ag-energiebilanzen.de/daten-und-fakten/zeitreihen-bis-1989/.

80. Rüdiger Graf, *Öl und Souveränität* (Berlin, 2014), ch. 6. See also Stephen G. Gross, *Energy and Power* (Oxford, 2023).

81. Eco-Archiv, 12/2006: Aktionswoche Verkehr und Umwelt, 1982, Umweltbundesamt, Bericht über den freiwilligen Sonntag am 27 September 1981. *Frankfurter Allgemeine Zeitung*, 25 September 1981; *Bild*, 27 September 1981.

82. Erhard Eppler, *Ende oder Wende* (Stuttgart, 1975), p. 18.

83. Stephen G. Gross, "Reimagining Energy and Growth," *Central European History* 50 (2017): 514–46 and now also his *Energy and Power.*

84. Eppler, "Umweltschutz ist kein Spleen gelangweilter Mittelständler," Sozialdemokratischer Pressedienst 37/248, 30 December 1982.

85. "Primärenergieverbrauch, alte und neue Bundesländer, 1950–94." See also T. Parrique et al., "Decoupling Debunked" (European Environmental Bureau, 2019).

86. For 2021, www.ag-energiebilanzen.de/daten-und-fakten/primaerenergieverbrauch/. As share of gross final energy consumption, renewables reach 20 percent, www.umweltbundesamt .de/daten/energie 25 March 2022. AGEB, Auswertungstabellen zur Energiebilanz Deutschland, 1990–2020, table 1.1. Destatis, *Datenreport 2021*, pp. 431–39.

87. World Economic Forum, *Fostering Effective Energy Transition* (Geneva, 2019), p. 11.

88. Friedrich-Ebert-Stiftung, *Die Energiepolitik der DDR*, pp. 24–25.

89. Hanna Brauers, "Natural Gas as a Barrier to Sustainability Transitions?," *Energy Research & Social Science* 89 (2022): 1–18; Ethik-Kommission, "Sichere Energieversorgung, Deutschlands Energiewende" (Berlin, 2011), p. 60; IEA, Germany 2020 (2020), p. 3; www.weforum.org/reports /fostering-effective-energy-transition/.

90. In 2020, Germans paid 31 cents per kilowatt-hour for their electricity, almost twice as much as people in France or Finland, where taxes and tariffs were lower. German industry paid a quarter less for its gas in 2019–20 than in 2013–14. Eurostat, Electricity prices for household consumers, 2022; Destatis, Daten zur Energiepreisentwicklung (2022), p. 17.

91. Hannß Carl von Carlowitz, *Sylvicultura oeconomica* (Leipzig, 1713; reprinted 2012), p. 105.

92. Elke Seefried, "Rethinking Progress: On the Origin of the Modern Sustainability Discourse, 1970–2000," *Journal of Modern European History* 13, no. 3 (2015): 377–400, esp. pp. 385–86.

93. World Commission on Environment and Development, *Our Common Future* (Oxford, 1987), p. 8.

94. Baden-Württemberg, Ministerium für Umwelt, Klima und Energiewirtschaft, *Indikatorenbericht 2019* (2019).

95. *The 2018 Peer Review on the German Sustainability Strategy* (chaired by Helen Clark), German Council for Sustainable Development (Berlin, 2018).

96. For the above, see bdew.de/service/daten-und-grafiken/entwicklung-beheizungsstruktur -wohnungsneubau/, 2 June 2022; KBA, Pressemitteilung no. 8/2021: Fahrzeugbestand; Umweltbundesamt, Energieverbrauch privater Haushalte, 1 July 2020.

97. Destatis, *Datenreport 2021*, pp. 433–35, 449–54.

98. Umweltbundesamt, *KonsUmwelt* (2020), pp. 24–25; Destatis, Pressemitteilung no. 081, 7 March 2019 (Flugverkehr).

99. F. Krausmann et al., "Growth in Global Materials Use, GDP and Population During the 20th-Century," *Ecological Economics* 68 (2009): 2696–2705. Trentmann, *Empire of Things*, pp. 664–75; E. Shove and F. Trentmann, eds., *Infrastructures in Practice: The Dynamics of Demand in Networked Societies* (London, 2019); www.demand.ac.uk.

100. Harry Lehmann interview, 13 April 2018, www.energiewinde.orsted.de.

101. Umweltbundesamt Präsident Dirk Messner, 15 March 2022, www.umweltbundesamt.de. In order to lower CO_2 emissions by 80 to 95 percent in 2050, buildings would need a total of 450 billion to 1,000 billion euros in additional investment, according to the scenarios by the German Energy Agency, dena-Leitstudie: *Integrierte Energiewende* (Berlin, 2018), p. 21.

102. BVerfG: Erste Senat, 24 March 2021, 1 BvR 2656/18. See further Stephan Lessenich, *Neben uns die Sintflut: Die Externalisierungsgesellschaft und ihr Preis* (Munich, 2016).

103. Umweltbundesamt, *KonsUmwelt*, p. 12.

104. Agora, *Das Klimaschutz-Sofortprogramm* (2021), p. 46.

105. *Global Commons Stewardship Index 2021* (2021), pp. 146–47.

106. Quoted in S. Bose et al., *Nach der Kohle II* (Rosa-Luxemburg-Stiftung, October 2020), p. 9.

107. H. Sander, "Ende Gelände," *Forschungsjournal Soziale Bewegungen* 30, no. 1 (2017): 26–36; R. Kaufer and P. Lein, "Widerstand im Hambacher Forst," *Forschungsjournal Soziale Bewegungen* 31, no. 4 (2018): 1–12; www.ende-gelaende.org.

108. J. de Moor et al., eds., *Protest for a Future II* (2020).

109. BMWK, "Überblickspapier Osterpaket," 6 April 2022, www.bmwk.de.

110. BUND, "Der Krieg in der Ukraine und seine Folgen in Deutschland," 21 March 2022, www .bund.net/service/publikationen.

111. Fatih Birol (IEA) in *Die Zeit*, 23 June 2022, p. 12.

112. StAHH: 44-5-2, no. 615, 29 November 1955, letter by Walter Roewer; Ortsamt Blankenese, minutes 23 February 1956; Schade to Roewer, 4 April 1956. *Norddeutsche Nachrichten*, 3 and 10 December 1955.

113. Cit. in Dieter Hartwig (Kriminalhauptkommissar), "Bedrohung durch 'Kampfhunde,'" *Unser Rassehund* 5 (1991).

114. StAHH: 327-1, no. 2030, Baubehörde, 9 December 1959.

115. StAHH: 327-1, no. 2030, Bezirksblätter, 29 May 1974; 16th conference, Gartenbauamtsleiter, September 1974; Bezirksamt 6, 19 August 1975. *Morgenpost*, 27 August 1975.

116. *Bild*, 28 August 1975.

117. *Frankfurter Allgemeine Zeitung*, 2 September 1975.

118. StAHH: 327-1, no. 2030, K. K. corresp. with Senat, 20 and 28 October 1975.

119. *Frankfurter Allgemeine Zeitung*, 7 August 1972.

120. Heinz Matrose, chair of the Dortmunder Verband für das deutsche Hundewesen, quoted in *Der Spiegel*, 21 July 1975. *Lebensmittelhandel*, 29 July 1972.

121. Y. Strengers et al., "Curious Energy Consumers," *Journal of Consumer Culture* 16 (2016): 761–80.

122. See www.dankundtreu.de; *Welt*, 24 November 1984 and 17 August 1985; *Hamburger Abendblatt*, 28 November 1998.

123. *Hamburger Fremdenblatt*, April 1931.

124. *Hamburger Abendblatt*, 9 July 1996; for the following: OVG RP, 7 May 1996–6 A 12926/95.

125. StAHH: 131-21, no. 1011, Veterinäramt, 20 October 1986; Vermerk, 10 March 1988; A. Klein to Senat, 25 August 1991. F.-J. Luettmann in *Deutsche Verwaltungspraxis*, September 1987; Hartwig, "Bedrohung."

126. See Veronika Settele, *Revolution im Stall* (Göttingen, 2020). Ruth Harrison, *Animal Machines* (London, 1964).

127. Settele, *Revolution im Stall*, quoted at p. 115. Patrice Poutrus, *Die Erfindung des Goldbroilers* (Weimar, 2002).

128. BArch Berlin: DL 102/543, "Entwicklung . . . Lebensgewohnheiten," 30 June 1971, p. 6.

129. Alfred Reckendrees, "Konsummuster im Wandel," *Jahrbuch für Wirtschaftsgeschichte* 2 (2007): 29–61.

130. StAHH: 352-6, no. 2882, BML, 14 February 1956 and 1958. See also *Stern*, 29 May 1955.

131. § 17 TierSchG.

132. Marianne Stock, "Tierschutz in der DDR" (PhD thesis, FU Berlin, 2014).

133. Niko Rittenau, at https://www.peta.de/kampagnen/speziesismus/; Peter Singer, *Animal Liberation* (New York, 1975).

134. BVerfG: Urteil des Ersten Senats vom 15. Januar 2002–1 BvR 1783/99, Rn. 1-61; Wissenschaftliche Dienste des Deutschen Bundestages, "Das verfassungrechtliche Spannungsfeld zwischen Religionsfreiheit und Tierschutz," Ausarbeitung WD 3–202/07.

135. *Deutschlandfunk*, 15 February 2002; David Smith, "'Cruelty of the Worst Kind': Religious Slaughter, Xenophobia, and the German Greens," *Central European History* 40, no. 1 (2007): 89–115; *taz*, 18 May 2002.

136. Destatis, Pressemitteilung no. N 046, 14 July 2021.

137. BMEL, Pressemitteilung no. 20/2022, 15 February 2022. For the above, see Bundesinformationszentrum Landwirtschaft, "Tierwohl—was heisst das konkret?," 18 May 2021; Deutscher Tierschutzbund, "Schwanzkupieren bei Schweinen," 12 April 2021; www.peta.de/themen/bio-eier/; Destatis, "Tiere und tierische Erzeugung" (May 2022). Jens Bülte, "Zur faktischen Straflosigkeit institutionalisierter Agrarkriminalität," *Goltdammer's Archiv für Strafrecht* 165 (2018): 35–56. See also www.organicdenmark.com (February 2022).

138. Wissenschaftlicher Beirat Agrarpolitik beim BMEL, *Wege zu einer gesellschaftlich akzeptierten Nutztierhaltung* (Berlin, 2015), p. 1.

139. In 2012, the Vegetarierbund Deutschland estimated 1,094 animals; *Deutsche Welle*, 10 January 2013. See also the *Fleischatlas* published by the Heinrich-Böll-Stiftung in 2013 and 2021.

140. BMEL, "Versorgung mit Fleisch: Fleischbilanz 2021 vorläufig." These figures are based on "*Verbrauch*" (consumption) and include bones; those for "*Verzehr*" (intake) are lower.

141. A. Stahl et al., "Changes in Food and Nutrient Intake of 6- to 17-Year-Old Germans," *Public Health Nutrition* 12, no. 10 (2009): 1912–23.
142. See www.smartproteinproject.eu: "What Consumers Want" (2021). In 2016, just under 1 million Germans described themselves as vegan or someone who largely avoids animal products; IfD Allensbach, Allensbacher Markt- und Werbeträger-Analyse (2016).
143. The German National Nutritional Survey (NVS) II, 2005–7, and the NEMONIT study 2005–15; see Max Rubner-Institut, ed., *Nationale Verzehrstudie II: Ergebnisbericht* (2008), pt. 2, esp. pp. 31–33, 44–45. M. Gose et al., "Trends in Food Consumption and Nutrient Intake in Germany Between 2006 and 2012," *British Journal of Nutrition* 115 (2016): 1498–1507; F. Koch et al., "Attitudes, Perceptions and Behaviours Regarding Meat Consumption in Germany," *Journal of Nutritional Science* 10 (2021): 1–9, with special thanks for further information to Carolin Krems, one of the lead researchers.
144. See MacGregor, *Germany*, pp. 174–79 ("One People, Many Sausages").
145. *Dialog über Deutschlands Zukunft: Ergebnisbericht* (2012).
146. Stadt Essen, *Einmal grüne Hauptstadt—Immer grüne Hauptstadt: 1. Fortschrittsbericht 2020*, pp. 32–34.
147. L. Graaf et al., "The Other Side of the (Policy) Coin: Analyzing Exnovation Policies for the Urban Mobility Transition in Eight Cities around the Globe," *Sustainability* 13, no. 9045 (2021); M. Müller and O. Reutter, "Course Change," *International Journal of Sustainable Transportation* (2021); M. Menendez and L. Ambühl, "Implementing Design and Operational Measures for Sustainable Mobility," *Sustainability* 14, no. 625 (2022); www.barcelona.cat/mobilitat/ca.
148. Projekt WindNODE, www.energie-und-kunst.de.
149. Futurium, Berlin, October 2022.
150. F. Trentmann and A. Carlsson-Hyslop, "The Evolution of Energy Demand," *Historical Journal* 61, no. 3 (2018): 807–39; www7.bbk.ac.uk/mce/.
151. Kopernikus-Projekte, ed., *Generation 2050* (2021), quoted at p. 45.
152. See www.utopiastadt.eu/zeitstrahl/.
153. K. Thieme and S. Middendorf, "Das Augsburger Schwabencenter," *Geographica Augustana* 23 (2017): 21–28; www.gruenes-schwabencenter.de/wz-program/; N. Hendriks and G. Pflitsch, "Local Agenda in Transition," in *Lessons Learnt*, ed. N. Stamm (Augsburg, 2021), pp. 51–60.
154. See www.futurzwei.org; H. Welzer and S. Rammler, eds., *Der Futurzwei Zukunftsalmanach 2013* (Frankfurt, 2013), and edns. 2015–16, 2017–18. See www.in-zukunft.org; H. Welzer, *Alles könnte anders sein* (Frankfurt, 2019).
155. J. Habermas, "Die neue Unübersichtlichkeit," *Merkur* 431 (January 1985): 1–14; English edn., "The New Obscurity," *Philosophy and Social Criticism* 11, no. 2 (1986): 1–18. See further Joachim Radkau, *Geschichte der Zukunft* (Munich, 2017), as well as R. Graf and B. Herzog, "Von der Geschichte der Zukunftsvorstellungen zur Geschichte ihrer Generierung," *Geschichte und Gesellschaft* 42 (2016): 497–515.
156. W. Kretschmann, *Worauf wir uns verlassen wollen* (Frankfurt, 2018), p. 117.

EPILOGUE: WHAT IS GERMANY FOR?

1. Deutscher Bundestag, WD 2–3000–028/19, 28 Februar 2019; Bundesministerium der Verteidigung, *Bericht zur materiellen Einsatzbereitschaft der Hauptwaffensysteme der Bundeswehr 2017*, p. 45.
2. In 2022, 9 percent of the electricity imported by Germany came from nuclear power in neighboring countries (especially France, Belgium, and Switzerland); in 2020 it was even 23 percent; Bundestag, WD 5–3000–095/22 (12 August 2022).
3. See https://www.bundesregierung.de/breg-de/suche/regierungserklaerung-von-bundeskanzler-olaf-scholz-am-27-februar-2022-2008356.
4. *Das Parlament*, 28 November 2022.
5. Scholz, 27 February 2022.
6. See https://www.unhcr.org/refugee-statistics/.

7. "Germany Mulls Sending Refugees to Africa," *Deutsche Welle*, 2 October 2022.
8. World Bank data, GDP growth (annual percentage); OECD income inequality data.
9. A. Dirk Moses, "The German Catechism," 23 May 2021, https://geschichtedergegenwart.ch/the-german-catechism/.
10. S. Friedländer et al., *Ein Verbrechen ohne Namen* (Munich, 2022); S. Neiman and M. Wildt, eds., *Historiker Streiten* (Berlin, 2022); F. Bajohr und R. O'Sullivan, "Holocaust, Kolonialismus und NS-Imperialismus," *Vierteljahresheft für Zeitgeschichte* 70, no. 1 (2022); Michael Rothberg, *Multidirectional Memory: Remembering the Holocaust in the Age of Decolonization* (Stanford, CA, 2009).
11. Forsa survey for RTL/ntv, 25 January 2023; cf. RTL/ntv Trendbarometer, 30 August 2022.
12. J. Matthes, "Wie abhängig ist die deutsche Wirtschaft exportseitig von China?," *ifo Schnelldienst* 73, no. 2 (2020); Vbw, "Geopolitische Herausforderungen und ihre Folgen für das deutsche Wirtschaftsmodell" (August 2022); *Die Zeit*, 11 August 2022, pp. 19–22; iwd, 26 August 2022; *The Economist*, 5 November 2022, p. 74.

Index

A NOTE ABOUT THE AUTHOR

Frank Trentmann is professor of history at Birkbeck, University of London, and at the University of Helsinki. Previously he taught at Princeton University. He was a Moore Scholar at Caltech and has been awarded the Whitfield Prize, the Austrian Science Book Prize, and the Humboldt Prize for Research. He was born in Hamburg and lives in London.

A NOTE ON THE TYPE

This book was set in Janson, a typeface long thought to have been made by the Dutchman Anton Janson. However, it has been conclusively demonstrated that these types are the work of Nicholas Kis (1650–1702), a Hungarian. The type is an excellent example of the Dutch types that prevailed in England up to the time William Caslon (1692–1766) developed his own designs from them.

Composed by North Market Street Graphics, Lancaster, Pennsylvania

Printed and bound by Berryville Graphics, Berryville, Virginia

Designed by Maggie Hinders